THOMPSON'S MODERN LAND LAW

Thompson's Modern Land Law

Seventh Edition

MARTIN GEORGE

LL.B *(Leicester)*; LL.M *(Nottingham)*,
Associate Professor of Property Law, University of Leicester

ANTONIA LAYARD

*BA (Oxon), MPA/MPH (Columbia), LLM (LSE), DPhil (Oxon),
Professor of Law, University of Bristol*

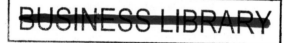

OXFORD
UNIVERSITY PRESS

OXFORD

UNIVERSITY PRESS

Great Clarendon Street, Oxford, OX2 6DP,
United Kingdom

Oxford University Press is a department of the University of Oxford.
It furthers the University's objective of excellence in research, scholarship,
and education by publishing worldwide. Oxford is a registered trade mark of
Oxford University Press in the UK and in certain other countries

Fourth edition 2009
Fifth edition 2012
Sixth edition 2017
Impression: 1

Public sector information reproduced under Open Government Licence v3.0
(http://www.nationalarchives.gov.uk/doc/open-government-licence/open-government-licence.htm)

Published in the United States of America by Oxford University Press
198 Madison Avenue, New York, NY 10016, United States of America

British Library Cataloguing in Publication Data
Data available

Library of Congress Control Number: 2019937520
ISBN 978-0-19-882802-0

Printed in Great Britain by
Bell & Bain Ltd, Glasgow

Preface

It has been a relatively short time since the last edition of this book was published in 2017, and yet a great deal has happened. First, and most importantly, we must pay tribute to Professor Mark Thompson, who was the author of this work from the first edition in 2001. Mark passed away in June 2017, shortly after work had been completed on the sixth edition with Martin George, and it is no exaggeration to say that working on the book during the last months of his life gave Mark vital purpose. We are deeply grateful that *Thompson's Modern Land Law* has now been entrusted to us, and we shall strive to develop the book over the coming years with the same rigorous and erudite approach that encapsulated all of Mark's work.

Second, of course, it is right to say *we* because Martin has been joined by Antonia Layard as the new co-author of the book. We have worked together before, and we are delighted to be a team once again. We have had many discussions about what our own approaches to land law can bring to *Thompson's Modern Land Law* in future editions, and we are looking forward to shaping the content in a way that makes sense in the twenty-first century, while retaining the doctrinal heart of the book. As Mark put it in the preface to the sixth edition, our overriding intention is 'to facilitate the understanding of a complex and important subject and to stimulate the reader to think critically about it, both in terms of what the law actually is and, importantly, what it should be.'

In order to assist law students and academics, we have made several key changes to the structure and format of the book for this edition. Readers will notice, perhaps with relief, that all of the sub-headings or sections in each chapter are now numbered, which will help to make reading lists, lecture handouts, essays and everything else that relies upon references much simpler to create and manage. This also has the associated effect of simplifying the book's footnotes, because a cross-reference can simply be to a number (e.g. see 3.1.2) rather than the full name of the section. Perhaps more importantly, we recognised at the start of our work on this edition that the book has grown steadily over the last eighteen years, and one of our primary aims was to address that trend. We have cut Chapter 6 on The Transfer of Freehold Land, because it seemed superfluous to the book's core themes, and also to the vast majority of undergraduate land law courses. This means that all of the chapters after Chapter 5 have now moved up one place, so we recommend consulting the Table of Contents if you used a previous edition of the book.

Proprietary estoppel, by contrast, has been given the opposite treatment: it now has a new chapter all of its own, with a great deal more commentary and analysis, reflecting properly the place of the topic in the modern land law. Licences, as a consequence, are also carved into a new, small chapter at the end of the book. There has also been considerable work on some of the bigger chapters, to make them more accessible and more readable. Chapter 5 on Registration of Title has had a structural makeover, with a refresh too for Chapter 10 on Leases. A plethora of smaller changes – too many to mention here – will also be noticeable, we hope, to both new and already-familiar readers of the book.

Although it has only been a couple of years since the sixth edition, a surprising number of new developments in the law have necessitated inclusion. The Supreme Court has confirmed the inherent validity of recreational easements in *Regency Villas v Diamond Resorts*, following the Court of Appeal decision that we discussed in the previous edition – a welcome result. So too has the European Court of Human Rights confirmed the Supreme Court's judgment in *McDonald v McDonald* on the right to a home under Article 8 of the European Convention on Human Rights and its application in cases involving private landlords. The Law Commission has also been busy, and we weave our analysis of their Report on *Updating the Land Registration Act 2002* into the book, and particularly Chapter 5. Most of the recommendations are entirely sensible, and it is expected that Government will set out their final conclusions in response the Report at some point in 2019 (timing, we suspect, will depend upon Brexit.) The Law Commission has been consulting or reporting on a range of other matters, such as business tenancies, commonhold, leasehold enfranchisement, the right to manage, and so on. We mention these as the need arises, but more detailed commentary will be deferred until they seem likely to become, or are, part of English land law.

One area that cannot seem to stem the flow of judgments is proprietary estoppel, and so many of the cases involve farms that we mused whether it might make more sense to rename Chapter 14 as the Law of Farms. What is clear is that these cases make proprietary estoppel no clearer, and our enlarged commentary attempts to find a principled path through it. For trusts of the family home, in the previous edition we lamented the decisions in *Stack v Dowden* and *Jones v Kernott* because they had not done what they had set out to do, and we pointed to many Court of Appeal decisions which demonstrate confusion and dissent. There has not been much development in our domestic courts, but the Privy Council in *Marr v Collie* has, we argue in Chapter 8, somehow managed to make the law even more confusing. More than ever, cohabitation and trusts of the family home are crying out for some sort of legislative intervention.

There are other new and interesting cases besides all of that, such as the Court of Appeal in *Baker v Craggs* correcting the error made at first instance on whether an easement can have overreaching effect, and the judgment in *Rashid v Nasrullah* on adverse possession and fraud. We leave it to you to find our commentary on these cases, as and when you have need of them.

All of this work means that we have incurred a number of debts. We would like to thank our excellent team at Oxford University Press, and particularly Felicity Boughton. We also thank Lucy Read, Sarah Parker, Abhishek Sarkari and Paul Nash. Writing a book is hard, but it is made both easier and more enjoyable by a great publisher. We are grateful to Alan Waltham once again for allowing us to use a Steggles painting for the cover. We have also benefitted from many conversations with our colleagues at Leicester and Bristol over the last couple of years, and our students too. It is not possible to list everyone who falls into that category, and so we name you in a manner akin to a discretionary trust: as belonging to that particular class. Above all, we would like to express our deepest appreciation to our families, who have been tremendously supportive during the writing process. Martin would like to thank Lisa, as well as Oscar, Evie and Henry. Antonia would like to thank Daisy, Nina and Ted, even though she still cannot convince them that land law is the best subject *ever*.

Between editions, we use Twitter as our primary method of updates for the book. You can find us @modernlandlaw.

We have attempted to state the law as at 18th February 2019.

Martin George
Antonia Layard

19th June 2019

Acknowledgements

Grateful acknowledgement is made to Janeta Waltham for permission to use *Aldeburgh*, c.1975, by Walter Steggles on the front cover of this book. Special thanks also go to Alan Waltham for providing us with this painting and the following biography about the artist.

Walter James Steggles (15 August 1908 to 5 March 1997)

Wally, as he was generally known, was born in Highbury north London: he was the eldest of five children born to Annie Elizabeth and Walter Steggles. His early years were spent at various addresses in London but during WW1 the family lived for a while in Bath whilst Walter senior was serving with the Royal Flying Corps in Northern France. Around 1920 the family moved back to Ilford where Wally finished his schooling. Aged fourteen he successfully applied for a job with Furness Withy & Co and he worked for them until he retired.

In May 1925 Wally joined the art classes at the Bethnal Green Men's Institute at Wolverley Street along with his younger brother Harold, later transferring their allegiances to the Bow and Bromley Evening Institute when their tutor, John Cooper moved there from Bethnal Green in 1926. Wally exhibited in the East London Art Club's exhibition at the Whitechapel Gallery in 1928. The East London Group, as it became known then transferred to the Alex. Reid and Lefevre gallery in November 1929 and Wally went on to exhibit at all eight shows that the Group held there up until 1936.

Like several other members of the Group, Wally exhibited widely in mixed shows from as early as 1929 and continued to do so up to and into World War Two. His crowning glory came in 1936 when he and fellow Group member Elwin Hawthorne were selected to represent Great Britain at the Venice Biennale that year. It was a great recognition of his talent in such a prestigious international arena but one which, in later life, he chose not to mention! Wally continued to paint almost up until his death in 1997: by his own admission, he couldn't stop!

Detailed Contents

Table of Cases

Table of Primary Legislation

Table of Secondary Legislation

Table of International Treaties and Conventions

Abbreviations of Academic Journals

A note on the abbreviations for academic journals we use in the footnotes. When we refer the reader to an article, we follow the convention of providing the author's name, together with the reference for the piece in its abbreviated form. For example, M.P. Thompson [2002] Conv. 174 refers you to the article on 'Wives, Sureties and Banks' by M.P. Thompson in *The Conveyancer and Property Lawyer* in 2002 at page 174.

To assist in the reader's research, we list here the abbreviations for the key journals we cite in the book, along with their corresponding full titles.

C.L.J.	Cambridge Law Journal
C.L.P.	Current Legal Problems
C.L.W.R.	Common Law World Review
Conv.	The Conveyancer and Property Lawyer
I.C.L.Q.	International & Comparative Law Quarterly
K.L.J.	King's Law Journal
L.M.C.L.Q.	Lloyd's Maritime & Commercial Law Quarterly
L.Q.R.	Law Quarterly Review
L.S.	Legal Studies
M.L.R.	Modern Law Review
N.I.L.Q.	Northern Ireland Legal Quarterly
O.J.L.S.	Oxford Journal of Legal Studies

1

Introduction to Property and Land

When people refer to property, they frequently mean a specific item or object. A person may point to a car or a watch and state: 'this is my property'. Such a statement actually incorporates two things.[1] The first is a possessive statement relating to the assertion of ownership; a concept which involves a person's relationship to a particular thing, and the term 'property' is frequently used in this sense.[2] The second sense in which the word 'property' is being employed is to identify a particular thing: a factual statement. Neither aspect of the term property is free from difficulty. To take the second limb of the use of the term 'property' first, the issue is what subject matter English law regards as capable of being the subject of ownership. Although the subject matter of this book is land, which as a commodity is readily accepted as being capable of being owned, it is desirable to delve a little into the issue of what is capable of being owned in order to understand better some of the abstract concepts that underpin land law. Before doing so, however, some discussion of the concept of ownership is appropriate.

1.1 Aspects of ownership

The concept of ownership is a difficult one. What one means by it may vary both with respect to different subject matter under consideration and also with regard to the approach of different legal systems to the same subject matter. As a concept, it is most helpfully seen as being a shorthand term to describe the various rights a person has in relation to a particular item. This idea is embraced in the analysis of ownership as consisting of a bundle of rights[3] or, perhaps more accurately put, the aggregate of legal relations[4] existing between a person and a particular item.

1.1.1 Limitations on use

While it is helpful to describe an owner of a particular thing as being the person possessed of the maximum number of powers over that item of property, it is wrong to conclude from this that that person is thereby enabled to do anything he or she likes with it.[5]

---

[1] See, e.g., A.W.B. Simpson (1964) 80 L.Q.R. 535 at 551. See also Harris, *Property and Justice* (Oxford, Clarendon Press, 1996), at 13.

[2] See, generally, K. Gray and S.F. Gray in Bright and Dewar (eds), *Land Law, Themes and Perspectives* (Oxford, Oxford University Press, 1998), 15 *et seq*; *Yanner v. Eaton* (1999) 201 C.L.R. 351 at 366 *per* Gleeson C.J., Gaudron, Kirby, and Hayne JJ.

[3] See, in particular, A.M. Honoré in Guest (ed.) *Oxford Essays in Jurisprudence* (Oxford, Oxford University Press, 1961), 107. See also G.P. Wilson [1957] C.L.J. 216 at 222–3; S.N. Glackin [2014] Legal Theory, 1.

[4] *Yanner v. Eaton, supra*, at 389 *per* Gummow J. See also Penner, *The Idea of Property in Law* (Oxford, Oxford University Press, 1997), 73, where the distinction is made between rights and privileges.

[5] This is described as 'totality ownership' by Harris, *Property and Justice*, 120, where it is rightly castigated as being 'a ridiculous Aunt Sally'.

Restraints on such use come, first, from the general law. So, for example, in a society such as the United States, where there exists only minimal control of the ownership of guns, a gun owner could not conceivably justify his shooting of another person by stating that he was merely using his own weapon; that is, exercising his powers of ownership.[6] Similarly, if one owns a car, one's use of it is constrained by the general law relating to matters such as the speed at which the car can be driven and the amount of alcohol that can be consumed before one can take control of it at all. Again, in the context of land, the use an owner can make of it is restricted by the need to comply with planning legislation on the one hand, and by the private law of nuisance on the other.

The above are examples of the general law restricting how a person can enjoy what may be regarded as being their own property, thereby preventing them from doing with it whatsoever they please. Such controls, albeit important, are largely outside the scope of this book. A second limitation on the powers that one may seek to exercise over property is that the law of a given country may not actually recognize the existence of a particular power. As an example of this, one may cite the ability, or lack of it, to make testamentary dispositions.[7] In England, the general principle is one of testamentary freedom: one can leave one's property to whomsoever one likes. That principle is, however, modified to a certain extent by the statutory provision[8] that enables certain people to claim against the estate of a deceased person if insufficient provision had been made for them by the testator. In other jurisdictions, the restrictions on leaving certain property to people outside a specified list of family members are more explicit, and, indeed, in this country, testamentary powers were initially limited, in that it was not possible to make any direct testamentary disposition of freehold land at all until 1540.[9] A third restriction on a person's power to use property in a particular way derives from the rights of other people.

1.1.2 Private law restraints

As will be seen, because of its essential nature, land is a commodity which lends itself particularly well to the creation of a diverse range of rights affecting it. Although this phenomenon is seen most readily in respect of land, it can occur, although normally to a much lesser extent, with other forms of property as well. So, for example, if one is the owner of a book one has largely unfettered powers of dealing with it. Those powers are curtailed in one potentially important way, however, in that, although the owner of the book may sell it, lend it, or destroy it, he cannot copy it.[10] To do so would infringe the property right of the owner of the copyright in that book, normally, but not invariably, the author or publisher of it.[11]

Ownership rights over property can perhaps best be seen as a series of open-ended powers over a particular item. It is not possible to comprise a complete, finite, list of such powers;[12] the extent or range of those powers will vary between different legal systems, in

---

[6] See P. Birks [1985] Acta Juridica, 1.   [7] See Harris, Property and Justice, at 35.

[8] Inheritance (Family Provisions) Act 1075, s. 1. For a full discussion of the issues involved in the application of this jurisdiction, see Ilott v. The Blue Cross [2017] UKSC 17.

[9] Statute of Wills 1540.

[10] See Lawson and Rudden, The Law of Property (3rd edn) (Oxford, Oxford University Press, 2002), 39. See also for a similar example involving a letter, Sir John Mummery in Barr (ed.), Modern Studies in Property Law (vol. 8) (Oxford, Hart Publishing, 2015), 3 at 5.

[11] See Bentley and Sherman, Intellectual Property (4th edn) (Oxford, Oxford University Press, 2012), 3. The ownership of the copyright may be transferred to a person unconnected with the creation of the work in question.

[12] See Penner, The Idea of Property in Law 73; K Campbell (1992) 3 KiCLi]. 79 at 91, LW, Harris in McCormick and Birks (eds) The Legal Mind: Essays for Tony Honoré (Oxford, Clarendon Press, 1986), 143 at 152. Contrast Honoré, Essays in Jurisprudence, at 113. See also Lawson, The Rational Strength of English Law (London, Stevens & Son, 1951), at 86 instancing the power to exclude, the power to alienate, and the power to enjoy.

terms of what powers are recognized by that system. The exercise of those powers can then be limited either by the state, which may stipulate how particular items of property can, or cannot, be enjoyed, or by the existence of other, private, rights over the property. So, at least in general terms, it can be said that there are no natural limits on the use privileges that stem from the concept of ownership, but that there are other important limitations, these being drawn from public laws and private agreement.[13] Nevertheless, it is helpful to focus a little on some of the core issues which are inherent in notions of ownership.

1.1.3 **The power to exclude**

A central feature of the idea of ownership is the power to exclude others from the particular item in question.[14] So, if A is, in the sense that English law embraces that concept,[15] the owner of a piece of land, he has the right to exclude everybody else from it. All people are, unless given permission to enter, or enjoying some other right of entry, excluded from the property and it is quite immaterial that they have never had any relationship with the person who owns the land. This is the trespassory aspect of ownership.[16]

As is evident from the above statement, there is a considerable caveat to the assertion that the power to exclude others is a core feature of the notion of ownership. In the context of land, this right to exclude obviously does not embrace those to whom the landowner has given permission to enter the property. Neither does it affect those who, through ownership of a relevant property right, have the right to enter. While it is true that the default position is that a landowner's right to exclude all from his home extends to representatives of the state,[17] it is also the case that the Home Office, in its work which informed the enactment of a legislative framework to enable the streamlining and regulation of the existing position,[18] was able to identify more than a thousand separate powers of entry to a person's property existing under UK legislation.[19] Such powers related to entry for specific purposes. A more general right of entry onto the land of others was conferred on the public at large by the Countryside and Rights of Way Act 2000,[20] which created a so-called 'right to roam' over certain types of land, the extent of such a right being defined in Part 1 of the Act.

These extensive inroads into the power of a property owner to exclude others from it are, in fact, indicative of the strength of this aspect of the concept of ownership; without specific exceptions being made, a landowner, and indeed the owner of other forms of property, has the right to prevent others from encroaching on that property. A related point is that, although the right to exclude is a core element of ownership, it is always open to the state to modify that right or, more radically, to remove ownership rights from a person altogether.[21] This latter event will occur if the state, in order to further some public purpose,[22] exercises a statutory right to purchase[23] land from a particular person

---

[13] S. Bright in Bright and Dewar, *Land Law*, 529 at 536.

[14] See Penner, *The Idea of Property in Law*, at 72.   [15] See Chapter 2.

[16] Harris, *Property and Justice*, 5.   [17] See *Entick v. Carrington* (1765) 2 Wils K.B. 274.

[18] See Protection of Freedoms Act 2012, ss 39–40.

[19] See Stone, *The Law of Entry, Search and Seizure* (5th edn) (Oxford, Oxford University Press, 2013), vi.

[20] For the increased recognition of generalized access to, and recreational rights over, land, see Gray and Gray, *Elements of Land Law* (5th edn) (Oxford, Oxford University Press, 2009), 10.6–10.7.52.

[21] This is referred to by Honoré, *Essays in Jurisprudence*, at 113 as the liability to execution.

[22] For a penetrating discussion of the use of such powers to further the commercial interests of private bodies, with particular reference to the United States, see K. Gray in Bright (ed.) *Modern Studies in Property Law* (vol. 6) (Oxford, Hart Publishing, 2011), 3.

[23] The requirement to compensate the landowner is long-standing and is now a requirement of Article 1 of the First Protocol of the European Convention on Human Rights, incorporated into English law by the Human Rights Act 1998, s. 1. See Chapter 3.

or body. Separate from this, and as part of the criminal process, the state has the power to confiscate a person's property[24] either in a generalized way by the imposition of a fine, or by a more specific order relating to particular identified property.[25] It is also the case that, under legislation, property can be transferred from one person to another without the consent of the former, examples of this being the power to reallocate property on divorce,[26] and the automatic vesting of a person's property in the trustee in bankruptcy following a bankruptcy order.[27]

All of this serves to demonstrate that, although English law has always placed great emphasis on the recognition and enforcement of property rights, it is wrong to regard such rights as being absolute and unassailable. Over very many years, such rights have been modified by legislation and, today, in considering the development of land law, one of the issues is the extent to which principles derived from the European Convention on Human Rights operate to do this, so as to prevent a person from enforcing a recognized property right.[28]

1.1.4 **The power to alienate**

The ownership of property amounts to wealth. Property has value in a number of ways. The item can simply be enjoyed for itself, as an item. An example of this is a work of art. In the case of land, enjoyment of the thing, itself, can entail it being used as a home. Alternatively, its principal value can be its capacity to produce income. In the case of land, its physical aspects can be exploited by means, for example, of farming. In the case of commercial or residential buildings they can be used to generate rental income. Indeed the desire to generate income from one's property, particularly at a time following the imposition of very low interest rates which have been in place since the financial crisis in the first years of the twenty-first century, has led to a proliferation of houses being acquired solely for the purpose of creating tenancies, this phenomenon being known as buy to let.

Whether property has been acquired principally so it can be enjoyed as an item, or a source of income, another aspect of its attraction is its tendency either to retain its capital value or, better still, for that value to increase.[29] For the owner to be able to realize the capital value of the property, it is, of course, necessary that he is able to alienate it by sale, thereby securing its exchange value.[30] It is also an aspect of ownership that a person may make a gift of his property, either while still alive or upon death,[31] and it is certainly the case that a normal incident of ownership is the power to alienate the item in question.[32] Recognizing this, the law is keen to strike out attempts to make property inalienable.[33]

---

[24] Such a power has existed since feudal times and was part of the law of escheat. See Chapter 2.

[25] See Proceeds of Crime Act 2002, Part 5 and, for a recent example, *Fletcher v. Chief Constable of Leicestershire Constabulary* [2013] EWHC 3357 (Admin). For a valuable discussion of the interrelationship between this Act and the Human Rights Act 2008 in respect of innocent volunteers of property, see *Sanam v. National Crime Agency* [2015] EWCA Civ. 1234 at [58]–[76] *per* Sir Terence Etherton QC.

[26] Matrimonial Causes Act 1973, s. 24.   [27] Insolvency Act 1986, s. 306.

[28] See Chapter 3.

[29] Some forms of property, for example gold, have no real use value and produce no income. They are acquired to seek to ensure the protection of the capital value of a person's possessions.

[30] For a detailed discussion of the importance of this, see J. Penner in Penner and Smith (eds), *Philosophical Foundations of Property Law* (Oxford, Oxford University Press, 2015), Chapter 11.

[31] The insistence by Penner, *The Idea of Property in Law*, at 88–96, that the power to alienate by gift should be distinguished from the power to do so by sale, the latter being part of the law of contract rather than the law of property, is puzzling. While the motivation for the two transactions is different, both rely on the power to alienate and, as such, both are part of the incidents of ownership.

[32] See *Doe d. Mitchinson v. Carter* (1798) 8 T.R. 57 at 60 *per* Lord Kenyon.

[33] See, e.g., *Re Brown* [1954] Ch. 39.

Nevertheless, it is possible that a person may have the right to exclude others from property but have very little, or indeed no, right to alienate the property while alive,[34] and only a very limited ability to do so on death and, indeed, in the case of certain lands held by the National Trust, no ability to alienate that land at all.[35]

1.1.5 **Land and property issues**

From the foregoing, it is apparent that the notion of ownership is a flexible one. At its core are the general powers to exclude the rest of the world from the thing in question and to be able to alienate it. From these core aspects, other powers of control and exploitation follow, powers which have been described as being part of 'the ownership spectrum'.[36] Because of the physical nature of land, the range of this spectrum is larger in respect of land than is the case with other forms of property. Particular features of land are that it is permanent and indestructible and, in the case of this country at least, where there is no scheme of land reclamation from the sea, finite: the amount of it will not increase. These characteristics make it both possible, and feasible, for ownership rights to be divided between different people, in some cases over successive generations, in a way that is not true with many other types of property.

1.2 **Possession**

One of the more important rights which can exist in relation to land is the right, physically, to possess it. This right can be shared amongst different people. Most obviously, more than one person can simultaneously have the right to possess. This will occur when there is concurrent ownership, such as a husband and wife together sharing the matrimonial home.[37] Alternatively, consecutive rights to possess the land can be created. A settlement of land can be created when land is transferred to A for life, thereafter to B. Such a settlement arose from a desire which, at one time at least, was very strong, to ensure dynastic succession to land. As will be seen at later stages in this book, English land law has been able to accommodate this situation and will recognize both A and B as having ownership rights in the land. A has the right to possess the land and to exclude others from it, but that right is limited to his lifetime. He is free to transfer that right to another person but all that he can transfer is his own, rather limited interest. B, on the other hand, does not have the right either to possess the land or to exclude others from it. He does, however, have a valuable interest in the land. After A's death, he, or possibly his successor, will acquire both of those rights. The law recognizes the value of B's interest, which he is free to alienate, by giving him the right to control A's use of the land.

Another common situation where a person cedes physical possession of land to another is when a lease is created. This is a commercial transaction where, for historical reasons, the landlord, or freeholder, is still, legally, regarded as being in possession of the property, his interest in that property being termed a reversion; his right, physically, to possess the land[38] reverts to him on the termination of the tenancy. Nevertheless, it is a transaction

---

[34] This was effectively the position of tenants who enjoyed security of tenure under the Rent Act 1977. They had a personal right of occupancy and the ability to exclude others, but no power to alienate the property during their lifetime.

[35] National Trust Act 1907, s. 21 and Sched. 1, Part 1.   [36] Harris, *Property and Justice*, at 5.

[37] See Chapter 7.

[38] Under the Law of Property Act (LPA) 1925, s. 201(1)(xix), possession is defined to include the receipt of rents and profits or the right to receive the same, thereby ensuring that, legally, a landlord is still regarded as being in possession of the land.

which results in more than one person concurrently owning interests in the property, those interests being akin to a form of ownership of it.

The preceding examples have focused on the possibility of dividing rights to possession of land amongst different people. Because the right to possession of land is regarded as one of the more important incidents of ownership, these types of situation are generally seen as the division of ownership rights between the parties involved. Other rights can, however, be created over land. For example, because of the nature of the property in question, it forms good security for a loan. Consequently, an important, and common, right to create over land is a mortgage, whereby the lender, or mortgagee, in return for his loan, acquires important rights over the land of the borrower or, as that person is referred to, the mortgagor.

The rights acquired by a mortgagee are sufficiently extensive to be able to regard him as having acquired ownership rights over the property. Indeed, as shall be seen, until 1925, the mortgagee did actually become the legal owner of the mortgaged property.[39]

1.3 Third-party rights

The previous section has been concerned, principally, with ownership rights. These rights, which can be divided between different people, tend to be open-ended in nature and relate to the control and management of the land. One of the key ownership rights, the right, physically, to possess the land, can be predetermined across more than one generation, so that a person is given a right to possess for the duration of his lifetime and, upon his death, the right to possess then passes to a nominated person. That person, as a result of his future right to possession of the land has, as will be seen, various powers to control the use of the land by the person currently entitled to possess that property.[40] The existence of such powers is necessary in order to protect his ownership rights in the same land. As well as ownership rights existing in relation to land, it is also common for people to have rights over land they do not own. These rights, which are essentially non-possessory in nature,[41] are quite tightly defined in scope. Broadly speaking, a principal, albeit not universal, characteristic of rights of this type, which are frequently referred to as third-party rights, is that the right is owned by one landowner and takes effect over the land of another. One example of such a right is a right of way one landowner has over nearby land. Such a right is termed an easement. A second instance is a right to prevent a neighbour from using his land in a particular way, for example for commercial purposes, or for the sale of intoxicating liquor. A right such as this is termed a restrictive covenant.

1.4 The conveyancing dimension

In view of the foregoing, it is evident that a number of people may, simultaneously, have interests in the same piece of land. A feature of the law of property is that these rights are binding not only upon the parties who were privy to their creation, and this is true of both ownership rights and of third-party rights. Rather, the rights which are created can affect successive owners of the relevant land. Thus, a right granted by the owner of a piece of land to a neighbour to cross it would have only limited utility if it was lost when that owner sold the land to another person. Unlike the law of contract, where the liabilities[42] under the

---

[39] See Chapter 11.   [40] See 2.6.3.1.   [41] See 12.1.4.6.

[42] Rights can now be conferred on someone who is not a party to the contract: Contracts (Rights of Third Parties) Act 1999. See *Prudential Assurance Co. Ltd v. Ayres* [2007] 3 All E.R. 946.

contract are personal to the parties who entered into that contract, once a particular right is recognized as part of the law of property or, as it is also put, as being a proprietary right, it takes effect against successive owners of the land in question. Those people are said to be bound by that right. So, in the above example, if certain conditions are satisfied, the new owner of the land will take subject to the right of way created by the former owner or, as that person is frequently referred to, his predecessor in title.

The fact that certain rights can be enforced against successive owners has important consequences. One such consequence is that the transfer of land is more complicated than the transfer of other forms of property, which are far less likely to be affected by the enduring rights of others. Ownership rights can, as has been seen, be fragmented and divided among different people. Again, a particular piece of land may be subject to a covenant restricting building upon it. From the point of view of a person buying that land, these are matters of major concern. A property developer will obviously not wish to buy a piece of land which is subject to an obligation prohibiting building upon it.

One of the tasks of land law is to seek to reconcile competing interests. On the one hand, people who enjoy rights in or over land wish to ensure that such rights remain in existence, whoever currently owns that land. On the other, people who buy land wish to acquire as many rights as possible in it and to be free of other people's rights, or at least be able to discover, as easily as possible, before buying the land, what those other rights are. The greater the protection given to people claiming rights in another's land, the more difficult it can be to enter into commercial transactions involving that land.

This tension between the protection of the use value of land, and the facilitation of the ability to sell it, its exchange value, which has been described as being the protection of dynamic security as opposed to static security,[43] lies at the heart of a number of policy issues affecting modern land law. The exchange value, also often referred to as the conveyancing dimension, is one which the law has traditionally favoured. So, for example, in a famous statement made in the 1960s, Lord Upjohn said, 'It has been the policy of the law for over a hundred years to simplify and facilitate transactions in real property.'[44] While it is undoubtedly true that this policy has been advanced over a prolonged period, both by statute and case law, as will be seen, the position is more nuanced than the statement would appear.

1.4.1 **The *numerus clausus* principle**

To facilitate conveyancing, the law has adopted a number of strategies. One of these is to limit the number of rights which are admitted to the category of proprietary rights: a strategy termed the *numerus clausus* principle.[45] Under this principle, while the law recognizes that landowners are free to enter into as many commercial transactions affecting the land as they please, and these transactions are, of course, entirely enforceable by the original parties to them, it constrains their ability to create new types of proprietary rights which will adversely affect future owners of the land.[46] The number of proprietary rights recognized by the law is limited, and it is not open to landowners to fashion new rights that will continue to affect the land through successive periods of ownership.[47] The traditional

---

[43] Cooke, *Land Law* (2nd edn) (Oxford, Clarendon Law Series, 2012), 9.

[44] *National Provincial Bank Ltd v. Ainsworth* [1965] A.C. 1175 at 1233.

[45] See B. McFarlane in Gravells (ed.), *Landmark Cases in Land Law* (Oxford: Hart Publishing, 2003), Chapter 1.

[46] See also M. Dixon in Tee (ed.), *Land Law: Issues, Debates, Policy* (Cullompton: Willan Publishing, 2001), Chapter 1.

[47] See *Keppel v. Bailey* (1833) 2 My & K 517 at 533 *per* Lord Brougham. For statutory endorsement of this principle, see LPA 1925, s. 4.

argument for this policy is that, were the law otherwise, and a wider variety of property rights were allowed to exist than is currently the case, it would adversely affect the alienability of land. This argument has met with an interesting, and sceptical, response, where the question was raised as to whether the existence of a greater number of rights binding the land to be sold should be reflected in the price of the land, rather than it being simply accepted that the existence of those rights would tend to make the land affected difficult to alienate.[48] In other words, matters such as this are best left to the market. Whatever the force of that argument, however, it was also recognized by the same author that the liberalization of the rules as to the ability to create new property rights might create problems in the future, in that an inability to terminate such rights might prevent desirable developments of that land many years after the particular obligation had been created:[49] a separate argument from the original, traditional, one of impeding the free alienability of land. The policy, which is very well established, seems to be sound.

Notwithstanding the existence of a strong principle against the creation of new species of property rights, an attempt was made to do just that in a series of cases which sought to establish the existence of a new right: the deserted wife's equity.[50] This attempt failed. As Lord Wilberforce put it:

> Before a right or interest can be admitted into the category of property, it must be definable, identifiable by third parties, capable in its nature of assumption by third parties, and have some degree of permanence and stability.[51]

Although this passage has been criticized as being somewhat circular,[52] the main feature of it, which is intended to limit the number of property rights, is the insistence that property rights need to be certain in nature and easily identifiable. Hence, although the courts have been prepared to recognize new instances of existing categories of right,[53] they have not, in recent times, created any new species of right, that task having been carried out by legislation.[54]

1.4.2 Formal requirements

Consistent with its policy of requiring property rights to be certain in nature, the law has also insisted upon certain formalities being observed before such rights could be created.[55] As a general rule, in order to transfer land or create an interest in it, one must use a deed.[56] A deed is a formal document which explicitly makes clear that it is intended to be a deed, is signed by the person making it in the presence of a witness who attests the signature, and is delivered as a deed.[57] Similarly, contracts for the sale of land, or an interest in land,

---

[48] B. Rudden in Bell and Eekelaar, *Oxford Essays in Jurisprudence* (3rd series) (Oxford: Oxford University Press, 1997), 239 at 246.

[49] Rudden, *Essays in Jurisprudence*, at 259.

[50] See, e.g., *Bendall v. McWhirter* [1952] 2 Q.B. 406; *Street v. Denham* [1954] 1 W.L.R. 624. See Chapter 4, Class F: A spouse's statutory right of occupation, p. 102.

[51] *National Provincial Bank Ltd v. Ainsworth, supra*, at 247–8.

[52] Gray and Gray, *Elements of Land Law*, 97–8. J.-P. Hinojosa [2000] Conv. 114 at 116–22.

[53] See 12.1.4.1.

[54] See Matrimonial Homes Act 1967, ss. 1 and 2; Land Registration Act 2002, s. 116.

[55] For a valuable discussion of the reasons for formal requirements, see P. Critchley in Bright and Dewar, *Land Law*, Chapter 20.

[56] LPA 1925, s. 52. There are a number of exceptions to this, the most important being a lease for a period of less than three years: ibid., s. 54(2).

[57] Law of Property (Miscellaneous Provisions) Act 1989, ss. 1–2 replacing the old requirement that, to be a deed, a document had to be signed, sealed, and delivered.

are required to be in writing.[58] In the future, it is intended that such formalities will be satisfied by electronic means,[59] but the essential need for formal requirements to be met will remain.

1.4.3 Registration

With a view to facilitating conveyancing, systems of registration were also introduced. The two main systems, which are mutually exclusive, provide, in one case, for various interests in the land of others to be registered, and, in the other, for the ownership of the land *itself* to be registered. This latter system of registration, termed registration of title, operates so that the registration entry for a piece of land records not only the registration of the ownership of it, but, subject to a category of interest termed 'rights which override registration',[60] also the interests which other people have over that land.

The purpose of the registration systems is to make it as straightforward as possible for a purchaser of land to discover, before buying the property, what rights he will take subject to and, in the case of registration of title, to assure him that the seller actually owns the land he is purporting to transfer. These systems undoubtedly facilitate the conveyancing process. This facilitation, however, comes at a price.

If a person has a right over another person's land then, from a conveyancing perspective, it is desirable that such a right is easily discoverable. The process devised to implement such a policy is to make as many rights as possible registrable. A purchaser may then easily discover[61] what rights affect the land which is being bought. If no rights have been registered, then the purchaser is entitled to assume that there are no such rights: the general sanction for a failure to register a registrable interest being that it is void against a purchaser of the land.[62] The difficulty with this is that a person who possesses a right may be quite unaware of registration requirements, particularly if the right in question has arisen in an informal situation. In such situations, especially where the person claiming the right actually lives in the property, the argument that the law should always favour simplification of conveyancing becomes less compelling.

The task of reconciling the competing interests of those claiming rights in land and the pressure to simplify conveyancing has become an issue of increased importance in modern times. How the law has approached this task will be examined fully in various parts of this book. In order to do this, it is first necessary to appreciate not only what constitutes land but also the principles upon which the ownership of land, and interests in land, are based.

1.5 Real property

Some legal systems, when classifying different forms of property, adopt a division between movable and immovable property. English law did not do this.[63] Rather, for historical reasons, the essential difference is between real property and personal property, with land coming into the former category, and all other forms of property into the latter.

---

[58] Ibid., s. 2. See 14.2.   [59] Electronic Communications Act 2000, s. 8(2)(a)(b).
[60] See Chapter 5.   [61] For the defects in the registration system, see Chapter 4.
[62] For a more detailed discussion of this, see Chapter 4.
[63] English law adopts this classification in cases involving the conflict of laws. See Hill and Ní Shúilleabháin, Clarkson and Hill, *The Conflict of Laws* (5th edn) (Oxford: Oxford University Press, 2016), 471–3.

1.5.1 **Origins of the distinction**

The basis for the distinction in English law between real property and personal property is rooted in history and rests upon the different remedies available in the event of interference with a person's rights to property. In the case of land, if a person was dispossessed by another he could bring an action to recover the thing itself and did not have to be content with damages for trespass. As what was recovered was the land itself, the type of action involved was termed a real action; that is, an action relating to the thing or, as it was put in Latin, the *res*. If, on the other hand, the wrongdoer had dispossessed a person of his horse, there was no right to recover the actual property;[64] the action was for damages only, the measure of those damages being, in general, the value of the property. Because of the nature of the actions, property which could be recovered by an action was termed real property. Other forms of property were categorized as personal property, or personalty. The classification was based upon the process of execution of a judicial order vindicating the right.[65]

1.5.2 **Proprietary and personal actions**

The existence of a specific right of recovery in the case of one type of property and the alternative remedy in the case of other types led to the English classification of property into being either real or personal. The original sharp edges of this distinction have been blunted over time, however, as the possibility of an award of damages rather than a form of specific enforcement in the case of real property,[66] and the reverse in the case of personal property, became established.[67] Nevertheless, the distinction was the basis of classification of property in this country. A rather different effect of this distinction has, however, also been made between what has been termed a property rule on the one hand, and a liability rule on the other. In the case of the former, if the holder of a particular right can refuse to release it to another person in return for a payment of money, then this is analysed as being a property right. If, however, that other person may, on the payment of compensation, the level of that compensation being set by a court or other adjudicator, override that person's right, then this is classified as being a liability right.[68] While plausible, and at times influential,[69] this classification is flawed and, potentially, highly misleading.[70] The main problem with it is the inherent confusion between the vindication or recognition of a right and the determination of the appropriate remedy for the wrong which has been committed. It obscures the essential difference between the creation of property rights, which endure through successive periods of ownership, and personal rights where, in general, liability is limited to the person privy to the creation of the particular right.

The hallmark of a property right is its enforceability against a person other than the one who was party to its creation. The issue is what has been described as the 'sphere of enforceability', not the order that the court will make'.[71] Personal liability, which must be distinguished from a personal property right, occurs when the person against whom the

---

[64] See Bridge, Gullifer, McMeel and Worthington, *The Law of Personal Property* (London: Sweet & Maxwell, 2013), 1–012. The position as to remedies has since been modified: see Common Law Procedure Act 1854, s. 78; Torts (Interference with Goods) Act 1977, s. 3.

[65] See T.C. Williams (1888) 4 L.Q.R. 394 at 398.

[66] See Chancery Amendment Act 1858, s. 2; Supreme Court Act (now Senior Courts Act) 1981, s. 50.

[67] See Common Law Procedure Act 1854, s. 78; Torts (Interference with Goods) Act 1977, s. 3.

[68] See G. Calabresi and A.D. Melamed (1971–2) 85 Harv. L.R. 1089, especially at 1105–6.

[69] See, e.g., S. Grattan in Hopkins (ed.) *Modern Studies in Property Law* (vol. 7) (Oxford: Hart Publishing, 2013), 376 at 383.

[70] See Harris, *Property and Justice*, at 148; Penner, *The Idea of Property in Law*, at 67.

[71] W.J. Swadling in Birks (ed.), *English Private Law* (Oxford, Oxford University Press, 2000), 4.48.

action is brought has, through some conduct on his part, occasioned liability to arise. A couple of examples may assist.

1.5.3 **Rights and remedies**

A has been granted a right of light by B over his (B's) land. B then starts to build in such a way as to obstruct that right. A clearly has a right of action against B, and that right may be enforced in one of two ways. The wrongful behaviour may be stopped by an injunction restraining B from interfering with that right, or it may be allowed to continue and A is compensated by the award of damages in lieu of an injunction.[72] At this stage, it is immaterial whether A is enforcing a proprietary right or a personal right. If, however, B has sold his land to C, and it is C who is infringing A's right to light then it is of critical importance as to whether or not A's right is a personal right or a proprietary right. If, as is quite possible, it is a proprietary right then A has a cause of action against C. Again, however, the remedy might be either an injunction or damages in lieu thereof. The key point is that the existence of the liability depends upon whether A has a property right. If he does, he can enforce it against C and then the nature of the remedy available, which is a secondary issue, does not alter the fact that the right which is being vindicated is a property right. The fact that the remedy may be pecuniary in nature and has the consequence of, in effect, securing the compulsory purchase of that right does not alter that original analysis. If, on the other hand, the original right in question is merely a personal right, then A has no remedy of any kind against C. Any rights he has are against B which, in the instant case, as B no longer owns the land, can only be pecuniary. This fundamental point can be reinforced by a second, seemingly obvious, scenario. E is injured by a car owned and driven by F. F later sells the car to G. E has only a personal right and that right is exercisable solely against F. He has no right at all against G, the current owner of the car.

1.5.4 **Tangible and intangible property**

A further division in the categorization of property is that between tangible and intangible property. The former category is self-explanatory and includes items such as a car or a television. Intangible property, also referred to as a *chose in action*, is something which is capable of exploitation. It is an object of wealth, but is not a physical entity.[73] The most valuable form of intangible property is that which is grouped under the generic heading of intellectual property, prominent examples of which are patents and copyrights.[74] The existence of copyright in an artistic or literary work entails the owner of that right being able to prevent other people from exploiting that work without permission.[75] It is normal for that permission to be given in return for payment, so that the owner of a copyright in a book will receive payment, termed royalties, on the sale of that book and will also be entitled to payments when parts of it are photocopied. Similarly, the composer or writer of songs will receive payments when their compositions are played, and such payments can form a very

---

[72] For the jurisdiction to award damages in lieu of an injunction, see 13.6.1.

[73] See Lawson and Rudden, *The Law of Property*, 20–9. The recent assertion that to exist as a property right it must be physically located, McFarlane, *The Structure of Property Law* (Oxford, Hart Publishing, 2008), 132 is untenable. For a discussion of intellectual property in this context, see Penner, *The Idea of Property in Law* (Oxford, Oxford University Press, 2000), 118–20 and for a critique of McFarlane's views, see S. Gardner in Hopkins (ed.) *Modern Studies in Property Law* (vol. 7), Chapter 15.

[74] See D.F. Libling (1978) 94 L.Q.R. 103 dealing principally with the concept of passing off, the action whereby one person is prevented from trading his property under the pretence that it is a different, and better known, brand.

[75] See, e.g., *Fisher v. Brooker* [2009] UKHL 41 at [8] *per* Lord Hope.

substantial income stream. The owner of the copyright will also be entitled to compensation if the rights inherent in that copyright are infringed by actions such as plagiarism, and this is true even if the plagiarism is not done intentionally, as can easily happen when part of an existing musical composition is incorporated into what is thought to have been an original composition. As such, these rights can have a significant capital value.

1.5.5 Leases

Today, leases are a common form of land holding and very much a part of land law. In the earliest days of the development of the subject, however, this was not so. At the outset, land law was based upon the feudal system.[76] One held land from a superior lord in return for the performance of various duties. How one held the land was indicative of one's status in society. A lease was seen as a commercial transaction and, as such, did not fit into the feudal system of landholding. Because of this, the relationship between the landlord and the tenant was not seen as being part of land law. A tenant who had been dispossessed could not, therefore, recover the land by bringing a real action and, as a result, a lease was classified as personal property.

In time, and in particular when the feudal system began to decay, it became increasingly unrealistic to view the lease in this way. Nevertheless, they were still regarded as being part of the law of personalty but, in recognition of the importance of the lease with regard to land, they are now termed chattels real. The term 'chattel' reflects the fact that leases were originally regarded as personal property, and the addition of the word 'real' recognizes the importance of the lease in land law.

1.5.6 The distinction today

The main reason for distinguishing between real property and personal property used to be that different rules of inheritance applied to the two types of property in the event of a person dying intestate. This is no longer the case and s. 46 of the Administration of Estates Act 1925 now provides for the devolution of a deceased's property upon intestacy. If a testator makes a will leaving real property to one person and personal property to another,[77] then the distinction will be important. Aside from that, the term 'real property' is used essentially to differentiate between what the law considers to be land and other forms of property.

1.6 The meaning of land

Land is defined elaborately by s. 205(1)(ix) of the Law of Property Act (LPA) 1925 to include not just the physical entity itself. Also within the definition are things such as mines and minerals found underneath the land, buildings on the land, and rights over land, such as easements, as well as some archaic rights derived from the feudal system such as an advowson, which is the right to present a clergyman to a living, which, for some reason, was classed as real property. The extent of ownership of land can now be more fully considered.

1.6.1 The extent of ownership

The extent of one's ownership of land is encompassed in the somewhat misleading Latin phrase, which dates back to at least the thirteenth century,[78] that: *cuius est solum eius est*

---

[76] See Chapter 2.   [77] See, e.g., *Re Hemphorne* [1938] 1 Ch. 208.

[78] See the analysis in *Bocardo SA v. Star Energy UK Onshore Ltd* [2011] 1 A.C. 380 at [18]–[28] *per* Lord Hope.

usque ad coelum et ad inferos. This means that he who owns the land owns everything 'up to the sky and down to the centre of the earth'.[79] Not surprisingly, such an extreme statement is not, particularly in the modern world, without its problems, and Lord Wilberforce commented that it was 'so sweeping, unscientific and unpractical that it is unlikely to appeal to the common law mind'.[80] More recently, in *Bocardo SA v. Star Energy UK Onshore Ltd*,[81] Aitkens J., sitting in the Court of Appeal, asserted that the maxim did not represent English law. On appeal, however, Lord Hope expressed the view that it was a little hasty to assert that the maxim was not part of the law, although he did concede that the principle was neither absolute nor consistent in its application between downward and upward ownership.[82] That said, the ownership of land beneath the surface has been of particular value to the super rich in London where, if money is no object and one cannot build upwards or sideways, there remains the possibility of extending the property by digging down.[83]

In terms of downward ownership,[84] this means that the landowner owns the mines and minerals contained in the land.[85] This is subject to statutory exceptions, so that coal, gas, and petroleum found under land are now subject to public ownership.[86] In *Bocardo*, the defendant had a licence to drill for oil. To extract the oil, it drilled under the claimant's land, at depths of up to 3,000 feet, and the claimant brought an action for trespass. This claim was upheld by the Supreme Court although, by a majority, only relatively nominal damages were awarded. In holding that the action, which occasioned no damage to the claimant's land, amounted to trespass,[87] the argument that the land was not owned by the claimant was rejected. Lord Hope accepted that the maxim could not apply literally, but that the facts of the instant case did not get anywhere near to approaching the point of absurdity. Where, as here, there were substances which could be exploited, this raised the question as to who, if anyone, was the owner of the strata where those substances were to be found. In his view, the only plausible candidate was the registered owner of the land above, a conclusion which was exactly in line with the maxim.[88]

As well as the strata beneath the surface of the land, items found buried in the soil, unless such items constitute treasure trove[89] belong to the owner of the land.[90] This is so, unless the previous owner of the object can be found. So, for example, in *Elwes v. Brigg Gas Co.*,[91] a prehistoric boat buried six feet below the surface of the land was held to belong to the landlord, as opposed to the tenant who had discovered it. The basis of this was not that

---

[79] *Corbett v. Hill* (1870) L.R. 9 Eq. 671 at 673 *per* Sir William James V.-C. (column of air above a room). See also *Mitchell v. Manley* [1914] 1 Ch. 438 at 450 *per* Cozens-Hardy M.R.

[80] *Commissioner for Railways v. Valuer-General* [1974] A.C. 328 at 351.

[81] [2010] 1 All E.R. 26 at [59].

[82] *Bocardo SA v. Star Energy Weald Basin Ltd* [2011] 1 A.C. 380 at [14].

[83] Dorling, *All that is Solid* (London, Allen Lane, 2014), 122.

[84] See J. Howell (2002) 53 N.I.L.Q. 268. For an interesting account of the extent of subterranean ownership of land, with particular reference to the Post Office, see A. Turner [2011] Conv. 465. See also J. Morgan (2013) 62 I.C.L.Q. 813 discussing carbon capture and storage.

[85] For a review of the some of the problems pertaining to this issue, see (2016) Law Com. Consultation Paper, No.227 at 3.15–3.67.

[86] Petroleum Act 1998, s. 2 (replacing earlier legislation); Coal Industry Act 1994, ss 7(3), 9.

[87] See also *Bulli Coal Mining Company v. Osborne* [1899] A.C. 351

[88] [2011] 1 A.C. 380 at [15]. See also *Gorst v. Knight* [2018] EWHC 613 (Ch) on the question of whether a long lease of a maisonette extended to the subsoil beneath it.

[89] For the definition of which, see Treasure Act 1996, ss 1–3. *Ex gratia* payments are normally made to the finder of treasure trove by the Secretary of State. For an excellent critique of the current law relating to treasure trove and its effect on archaeological practice, see J. Bray [2013] Conv. 265.

[90] For a critical discussion of this, see N.E. Palmer in Meisel and Cook (eds), *Property and Protection: Essays in Honour of Brian Harvey* (Oxford, Hart Publishing, 2000), Chapter 1.

[91] (1886) 33 Ch.D. 562. See also *South Staffordshire Water Co. v. Sharman* [1896] 2 Q.B. 44 (rings found in mud at the bottom of a pond were part of the land); *Waverley Borough Council v. Fletcher* [1996] Q.B. 334.

the item had become part of the land.[92] Indeed, had that been the case the identity of the original owner of the item would have been irrelevant.[93] Rather it was that, as the landlord was in possession of the land, including that part of the land which was below the surface, at the time when the lease was granted, he was regarded as being in possession of the chattel, and so had a better claim to it than the tenant.[94] It was quite immaterial to this finding that, until the boat was discovered, the landlord was unaware of its existence.

1.6.2 Items found on the land

Although not directly relevant to the issue of the extent of land ownership, it is convenient at this stage to consider the related issue of the ownership of chattels found on the land. In the case of objects found on the surface of the land, a distinction is drawn between situations when the object is found by a person who is on the land lawfully and where it is found by a trespasser. This issue was fully reviewed by the Court of Appeal in *Parker v. British Airways*.[95] The plaintiff was in the executive lounge at an airport when he found a bracelet on the floor. He handed it in to one of the airport staff, together with his name and address, and asked them to contact him if the owner could not be found. He later discovered that the defendants had sold the bracelet for £850 and he claimed to be entitled to the money. His claim succeeded.

To the evident surprise of Donaldson L.J., who gave the leading judgment, the law with regard to this issue was unclear. Having reviewed the authorities, he first of all recognized that, if the true owner of the property came forward, that person would have the best claim of all to the property.[96] The contest, therefore, is not generally to determine, absolutely, who is the owner of the chattel in question. The issue is simply, as between two claimants, which of them has the better right to it. As will be seen, this is an approach applied generally in disputes to rights to possession in land law cases.[97] He then articulated the relevant principles to be applied.

First, he stated that the finder of a chattel acquires no rights over it unless it has been abandoned[98] or lost and then taken into his care and control.[99] If the finder is a trespasser, or has a dishonest intent, then, in his view that person acquires only very limited rights. The weakness of these rights is manifest only against the true owner of the property and, it seems, the occupier of the land. As against other people, the fact of possession confers on the person a possessory title, which is good against them. This latter point is illustrated by *Costello v. Chief Constable of Derbyshire Constabulary*.[100] The police lawfully took possession of a car in the belief that it had been stolen. At the time when they did this, the car was in the possession of the claimant. When, in 1997, the statutory purpose for which

[92] (1886) 33 Ch.D. 562 at 566 *per* Chitty J., although contrast *City of London Corporation v Appleyard* [1963] 1 W.L.R. 982 at 987 *per* McNair J.

[93] See also McFarlane, *The Structure of Property Law*, 156–8.

[94] See Hickey, *Property and the Law of Finders* (Oxford: Hart Publishing, 2010), 28–49.

[95] [1982] Q.B. 1004. See S.A. Roberts (1982) 45 M.L.R. 683.

[96] *Moffatt v. Kazana* [1969] 2 Q.B. 152.

[97] See Chapter 7.

[98] For an interesting, comparative, analysis of the proprietary consequences of abandonment, see J. Griffiths-Baker (2007) 36 C.L.W.R. 16. See also, A.H. Hudson (1984) 100 L.Q.R. 110, although contrast R. Hickey [2016] Conv. 28. For the problems associated with the practice known as freeganism, that is taking goods, often food, which appear to be abandoned, see S. Thomas (2010) 30 L.S. 98.

[99] [1982] Q.B. 1004 at 1017. For justified criticism of the need for the chattel to have been lost or abandoned with respect to a claimant who asserts title after the chattel has been found, see Hickey, *Property and the Law of Finders*, Chapter 4; Roberts (1982) 45 M.L.R. 007.

[100] [2001] 3 All E.R. 150. See also *Webb v. Chief Constable of Merseyside Police* [2000] Q.B. 427. See G. Battersby (2002) 65 M.L.R. 603.

the police were authorized to hold the car had been exhausted, the claimant demanded its return. The police refused to return the car on the ground that the claimant knew it to have been stolen. The Court of Appeal decided in favour of the claimant. According to Lightman J.:

> The fact of possession of a chattel of itself gives to the possessor a possessory title and the possessor is entitled to rely on such title without reference to the circumstances in which such possession was obtained; his entitlement to do so is not prejudiced by the fact that he obtained such possession unlawfully or by an illegal transaction.[101]

On this basis, it was held that the claimant had a better right to the car than did the police and they were ordered to return the car to him.

Ultimately, the issue in cases of this nature is who has the better right to the chattel in question. The finder of a lost or abandoned chattel will have a better right to it than everyone other than the true owner of the property,[102] unless the occupier of the land on which the item was found has a better right to it. To establish a better right than the finder, the occupier must have manifested an intention to exercise control over the land and the things which might be found upon it.[103]

1.6.3 **Degree of control**

This issue, the degree of control exercised over the place where the property was found, is the most contentious part of this area of the law. As a result it is difficult to disagree with the sentiment that, in practice, the judges have, first, decided where the merits of the case lay and then concealed that policy decision behind a finding as to whether or not the occupier did or did not have possession of the disputed item.[104] The law would be a lot easier to apply, and arguably more coherent, if it had simply opted for holding that either, in all cases, the finder of a lost object, wherever found, had a good title against all the world save for the true owner or, alternatively, that in such circumstances, title should vest in the possessor of the land on which it was found.[105] This course has not been taken and, instead, one is left with a test which is difficult to apply, in that it focuses on the degree of control over the property exercised by the owner of it.

1.6.3.1 **Finders**

An early decision which favoured the finder is the famous, and much criticized,[106] case of *Bridges v. Hawkesworth*.[107] The plaintiff, a travelling salesman, found a parcel on the floor in a public part of a shop. He immediately showed it to the shop assistant and it was discovered that it contained £65 in banknotes. The parcel was left with the defendant, the shopkeeper, and three years later when attempts to trace the true owner had failed, the

---

[101] [2001] 3 All E.R. 157. Contrast *Hibbert v. McKiernan* [1948] 2 K.B. 142, where the notion that a thief could obtain any sort of title was regarded as 'fantastic': at 151 *per* Humphreys J. For similar hostility to such an outcome, see R. Hickey in Hopkins, *Modern Studies in Property Law*, Chapter 18 and in Douglas, Hickey, and Waring, *Landmark Cases in Property Law* (Oxford, Hart Publishing, 2015), 131 at 148–9.

[102] See *Armorie v. Delamirei* (1722) 1 Str. 505. (Chimney sweep finding a jewel in a chimney had a better right to it than the jeweller to whom he had entrusted it.)

[103] *Parker v. British Airways Board* [1982] Q.B. 1004 at 1007–8 *per* Donaldson L.J.

[104] D.R. Harris in A.G. Guest (ed.), *Essays in Jurisprudence*, 69 at 84.

[105] See *Hannah v. Peel* [1905] K.B. 509 at 513 *per* Birkett J.

[106] See, e.g., A. G. Goodhart (1928) 3 C.L.J. 195, who argued, at 202–3, that the case was wrongly decided. It was described as a 'much-battered case' in *Hibbert v. McKiernan, supra*, at 149 *per* Lord Goddard C.J.

[107] (1851) 21 L.J.Q.B. 75.

plaintiff sued for the recovery of the money. It was held that the general rule of law was that the finder of a lost article is entitled to it against all persons except the true owner. This general rule was applicable save where the goods in question had, before they were found, been taken into the custody of the landowner or within the protection of his house, neither of which had occurred in *Bridges v. Hawkesworth* itself.[108]

As against this, however, was the approach taken in *South Staffordshire Water Company v. Sharman*.[109] This case concerned a dispute as to the entitlement to rings found stuck in mud at the bottom of a pool. It was held that the freeholder of the land had a better right to the rings than the person who had found them. In reaching this conclusion, Lord Russell C.J. distinguished *Bridges v Hawkesworth* on the basis, even though this had not been a ground for the decision, that in that case the bundle of notes had been dropped in a place to which the general public had access and over which the shopkeeper did not exercise any control. In his view,

> the general principle seems to be that where a person has possession of house or land, with a manifest intention to exercise control over it and the things which may be upon it or in it, then, if something is found on that land, whether by an employee of the owner or by a stranger, the presumption is that possession of that is in the owner of the *locus in quo*.[110]

Although this question of the degree of control over the land or, more accurately, the items left on it had re-emerged to arrive at different results as to the entitlement to such items,[111] the position, at least until *Parker*, seemed to be that 'There is a consistent line of cases which shows that there is a legal presumption that the owner of the land is the owner of the chattels found on the land'.[112] Nevertheless, in *Parker* it was held that, although access to the executive lounge was limited to first-class customers, because no attempt was made to search for lost articles there was, as such, no attempt to exert control over such property. The result was that the person finding the bracelet had a better right to it than the owner of the land on which it was found.

It is easy to see that the resolution of disputes of this nature by recourse to a test based on the degree of control exercised over lost items may be fraught with difficulty, both as to what part of a shop a member of the public is entitled to go into without express permission (a changing room perhaps), or the general control which the landowner seeks to exercise over lost goods. (Would a notice requesting customers to hand in any lost items suffice to assert such control?)[113] The issue of claims to chattels found on another person's land was considered again in *Waverley Borough Council v. Fletcher*.[114] The plaintiff council owned an open access park. It was council policy not to allow people to use metal detectors in the park and this policy was implemented not by the enactment of byelaws but by placing prohibitory notices in the park, although it was admitted that these notices were often pulled down. The defendant, who was unaware of the council's policy, used his detector in the park and was thus able to discover a medieval bronze brooch some nine inches below the surface of the land, which he recovered by digging it up. He offered it to the coroner as treasure trove but the offer was declined. The council then claimed to be

---

[108] Ibid. at 78 *per* Patteson J.   [109] [1896] 2 Q.B. 44 .   [110] Ibid. at 47.

[111] Compare *Hibbert v. McKiernan, supra* (trespasser on golf course guilty of stealing lost golf balls from the owner of the course) and, to the same effect, *R. v. Rostron (Terry)* [2003] EWCA Civ. 2206 with *Hannah v. Peel* [1945] K.B. 509. (Soldier occupying a house which had been requisitioned in World War Two had better title to a lost brooch than the owner of the house who had never actually possessed it.)

[112] *Re Cohen* [1953] Ch. 88 at 92–3 *per* Vaisey J. See also *Johnson v. Pickering* [1907] 2 K.B. 437 at 444–5 *per* Lawrance J.

[113] See also Goodhart, (1928) 3 C.L.J. 195, at 199–200.

[114] [1996] Q.B. 334. See J. Stevens [1996] Conv. 216.

entitled to the brooch and the action was resisted by the defendant. The Court of Appeal found in favour of the council.

Auld L.J. restated the views expressed in *Parker*. He said that where an article is found in or attached to the land then, as between the owner or lawful possessor of the land and the finder of the article, the owner or possessor of the land has the better title to it. When the article is unattached to the land then, as between these two rival claims, the finder has the better right to the article unless the possessor of the land has exercised such manifest control over the land as to indicate an intention to control the land and anything which might be found upon it.[115] In the present case, the finder lost his claim on two grounds. First, because the brooch was found under the ground this, of itself, meant that the owner of the land had the better right to it. Second, although the public had a right of general access to the park, that right did not extend to digging,[116] so that activity of this sort, which was outside the scope of the general licence to use the park, made the claimant a trespasser with the result that any claim by the finder to the chattel was weaker than that of the occupier of the land.

1.6.3.2 Trespassers

It will be observed that, in both *Parker v. British Airways* and *Waverly Borough Council v. Fletcher*, the status of the finder was considered to be important; if the finder was a trespasser then his claim to the chattel is said to be weaker than that of the occupier of the land. This seems highly questionable. As has been pointed out, if in *Parker*, the finder had simply put the brooch in his pocket and had not alerted the British Airways staff of his find then, although he might be said to have been behaving dishonestly, it is difficult to see why that should enhance the claim of British Airways to the brooch.[117] Similarly, if a friend of Mr Parker who was flying economy class accompanied him into the executive lounge, where he was not entitled to be, and he found the brooch, it is not at all obvious why his claim to it, as against British Airways, should fail. It is true that in cases of trespass, the occupier of the land may find it easier to show the requisite degree of control to establish possession of the chattel and to be able to assert a stronger title to it than the finder, but if he cannot do this, then the title of the finder should be stronger than that of the occupier of the land regardless of the legal status of the finder. Distaste for dishonest people and for trespassers should not alter the general principles applicable when resolving disputes between the occupier of land and a person who finds chattels on that land as to who has the better title to the particular object in question.[118]

One purported justification for this position that, because 'every householder or occupier of land intends to exclude thieves and wrongdoers from the property occupied by him, and this confers on him a special property in good found on his land',[119] fails to convince. An assertion of the existence of some special property serves simply to disguise the fact that there is no orthodox justification for the proposition in question. It would be better, rather than adopting various mental contortions, to adopt a general view that, in all cases, the owner or occupier of land has a better right to it than any person who finds it:[120] an outcome which might make it more likely for the person who lost the item to be reunited with it.

---

[115] *Waverly Borough Council v. Fletcher* [1996] Q.B. 334 at 336.

[116] Cf. *The Calgarth* [1927] P. 93 at 110 *per* Scrutton L.J.

[117] Battersby, (2002) 65 M.L.R. 604–5. See also Roberts, (1982) 45 M.L.R. 687–8; Hickey, *Property and the Law of Finders*, 132–5.

[118] In *Parker*, Sir David Cairns reserved his opinion on this matter: see [1982] Q.B. 1004 at 1021.

[119] *Hibbert v. McKiernan, supra*, at 150 *per* Lord Goddard C.J.

[120] See also D.R. Harris, *Essays in Jurisprudence*, at 93.

1.6.4 **Airspace**

In this context, the maxim that he who owns land does so up to the sky and down to the centre of the earth is particularly apt to mislead, and it has been accepted that it is not generally applicable in respect of upwards ownership.[121] Nevertheless, it has long been accepted that a physical incursion into the airspace over a person's land is capable of amounting to a trespass. So, in *Kelsen v. Imperial Tobacco Co. (of Great Britain and Ireland) Ltd*,[122] a mandatory injunction was granted to secure the removal of an advertising sign which infringed the airspace above the plaintiff's single-storey shop.

It was made clear that the basis of the cause of action was in trespass rather than nuisance;[123] that it was in respect of the intrusion onto the property and not because it affected the enjoyment of the land in any way. On this basis, it was accepted that a landowner had the right to object to someone putting anything, such as a wire, over his land at any height.[124] Similarly, a landowner, provided he does not, himself, have to trespass on his neighbour's land to do it, has the right to lop overhanging branches,[125] but, if this is done, any fruit, or suchlike, remains the property of the neighbour.[126]

1.6.5 **Aircraft**

If one takes the maxim to its logical extreme, difficulties would be faced in the context of overflying aircraft. In the case of civil aircraft, the matter is regulated by statute. Section 76 of the Civil Aircraft Act 1982 provides that no action for trespass or nuisance is available for the flight of aircraft over land at a reasonable height, provided that the proper regulations have been observed. This would seem to reflect the general law, because as long ago as 1815, in a judgment which was admittedly unsympathetic to the notion that a landowner also owns the airspace over the land, it was said that a balloonist would not be liable in trespass for flying over a person's land.[127] This was confirmed in *Bernstein of Leigh (Baron) v. Skyviews & General Ltd*,[128] where the defendant flew a light aeroplane over the plaintiff's country house to photograph it and then sell the photograph to him. The plaintiff sued for trespass and breach of privacy. He lost. Starting from the premise that it would be an absurdity to imagine that an action for trespass could be brought each time a satellite passes over a suburban garden,[129] Griffiths J. thought that the maxim could not be applied literally and that what was involved was 'to balance the rights of an owner to enjoy the use of his land against the rights of the general public to take advantage of all that science now offers in the way of air space'.[130] In determining where that balance lay,

---

[121] *Bocardo SA v. Star Energy UK Onshore Ltd* [2011] 1 A.C. 380 at [26] *per* Lord Hope.

[122] [1957] 2 Q.B. 334. It remains a matter of discretion as to whether an injunction is an appropriate remedy on the facts. See *Woolerton & Wilson Ltd v. Richard Costain Ltd* [1970] 1 W.L.R. 411 and *Trenbath Ltd v. National Westminster Bank Ltd* (1979) 39 P & CR 104; *Anchor Brewhouse Developments Ltd v. Berkley House (Developments) Ltd* [1987] 2 E.G.L.R.173. For a fuller discussion of this important general issue, see Chapter 14, Damages in lieu, pp. 543–5.

[123] *Kelsen v. Imperial Tobacco Co. (of Great Britain and Ireland) Ltd* [1957] 2 Q.B. 334 at 345 *per* McNair J., disapproving *dicta* in *Pickering v. Rudd* (1813) 4 Camp. 219. See also *Gifford v. Dent* [1926] W.N. 336.

[124] See *Wandsworth District Board of Works v. United Telephone Company Co. Ltd* (1884) 13 Q.B.D. 904 at 919 *per* Bowen L.J. The case turned on the meaning of 'street'.

[125] *Lemmon v. Webb* [1895] A.C. 1. Owing to the differing size of a tree over the requisite twenty-year period, it is very difficult to obtain a prescriptive right to have branches overhanging a neighbour's land: ibid. at 6 *per* Lord Herschell L.C. For prescription, see 12.6.

[126] *Mills v. Brooker* [1919] 1 K.B. 555. It is immaterial whether the fruit falls off the tree naturally or by the result of some physical act. ibid. at 558 *per* Lush J.

[127] *Pickering v. Rudd* (1815) 4 Camp. 219 at 221 *per* Lord Ellenborough.

[128] [1978] Q.B. 474.   [129] Ibid. at 487.   [130] Ibid. at 488.

relevant criteria would include the height at which the plane flew and whether or not what occurred amounted to a form of constant surveillance which, he thought, might be actionable in nuisance.[131] While an argument based upon trespass would still fail on the facts if they recurred today, it is possible, depending upon what was actually photographed, that an action could now be brought either for breach of confidence[132] or under the emerging tort of breach of privacy.[133]

1.6.6 **Flats**

Particular problems can arise when a building is divided horizontally rather than vertically. This is the normal situation when one is considering a flat. In such cases, unless one is talking about a ground floor flat, what is in question is the ownership of a block of space[134] surrounded by other flats. While it is possible for such property to be owned in the same way as a house, such a form of ownership being, in the present context, known as a flying freehold,[135] there are serious practical problems relating to ownership of this type of property.[136] The principal problem is, when considering properties of this nature that it is desirable to create a system of mutual obligations, such as the liability to contribute to the cost of maintenance of the common parts of the building and the lift. Insofar as freehold ownership is concerned, it is extremely difficult to ensure that such obligations remain binding upon successive owners of the flats[137] and, for this reason, it is usual to find that such properties are dealt with by the creation of a lease.[138] In the future, some of these problems may be resolved by the implementation of the new scheme of landholding, termed commonhold,[139] although the very low uptake of this new scheme indicates that is very unlikely.

1.6.7 **Water**

Water lying on the land itself is not regarded as being capable of separate ownership, so that any right of public navigation is not regarded as a right over the water but as a right over the land underneath the water.[140] That said, the owner of land upon which there is water does have rights over that water, such as the right to fish. Where a river flows between two plots of land, the owner of each bank has rights up to the middle of the river. In terms of the abstraction of water, this is now governed by the Water Resources Act 1991, which limits the amount of water that can be abstracted.

---

[131] Ibid. at 489.

[132] See *Hellewell v. Chief Constable of Derbyshire* [1995] 1 W.L.R. 804 at 807 *per* Laws J.; M.P. Thompson [1995] Conv. 404. For recent discussions of the impact of the Human Rights Act 1998 and the relationship between breach of confidence and privacy, see *Douglas v. Hello! Ltd* [2001] Q.B. 967. Contrast *A v. B (a company)* [2002] 2 All E.R. 545. See now *Campbell v. Mirror Group Newspapers Ltd* [2004] 2 A.C. 457; *Mosley v. News Group Newspapers Ltd* [2008] EWHC 1777 (Ch).

[133] See, e.g., Witting, *Street on Torts* (14th edn) (Oxford: Oxford University Press, 2014), Chapter 22.

[134] See K. Gray [1991] C.L.J. 252. See also *Eason v. Wong* [2017] EWHC 209 (Ch).

[135] For the position in Lincoln's Inn, see Lincoln's Inn Act 1860. For discussion of the meaning of the term 'freehold', see Chapter 2.

[136] See *Stadium Capital Holdings v. St Marylebone Properties Co Plc* [2009] EWHC 2942 (Ch) at [26], where Sir Donald Rattee considered the ownership of airspace separate from ownership of the land underneath 'a very strange concept'.

[137] See 13.8.

[138] This, too, is not without its problems. See D. Clarke in Bright and Dewar, *Land Law*, Chapter 15.

[139] See Commonhold and Leasehold Reform Act 2002 and Chapter 14.

[140] *Attorney-General, ex rel. Derwent Trust Ltd v. Bortherton* [1992]1 A.C. 425 at 441 *per* Lord Goff. For a fascinating account of the development of different approaches to issues involving water and land, see Dame Mary Arden, in Bright and Dewar, *Land Law*, Chapter 3.

In cases where the land is bounded with water which over the years ebbs and flows, then, if there is a fixed boundary, that is conclusive of the matter.[141] If this is not the case, then the boundary will move with the water, so that the land will either increase or diminish in size accordingly,[142] a process known as accretion, or diluvion, respectively. For this process to occur, however, it is necessary that the process is gradual and imperceptible. If there is a specific moment when two separate pieces of land, such as a sandbank and the foreshore become connected, then accretion will not occur, and so the boundary will not be regarded as having moved.[143]

1.6.8 Wild animals

Wild animals do not belong to anyone. The owner of the land on which they are has the right to catch or kill such animals and, when killed, the carcass belongs to the landowner, regardless of who killed it.[144]

1.6.9 Human remains

Following the discovery of the remains of Richard III under a council car park in Leicester, a dispute arose as to where those remains should be reinterred. They had previously been buried in the Grey Friars Priory following the Battle of Bosworth and were discovered following an archaeological investigation conducted by the University of Leicester. Following the identification of the remains, the Plantagenet Society, which sought to represent the interests of a number of distant collateral relatives of the king, was formed to challenge the lawfulness of the licence granted by the Ministry of Justice to the University of Leicester, which required the University to reinter the remains of the king in Leicester Cathedral. The members of the Society strongly favoured reinterment taking place at York. At a late stage in the proceedings, Leicester City Council intervened, arguing that, as the owner of the land under which the remains were discovered, it was the 'legal sentinel' of them, this claim seemingly based upon an argument that it was the owner of them. This claim, which was variously described as being 'unnecessary, unhelpful and misconceived',[145] was based upon the fallacy that a human corpse is capable of ownership. Although, clearly, it has physical characteristics, it has long been a principle of common law that there is no property in a corpse[146] and, perhaps belatedly recognizing this, the Council ultimately withdrew this argument. The dispute was, therefore, resolved without recourse to arguments about ownership, and the king's remains were ultimately laid to rest in Leicester Cathedral in the summer of 2015.

1.7 Items attached to the land

It is a general maxim of English land law that 'quicquid planatur solo, solo cedit'.[147] This means that whatever is attached to the soil becomes part of it. The application of this maxim leads to an important distinction between what are known as fixtures and fittings.

---

[141] Baxendale v. Instow Parish Council [1982] Ch. 14.
[142] Southern Centre of Theosophy Inc. v. State of South Australia [1982] A.C. 706. See R.E. Annand [1982] Conv. 208; W. Howarth [1986] Conv. 247.
[143] See Lynn Shellfish Ltd v. Loose [2016] UKSC 14 at [78] per Lord Neuberger.
[144] Blades v. Higgs (1865) 11 H.L.C. 349.
[145] R (On the Application of the Plantagenet Alliance) v. Secretary of State for Justice [2014] EWHC 1662 (Admin) at [164].
[146] See Hardcastle, Law and the Human Body (Oxford, Hart Publishing, 2007), 25–8.
[147] A maxim apparently first coined in Marshall v. Lloyd (1837) 2 M. & W. 450 at 459 per Parke B. See P. Luther (2004) 24 O.J.L.S. 597 at 600.

The essence of the distinction between the two is that a fixture is something which, due to the manner and purpose of its attachment to the land, becomes part of the land itself, whereas fittings are chattels which are physically in the property and, in some cases, attached to it but are not considered to be a part of it. As will be seen, an important aspect in deciding whether or not a particular item is a fixture is the degree of physical attachment to the land. Before considering the distinction between the two, it is necessary to have regard to a third category; items which are brought onto the land and become part of it, without properly being regarded as fixtures at all.

1.7.1 **Part of the land**

The issue arose in *Elitestone Ltd v. Morris*.[148] The plaintiffs owned land on which were constructed wooden bungalows. The bungalows rested upon concrete pillars which were attached to the land and to remove them would have required their demolition. The issue arose as to whether the defendant's bungalow was a building or a chattel. The House of Lords held unanimously that the building was part of the land. Lord Lloyd adopted the tripartite analysis put forward in a leading text that:

> An object which is brought onto land may be classified under one of three broad heads. It may be (a) a chattel; (b) a fixture; or (c) part and parcel of the land itself. Objects in categories (b) and (c) are treated as being part of the land.[149]

Pointing out that the building in question was not like a Portakabin or a mobile home,[150] Lord Lloyd took the view that it was not really apposite to consider whether or not the bungalow was a fixture. He thought that the issue of whether an item was a fixture arose when it was attached to a building; when one was considering whether the structure itself was part of the land, different considerations applied. This point was also made in *Holland v. Hodgson*,[151] where Blackburn J. explained that:

> blocks of stone placed one on top of another without any mortar or cement for the purpose of forming a dry stone wall would become part of the land, though the same stones, if deposited in a building yard and for convenience sake stacked on top of each other in the form of a wall, would not.

The issue in cases of this nature is not the subjective intention of the party constructing the item in question; rather it is 'whether the object is designed for the use or enjoyment of the land or the more complete or convenient use or enjoyment of the thing itself'.[152] With regard to fixtures, an important issue will be the damage that would be done to the remaining property by removing the particular item, and the more difficult it is to remove the disputed item intact, the more likely it is that it will be held to be part of the land.[153]

---

[148] [1997] 1 W.L.R. 687; H. Conway [1998] Conv. 418; P. Luther (2008) 28 L.S. 574. See also *Spielplatz Ltd v. Pearson* [2015] EWCA Civ. 804 (wooden chalets held to be part of the land).

[149] Woodfall, *Landlord and Tenant* (London: Sweet & Maxwell, Looseleaf), vol. 1, para. 13.131, cited at [1997] 1 W.L.R. 687 at 691.

[150] [1997] 1 W.L.R. 687 at 690. Similarly, a moveable houseboat is not regarded as being part of the land. See *Chelsea Yacht and Boat Co. Ltd v. Pope* [2000] 1 W.L.R. 1941; M.P. Thompson [2001] Conv. 417. For a more marginal example of this, see *Mew v. Tristmere Ltd* [2011] EWCA Civ. 912.

[151] (1872) L.R. 7 C.P. 328 at 335.

[152] *Elitestone Ltd v. Morris, supra*, at 698–9 *per* Lord Clyde. See also *Spielplatz Ltd v. Pearson, supra*, at [41] *per* Rimer L.J.

[153] See, generally, *Wessex Reserve Forces and Cadets Association v. White* [2005] EWHC 982 (Q.B.) at [21]–[61] *per* Mr Michael Harvey Q.C., affmd [2005] EWCA Civ. 1744. See also *Lictor Anstalt v. Mir Steel UK Ltd* [2014] EWHC 331 (Ch) at [187] *per* Asplin J.

1.8 **Fixtures**

The issue of whether a particular item is regarded as being a fixture is potentially important to a number of people. If a person has contracted to sell a house, then it is quite clear
that, after the contract has been made, the seller cannot remove any items from the property and is liable to the purchaser should he do so.[154] Rather more contentiously, in *Taylor
v. Hamer*,[155] the majority of the Court of Appeal held that the seller was liable for the removal of flagstones, which were undoubtedly fixtures, when the stones had been removed
after an agreement in principle had been reached concerning the sale of the property but
before a binding contract had been entered into. This decision goes further than previous
authority, and is unusual. A few days before the contract had been formed, the vendor had
given a highly misleading answer to a question directly concerning the disputed flagstones
and this aspect of the case clearly weighed heavily with the majority of the court. Indeed,
subsequently, this was seen as being an integral part of the reasoning and the proposition
that there is a wider principle that a vendor may not remove fixtures prior to the formation of a contract of sale was denied.[156] Despite some wide statements made in *Taylor*[157]
that a vendor may not remove fixtures prior to entry into a contract, this is unlikely to be
followed, particularly as the leading work on the subject has said of the case that 'it seems
so anomalous, although meritorious, that it cannot comfortably be incorporated into any
existing account of the law'.[158] Clearly, however, the avoidance of disputes of this nature
is desirable, and it is now normal practice, as part of the Conveyancing Protocol, for the
seller to complete, prior to entry into the contract, a questionnaire detailing which common household items are to be included in the sale and this then becomes the basis of
what is included in the contract.

If the property is mortgaged, then the mortgage extends to all fixtures,[159] even those
which were affixed after the mortgage was created.[160] Again, if a situation, termed a settlement, is in existence whereby, for example, land is left to A for life thereafter to B, on A's
death, fixtures will pass to B and will not pass under A's will or upon his intestacy. Finally,
when property is leased, items which are fixtures become part of the land and will pass
to the landlord on the termination of the lease. An unusual example of this occurred in
The Creative Foundation v. Dreamland Leisure Ltd.[161] The claim was for the delivery up
of a section of the wall of a house, which had been rented, and on which the urban artist,
Banksy, had painted a mural. That wall was removed by the tenant and replaced by a mu-
ral-free wall and the original was transported to New York where its value was estimated as
being between £300,000 and £470,000. It was held that the default position was that every
part of the demised property belonged to the landlord[162] and, as this included the original
wall, he had a better right to the mural than the tenant.

In this case the mural was a fixture and, therefore, become part of the land and, consequently, belonged to the landlord. Although, as a general proposition this is true, there
does exist a right enjoyed by tenants to remove certain types of fixture. This right relates to

---

[154] See, e.g., *Phillips v. Lamdin* [1949] 2 K.B. 33 (ornate Adam door).
[155] [2003] 1 E.G.L.R. 103. For criticism, see C. McNall [2003] Conv. 432.
[156] *Sykes v. Taylor-Rose* [2004] EWCA Civ. 299 at [15] *per* Sir William Aldous, quoting the trial court
judge. This aspect of the decision was not appealed. See also, to similar effect, *Wickens v. Cheval Property
Developments Ltd* [2010] EWHC 2249 (Ch).
[157] [2003] 1 E.G.L.R. 103 at [93] *per* Sedley L.J.
[158] Ferrand, Clarke et al., *Emmet and Farrand on Title* (London: Sweet & Maxwell, looseleaf) para. 4.001.
[159] LPA 1925, s. 62(1); *Botham v. TSB Bank plc* (1997) 73 P. & C.R. D1.
[160] *Reynolds v. Ashby & Son* [1904] A.C. 466.   [161] (2015) EWHC 2556 (Ch).
[162] Ibid. at [55] *per* Arnold J.

items affixed by the limited owner, or the tenant, and so would not impact on the case just considered. The rationale for the existence of this right, and its scope, will be considered shortly.

1.8.1 **The distinction between fixtures and fittings**

In answering the question as to whether a particular item is a fixture it is traditional to consider two issues:

(i) the degree of annexation of the object to the land; and

(ii) the purpose of annexation.[163]

1.8.1.1 **The degree of annexation**

As a general rule, unless an item is physically attached to the land, it will not be considered to be a fixture. Items which rest on the property by their own weight, such as a 'Dutch barn',[164] are unlikely to be regarded as fixtures. Similarly, a greenhouse which is not physically attached to the land is also not likely to be seen as a fixture and this is particularly true if it is normal practice to move the greenhouse periodically to various sites on the land.[165] It is not the case, however, that physical attachment is necessarily essential for an item to be regarded as being part of the land. As has been seen, if a structure, such as a dry stone wall or a pre-constructed bungalow, cannot be removed without destroying that structure then it is likely that it will be regarded as being a part of the land. It is not seen as helpful to describe it as a fixture.[166] While is possible that self-standing objects, such as statues, could be regarded as fixtures, this will only be the case if they are regarded as an integral part of the architecture.[167] In the light of the modern approach to this issue, it is improbable that this will be held to be the case.[168]

1.8.1.2 **The purpose of annexation**

Although it is generally true to say that an item will not be regarded as a fixture unless it is physically attached to the land, that alone is insufficient; the court will also look at the purpose of the annexation to determine whether something is, or is not, a fixture and, in deciding this matter, how the parties choose to describe a particular object is not determinative.[169] The court will take an objective view of the matter. This can cause problems for suppliers of goods on hire-purchase agreements, who seek to retain ownership of the product until all the payments have been made. If the installation of the chattel in question is such that it becomes a fixture, then it will become part of the land and, consequently,

---

[163] See *Holland v. Hodgson* (1872) L.R. 7 C.P. 328 at 334 *per* Blackburn J. For an interesting historical account of the development of this test, see P. Luther (2004) 24 O.J.L.S. 597.

[164] See *Wiltshear v. Cottrell* (1853) 1 E. & B. 674.

[165] See *H.E. Dibble Ltd v. Moore* [1970] 2 Q.B. 181 at 187 *per* Megaw L.J. See also *Deen v. Andrews* [1986] 1 E.G.L.R. 262. As a general proposition, when it is envisaged that an item will be moved regularly, it is very unlikely that that item will be regarded as being a fixture. See *Hynes v. Vaughan* (1985) 50 P. & C.R. 444 (growing frame and garden sprinkler).

[166] *Elitestone Ltd v. Morris* [1997] 1 W.L.R. 687; *Spielplatz Ltd v. Pearson* [2015] EWCA Civ. 804.

[167] See *D'Eyncourt v. Gregory* (1866) L.R. 3 Eq. 382; *Re Lord Chesterfield's Settled Estate* [1911] Ch. 237.

[168] See *Berkley v. Poulett* [1977] E.G.D. 754; *London Borough of Tower Hamlets v. London Borough of Bromley* [2015] EWHC 1954 (Ch) at [16]–[17] *per* Norris J. (Henry Moore sculpture held to be a chattel). For an interesting discussion, including whether such a sculpture should be considered as being part of the land rather than a fixture or fitting, see M. Iljadica [2016] Conv. 242.

[169] *Melluish v. B.M.I. (No. 3) Ltd* [1996] A.C. 454 at 473 *per* Lord Browne-Wilkinson. See also *Lictor Anstalt v. Mir Steel UK Ltd* [2014] EWHC (Ch) at [165] *per* Asplin J. The approach taken to this issue in *Hamp v. Bygrave* [1983] E.G.D. 1000 must now be regarded as wrong.

part of the security of the house if the house is mortgaged.[170] Nevertheless, how the parties regard a particular item can have some effect, so that if a vendor and purchaser agree that certain items are fixtures, the vendor will not, after a contract of sale has been made, be able to remove them.[171]

In drawing the line between fixtures and fittings, the modern tendency is to place considerably more emphasis on the purpose of annexation than on the method of attachment. That said, the issue remains whether the item in question is properly to be regarded as part of the building.[172] In determining this matter, attitudes have changed to reflect the fact that the manner in which ornaments have been put up is different from that which occurred in the past, with the result that less disruption is now necessary to the building in order to remove them than was previously the case.[173] So, in *Leigh v. Taylor*,[174] a tapestry attached by tacks to wooden frames was held not to be a fixture, the purpose of the attachment to the building being to enable the tapestry to be enjoyed as an ornament rather than to enhance the building.

This approach was continued in *Berkley v. Poulett*,[175] where the principal issues of dispute were whether paintings screwed into recesses in a wall, a large sundial on a plinth, and a statue weighing half a ton were fixtures. The Court of Appeal held that they were not. Scarman L.J. considered that the starting point in determining this issue was *Leigh v. Taylor* and the essential issue to be determined was whether the purpose of the annexation was to enjoy the pictures as pictures or to enhance the structure of the building. Conceding that the law in this area was frequently more difficult to apply than to state, and that 'a degree of annexation which in earlier times the law would have treated as conclusive may now prove nothing',[176] he concluded that the pictures remained as chattels. They were put on the wall to be enjoyed as pictures and how a workman chose to solve the problem of how they should be fixed to the walls was not decisive in determining their status. That they could be removed with comparative ease and without significant damage to the building[177] militated against them being fixtures. Similarly, the statue and sundial, which both rested by their own weight, were also regarded as chattels.

1.8.1.3 Household items

The most detailed consideration of which ordinary household items were fixtures occurred recently in *Botham v. TSB Bank plc*,[178] where the Court of Appeal had to consider the status of some 109 different items in a flat, the issue being whether they were included as part of the security for a loan, which would have been the case if the items were fixtures. The items were placed into nine different categories, of which eight were in dispute. It is not essential to enumerate each item to obtain the gist of the approach taken. The more important items were fitted carpets, curtains, light fittings, gas fires, and kitchen appliances, but the dispute also extended to more mundane items such as towel rails, lavatory roll holders, and soap dishes.

Quoting extensively from *Berkley v. Poulett*, Roch L.J. giving the leading judgment approached the problems by asking, in essence, whether the purpose of the attachment was to allow the chattel to be enjoyed as a chattel or was designed to improve the building.

---

[170] *Botham v. TSB Bank plc* (1977) 73 P. & C.R. D1; *Melluish v. B.M.I. (No. 3)* [1996] A.C. 454.
[171] *Hamp v. Bygrave* [1983] E.G.D. 1000.
[172] *D'Eyncourt v. Gregory* (1866) L.R. 3 Eq. 382 at 396 *per* Lord Romilly M.R.
[173] *Leigh v. Taylor* [1902] A.C. 157 at 161 *per* Earl of Halsbury L.C.
[174] [1902] A.C. 157. See also *Re Falbe* [1901] 1 Ch. 523.
[175] (1976) 241 E.G. 911.   [176] Ibid. at 913.
   In contrast, some Chinese prints which were stuck to the wall and could not be removed without ripping off the wallpaper were conceded to be fixtures.
[178] (1997) 73 P. & C.R. D1. See M. Haley [1998] Conv. 137.

On this basis, items such as fitted carpets,[179] which can easily be removed, and curtains, were seen as chattels. Conversely, the various items of bathroom furniture, compendiously described as ironmongery, were regarded as fixtures, as their purpose was to improve the bathroom as a bathroom and, indeed, make it usable as such. Other items came into a greyer area.

With regard to kitchen equipment, gas fires, and lighting, much depended upon how they were fitted. For example, an oven can be free-standing and attached to the building by either an electricity cable or gas pipe, or it can form an integrated part of the kitchen, as is the case where it is a fitted unit. If the former is the case, the item will remain a chattel; if the latter, which will require considerable damage to the fabric of the kitchen to secure its removal, it will be regarded as a fixture. An essentially similar test is applied to items such as fires and lights. If the item in question is integrated into the structure of the building, so that its removal will occasion difficulty, then the item would, *prima facie*, be a fixture.[180]

What the cases show is that, where possible, it is highly desirable to stipulate in a contract of sale which items are to be included and which are to be excluded from the sale.

1.8.2 The removal of fixtures

The effect of a chattel becoming a fixture is that, if the person who attaches the item to the property has only a limited interest in that property, which will be the case if that person has only a lease, or is entitled to that property only for his lifetime, that person being termed a tenant for life or life tenant, then they will lose the ownership of that item. Either the landlord or the person entitled to the land after the death of the tenant for life will acquire the item after the termination of the prior interest. This may not, however, be universally desirable in that the rule may provide a disincentive for certain limited owners of property to use the land to its best effect. This is particularly the case with regard to tenancies when, in order to pursue a business, a tenant may wish to install equipment or other items which would ordinarily become fixtures. If these passed to the landlord on the termination of the lease, a tenant may be disinclined to do this. To avoid this difficulty certain limited owners have the right to remove certain fixtures.

1.8.2.1 Tenant's fixtures

As a general rule, if a tenant attaches items to the property which is being leased in such a way that they become fixtures, then they will become part of the land and so the landlord will be entitled to them at the end of the lease. To avoid this consequence, certain items are designated as 'tenant's fixtures', which the tenant, subject to any terms in the lease to the contrary,[181] is entitled to remove during the subsistence of the lease. They can also be removed at the end of the lease and, indeed, thereafter, if the tenant remains in possession of the property under statute.[182] Where the tenancy is terminated without giving the tenant a reasonable time to remove the fixtures, then that time is afforded to him to effect their removal.[183] Any damage done by the tenant in either installing or removing the fixtures must be made good.[184] If the tenant does not exercise his right to remove such fixtures, then the items will be regarded as belonging to the landlord.

---

[179] *Young v. Dalgety plc* [1987] 1 E.G.L.R., which accepted fitted carpets as being fixtures, was disapproved.
[180] See also *Hamp v. Bygrave* [1983] E.G.D. 1000, where patio lights were conceded to be fixtures.
[181] See *Peel Land Property (Ports No.3) Ltd v. TS Shearness Ltd* [2014] EWCA Civ. 100.
[182] See *Poster v. Slough Estates Ltd* [1969] 1 Ch. 495; *New Zealand Government Property Corporation v. H. M. & S. Ltd* [1982] Q.B. 1145.
[183] *Smith v. City Petroleum Co. Ltd* [1940] 1 All E.R. 260.
[184] *Mancetter Developments Ltd v. Garmanson Ltd* [1986] Q.B. 1212.

Tenant's fixtures are divided into three types: trade fixtures, ornamental fixtures, and agricultural fixtures.

1.8.2.2 Trade fixtures

There is a tendency when considering what amounts to a tenant's fixture to run together the separate questions of whether the particular item is a fixture at all and whether or not it can be removed.[185] While this is understandable when the issue is as to whether the landlord or the tenant is entitled to a particular item, it is not without its difficulties. First, it can lead to subsequent confusion, outside the context of landlord and tenant, as to the status of a particular item.[186] Second, it can be important from a tax point of view to determine who owns a particular item at a given time,[187] and, third, the issue may be relevant in the context of rent reviews. Rent review clauses are common in commercial leases. They are included in long leases, so that the rent which was originally agreed to be payable can be adjusted, in order to reflect the prevailing market conditions. If specific mention is made in a rent review clause to fixtures,[188] then the task of determining what are actually fixtures is obviously important.

The first task is then to determine whether or not the item in question is a fixture. In so doing, one must look to see 'what is the physical extent of the item; can it be physically severed and, if so, with what degree of difficulty?; what is the effect of severance on the premises which remains and is that effect remediable?; what is the effect of severance on the item itself and is that effect remediable?; does the item when severed retain its essential character and utility?'[189] On this basis, machines weighing 50 and 100 tons respectively, but resting under their own weight, were regarded as chattels, whereas a crane running on a track, and indeed the track itself, were held to be fixtures.[190]

It has long been accepted that items attached to the land in order that the tenant can carry out his trade can be removed and so, it has been held, the fittings of a public house can be removed by the tenant.[191] Other examples of trade fixtures are vats, steam engines, and boilers and other articles of this type.[192]

1.8.2.3 Ornamental fixtures

An article which can be removed whole, without substantial damage to the building, has traditionally been regarded as an ornamental fixture, which the tenant can remove.[193] In view of the modern approach to fixtures, which emphasizes the purpose of annexation, it is likely that this would not, today, be regarded as a proper exception, the real question being whether the item is a fixture at all.

---

[185] For an excellent example of the care taken to distinguish the two things, see *Peel Land and Property (Ports No.3) v. TS Shearness Ltd* [2013] EWHC 1658 (Ch) at [69] *per* Morgan J., rvsd in part on the issue of the construction of the lease at [2014] EWCA Civ. 100.

[186] See the discussion of *Webb v. Frank Bevis Ltd* [1940] 1 All E.R. 247 in *Elitestone Ltd v. Morris* [1997] 1 W.L.R. 687 at 691 *per* Lord Lloyd.

[187] See *Melluish v. B.M.I. (No. 3) Ltd* [1996] A.C. 454.

[188] See, e.g., *National Grid Co. plc v. M25 Group Ltd* [1999] 1 E.G.L.R. 65. *Prima facie* a rent review should not take account of the value of tenant's fixtures: *Young v. Dalgety plc* [1987] 1 E.G.L.R. 116.

[189] *Peel Land and Property (Ports No.3) v. TS Shearness Steel Ltd* [2013] EWHC 1658 (Ch) at [103] *per* Morgan J., a passage unaffected by the partial reversal of the actual decision at [2014] EWCA Civ. 100.

[190] Contrast, albeit not in the context of tenants' fixtures, *Lictor Anstalt v. Mir Steel UK Ltd* [2014] EWHC 3316 (Ch), where a hot strip mill attached to the land by heavy bolts, and which would take about two years to remove, was held to be part of the land.

[191] *Elliott v. Bishop* (1854) 10 Exch. 496.

[192] See Harpum, Bridge and Dixon, *Megarry and Wade: Law of Real Property* (8th edn) (London: Sweet & Maxwell, 2012), para. 23–014.

[193] *Martin v. Roe* (1857) 7 E. & B. 237.

1.8.2.4 Agricultural fixtures

The position of a farm tenant is governed by s. 8 of the Agricultural Tenancies Act 1995, a provision which gave greater rights for tenants to remove fixtures than had previously been the case.[194] Under the section, the tenant can, subject to certain exceptions, remove any fixture (of whatever description), affixed, whether for the purposes of agriculture or not, to the holding under a business farm tenancy, and any building erected by him on the holding.

This right may be exercised at any time during the subsistence of the tenancy, or at any time after its termination, provided that he remains in possession as a tenant. Unlike the position with other tenancies, the fixtures remain the property of the tenant while he continues to have the right to remove it. When removing the fixture, he must not cause avoidable damage and, in any event, must make good any damage caused by the removal of the fixture.[195]

1.8.2.5 Life tenants

A person who has a life interest in property—a life tenant—is in much the same position as a tenant under a lease, save that the provisions of the Agricultural Tenancies Act 1995 will not apply.

1.9 Incorporeal hereditaments

The previous discussion has related, with the possible exception of airspace, to tangible property. The definition of land extends also to intangible rights, known as incorporeal hereditaments. This, in essence, refers to rights over another person's land, such as an easement. A classic example of an easement is the right to cross a neighbour's land. Such a right is regarded as being land, so that if the owner of the land with the right to cross his neighbour's property sells his land to another person, that purchaser,[196] will acquire, together with that land, the right to cross the neighbour's land.[197] The question may also arise as to when a person who acquires the land over which the right is enjoyed must also give effect to that right—whether they are bound by the easement, in other words. We consider the law of easements in Chapter 12.

---

[194] Cf. Agricultural Holdings Act 1986, s. 10.　　[195] Agricultural Tenancies Act 1995, s. 8(3), (4).
[196] Formally known as the 'successor in title'.　　[197] LPA 1925, s. 62(1).

2

Tenure and Estates

When people describe their relationship with property, it is common to speak of owner-ship of the item in question. With regard to land, although such usage is normal, techni-cally, it is inaccurate. This is because of the doctrines of tenure and estates. The former notion is now, essentially, of historical interest and of little contemporary significance; the latter concept remains, however, a theoretical pillar of land law.

2.1 Tenure

In the early eleventh century, there existed a rudimentary system of strip farming in England. After the Norman invasion in 1066, a rigorous feudal structure was imposed upon the country. A central feature of this system, which is common to other systems where there is a human ruler in the person of a monarch, emperor, or khan, was that the land was seen as belonging to the king, that person being the representative of divine power on earth.[1] The king who, by the conquest or acquisition of the country, had suc-ceeded to the rights of his Anglo-Saxon predecessors,[2] then proceeded to grant tracts of land to his principal supporters, who held the land from the Crown. In return for this grant, they provided various services.[3]

The people to whom land was granted directly by the king were termed tenants in chief. They, in turn, granted part of the land to someone else, again in return for feudal services. This process could then be continued to create further holdings, a process known as sub-infeudation. This process led to the formation of a feudal pyramid or ladder, which is illustrated in Figure 2.1.

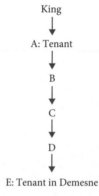

Fig. 2.1 The feudal pyramid or ladder

[1] Linklater, *Owning the Earth: The Transforming History of Land Ownership* (London, Bloomsbury Publishing Ltd, 2013), 26.
[2] Digby, *An Introduction to the History of the Law of Real Property* (3rd edn) (Oxford, Clarendon Press, 1884), 33–4.
[3] See, generally, Simpson, *A History of the Land Law* (2nd edn) (Oxford, Oxford University Press, 1986), Chapter 1.

The person at the bottom of the ladder was termed the tenant in demesne and those between that person and the tenant in chief were termed mesne[4] lords. Central to the system was that the land was enjoyed in return for services. A person held land from another, this being the origin of the term 'tenure', which derives from the Latin *tenere*, to hold. These terms on which the land was held varied both in nature and in prestige. The types of tenure were divided into free and unfree tenures.

2.1.1 Free tenures

Free tenures were divided into tenures of chivalry, spiritual tenures, and socage.

2.1.1.1 Chivalry

This form of tenure was divided into two main types: grand sergeanty and knight's service. The former involved the tenant performing personal tasks for the king and were, in the main, regarded as being highly honourable.[5] Somewhat surprisingly, some continue to the present day so that, as an aspect of feudal service, an embroidered glove was presented by, or on behalf of, the Lord of the Manor of Worksop at the coronations of George VI and Elizabeth II.[6] Knight service was, as the name suggests, the provision of armed knights for a period of a year.

2.1.1.2 Spiritual tenancies

This, again, as the name implies, was the holding of lands in return for the performance of divine services for the grantor.[7]

2.1.1.3 Socage

This was a form of tenure which, in essence, did not fall into any of the other categories and consisted principally of the provision of agricultural services, but could also involve non-personal services for the king. Over time, it became the most common form of tenure.

2.1.2 Unfree tenures

The essence of an unfree tenure was that the services of the tenant were not known from day to day; the tenant had to perform such tasks as he was instructed to do. Originally, this was known as villein tenure, but this form of landholding gradually died out to be superseded by copyhold, a form of landholding which did not entirely disappear until 1925.[8]

2.2 Incidents of tenure

The feudal system carried with it a number of consequences which helped to shape modern law. In addition to the services which had to be performed in return for the grant of

---

[4] Pronounced 'mean'.

[5] For amusing and outlandish forms of tenure, some of which were certainly not honourable, see Megarry, *Miscellany-at-Law* (London, Stevens & Sons Ltd, 1955), 154–7. Services of a non-personal kind were referred to as petty sergeanty.

[6] Simpson, *A History of the Land Law*, 10–11.

[7] This form of service was subdivided into divine service and frankelmoign. See Harpum, *Megarry and Wade's Law of Real Property* (6th edn) (London, Sweet & Maxwell, 2000), 21–2, a fuller account than is contained in Harpum, Bridge, and Dixon, *Megarry and Wade's Law of Real Property* (8th edn) (London, Sweet & Maxwell, 2012).

[8] LPA 1925, s. 202. For details of these and other forms of miscellaneous tenures, see Harpum, Megarry, and Wade, *Law of Real Property*, 22–8.

land,[9] the superior lord was entitled to a number of benefits upon the death of the tenant. As will be seen, it was a desire to avoid such death duties that was a powerful spur to the creation of the trust.

2.2.1 Escheat

A further aspect of the system of tenure is the existence of the doctrine of escheat.[10] Under the feudal system of land holding, all land in England was held of some lord, the original grant having derived from the Crown.[11] If this grant terminated, then the land would revert to the superior lord, this process being termed escheat. Escheat occurred for one of two reasons. The first, which is now obsolete, related to the commission of a felony. Under this aspect of the rule, if a tenant was guilty of a felony or petit treason, the effect was to deprive him of his lands, which would then vest in his lord. This, it should be appreciated, was not necessarily the king. While later, when the feudal system had withered, it was common for tenants to hold directly from the Crown, and the effect of escheat was that the land returned to the king, the effect of escheat was that the land fell back to the superior lord. Escheat had also to be distinguished from forfeiture. In cases of high treason, the lands of the traitor were forfeit to the Crown, and not to the superior lord, a quite different process from escheat.[12] Both escheat and forfeiture resultant on the commission of crime have ceased to exist.[13]

The other form of escheat occurred when a tenant died without heirs. In the case of individuals, this occurred in the case of a person dying without heirs prior to 1925.[14] A modern example of this occurred in *Re Lowe's Will Trusts*.[15] A firm of solicitors had been collecting rents from a tenant in respect of a property of which the last known devise had occurred in 1851. Nobody had laid any claim to the rent, and extensive searches had failed to locate anyone who might claim to be entitled to the freehold. As a consequence, the land had passed to the Crown by escheat, the possibility of there being a mesne lord who might be entitled 'is one that is so remote that it may be wholly ignored'.[16]

Cases of escheat involving individuals are rare. Less so are instances involving companies.[17] This may occur when a company goes into liquidation and the liquidator disclaims a freehold previously held by the company.[18] Similarly, if a company is otherwise dissolved without the prior distribution of its assets,[19] land held by the company will, by virtue of s. 1012 of the Companies Act 2006, be deemed to be *bona vacantia* (ownerless goods) and, as such, vest in the Crown. The Crown, may, however, under s. 1013 of the Act disclaim property which would otherwise vest in it. The effect of any such disclaimer is limited, however, because, if that course of action is taken, title to the land will still vest in the

---

[9] Some of which are still referred to in current legislation. See, e.g., Land Registration Act (LRA) 2002, Scheds 1 and 3.

[10] For an informative account of this doctrine, see F.W. Hardman (1886) 4 L.Q.R. 318.

[11] *A.G. for Ontario v. Mercer* (1883) 8 App. Cas. 767 at 771–2 *per* Earl of Selborne L.C.

[12] See Hardman, (1886) 4 L.Q.R. 318, 323–4.

[13] See Corruption of Blood Act 1814; Forfeiture Act 1870.

[14] In such cases after 1925, see Administration of Estates Act 1925, s. 4; LRA 2002. s. 82.

[15] [1973] 1 W.L.R. 882. '[B]y a happy chance the topic has arisen from the past in connection with premises known as the Phoenix Inn': at 884 *per* Russell L.J.

[16] Ibid., at 886 *per* Russell L.J.

[17] Apparently there are around 500 such cases a year: (2001) Law Com No. 271, paras 11.1–11.38.

[18] Under the Insolvency Act 1986, s. 178. See *Semilla Properties Ltd v. Gesso Properties (BVI) Ltd* [1995] B.C.C. 793, a decision containing a thorough review of escheat.

[19] See *Re Strathblaine Estates Ltd* [1948] Ch. 228.

Crown by virtue of the doctrine of escheat.[20] Escheat will also operate to vest title in the Crown in the case of the dissolution of a company incorporated overseas which owned land in this country.[21]

2.3 **The dismantling of tenure**

The feudal system of landholding had a number of disadvantages, a notable one being its cumbersome nature. To collect undelivered incidents, which increasingly became the most important aspect of the feudal system, an action had to be brought against the person in possession of the land. That person then had a remedy against his lord. As the rungs grew in the feudal ladder the system became increasingly unwieldy, with the result that further subinfeudation became increasingly unpopular and led to the enactment of the statute, *Quia Emptores* 1290. This provided for the substitution of tenants rather than the creation of a further rung in the feudal ladder. The statute effectively put an end to any further process of subinfeudation.

This statute, together with the increased commutation of feudal services by the payment of money, such payments being termed scutage in the case of knight service, and quit rents in respect of other feudal dues, led to the withering away of the rungs in the ladder. Over time, the money payments ceased to be worth collecting, and therefore lapsed. Coupled with the conversion of all tenures, except frankelmoign and copyhold (respectively, a form of spiritual tenure and a form of tenure peculiar to certain manors), into free and common socage by the Tenures Abolition Act 1660, the end of the feudal pyramids became inevitable, so that, today, a person who owns a house is, in fact, a tenant in chief holding from the Crown. It is readily assumed that if a person died without heirs, he was not holding the land from another lord and so the land will pass to the Crown.[22]

One, perhaps surprising, paradox concerns leasehold property. The feudal system of landholding had, as an important element of it, the identification of one's status in society: that status being coloured to a large extent by where one was in the feudal pyramid and the nature of the services which were required. The lease, whereby the land was used for exclusively commercial purposes, was outside this system with the consequence that a lease was not originally regarded as being real property at all.[23] Therefore, the statute *Quia Emptores* did not apply to leasehold property and so did not prevent a different process of subinfeudation, where sub-leases are created. So, a person who has a ninety-nine-year lease can carve out of that interest a lesser interest, say, of fifty years, the result being described diagrammatically in Figure 2.2.

The tenant occupies a position akin to that of a feudal mesne lord; he holds as tenant from the head landlord but is, himself, the landlord of the sub-tenant.

Fig. 2.2 Lease and sub-lease

---

[20] See *UBS Global Asset Management (UK) Ltd v. Crown Estate Commissioners* [2011] EWHC 3368 (Ch); *Quadracolour Ltd v. Crown Estate Commissioners* [2013] EWCA Civ. 4842. See also D.W. Elliott (1954) 70 L.Q.R. 25. For possible reasons why the Crown may disclaim property which will ultimately pass to it by escheat, see Harpum, Bridge, and Dixon, *Law of Real Property*, 2.023–2.024.

[21] *In the Matter of Fivestar Properties Ltd* [2015] EWHC 2782 (Ch).

[22] See *Re Lowe's Will Trusts* [1973] 1 W.L.R. 882 at 886 *per* Russell L.J.   [23] See 1.5.5.

With regard to holdings within the feudal system, the rungs between the person in possession of the land and the Crown withered away and it is now assumed that an owner of land holds directly from the Crown as tenant in chief but without the provision of any services in respect of that holding. The effect of the statute *Quia Emptores* is that, when a house is sold, the purchaser replaces the vendor as the tenant in chief, holding the land directly from the Crown. How best to describe the interest that the Crown has will be considered shortly after a discussion of the concept of estates: a concept which still underpins land law.

2.4 Estates

The doctrine of tenure is now almost entirely of historical interest. The main reasons for saying anything about it today are, first, to point to the different importance attached to one's relationship with land, as opposed to other forms of property. While it was, and of course still is, a source of wealth, it was also indicative of one's status in society. Its other principal value, however, is to allow one to become accustomed to the idea that land ownership is not an absolute thing. It remains theoretically true to say that all land is held from the Crown. The idea that one does not actually own the thing itself but rather has an interest in it, is also what underlies the theoretical basis of landholding in this country: the estate, the development of which in part at least, it has been said,[24] was forced upon the common lawyers by the theoretical difficulties caused by the doctrine of tenure. An estate is an abstract entity which defines the rights that the owner of an estate has in relation to the land in question.

2.5 The nature of an estate

It is common to talk of a person owning an item of property. As discussed in Chapter 1, the use of such a term is a form of shorthand; it is a means of describing the rights or powers which a person has over a particular item. If one speaks of ownership of a car, then one can readily appreciate the rights which one has over it. The owner can drive it, sell it, lend it to others, and maintain an action against any person who damages it, or otherwise infringes his ownership rights. There are, of course, restrictions on what the owner of a car can do with it. Such restrictions are not so much a matter of private ownership; rather they are matters imposed by the state or by the general law. So, for example, a car must be taxed and insured; the speed limits must be observed; one should not drive having consumed more than a specified amount of alcohol; and, in driving the car, one must take reasonable care not to injure other people or other people's property.

Similar observations can be made about land ownership. The 'owner' of land can exercise a wide variety of rights over it, the range of these rights, owing to the physical nature of the property in question being, in practical terms, rather wider than those enjoyed by a car owner. For example, although car leasing arrangements certainly exist, such arrangements are far less prevalent than is the case with land. Similarly, a long-term mortgage of land is a commonplace, something not really possible with cars. Again, however, there are restrictions on how one can enjoy the land. In the main, these, again, are matters imposed by the state and the general law. Thus, for example, there are restrictions imposed by planning legislation on how one can develop land or alter its use. In terms of the general law, an

---

[24] Simpson, *A History of the Land Law*, 1, although cf. Digby, *An Introduction to the History of the Law of Real Property* (3rd edn) (Oxford, Clarendon Press, 1884), 27, where it is said that the doctrine of estates predated the Norman Conquest.

owner of land is restricted by the law of nuisance as to how the land is enjoyed; its use must not cause unreasonable interference with the enjoyment of land by a neighbour.

One speaks of ownership of a car yet, in the context of land, one does not, technically, refer to ownership of the land; instead, an abstract entity,[25] known as an estate, was created and one's ownership rights are defined by this abstract entity. Of this entity, it was said that 'the land itself is one thing, and the estate in land is another thing, for an estate in the land is a time in the land, or land for a time, and there are diversities of estates, which are no more than diversities of time'.[26] As is evident from this statement, the main defining aspect of the estate is its temporal nature: the length of time that the land would be enjoyed,[27] and an integral part of this matter was the question of whether the rights over the land were inheritable and, if so, by whom. A natural question is why this occurred; what is the point of this abstract entity?

First, the doctrine of estates seems to be a logical consequence of tenure. As the theory underpinning English land law is that all land is held from the Crown,[28] originally, in return for the performance of services, it is difficult to say that the tenants actually owned the land itself; rather, they held an interest or estate in the land. The second reason is more practical. This is that certain incidents of ownership can be divided between different people at different times. The doctrine of estates facilitates this process.

2.6 Freehold estates

Traditionally, estates are defined in terms of their duration. A freehold estate is one whose actual duration cannot be known, with certainty, at the outset. One knows its theoretical duration but cannot know, in advance, when the event will occur which will cause the estate to end. Originally, at common law, there were two freehold estates: the fee simple and the life estate. To these estates, a third, the fee tail, was later added by statute.

2.6.1 The fee simple

The word 'fee', in the context of estates, means that it is inheritable.[29] The word 'simple' indicates that the right to inherit the property is unrestricted. So, it was said, 'a fee simple, and that is, where lands are given to a man and his heirs absolutely without any end or limitation put to the estate, for (fee) is an inheritance . . . and (simple) is that which is pure and perpetual, so that inasmuch as he has an absolute estate of perpetuity in the land, such estate is properly termed a fee-simple'.[30] This means that, if a person with a fee simple estate dies intestate, the land can be inherited by any heir. This includes lineal heirs such as sons, daughters, and grandchildren, as well as collateral heirs, such as cousins, nephews, and nieces.

Because the fee simple could pass to any heir, however remote, it is highly unlikely that it will ever end. In consequence, it is the largest estate that it is possible to own and, in

---

[25] See Lawson, *The Rational Strength of English Law* (London, Stevens, 1951), 87.

[26] *Walsingham's Case (1573) 2 Plowd.* 547 at 555.

[27] See Lawson and Rudden, *The Law of Property* (3rd edn) (Oxford, Clarendon Law Series, 2002), 79; P. Birks in Bright and Dewar, *Land Law, Themes and Perspectives* (Oxford, Oxford University Press, 1998), 462–7.

[28] To improve the accuracy of the register of title, the Queen may now grant an estate to herself: LRA 2002, s. 79.

[29] See Pollock and Maitland, *The History of English Law* (2nd edn) (vol. 1) (Cambridge, Cambridge University Press, 1898), 234–5.

[30] *Walsingham's Case, supra,* at 557.

reality, is akin to outright ownership of the land. As such, the owner of the fee simple is, in general, unrestricted as to what he can do with the land. Such restrictions as there are derive in the main from the general law relating to planning[31] and nuisance.

Some restrictions on the enjoyment of the land can be caused by the creation of third party rights over it. For example, the owner of a fee simple in land has the right to sue people who trespass on that land. If, however, he has granted a neighbour a right of way over the land, then clearly, he cannot bring an action in trespass against the person who exercises that right. To that extent, he has modified one of the rights of the fee simple owner, which is to restrain all other people from coming on to the land,[32] because he has given his neighbour the right to cross the land in accordance with the right. Similarly, the owner of the fee simple may covenant with a neighbour that the property will only be used as a private residence. The effect of this is that the right, which is normally an incident of ownership of the fee simple, to use the land for whatever purpose one likes, has, to an extent, been lost. On the other side of the same coin, the neighbour, as part of his owner- ship of land, has acquired a right over the affected land; in the first instance a right to cross another person's land and, in the second, the right to restrain his neighbour's use of that land.[33] One can envisage an estate as a metaphorical receptacle, the ownership of which carries various rights over the land in question. Various rights can, however, be removed from that receptacle and given to holders of other estates.

2.6.1.1 The position of heirs

The fee simple is defined in terms of its potential duration. In theory, it is likely never to end as it can be passed to any heir of the owner of it. This is not to say that the potential heirs have any rights in the property while the owner of the fee simple is alive. They merely have a hope[34] of succeeding to the property. As such, they have no right to control how the holder of the fee simple uses the land. This point is reflected in the difference between words of purchase (purchase here not being used in its normal meaning of buying but meaning, instead, taking hold of) and words of limitation.

Traditionally, the way in which a fee simple was created was to grant the land 'to A and his heirs'. This gave no estate to A's heirs; rather it defined the estate that A has. The first part of the phrase is regarded as words of purchase, the words which grant the estate to A; the latter part as words of limitation—they define the estate that A has.

In the past, a good deal of technicality hinged upon the correct wording being used and a failure to do so resulted in lesser estates than a fee simple being created.[35] Happily, these difficulties are a thing of the past because s. 60 of the Law of Property Act (LPA) 1925 pro- vides that 'a conveyance of freehold land to any person without words of limitation, or any equivalent expression, shall pass to the grantee the fee simple or other the whole interest which the grantor had power to convey in such land, unless a contrary intention appears in the conveyance'. This means simply that, whatever interest the grantor has, a conveyance will, unless there are words to the contrary in that conveyance, operate to transfer that interest. The distinction between words of purchase and words of limitation does retain some importance, however, in that, technically, a person who is granted land by the act of another party is a purchaser. This, contrary to common parlance, does not mean that the

---

[31] Such public control of land which restricts the rights of owners now has to be considered in the context of the European Convention on Human Rights, incorporated into English law by the Human Rights Act 1998. See J. Howell [1999] Conv. 287; K. Gray in Tee, *Land Law: Issues, Debates, Policy* (Cullompton: Willan Publishing, 2002), Chapter 7.

[32] See 1.1.3.

[33] For the substantive law of easements and covenants, see Chapters 12 and 13.

[34] Sometimes referred to by its Latin form as a *spes*.

[35] See Megarry and Wade, *Law of Real Property*, 3–023–3–034.

grantee has necessarily given value for the transfer. To signify that value or consideration has been given for the transfer, the correct expression is 'sold and conveyed'.

A second point concerning the position of heirs with regard to the fee simple estate concerns the situation where that estate is transferred. Logically, if A holds a fee simple in land and transfers it to B then the duration of the estate should be determined by the continued existence of A's heirs rather than those of B. Presumably for practical reasons, this position was abandoned by 1306,[36] so that in the example given above, the measuring aspect of the estate becomes B's heirs and not those of A.

2.6.2 **Qualified fees simple**

The fee simple outlined above is not qualified, or cut down in any way. It is therefore referred to as a fee simple absolute. It is possible, however, for the fee simple to be cut down. As an example of this, land can be granted to a person in fee simple or until he becomes a solicitor. Such a grant may, in fact, be absolute because the determining, or terminating, event may never happen. If the person does become a solicitor, however, his interest will terminate and the land will pass to someone else. That person has a contingent interest in the land; it is contingent upon that determining event actually occurring. Because the original estate which was granted is liable to be terminated for a reason other than the death without heirs of the holder of it, it is not a fee simple absolute but is a qualified fee simple.

In modern times, it is quite rare for such an interest to be created with respect to land. More commonly, such interests are created in respect of money, where a person is given a life interest in money determinable upon that person becoming bankrupt or suffering any act or thing which causes him to cease to be entitled to the income, such interests being known as protective trusts.[37]

A further example of a contingent interest would be where a testator leaves land in his will 'to the first of my children to become a barrister'. When the testator dies, he may have a number of children, none of whom, as yet, have qualified to be a barrister. As such, none of them are entitled to the land; they merely have a hope of one day satisfying the condition inherent in the will and taking the land. Until that event occurs, some other person is entitled to the land. That person would be either the person identified in the will or, if there is no such person, whoever is entitled, on intestacy, to the deceased person's property. That person's interest in the property is also determinable, in that as soon as one of the testator's children qualified as a barrister, that person would become entitled to the land and would acquire a fee simple absolute.

A problem with transactions of this nature, particularly when the contingencies in question are more complicated than the example just referred to, is that one might have to wait a considerable period of time to see whether or not the contingency has occurred and the person entitled to the land upon the event occurring has the estate vested in him. To circumvent this problem, a complex body of law, which is a combination of common law and statute,[38] developed to fix a time limit by which the contingency must occur. The details of these rules are outside the scope of this book.[39] The Law Commission recommended a legislative simplification of this highly complex body of law[40] and, in respect

---

[36] See Harpum, Bridge, and Dixon, *Law of Real Property*, 3–005.
[37] See Trustee Act 1925, s. 33. For the concept of the trust, see Chapter 3.
[38] Perpetuities and Accumulations Act 1964.
[39] For details of the rules, see Harpum, Bridge, and Dixon, *Law of Real Property*, Chapter 9; Maudsley, *The Modern Law of Perpetuities* (London, Butterworths, 1979).
[40] (1998) Law Com. No. 251. See P. Sparkes [1995] Conv. 212; (1998) 12 Trust Law International 148.

of instruments taking effect after the Perpetuities and Accumulations Act 2009 came into force, a more straightforward perpetuity period of 125 years has been introduced.[41]

2.6.3 **The life estate**

One of the more important rights that the owner of a fee simple has is the right, physically, to possess the land. One of the principal flexibilities of the doctrine of the estate is that particular rights can be separated out from the bundle of rights that the fee simple owner has and become, themselves, the subject of ownership. The right to possess the land is one of the more important rights which a landowner has. This right can be separated from the bundle of rights and become, itself, the subject matter of ownership. Thus, A can be given a life estate in land, remainder to B in fee simple. This means that, for the duration of A's life, it is A who has the right to possess and enjoy the land.

The duration of the life estate is self-explanatory; it continues for as long as A, who is termed the life tenant or tenant for life, continues to live. Various consequences flow from the existence of this more limited estate. First, the principal right that the tenant for life enjoys is the right, physically, to possess and enjoy the land in his lifetime. Upon his death, however, that right will pass to B. Unlike the position considered earlier, where land is settled to the first of a person's sons to become a barrister, where that qualifying event is not certain to happen, it is inevitable that A, at some time, will die and that B or his heirs will become entitled to the property. B does not, therefore, have a contingent interest in the property. The only element of futurity about B's interest in the land is his right, physically, to possess it. To distinguish his position from that of the holder of a contingent interest in land, B's estate is said to be vested in interest. Because, unlike the holder of a contingent interest, B's right to possess the land at some time in the future is certain, his estate is said to be vested in interest, and is termed a fee simple in remainder. A, as the person entitled to possess the property during his lifetime, is said to have an interest in possession. When A dies, the prior estate comes to an end and B's estate is now said to fall into possession. His fee simple is no longer subject to any qualification and becomes absolute.

A second element of the life estate is that, unlike the position with the fee simple, the determining event of A's estate is quite simple to identify. Whereas, if land is granted to X in fee simple, it will not be practical to consider when all X's heirs have died, so that, if X transfers his fee simple to Y, the duration of Y's estate is determined by the continued duration of Y's heirs and not X's, this is not the case with the life estate. It is easy to determine when the life tenant dies so that if A transfers his life estate to C, the rights that C obtains are determined by the longevity of A, not C. What C has acquired is termed an estate *pur autre vie*: an estate for the life of another.

A final point to make about the nature of the life estate is that, because A's right to enjoy the land is limited to his lifetime, his rights over that land are correspondingly limited. As it is certain that B will be entitled to the land upon A's death, B has legitimate concerns as to how A uses the property during his lifetime. To protect B's interest, the doctrine of waste was developed. The idea underlying this doctrine is that the holder of the life interest may use, but not use up, the property. Put another way, he is entitled to the income produced by the property but is not entitled to diminish its capital value.[42]

2.6.3.1 Waste

Technically, what is meant by waste is a change in the use of land. Such a change can amount to an improvement in the land, known as ameliorating waste, or it can cause the

---

[41] Perpetuities and Accumulations Act 2009, ss 5, 15.
[42] See Lawson and Rudden, *The Law of Property*, 98.

property to deteriorate. A life tenant is not liable for ameliorating waste.[43] Neither is he liable, unless the contrary is specifically stated,[44] for what is termed permissive waste. What is meant by permissive waste is the natural deterioration of the property caused, for example, by the failure to repair buildings or clean out ditches.[45] He is, however, liable for voluntary waste, which is, as the name suggests, an act performed by the life tenant, such as felling timber, which reduces the value of the property.[46]

It was not uncommon, however, when creating a life estate, to stipulate that the life tenant was not impeachable; that is, liable for waste. Such a clause did not, however, give the life tenant *carte blanche* to enjoy the property. The body of law known as equity, which developed to modify the common law,[47] would intervene to make liable a life tenant who was unimpeachable for waste if what was done amounted to devastation of the property. An example of equitable waste occurred in *Vane v. Lord Barnard*,[48] where the life tenant was held liable for stripping a house of lead, iron, and glass, the value of which was the then massive sum of £3,000.

2.6.4 **The fee tail**

The only freehold estates which existed from the outset were the fee simple and the life estate. Neither of these estates permitted the realization of what was for some a strongly held aspiration, which was to ensure that land remained within the family from generation to generation. To accommodate this desire, the Statute *De Donis Conditionalibus* 1285 was enacted, its effect being to create a new estate, the fee tail. The term 'fee' again indicates that the estate is inheritable; the word 'tail', which derives from the French word '*taille*', indicates that the range of those who may inherit the estate is cut down. In the case of the fee simple, any relation of the holder of the estate can inherit it on his death. In the case of the fee tail, only lineal descendants can inherit. The range of potential descendants could be cut down further, for example by stipulating that only the male heirs can own the property, such a settlement being termed a tail male.

The introduction of the fee tail led to a conflict of aspirations with regard to the use of the land. On the one hand was the aspiration which prompted the enactment of the Statute *De Donis* in the first place, the wish for a legal mechanism to be created which would facilitate the intergenerational transfer of a particular parcel of land within the same family; on the other was the emerging desire for land to be freely alienable. Once a fee tail had been created then, unless it could somehow be upgraded into a fee simple, its transferability was limited. The reason for this was that, *mutatis mutandis* with the situation pertaining to the life estate, if A had a fee tail and transferred it to B, its duration would be measured by the continuation of A's heirs, not by those of B. What B would acquire was termed a base fee.

To enable land to be freed from the constraints imposed by the existence of a fee tail, two devices were developed to enable a fee tail to be enlarged into a fee simple. The process involved is termed barring the entail. The two devices, which were both highly artificial, were known respectively as suffering a recovery or levying a fine. The essential difference between the two actions lay in the identity of the person seeking to bar the entail. If a settlement was created whereby the land was granted to A in fee tail, remainder to B, then A, whose interest was in possession, could suffer a recovery. The

---

[43] *Doherty v. Allman* (1879) 3 App. Cas. 709. [44] *Re Cartwright* (1899) 41 Ch.D. 532.

[45] *Sticklehorne v. Hatchman* (1586) Owen 43; *Powys v. Blagrave* (1854) 4 De G.M. & G. 448.

[46] See *Honywood v. Honywood* (1874) L.R. 18 Eq. 306, a decision which contains an interesting account as to which trees constitute timber, at 309–11 *per* Sir George Jessel M.R. See also *Pardoe v. Pardoe* (1900) 82 L.T. 549.

[47] For the development of equity, see Chapter 3. [48] (1716) 2 Vern. 738.

effect of this was to enlarge A's interest into a fee simple, thereby defeating any chance B might have of succeeding to the property. If, however, the settlement was to A for life, remainder to B in fee tail, then B was not in possession of the land. Unless B could secure A's co-operation, his only recourse, while A was alive, was to levy a fine and this would create a base fee.[49] Although entirely artificial, these methods of barring entails were popular in that they enabled people to enlarge their estates into a fee simple. To reflect this, the law was put on a statutory footing by the Fines and Recoveries Act 1833, which provided new methods of barring an entail but with the same effects as described above. It was not then possible to bar an entail by will, but this was later made possible by s. 176, LPA 1925.

It is the case today that the desire to attempt to secure intergenerational transfers of land by the use of the fee tail is not nearly as strong as was previously the case. Acknowledging this, it is no longer possible to create a new fee tail, and any attempt so to do will instead create a fee simple.[50] Existing fees tail are not affected by this legislation.

2.6.4.1 Unbarrable entails

The whole process of barring entails was to enable land to become more freely alienable, a fee simple being far more attractive to a potential purchaser than a base fee. The effect of barring the entail, of course, affected later generations, who could no longer rely upon the land descending down the family line. It was not possible for individuals to create an unbarrable entail but certain entails became unbarrable by statute. Instances of this are, first, when, as a reward for services rendered, a fee tail was created by the Crown, in whom the fee simple in remainder was vested and, second, when a special Act of Parliament is passed to create an unbarrable entail, as occurred to reward the first Duke of Marlborough.[51] The existence of such an entail can create problems, however, where the heir apparent is unsuitable to manage the estate on the death of his father, and in such situations the court has jurisdiction under s. 64 of the Settled Land Act 1925 to vary the settlement.[52]

2.7 The coexistence of estates

It is fundamental to the understanding of the doctrine of estates to appreciate that they coexist simultaneously with regard to the same plot of land. The largest estate is the fee simple and it is from this estate that the smaller estates are carved. Some examples can be given.

1. X has a fee simple in land and grants his son, S, a life interest in it. That settlement does not exhaust X's interest in the property, so that, on S's death, the land will revert back to X or if, as is likely, X has already died, to whoever is next entitled in descent from X. Diagrammatically, the position is shown in Figure 2.3.

S (Life Interest) ⟶ X (Fee Simple in Reversion)

Fig. 2.3 Life interest

[49] For a fuller account, see Harpum, Bridge, and Dixon, *Law of Real Property*, 3–080–3–083.
[50] Trusts of Land and Appointment of Trustees Act 1996, Sched. 1, para. 5. But see E. Histed (2000) 116 L.Q.R. 445 who argues that, despite the Act, it may be possible to create a new fee tail. Such an argument is highly unlikely to prevail.
[51] 3 and 4 Anne, c. 6 (1704); 5 Anne, c. 3 (1706).
[52] *Hambro v. Duke of Marlborough* [1994] Ch. 158. See E. Cooke [1994] Conv. 492.

2. X has a fee simple and, by will, leaves the land to his widow, W, for life, thereafter to his son, S, in fee simple. Such a settlement will, on X's death, exhaust his interest in the property, leaving W with a life estate and S with a fee simple in remainder. The term remainder is used, as opposed to reversion, because S's interest is what remains out of the settlement made by X, whereas in the first example, X's interest in the land reverts back to him. Diagrammatically, the position is shown in Figure 2.4.

W (Life Interest) $\longrightarrow$ S (Fee Simple in Remainder)

Fig. 2.4   Life interest and fee simple

3. X has a fee simple and creates a settlement under which he grants the land to his wife, W, for life, thereafter to his son in fee tail. In this situation, X has not exhausted his fee simple; what he has created is a life estate for W, a fee tail in remainder for S and a fee simple in reversion for himself. Diagrammatically, the position is shown in Figure 2.5.

W (Life Interest) $\longrightarrow$ S (Fee Simple in Remainder) $\longrightarrow$ X (Fee Simple in Reversion)

Fig. 2.5   Life interest, fee tail, and fee simple

It is important to realize that in all the examples given the parties each have estates in land, although in the case of some of them their right, physically, to possess that land will not arise until the future. Their interests exist, however, from the date of their creation. So, for instance, in the first example, X has a fee simple in reversion. If, before the death of himself and his son, he makes a will leaving all his property to Y, then, on his death, that reversion will pass to Y, so that on S's death, Y will be entitled to the land.

Again, if one considers example 2, both W and S have interests in the land which they are free to deal with. W could, for example, sell her interest to P. P's right to the land is determined by W's lifetime, it is a tenancy *pur autre vie* and, as such, is unlikely to be an attractive proposition to a purchaser. S, who has the fee simple in remainder, has the more valuable interest, but a purchaser would not be able to possess the land until W dies. Its potential value to a purchaser would depend upon an actuarial assessment of W's life expectancy.

Finally, in example 3 all the parties, X, W, and S, have estates in the property. X's interest, while existing, is of minimal value as the fee tail may not come to an end, thereby preventing the fee simple from falling into possession. Moreover, after W's death, it would always be possible for S, or one of his successors, to bar the entail which would convert the fee tail into a fee simple and put an end to X's reversionary interest.

A final point to make in the present context is that, whenever there exists a succession of interests, the finishing point is always the fee simple. The reason for this is because it is the largest estate out of which all other estates are carved. So, in example 3, X has a fee simple in reversion because, having initially had vested in him a fee simple in possession, he has failed to dispose entirely of his interest in the property. In the second example, on the other hand, he has divested himself entirely of his interest in the land. A succession of estates will, therefore, always end with a fee simple, which will either be in reversion or in remainder.

2.7.1 **The position of the Crown**

At the time of the Norman Conquest, to say that the land in England was owned by the king was not misleading; certainly it represented through the existence of the feudal system an important source of revenue and power. As the feudal system declined, however, the statement, albeit still commonly seen today,[53] that all land in England and Wales is owned by the Crown seems quite odd and, to one leading legal historian, was a 'dogma of very modern appearance'.[54] While not denying that all land is held of the Crown, the modern, and more accurate, analysis of the position of the Crown is to say that what is held is what is termed a radical title to the land, rather than ownership: a statement of political sovereignty rather than proprietorship.[55] The radical title theory was accepted by the High Court of Australia in *Mabo v. Queensland (No. 2)*,[56] where it was held that the native rights of Aborigines to various islands established well before the colonization of those islands had survived that process, and remained in existence. While it was accepted that, as a consequence of colonization, the ultimate title to the lands vested in the Crown, it did not follow from this that pre-existing rights were extinguished.

The idea that what is possessed by the Crown is a radical title based on sovereignty rather than being some form of vestigial ownership is realistic. Certainly the interest that the Crown has in the land carries with it none of the incidents of ownership and, so, to describe the position as a form of vestigial ownership is not particularly meaningful. When one considered the law of escheat, it is tempting, but wrong, to see that as an instance of land reverting to the Crown. That would be the case if the tenant held directly from the Crown but would not be so if the land was held from some other superior lord. In such cases, neither the Crown, nor the superior lord, held any kind of reversion on the fee simple. Such a concept simply did not exist,[57] While it is true that, in *Mabo*, the court could have held that the Crown had acquired a form of ownership of the land but had nevertheless taken subject to pre-existing rights, much the more realistic view of things, particularly in the modern world is to see the Crown as holding a radical title to the land, rather than some form of ownership which has no discernible content.

2.8 Possession

The foregoing discussion of estates has tended to presuppose that the person creating the various estates in land was, in fact, entitled to do so. For various reasons, however, this might not be the case. English law has never embraced the concept of absolute ownership of land. The closest it has come to doing so is when a person is registered as the proprietor of land with an absolute title. Even then, however, as will be seen, that person's title is not indefeasible.[58] Where title to the land is unregistered, this is even more the case. All that a person can do is to demonstrate that he has the better right to possess the land than anyone else. To do this, he must show a convincing documentary title to the property, which will establish how, through various transactions in the past, the land came to be vested in him. Even such a process cannot, however, prove conclusively that no better title to the land exists. This proposition was explained engagingly in the following terms:

> To make better rights impossible the proof would have to start with the grant to Adam and Eve, but even then this was save and except the Garden of Eden, and one is not even sure if they took as joint tenants or tenants in common . . . [59]

---

[53] See, e.g., Harpum, Bridge, and Dixon, *Law of Real Property*, 2.001; and the 5th edition of this work, 24.

[54] Simpson, *A History of the Land Law*, 46.

[55] See Gray and Gray, *Elements of Land Law* (5th edn) (Oxford, Oxford University Press, 2009), 1.3.4.

[56] (1992) 175 C.L.R. 1. See also *Tijani v. Secretary, Southern Nigeria* [1921] A.C. 399 at 404 *per* Viscount Haldane.

[57] Hardman, (1886) 4 L.Q.R. 310, 322, See also A.-G. for Ontario v. Mercer (1883) 8 App. Cas. 767 at 772 *per* Earl of Selborne L.C.; K. Campbell (1992) 3 K.K.L.J. 79 at 93–4.

[58] See Chapter 5.

[59] Farrand, *Contract and Conveyance* (4th edn) (London, Oyez Longman, 1983), 85. For the distinction between joint tenants and tenants in common, see Chapter 9.

English law has traditionally adopted a pragmatic approach to ownership rights with regard to land, although that tradition has changed markedly with the spread of registration of title. The traditional approach was to afford particular importance to the issue of who was in possession of it. The importance of possession was reflected in the medieval doctrine of seisin, so that the person who was in peaceful possession of the land was said to be seised of it and, from that, it was presumed that that person held the land in fee simple.[60] This was particularly important during the feudal period, because the various feudal incidents were levelled against the person who had seisin.[61]

This element of seisin is no longer of any consequence, but the importance of possession of the land remains, in that it is assumed that the person in physical possession of the land is rightfully there. Such a person can bring an action against anyone who interferes with his enjoyment of the land, except someone who can show a better right to possess it. In that sense, title to land is relative.[62] If A sues B for trespass, it is no defence to argue that A is not entitled to be in possession of the land. As the person in possession, A has a better right to the land than B. Possession, therefore, raises the presumption that the possessor of the land has a fee simple in that land,[63] unless and until some other person establishes a better right to it.[64] In time, the possession, originally wrongful, may be sufficiently prolonged to prevent anyone else from successfully challenging the possessor's right to the land, although, as will be seen, this principle has been drastically curtailed by the provisions of the Land Registration Act (LRA) 2002.[65]

The power of a person in possession of land to recover that possession as against anyone who cannot show a better right to that land was squarely based on the importance that the common law attached to the very fact of possession, and the action for ejectment was based on the recovery of possession. In modern times, however, the issue is less the fact of possession than the right to it. In *Manchester Airport Plc v. Dutton*,[66] the claimant had a licence to occupy a wood adjoining the airport, the purpose of the licence being to enable it to fell trees which were obstructing the flight path of a runway. Prior to occupation having been taken, protesters occupied the land and an action was brought to obtain possession, thereby removing the demonstrators. The action succeeded despite the claimant neither being in possession of, nor owning an estate in, the land. While it is true that, historically, a successful claimant would have needed to satisfy one of these criteria in order to bring an action for possession,[67] this was not considered by the majority to be essential. Seeing such an argument as involving 'the rattle of mediaeval chains',[68] the case was treated as being one as deciding which of two claimants had the better right to occupy the land.[69] As between the airport who, albeit not in occupation, had a licence to occupy and the actual occupiers, who were trespassers, the former had the better right, which the law protected. It did not matter that the occupier's right did not, of itself, amount to a recognized property right.[70]

---

[60] See J. Williams, *The Seisin of the Freehold* (London, H. Sweet, 1878), 7.

[61] See Harpum, Bridge, and Dixon, *Law of Real Property*, 45–7.

[62] See *Asher v. Whitlock* (1865) L.R. 1 Q.B. 1 at 5 *per* Cockburn C.J.; *Ocean Estates Ltd v. Pinder* [1969] 2 A.C. 19 at 24–5 *per* Lord Diplock; and *Turner v. Chief Land Registrar* [2013] EWHC 1382 (Ch) at [15] *per* Roth J.

[63] See E. Cooke (1994) 14 L.S. 1 at 4–5.

[64] See *Alan Wibberley Building Ltd v. Insley* [1999] 1 W.L.R. 894 at 898 *per* Lord Hoffmann.

[65] See Chapter 6.   [66] [2000] Q.B. 133.

[67] See the measured discussion of this case by E. Paton and G. Seabourne [1999] Conv. 535.

[68] [2000] Q.B. 133 at 148 *per* Laws L.J.

[69] See also the supportive comments in *Mayor of London v. Hall* [2010] EWCA Civ. 817 at [27] *per* Lord Neuberger M.R.

[70] The highly critical commentary on this case by W. Swadling (2000) 116 L.Q.R. 354 at 360 incorrectly asserts that the analysis involves according the status of a property right to a licence. For a full discussion of licences, see Chapter 15.

2.9 Leasehold estates

The other estate known to the law is the leasehold estate. As the law developed in the context of the feudal system, the lease, being a commercial transaction, was not regarded as being an estate at all, precisely because it was an economic relationship rather than a feudal relationship of subservience and protection, sealed by homage.[71] It was seen as personal property and the tenant was not regarded as being seised of the property. The owner of the freehold estate, who created the lease—the landlord—was regarded, legally, as being in possession of the land, something which is true to this day, as possession is defined to include the receipt of rents and profits or the right to receive the same.[72] Somewhat misleadingly, however, when compared to the use of the term in the context of freehold estates, the landlord's interest is described as a reversion. Although, legally, he is considered to be in possession of the land, while the lease continues, he cannot possess the land physically.

Despite the historical origins of the lease being outside the law of real property, it has been recognized for a considerable period of time that it is an important form of landholding. To reflect this fact, leases are now classified as chattels real, are invariably regarded as forming part of the law of real property, and will be considered in a subsequent chapter of this book.[73]

---

[71] Simpson, *A History of the Land Law*, 73.   [72] LPA 1925, s. 205(1)(xix).
[73] See Chapter 10.

3

Law, Equity, and Human Rights

This chapter considers two important areas of law that connect to, but remain conceptually distinct from, land law. The first is equity, which has intervened in English land law for a very long time, and it is now axiomatic that land law cannot be understood without an appreciation of equity and the law of trusts. The second area, human rights, is a much more recent subject to emerge in real property cases, and its impact thus far remains limited. They shall be considered in turn.

3.1 The historical basis of equity

As the English legal system developed, it was based upon local courts and the Royal Courts: the Courts of Common Law. At the outset, the system was bedevilled by excessive formality. As is the case today, an action had to be initiated by the service of a writ. Unlike modern times, however, this was a highly technical process in the medieval period. Writs were issued through the office of the Chancellor, at the time the King's chief minister and legal adviser. In order to seek different sorts of relief, different writs had to be issued. This caused difficulty, because fitting one's case into a particular legal form of relief was not always straightforward and, if the wrong writ was issued, the action would be discontinued and the litigant would have to recommence the action.[1] Further problems arose if there was not in existence an appropriate writ with which to initiate the particular action. Even if the Chancellor could be persuaded to issue a new writ, and his power to do so was limited,[2] it was not certain that a court would accept its validity.

In addition to the problems caused by the excessive formality, which was an inherent part of the system, difficulties also arose because of the nature of the local courts. The possibility arose that certain powerful opponents could exert undue influence in a particular case, with the possibility that a litigant might have the law on his side, but be unable to vindicate that right in the local court.[3]

3.1.1 Petitions to the king

Because of the problems inherent in the legal system, a good deal of dissatisfaction with it developed. As a result of this sense of grievance, disappointed litigants began the process of petitioning the king directly, the king being regarded as the fount of justice. These petitions were heard by the King's Council, of which the Chancellor was a prominent member.

---

[1] This degree of formality died out as a result of the Common Law Procedure Act 1852 and the Judicature Acts 1873–1875.

[2] See Harpum, Bridge, and Dixon, *Megarry and Wade's Law of Real Property* (8th edn) (London, Sweet & Maxwell, 2012), 5–003.

[3] See Maitland, ed. Brunyate, *A Course of Lectures on Equity* (Cambridge, Cambridge University Press, 1936), 4–5.

In time, these petitions were addressed directly to the Chancellor, who would determine the case.

The office of Chancellor was frequently held by an ecclesiastic.[4] This background was important because cases were frequently decided on the basis of an appeal to conscience and, as an ecclesiastic often trained in 'canon' or church law, the Chancellor would be familiar with disputes concerning the state of a man's soul, or good conscience. Such an approach to the exercise of jurisdiction was, of course, unpredictable in nature. What is unconscionable to one mind may be acceptable to another. Such a system, which gave a seemingly unfettered discretion to the Chancellor, could not be tolerated as a rational system of law, and so the principles upon which the Chancellor would intervene became established and developed into a coherent body of law, known as equity.[5] Equity, as a body of law based upon the notion of conscience, continues to have an important effect.

As the principles upon which equity would intervene became systematized, so the administration of the jurisdiction was also put on an organized footing. The task of resolving disputes of this nature was not confined to the Chancellor. Various judges were appointed to exercise the equitable jurisdiction, sitting in what became known as the Court of Chancery. Later, when the court system was reformed, what was the Court of Chancery became a separate division of the High Court and is termed, simply, the Chancery Division.[6]

3.1.2 Equity acts *in personam*

In order to grasp the nature of equitable intervention, it is necessary to appreciate the technique employed, first by the Chancellor, and then by the Court of Chancery. The Chancellor did not disregard the common law. To the contrary, the common law position would be recognized and regard then had to the merits of the particular case to determine if it was conscionable for one party to rely on it. If it was not, then that party would be personally ordered to do something, or to refrain from doing so.

A good example of this occurred in *Penn v. Lord Baltimore*.[7] A dispute arose as to the boundary between Maryland and Pennsylvania and this led to an agreement being arrived at between the plaintiff and defendant. When the plaintiff sought to enforce the agreement, the argument was raised that the court lacked the jurisdiction to determine a boundary dispute in land situated overseas.[8] This was not, however, seen as a major problem. Lord Hardwicke L.C. said: 'The conscience of the party is bound by this agreement and being within the jurisdiction of this court . . . which acts *in personam*, the court may properly decree it as an agreement.'[9] In other words, because the defendant's conscience was affected by the agreement, he was ordered to implement it. This order is now known as specific performance.

Penn is illustrative of a number of things. First, the nature of the remedy can be seen to be an order directed specifically at an individual: an instance of equity acting on the person. Second, it was made clear in the judgment that the reason why equity intervened was because the common law was inadequate to provide a solution; the award of damages, a monetary form of compensation and the only remedy which the common law could grant, would not have been adequate.[10] Finally, it points to what became a source of tension and

---

[4] Probably the best known of the holders of the Office of Chancellor was Sir, later St, Thomas More who ironically was not from an ecclesiastical background.

[5] For the comments of Lord Eldon L.C. on the demise of a general discretionary approach, see *Gee v. Pritchard* (1818) 2 Swans. 402 at 414.

[6] Supreme Court Act 1981, s. 5.

[7] (1750) 1 Ves. Sen. 444. See also *Luxe Holding Ltd v. Midland Resources Ltd* [2010] EWHC 1908 (Ch) at [28]–[46] *per* Roth J.

[8] With regard to this land, that jurisdiction rested with the king in council.

[9] (1750) 1 Ves. Sen. 444 at 447–8.   [10] Ibid. at 446. See 3.1.4.

conflict within the legal system. The more that the Chancery judges intervened when the common law was perceived to be inadequate, the greater was the irritation of some common law judges; a factor which led to a struggle between judges as to which system was to have supremacy: law or equity.

3.1.3 **Conflict between law and equity**

This, in truth, was a somewhat arid debate. For equity to have any role at all, it must have precedence when common law and equity took a different view of a situation. This proposition is what lay behind Maitland's oft-quoted proposition that equity had come not to destroy the law, but to fulfil it.[11] This means that equity recognizes what the position is but intervenes to modify its effect in the exercise of its jurisdiction. Equity could not operate without the prior existence of the law; its role then became to intervene to complement the law.

As equity developed, it was administered in a different court from the common law courts, thereby leading to prolonged litigation; a case was brought, first, in the common law court and then the action continued until its final resolution in Chancery. This was clearly inefficient and, to obviate this, moves were made to fuse the administration of the two systems, culminating in the Judicature Acts 1873 and 1875.

Under the Acts, now superseded by the Supreme Court Act 1981, the separate courts were abolished to be replaced by the Supreme Court of Judicature, consisting of a High Court made up of Divisions, the assignment of the workload being done on the basis of convenience, the determining factor being the subject matter of the dispute. However, whatever the nature of the dispute, any point of law or equity could be determined by any Division. Moreover, it was provided by s. 25(11) of the Supreme Court of Judicature Act 1873 that:

> Generally, in all matters not hereinbefore particularly mentioned in which there is any conflict or variance between the rules of equity and the rules of common law with reference to the same matter, the rules of equity shall prevail.

The effect of this provision, which finally determined the supremacy of equity, is well illustrated in the leading case of *Walsh v. Lonsdale*.[12] The defendant, the landlord, agreed in writing to grant the plaintiff, the tenant, a seven-year lease. It was a term of the lease that the landlord could demand one year's rent in advance. A deed was not executed so that, at law, there was not a seven-year lease. The tenant nevertheless took possession and paid rent quarterly in arrears. The landlord then, as the agreement envisaged, demanded payment of a year's rent in advance and, when the tenant refused, he purported to exercise the remedy of distraint: the seizing of the tenant's goods to the value of the rent which was owed. The tenant disputed the landlord's right to do this and sued for trespass.

The competing arguments of the two parties rested on the different view taken of the transaction by law and equity. At law, because there was no deed, there could not be a seven-year lease. Because the tenant had gone into possession and paid rent, the law implied that there was a periodic tenancy from year to year, which could be terminated by giving six months' notice to quit.[13] The requirement to pay a year's rent in advance was inconsistent with the tenant's ability to terminate the lease by giving six months' notice to end the lease and, therefore, it was argued that the distress was unlawful. Equity, on the

---

[11] Maitland, *A Course of Lectures on Equity*, 17.
[12] (1882) 21 Ch.D. 9. The case is discussed further at 10.7.
[13] For this aspect of the case, see 10.10.

other hand, takes a more relaxed view as to the need for formality and considered that there was a valid seven-year lease. Insofar as law and equity differed as to how the transaction was viewed, equity prevailed. A seven-year equitable lease existed and, consequently, what the landlord had done was lawful. As Sir George Jessel M.R. put it: 'There is only one court and the equity rules prevail in it.'[14]

Although this is rightly considered to be a leading case on the effect of the Judicature Acts in fusing the administration of law and equity, it should be appreciated that the result would have been the same prior to the Act: the litigation would simply have been more prolonged. The plaintiff would have brought his case in the common law courts and won. The defendant would then have sought in Chancery an injunction to restrain him from enforcing his judgment and would also have won. By fusing the administration of the two systems, the case is now disposed of by one court rather than two.

3.1.4 **Equitable remedies**

A central feature of equitable intervention is the nature of the remedies afforded. Equity acts on the person by issuing an order to do something or to refrain from doing something. The former remedy is most commonly associated with specific performance, whereby one party to a contract is ordered to fulfil the obligations which have been created, but can also be the subject of a mandatory injunction, whereby the defendant is ordered to undo a wrong he has committed, such as building in contravention of a restrictive covenant.[15] An order to refrain from doing something is called an injunction. In the event of non-compliance with either order, the defaulting party is in contempt of court and, as a result, is subject to punitive sanctions.

The principal equitable remedies of specific performance and the injunction are integral parts of the equitable process. The availability of either remedy is predicated upon the common law being unable, through the award of damages, to provide an adequate remedy for the wronged party. If, for example, A contracts with a car dealer to buy a mass-produced car and, in breach of contract, the dealer fails to deliver it, A is adequately compensated by an award of damages; he can easily use the monetary award to buy a car of the same type from another source. If, however, the subject matter of the contract is for the purchase of a rare item, such as an original Van Gogh, then damages cannot compensate entirely for the failure to deliver. The buyer wants the actual painting. In recognition of this fact, equity would normally award specific performance of this type of contract and the seller would be ordered to deliver the painting in return for the purchase price.[16] In the context of land, it has long been assumed that damages are not an adequate remedy for the non-performance of a contract of sale and so a contract to create, or transfer, an interest in land is, *prima facie*, liable to be enforced by a decree of specific performance.

Although specific performance is generally available as a remedy for contracts for the sale of land, or the creation of interests in land, the decree is not automatic. Equitable remedies are awarded at the discretion of the court,[17] and factors may be present which would cause a court to decline to order specific performance. For example, if the completion of a contact to sell land to B would entail the breach of a prior contract to sell that land to A, then specific performance will not be ordered in favour of B.[18] Alternatively, if

---

[14] (1882) 21 Ch.D. 9 at 14.   [15] See, e.g., *Wakeham v. Wood* (1982) 43 P. & C.R. 40.

[16] Contrast *Cohen v. Roche* [1927] 1 K.B. 169, where specific performance of a contract to deliver ordinary chairs was refused, with *Behnke v. Bede Shipping Co.* [1927] 1 K.B. 649, where specific performance of a contract to sell a ship was ordered, regard being had to the particular value of the ship in the matter.

[17] See *Haywood v. Cope* (1858) 25 Beav. 140 at 141 *per* Sir Samuel Romilly M.R.; *White v. Damon* (1801) 7 Ves. Jun. 31 at 35 *per* Lord Eldon L.C.

[18] See *Warmington v. Miller* [1973] 2 All E.R. 372.

performance of the contract would require constant supervision by the court,[19] or such an order would cause exceptional hardship,[20] the remedy will also be refused.

3.1.5 **The creation of equitable interests**

The availability of specific performance in the context of contracts for the sale of land is important. This is because of an important maxim of equity which is that equity looks on that which ought to be done as already having been done. This is the basis of the decision in *Walsh v. Lonsdale*[21] where, because there was a contract to grant a seven-year lease, it gave rise in equity to a seven-year lease. The basis of this was that equity would have awarded specific performance of this contract. Pending the actual award of the decree, which would have led to the creation of a legal lease, equity anticipates the making of such an order and considers the lease already to have been created.

This doctrine, which is applicable to contracts to create other interests in land,[22] is an important source of the creation of equitable interests in land; that is interests in land whose existence depends upon the rules of equity rather than those of the common law. An essential part of the reasoning process is that for the equitable interest to arise, the remedy of specific performance must be available. Because all equitable remedies are discretionary,[23] a reason may exist why that remedy is not available and, if this is the case, the equitable interest in question will not be created.[24]

3.2 **The trust**

The original basis upon which equity intervened was to enforce obligations of conscience and to redress defects in the common law. What also emerged from the intervention of equity was its most important theoretical and practical development: the trust.

3.2.1 **The use**

The precursor of the trust was a device termed the use. From early days, the practice developed of land being conveyed to a person, T, for the use of another person, B. The effect of this at law was quite straightforward. T was the legal owner of the property and the obligation accepted on behalf of B was disregarded by the common law. Equity, however, took a different view of the matter. Because T had accepted the undertaking to hold the land to the use of B, it was considered unconscionable for T to renege on that obligation. His conscience was affected and equity compelled T to comply with the use. In this way, equity ensured that B enjoyed the benefit of the land.

---

[19] *Co-operative Insurance Society Ltd v. Argyll* [1998] A.C. 1. For a valuable critique of this decision, see A. Tettenborn [1998] Conv. 23.

[20] *Patel v. Ali* [1984] Ch. 283.

[21] (1882) 21 Ch.D. 9.

[22] See *McManus v. Cooke* (1887) 35 Ch.D. 681; *United Bank of Kuwait v. Sahib* [1997] Ch. 107, where there was held not, in fact, to be a contract to create a mortgage. See 11.4.4.2.

[23] The court has a jurisdiction, in appropriate cases, to award damages in lieu: Chancery Amendment Act 1858 (Lord Cairns' Act); Supreme Court Act 1981, s. 50. For the award of such damages, see *Shelfer v. City of London Lighting Co.* [1895] 1 Ch. 287; *Jaggard v. Sawyer* [1995] 1 W.L.R. 269. See J.A. Jolowicz [1975] C.L.J. 224; P.H. Pettit [1977] C.L.J. 369, [1978] C.L.J. 51. See 13.6.1.

[24] See *Bell Street Investments v. Wood* [1970] E.G.D. 812; *Warmington v. Miller* [1973] 2 All E.R. 272. See 10.7.2.

Before considering how the early use developed into the modern trust, it is as well to question why people should have adopted this procedure. If it was intended that B should benefit from the land, the obvious question is why not transfer the land to him directly and forego the somewhat artificial procedure of transferring the land to T to be held to the use of B. There were a number of reasons why this procedure was adopted. Some had a slightly romantic air to them; others were more prosaic.

3.2.1.1 Reasons for the use

One of the reasons for putting land into use was when the owner of it was going to go abroad to fight in the crusades. In such circumstances, the land was transferred to a nominee to hold the property for the use of the departing knight. A second, rather more meretricious, reason concerned certain people who were in religious orders. Some religious orders had taken vows of poverty and, because of these vows, the monks could not own land. To circumvent this difficulty, land could be conveyed to a nominee to be held to the use of the monks. Technically, therefore, because the legal title was not vested in the monks, the legal ownership being in the nominee, the vow of poverty had not been broken but they, nevertheless, enjoyed the benefit of the land because equity would enforce the use. As it was engagingly put, 'Like horses, which used but did not own their stables, the friars used, but did not own, the buildings they occupied.'[25] The third main reason for employing the use was succession, and the closely related issue of tax.

3.2.1.2 Feudal dues

An inherent part of the feudal system was that the person who was to inherit the land was determined by the estate which was owned, it not being possible to leave land by will. Coupled with this was the incidence of onerous feudal dues which became payable to the superior lord upon the death of the tenant. The device of the use was central to the twin aims of allowing, in effect, land to be left by will,[26] and, at the same time, avoiding the payments of these feudal dues; a practice described as 'having reached a [level of] perfection which a modern income tax practitioner might well envy.'[27] The scheme adopted was for land to be transferred to a number of people, say, T1, T2, T3, and T4, to be held to the use of B and his heirs. The effect of this was that the legal title to the land would be vested in the name of these four people subject to their obligation, enforceable in equity, to honour the use in favour of B. When B died, because the use was in favour of B and his heirs, the land would now be held for the benefit of that heir. The important point was that, at law, nothing of significance had happened. The legal title remained vested in T1, T2, T3, and T4. Consequently, although the actual benefit of the land had passed, by inheritance, to B's heir, because this had not happened at law, the feudal incidents were not payable. Also, the person named as the beneficiary of the use upon the death of B could be someone who would not otherwise have been entitled to take over the estate, thereby allowing an indirect form of testamentary freedom to occur.

Of course, T1, T2, T3, and T4 were not immortal. It was unlikely, however, that all of them should die simultaneously, thereby causing the legal title to pass by inheritance. Instead, when one of the legal owners died, the remaining three would retain the legal ownership or title to the land[28] and the person would simply be replaced. So, on the death of T1, the position would be that T2, T3, and T4 would be the legal owners of the land. T5 would then be added to the

---

[25] Simpson, *A History of the Land Law* (2nd edn) (Oxford, Oxford University Press, 1986), 174.

[26] See A.D. Hargreaves in Warmington (ed.), *Stephen's Commentaries on the Law of England* (vol. 1) (London, Butterworths, 1950), 117; Simpson, *A History of the Land Law*, 181–2.

[27] Simpson, *A History of the Land Law*, 22–3.

[28] This depended upon the land being conveyed to them as joint tenants, a concept which will be fully explained in Chapter 9.

number of legal owners. By topping up the legal owners in this way, it was ensured that, barring catastrophe, the payment of the feudal dues incident upon death was avoided.

3.2.2 The Statute of Uses 1535

For the leading barons, the use was a very welcome device in that it enabled them to avoid paying feudal incidents to the king. While it was true that their own tenants could utilize the use to avoid similar payments, the use was nevertheless highly popular. For the king, however, the use had no advantages. As the king was at the apex of the feudal pyramid, the ultimate lord and tenant of no one, the employment of the use deprived him of valuable resources while conferring no advantages upon him. In an effort to emasculate the use, which was an extremely popular device,[29] Henry VIII forced through a very unwilling Parliament the Statute of Uses in 1535.

The effect of the statute was to 'execute' the use. The purpose of this was to make the ostensible tenant in every case also the legal tenant, liable to his lord for all the feudal services and incidents.[30] If land was conveyed to T1, T2, T3, and T4 to the use of B and his heirs, then the statute operated to execute the use and cause the legal title to the land to vest in B. So, when B died, the land would pass by inheritance to his heir and feudal dues would now be payable.

3.2.2.1 The use upon a use

Faced with a potentially lethal attack upon a popular concept, lawyers employed a degree of ingenuity to sidestep the statute and to resurrect the use. The method adopted was to employ two uses: the use upon a use. What this amounted to was that if one was trying to ensure that C obtained the benefit of the land, it would be conveyed to A and his heirs to the use of B and his heirs to the use of C and his heirs. It was eventually held that while the statute operated to execute the first use, thereby transferring the legal title to B, it did not operate to execute the second use, with the result that equity recognized the obligation imposed upon B.

The acceptance of this device demonstrated the enthusiasm of lawyers to reintroduce a popular device, because the reasoning employed to achieve this goal is manifestly threadbare. This reasoning was less controversial than might be supposed in that, with the decline in the feudal system, the avoidance of feudal dues was less of a motivation for the employment of the use than was previously the case. Be that as it may, it enabled the use to continue. In time, however, the second use changed its name and the practice developed of terming the second use a trust. Land was then conveyed to A and his heirs unto the use of B and his heirs on trust for C and his heirs. The Statute of Uses was repealed in 1925[31] and what one does now is simply convey the land to B in fee simple upon trust for C. B is termed the trustee and C the beneficiary.

3.2.3 Formality

To create a trust of personalty, no formality is required. A trust can be created orally. All that is necessary is for a court to be satisfied that the person intended to create a trust.[32]

---

[29] The Statute of Uses was said to be an excuse for, if not one of the causes of, the Pilgrimage of Grace: Maitland, *A Course of Lectures on Equity*, p. 35.

[30] Digby, *An Introduction to the History of the Law of Real Property* (3rd edn) (Oxford, Clarendon Press, 1884), 302.

[31] LPA 1925, Sched. 7.

[32] See, e.g., *Paul v. Constance* [1977] 1 W.L.R. 527; *Rowe v. Prance* [1999] 2 F.L.R. 787. For criticism of the latter decision, see S. Baughen [2000] Conv. 58.

Provided, then, that the subject matter and the objects of the trust are sufficiently certain, a trust will be created. This is not the case with land. Section 53(1)(b) of the Law of Property Act (LPA) 1925 provides that:

> a declaration of trust respecting any land or interest therein must be manifested and proved by some writing signed by some person who is able to declare such trust or by his will.

This formal requirement, it should be noted, is evidentiary, so that it is not necessary that the declaration itself should be in writing. More importantly, resulting and constructive trusts are exempt from the requirement that there be written evidence of the trust.[33] These trusts have particular importance in the context of disputes as to ownership of the family home,[34] but are relevant also to some other areas of land law. Although the operation of these trusts will be considered in detail later in the book, it is convenient to say something about the nature of these trusts at this stage.

3.2.3.1 Resulting trusts

The essential nature of the resulting trust is that it arises when the legal title is put into the name of one person but it is not intended to make an out and out gift to that person.[35] In the context of land law, the main relevance of the resulting trust is when land is conveyed into the name of one person but another person has contributed to the purchase price. So, if a house is bought outright for £100,000 and A provides £10,000 and the balance of £90,000 is supplied by B, into whose name the house is conveyed, equity presumes that A did not intend to make B a gift of the £10,000. Despite the lack of writing normally required to create a trust, a resulting trust will arise whereby A will get an equitable share in the property commensurate with the size of the contribution to the purchase price. In this case, B will hold the property on trust for himself and A in the proportion of 90 per cent to 10 per cent.[36]

3.2.3.2 Constructive trusts

The constructive trust is a trust imposed by equity as a response to inequitable conduct on the part of the holder of the legal title to the property.[37] This, it will be appreciated, is a somewhat vague definition which says nothing of when conduct will be regarded as being inequitable. The constructive trust has a wide role to play in the resolution of disputes concerning all types of property. In the context of land law, somewhat ironically, its main role is to prevent one person, C, going back on an oral undertaking that he would hold the land on trust for another person, D, in circumstances when it would be unconscionable to allow C to rely on the lack of writing which would normally be required to create such a trust. The reason that this is described as ironic is that the case which is generally taken as the progenitor of this line of jurisprudence, *Rochefoucauld v. Boustead*,[38] was very arguably decided as an instance of an express rather than a constructive trust.[39] Nevertheless, in modern times in a situation where C assures D that she will have a beneficial interest in land, and D relies on that assurance, a constructive trust will be imposed so that C is

---

[33] LPA 1925, s. 53(2).   [34] See Chapter 8.

[35] See Chambers, *Resulting Trusts* (Oxford, Clarendon Press, 1997), 5. Contrast W. Swadling (2008) 124 L.Q.R. 72 at 85 *et seq.*

[36] See, e.g., *Re Rogers' Question* [1948] 1 All E.R. 328. The role of the resulting trust in the context of the family home has become much diminished. See Chapter 8.

[37] See P. Millett (1995) 9 Trust Law International 35 at 39.

[38] [1897] 1 Ch. 196

[39] See W. Swadling in Mitchell (ed.), *Constructive and Resulting Trusts* (Oxford, Hart Publishing, 2010), Chapter 3, although see G. Allen (2015) 36 Journal of Legal History 43, especially at 72–82.

required, notwithstanding the failure to comply with the statutory formalities required for the creation of a trust of land, to give effect to that assurance.[40] More recently, however, the courts have adopted a rather wider rationale for the imposition of a constructive trust. The ramifications of this will be considered fully in the discussion of ownership of the family home.[41]

3.2.4 Equity follows the law

It is important to appreciate that, as the trust concept developed, equity never disputed that the trustee was the legal owner of the land. Equity took the view, however, that the trustee was required to use the land for the benefit of the beneficiary. From there it was but a short step, when land is conveyed to T on trust for B, to say that, although T was the legal owner of the land, because the real enjoyment of the land belonged to B, B was regarded as the equitable owner of it. Various consequences flowed from this. T is the legal owner of the property but is required to use that property for B's benefit. To ensure that this is the case, equity imposes various obligations, termed fiduciary obligations, on the trustee as to how that property is used. For example, T cannot use his position as the legal owner of the property for personal gain and, if he does, equity will require him to hold that profit on a constructive trust for the beneficiary because his action is regarded as an abuse of his fiduciary position.[42]

Having accepted the notion of equitable ownership of land, the next question is to determine the nature of that ownership. At law, a person does not actually own the land itself; rather he owns an estate in land, originally either a fee simple, a fee tail, or a life estate. Equity followed the same theoretical framework. So, as the common law enabled land to be settled upon A for life, to B in fee tail, remainder to C in fee simple, equity also allowed these interests to be held on trust. The effect of this is that legal estates have their counterparts in equity, so one could have equitable life estates, fees tail, and fees simple. This mirroring of the common law estates is an application of an important principle, applicable to many areas of land law, that principle being that equity follows the law.

The trust is a legal device which is widely used and embraces all sorts of property and not just land. It nevertheless occupies a pivotal role in land law. Although it is commonly the case that a legal owner of land does not hold the land on trust for anyone, this is not necessarily the case. If the legal owner of the property does not hold on trust for anyone else, it is misleading to refer to him as the owner in equity as well as at law because in this situation there is no trust in existence, and consequently no separate equitable title.[43] To emphasize that there is no trust in existence, it is common to refer to this person as being the legal and beneficial owner of the land. While the legal owner may be solely entitled to the land for his own benefit, this is not necessarily the case. He may hold the land on trust for another person altogether,[44] or for himself and another person, a case where there is sole ownership at law but co-ownership in equity.[45] In these cases, the legal owner is not the sole beneficial owner and it is then necessary to locate the equitable ownership of the property.

---

[40] See, e.g., *Bannister v. Bannister* [1948] 2 All E.R. 133; *Grant v. Edwards* [1986] Ch. 638. See 8.7.3.

[41] Chapter 8.

[42] See *Boardman v. Phipps* [1967] 2 A.C. 46, which involved a very strict application of this principle. See, generally, *Attorney-General of Hong Kong v. Reid* [1994] 1 A.C. 324.

[43] See *Westdeutsche Landesbank Girozentrale v. Islington London Borough Council* [1996] A.C. 669 at 706 *per* Lord Browne-Wilkinson.

[44] See, e.g., *Hodgson v. Marks* [1971] Ch. 892.

[45] See, e.g., *Williams & Glyn's Bank Ltd v. Boland* [1981] A.C. 487.

3.2.5 The imposition of a trust

Normally, if the legal owner, or owners, of the property are also beneficially entitled to that property, it is misleading to talk of them being the equitable owners. Ordinarily, there would not be a trust in existence as there are no outstanding equitable interests. An extremely important exception to this occurs in the case of co-ownership at law. In this case a trust of land is imposed by statute, so that if A and B are co-owners at law, they hold the land on trust for themselves in equity.[46] The reason for this derives from the nature of co-ownership. In the case of co-owners of land, the co-owners can be either joint tenants or tenants in common. These concepts will be explained more fully in a later chapter.[47] For present purposes, it is sufficient to say that if a joint tenancy is in existence, the co-owners are regarded as being one legal unit and, as individuals, they own no specific share in the property. If they are tenants in common, they do own separate shares in the property, but those shares are not physically divided. For example, A can own a 60 per cent share of the property and B a 40 per cent share and, when the property is sold, they will divide the proceeds of sale in those proportions. At law, it is only possible for co-owners to hold the property as joint tenants, whereas, in equity, they can be either joint tenants or tenants in common. To recognize this, a trust is always imposed in the case of legal co-ownership, even when the only beneficiaries are the legal co-owners. So, it is quite possible, and indeed common, for A and B, who are joint tenants at law, to hold a house on trust for themselves as joint tenants in equity so that, perhaps counter-intuitively, the position at law and in equity is exactly the same. In this context, it is perfectly correct to say that A and B hold land on trust for themselves.

3.3 Other equitable interests

Although the trust is probably equity's greatest creation, the intervention of equity was not limited to that. There were other areas of land law where the common law position was considered to be defective or oppressive and so equity intervened to mitigate the harshness of the law. A notable example is the law of mortgages.[48] As well as modifying the common law, equity also recognized other rights which did not amount to the beneficial entitlement to the land.

3.3.1 The creation of equitable rights

There are a number of ways in which an equitable interest can be created. These can be enumerated here and elaborated hereafter.

1. **Lack of formality.** As a general proposition, in order to create a legal interest in land, a deed must be used.[49] Equity, however, takes a more relaxed view of formalities. An attempt to create a legal interest which fails due to the lack of a deed is, by a fiction, regarded as a contract to create that interest.[50] Provided specific performance is available, then, on the basis that equity looks on that which ought to be done as already being done,[51] an equitable right would be created. For such a view to be taken, however, it is essential that there is in being a contract. For many centuries, it was possible for there to be in existence an oral contract for the sale of land, or an interest in land. Such contracts could not be sued upon, however, unless they were either evidenced in writing or supported by an act of part

---

[46] Trusts of Land and Appointment of Trustees Act 1996, s. 5, Sched. 2.
[47] See Chapter 9.   [48] See Chapter 11.   [49] LPA 1925, s. 52(1).
[50] *Parker v. Taswell* (1858) 2 De G. & J. 559.   [51] See 3.2.

performance.[52] Since the enactment of s. 2 of the Law of Property (Miscellaneous Provisions) Act 1989, however, a contract for the sale of land can only be made in writing. There is no longer any such thing as an oral contract for the sale of land. This means that, to create an equitable interest in land in this way, the formal requirements of s. 2 must be met.[53] If they are not, an equitable interest will not arise directly, although rights may be acquired through the medium of estoppel.[54]

2. **Possession of an equitable interest.** If a person has only an equitable estate in land, then the only interests he can create over that land are, themselves, equitable. The holder of an equitable estate cannot, as a matter of general principle, create a legal estate or interest.[55]

3. **Time.** As will be seen in Chapter 4, the legislation of 1925 provided that, to exist as a legal interest, the right in question must exist for the equivalent of a fee simple absolute in possession or a term of years. If, for example, a person purports to create a right of way for life, that easement can only be equitable.

4. **Right only recognized in equity.** There are certain recognized property rights which were the creation of equity. A good example of such a right is a restrictive covenant where, for instance, one landowner covenants with his neighbour that he will only use the land as a private residence. Such a covenant is capable of existing as a property right[56] but has only ever been recognized in equity.

3.4 The enforceability of legal and equitable rights

In the law of contract, the doctrine of privity was to the effect that only the parties to a contract could sue or be sued upon it. Nowadays, with regard to who can sue on the contract, the position has been changed considerably by the Contracts (Rights of Third Parties) Act 1999 so as to enable a person who is not a party to the contract, but for whose benefit the contract is made, to bring an action on it. It remains axiomatic, however, that a person who is not a party to a contract cannot be sued upon it.[57] In land law this is not the case. If something is recognized as a property right, then parties other than those who are privy to its creation will be affected by it.[58] If a right of way has been created, successive owners of the land affected by that right will have to give effect to it or, as is also said, will take subject to the right or be bound by it. On the other side of the coin, the issue will arise as to the circumstances when a person who acquires land acquires, also, rights over another person's land. Of these two issues, it is the circumstances when a person takes subject to rights which is the most contentious and, in determining this issue, it was always vital to distinguish between legal and equitable rights, although this previously fundamental distinction is less important under the system of registration of titles to land.

---

[52] Statute of Frauds 1677, s. 4; LPA 1925, s. 40(1)(2).

[53] *United Bank of Kuwait plc v. Sahib* [1997] Ch. 107. For criticism, see M.P. Thompson [1995] Conv. 465, commenting on the decision at first instance.

[54] See *Halifax Plc v. Curry Popeck (A Firm)* [2008] EWHC 1692 (Ch) at [15] *per* Norris J. and Chapter 14.

[55] *Cook v. The Mortgage Business Plc* [2012] EWCA Civ. 17 at [59] *per* Etherton L.J. affmd without reference to this issue, sub nom, *Scott v. Southern Pacific Mortgages Ltd* [2014] UKSC 52, although see at [112] *per* Lady Hale. See also *Skelwith (Leisure) Ltd v. Armstrong* [2015] EWHC 2830 (Ch) at [52]–[59] *per* Newey J.

[56] *Tulk v. Moxhay* (1843) 2 Ph. 773. See Chapter 13.   [57] *Dunlop v. Selfridge* [1915] A.C. 847.

[58] This difference between personal and property rights has been described as 'the doctrinal cleavage': J.W. Harris in Bell and Eekelaar (eds), *Oxford Essays in Jurisprudence* (3rd series) (Oxford, Oxford University Press, 1987), 167 at 181.

3.5 Legal rights

If a legal right affects land then any person who acquires that land will be bound by that right. It is immaterial whether or not he had prior notice of it. A legal right binds the world. This is well illustrated by *Wyld v. Silver*.[59] A property developer bought land and had obtained outline planning permission to build five houses. It then transpired that, under a private Act of Parliament of 1799, the villagers had been given the right to hold an annual fair or wake on the land on the Friday in Whit week, although the last known occasion when this right had been exercised was in 1875. It was nevertheless held that an injunction should be granted to restrain the planned building so as not to interfere with the legal right of the villagers to hold a fair. The fact that the purchaser neither knew, nor could have known, of this right was immaterial. Because it was a legal right, the purchaser, despite enjoying the unqualified sympathy of Russell L.J.,[60] was bound by it.

The case also illustrates a second point. In *Wyld v. Silver*, the builder had acquired outline planning permission to build. Although this is necessary in order for the proposed development to be lawful, alone it is not sufficient. The fact that planning permission has been granted will not override an individual's property right to object to what has been permitted by the local authority.[61]

3.6 Equitable rights

Unlike legal rights, equitable rights are not automatically binding on a successor in title to the land affected. The original basis of equitable intervention was that the conscience of a landowner had been affected by some undertaking that had been entered into. The next question was to determine the circumstances in which the conscience of a successor in title would also be regarded as being affected by the particular obligation. The answer to this came in an essentially negative form. An equitable interest would be binding upon the whole world, except a bona fide purchaser of a legal estate for value without notice of the equitable interest.

In *Pilcher v. Rawlins*,[62] the legal owner of land, which was already subject to an equitable mortgage, created a legal mortgage and the issue was whether the second mortgagee, who had a legal estate in the land, took subject to the first mortgage, which was an equitable interest in the land. When creating the legal mortgage, the landowner, by suppressing relevant documents, had been able to create the impression that the land was free of any incumbrance. The second mortgagee neither knew of, nor had any means of discovering, the prior equitable mortgage which, for this reason, was held to be void against him. The position was that 'such a purchaser's plea of a purchase for valuable consideration without notice is an absolute, unqualified plea to the jurisdiction of this court'.[63] To sum up, the essential difference between legal and equitable rights is that legal rights are enforceable against the whole world, whereas equitable rights are enforceable against the whole world, except the bona fide purchaser of the legal estate for value without notice. What must now be considered is what must be established before a person is regarded as being a bona fide purchaser (as the term is usually abbreviated).

---

[59] [1963] Ch. 243.   [60] Ibid. at 268.
[61] See also *Wheeler v. J.J. Saunders Ltd* [1996] Ch. 19; *Turner v. Pryce* [2008] 1 P. & C.R. D. 52. See M.P. Thompson [1995] Conv. 239 at 242–4.
[62] (1872) 7 Ch. App. 259.   [63] Ibid. at 268–9 *per* James L.J.

3.6.1 **Bona fide**

Although it has been said that good faith is an independent part of the definition,[64] no example appears to exist where this seems to play any separate role. All that it appears to do is to emphasize that the purchaser must be without notice of the relevant equitable interest.

3.6.2 **Purchaser for value**

As was explained in Chapter 2,[65] the term 'purchaser' is a technical term and does not, as it does in common parlance, carry the necessary implication that the transfer was for value. A purchaser is a person who acquires property through the act of the parties and not by operation of law. A person who acquires property under a will is, therefore, a purchaser but someone who succeeds to property on intestacy is not. In neither case, however, has the person given value and will, therefore, be bound by any equitable interests regardless of notice.

Value includes more than money and this can be anything that the common law would regard as being good consideration. As is the case in the law of contract, the consideration need not be adequate, so that a purchase at an undervalue is, nevertheless, for value.[66] In addition to what common law regards as consideration, equity regards an ante-nuptial agreement made in contemplation of marriage to transfer property as being for value. Such agreements must, today, be very rare.

3.6.3 **Legal estate**

To take free of an equitable interest, the purchase must be of a legal estate. This obviously includes the purchase of a freehold estate, but also includes the purchase of a lease and, most importantly, a mortgage. This is because a mortgage, when it has been created by a charge by deed expressed to be by way of legal mortgage, which is the usual method of creating a legal mortgage, is given the same protection as if the mortgage had been created by a 3,000-year lease[67] and, as a result, is treated as being a purchase of a legal estate.

If the purchaser acquires only an equitable estate, as would be the case upon the creation of an equitable mortgage,[68] the contest for priority is between two equitable rights. In such a case, the normal rule is that, when the equities are equal, the first in time will prevail.[69] What will cause the equities to be unequal is when the holder of the first equitable interest allows the holder of the legal estate to appear to be absolutely entitled to the property, thereby allowing the subsequent person to act to his detriment.[70] An example of this occurred in *Freeguard v. Royal Bank of Scotland plc.*[71] Mr and Mrs Freeguard owned land situated near other land which they had sold to a Mr Edgar, a property developer. To disguise their interest in the retained land, they sold it to the developer, having lent him the money to finance the purchase. They were granted an option to repurchase the land, but did not protect that

---

[64] *Midland Bank Trust Co. Ltd v. Green* [1981] A.C. 513 at 528 *per* Lord Wilberforce.

[65] See 2.6.1.1.

[66] *Bassett v. Nosworthy* (1673) Rep. T. Finch 102; *Midland Bank Trust Co. Ltd v. Green* [1981] A.C. 513.

[67] LPA 1925, s. 87(1)(a). See 11.4.1.

[68] See *McCarthy & Stone Ltd v. Julian S. Hodge & Co. Ltd* [1971] 1 W.L.R. 1547 at 1555.

[69] Ibid. at 1554 *per* Foster J. See also *Flinn v. Pountain* (1889) 60 L.T. 484 at 486 *per* North J.; *Sainsbury's Supermarkets Ltd v. Olympia Homes Ltd* [2005] EWHC 1235 (Ch) at 79 *per* Mann J.; *Halifax Plc v. Curry Popeck (A Firm)* [2008] EWHC 1692 (Ch) at [24]–[25] *per* Norris J.; *Rees v. Peters* [2011] EWCA Civ. 386 at [24] *per* Sir Andrew Morritt C. See also LRA 2002, s. 28.

[70] See *Abigail v. Lapin* [1934] A.C. 491 at 507 *per* Lord Wright.

[71] (2000) 79 P. & C.R. 81.

option in the appropriate manner by registration. He subsequently created an equitable mortgage in favour of the bank and the issue was whether the equitable interest which arose as a result of the creation of the option had priority over the, later, equitable mortgage. It was held that it did not. While refusing to stigmatize the transaction between the Freeguards and Mr Edgar as a sham,[72] Robert Walker L.J. considered it to be 'designed, if not to deceive, at any rate to give to the world . . . the impression that he was the unencumbered owner of the . . . strip and could deal with it as he pleased'.[73] This conduct caused the normal priority rule to be displaced, so that the bank took free from the prior equitable interest.

A similar line of reasoning has been employed in a superficially similar situation, whereby the legal title to a house is in the name of one person but there exists co-ownership in equity, and the legal owner creates a mortgage over the property. The question which then arises is whether the beneficial co-owner can enforce her right against the mortgagee; whether the equitable interest is binding on the purchaser of a legal estate. This is an issue of considerable theoretical and practical importance. In some cases, the holder of the beneficial interest has been prevented from asserting the priority of that interest precisely because she has allowed the legal owner of the house to present himself to the outside world as being the unencumbered owner of the property.[74] This line of cases represents a significant, and it will be argued, generally justifiable restriction on the enforceability of equitable interests against institutions who lend money against the security of real property. This issue will re-emerge at various parts of this book and will be dealt with in more detail when considering the rights and potential liabilities of mortgagees, in the context of co-ownership.[75]

There are three other exceptions to the normal rule whereby, as between two competing equitable interests, the first in time prevails. These are:

1. **Better right to legal estate.** If the purchaser of an equitable estate has, as a result of his purchase, a better right to the legal estate than the holder of the prior equitable interest, he will take free from it. An example of this occurred in *Assaf v. Fuwa*,[76] where land was conveyed to a trustee, who is, it will be recalled, the legal owner of the property and so can be classed as a bona fide purchaser. The trustee did not have notice of the equitable interest, and so the beneficiary under the trust, who had the right to have the legal estate conveyed to him, was held to take free of it.

2. **Later acquisition of the legal estate.** A purchaser of an equitable estate without notice will take free from a prior equitable interest if he subsequently acquires the legal estate, even if, when he does so, he then has notice of it.[77] This is so unless he knowingly acquires the legal estate in breach of trust, in which case he will take subject to the interests under that trust.[78]

3. **Mere equities.** A purchaser of an equitable estate will take free of 'mere equities' of which he has no notice. Mere equities are equitable rights which fall short of being a full equitable interest in land[79] and, in essence, amount to claims to equitable relief. Examples of such equities are the right to have an instrument set aside on the ground of mistake,[80] or a transaction set aside because of fraud.[81] While such an equity is

---

[72] Ibid. at 84 *per* Robert Walker L.J. For sham transactions, see 5.5.1.   [73] Ibid. at 89.
[74] This line of cases starts with *Bristol and West Building Society v. Henning* [1995] 1 W.L.R. 778 and currently extends to *Wishart v. Credit and Mercantile plc* [2015] EWCA Civ. 655.
[75] See 11.6.8.   [76] [1955] A.C. 215.   [77] *Bailey v. Barnes* [1894] Ch. 25.
[78] *McCarthy & Stone Ltd v. Julian S. Hodge & Co. Ltd* [1971] 1 W.L.R. 1547.
[79] Where title is registered, these equities are interests capable of binding successors in title: LRA 2002, s. 116. See 5.1.5.3.
[80] *Smith v. Jones* [1954] 2 All E.R. 823.   [81] *Ernst v. Vivian* (1863) 33 L.J. Ch. 513.

capable of binding a purchaser,[82] a purchaser of an equitable estate without notice will take free from it.[83]

3.6.4 **Without notice**

The final element of the notion of the bona fide purchaser is that he is without notice. This is also the part which has generated the greatest debate. There are three forms of notice: actual notice, constructive notice, and imputed notice, which will be examined in turn.

3.6.4.1 **Actual notice**

As a result of the system of registration of land charges, to be discussed in Chapter 4, actual notice has increased in importance. This is because the effect of registration is that a purchaser is deemed to have actual notice of any matter which has been registered,[84] irrespective of his true state of mind. Prior to this legislative change, however, this form of notice was considerably less important, and certainly less litigated, than other sources of notice, since disputes normally centred on what a purchaser should have known rather than what he did know. A person was regarded as having actual notice of a matter if information about it had come to his attention from a reputable source and not simply from casual conversations.[85]

3.6.4.2 **Constructive notice**

If a purchaser of a legal estate was only bound by equitable interests, the existence of which he was actually aware, then it would be in his interest to know as little as possible prior to making the purchase. This would make equitable interests highly vulnerable. To avoid this, equity developed the doctrine of constructive notice. Under this doctrine the question which had to be considered is what the purchaser should have known.[86] The test which came to be adopted, and which was confirmed by statute,[87] was to consider what a purchaser should have discovered by making reasonable enquiries. The relevant test is now that contained in s. 199, LPA 1925, which provides that:

> a purchaser is not to be prejudicially affected by notice of . . . any instrument or matter unless it is within his own knowledge, or would have come to his knowledge if such inquiries and inspections had been made by him as ought reasonably to have been made by him.

The issue to be addressed is what enquiries a purchaser ought reasonably to make, assuming that such enquiries would have revealed the necessary knowledge.[88] The two main sources of information were investigation of title and a physical inspection of the property.

Investigation of title

Although it is true to say that when title is unregistered possession of land is indicative of ownership in fee simple, 'no man in his senses would take an offer of purchase from a man merely because he stood on the ground'.[89] Such a person might be a tenant or even a squatter. The essence of unregistered conveyancing was that the seller of the land would

---

[82] See, e.g., *Blacklocks v. J.B. Developments (Godalming) Ltd* [1982] Ch. 183.
[83] See, generally, *Latec Investments Ltd v. Hotel Terrigal Pty Ltd* (1965) 113 C.L.R. 265.
[84] LPA 1925, s. 198.   [85] *Lloyd v. Banks* (1868) L.R. 3 Ch. App. 488.
[86] For an historical account, see J. Howell [1997] Conv. 431.
[87] Conveyancing Act 1882, s. 3(1). This was regarded as being confirmatory of the general law in *Hunt v. Luck* [1901] 2 Ch. 428 at 435 *per* Vaughan-Williams L.J.
[88] See *Kemmis v. Kemmis* [1988] 1 W.L.R. 1307 at 1319 *per* Purchas L.J.
[89] *Hiern v. Mill* (1806) 123 Ves. 113 at 122 *per* Lord Erskine.

be required to deduce his title to the land and the purchaser would then investigate it. This entailed the provision of documentary evidence to give a convincing historical account of how the land came to be vested in the vendor. This, ordinarily, meant going back in time to a conveyance on sale of the land which was at least[90] fifteen years old,[91] this document being known as the root of title. The vendor must then also reveal, and the purchaser investigate, every transaction, such as a conveyance or event, for example death, marriage, or bankruptcy, relevant to the transmission of the legal estate, from the root of title to the present day.[92] Should the purchaser not carry out this process in full, he would be deemed to have constructive notice of any equitable interest which would have been discovered had such an investigation been properly conducted.[93] Because of the implementation of the system of the registration of land charges and the spread of registration of title, this form of constructive notice is almost entirely obsolete.

Inspection of the land: the rule in Hunt v. Luck

Possibly the first judicial recognition that a purchaser may be regarded as having constructive notice of the rights of occupiers of the land occurred in *Taylor v. Stibbert*,[94] where it was recognized that when land was occupied by tenants, a purchaser was bound to enquire as to what rights the tenants had in the property. This approach became known as the rule in *Hunt v. Luck*, where it was said that:

> . . . if a purchaser or a mortgagee has notice that the vendor is not in possession of the property, he must make enquiries of the person in possession—of the tenant in possession—and find out from him what his rights are, and if he does not choose to do that, then, whatever title he acquires as purchaser or mortgagee will be subject to the title or right of the tenant.[95]

The rule in *Hunt v. Luck*, whereby a person is fixed with constructive notice of the rights of persons in actual possession of the land, seems eminently sensible. In the situation in which the rule was formulated, the vendor himself did not physically occupy the land which was being sold.[96] As a matter of common sense, in this situation one would enquire of the people who did possess the land what their rights were and, if a purchaser did not do this, then it is perfectly reasonable to hold that he has constructive notice of those rights. What causes rather greater problems is the situation where the vendor is in occupation of property which he shares with others. The question is whether a purchaser should make enquiries of these other occupiers or, put another way, whether he would have constructive notice of any rights those people possess.

Shared occupation

There can be little doubt that, as the doctrine of constructive notice was being developed, a purchaser would not have been expected to make enquiries of occupiers of the property

---

[90] The likelihood of finding such a document exactly fifteen years old was slim, so in practice this document would be older: see *Re Cox and Neve's Contract* [1891] 2 Ch. 109 at 118 *per* North J.

[91] The original period at common law was sixty years, that period being successively reduced: see Vendor and Purchaser Act 1874, s. 1; LPA 1925, s. 44(1) and LPA 1969, s. 23. For an interesting account of the development of this area of law, see (1966) Law Com. No. 9, especially paras 15–36.

[92] See Williams in Williams and Lightwood (eds), *Vendor and Purchaser* (4th edn) (London, Sweet &. Maxwell, 1936) 123.

[93] *Re Nisbett and Pott's Contract* [1906] 1 Ch. 386.

[94] (1794) 2 Ves. Jr 438 at 440 *per* Lord Loughborough. See also *Barnhart v. Greenshields* (1853) 9 Moo. P.C. 18 at 32–3.

[95] [1901] 2 Ch. 428 at 433 *per* Vaughan-Williams L.J.

[96] See also *Daniels v. Davison* (1809) 16 Ves. Jun. 249 at 252.

other than the vendor when the vendor was also in occupation of the land.[97] The problem did not seem to have arisen, however; the reason probably being that, in the nineteenth century, it would have been highly unlikely that a person sharing a house with a vendor would have had an equitable interest in it. In modern times, however, it is common for wives, or unmarried partners, to go out to work and contribute to the purchase of the house[98] and so the issue became very much a live one.

Caunce v. Caunce[99] involved what was to become a familiar scenario. A matrimonial home was legally in the sole name of Mr Caunce but his wife, having contributed to the purchase of it, was an equitable co-owner of it.[100] He mortgaged the house to the bank without telling her that he had done so. The bank, when granting the mortgage, made no enquiries of her. When he defaulted on the mortgage and the bank sought possession, the issue was whether or not the bank was bound by her equitable interest, which turned, of course, on whether it had constructive notice of her interest in the property.

In a judgment which was, initially, warmly welcomed by conveyancers,[101] Stamp J. held in favour of the bank. In his opinion, it was quite unreasonable to expect a bank to make enquiries beyond the legal owner of the property, taking the view that 'it is not in the public interest that bank mortgagees should be snoopers and busybodies in relation to wholly normal transactions of mortgage'.[102]

The appeal to public interest in this case involves the reiteration of a policy statement articulated previously in the House of Lords. In *National Provincial Bank Ltd v. Ainsworth*,[103] Lord Upjohn famously remarked that, 'It has been the policy of the law for over a hundred years to simplify and facilitate transactions in real property.' What this means, in the present context, is that it is contrary to this policy to allow people with informally created rights in land to assert those rights against institutions who lend money against the security of a house. To decide in favour of banks in situations such as these means that their task when lending money is easier than it would otherwise be. Provided that the legal owner lives in the property in question, enquiries need not be addressed to any other occupier. This reduces the transaction costs involved and enhances the security of the mortgagee's position. On the other hand, it necessarily involves reducing the residential security of those who, for whatever reason, are equitable rather than legal co-owners of the property,[104] and have not been consulted about the transaction in question. This, in stark form, is the tension between the exchange value and the use value of land: the conflict between dynamic and static security, with the judgment, emphatically, endorsing the former value.

The approach taken by Stamp J. was consistent with the view that was taken in the early development of constructive notice and was that, 'the vendor being in possession, the presence of his wife or guest or lodger is not inconsistent with the title offered'.[105] This view, which found a ready echo in some quarters, it actually being said that a wife's occupation of a matrimonial home should be regarded as being a shadow of that of her husband,[106] construed the ambit of constructive notice narrowly. In so doing, Stamp J.'s

---

[97] See R.H. Maudsley (1973) 36 M.L.R. 25 at 33; M.P. Thompson [1984] Conv. 362 at 367.

[98] See the comment in *Williams & Glyn's Bank Ltd v. Boland* [1981] A.C. 487 at 508 *per* Lord Wilberforce.

[99] [1969] 1 W.L.R. 286.   [100] See 8.6.

[101] See Barnsley, *Conveyancing Law and Practice* (1st edn) (London, Butterworths, 1973), 333.

[102] [1969] 1 W.L.R. 286 at 294.   [103] [1965] A.C. 117 at 1233.

[104] The fact that Mrs Caunce was not a legal co-owner seemed to influence the judge against her, in that she allowed a position to exist whereby her husband could present himself to the world as the absolute owner of the property: see [1969] 1 W.L.R. 286 at 290 and 292. See also *Abbey National Building Society v. Cann* [1991] 1 A.C. 56 at 94 *per* Lord Oliver and the position where the contest is between two equitable interests. See 4.3 and 11.6.8.

[105] [1969] 1 W.L.R. 286 at 294.

[106] See *Bird v. Syme-Thomson* [1979] 1 W.L.R. 440 at 444 *per* Templeman J.

approach was to take the view that s. 199, LPA 1925, and its predecessor, s. 3(1) of the Conveyancing Act 1882, had been intended to restrict rather than extend the scope of constructive notice,[107] with the result that his conclusion appeared, as a matter of analysis, to have been amply justified in terms of what would, in the nineteenth century, have been considered to be the extent of reasonable enquiries. It failed, however, to give weight to the idea that notions of reasonableness may change over time, as the nature of society changes. In particular, it gave little weight to the expectation of security in a home that a co-owner might legitimately hold. It was perhaps unsurprising that what might be regarded as the conservative conveyancing-based approach did not ultimately prevail.

The retreat from Caunce

Soon after *Caunce* was decided, the position of occupiers who shared the property with the legal owner was reconsidered, albeit in a different context. In *Hodgson v. Marks*,[108] a man, who was originally a lodger in the house in question, became the legal owner of it, but he held the property on trust for an elderly woman who had previously held the legal title and who lived in the house at all material times. He transferred the house to a purchaser who, in turn, created a mortgage over it. The issue was whether the woman's equitable interest in the house was binding upon the purchaser.

Because the title to the house in question was registered, the determination of this issue raised a similar, but not identical, question to that which was addressed in *Caunce*. Whether or not the woman's interest was binding upon a purchaser depended upon whether she was to be regarded as having been in actual occupation of the house, within the meaning of s. 70(1)(g) of the Land Registration Act (LRA) 1925, rather than whether reasonable enquiries would have revealed the existence of her interest.[109] Reversing the first instance decision, which was based on the interpretation of 'actual occupation' as meaning 'actual and apparent occupation', the Court of Appeal held that she was and that the purchaser took subject to her interest.

Although Russell L.J. was prepared, without deciding, to construe the phrase 'actual occupation' in such a way that it would equate with the ambit of constructive notice,[110] he did not think that this would help the purchaser. He thought, as a matter of fact, that the woman was in actual occupation of the land and that the addition of the adjective 'apparent' added little if anything to the meaning of the words 'actual occupation'. Had the issue been whether the purchaser had constructive notice of the woman's rights, it is fairly clear that he would have held that he did because, when commenting on *Caunce*, he said:

> In that case the occupation of the wife may have been rightly taken to be not her occupation but that of her husband. In so far, however, as some phrases in the judgment might appear to lay down a general proposition that inquiry need not be made of any person on the premises if the proposed vendor himself appears to be in occupation, I would not accept them.[111]

Although prepared to countenance the actual result in *Caunce*, it was clear that the Court of Appeal was not prepared to accept as a general proposition that the ambit of reasonable enquiries did not extend to asking occupiers of the land what, if any, interests they had in it. In the light of this, it was, perhaps with the benefit of hindsight, fairly obvious that the exclusion of wives from the class of people to whom questions needed to be addressed was unlikely to survive for long. Leaving aside the inherent unattractiveness of singling out one particular type of occupier in this way, to do so was not very helpful to a purchaser because this exclusion of wives would necessitate an enquiry as to whether an occupant was in fact

---

[107] [1969] 1 W.L.R. 286 at 293.   [108] [1971] Ch. 892.   [109] See 5.1.5.3 The 'actual occupation'.
[110] [1971] Ch. 892 at 931.   [111] Ibid. at 934–5.

married to the vendor or was merely living with him; not the sort of enquiry that the law should require a purchaser to make.[112]

The criticisms made of *Caunce* in *Hodgson v. Marks* found strong support in the House of Lords in *William & Glyn's Bank Ltd v. Boland*,[113] a case involving substantially the same facts as *Caunce* but which, again, concerned registered land. Lord Wilberforce, in deciding that Mrs Boland was in actual occupation of the house, aligned himself with the criticisms made of *Caunce*. He was also quite unprepared to treat wives as being, legally, the shadow of their husbands, an attitude he condemned as being 'heavily obsolete', thereby effectively removing the cautiously stated qualification expressed by Russell L.J.[114] Lord Scarman, while recognizing that he did not have to decide the point, expressed himself to be far from certain that *Caunce* had been correctly decided.[115] The upshot was that it became overwhelmingly apparent that a purchaser would, in principle, have constructive notice of the rights of occupiers who shared the property with the vendor.

The post-Boland approach to constructive notice

There was soon afterwards an acceptance by the Court of Appeal that the *dicta* in *Boland* had had the effect that the restrictive approach taken in *Caunce* was no longer applicable and that the ambit of reasonable enquiries extended to making enquiries of all occupiers of the property, despite the vendor also being in occupation.[116] The full extent of the purchaser's task was considered in *Kingsnorth Trust Ltd v. Tizard*.[117] A house was in the sole name of Mr Tizard, although it was conceded that his wife was an equitable co-owner of it. They had separated and she lived with her sister and only stayed in the house when he was not there. She did, however, visit the house on a daily basis to collect their two children for school. He applied for a loan to be secured by a mortgage against the house. On his application form, he stated that he was single. A surveyor was instructed to inspect the house and to interview Mr Tizard, where he was told that the house was untidy because Mrs Tizard had recently left. In his report, the agent stated that Mr Tizard was single and occupied the house with his two children. After the mortgage was granted and Mr Tizard had defaulted on the repayments, it was held that the mortgagee was bound by Mrs Tizard's equitable interest on the basis that it had constructive notice of it.

Of more general importance, it was held that, in the light of the approach taken in *Boland*, the decision in *Caunce* could no longer stand. It was accepted that reasonable enquiries now embraced making enquiries of all occupants of the house, whether or not the vendor was himself in occupation of it. This seemed inevitable and represents a welcome recognition that people living with the legal owner of a house may have an interest in it and that those rights are deserving of protection when the property is mortgaged without their consent. Less welcome were some of the judge's comments on the ambit of reasonable enquiries. He expressed the view that, if the purpose of an inspection of the property is to ascertain the existence of other occupiers, then an inspection at a time pre-arranged with the vendor might not be sufficient.[118] This goes too far. While the actual decision might, on the facts, have been justified, in that the agent was put on notice that Mrs Tizard had only recently left the house and so might well have had an interest in it,[119] the requirement that an inspection of the property should take place at an unannounced time goes well beyond what might be regarded as a reasonable enquiry.

---

[112] *National Provincial Bank Ltd v. Ainsworth* [1965] A.C. 1175 at 1234 *per* Lord Upjohn. See 11.6.8.1.
[113] [1991] A.C. 487. [114] Ibid. at 505. [115] Ibid. at 511.
[116] *Midland Bank Ltd v. Farmpride Hatcheries Ltd* [1981] 2 E.G.L.R. 147. The interest claimed in this case has since been held not to be an interest in land and so the point need not actually have arisen: *Ashburn Anstalt v. W.J. Arnold* [1989] Ch. 1. For contemporary comment, see R.E. Annand [1982] Conv. 67.
[117] [1986] 1 W.L.R. 783. [118] [1986] 1 W.L.R. 783 at 794–5.
[119] See M.P. Thompson [1986] Conv. 283 at 285.

On the other hand, what seems to be an unduly relaxed view as to the ambit of constructive notice was taken in *Le Foe v. Le Foe*.[120] One of the issues in this case was whether a mortgage created by Mr Le Foe should be set aside under s. 37 of the Matrimonial Causes Act 1973 on the basis that the bank had notice of his intention to defeat his wife's claim for financial relief under that Act.[121] The judge held that it did not but considered, also, whether the bank would have had constructive notice of her presence in the house. As to this, despite expressing the view that the person who inspected the property on behalf of the bank could hardly have failed to notice evidence of her presence in the house,[122] he considered that it would not have done. The reason for this surprising conclusion appeared to be that the remit of the person instructed to inspect the house was limited to assessing its value. On this basis the judge expressed the view, albeit *obiter*, that, had the point been in issue, he would not have considered the bank, through its representative, to have had constructive notice of her presence.[123]

This seems remarkably generous to the purchaser,[124] and is out of line with recent authority. When, as in this case, it is evident that the borrower is sharing accommodation with another person then, as between the bank and that person, reasonable enquiries should extend to asking that person what, if any, interest they have in the property. The instructions given by the bank to its representative should not limit what are, for the purposes of constructive notice, reasonable enquiries.

Although the importance of the doctrine of constructive notice, *per se*, has receded considerably as a consequence of the spread of registration of title,[125] the question of what is comprehended by reasonable enquiries remains important. This is because on a transfer of land when title is registered, the transferee will take the land subject to an interest of a person in actual occupation of the land, provided that the fact of occupation would have been obvious on a reasonably careful inspection of the land: a term which is clearly highly redolent of the ambit of constructive notice.[126] The *dicta* in *Tizard* appear to take too stringent a view of what is reasonable, whereas those in *Le Foe* appear to err in the other direction.

The nature of the transaction

The doctrine of notice is traditionally concerned with determining whether or not a purchaser of a legal estate is bound by a prior equitable interest. Its role may, however, be wider than this[127] and involve situations where what is in issue is where a transaction is entered into in circumstances where some wrong, such as misrepresentation or undue influence, has been exerted on one of the parties to it. This has become a major issue in the context of the law of mortgages and will be analysed fully in Chapter 12.

3.6.4.3 Imputed notice

Under s. 199(1)(ii)(b), LPA 1925, a purchaser will be regarded as having notice of any matter which has, in respect of the same transaction in which the question arises, come to the knowledge of his solicitor or other agent or would have come to the knowledge of the solicitor or agent had that person made such enquiries as should reasonably have been made.

Ordinarily, the person most likely to acquire notice is the purchaser's solicitor.[128] As the section makes clear, however, knowledge which has either been acquired, or should have

---

[120] [2001] 2 F.L.R. 970. Permission to appeal was originally granted, [2001] EWCA Civ. 1789 but subsequently withdrawn: [2001] EWCA Civ. 1870.

[121] For the relevance of constructive notice in this context, see *Kemmis v. Kemmis* [1988] 1 W.L.R. 1307. See J.E.S. Fortin [1989] Conv. 204.

[122] [2001] 2 F.L.R. 970 at 988 *per* Nicholas Mostyn Q.C.   [123] Ibid. at 989.

[124] See M.P. Thompson [2002] Conv. 273 at 283–4.   [125] See Chapter 5.

[126] LRA 2002, ss 29 and 30; Sched. 3, para. 2. See 5.1.5.3.   [127] See J. Howell [1996] Conv. 33.

[128] For an example, see *Bank of Credit and Commerce International SA v. Aboody* [1990] 1 Q.B. 923 at 971 *per* Slade L.J. On imputed notice generally, see S. Nield [2000] Conv. 196.

been acquired, by any agent, will be imputed to the principal. So, in *Kingsnorth Trust Ltd v. Tizard*,[129] notice was imputed to the finance company on account of constructive notice acquired by a surveyor instructed by them to inspect the property.

A limitation on imputed notice is that the notice must have been acquired in respect of the same transaction. This was introduced because otherwise, if a solicitor had acquired notice in a previous transaction, this notice could be imputed to his present client,[130] an undesirable state of affairs[131] which could dissuade purchasers from employing local solicitors who may have acquired notice of matters when dealing, in the past, with the property in question.

Involvement in different stages of transaction

The requirement that notice be acquired in the same transaction would mean that, if a solicitor is acting for both parties, any notice he acquires will be imputed to them both.[132] Some difficulty has arisen, however, when a solicitor acts for both parties but his involvement with each of them occurs at a different stage in the transaction, or when he performs different roles for the two parties. In *Halifax Building Society v. Stepsky*[133] a solicitor knew that the stated reason being given by a married couple for a loan was not true. Had the real reason been known, the mortgagee would have been put on notice that the wife's agreement to the proposed mortgage might have been obtained by misrepresentation or undue influence. When, subsequently, the same solicitor was instructed to act for the bank in respect of the mortgage, he did not inform the bank of what he knew and that knowledge was not imputed to them. This seems correct, in that, although the solicitor was acting for both parties to a transaction, he did so at significantly different times and when he acted for the wife, he was not, at the time, also the agent for the bank.[134]

The role of imputed notice can be confused in cases of this nature. In *Barclays Bank plc v. Thomson*,[135] a wife claimed that a mortgage was not binding on her as she claimed that the bank had notice of the fact that her signature to the mortgage had been obtained by misrepresentation and undue influence. The bank had instructed the solicitor who was acting for the husband to explain the charge to the wife and also to secure its registration. She claimed that the advice given to her by the solicitor was deficient and that knowledge of that deficiency should be imputed to the bank.

Deciding in favour of the bank, the Court of Appeal rejected that argument. Such a conclusion seems inevitable as imputed notice should not be relevant to a situation such as this and it is perhaps unfortunate that the case was presented, at least in part, on this basis. Whether a solicitor ought to know that his advice is inadequate is hardly knowledge that can be imputed to the bank.[136] Rather, the case is really about whether or not the bank took adequate steps to ensure that she received proper, independent advice, that is, from a source other than the husband's solicitor, as to which, the decision was arguably overly lenient to the bank.[137]

---

[129] [1986] 1 W.L.R. 743.   [130] *Hargreaves v. Rothewell* (1836) 1 Keen 154.

[131] See *Re Cousins* (1886) 31 Ch.D. 671 at 676–7 *per* Chitty J.

[132] *Sharpe v. Foy* (1868) 4 Ch. App. 35; *Meyer v. Chartres* (1918) 34 T.L.R. 589.

[133] [1997] 1 All E.R. 46. See also *The Mortgage Business Plc v. Green* [2013] EWHC 4243 (Ch) at [40]–[50] *per* Morgan J.

[134] See also *Midland Bank plc v. Serter* [1995] 1 F.L.R. 1034 at 1045 *per* Glidewell L.J., although contrast *Barclays Bank plc v. Thomson* [1997] 4 All E.R. 816 at 826 *per* Simon Brown L.J., criticized by M.P. Thompson [1997] Conv. 216 at 219.

[135] [1997] 4 All E.R. 816.

[136] See ibid. at 829 *per* Morritt L.J. See also *Royal Bank of Scotland v. Etridge (No. 2)* [2001] 4 All E.R. 449 at 472 *per* Lord Nicholls.

[137] See M.P. Thompson [1997] Conv. 216 and 11.5.7.3.

3.6.4.4 Successors in title

If land has been conveyed to a bona fide purchaser who consequently is not bound by a prior equitable interest, the question can arise as to whether a subsequent purchaser who does have notice of it will be bound; whether the equitable interest will be revived. This point arose in *Wilkes v. Spooner*,[138] where the court held that it was not. Once the land has been conveyed to a bona fide purchaser, any equitable interests are overridden and, thereby, removed from the land. The only exception to this is when the land is subsequently conveyed to a person who had previously owned the land and who was, at that time, bound by the interest in question.

3.7 Human rights

A further, more recent, influence on land law is the human rights legislation.[139] Under s. 3(1) of the Human Rights Act 1998, which incorporated the European Convention on Human Rights into English law, a court is obliged to read primary and secondary legislation in a way which is compatible with Convention rights. This has entailed the courts adopting a new approach to statutory interpretation.[140] In *Ghaidan v. Godin-Mendoza*,[141] Lord Nicholls said that:

> the application of section 3 does not depend upon the presence of ambiguity in the legislation being interpreted. Even if construed according to ordinary principles of interpretation, the legislation admits of no doubt, the section may none the less require the legislation to be given a different meaning.

On this basis, the expression 'living with the tenant as his/her wife or husband'[142] was interpreted, Lord Millett dissenting, to include a cohabiting homosexual couple. The reason for this was that an interpretation which limited the meaning of this phrase to heterosexual couples would have been discriminatory and in contravention of art. 14, which prohibits discrimination on, *inter alia*, grounds of sexual orientation.

While it is clear that the section can have a significant effect on the tenets of statutory interpretation, it does not empower the courts to disregard clear statutory provisions. Thus, under s. 89 of the Housing Act 1980, after making a possession order, the giving up of possession may not be postponed for more than fourteen days or, in cases of exceptional hardship, to a date no later than six months after the making of the order. Even were this to be considered incompatible with the Convention, it would not be possible, in the teeth of such clear language, to construe this provision in a way so as to extend the period of postponement.[143]

3.7.1 Statutory interpretation

That s. 3 of the Human Rights Act 1998 does not empower a court to effectively rewrite legislation was emphatically endorsed by the Supreme Court in *McDonald v. McDonald*.[144] Lord

---

[138] [1911] 2 K.B. 473.

[139] See generally Allen, *Property and the Human Rights Act* (Oxford, Hart Publishing, 2005).

[140] See A. Kavanagh (2004) 24 O.J.L.S. 259. It is clear that, although the Act refers to legislation, this principle applies to domestic law as a whole: see *Doherty v. Birmingham City Council* [2009] A.C. 367 at [67] *per* Lord Scott.

[141] [2004] 2 A.C. 557 at [29]. See also *R. v. A. (No.2)* [2002] 1 A.C. 45.

[142] Rent Act 1977, Sched. 2, para. 2(2).

[143] *London Borough of Hounslow v. Powell* [2011] UKSC 8 at [62] *per* Lord Hope.

[144] [2016] UKSC 28 at [69], applying *Ghaidan v. Godin-Mendoza* [2004] A.C. 557 at [121] *per* Lord Rodger. On appeal, the European Court of Human Rights entirely agreed with the Supreme Court's analysis: *F.J.M. v UK.* [2018] App No 76202/16

Neuberger and Lady Hale, with whom the other members of the Supreme Court agreed, stressed that 'there is a difference between interpretation, which is a matter for the courts and others who have to give effect to legislation, and amendment which is a matter for Parliament'. Although this distinction may be easier to state than to apply, the underlying rationale is to consider whether the grain of the legislation is consistent with a wider approach to interpretation than, prior to the enactment of s. 3, would have been possible. Hence, on this basis, it is possible to give a more expansive interpretation to the expression 'living together as husband and wife' contained in the Rent Act 1977, so as to interpret it to extend to people who, at the time, were legally incapable of marrying each other. It is not possible, however, as a matter of interpretation, to construe a definite time limit on the extent to which a grant of possession may be granted effectively to be ignored. This limitation on the width of the new approach to statutory interpretation needs to be borne in mind when regard is had to some of the wider views of the approach to be taken as to the effect of s. 3.

An articulation of the wider approach occurred in a dissenting speech in *Hounslow London Borough Council v. Qazi*,[145] where Lord Steyn was critical of an analysis which allowed domestic notions of title, legal and equitable rights, and interest, to colour the interpretation of art. 8.[146] Instead, he considered that:

> Nowhere in our legal system is a literalistic approach more inappropriate than when considering whether a breach of a Convention right may be removed by interpretation under section 3. Section 3 requires a broad approach concentrating, amongst other things, in a purposive way on the importance of the fundamental right involved.[147]

Had this approach been followed, it would have had the potential to alter significantly our traditional understanding of property rights which have been developed over centuries. It raised the prospect of a decision being arrived at on the application of normal principles of property law and that decision then being trumped by an appeal to a Convention right. As will be seen, as the law has developed this very expansive approach to statutory interpretation has not been adopted, and so, private individuals and companies have not found that their pre-existing property rights have been significantly affected by the human rights jurisprudence. As one might expect, however, the Convention has had an impact on the enforcement of property rights by public authorities, although it must be said that this has been of greater theoretical than practical importance.

3.7.2 Convention rights

Of the various rights contained within the Convention, there are two,[148] in particular, which may be engaged in disputes pertaining to matters within the scope of this book. The first is art. 1 of the First Protocol, which provides that, subject to some qualifications, everyone is entitled to the peaceful enjoyment of his possessions.[149] Second, and of considerable significance, is art. 8, which provides that:

(1) Everyone has the right to respect for his private and family life, his home and his correspondence;

---

[145] [2004] 1 A.C. 983.   [146] Ibid. at [27].

[147] Ibid. at [41]. For a strong, and convincing, critique of this dictum, see J. Howell (2007) 123 L.Q.R. 618.

[148] Article 6, which affords the right to a fair and impartial trial may also be relevant, but is not of central concern to the issues considered in this section.

[149] *King v. Environment Agency* [2018] EWHC 65 (QB) is one recent example, where the court held that the Environment Agency's policy of using the claimant's land for flood mitigating did not breach the claimant's A1P1 rights, as they must be balanced with the public interest.

(2) There shall be no interference by a public authority with the exercise of this right except such as in accordance with the law and is necessary in a democratic society in the interests of national security, public safety or the economic well-being of the country, for the prevention of disorder or crime, for the protection of health or morals, or for the protection of the rights and freedoms of others.

Reliance has been placed on this provision in a number of different contexts, and will be dealt with as and when they arise, rather than being collected in a somewhat miscellaneous group. Recent developments have, however, necessitated a discussion of the general approach to the issue of the impact of human rights considerations on the law of property and, in particular, on the question of the right to possession.[150]

3.7.3 Possession actions and human rights

A fundamental issue which has repeatedly exercised the courts has been when a local authority brings an action for possession in circumstances where, as a matter of general property law, the occupier has no legal right to remain in the property. The question which has arisen is whether, despite that entitlement to possession, a defence can be raised on the basis of art. 8. After a prolonged debate at the highest judicial level, the question has been answered in the affirmative by the Supreme Court in *Manchester City Council v. Pinnock*.[151]

In 1978, Mr Pinnock was granted a secure tenancy of a property, where he lived with his partner and, from time to time, their children. In 2005, the council brought possession proceedings, this action being prompted as a result of serious anti-social behaviour by his children and partner. Perhaps as a consequence of his prolonged residence and the fact that he had not, himself, been guilty of anti-social behaviour, a possession order was not granted and, instead, a demotion order was made. This type of order,[152] which can only be made if one of a number of criteria relating to antisocial behaviour is satisfied and it is, separately, considered to be reasonable to make the order, has the effect of removing secure status from the tenant for a period of one year. During that period, the council can bring possession proceedings and, if it does so, must follow a prescribed procedure,[153] which involves giving reasons why the proceedings are being brought and notification of a right to request a review. It is then for the county court to make an order for possession and it is provided by s. 143D of the Housing Act 1996 that the court must make an order if it is satisfied that the statutory procedure has been followed. In the present case, following further misconduct on the part of members of Mr Pinnock's family, this procedure was followed and an order for possession was made. Mr Pinnock appealed, contending that his rights under art. 8 had been violated. This contention was upheld by the Supreme Court although, on the facts, the appeal was dismissed.

The point of principle centred on the role of the county court. Under the legislation, it appeared that this was confined to ascertaining that the correct procedure had been followed by the local authority. If it had been, a possession order had to be made: the local authority had an absolute right to possession. The argument for the tenant, which

---

[150] Article 8 can also be engaged as a result of action by a public body falling short of a possession action. See, e.g., *Lane v. London Borough of Kensington and Chelsea London Borough Council* [2013] EWHC 1320 (Ch) (felling a tree in a garden).

[151] [2010] UKSC 45. See also *London Borough of Hounslow v. Powell* [2011] UKSC 8; M.P. Thompson [2011] Conv. 421; S. Bright in Gravells (ed.) *Landmark Cases in Land Law* (Oxford, Hart Publishing, 2013), Chapter 11.

[152] Introduced by the Anti-social Behaviour Act 2003, s. 15.

[153] Housing Act 1996, s. 143.

was accepted by the Supreme Court, was that, even when a local authority had an absolute right to possession, in order to satisfy art. 8(2) of the Convention, the question as to whether the grant of possession was necessary or, as the test has become, whether making such an order was proportionate was relevant. The actual appeal was, however, dismissed, it being held that, as the facts were largely undisputed, there was no need to remit the case to the county court to consider the proportionality of the possession order; on the facts, such an order was considered to be amply justifiable.

It is now clear that, at least so far as actions brought by public bodies are concerned, it will be possible for an occupier of land, who has no legal right to possession, to be able to defend a possession action on the basis that an order for possession is disproportionate. This raises three issues. First, one has to determine what the judicial stance is towards the issues of proportionality and, in particular, how likely it is that an argument based on art. 8 will succeed. The second issue is whether the proportionality argument is applicable only to landowners who are public authorities, or whether it is applicable to all landowners seeking possession. Third, and this relates also to the second issue, the question arises as to whether the effect of the Convention is to change substantive land law, or whether its impact relates to the ability to enforce recognized rights. To address these issues, it is necessary to consider the underlying basis of the decision in *Pinnock* and how the law has developed to its current state.

3.7.4 **The increased recognition of human rights**

In arriving at the position that occupiers of land may be able to rely on an art. 8 defence to possession proceedings, there has been a considerable prior debate involving both the English courts and the European Court of Human Rights. The starting position is the House of Lords decision in *Harrow London Borough Council v. Qazi*.[154] Mrs Qazi, one of two joint tenants of a council house, left the property and, having done so, served a notice to quit on the landlord. This had the effect of terminating the tenancy,[155] with the result that the remaining joint tenant, her estranged husband, had no legal right to remain in the property. The House of Lords was unanimous that, as Mr Qazi occupied the house as his home, art. 8 was engaged. By a bare majority, however, it was held that there was no need to remit the case to the county court to consider whether the grant of possession could be justified under art. 8(2). This was because 'article 8(2) *is* met where the law affords an unqualified right to possession on proof that the tenancy has been terminated'.[156] Put another way, the balancing act envisaged by art. 8(2) is carried out by the law of property and, once that has provided the answer, there is no further balancing to do.[157] That said, the action of the local authority in bringing possession proceedings was, as is the case with other actions by public bodies, amenable to judicial review; an important caveat, in that this remedy is not available to regulate the actions of private individuals and the availability of this remedy is also key in establishing the grounds on which the courts could intervene.

The minority took the view that, even when a proprietary right to possession had been established, it would still be possible for an individual to argue, on the particular facts of a case, that art. 8(2) could require the issue of proportionality to be addressed, although it was conceded that it would only be in exceptional cases that such an argument would succeed.[158] This

---

[154] [2004] 1 A.C. 983. See S. Bright (2004) 120 L.Q.R. 398.

[155] See 10.10.2.

[156] [2004] 1 A.C. 983 at [78] *per* Lord Hope. Lord Hope's italics. For the view that this represented a wrong turn in the development of the law, see Lord Walker in Hopkins (ed.) *Modern Studies in Property Law* (vol. 7) (Oxford, Hart Publishing, 2013), 3 at 13.

[157] [2004] 1 A.C. 983 at [103] *per* Lord Millett.   [158] Ibid. at [25] *per* Lord Bingham.

aspect of the law will be considered shortly. What the majority decision clearly established, however, was that 'as a matter of human rights law, Art.8 was not available as a defence to possession proceedings brought to enforce the ordinary property rights of a local authority'.[159]

3.7.5 **The retreat from** *Qazi*

The position laid down in *Qazi* soon had to be modified. This was as a result of the decision of the European Court of Human Rights in *Connors v. United Kingdom*.[160] This case arose out of a decision by a local authority to bring possession proceedings against a gypsy who, save for a short interruption, had been living on the authority's land for over sixteen years. He occupied the land under a licence agreement. When this licence was revoked the effect was that he had no legal right to remain. Following an unsuccessful application by Mr Connors for permission to seek judicial review, the county court granted a possession order and Mr Connors brought proceedings in Strasbourg alleging an infringement of his human rights. The European Court upheld his claim.

Underlying the decision of the council to seek possession was its view, although this was strongly contested, that Mr Connors and his family had been guilty of various acts of anti-social behaviour. No opportunity was given for a court to determine the actual facts, because the procedure adopted by the council of determining the licence and seeking summary possession obviated the need to do so. As a matter of law, it was entitled to possession because, unlike other occupiers of mobile homes, gypsies occupying local authority property did not enjoy security of tenure. The European Court was critical of a situation whereby a local authority could obtain possession of a person's home without any investigation of the factual position and concluded that his rights had been infringed.

The impact of the decision in *Connors* was first considered by the Court of Appeal in *Leeds City Council v. Price*,[161] a case also involving gypsies, and it was considered that, as a result of that case, the decision in *Qazi* was incompatible with the Convention. The Court, nevertheless, considered itself to be bound by *Qazi* and followed it: a course of action which was subsequently expressly approved by the House of Lords.[162] As to the merits, this was reconsidered by a seven-member panel of the House of Lords in the conjoined appeals in *Price* and *Kay v. London Borough of Lambeth*.[163]

In *Price*, the House unanimously rejected the argument that art. 8 had been infringed. This was because the occupation in this case had only been for a period of two days and this was insufficient to establish that the property was occupied as a home: art. 8 was not, therefore, engaged at all.[164] In *Kay*, however, there had been a sufficiently prolonged occupation of the property to establish that it was the defendant's home, and the issue of whether the reasoning employed in *Qazi* could survive the decision in *Connors* had to be addressed. With some modification of the earlier decision, a bare majority held that it could.

3.7.6 **The gateway approach**

Kay involved a situation where, as a matter of law, the local authority had an unqualified right to possession and the occupier ran the same argument that had failed in *Qazi*: that

---

[159] *Birmingham City Council v. Bradney* [2004] H.L.R. 27 at [15] *per* Mummery L.J.

[160] (2005) EHHR 9.   [161] [2005] 3 All E.R. 573.

[162] *Kay v. London Borough of Lambeth* [2006] 2 A.C. 465 at [43] *per* Lord Bingham.

[163] [2006] 2 A.C. 465.

[164] Where land is occupied as part of a demonstration, it will be difficult to establish that the property is occupied as a home, with the consequence that art. 8 will not be engaged: see *The Mayor of London v. Samede* [2012] EWCA Civ. 160 at [50] *per* Lord Neuberger M.R.; *Manchester Ship Canal Developments Ltd v. Persons Unknown* [2014] EWHC 645 (Ch) at [38] *per* H.H. Judge Pelling Q.C.

to grant possession without adverting to his personal circumstances infringed his rights under art. 8. The leading speech, which rejected this argument, was given by Lord Hope. Upholding the essential reasoning in *Qazi*, he nevertheless, to an extent, modified it. In his view, art. 8 could be relied upon in two situations, later termed gateways (a) and (b).[165] Under the first of these gateways, the occupier could argue that the substantive law which afforded the authority the right to possession was, itself, challengeable as being inconsistent with the Convention. In such circumstances the court should, if possible, apply s. 3 of the Human Rights Act 1998 and construe the legislation in a way which was compatible with the Convention. If that was not possible, the proceedings should be adjourned to the High Court to determine the issue of compatibility with the Convention and, if the law was not so compatible, a declaration to that effect should be made.[166] The alternative argument, gateway (b), was to challenge the decision of the local authority on the basis that, notwithstanding its unqualified right to possession, to seek to enforce that right would amount to an abuse of its powers.[167] Such an attack on the decision-making process could only succeed, however, if the decision was one which no reasonable person would consider to be justifiable: the public law test of *Wednesbury* unreasonableness.[168]

Applying this to the facts of *Connors*, both gateways appeared to be open. First, the legislative regime which was then in place discriminated against gypsies who, unlike other occupiers of mobile homes, were not afforded any security of tenure:[169] a position which could amount to an infringement of a different article of the Convention, in this case art. 14.[170] Second, although the council had the right to terminate the licence, the view was expressed that, given the length of the period of occupation that the defendants had enjoyed, it would be grossly unfair to take such action without having to make good any underlying reason for doing so.[171]

An important point to stress about this reasoning is that it should be appreciated that if the substantive law affords a local authority an unqualified right to possession, that does not entail, of itself, that that law is incompatible with the Convention. Were this to be the case, gateway (b) would be redundant. There would be no reason to insist that the decision to enforce this right was an abuse of power: the very existence of the right would contravene the Convention. Hence, it has been cogently argued that the effect of the decision in *Pinnock* is effectively to remove the gateway (a) defence in practically all possession cases.[172] For gateway (a) to be an issue, it must have been the case that the substantive law infringed some other Convention right: an important point to appreciate when assessing the impact of the decision in *Pinnock*.

3.7.7 The widening of the grounds for review

Prior to the Supreme Court finally abandoning the position laid down in *Qazi*, the House of Lords had a final opportunity to review this area of law in *Doherty v. Birmingham City Council*.[173] The council brought summary possession proceedings against a gypsy family who had occupied council property for over seventeen years, it having terminated their licence to occupy. The reason why the council had done this was not because of

---

[165] See I. Loveland [2009] Conv. 396; M. Davis and D. Hughes [2010] Conv. 57.
[166] See Human Rights Act 1998, s. 4.
[167] *Kay v. London Borough of Lambeth* [2006] 2 A.C. 573.
[168] *Associated Provincial Picture Houses Ltd v. Wednesbury Corp* [1948] 1 K.B. 223.
[169] This position has now been remedied by the Housing and Regeneration Act 2008, s. 318, Sched. 16.
[170] See *Doherty v. Birmingham City Council* [2009] A.C. 367 at [25] *per* Lord Hope, albeit conceding that the European Court had not decided that this was the case.
[171] *Kay v. London Borough of Lambeth* [2006] 2 A.C. 367 at [210] *per* Lord Brown.
[172] D. Cowan and C. Hunter (2012) 75 M.L.R. 78 at 84.   [173] [2009] A.C. 367.

any misconduct on the part of the family, but because it wanted to redevelop the land. Following *Qazi*, possession was ordered and the defendants appealed. The appeal was allowed, and the case was remitted to a High Court judge to consider the reasonableness of the council's actions having regard to its stated reason for seeking possession and the length of occupancy of the defendants: in effect gateway (b). As to the more substantive elements of the decision, despite some forthright statements, the effect of the judgments was not that easy to state.

In deciding whether a court was required to have regard to the issue of proportionality when considering whether a council had an unqualified right to possession, the House was pressed with another decision of the European Court, *McCann v. United Kingdom*.[174] In that case, following issues concerning domestic violence, Mrs McCann left the council house she had shared with her husband. At the instigation of the council, she served a notice to quit, thereby terminating the tenancy. The council then obtained possession and Mr McCann pursued the matter in Strasbourg, where it was held that there had been an infringement of his right under art. 8.

In upholding the claim, the Court noted that, by persuading Mrs McCann to serve a notice to quit, the council had sidestepped the need to bring possession proceedings under s. 84 of the Housing Act 1985. Doing this obviated the need to satisfy a court that an order for possession was reasonable: a task which would have required the facts to be ascertained and the merits of the case to be assessed.[175] It went further than this, however, commenting that the decision in *Connors* was not confined to gypsies or to cases where the substantive law was challenged as being incompatible with the Convention. Instead, it considered that the loss of one's home was a major interference with a person's right and this should require the proportionality of the measure to be determined by an independent tribunal, notwithstanding that, under the general law, the occupier had no legal right to be on the property.[176] Having said that, however, the actual decision that there had been a violation of art. 8 was based on the procedural aspect only, and it was stressed that it was far from clear that had a domestic tribunal been in a position to assess the proportionality of the eviction the possession order would not still have been granted.[177]

While the writing on the wall of the Strasbourg jurisprudence seemed to be clear that the philosophy underlying *Qazi* was not acceptable, the House of Lords in *Doherty* made one last-ditch attempt to hold the line it had previously laid down. The European Court's judgment in *McCann* was given fairly short shrift. Lord Hope considered that the failure of that Court to articulate any criteria as to what the exceptional circumstances might be which could cause a possession order to be refused made the guidance almost useless,[178] and indicated that English courts should continue to follow the decision in *Qazi*. He reiterated that, if a local authority had an unqualified right to possession then, unless that right could be challenged on the basis that the relevant legislation was, itself, incompatible with the Convention, it 'is not open to the court . . . to hold that the exercise of that right should be denied because of the occupier's personal circumstances'.[179] Any such challenge must be on public law grounds, that the decision of the public authority amounted to an abuse of its powers on the basis that it was a decision that no reasonable person would consider to be justifiable: that it was *Wednesbury* unreasonable.

---

[174] [2008] H.L.R. 40.

[175] This was considered to be an important consideration in *Wandsworth London Borough Council v. Dixon* [2009] EWHC 27 (Admin) at [51] *per* Judge Bidder Q.C.

[176] *McCann v. United Kingdom* [2008] H.L.R. 40 at [50].   [177] Ibid. at [59].

[178] *Doherty v. Birmingham City Council* [2009] A.C. 367 at [20]. See also the comments, at [82], of Lord Scott on the failure of the European Court to appreciate the procedural protection which was already available in England in this type of case.

[179] Ibid. at [22].

Having reaffirmed the essential approach in *Qazi*, as modified by what he had said in *Kay*, however, Lord Hope appeared to widen the basis on which a public law challenge could be made. He said:

> I think that . . . it would be unduly formalistic to confine the review strictly to traditional *Wednesbury* grounds. The considerations that can be brought into account in this case are wider. An examination of the question whether the council's decision was reasonable, having regard to the aim which it was pursuing *and to the length of time that the first defendant and his family have been living on the site would be appropriate.*[180]

It will be appreciated that, although Lord Hope had expressly discounted the relevance of the personal circumstances of the occupier, his acceptance that the length of the period of residence was a relevant consideration in determining the reasonableness of the council's action does actually amount to a consideration of one such personal circumstance. This, together with the comments of Lords Walker and Mance that the decisions of local authorities to enforce an unqualified right to possession could be challenged on grounds wider than the traditional test of *Wednesbury* unreasonableness[181] meant that, despite the strong reaffirmation of *Qazi*, English law was moving towards an approach more consistent with that taken in Europe.

3.7.8 **The abandonment of *Qazi***

Despite protestations to the contrary, it was evident that English law had moved towards a position with regard to possession proceedings brought by local authorities which was more consistent with that taken in Europe than had previously been the case. The extent of convergence was, however, unclear. Thus in *Taylor v. Central Bedfordshire Council*,[182] Waller L.J. said 'that the question whether a decision of a public body is "reasonable" post-*Doherty* goes beyond the question whether it is rational', but commented that there 'does appear to have been a tension between the House of Lords as to the proper approach to Article 8, and those of ECtHR, but hopefully the divergence is less serious than some would suggest'.[183] How far the divide might have been bridged by the English courts acting alone is speculative, but also became academic, in the light of the decision of the European Court of Human Rights in *Kay v. United Kingdom*,[184] which, following the dismissal of his appeal by the House of Lords, held that there had been an infringement of the applicant's rights under art. 8 and awarded him compensation.

While the European Court accepted that the distance between conventional judicial review grounds and Human Rights Act grounds appeared to have narrowed, it was also noted that the extent to which those grounds could be said to encompass proportionality was unclear.[185] Moreover, it was critical that the facts which it considered to be relevant to that issue had not been considered by the county court. The matters to which the court considered that regard should have been had included such things as the lengthy period of occupation, the improvement works carried out to the property, the factual correctness (or otherwise) of the authority's reasons for seeking possession, and whether there

---

[180] Ibid. at [55]. Emphasis supplied. For the importance of the length of occupation, see *Stokes v. London Borough of Brent* [2009] EWHC 1426 (Ch) at [49]–[50] *per* King J.

[181] [2009] A.C. 367 at [135] and [162]. For an example of such a case based upon procedural defects, see *Eastlands Homes Partnership Ltd v. Whyte* [2010] EWHC 695 (QB).

[182] [2010] 1 W.L.R. 446 at [44].

[183] Ibid. at [26], although see *Salford City Council v. Mullen* [2010] EWCA Civ. 336 at [61] *per* Waller L.J.

[184] [2011] H.L.R. 2. See S. Nield [2010] Conv. 498.   [185] [2011] H.L.R. 2 at [54].

actually was a need for vacant possession. The overriding principle was stated as being that:

> Any person at risk of an interference of this magnitude should . . . be able to have the pro-
> portionality of the measure determined by an independent tribunal in light of the relevant
> principles under Article 8 of the Convention, notwithstanding that, under domestic law, his
> right to occupation has come to an end.[186]

This decision meant the English courts had to accept either that there was a rift between English law and the European Court of Human Rights as to the scope of art. 8 of the Convention, or it had to accept that the law as laid down in *Qazi* was wrong. Accepting the seemingly inevitable, a nine-member panel of the Supreme Court in *Manchester City Council v. Pinnock*[187] took the latter option.[188] In so doing, a number of issues emerged which will be considered in turn.

3.7.9 Introducing proportionality

Having accepted that as a result of the European ruling in *Kay* the proportionality of making a possession order was now an issue, the first question was how to introduce this in the context of the legislative provisions relevant to the demoted tenancy procedure. It will be recalled that under the Act, the role of the county court was to ascertain that the local authority had followed the correct procedure. If it was satisfied that this was the case, then under s. 143D of the Housing Act 1996 the court must make an order for possession. Giving the judgment of the Court, Lord Neuberger found a neat solution. When deciding whether to institute possession proceedings and, where requested, to establish a review, the local authority is under a duty, as a public body, to consider whether it is proportionate that possession be obtained. The role of the county court is to establish that the correct procedure has been lawfully carried out. To this end, it must be able to satisfy itself that the making of an order was proportionate. Accordingly, s. 149D of the Act was construed to allow the county court 'to consider and, where appropriate, to give effect to, any article 8 defence which the defendant raises in the possession proceedings'.[189] In short, it is now open to county court judges to consider the factual basis of an authority's action and then, notwithstanding that under domestic law the authority has an unqualified right to possess the property, to decide whether the making of a possession order is proportionate. This gives rise to the related questions as to the impact of this on the conduct of possession proceedings, and to what matters the court will have regard in considering proportionality.

3.7.10 Assessing proportionality

In *Qazi* Lord Millett stressed that the issue of principle which divided the House was a narrow one, but one which he considered to be of considerable practical importance.[190] The practical issue was articulated by Lord Hope who said the point of automatic possession proceedings was to provide a quick and reliable way of evicting tenants whose leases have terminated, and that to confer on county court judges a discretion to not order possession on the ground of proportionality would be inimical to that policy.[191] While it is

---

[186] Ibid. at [68].   [187] [2010] 3 W.L.R. 1441.
[188] For the reasons, see at [48] *per* Lord Neuberger.
[189] Ibid. at [79]. See also in respect of the similar legislative provisions with respect to introductory tenancies *London Borough of Thomston v. Powell* [2011] 2 W.L.R. 287 at [56] *per* Lord Hope. See also *McDonald v. McDonald* [2016] UKSC 28 at [64]–[67] *per* Lord Neuberger and Lady Hale.
[190] *Harrow London Borough Council v. Qazi* [2004] 1 A.C. 983 at [85].   [191] Ibid. at [38].

true that the possession proceedings may be complicated to an extent by the admission of a criterion of proportionality as a potential defence, Lord Neuberger in *Pinnock*[192] was clearly mindful of this consideration when he considered how such cases should proceed. In his view, art. 8 need only be considered by the court if it is raised by the residential occupier. If it is not, it would seem that summary judgment should be given. If, however, the matter is raised, the judge should consider the matter on a summary basis and:

> if, as no doubt will often be the case, the court is satisfied that, even if the facts relied on are made out, the point would not succeed, it should be dismissed. Only if the court is satisfied that it could affect the order that the court might make should the point be further entertained.[193]

Throughout the debate as to the applicability of an art. 8 defence, it has been stressed, even by those by judges who at the outset were in the minority as to the need to consider the issue of proportionality as a defence to a possession action, that it would only be in exceptional cases that this defence would prevail.[194] This stance was emphasized in *Pinnock*, where Lord Neuberger, while preferring to eschew the expression 'exceptional circumstances',[195] made it clear that, as a defence, it was one which was unlikely to be of wide application. What this might mean was developed in *London Borough of Hounslow v. Powell*.[196] Lord Phillips took the view that the effect of art. 8 was that, when a local authority sought to exercise its right to possession, the existence of that right was not, of itself, a sufficient ground for possession to be granted.[197] Rather, the obtaining of possession should be pursuant to the specified legitimate aims of its housing policy, and possession should be a proportionate means of achieving those aims. If there are disputed issues of fact, the occupier should be entitled to have any such issue determined by an independent tribunal.[198] Having said that, however, he went on to emphasize that the prospects of success for an occupier relying solely on art. 8 to defend a possession action were remote. He said:

> It is likely to be a rare case, particularly as the defendant has a right to a review, where the defendant will be in a position to demonstrate that there are substantial grounds for attacking the authority's findings of fact, or the decision based on them. I note that . . . the Strasbourg Court accepted that it would only be in very exceptional cases that an applicant would succeed in raising an arguable case which would require the court to examine the issue and that in the great majority of cases it would be possible for possession orders to be made in summary proceedings.[199]

3.7.11 Exceptional cases

Since the decision in *Pinnock*, it has been made increasingly clear that that the occupier has a very high bar to surmount in order to establish that there is an arguable case that the granting of possession would be disproportionate and, therefore, in breach of art. 8.[200]

---

[192] *Manchester City Council v. Pinnock* [2010] UKSC 45.
[193] Ibid. at [61].   [194] *Harrow London Borough Council v. Qazi, supra*, at [25] *per* Lord Bingham.
[195] *Manchester City Council v. Pinnock, supra*, at [64].   [196] [2011] UKSC 8.
[197] Ibid. at [90].   [198] Ibid. at [73].
[199] Ibid. at [94]. As to the need for the right of the occupant to procedural fairness in the determination of disputed issues, see also *R (on the application of ZH and CN) v. London Borough of Newham* [2014] UKSC 62 at [63] *per* Lord Hodge.
[200] See, for example, *R. (on the application of ZH and CN) v. London Borough of Newham, supra*, at [65] *per* Lord Hodge; *The Riverside Group Ltd v. Thomas* [2012] EWHC 169 at [38] *per* Ryder J.; *Fareham Borough Council v. Miller* [2013] EWCA Civ. 159 at [21] *per* Patten L.J.; *Hampson v. Orchid Runnymede Ltd* QB/2015/0285 at [32] *per* Simler J.

Very little guidance was given, however, as to what criteria might need to be met in order to overcome this hurdle. In *Pinnock*,[201] Lord Neuberger was content to leave this to the good sense and experience of County Court judges,[202] and the prevailing judicial attitude since then would seem to indicate that the only serious prospects of a successful argument based upon art. 8 would appear to lie in either establishing a procedural irregularity, or the lack of a reason, other than the mere existence of a right to possess, for enforcing the right to possession. Certainly, it is easier to state what grounds are likely to result in failure than when an art. 8 defence is likely to succeed.

3.7.12 Judicial discretion

In *Pinnock* itself, Lord Neuberger referred to cases where, in order to obtain a possession order, the local authority must, in addition to establishing a ground for possession, also satisfy the court that it is reasonable to make such an order. In such cases, he said that that there was no room for a separate defence of proportionality: if it is reasonable to make an order for possession it cannot be arguable that it is in some way disproportionate to do so.[203] This must be right. Similarly, it is suggested, if legislation makes clear that possession is to be granted unless the circumstances are exceptional, as, for example, is the case under s. 335A of the Insolvency Act 1986,[204] then it should also be the case that there is no further argument to be made as to proportionality. The legislature has enacted that, while there is no absolute right for the trustee in bankruptcy to secure a judicial order that the bankrupt's home be sold, it has also made it clear where the balance should be struck between the realization of assets on behalf of creditors and the enjoyment of the property as a home by the bankrupt and, perhaps more pertinently, members of his or her family. Where Parliament has expressly struck a balance in this way, this should be regarded as being within the margin of appreciation applicable to member states in the fulfilment of their obligations and, consequently, should be immune from attack on the basis of proportionality under art. 8.[205]

3.7.13 Status of occupier

Although the entire discussion to date has centred on the position when the local authority has, under domestic property law principles, an unfettered right to possession of the property and, consequently, the occupier has no legal right to remain in it, the courts do distinguish between situations where the initial occupation was lawful and those where it was not. This latter position will occur when the occupier has, throughout the period of occupation, been a trespasser. In this situation, it has been made very clear that, while not impossible, it is very hard to envisage circumstances whereby the occupier will be able to

---

[201] [2010] UKSC 45 at [57], although see *Birmingham City Council v. Lloyd* [2012] EWCA Civ. 969 at [12], where Lord Neuberger M.R. added his voice to those who had emphasized that it was only in 'very highly exceptional circumstances that it would be appropriate for the court to consider a proportionality argument'. See also *McDonald v. McDonald* [2016] UKSC 28 at [73] *per* Lord Neuberger and Lady Hale.

[202] This led to the justified criticism that this left those judges rather in the dark as to what a seriously arguable case might look like: D. Cowan and C. Hunter (2012) 75 M.L.R. 78 at 86.

[203] *Manchester City Council v. Pinnock* [2010] UKSC 45 at [55]–[56]. See also *McDonald v. McDonald* [2014] EWCA Civ. 1049 at [16] *per* Arden L.J. affmd on appeal at [2016] UKSC 28.

[204] See 9.8.5. Precisely this point was also made some years earlier in the context of possession actions brought by mortgagees: see *Barclays Bank Plc v. Alcorn* [2002] EWHC 498 (Ch) at 26 *per* Hart J. See 11.6.2.2.

[205] See also *Akerman-Livingston v. Aster Communities* [2015] UKSC 15 at [51] *per* Lord Neuberger and *McDonald v. McDonald* [2016], *supra*, at [45] *per* Lord Neuberger and Lady Hale.

rely on art. 8 to defend a possession action. In *Birmingham City Council v. Lloyd*,[206] Lord Neuberger M.R. said of this:

> It would, I accept, be wrong to say that it could never be right for the court to permit a person, who had never been more than a trespasser, to invoke Article 8 as a defence against an order for possession. But such a person seeking to raise an Article 8 argument would face a very uphill task indeed, and, while exceptionality is rarely a helpful case, it seems to me that would . . . require the most extraordinarily exceptional circumstances.

The possibility of a person who has entered the land as a trespasser being able to rely on art. 8 would, therefore, although not impossible, at least in theory, appears to be almost vanishingly small.[207]

3.7.14 **Personal circumstances**

In deciding whether or not it is proportionate to make a possession order and, taking on board that the task of the occupier to persuade a court that the case is exceptional will be very difficult, one might have thought that the personal circumstances of that person and, presumably, his or her family would be highly relevant considerations. This, however, is not the case. In *Corby Borough Council v. Scott*,[208] the Court of Appeal rejected an argument that, in assessing whether the making of a possession order was proportionate, regard should be had to the fact that the defendant, in this case a woman who had entered the property as an introductory tenant, had a drink problem and had also been the victim of a very serious assault. The existence of these circumstances did not mean that she had even an arguable case that the enforcement of a right to possession was disproportionate. The tenancy had been terminated because of problems with rent arrears and complaints by neighbours relating to loud parties which took place at the house. According to Lord Neuberger M.R.:

> The principal fact relied upon . . . namely that Ms Scott had been subject to a murderous attack in July 2010, appears to me to be simply irrelevant to the issue of Article 8 proportionality. The attack, although no doubt a shocking experience, simply had nothing to do with the claim for possession, or the respect to which Ms Scott is untitled under Article 8 for her home.[209]

Lord Neuberger elaborated on this in *West Kent Housing Association v Hayward*, a case decided together with *Scott*, saying that:

> I consider that *Corby B.C. v. Scott* emphasises that, in such a case, a judge (i) should be rigorous in ensuring that only relevant matters are taken into account on the proportionality issue, and (ii) should not let understandable sympathy for a particular tenant have the effect of lowering the threshold identified by Lord Hope in *Powell*. As for [the present case], it seems to me to emphasise the height of that threshold, or, to put it another way, how exceptional the facts relied on by any residential occupier must be, before an Article 8 case can have a real prospect of success.[210]

---

[206] [2012] EWCA Civ. 969 at [18]. See also, to the same effect, *Thurrock Borough Council v. West* [2012] EWCA Civ. 1435 at [31] *per* Etherton L.J.

[207] Although see the discussion by R. Walsh (2015) 131 L.Q.R. 585.

[208] [2012] EWCA Civ. 276.   [209] Ibid. at [24].   [210] Ibid. at [35].

3.7.15 Disability

It is clear that, for a defence based upon art. 8 to succeed, any personal circumstances relied upon must be relevant to the possession order; that the facts of the case are highly unusual does not mean that a possession order is disproportionate. The question is not whether the facts are exceptional; the test of exceptionality relates to outcome.[211] In *Scott*, the fact that she had been a victim of a serious assault did not relate to whether there was a particular need for her to continue her occupation of her current accommodation. What may be more relevant is if the occupier suffers from a disability although, even then, that will not necessarily mean that it will be disproportionate to make a possession order.

In *Pinnock*, Lord Neuberger accepted as well made the argument put forward by the Equality and Human Rights Commission that proportionality may become a live issue in the case of occupiers who are vulnerable by reason of mental illness, ill-health, and frailty.[212] Despite this comment, however, it is now apparent that disability, *per se*, cannot be relied upon to anchor a defence under art. 8. This emerged from the decision in *JL v. Secretary of State for Defence*.[213]

The claimant sought judicial review to challenge a decision to enforce a possession order against her. She was married to an army officer. He was an alcoholic, who was violent towards her and abusive to one of her two daughters. In addition to having an abusive husband, she also suffered from substantial disabilities which, amongst other things, entailed that she had to use a wheelchair. She lived with her two daughters, one of whom had mental health problems and the other acted as carer, both for the claimant and also for her own son who suffered from Crohn's disease. Following a court martial, her husband resigned from the army and this ended any duty which the Ministry of Defence had to provide accommodation for her and her daughters. She was nevertheless, on compassionate grounds, allowed to continue in occupation of MoD property on what was described as a temporary basis. Notwithstanding all of this, Ms Ingrid Simler Q.C., sitting as a Deputy High Court judge, held that it was not disproportionate within the meaning of art. 8 to enforce the possession order.

A number of points should be made about what, at first blush, appears to be a somewhat surprising decision. First, although the Ministry of Defence is unquestionably a public body and so directly affected by the Human Rights Act, it does not, as the judge pointed out, have the public function of providing social housing. That responsibility rests with the city council:[214] a point which is even more formidable when consideration is given to the position of private landlords. Secondly, it was accepted on all hands that, even had a proportionality defence succeeded, this would not have entitled the claimant to remain in the property indefinitely,[215] and that it might take a significant period of time for the council, even though it had categorized the family as belonging to the highest category of housing priority, to identify or adapt a property to be a suitable permanent alternative. It was also relevant that the Ministry had waited for over a year before seeking to enforce the possession order and that it had repeatedly warned her that it would not be prepared to house her indefinitely. Moreover, given the long-standing nature of her own and her family's problems, coupled with the position that she was not entitled to remain in the property indefinitely, enforcing possession at the present time would not have any greater impact than would be the case in a further three, six, or even twelve months' time.[216] From the

---

[211] Ibid. at [27].   [212] [2010] UKSC 45 at [64].   [213] [2012] EWHC 221 (Admin).

[214] Ibid. at [77].

[215] See also to the same effect, *Thurrock Borough Council v. West* [2012] EWCA Civ. 1435 at [31] *per* Etherton L.J. It was stressed in *McDonald v. McDonald* [2016], *supra*, on the basis of evidence supplied by Shelter, that such an order would hardly ever be made: [73] *per* Lord Neuberger and Lady Hale.

[216] [2012] EWHC 221 (Admin) at [82].

point of view of the Ministry, there were two legitimate aims; first, it had the right under domestic law to possession of the property and, second, it had a general duty to manage service properties and the Ministry's resources more generally and this militated against providing accommodation to people who were not entitled to it.[217] For all these reasons, the judicial review application failed.

3.7.16 Equalities Act

Some of the reasoning in this case would clearly not apply when the landlord is a local authority which has duties in respect of social housing. Nevertheless, one can see that the fact that the occupier suffers from disabilities will not necessarily mean that it is disproportionate for a possession order to be made. This was recognized by the Supreme Court in *Akerman-Livingston v. Aster Communities Ltd*,[218] where it was also decided that the approach to be taken in possession cases differed depending upon whether the occupier relied on art. 8 of the European Convention or, instead, prayed in aid the provisions of the Equalities Act 2010.

The case concerned a man who had, through an agreement between the local authority and a housing association, been provided with temporary accommodation under s. 193 of the Housing Act 1996. He suffered from a complex form of Post Traumatic Stress Disorder, the effect of which made him a highly vulnerable person with considerable sensitivity as to where he lived. This was manifested by his refusal to accept several offers of alternative accommodation. In the end this led to possession proceedings being brought and the issue for the Supreme Court was whether the proportionality test contained within art. 8 was the same as the duties imposed by the Equalities Act 2010. It was unanimously held that it was not, and that an occupier had considerably more rights under the domestic legislation than under the Convention.

3.7.17 Ambit of the Equalities Act

As was pointed out in *Ackerman-Livingston*, the duties under the 2010 Act unequivocally apply to both public and private landlords, whereas it is now clear that, in the case of art. 8, the proportionality defence is confined to the former category of landowners. The actual duty imposed by the Act is not to discriminate against a person who has a protected characteristic, one of which is defined as disability,[219] a requirement which was clearly satisfied in the present case. The range of activities where discrimination is made unlawful includes eviction from occupied property.[220] What this means is defined by s. 15(1)(a) and (b) of the Act as being that a person (A) discriminates against a disabled person (B) if he treats B unfavourably because of something arising in consequence of B's disability, and A cannot show that the treatment is a proportionate means of achieving a legitimate aim. Moreover, once there are facts from which the court could decide, in the absence of any other explanation, that person (A) has contravened the duty imposed by s. 15, the onus of proof is then placed upon A to show that he or she did not, in fact, contravene the section: that is that there was not discrimination on the ground of disability.[221]

The effect of these provisions, together with the duty on the managers of property to make reasonable adjustments to accommodate the needs of a disabled occupier, led Lady Hale to stress the important differences between a defence based simply on proportionality under the Convention and that based upon the 2010 Act. She said:

---

[217] Ibid. at [75]. [218] [2015] UKSC 15. [219] Equalities Act 2010, s. 4.
[220] Ibid., s. 35(1)(b). [221] Ibid., s. 136(2), (3).

> When a disability discrimination defence is raised, the question is not simply whether the social landlord is entitled to recover the property in order to fulfil its or the local authority's public housing functions, but also whether the landlord of the local authority has done all it can reasonably be expected of it to accommodate the consequences of the disabled person's disability and whether, at the end of the day, the 'twin aims' are sufficient to outweigh the effect upon the disabled person. These are questions which the court is well-equipped to address.[222]

Building on this, Lord Neuberger, having reiterated views he had expressed in other cases as to how difficult it is for a tenant, successfully, to raise a pure proportionality defence under art. 8,[223] said:

> Accordingly, it appears to me clear that it is wrong to equiperate, either procedurally or substantively, a defence under section 35(1)(b) to a possession action with a defence under article 8 to a possession action. Provided that a defendant establishes that the landlord is (or at a summary stage, may well be) seeking to evict him 'because of something arising in consequence of [his] disability', the landlord faces a significantly more difficult task in having to establish proportionality than does a landlord who faces an Article 8 defence.[224]

The obvious impact of this decision is that what, at one time, was thought to be the most likely basis on which to rest an art. 8 defence, disability, will now be pursued under the provisions of the Equality Act 2010, making it more difficult to see when such a defence based upon art. 8 is likely to succeed.

3.7.18 **Procedural issues**

As has been seen, the prospect of a successful art. 8 defence being raised to defeat a possession action brought by a local authority which is entitled, as a matter of law, to possession of that property, is extremely small and, now that disability cases are much more likely to be contested under the Equalities Act than under the Human Rights Act, this is even more the case. This leaves the question as to when a proportionality defence might succeed. In the past, where defences have succeeded it has been the case that local authorities have either not made out a proper case for bringing the possession action, or, at least arguably, have attempted to manipulate the law to facilitate their right to possession. Thus in *Connors v. United Kingdom*,[225] a local authority adopted a procedure which avoided any determination of disputed facts concerning anti-social behaviour by relying on a right to bring summary possession proceedings. Its ability to do so was based on the then existing law which was discriminatory against gypsies, and so in contravention of art. 14 of the Convention. Because the local authority had precluded any factual investigation of the facts underlying the possession proceedings, it was held that the human rights of the claimants had been infringed.

Similarly, in *McCann v. United Kingdom*,[226] a local authority persuaded one joint tenant to serve a notice to quit, the effect of which was to terminate the joint tenancy and confer upon the authority an absolute right to possession. The adoption of this procedure enabled the authority to sidestep the need to bring possession proceedings when the reasonableness of such an order would be in issue.[227] This means of avoiding any consideration of the underlying facts of the case amounted, effectively, to an abuse of process and,

---

[222] [2015] UKSC 15 at [32].   [223] Ibid. at [51].   [224] Ibid. at [58].
[225] (2005) EHHR 9. See also *Doherty v. Birmingham City Council* [2009] A.C. 367.
[226] [2008] H.L.R. 40.   [227] Housing Act 1985, s. 84.

consequently, a breach of art. 8. Indeed, notwithstanding comments about the need to assess the personal circumstances of occupiers, it seems probable that the prospects of a successful defence based on art. 8 to a possession action brought by a local authority is dependent upon the decision-making process of that authority, rather than the individual circumstances of the case.

3.7.19 Proportionality and private landowners

The discussion to date has centred solely on the possession actions brought by public bodies, to whom the provisions of the Human Rights Act are directly applicable. Now that it has been established that an art. 8 defence can be run to defend such possession actions, the question arises whether this is also the case when the action for possession is brought by a private individual.

As the debate as to the potential impact of art. 8 developed, the proponents of that debate were, initially at least, quite clear that their analyses of the situation were directed only to public authorities. Lord Bingham, in *Qazi*, was explicit that 'nothing I have said in this opinion should be understood as applying to any landlord or owner which is not a public authority'.[228] Lord Neuberger in *Pinnock* also reserved his opinion on this matter, expressly leaving open the question as to whether the reasoning of the Supreme Court was applicable to private as well as public landowners, although he did point out that to hold that it did would raise a separate argument that this would infringe landowners' rights under art. 1 of the First Protocol.[229]

The argument that art. 8 should be relevant to proceedings brought by private landowners has two separate, albeit related, strands. The first derives from s. 6(1) of the Human Rights Act, which provides that it is unlawful for a public authority to act in a way which is incompatible with a Convention right. Section 6(3)(a) then defines a public authority to include a court or tribunal. This leads to the argument that in deciding any case, such as a possession action brought by a private landlord, a court must only make such an order if to do so is proportionate; that is, the proportionality test should be as applicable to private landowners as it is to public bodies.

3.7.20 Substance or procedure?

To resolve this important question, it is important to be clear as to the basis on which the courts have introduced the art. 8 defence of proportionality. One way of looking at the impact of the article is to see the effect of *Pinnock* as altering the substantive law by creating, in effect, a freestanding defence to any possession action underpinned by the concept of proportionality. If this was the case, and such an argument was flatly rejected by the House of Lords in *Kay*,[230] then its effect would be to 'create an extensive reservoir of entitlement which would wreak havoc within substantive property law'.[231] This is because the substantive law would be the same irrespective of the identity of the landowner. Precisely this argument has been raised. It has been contended that the effect of art. 8 is to modify the

---

[228] *Harrow London Borough Council v. Qazi* [2004] 2 A.C. 983 at [23].

[229] *Manchester City Council v. Pinnock* [2010] UKSC 45 at [4] and [50]. For a further example of judicial fence-sitting with regard to this issue, see *Sun Street Property Ltd v. Persons Unknown* [2011] EWHC 3432 (Ch) at [28] *per* Roth J.

[230] *Kay v. London Borough of Lambeth* [2006] 2 A.C. 465 at [207] *per* Lord Brown.

[231] See A. Goymour [2006] C.L.J. 696 at 706, although for a very different approach by the same author, see A. Goymour in Hoffman (ed.), *The Impact of the UK Human Rights Act on Private Law* (Cambridge, Cambridge University Press, 2011), Chapter 12.

general principles of property law in such a way that the identity or status of the claimant is irrelevant: the real 'defendant', it is argued, is the substantive law itself.[232] This argument which, it is suggested, is supported neither by precedent nor by principle, has been rejected by the Supreme Court in *McDonald v. McDonald*,[233] and recently rejected again by the European Court of Human Rights on appeal in the same case.[234]

Before looking at the decision in *McDonald*, it is as well to see why it is that the scope of art. 8 should be limited to landowners who are public bodies. From the very outset of the debate as to the role of art. 8, the substance of it has related to the supervisory role of the courts with regard to decision-making by public bodies. In *Qazi*, the scope of that intervention was limited by the majority to the traditional role of judicial review of the decision to initiate possession proceedings.[235] As the indirect dialogue with Strasbourg continued, while it was true to say that the grounds on which such review would be available progressively widened, it remained the case that the focus of attention was on the decision to enforce the right to possession. This was the case unless, separately, an attack could be made on the substantive law that afforded the right to possession in the first place: a state of affairs which led to the dual-track approach of gateways (a) and (b). This dichotomy would have been completely unnecessary had the position been that the effect of art. 8 was to alter the substantive law so that the absolute right to possession recognized by the law of property had been diluted.

The essential point to recognize is that 'the central bone of contention is not the substance of established property rules themselves but the process by which those property rules are asserted and reconciled'.[236] This is apparent from the analysis of the European Court of Human Rights itself, whose concern has not been with the content of the substantive domestic law but has been with the procedural safeguards afforded to residential occupiers. This was made clear both in *McCann v. United Kingdom*[237] and in *Kay v. United Kingdom*.[238] In the latter case, the Court welcomed the fact that the English courts had widened the grounds for judicial review from the very narrow base of *Wednesbury* unreasonableness but considered that, at the time when the actual case was decided in England, the majority view did not extend to allowing a defendant to argue that the public body had been acting in a way that was disproportionate and, as a result, was in breach of the Convention.

3.7.21 Supervisory role

Of course, a public or private body with the right to possess land which is in the occupation of another does not have to exercise that right. In the case of public bodies, however, the decision-making process involved in enforcing that right has always been amenable to judicial review. As a result of *Pinnock*, it is now clear that that decision-making process must be compliant with the Convention and must be a proportionate action.[239] In the case of private landowners, however, there is no such constraint. This was spelled out explicitly in *Central Bedfordshire Council v. Taylor*.[240] Commenting on the decision in *Docherty*, Waller L.J. said:

---

[232] I. Loveland (2011) EHRLR 151 at 158. See also M. Davis and D. Hughes [2010] Conv. 57 at 72.
[233] [2016] UKSC 28.   [234] *F.J.M. v. UK* [2018] App No 76202/16.
[235] See *Harrow London Borough Council v. Qazi* [2004] 1 A.C. 983 at [109] *per* Lord Millett.
[236] S. Nield in Bright (ed.), *Modern Studies in Property Law* (vol. 6) (Oxford, Oxford University Press, 2011), 101 at 112.
[237] [2008] 47 EHHR 913 at [55].   [238] [2011] H.L.R. 2.
[239] See the comments in *Doherty v. Birmingham City Council* [2009] A.C. 367 at [121] *per* Lord Walker.
[240] [2009] EWCA Civ. 613 at [18]. Emphasis added.

> I can start by emphasising that if the landowner were a private landowner there would be no question of that landowner being required to take account of the personal circumstances of the trespassers. The court would be bound to make an order for possession. *It is because the council are a public authority and its decisions are susceptible to judicial review that there can be any question of the appellants being able to raise what is loosely called an Article 8 defence.*

This is entirely consistent with the normal judicial attitude to the enforcement of private property rights. In such cases, it has been said that:

> There is no concept that is more fundamental than a right of property. Where it exists, it is for the owner to exercise it as he pleases. He does not need the permission of the court, nor is it subject to the court's discretion . . . These are rights which the court must respect and which it will enforce if asked to do so.[241]

Despite the existence of various judicial statements expressing considerable scepticism as to whether a private landowner could, when seeking to enforce a proprietary right to possession, be met with an art. 8 defence, in *Malik v. Fassenfelt*,[242] Sir Alan Ward took a different view. While he conceded that, because a private landowner is not a public authority and is not, therefore, obliged to respect the human rights of a trespasser under art, 8, he thought it to be common ground that, because the court is a public body, it is obliged to act in a way which is consistent with the European Convention. In his view, this meant, in effect, that the private landowner was, through this indirect method, potentially subject to an art. 8 defence.

The comment that this position represented common ground is surprising. It is contrary to the general tenor of judicial statements with regard to this matter and was also treated with considerable caution by the other members of the court in *Malik* itself.[243] Be that as it may, the matter has now been laid to rest by the Supreme Court in *McDonald v. McDonald*,[244] although, perhaps surprisingly, there is no discussion of earlier judicial comments on this important issue.

The landlords in this case were Mr and Mrs McDonald, and the tenant was their daughter, Fiona, who held under an assured shorthold tenancy. She suffered from a severe form of mental disorder, that disorder being of such gravity that the psychiatric evidence was that forcing her to move home, even were it possible to find accommodation for her, would probably require her admission to hospital and could also lead to self-harm and the risk of suicide.[245] The house had been acquired on a buy-to-let basis, the object of the exercise being to provide a home for Fiona. The purchase price was provided by a company, CHL. The plan was to repay the loan through housing benefit payable to Fiona. This plan did not work and arrears accrued. CHL appointed a receiver who, as they were entitled to do, terminated the tenancy. The consequence of this was that there now existed a mandatory ground for possession[246] in favour of the parents who, although the litigation was instigated by the receiver, were, technically, the claimants in the case. The first, and arguably most important issue to be raised was whether art. 8 had a direct effect on private landowners.

---

[241] *Fischer v. Brooker* [2009] 1 W.L.R. 1764 at [8] *per* Lord Hope. The case concerned intellectual property rights.

[242] [2013] EWCA Civ. 798 at [8]. See also, to similar effect, *Manchester Ship Canal Developments Ltd v. Persons Unknown* [2014] EWHC 645 (Ch) at [46] *per* HH Judge Pelling, although these remarks are hard to reconcile with his earlier comments at [38].

[243] [2013] EWCA Civ. 798 at [45]–[47] *per* Lord Toulson, and at [51] *per* Lloyd L.J.

[244] [2016] UKSC 28. See S. Nield [2017] Conv. 60. For critical comment of the Court of Appeal decision, [2014] EWCA Civ. 1049, see E. Lees (2015) 131 L.Q.R. 34, and particularly S. Nield [2015] Conv. 77.

[245] [2016] UKSC 28 at [7] *per* Lord Neuberger and Lady Hale.

[246] Housing Act 1998, s. 21.

The clear decision was that it did not. At the outset, it was agreed that, if the outcome of the case was that private landowners were affected in this way, then this would mean that 'a judge invited to make an order for possession against a residential occupier by a private sector landlord would . . . have to balance the landlord's [Article 1 Protocol 1] rights against the occupier's article 8 rights. Either party would have a potential claim against the United Kingdom in Strasbourg if the balance were struck in the wrong place.'[247] This is not, of itself, that convincing, in that the striking of balances between competing rights is part of the bread and butter of the judicial process. This was indeed recognized when it was pointed out that the development of a right of privacy from the already developing case law based upon breach of confidence involves the striking of balance between the competing Convention rights of privacy (embraced in art. 8) on the one hand and freedom of speech (encompassed in art. 10) on the other.[248] What, however, this *dictum* does clearly recognize is that, unlike public authorities, private landlords also have rights entitled to protection under the Convention. To impose the same obligations with regard to the recovery of possession as is now the case with public authorities is therefore hard to justify.

More compelling is the attitude of the Supreme Court to the proper applicability of the Convention. In its view, under s. 6(1) of the Human Rights Act 1998, the Convention was only applicable to a public authority because 'the Convention is intended to protect individual rights against infringement by the state or its emanations.'[249] Continuing with this theme, the Supreme Court considered the respective role of the domestic legislature. Lord Neuberger and Lady Hale said that:

> it would be unsatisfactory if a domestic legislature could not impose a general set of rules protecting residential tenants in the private sector without thereby forcing the state to accept a super-added requirement of addressing the issue of proportionality in each case where possession is sought. In the field of proprietary rights between parties neither of whom is a public authority, the state should be allowed to lay down rules which are of general application and certainty of outcome. These are two essential ingredients of the rule of law, and accepting the appellant's argument in this case would involve diluting those rules in relation to possession actions in the private sector.[250]

The European Court of Human Rights *in F.J.M. v. UK*, the appeal from *McDonald*, squarely agreed with the Supreme Court's position. The European Court remarked that:

> . . . while the applicant's particular circumstances are undoubtedly deserving of sympathy, having regard to the considerations set out above they cannot justify the conclusion that in cases where a private sector landlord seeks possession, a residential tenant should be entitled to require the court to consider the proportionality of the possession order.[251]

Following the decisions of the Supreme Court and European Court of Human Rights, it can be stated with confidence that art. 8 does not confer any direct rights enforceable against a private landlord; a position which is much to be welcomed.

3.7.22 Related issues

A principal argument propounded by those that favour the view that art. 8 and, of course, other Convention rights, should be universally applicable is founded on s. 6 of the Human

---

[247] [2016] UKSC 28 at [39] *per* Lord Neuberger and Lady Hale.   [248] Ibid. at [46].
[249] Ibid. at [37].   [250] Ibid. at [43]. See also the remarks at [41].
[251] [2018] App No 76202/16 at [45].

Rights Act 1988. This section makes it unlawful for a public body to act in a way which is incompatible with Convention rights. This provision has been used as the basis for arguments that the Convention has, in effect, created a backstop of proportionality to be used by one private individual against another. Although the Supreme Court did not advert to the substantial academic literature devoted to this topic, its conclusion was succinct. The *dictum* of Lord Millett in *Harrow London Borough Council v. Qazi*[252] that, the court 'is "merely" the forum for the determination of the civil right in dispute between the parties' and 'once it concludes that the landlord is entitled to an order for possession, there is nothing further to investigate' was accepted as an accurate statement of the law.[253]

A little more flesh was put on this when considering the basis of judicial intervention in art. 8 cases. As has been seen, as the law developed, the concept of proportionality embraced by that article is given effect by the supervision of the behaviour of public authorities. In effect, the criteria by which decisions by those bodies are susceptible to review have been widened from an original basis of rationality and the adherence to proper procedures to include proportionality. In the case of private individuals, however, the basis of decisions made to enforce property rights is not the subject of judicial review; it is up to such people to make such decisions as they see fit and, consequently, their ability to enforce property rights is unaffected by art. 8.[254]

3.7.23 Defects in the substantive law

A situation where a private landowner may be restricted in his ability to obtain possession of land is where the law which entitles him to do is itself open to objection on the basis that it contravenes the Convention. A good example of this occurred in *Ghaidan v. Godin-Mendoza*.[255] A private landlord sought possession of property after the death of a tenant. This was resisted by the homosexual partner of the deceased. Had the couple been heterosexual, the defendant would have succeeded to the tenancy as the survivor of a couple who had been living together as husband and wife. To avoid the statute[256] from causing discrimination against the defendant on the ground of sexual orientation, which would infringe art. 14 of the Convention, the House of Lords, following s. 3 of the Human Rights Act 1998, construed the expression 'living together as husband and wife' to include a homosexual couple. This is illustrative of how the Human Rights Act has had a very significant impact on the principles of statutory interpretation so that the substantive law is interpreted in a way which is consistent with the Convention.

Although this new principle of interpretation is highly significant, as has been seen, there are limits to it. So, for example, where a statutory provision stipulates a specified time limit under which possession can be postponed, it is not possible to interpret such a provision to mean that an order may be suspended beyond that period. What is, perhaps, more difficult is the situation where, under a common law principle, a claimant is entitled to possession of property. The argument which has arisen is that, for the court to fulfil its obligation to act in way which is in accordance with the Convention, it should alter the substantive common law so as to be compliant. Underlying such an argument is that it is not the identity of the claimant which is in issue; rather it is the law itself, which will be the same whoever is seeking to enforce it.

This argument has been put most forcefully in the context of the common law rule that a notice to quit served by one tenant upon the landlord has the effect of terminating that

---

[252] [2004] 1 A.C. 983 at [108]–[109].
[253] [2016] UKSC 28 at [44] *per* Lord Neuberger and Lady Hale.   [254] Ibid. at [64].
[255] [2004] 2 A.C. 557.   [256] Rent Act 1977, Sched. 1, paras 2, 3.

tenancy, regardless of the wishes of the other tenant.[257] This is a long-standing common law rule[258] which, it has been argued, should be changed by the courts because it infringes art. 8, the argument being that it does so because it allows one person, by unilateral action, to deprive another of his or her right to a home without there being any question of the proportionality of this being considered.

3.7.24 The role of property law

At the outset, one should say that, were this argument to prevail, then it would do so regardless of the personal circumstances of any of the occupiers of the property. Moreover, the argument would appear to apply in any situation whereby the rules of property law dictate that a person's interest in a property, which of course can include their right to live in it, would be terminated as a result of some event: an event which will usually, albeit not in the present situation, involve the acquisition of the property by a third party. In each case, however, the rules of property law have developed so as to balance competing interests. While views may differ as to whether the balance has always been struck in the correct place, the balancing act has already occurred and this should be sufficient to establish that the substantive law is proportionate,[259] and therefore not susceptible to challenge under the Human Rights Act.

This is the conclusion reached by the Supreme Court in *Sims v. Dacorum Borough Council*.[260] Mrs Sims, who had suffered acts of violence at the hands of her husband, served a notice to quit on the housing association from whom she and her husband had held a joint periodic tenancy. Upholding the decision of the Court of Appeal, where trenchant statements can be found excoriating the argument that the existing law was in contravention of art. 8,[261] it was held that the common law rule that a periodic tenancy is brought to an end by the unilateral act of the service of a notice to quit did not infringe art. 8. Lord Neuberger considered that the rule, the substance of which was specifically adverted to in the lease signed by both parties to the lease, was, itself, not unreasonable. Were it otherwise, one effect would have been that a person in the position of Mrs Sims would be tied to the continuation of a lease against her will.[262] The argument that her action in serving a notice to quit, thereby putting his right of occupation at risk, involved an infringement of art. 8 was seen as going much further than anything warranted by the jurisprudence of the European Court in Strasbourg and, therefore, effectively untenable.[263]

The Human Rights Act has undoubtedly had a major impact on English law. In the sphere of property law, however, although the decision in *Pinnock* is of considerable theoretical importance, its practical effect is likely to be minimal. This is, first, because although it allows art. 8 of the Convention to be used as a defence in possession proceedings, the subsequent Supreme Court decision in *McDonald v. McDonald* and European Court of Human Rights decision in *F.J.M v. UK* have established that this defence is confined to actions brought by public bodies and that its main scope is the exercise of the decision to enforce a right to possession. Although the personal circumstances of the occupier are relevant factors in the exercise of that discretion, it is not enough that such circumstances

---

[257] See I. Loveland [2013] EHLR 573.

[258] It dates back to *Doe d. Aslin v. Summerset* (1830) 1 B. &. Ad. 135 and has been consistently reaffirmed since then, notably by the House of Lords in *Hammersmith and Fulham London Borough Council v. Monk* [1992] 1 A.C. 478.

[259] See also A. Goymour in Hoffman, *The Impact of the UK Human Rights Act on Private Law*, 249 at 285.

[260] [2014] UKSC 63.

[261] See [2013] EWCA Civ. 12 at [27]–[30] and [34]–[36] *per* Mummery L.J.

[262] Ibid. at [17].   [263] Ibid. at [22].

exist; those circumstances must be relevant to the possession action. This is most likely to be the case when the defendant, or his or her family, suffer from some form of disability. Even if such circumstances exist, it is apparent that the defendant has a much better prospect of defending the action by relying on the provisions of the Equalities Act rather than art. 8. Finally, an argument that the substantive law contravenes the Human Rights Act and must, therefore, be altered would appear to be doomed to failure, unless the reason for such a finding is that it is contrary to some article other than art. 8. The fact that the law is that a particular landowner has an unqualified right to possession does not mean that there is an infringement of art. 8.

Throughout the debate as to the applicability of art. 8 when a person has a proprietary right to possession of land, there has been a recognition that the issue is of much greater theoretical importance than practical application. As was said in a different, albeit not unrelated, context, 'The point, though one of principle, is a narrow one. It is the difference immortalised in *H.M.S. Pinafore* between "never" and "hardly ever" . . . [and] the cases in which it could properly be applied must be extremely rare.'[264] This is equally the case with regard to the scope of art. 8 to affect possession actions involving land.

---

[264] *National Carriers Ltd v. Panalpina (Northern) Ltd* [1981] A.C. 675 at 688–9 *per* Lord Hailsham. For the context, see 10.8.4.

4

Unregistered Land and the 1925 Legislation

In 1925, substantial legislation was enacted which recast land law in this country. Surprising though this may seem, this legislation, now nearly one hundred years old, continues to provide the skeleton on which modern land law is based. Of course, over the years, many developments, both statutory and judicial, have occurred since that date, but the essential framework remained intact until the enactment of the Land Registration Act (LRA) 2002, legislation which replaced, and substantially modified, the LRA 1925. Although the 2002 Act will, for the future, be the principal piece of legislation relating to land ownership in this country, a good deal of the theoretical underpinning of the subject will remain that provided by the 1925 legislation and, in particular, the Law of Property Act (LPA) 1925.[1]

4.1 The legislative background

A feature of the doctrine of estates was that it allowed for the fragmentation of ownership rights amongst various people. In addition to the existence of legal estates there existed their equitable counterparts. As well as it being quite possible for a number of estates to exist simultaneously with respect to the same plot of land, there could also exist a number of different third party rights over that land, such as easements and restrictive covenants. Moreover, there was considerable formality and artificiality involved with the creation of interests in land, with the result that, to quote a memorable phrase attributed to Lord Westbury, titles to land depended on the interpretation of deeds which were 'difficult to read, disgusting to touch, and impossible to understand'.[2] This problem, coupled with the complexity of the substantive law itself,[3] was the principal reason for a special rule affecting contracts for the sale of land. This rule[4] limited the damages recoverable for the breach of such a contract by the vendor, if the breach was occasioned by his inability to convey that which he had contracted to convey because his title to it was defective.

Various attempts were made to simplify and add security to the conveyancing process, measures which included the registration of deeds[5] and the registration of incumbrances affecting the land. The ultimate goal, however, was to facilitate the registration of title to land, whereby a person's ownership of the land would be entered upon an official register,

---

[1] On the legislative background, see Anderson, *Lawyers and the Making of English Land Law 1832–1940* (Oxford, Oxford University Press, 1992).

[2] See *Wroth v. Tyler* [1974] Ch. 30 at 56 *per* Megarry J.

[3] See Law Reform Commission of British Columbia, Report on the Rule in *Bain v. Fothergill* (1976) 6 cited in (1987) Law Com. No. 166, Appendix C, para. 3.7.

[4] *Flureau v. Thornhill* (1776) 2 Wm. Bl. 1078; *Bain v. Fothergill* (1874) L.R. 7 H.L. 158. This rule was not finally abolished until 1989: LP(MP)A 1989, s. 3, implementing (1987) Law Com. No. 166.

[5] See J. Howell [1999] C.L.J. 366.

and the third-party rights affecting that land would also be entered on that register. For this process to happen, however, it was necessary to simplify the substantive law relating to land.[6] To this end, a series of reforming statutes was enacted,[7] culminating in the largely consolidating legislation of 1925, which is sometimes referred to as the Birkenhead legislation, after its principal architect.[8]

The aim of this chapter is to explain the main strategies of the 1925 legislation. This will focus, principally, on its effect on unregistered land. Although this form of land ownership, whereby a person proves his entitlement to land by reference to the title deeds, will soon be superseded by the universal spread of registration of title, it remains relevant and will continue to do so for a number of years to come. The next chapter will consider the system of registration of title. For many years, the Act concerned with registration of title was the LRA 1925. This legislation has now been superseded by the LRA 2002.

4.2 Land law after 1925

Lord Birkenhead, who piloted the earlier legislation through Parliament, described its policy in the following terms. He said:

> Its general principle is to assimilate the law of real and personal estate and to free the purchaser from the obligation to enquire into the title of him from whom he purchases, any more than he would have to do if he were buying a share or a parcel of stock.[9]

To seek to achieve what was probably an unattainable goal, various strategies were adopted. As well as ridding the law of some of the more technical and artificial aspects,[10] various substantive themes can be seen. These can be outlined as follows.

4.2.1 Reduction in legal estates and interests

Prior to 1926, when the legislation came into force, various different estates could exist at law. Section 1 of the LPA 1925 reduced the number of legal estates which could exist to two: the fee simple absolute in possession and the term of years absolute. The former expression has already been discussed[11] and the latter relates to leases. All other estates in land can now exist only in equity. In addition to this, the number of legal interests, which would bind a purchaser of land, irrespective of notice, was also reduced.

4.2.2 Registration of land charges

The reduction of the number of legal estates and interests in land led to a corresponding increase in the number of equitable interests. Prior to 1925, the question of whether or

---

[6] Hayton, *Registered Land* (3rd edn) (London, Sweet & Maxwell, 1981), 8–14.

[7] Notably, the Vendor and Purchaser Act 1874, the Conveyancing Act 1881, the Settled Land Act 1882, and the LPA 1922 and 1924.

[8] See Campbell, *F.E. Smith First Earl of Birkenhead* (London, Jonathan Cape, 1983), 483–6. The Lord Chancellor when the 1925 legislation was enacted was Lord Cave L.C.

[9] Letter to *The Times*, 15 December 1920, cited in Campbell, *F.E. Smith First Earl of Birkenhead*, 485.

[10] For example, the rule in *Shelley's Case* (1581) 1 Co. Rep. 88b, described as being 'one of the most difficult and by far the most notorious of the rules of the old law of real property'. Hargreaves in Warmington (ed.), *Stephen's Commentaries on the Laws of England* vol. 1 (London, Butterworths, 1950), 166 was abolished: LPA 1925, s. 131 and the Statute of Uses 1535 was finally repealed: LPA 1925, Sched. 7, thereby making the creation of trusts of land more straightforward.

[11] See 2.6.1.

not a purchaser would be bound by equitable interests turned on whether he was able to establish that he was a bona fide purchaser of a legal estate without notice. This entailed him having to establish that he had made all the enquiries which the law considered ought reasonably to have been made when purchasing land. To facilitate the purchaser's task, and also to assist a holder of an equitable interest to be able securely to protect that right, provision was made for such rights to be made registrable as land charges. The aim of this was to enable a purchaser, by the relatively simple means of requisitioning an official search of the land charges register, to be able to discover to what third party rights the property he was buying would be subject.

4.2.3 Registration of title

As indicated earlier, one of the principal reasons for reforming the substantive law was to promote the spread of registration of title. The traditional method of establishing that the vendor owned the land which he was purporting to sell was to examine the title deeds, the purpose of which was to show a convincing account of the devolution of the property in the past to establish his right to deal with the land. This was a time-consuming business and one where mistakes could be made, so that security of title was not guaranteed. Registration of title is an idea designed to make this process obsolete. Once title to the land is registered, a central idea of the system is that the state will guarantee that the register is accurate in terms of who owns the land. The register also give a definitive account as to what third party rights the land is subject. There is, however, an extremely important exception to this and this relates to a category of right, formerly known as overriding interests and now, considerably less elegantly, as 'unregistered interests which override registration'.[12] As the name suggests, these are rights which will bind a purchaser of the land despite not being noted on the register of title.

4.2.4 Extension of overreaching

The existence of a large number of freehold estates in relation to the same property was normally indicative of there being a family settlement. A settlement to A for life, to B in fee tail, to C in fee simple would normally take place within a family unit. That being the case, it is unlikely that any of A, B, or C would have paid money to acquire their interests in the land. The effect of the settlement, however, made it extremely difficult for the land to be sold, for the simple reason that none of the estate owners held an estate that would be particularly attractive for a purchaser to buy. If, for example, A sold his interest, then all that a purchaser would acquire was an estate *pur autre vie*; his interest in the land would terminate upon the death of A. Again, if either B or C sought to alienate their interests, then a purchaser would have to wait until that interest fell into possession before the land could actually be enjoyed and, in the case of C, there would be no guarantee that this would necessarily ever happen at all.

To enable land, subject to a settlement such as this, to become marketable, a mechanism was imposed to enable the land to be sold. A, who is termed the tenant for life, is given a legal fee simple but, to safeguard the position of B and C, two trustees had to be appointed to receive the purchase money when the land was sold. The purchaser would take a conveyance from A and pay the purchase money to the trustees. That money would be invested and A would receive the income, that money representing his life interest in the land. On A's death the money would then pass in accordance with the settlement.

---

[12] LRA 2002, Scheds 1 and 3. For a full discussion of these matters, see Chapter 5.

In this way, the interests in the land are converted into money. This process is termed 'overreaching'.[13]

4.2.5 **Reform of co-ownership**

It is common for land to be co-owned, the most common situation probably being when a family home is owned by a married couple. Under the law as it existed prior to 1925, it was possible for the legal ownership of the land to become fragmented between numerous people, with obvious attendant conveyancing difficulties. To avoid these difficulties, the law was altered, limiting to four the number of people who could be legal owners of land. The legal owners could then hold the property on trust for any number of equitable co-owners.[14] Provided that the purchase money is paid to the legal co-owners, the purchaser need not concern himself with the interests of the equitable co-owners, whose interests will be overreached,[15] that is, their interests will take effect against the proceeds of sale of the property.[16]

4.2.6 **Mortgages**

A mortgage is a loan secured against land. Under the old law, the security was given by conveying the land to the mortgagee, the land being reconveyed upon the repayment of the loan. This, of course, was highly artificial and disguised the true nature of the transaction. After 1925, a mortgage could be created either by executing a charge by way of legal mortgage, by which the lender, or as he is technically referred to, the mortgagee, acquires the right to take possession of the mortgaged property and, if the mortgage is not repaid, to sell the property, or by creating a 3,000-year lease,[17] although where title is registered, it is no longer possible to utilize the latter method to create a mortgage.[18] In both cases, the fee simple remains with the borrower, the mortgagor.

4.2.7 **Capacity**

Section 1(6) of the LPA 1925 provides that a legal estate is not capable of being held by a minor. The general rule is clear that a person below the age of eighteen lacks the capacity to own a legal estate.[19] If, however, by some mistake, a person below that age is registered as the proprietor of land with an absolute title, then the provisions of the LRA 2002 would appear to clothe that person with the legal title, notwithstanding s. 1(6) of the earlier Act.[20]

---

[13] See also Lawson, *The Rational Strength of English Law* (London, Stevens & Son, 1951), 92–3. For settlements created after 1996 a new regime was introduced by the Trusts of Land and Appointment of Trustees Act (TOLATA) 1996. See Chapter 9.

[14] LPA 1925, s. 34(2). The Law Commission has recommended that, in respect of housing tenancies, this restriction should be abolished: (2003) Law Com. No. 284, para. 11.12.

[15] *City of London Building Society v. Flegg* [1988] A.C. 54; *State Bank of India v. Sood* [1997] Ch. 276. See 7.8.

[16] While at first instance in *Baker v. Craggs* [2016] EWHC 3250 (Ch), overreaching was held to have happened upon the grant of an easement, in the Court of Appeal, order was restored. The court held that overreaching had not occurred as the grant of an easement to a purchaser of land is not a conveyance of a legal estate in land within the meaning of section 1(1) LPA 1925 and so was not capable of being overreached, *Baker v. Craggs* [2018] EWCA Civ 1126. See J. Roche [2018] CLJ 600.

[17] LPA 1925, s. 85. See Chapter 11.   [18] LRA 2002, s. 23(1).

[19] If land is conveyed to a minor before 1997, the land will be regarded as settled land: Settled Land Act 1925, ss 1, 26. If this occurs after this date, the land will be held on a trust of land. See Chapter 7.

[20] See 5.2.6.

The Law Commission has recently recommended that letting contracts should be able to be entered into with minors aged sixteen and seventeen.[21] This is sensible when one bears in mind that people of that age can marry,[22] and it makes little sense for the law then to preclude them from the legal ownership of a place in which to live, although this yet to be implemented proposal relates only to leasehold and not to free-hold property.

4.2.8 Reduction in legal estates

Section 1 of the LPA 1925 provides that the only estates in land which are capable of subsisting or being created at law are:

(a) an estate in fee simple in possession; and

(b) a term of years absolute.

Section 1(2) also limits the number of legal interests in land capable of subsisting or being conveyed. Of these interests, the most important are:

(a) an easement right or privilege in or over land for an interest equivalent to an estate in fee simple absolute in possession or a term of years absolute;

(b) a rentcharge in possession issuing out of or charged on land being either perpetual or for a term of years absolute;

(c) a charge by way of legal mortgage;

(d) rights of entry exercisable over or in respect of a term of years absolute or annexed, for any purpose, to a legal rentcharge.

It is provided by s. 1(3), LPA 1925 that all other estates, interests, or charges in or over land shall take effect as equitable interests.

Before elaborating on these crucial definitions, some preliminary points should be made.

4.2.9 Capable of existing as legal estates

Section 1 of the Act lays down which estates are *capable* of existing as legal estates. It is not the case, however, that because a particular interest falls within that definition it will necessarily be legal. In general, to create a legal estate or interest in land one must use a deed.[23] If a deed is not used, then unless the transaction in question is exempt from this formal requirement,[24] no legal estate or interest will be created. The purported grant may, however, take effect in equity. A term of years absolute, or lease, may therefore be either legal or equitable.

4.2.10 Estates and interests

Section 1 of the Act refers separately to estates and interests. This is a helpful division, in that the concept of an estate connotes ownership rights in land, which are possessory in nature, either immediately or at some time in the future, whereas the idea of an interest in land generally means rights over another person's land.

---

[21] (2003) Law Com. No. 284, para. 3.18.   [22] See Marriage Act 1949, s. 2.
[23] LPA 1925, s. 52(1).   [24] Ibid., s. 53(2). For prescriptive rights, see 12.6.

4.3 Legal estates

4.3.1 The fee simple absolute in possession

A central plank in the strategy was to make the basis of conveyancing the fee simple absolute. Hence this is now the only legal freehold estate which can exist. The nature of a fee simple absolute in possession has already been considered. Outside the definition would be estates such as a life estate, a fee tail, or a base fee, which can now only take effect in equity. Similarly, a fee simple which will determine upon the occurrence of a particular event, for example to A in fee simple or until he becomes a solicitor, is not a fee simple absolute because of the existence of the determining element.

Some problems were occasioned, however, with regard to certain types of determinable fees simple and, in particular, the situation where land was subject to a rentcharge. The practice developed in some parts of the country whereby land would be conveyed subject to a rentcharge, which is an obligation on the part of the landowner to pay an annual sum of money charged on the land. The normal sanction for non-payment was that the owner of the rentcharge had the right to re-enter the land and to determine the fee simple. This type of device would prevent the original fee simple from being legal as, because it was liable to be determined, it was not absolute. This problem was solved by the Law of Property (Amendment) Act 1926, which amended s. 7(1) of the 1925 Act to provide that a fee simple subject to a legal or equitable right of re-entry is for the purposes of the Act a fee simple absolute.[25] The importance of this is diminished, however, because the ability to create new rentcharges was severely restricted by s. 2 of the Rentcharges Act 1977 and those already in existence at the time that the Act was passed will be extinguished sixty years from the passing of the Act or when the rentcharge first became payable, whichever is the later.[26]

A fee simple is in possession unless it is subject to some prior freehold estate, such as a life estate. Any fee simple in remainder cannot, therefore, be legal. Possession does not necessarily entail physical possession. If the owner of a fee simple creates a lease, the fee simple remains in possession because possession is defined to include the right to receive rents and profits.[27]

4.3.2 The term of years absolute

A term of years absolute is a lease. The definition is somewhat unhelpful as term of years includes periods of less than a year, as well as periods from year to year.[28] This latter concept occurs when a lease is granted initially for a specific period, such as one year, and at the end of that period it is renewed automatically for a further period. Such leases will continue indefinitely until either the landlord or the tenant brings it to an end by a process of serving a notice to quit upon the other. What the definition entails is that there is a term which is either certain at the outset,[29] or is capable of being made certain upon the service of a notice to quit.[30]

The word 'absolute' appears to have no discernible meaning in that a lease which is determinable on the occurrence of a particular event, or is liable to forfeiture—that is where the lease can be brought to a premature end by the landlord consequent upon a breach by the tenant of one of the terms of the lease—is, nevertheless, a term of years absolute.

---

[25] Law of Property (Amendment) Act 1926, s. 7, Sched.   [26] Rentcharges Act 1977, s. 3(1).
[27] LPA 1925, s. 205(1)(xix).   [28] Ibid., s. 205(1)(xxvii).
[29] For a full discussion of this issue, see 10.3.1.
[30] *Prudential Assurance Co. Ltd v. London Residuary Body* [1992] 2 A.C. 386. See 10.4.2.1.

A term of years need not take effect in possession, so that a lease granted today to commence in five years' time is perfectly valid. A lease which is to take effect more than twenty-one years from the date of its creation is, however, void.[31]

4.4 Legal interests

Various interests are capable of taking effect as legal interests in land. They are defined by s. 1(2), LPA 1925 and the most important of these are as follows.

4.4.1 Easements, rights, and privileges

An easement, right, or privilege in or over land for an interest equivalent to a fee simple absolute in possession or a term of years absolute is capable of taking effect as a legal interest. An easement is normally a positive right to do something over nearby land, such as the exercise of a right of way over it. Less commonly, it can amount to a restriction on another's use of his own land. This will be the case if there is in existence an easement of light which will restrict a landowner's ability to build on his own land, if the effect of so doing would be to obstruct the flow of light. Also within the definition is a *profit à prendre*.[32] This is the right to go onto another person's land and to take something from the land, examples of this including the right to take wood, or fish, these being termed estovers, and rights of piscary,[33] respectively.

For either interest to be legal, their duration must be equivalent to a fee simple absolute or to a term of years absolute. An easement for life, if such a right is actually an easement at all,[34] is, therefore, necessarily equitable.

4.4.2 Rentcharges

A rentcharge is a right for the owner of it to receive a periodical payment from the owner of the burdened land. This right is independent of any other interest in the land. To be legal, a rentcharge must be perpetual, the term 'perpetual', for some reason, being used instead of the more normal expression, 'fee simple absolute', or it must subsist 'for a term of years absolute'. While it must also take effect in possession, possession in this context has a wider meaning than normal; it includes a situation where it becomes payable at some time in the future, after its creation, provided that it does not take effect upon the determination of some prior interest.[35]

Subject to limited exceptions,[36] no new rentcharges may be created after 1977 and rentcharges still in existence, having been created prior to that date, will expire, at the latest, by 2033.[37]

4.4.3 A charge by way of legal mortgage

A mortgage is one of the most important interests affecting land and will be considered in Chapter 11.

---

[31] LPA 1925, s. 205(1)(xxvii).   [32] For easements and profits, see Chapter 12.
[33] Such rights remain potentially very important: see *Lynn Shellfish Ltd v. Loose* [2016] UKSC 14
[34] For the view that it is not, see D.G. Barnsley (1999) 115 L.Q.R. 89.
[35] Law of Property (Entailed Interests) Act 1932, s. 2.   [36] See 13.8.5.
[37] Rentcharges Act 1977, ss 2, 3.

4.4.4 **Rights of re-entry**

A right of re-entry is normally annexed to a leasehold estate to enable the landlord to determine the lease upon the tenant's failure to comply with the covenants contained in the lease. A right of re-entry is the normal sanction in respect of a failure to comply with the terms of a rentcharge. On the exercise of that right the fee simple against which the rentcharge takes effect is terminated.

4.5 **Equitable rights**

Unless a right in land falls within one of the definitions given above, it cannot be a legal right and must, therefore, be equitable. The types of equitable interest in land, however, differ in nature. Although there is no formal statutory division of equitable interests, they fall within two broadly defined groups: family interests and commercial interests. The general scheme of the legislation was to make the former type of interest overreachable and the latter type registrable.

4.5.1 **Family interests**

If one returns to the settlement considered earlier, where land is settled on A for life, to B in fee tail, remainder to C in fee simple, it should be apparent that, after 1925, neither A, B, nor C have legal interests in the property. Neither A nor B has a fee simple in the land. C does have a fee simple but it is not in possession. The effect of s. 1, LPA 1925 was to ensure that all three would now have equitable estates in the land.

The fee simple absolute in possession was made the only legal, freehold estate in land and was intended to be the subject matter of a conveyance. Yet, in this situation, nobody would be entitled to such an estate in his own right. To fill this gap, the original solution[38] imposed by the Settled Land Act (SLA) 1925 was to require a vesting deed to be executed, the effect of which would be to vest in A, the tenant for life, a legal fee simple. That fee simple is then held by A on trust for those, including himself, entitled under the settlement. To prevent A from selling the property and then misapplying the purchase money, two trustees would be appointed and any purchase money paid to them. On a conveyance by A, the purchaser, provided that he paid the money to the trustees, would take free of the interests behind the settlement which would attach to the proceeds of sale. What this means is that the trustees would invest the capital money which was realized by the sale of the land. They would then pay the interest to A, this representing what was his estate in the land. On A's death, B, if still alive, would be entitled to the interest and, on B's death, or, if B had predeceased A, B's lineal heir would be entitled to that money. Provided that the fee tail had not been enlarged into a fee simple then, on the failure of B's lineal heirs, C would be entitled to the capital sum. In this way, the interests which were previously interests in land become interests in money and those interests are said to have been overreached.

The result of this procedure is that A can, in a sense, effect the compulsory purchase of the interest of B and C. While, at first sight, this can appear to be harsh on them, this is not really so; given the type of interests that the various characters have in the property, it is unlikely that they will have paid to acquire them. The interests will almost inevitably have been created as part of a family settlement and, in the interests of making the land marketable, this procedure was made available to allow the family interests to be overreached.[39]

---

[38] Such settlements, if created after 1996, are now governed by the TOLATA 1996, s. 2.

[39] Overreaching can also occur in different contexts, most notably on a sale by a mortgagee. See LPA 1925, s. 104, see 11.6.5.1.

4.5.2 **Commercial interests**

A person may own land and covenant with his neighbour that he will only use the land as a private residence. This obligation, termed 'a restrictive covenant', is, if certain criteria are satisfied,[40] capable of creating an equitable burden affecting the land of the covenantor and is able to affect subsequent purchasers of the land. It should be apparent that this type of right, which affects the value of the burdened land, is unlikely to have been granted for nothing. It will have been paid for, either as an independent transaction or, more likely, as part of a commercial transaction involving the sale of the land in question. Moreover, it is not the sort of right which can sensibly be transferred to money.[41] While it can readily be seen that one can have a life interest in a capital fund, the effect of which is that the tenant for life enjoys the income produced by the investment of that fund, one cannot intelligibly be said to enjoy a restrictive covenant over money. To retain its utility, it must remain attached to the land through successive periods of ownership. It is a commercial interest in land which cannot be overreached, and its enforceability is made dependent upon registration. A basic strategy of the 1925 legislation was to categorize equitable interests into family interests, which, by implementing the correct conveyancing procedure, can be overreached, and commercial interests, which would depend for their enforceability upon registration. If such a scheme was all-embracing, the purchaser's task would be relatively straightforward. Where land was subject to family interests, his task would be simply to ensure that the correct procedures are followed; in the case of commercial interests, he would simply have to ascertain what interests had been registered, in order to know, before buying the land, to what incumbrances it would be subject. As will be seen, however, this dichotomy is not exhaustive of equitable interests. There exists a third category of interest which is neither overreachable nor registrable, the enforceability of which depends upon the traditional doctrine of notice.[42]

4.6 **Land charges registration**

An aim of the legislation was to make the enforceability of various rights dependent upon registration. To this end, the Land Charges Act (LCA) 1925, which has since been superseded by the LCA 1972, was enacted. This Act established five separate registers, of which the most important is the land charges register. The remainder of this chapter will be confined to this most important category established by the land charges legislation, the land charges register.[43]

Before considering the structure and working of the system, a number of preliminary points may be made. First, one must distinguish land charges registrable under the 1972 Act from local land charges registrable under the Local Land Charges Act 1975. Local land charges relate to various charges, normally either of a financial nature or restrictive of land use, imposed on land in favour of local authorities. Second, and more importantly, it is essential not to confuse the registration of land charges with registration of title. The registration of land charges concerns land where the title is still evidenced by deeds. Registration of title is a system of land ownership whereby the actual title to the land is registered and where recourse to the deeds is no longer

---

[40] See Chapter 13.

[41] See *Birmingham Midshires Mortgage Services Ltd v. Sabherwal* (1999) 80 P. & C.R. 256 at 263 *per* Robert Walker LJ.

[42] See 4.5.

[43] For the other registers, see Thompson, *Barnsley's Conveyancing Law and Practice* (4th edn) (London, Butterworths, 1996), 390–1.

necessary, or, indeed, possible. Under this system, which will eventually replace almost entirely the unregistered, or deeds-based system of land ownership, the register gives an authoritative version of the ownership of the land itself and, subject to a category of rights, originally termed 'overriding interests', will reveal the obligations to which the land is subject.[44] A separate register of third party rights affecting the land is unnecessary.

Ultimately, the land charges system will become obsolete. As virtually all titles become registered, all transactions conducted under the old system of establishing title to the land by reference to the title deeds, where searches in the land charges register are necessary, are now, by force of law, to be followed by the immediate registration of title. This means that the deeds will not normally[45] be used again to provide evidence of ownership of the land in question. At present, and this will also be true for some time to come, the system remains important, albeit less so than was previously the case. In 2015/2016, there were over 42,500 registrations of new land charges, and over 172,000 full official searches made.[46] The remainder of this chapter is concerned with the operation of the system of land charges, and relates to land where the title is not registered.

4.6.1 Basic principles

It may be helpful, at the outset, to state the two basic principles which apply to the registration of land charges. These are that:

(i) the registration of a land charge constitutes actual notice of the interest registered;[47] and

(ii) non-registration of an interest against a particular type of purchaser will make it void against certain types of purchaser.[48]

4.7 Registration under the Land Charges Act

Under s. 1, LCA 1972, the registrar is required to keep five registers and an index. The five registers are:

(i) a register of land charges;

(ii) a register of pending land actions;

(iii) a register of writs and orders affecting land;

(iv) a register of deeds of arrangement affecting land;

(v) a register of annuities.

The five registers are kept in computerized form at the Land Charges Department at the Land Registry in Plymouth.[49] Of the five registers, the most important is the first named, the land charges register, and this is the only one of the registers which will be discussed.

---

[44] See Chapter 5.

[45] The deeds may, however, be relevant to help to resolve boundary disputes or when there is a dispute as to the possible alteration of the register. See 5.4.

[46] Land Registry Annual Report 2015/2016, p. 99.   [47] LPA 1925, s. 198.   [48] LCA 1972, s. 4.

[49] For an account of how the system worked prior to computerization, see *Oak Co-operative Building Society v. Blackburn* [1967] Ch. 730 at 741 *per* Russell L.J.

4.7.1 **Land charges**

This is far and away the most important of the registers. Matters registrable as land charges are placed into one of six categories, labelled A to F, some of these categories themselves being subdivided. The various land charges are defined in s. 2 of the Act.

4.7.1.1 **Class A**

This class consists of financial charges on land created pursuant to a statute on the application of some person. An example is a charge obtained by a landlord in respect of compensation paid to his tenant for improvements to business premises.[50]

4.7.1.2 **Class B**

This group consists of charges, not being local land charges, which are imposed automatically by statute, an example being a legal aid charge in favour of the Legal Services Commission in respect of property recovered or preserved by a legally aided litigant.[51]

4.7.1.3 **Class C**

This category is one of the most important classes of land charge and is subdivided into four sub-categories.

Class C(i): A puisne mortgage

A puisne mortgage[52] is a mortgage not protected by a deposit of title deeds relating to the legal estate affected. This type of mortgage is a legal interest in land but, for it to be enforceable against purchasers of the estate affected, it must be protected by registration. As such, this is an exception to the general principle that legal rights bind the world, regardless of notice. The reason for this exception is entirely pragmatic.

Prior to 1925, the traditional way of creating a mortgage was to convey the land to the mortgagee as security for the loan, and the land was reconveyed when the loan was repaid. As the legal owner of the land, the mortgagee was entitled to the title deeds. Moreover, if land had been mortgaged in this way, it was not possible to create a second legal mortgage as, the land having already been conveyed to the first mortgagee, it could not be conveyed a second time to a subsequent lender. After 1925, to create a legal mortgage, one executes a charge by way of legal mortgage[53] and the mortgagor retains the legal estate. It is possible, therefore, for him to create subsequent legal mortgages.

The first mortgagee is entitled to possession of the title deeds and this alerts subsequent lenders to the fact that the land is already subject to a mortgage. Unless any subsequent mortgages were registered, however, one could not know if the land was subject to more than one mortgage and it would be unsafe to lend money against the security of the land. For this reason, a legal mortgage not protected by a deposit of title deeds is registrable as a land charge.

Class C(ii): A limited owner's charge

A limited owner's charge is an equitable charge acquired by a tenant for life or statutory owner when that person discharges tax liability[54] payable on the death of the previous tenant for life out of his own resources rather than from the settled property.

---

[50] Landlord and Tenant Act 1927, s. 12 and Sched. 1, para. 7. The full list of such charges is contained in LCA 1972, Sched. 2.

[51] Legal Aid Act 1988, s. 16. See *Hanlon v. Law Society* [1981] A.C. 124; *Curling v. Law Society* [1985] 1 W.L.R. 470; *Davies v. Legal Aid Board* [1996] 4 All E.R. 271.

[52] Pronounced 'puny'.   [53] LPA 1925, s. 85. See 11.4.

[54] LCA 1972, s. 3(4)(ii) as amended by Capital Transfer Tax Act 1984, Sched. 8, para. 3. The tax is now termed Inheritance Tax: Finance Act 1986, s. 100.

Class C(iii): General equitable charge

This is a residuary category which is defined in a negative way, by reference to what it is not. It is an equitable charge which:

(a) is not secured by a deposit of documents relating to the legal estate affected; and

(b) does not arise or affect an interest arising under a trust of land or a settlement; and

(c) is not a charge given by way of indemnity against rents equitably apportioned on land in exoneration of other land and against the breach or non-observance of other covenants or conditions; and

(d) is not included in any other class of land charge.[55]

As can be seen, this is something of a 'sweeper' category. It includes an unpaid vendor's lien,[56] which is a charge that a vendor has against the land which he has sold in respect of which some, or all, of the purchase money remains outstanding. It also includes annuities created after 1925. An annuity is a charge against land to produce an annual income and is rarely, if ever, encountered today.

Class C(iv)

Estate contract

The estate contract is one of the more important categories of land charge. It is defined by s. 2(4)(iv) of the Act as being:

> . . . a contract by an estate owner to have a legal estate conveyed to him to convey or create a legal estate, including a contract conferring either expressly or by statutory implication a valid option to purchase, a right of pre-emption or any other like right.

A contract to purchase land is obviously within the terms of the definition. In the case of contracts made after 1989, it is now essential that they are made in writing and signed by both parties.[57] An agreement which does not comply with these formalities is non-contractual in nature and cannot be registered. A conditional contract, such as where the contract is conditional upon the purchaser obtaining planning permission,[58] is apparently registrable[59] even though the condition has not, at the time, been satisfied.[60]

A contract to create a lease is registrable as a C(iv) land charge, so that a lease which should have been granted by deed and which satisfies the formal requirements of s. 2 of the Law of Property (Miscellaneous Provisions) Act (LP(MP)A) 1989, which means that it must be in writing and signed by both landlord and tenant, will be registrable.

Options to purchase

An option to purchase is a right given by the owner of land to another person, within a stated period of time, to purchase the land. Upon the grant of the option neither side is committed to a purchase. The contract of sale arises when the grantee of the option exercises it, thereby causing a binding contract to be created between the landowner and the grantee of the option. An option to purchase is registrable as a land charge, although once

---

[55] LCA 1972, as amended by TOLATA 1996, s. 25, Sched. 3, para. 12(1)(2).

[56] *Uziell-Hamilton v. Keen* (1971) 22 P. & C.R. 655. For a discussion of this lien, see D.G. Barnsley [1997] Conv. 338.

[57] LP(MP)A 1989, s. 2.   [58] See, e.g., *Batten v. White* (1960) 12 P. & C.R. 66.

[59] *Haselmere Estates Ltd v. Baker* [1982] 1 W.L.R. 1109 at 1118–19 *per* Sir Robert Megarry V.-C. See also *Williams v. Burlington Investment Ltd* (1979) 121 S.J. 424.

[60] For an argument that such a contract should not be regarded as registrable, see R.J. Smith [1974] C.L.J. 311 at 314.

it has been registered, it is unnecessary to register, separately, the contract of sale which is created upon the exercise of the option.[61]

A lease may give to the tenant the option at the end of the period granted the right to renew that lease for a further term. Although it has been argued that it should not be necessary for such an option to be registered,[62] it is now clear that, for such an option to bind a purchaser of the landlord's reversion, the option must be registered as a land charge.[63] Similarly, a lease may contain a term that, if the tenant wishes to assign his lease—that is, to transfer it to another person—he must first offer to surrender it—that is, give it up—to the landlord. Such a clause is also registrable as a C(iv) land charge.[64]

Rights of pre-emption

Although express reference is made in the Act to a right of pre-emption, that is a right of first refusal should an owner of land decide to sell it, the position is not straightforward. In *Pritchard v. Briggs*,[65] the Court of Appeal held that, contrary to what the framers of the legislation had thought, a right of pre-emption is not an interest in land.[66] This was because, unless the owner of the land decides that he will sell it, the holder of the right of pre-emption has no right to insist upon the land being conveyed to him. This contrasts with an option to purchase where, on the exercise of the option, the grantee has a contractual right to the property. The majority[67] further held, however, that, when the condition precedent to the right of pre-emption becoming enforceable is satisfied, that is when the vendor decides to sell the land, the right does then become an interest in land and is, therefore, registrable.

In the case of *Pritchard v. Briggs*, an option to purchase was granted subsequent to the creation of a right of pre-emption. Despite the right of pre-emption having been registered, it was held not to be binding on the grantee of the option. On the exercise of the option, the condition precedent to the right of pre-emption was not satisfied as the vendor had not decided to sell the land; he was required to sell it by the exercise of the option by the grantee. In most cases, however, registration of the right of pre-emption will adequately protect the holder of the right because, if the vendor chooses to sell the property, the condition precedent to the right of pre-emption will be satisfied and the holder of that right is now in a position to enter into a binding contract for the sale of the land in question.

Mortgage by deposit of title deeds

A traditional method of creating an equitable mortgage was to deposit with the lender of money the title deeds to land, such a deposit acting as security for the loan. The basis of such a transaction being regarded as an equitable mortgage is that, provided the necessary statutory formalities are complied with,[68] it is seen as a contract to create a legal mortgage.[69] As such it is a contract to create a legal estate and is registrable as a C(iv) land charge and is not registrable as a C(iii) land charge.[70]

---

[61] *Armstrong & Holmes v. Armstrong and Dodds* [1994] 1 All E.R. 826. See N. Gravells [1994] Conv. 483.

[62] See M.P. Thompson (1981) 125 S. J. 816. See 10.9.1.2.

[63] *Beesly v. Hallwood Estates Ltd* [1960] 2 All E.R. 314, affirmed on other grounds [1961] Ch. 105; *Taylors Fashions v. Liverpool Victoria Trustees Ltd* [1982] 1 Q.B. 133n; *Phillips v. Mobil Oil Co. Ltd* [1989] 1 W.L.R. 888; *Markfaith Investments Ltd v. Chap Hua Flashlights Ltd* [1991] 2 A.C. 43 at 58–9 *per* Lord Templeman.

[64] *Greene v. Church Commissioners for England* [1974] Ch. 467.

[65] [1980] Ch. 338. See H.W.R. Wade (1980) 96 L.Q.R. 488; J. Martin [1980] Conv. 433. But contrast *Dear v. Reeves* [2002] Ch. 1, a case on the Insolvency Act 1986, s. 436, where it was said that the reasoning in the judgments in *Prichard v. Briggs* may need reconsideration: [2002] Ch. 1 at 10 *per* Mummery L.J.

[66] See also *Cosmichome Ltd v. Southampton City Council* [2013] EWHC 1378 (Ch) at [59]–[60] *per* Sir William Blackburne.

[67] Templeman and Stephenson L.JJ.; Goff L.J. dissenting   [68] LP(MP)A 1989 s. 2.

[69] *Habib Bank of Kuwait plc v. Sahib* [1996] 3 All E.R. 215. See 11.4.4.2.

[70] An equitable charge on an equitable interest is registrable as a Class C(iii) land charge: *Property Discount Corpn Ltd v. Lyon Group Ltd* [1981] 1 All E.R. 379 at 383 *per* Brightman L.J.

Class D(i): HMRC land charge

The Commissioners for HMRC may register a charge for unpaid inheritance tax in respect of freehold land.[71]

Class D(ii): restrictive covenants

A restrictive covenant is registrable as a D(ii) land charge. This does not include either covenants created before 1926 or covenants between landlord and tenant.[72] The enforceability of the former category depends upon the old doctrine of notice. In the case of restrictive covenants contained in leases, their enforceability will depend either upon the rules which relate to the running of covenants in leases[73] or, if these do not cause the burden of the covenant to run, upon the doctrine of notice.

There is some disagreement as to whether restrictive covenants arising under a scheme of development are registrable as land charges. A scheme of development, to be discussed in a later chapter,[74] involves a situation where land is sold off in individual lots and an attempt is made to impose mutually enforceable restrictive covenants upon the purchasers of the individual lots. While there are practical arguments for suggesting that they are not registrable,[75] there is nothing actually in the Act to exclude such covenants which, in principle, would seem to be registrable.[76]

Class D(iii): Equitable easements

An equitable easement[77] is defined as being an easement, right, or privilege affecting land created or arising on or after 1 January 1926, and being merely an equitable interest. This will include easements which are not equivalent to a fee simple absolute in possession or a term of years. An easement for life will, if contrary to the views of some it is capable of existing as an easement at all,[78] therefore, be registrable. Also registrable will be a specifically enforceable contract to create an easement.[79]

The definition of this category of land charge includes a 'right or privilege affecting land'. These words are construed narrowly so that the right in question must have the essential characteristics of an easement[80] in order to be registrable. Accordingly, a requisition of land under Defence Regulations,[81] a right to remove fixtures at the end of a lease,[82] and an equitable right of re-entry to secure compliance with covenants contained in an assignment of a lease[83] have all been held not to be registrable as equitable easements. Neither has a claim arising under the principles of estoppel.[84] The enforceability of such rights against a purchaser is dependent upon the old doctrine of notice.

Class E

This is an annuity created before 1926 and not registered in the register of annuities.

---

[71] LCA 1972, s. 2(5) as substituted by the Inheritance Tax Act 1984, s. 276, Sched. 8, para. 3.
[72] LCA 1972, s. 2(5).   [73] See 10.9.   [74] See Chapter 13.
[75] Thompson, *Barnsley's Conveyancing Law and Practice*, 388–9.
[76] R.G. Rowley (1956) 20 Conv. (N.S.) 370 at 371–3.
[77] See D.G. Barnsley (1999) 115 L.Q.R. 89.   [78] Ibid.
[79] See *E.R. Ives Investment Ltd v. High* [1967] 2 Q.B. 379. Arguably, it is also registrable as an estate contract. See *Huckvale v. Aegean Hotels Ltd* (1989) 58 P. & C.R. 163 at 165; E.O. Walford (1947) 11 Conv. (N.S.) 165 at 176.
[80] See Chapter 12.   [81] *Lewisham Borough Council v. Moloney* [1948] 1 K.B. 50.
[82] *Poster v. Slough Estates Ltd* [1969] 1 Ch. 495.
[83] *Shiloh Spinners Ltd v. Harding* [1973] A.C. 691.
[84] *E.R. Ives Investment Ltd v. High* [1967] 2 Q.B. 379. For the doctrine of proprietary estoppel, see Chapter 14.

Class F: A spouse's statutory right of occupation

The Class F land charge was created as a legislative response to the House of Lords decision in *National Provincial Bank Ltd v. Ainsworth*.[85] Prior to this decision there had been a controversial line of authority[86] where it was held that a wife who had been deserted by her husband had an equitable right to remain in the matrimonial home. This right, which had been considered to be some form of equitable property right, was held to be binding upon mortgagees. In *Ainsworth*, however, the House of Lords held that there was no such right known to law and, therefore, no possibility of mortgagees being bound by it.

This decision was seen as leaving wives in an unacceptably exposed position and a Private Member's Bill was guided through Parliament to become the Matrimonial Homes Act 1967.[87] Under the terms of this Act a spouse, and now also a person in a registered civil partnership,[88] was given a statutory right not to be excluded from the matrimonial home and, if not in possession of it, the right, with the leave of the court, to enter the matrimonial home.[89] This right will, if registered,[90] be binding also upon a purchaser and on a trustee in bankruptcy.[91]

The court has the power to regulate the statutory right, so that if registration is motivated by spite, the court will order its removal.[92] The court has wide regulatory powers in respect of matrimonial rights[93] and, in exercising these powers the court is directed to have regard to various factors, including the housing needs and resources of the parties[94] and any relevant child, the health, safety, and well-being of the parties and any relevant child, and the conduct of the parties towards each other.[95]

The 1967 Act provided some modest reform of this area and afforded some protection to spouses who are not legal co-owners of the matrimonial home. The statutory right of occupation can be a powerful weapon in the hands of a spouse, giving her potentially a power of veto over a proposed transaction affecting the matrimonial home.[96] On the other hand, however, the enforceability of this right as against a purchaser is made dependent upon registration.[97] Unless the wife (or husband) is in receipt of legal advice, the most likely occasion for this being if there are marital difficulties, she is highly unlikely to have heard of the statutory right of occupation, let alone the need to protect it by registration. By the time this has been discovered, the house may already have been mortgaged, in which case her right will not be binding upon the mortgagee.

The history of the Class F land charge reveals an underlying tension between protecting the rights of occupiers and promoting the security of conveyancing transactions. Had the existence of the deserted wife's equity been upheld in the House of Lords, there would have been recognized an informal right in land which was potentially binding upon a purchaser but was not registrable. The purchaser could not then rely on the simple expedient of searching the register to discover the existence of all equitable rights to which the property was subject. Instead, he would need to make additional enquiries, thereby complicating

---

[85] [1965] A.C. 1175.

[86] *Bendall v. McWhirter* [1952] 2 Q.B. 406; *Street v. Denham* [1954] 1 W.L.R. 624. See R.E. Megarry (1952) 68 L.Q.R. 379.

[87] The relevant legislation is now the Family Law Act 1996. See, generally, M.P. Thompson in Meisel and Cook (eds), *Property and Protection: Essays in Honour of Brian Harvey* (Oxford, Hart Publishing, 2000), 157 at 158–61.

[88] Civil Partnerships Act 2004, s. 101.   [89] Family Law Act 1996, s. 32.

[90] The right can be registered before a court has granted leave: *Watts v. Waller* [1973] Q.B. 133. See, generally, D.G. Barnsley [1974] C.L.P. 76; D.J. Hayton [1976] C.L.P. 26.

[91] Insolvency Act 1986, s. 336(2).   [92] *Barnett v. Hassett* [1981] 1 W.L.R. 1385.

[93] Family Law Act 1996, s. 33(3).

[94] This would seem to include a purchaser who has taken subject to the right: *Kashmir Kaur v. Gill* [1988] Fam. 110.

[95] Family Law Act 1996, s. 33(6).   [96] For a graphic example, see *Wroth v. Tyler* [1974] Ch. 30.

[97] Where title is registered, the statutory right of occupation must also be registered if it is to bind a purchaser. See Family Law Act 1996, s. 31(10)(b) and 5.1.5.3—Rights incapable of overriding.

the conveyancing process. It is clear that a desire to avoid any such complication was an important factor in the decision-making process in *Ainsworth*, Lord Upjohn commenting that it had been the policy of the law for over a hundred years to simplify and facilitate the conveyancing process;[98] a policy objective which would have been hindered had the case been decided the other way.

The legislative response to the decision was consistent with this general policy. Although a wife is given the statutory right to occupy the matrimonial home, its enforceability is made dependent upon registration. The effect of this is that, in general, the conveyancing process will continue to operate smoothly and the reliability of the register of land charges is enhanced. There is a cost to this, however, which is that people who are not familiar with the registration system are, through a failure to protect their rights by registration, at risk of losing those rights, and also their homes, because of ignorance of the need to register. As will be seen, this tension between the competing interest of protecting the rights of occupiers and enhancing the security of conveyancing transactions has continued to be an important one in the law.

4.8 The registration of land charges

Having considered the different classes of land charge, it is now necessary to consider the system in operation.

4.8.1 The effect of registration

The effect of registration of a land charge is determined by s. 198, LPA 1925, which provides that:

> The registration of any instrument or matter . . . shall be deemed to constitute actual notice of such instrument or matter, and of the fact of such registration, to all persons and for all purposes[99] connected with the land affected, as from the date of registration or other prescribed date and so long as the registration continues in force.

This important provision is central to the working of the Act. If an interest has been registered correctly as a land charge, then, subject to one exception,[100] a purchaser cannot claim not to have notice of it. Registration constitutes notice. The purpose of the legislation is to do away with the uncertainties attendant on the old doctrine of notice in respect of matters which are registrable. Registration supplies a different form of notice. If, however, something is registered as a land charge, this does not guarantee the validity of the right in question, so that, if something is registered which is not actually an interest in land, registration will not confer validity upon it.[101]

4.8.2 Registration against names

The most serious defect in the whole system of registration of land charges is the method of registration. Section 3(1) of the LCA 1972 provides that:

> A land charge shall be registered in the name of the estate owner intended to be affected.

---

[98] [1965] A.C. 1175 at 1233.

[99] There are statutory exceptions to this: LPA 1969, s. 24, removing the problem caused by the decision in *Re Forsey and Hollebone's Contract* [1927] 2 Ch. 379, a decision disapproved in *Rignall Developments Ltd v. Halil* [1987] 1 E.G.L.R. 193; s. 25(2) (compensation for undiscoverable land charges).

[100] This is if an official search fails to reveal a properly registered land charge: LCA 1972, s. 10(4).

[101] Cf. *Cator v. Newton* [1940] 1 Q.B. 415 (registration of a positive covenant on the register of title).

The requirement that a land charge be registered against the owner of the land, at the time when the charge was created, rather than against the land itself, has created a number of avoidable difficulties. Even without these difficulties, this requirement does not avoid both the registration and the application for a search having to give the accurate address of the property, as it will be appreciated that registration against the name of John Smith, without any description of the property to be affected, would be pointless.

4.8.2.1 **What name?**

Registration of a land charge must be against the correct name of the estate owner. This has been held to mean the version of the name, or names, as it appears in the title deeds and not as it may appear in other contexts, such as a birth certificate.[102] This may be easier said than done. In *Diligent Finance Co. Ltd v. Alleyne*,[103] a wife sought to register a Class F land charge against her husband, whom she knew by the name Erskine Alleyne. Unknown to her, he had a middle name, Owen. The finance company searched against the full, correct version and obtained a clear certificate of search, and her attempted registration was held to have been ineffective.

The problems involved in getting the names right, a problem described as 'the tip of a fairly large iceberg',[104] emerged again in the near farcical case of *Oak Co-operative Building Society v. Blackburn*.[105] Mr Blackburn's real name was **Francis David** Blackburn. A land charge was registered against the name **Frank** David Blackburn, which was the name under which he traded. A search was then requisitioned against the name Francis **Davis** Blackburn; in other words, both the registration and the search used the wrong names. It was held that a purported registration against what can be regarded as a fair approximation of the estate owner's correct name was effective against a person who either did not search at all, or who had requisitioned a search against an incorrect version of the name.

This was a pragmatic rather than a logical solution. If a person has registered a land charge against the wrong name then, unless the person requisitioning the search replicated that error, the land charge could not have been discovered. Yet, the result is not unreasonable as the task of the person seeking to register a land charge against an estate owner is more difficult than is the task for the person making a search against that person. Someone registering a land charge against a person may not have the latter's co-operation in so doing. It may be a hostile act, in which case access to the title deeds will not be available and the prospect of getting the name wrong is increased. A person requisitioning a search would normally be engaged in a transaction with the estate owner, who will be co-operative and allow him access to the deeds. There is, therefore, very little excuse for the person searching to get the name wrong. This problem would not have occurred, however, if registration was against the land rather than the estate owner.

4.8.2.2 *Who is the estate owner?*

A second, related, problem is to establish who the estate owner actually is at the relevant time. This problem was seen in *Barrett v. Hilton Developments Ltd*,[106] where A contracted to sell land to B, who, before the completion of that contract, had contracted to sell the same land to C. C registered his estate contract against B but this was invalid because the estate owner at the time was not B but A. A similar difficulty could occur when an estate owner died, in that registration should be against his personal representatives.[107] If he died

---

[102] *Standard Property Investment plc v. British Plastics Federation* (1985) 53 P. & C.R. 25.
[103] (1972) 23 P. & C.R. 346.   [104] Ruoff, *Searching without Tears* (London, Oyez, 1974), 49.
[105] [1968] Ch. 730.   [106] [1975] Ch. 237.
[107] These are the people in whom the property of a deceased will vest pending the implementation by them of his will.

intestate, until 1995 it was the case that the deceased's property vested in the President of the Family Division of the High Court and so any land charge would need to be registered against that person. Thereafter the property vests in the Public Trustee.[108] This particular problem has now been eradicated in that s. 15, LP(MP)A 1994 amended the LCA 1972 to permit registration of a land charge against a person who has died.[109]

4.8.2.3 Undiscoverable land charges

A further difficulty that was caused by requiring land charges to be registered against the name of the estate owner is that the possibility may arise of a purchaser being deemed to have notice of a land charge which he could not actually discover. This possibility arose owing to a combination of registering against names, the effect of s. 198, LPA 1925, and the method of investigating title to unregistered land. The problem is best illustrated by an example.

1925 A conveyed to B

1935 B conveyed to C

1945 C conveyed to D

1955 D conveyed to E

1965 E conveyed to F

1975 F conveyed to G

1996 V inherited the property from G[110]

2017 V contracts to sell the property to P.

In this example, the entire list of transactions affecting the land since 1925 is given. It is possible that a land charge was registered against any of the different people from that date, when they owned the land. Suppose, for example, that the conveyance in 1935 from B to C contained a restrictive covenant and that that covenant was duly registered against the name of C. The fact that the land charge had been properly registered means that P will be deemed to have actual notice of it. This means that, on completion of the V–P transaction, P will be bound by the covenant. The problem is that he may have had no way of discovering it.

When investigating title, a purchaser must go back to a good root of title which is at least fifteen years old.[111] In the example given above, this is the 1975 conveyance between F and G. Although this conveyance is over forty years old, it is the first conveyance which is at least fifteen years old. He will then discover that, at various times, F, G, and V were estate owners of the land and be able to requisition searches against them. He will not, however, discover who owned the land previously and will be unable to search against them. He runs the risk, therefore, of being bound by a land charge, the existence of which he could not have discovered. This risk, in theory at least, grows as the period of time between 1925 and what will constitute a good root of title grows.[112]

This problem, which was a direct consequence of registration being against names of estate owners rather than against the land itself, was appreciated a long time ago and the

---

[108] Administration of Justice Act 1925, s. 9, as substituted by the LP(MP)A 1994, s. 14(1). For a discussion of the difficulties caused by death, see A.M. Prichard [1979] Conv. 249.

[109] LCA 1972, s. 3(1)(A).

[110] At that time, the transmission of land by means of an assent, the procedure by which land is transferred on death, did not trigger compulsory registration of title. See 5.2.1.

[111] LPA 1969, s. 23.

[112] The problem has been likened to 'the conveyancing equivalent of a Franckenstein's [sic] monster, which with the passing years would become not only more dangerous but also more difficult to kill': H.W.R. Wade [1956] C.L.J. 216.

only palliative for it was seen to be compensatory, it not being realistic to unscramble the whole system.[113] A compensation scheme was established in 1969.

4.8.2.4 Compensation

Under s. 25, LPA 1969, a purchaser may claim compensation if various conditions are satisfied, the principal ones being that he had no actual knowledge of the charge[114] and that the charge was registered against the owner of an estate who was not, as owner of any such estate, a party to any transaction, or concerned in any event, comprised in the relevant title. This means that the purchaser has investigated back to a good root of title and could not have discovered the land charge by searching against the names of people revealed to have been estate owners from then to the present day. In the example given above, because C is not a name which would be revealed by an investigation of the relevant title, P would be entitled to compensation under the Act.

Given the scale of the theoretical risk of undiscoverable land charges, it may, at first sight, seem surprising that there appear to have been very few claims for compensation under this legislation.[115] There appear to be two main reasons for this. First, on each transaction involving the land since 1925, the purchaser would have made a land charges search and would discover land charges registered at an earlier time and this information could be passed on to later purchasers. Second, the problem has been assuaged by the spread of registration of title. It has been the case that, since 1989, every conveyance on sale of unregistered land must be completed by registration of title.[116] If, as is likely, the land charge was not discovered when title is registered, it would not have been entered on the register, with the result that the registered proprietor would have taken free from it. If it is sought, subsequently, to enforce the right protected by the land charge, the person seeking to enforce that right will have to proceed by way of rectification of the register[117] and the compensation scheme devised by the 1969 Act will not be relevant.[118]

The problems with land charges and other, more technical matters affecting leasehold property[119] were a direct consequence of a flawed system based on registration of third-party rights against the name of the estate owner rather than the land itself. Some other aspects of the system, however, raise issues which remain highly relevant to the system of registered titles and it is instructive to see how these were dealt with under the land charges system.

4.8.3 The effect of non-registration

Just as the effect of registration of land charges is clear, so, too, is the consequence of non-registration. Although there are some differences between the different classes of land charge, the essential consequence of non-registration is that the particular land charge becomes void for non-registration against a purchaser for value,[120] such persons including, of course, a lessee and a mortgagee.[121] The differences relate to the different type of purchaser with respect to particular land charges. Some land charges are void for non-registration

---

[113] Report of Committee on Land Charges 1956 (Cmd. 9825) (The Roxburgh Committee).

[114] The effect of LPA 1925, s. 198, which deems a person to have actual notice of any matter registered as a land charge, is disregarded in determining whether a purchaser actually knew of the land charge: ibid., s. 25(2). Whether the purchaser knew of the matter is a matter of fact decided without reference to s. 198.

[115] For the first such claim, see Chief Land Registrar's Report (1988–89), para. 56.

[116] See 5.2.1.   [117] See 5.4. See also *Horrill v. Cooper* (2000), Unreported, Court of Appeal.

[118] See 5.1.5.3.

[119] Most notably the issues associated with what is known as the rule in *Patman v. Harland* (1881) 17 Ch.D. 353. See the fifth edition of this book, p. 100.

[120] LCA 1972, s. 4.   [121] Ibid., s. 17(1).

against a purchaser for value of any interest in the land, whereas, in the case of other land charges, they are void against the purchaser of a legal estate for money or money's worth. Class C(iv) and Class D[122] fall into the latter category. This division seems needlessly complex, although no particular problems seem to have arisen in consequence of it.

Two initial points can be made. If the purchaser has not given value, perhaps because he has inherited the property, or has been given it, then he will still be bound by an interest which is registrable but not registered. Second, if the land charge is void for non-registration as against a purchaser for value, it will not be binding on a successor in title of that purchaser, even if that person is not, himself, a purchaser for value.

The consequence of a land charge being void for non-registration is underlined by s. 199(1), LPA 1925, which provides that:

> A purchaser shall not be prejudicially affected by notice of—
> any instrument or matter capable of registration under the provisions of the Land Charges Act 1972 . . . which is void or not enforceable as against him under that Act . . . by reason of the non-registration thereof.

The operation of these provisions was considered by the House of Lords in the leading case of *Midland Bank Trust Co. Ltd v. Green*.[123] Walter Green granted his son, Geoffrey, an option to purchase agricultural land, of which he was a tenant, for the sum of £22,000. This option was exercisable for a period of ten years. Some six years later, when the value of the land had nearly doubled in value, Walter 'met a lawyer somewhere or other and told him of the option'.[124] After this meeting he consulted another solicitor and, within three days thereafter,[125] he conveyed the land to his wife, Evelyne, for £500. The principal issue in the litigation was whether the option to purchase the land, which by then was worth in excess of £450,000, was binding upon Evelyne who, it was accepted, knew of the existence of the option, despite it having not been registered.

The majority of the Court of Appeal had held the option to be enforceable despite it not having been registered. One basis for this decision was that, because £500 was a substantial undervalue, Evelyne should not be classified as a purchaser for money or money's worth.[126] An alternative reason was that one could not rely upon the statute as to do so would have been fraudulent; fraud in this context, according to Lord Denning M.R., being 'any dishonest dealing done so as to deprive unwary innocents of their rightful dues'.[127] The House of Lords unanimously reversed this decision and held that the option was void for non-registration.

4.8.3.1 The irrelevance of good faith

The only speech was delivered by Lord Wilberforce, who applied traditional concepts of the doctrine of consideration and refused to consider its adequacy. In his view, £500 clearly represented money or money's worth.[128] He also declined either to read the notion

---

[122] Except for the Class D(i) charge, which is void against a purchaser of any estate: ibid., s. 4(6).

[123] [1981] A.C. 513. See also *Hollington Bros v. Rhodes* [1951] 2 All E.R. 487; *Markfaith Investments Ltd v. Chap Hua Flashlights Ltd* [1991] 2 A.C. 43. For a full analysis of issues relating to the non-registration of registrable interests, see M.P. Thompson in Gravells (ed.), *Landmark Cases in Land Law* (Oxford, Hart Publishing, 2013), Chapter 7.

[124] *Midland Bank Trust Co. Ltd v. Green* [1980] Ch. 590 at 620 *per* Lord Denning M.R.

[125] 'Never in the history of conveyancing has anything been done so rapidly': ibid. at 621 *per* Lord Denning M.R. Cf. *Miles v. Bull* [1969] 1 Q.B. 255. at 260, where contract and completion occurred on the same day.

[126] [1980] Ch. 590 at 624 *per* Lord Denning M.R.; at 628 *per* Eveleigh L.J.

[127] Ibid. at 625.

[128] [1981] A.C. 513 at 532. Cf. *Nurdin & Peacock plc v. D.B. Ramsden & Co. Ltd* [1999] 1 E.G.L.R. 119 at 123 *per* Neuberger J.

of good faith into what he regarded as clear legislation or to disallow the purchaser from relying on the legislation on the basis that the transaction was fraudulent. By fraud was meant something similar to the more colourful language of Lord Denning that, if the motive underlying the transaction was to defeat an unregistered interest, then this was fraudulent.[129] Taking the view that there may be mixed motives underlying a particular transaction,[130] Lord Wilberforce saw such a test as being unworkable. Accordingly, the legislation was given its plain meaning with the result that, despite having actual knowledge of the unregistered land charge, the purchaser took free from it.

Not surprisingly, this decision attracted criticism, one commentator asking when discussing a case raising a similar issue,[131] 'would it really cause the collapse of civilised conveyancing if the . . . statutes were altered to make actual notice of an unprotected interest binding upon a purchaser?'[132] While such views are readily understandable, in that the mother's case seemed to be short of merit and that the land charges legislation was being construed in what might be termed an amoral way, there is also a good deal to be said in favour of the approach taken.

First, the decision brings certainty into this branch of the law. While certainty is not necessarily an overriding goal, and the facts of *Green* were such that one would instinctively sympathize with the plaintiff, other cases where issues of good faith might arise may well involve less dramatic facts and a less substantial undervalue.[133] In such circumstances, the temptation to water down the clarity of the legislative provision of the legislation may be less strong and the results less predictable.

A second point is that the plaintiff is usually not without a remedy in this type of case. In *Green* itself, as one would expect in a commercial transaction of this nature, legal advice had been taken. Insisting that rights such as an option to purchase should be registered if they are to be enforceable against third parties should not cause undue hardship, as one would expect a competent solicitor to ensure that it was protected in this way. Indeed, the failure to do so led to a successful action for substantial damages.[134] It should also not be forgotten that the father who, in breach of his obligation to his son, conveyed the land to his wife would also have been personally liable to his son for breach of contract although, admittedly, given the sums involved, this was probably not a cause of action worth pursuing.

4.8.3.2 The economic torts

A final potential cause of action, which was assumed to be available on the facts of *Green*, was to pursue an action in tort against the parents for conspiracy.[135] This assumption seems questionable for two reasons. First, an essential ingredient of this tort is to be able to identify a predominant intention to injure.[136] Yet, it was precisely the difficulty in isolating an intention of this type that led to Lord Wilberforce rejecting the test of fraud as

---

[129] *Re Monolithic* [1915] 1 Ch. 643 at 669–70 *per* Phillimore L.J. See also M.P. Thompson [1985] C.L.J. 280 at 280–4.

[130] [1981] A.C. 513 at 530. See also [1980] Ch. 590 at 625 *per* Eveleigh L.J.

[131] *Peffer v. Rigg* [1977] 1 W.L.R. 285. See 3.3.1.

[132] S. Anderson (1977) 40 M.L.R. 600 at 606. See also B. Green (1981) 97 L.Q.R. 518 at 520.

[133] For the difficulties which can arise in deciding whether a particular purchase price was an undervalue, see *Haque v. Khan* [2016] EWHC 1950 (Ch) at [51] *per* Henderson J.

[134] See *Midland Bank Trust Co. Ltd v. Hett, Stubbs and Kemp* [1979] Ch. 384. See also *Midland Bank Trust Co. Ltd v. Green* [1981] A.C. 513 at 526 *per* Lord Wilberforce, although contrast *Bell v. Peter Browne & Co.* [1990] 2 Q.D. 195.

[135] *Midland Bank Trust Co. Ltd v. Green (No. 3)* [1982] Ch. 529.

[136] See *Lonrho Ltd v. Shell Petroleum Co. Ltd* [1982] A.C. 173 at 189 *per* Lord Diplock. See, also, *Meretz Investments N.V. v. ACP Ltd* [2007] EWCA Civ. 1303 at [172] *per* Toulson L.J.

being an intention to defeat an unregistered interest, thereby injuring the holder of the right. Isolating this intention can be no easier a task if the cause of action is in tort. Second, the land charges legislation is designed to answer questions as to when a purchaser takes subject to a prior interest in land. It makes little sense to hold, as a matter of property law, that the purchaser takes free from an interest and then to hold that person liable in tort in respect of the same right. It is suggested that the economic torts should not have a role to play in this context.[137]

A second economic tort which might appear to be relevant in circumstances such as those which occurred in *Green* is that of procuring a breach of contract. The essence of this tort is that there is in existence a contract between A and B and then C does some act in the knowledge that this will cause A to breach his contract with B.[138] The argument is, in a case such as *Green*, that the purchase of the farm by Evelyne would, necessarily, and to her full knowledge, involve Walter being in breach of contract to Geoffrey. Despite this argument being accepted as correct by Asplin J. in *Lictor Anstalt v. Mir Steel UK Ltd*,[139] it is suggested that it is wrong in principle, and for much the same reasons as those which relate to the tort of conspiracy.

In the first place, one should look at context. The tort of procuring breach of contract has been created to deal with situations where the general law is that C does not take subject to a contract between A and B. Indeed, the law of privity is to the effect that C is not affected by any such prior contract. The involvement of the law of tort is, to an extent, an exception to this basic principle of the law of contract. It should not be applicable however, when its effect would be to undermine the law of property. To a considerable extent, the law of property is concerned to decide the circumstances in which a purchaser is bound by a prior interest. To hold, on the same facts, that the purchaser is liable in tort to the person who has failed to protect his equitable interest when the law of property holds that the purchaser is not liable negates the principles of property law which have been developed over centuries. Such an outcome needs to be squarely addressed and justified.

A second point is that, for a person to be liable in tort for procuring a breach of contract, that person must, of course, be aware of the existence of that contract. Once, as was the case with *Green*, the contract was completed, the prior interest became void for non-registration.[140] As noted previously, the consequence of this is that, by dint of s. 199(1), LPA 1925, a purchaser is not to be prejudicially affected with notice of any matter which is void against him for non-registration. The effect of these two provisions should be sufficient to prevent a constituent part of the tort from being established: that the purchaser knew about the prior contractual right. In *Lictor Anstalt*, the judge, when addressing the issues of the state of mind of the purchaser, and the possible defence of justification, appeared to address the issue from the standpoint of the purchaser's state of mind prior to the transaction. If, however, as should be the case, the focus is on the position after the sale, then the relevant statutory provisions, and the policy underlying them, should have led to the conclusion that the purchaser was immune from a separate action in tort.[141]

4.8.3.3 Payment of purchase price

Midland Bank Trust Co. Ltd v. Green was followed recently in a less clear context in *Lloyds Bank plc v. Carrick*.[142] Mrs Carrick contracted orally[143] to buy a long leasehold of

---

[137] See R.J. Smith (1977) 41 Conv. (N.S.) 318; M.P. Thompson [1985] C.L.J. 280 at 293–5.

[138] See *OBG v Allen* [2008] 1 A.C. 1 at [39] *per* Lord Hoffmann.

[139] [2014] EWHC 3316 (Ch).   [140] LCA 1972, s. 4(6).   [141] See also 5.5.3.1.

[142] [1996] 4 All E.R. 630. See M.P. Thompson [1996] Conv. 295; P. Ferguson (1996) 112 L.Q.R. 549.

[143] The agreement pre-dated the coming into force of the LP(MP)A 1989, s. 2, when oral contracts for the sale of land could be made. See Chapter 14.

a maisonette from her brother-in-law. She paid the purchase price in full and went into sole possession.[144] The legal title was never, however, conveyed to her. Some time later, the brother-in-law mortgaged the property to the bank and, when he defaulted on the repayments, the bank sought possession, an action resisted by Mrs Carrick. It was held, following *Green*, that the contract was void against the bank for want of registration and so the bank was entitled to possession.

Had the contract in this case been entirely executory, then the case would, indeed, have been on all fours with *Green*. It is suggested, however, that the fact that the purchase price had, in this case, been paid in full should have made a material difference to the decision. While it is true to say that the existence of an enforceable contract of sale did, in itself, give rise to an equitable interest in favour of Mrs Carrick,[145] the fact that she had paid the entire purchase price meant that her brother-in-law would hold the property on a bare trust for her, thus making her the equitable owner of the lease.[146] The nature of this interest is different in nature from that which arises from an enforceable contract of sale and, it is thought, the bank should have been held to have been bound by this interest, which would not have been registrable.

4.8.3.4 Actual occupation

A feature of both *Midland Bank Trust Co. Ltd v. Green* and *Lloyds Bank plc v. Carrick* is that, in each case, the person seeking to enforce the right was in actual occupation of the land at all material times. The fact that this had no bearing on the outcome of the litigation highlights, as was pointed out in *Carrick* itself,[147] an anomalous difference between the unregistered and registered land systems. Had title to the land been registered, then the fact that Mrs Carrick was in actual occupation of the land would have meant that her interest in the land would have been binding on the bank; the existence of her right, coupled with actual occupation of the land would have meant that she would have had an overriding interest,[148] or, as this concept is now termed, an unregistered interest which overrides a registered disposition.[149]

When title to the land is registered, then, in general, if the person with a right over another's land is in actual occupation of that land, this is an alternative to registration as a means of ensuring its enforceability against purchasers.[150] As such, the importance of actual occupation is that it provides a form of safety net against the consequences of non-registration of rights. Where title to the land is unregistered, almost certainly as a result of a legislative mishap,[151] no such alternative form of protection is available.

The result of this is that, if an interest is registrable but not registered, the fact that the owner of that interest is in actual occupation of the relevant land is irrelevant. It is unfortunate that a morally neutral matter such as whether or not title to land is registered should have such a decisive effect on the outcome of disputes of this nature. It is suggested that the registered land position is preferable, reflecting as it does the modern tendency to afford greater protection to the rights of people who actually occupy the land.

---

[144] For a similarly cavalier approach to the conveyancing process by the late actor, Kenneth More, see Kenneth More, *More or Less*, an autobiography, 194.

[145] See the sixth edition of this work: The effect of the contract at 220–5.

[146] See *Bridges v. Mees* [1957] Ch. 475.

[147] [1996] 4 All E.R. 630 at 642 *per* Morritt L.J.

[148] LRA 1925, s. 70(1)(g). See *Bhullar v. McArdle* [2001] EWCA Civ. 557, where such a claim failed because the person was not in actual occupation of the land.

[149] LRA 2002, Sched. 3.

[150] LRA 1925, s. 70(1)(g); *Williams & Glyn's Bank Ltd v. Boland* [1981] A.C. 487. See 5.1.5.3—The upgrading of rights.

[151] Earlier legislation did provide protection for people in actual occupation. See LPA 1922, ss 14, 32, Sched. 7; H.W.R. Wade [1956] C.L.J. 216 at 228.

4.9 **Unregistrable interests**

In reforming the substantive law as it affects unregistered land, a principal stratagem was to fit equitable interests into one of two categories: those which were overreachable and those which were registrable. Had this compartmentalization been complete, a purchaser of land would be able to be assured that, provided where necessary he operated the over-reaching machinery correctly, he would take subject only to those equitable interests which had been correctly registered and the limited number of legal interests which remained in existence. He could be unconcerned with any other rights. This scenario has not occurred, however, as not all equitable rights fall into one of these categories.

It can be stated at the outset that the legislation itself envisaged that some equitable interests would fall into a residuary category where their enforceability against a purchaser was made dependent upon the unreformed doctrine of notice, an example being a restrictive covenant created before 1926.[152] Other rights, however, came to be recognized as having the capacity to affect purchasers without being registrable. At first, such rights were limited to relatively arcane matters, such as a tenant's right to remove fixtures at the end of the lease[153] or an equitable right of re-entry.[154] Of much greater significance were rights arising under trusts and rights arising through estoppel.

4.9.1 **Informal rights**

A phenomenon which, in recent times, has frequently exercised the courts is where a house has been conveyed into one person's name but another person has an equitable interest in it. This situation will most frequently arise where the two parties are either married or are involved in a stable relationship. The normal scenario is when the legal title to a house is in the name of the man and his partner is an equitable co-owner of it. He then, without consulting her, mortgages the property and then defaults on the mortgage repayments. The issue then becomes whether or not her interest is binding upon the mortgagee.

The difficulty for the mortgagee is that the framework of co-ownership of land is predicated upon the notion that the legal title is vested in two legal owners. If that is the case then, on a conveyance by the two legal owners, any equitable co-ownership interests will be overreached and attached to the purchase money.[155] Where the correct overreaching machinery is not operated, which will be the case when there is only one legal owner of the land, there is no land charge which would include the rights of an equitable co-owner.[156] The determination of the issue of whether such an interest is binding on a purchaser is then governed by the traditional doctrine of notice.

Where a person has become an equitable co-owner in circumstances such as those outlined above, she will have acquired her interest under a trust. This trust will normally have arisen as a result of her contributing financially to the acquisition of the house; for example, by using her salary to help meet the mortgage repayments.[157] It is also possible that an interest may be acquired in the property without making direct contributions to the purchase of the house, relying on this occasion on the doctrine of equitable estoppel which, in the present context, is a doctrine which bears a close affinity to the law of trusts.[158]

Equitable estoppel, which will be examined in depth in subsequent chapters, is a flexible doctrine, whereby one person acquires rights over another's land by relying upon the

---

[152] LPA 1922, s. 3.   [153] *Poster v. Slough Estates Ltd* [1969] 1 W.L.R. 1807.

[154] *Shiloh Spinners Ltd v. Harding* [1973] A.C. 691. See P.B. Fairest [1973] C.L.J. 218.

[155] *City of London Building Society v. Flegg* [1988] A.C. 54. See 4.2.4.

[156] This is also true in the rarer situation where a legal owner holds the land on a bare trust for another. Cf. *Hodgson v. Marks* [1971] Ch. 892.

[157] See Chapter 8.   [158] See Chapter 14.

expectation either that they will acquire, or already have, an interest in that person's land, in circumstances when it would be inequitable for the latter to deny some effect to such an expectation. Although not entirely uncontroversial,[159] it seems probable that such rights are capable of binding purchasers and that their enforceability will depend upon the doctrine of notice. This view is reinforced by the recognition in s. 116, LRA 2002 that such rights are, for the purposes of registered land, capable of binding purchasers of that land. It is unlikely that a different view will be taken when title is unregistered.

When faced with the question of the enforceability of rights of this nature, the original judicial attitude was to give the doctrine of notice a narrow ambit, holding that a purchaser did not have notice of the rights of a person who was sharing occupation of a house with the legal owner of it, thereby enhancing the security of the conveyancing transaction.[160] Latterly, however, a different line has been taken, with the courts being prepared to hold a purchaser to be fixed with notice of the rights of such occupiers.

The recent trend of judicial decisions has been to protect the rights of occupiers of land. Such a trend could be reversed by legislation, by making rights of this nature registrable so that, if not registered, they would be void as against purchasers. If such a course was taken, it would give priority to the conveyancing dimension and make it more true than it is currently to say that equitable rights are either overreachable or registrable. To adopt such a course would necessarily entail a number of people having their homes put at risk through the activities of the person with whom they share the property. Cases of this type tend, generally, to involve the acquisition of rights through highly informal transactions of a non-commercial nature, where it is highly unlikely that legal advice would be taken. To insist upon such rights being registrable would, in most cases, mean that they would not be binding upon mortgagees. Clearly, this involves a policy issue as to which of two competing interests should be afforded priority and, indeed, where the balance should be struck between them. The resolution of this issue has underpinned a considerable amount of litigation in this area and will be considered in detail when considering the law relating to mortgages.[161]

4.10 The classification of interests

Having analysed the legislative reform of unregistered land, it may be useful to tabulate how the various interests can be classified resulting from the reduction of the number of legal estates and interests and the treatment of equitable interests.

(i) **Legal estates.** These are the fee simple absolute in possession and the term of years absolute.

(ii) **Legal charges.** These are mortgages.

(iii) **Legal interests.** This group principally involves easements and profits.

(iv) **Equitable interests.** This group divides into three categories:

    (a) **Overreachable interests.** These family-type interests will be transferred from land to money, provided that the correct machinery is employed.

    (b) **Registrable interests.** These equitable interests will, if registered, bind a purchaser. If not registered, they will be void against a purchaser for money or money's worth.

    (c) **Residual category.** This is a category of equitable right which is neither overreachable nor registrable but depends for its enforceability against purchasers on the traditional doctrine of notice.

---

[159] See Chapter 14.   [160] See 3.6.4.2—Shared occupation.   [161] See Chapter 11.

5

Registration of Title

After an initial scheme allowing for voluntary title registration, and compulsory registration in London in 1898, compulsory registration of title was introduced for all of England and Wales by the Land Registration Act 1925. The LRA was accompanied by the simplification of the basic doctrines of substantive land law, through the Law of Property Act 1925. Yet for reasons that will become apparent, it has taken many years for compulsory registration to be implemented and even though the past few years have seen a concerted legislative attempt to accelerate the process of ensuring that the title to all land in England and Wales is registered, there is still some way to go before all titles are registered. The Land Registry's Annual Report of 2017/18[1] reveals that there are around 25 million separate registered titles, amounting to nearly 85 per cent of England and Wales. It remains to be seen whether the remaining 15 per cent can be registered by the target date of 2030.[2]

For nearly one hundred years, the law governing land registration was underpinned by the LRA 1925, as amended.[3] In 1998, a joint report by the Law Commission and the Land Registry proposed a radical overhaul of the system.[4] In 2001, a further joint report was published after consultation, entitled: *Land Registration for the Twenty First Century: A Conveyancing Revolution*.[5] As the title to this report suggests, the changes introduced were intended to be substantial and were implemented by the LRA 2002.[6] While it may be an overstatement to say, as the Law Commission did in 2001, that the changes made by the LRA 2002 'are likely to be more far-reaching than the great reforms of property law that were made by the 1925 legislation',[7] it is undoubtedly the case that the LRA 2002 has, to a considerable extent, reshaped the terrain of modern land law.

One of the principal ambitions underlying the LRA 2002 was a shift to compulsory electronic conveyancing,[8] which has not yet come into effect, so the revised legislation is perhaps not as revolutionary as its architects claimed. The LRA 2002 has also failed to resolve some of the problems which had emerged under the LRA 1925 that it replaced as well as creating some difficulties that had not previously been evident.[9] The existence

---

[1] HM Land Registry, *Annual Reports and Accounts 2017–18: Transformation Underway* (HMLR, London), 11,

[2] Ibid, 21.

[3] The main amendments were implemented by the LRAs 1936, 1986, 1988, and 1997.

[4] (1998) Law Com. No. 254.   [5] (2001) Law Com. No. 271.

[6] For helpful accounts of the new law, see Harpum and Bignell, *Registered Land, The New Law* (Bristol, Jordans, 2002) and Abbey and Richards, *Blackstones Guide to the Land Registration Act 2002* (Oxford, Oxford University Press, 2002). See also E. Cooke, *The New Law of Land Registration* (Oxford, Hart, 2003) and E. Cooke [2002] Conv. 11. Charles Harpum was a member of the Law Commission throughout the period when these reports were prepared.

[7] (2001) Law Com. No. 271, para. 1.1.

[8] See S. Gardner [2013] Conv. 530 at 536 who comments, with some justification, that, 'the arguments proposing the [LRA 2002] strike me as made in a more technocratic (obsessed with computers) than an ethically or politically substantive vein'.

[9] See the comments in *Knights Construction (March) Ltd v. Roberto Mac Ltd* [2011] 2 EGLR 123 at [89] *per* Mr Michael Mark, sitting as a Deputy Adjudicator. See also Gardner who, in a somewhat exaggerated fashion, describes the LRA 2002's scheme as 'a tragic mess': [2013] Conv. 530 at 635.

of some of these problems led to the Law Commission revisiting the subject of registration of title, publishing a Consultation Paper Updating the *Land Registration Act 2002: A Consultation Paper* in 2016,[10] and then its report *Updating the Land Registration Act 2002* in 2018.[11] The report contains fifty-three recommendations for reform as well as a Land Registration (Amendment) Bill to give effect to its recommendations which would, as its name illustrates, amend the LRA 2002, rather than providing a free-standing statute.[12] In its interim response in early 2019, the government has said that 'many of the report's recommendations are likely to be acceptable in principle'. It plans to respond in detail in the summer of 2019.

The main provisions of the LRA 2002 came into force towards the end of 2003. While the LRA 2002 repealed the LRA 1925 in its entirety,[13] some reference will need to be made to the earlier legislation both in order to understand the new law as well as to explain some of the transitional provisions that had to be introduced by the new regime.

5.1 The basics of registration of title

The principal ambition of registration of title is to facilitate the security of land ownership and transfer:

> The essential purpose of the scheme created by the [Land Registration Act 2002] is to provide a system of state-guaranteed registered title. Subject to exceptions, the register is intended to provide a comprehensive and accurate reflection of the title to registered land at any given time, so that it is possible to investigate title on line with the 'minimum of additional enquiries and inspections'.[14]

Under the unregistered system, the seller of land has to give a convincing historical account of his right to sell it. This entails an inspection of the title deeds to prove, so far as possible, that the purchaser's right to enjoy the land will not subsequently be disturbed by others. Elaborate enquiries, admittedly made easier by the system of the registration of land charges, have to be made to discover what third-party rights affect the land in question. This process is repetitive and not entirely secure. For example, a purchaser will be bound by legal third-party rights regardless of whether he knew, or even could have known, about them.[15]

To replace this laborious process, the fundamental idea behind the system of registration of title was that title to the land itself should be registered, rather than requiring certain equitable[16] third-party rights affecting land the land charges system to be registrable as under the land charges system. The registered title replaces the evidence of entitlement to the land that was previously provided by the title deeds.

As will be seen, however, the system of registration of title does more than replace one form of evidence of entitlement to the land with another. It is the very fact of registration of title that operates to confer a legal estate in the land, a phenomenon that has led to the

---

[10] (2016) Law Com. Consultation Paper, No. 227. Hereafter Law Commission Consultation Paper (2016).

[11] (2018) Law Com. No. 308. Hereafter Law Commission Report (2018).

[12] N. Hopkins and J. Griffin, 'Updating the Land Registration Act 2002' (2018) Conv. 207.

[13] LRA 2002, s. 135, Sched. 13.

[14] *Chief Land Registrar v. Franks* [2011] EWCA Civ. 772 at [25] *per* Rimer L.J. See also Law Commission Consultation Paper (2016), para. b.b 'An underlying purpose of the LRA 2002 is for the register to be a complete and accurate statement of title.'

[15] See, e.g., *Wyld v. Silver* [1963] Ch. 243. For further analysis, see 3.5.

[16] One legal right, the puisne mortgage, was also made registrable as a land charge: see 4.7.1.3.

operation of the system being termed 'title by registration' rather than registered land.[17] In addition, third-party rights affecting the land are entered on to the register so that, by the relatively simple process of inspection of the register, a purchaser can ascertain both who owned the land and the rights to which it would be subject. As part of this process, the legislation also introduces a scheme to ascertain the relative priority of various, potentially competing, interests in the land, based largely on registration. Finally, the accuracy of the register is backed by a state guarantee.

5.1.1 **The relationship between unregistered and registered land**

The unregistered and registered land systems are both concerned with establishing who has title to any land and with priority; that is, the order in which interests are enforceable and which interests prevail over others. The concept of notice, that underpins priority rules for unregistered land, is (ostensibly) not required for registered land.[18] It has long been recognized that problems that can occur in either system of land ownership may be resolved differently depending upon whether or not title is registered.[19] When title is registered, the issue of the binding effect of third-party rights is dependent upon whether they have been registered or take effect as an interest overriding registration.[20] This contrasts starkly with the sharp divide in unregistered land between legal and equitable interests; a distinction, it has been argued, which will cease to be relevant once registered title is universal.[21]

A second difference between registered and unregistered land is that, in the registered system, the fact that a person is registered as proprietor of land is sufficient to confer the legal title[22] on him notwithstanding the fact that the person who purported to transfer title to him did not, himself, have title to that land. This is a major exception to a cardinal principle underlying a good deal of English law: *nemo dat quod non habet*, or one cannot give what one does not own.[23]

A third difference between the registered and unregistered land systems is that the law relating to adverse possession underwent significant changes as a result of the LRA 2002, so that it is much more difficult to acquire title to registered land by long-term possession of it than is the case when title is not registered:[24] in some ways, a rational consequence of the former system being based upon registration, while unregistered land has, as its underlying basis, the fact of possession.[25]

These considerations have led to the statement that the differences between the two systems are substantive and not confined merely to the machinery of conveyancing;[26] a point of view which seeks largely to disregard what might be termed general property law principles in favour of seeing the system of registration of title as a unitary whole. In

[17] Section 58, LRA 2002.This 'title guarantee', according to the Law Commission, 'presents little in the way of risk, because the person's title is conclusive and guaranteed by HM Land Registry' (*Updating the Land Registration Act* 2002, 93). This expression appears to have been coined in the Australian case of *Breskvar v. Wall* (1971) 126 C.L.R. 376 at 385 *per* Barwick C.J. See Cooke, *The New Law of Land Registration*, 3. For a strong critique of this concept, see A. Goymour [2013] C.L.J. 617.

[18] The detail of Sched. 3, para. 2, LRA 2002, especially (c), arguably still imports some elements of notice.

[19] See, for example, *Lloyds Bank plc v. Carrick* [1996] 4 All E.R. 630 at 642 *per* Morritt L.J.

[20] See 5.2.6.3.

[21] See R.J. Smith in Tee (ed.) *Land Law: Issues, Debate, Policy* (Cullompton, Willan Publishing, 2002), Chapter 2. Cf. Cooke, *The New Law of Land Registration*, 4.

[22] As to the position with regard to the equitable title, see 5.2.6.2.

[23] See 5.2.6 for the 2018 Law Commission proposals.   [24] See Chapter 6.

[25] See (2001) Law Com. No. 271, para. 1.13.

[26] Harpum, Bridge, and Dixon, *Megarry and Wade, The Law of Real Property* (8th edn) (London, Sweet & Maxwell, 2012), para. 7–001.

2016, the Law Commission stressed the importance of a system of land registration: 'the LRA 2002 forms a complete and stand-alone system for dealings in registered land. It is not always appropriate, or helpful, to make comparisons at a micro level with the position in unregistered land.'[27] This statement of a self-contained system was echoed in judicial comments. In *Scott v. Southern Pacific Mortgages Ltd*,[28] Lady Hale said:

> It is important to bear in mind that the system of land registration is merely conveyancing machinery. The underlying law relating to the creation of estates and interests in land remains the same. It is therefore logical to start with what proprietary interests are recognised by the law and then to ask whether the conveyancing machinery has given effect to them and what the consequences are if it has not. Otherwise we are in danger of letting the land registration tail wag the land ownership dog.

Put in such stark terms, and given some of the differences between the two systems adverted to in the previous paragraph, this is a surprising *dictum*.[29] It nevertheless contains a strong element of truth to it. For example, the LRA 2002 does not redefine the content of various property rights: these are still determined by the general principles of land law. Accordingly, the nature of an easement is not dependent on whether or not title is registered: this is a matter of the general law.[30]

However, as the Law Commission explained in its 2018 report, it would go too far to say that the 'law of property' and the 'law of land registration' are conceptually distinct:

> The LRA 2002 is the primary statute that governs land registration, but land registration does not exist in a vacuum. It has never been intended that the LRA 2002 or the legislation it succeeded should provide a self-contained legal 'code' for land registration. Land registration law developed from, and depends upon, the general law of property.[31]

Sometimes, for example, in defining what is meant by 'valuable consideration', it is, according to the Law Commission, better to look to general law, rather than develop 'land registration only' definitions.[32]

Lastly, the impact of general property law principles can be seen when the dispute concerns possible alteration or rectification of the register. If a person is wrongly registered as the proprietor of land, it is true that, pending any alteration or rectification of the register, that person is the owner of the land. Clearly, though, the decision as to whether the register should be amended will depend on what the position would have been had title not been registered. To some extent, therefore, despite the two systems being to a considerable extent mutually exclusive (and this is particularly the case when it comes to a consideration of issues such as the enforceability of third-party rights) it remains the case that the registered land system is underpinned in part by general principles of property law.[33] The unregistered system will, as long as it continues, often provide a comparison for registered land.

5.1.2 Three underlying principles

There are three basic principles, as articulated by Theodore Ruoff, a former Chief Land Registrar,[34] which underlie the land registration system:

---

[27] Law Commission Consultation Paper (2016), para 11.27   [28] [2014] UKSC 52 at [96].
[29] For criticism, see N. Hopkins [2015] Conv. 245 at 252.
[30] See Chapter 12.   [31] (2018) Law Com. No. 380, [2.10].   [32] (2018) Law Com. No. 380, [2.11].
[33] See also A. Nair in S. Bright (ed), *Modern Studies in Property Law (Vol. 6)* (Hart Publishing, 2011), 263, at 265; A. Goymour [2015] Conv. 253 at 259.

(i)   the mirror principle;

(ii)   the curtain principle; and

(iii)   the insurance principle.[35]

We will consider each of these in turn.

5.1.2.1 The mirror principle

In 2018, the Law Commission defined the mirror principle as:

> One of the three basic principles underpinning title registration. This principle reflects the aim that the register provides an accurate and complete reflection of property rights in relation to a piece of land. This aim sometimes gives way to countervailing policy choices.[36]

This means that the register should reflect accurately the position with regard to the ownership of land and the third party rights affecting it. This explicit recognition to 'countervailing policy choices' (for example, in relation to overriding interests[37]) is slightly less dogmatic than the restatement of the principle was restated in the 2001 joint report, where it was said that:

> The fundamental objective of the [Act] is that, under the system of electronic dealing with land that it seeks to create, the register should be a complete and accurate reflection of the state of the title to land at any given time, so that it is possible to investigate title to land on line, *with the absolute minimum of additional enquiries and inspections.*[38]

The italicized part of the quotation from the 2001 joint report between the Law Commission and the Land Registry acknowledges what was recognized by Ruoff himself: the mirror principle is not an inviolate one. It has always been the case that a certain category of interests, first termed overriding interests, and now referred to, rather more clumsily, as interests which override either first registration or registered dispositions,[39] will bind a purchaser of registered land. These are interests which do not appear on the register of title but to which the registered proprietor will be subject. The 2001 joint report recognized that this category of interest was a major impediment to the achievement of a complete and accurate register.[40] It was also recognized, however, that there are certain types of right which it is not reasonable to expect to be protected on the register.[41] The existence of this category of right is, therefore, a fairly large exception to the mirror principle.[42]

  A second major limitation on the accuracy of the reflection provided by the register of title is the jurisdiction to make alterations to, or rectification of, that register of title. The body of the LRA 2002 operates in a positive way to confer a large variety of ownership rights on the registered proprietor. Under the Schedules to the LRA 2002, however, there exists a wide-ranging jurisdiction to make changes to the register, thereby making titles conferred by the LRA 2002 defeasible:[43] a situation which can certainly be defended, but

---

[34] Albeit when describing the system as it operated elsewhere in the Commonwealth rather than the rather more flexible one in existence in this country. See the comments in *Cherry Tree Investments Ltd v. Landmain Ltd* [2012] EWCA Civ. 736 at [127] *per* Lewison L.J.

[35] Ruoff, *An Englishman Looks at the Torrens System* (Sydney, Law Book Co., 1957), 8.

[36] (2018) Law Com. No. 380, xv.   [37] See 5.1.5.3.

[38] (2001) Law Com. No. 271, para. 1.5. Emphasis added.   [39] LRA 2002, Scheds 1 and 3.

[40] (2001) Law Com. No. 271, para. 2.24. See also *Secretary of State for the Environment, Transport and the Regions v. Baylis (Gloucester) Ltd* (2000) 80 P. & C.R. 324 at 338 *per* Mr Kim Lewison Q.C., sitting as a High Court judge.

[41] (2001) Law Com. No. 271, para. 2.25.   [42] See 5.1.5.3.

[43] See A. Goymour [2013] C.L.J. 617 at 625.

is not readily consistent with the so-called mirror principle. A third limitation is the effect of the curtain principle, which keeps beneficial interests off the title. This is the second principle, which we will now consider.

5.1.2.2 The curtain principle

In 2018 the Law Commission defined the curtain principle as saying:

> that a curtain is drawn across the register against any trusts. Hence, the register does not record beneficial ownership of land.[44]

Equitable interests are 'curtained off' on the register. As was explained in Chapter 4, there is authority and some practice that equitable interests in land can be divided into commercial interests and family interests.[45] Family interests will, provided that the correct machinery is operated, be overreached on a conveyance of the land and will not prejudicially affect a purchaser.[46] The curtain principle in registered land is an application of this distinction. The details of equitable interests affecting registered land which will be overreached by a disposition of that land are kept off the register of title; purchasers need not look behind the curtain. Their existence is protected by alerting the purchaser to what formalities have to be complied with to ensure that those interests are overreached, so that the equitable interest is transferred from the land into the purchase money.[47]

5.1.2.3 The insurance principle

In 2018 the Law Commission defined the insurance principle as follows:

> The register operates as a guarantee of title. The insurance principle means that if the register is shown to be incorrect, those who suffer loss as a result are compensated by HM Land Registry.[48]

The insurance principle underpins the provision by the state of a financial guarantee. The essence of this guarantee is said to be 'that the mirror that is the register is deemed to give an absolutely correct reflection of title but if, through human frailty, a flaw appears, anyone who suffers loss must be put in the same position, so far as money can do it, as if the reflections were a true one. A lost right is converted into hard cash.'[49]

The basic idea is straightforward. The state, through the medium of the Land Registry, provides insurance cover to people who either conduct transactions involving registered land or, perhaps less obviously, are affected by transactions conducted by other people that affect land in which they have an interest. The operation of this principle is not, however, as clear as the basic articulation of it would appear.

In the first place, due in large part to the drafting of the relevant provisions in the LRA 2002, the circumstances when a change[50] to the register may be made are unclear and have been the subject of considerable debate. Turning to the other side of the coin, there are situations when the register is changed but no indemnity is payable on the basis that the change has not caused loss to anyone. While this seems eminently reasonable, as will be seen it is by no means uncontroversial as to when it is that loss has or has not been occasioned in the exercise of judicial discretion as to making changes to the register.

---

[44] (2018) Law Com. No. 380, xii.   [45] See 4.5.   [46] Law of Property Act (LPA) 1925, ss 2 and 27.
[47] See 5.1.5.3—Restrictions.   [48] (2018) Law Com. No. 380, xiv.
[49] Knight AM Highchman *Looks at the Torrens System*, 15. See also *Chief Land Registrar v. Franks* [2011] EWCA Civ. 772 at [70] *per* Rimer L.J.
[50] This word, which is not used in the Act, is employed to embrace both alteration and rectification, which involve different issues: see 5.4.

The various uncertainties pertaining to the state guarantee of title will be addressed later in this chapter. Perhaps more fundamental is the question as to whether such a guarantee should exist at all. The reason for the creation of a state guarantee of title is to enable people involved in commercial transactions involving land to be able to deal with that land, secure in the knowledge that the register is accurate but that, if it is not, appropriate compensation will be paid. This means, as the Law Commission pointed out, that the Land Registry is in the unique position of having the liability of an insurer, without being in the business of insurance.[51] It can be exposed to a significant financial risk without any means of setting an appropriate premium. Moreover, the reason for most payments by the Land Registry has been because of the perpetration of fraud.[52] Fraud, of course, is a potential scourge of all commercial transactions but it is only in the context of land transactions that the state acts as an insurer for the victim, who has paid no premium for such protection. It should also be appreciated that the fraud normally involves impersonation or forgery, neither of which relate to the general issue of the accuracy of the register. Nevertheless, there are no plans to do away with the state guarantee, which is intended to provide confidence in the market concerning land.

5.1.3 **The Land Registry**

Section 1 of the LRA 2002 provides that there will be a register of title kept by the registrar.[53] The business of registration under the LRA 2002 is carried out by an office termed Her Majesty's Land Registry. The Land Registry consists of the Chief Land Registrar, who is appointed by the Lord Chancellor, and the staff appointed by the Registrar.[54] Until 1990, the Chief Land Registrar had to be a solicitor or barrister of at least ten years' standing, and he played an important role in the resolution of disputes and the interpretation of the legislation.[55] Upon the Land Registry becoming an executive agency,[56] the requirement that the Chief Land Registrar be legally qualified was removed,[57] and the principal legal tasks once performed by that official were undertaken by the Solicitor to the Land Registry.[58] This role was superseded by the creation of a new office, independent from the Land Registry, which was led by an official with the title of the Adjudicator, who had to be a solicitor or barrister of at least ten years' standing.[59] The post of Adjudicator was, itself, abolished in 2013 and the functions of the office were passed to the First-tier tribunal.[60]

The main functions of registration are performed by Land Registry offices, formerly District Land Registries, established by s. 132, LRA 1925.[61] At the various Land Registry

---

[51] Law Commission Consultation Paper (2016), para. 14.11.

[52] Ibid. Table 1, at para. 14.34.   [53] This was also a requirement under the LRA 1925.

[54] LRA 2002, s. 9(9).

[55] Successive holders of this office published a regularly updated reference work on Land Registry law and practice. The current edition is Ruoff and Roper, *The Law and Practice of Registered Conveyancing* (London, Sweet & Maxwell, looseleaf).

[56] The government, despite strong and widespread criticism, was committed to the privatization of the Land Registry: see generally, H. Cromerty, Briefing Paper No. 07556, April, 2016. Despite this public commitment, however, a plan to implement this by a clause in the draft Neighbourhood Planning and Infrastructure Bill introduced to Parliament in September 2016 has been dropped. For more on the privatization proposals see (2018) Law Com. No. 380, [1.18–1.23].

[57] Courts and Legal Services Act 1990, s. 125(2)(7), Sched. 17, para. 3; Sched. 20, replacing Administration of Justice Act 1956, s. 53.

[58] Land Registry (Solicitor to HM Land Registry) Rules 1990, rr. 3, 4; Land Registration (Conduct of Business) Regulations 2000, reg. 3.

[59] LRA 2002, s. 107, repealed by Transfer of Tribunal Functions Order 2013 (S.I. 2013/1036).

[60] Transfer of Tribunal Functions Order 2013 (S.I. 2013/1036). For a critical account of this change and, in particular, the propensity to increase the number of disputes, see K. Harrington and C. Auld [2016] Conv. 19.

[61] See now LRA 2002, s. 100(3).

offices are kept and maintained a register of title to freehold and leasehold land which, since 1982, can be kept in documentary form.[62] It is also important for people dealing with land to know if it is already registered. To this end, also kept at the Registry is a map, formerly known as the public index map, but now simply termed the Index. This enables it to be ascertained whether any registered estate relates to the land and how any registered estate that relates to the land is identified for the purposes of the register.[63]

For many years, the register, as opposed to the public index map, was not open to public inspection; it could only be inspected with the written authority of the proprietor or his solicitor.[64] Following an earlier Law Commission Report,[65] the position was changed by s. 1(1), LRA 1988 to enable open access to the register.[66]

HM Land Registry has become extraordinarily profitable, making a net operating surplus of £53,545,000 in 2016–17, from which it paid the Treasury a dividend of £38,706,000, and retained the remaining surplus of £24,839,000.[67] As well as providing resources for the state guarantee, including in cases of fraud, these profits have underpinned economic arguments in favour of privatization.[68]

5.1.4 The register of title

The registrar must keep a *register of title*,[69] where freehold and leasehold estates in land are recorded. A property subject to a lease for more than seven years will have two: one freehold title and one leasehold title (if there are further long leases, there may be more titles). Each title is divided into three constituent parts: the property register, the proprietorship register, and the charges register.

5.1.4.1 The property register

This part of the register gives a verbal description of the property consisting of a physical and legal description. The physical aspect of the description makes reference to a title plan. The description of the property will note the boundaries although, unless the boundaries are shown as being fixed, which is extremely rare,[70] then the boundaries are general boundaries: that is they do not determine the exact line of the boundary.[71] In the event of a boundary dispute,[72] the conveyance of the property prior to registration of title may then be relevant,[73] as will the normal presumptions made for the resolution of such disputes.[74] The fixing of boundaries does not prevent the operation of accretion or diluvion.[75]

---

[62] LRA 1925, s. 1 as amended by Administration of Justice Act 1982, s. 66. The form in which information included in the register is to be kept will be governed by Land Registration Rules made under the Act: LRA 2002, s. 1(2).

[63] LRA 2002, s. 68(1).   [64] LRA 1925, s. 112, as originally enacted.

[65] (1986) Law Com. No. 148.

[66] Exemptions are available from this in respect of confidential information: LRA 2002, s. 66(2).

[67] HM Land Registry, *Annual Reports and Accounts 2017–18: Transformation Underway* (HMLR, London), 93.

[68] Hannah Cromarty, House of Commons Library Briefing Paper No. 07556 Land Registry Privatisation.

[69] LRA 2002, s. 1 and Land Registration Rules 2003. The Registrar should also keep a register of cautions against first registrations.

[70] Rules to govern fixing the exact boundaries have been made under the LRA 2002, s. 60(3). See Land Registration Rules 2003, Part 10.

[71] LRA 2002, s. 60(1)(2).

[72] Whether the issue can properly be termed a boundary dispute or is a more substantive dispute as to the ownership of an area of land can be a vexed one, with important consequences: see Boundary disputes, 183.

[73] See *Lee v. Barrey* [1957] Ch. 251; *Derbyshire County Council v. Fallon* [2007] EWHC 1326 (Ch); *Wilkinson v. Farmer* [2010] EWCA Civ 1110.

[74] See *Alan Wibberley Buildings Ltd v. Instey* [1999] 1 W.L.R. 894 (the hedge and ditch presumption); J. Cross and G. Broadbent [2000] Conv. 61.

[75] LRA 2002, s. 61(1).

Accretion is when land is bounded by water and that water recedes, and diluvion is the converse situation. The boundary then moves to where the new waterline is.[76]

The legal description of the property will indicate the interest that is held and any appurtenant rights, such as the benefit of easements or covenants. If mines and minerals have previously been excluded, this will be recorded in this part of the register.

5.1.4.2 The proprietorship register

This part of the register states the name and address of the proprietor and the nature of the title. In the case of freehold land, this will indicate whether it is absolute, qualified, or possessory. In the case of leasehold titles, there is a similar gradation, in that case the title being either absolute, good, qualified, or possessory leasehold.[77] Also included in the proprietorship register are any restrictions which affect the ability of the proprietor to deal with the property.

5.1.4.3 The charges register

This part of the register is concerned with third party rights that adversely affect the property, such as covenants, easements, and mortgages. Matters that are registrable as land charges, where title to the land is unregistered, should appear in this section of the register. It is important to appreciate that, when title is registered, the enforceability of such rights no longer depends upon the registration of that interest as a land charge; the enforceability depends upon it either being entered on the register or it taking effect as an interest which overrides registration. The two systems are mutually discrete. There are now two issues. The first is whether or not a particular interest is registrable and, if so, whether it is registered. The second is whether it is categorized as an interest which overrides registration.[78] If it is, it will be binding on a purchaser despite non-registration.

5.1.5 The structure of registration

One central distinction in the registration system is between registration of title for the first time (known as 'first registration') and registration of something that is done to the piece of land (known as a 'dealing' or a 'disposition'). First registration is when title, usually for a freehold or leasehold estate[79], is registered for the first time, moving from unregistered to registered land. Once a title is registered, s. 58 LRA 2002 provides that the legal estate 'shall be deemed to be vested in him [the registered proprietor] as a result of registration'.

A registrable disposition is when something happens to registered land which is 'registrable', including a transfer of freehold land, the grant of a lease for more than seven years, or a registered charge (mortgage).[80] The LRA 2002 establishes a system to identify the effect of dispositions on priority.[81]

Registered titles and dispositions may be subject to third party interests, both at first registration and when dispositions are registered. Third-party interests can be protected under the LRA 2002 by notices or restrictions.[82] Titles and dispositions may also, however, be affected by 'unregistered interests that override', often called overriding interests, under Sched. 1 for land undergoing first registration and Sched. 3 for registrable dispositions.

---

[76] See *Southern Centre of Theosophy Inc. v. State of South Australia* [1982] A.C. 706 at 712 *per* Lord Wilberforce; *Lynn Shellfish Ltd v. Loose* [2016] UKSC 14 at [78] *per* Lord Neuberger.

[77] See 5.1.5.1.

[78] A registrable interest may become one which overrides registration if the holder of that interest is also in actual occupation of the affected land: see 5.1.5.3—The upgrading of rights.

[79] LRA 2002, s. 3.   [80] The whole list is set out in LRA 2002, s. 27(2).

[81] LRA 2002, ss 28–30.   [82] LRA 2002, Part 4.

5.1.5.1 First registration

Although it is common, as a form of shorthand, to speak of registered land, this technically is inaccurate. What is registered is not the land, but title to it. Only certain estates and interests are registrable with separate titles. One must keep separate the ideas of registration with an independent title from matters which can be registered so as to affect that title. First registration is set out in Part 2 of the LRA 2002.

Traditionally, it was the case that only certain legal estates in land and rentcharges could be substantively registered with a separate title.[83] The list has now been expanded and the following interests are now capable of registration:

(i)   freehold and leasehold estates in land;

(ii)   a rentcharge;

(iii)   a franchise;

(iv)   a *profit à prendre* in gross.[84]

Registration can be either voluntary or compulsory if one of the 'triggers' for registration, set out in s. 4(1) LRA 2002, occur.[85] The most important titles to be registered are unregistered freehold and leasehold estates.

Freehold estates

A person who holds a freehold estate in unregistered land may apply to be registered as proprietor of that estate. Under s. 3(2), LRA 2002, a person who is entitled to have a legal estate vested in him may also apply to be registered. Thus, if land is held on a bare trust for a person, the beneficiary may apply to be registered as proprietor. This does not extend, however, to a person who is entitled to have an estate vested in him by reason of a contract to purchase that land.[86] He should first have the land conveyed to him, pursuant to the contract, and then apply for registration. Where freehold titles are concerned, in the overwhelming majority of cases when application is made for first registration of title, the applicant is registered with an absolute title. There are, however, lesser titles which can now be considered.

Qualified titles

When an application is made for registration with an absolute title, it may emerge that there is a defect in title such that an absolute title cannot be registered. In such a case, it is provided by s. 9(4), LRA 2002 that, if the registrar is of the opinion that the person's title to the estate has been established only for a limited period or subject to certain reservations which cannot be disregarded, the applicant may be registered with a qualified title. The effect of registration with a qualified title is the same as registration with an absolute title, except that it does not affect the enforcement of any estate, right, or interest that appears from the register to be excepted from the effect of registration.[87]

Possessory titles

A possessory title is applied for when the applicant is unable to produce the title deeds to the property. This will normally be the case when the title is based upon a squatter's adverse possession of unregistered land.[88] The effect of the grant of a possessory title is that, subject to any pre-existing rights, the registration has the same effect as registration with an absolute title.[89] What this means is that there is no guarantee as to what rights the land

---

[83]   LRA 1925, s. 2.   [84]   LRA 2002, s. 3.   [85]   This is explained further in 5.2.1 below.

[86]   LRA 2002, s. 3(2)(6).   [87]   LRA 2002, s. 11(6).

[88]   For the position when adverse possession is established against a registered proprietor, see 6.7.2.

[89]   LRA 2002, s. 12(7).

is subject prior to registration, so that a proprietor with a possessory title will be bound by any existing restrictive covenants.

Leasehold estates

In unregistered land, provided that the lease in question satisfies the definition of a term of years absolute, it can subsist as a legal estate in land. One of the purposes of registration of title is to facilitate dealings in land. As short leases are frequently not the subject of dealings, it would make little sense to make all such leases registrable. In any event, to make any lease of whatever duration registrable would clog up the system.[90] Accordingly, only certain leases are registrable.

At one time, the position with regard to the registration of leases was unnecessarily complex. It was simplified in 1996, however, so that the position which was then introduced was that a leasehold interest of not less than twenty-one years was registrable.[91] On reflection, this period was considered to be too long,[92] and it is now the case that leases of more than seven years are registrable with their own title.[93] Shorter leases that are discontinuous, which is the case with time-sharing agreements, are also made registrable. The Lord Chancellor is empowered, after consultation with such persons as he considers appropriate, to reduce this term,[94] and it was envisaged that, when electronic conveyancing became compulsory, the term would be reduced to three years.[95] As the prospect of compulsory e-conveyancing has receded, the Law Commission is now of the view that the current position should be maintained.[96] There are four classes of leasehold title: absolute, good, qualified, and possessory. Of these titles, the only one which is not a counterpart of a freehold title is the good leasehold title.

Absolute leasehold title

An absolute leasehold title can only be registered if the registrar is satisfied as to the freehold title out of which the lease has been granted. The problem here was that, on the grant of a lease, the tenant, unless the contract provided to the contrary, did not have the right to investigate the freeholder's title[97] and, therefore, could not supply the registrar with the requisite evidence of that title. In this event, the applicant would be registered with a good leasehold title. The effect of registration is that there is no guarantee of the landlord's right to grant the lease, and the tenant will take subject to any interests affecting the freehold.[98] This title is, therefore, inferior to an absolute leasehold title.

This problem has been alleviated in two ways. Since 1998, the register of titles has been open to inspection.[99] If the freehold title out of which the lease is to be granted is itself registered, then the problem of establishing evidence of the freehold title has disappeared. Second, para. 2 of Sched. 11 to the LRA 2002 has altered the rules concerning the investigation of the freehold title on the grant of the lease. The position now is that, on the grant of a lease that will trigger compulsory first registration of title, the tenant will be entitled to register the freehold title out of which the lease is being granted, unless there is a contractual provision to the contrary.[100] Accordingly, in the future, the registration of good leasehold titles will become less common.

---

[90] This reason will be less cogent should electronic conveyancing ever be made compulsory.
[91] LRA 1986, s. 2, replacing LRA 1925, s. 8, implementing proposals contained in (1983) Law Com. No. 125.
[92] (2001) Law Com. No. 271, para. 3.17.
[93] Unless the leasehold estate is vested in him as mortgagee where there is a subsisting right of redemption: LRA 2002, s. 1(5). See 5.2.1.
[94] LRA 2002, s. 118(1)(3).   [95] (2001) Law Com. No. 271, para. 3.17.
[96] Law Commission Consultation Paper (2016), para. 3.68.   [97] LPA 1925, s. 44(2).
[98] LRA 2002, s. 12(6).   [99] LRA 1998, s. 1. See now LRA 2002, s. 66.
[100] LPA 1925, s. 44(11). This presupposes that the grant of the lease is preceded by a contract, which is not always the case.

Upgrading of titles

Provision is made by s. 62, LRA 2002 for the registrar to upgrade various titles which have already been registered. It was previously the case that only the registered proprietor could apply for title to be upgraded,[101] but, under s. 62(7) of the Act, the class of potential applicants has been widened to include a person entitled to be registered as proprietor of the estate, the proprietor of a registered charge affecting that estate, and a person interested in a registered estate which derives from that estate.

If the title is freehold, then a qualified or a possessory title can be upgraded to an absolute title. In the case of a possessory title, if that title has been registered for a period of at least twelve years, it may be upgraded to an absolute title. Where the title is leasehold, then a qualified or possessory title can be upgraded to a good leasehold if the registrar is satisfied as to the title to the estate and to absolute leasehold if he is satisfied both as to the title to the estate and to the title to the freehold. Again, in the case where title to a possessory leasehold title has been registered for at least twelve years, then the registrar may enter it as a good leasehold title if satisfied that the proprietor is in possession of the land.[102]

The effect of the upgrading of a title is laid down by s. 63, LRA 2002. In the case of registration of either a freehold or leasehold estate being entered as an absolute title, the proprietor ceases to hold the estate subject to any estate, right, or interest whose enforceability was preserved by virtue of the previous entry about the class of title. The same applies in the case of the registration of a good leasehold title, except that the entry does not affect the enforcement of any estate, right, or interest affecting the title of the lessor to grant the lease. A consequence of the upgrading of a title may be to cause loss to a person who, prior to the upgrading of the title may have had an interest affecting that property. If this occurs, then the person who suffers loss is entitled to be indemnified.[103]

5.1.5.2 Dispositions

Once a title is registered, dispositions in relation to it must be registered if they are to take effect at law and not merely in equity.[104] Registrable dispositions are defined as 'a disposition which is required to be completed by registration under section 27'[105] and include transfers of the legal estate or the creation of legal estates, interests, or charges. Dispositions are set out in Part 3 of the LRA 2002.

Owner's powers

The LRA 2002 introduced the concept of 'owner's powers' to protect registered proprietors since, if a registered proprietor makes a disposition that he has no power to make, the disponee's title could be vulnerable, notwithstanding its registration. The concept of owner's powers also provides protection for disponees since unless a restriction is entered on the register, restricting the registered proprietor's powers, the disponee's title cannot be challenged on the ground that the registered proprietor had no power to make the disposition. This has a further benefit in that the registration of the disposition cannot consequently be a mistake that is capable of rectification.

Under s. 23(1) LRA 2002, the owner's powers in relation to a registered estate are more limited than those under the LRA 1925.[106] They consist of:

(a) power to make a disposition of any kind permitted by the general law in relation to an interest of that description, other than a mortgage by demise or sub-demise, and

(b) power to charge the estate at law with the payment of money.[107]

---

[101] LRA 1925, s. 77.   [102] LRA 2002, s. 62(1)–(6).   [103] LRA 2002, Sched. 8, para. 2. See 5.4.8.
[104] LRA 2002, s. 27(1).   [105] LRA 2002, s. 132(1).   [106] LRA 1925, s. 18.
[107] Similar provisions exist in respect of owners of a registered charge: LRA 2002, s. 23(2).

A person is entitled to exercise these powers in relation to a registered charge or estate if he is either the registered proprietor or entitled to be so registered.[108] As far as the disponee is concerned, s. 26 LRA 2002 provides that a person's right to exercise an owner's powers in relation to a registered estate or charge is to be taken to be free from any limitation affecting the validity of the disposition, unless that limitation is reflected by an entry in the register or is imposed by the LRA 2002.

The effect of these provisions is to prevent an argument being raised that a particular disposition by a registered proprietor is ineffective on account of a lack of power to implement it. If the consent of a particular person is required for a particular transaction[109] then, unless the need for this consent is referred to in a restriction entered on the register, the title of the disponee will not be impeachable on the ground that the requisite consent has not been obtained. The transferors will be liable to the person whose consent was necessary,[110] but the disponee's title will not be affected.

The power given by s. 26 LRA 2002 is to make a disposition of any kind permitted by the general law. Hence, an equitable mortgagee does not have the power to transfer the legal estate of the mortgagor because, under the general law, a holder of an equitable estate cannot transfer a legal title.[111] Of potentially greater significance is the need to ensure that the overreaching machinery, which is part of the general law affecting the rights of an owner, is complied with. If there is a sole registered proprietor but there exists co-ownership in equity, then a disposition by the sole trustee, while sufficient to vest the legal title in the disponee, will not overreach the beneficial interests existing behind the trust.[112] If the beneficiary is in actual occupation of the property, that interest will override a registered disposition.[113]

5.1.5.3 Protecting third-party interests

Third-party interests should be entered on the register against the title they burden (usually a freehold or a leasehold estate). If third-party interests are entered in the correct way, they will have priority against the registered proprietor and bind them. If the third-party interests are not entered in the required way, they may still be overriding interests (under Scheds 1 or 3 of the LRA 2002) but this may just be a matter of luck.

The LRA 1925 used the term 'minor interests' to define third-party rights affecting land that were not overriding interests. This naming was not taken up by the LRA 2002, which also reduced the four ways in which third-party rights could be protected on the register (restrictions, inhibitions, notices, and cautions) to two (restrictions and notices). As the 2002 LRA does not operate retrospectively and many titles will have been registered long before 2003 when the Act came into force, it remains necessary to have some regard to the old regime under the 1935 as well. The next section will first set out the four ways in which third-party interests could be protected under the LRA 1925 before turning to protection under the LRA 2002.

Protecting third-party interests under the LRA 1925

Before the changes made by the LRA 2002 came into force, there were four ways in which third-party interests in land could be protected. These were restrictions, inhibitions, notices, and cautions.

---

[108] Ibid., s. 24.   [109] As may well be the case under the TOLATA 1996, s. 10.

[110] LRA 2002, s. 26(3).

[111] See *Skelwith (Leisure) Ltd v. Armstrong* [2015] EWHC 2830 (Ch). For a full discussion which culminates in a proposal to reverse this, see Law Commission Consultation Paper (2016), paras 5.35–5.62.

[112] See 7.5.6.

[113] *Williams & Glyn's Bank Ltd v. Boland* [1981] A.C. 487.

Restrictions

A restriction, as the name suggests, is a limitation on the power of the registered proprietor to deal with the property.[114] Unless the terms of the restriction are complied with, the registrar will not register the disponee of the property. The function of a restriction is largely to protect family interests relating to land that can, if the proper machinery is operated, be overreached. Where, for example, land is subject to a settlement, a restriction will be entered to the effect that no disposition by a sole registered proprietor shall be registered unless the capital money which arises is paid to two trustees. Again, when two or more persons are registered as the proprietor of an estate in land, the registrar is obliged to enter a restriction to ensure that interests which are capable of being overreached on a disposition of the estate are indeed overreached.[115] This will be the case when, on the death of one of the co-owners, beneficial co-ownership will continue, and, to effect overreaching, a second legal owner of the property must be appointed.[116] In these cases, the nature of the beneficial interests is not disclosed; an intending purchaser is simply informed as to how the conveyancing procedure is to be operated for those equitable interests to be overreached. This is what is meant by the curtain principle.

The restriction, as described above, is being used to ensure that the overreaching mechanisms are operated correctly. It can also perform other functions. In particular, the Act itself mentions other situations where a restriction may be registered. These include where notice must be given to a person prior to a disposal of the property, the need to obtain a person's consent to the disposal, and the need for an order by the court or registrar.[117]

Inhibitions

An inhibition was an entry made by the court or the registrar on the application of any person interested in the land.[118] The purpose of such an entry was to inhibit the occurrence of any event specified in the inhibition. Such entries were rare and were intended to provide protection in cases where fraud or suchlike was suspected.[119] In the case of a bankruptcy order, the registrar would automatically enter a bankruptcy inhibition restraining any dealing with the land until the trustee in bankruptcy was registered as the proprietor.[120]

Notices

A notice is the most effective way of protecting an interest in another person's land. A disposition by the proprietor will take effect subject to all entries, rights, and claims which are protected by the entry of a notice on the register.[121] This is subject to an important qualification. This is that the right which is sought to be protected must be a valid right, as the fact that the interest is the subject of a notice does not necessarily mean that the interest which it seeks to protect is valid.[122]

The registration of a notice was generally a co-operative act, in that the registered proprietor had to agree to its registration. Accordingly, it was unusual for there to be any dispute as to the validity of the interest in question. There is now, however, a new type of notice, a unilateral notice, to be discussed below, where the proprietor's consent to its registration is not required and, in this context, disputes have occurred.[123]

---

[114] LRA 2002, s. 40.   [115] Ibid., s. 44(1).   [116] See 7.8.2.   [117] LRA 2002, s. 40(3).
[118] LRA 1925, s. 57.   [119] See *Ahmed v. Kendrick* (1987) 56 P. & C.R. 120.
[120] LRA 1925, s. 61, as amended by Insolvency Act 1986, s. 235(1), Sched. 8, para. 6(3).
[121] LRA 2002, s. 29. It is not necessary in order to maintain priority that the precise nature of the interest to be protected is identified: see *Bank of Scotland Plc v. Joseph* [2014] EWCA Civ. 28.
[122] LRA 2002, s. 32(3). See also *Kitney v. M.E.P.C. Ltd* [1977] 1 W.L.R. 981.
[123] See 5.1.5.3—Agreed and unilateral notices.

The LRA 1925 contained a list of interests which could be protected by a notice.[124] The LRA 2002 operates in the opposite way and lists in s. 33 the interests which cannot be protected in this way. They are, first, an interest under a trust of land or a settlement under the Settled Land Act (SLA) 1925. These are family-type interests which will be overreached on a disposition and should be protected by a restriction. The remaining interests which cannot be protected by the entry of a notice are leases of three years or less, which take effect in possession, a restrictive covenant between landlord and tenant, which relates to the property which has been leased, an interest capable of being registered under the Commons Registration Act 1965, and rights relating to coal or coal mines.

Cautions

The entry of a notice, as has been seen, is frequently effected with the consent of the registered proprietor. A caution, on the other hand, was non-consensual and could be seen as a hostile act. There were two types of caution, although they performed the same function. First, for unregistered titles, a caution could be lodged against first registration.[125] Second, for registered titles, a caution could be lodged against dealings. It is this latter form of caution which is of current concern.

The purpose of lodging a caution against dealings was to protect a claimed proprietary right in another person's property, such as a contract to buy the land or a lien over it.[126] The effect of registering a caution was not, of itself, to validate the claim. Once a caution had been registered, no dealing with the land was to be registered until notice of that proposed dealing had been served on the cautioner. He then had fourteen days in which to object to the registration. If the cautioner did not object within that period, then registration would occur and the caution was removed from the register; it was said to have been 'warned off'.[127] If the cautioner responded, then the registrar would determine the matter and either, if the claim could not be sustained, remove the caution, or, alternatively, an appropriate entry was made on the register to give effect to the interest.

The protection afforded by a caution was inferior to that given by a notice. The registration of a notice secured the priority of the relevant interest against a disponee of the land, whereas the registration of a caution did not, of itself, confer priority on the claim[128] but merely afforded the right to be heard.[129] Nevertheless, its existence cast 'a dark shadow on the property [and] paralyses dealings in it'.[130] Consequently, there grew up a body of case law dealing with the issue of the speedy removal of them,[131] and the approach taken in that line of authority continues to be relevant to the new procedures pertaining to unilateral notices.

Protection for third-party interests under the LRA 2002

The LRA 2002 established a new regime for the protection of third-party rights.

Inhibitions and cautions

Although existing inhibitions and cautions under the LRA 1925 continue to have effect,[132] the LRA 2002 does not enable new inhibitions to be registered; the role of the inhibition is subsumed into the restriction. It is also not possible to register new cautions against dealings, although cautions against first registration may still be registered (with a separate register held for cautions against first registration).[133]

---

[124] LRA 1925, s. 49.   [125] See 5.2.5.   [126] See *Lee v. Olancastle* [1997] N.P.C. 66.

[127] LRA 1925, s. 54(2); Land Registration Rules 1925, r. 218.

[128] *Clark v. Chief Land Registrar* [1994] Ch. 370.

[129] See *Barclays Bank Ltd v. Taylor* [1974] Ch. 137 at 147 *per* Russell L.J.

[130] *Tiverton Estates Ltd v. Wearwell* [1974] Ch. 146 at 156 *per* Lord Denning M.R.

[131] See the fifth edition of this book, p. 133.   [132] LRA 2002, Sched. 12.

[133] Sched. 12, para. 4. LRA 2002, s. 19.

Restrictions

The only methods available for protecting third-party rights on the register under the LRA 2002 are the restriction and the notice. The role of the restriction has not changed with the introduction of the 2002 legislation and s. 42 LRA 2002 provides that a restriction *may* be entered by the Registrar in three sets of circumstances:

(1) to prevent invalidity or unlawfulness in relation to dispositions of a registered estate or charge;

(2) to secure overreaching where appropriate; and

(3) to protect a right or claim in relation to a registered estate or charge.

The key point to remember is that while a notice protects priority, a restriction regulates when the registered estate or charge may be the subject of an entry in the register. Restrictions can limit owners powers significantly and in 2018, the Law Commission reported that that 'disputes about restrictions make up approximately 15 to 20% of the referrals made to the Tribunal'.[134]

Agreed and unilateral notices

Under the LRA 1925, the registration of a notice was normally a consensual matter. Under s. 34(2), LRA 2002, a notice may now be either an agreed notice or a unilateral notice. The agreed notice may be registered only if either the applicant is the registered proprietor, or a person entitled to be registered as such proprietor, or, alternatively, if such a person consents to the entry, or the registrar is satisfied as to the validity of the applicant's claim.[135] A unilateral notice is designed to replace the caution against dealings, and has been employed to protect an alleged lien over the land,[136] a pending land action,[137] and an alleged contract to purchase the relevant property.[138]

When a person applies for the registration of a unilateral notice the registrar must give notice to the registered proprietor of the entry. The registered proprietor, or the person entitled to be so registered, may then apply to the registrar for the cancellation of the notice.[139] If such an application is made, the registrar must serve on the person who lodged the entry notice of the application for cancellation. If there is no response to this notice within fifteen working days, the entry will be cancelled.[140]

It may be the case that, at a hearing of the matter, issues arise that cannot quickly be resolved. In such cases, in the event of an application to have the notice removed, the approach that is to be taken in determining whether or not to order the vacation is to decide on the basis of the balance of convenience.[141] This is very similar to what occurred under the previous regime, when it was said to the cautioner that:

> You may keep the caution on the register if you undertake to pay any damages caused by its presence if it was afterwards held that it was wrongly entered. But if you are not prepared to give such an undertaking, then the caution must be vacated.[142]

---

[134] (2018) Law Com. No. 380, 205.   [135] LRA 2002, Sched. 12, s. 34(3).

[136] *Donnelly v. Weybridge Construction Ltd* [2006] EWHC 348 (T.C.C.).

[137] *Godfrey v. Torpey* [2006] EWHC 1423 (Ch).

[138] *Loubatieres v. Mornington Estates (UK)* [2004] EWHC 825 (Ch). It is not essential that the interest involved is precisely identified: See *Bank of Scotland Plc v. Joseph* [2014] EWCA Civ. 28.

[139] LRA 2002, ss 35, 36.

[140] Ibid., s. 36(2), (3). Land Registration Rules 2003, r. 53. This effectively, is the 'warning off' procedure that operated under the old system of cautions. The difference is that such matters are now likely to be dealt with before there is any dealing with the land, and so the system is more satisfactory than that which it replaced.

[141] *Donnelly v. Weybridge Construction Ltd, supra,* at [18] per H.H.J. Peter Coulson Q.C.

[142] *Tiverton Estates Ltd v. Wearwell, supra,* at 161–2 per Lord Denning M.R. See also *Tucker v. Hutchinson* (1987) 54 P. &. C.R. 106; *Alpenstow Ltd v. Regalia Properties Ltd* [1985] 1 W.L.R. 271.

Under the LRA 2002, a notice has been removed when the person seeking to maintain its presence has been unable to give a meaningful undertaking in damages to compensate for the wrongful maintenance of it,[143] a criterion which is also used in exercising the more general jurisdiction to grant interlocutory injunctions.[144]

Unregistered interests that override (overriding interests)

Unregistered interests that override are usually called overriding interests, as they were under the LRA 1925.[145] They are estates, rights, and interests that have not been protected in the register yet still override either first registration or a disposition of a registered estate and are set out in Sched. 1 (for first registration) and Sched. 3 (for dispositions).

Overriding interests reflect social and economic concerns and in 2018 the Law Commission called them 'countervailing policy choices'.[146] The Law Commission suggested that 'an interest should only have overriding status if protection against buyers is needed, but if it is neither reasonable to expect nor sensible to require any entry in the register'.[147]

More interests override first registration than override a registered disposition. The justification for this broader approach for first registration is twofold: First, that 'a first registration should not affect the priority of interests adverse to the estate as the priority of interests has already been settled by a previous transfer under the principles of unregistered conveyancing'. And second, 'because a registered disposition does indeed result in a change of estate owner and also because of the Act's general policy of encouraging the registration of adverse rights—and hence their removal as overriding rights'.[148]

Schedule 1, LRA 2002: UNREGISTERED INTERESTS WHICH OVERRIDE FIRST REGISTRATION

1   A leasehold estate in land granted for a term not exceeding seven years from the date of the grant, except for a lease the grant of which falls within section 4(1)(d), (e) or (f).

1A   A leasehold estate in land under a relevant social housing tenancy.

2   An interest belonging to a person in actual occupation, so far as relating to land of which he is in actual occupation, except for an interest under a settlement under the Settled Land Act 1925 (c. 18).

3   A legal easement or profit a prendre.

4   A customary right.

5   A public right.

6   A local land charge.

7   An interest in any coal or coal mine, the rights attached to any such interest and the rights of any person under section 38, 49 or 51 of the Coal Industry Act 1994 (c. 21).

8   In the case of land to which title was registered before 1898, rights to mines and minerals (and incidental rights) created before 1898. Commencement Sch. 1 para. 8: October 13, 2003 (SI 2003/1725 art. 2(1))

9   In the case of land to which title was registered between 1898 and 1925 inclusive, rights to mines and minerals (and incidental rights) created before the date of registration of the title.

---

[143] See *Williams v. Seals* [2014] EWHC 3708 (Ch) at [36] *per* David Richards J.; *Swiss Cottage (40) Properties Ltd v. Primestate Investments Ltd* [2015] EWHC 2977 (Ch). If a person registers or maintains an entry without reasonable cause, he is potentially liable in damages: LRA 2002, s.77.

[144] See *Nugent v. Nugent* [2013] EWHC 4095 (Ch) at [50] *per* Morgan J.

[145] Section 3(xvi), LRA 1925.   [146] Law Com. No. 380, xv.   [147] Law Com. No. 380, 229.

[148] Ruoff and Roper, *The Law and Practice of Registered Conveyancing*, 10.044.

Schedule 3: UNREGISTERED INTERESTS WHICH OVERRIDE REGISTERED DISPOSITIONS

1   A leasehold estate in land granted for a term not exceeding seven years from the date of the grant, except for– (a) a lease the grant of which falls within section 4(1)(d), (e) or (f); (b) a lease the grant of which constitutes a registrable disposition.

1A A leasehold estate in land under a relevant social housing tenancy.

2   An interest belonging at the time of the disposition to a person in actual occupation, so far as relating to land of which he is in actual occupation, except for– (a) an interest under a settlement under the Settled Land Act 1925 (c. 18);

   (b) an interest of a person of whom inquiry was made before the disposition and who failed to disclose the right when he could reasonably have been expected to do so;

   (c) an interest– (i) which belongs to a person whose occupation would not have been obvious on a reasonably careful inspection of the land at the time of the disposition, and (ii) of which the person to whom the disposition is made does not have actual knowledge at that time;

   (d) a leasehold estate in land granted to take effect in possession after the end of the period of three months beginning with the date of the grant and which has not taken effect in possession at the time of the disposition.

2A (1) An interest which, immediately before the coming into force of this Schedule, was an overriding interest under section 70(1)(g) of the Land Registration Act 1925 by virtue of a person's receipt of Land Registration Act 2002 Page 93 rents and profits, except for an interest of a person of whom inquiry was made before the disposition and who failed to disclose the right when he could reasonably have been expected to do so. (2) Sub-paragraph (1) does not apply to an interest if at any time since the coming into force of this Schedule it has been an interest which, had the Land Registration Act 1925 (c. 21) continued in force, would not have been an overriding interest under section 70(1)(g) of that Act by virtue of a person's receipt of rents and profits.

3   (1) A legal easement or profit a prendre, except for an easement, or a profit a prendre which is not registered under Part 1 of the Commons Act 2006, which at the time of the disposition– (a) is not within the actual knowledge of the person to whom the disposition is made, and (b) would not have been obvious on a reasonably careful inspection of the land over which the easement or profit is exercisable. (2) The exception in sub-paragraph (1) does not apply if the person entitled to the easement or profit proves that it has been exercised in the period of one year ending with the day of the disposition.

4   A customary right.

5   A public right.

6   A local land charge.

7   An interest in any coal or coal mine, the rights attached to any such interest and the rights of any person under section 38, 49 or 51 of the Coal Industry Act 1994 (c. 21).

8   In the case of land to which title was registered before 1898, rights to mines and minerals (and incidental rights) created before 1898. Land Registration Act 2002

9   In the case of land to which title was registered between 1898 and 1925 inclusive, rights to mines and minerals (and incidental rights) created before the date of registration of the title.

The LRA 2002 narrowed overriding interests as they are an obstacle to 'achieving a conclusive register' (one of the LRA's objectives as set out in its preamble). However, although overriding interests 'crack' the mirror of registration, these interests have important social and economic justification. The three categories of overriding interests for land that is already registered are: short lease, interests of persons in actual occupation, and easements.[149] The first two categories, short leases and interests of persons in actual oc-cupation, often apply to people in their homes and there has been a longstanding com-mitment to protect these types of unregistrable interests even if they cannot be seen on the register for policy reasons. Similarly, legal easements continue to be overriding given their wider social benefit. We will now consider each of these three categories of overrid-ing interest in turn.

Leases for less than seven years

Under the LRA 1925, only leases granted for a period of more than twenty-one years were capable of substantive registration. As a corollary to this, it was provided that leases granted for a period not exceeding twenty-one years took effect as overriding interests.[150] The word 'granted' is important as this meant that only legal leases came within this cat-egory of overriding interest,[151] and this is still the case under Scheds 1 and 3. Equitable leases are likely to be binding upon a registered proprietor, however, as it is probable that the tenant will be in actual occupation of the land and so protected under the next cat-egory of overriding interest.[152]

Under the LRA 2002, on the grant of a lease for more than seven years, the tenant should apply for registration of the title to that lease.[153] Consistently with the previous treatment of this issue, a lease granted for a period not exceeding seven years[154] will normally override registration and so bind the proprietor, both on first registration[155] and on a subsequent disposition.[156] There are, however, exceptions to this. The grant of certain leases not ex-ceeding seven years triggers the obligation for those leases to be registered with their own titles. These leases are listed in s. 4, LRA 2002, of which the most important concerns a lease which takes effect in possession after the end of a period of three months beginning with the date of the grant.[157] Such a reversionary lease is required to be registered and, conse-quently, will not override registration.[158] This may cause problems with certain student lets, where it is not uncommon for a lease to be granted in March to take effect in possession in September. This lease should now be registered with its own title,[159] and such a lease will not override registration. So, if a purchaser buys the freehold, prior to the lease falling into pos-session, he will take free of that lease.[160] If the disposition takes place after the tenants have gone into possession, then the tenants' rights will normally be overriding as they are in ac-tual occupation of the property and have an interest 'at the time of disposition' (their lease).

The LRA 2002 makes specific transitional provision for certain leases. If, before the LRA 2002 came into force, a person had been granted a lease of less than twenty-one years, that lease would have taken effect as an overriding interest.[161] This position is retained by para. 12 of Sched. 12 to the LRA 2002, which continues the overriding status of leases which were previously overriding interests under the LRA 1925. This transitional period will cease to have effect in 2023, which is twenty years after the commencement of the LRA 2002 and by which time any such leases will have expired.

---

[149] LRA 2002, Sched. 3, para 2.   [150] LRA 1925, s. 70(1)(k).

[151] *City Permanent Building Society v. Miller* [1952] Ch. 840. See also, in a different context, *Truro Diocesan Board of Finance v. Foley* [2008] EWCA Civ. 1162.

[152] LRA 2002, Sched. 1, para. 2; Sched. 3, para. 2, respectively.   [153] Ibid., s. 4(1)(c).

[154] In the case of a relevant social housing tenancy, a lease of any period may override: Localism Act 2011, s. 137(5), amending LRA 2002, Scheds 1 and 3.

[155] LRA 2002, Sched. 1, para. 1.   [156] Ibid., Sched. 3, para. 1.

[157] Ibid., s. 4(1)(d). The other exceptions are contained in paras (e) and (f).

[158] Ibid., Sched. 1, para. 1; Sched. 3, para. 1.   [159] See 5.2.1.2.

[160] If the lease has yet to fall into possession, it cannot be an overriding interest, even if the prospective tenant has been allowed in occupation of the property: LRA 2002, Sched. 3, para. 2(d).

[161] LRA 1925, s. 70(1)(k).

Interests of persons in actual occupation

The 2002 LRA provisions on the overriding effects of persons with interests and in actual occupation were modelled on s. 70(1)(g), LRA 1925, with the words 'actual occupation' conventionally construed in the same way as they were under paragraph (g). Section 70(1) (g) defined as an overriding interest 'the rights of every person in actual occupation of the land or in receipt of the rents and profits thereof, save where enquiry is made of such person and the rights are not disclosed'. Its purpose was to provide a safety net in terms of the protection of people who have rights in property and who actually occupy it, or, as it was put by Lord Denning M.R., 'to protect a person in actual occupation from having his rights lost in the welter of registration'.[162]

There were two components to the operation of this paragraph, and this remains the case under the modified versions of it contained in the LRA 2002. These are the establishment of a right and the requirement that the holder of the right be in actual occupation of the land. These matters will be addressed in turn.

The right

It is not the fact that a person is in actual occupation of another person's land that gives him an interest overriding registration. He must also establish that he has a right in that property. To ascertain what rights override registration, regard must be had to the general law. If, as a matter of general principle, a right is not regarded as being a property right, then despite the holder of that right being in actual occupation, it will not override registration and will not, therefore, bind the new registered proprietor of the land.[163] So, for example, in *National Provincial Bank Ltd v. Ainsworth*,[164] the House of Lords held that the 'deserted wife's equity' was not an interest in land, a finding which precluded the wife in that case from being able to establish an overriding interest in the property. With the coming into force of s116 LRA 2002, it is also clear that estoppels and 'mere equities' have the requisite proprietary character to be capable of being 'interests' within Sched. 3, para. 2, LRA 2002 and so overriding.[165]

Rights incapable of overriding

Certain rights are not capable of being overriding. The LRA 2002 specifies two such interests. First, an interest under a settlement under the SLA 1925 cannot be overriding.[166] This Act deals mainly with successive interests in land and, after 1997, would take effect under a trust of land.[167] Second, in the case of a transfer of registered land, a reversionary lease which takes effect in possession more than three months beginning with the date of the grant and which has not taken effect at the time of the disposition cannot override a registered disposition.[168]

There are two further interests which cannot override either registration or a registered disposition. The first of these is a spouse's statutory right of occupation.[169] The spouse's statutory right of occupation was first introduced as a direct response to the decision in *Ainsworth*, where the House of Lords held that the so-called deserted wife's equity was not capable of taking effect as an overriding interest. If it is correct to describe this right as an equity, then, read literally, s. 116, LRA 2002 would appear to allow such a right to

---

[162] *Strand Securities Ltd v. Caswell* [1965] Ch. 958 at 979.
[163] See *Scott v. Southern Pacific Mortgages Ltd* [2014] UKSC 52 at [59] per Lord Collins.
[164] [1965] A.C. 1175. See L. Tee [1998] C.L.J. 328 at 331 *et seq.*
[165] Explanatory Notes to the LRA 2002, paras 184 and 185.
[166] LRA 2002, Sched. 1, para. 2; Sched. 3, para. 2(a).
[167] Trusts of Land and Appointment of Trustees Act (TOLATA) 1996, ss 1, 2(1). See 7.6.1.
[168] LRA 2002, Sched. 3, para. 2(d).   [169] Family Law Act 1996, s. 31(10)(b).

override.[170] Finally, s. 20(6) of the Landlord and Tenant (Covenants) Act 1995 provides that the right to what is termed an overriding lease[171] is not capable of being an overriding interest.

The upgrading of rights

The LRA 1925 divided interests in registered land into either minor or overriding interests. With minor interests defined by s. 3(xv) of that Act, the question arose whether an interest defined as a minor interest would be transformed into an overriding interest if the owner of that right was in actual occupation of the land affected by it. This matter was squarely raised in *Williams & Glyn's Bank Ltd v. Boland*.[172] Mr Boland was the sole registered proprietor of the matrimonial home, although it was conceded that his wife[173] was a beneficial co-owner of it. The effect of this was that he held the house on trust for himself and his spouse.[174] Mr Boland mortgaged the house to the bank. Mrs Boland argued that, as she had an equitable interest in the house and was in actual occupation of it, she had an overriding interest binding on the bank. The bank countered by arguing that, because the type of interest which she had in the land was within the definition of a minor interest, it could not take effect also as an overriding interest. Despite finding this argument to be 'formidable',[175] Lord Wilberforce rejected it. In his view, if a person held a minor interest in land and was also in actual occupation, there was every reason why that right should acquire the status of an overriding interest.[176]

Boland was a seminal decision that established, for the purposes of the LRA 1925, an important equation:

$$\text{Minor interest} + \text{actual occupation} = \text{overriding interest}$$

Under the LRA 2002, this equation exists in substance, but not in form. There is a distinction between interests that are subject to an entry on the register and interests that override first registration or a registered disposition. However, provided that a right is capable of being protected by an entry on the register, and is not specifically excluded from being able to override, then, if the holder of the right is in actual occupation of the property, that right will be protected and will override either first registration or a registered disposition.[177] In other words, the substance of the decision in *Boland* is retained.

It should be appreciated that the right which is overriding need not, of itself, confer the right of occupation.[178] In *Webb v. Pollmount*,[179] a tenant, as one of his rights under the lease, had the option to purchase the freehold. Because the tenant was in actual occupation of the land, the option was held to be an overriding interest binding upon a purchaser of the landlord's reversion. In other words, the tenant was entitled to purchase the freehold from him. It was immaterial that his right of occupation derived from the lease and not

---

[170] Though contra see Smith in *Land Law: Issues, Debate, Policy* at 36 and the 6th edition of this book.

[171] For the nature of such leases, see 10.9.2.3.

[172] [1981] A.C. 487. See also *Haque v. Raja* [2016] EWHC 1950 (Ch) at [44] *per* Henderson J., where the absence of actual occupation was fatal to any claim to possession of an overriding interest.

[173] The fact that she was his wife was irrelevant to the decision. Her case was based upon her being an equitable co-owner of the property, not on her status as a spouse.

[174] In *Boland*, it was a trust for sale under the SLA 1925, s. 36(4). The property would now be subject to a trust of land: TOLATA 1996, s. 25(1), Sched. 3, paras 2(1), 11(b).

[175] [1981] A.C. 481 at 506.

[176] Ibid. at 507. As Lord Wilberforce recognized, this conclusion was consistent with earlier authority such as *Bridges v. Mees* [1957] Ch. 475 and *Hodgson v. Marks* [1971] Ch. 892.

[177] If the person is not in actual occupation then, to bind a purchaser, it must be registered. See, e.g., *Haque v. Raja* [2016] EWHC 1950 (Ch) at [44] *per* Henderson J.

[178] Cf. S. Baughen [1991] Conv. 116. Although some concern has been expressed about this, the Law Commission has not recommended changing it: LCCP Law Commission Consultation Paper (2016), paras 11.22–11.24.

[179] [1966] Ch. 58.

from the option. Provided that the occupier of land has proprietary rights in it, which in this case included the option, then the effect of actual occupation will make those rights overriding.

The 'actual occupation'

While actual occupation of land without ownership of a right will not create an interest overriding registration, the converse is also true; in addition to the possession of a right, the person must also be in actual occupation of the land. What was meant by the phrase 'actual occupation' within the meaning of paragraph (g) was a matter of some controversy and, despite the reform contained in the LRA 2002, the matter is not free from doubt. The word 'occupation' has been said to be capable of meaning different things in different contexts,[180] 'some of which can differ quite subtly from others, and its precise meaning in any case is thus particularly prone to be governed by its context'.[181] In the present context, initially, the courts were keen to assimilate the meaning of the words 'actual occupation' with the concept of constructive notice.

In *Hodgson v. Marks*,[182] the question was whether an elderly woman, who held a beneficial interest in a house, was in actual occupation of it within the meaning of the LRA 1925 when she shared the accommodation with the registered proprietor. At first instance, Ungoed-Thomas J. held that she was not. He considered that actual occupation should be construed to mean 'actual and apparent occupation'[183] and, because the registered proprietor was also in occupation, he considered her occupation not to be apparent. On appeal, however, this was rejected. Russell L.J. declined to gloss the wording of the legislation in this way. He preferred to give the words their literal meaning and treat the question of whether a person was in actual occupation as being one of fact.[184] As, factually, the elderly woman was in actual occupation of the house, it was held that she had an overriding interest in it.

This approach was continued in *Williams & Glyn's Bank Ltd v. Boland*, where it was held that a wife who shared occupation of the matrimonial home with her husband was in actual occupation of it. The argument that a wife could not, as a matter of law, be regarded as being in actual occupation of the shared matrimonial home in her right, because of a fictitious unity between husband and wife, so that her occupation was to be regarded as being a shadow of his,[185] was condemned as being 'heavily obsolete'.[186] Of more general interest was the approach taken to the construction of the phrase 'actual occupation' as used in the LRA 1925.

Lord Wilberforce expressly declined to construe the meaning of actual occupation so as to make it correlate to the ambit of constructive notice in unregistered land. He emphasized this by saying that 'the law as to notice as may affect purchasers of unregistered land, whether contained in decided cases, or in a statute has no application even by analogy to registered land'.[187] He underlined this still further, by going on to say that, 'In the case of unregistered land, the purchaser's obligation depends upon what he had notice of—notice actual or constructive. In the case of registered land, *it is the fact of occupation that matters*'.[188]

---

[180] *RCC v. Newnham College, Cambridge* [2008] UKHL 23 at [9] *per* Lord Hoffmann. See, also, *Madrassa Anjuman Islamia of Kholwad v. Municipal Council of Johannesburg* [1922] 1 A.C. 500 at 504 *per* Viscount Cave; *Southern Water Authority v. Nature Conservancy Council* [1992] 1 W.L.R. 775 at 781 *per* Lord Mustill.
[181] *RCC v. Newnham College, Cambridge, supra* at [56] *per* Lord Neuberger.
[182] [1971] Ch. 892.   [183] Ibid. at 916.   [184] Ibid. at 931–2.
[185] An expression used in *Bird v. Syme-Thomson* [1979] 1 W.L.R. 440 at 444 *per* Templeman J.
[186] *Williams & Glyn's Bank Ltd v. Boland* [1981] A.C. 487 at 504 *per* Lord Wilberforce.
[187] Ibid.   [188] Ibid., emphasis supplied. See also at 511 *per* Lord Scarman.

Absolutism or constitutionalism?

The comments of Lord Wilberforce, and by others made in similar vein,[189] represented the high point of what has been termed the absolutist view of what constituted actual occupation; that the determination of whether or not a person was in actual occupation of land was a matter of fact, and did not depend upon the discoverability of that fact. Others took the view that because paragraph (g) was intended to encapsulate the unregistered land concept of constructive notice, which derives from the rule in *Hunt v. Luck*,[190] in determining whether a person was in actual occupation of land, regard should be had to whether that occupation could be discovered by making reasonable enquiries and inspections.[191] This approach, termed the constitutionalist view, also has judicial support.[192]

In truth, this was probably rather an academic debate in that the scope of constructive notice had widened considerably since the rule in *Hunt v. Luck* was formulated.[193] In particular, it has now been accepted that, if a person with a beneficial interest in a house shares that accommodation with the sole legal owner of it, a purchaser would be fixed with constructive notice of that person's rights unless enquiries had been addressed to that occupier.[194] Had the legislation insisted that the occupation had to be actual and apparent, the result in most cases would have been the same.[195] The approach of the LRA 2002, to be considered shortly, in respect of interests which override registered dispositions adopts the constitutionalist view with respect to the binding effect of the right in question[196], stressing discoverability, even though the section adopts an absolutist position for the meaning of actual occupation. This is because it is provided by para. 2 of Sched. 3 to the LRA 2002 that, to bind a purchaser, the interest must belong to a person in actual occupation *and* that occupation must be obvious on a reasonably careful inspection of the land. It must follow that there can be some instances when a person is in actual occupation of land, but that fact was not obvious on a reasonably careful inspection.[197] Consequently, it is no longer the case that the finding that a person was in actual occupation will be determinative of whether the right of that person will override.

Nature of the property and intermittent occupation

Situations which have caused difficulty in the past have arisen where either the nature of the property in question is such that what might be regarded as normal occupation of it may be difficult or, alternatively, the person claiming to have been in occupation is either an intermittent occupier or is absent from the property for prolonged periods of time. Where the property in question is not residential, such as a lock-up garage, then the

---

[189] *Hodgson v. Marks* [1971] Ch. 892 at 932 *per* Russell L.J.; *Kling v. Keston Properties Ltd* (1989) 49 P. & C.R. 212 at 222 *per* Vinelott J.

[190] [1902] 1 Ch. 428. See, e.g. *National Provincial Bank Ltd v. Ainsworth* [1965] A.C. 1179 at 1259 *per* Lord Wilberforce; *Abbey National Building Society v. Cann* [1991] A.C. 56 at 87 *per* Lord Oliver.

[191] P. Sparkes [1989] Conv. 342; Sparkes, *A New Land Law* (2nd edn) (Oxford, Hart Publishing, (2003), 281.

[192] See, e.g., *Lloyds Bank plc v. Rosset* [1989] Ch. 350 at 377 *per* Nicholls L.J.; at 397 *per* Mustill L.J. (dissenting on the facts); at 403 *per* Purchas L.J., reversed on an unrelated point [1991] 1 A.C. 107. For criticism of these views see R.J. Smith (1988) 104 L.Q.R. 507; M.P. Thompson [1988] Conv. 453. See, however, *Malory Enterprises Ltd v. Cheshire Homes (U.K.) Ltd* [2002] 3 W.L.R. 1 at 21 *per* Arden L.J.

[193] See 3.6.4.2—Inspection of the land: the rule in *Hunt v. Luck*.

[194] *Kingsnorth Finance Co. Ltd v. Tizard* [1986] 1 W.L.R.783; *Midland Bank Ltd v. Farmpride Hatcheries Ltd* [1981] 260 E.G. 493. Contrast *Le Foe v. Le Foe* [2001] 2 F.L.R. 970 at 988 *per* Mr Nicholas Mostyn Q.C., sitting as a High Court judge, criticized by M.P. Thompson [2001] Conv. 273 at 283.

[195] See L. Tee [1988] C.L.J. 328.

[196] Although see the counter-argument by N. Jackson (2001) 119 L.Q.R. 660 at 665 *et seq.*

[197] For a good example of this, see *Knights Construction (March) Ltd v. Roberto Mac Ltd* [2011] 2 E.G.L.R. 123 at [50] *per* Mr Michael Mark.

parking of a car in it can be regarded as amounting to actual occupation.[198] Again, when the condition of the property is such that it cannot physically be occupied, the presence of builders under the supervision of the right holder will also amount to actual occupation,[199] as will the enclosure of an area of land for use by the tenants of adjoining property to dry washing.[200] It has also been accepted that a person may be in actual occupation through the medium of an agent, such as a caretaker,[201] but not through the presence of a licensee, who is not a representative occupier.[202] In any event, however, to establish actual occupation in the first place, there must be some degree of permanence and not merely a fleeting presence, such as will occur when a prospective purchaser is allowed access to the property prior to its purchase.[203]

Cases where the person claiming to be in actual occupation of a house but physically absent from it at the relevant time have also created difficulty. Clearly, it is not necessary for continuous physical presence to be maintained for actual occupation to be established so that, if for example, the transaction occurred when a beneficial co-owner was in hospital having a baby, this would not prevent her from being in actual occupation of the house.[204]

The issue of intermittent occupation was considered by the Court of Appeal in *Link Lending Ltd v. Bustard*.[205] The case concerned whether a person's beneficial interest in a house was binding on a mortgagee, and this turned on whether or not Ms Bustard was to be regarded as being in actual occupation of it. She had been compulsorily detained in a psychiatric hospital for over a year under the Mental Health Act during the relevant period. She did not actually live in the property, although she retained some furniture there and made supervised visits to the house on a weekly basis. It was held that she was in actual occupation. Mummery L.J. rejected any attempt to lay down any single test for determining whether a person was in actual occupation. Instead he adverted to various criteria to which consideration should be given. These included the degree of permanence and continuity of presence of the person concerned; the intentions and wishes of that person; the length of absence from the property and the reason for it, and the nature of the property and personal circumstances of the person concerned.[206] Ms Bustard was absent on an involuntary basis from the property and always intended to return to it.[207] By way of contrast, in *Stockholm Finance Ltd v. Garden Holdings Ltd*,[208] a Saudi princess had been absent from the property for over a year and, although she retained furniture in it, seemed to regard the flat as an alternative home, and this was not sufficient to amount to actual occupation. Similarly, in *AIB Group (UK) Ltd v. Turner*,[209] a person who spent most of the year in Barbados, a place she regarded as her permanent residence, and only visited

---

[198] *Kling v. Keston Properties Ltd* (1989) 49 P. & C.R. 212. Cf. *Epps v. Esso Petroleum Ltd* [1973] 2 All E.R. 465.

[199] *Lloyds Bank Plc v. Rosset* [189] Ch. 350, reversed on a different point: [1991] A.C. 107; *Thomas v. Clydesdale Bank Plc* [2010] EWHC 2755 (QB). See also *Malory Enterprises Ltd v. Cheshire Homes (UK) Ltd* [2002] Ch. 216 at [82] *per* Arden L.J.

[200] *Knights Construction (March) Ltd v. Roberto Mac Ltd, supra,* at [51] *per* Mr Michael Mark.

[201] *Abbey National Building Society v. Cann* [1991] A.C. 56 at 93 *per* Lord Oliver.

[202] *Strand Securities Ltd v. Caswell* [1965] Ch. 958 at 981 *per* Lord Denning M.R. See *Thompson v. Foy* [2009] EWHC 1076 (Ch) at [127] *per* Lewison J., approved in *Link Lending Ltd v. Bustard* [2010] EWCA Civ. 424 at [31] *per* Mummery L.J.

[203] *Abbey National Building Society v. Cann* [1991] A.C. 56 at 93 *per* Lord Oliver. See, also, albeit in a different context, *RCC v. Newnham College, Cambridge* [2008] UKHL 23 at [31] *per* Lord Hope.

[204] *Chhokar v. Chhokar* [1984] F.L.R. 313.

[205] [2010] EWCA Civ. 424.

[206] Ibid at [77] See also *Baker v. Craggs* [2016] FWHC 3250 (Ch) at [12] *per* Newey J.

[207] Although see *Haque v. Raja* [2016] EWHC 1950 (Ch) where a person serving a two year prison sentence was held not to be in actual occupation.

[208] [1995] N.P.C. 162.   [209] [2015] EWHC 3994 (Ch).

the house in which she claimed to have an interest binding on a mortgagee on a sporadic basis, was held not to be in actual occupation of it.[210]

Obviously, in answering the question as to whether a person is in actual occupation of property, the issue of intention is important.[211] For example, a person may have left furniture in a house in one case because he intends to return to live in it and, in another, permission is given merely to store the goods and there is no intention to live there. In the former case it is reasonable to regard the person as being in actual occupation of the property, whereas in the second it is not. Intention to occupy on its own, however, should not be enough, and, in the case of prolonged absences, it is thought that, as well as an intention to return, some physical manifestation of that intention should be necessary,[212] although this will also clearly be relevant to the issue of discoverability, to be considered shortly.

Additional rules on interests of persons in actual occupation under Schedule 3

Paragraph 2 of Sched. 3 to the LRA 2002 sets out additional criteria for interest + actual occupation for an unregistered interest which will override registered dispositions:

> An interest belonging at the time of disposition to a person in actual occupation, so far as relating to land of which he is in actual occupation, except for—
>
> . . .
>
> (b) an interest of a person of whom inquiry was made before the disposition and who failed to disclose the right when he could reasonably have been expected to do so;
>
> (c) an interest—
>
>   (i) which belongs to a person whose occupation would not have been obvious on a reasonably careful inspection of the land at the time of the disposition,[213] and
>
>   (ii) of which the person to whom the disposition is made does not have actual knowledge at the time, and
>
> . . .

Inquiry

In respect of any inquiry under Sched. 3, para. 2(b), it should be made to the occupier, and not the owner, since: 'reliance on the untrue *ipse dixit* of the vendor will not suffice'.[214] In *HSBC Bank v. Dyche*,[215] the bank was prepared to accept that a forged lease shown to it by the mortgagor was an adequate explanation of the right of an occupier and did not ask that person what right, if any, he actually had in the property. The bank was subsequently held to be bound by Mr Dyche's beneficial ownership of the property, as it should have asked the question directly of Mr Dyche. The bank, as legal owner, held the property on a constructive trust for Mr Dyche.

---

[210] The case should have been decided on a quite different point that, as the mortgage had been executed by the two legal owners, any interest she had in it should have been held to have been overreached. Amazingly, this fairly elementary point was totally overlooked. See M. Dixon [2016] Conv. 81; and 7.5.5.

[211] See B. Bogusz [2014] Conv. 27.

[212] *Thompson v. Foy* [2009] EWHC 1076 (Ch) at [127] *per* Lewison J. See also *Chhokar v. Chhokar* [1984] F.L.R. 313 at 317 *per* Ewbank J., a point not considered on appeal. See also the helpful discussion of a similar issue in the context of what is now Rent Act 1977, s. 2 in *Brown v. Brash* [1948] 2 K.B. 247 at 254–5 *per* Asquith L.J. and *Hoggett v. Hoggett* (1980) 39 P. & C.R. 121 at 127 *per* Sir David Cairns.

[213] It is, perhaps, symptomatic of some of the less than user-friendly drafting of the Act that a double negative is employed.

[214] *Hodgson v. Marks* [1971] Ch. 892 at 932 *per* Russell L.J., who also commented that he shed no tears for a building society who had done that and had been lied to.

The second aspect of para. (b) is that a person cannot assert an overriding interest if an enquiry is addressed and that person fails to reply when it is reasonable do so.[216] In most cases, this should not be an issue. If, however, an enquiry is made of a person in inappropriate circumstances such as a social event, then this will not satisfy the terms of the paragraph.[217] Second, when any such enquiry is made, care should be taken that the person of whom the enquiry is made is not potentially subject to undue influence by other parties involved in the transaction.

Obvious and actual knowledge

The requirement that the interest 'would not have been obvious on a reasonably careful inspection of the land at the time of disposition' and 'of which the person to whom the disposition is made does not have actual knowledge at the time' has been said to be 'an extraordinary restriction', which re-introduces the concept of constructive notice.[218] The 2001 joint report before the LRA 2002 insisted, however, that the 'test is not one of constructive notice of the occupation. It is the less demanding one (derived from the test applicable to intending buyers of land) that it [the fact of occupation] should be obvious on a reasonably careful inspection of the land.'[219]

Obvious

The test in para. ?, as the joint report was at pains to point out, is not whether the right is obvious; it is whether the fact of occupation is obvious.[220] This, however, leaves open the questions of what is a reasonably careful inspection of land and, then, what should be considered to make the fact of occupation obvious.

As to what constitutes a reasonably careful inspection of the land, the answer to this must be dependent upon what the inspection is intended to achieve. In this day and age, an inspection limited solely to ascertain the monetary value of the property[221] will surely not exhaust what is meant by a reasonably careful inspection. Rather, when one has regard to the 'extension, beyond the paterfamilias, of rights of ownership following from the diffusion of property and earning capacity',[222] one would anticipate that a reasonably careful enquiry should extend to seeking to establish whether there is an occupier of the property other than the registered proprietor. So, if an inspection of the property reveals some evidence of another person's presence, such as clothes, this should, it is thought, make the fact of actual occupation obvious within the meaning of the Act.[223]

The case of *Link Lending Ltd v. Bustard*[224] should have provided an opportunity to discuss this issue. In this case the person claiming to have an overriding interest was only in intermittent occupation of the house. Unfortunately, the bank did not rely on whether or not the occupation would have been obvious on a reasonably careful inspection of the property. This was because it accepted that the only inspection actually carried out was a 'drive-by' inspection done for the purpose of valuation and, therefore, inadequate.[225] This misses the point. The statute does not require that an inspection be made; it is a requirement that the fact of occupation *would* have been obvious on a reasonably careful

---

[215] [2009] EWHC 2954 (Ch).

[216] For an example, see *Mortgage Express v. Lambert* [2016] EWCA Civ. 555.

[217] See *Begum v. Issa* (2014) Case No: 3 NE 3007 at [100] *per* HH Judge Behrens (Leeds County Court).

[218] *Ferrand, Clarke et al., Emmet and Farrand on Title* (19th edn) (London, Sweet & Maxwell, Looseleaf), 5.105.

[219] (2001) Law Com. No. 271, para. 8.62(2).   [220] Ibid., para. 8.62.

[221] Although, see the extremely lax approach adopted with regard to this point in *Le Foe v. Le Foe* [2001] 2 F.L.R. 970 at 988 *per* Mr Nicholas Mostyn Q.C.

[222] *Williams & Glyn's Bank Ltd v. Boland* [1981] A.C. 487 at 508–9 *per* Lord Wilberforce.

[223] See *Le Foe v. Le Foe, supra*, at 988.   [224] [2010] EWCA Civ. 424.

[225] Ibid. at [12] *per* Mummery L.J.

inspection. If it would not, then it should be completely immaterial whether any inspection was cursory, or even took place at all. The establishment of the fact of actual occupation and the determination of the obviousness of that occupation are separate questions.[226]

A person whose physical presence in the property is intermittent may well be held to be in actual occupation of that property, although the fact of occupation may not have been obvious on a reasonably careful inspection of the property. If that is the case, then the interest will not override. So, for example, in *Knights Construction (March) Ltd v. Roberto Mac Ltd*,[227] the parking of cars and the placing of waste bins on what appeared to be uncultivated waste land was considered to be occupation of that land, but occupation that would not have been obvious on a reasonably careful inspection.

It is plain that the absolutist view of the meaning of actual occupation no longer represents the law.[228] Although the wording of para. 2 is not as clear as it might be, it is suggested that the constitutionalist interpretation employed with regard to s. 70(1)(g), LRA 1925 is now the position and that, despite the protestations of the authors of the joint report, the test of whether a purchaser will take subject to the rights of an occupier is, in substance if not in form, that of constructive notice. If this is correct, then it would seem that the judicial comments favouring the constitutionalist approach remain good law.

Actual knowledge

Finally, even if the right would not have been obvious on a reasonably careful inspection of the land, if the person to whom the disposition is made actually knows of the existence of the right held by the person in actual occupation of the land, then the right will override the registered disposition.[229] This was considered in *Thomas v. Clydesdale Bank Plc.*,[230] where the issue arose as to whether a woman had an overriding interest binding on a mortgagee. Ramsey J. thought that, as the bank was aware that the borrower had a new partner who was prepared to contribute in the region of £100,000 to the property which was to become the family home, she had a reasonable prospect of showing that the bank had actual knowledge of her interest.[231]

It must be said that this is a very curious provision. First, it seems odd that, in a system that places such emphasis on registration, the state of mind of a purchaser should be an important criterion in the determination of whether or not an interest is binding upon him. As will be seen, this is true not only in the case of the rights of occupiers, but applies also to other interests which override registered dispositions.[232] A second point to make is that what is relevant is actual knowledge of the interest, not actual knowledge of the fact of occupation. As will be seen, the fact that a purchaser has actual knowledge of an interest that should have been protected by registration will not mean that he will be bound by that interest. If, however, the owner of that interest is in intermittent, or occasional, occupation of the relevant property, so that occupation as a matter of fact has been established but the existence of that fact would not have been obvious on a reasonably careful inspection of the land, then the interest will bind a purchaser who has knowledge of the right. The distinction is more than a little puzzling.

---

[226] See *Thompson v. Foy* [2009] EWHC 1076 (Ch) at [132] *per* Lewison J.; *Thomas v. Clydesdale Bank Plc* [2010] EWHC 2755 (QB) at [40] *per* Ramsey J.

[227] [2011] E.G.L.R. 123 at [50].

[228] Although see the counter-argument by N. Jackson (2003) 119 L.Q.R. 660 at 665 *et seq.*

[229] LRA 2002, Sched. 3, para. 2(c)(ii).   [230] [2010] EWHC 2755 (Ch) at [49].

[231] Because the purpose of the loan was to pay off a mortgage used to finance the acquisition of the house, the bank's interest should, on this ground, have had priority: see *Equity and Law Home Loans Ltd v. Prestidge* [1992] 1 W.L.R. 13; and 11.2.1.

[232] See generally 5.1.5.3.

Occupation of part of the property

An issue that arose on the construction of s. 70(1)(g), LRA 1925 was whether, if the occupier of land which forms part of a larger plot enjoys rights over that larger part, he also enjoyed an overriding interest over the unoccupied part. In *Wallcite Ltd v. Ferrishurst Ltd*,[233] the occupier of premises which adjoined a garage had a right affecting both the premises and the garage. It was held that, because he was in actual occupation of part of the property, he had an overriding interest affecting both the premises and the garage. This conclusion would lead to the somewhat startling, if unlikely, result that if a tenant of a flat in The Barbican had an option to purchase the freehold of the entire complex then that option would be an overriding interest.[234] This was considered to be unacceptable,[235] and the position under the LRA 2002 is that the right will affect only the part of the land which is actually occupied. This is so, both on first registration and on a registered disposition.[236]

Date of actual occupation

An important issue is that of the date when the person claiming to have a right overriding a registered disposition must be in actual occupation. When registered land is being transferred, this is a two-stage process.[237] The transferor executes a document termed a transfer in favour of the transferee. The transferee then applies to be registered as the new proprietor. The legal title will not pass to the transferee until registration occurs.[238] There is a period of time between these two events and the possibility exists that a third person with an interest in the property may go into occupation of it during this period and thereby establish an interest overriding the registered disposition. This period is known as the 'registration gap'.

This potential problem had also existed with respect to s. 70(1)(g), LRA 1925 but was resolved by the House of Lords in *Abbey National Building Society v. Cann*,[239] where it was held that, for the purpose of para. (g), the relevant date is the date of the transfer and not the date of registration. Paragraph 2 of Sched. 3 to the LRA 2002 refers to the person being in actual occupation at the time of the disposition. This approach was confirmed as synonymous with the date of the transfer by the Supreme Court in *Scott v. Southern Pacific Mortgages Ltd*.[240] This was a test case involving a Mrs Scott, which concerned a scheme whereby owners of properties in the North East sold the freehold of their houses at a discounted price to a company, NEPB, and then rented them back. The aim of these transactions was to raise capital while securing their continuing occupation of their homes. To that end, what was agreed with NEPB was that Mrs Scott would have long-term occupation rights and that she would have a discounted rent. Unfortunately, and unbeknown to her, in order to raise the finance to purchase the various properties, NEPB mortgaged the properties. The transfer of the legal title and the creation of the mortgage were, effectively, simultaneous transactions. The question was whether Mrs Scott had an interest binding on the mortgagee. The Supreme Court held that she did not.

The basis of the decision in *Scott* was that, pending the completion of the transaction between Mrs Scott and NEPB, any rights she had against them were entirely personal.

---

[233] [1999] 1 All E.R. 977. See S. Pascoe [1999] Conv. 144.

[234] Ibid. at 990 *per* Robert Walker L.J.   [235] (2001) Law Com. No. 271, para. 8.58.

[236] LRA 2002, Sched. 1, para. 2; Sched. 3, para. 2. See *Thompson v. Foy* [2009] EWHC 1076 (Ch) at [128]–[129] *per* Lewison J.

[237] Should Part 8 of the LRA 2002 ever be brought into force and electronic conveyancing is made compulsory, there will only be one stage as the disposition and its registration will be simultaneous. See 5.1.6.

[238] LRA 2002 s. 27(1).

[239] [1991] A.C. 56. Contrast *Barclays Bank plc v. Zaroovabli* [1977] 1 All E.R. 19, in respect of a different overriding interest (a lease).

[240] [2014] UKSC 52. See M. Dixon [2014] Conv. 461; N. Hopkins [2015] Conv. 245.

Whatever property rights she acquired through her agreement with NEPB did not become proprietary rights until the transfer of the property to NEPB. Because that transfer, and the creation of the mortgage were regarded as simultaneous transactions, there was no pre-existing property right in existence prior to the creation of the mortgage. So, although Mrs Scott was in actual occupation at all material times, she did not have any rights capable of binding a mortgagee when that mortgage was created as an inherent part of the purchasing process.[241]

This gives rise to a related point. If the person is in actual occupation at the time of the disposition, his interest will continue to override the registered disposition, notwithstanding that, subsequently, the property is vacated.[242] Although the point was left open in *Thompson v. Foy*,[243] it would seem that, if the occupier ceased to be in actual occupation between the date of the disposition and that of its registration, the interest will still override.

Receipt of rents and profits

Possession, for the purposes of the LPA 1925, includes the receipt of rents and profits or the right to receive the same.[244] Perhaps for this reason, s. 70(1)(g), LRA 1925 included, in addition to the rights of people in actual occupation of the land, the rights of those in receipt of rents and profits.[245] While one can appreciate why the rights of people who actually occupy land should nevertheless have their unregistered rights in it protected as a consequence of their occupation, it is not easy to see why someone who does not occupy property but instead derives profit from it should be spared the normal consequence of a failure to register a registrable interest.[246] The LRA 2002 does not allow the receipt of rent and profits as an alternative to actual occupation of the land. So as not to deprive people in this position of their established rights, however, transitional provisions are in place. Paragraph 8 of Sched. 12 to the LRA 2002 introduces two new paragraphs into Sched. 3.[247]

The effect of these paragraphs is that, if immediately prior to the coming into force of Sched. 3 a person held an overriding interest as a result of being in receipt of rents and profits, then that right will continue to override a registered disposition. If, however, a person becomes entitled to rents and profits after the Schedule came into force, then the right which he has in the land will not enjoy overriding status.

The protection of occupiers

It was undoubtedly the case that the House of Lords decision in *Williams & Glyn's Bank Ltd v. Boland*[248] generated considerable interest and controversy. In particular, it established that occupiers of property, provided that they were adults,[249] could establish an overriding interest in that property despite the fact that the registered proprietor was also in occupation of it. The conveyancing implications of this were regarded as being extremely serious. The reliability of the register was undermined and, to satisfy himself that there were no

---

[241] See further 11.6.8.3.

[242] *London and Cheshire Insurance Co. Ltd v. Laplagrene Property Co. Ltd* [1971] Ch. 499.

[243] [2009] EWHC 76 (Ch) at [122]–[126].   [244] LPA 1925, s. 3(xvii).

[245] If rent is reserved but not paid, the person entitled to the rent does not have an overriding interest: *E.S. Schwab & Co. Ltd v. McCarthy* (1975) 31 P. & C.R. 196. See also *Strand Securities Ltd v. Caswell* [1965] Ch. 958.

[246] Although see L. Tee [1998] C.L.J. 328 at 348.

[247] Would the legislation not be more 'user-friendly' if these provisions were contained in Sched. 3 itself, rather than being cross-referenced in this way?

[248] [1981] A.C. 487.

[249] *Hypo-Mortgage Services Ltd v. Robinson* [1997] 2 F.L.R. 71. The blanket statement denying protection to all minors is probably too sweeping, particularly when regard is had to the fact that minors aged sixteen have the capacity to marry. See also on the capacity to give consent, admittedly in a different context, *Gillick v. West Norfolk and Wisbech Area Health Authority* [1986] A.C. 112.

adverse rights affecting the property, the purchaser would have to depart 'from the easy-going practice of dispensing with enquiries beyond that of the vendor'.[250]

In reaching this decision, the House of Lords was clearly mindful of the tension existing between the conflicting policies of, on the one hand, protecting the rights of people whose principal interest in the property was its use as a home and, on the other, the facilitation of conveyancing; an interest which is enhanced by confining the ambit of interests which override registered dispositions as narrowly as possible. The conclusion reached in *Boland* was to favour the former interest.[251] This tension has permeated the law for a considerable period of time and has usually become apparent when the contest is between the occupier of a home and a mortgagee, who has lent money against the security of a house. This issue will be returned to, therefore, when considering possession actions brought by mortgagees.

Easements and profits à prendre

The status of easements and profits was formerly governed by the obscurely drafted s. 70(1)(a), LRA 1925, under which it was eventually established that both legal and equitable easements[252] and profits were overriding interests. The position has been affected considerably by the LRA 2002, which deals differently with the position on first registration of title and registered dispositions and contains also transitional provisions. These will be dealt with in turn.

A legal easement or profit will override first registration.[253] It was a conscious decision to exclude equitable easements and profits from overriding status on first registration of title.[254] Although welcome, this was not actually necessary, in that equitable easements could not have bound a first registered proprietor. This is because, when title is unregistered, an equitable easement is registrable as a Class D(iii) land charge and would be void as against a purchaser for money or money's worth if not registered.[255] It could not, therefore, take effect as an overriding interest on an application for first registration which followed a conveyance on sale.

Easements and profits affecting registered land are affected by s. 27 and Scheds 3 and 12, LRA 2002. The effect of s. 27(d) and (e) is to prevent express grants or reservations of easements or profits from taking effect as interests which override registration because they are, themselves, dispositions which require to be completed by registration. Excluded from the effect of this section are easements or profits which are created as a result of the operation of s. 62, LPA 1925.[256]

The combined effect of s. 27 and Sched. 3 is to reduce significantly the types of easement and profit that can override a registered disposition. First, only legal easements and profits can override. Second, the express creation of such interests are registrable dispositions and so cannot override a registered disposition. The effect of this is that the only legal easements which can override a registered disposition are those which are created by prescription, that is long user,[257] or by implication. To repeat, express easements must themselves be completed by registration against the title of the burdened land.[258]

---

[250] [1981] A.C. 487 at 508 *per* Lord Wilberforce.   [251] See, especially, ibid. at 510 *per* Lord Scarman.

[252] *Celsteel Ltd v. Alton House Holdings Ltd* [1985] 1 W.L.R. 204 (reversed, in part, on another point: [1986] 1 W.L.R. 512); *Thatcher v. Douglas* (1996) 146 N.L.J. 282; *Sommer v. Sweet* [2005] EWCA Civ. 227. See M.P. Thompson [1986] Conv. 31; M. Davey [1986] Conv. 296.

[253] LRA 2002, Sched. 1, para. 3.   [254] (2001) Law Com. No. 271, para. 8.24.

[255] LCA 1972, ss 2(5), 4(6). See also *Sainsbury's Supermarkets Ltd v. Olympia Homes Ltd* [2005] EWHC 1235 (Ch) at para. 53 *per* Mann J.

[256] LRA 2002, s. 27(7). This section operates to imply words into conveyances, with the result that a purchaser of part of a vendor's land may acquire easements over the land which was retained. This provision will be fully explained in Chapter 12.

[257] See 12.6.   [258] Section 27(d) and (e) LRA 2002.

In the case of easements and profits which are capable of overriding a registered disposition, the LRA 2002 imposes further limitations on their ability so to do. Except in the case of easements or profits which are registered under the Commons Registration Act 1965, an easement will not override a registered disposition if it was not within the actual knowledge[259] of the person to whom the disposition is made, and would not have been obvious on a reasonably careful inspection of the land over which the easement or profit is exercisable. These qualifications do not apply if the person entitled to the easement or profit proves that it has been exercised in the period of one year ending with the disposition.[260] The purpose of these provisions is to reduce the likelihood of a purchaser of land being bound by an easement that is difficult to discover and has not been exercised for a long period of time, but has not necessarily been abandoned.[261]

Actual occupation

At one time it was thought to be highly unlikely that an easement could achieve overriding status as a result of the owner of the right being in actual occupation of the servient land affected, and thus come within Sched. 3, para. (2). This was because the nature of an easement was generally thought to entail the right to do something on the servient land rather than to occupy it.[262] The House of Lords in *Moncrieff v. Jamieson*,[263] however, has widened the scope of the type of right which can qualify as an easement, and it would now seem to be quite possible for an easement to secure overriding status because the holder of it is regarded as being in actual occupation of the servient land. That said, in the case of the exercise of an easement such as a right of way (as distinct from a right of parking or storage), that use will not be regarded as actual occupation of the servient tenement,[264] so that cases where the owner of an easement can be said to be in actual occupation of the servient land are likely to be rare.

Other unregistered interests which will override

The remaining unregistered interests which will override are common to both Scheds 1 and 3.

(4) a customary right;

(5) a public right;

(6) a local land charge;

(7) an interest in any coal or coal mine, the rights attached to any such interest and the rights of any person under section 38, 49, or 51 of the Coal Industry Act 1994;

(8) in the case of land to which title was registered before 1898, rights to mines and minerals (and incidental rights) created before 1898;

(9) in the case of land to which title was registered between 1898 and 1925 inclusive, rights to mines and minerals (and incidental rights) created before the registration of the title.

---

[259] This is another instance of the LRA 2002 making the issue of the actual knowledge of a purchaser an important criterion.

[260] LRA 2002, Sched. 3, para. 3(1)(2).   [261] See (2002) Law Com. No. 271, paras 8.70–8.73.

[262] See M.P. Thompson [1988] Conv. 31 at 36.   [263] [2007] 1 W.L.R. 2620. See Chapter 12.

[264] See *Chaudhury v. Yavuz* [2011] EWCA Civ. 1314 at [27]–[36] *per* Lloyd L.J.

5.1.6 **Electronic conveyancing**

Central to the joint report which led to the enactment of the LRA 2002 was the ambition that all dealings involving registered land should be conducted electronically.[265] Currently, the transfer of registered land involves two stages.[266] First, there is a transfer by the registered proprietor in favour of the transferee. The transferee then applies to the registry to be registered as the new proprietor. Until the transferee is registered as the new proprietor, the legal title does not pass.[267] There is, however, a gap between these two events, dubbed 'the twilight zone'[268] and referred to in conveyancing circles as 'the registration gap'. A principal aim of the move to e-conveyancing was to close this gap and make the transfer and registration of a transaction simultaneous.

The Law Commission in 2018 declined to make any legal recommendations on the registration gap, despite acknowledging the practical difficulties, concluding that: 'the only viable means of reducing, and ultimately closing, the registration gap is through electronic conveyancing'.[269] Their reasons for this conclusion is that, in their words: '[t]he only way to solve the registration gap is to close it. The only legal reform that can close the registration gap would be to reverse s. 27(1) to provide that legal title passes on completion, not registration. This is not an option: legal title vesting on registration is the bedrock principle of registered land. Reversing it would be to undermine the entire scheme of the LRA 2002.'[270] For as long as there is no e-conveyancing then, the registration gap will continue.

5.1.6.1 **E-conveyancing**

The most far-reaching change the LRA 2002 was intended to implement is contained in s. 93. This provision, had it been brought into force, would not have provided an alternative method of transferring or creating interests in land to that which currently exists. The electronic procedure would have become mandatory.

Section 93 provides that:

> A disposition to which this section applies, or a contract to make such a disposition, *only has effect if it is made by electronic form* and, if when the document purports to take effect—
>
> (a) It is electronically communicated to the registrar, and
>
> (b) The relevant registration requirements are met.[271]

The section applies to the disposition of a registered estate or charge or an interest which is the subject of a notice in the register, where the disposition is of a description specified in the rules.[272] The relevant registration requirements are then listed in Sched. 2.

The combined effect of the section and the Schedule would be that it would only be possible to create or transfer various interests in land by electronic means which are communicated to the registrar; the creation of the electronic document and the communication to the registry would be simultaneous.

---

[265] See (2001) Law Com. No. 271, paras 1.2, 1.8 and 1.12. For the detailed proposals, see Part XIII of the Report. For a helpful discussion, not least of the technical aspects of this, see D. Capps [2002] Conv. 443. See also C. Harpum in E. Cooke (ed.), *Modern Studies in Property Law. Vol. 1: 2000* (Oxford, Hart Publishing, 2001), Chapter 1; R. Parry [2003] Conv. 215.

[266] This transaction is, of course, often preceded by a contract of sale.

[267] LRA 2002, s. 27(1).   [268] Harpum and Bignall, para. 2.24.   [269] Law Com. No. 380, 112.

[270] Law Com. No. 380, 112. See above section: *Additional rules on interests of persons in actual occupation under Schedule 3.*

[271] Emphasis supplied.   [272] LRA 2002, s. 93(1).

The provisions of the Act dealing with e-conveyancing were intended to apply to various dispositions affecting the land. These are:

(i) a disposition of a registered interest or charge,

(ii) a disposition of an interest which is the subject of a notice in the register, or

(iii) a disposition of an interest which is the subject of a notice in the register, which is of a kind specified by the rules.[273]

Two key points need to be made about these provisions. First, s. 93(3) makes clear that the imposition of compulsory electronic formalities was to apply not only to actual dispositions but also to contracts to make such dispositions. Second, it was also made clear that dispositions to which the section applies but which do not comply with its requirements have no effect. In its 2018 report, and draft Bill, the Law Commission has proposed an additional provision to enable e-conveyancing to be introduced without simultaneity of completion and registration.[274] It will be interesting to see whether the government agrees.

5.1.6.2 The consequences of non-compliance

For very many years, to create most legal interests in land, it was necessary to use a deed. A failure to do so was not, however, fatal to the creation of an equitable interest. If a deed was not used then, provided other formal requirements were met, the intended transaction was seen as a contract to create whatever interest was intended. Provided specific performance was available, an equitable interest would be created.[275] Such an argument would not be sustainable under e-conveyancing. The distinction between legal and equitable interests would, to a considerable extent, disappear.

It is not hard to envisage, however, that cases could come before the courts where the parties have not complied with the requirements to use electronic documents and electronically communicated the disposition to the registrar but have, nevertheless, acted in the belief that their intended transaction had legal efficacy. In such circumstances, one would envisage that the principles of estoppel would be applicable, and that there may emerge a proliferation of such claims.[276] Given the highly conservative approach taken in some quarters to allowing the perception that estoppel may be able to outflank the formal requirements of s. 2 of the Law of Property (Miscellaneous Provisions) Act 1989—a provision dealing with the formal requirements for the creation of a contract for the sale of land[277]—it may be the case that the courts would not accept this argument, although the better view is that they should do so.

A further point is that these new provisions do not apply to the creation of trusts. It will, therefore, still be open to a person to argue that they have an interest in another person's land under a trust and such a trust may override a registered disposition.

5.1.6.3 Non-implementation of e-conveyancing

As indicated above, the introduction of e-conveyancing was a central plank of the reforms recommended in the joint report that formed the basis of the LRA 2002. The e-conveyancing provisions were not brought into force alongside the other parts, it being recognized that it would take time to put the necessary infrastructure in place. Although work was

---

[273] LRA 2002, s. 91(2).   [274] (2018) Law Com. 308, 444.   [275] See 3.3.1.

[276] See M. Dixon in Cooke (ed.), *Modern Issues in Property Law Vol 0.2: 2002* (Oxford, Hart Publishing, 2003), Chapter 9. See Chapter 14.

[277] See *Yeoman's Row Management Ltd v. Cobbe* [2008] UKHL 1139 at [29] *per* Lord Scott.

done to seek to achieve this end, the Land Registry halted the development of an electronic transfer system in 2011. In 2017, the government promised to support HM Land Registry's work 'to facilitate a transition to digital registration and e-conveyancing'.[278] In 2018 the Law Commission proposed non-simultaneous e-conveyancing, keeping simultaneity (and the elimination of the registration gap as the ultimate goal) but adopting incremental development in the meantime.[279]

5.2 First registration of title

Although the principle of compulsory registration of title was introduced in 1925, the registration of titles to land took time. It was provided by s. 120, LRA 1925 that, by Order in Council, a particular area could be designated as being of compulsory registration of title. Over time, the areas of compulsory registration were extended, the process resembling the construction of a patchwork quilt. This process was completed on 1 December 1989, when the whole of England and Wales was designated as an area of compulsory registration of title,[280] each geographical area being served by a District Land Registry (now Land Registry offices).

Simply because land is situated in an area of compulsory registration of title does not mean that the landowner is required to register the title to it. The requirement to do so applies only on the occurrence of certain triggering events. It has always been possible to register the title voluntarily, however, and inducements are provided in the form of reduced fees to encourage people to do this, thereby helping to accelerate the spread of registration of title.[281]

5.2.1 Triggering events

Registration is made compulsory when specified transactions ('triggers') involve the land. For many years, triggering events were either a conveyance on sale of a fee simple, or the grant or assignment of a lease of more than twenty-one years. This short list meant that land could be in an area of compulsory registration of title for a very long time before there was any requirement for title to it to be registered. The land might remain unsold for many years and pass down the family by inheritance. In order to accelerate the spread of registration of title,[282] the number of transactions which would trigger the compulsory registration of title was extended considerably by s. 1, LRA 1997. In particular, the requirement to register title was extended to occasions when land passed by inheritance;[283] a factor which has obviously accelerated the achievement of the goal of universal registration of title.[284] The requirement to register title was further extended by the LRA 2002 and the list of triggering events is now to be found in s. 4.[285]

Under s. 4(1) of the Act, the requirement of registration applies on the occurrence of any of the following events:

---

[278] Fixing our Broken Housing Market (2017) Cm 9352, para 1.18
[279] (2018) Law Com. No. 380, 443.
[280] Registration of Title Order 1989 (S.I. 1989/1347).
[281] Land Registration Fees Order 2001 (S.I. 2001/1179), art. 2(5). For the power of the Lord Chancellor to prescribe fees, see LRA 2002, s. 102.
[282] (1995) Law Com. No. 154, a paper published jointly by the Law Commission and the Land Registry.
[283] LRA 1997, s. 1(6).
[284] This may still not be achieved for some time, as companies can hold unregistered land for prolonged periods and there will not be an inheritance of it. This is also true of local authorities.
[285] The Lord Chancellor is empowered to add to the triggering events: LRA 2002, s. 5(1).

(a) the transfer of a qualifying estate—

    (i) for valuable or other consideration, by way of gift or in pursuance of an order of any court,

    (ii) by means of an assent (including a vesting assent);[286] or

    (iii) giving effect to a partition of land subject to a trust of land; . . .

(b) the transfer of an unregistered legal estate in land in circumstances where section 171A of the Housing Act 1985 applies (disposal by landlord, which leads to a person no longer being a secure tenant);

(c) the grant out of a qualifying estate of an interest in land—

    (i) for a term of years absolute of more than seven years from the date of the grant, and

    (ii) for valuable or other consideration, by way of gift or in pursuance of an order of any court;

(d) the grant out of a qualifying estate of an estate in land for a term of years absolute to take effect in possession after the end of a period of three months beginning with the date of the grant;

(e) the grant of a lease in pursuance of Part 5 of the Housing Act 1985 (the right to buy) out of an unregistered legal estate in land;

(f) the grant of a lease out of an unregistered legal estate in land in such circumstances as are mentioned in paragraph (b);

(g) the creation of a protected first legal mortgage of a qualifying estate.

Section 4(2) defines a qualifying estate as being an unregistered legal estate, which is either a freehold estate in land, that is a fee simple absolute in possession, or leasehold estate in land for a term which, at the time of the transfer, grant, or creation, has more than seven years to run.

Before expanding on this definition, it is convenient to mention some events that are specifically excluded from being triggering events. These are the assignment of a mortgage term, or the assignment or surrender of lease to the owner of the immediate reversion where the term is to merge in that reversion.[287] The latter event is a means by which a lease can come to an end, the tenant giving up, and the landlord accepting, the lease prior to its coming to the end of its natural term.[288] A further excluded event is the creation of a lease in order to create a mortgage. One way of creating a legal mortgage was by the creation of a long lease in favour of the lender, the mortgagee. It is no longer possible to create a mortgage of registered land in this way.[289]

The LRA 2002 goes on to define what constitutes a triggering event. First, if the estate transferred or created has a negative value, it is nevertheless to be regarded as having been transferred or granted for valuable consideration.[290] Such an event is likely to occur when the extent of the repairing obligations in a lease means that the cost of complying with such obligations exceeds the value of the lease itself. Second, a transfer or grant by way of gift expressly includes the constitution of a trust where the settlor does not retain the whole of the beneficial interest. This would include a situation where a person who is the sole owner of

---

[286] An assent is the process by which the personal representatives of a deceased person vest the property in the person entitled under the will. In cases of intestacy, the assent is executed by the administrators of the estate.

[287] LRA 2002, s. 4(4).   [288] See 10.10.4.   [289] LRA 2002, s. 23(1).   [290] Ibid., s. 4(6).

a house, on getting married, transfers the house into their joint names. A further event that triggers compulsory registration is a transaction uniting the legal and beneficial titles where the settlor, on the constitution of the trust, did not retain the entire beneficial interest.[291]

5.2.1.1 Protected mortgages

A protected mortgage (in s. 4(1)(g)) is defined by s. 4(8) as being a legal mortgage if it takes effect on its creation as a mortgage to be protected by the deposit of documents relating to the mortgaged estate. A first legal mortgage is one which, on its creation, ranks in priority ahead of any other mortgages then affecting the mortgaged land. This aspect of the law of mortgages will be explained in Chapter 11.

5.2.1.2 Reversionary leases

One of the main changes introduced by the LRA 2002 was to reduce the length of leases which are required to be registered from twenty-one years to a period of seven years. What should not be overlooked, however, is that on the grant of a lease to take effect in possession after the end of the period of three months beginning with the date of the grant, this lease is required by s. 4(1)(d) of the Act to be registered. This type of lease is termed a reversionary lease and it is immaterial for how long the lease is to last. The width of this provision is unfortunate. It is by no means uncommon for student leases to be granted in March or April, to take effect in possession in September and to be for a period of one year.[292] Such a lease is now the subject of compulsory registration. One suspects strongly that registration will not occur.

5.2.2 Duty to register

Section 6 of the LRA 2002 imposes a duty to register on the occurrence of one of the events specified in s. 4. This duty is generally imposed upon the transferee of the relevant estate. In the case of the creation of a protected first mortgage, s. 4(1)(g), LRA 2002 imposed the obligation to apply for registration upon the mortgagor (that is, the borrower). This potentially created a problem for the mortgagee in ensuring that the mortgagor did this.[293] This potential difficulty has been removed as under a rule made under s. 6(6) of the Act, the mortgagee may make an application in the name of the mortgagor for the estate charged to be registered, whether or not the mortgagor consents.[294]

5.2.3 Effect of non-registration

The Act makes registration of title compulsory on the occurrence of one of the events set out in s. 4. The original legislation simply enacted that if, after two months from the date of the conveyance no application had been made for registration, then the conveyance would be void. This provision was thought to give rise to potential problems.[295] The consequence of non-registration was later spelled out more explicitly in amending legislation,[296] and the matter is now governed by s. 7, LRA 2002.

[291] Ibid., s. 4(7).

[292] This point is also taken by Smith, *Property Law* (8th edn) (Harlow, Longman, 2014), 242. For other problems with this type of lease, see 10.6.2.3.

[293] For the considerable problems caused by a failure to make a proper application for first registration, see *Sainsbury's Supermarkets Ltd v. Olympia Homes Ltd* [2005] EWHC 1235 (Ch).

[294] Land Registration Rules 2003, r. 21.

[295] See D.G. Barnsley (1968) Conv. (N.S.) 391 at 401, although see *Pinekerry Ltd v. Kenneth Needs (Contractors) Ltd* (1992) 64 P. & C.R. 245 at 247.

[296] LRA 1997, s. 1.

Section 7 LRA 2002 provides that unless, within two months of the disposition,[297] an application is made for registration,[298] then, if the disposition purports to transfer the legal estate, the title to the legal estate will revert to the transferor, who will hold it on a bare trust for the transferee.[299] In the case of grant or creation of a lease or a mortgage, the effect of non-registration is to treat what has happened as a contract for valuable consideration to grant or create the particular interest.[300] If either of these consequences occurs, then the cost of retransferring, regranting, or recreating the legal estate will fall upon the person who failed to register the title.[301]

The consequence of a failure to register is that the transferee is in danger of losing priority to an interest which is created subsequent to the disposition. It is true that, in most cases, the transferee will be in actual occupation of the land in question and that occupation will afford protection to the right as against a subsequent transferee of the property,[302] but this is unlikely to be the case where the disposition in question is a mortgage. In that event, a failure to apply for registration of title may cause the mortgagee to be bound by interests created subsequent to the mortgage; a position which would not have happened had a timely application for registration been made.[303]

5.2.4 **The process of registration**

Once one of the triggering events has occurred, an application for registration must be made within the two-month period. If the transaction is a conveyance on sale, then the traditional method of investigation of title will be employed; the purchaser will peruse the title deeds and make the normal searches in the land charges registry. When the process has been completed, and the land conveyed to the purchaser, this process is repeated in the registry. If the registrar is satisfied that the title is such as a willing buyer could properly be advised by a competent solicitor to accept, then the applicant for first registration will be registered with an absolute title. In deciding this question, the registrar may disregard the fact that the title may be open to objection if he is of the opinion that the defect will not cause the holding under the title to be disturbed.[304] This latter provision is designed to enable the registrar to register the applicant with an absolute title, despite there being technical objections to the title deduced. The registrar is prepared to take a robust view as to when a defect is merely technical; so much so, that it was said that the Chief Land Registrar 'does everything in his power to grant the best kind of title whenever possible. As a result, it is not perhaps surprising that under the policy of a liberal insurance of title, flaws that are hidden at the time of first registration sometimes appear later on.'[305]

---

[297] LRA 2002, s. 6(5). The registrar is empowered by s. 6(5) to extend this period, if satisfied that there is a good reason for so doing. In practice, the registrar is normally willing to grant an extension: Ruoff and Roper, *The Law and Practice of Registered Conveyancing*, 11.13.

[298] A misdescription of the property in the application does not amount to a failure to apply: *Proctor v. Kidman* (1985) 51 P. & C.R. 647.

[299] LRA 2002, s. 7(2)(a). The possibility of the estate reverting is disregarded for the purpose of determining whether a fee simple is a fee simple in possession: ibid., s. 7(4). See 4.3.1. For a good example of the reversion of the estate, see *Sainsbury's Supermarkets Ltd v. Olympia Homes Ltd, supra.*

[300] LRA 2002, s. 7(2)(b).   [301] Ibid., s. 8.

[302] See 5.1.5.3—Interests of persons in actual occupation.

[303] See *Barclays Bank plc v. Zaroovabli* [1997] 1 All E.R. 19, although not a case concerning first registration of title.

[304] LRA 2002, s. 9(2)(3).

[305] T.B.F. Ruoff (1956) Conv. (N.S.) 302 at 307. For criticism of this general policy, see C.T. Emery (1976) 40 Conv. (N.S.) 122.

Any refusal by the registrar to register the applicant with an absolute title cannot, apparently, be appealed against directly,[306] although the matter would seem to be amenable to judicial review and may, in the future, be dealt with in rules promulgated under the LRA 2002.[307] If, in separate proceedings, a court has held a title to be free from objection, and such that it can be forced upon a reluctant purchaser, then it is considered to be inconceivable that the Registry will decline to register the purchaser with an absolute title.[308]

5.2.5 Cautions against first registration

An application for first registration of title may affect the rights and interests of other people with interests in the land. Provision is made for those people to lodge a caution against first registration of title. The effect of the registration of such a caution is that, when an application is made for registration of title, the registrar must give the cautioner notice of the application for registration and of his right to object to the registration.[309] The cautioner is then given a period of fifteen working days from the issue of the notice to exercise his right to object to the application or to give the registrar notice that he does not intend to do so.[310] The registrar cannot determine an application for first registration until the period specified in the rules has expired. If the period expires without there being any response from the cautioner, then the registrar will proceed to determine the application for registration. If the cautioner objects to the application, then, unless the registrar is satisfied that the objection is groundless,[311] or it can be disposed of by agreement, the matter must then be referred to the First-tier tribunal,[312] who may determine any dispute between the parties.[313]

A person may lodge a caution against first registration if he claims to be either the owner of a qualifying estate or entitled to an interest affecting a qualifying estate. A qualifying estate is either an estate in land, a rentcharge, a franchise, or a profit in gross. An interest in land is defined by s. 132(3)(b), LRA 2002 to mean an adverse right affecting the title to the estate or charge. This will necessarily include matters registrable under the Land Charges Act (LCA) 1972, and the possibility of lodging a caution against first registration to protect such a right is seen as a means of conferring additional protection upon such rights. What is essential is that the claim should relate to the land itself. If the claim, should it succeed, is likely to be met by an order for the payment of money, as would frequently be the case if an action is brought under the provisions of the Inheritance (Provision for Family and Dependants) Act 1975, then the registration of a caution is inappropriate.[314]

---

[306] *Dennis v. Malcolm* [1934] Ch. 244, although see *Quigly v. Chief Land Registrar* [1992] 1 W.L.R. 834 at 837 *per* Millett J.

[307] LRA 2002, s. 14.

[308] *M.E.P.C. Ltd v. Christian-Edwards* [1981] A.C. 205 at 220–1 *per* Lord Russell, a case concerning the enforceability of an uncompleted contract made in 1911 to buy land contracted to be sold in 1973.

[309] LRA 2002, s. 16(1).

[310] Land Registration Rules 2003, r. 53(1). At the request of the cautioner, this period can be extended to a maximum of thirty working days: r. 53(1)(2).

[311] This is a very low bar, which has the effect of increasing the need for judicial involvement in disputes: see *Silkstone v. Tatnall* [2010] EWHC 127 (Ch) at [17] *per* Floyd J. and, for a full consideration of the adjudication process, K. Harrington and C. Auld [2016] Conv. 19. It has been provisionally recommended that a higher standard should be introduced: Law Commission Consultation Paper (2016) para. 9.105.

[312] LRA 2002, s. 73(7)(b)(i).

[313] See *Jayasinghe v. Liyange* [2010] EWHC 265 (Ch); *Chief Land Registrar v. Silkstone* [2011] EWCA Civ. 801.

[314] See *Williams v. Seals* [2014] EWHC 3708 (Ch) at [32] *per* David Richards J.; *Zeckler v. Kylun Ltd* [2015] EWHC 2977 (QB).

It should be appreciated, however, that the lodging of a caution against first registration is an additional method of affording protection to a matter which is registrable as a land charge. It is not an alternative to it. In *Sainsbury's Supermarkets Ltd v. Olympia Ltd*[315] the claimant sought to protect an option to purchase by the lodging of a caution against first registration but did not also register a land charge. As was pointed out by Mann J., this was insufficient. The reason for this is that the effect of s. 4(6) of the LCA 1972 is that the option became void for non-registration on the occasion of the conveyance for money or money's worth, an event which preceded the application for first registration.[316] This point is reinforced by s. 16(3), LRA 2002, which specifically provides that a caution against first registration has no effect on the validity of any interest of the cautioner in the legal estate to which the caution relates: that is, it does not confer validity on a claim which is not otherwise valid.[317] What it does is to allow the cautioner to substantiate a claim to have a right in another person's land. The existence of such a caution is revealed by searching the register of cautions, which the registrar is obliged to maintain in the Index.[318]

The existence of a caution against first registration may, however, prejudicially affect the owner of the land to which the caution relates. Its existence may well impair his prospects of selling the land, as no purchaser wishes to buy a law suit. To reflect this, a cautioner owes a statutory duty to the owner of the estate affected not to lodge a caution without reasonable cause.[319] The owner of the estate may also apply for the cancellation of a caution. If this is done, then the registrar must serve notice on the cautioner and must also inform him that, if he does not exercise his right to object within fifteen working days, the caution will be cancelled.[320]

5.2.6 Registration with an absolute title

The overwhelming majority of applications for first registration of a freehold title result in the applicant being registered as proprietor with an absolute title. The key provision is s. 11, LRA 2002. This provides that:

(1) The estate is vested in the proprietor together with all interests subsisting for the benefit of the estate.

(2) Registration with absolute title has the effect described in subsections (3) to (5).

(3) The estate is vested in the proprietor together with all interests subsisting for the benefit of the estate

(4) The estate is vested in the proprietor subject only to the following interests affecting the estate at the time of registration—

    (a) interests which are subject to an entry in the register in relation to the estate,

    (b) unregistered interests which fall within any of the paragraphs of Schedule 1, and

    (c) interests acquired under the Limitation Act 1980 of which the proprietor has notice.

(5) If the proprietor is not entitled to the estate for his own benefit, or not entitled solely for his own benefit, then, as between himself and the persons beneficially entitled to the estate, the estate is vested in him subject to such of their interests as has notice of . . . [321]

---

[315] [2005] EWHC 1235 (Ch).   [316] Ibid. at para. 53.

[317] See also *Kitney v. M.E.P.C. Ltd* [1977] 1 W.L.R. 981. In *Turner v. Chief Land Registrar* [2013] EWHC 1382 (Ch), it was said, at [30] *per* Roth J., to be fundamental that a caution gives no interest in land but is only a procedural safeguard.

[318] LRA 2002, ss 19, 68(1)(c).   [319] Ibid., s. 77(1)(2).

[320] Ibid., s. 18; Land Registration Rules 2003, r. 53. As to the resolution of such disputes, see 5.1.5.3—Agreed and unilateral notices.

[321] LRA 2002, s. 11(3)(4)(5). The last provision relates to a situation where the proprietor holds the land on trust for others.

This provision is fundamental to the working of the system. It operates at two levels. First, it has a credit side, stipulating what it is that the statute gives to the registered proprietor by the workings of 'statutory magic', and, second, it makes clear the third-party rights to which he takes subject.[322]

5.2.6.1 The statutory magic

A central feature of property law in general is encapsulated in the Latin phrase, *nemo dat quod non habet*: one cannot give what one does not own. Under the unregistered land system, if a person purported to convey either more land than he actually owned, or land to which he had no title at all, the conveyance would be void in respect of that piece of land. Whether or not the purchaser either could, or should, have known of this is quite immaterial.

Section 5 of the LRA 1925 operated to create a major exception to this principle of *nemo dat*, a practice illustrated in *Re 139 High Street, Deptford*,[323] where a vendor purported to convey to a purchaser a shop, together with an annexe. The purchaser was registered as the proprietor with an absolute title of both the shop and the annexe. In fact, the annexe did not belong to the vendor but to a third party. The litigation concerned an attempt by the third party to secure the rectification of the register, so as to have the land returned to him. The point, for present purposes, is that what was once termed 'the statutory magic'[324] had operated to vest in the registered proprietor the legal estate to the land, even though the person who had purported to transfer the land to him did not own the land which he had purported to convey.

The LRA 2002 made this change even clearer. In addition to s. 11 LRA 2002, which operates to vest title in the registered proprietor, s. 58(1) provides that:

> If, on the entry of a person in the register as the proprietor of a legal estate, the legal estate would not otherwise be vested in him, it shall be deemed to be vested in him as a result of the registration.

The effect of s. 58 LRA 2002 was seen in *Knights Construction (March) Ltd v. Roberto Mac Ltd*.[325] The voluntary registration of a piece of land occurred in 2007 and, in error, the registration included land owned by the applicant. The registered title was transferred to the respondent who proceeded to enclose the disputed plot by fencing it. The applicant who, until this happened, had been justifiably ignorant of what had occurred at the Land Registry, then sought rectification of the register to recover the land. Both of these cases involved situations where a person who, had title not been registered, would have been able to establish a better right to the land than the person who had been registered as proprietor of it, and the actions were brought to undo the effect of the two statutory provisions.

In each case, the outcome was that the register was changed so as to re-vest the title to the land to the person who had, as a consequence of the registration procedure, and through no fault of their own, lost title to the land. In each case, compensation was, at least in principle, available to the registered proprietor who had subsequently lost what registration had conferred. This is illustrative of one of the principles underpinning the system

---

[322] See Section 5.2.6.1 below. [323] [1951] Ch. 884.

[324] Ruoff and Roper, *The Law and Practice of Registered Conveyancing* (5th edn, 1986), 70, a process now less graphically, termed 'automatic vesting': para. 2.08. For more recent use of the older expression, see *Pick v. Chief Land Registrar* [2011] EWHC 206 (Ch) at [7] *per* Proudman J.

[325] [2011] E.G.L.R. 123.

of registration of title, the insurance principle,[326] whereby, as a general rule, persons who suffer loss as a result of the registration process obtain compensation from central funds.

A number of initial points should, however, be observed about this process. First, in the *Deptford* case, the person against whom rectification was sought was the first registered proprietor. As such, there had been no prior reliance on the accuracy of the register. This was a conveyancing mistake, which, because the mistake had not been revealed prior to registration, enabled the proprietor to come within the protective umbrella of the insurance principle. In *Knights Construction*, however, the proprietor had relied upon the register, the error having occurred prior to the transfer to him. As such, that proprietor's ability to resist a rectification action should, as a purchaser for value, have been stronger than was the case in *Deptford*, the policy of the legislation being seen as being to provide protection for just such a person.[327]

In both cases, one should consider also the impact of the registration provisions on the person who, because of the effect of wrongful registration was deprived of his land. It has been said that this divestment of title, without the owner's consent, 'seems anathema to democratic ideals of private ownership.'[328] This is a dilemma that lies at the heart of the system of registration of title. To what extent should the system seek to preserve the integrity of the register,[329] when an important outcome of doing so is to effect the compulsory transfer of one person's land to another? The Law Commission has considered these questions around the *nemo dat* principle in its 2018 report. Its conclusion is that the common law principle of *nemo dat* should not limit owner's powers, particularly given the intention behind the LRA 2002 to extend owner's powers to persons entitled to be registered as the proprietor. The Law Commission has consequently recommended, not without some controversy, that the common law *nemo dat* principle should be eliminated in relation to persons entitled to be registered as proprietor. If adopted, this recommendation would mean that the LRA 2002 would confirm that in the case of a person entitled to be registered as the proprietor, owner's powers are not limited by reason only of the fact that the person is not yet registered as the proprietor and so merely has an equitable, rather than a legal, title. Such a change would, as the Law Commission acknowledges, have consequences for cases such as *Scott v Southern Pacific Ltd*; however, it couples its call for reform on owner's powers with recommendations on priority for unregistrable leases and mortgages to create a form of balance in *Scott*-type situations.[330]

In seeking to resolve this problem, consideration needs also to be given to when compensation is awarded to the various people who are inevitably affected when things go wrong. These issues will be returned to when considering the jurisdiction to alter or rectify the register at 5.4.1 below.[331]

5.2.6.2 Equitable title

Section 58 of the LRA 2002 is quite explicit that the proprietor of a legal estate is deemed to have the legal estate vested in him, notwithstanding that, apart from the fact of registration,

---

[326] For a memorable example of this principle, see the reference to *Haigh's Case*, in Ruoff and Roper, *The Law and Practice of Registered Conveyancing*, para. 40.13, where the notorious 'acid bath murderer' also forged conveyances from his victims and secured himself as proprietor of their properties. Apparently the personal representatives of the victims did not want the land back and were happy to receive an indemnity: see T.B.F. Ruoff (1956) 20 Conv. (N.S.) 302 at 309.

[327] For a different view, see S. Cooper (2015) 131 L.Q.R. 108.

[328] A. Goymour [2013] C.L.J. 617 at 623. See, to much the same effect, S. Gardner [2013] Conv. 530 at 538.

[329] For a strong statement in favour of such a policy, see *Banwaitt v. Dewji* [2015] EWHC 3441 (Ch) at [38] *per* Master Matthews.

[330] (2018) Law Com. Rep. 380. Chapters 5 and 8.

[331] See 5.4 - Alteration and indemnity.

that estate would be vested in someone else. Save for limited examples,[332] the fact of registration is conclusive as to the location of the legal title: it is vested in the registered proprietor. Unfortunately, neither the LRA 1925 nor the LRA 2002 dealt explicitly with the ownership of the equitable title.

This issue arose in *Epps v. Esso Petroleum Ltd.*[333] By mistake, a strip of land was purported to be conveyed twice by the same person. On the occasion of the second conveyance, which was of course void, the person to whom the strip had purportedly been conveyed was registered as the proprietor of it. The action was brought by the people who derived title from the person to whom the first conveyance was made: that is the people who, had title not been registered in the name of the wrong person, would have been the owners of it.

One of the arguments employed by the plaintiffs to secure the restoration of the land to them was that they had an overriding interest in it. Although it was accepted that the effect of s. 5, LRA 1925 was to vest the legal title in the registered proprietor, it was contended that the equitable title was not but, instead, was retained by the first purchaser of the strip and had then passed to them as successors in title. It was then argued that, because they were in actual occupation of the land, that interest took effect as an overriding interest binding upon the registered proprietor.[334] Although the argument failed on the facts, in that it was held that they were not in fact in actual occupation of the disputed strip, the premise upon which it was based appeared to have been accepted. Had Templeman J. not accepted the argument that the effect of registration of the wrong person as proprietor of the land was to vest only the legal title, but not the beneficial ownership, the point as to whether or not the plaintiffs were in actual occupation of the strip would not have arisen. They would not have had any interest in the property. The case seems to accept, therefore, that the curative effect of registration is only to vest the legal title in the person wrongly registered as the proprietor, but not the equitable title.

This is wrong in principle.[335] If the argument that the effect of registration is merely to clothe the registered proprietor with the bare legal title to the land, but leaves the beneficial title outstanding is correct, this would have serious consequences. Under the rule in *Saunders v. Vautier*[336] a beneficiary of full age under a bare trust can insist that the trustee transfers the legal title to him. In the present context, this would mean that the person who had lost the legal title to the land, as a result of another person being mistakenly registered as the proprietor of it, could simply call for the land to be reconveyed to him. This would undermine completely the whole basis of the conclusiveness of the register. The LRA 2002 does not, as it could have done, deal explicitly with this point, albeit the terms of s. 11(3), which operate to vest in the proprietor all interests subsisting for the benefit of the estate, would seem to have this effect. Much the better view is that first registration of title vests in the registered proprietor both the legal and the equitable titles to the land.[337]

---

[332] See Ruoff and Roper, *The Law and Practice of Registered Conveyancing*, para. 2.09, instancing matters such as the death or bankruptcy of the proprietor. In the case of bankruptcy, see LRA, s. 27(5) and *Pick v. Chief Land Registrar* [2011] EWHC 206 (Ch) at [7] *per* Proudman J.; *Re The Keepers and Governors of the Possession, Remains and Goods of the Free Grammar School of John Lyon v. Helman* [2014] EWCA Civ. 17

[333] [1973] 1 W.L.R. 1071. See also *Gardner v. Lewis* [1998] 1 W.L.R. 1535 at 1538 *per* Lord Browne-Wilkinson. Cf. *Blacklocks v. J.B. Developments (Godalming) Ltd* [1982] Ch. 183.

[334] See 5.1.5.3—The upgrading of rights.

[335] For a convincing critique, see S.N.L. Palk (1974) 38 Conv. (N.S.) 236. See also the comments in *Malory Enterprises Ltd v. Cheshire Homes Ltd* [2002] Ch. 216 at 232 *per* Arden L.J.

[336] (1841) Beav. 115.

[337] See, generally, C. Harpum in Getzler (ed.), *Rationalizing Property, Equity and Trusts: Essays in Honour of Edward Burn* (London: LexisNexis, 2003), 187. The interesting article on the role of resulting trusts in registered land, D. Wilde [1999] Conv. 382 is not germane to this issue because, *ex hypothesi*, the transferor never held either the legal or equitable titles to the property. For the related issue concerning transfers of registered land, see 5.3.6—Forgery.

5.2.6.3 Third-party rights binding on first registration

Section 11 of the LRA 2002 operates positively to vest the legal and equitable titles to freehold estates in the registered proprietor. It also stipulates to what rights the land is subject, namely, third-party entries noted on the register, unregistered interests which fall within any of the paragraphs of Sched. 1 (overriding interests), and interests acquired under the Limitation Act 1980, of which the proprietor has notice.

5.3 Dispositions

When a title is registered, dealings with it must be completed by registration. This is dealt with explicitly by s. 27(1), LRA 2002, which provides that if a disposition of a registered estate or registered charge is required to be completed by registration, it does not operate at law until the relevant registration requirements are met. Until application is made for registration, the transfer operates only in equity.[338] The dispositions required to be completed by registration are then listed in s. 27(2). This list includes a transfer, the grant of various leases, the grant of easements and rentcharges, and the grant of a legal charge. With regard to leases, it is important to distinguish between situations when a leasehold estate is registered and when it is not. When a leasehold estate is registered and that lease is then assigned, then that assignment must be registered. It is immaterial how many years remain under the lease. The assignment is a transfer. So if the residue of a registered lease with six years remaining is assigned, that assignment must be completed by registration. Despite the fact that the term is for less than seven years, it will not take effect as an interest overriding registration.[339] When what is in question is the grant of a new lease, the leases which must be completed by registration are those which exist as registrable interests.[340]

Having contracted to purchase the particular estate in question, the purchaser will requisition an official search of the register.[341] Provided that he is in good faith and the application for registration is made within the priority period,[342] this period currently being thirty working days from the time when the search application is deemed to have been delivered,[343] he will take free from any interests registered between the date of the search and the application for registration.[344] Good faith, in this context, appears to mean only that the purchaser is acting honestly,[345] a requirement which is not precluded simply because he has notice of a competing claim.[346]

If the official search certificate is incorrect, the position is different from that which pertains with regard to unregistered land. When title is unregistered, it is provided by s. 10(4)

---

[338] See *Barclays Bank plc v. Zaroovabli* [1997] Ch. 321 (creation of a mortgage); *Scribes West Ltd v. Relsa Anstalt* [2004] EWCA Civ. 1744 (transfer of freehold reversion); *Baker v. Craggs* [2016] EWHC 3250 (Ch) at [10] *per* Newey J. See also *Skelwith (Leisure) Ltd v. Armstrong* [2015] EWHC 2830 (Ch).

[339] LRA 2002, Sched. 3, para. 1(b).

[340] See 5.1.5.1—Leasehold estates.   [341] LRA 2002, s. 70.

[342] It is not sufficient if the transaction is completed within the priority period. An application must be made for registration of title: see *Howell v. Murray* (1990) 61 P. & C.R. 18.

[343] Land Registration (Official Searches) Rules 1993, r. 3. The Lord Chancellor is empowered to make rules in respect of priority periods: LRA 2002, s. 72(6)(7).

[344] LRA 2002, s.72(1)(2). See *Meretz Investments N.V. v. ACP Ltd* [2007] EWCA Civ. 1303 at [18] *per* Arden L.J. If not, he will be bound by that interest: see *Baker v. Craggs* [2016] EWHC 3250 (Ch) (Easement). To hold, as was done in this case, that the easement overreached a prior, unprotected contract of sale, seemed unnecessarily confusing and has now been found to be incorrect by the Court of Appeal: [2018] EWCA Civ. 1126.

[345] Land Registration (Official Searches) Rules 1993, r. 2(1).

[346] *Smith v. Morrison* [1974] 1 W.L.R. 659.

of the LCA 1972 that the certificate shall be conclusive, so that if the search erroneously fails to reveal the existence of a registered land charge, the purchaser will take free from it.[347] When title is registered, it is the actual state of the register which is conclusive and so, in *Parkash v. Irani Finance Co. Ltd*,[348] a purchaser took subject to a caution even though the search had failed to reveal it. The purchaser's remedy in this situation is to obtain an indemnity.[349]

5.3.1 Priority

As the Law Commission noted in 2016:

> Priority is a central concept in land law. Because English law allows for the presence of so many enforceable interests in land, the law has to develop complex rules for regulating their priority, in other words for determining the order in which interests in land are enforceable and which interests prevail over others.[350]

The LRA 2002 purports, first, to set down a 'basic rule' to govern priorities (s. 28 LRA 2002) and then goes on to deal with the effect of dispositions for value on that position (s. 29 LRA 2002 and, for charges, s. 20 LRA 2002).

5.3.2 Basic rule

The 'basic rule' of 'first in time' is laid down by s. 28, LRA 2002. This provides that:

> (1) Except as provided by sections 29 and 30, the priority of an interest affecting an interest or charge is not affected by a disposition of the estate or charge.
>
> (2) It makes no difference for the purposes of this section whether the interest or disposition is registered.

What this means is that, unless the order of priorities is affected by a disposition which comes within the terms of either s. 29, which deals with dispositions for valuable consideration of a registered estate, or s. 30 which is concerned with registered charges, the question of priorities is resolved on the basis that the interest which is created first has priority. The basic rule is that created 'first in time' has priority. This position is potentially unfair, however, as demonstrated by the Law Commission. The scenario envisaged is this:[351]

Interest 1 created;

Interest 2 created;

Interest 2 noted on the register;

Interest 1 noted on the register;

Under s28, Interest 1 has priority.

Where there is no valuable consideration, since protecting an interest, such as a contract to create a lease,[352] by noting it on the register is not a disposition within the meaning of

---

347 See 4.8.1.   348 [1970] Ch. 101.

349 LRA 2002, Sched. 8, para. 1(1)(c). See *Prestige Properties Ltd v. Scottish Provident Institution* [2003] Ch. 1.

350 Law Commission Consultation Paper (2016), para. 2.56.   351 Ibid., para. 6.30.

352 This is not included in s. 27(2) LRA 2002 and so not a 'registrable disposition' for the purposes of s. 29 LRA 2002. See *AZ Dominion Homes Ltd v. Price Evans Solicitors* [2015] EWHC 2490 (Ch).

either ss 29 or 30, the basic rule applies, and so the order of priority is interest 1 followed by interest 2. This can be unfair on the holder of interest 2 who, when that interest was acquired, could not have discovered the prior interest. In 2018, the Law Commission has declined, however, to recommend any reform of these rules on the basis that it found no evidence of widespread problems and 'by and large, the current priorities work in practice'.[353]

5.3.3 Registrable disposition and valuable consideration

There is an exception to the 'basic rule', set out in s. 29, LRA 2002. This provides that: 'If a registrable disposition of a registered estate is made for valuable consideration, completion of the disposition by registration has the effect of postponing to the interest under the disposition any interest affecting the estate immediately before the disposition whose priority is not protected at the time of registration.' Section 29 effectively reverses the basic priority rule in s. 28, so that a later registered disposition will take priority over an earlier unregistered interest *if* it is made for valuable consideration. The disposition that is *registered* first *if* there is valuable consideration. The same principle underpins s. 30 LRA 2002 in relation to charges—that is, mortgages—so that if there is valuable consideration the interest that is the 'first registered' will have priority.

5.3.3.1 Valuable consideration

What then is 'valuable consideration'? The definition in the LRA 2002 excludes voluntary transfers, whether during the transferor's lifetime or by will as well as marriage consideration and a nominal consideration in money.[354]

Critics have long argued that nominal consideration should not be excluded from this definition since it is because it is very difficult to know precisely what is meant by 'nominal'. In 2018 the Law Commission recommended that nominal consideration be removed from the definition of 'valuable consideration' for the purposes of s. 29 LRA 2002.[355] So however much 'nominal consideration' might be, it would not be excluded from 'valuable consideration'. This would be a pragmatic and practical reform.

5.3.4 Postponement of interest

Section 29 states that the completion by registration of a disposition for value has the effect of postponing to the interest under the disposition any interest affecting the estate immediately before the disposition whose priority was not protected at the time of registration. The word 'postponement' is very curious and is not one generally used when dealing with the subject of priorities. This has led to the question being raised whether the postponement is confined to the estate of a disponee for value, so that the unprotected interest may be revived subsequently.[356] The issue was considered by the Law Commission in 2016, which gave the following scenario:

A is a registered proprietor of land and enters into a restrictive covenant with his neighbour, Z. The covenant is not noted on A's title. A then transfers the land to B, who is

---

[353] (2018) Law Com. No. 380, 131.

[354] LRA 2002, s. 132(1).

[355] (2018) Law Com. No. 380, 150. The Law Commission does not, however, propose changing the definition of 'valuable consideration' in s. 86 LRA 2002 (bankruptcy of the registered proprietor) given the interplay between insolvency and land registration law.

[356] This is explored by M. Dixon (2009) 125 L.Q.R. 401 at 405–8, who, having raised the point, concludes that the better view is that this is not the case.

registered as the new proprietor. The effect of s. 29 is that Z's interest is postponed to that of B. B is therefore not bound by the covenant. B then dies and leaves his property to C. Because C is not a transferee for value, s. 29 does not apply and the question which is put is whether the basic rule laid down by s. 28 now applies, in which case, as Z's interest pre-dates that of C, is C bound by the covenant?[357]

While the drafting of this important part of the LRA 2002 leaves a good deal to be desired, it is suggested that the answer is that C is not bound by the covenant. The rule derived from the general law is that an equitable interest is void as against a purchaser for value. If, subsequently, that person transfers the land to a person who did have notice of the prior equitable interest then, as was decided in *Wilkes v. Spooner*,[358] the equitable right is not revived. The same result would have occurred had the transferee in that case not provided consideration rather than what actually happened which was that the second transferee had provided consideration but had notice of the interest. While the use of the unfamiliar language of postponement in s. 29 is unfortunate, it is thought that the rule in *Wilkes v. Spooner* is analogous and, in the example given by the Law Commission, the transferor A would not transfer to B a worse title than that which he had himself acquired, so that B would not be bound by Z's covenant.[359]

5.3.5 Interests binding on a registrable disposition

An interest is protected if:

(i) it is a registered charge or the subject of a notice on the register;

(ii) it falls within any of the paragraphs of Sched. 3 (and is an interest that overrides); or

(iii) it appears from the register to be excepted from the effect of registration; and

(iv) in the case of a disposition of a leasehold estate, if the burden of the interest is an incident of the estate.

The first two paragraphs are self-explanatory. The registered proprietor takes subject to interests noted on the register and to interests which override registered dispositions. The third paragraph is relevant to situations where the proprietor is not registered with an absolute title and so the purchaser takes subject to the interests excepted from registration. The final paragraph means simply that the purchaser of a leasehold estate takes subject to the obligations imposed by the lease.

Although these provisions appear to be clear enough, there is the scope for fraud.

5.3.6 Forgery

The conclusiveness of s. 58 LRA 2002 means that if an estate owned by A is fraudulently transferred to B and he is then registered as the registered proprietor, B becomes the owner. The 'statutory magic' of land registration takes effect. This is not an absolute guarantee and can be challenged. This is known as the 'indefeasibility question' and has for some time now been a topic of interest for the Law Commission.

Such fraudulent behaviour underlay the dispute in *Malory Enterprises Ltd v. Cheshire Homes (U.K.) Ltd*,[360] where A was the registered proprietor of land and B, by fraud, secured

---

[357] Law Commission Consultation Paper (2016), para. 8.8.

[358] [1911] 2 K.B. 473 C.A. 2 6 4 4

[359] This view is supported by *Halifax Plc v. Curry Popeck* [2008] EWHC 1692 (Ch).

[360] [2002] Ch. 216. For critical analysis, see C. Harpum in Getzler (ed.), *Rationalizing Property, Equity and Trusts: Essays in Honour of Edward Burn* (London, LexisNexis, 2003), 187 at 199–203.

a land certificate for this land in its own name. B then executed a transfer of that land to C, who was registered as the proprietor.[361] A then sought and obtained rectification of the register to recover the land.

The Court of Appeal analysed the effect of the forgery in the context of the provisions of the LRA 1925. Arden L.J. held that the purported transfer could not, in law, have had any effect because B was not the proprietor of the land, and thus had no right to execute it. C, however, had become the registered proprietor and one then had to consider what the effect of that registration was. This was governed by s. 69 of the 1925 Act, which provided that 'the proprietor of land shall be deemed to have vested in him, where the legal estate is freehold, the legal estate in fee simple'. This section, she observed, unlike s. 5 of the Act which dealt with first registration of title, did not state that the fee simple was vested in the proprietor 'together with all rights, privileges and appurtenances'. She concluded, as a result, that C as registered proprietor held the legal estate, but that the beneficial interest was held by A, who was previously the registered proprietor.[362]

The person entitled to exercise owner's powers in relation to a registered estate conferred by s. 23, LRA 2002 is either the registered proprietor or the person entitled to be registered as proprietor.[363] Manifestly, this does not include the forger. Second, s. 26, which is headed 'Protection of disponees', would not appear to be relevant, as this protects the disponee in respect of any limitation of a person's right to exercise owner's powers. This would not seem apt to cover the case where the person purporting to exercise these rights has no power at all to exercise them. Third, the protection afforded to a purchaser of registered land by s. 29 proceeds on the basis of there having been a registrable disposition. In *Malory*, the Court of Appeal held that the forged disposition was not a disposition, with the consequence that s. 20, LRA 1925, which provided protection on a registered proprietor following a disposition to him for valuable consideration, did not apply. The same reasoning would seem to apply to s. 29, LRA 2002.

Registration of C did, however, occur. Under the LRA 1925 the effect of this was indisputably to vest the legal title in it. The same result is confirmed by s. 58, LRA 2002, which provides that:

> If, on the entry of a person on the register as the proprietor of a legal estate, the legal estate would not otherwise be vested in him, it shall be deemed to be vested in him as a result of registration.

While this section makes it clear that the legal title is vested in the transferee, no mention is made of the beneficial interest. Accordingly, the reasoning employed in *Malory* would appear to be equally applicable to the provisions of the LRA 2002: if the purported disposition is a forgery, the registered disponee will hold the property on trust for the person who, as a result of the forgery, has been wrongly been deprived of the legal title.[364] The consequence of this is that, if A is the registered proprietor, and B forges a transfer in favour of C, who is registered as the new proprietor, C will hold the property on trust for A. It was pointed out at first instance in *Malory* that, as such, C could simply be called upon to execute a transfer to A.[365] C, an entirely innocent victim of the fraudster, will then lose his estate in land despite having paid a market price for the property. Moreover, C would

---

[361] For the relative ease of making fraudulent transfers, see P.H. Kenny [2007] Conv. 195.

[362] [2002] Ch. 216 at 232. On the operation of s. 69 see also *Rashid v. Nasrullah* [2018] EWCA Civ. 2685

[363] LRA 2002, s. 24.

[364] This was accepted as being the case in *Malory*, itself, as well as in *Fitzwilliam v. Richall Holdings Services Ltd* [2013] EWHC 86 (Ch) at [81] *per* Newey J.; *Park Associated Developments Ltd v. Kinnear* [2013] EWCA Civ. 3617 (Ch) at [10]–[11] *per* Newey J.

[365] See [2002] Ch. 216 at 224.

not appear to be entitled to any indemnity because, first, the deprivation of the legal title in favour of the beneficial owner would not occasion him any loss, and, second, the ability of A to call for the legal estate to be vested in him is not dependent upon the statutory provisions to rectify the register.[366] Instead, it is an inherent part of the general law whereby a beneficiary has the right to compel the trustee to transfer the legal title to him.[367]

The decision in *Malory* was followed, albeit with some reluctance, at first instance[368] but has since been repudiated by the Court of Appeal in *Swift 1st Ltd v. Chief Land Registrar*.[369] This case concerned forgery whereby the forger had purported to create a legal charge[370] over the property, which was duly registered. The issue in the litigation was whether the chargee, after the charge was removed from the register of title, was entitled to an indemnity. Had the decision in *Malory* been followed, it would not have been, as it would only have held a bare legal title to the charge. The Court of Appeal declined to follow its earlier decision in *Malory*, being of the view that it had been decided *per incuriam*. The Court of Appeal in *Swift* held that had the court in *Malory* had regard to s. 114, LRA 1925, it would not have held that the beneficial interest did not pass to the registered proprietor and, consequently, declined to follow its earlier decision. For the time being at least,[371] it is now established that a forged disposition will operate to vest in the disponee, once that person's interest has been entered on the register, both the legal and beneficial ownership.

This is to be welcomed. As noted previously, after some uncertainty, it is now accepted that on first registration of title, the proprietor is vested with both the legal and equitable title, despite the fact that the person who conveyed the land had no title to it.[372] It would make little sense for there to be a fundamental difference in this regard between a first registered proprietor, who was a victim of forgery, and a subsequent proprietor who had fallen prey to the same type of behaviour. Second, had the decision in *Malory* stood, then the provisions in the LRA 2002 dealing with alteration of the register and indemnity would be completely bypassed. The person who had, as a result of the forgery, either lost legal title to the land or, through no act of his own, found that his title was now subject to a mortgage could simply call upon the new proprietor, who is also a victim of fraud, to undo what had been done without recourse to the relevant statutory provisions. Moreover, the provision in para. 1(2) of Sched. 8 to the LRA 2002, which provides the criteria for the award of an indemnity, makes specific provision to protect a registered proprietor who is the victim of fraud.[373] This provision would be completely redundant had the decision in *Malory*, that a person registered as proprietor of an estate or charge following a forged disposition had only the legal title and not the beneficial title, been allowed to prevail.

5.4 Alteration and indemnity

One of the effects of the LRAs 1925 and 2002 is to provide certainty as to the ownership of the land. If a person is registered as proprietor with an absolute title then, whatever the position might have been had title been unregistered, the proprietor is the owner of that land. Of course, mistakes may happen. A situation may occur when the person who has been

---

[366] See 5.4.   [367] This is the rule in *Saunders v. Vautier* (1841) Cr. and Ph. 240.
[368] *Fitzwilliam v. Richall Holdings Ltd, supra; Park Associated Developments Ltd v. Kinnear, supra.* For a barrage of criticism of the former decision, and those which followed it, see E. Cooke [2013] Conv. 344 and [2014] Conv. 444; M. Dixon [2013] 129 L.Q.R. 148; E. Lees (2013) 76 M.L.R. 924. For a very different view, see S. Gardner [2013] Conv. 530.
[369] [2015] EWCA Civ. 330, See E. Lees (2015) LQR 515.
[370] In fact, more than one charge had been created but the money raised by the final charge had been used, in part, to discharge the earlier mortgages.
[371] For surprisingly fierce criticism of the decision in *Swift*, see *Emmet and Farrand on Title*, para. 9.009.01
[372] See 5.2.6.2.   [373] See further 5.4.

registered as proprietor may not actually be entitled to the land because the person who conveyed it to him was not, himself, the owner of it.[374] To deal with problems such as this, and other, less fundamental errors, jurisdiction exists for these matters to be corrected.[375]

The existence of this jurisdiction means that, in principle, 'the system of land registration provides for only qualified indefeasibility of title'.[376] There are two sides to this. First, if there exists the possibility of changes being made, it is not true to say that a person can always place an unqualified reliance on the accuracy of the register. Leaving aside the possibility of being bound by overriding interests which, by definition, are interests which do not appear on the register of title, there remains the possibility that the register may be changed to recognize as valid claims by other people. On the other hand, if no such jurisdiction existed, the effect of the system of registration of title would be to deprive those people of pre-existing rights in property as a consequence of transactions to which they were not a party: a state of affairs which is difficult to justify.[377]

As well as there being in existence the power to change the register, there is also a complementary jurisdiction to award an indemnity to people who suffer loss as a result of a change being made to the register or, alternatively, suffer loss because such a change has been refused. The availability of indemnities is what underpins the insurance principle underlying the registered land system.

5.4.1 **Alteration and rectification**

The LRA 2002 distinguishes between alteration and rectification, both of which are governed by Sched. 4.[378] The term rectification is limited to situations where, first, the change involves the correction of a mistake and, second, that the effect of the correction is that it adversely affects the title of a registered proprietor.[379] Alteration is wider than this and includes any changes which are made to the register that do not adversely affect the title of a registered proprietor.[380] This distinction is important because the indemnity provisions contained in Schedule 8 are relevant to cases of rectification but not to alterations. To reiterate, rectification is a process the effect of which prejudicially affects a registered proprietor. Because of that, compensation in the form of an indemnity is regarded as being appropriate. Other alterations can be made to the register which do not operate to prejudicially affect the registered proprietor and, as a result, no indemnity is payable.

5.4.2 **Jurisdiction to alter the register**

The court may make an order for the alteration of the register in one of three situations. These are:

(i) correcting a mistake;

(ii) bringing the register up to date; and

(iii) giving effect to any estate, right or interest excepted from the effect of registration.[381]

---

[374] See, e.g., *Re 139 High Street, Deptford* [1951] Ch. 884.

[375] The terms 'correction' and 'change' are used at this stage because 'alteration', which might otherwise be used, has a technical meaning under the LRA 2002.

[376] *Gold Harp Properties Ltd v. MacLeod* [2014] EWCA Civ. 1084 at [23] *per* Underhill L.J.

[377] For excellent discussions which highlight the potential injustice caused to such people, see E. Lees (2013) 76 M.L.R. 62; S. Gardner [2013] Conv. 530, especially at 536 and A. Goymour [2013] C.L.J. 617. For a related discussion, which is critical of what is perceived to be the undue protection given to purchasers, see S. Cooper (2015) 131 L.Q.R. 108. See also the comments of Mummery L.J. in *Parshall v. Hackney* [2013] EWCA Civ. 240 at [62].

[378] Section 65.   [379] LRA 2002, Sched. 4, para. 1.

[380] See *Prashar v. Tunbridge Wells Borough Council* [2012] EWHC 1734 (Ch) at [8] *per* Mr Alan Stanfield Q.C., sitting as a Deputy High Court judge.

[381] Under para. 2 of Sched. 4 to the LRA 2002.

Paragraph 2 of Sched. 4 to the LRA 2002 also provides that an order made under this paragraph has effect when served on the registrar to impose a duty on him to give effect to it.[382]

Paragraph 5 of the Schedule confers on the registrar the same jurisdiction as is conferred upon the court, by para. 2 of the Schedule, with the additional power to remove superfluous entries from the register. Unless the registered proprietor is in possession of the land, in which case there are restrictions on the power to order the alteration of the register, so that the case comes within either para. 2 or para. 5, then, unless there are exceptional circumstances, an order must be made.[383] In other words, assuming that one of the criteria for alteration is satisfied, if the proprietor is in possession of the land, there is a presumption against alteration, whereas if he is not, then the presumption is in favour of such an order.[384] In applications made to the registrar, if agreement cannot be reached between the parties, then the matter is referred to the First-tier tribunal.[385]

5.4.3 Mistake

Under the LRA 1925, the power was given to rectify the register if one of a number of grounds was established. In a misguided attempt to encapsulate the previous law within one general definition, the LRA 2002 confers jurisdiction to rectify the register for the purpose of correcting a mistake. What is meant by the word 'mistake' is, however, far from clear.[386] This lack of clarity has come to the fore in the important situation when the parties to the rectification action are not the original parties to the transaction which has led to rectification proceedings. The problem has tended to arise in cases of fraud, although the attendant problems are not limited to this type of case. Various scenarios can occur.[387]

- The first is a 'two party' mistake; for example, where A was the registered proprietor[388] and, for some reason, be it fraud or a more honest mistake, B becomes the proprietor of part or all of the land of which A was previously registered proprietor.[389] The action is between A and B.

- The second is a 'three party mistake' where C is the registered proprietor. D then impersonates C and purports to transfer the land to E.[390] This time, the proceedings will be between C and E, both of whom may be innocent of any wrongdoing, although it may be the case that E has been guilty of a lack of proper care.

- These scenarios can escalate. For example, F is the registered proprietor. By reason of fraud or some other cause, G is wrongly registered as the proprietor. G then transfers title to H who is registered as proprietor. H also creates a charge in favour of a bank. In this scenario, the action for alteration is brought by F against both H and the bank. How these different scenarios are treated will be considered shortly. First, consideration can be given to mistakes which do not go to the question of title, insofar as that term relates to ownership of the land itself.

---

[382] LRA 2002, Sched. 4, para. 2.

[383] Ibid., paras 3(3), 5(3); Land Registration Rules 2003, r. 126.

[384] *Gold Harp Properties Ltd v. MacLeod* [2014] EWCA Civ. 1084 at [21] *per* Underhill L.J.

[385] LRA 2002, s. 73(7).

[386] For a helpful discussion of the various meanings of mistake, see S. Cooper [2013] C.L.J. 341 and Cooper [2018] Conv. 225.

[387] The various scenarios were first discussed at length in the important articles referred to in n. 393.

[388] The same problems may occur when the error occurs on first registration of title and where A, prior to the registration of B as proprietor, was the owner of the land.

[389] For the very rare situation where both A and B were, simultaneously, registered as proprietors of the same land, see *Parshall v. Hackney* [2013] EWCA Civ. 240. For critical comment, see L. Xu [2013] 129 L.Q.R. 477; K. Lees [2013] Conv. 222.

[390] See *Malory Enterprises Ltd v. Cheshire Homes (UK) Ltd* [2002] Ch. 216.

5.4.3.1 **Mistaken entries or omissions**

Under the LRA 1925, jurisdiction existed to order rectification if a person was aggrieved by an entry or omission on the register.[391] This would be apt to cover the situation to give effect to a land charge which had been correctly registered under the LCA 1972 and which, for some reason, had not been included on the register of title.[392] This may occur when the land charge was behind the root of title and has only come to light some time after registration of title has occurred. This would now appear to come within the meaning of mistake although, as the proprietor is likely to be in possession of the land, it is improbable that rectification will be ordered.[393]

It has been suggested that rectification could have been ordered under s. 82, LRA 1925 to give effect to an unprotected minor interest which had become void for non-registration against a registered proprietor.[394] This always seemed unsound as it would make little sense to hold first that a proprietor had taken free from an interest and then to rectify the register to give effect to that same interest.[395] The argument that the register should be rectified in these circumstances seems to be even less tenable under the LRA 2002 as it is impossible to see what mistake has been made.

While provision has, since the outset, been made for the register to be rectified in the case of fraud, the 1925 LRA construed this to mean a fraud perpetrated on the Registry[396] so that, if a transfer occurred as a result of fraud practised on the transferor, in the sense that the transaction was voidable rather than void, rectification would not be ordered under the statute.[397] In such circumstances, the aggrieved person should seek to have the transfer set aside and, this having been done, secure the alteration of the register to bring it up to date.[398] If a conveyance or, more likely, a mortgage is forged,[399] then jurisdiction would have been available to rectify the register as the fraud would have been practised on the Registry. Under the LRA 2002, because a forged document had been lodged at the Registry, the ensuing registration would be mistaken and so the register could be rectified in order to correct that mistake. Clearly, in these circumstances, the forger would not be entitled to any indemnity.

Recent cases have elaborated on this question of a mistaken entry, both accidental in *NRAM v. Evans* and a deliberate forgery in *Antoine v. Barclays*. In *NRAM Ltd v. Evans*, the Bank (Northern Rock) had made an administrative error by mistakenly lodging a form (called an e-DS1 discharge form) with the Land Registry with respect to a mortgage taken out by Mr and Mrs Evans.[400] The key question for the Court of Appeal was whether the subsequent re-registration of the charge constituted the rectification of a mistake or whether the re-registration was an update to the register. Was the purpose behind the alteration to bring the register up to date[401] or was it to correct a mistake?[402] There is no definition of a 'mistake' in the LRA 2002.[403]

---

[391] LRA 1925, s. 82(1)(b).

[392] See *Rees v. Peters* [2011] EWCA Civ. 836. Cf. *Horrill v. Cooper (2000)* Unreported, Court of Appeal.

[393] See 5.4.7.

[394] See R.J. Smith (1977) 93 L.Q.R. 341 at 343–5; *Orakpo v. Manson Developments Ltd* [1977] 1 All E.R. 666 at 678 *per* Buckley L.J., affirmed without reference to this point: [1978] A.C. 95.

[395] D.C. Jackson (1978) 94 L.Q.R. 239 at 244; M.P. Thompson [1985] C.L.J. 280 at 299–301.

[396] *Norwich & Peterborough Building Society v. Steed* [1993] Ch. 116 at 134 *per* Scott L.J.

[397] Ibid. at 137 *per* Scott L.J. not following *Re Leighton's Conveyance* [1936] 1 All E.R. 667. See C. Davis [1992] Conv. 293.

[398] See 5.4.2. Bringing the register up to date.

[399] See *First National Securities Ltd v. Hegerty* [1985] Q.B. 550; *Ahmed v. Kendrick* (1987) 56 P. & C.R. 120. Cf. *Mortgage Corporation Ltd v. Shaire* [2001] Ch. 743, criticized by M.P. Thompson [2000] Conv. 329 at 331–2.

[400] [2018] 1 W.L.R. 639.   [401] Paragraph 2(1)(b) of Sched. 4 of the Land Registration Act 2002.

[402] Paragraph 2(1)(a) of Sched. 4.

[403] For a contrast with the 1925 LRA see Thompson, 6th edition. The Law Commission has declined to recommend the introduction of a statutory definition of mistake into Sched. 4 although it proposes some clarifications, Law Com. No. 380, 254.

To answer the question of whether this was a 'mistake' (and so capable of being a rectification, entitling the Evans' to an indemnity), Kitchen L.J. relied on the distinction between void and voidable dispositions.[404] He held that while a void disposition should not have been made at the time and is a mistake, a voidable transaction, in contrast, is correct at the time it is made and is therefore not a mistake. Here the lodging of the e-DS1 form was a voidable transaction and so not a mistake.

Timing is key here, since the register should be accurate at the time it is consulted. If it is inaccurate at that time, then a rectification may be required. If the register is accurate, according to the known facts, then there is no question of rectification and indemnity is not appropriate. The register may subsequently be altered but it was accurate at the time it was consulted. As Kitchen L.J. concluded:

> a voidable disposition is valid until it is rescinded and the entry in the register of such a disposition before it is rescinded cannot properly be characterised as a mistake. It may be the case that the disposition was made by mistake but that does not render its entry on the register a mistake, and it is entries on the register with which Schedule 4 is concerned.

In other words, an entry cannot retroactively become a mistake. The register should be a complete statement of title at the time (the mirror principle).[405]

This approach that the registration of a voidable disposition before it is rescinded is not a mistake was followed in *Antoine v. Barclays Bank & the Chief Land Registrar*.[406] Here the Court of Appeal held that an entry on the Land Register pursuant to a Court Order obtained using forged documents, and which had not been set aside at the time of registration, does not give rise to a 'mistake' so there was no proper basis to rectify the Register.

In *Antoine* loan documents had been forged but the basis for the registration was a Vesting Order granted by a court based on defaulted loan repayments for the property to be transferred to him and the application was accepted based solely on the Vesting Order. The forged documents were not considered. The Land Registrar was obliged to register the Vesting Order and it was outside the Registrar's powers to explore the validity of the Vesting Order which was valid and effective at the time and hadn't been set aside. Relying on the importance of the policy that the register should be a complete and accurate statement, as well as the effect of s. 58 LRA 2002 on conclusiveness, Asplin L.J. rejected the argument that the registration based on underlying documents that had been forged, but still produced a valid vesting order, was a 'mistake' for the purposes of Sched. 4 LRA 2002. She emphasized that: '[t]he mistake must be as to the state of the Register. The focus therefore, is upon the Register and not the underlying disposition in relation to the property.'[407]

Antoine v. Barclays is a decision that can provide succour to lenders as they can make loans that will not later be found to rest on 'mistakes' in circumstances such as these. However, Trevor Antoine, who would have owned the house had the forged documents been held to underpin a 'mistake' received nothing despite the fraud. As the Court of Appeal found no mistake, no indemnity was payable. Giving judgment, Asplin L.J. concluded that she 'accepted that the outcome, from Mr Antoine's perspective, is unfortunate', even though in *NRAM Ltd v. Evans*, the Court of Appeal had endorsed the view that there is a mistake if the registrar makes, fails to make, or alters an entry in the register but would not have done so if he or she had known the true or full facts. Of course, the mistake was not made by the Land Registry (there being insufficient time or resources to check the

---

[404] This has been called an 'outrageous' distinction. For a discussion see *Antoine v. Barclays & the Chief Land Registrar* at [30–8].

[405] Citing Ruoff and Roper, *The Law and Practice of Registered Conveyancing*, 46.009.

[406] [2018] EWCA Civ. 2846.   [407] Ibid. at [40].

propriety of underlying documents for vesting orders such as these). However, these administrative shortcuts might be thought to fall unfairly on victims of fraud. While, the Law
Commission has been clear that land registration is not a closed system, so far it does not
seem clear how a remedy for these types of disputes might be found.[408]

5.4.3.2 Transfer to third party

Another problematic scenario is where the fraudster operates to transfer title to an innocent third party rather than to himself: the second of the scenarios envisaged above.
This problem was considered by the Court of Appeal in *Malory Enterprises Ltd v. Cheshire
Homes (UK) Ltd*[409] Company A was the registered proprietor of land. By means of forgery,
B, an entity masquerading as company A, purported to transfer the land to company C,
who was registered as proprietor. When A sought to correct the position, it was held that,
as B was not the registered proprietor, it did not have the statutory powers conferred on
that person by the Act. Moreover, the effect of registration was to confer the legal title
upon C while leaving the beneficial title in A. The upshot of this was that A, as the absolute
beneficial owner, could simply call on C to transfer the legal title to it. Changing the register to reflect this would amount to bringing it up to date,[410] which amounts to alteration
rather than rectification, with the result that that no indemnity would be payable to C.

The decision that A was entitled to recover the land is reasonable because, otherwise,
the registration procedure would have operated to deprive A of its land, through no fault
or even involvement of its own: a result which is difficult to defend. The reasoning process
creates difficulty, however, in that, although it enabled the restoration of the status quo
ante, it afforded no compensation to the person who was deprived of what the registration of title had conferred upon him. This is because of para. 1(3) of Sched. 8 to the LRA
2002, which provides that no indemnity is payable until a decision has been made to alter
the register for the purpose of correcting a mistake; and the loss suffered by reason of the
mistake is to be determined in the light of that decision. If it is decided that no mistake
has been made at all, then no indemnity is payable to the person who has lost the land of
which he was registered as proprietor. This significantly undermines the state guarantee of
title, which is one of the principles underlying the scheme of registration of title.

The subsequent overruling of *Malory* by the Court of Appeal in *Swift 1st Ltd v. Chief
Land Registrar*[411] on the basis that the former decision was reached *per incuriam* is to be
welcomed. If a case like *Malory* reoccurred then, subject to a determination of whether
the claim to rectification could take effect as an overriding interest,[412] the position would
be that rectification could still be ordered, this time on the basis of the correction of a
mistake.

5.4.3.3 Transactions following earlier forgery or mistake

A further problem which has arisen is the situation encapsulated in the third scenario envisaged earlier, where A is the registered proprietor. Because of fraud, or some other error,
B, wrongly, replaces A as the registered proprietor. B then transfers the title to C, who is
registered as the new proprietor. C also creates a mortgage in favour of a bank, who is
registered as the proprietor of a charge. When all of this comes to light, A seeks to have the
register rectified. The problem is to identify whether the registration of C and the bank has
been the result of a mistake. While it is true that the original registration of B could properly be described as being the result of a mistake, the same is not true of the registration

---

[408] Since there was no mistake, this type of situations would not benefit from the Law Commission's
recommendations on reform for mistake. (2018) Law Com. No. 380, Recommendations 22 and 23.
[409] [2002] Ch. 216.   [410] See 5.4.4.   [411] [2015] EWCA Civ. 338.   [412] See 5.4.5.1.

of C and the bank. Precisely because B was the registered proprietor, he had the powers conferred by the LRA 2002 (the 'statutory magic' and the operation of s. 58 LRA 2002) and so the registration of C and the bank, pursuant to a transfer and the creation of a charge by C, was not a mistake by anyone.[413] The alternative view was that the original mistaken registration of B continued to be effective and, consequently, subsequent dealings which followed sequentially from that original registration continued to be tainted by the original mistake and, so, jurisdiction existed to correct that mistake.[414]

This issue, which was described as being 'one which raised considerable difficulty',[415] is as it determines whether there is any jurisdiction to rectify the register at all. If the answer to this question is 'no', this would mean that there is no jurisdiction to award an indemnity to A, to give him, in effect, compensation in lieu of the return of the land which has been taken from him. That outcome may amount to a breach of art. 1 of the First Protocol to the European Convention on Human Rights.[416] Happily this, and another important issue which the Act had failed to clarify, has been settled in the seminal decision in *Gold Harp Properties Ltd v. MacLeod*.[417]

5.4.3.4 Continuing mistake: *Gold Harp Properties v. MacLeod*

The claimants, two teachers, held leases for 135 years in respect of roof space in a large house. The original landlord, as part of a scheme to enable him to acquire that space which he intended to redevelop, orchestrated a series of events designed to achieve that end without compensating his tenants. First, he transferred the freehold to his son who, it was found, operated entirely at the behest of his father. A firm of bailiffs were then instructed to effect a formal re-entry of the property[418] on the ground that payment of the ground rent was three months in arrears. A statutory declaration was made that the original leases had been determined by peaceable re-entry. Upon receipt of this declaration, the Land Registry closed the titles of the tenants. The son then granted a long lease of the entire roof space to a company and this lease was duly registered. The lease was assigned on two occasions, the ultimate assignee being Gold Harp. Although the assignment was said to have been in consideration of £150,000 there was no evidence that this had ever been paid. Gold Harp was a company controlled by the original freeholder. While one might have thought that there would have been a strong argument that the various transactions could have been set aside on the ground that they were shams,[419] the claimants instead argued that the register should be rectified to correct a mistake. The mistake in question was that the information contained in the statutory declaration was wrong in that the landlord had not been entitled to terminate the lease. The difficulty was that, assuming the transactions were genuine, the registration of Gold Harp was not, itself, a mistake; that mistake had occurred earlier.

Having engaged in an extensive review of the authorities, including the views of various adjudicators, Underhill L.J. concluded that, although the subsequent registration could not be regarded as having been a mistake, the correct interpretation was essentially to

---

[413] This view was accepted by the Court of Appeal in *Barclays Bank Plc v. Guy* [2008] EWCA Civ. 452.

[414] For support for the continuing mistake theory, see *Quinto v. Santiago Castillo Ltd* [2008] Privy Council Appeal No. 27 at [38]–[39] *per* Lord Phillips; *Odugwu v. Vastguide Ltd* [2009] EWHC 3565 (Ch). See also the comments in an unsuccessful attempt to reopen earlier litigation in *Guy v. Barclays Bank Plc* [2010] EWCA Civ. 1396 at [35] *per* Lord Neuberger M.R.

[415] *Paton v. Todd* [2012] EWHC 1248 (Ch) at [50] *per* Morgan J. For a valuable analysis of the conflicting views and consequences thereof, see E. Lees (2013) 76 M.L.R. 62 at 65–75.

[416] See *Knights Construction (March) Ltd v. Roberto Mac Ltd* [2011] 2 EGLR. 124 at [126]–[129] cited with approval in *Gold Harp Properties Ltd v. MacLeod* [2014] EWCA Civ. 1084 at [80] *per* Underhill L.J.

[417] [2014] EWCA Civ. 1084. For a valuable discussion, see A. Goymour [2015] Conv. 253.

[418] See 10.10.3.2.   [419] See 10.3.4.1.

adopt the view that the original mistake, in this case the wrongful closure of the title to the claimants' leases, continued to operate. This meant that the court had jurisdiction to rectify the register, a decision which led to the remaining difficult problem: determining the effect of rectification.

5.4.3.5 **The effect of rectification: prospective or retrospective change?**

Once it was decided that the register should be rectified, this led to the difficult issue as to the time from which that rectification should take effect. It was argued for the defendants that, if rectification was ordered, it should take effect prospectively, that is from the date of rectification. In support of this argument was cited para. 8 of Sched. 4 to the LRA 2002, which provides that the powers under the Schedule to alter the register, so far as relating to rectification, extend to changing *for the future* the priority of any interest affecting the registered estate or charge concerned. This, coupled with the decision in *Freer v. Unwins*,[420] and *dicta* in *Malory Enterprises Ltd v. Cheshire Homes (UK) Ltd*,[421] provided support for the proposition that any order for rectification should take effect from the date of the order and not before.

The problem with this argument was that, if correct, any rectification of the register would confer no benefit on the claimants. Before the mistake was made, the long leases, which may be termed interest one, were correctly registered. After they were wrongly closed, and the new lease, interest two, was registered, and this was then the only existing interest. If the register was rectified with effect from the date on which the order was made, the order of priority would be interest two followed by interest one. Rectification would then have been entirely valueless from the perspective of the holders of interest one. To avoid this conclusion, and following a detailed discussion of various authorities and the rival views of practitioner texts,[422] Underhill L.J. was able to conclude that in order for rectification to correct the mistake, it was necessary for the rectification to operate from the date the mistake was made. The effect of this was to create the order of priority: the teachers' leases followed by Gold Harp's.

While the decision in *Gold Harp* has done much to bring sense to an important aspect of registered land, the Law Commission has recognized that there remain problems in particular if interests are acquired after the mistake. The most difficult area is where A is registered as proprietor. Then, by fraud, or other mistake, B wrongly becomes registered as proprietor of the land. B then transfers the land for value to C, who creates a mortgage in favour of a bank. The claim for rectification is, in this case, brought by A against C and the bank. Should the register be rectified in these circumstances? In 2016 the Law Commission accepted the view of 'mistake' as applied in *Gold Harp*, recommending that the register should *not* be rectified so as to prejudice the registered proprietor who is in possession of land without that proprietor's consent, except where (a) the registered proprietor caused or contributed to the mistake by fraud or lack of proper care, or (b) less than ten years have passed since the original mistake and it would be unjust to rectify the register.[423] In 2018, the Law Commission returned to this approach, endorsing the outcome in *Gold Harp* so that where the register is rectified to reinstate a derivative interest, the rectification can also restore the priority of the interest. It recommended that the legislation should be amended to provide that:

---

[420] [1976] Ch. 288.

[421] [2002] Ch. 216 at [79] *per* Arden L.J. Clarke and Schiemann L.JJ. expressly reserved their opinions on this point, at [87] and [90] respectively.

[422] *Emmet and Farrand on Title*, 9.027–9.028, favouring retrospectivity, and Ruoff and Roper, *The Law and Practice of Registered Conveyancing*, 46–0170–18 to the opposite effect. This latter view was also supported by Megarry and Wade, *The Law of Real Property*, 7–136.

[423] Law Commission Consultation Paper (2016), no. 227, para. 13.120.

> the LRA 2002 provides that where the registration of a registered proprietor is held to be a mistake, registration of any estates or charges granted by the registered proprietor, and any entry made in the register in respect of a derivative interest granted by the registered proprietor, should also be classed as a mistake.[424]

The Law Commission drew a distinction between rectification being 'backward-looking', which it recommended, so the priority that, in this case, B's lease should have had, can be assessed and rectified. It did not think, however, that rectification should be retroactive. Although the lease was erroneously removed from the register, this does not mean that, for example, B could now sue any occupier who has been there instead of B in trespass.[425]

The Law Commission also recommended a ten-year 'long stop' for rectification, recommending that after this time rectification should not be granted even if there was a mistake. This proposal, which adopts the time period that is now in place in cases of adverse possession, is broadly seen to advocate a reasonable compromise between the recognition of the enduring rights of the original landowner and the person who has relied on the register to assure himself that the transferor owns the land he is transferring. Indeed, unlike the other scenarios considered above, this is truly a case of a transferee placing reliance on the actual state of the register of title. In other cases of fraud, the problem has generally been that the transferee has been misled so as to believe that the person with whom he is dealing is actually the person named as the proprietor on the register of title. This type of fraud, which is based upon impersonation, occurs throughout the commercial world. What is particular to land is that there is state-backed insurance against certain fraudulent dealings with this form of property, whereas there is no such safety net in existence in respect of other forms of property.[426]

5.4.4 Alteration

This innocuous-looking provision in LRA 2002, Sched. 4, para. 2 is an example of alteration of the register and not rectification. The significance of this distinction is that, unlike the position when the register is rectified, no indemnity is payable after the register is altered. Because no indemnity is payable if the register is altered under this head, it is important to be clear as to the scope of it. Unfortunately, the matter is not as clear as one would like.

The ambit of the expression of bringing of the register up to date is apt to cover the situation where, perhaps through marriage or death, the names in the proprietorship register are changed to reflect the current position.[427] Also within the scope of this provision are rights that arise after registration, such as when an easement by prescription is established, and the register is then altered to reflect the true position.[428] Perhaps less obviously, it will also include the entry onto the register of what was previously an interest which has overridden registration.

In *Chowood v. Lyall (No.2)*,[429] which was decided under the previous legislation,[430] the register was rectified to give effect to a possessory title established over part of the land that had been included in the title of the registered proprietor. Under the LRA 1925 Act, the change to the register was termed rectification. Under the LRA 2002 the outcome

---

[424] (2018) Law Com. No. 380, 279.   [425] (2018) Law Com. No. 380, 284.

[426] (2018) Law Com. No. 380, 267.

[427] Jurisdiction to alter the register to correct a mistaken address is also, apparently, conferred by this provision. See *Isaaks v Charlton Triangle Homes Ltd* [2015] EWHC 2611 (Ch).

[428] See 12.6.   [429] [1930] 2 Ch. 156.

[430] LRA 1925, s. 83(2), which, unlike the current legislation, makes specific provision for rectification to give effect to an overriding interest.

would now be alteration of the register, not rectification. This is because, as a registered proprietor will always take subject to an interest which overrides registration, the entry of the matter on the register serves only to recognize the existing position. It does not put the registered proprietor in any worse position than was the case prior to the change to the register.[431] For this reason, if the register is altered to give effect to an overriding interest, the registered proprietor suffers no loss and is not, therefore, entitled to any indemnity.[432]

5.4.5 Fraud

In *Malory Enterprises Ltd v. Cheshire Homes (UK) Ltd*,[433] the Court of Appeal held that the effect of the forgery was simply to clothe C with the legal title. The upshot of this finding was that, because C held the land on a bare trust for A, A could simply call for A to re-transfer the legal title to it. Had this case been decided under the LRA 2002, the order of the court for C to do that would therefore have amounted to the bringing of the register up to date. As a result, C would not have been entitled to an indemnity: a conclusion widely felt to be inimical to the state guarantee of title, something which is regarded as one of the underpinning principles of the land registration system. In *Swift 1st Ltd v. Chief Land Registrar*,[434] the Court of Appeal declined to follow *Malory* on this point, considering it to have been decided *per incuriam*.[435] This does not, however, resolve all the problems concerning the alteration of the register and any possible indemnity.

5.4.5.1 Claim to rectification and overriding status

There was a second aspect of the decision in *Malory*, which, arguably, still represents the law and, if it does, could operate in much the same way as the now discredited main ground of the decision. This ground for the decision, described by the Law Commission as 'The *Malory* 2 argument',[436] was that the claimant's case for rectification, to undo the effect of the forgery, took effect as an overriding interest. The basis of this argument was that a claim to rectify the register was proprietary in nature and, if the claimant was also in actual occupation, that right took effect as an overriding interest. While this argument was accepted in *Malory*, it is argued that it is wrong in principle.

The first objection relates to the nature of the right. Under both the LRA 1925 and the LRA 2002, there is no absolute right to rectification of the register. A discretion exists as to whether this should be ordered. This claim is, therefore, akin to the existence of a mere equity.[437] Unlike the position under the LRA 1925, the provisions of which were applicable in *Malory*, s. 116, LRA 2002 provides that a mere equity is capable of subsisting as an interest which can override registration. This does not, however, conclude the matter. All that s. 116 can do is to enable a particular claim to take effect against a transferee for value; it cannot, or at least should not, upgrade the nature of the claim itself. So if A has a discretionary claim to rectify the register against B, and B transfers the land to C, it is very difficult to see how what was discretionary against B can be upgraded to a right as against C. C should not be in a worse position than was the person who transferred the land to him, B. This was seemingly recognized in *Malory*, when Arden L.J. said that there is 'a distinction to be drawn between a right to seek rectification and the fulfilment of that right'.[438] This must mean that the claim to rectification against C remains a matter of

---

[431] See *Re Chowood's Registered Land* [1933] Ch. 574 at 582 *per* Clauson J.
[432] Ibid.   [433] [2002] Ch. 216.   [434] [2015] EWCA Civ. 330.
[435] For a discussion of the debates around *Malory* see *Rashid v. Nasrullah* [2018] EWCA Civ. 2685.
[436] Law Commission Consultation Paper (2016), para. 13.60.
[437] See 3.6.3.   [438] [2002] Ch. 216 at [67].

discretion and does not become a right and, consequently, to describe it as an overriding interest in not very meaningful.

A second objection to holding that the claim to rectification took effect as an overriding interest in *Malory* is that it did not predate the registration of the proprietor against whom rectification was sought.[439] This argument was raised but rejected in *Malory*, where Arden L.J. said:

> Nor do I accept the argument that the right to seek rectification comes into existence only after Cheshire is registered. The registration of Cheshire give rise to the right to seek rectification at the same time as, and as part of, the same transaction. I do not consider that the registration can be treated as predating the right to seek rectification in this way.[440]

This is very difficult to follow. On the facts of *Malory*, the claim to rectification could only come into being when the transferee was registered as the proprietor of land. It could not possibly predate that moment in time. To say that a transferee is bound by an interest that did not, and could not, exist prior to that registration is meaningless. Moreover, the reasoning is completely at odds with that taken by the Supreme Court in *Scott v. Southern Pacific Mortgages Ltd*,[441] where, on a somewhat simplified version of the facts, it was held that a mortgagee was not bound by a tenancy which had been purported to have been created by the mortgagor prior to the transfer of the legal title against which the mortgage took effect. The Court refused to accept that the tenancy had come into being a fraction of a second prior to the creation of the mortgage and so had priority to it. It cannot be the case that a claim to rectification which, by definition, cannot predate the registration of the transferee can take effect as an overriding interest when that is not the case with respect to an interest which, purportedly, was created prior to that event taking place. The provisional recommendation of the Law Commission in 2016 was that the right to seek alteration or rectification of the register should not be capable of taking effect as an interest which overrides registration.[442] In 2018, the Law Commission went further still, recommending that the ability to seek rectification under Sched. 4 should not be considered a proprietary right at all (and so cannot be overriding).[443]

5.4.6 Boundary disputes

When title to land is registered, the land is identified by reference to a title plan. In the vast majority of cases, the boundaries are what are termed 'general boundaries'; that is, they do not determine the exact line of the boundary between two adjoining properties.[444] The accuracy of the boundaries is only guaranteed in the fairly rare situation when the boundaries are shown as being fixed. As is notorious, neighbours can engage in extraordinarily acrimonious, and extremely expensive, disputes as to the ownership of seemingly very small amounts of land. The resolution of such disputes may involve either the determination of the proper location of a boundary or, alternatively, what might be the real issue is whether, by mistake, a person has been registered as proprietor of an area of land when this should not have occurred. If it is found that the boundary has been located in the wrong position then, save in exceptional circumstances, the plan will be altered to relocate

---

[439] See E. Cooke [2014] Conv. 441 at 447; P. Milne [2015] Conv. 356 at 362.
[440] [2002] Ch. 216 at [69].
[441] [2014] UKSC 52. See also *Abbey National Building Society v. Cann* [1991] 1 A.C. 56.
[442] Law Commission Consultation Paper (2016), para. 13.76.
[443] (2018) Law Com. No. 380, 257.
[444] LRA 2002, s. 60(1), (2).

the boundary to the correct position.[445] While, in a sense, this causes loss to the losing party, this will not warrant the payment of an indemnity because there was no initial guarantee as to the accuracy of the boundary. On the other hand, if the real issue is not the actual location of the boundary, but a substantive measurement of a plot of land, then a correction of the register will amount to rectification and not alteration,[446] with the result that an indemnity may be available to the losing party.

At times, this distinction, albeit a potentially important one, may be easier to state than to apply[447] and, perhaps surprisingly, is not determined by the area of land at issue. Thus, in *Prashar v. Tunbridge Wells Borough Council*,[448] the area in dispute was substantial and ran for almost the entire length of the respective titles of the two parties. By way of contrast in *Parshall v. Hackney*,[449] two people had been simultaneously registered as proprietors of a triangle of land that was less than two metres across and only four metres long. There was no dispute as to where the original boundary was; what had happened was that the Land Registry had erroneously included the disputed triangle in both titles and the case was, quite rightly,[450] treated as a case involving the exercise of discretion as to whether or not the register should be rectified to correct a mistake.[451] The most helpful way of distinguishing between the two situations is whether recourse is had to the general common law presumptions to resolve the dispute, so that what is really at issue 'is simply to give a more accurate delineation of a general boundary'.[452]

However in *Rashid v. Nasrullah*, the Court of Appeal held that *Parshall v. Hackney* was incompatible with *Pye v. Graham*,[453] confirming that dispossession does not need to be unlawful in order for time to run, and purported to overrule it.[454] The practical consequence of *Rashid v. Nasrullah* is that someone who has a wrongly registered title in their name can acquire a good title by adverse possession, benefiting people inadvertently affected by registration errors. King and Peter Jackson L.JJ. went further by noting that while there are some categories of people in whose favour time cannot run (trustees, tenants, and licensees), there is 'no policy logic' to expand these categories to include the registered owner. While the Court of Appeal expressed sympathy for the original owner, it held that he had lost his land as a result of not challenging the adverse possession within the requisite period and this would have happened whether or not the squatter 'for good measure forges a transfer document' as well.[455]

5.4.6.1 Exceptions from registration

If a person is registered with a title less than absolute, then he takes subject to various interests which were excepted from registration.[456] When it is discovered what those interests are, the register may be altered to enable the register to reflect more accurately the true position.

---

[445] Land Registration Rules 2003, r. 126. As to what can constitute exceptional circumstances, see *Derbyshire County Council v. Fallon* [2007] EWHC 1236 (Ch) discussed by M. Dixon [2008] Conv. 238.

[446] See *Knights Construction (March) Ltd v. Roberto Mac Ltd* [2011] 2 E.G.L.R. 123 at [39] *per* Mr Michael Mark.

[447] See Law Commission Consultation Paper (2016), para. 15.32.

[448] [2012] EWHC 1734 (Ch).   [449] [2013] EWCA Civ. 240.

[450] Contrast K. Lees [2013] Conv. 222 at 225 who argues, based largely and erroneously on the size of the disputed plot, that this case should have been treated as a boundary dispute.

[451] For a highly critical discussion of this, see L. Xu (2013) 129 L.Q.R. 477, especially at 479–80.

[452] *Drake v. Fripp* [2011] EWCA Civ. 1279 at [22] *per* Lewison L.J., where the amount of land 'lost' as a result of the resetting of the boundary was 1.5 acres, some 6 per cent of the total acreage comprised in the registered title.

[453] [2002] UKHL 30.   [454] [2018] EWCA Civ. 2685.

[455] [2018] EWCA Civ. 2685 at [81].   [456] See LRA 2002, s. 11(6)(7).

5.4.6.2 Removal of superfluous entries

The registrar is given jurisdiction to remove superfluous entries on the register. Examples of when this jurisdiction may be exercised are when a restriction has been entered on the register to freeze all dealings with a registered estate, but the circumstances which made that precaution necessary have passed; an interest protected by one entry was adequately protected by another; and a restriction on the powers of a registered proprietor has ceased to apply.[457]

5.4.7 Restrictions on jurisdiction to alter the register

As was the case under the LRA 1925, the jurisdiction to order the alteration of the register is seriously limited when the registered proprietor is in possession of the property. Under para. 3(2) of Sched. 4 to the LRA 2002, if an alteration affects the title of a registered estate in land, no order may be made under para. 2 without the proprietor's consent in relation to land in his possession unless either he has by fraud or lack of proper care caused or substantially contributed to the mistake or, if for any other reason, it would be unjust for the alteration not to be made.

Before looking more closely at this provision, one important preliminary point should be made. The additional protection afforded to a proprietor in possession extends to rectification of the register; it does not relate to an alteration of the register which does not prejudicially affect him.[458] So, if the land is subject to an interest which overrides a registered disposition, and the register is altered to reflect the true position, the alteration has not affected the title of the registered proprietor. Consequently, alteration will be ordered whether or not the proprietor is in possession. This point was dealt with explicitly under the previous legislation[459] but implicitly by the LRA 2002.

5.4.7.1 Alterations on the basis of possession

Under s. 131(1), LRA 2002, a registered proprietor is in possession of land if it is physically in his possession,[460] or in that of a person who is entitled to be registered as the proprietor of a registered estate. The section then goes on to make specific provision for certain relationships. Section 131(2) provides that, when land is in the physical possession of the second-named person, then the first-named person is to be treated for the purposes of subsection (1) as being in possession. These are:

(a) landlord and tenant;

(b) mortgagor and mortgagee;[461]

(c) licensor and licensee; and

(d) trustee and beneficiary.

A squatter is not regarded as being in possession.[462]

---

[457] (2001) Law Com. No. 271, para. 10.19.
[458] See *Derbyshire County Council v. Fallon* [2007] EWHC 1326 (Ch) at [27] *per* Mr Christopher Nugee Q.C.
[459] LRA 1925, s. 82(3).
[460] The previous position, laid down in *Kingsalton v. Thames Water Developments Ltd* [2002] 1 P. & C.R. 15, that a person was considered to be in possession of the land simply because he was the registered proprietor of it, has been reversed by this section.
[461] This reverses the previous position as exemplified in *Hayes v. Nwajiaku* [1994] E.G.C.S. 106.
[462] LRA 2002, s. 133(3).

5.4.7.2 Lack of proper care

As originally drafted, the register could be rectified against a registered proprietor in possession who had contributed to the error. This meant that, if a person lodged an inaccurate conveyance, then he would be regarded as having contributed to the error with the result that he did not enjoy the protection afforded to proprietors in possession.[463] The introduction of the requirement of fraud or lack of proper care removed this difficulty. Although the issue of a lack of proper care relates to the proprietor against whom rectification is sought, if the person seeking rectification has, through a lack of proper care facilitated the dishonest dealings by others, this will militate against an order being made in his favour.[464]

5.4.7.3 Unjust not to rectify

The onus is on the person seeking rectification against a proprietor in possession to show that it is unjust not to rectify. This is not easy to satisfy. In particular, the mere fact that the wrong person has been registered as the proprietor of the land will not, of itself, mean that it is unjust not to rectify.[465] Instances where it has been considered to be unjust not to rectify the register have included a situation where a purchaser was perfectly well aware of the existence of a land charge which, owing to a mix up, was not revealed by a search in the land charges register.[466] Another occurred in *Johnson v. Shaw*,[467] where the paper title had been held for many years by the person seeking rectification and the land had continued to be used by him. This, coupled with the fact that the registered proprietor had contributed to the mistake, led to rectification being ordered.[468] Again, in *James Hay Pension Trustees Ltd v. Cooper Estates Ltd*,[469] rectification was ordered to remove a 14-foot strip of land from the title of a proprietor in possession. The reason it was considered to be unjust not to rectify was that the proprietor was 'the accidental owner of a small parcel of land which it never intended to acquire and which is of no use to it save as a means of extracting a ransom payment . . . , a stand which however legitimate commercially does not commend itself to this court as in any way meritorious'.[470]

The decision in *Sainsbury's Supermarkets Ltd v. Olympia Homes Ltd*[471] provides an interesting example of the exercise of this jurisdiction. A Mr Hughes bought land from British Gas and applied for first registration of title. Because he failed to respond to requisitions on title made by the Land Registry, this application lapsed. The consequence of this was the legal title revested in British Gas, leaving Mr Hughes with only the equitable title to the land. A little later, he entered into a complex arrangement with Sainsbury's, the effect of which was to create an option to purchase part of the land. Sainsbury's sought to protect this option by lodging a caution against first registration. This, however, was inapposite. What should have been done was to register a land charge.[472] Later still, a charging order was obtained against Mr Hughes's property in respect of a debt in excess of £3.75 million. The property was then sold to Olympia, who were registered as proprietors of the land. Sainsbury's, on being notified of the application for registration, did not respond and the

---

[463] See S. Cretney and G. Dworkin (1968) 84 L.Q.R. 528.

[464] See *Nouri v. Marvi* [2005] EWHC 2996 (Ch) at [51] *per* Judge Rich Q.C.

[465] See *Epps v. Esso Petroleum Ltd* [1973] 1 W.L.R. 1071; *Kingsalton v. Thames Water Development Ltd* [2002] 1 P. & C.R. 15.

[466] *Horrill v. Cooper* (1998) 78 P. & C.R. 293.   [467] [2004] 1 P. & C.R. 10.

[468] See also the robust approach to this matter in *Mannion v. Baxter* [2011] EWCA Civ. 120 at [41]–[42] *per* Jacob L.J.

[469] [2005] EWHC 36 (Ch).   [470] Ibid. at [41] *per* Hart J.

[471] [2005] EWHC 1235 (Ch). See M. Dixon [2005] Conv. 447.

[472] Whether this should have been registered against Mr Hughes or British Gas would seem to have depended on the precise time when the legal title revested in the latter: a further illustration of the problems of registration of land charges being against the name of the estate owner. See 4.8.2.

option was not entered onto the register of title. The action arose when Sainsbury's sought rectification of the register to give effect to the option.

Amongst the complications of this case was that Olympia should not have been registered as proprietors at all. This was because when the charging order was made, Mr Hughes did not own the legal estate in the land, the title having revested in British Gas. Consequently when the sale was ordered, all that he could transfer was his own equitable interest in the property. The registration of Olympia as proprietors was a mistake. The whole transaction between the creditor enforcing its security and Olympia was predicated on the basis that the option in favour of Sainsbury's was enforceable, and the purchase price reflected this. To have held the option not to be binding would have occasioned Olympia a considerable windfall, and this was considered to be unjust. Consequently Mann J. ordered rectification. This was not done on the basis simply that Olympia had notice of an unregistered interest. To have done so would undermine the registration provisions, whereby a purchaser takes free of unregistered interests. The facts went beyond that and the case provides a good example of the proper exercise of discretion.

5.4.7.4 Human rights

If a person fails to secure rectification of the register to reflect the fact that, owing to some mistake, the wrong person has been registered as the proprietor of the land, then the effect will be that he has, as a result of the registration process, been deprived of land which he previously owned. In *Kingsalton v. Thames Water Developments Ltd*,[473] it was argued that this contravened art. 1 of the First Protocol of the European Convention on Human Rights, the argument being that such a decision would deprive the company of its possessions. This was rejected. The power to decline rectification was considered to have been given for the legitimate aim in the public interest of enhancing the security of the land registration system and, having regard to the fact that the unsuccessful claimant would be entitled to an indemnity payment, no breach of the Convention was established.[474]

5.4.8 Indemnity

A remedy, which is complementary to that of alteration of the register, is the payment of an indemnity.[475] Because there is a discretion as to whether or not to alter the register, provision is made both for the payment of an indemnity when loss is suffered as a result of rectification and also when loss occurs when rectification is refused.[476]

5.4.8.1 Loss due to rectification

A person suffering loss as a result of rectification of the register is, in general, entitled to be paid an indemnity, this indemnity being paid from public funds. Thus, in a case such as *Re 139 High Street, Deptford*,[477] an indemnity was paid to a person who had wrongly been registered as proprietor of an annexe, and against whom rectification was ordered to restore the property to the person who, had title not been registered, would have been

---

[473] [2002] 1 P. & C.R. 15.

[474] Ibid. at para. 30 *per* Peter Gibson L.J.; at para. 45 *per* Arden L.J. See also Chapters 6 and 3 on adverse possession and human rights respectively.

[475] In 2015/16 a total of £8.3 million was paid under the indemnity provisions: Land Registry Annual Report 2015/16, 24.

[476] LRA 2002, Sched. 8, para. 1. An indemnity may also be paid when rectification is ordered but the person in whose favour rectification is ordered still suffers loss, thus dealing with the problem illustrated by *Freer v. Unwins* [1976] Ch. 288 although, in the light of the decision in *Gold Harp Properties Ltd v. MacLeod* [2014] EWCA Civ. 1084, this particular problem is unlikely to recur. See also 5.4.3.5.

[477] [1951] Ch. 884.

the owner of it. The position contrasts with that which pertains when title is unregistered. In that case, if a person had purported to convey land which he did not own, the conveyance would have had no effect and the purchaser would have paid money but got no title to the land. Where title is registered, he first gets title to the land and, if he is deprived of that land, by rectification, he is compensated from public funds; this is an example of the insurance principle.

5.4.8.2 Loss

As has been seen,[478] Sched. 4 to the Act distinguishes between rectification and alteration of the register. The former is a process by which mistakes can be corrected and which adversely affect the title of a proprietor, thereby causing loss. This is not the case when alteration occurs. An indemnity is only payable if either loss is caused by rectification, or by a mistake the correction of which would involve rectification. This latter provision provides, somewhat more elliptically than did its predecessor,[479] for an indemnity to be paid to a person who suffers loss when a mistake has occurred but, in the exercise of discretion, it is decided not to rectify the register. In plain English, this allows an indemnity to be paid to a person who suffers loss when, in the exercise of discretion, the register is not rectified to correct a mistake. The distinction between rectification and alteration adverted to earlier is, therefore, of considerable theoretical and practical importance.

5.4.8.3 Fraud or lack of proper care

If a person suffers loss as a result of rectification, he is not entitled to an indemnity on account of his loss suffered as a result of his own fraud or lack of proper care. Where the loss is caused partly by his own lack of proper care, any indemnity payable shall be reduced to such an extent as is just and equitable having regard to his share in the responsibility for the loss; in effect a defence of contributory negligence.[480] An example may assist.

Let us suppose a case where money is borrowed from a mortgagee by a person impersonating the proprietor or one of the proprietors. The signature on the mortgage is forged but, when it is lodged at the Registry, the charge is registered. When the fraud is discovered, the application for rectification is successful and the charge is removed from the register. If the mortgagee, who has now lost the security for the loan, seeks an indemnity, then it is thought that much will depend upon the precautions, such as the requiring of the production of passports, which were taken when obtaining the signatures to ensure that the person or persons signing the mortgage deed were who they were claiming to be.[481]

5.4.8.4 The quantum of indemnity

The amount payable as an indemnity is governed by Sched. 8, para. 6, which distinguishes between the amount payable when rectification is ordered and when it is not. In the former situation, the amount payable in respect of the loss of an estate, interest or charge is the value of that interest immediately before rectification is ordered. That is its current market value. When rectification is refused, however, as is likely to be the case when the proprietor is in possession of the land, the amount payable as an indemnity is the value at the time when the mistake was made. While logical, this is arguably unfortunate. It may be the case that the error is not discovered for some time and, if in the exercise of his discretion the adjudicator declines to rectify the register, the claimant will get an indemnity to reflect the value of the land at the time when the original error was made and not the date

---

[478] See 5.4.1.   [479] LRA 1925, s. 83.

[480] LRA 2002, Sched. 5, para. 5(1)(2). See *Dean v. Dean* (2000) 80 P. & C.R. 457.

[481] For a detailed discussion of identity issues, see Law Commission Consultation Paper (2016). paras 14.62–14.126.

of the adjudication. Given the substantial rise in the value of land, this may be a significant undervalue.

This problem was more acute as the claim to an indemnity is a contract debt and so liable to become statute barred under the Limitation Act 1980. This occurred in *Epps v. Esso Petroleum Ltd*,[482] where the fact that the claimant for rectification would receive no indemnity if the register was not rectified was unsuccessfully argued to mean that it would be unjust not to rectify the register. This particular problem is now less serious as it is provided by Sched. 8, para. 8 that, for the purpose of the Limitation Act 1980, the cause of action arises at a time when the claimant either knows or, but for his own default, might have known of the existence of the claim and rules may be made for the payment of interest on the indemnity.[483] The disparity between indemnity payable in case of rectification and non-rectification is not something which contravenes the European Convention on Human Rights,[484] although it nevertheless seems unfair. The Law Commission's proposal that, in all cases, the valuation of the land should be capped at the time when the hearing takes place[485] is welcome.

5.5 Notice of unprotected interests

In any system of registration, the question will arise as to what the position is when an interest which is registrable is not registered, but the purchaser has notice of it.[486] The provisions of the LRA 1925 appeared to provide a clear answer: that the purchaser was not bound.[487] Initially, this was also the approach of the judiciary. In *De Lusignan v. Johnson*,[488] a claim that a registered chargee was bound by an unregistered interest, of which he had prior notice, was struck out as disclosing no cause of action.

This has raised the interesting question of the extent to which the priority provisions in the LRA 2002 are affected by what might be termed general equitable principles.[489] In particular, is there a role in this context for the prevention of what is sometimes perceived as fraud? To answer this, it is important to try and identify what, if anything, is actually meant by fraud in the present context.[490] To do this, three issues will be considered: (1) the nature of the transaction; (2) an agreement by the purchaser to take subject to a particular interest; and (3) the potential role of personal remedies against a purchaser in relation to a transaction where he is aware of a prior unprotected interest.

5.5.1 Sham transactions

It is clearly established that, if a particular transaction is not genuine, a person who claims to be a purchaser for value and consequently takes free from an unprotected interest will not be allowed to do so. A classic example of this occurred in *Jones v. Lipman*.[491] The

---

[482] [1973] 1 W.L.R. 1071.   [483] LRA 2002, Sched. 8, para. 9.

[484] *Kingsalton v. Thames Water Developments Ltd* [2002] 1 P. & C.R. 15 at para. 45 *per* Arden L.J.

[485] LCCP Law Commission Consultation Paper (2016), para. 14.155.

[486] For a fuller discussion of this issue, see M.P. Thompson in Gravells (ed.), *Landmark Cases in Land Law* (Oxford, Hart Publishing, 2013), 155 at 164–78.

[487] LRA 1925, s. 20.   [488] (1973) 230 E.G. 499.

[489] [1977] 1 W.L.R. 285. For criticism, see D.J. Hayton [1977] C.L.J. 277; D.C. Jackson (1977) 94 L.Q.R. 239, especially at 242; R.J. Smith (1977) L.Q.R. 341; M.P. Thompson [1985] C.L.J. 280 at 285 and 289. Cf. S. Anderson (1977) 40 M.L.R. 600 at 606.

[490] See, general, M.P. Thompson [1985] C.L.J. 280, P.J. Cooke and D. O'Connor (2004) 120 L.Q.R. 640. M. Harding and M. Bryan in Dixon (ed.), *Modern Studies in Property Law* (vol. 5), (Oxford, Hart Publishing, 2009), Chapter 1.

[491] [1962] 1 W.L.R. 832. See also *Buckinghamshire County Council v. Briar* [2002] EWHC 2821 (Ch).

defendant, in order to escape a contract of sale which he had made, transferred the property to a company which he controlled. As the company was considered to be 'a device and a sham, which he holds before his face in attempt to avoid recognition by the eye of equity',[492] specific performance was ordered against the company, despite the original contract not having been protected by registration.

Cases such as this, while clearly correct, are highly unusual.[493] The fact that a sale is at an undervalue will not, of itself, mean that it is a sham. Thus in *Midland Bank Trust Co. Ltd v. Green*,[494] the fact that the transaction was between husband and wife, and at an undervalue, did not mean that the transaction was a sham. For such a finding to follow, the parties must be seeking to give the impression of a genuine transaction having taken place when that is not in fact true.[495] What will be key to this is whether or not the purported vendor, in reality, retains control over the property after the purported transaction has occurred. In *Green*, the purchase money changed hands and the conveyance occurred. These factors militated against the transaction being considered a sham.[496] So, although a transaction which is later stigmatized as a sham will not result in the defeat of a prior unprotected interest, it will only be in very rare cases that a transaction will be classified in this way.

5.5.2 **Agreement**

It is clear that, in certain circumstances, a purchaser of registered land can be subjected to a constructive trust. Cases such as these should have nothing to do with registration issues. A good example of this occurred in *Arthur v. Attorney-General of the Turks and Caicos Islands*.[497] Property was sold by the Crown to the defendant, who was registered as proprietor. Immediately afterwards, he resold the property to a purchaser for a very substantial profit. The defendant had been able to carry out these transactions because he had been given the opportunity to purchase the property by a minister, who had also supplied him with inside information, and who had operated corruptly. No action was brought against the current proprietor of the land who had bought the land from the defendant. Instead, the claim was that the defendant held the proceeds of sale of the land on trust for the Crown. This claim was defended on the basis that he had taken the land free from any interest of the Crown because he was a registered proprietor of the land, and any interest which the Crown had was not binding upon him because it had not been protected by registration.[498]

As an argument, this was misconceived because, until the transfer of the property to the defendant, there was no prior interest which could be binding upon him. The obligation in equity arose entirely because of the abuse of a fiduciary position by the minister, the result of which would be that he would hold any property which he acquired as a result of that abuse on constructive trust.[499] 'The intervention of equity in such cases does not reflect any pre-existing obligation but comes about solely because of the misapplication of

---

[492] [1962] 1 W.L.R. 832 at 836 *per* Russell L.J.

[493] Although for a more recent example, see *Halifax Plc v. Curry Popeck (A Firm)* [2008] EWHC 1692 (Ch).

[494] [1981] A.C. 513.

[495] See *Snook v. London and West Riding Investment Co. Ltd* [1967] 2 Q.B. 786 at 802 *per* Diplock L.J. (a hire purchase case). See also the comments in *Beerjeraz v. Dubee* [2012] UKPC 22 at [35] *per* Lord Mance.

[496] See the comments at first instance by Oliver J. [1980] Ch. 590 at 613. In *Peffer v. Rigg* nobody suggested that the transaction was a sham.

[497] [2012] UKPC 30.   [498] Ibid. at [11] *per* Sir Thomas Etherington.

[499] See *FHR European Ventures v. Cedar Capital Partners* [2014] UKSC 17, and J. Glister and J. Lee, *Hanbury and Martin, Modern Equity* (20th edn) (London, Sweet &. Maxwell 2015), 22–017–22–032.

the assets.'[500] The liability of the defendant, who no longer owned the property, was on the basis of knowing receipt of property transferred to him in breach of trust.

The potential liability of a purchaser on the basis of knowing receipt is an important one which will be addressed shortly. First, however, it should be stressed that this case was not one whereby a pre-existing proprietary claim which had not been protected by registration was enforced against a purchaser; it was a case where the involvement of the defendant in a particular transaction was what gave rise to the liability in equity. This is an important distinction.

5.5.3 Taking subject to an interest

Another area which has been considered by the courts is the comparatively rare one where a purchaser agrees with the vendor to take subject to a third party right which, absent such agreement, would not be binding on him. This occurred in *Lyus v. Prowsa Developments Ltd*[501] Land was mortgaged to a bank. The registered proprietor then contracted to sell it to the plaintiff. Before that contract could be completed, however, the bank exercised its power of sale over the property, and sold it to D1, who in turn sold the land to D2. Although it was clearly the case that, because the mortgage had priority over the subsequent contract of sale, the bank could have sold the property free from the plaintiff's contractual right,[502] it chose, at least so far as it could, not to do so.[503] Instead, each successive sale was made expressly subject to the rights of the plaintiff. Dillon J. ordered specific performance of the contract.

The reasoning was that, because the purchaser had expressly agreed to take subject to the plaintiff's right, it would be inequitable for him to renege on that undertaking, and, to prevent this from happening, a constructive trust was imposed. While this reasoning appears to be attractive, and has secured the approval, albeit *obiter*, of the Court of Appeal,[504] it has subsequently been made evident that it is to be applied extremely narrowly. In *Lloyd v. Dugdale*,[505] Sir Christopher Slade was clear that, for a constructive trust to arise, it is essential that there be an undertaking to give effect to a new obligation, and notice of its existence is not sufficient.[506] Even construed narrowly, however, there are serious difficulties with it.[507] The essential proposition which was accepted was that if A and B contract, and that contract seeks to confer rights on C, then a constructive trust should be imposed to give effect to that agreement. This would seem to conflict with the doctrine of privity of contract,[508] which prevailed at the time when this case was decided.

The particular problem thrown up by *Lyus v. Prowsa Developments Ltd* would now be resolved by s. 1 of the Contracts (Rights of Third Parties) Act 1999. Under this section, where two parties to a contract seek to confer rights upon a third party, then that party may sue upon that contract and the remedies available may include specific performance. The more general issue remains, however, which is the extent to which seemingly clear statutory provisions should be undermined by the application of general equitable principles.

---

[500] *Williams v. Central Bank of Nigeria* [2014] UKSC 10 at [9] *per* Lord Sumption.
[501] [1982] 1 W.L.R. 832.
[502] See also *Valais v. Clydesdale Bank Plc* [2011] EWHC 94 (Ch).
[503] For criticism of this decision which, if effective, operated to the detriment of other creditors, see P. Jackson [1983] Conv. 64 at 67.
[504] *Ashburn Anstalt v. Arnold* [1989] Ch. 1 at 24 *per* Fox L.J.
[505] [2002] 2 P. & C.R. 13 at [52].
[506] See also *Chattey v. Farndale Holdings Ltd* (1996) 75 P. & C.R. 298 at 317 where Morritt L.J. stressed that notice of a prior interest would, on its own, be insufficient to give rise to a constructive trust.
[507] For a different view, see B. McFarlane (2004) 120 L.Q.R. 667, although the difficulty with privity remains.
[508] See M.P. Thompson [1988] Conv. 201 at 206.

The problem of the role, if any, actual notice of an unprotected interest should play in a system of registration is a thorny one, but the use of the constructive trust in *Lyus v. Prowsa* has failed to attract support. Thus, in *Chaudhary v. Yavuz*,[509] Lloyd L.J. pointed out that he knew of no English case where the reasoning employed in *Lyus v. Prowsa* had been used to make binding on a purchaser an interest which was void against him for non-registration and, in the light of these comments, in *Groveholt Ltd v. Hughes*,[510] David Richards J. said of *Lyus* that it 'must be regarded as being on the outer edge of the circumstances in which a constructive trust will be found to exist'.

In unregistered land, the House of Lords declined to apply a gloss to the provisions of the LCA 1972, so as to introduce any notion of good faith.[511] *Peffer v. Rigg*, while dealing with the provisions of a different statute, embraces a totally different philosophy from that adopted by the House of Lords and the question remains as to which of the two should prevail, a question which becomes increasingly pertinent as the total replacement of the unregistered land system is now a foreseeable event. In approaching this question, it is apposite to bear in mind that 'since in matters relating to title to land certainty is of prime importance, it is not desirable that constructive trusts of land should be imposed in reliance on inferences from "slender material" '.[512]

5.5.3.1 Personal liability

In its Third Report, the Law Commission did advocate that a purchaser should be required to be in good faith but, beyond a statement that this should not be equated simply with notice of an unprotected interest, little guidance was given as to what this might mean.[513] This important matter was not pursued in the most recent reports and the LRA 2002 does not specifically deal with this issue. What appeared to have been intended was that the disponee's title should not be impeachable in the sense that he would take free from the particular unprotected interest, but that he should, in appropriate cases, be personally liable for complicity in any breach of trust. The example which is given is a case where A and B hold land on trust and have limited powers of disposition. They then transfer the property to C in circumstances that were prohibited by the trust. C knows of this. The effect of the statutory provisions is that C's title is unimpeachable, yet, it is argued, there is no obstacle in holding C to be personally liable for the knowing receipt of trust property transferred in breach of trust.[514] It is hoped, for a number of reasons, that this suggestion is not taken up by the courts.

5.5.3.2 Knowing receipt

It is perfectly true that a registered proprietor with an absolute title may be subject to personal liability in respect of his acquisition of the title.[515] Where that liability has been recognized, however, is in respect of a wrong committed by the transferee as against the transferor.[516] The point is 'that the continued existence of rights of action of a personal

---

[509] [2011] EWCA Civ. 1314 at [61].   [510] [2012] EWHC 3351 (Ch) at [16].

[511] *Midland Bank Trust Co. Ltd v. Green* [1981] A.C. 513.

[512] *Lloyd v. Dugdale* [2002] 2 P. & C.R. 13 at [52] *per* Sir Christopher Slade.

[513] (1987) Law Com. No. 158, paras 4.14–4.17. See R.J. Smith [1987] Conv. 334 at 337; R.J. Smith in Jackson and Wilde (eds), *The Reform of Property Law* (Aldershot, Dartmouth, 1997), 129 at 133–7. For an argument sympathetic to the introduction of notions of good faith, see J. Stevens in Meisel and Cook (eds), *Property and Protection: Essays in Honour of Brian Harvey* (Oxford, Hart Publishing, 2000), 177.

[514] (2001) Law Com. No. 271, para. 4.11.

[515] For a general discussion of knowing receipt, see M. Conaglen and A. Goymour in Mitchell (eds) *Constructive and Resulting Trusts* (Oxford, Hart Publishing, 2010), 159.

[516] [2012] UKPC 30. See *Frazer v Walker* [1967] A.C. 569; *Creque v. Penn* [2007] UKPC 44.; *Arthur v. Attorney-General for the Turks and Caicos Islands* [2012] UKPC 30.

nature, *as between the original parties to a land transaction*, is not inconsistent with the LRA'.[517] Where the dispute is not confined to the original parties to the transaction, however, the situation is not the same. As was explained in *Creque v. Penn*,[518] '[t]he position as against a third party (such as a mortgagee or a later purchaser deriving title from the original purchaser) would be quite different, because then it would be a matter of title, not personal liability'.

This point was also emphasized over a century ago. In *Assets Co. Ltd v. Mere Roihi*,[519] in an important passage, Lord Lindley said:

> If the alleged [beneficiary] is a rival claimant, who can prove no trust apart from his own alleged ownership, it is plain that to treat him as a beneficiary is to destroy all benefit from registration. Here the plaintiffs set up an adverse title and nothing else; and to hold in their favour that there is any resulting or other trust entitling them to the property is, in their Lordships' opinion, to do the very thing which registration is designed to prevent.

If one returns to the example, it should first be emphasized that the principles enshrined in the LRA 2002 make it clear that, as a matter of property law, the disponee takes free from the unprotected interest. To hold that he is personally liable to the holder of the unprotected interest undermines this principle. To say that liability is personal and not proprietary 'masks the reality that the purchaser will barely spot the difference: liability feels the same by which ever route it arrives'.[520] This point can be reinforced by enquiring as to what the basis of this personal liability is.

In trust law, a person who receives trust property in breach of trust, and subsequently disposes of that property, can, in principle, be personally liable to the beneficiary on the basis of knowing receipt. His liability is personal in the sense that, because he no longer holds the disputed property, he cannot hold it on trust. His liability is an obligation to account on the basis of what has been termed ancillary liability, that liability stemming from his wrongful disposal of the trust property.[521] Indeed, it is central to this form of liability that the person to whom liability is sought to be established no longer holds the trust property. If, on the other hand, he still has the property then, unless he is a bona fide purchaser, he will be liable to return the trust property and pending that return will be bound by the original trust; he will hold the property on trust for the wronged beneficiary.[522]

When liability is imposed upon a person who previously held trust property, a crucial issue is whether that person has behaved unconscionably in respect of the dealings with that property and this, in turn, will depend upon the extent of his knowledge of the transaction being in breach of trust.[523] If that person was not bound by the trust in the first place as a matter of property law, then, as the High Court of Australia made clear in *Farah Constructions Pty Ltd v. Say-Dee Pty Ltd*,[524] his subsequent disposal of that property cannot give rise to personal liability on the basis of knowing receipt. Consequently, it is argued, there is no role to play in the present context for the equitable doctrine of knowing receipt.

---

[517] *Creque v. Penn, supra*, at [15] *per* Lord Walker.   [518] Ibid. at [10] *per* Lord Walker.

[519] [1905] A.C. 176 at 204–5.

[520] Smith, *Property Law* (8th edn) (Harlow, Pearson Educational, 2014), 256.

[521] See *Paragon Finance Plc v. D B Thakerar &. Co. (a firm)* [1999] 1 All E.R. 400 at 412 *per* Millett L.J., cited with approval in *Williams v. Central Bank of Nigeria* [2014] UKSC 10 at [26] *per* Lord Sumption.

[522] See Glister and Lee, Hanbury and Martin, *Modern Equity* (20th edn) (London, Sweet & Maxwell, 2015), para. 25–002.

[523] See *Bank of Credit and Commerce International (Overseas) Ltd v. Akindele* [2001] Ch. 437 at 455 *per* Nourse L.J.; *Twinsectra Ltd v. Yardley* [2002] 2 All E.R. 377, criticized by M.P. Thompson [2002] Conv. 387 at 394–5.

[524] (2007) 230 C.L.R. 89 at [193].

Instances of personal liability

A good example of where there is scope for imposing personal liability occurred in *HSBC Bank Ltd v. Dyche*.[525] Mr and Mrs Dyche were the registered proprietors of a house, but held it on constructive trust for her father, Mr Collelldevall. As part of a divorce settlement, they transferred the title to her in consideration of £5,000. She then mortgaged the house to the bank, having explained her father's presence in it by showing a tenancy agreement with him. This was a forgery. It was held that the bank was bound by Mr Collelldevall's interest in the property. In reaching this conclusion Judge Purle attached significance to the fact that, as Mrs Dyche knew that the transfer to her was in breach of trust, this meant that she was not acting in good faith and so would not take free from a beneficial interest existing behind a trust of land, as a purchaser normally would if the transfer is executed by two trustees.[526]

This reasoning must, however, be read in the context of the facts of the case, and should certainly not be seen as introducing a general requirement of good faith: a general requirement which is unsupportable. On the facts, Mrs Dyche was a co-trustee prior to the transaction and, therefore, could not use the overreaching machinery to convey the property to herself to escape her own trusteeship. After she became the sole proprietor of the house, she continued to be bound by the trust obligation. That obligation was held to be binding on the bank because, as in *Boland*,[527] the mortgage was executed by only one legal owner, and the beneficial owner was in actual occupation at the relevant time.

Far less easy to justify is some of the reasoning employed in *Haque v. Raja*.[528] The claimant asserted that his former wife,[529] D1, held a property on trust for him. That interest was not protected on the register of title. D1 transferred the property to D2 for a purchase price of £135,000,[530] this, it being argued, representing an undervalue. The claimant was not in actual occupation of the property and so could not argue that he had an overriding interest. Despite the interest not being protected on the register or taking effect as an overriding interest, it was argued that an interlocutory injunction restraining D2 from dealing with the property, which had previously been granted, should be maintained. This was because D2 should be regarded as having taken subject to the claimant's interest, the thrust of the argument being that D2 took subject to that interest because of his prior knowledge of it. This argument failed.

It was argued that, because the transfer had only been executed by one legal owner, the effect of *Williams & Glyn's Bank v. Boland*[531] was that his interest had not been overreached. This was rejected by Henderson J., who held that unless an interest such as that asserted by the claimant was either protected on the register or took effect as an overriding interest, the effect of s. 29, LRA 2002 was that the interest was not binding on a transferee for value. This should have been enough to dispose of the case. Unfortunately the judge, again without reference to authority, said, under the general heading of 'knowing receipt' that:

---

[525] [2009] EWHC 2954 (Ch). For criticism of the reasoning, albeit not the result, see M. Dixon [2010] Conv. 1; N.P. Gravells [2010] Conv. 169.

[526] [2009] EWHC 2954 (Ch) at [38]–[40].

[527] *Williams & Glyn's Bank v. Boland* [1981] A.C. 487.

[528] [2016] EWHC 1950 (Ch).

[529] This was a marriage at first recognized and then dissolved under Sharia law but not recognized under English law. Nothing turned on the marital status of the parties.

[530] Although this was less than the sum originally paid for the property, given the history of it since its acquisition, it was not clear that this amounted to an undervalue: ibid. at [51] *per* Henderson J.

[531] [1981] A.C. 483.

> If the requisite degree of knowledge on the part of [D2] is established, his liability as a constructive trustee arises as a matter of law and attaches to the Property while it remains in his ownership. It is a liability which affects his conscience directly, and is not dependent upon the survival of the claimant's original beneficial interest which binds the Property in his hands. This way of putting the claim is therefore unaffected by the technicalities of overreaching and land registration.[532]

Although the claim failed because it had not been established that D2 actually had the requisite knowledge of the claimant's interest,[533] this should not have been a relevant issue. The language employed in this case is redolent of the discredited reasoning employed in *Peffer v. Rigg* and is wrong. It is somewhat meaningless to say that, as a matter of property law, a purchaser takes free from an unregistered interest and, in the next breath, to impose a new constructive trust upon him, that trust being based upon broad concepts of unconscionability which the legislation was designed to eradicate. It is submitted that this section of the judgment is *per incuriam* and wrong.

5.5.4 Equitable concepts

It is always tempting to temper the stark nature of registration systems by the introduction of general equitable interests so as to avoid seemingly unmeritorious purchasers taking advantage of those provisions to take free from unprotected interests of which they are aware prior to the purchase. Indeed, such a course of action has been taken in other jurisdictions, where a purchaser who is considered to be fraudulent is not able to rely on these provisions to take free from unprotected interests. This has not led to a resolution of all the problems because the determination of what is meant by fraud has not proved to be an uncontroversial task.[534] In this country, the legislation makes the position quite clear and an appeal to general notions of equity is unhelpful.[535] More importantly, it risks the law relating to this important issue becoming incoherent. An important role of property law is to determine which of two competing claims has priority over the other. To reach a conclusion that, under the principles of property law, the order of priority is A followed by B and then, by recourse to an appeal to general, although ill-defined, equitable principles to reverse that order of priority undermines the principles of property law which have evolved to determine this very question. To do this is classically an instance where to make available so many different remedies for the same misapplication of property makes the law unnecessarily complex,[536] and lacking in internal coherence. It is already the case that the insistence of the legislation on the need to register an interest in another person's land is modified considerably by the fact that those rights will, generally speaking,[537] be enforceable if, notwithstanding a failure to register, the holder of that right is in actual occupation of the relevant land. If the holder of the right is not in actual occupation, it is not unreasonable to insist that, for that right to be enforceable against a transferee for value, it should be registered. It is suggested that attempts to water this down are unprincipled and can lead to uncertainty in an area of law where that quality is traditionally highly valued.

---

[532] [2016] EWHC 1950 (Ch) at [47].

[533] Ibid. at [50].

[534] See, e.g., *Bahr v. Nicolay (No.2)* (1988) 164 C.L.R. 604. See the discussions by E. Cooke and P. O'Connor (2004) 120 L.Q.R. 640 and M. Harding and M. Bryan in Dixon (ed.) *Modern Studies in Property Law* (vol. 5) (Oxford, Hart Publishing, 2009), Chapter 1.

[535] See also *Halifax Plc v. Curry Popeck (A Firm)* [2008] EWHC 1692 (Ch) at [48]–[52] *per* Norris J.

[536] See *Paragon Finance Plc v. D B Thakerer & Co. (A firm)* [1999] 1 All E.R. 400 at 414 *per* Millett L.J.

[537] For an important exception to this, see 11.6.8.5—Legal co-ownership.

6

Adverse Possession

One of the more peculiar features of the law of property is the idea that title to land can be acquired by a mere trespasser's possession of it. The legal, or paper, owner who has been dispossessed is unable, after a specified period, to defeat the trespasser's claim, and so their title is extinguished. This is law at a primal level;[1] the uncontested and long use of land is seen as more valuable, more worthy of recognition, than the formal ownership of land reflected in deeds and registers. English land law has historically enabled the acquisition of title by adverse possession through two complementary concepts: the relativity of title, and the principle of limitation.

6.1 The relativity of title

Ownership of land is a relative concept.[2] If a court is faced with a dispute as to the entitlement to possession of land, its task is not to make a definitive determination as to who is the owner of it. Its task is simply to determine which of the two claimants has a better right to possess it. This central point was made over two hundred years ago, when Lord Mansfield said that:

> the plaintiff cannot recover but upon the strength of his own title. He cannot found his claim upon the weakness of the defendant's title. For possession gives the defendant a right against every man who cannot show a good title.[3]

This emphasizes that the court is concerned only to determine the relative strengths of the claims to possession of the land. For example, if A has taken possession, or is entitled to take possession under a licence,[4] then A can recover possession as against B, unless B can show that A's right is, as against him, statute barred. It is quite irrelevant that B can prove that A had no right to possession in the first place, or that his claim to possession did not

---

[1] As Oliver Wendell Holmes said, '[a] thing which you have enjoyed and used as your own for a long time . . . takes root in your being and cannot be torn away without your resenting the act and trying to defend yourself, however you came by it'. See (1897) 10 Harv. L Rev 457 at 477.

[2] In *Berrisford v. Mexfield Housing Co-operative Ltd* [2011] UKSC 52 at [65], this principle was described by Lord Neuberger as being 'the traditional bedrock of English land law'.

[3] *Roe D. Haldane v. Harvey* (1769) 4 Burr. 2484 at 2487.

[4] See *Dutton v. Manchester Airport plc* [2000] 1 Q.B. 133. See E. Paton and G. Seabrooke [1999] Conv. 535. If a person has, by licence, only a right of access to property, he does not have the right to bring an action for trespass: *Countryside Residential (North Thames) Ltd v. Tugwell* (2000) 34 E.G. 87. See W. Swadling (2000) 116 L.Q.R. 254.

confer any proprietary right on him,[5] and that C had a better right to possession than either of them.[6] As the person in prior possession, A has a better right to possess the land than does B and it is this claim with which the court is concerned.

The importance of the relativity of title in modern land law was stressed again in *Harrow London Borough Council v. Qazi*.[7] Lord Millett explained the position in the following terms:

> A person who is in actual possession of land is entitled to remain in peaceful enjoyment of the property without disturbance by anyone except a person with a better title to possession. It does not matter that he has no title. A squatter can maintain an action for trespass. He cannot be evicted save at the suit of a person with a better right to possession, and even then that person must rely on the strength of his own title and not the weakness of the squatter's.

In general, proof that a third party has a better right to the land is immaterial.[8] The only time that such a plea will be relevant is if C is in possession of land and D, who has not, himself, been in prior occupation of the land, brings an action to recover it from C. In such a case, C can rely on the fact that D has no right to the land because E is entitled to it. This, however, serves only further to illustrate that the task of the court is to weigh the strengths of the competing claims to the land. As C is in possession, for D to recover the land, he must show a better right to it than C and this he cannot do if all that C can show is that D has no such right because E has a better right to it. The fact that E might have a better right to the land than C is of no assistance to D's claim to possession.

6.2 The principle of limitation

The concept of all titles being relative to the strength of the claim to possession allows the common law to deal with land disputes in a more nuanced way than legal systems which enforce a notion of absolute ownership, but it also leads to a difficulty: a possessor of land can always, by definition, be beaten by the stronger claim of some prior possessor. In order to prevent constant uncertainty over the question of entitlement to land, it became necessary to invoke a principle of limitation in claims for the possession of land. This means that, as is the case with other causes of action, an action to possess land can, after a period of time, become statute barred. In the case of actions in contract and tort, the essence of statutes of limitation is that a particular remedy has been lost. In the case of land, the effect of limitation is more profound. The essential reason for this is that once the right to recover possession has been lost, a statute of limitations provides that the title of that person to the land is extinguished.[9] The corollary to this is that the person who has taken possession acquires rights of ownership. As such, although the working of the limitation period is essentially negative in nature, operating to extinguish the title of the paper owner of the land, it is also a means of acquiring title to property, albeit in a non-consensual manner.

---

[5] Ibid. Contrast the position in the law of nuisance, where, to bring a claim, the plaintiff must establish a proprietary interest in the land: see *Hunter v. Canary Wharf* [1997] A.C. 635.

[6] See *Marsden v. Miller* (1992) 64 P. & C.R. 239 at 240 *per* Scott L.J., pointing out that in the case before him the identity of the paper owner of the disputed land was unknown.

[7] [2001] 1 A.C. 003 at 1015. See also *Ocean Estates Ltd v. Pindes* [1969] 2 A.C. 19 at 25 *per* Lord Diplock

[8] It is relevant if the person in possession shows that he is there as the agent of a person with the paper title to the land. See *Rosenberg v. Cook* (1881) 8 Q.B.D. 162.

[9] Section 17 of the Limitation Act 1980. See 6.7.

6.3 Relativity, limitation, and registration

The relativity of title and the principle of limitation act in concert to form the basis of the law on adverse possession in unregistered land, but they sit unhappily in a registered title system. The transformations wrought by the LRA 2002 provide us with a concept close to absolute ownership of land; s. 58 explicitly states that registration is *conclusive* as to ownership. Although there remains a possibility that the register could be rectified or altered, which means that title remains relative to a degree,[10] it is otherwise difficult to see why possession of land for however long should, in theory, take priority over the conclusiveness of the register. Title, in other words, is granted through registration, and not through possession and concomitant extinguishment by limitation, so why should a period of adverse possession have any effect on the registered title? Except in the case of boundary disputes, where the normal position is that the registered title does not guarantee the precise location of the boundaries,[11] there is no curative effect in respect of possessory titles. In fact, the converse is the case. The existence of possessory titles undermines the reliability of the register, in that the person registered as the proprietor and the person entitled to the enjoyment of the land are different.

This begs the question why adverse possession is allowed in registered land at all, and the answer must lie in something more elemental than the reliability of the register. It has been argued that a deep and long-term connection to land inculcates a part of human identity or personhood. As Margaret Radin put it, '[m]ost people possess certain objects they feel are almost part of themselves. These objects are closely bound up with personhood because they are part of the way we constitute ourselves as continuing personal entities in the world.'[12] The strength of one's connection to property can be gauged by the pain that would be felt by its loss. If, therefore, an owner cares insufficiently about their land so that someone else can come to possess it for a long period of time, the law allocates the loss to the person who will suffer the least because of it: the neglectful owner.[13]

These fundamental ideas on personal connections to property mean that adverse possession has survived the reform of the law, but only just; the infallibility of the register takes priority in a system that grants title to land by registration. The law on adverse possession has, therefore, been entirely recast under the LRA 2002, with the odds now heavily stacked against the mere trespasser in attempting to register title. Importantly, the possession of land for a period of time can no longer, of itself, bar the rights of the registered owner, and the statute of limitations is expressly disapplied under the LRA 2002.[14] This means that, while the substantive law on how adverse possession is *established* applies to all claims, the *effect* of adverse possession is markedly different between the unregistered and registered systems, and must therefore be dealt with separately.

6.4 Establishing adverse possession

The concept of adverse possession involves two elements. These are the dispossession or discontinuance of possession by the owner, and the requisite possession by the squatter.

---

[10] See, e.g., *Re 139 High Street, Deptford* [1951] Ch. 884; see also 5.4.
[11] See 5.4.6.　　[12] M.J. Radin 34 Stanford L Rev 957 (1982) at 957.
[13] See generally J.E. Stake (2001) 89 Geo LJ 2419; K. Gray and S. Gray, *Elements of Land Law* (5th edn, Oxford, Oxford University Press, 2009), 1162.
[14] LRA 2002, s. 96. See 6.7.3.4.

6.4.1 **Dispossession or discontinuance**

The starting point in establishing a claim to adverse possession is to show that the paper owner has either been dispossessed or has discontinued his occupation of the land. In *Rains v. Buxton*,[15] Fry J. explained the fairly obvious distinction between the two as being that 'the one is where a person comes in and drives out the others from possession, the other is where the person in possession goes out and is followed into possession by other persons'.

Adverse possession cases normally involve the latter scenario, as, if a person is forcibly evicted from property, the matter is unlikely to lie uncontested for a period of twelve years. The normal situation is where land has been unused by the owner of it and the squatter then argues that he has taken over the land. Discontinuance must, nevertheless, be established and relatively minor acts by the owner of it are likely to be regarded as negating this requirement,[16] although merely leaving chattels on open land is not enough to maintain possession of it,[17] and neither is the sporadic draining of water on the land in question.[18]

6.4.2 **Adverse possession**

For the owner's title to be potentially defeated, more than a mere discontinuance of possession must be shown; a squatter must establish a period of adverse possession. This involves a number of matters. First, the squatter must establish possession as a fact. Second, he must show the requisite intention with regard to that possession and, finally, he must show the possession to be adverse, the final requirement overlapping to a degree with the second.

6.4.2.1 **Factual possession**

The squatter must establish an appropriate degree of physical control over the property in question[19] in order to be regarded as being in possession of it.[20] In considering what amounts to a sufficient degree of physical control, the courts will apply an objective test, which relates to the nature and quality of the land in question and is not subject to any variation accorded to the resources and status of the individual parties to the case.[21]

In applying this objective standard, the most obvious act of possession is the physical enclosure of the land by fencing.[22] Fencing alone will not necessarily be sufficient, however, as if the purpose of erecting gates or fences is to protect a right of way, then the erection of the fences will not be considered as taking possession of the land.[23] It may also be the case that the purpose of the fence is to keep livestock from straying. If this is the case, then this will not be regarded as the taking of possession.[24] The reason for this is that '[a] fence is a barrier. It keeps things in and it keeps things out. No doubt it is reasonable to

---

[15] (1880) 14 Ch.D. 537 at 540.

[16] See *Powell v. McFarlane* (1977) 38 P. & C.R. 450 at 472 *per* Slade J.

[17] See *London Borough of Tower Hamlets v. Baker* [2005] EWCA Civ. 923 at [60] *per* Neuberger L.J.

[18] *J Alston & Sons Ltd v. BOCM Pauls Ltd* [2008] EWHC 3310 (Ch) at [77] *per* H.H.J. Marshall.

[19] In the case of a house, it is possible to establish adverse possession of a discrete part of a house: *Ramroop v. Ishmael* [2010] UKHL 14 at [25] *per* Lord Walker.

[20] *Powell v. McFarlane* (1977) 38 P. & C.R. 450 at 470 *per* Slade J. See also *Tennant v. Adamczyk* [2005] EWCA Civ. 1239 at [22] *per* Mummery L.J.

[21] *West Bank Estates Ltd v. Arthur* [1967] A.C. 665 at 678–9, *per* Lord Wilberforce. See also *J.A. Pye (Oxford) Ltd v. Graham* [2003] 1 A.C. 419.

[22] *Seddon v. Smith* (1877) 36 L.T. 168. If the fence is pulled down by the owner, however, this will be of little use as an act of possession: See *Marsden v. Miller* (1992) 61 P. & C.R. 239.

[23] See *Littledale v. Liverpool College* [1900] 2 Ch. 19; *George Wimpey & Co. Ltd v. Sohn* [1967] Ch. 487.

[24] *Inglewood Investment Co. Ltd v. Baker* [2003] 1 P. & C.R. 23, where the evidence was that, if the livestock had been cattle as opposed to sheep, the fencing would not have been put up. See at [30] *per* Aldous J.

assume that a person who maintains a fence is doing so for both purposes, but that is not necessarily so.'[25]

Although the physical enclosure of the land is, generally, the most unequivocal way of taking possession of it, it is not an essential act; indeed, the property may be such that it is not capable of being enclosed, but a person may, by his acts in relation to it still take possession of it.[26] It was made clear in *Greenmanor Ltd v. Pilford*[27] that there is no requirement on the adverse possessor to enclose the land in such a way and to such an extent that nobody could gain access except with their permission. Similarly, in *Wata-Ofei v. Danquah*,[28] it was stressed that the acts necessary to take possession of land will vary depending upon the land in question, so that, in the case of vacant and unenclosed land, which is not being cultivated,[29] there is very little that can be done to it to indicate that it has been possessed.[30] Consistent with this, it was held in *Red House Farms (Thorndon) Ltd v. Catchpole*[31] that the use of waste land for shooting was a sufficient act to constitute possession. Most recently, the Court of Appeal in *Thorpe v. Frank*[32] held that what constituted a sufficient degree of exclusive physical control so as to satisfy the requirement of factual possession was dependent upon the nature of the land in question, and the usage to which the land was put. The focus, said McCombe L.J., should be on what the occupier might be expected to do in the particular circumstances, and not only on the steps the occupier took to exclude others.[33] In *Thorpe v. Frank* itself, this meant that paving the land in question qualified as factual possession.

Much will depend upon the facts of each case as to whether or not the acts relied upon with respect to the disputed land will be regarded as sufficient to amount to possession of it. It is not necessary for the act relied upon to inconvenience the owner,[34] but, as is to be expected, the more inconvenience caused to the owner the more likely it is that an action will be brought against the squatter within the twelve-year period. Acts which are considered to be trivial acts of trespass will not suffice to constitute possession,[35] unless the nature of the disputed land is such that what otherwise would be regarded as a trivial act is the only sensible use of the land.[36] Equally, the judge in *Heaney v. Kirkby*[37] emphasized that 'what matters is an objective assessment of the circumstances and all the circumstances taken as a whole', and that it is 'not a question of taking isolated items' in order to avoid a finding of factual possession.

6.4.2.2 Open enjoyment

Although it has been said that adverse possession must be open,[38] the better way of putting it is that the possession must not be concealed or fraudulent. If the squatter's action is

---

[25] *Trustees of the Michael Batt Charitable Trust v. Adams* (2001) 82 P. & C.R. 406 at 415 *per* Laddie J. See also *Chambers v. London Borough of Havering* [2011] EWCA Civ. 1576 at [37]–[40] *per* Etherton L.J.

[26] See *Prudential Assurance Co. Ltd v. Waterloo Real Estate Inc.* [1999] 2 E.G.L.R. 85 and *Palfrey v. Wilson* [2007] EWCA Civ. 94 (in both cases a party wall was held to have been adversely possessed).

[27] [2012] EWCA Civ. 756.   [28] [1961] A.C. 1238.

[29] For possession by cultivation, see *Hicks Development Ltd v. Chaplin* [2007] EWHC 141 (Ch); *J. Alston &. Sons Ltd v. BOCM Pauls Ltd* [2008] EWHC 3310 (Ch); *Chambers v. London Borough of Havering* [2011] EWCA Civ. 1576 at [48] *per* Lewison L.J., although see our analysis at 12.1.4.8.

[30] *Hicks Development Ltd v. Chaplin* [2007] EWHC 141 (Ch) at 1243 *per* Lord Guest. See also *Bristow v. Corrican* (1878) 3 App. Cas. 641 at 657 *per* Lord Hatherley.

[31] [1977] 2 E.G.L.R. 125. Contrast *Inglewood Investment Co. Ltd v. Baker* [2003] 1 P. & C.R. 23 at [35] *per* Aldous J.

[32] [2019] EWCA Civ. 150.   [33] Ibid. at [42].

[34] See *Trealor v. Nute* [1976] 1 W.L.R. 1295; *Williams v. Usherwood* (1981) 45 P. & C.R. 235.

[35] See *Williams Bros District Suppliers Ltd v. Raftery* [1958] 1 Q.B. 159; *Tecbild Ltd v. Chamberlain* (1969) 20 P. & C.R. 633.

[36] See *Mayor of London Borough of Hounslow v. Minchinton* (1997) 74 P. & C.R. 221 at 233 *per* Millett L.J.

[37] [2015] UKUT 0178 (TCC) at [38] per Judge Roger Kay Q.C.

[38] *Browne v. Perry* [1991] 1 W.L.R. 1297 at 1302 *per* Lord Templeman.

based upon fraud, deliberate concealment, or the consequence of a mistake, the time will not begin to run, unless the owner has, or could have, discovered the fraud, concealment, or mistake by reasonable diligence[39] and the onus of proof with regard to these matters is on the owner.[40] For adverse possession to be established, it is not necessary that the owner of the land is actually aware of the fact that the land is in another person's occupation.[41] Nevertheless, because of the need for the squatter to prove the requisite intention to possess, it will only be on very rare occasions that a squatter will be regarded as having been in adverse possession when that fact is not readily discoverable from an inspection of the land. It remains the case, however, that the test is simply to ask if the squatter is in possession.

The matter was considered in *Purbrick v. London Borough of Hackney*.[42] The property in question was what appeared to be a burnt-out shell of a building which had survived demolition and had stood derelict for years. The squatter made an increasing amount of use of it over the years, although he admitted that, at first, he had sought to maintain a low profile, in case the owner saw him and tried to prevent his activity.[43] It was nevertheless held that the squatter was in possession. Keeping a low profile was not regarded as being the same as either fraud or concealment. The question is essentially factual and, on the facts of this case, it was said that 'to an ordinary speaker of English and, indeed, to any property lawyer—who many would say are not ordinary speakers of English—Mr Purbrick would appear to have been, at least on the face of it, in possession'.[44] Once that was established, this was sufficient to constitute the fact of possession, and any supposed test based upon how the position might have appeared to an objective observer was rejected.[45] Quite simply, it is 'wrong to formulate the legal test by reference to what the paper owner, or anyone else, might have inferred from a visit to the property'.[46]

6.4.2.3 The intention to possess

As well as factually being in possession of the land, the squatter must also have the requisite intention to possess it: the *animus possedendi*.[47] Quite what it is that the squatter must intend to do, however, has for some time been a matter of contention. In *Littledale v. Liverpool College*,[48] Lindley L.J., in an influential dictum, insisted that the squatter must not intend simply to possess the land; it was necessary to intend also to exclude everyone else, including the true owner, from the property. This requirement was open to both theoretical and practical objections. The former related to the change in the law brought about in 1833. Until the Real Property Limitation Acts of 1833 and 1874, the rights of the owner of the paper title were not regarded as having been interfered with unless he had been ousted by the squatter. Where a squatter had taken possession of land without ousting the true owner, this was considered to be 'non-adverse' possession.[49] In 1833, the cause of action was deemed to accrue on the dispossession of, or discontinuance by, the

---

[39] Limitation Act 1980, s. 32(1).   [40] *Rains v. Buxton* (1880) 14 Ch.D. 537 at 540 *per* Fry J.

[41] *J. Alston & Sons Ltd v. BOCM Pauls Ltd* [2008] EWHC 3310 (Ch) at [114] per H.H.J. Hazel Marshall. Cf. *Powell v. McFarlane* (1977) 38 P. & C.R. 452, where the claim of adverse possession failed on the facts.

[42] [2004] 1 P. & C.R. 34. See also *Wretham v. Ross* [2005] EWHC 1259 (Ch).

[43] [2004] 1 P. & C.R. 34 at [5] *per* Neuberger J.   [44] Ibid. at [18].

[45] Ibid. at [27]. For an argument to the contrary, see Jourdan, *Adverse Possession* (London, Butterworths LexisNexis, 2002), 155–8.

[46] *Wretham v. Ross* [2005] EWHC 1259 (Ch) at 3 *per* David Richards J. accepting the argument of counsel.

[47] *Powell v. McFarlane, supra*, at 470 *per* Slade L.J.

[48] [1900] 1 Ch.D. 19 at 23. For an interesting discussion of the introduction of this requirement, and its origins in German law, see O. Radley-Gardner (2005) 25 O.J.L.S. 727.

[49] See *Paradise Beach and Transportation Co. Ltd v. Price-Robinson* [1968] A.C. 1072 at 1082 *per* Lord Upjohn; M. Dockray [1982] Conv. 256 at 258.

paper owner[50] and from that time on, the question was simply whether the squatter had taken possession of the disputed land; it was not necessary to show an intention to oust the holder of the paper title.[51]

Despite this, the idea that the squatter must intend to exclude everyone, including the true owner, gained currency.[52] Nevertheless, it was contrary to principle and, moreover, erected an artificial barrier in the way of a squatter seeking to establish a possessory title as it required him to show 'little more than a private intention to do something which [he] is not required to attempt and which, in most cases, he could not lawfully or practically do'.[53]

This latter point is important as, if a squatter knows that the land he is occupying does not belong to him, he knows that he is not able to exclude the true owner. Nevertheless, such a person is able to acquire a possessory title and his willingness to pay for the right to occupy the land, if requested to do so will not prevent the squatter from being in adverse possession.[54] Similarly, an attitude by the squatter that he would leave the property if asked to do so would render him a 'candid squatter',[55] but would not prevent him from having the requisite intention to possess. The practicalities involved led to a more cautious statement of principle in *Powell v. Macfarlane*,[56] where Slade J. said:

> [T]he *animus possedendi* involves the intention, in one's own name, and on one's own behalf, to exclude the world at large, including the owner with the paper title if he be not himself the possessor, *so far as is reasonably practicable and so far as the law will allow him.*

More recent statements as to what it is that the squatter must intend to do, were made in *Buckinghamshire County Council v. Moran*,[57] where Slade L.J. stressed that what is required is that the squatter must intend to possess the land. That position was itself attacked and the argument advanced that not only must the squatter intend to exclude everyone, including the true owner from the land, he must intend actually to own it.[58] This dispute has now been authoritatively resolved by the House of Lords in *J.A. Pye (Oxford) Ltd v. Graham*,[59] where it was held that the requisite intention was the intention to possess.

Intention to possess and not to own

The dispute involved 25 hectares of agricultural land in Berkshire of which, at all material times, Pye was the registered proprietor. In 1977, Pye sold farmland, that land being acquired by the Grahams in 1982. The disputed area was retained by Pye, who intended, in the future, to develop it. From 1982, the Grahams used their own farmland together with the disputed land for farming purposes. Early in 1983, Pye and the Grahams entered into a written agreement to confer grazing rights on the land. On the expiry of this agreement, Pye's surveyor wrote to the Grahams requiring them to vacate the land. He also wrote to Pye asking if they could be granted a new tenancy but Pye declined on the basis that they

---

[50] Real Property Limitation Act 1833, s. 3.

[51] See *Culley v. Doe d. Taylerson* (1840) 11 Ad. & El. 1008 at 1015 *per* Lord Denman C.J.

[52] See, e.g., *Battersea Freehold and Leasehold Co. Ltd v. The Mayor and Burgesses of the London Borough of Wandsworth* (2001) 82 P. & C.R. 137 at 144 *per* Rimer J.; *Trustees of the Michael Butt Charitable Trust v. Adams* (2001) 82 P. & C.R. 406 at 412–13 *per* Laddie J.

[53] Dockray [1982] Conv. 256 at 261.

[54] *Ocean Estates Ltd v. Pinder* [1969] 2 A.C. 19 at 24. See also *The Mayor and Burgesses of Lambeth v. Blackburn* (2001) 82 P. & C.R. 494; *J.A. Pye (Oxford) Ltd v. Graham* [2003] 1 A.C. 419 at 429 *per* Lord Browne-Wilkinson.

[55] *J. Alston & Sons Ltd v. BOCM Paul Ltd* [2008] EWHC 3310 (Ch) at [105] *per* H.H.J. Hazel Marshall.

[56] (1977) 38 P. & C.R. 452 at 470. Italics supplied.

[57] [1990] Ch. 623 at 636.

[58] L. Tee [2000] Conv. 113. For a convincing refutation, see O. Radley-Gardner and C. Harpum [2001] Conv. 155.

[59] [2003] 1 A.C. 419. See M.P. Thompson [2002] Conv. 480.

wanted the land to be vacant when they applied for planning permission. Thereafter, the Grahams in 1984 paid Pye £1,100 to buy crops on the land and, on several occasions, wrote to Pye asking for a new licence. None of these letters was answered and the last such letter was written in May 1985. Thereafter, until 1999, the Grahams continued to farm the land and it was held that, by then, a possessory title had been obtained.

Once it had been found that the Grahams were in factual possession of the land,[60] the issue turned to the intention of the occupier and, in particular, that of the Grahams' son, Michael, who, until his death in 1998, had carried out most of the farming activity. It was accepted that Michael was quite well aware that Pye could have repossessed the property and, if asked, would have been prepared to pay to be allowed to continue in occupation of it. The argument that this prevented the acquisition of a possessory title was rejected: what was required was the intention to possess the land. It was not necessary to have the further intention of excluding the owner or of being the owner of the land.[61] On the facts, this intention was plainly established.

To establish the requisite intention to possess the land, it is not necessary that his intention need in any way be hostile to the paper owner. Indeed, it may be the case that he mistakenly believes that he actually owns the land in question,[62] or holds the property under a lease,[63] in which case the requisite intention to possess will be easy to establish.[64] To establish the intention to possess, the squatter must rely on the nature of the acts themselves. His own evidence given at trial as to what his intention was at the time when he started to make use of the land in question is regarded as being of little weight, as it is likely to be self-serving.[65] The acts relied upon 'must be unequivocal in the sense that his intention to possess has been made plain to the world. If his act is equivocal and his intention has not been made plain, his claim will fail.'[66]

6.4.2.4 Possession must be adverse

The Act requires that, before time will begin to run in favour of a squatter, he must be in adverse possession of the land.[67] What this means 'is possession which is inconsistent with and in denial of the true owner. Possession is not normally adverse if it is enjoyed with the consent of the owner.'[68] Central to the concept is, therefore, permission.

6.4.2.5 Permission

It is axiomatic that time does not begin to run in favour of a person in possession of another person's land if he is there with the latter's permission,[69] or if he believes that he has the owner's permission.[70] In this situation, he is a licensee and 'time can never run in favour of a person who occupies or uses land by licence of the owner with the paper title and whose licence has not been duly determined'.[71] So, if a former tenant is given permission

---

[60] This, somewhat remarkably, was found not to be the case in the Court of Appeal: [2001] Ch. 804 at 814–15 *per* Mummery L.J.

[61] [2003] 1 A.C. 419 at 437 *per* Lord Browne-Wilkinson.

[62] *Armbrister v. Lightbourn* [2012] UKPC 40.   [63] *Ofulue v. Bossert* [2008] EWCA Civ. 7.

[64] See *Pulleyn v. Hall Aggregates (Thames Valley) Ltd* (1992) 65 P. & C.R. 452.

[65] *Bolton Metropolitan Borough Council v. Musa* (1998) 64 P. & C.R. D. 36 at 37 *per* Peter Gibson L.J. See also the remarks in *J.A. Pye (Oxford) Ltd v. Graham* [2003] 1 A.C. 419 at 443 *per* Lord Browne Wilkinson.

[66] *Prudential Assurance Co. Ltd v. Waterloo Real Estates Inc.* [1999] 2 E.G.L.R. 85 at 87 *per* Peter Gibson L.J.

[67] Limitation Act 1980, Sched. 1, para. 8.

[68] *Ramnarace v. Lutchman* [2001] 1 W.L.R. 1651 at 1654 *per* Lord Millett.

[69] See *Hughes v. Griffin* [1969] 1 W.L.R. 23; *J.A. Pye (Oxford) Ltd v. Graham* [2003] 1 A.C. 419 at 434 *per* Lord Browne Wilkinson.

[70] *Clowes Development (UK) Ltd v. Walters* [2005] EWHC 669 (Ch) at [40] *per* Hart J.

[71] *Powell v. McFarlane* (1977) 38 P. & C.R. 452 at 459 *per* Slade J. See also *Buckinghamshire County Council v. Moran* [1990] Ch. 623 at 626 *per* Slade L.J.; *Clarke v. Swaby* [2007] UKPC 1 at [11] *per* Lord Walker.

on the termination of the lease to remain in the property rent free, he will not be in adverse possession of the land.[72]

The question of whether possession was adverse arose in *Hyde v. Pearce*.[73] A purchaser bid successfully for a property at auction and paid a deposit. He was then allowed into possession. It was clear that, at this stage, he was a licensee.[74] A dispute arose between the parties because part of the land contracted to be sold had previously been conveyed to another party and agreement could not be reached as to an appropriate abatement of the purchase price. The vendor asked the purchaser to return the keys but he did not reply and there matters rested until, fourteen years later, the vendor, during the temporary absence of the purchaser, sold the property to a third party. The first purchaser claimed to have a possessory title to the land. His claim failed. Despite accepting that the licence to occupy had been terminated, the Court of Appeal held that he was not in adverse possession because he was there under the contract, which had not been terminated, and so had an equitable interest in the land, with the result that his possession was not adverse. This seems highly questionable. As his licence had been revoked, he did not have the right to be in possession of the land and, as he was there without permission, he should, it is submitted, have been held to have established a possessory title. Certainly, the case sits uneasily with *Bridges v. Mees*,[75] where a purchaser went into possession having paid all the purchase money but where the land had not been transferred to him. There, the judge had no difficulty in finding him to have been in adverse possession, although, as the vendor, having received the full purchase price, would have held the property on a bare trust for the purchaser, it is clear that the purchaser in this case had a much stronger right actually to take possession than did the purchaser in *Hyde v. Pearce*.

The facts of *Parshall v. Hackney*[76] presented a particularly unusual problem: where land had been incorrectly registered under two titles, with two separate owners, could it be said that one of the registered proprietors can dispossess the other through a period of adverse possession? The Court of Appeal held that this was logically impossible, because the taking of possession by a registered owner was not unlawful, and thus could not be adverse to the other registered owner. Until the register had been rectified to reflect only one owner, the question as to whether that owner's right to recover the land from an adverse possessor is statute barred was irrelevant. This interpretation of adverse—that possession must be *unlawful* for time to begin to run—was recently rejected by the Court of Appeal in *Rashid v. Nasrullah*.[77] The original proprietor of the land in question was deprived of his title by a forged transfer in 1989, supported by fraudulent documents, to the appellant's father. The father then transferred the land to his son by way of gift, and the son was complicit in the fraud by which the land had been obtained. Twenty years later, the original registered proprietor applied for rectification of the register, and the question for the court was whether the claim for rectification could be defeated by adverse possession on the current of the current registered owner. The argument by the original registered proprietor, based on *Parshall v. Hackney*, was that as the appellant son had registered title (albeit procured through fraud), his possession was not unlawful. In other words, as long as he was the registered owner, his possession was lawful and so could not be adverse to the original owner.

---

[72] *Smith v. Lawson* (1997) 74 P. & C.R. D. 34.

[73] [1982] 1 W.L.R. 560 described as 'an odd little case' at 562 *per* Templeman L.J.

[74] When a person is negotiating to acquire an interest in land goes into possession, it is normal for a court to consider him to be an implied licensee. See *Sandhu v. Farooqui* [2004] 1 P. & C.R. 3; *Colin Dawson Windows Ltd v. King's Lynn and West Norfolk Borough Council* [2005] 2 P. & C.R. 19 at [39] *per* Rix L.J.

[75] [1957] Ch. 475, not cited in *Hyde v. Pearce*.

[76] [2013] EWCA Civ. 240. See K. Lees [2013] Conv. 222; L. Xu (2013) 129 L.Q.R. 477.

[77] [2018] EWCA Civ. 2685.

Lewison L.J. rejected that argument, and stated that the correct question is simply whether there was a taking of possession without the consent of the true owner. To introduce the idea that the possession had to be unlawful to qualify as adverse was wrong, and irreconcilable with the decision of the House of Lords in *J.A. Pye (Oxford) Ltd v. Graham.*[78] As a result, the appeal in *Rashid v. Nasrullah* was allowed and the fraudster's son, the current registered proprietor, could claim title by adverse possession.[79]

6.4.2.6 Licence to occupy

A second issue which can cause difficulty is where the owner purports to grant a licence to an occupier after possession has been taken. This occurred in *B.P. Properties Ltd v. Buckler.*[80] Land had been occupied by the defendant's family since 1916, originally on a yearly tenancy. This lease was surrendered and a new periodic tenancy arose. No rent was paid and, in 1955, a possession order was obtained and enforced against all the property except, for compassionate reasons[81] a farmhouse and garden. The family remained in possession and, in December 1962, another possession order was issued but not enforced. Early in 1974, possession proceedings were again started but were not pursued. The land was then sold to the plaintiff who, in October 1974, one month short of twelve years from the date of the possession order having been obtained in 1962, wrote to the defendant's mother giving her permission to remain in the property, rent free, for the rest of her life. This offer was neither accepted nor rejected. After she died, the plaintiff brought possession proceedings against the son, who claimed to have a possessory title. His defence failed. The Court of Appeal held that the effect of the letter to his mother was that, from that point, she occupied the property as a licensee and was not, therefore, in adverse possession.

While the actual decision can just about be justified on the basis that the letter could be construed as the grant to the mother of a life interest in the property,[82] the actual ground for the decision seems to be wrong. Once a person is in adverse possession, it should not be open to the owner to convert the squatter into a licensee by the unilateral act of authorizing his presence. It was said in *Zarb v. Parry*[83] that if the owner of the paper title planted a flag on the disputed land, put up a notice or made an oral declaration of ownership, this would not prevent the squatter from continuing to be in adverse possession, and neither should it convert that possession into permissive occupation. For that to happen, it is thought that it should be necessary for the squatter to accept that he is there with permission. In *Smith v. Molyneaux,*[84] however, the Privy Council held that the Court of Appeal below had erred in holding that permission could not be given unilaterally by the owner of land and that it required to be acknowledged by the occupier. The Privy Council pointed to *B.P. Properties Ltd v. Buckler* as authority for the principle that a unilateral notice by the landowner was effective, regardless of whether it is acknowledged by the squatter, which meant that the appeal was allowed and the claim for adverse possession failed. The permission itself was never in writing, and instead Mr Smith asserted that it was given in conversation to the squatter, Mr Molyneaux, which he in turn denied. The

---

[78] [2003] 1 A.C. 419. See M.P. Thompson [2002] Conv. 480.

[79] It is not clear on what basis the Court of Appeal in *Rashid* legitimately declined to follow *Parshall*. As a matter of precedent, the Court of Appeal is bound by its own previous decisions unless they are *per incuriam*, or cannot stand with a subsequent decision of the House of Lords. The issue with *Parshall* is that Mummery L.J. referred to *Pye v. Graham* extensively, and so it cannot be said to be *per incuriam*, and of course *Pye* was handed down prior to *Parshall*. It would therefore be rather surprising if *Rashid* did not result in further litigation.

[80] [1987] 55 P. & C.R. 337. *Phil Ltd v. Hindustan*, see II, Wallace [1991] Conv. 196, although see *Clowes Development (UK) Ltd v. Walters* [2005] EWHC 669 (Ch) at [44] *per* Hart J.

[81] (1987) 55 P. & C.R. 337 at 339 *per* Dillon L.J.   [82] See Wallace [1994] Conv. 196 at 203.

[83] [2011] EWCA Civ. 1306 at [43] *per* Arden L.J.   [84] [2016] UKPC 35.

question of whether permission was ever given was the subject of lengthy proceedings at first instance, with the trial judge ultimately preferring the landowner's testimony and witness statement.

The effect of the decision in *Smith v. Molyneaux* is troubling, because it means that once a landowner has successfully argued that permission had been orally given at some point during the period of possession relied upon, that permission will then be effective in the absence of any acknowledgement by the squatter. The squatter has neither, according to his own mind, been given permission, nor acknowledged that permission. It is difficult to conceive of what else the squatter might have done to ensure his possession remained adverse, and it cannot be right that the core question of permission is entirely and only in the hands of the landowner.

If the squatter is well aware that he occupies the property only by virtue of the local authority's consent, through a housing co-operative, and knows that he is among the classes of people intended to benefit under the local authority scheme, *Smart v. Lambeth LBC*[85] demonstrates that adverse possession cannot be established simply because the squatter had not signed the original agreement.

Where there is an acknowledgement of the owner's title, through the acceptance of a licence, but the requisite period of adverse possession had been completed prior to that acceptance, the licence will not negate that previous possession. In *Mitchell v. Watkinson*,[86] the defendants occupied the land without a written lease from 1974 to 1990, but accepted a licence from the freehold owner in 1990. The High Court held that the claimant's action for possession failed because the defendants had already completed twelve years of adverse possession, and the freehold owner's title had been duly extinguished in 1986 by virtue of the rules in the Limitation Act 1980.[87]

6.4.2.7 Implied permission

It is no longer the case that, because the use of the property by a squatter is not inconsistent with some planned future use of the land by the title owner, that possession must be attributed to a licence. It is, nevertheless, possible that a licence to occupy can be implied. This issue was addressed in *J. Alston &. Sons Ltd v. BOCM Paul Ltd*[88] S was originally a licensee of the disputed land. When that land was transferred to a new owner, the effect was to revoke the licence. Because the original occupation was permissive, it was argued that the continued occupation by the squatter after the licence had ended should be regarded as being under an implied licence and, therefore, permissive. This was rejected.

Judge Marshall accepted as axiomatic that if a person holds over after a permission to occupy has come to an end, the mere fact that the title owner does not object amounts to acquiescence and not implied permission, and that the two are different. Mere acquiescence is not sufficient to defeat a squatter's claim.[89] For a court to find the existence of a licence to occupy, this must be established as a matter of fact.[90] For a licence to be implied there must be some overt evidence of the fact of the licence being communicated with the licensee. Cases where such a licence has been implied without there being direct communication between the owner and the squatter have fallen into two groups.[91] These are when the occupation was pending negotiation of the grant of an interest in the land,[92] or where the history of the matter has shown that there was a specific intention of the owner to evict the occupier, followed by express reconsideration and change of stance, so that

---

[85] [2013] EWCA Civ. 1375.   [86] [2013] EWHC 2266 (Ch).

[87] Although title was registered, as the period of adverse possession took place before the coming into force of the LRA 2002, those rules did not apply. See 6.7.2.

[88] [2008] EWHC 3310 (Ch).   [89] Ibid. at [129].   [90] Ibid. at [117].   [91] Ibid. at [137].

[92] *Colin Dawson Windows Ltd v. King's Lynn and West Norfolk Borough Council* [2005] 2 P. &. C.R. 19.

it was obvious that the continued occupation was permissive.[93] In cases that do not fall into either of these categories, it will, in most cases, be necessary for the permission to be communicated to the occupier and, it is suggested, the occupier must accept that the occupation is permissive.

6.4.2.8 Intention of the owner

A further difficulty caused by the need for possession to be adverse arose where the owner had a future use in mind for the land, and where the nature of the occupation by the squatter was not inconsistent with that intended use. The point arose in *Leigh v. Jack*.[94] The dispute focused on a strip of land on which the owner, at some time in the future, intended to construct a street. The squatter had stored material from his factory on the strip, thereby making it inaccessible to pedestrians, and erected fences at each end. This was held not to amount to adverse possession. In a much-quoted dictum, Bramwell L.J. said:

> in order to defeat a title by dispossessing the former owner, acts must be done which are inconsistent with his enjoyment of the soil for the purposes which he intended to use it: that is not the case here, where it is the intention of the plaintiff and her predecessors in title not either to build upon or cultivate the land, but to devote it at some time to public purposes.[95]

Although influential, the meaning of this dictum was not clear. It could be taken to establish that, if the owner of the land had some future use for it which was not precluded by the acts of the squatter, then his actions could never amount to adverse possession, although, if that was the case, the basis of any such rule would become important. Alternatively, it may have meant that, in these circumstances, it is merely more difficult for the squatter to establish the requisite *animus possedendi* for his occupation to amount to adverse possession. Various interpretations were put forward in the controversial case of *Wallis & Cayton Bay Holiday Camp Ltd v. Shell-Mex & B.P. Ltd*.[96]

The squatter performed extensive acts on the disputed land which was owned by a petrol company that intended, at a later date, to construct a road and a garage on the land, although the latter plan was subsequently abandoned. After twelve years, the squatter claimed to be entitled to the land, a claim rejected by the majority[97] of the Court of Appeal.

After referring to a number of authorities, including *Leigh v. Jack*, Lord Denning M.R. said:

> The reason behind the decisions is because it does not lie in that other person's mouth to assert that he used the land of his own wrong as a trespasser. Rather his user is to be ascribed to the licence or permission of the true owner.[98]

6.4.2.9 Ascribed licence

This dictum is manifestly heretical; the whole basis of adverse possession is that the squatter used the land as a trespasser and, so, to imply a licence, without any factual basis for so doing, would make it impossible for a claim of adverse possession to succeed.[99] What

---

[93] *Hicks v. Chaplin* [2007] 1 E.G.L.R. 1.   [94] (1879) 5 Ex. D. 264.

[95] (1879) 5 Ex. D. 264 at 273.   [96] [1975] Q.B. 94.

[97] The cogent dissenting judgment of Stamp L.J. was approved in *Buckinghamshire County Council v. Moran* [1990] Ch. 623 at 640 *per* Slade L.J.

[98] *Wallis & Cayton Bay Holiday Camp Ltd v. Shell Mex & B.P. Ltd* [1975] Q.B. 91 at 103. Contrast *Buckinghamshire County Council v. Moran* [1990] Ch. 623 at 644 *per* Nourse L.J. accepting that adverse possession is predicated on 'possession as of wrong'.

[99] See *Ramnarace v. Lutchman* [2001] 1 W.L.R. 1651 at 1655 *per* Lord Millett.

was less clear, however, was whether what was being done was to introduce a new, and wholly unjustifiable, rule into the law relating to adverse possession, or whether what was being done was to apply *Leigh v. Jack*, by explaining it in a totally unorthodox fashion. One view of that decision was that, if the owner of the land had some future plans for it, and those plans were not precluded by the squatter's activities, then his possession could not be adverse,[100] the basis of this rule being the novel, and fictitious, licence implied by Lord Denning.

The issue of whether Lord Denning's judgment was, in effect, a novel interpretation of *Leigh v. Jack* or, rather, a complete innovation, became important because of the manner of the legislative response to the decision. Schedule 1, para. 8(4) to the Limitation Act 1980 provides that:

> For the purpose of determining whether a person occupying any land is in adverse possession of the land it shall not be assumed by implication of law that his occupation is by permission of the person entitled to the land merely by virtue of the fact that his occupation is not inconsistent with the latter's present or future enjoyment of the land.
>
> This provision shall not be taken as prejudicing a finding to the effect that a person's occupation of any land is by implied permission of the person entitled to the land in any case where such a finding is justified on the actual facts of the case.

The effect of this provision was to make Lord Denning's approach untenable. For a licence to be implied, there must have been 'some overt act by the land owner or some other demonstrable circumstance from which the inference can be drawn that permission was in fact given. It is however, irrelevant whether the users were aware of those matters . . . [provided that] a reasonable person would have appreciated that the user was there with the permission of the land owner.'[101] Where it was not possible to imply a licence on the facts of the case, however, what was considerably less clear was the continuing status of *Leigh v. Jack*. Put another way, the issue remained whether, disregarding the implied licence theory, a person, whose occupation of land was not inconsistent with the projected use of that land by the owner, would be regarded as being in adverse possession. The issue was fully ventilated in the leading case of *Buckinghamshire County Council v. Moran*.[102]

Land owned by the council had been encroached upon for over twelve years by the defendant, an adjoining landowner, and his predecessor in title. Extensive use had been made of the land and access to it was possible only from the defendant's house. The council, who intended to use the land in the future for a proposed road diversion, argued that the defendant had not established adverse possession because the use to which the defendant had put the land was not inconsistent with their proposed future use of it.

6.4.2.10 Intention of the squatter

This was rejected by the Court of Appeal, who decided in favour of the defendant. It was held that what was crucial was the intention of the squatter, not that of the landowner. What must be established is that the squatter has the relevant intention to possess, in the sense of excluding all other people from the property. In the instant case, the defendant was aware of the planned use of the land by the council[103] but was, nevertheless, held to be in adverse possession of it, the placing of a lock and a chain and a gate amounting to a final

---

[100] This was the basis of Ormrod L.J.'s judgment in favour of the petrol company. See also *Williams Bros Direct Supply Ltd v. Raftery* [1958] 1 Q.B. 159 at 173 *per* Sellers L.J.

[101] *Lambeth London Borough Council v. Rumbelow* (2001), unreported *per* Etherton J., approved in *Bath and North Somerset District Council v. Nicholson* [2002] 10 E.G.C.S. 156 *per* Mr Kim Lewison Q.C.; *Colin Dawson Windows Ltd v. King's Lynn and West Norfolk Borough Council* [2005] 2 P. &. C.R. 19 at [34] *per* Rix L.J.; *Bradford Estates (1983) Co. Ltd v. Taylor* [1996] 2 P. &. C.R. 5 at [23] *per* Sir Martin Nourse.

[102] [1990] Ch. 623.   [103] Ibid. at 640 *per* Slade L.J.

unequivocal demonstration of the defendant's intention to own the land.[104] The intention of the paper owner with regard to the future use of the land is relevant only insofar as the squatter is aware of that intention. Even then, as *Moran* itself demonstrates, this knowledge does not preclude the establishment of adverse possession. Rather, its relevance relates to the state of mind of the squatter who, if he actually intends to use the land so as not to interfere with the owner's planned use of the land, is likely not to have the requisite *animus possedendi* to achieve adverse possession.

It has been made clear by the House of Lords in *J.A. Pye (Oxford) Ltd v. Graham* that the 'suggestion that the sufficiency of the possession can depend on the intention not of the squatter but the true owner is heretical and wrong',[105] and this view has recently been endorsed by the Privy Council in *Smith v. Molyneaux*. It was said that, '[t]he concept of implied licence in law now forms no part of the common law. The Board considers that any spectre which remains of this concept should be firmly laid to rest'.[106] The Privy Council also made clear in *Wills v. Wills* that the original formulation of this principle in *Leigh v. Jack* was wrong.[107] It was considered to be 'an attempt to revive the pre-1833 concept of adverse possession requiring inconsistent user',[108] and was never a correct statement of the law. In Lord Browne-Wilkinson's view, it would have been better if the term 'adverse possession' had not been used by s. 10 of the Limitation Act 1939, and repeated in Sched. 1, para. 8 of the Limitation Act 1980, as its continued use caused the two heresies concerning the respective intentions of the squatter and the paper owner to be perpetuated.[109] While it is now probably too late to expect the expression ever to disappear from use,[110] the decision in *Pye* has done much to clarify the meaning of the term. It makes clear that what is required is factual possession of land by the squatter, without the permission, express or implied, of the paper owner, with the intention to possess that land.[111] The future plans of the paper owner are not relevant.

6.5 Human rights and adverse possession

The enactment of the Human Rights Act 1998 has led to the question being raised as to whether the law regarding limitation of actions in respect of land was compatible with the Act. There are two rights in the European Convention on Human Rights that have particular relevance to adverse possession claims: Art. 1 of the First Protocol to the Convention, which protects a person's right to the peaceful enjoyment of their possessions, and Art. 8 of the Convention, which protects a person's right to their home. The questions that arise are, first, whether the law of adverse possession is in violation of the registered proprietor's right to peaceful enjoyment of their possessions under Art. 1 of the First Protocol. Second, to what extent can the squatter rely upon Art. 8 to resist an action for possession brought

---

[104]   Ibid. at 642 *per* Slade L.J.

[105]   [2003] 1 A.C. 419 at 438 *per* Lord Browne-Wilkinson. Considerable reliance was placed on a valuable article by M. Dockray [1982] Conv. 256 and 'a remarkable judgment' at first instance *Powell v. McFarlane* (1977) 38 P. & C.R. 452: ibid. at 432.

[106]   [2016] UKPC 36 at [23] *per* Dame Mary Arden. See also *Chambers v. London Borough of Havering* [2011] EWCA Civ. 1576 at [35] *per* Etherton L.J.

[107]   *Wills v. Wills* [2004] 1 P. & C.R. 37 at [29] *per* Lord Walker, approving statements to this effect in *Buckinghamshire County Council v. Moran* [1990] Ch. 623 at 645 *per* Nourse L.J. See also *Mayor of London Borough of Hounslow v. Minchinton* (1997) 74 P. & C.R. 221 at 227 *per* Millett L.J. For the somewhat startling suggestion, based on alternative reports of this decision, that Bramwell L.J. did not actually say what has been attributed to him, see A. Claherty and D. Fox [2006] C.L.J. 558 at 560.

[108]   [2003] 1 A.C. 419 at 438.   [109]   Ibid.

[110]   See LRA 2002, Sched. 6, para. 11(1).

[111]   See also *J. Alston & Sons Ltd v. BOCM Ltd* [2008] EWHC 3310 (Ch) at [99] *per* H.H.J. Hazel Marshall.

by the registered proprietor which would require the squatter to leave their home? These questions will be considered in turn.

6.5.1 Registered proprietors and Article 1 of the First Protocol

When the issue of whether the law which enabled a registered proprietor of land to lose his title to it as a result of adverse possession infringed the human rights of the proprietor was first addressed, such discussion was *obiter*. This was because the Human Rights Act 1998, which came into force in 2000, did not operate retrospectively, and the cases where the matter arose predated the implementation of the Act. Nevertheless, a consensus emerged that English law was compliant with the Convention. This was either because Art. 1 of the First Protocol was not engaged at all,[112] or, even if it was, the law was justifiable in the public interest. The justification was that the law was 'reasonably required to avoid the real risk of injustice in the adjudication of stale claims, to ensure certainty of title and to promote social stability by the protection of the established and peaceable possession of property from the resurrection of old claims.'[113]

Notwithstanding this consensus, in *Beaulane Properties Ltd v. Palmer*,[114] Mr Nicholas Strauss Q.C., sitting as a Deputy High Court judge, came to a different conclusion. Taking the view that 'the pre-2003 law caused hardship to the registered proprietor, and gives unwarranted windfalls to undeserving land thieves',[115] he decided that English law, as it pertained to registered land, was incompatible with the Convention. Having reached this conclusion, he then felt free not to follow a recent House of Lords decision,[116] and, instead, applied a discredited analysis of the law to arrive at a result favourable to the registered proprietor.

The approach taken to this matter in *Beaulane* was, potentially, a source of considerable confusion and is open to the criticism that it is not open to a first instance judge to disregard a decision of the House of Lords on the basis that he considers that it is inconsistent with decisions of the European Court of Human Rights.[117] The folly of adopting this course on his own interpretation of the Convention when there was not even a European Court judgment dealing with the matter was highlighted when it subsequently transpired that his interpretation of the Convention was wrong.[118]

In *J.A. Pye (Oxford) Ltd v. United Kingdom*,[119] the Grand Chamber of the European Court of Human Rights considered whether a company, which had, as a result of the Limitation Act 1980, lost title to 25 hectares of land to which it was the registered proprietor, had suffered an infringement of its human rights. By a majority of ten votes to seven, and arriving at a different conclusion to that reached by the Chamber of the Court which had heard the case at first instance,[120] the full Court held that it had not.

---

[112] *Family Housing Association v. Donnallen* [2002] 1 P. & C.R. 34 at [15] *per* Park J.; *J.A. Pye (Oxford) Ltd v. Graham* [2001] Ch. 844 at [822] *per* Mummery L.J.

[113] *J.A. Pye (Oxford) Ltd v. Graham, supra*, at [823], *per* Keane L.J. The comments on the Convention were unaffected by the reversal of the actual decision. [2003] 1 A.C. 419.

[114] [2005] 4 All E.R. 461. See M.J. Dixon [2005] Conv. 345.

[115] [2005] 4 All E.R. 461 at 509.

[116] *J.A. Pye (0xford) Ltd v. Graham* [2003] 1 A.C. 419.

[117] See the comments in *Kay v. London Borough of Lambeth* [2006] UKHL 10 at [40]–[45] *per* Lord Bingham of Cornhill. Cf. *Ofulue v. Bossert* [2008] EWCA Civ. 7 at [9] *per* Arden L.J., affmd without reference to this issue: [2009] UKHL 16.

[118] For further criticism of *Beaulane* in its analysis of the substantive law, and its approach to precedent, see the 4th edn of this work at pp. 229–31.

[119] (2007) (Application No 44302/02). See E.J. Cooke (2008) 59 N.I.L.Q. 149.

[120] [2005] 49 E.G. 90.

In reaching this decision, it was held that, because the proprietor had lost the title to his land through adverse possession, Art. 1 of the Convention was engaged. The view taken, however, was that the effect of the Limitation Act was not to operate as a deprivation of a person's possessions within the meaning of the second sentence of the first paragraph of Art. 1, but as a control of the use of land within the meaning of the second paragraph.[121] The issue then became whether the working of English law was within an acceptable margin of appreciation. As to this, the majority view was that 'the existence of a 12 year limitation period for actions for recovery of land as such pursues a legitimate aim in the general interest',[122] and that 'Even where title is registered, it must be open to the legislature to attach more weight to lengthy, unchallenged possession than to the formal act of registration.'[123] The argument that the company's rights had been infringed because it had lost the title to its land without compensation received short shrift. The Court took the view that, although the land lost, particularly if it had development potential, would have been worth a substantial amount of money, this could not affect the outcome of the case. If limitation periods are to fulfil their purpose, this will always be the case, and must apply whatever the size of the claim.[124]

The decision of the Grand Chamber in *Pye (Oxford) Ltd v. United Kingdom* completely undermined the decision in *Beaulane Properties Ltd v. Palmer*. Although in *Ofulue v. Bossert*,[125] Arden L.J. somewhat enigmatically declined to comment on the decision, save to say that leave to appeal out of time was being sought in that case, the decision of the House of Lords in *Pye* was followed. It now seems clear that *Beaulane* is wrongly decided,[126] and that the English law of adverse possession as it affects registered land is compliant with the European Convention on Human Rights, and it is also clear that the full authority of the House of Lords in *Pye* has been restored.[127]

6.5.2 **Squatters and Article 8**

As will be seen, the reforms enacted by the LRA 2002 have made it considerably more difficult for a squatter to acquire a possessory title to registered land than was previously the case. This raises the question as to whether a squatter who has occupied property as a home over a prolonged period can, notwithstanding the fact that he has no legal right to be on the land, nevertheless resist a possession action by the legal owner on the basis of the squatter's right to a 'home' under Art. 8 of the European Convention. The effect of the Supreme Court decision in *Manchester City Council v. Pinnock*[128] is that the answer to this must, in principle, be in the affirmative.

Pinnock decided that a person who occupies property as a home can rely on Art. 8 of the European Convention to resist a possession action, even if he has no legal right to be on the property. The question of proportionality may be raised. While, admittedly, this was held to be the case where the initial possession was lawful, it is hard to see why that fact should disentitle the squatter from raising the same argument. This matter was adverted

---

[121] *Pye (Oxford) Ltd v. United Kingdom, supra*, at [66].
[122] Ibid. at [70].   [123] Ibid. at [74].   [124] Ibid. at [85].
[125] [2008] EWCA Civ. 7 at [54]. See M.J. Dixon [2008] Conv. 160.
[126] The Land Registry now applies the law as it would have done prior to the decision in *Beaulane*: Land Registry Practice Guide No 5 (updated 10 December 2018).
[127] See *National Westminster Bank Plc v. Ashe* [2008] EWCA Civ. 55 at [92] *per* Mummery L.J., admittedly without reference to *Beaulane*. See also *Ofulue v. Bossert* [2009] UKHL 16 at [67], [90] *per* Lord Neuberger; *Higgs v. Leshal Maryas Investment Company Ltd* [2009] UKPC 47 at [57] *per* Lord Scott.
[128] [2010] UKSC 45. For a full discussion of this decision, see Chapter 3 and M.P. Thompson [2011] Conv. 421.

to by Lord Bingham in *Kay v. Lambeth London Borough Council*[129] who, after referring to the test of proportionality, said:

> Rarely, if ever, could this test be satisfied where squatters occupy the land of a public authority which they do not and ... never had any right to occupy, *and the public authority act timeously to evict them* ... [I]t is very hard to imagine circumstances in which a court could properly give squatters of the kind described above anything more than a very brief respite.

This, it will be observed, relates to public authorities who act expeditiously to regain possession. When a squatter, perhaps with a family, has occupied local authority property for a period of many years, then it would seem that the issue of the proportionality of the possession proceedings could be raised, and any personal circumstances of the occupiers brought into play. That said, it is likely that the legal owner's entitlement to possession would be a proportionate means of giving effect to their respective rights; even where a squatter's right under Art. 8 is engaged, therefore, it would need to raise exceptional facts so as to make the legal owner's possession disproportionate.

The court in *Pinnock* expressly reserved the question of whether a squatter's Art. 8 rights could be invoked against a private landowner. It is generally thought that rights under the European Convention do not have 'horizontal effect', which is to say that they cannot be enforced directly between private parties, rather than against a public authority. In *Malik v. Fassenfelt*,[130] however, Sir Alan Ward suggested that the squatter's Art. 8 rights could be enforced against the private landowner, as the court itself was acting as a public authority under s. 6(3)(a) of the Human Rights Act 1998. If this were correct, the implications for property litigation would be significant, because most relationships in dealings with land—landlord and tenant, mortgagee bank and mortgagor, trustee and beneficiary, and so on—revolve around someone's home. Fortunately, this issue of the horizontal effect of human rights in private land disputes has recently been addressed by the Supreme Court in *McDonald v. McDonald*.[131] The appellant's parents had purchased a house, with the help of a loan, for their daughter to live in, under a tenancy. The parents' business failed and they defaulted on their loan repayments, with the inevitable consequence that receivers stepped in to repossess the house. The primary question for the court was whether it should, when entertaining a claim for possession by a private sector owner against a residential occupier, be required to consider the proportionality of evicting the occupier. The Supreme Court unanimously answered in the negative. They held that it was:

> not open to the tenant to contend that article 8 could justify a different order from that which is mandated by the contractual relationship between the parties, at least where, as here, there are legislative provisions which the democratically elected legislature has decided properly balance the competing interests of private sector landlords and residential tenants.[132]

The relevant provisions of domestic law which regulate when a private sector landlord can seek repossession reflect the state's assessment of where to strike the balance between the Art. 8 rights of residential tenants and the Art. 1 Protocol 1 rights of private landlords. To allow an Art. 8 argument for the tenant would also potentially be an unjustified interference of the landlord's Art. 1 Protocol 1 rights, resulting in a messy and unpredictable battle between two human rights in circumstances that domestic law expressly covers.[133]

---

[129] [2006] 2 A.C. 465 at [37], italics supplied.   [130] [2013] EWCA Civ. 798.

[131] [2016] UKSC 28. Noted S. Nield [2017] Conv. 60.

[132] Ibid. at [40] *per* Lord Neuberger and Lady Hale.

[133] The European Court of Rights agreed with the Supreme Court's analysis: *F.J.M. v. U.K.* [2018] App. No. 76202/16.

Following *McDonald*, it seems reasonable to conclude that the relevant provisions of the LRA 2002, and equally the Limitation Act 1980, perform that same function for the law of adverse possession in reflecting the democratically elected legislature's assessment of a squatter's Art. 8 rights, and a legal owner's Art. 1 Protocol 1 rights. If correct, it would mean that a squatter will be unable to argue that a court should assess the proportionality of evicting him if the private legal owner brings an action for possession.

6.6 Adverse possession and the criminal offence of squatting

It has long been the case that where a trespasser fails to leave someone else's home if required to do so by the owner of that home, they commit a criminal offence.[134] The homeowner is entitled to use reasonable force to eject the trespasser, who can also be arrested if they do not leave.

The recent decline in popular support for the unauthorized acquisition of land, reflected in the reforms to adverse possession wrought by the LRA 2002, triggered a media-led campaign against squatters; neither the criminal or civil law, the newspapers claimed, went far enough in protecting law-abiding homeowners from squatters and their 'particularly nasty variety of land theft'.[135] Despite criticism that the creation of a new criminal offence was both unnecessary and unjustified,[136] the offence of 'squatting in a residential building' was introduced in 2012.

6.6.1 Squatting in a residential building

Under s. 144(1) of the Legal Aid, Sentencing and Punishment of Offenders Act 2012, a person commits an offence if:

(a) the person is in a residential building as a trespasser having entered it as a trespasser,

(b) the person knows or ought to know that he or she is a trespasser, and

(c) the person is living in the building or intends to live there for any period.

Given that the rules of adverse possession require a squatter to occupy the land without the permission of the owner and with an intention to possess, any attempt to commence a period of adverse possession in someone's home is likely to simultaneously constitute an offence under s. 144. That, in turn, raises an important question: can a squatter rely on a period of occupation of land to claim title by adverse possession when that occupation will also be a criminal offence? This was the precise issue recently before the Court of Appeal in *Best v. Chief Land Registrar*.[137] Mr Best had commenced building work on an empty, vandalized house in 1997. Title to the property was registered, and the house qualified as a 'residential building' under s. 144. The owner had died, and her son had not been seen since 1996. Mr Best had treated the house as his own since 2001, and it was not disputed that he satisfied the requisite period of ten years of adverse possession under para. 1,

---

[134] Most recently by virtue of the Criminal Law Act 1977, s. 7. We use the simple term 'homeowner' in this section to encompass 'displaced residential occupier' and 'protected intending occupier' under the 1977 Act, defined in ss 12 and 12A respectively.

[135] 'Squatting Laws Endorse Theft', *The Telegraph*, 27 February 2011, http://www.telegraph.co.uk/news/uknews/law-and-order/8349685/Squatting-laws-endorse-theft.html.

[136] Our 'Media and Politicians are Misleading about Law on Squatters', *The Guardian*, 25 September 2011. The letter was signed by over 160 lawyers, academics, and policy-makers: https://www.theguardian.com/society/2011/sep/25/squatting-law-media-politicians.

[137] [2015] EWCA Civ. 17. See M. West [2015] Conv. 432; T. Dunk [2016] Conv. 331.

Sched. 6, LRA 2002 before making his application for registration in 2012. The Chief Land Registrar refused Mr Best's application, on the basis that Mr Best putatively committed an offence, in the Registrar's view, under s. 144 every time he was in the house,[138] and adverse possession could not succeed where the occupation relied upon for a claim under the LRA 2002 was a criminal offence.

As authority for his decision, the Registrar cited *R (on the application of Smith) v. Land Registry*,[139] where the court had held that adverse possession of a highway could not be established where it was subject to a public right of way,[140] and to obstruct the public highway would be a criminal offence.[141] The judge in *Smith* had distinguished *Bakewell Management v. Brandwood*[142] on the basis that the owner of the highway could not consent to its obstruction—it could not be made lawful by simple authority.

Mr Best successfully sought judicial review of the Registrar's decision, and the matter was heard first by Ouseley J. in the High Court[143] before reaching the Court of Appeal. The Registrar's case was simple: it is a fundamental principle of law that 'no court will lend its aid to a man who founds his cause of action upon an immoral or an illegal act'.[144] Both the High Court and Court of Appeal agreed that the illegality principle could be relevant to Sched. 6, LRA 2002, but what effect it had must come down to the balancing of competing public policy considerations which underpin, on the one hand, the law relating to adverse possession and, on the other, the criminal offence of squatting.[145] In other words, everything depends upon context. Sales L.J. considered that Parliament did not intend s. 144 to impact on the law of adverse possession; it was created for deterrence, and the relatively easy removal of trespassers. The Registrar's reliance on *Smith* was misplaced, it was held, as the decision in *Bakewell Management* was analogous to *Best*: a person does not commit an offence under s. 144 if permission to be on the land is given—the paper owner can authorize the trespass.

As a result, the Court of Appeal overturned the Registrar's decision, so that Mr Best could legitimately apply for registration of title under Sched. 6. In a somewhat surprising twist, because the deceased owner's son was not entitled to give a counter-notice under Sched. 6, para. 3, he could not object to Mr Best's application, and so the Chief Land Registrar was directed to give effect to Mr Best's application for title by adverse possession as if Mr Curtis' application had never been made.[146] *Best* is a welcome result for the clarity of the law, and emphasizes the continuing importance of adverse possession in a registered title system, but it is also likely to lead to further calls to remove entirely the ability of squatters to claim ownership of land.[147] The debate is far from over.

---

[138] The Registrar took the view that the s. 144 offences took place every time Mr Best was physically in the house from 1 September 2012 (the date on which s. 144 came into force) to 27 November 2012 (the date Mr Best applied to be registered as proprietor).

[139] [2009] EWHC 328 (Admin). The point was not taken up by the Court of Appeal: [2010] EWCA Civ. 200.

[140] See, however, the decision in *Port of London Authority v. Ashmore* [2009] EWHC 954 (Ch), where it was conceded that a public right of navigation over the Thames would not prevent Mr Ashmore from acquiring title by adverse possession to the river bed over which his barge was moored. For further discussion of both *Smith* and *Ashmore*, see M. George [2009] L.M.C.L.Q. 427.

[141] Highways Act 1980, s. 137(1).   [142] [2004] UKHL 14. See the discussion in 6.7.1.3—Public rights.

[143] [2014] EWHC 1370 (Admin).

[144] *Holman v. Johnson* (1775) 1 Cowp. 341 at 343 *per* Lord Mansfield.

[145] See [2015] EWCA Civ. 17 at [70] per Sales L.J. See also *Rashid v. Nasrullah* [2018] EWCA Civ. 2685 at [74], where Lewison L.J. said that 'bad people are entitled to the benefit of limitation periods'.

[146] *Best v. Curtis* [2016] EWLandRA 2015_0130 (FTT) (decision of Principal Judge Elizabeth Cooke in the Property Chamber, Land Registration First-Tier Tribunal, 11 April 2016). Noted R. Hickey [2017] Conv. 53.

[147] The *Daily Mail* picked up the story of Mr Best's successful registration: 'How the squatter who "stole" a pensioner's 3-bedroom house with the blessing of the law cost you £250,000', 20 May 2016, http://www.dailymail.co.uk/news/article-3601741/Squatter-stole-pensioner-s-three-bedroom-house-blessing-law-cost-250–000.html.

6.6.2 **Adverse possession and easements**

Easements are property rights which one landowner has over a neighbour's land—a right of way is one example. Necessarily, the existence of an easement acts as a constraint on what the neighbour can do with his land. Now that it is much more difficult for a squatter to acquire a possessory title, a person who has enjoyed the use of someone else's land may find it more advantageous to argue that the use led to the creation (by prescription or 'long use') of an easement, rather than a right of adverse possession. The question therefore arises how extensive the inference caused by an easement can be, and what differences lie between the extent and scope of easements on the one hand, and adverse possession on the other. This issue is fully discussed in Chapter 13.[148]

6.7 **The effect of adverse possession**

There are three different regimes which govern the effect of a period of adverse possession on the title. First, unregistered land is governed by the Limitation Act 1980. Second, registered land where the period of adverse possession was completed prior to 13 October 2003 is governed by rules derived from the LRA 1925. Third, registered land where the period of adverse possession is completed after 13 October 2003 is governed by the LRA 2002.

6.7.1 **Unregistered land**

The consequence of a squatter achieving the requisite period of adverse possession is a combination of statute and common law. The statute has a negative impact whereas the common law view is more positive in its impact. The negative side of adverse possession is established by s. 17 of the Limitation Act 1980, which provides that 'subject to section 18 of that Act,[149] at the expiration of the period prescribed by this Act for any person to bring an action to recover land . . . the title of that person to the land is extinguished'.

It should be noted that it is not simply the remedy that is extinguished. The effect of the statute is to extinguish the right which previously existed so that, in principle, an acknowledgement by the squatter of the paper owner's title after the limitation period has expired should have no effect; that which has been extinguished cannot subsequently be resuscitated. It is possible, however, for this effect to be achieved indirectly through a genuine compromise agreement to resolve a dispute between the parties after the twelve-year period has elapsed.[150] It is also possible for a squatter to be estopped from asserting a possessory title,[151] although more than the mere acknowledgement of title will be necessary for this result to occur.[152] Under the new law, whereby the period of adverse possession has to be proximate to the application for registration,[153] this latter issue will not arise.

6.7.1.1 **The rationale of a limitation period in unregistered land: security of title**

When title is unregistered, the method by which a vendor proves to a purchaser his right to sell it is to give an historical account of how title to the property came to be vested in him.[154] At one time, the period of investigation was sixty years. This period of investigation has, over a period of time, been reduced, so that the current period of investigation is

---

[148] See 6.6.2.   [149] This relates to settled land and land held upon trust.
[150] *Colchester Borough Council v. Smith* [1992] Ch. 421. For cogent criticism, see A.R.H. Brierly [1991]
[llllv 39/
[151] *St Pancras and Humanist Housing Association Ltd v. Leonard* [2010] EWCA Civ. 1442.
[152] See *J. Alston & Sons Ltd v. BOCM Pauls Ltd* [2008] EWHC 3310 (Ch) at [109] *per* H.H.J. Hazel Marshall.
[153] LRA 2002, Sched. 15, para.1. See 6.7.3.5.   [154] See 3.6.4.2—Investigation of title.

one of at least fifteen years.[155] This reform, aimed at facilitating conveyancing, was made possible, in part, by changes to the law relating to limitation periods in respect of land actions.[156] In short, the early law on the subject was such that a purchaser had to engage in a very lengthy investigation of title as, owing to mistakes which might have been made in the past, a person may still, many years later, be able to substantiate a claim to the land. The effect of changes to the law relating to the law of limitation meant that it was safer for a purchaser to accept a shorter period title than it was in the past, secure in the knowledge that any rights accrued in the past would now have been extinguished by the passage of time.[157] The effect of limitation in the case of unregistered land was, therefore, to add security to titles, with the result that it has been described as being 'absolutely fundamental to unregistered conveyancing'.[158]

A second, related, point concerns boundary disputes. A not infrequent bone of contention between neighbours is where, legally, the boundary lies between two adjoining properties. When such disputes arise, they can frequently generate 'a particularly painful form of litigation. Feelings can run high and disproportionate amounts of money are spent.'[159] If a fence is erected in a place other than where the legal boundary actually is, then some of the neighbour's land will have been wrongfully enclosed. At the end of the limitation period, the person whose land is on the wrong side of the fence will find that his action to recover the land will have been statute barred, thereby in most cases avoiding long and expensive litigation to determine the precise location of the boundary.[160]

As against these arguments, the fact remains that the result of the establishment of a possessory title is that one person, the squatter, obtains land from another, the owner of the paper title, without having to pay anything for it. This was put in graphic terms in *Lambeth Borough Council v. Bigden*,[161] where, had the claim to a possessory title succeeded, 'millions of pounds of public housing stock in one of the poorest boroughs in the country [would have] passed gratis into private ownership'. Not surprisingly, this has evoked expressions of distaste, a factor which has been said to have caused the courts to put glosses on the law, to avoid deciding in favour of the squatter.[162] This evident distaste has led to the squatter being described as a 'thief of the land'.[163] In similar vein, unhappiness has been expressed 'with a jurisprudence that allows squatters to acquire title to land knowing full well that the land belongs to another'.[164] Nor are such claims rare. In the debates on the Land Registration Bill, it was revealed that each year there are some 20,000 applications to the Land Registry by people asserting possessory rights, and of those some 15,000 are successful.[165]

---

[155] LPA 1925, s. 44, as substituted by LPA 1969, s. 23.

[156] See Dockray [1982] Conv. 256 at 277–84. The Limitation Act 1833 was an important piece of reforming legislation.

[157] See, e.g., *Re Atkinson and Horsell's Contract* [1912] 2 Ch. 1.

[158] Baroness Scotland, Hansard, H.L. vol. 627, col. 1379.

[159] *Alan Wibberley Building Ltd v. Insley* [1999] 1 W.L.R. 894 at 895 *per* Lord Hoffmann. See also *Palfrey v. Wilson* [2007] EWCA Civ. 94; *Haycocks v. Neville* [2007] EWCA Civ. 78 at [22] *per* Lawrence Collins L.J.

[160] For a graphic illustration, involving a very small amount of land, see *Hawkes v. Howe* [2002] EWCA Civ. 1136. See also *Steward v. Gallop* [2010] EWCA Civ. 823, where the parties agreed that the value of the disputed land was nil, but each had incurred costs in excess of £100,000 in fighting the case!

[161] (2000) 33 H.L.R. 478 at 483 *per* Mummery L.J., although one can also point to the sustained neglect in the management of their property which would enable such a claim to succeed. For an interesting discussion of what they term 'urban squatting', see N. Cobb and L. Fox (2007) 27 L.S. 236.

[162] See *Purbrick v. London Borough of Hackney* [2003] EWHC 1871 (Ch) at [7] *per* Neuberger J.

[163] E.J. Cooke [1999] Conv. 136 at 142. See also *J.A. Pye (Oxford) Ltd v. Graham* [2000] Ch. 676 at 709 *per* Neuberger J., views endorsed on appeal at [2003] 1 A.C. 419 at 426 *per* Lord Bingham.

[164] L. Tee [2002] Conv. 50.

[165] Baroness Scotland, Hansard, H.L. vol. 627, col. 1332.

6.7.1.2 Limitation under the 1980 Act

Section 15 of the Limitation Act 1980 provides that no action shall be brought by any person to recover any land after the expiration of twelve years from the date on which the right of action accrued to him, or if first accrued to some person through whom he claims, that person. The Act refers to the right of action accruing to some person through whom the person seeking to recover the land claims. Thus, if A was dispossessed by S four years prior to B acquiring the title from A, B has a further eight years in which to bring his action against S to recover the land. The converse situation is also true. Suppose C was dispossessed by D four years previously and then D is dispossessed by E, who occupies the land for a further eight years. At this stage, C's cause of action will be barred and so he cannot recover the land from E.[166] D, however, who was in possession of the land before E will be able to recover the land from him, provided that he brings the action within the next eight years, as his right of action accrued four years ago.[167] The general period of limitation under the 1980 Act is twelve years. There are some limited exceptions to this, of which the most important is that when the land is owned by the Crown, the period is thirty years.[168]

6.7.1.3 The accrual of a right of action

For time to begin to run in favour of the claimant, who is normally referred to as the squatter, certain conditions laid down by s. 15 and Sched. 1 to the Act must be satisfied. The two main requirements are that:

(i) the owner of the land who is entitled in possession has been dispossessed or has discontinued his possession; and

(ii) some other person has gone into adverse possession of the land.

The various issues raised by these requirements will be considered in turn.

Entitled in possession

The Limitation Act refers to a person who is entitled in possession. Provision is made for the position of those who have future interests in the land and the squatter went into possession of the land before that interest fell into possession. Section 15(2) of the Act provides that time begins to run from the date when the squatter took possession. No action can then be brought by the holder of the future interest twelve years from that date or six years from the date when his interest fell into possession, whichever is the longer. So, if land is held by A for life, remainder to B in fee simple, and S takes possession while A is still alive, B must bring an action for possession within either twelve years of S taking possession or six years after A's death, whichever is the later. The purpose of this provision is to prevent the interest of the holder of a future interest being barred before it has actually come into possession. In such circumstances, the squatter may find that, despite having been in adverse possession for longer than twelve years, his right to continued possession is defeated by the holder of a future interest bringing possession proceedings.

Independent title

The rights acquired by a squatter derive from the relative nature of title to land. A person in possession of land has rights good against anyone except a person with a better right

---

[166] See *Chambers v. London Borough of Havering* [2011] EWCA Civ. 1576 at [52] *per* Lewison L.J.

[167] See generally, *Asher v. Whitlock* (1865) L.R. 1 Q.B. 1. See also *Sze To Chan Keung v. Kung Kwok Wai David* [1997] 1 W.L.R. 1232, which was, incidentally, the last appeal to the Privy Council from Hong Kong: see at 1233 *per* Lord Hoffmann.

[168] Limitation Act 1980, s. 25; Sched. 1, paras 11 and 12. It is not necessary that the Crown is the owner of the land throughout the thirty-year period. See *Hill v. Transport for London* [2005] 3 All E.R. 677.

to that land, that person being the rightful owner. If 'the rightful owner does not come forward and assert his title by process of law within the period prescribed by the Statute of Limitations applicable to the case, his right is forever extinguished, and the possessory owner acquires an absolute title'.[169] This title is quite independent from the title held by the person who has been dispossessed. In no sense does the squatter obtain a form of 'parliamentary conveyance'[170] of the estate of the person dispossessed.

The squatter occupies the land as a fee simple owner, whose right of occupation is only liable to be defeated by the holder of a person with a better right to the land. This is, until the limitation period has expired, the person with the superior title to the land. When his right to possession has been defeated, the squatter's possessory title is a fee simple, quite independent from that of the person he has dispossessed. He is not, however, a purchaser of the land for value. Accordingly, he will be bound by any equitable interests affecting the land regardless of notice.[171]

Interruption of time during the limitation period

Once time has begun to run, it does not matter if the first squatter is dispossessed by a second squatter. As against the owner, the two periods of time will be aggregated and, as against him, time will not stop running just because the squatter has, himself, been dispossessed. Where, however, the squatter gives up possession, or possession is recovered by the owner,[172] even temporarily, and he is not replaced by another squatter, the running of time will be interrupted and the full period of time will need to be established from the date when he retakes possession.[173]

Acknowledgement of title

The running of time will also be interrupted if the squatter acknowledges the title of the paper owner or pays part of the principal or interest due under a debt.[174] To be an effective acknowledgement of the owner's title, that acknowledgement must be in writing and signed by the person making it, or his agent, to the person entitled to the land, or to his agent.[175] An oral acknowledgement of the title will not suffice to stop time running; to allow this to have effect would lead to unnecessary disputes as to what was or was not said over the course of a long period of time.[176] The effect of a written acknowledgement of the owner's title is not suspensory. Once such an acknowledgement is made, then, for a possessory title to be established, the full limitation period must be established from that date.[177]

To interrupt the running of time, it is not necessary that the acknowledgement of the owner's title be explicit. Indeed, it is unlikely to be so.[178] An acknowledgement can be implicit, good examples of this being where the squatter offers to purchase the property,[179] or

---

[169] *Perry v. Clissold* [1907] A.C. 73 at 79 *per* Lord Macnaghten.

[170] *Tichborne v. Weir* (1892) 67 L.T. 735 at 737 *per* Bowen L.J.

[171] *Re Nisbet and Potts' Contract* [1906] 1 Ch. 386.

[172] See *Zarb v. Parry* [2011] EWCA Civ. 1306 at [29]–[44] *per* Arden L.J.

[173] *Generay v. The Containerised Storage Co. Ltd* [2005] EWCA Civ. 478. The squatter erected a fence temporarily excluding himself from part of the land he had previously occupied.

[174] Limitation Act 1980, s. 29.

[175] Ibid., s. 30. See O. Radley-Gardner and C. Harpum [2001] Conv. 155 at 164–72.

[176] See *Browne v. Perry* [1991] 1 W.L.R. 1297 at 1301–2 *per* Lord Templeman.

[177] Limitation Act 1980, s. 29(2)(a). For an example of this, see *J.A. Pye (Oxford) Ltd v. Graham* [2003] 1 A.C. 419.

[178] Although see *Lambeth London Borough Council v. Archangel* [2002] 1 P. & C.R. 18, where a letter from the squatter referred to Lambeth's property.

[179] *Edgington v. Clark* [1964] 1 Q.B. 367.

to rent it,[180] or enquires as to whether the owner intends to sell the property.[181] This is so, unless the offer is made 'without prejudice', when such correspondence is not admissible as evidence.[182] Similarly, a written request to the owner of the land to take steps to stop the property from being vandalized should suffice to interrupt the running of time. In all of these cases, the requests carry with them an implicit acknowledgement that the addressee has a better title to the land.[183]

Section 29(2) of the Limitation Act 1980 requires that the acknowledgement of the paper owner's title be made by the person in possession of the land. The meaning of this was considered in the interesting case of *London Borough of Tower Hamlets v. Barrett*.[184] The Barretts were the tenants of a pub. Adjoining the property was open land, the registered proprietor of which was the local authority. The Barretts were found to be in adverse possession of the land. One of the issues which arose in the case was the effect of written negotiations between the landlord of the Barretts, Trumans Brewery, and the local authority with regard to Trumans acquiring the land. It was held that this did not amount to a written acknowledgement of the local authority's title. This was because the meaning of possession in the section was taken to mean physical possession and the brewery was not in possession. The Barretts were.[185] While plausible, it is suggested that this is unsound. In the first place, possession is normally defined to include the receipt of rents and profits,[186] and it is not clear why this should not apply in the present context. Second, the effect of the adverse possession by the Barretts was to acquire title on behalf of Trumans[187] and it seems to be very strange that the brewery, having acknowledged in writing the title of the local authority, should subsequently be held to have acquired a possessory title to it.[188]

If the paper owner obtains a possession order, this will stop time running,[189] but a letter demanding that the squatter vacate the premises will not.[190] Neither will the service of a writ seeking possession stop time running,[191] unless the action is proceeded with, so that if the writ is served eleven years and six months after the squatter has taken possession, but the case is not actually heard until the full twelve years has elapsed, the service of the writ will be regarded as having interrupted the running of time. The fact that unilateral demands for possession will not stop time running, however, casts further doubt on the correctness of the decisions in *B.P. Properties Ltd v. Buckler*[192] and *Smith v. Molyneaux*[193] that a unilateral permission to occupy given to a squatter after he has taken possession, can stop time running for the purposes of the Limitation Act 1980.[194]

The implementation of the rules contained in the Limitation Act 1980 to unregistered land is, in part, dependent upon the nature of the proprietary interests of either

---

[180] *Lambeth London Borough Council v. Bigden* (2000) 33 H.L.R. 478. *R. v. Secretary of State for the Environment, ex parte Davies* (1990) 61 P. & C.R. 487, although disapproved in *J.A. Pye (Oxford) Ltd v. Graham, supra*, at 438 *per* Lord Browne-Wilkinson, is defensible on this basis. See also *Rehman v. Benfield* [2006] EWCA Civ. 1392.

[181] *Allen v. Matthews* [2007] EWCA Civ. 216, the background to this case being said to have been 'one of violence and crime' at [6] *per* Lawrence Collins L.J.

[182] *Ofulue v. Bossert* [2009] UKHL 16.

[183] Cf. *Pavledes v. Ryesbridge Properties Ltd* (1989) 58 P. & C.R. 459 at 480 *per* Knox J., who seemed to think that such action gave rise to different considerations when considering a person's intention to possess as opposed to an acknowledgement of title. This seems doubtful.

[184] [2005] EWCA Civ. 923.   [185] Ibid. at [95]–[99] *per* Neuberger L.J.

[186] Law of Property Act (LPA) 1925, s. 205(2)(xix).   [187] See 6.7.1.3—Tenancies.

[188] This did not actually happen in the present case, as the brewery had transferred the land to the Barretts.

[189] *B.P. Properties v. Buckler* (1987) 55 P. & C.R. 337.

[190] *Mount Carmel Investments Ltd v. Peter Thurlow Ltd* (1988) 57 P. & C.R. 396; *Ramnarace v. Lutchman* [2001] 1 W.L.R. 1651 at 1659 *per* Lord Millett.

[191] *Markfield Investments Ltd v. Evans* [2001] 2 All E.R. 738.

[192] (1987) 55 P. & C.R. 337. See 6.4.2.6.

[193] [2016] UKPC 35.   [194] See M.P. Thompson [2001] Conv. 341 at 346–7.

the dispossessed or the adverse possessor. Four alternatives are particularly worthy of note: first, what is the effect of a period of adverse possession of land subject to a tenancy? Second, can a trustee acquire a possessory interest against his beneficiary? Third, can a mortgagor claim title by adverse possession against the mortgagee bank? Fourth, is adverse possession of a public highway possible? These questions will be addressed in turn.

Tenancies

A squatter may go into possession when the land is subject to a tenancy. This adverse possession will operate against the tenant but will not do so against the owner of the reversion. Although the landlord is regarded as being in possession of the land, because he is in receipt of the rents and profits,[195] in the present context his claim to physical possession is what is important and so 'the landlord's right of action accrues when, but only when, the lease ends and the landlord's reversionary estate falls into possession'.[196]

It is possible for a tenant to be in adverse possession of a property. He cannot, however, acquire a possessory title of the property which is subject to the lease,[197] as he cannot deny his own landlord's title.[198] If he does not pay rent, however, then the landlord's right to bring an action in respect of the arrears will be barred after six years.[199] The tenant can acquire a possessory title against his landlord if he remains in possession of the property, without paying rent, after the lease has terminated. In the case of a written periodic tenancy, time starts to run from the termination of the lease, that occurring when either party has served upon the other a notice to quit.[200] In the case of an oral periodic tenancy, or one arising by implication, time begins to run from the end of the first period or, if rent is paid subsequently, from the last payment of rent.[201] In the case of a tenancy at will, which, as the name suggests, is a lease which either party can, at any time, terminate,[202] time will begin to run in favour of the tenant when the lease is determined.[203]

If a tenant occupies land owned by a third party, there is a rebuttable presumption that the occupation is on behalf of the landlord.[204] So, in *London Borough of Tower Hamlets v. Barrett*,[205] a tenant of a pub occupied adjoining land for the requisite period of time. It was held that the possessory title was acquired on behalf of the landlord. When, however, the landlord transferred the freehold of the pub to the tenant, this operated also to transfer the area of land to the tenant who was able, therefore, to resist a possession action brought by the local authority. This presumption is rebuttable and the further the land is away from that which is subject to the tenancy, the more likely it is to be rebutted.[206] If the tenant occupies other land, which is also owned by the landlord, a similar presumption applies, so that the land is regarded as being subject to the terms of the original lease.[207]

---

[195] LPA 1925, s. 205(1)(xix).

[196] *Chung Ping Kwan v. Lam Island Development Co. Ltd* [1997] A.C. 38 at 46 *per* Lord Nicholls.

[197] If the person occupies in the mistaken belief that he has a tenancy, he may acquire a possessory title against the freeholder. See *Ofulue v. Bossert* [2008] EWCA Civ. 7.

[198] A tenant in occupation under a tenancy granted contrary to a term in a mortgage will not be in adverse possession as against the mortgagee: see *Carroll v. Manek* (1999) 79 P. & C.R. 173 at 185 *per* Judge Hicks.

[199] Limitation Act 1980, s. 19. If rent is paid to a person other than the landlord, time will begin to run against the owner of the reversion in favour of the person in receipt of the rent: Sched. 1, para. 6.

[200] See 10.10.2.   [201] Limitation Act 1980, Sched. 1, para. 5(1)(2).

[202] See 10.10.4.   [203] *Colchester Borough Council v. Smith* [1991] Ch. 448 at 481 *per* Ferris J.

[204] *King v. Smith* [1950] 1 All E.R. 553; *Smirk v. Lyndale Developments Ltd* [1975] Ch. 317 at 323–31 *per* Sir John Pennycuick V.-C., reversed on the facts but approved on this point, ibid. at 337 *per* Lawton L.J.

[205] [2005] EWCA Civ. 923.

[206] Ibid. at [31] *per* Neuberger L.J.

[207] *J.F. Perrot & Co. v. Cohen* [1958] 1 K.B. 705.

When a squatter takes possession of land held previously by a tenant, again he takes possession as a fee simple owner and the title of the tenant is extinguished after the requisite twelve-year period. His position with regard to the freeholder is more complicated. What is clear is that time does not begin to run as against the freeholder until the lease has expired; until that time, he has no right to physical possession of the land.[208] When the lease expires, however, then, despite the squatter possessing the land as owner of a fee simple, the landlord will have the right to recover possession from the squatter because the landlord's right to the land is better than his.[209] The position while the lease continues to exist creates more difficulty.

While the lease is subsisting, the original contractual tenant remains liable to the landlord under the terms of that lease because there exists privity of contract between them. Because the effect of adverse possession is not to operate as a parliamentary conveyance, the effect of the squatter barring the title of the tenant is to make him not liable under the covenants contained in the lease.[210] An indirect method of enforcing these covenants is available, however, as, if the lease contains a forfeiture clause, the landlord can forfeit the lease as against the original tenant for breach of covenant, thereby ending that tenancy. The result of doing this is that, as against the squatter, who cannot apply for relief against forfeiture,[211] the landlord is now entitled to possession of the property. What has occasioned rather more controversy is to establish the respective positions of the landlord and the squatter when the tenant purports to terminate the lease after his title has been barred by a squatter.

Surrender of lease

This issue occurred in the leading case of *Fairweather v. St Marylebone Properties Ltd*,[212] where it was held by a bare majority of the House of Lords that a surrender of a lease by a tenant whose title was barred by the adverse possession of a squatter had the effect that the landlord was at that point entitled to possession of the property as against the squatter. This decision has been subjected to what has been termed a 'powerful critique'.[213] The essence of that critique is, indeed, plausible. Its basis is that the effect of the limitation period having expired is that the title of the tenant is extinguished,[214] and therefore he has nothing to surrender to the landlord. As he could not evict the squatter once the limitation period had expired, he should not be able to confer such a right upon the landlord.[215] He cannot transfer what he has not got.[216]

While persuasive, the argument is not compelling. As the majority in *Fairweather* pointed out, although the effect of the Limitation Act is to extinguish the tenant's title, it is evident that the title is not extinguished for all purposes. Were it otherwise, then when the tenant's title was barred by adverse possession, the landlord would be entitled to possession and the tenant would cease to be liable on the covenants in the lease, which, everyone

---

[208] *Chung Ping Kwan v. Lam Island Development Co. Ltd* [1997] A.C. 38 at 46 *per* Lord Nicholls. See 6.7.1.3—Tenancies.

[209] *Taylor v. Twinberrow* [1930] 2 K.B. 16.

[210] *Tichborne v. Weir* (1892) 67 L.T. 735. If the squatter actively takes advantage of covenants in the lease, he may then be estopped from denying that he is liable under other terms of that lease: *Tito v. Waddell (No. 2)* [1977] Ch. 106 at 299–302 *per* Megarry J.

[211] *Tickner v. Buzzacott* [1965] Ch. 426; D.G. Barnsley (1965) 28 M.L.R. 364. For forfeiture of leases, see 10.10.3.

[212] [1963] A.C. 510.

[213] *Chung Ping Kwan v. Lam Island Development Co. Ltd* [1997] A.C. 38 at 47 *per* Lord Nicholls, referring to H.W.R. Wade (1962) 78 L.Q.R. 541. The Privy Council found it unnecessary to express a view as to whether the decision in *Fairweather* was correct.

[214] Limitation Act 1980, s. 17.   [215] See Wade (1962) 78 L.Q.R. 541 at 552.

[216] Ibid. at 559.

agrees, is not the case. Moreover, if the original lease contained a break clause, giving either side the option to bring a fixed term tenancy to a premature end, and the landlord exercised this clause as against the original tenant whose interest had become statute barred, it should be the case that the landlord is now entitled to possession as against the squatter. The fact that adverse possession operates to extinguish the tenant's title *vis-à-vis* the squatter but does not do so *vis-à-vis* the landlord,[217] does seem to lead to the conclusion reached by the majority that it is open for the original tenant and the landlord to collude to defeat the squatter's title.

Trustees

As a matter of general principle, a trustee cannot acquire a possessory title against his beneficiary.[218] A consequence of this is that, because land which is subject to co-ownership is held on trust,[219] one co-owner cannot acquire a possessory title against the other.[220]

Mortgagors

Under the general law of mortgages, the mortgagee—that is, the lender—is entitled as from the date of the mortgage to possess the mortgaged property.[221] Ordinarily, the mortgagee does not exercise this right and, instead, it is the mortgagor—that is, the borrower—who is in possession. In *National Westminster Bank Plc v Ashe*,[222] the mortgagor had been in possession of the property for twelve years, during which time he had neither made any payments under the mortgage nor in any other way acknowledged the rights of the mortgagee. It was held that 'even though it may come as an unpleasant surprise to the Bank and other mortgagees that their mortgagors are in adverse possession',[223] this was the outcome which had occurred, and the registered charge was removed from the mortgagor's register of title. The bank raised concerns that a decision to this effect could lead to many mortgagees losing their security. This fear was, quite rightly, seen as an exaggeration, in that it will surely not be common for a lender to allow a mortgagor to remain in possession for twelve years without either receiving any payment or taking other steps to enforce its security. Furthermore, even if a bank is prepared to allow a defaulting mortgagor to remain in the property, it is quite easy for it to prevent the mortgagor from acquiring a possessory title, by ensuring that he acknowledges the mortgagee's title.[224]

Public rights

It is not possible to obtain a possessory right as against a public highway,[225] although one can acquire such a right to land beneath the surface of the highway, such as might occur in the case of a cellar.[226] Similarly, one can acquire a possessory right to a river bed, despite there being a public right of navigation on the river, which will continue notwithstanding the position with respect to the land below it.[227]

---

[217] [1963] A.C. 510 at 544 *per* Lord Denning.

[218] Limitation Act 1980, s. 22(2); *J.A. Pye (Oxford) Ltd v. Graham* [2003] 1 A.C. 419 at 434 *per* Lord Browne-Wilkinson.

[219] See Chapter 9.

[220] *Re Landi* [1939] Ch. 828. For the different position in Jamaica, see *Wills v. Wills* [2004] 1 P. & C.R. 37.

[221] See *Four-Maids Ltd v. Dudley Marshall (Properties) Ltd* [1957] Ch. 317; and 11.6.2.1.

[222] [2008] EWCA Civ. 55.   [223] Ibid. at [88] *per* Mummery L.J.

[224] Ibid. at [6]–[19] *per* Mummery L.J. For acknowledgement of title, see 6.7.1.3—Interruption of time during the limitation period.

[225] *R. (on the application of Smith) v. Land Registry* [2010] EWCA Civ. 200.

[226] Ibid. at [19] *per* Arden L.J.

[227] *Roberts v. Swangrove Estates Ltd* [2007] 2 P. & C.R. 326; *Port of London Authority v. Ashmore* [2010] EWCA Civ. 30. For analysis, see M. George [2009] L.M.C.L.Q. 427.

6.7.2 **Adverse possession in registered land under the LRA 1925**

Where title is registered, if twelve years of adverse possession has been completed before 13 October 2003,[228] the same basic principle of limitation applies as it does to unregistered title. These claims were originally governed by s. 75, LRA 1925, which replaced the extinguishment of title with the imposition of a trust:

> 75 –(1) The Limitation Acts shall apply to registered land in the same manner and to the same extent as those Acts apply to land not registered, except that where, if the land were not registered, the estate of the person registered as proprietor would be extinguished, such estate shall not be extinguished but shall be deemed to be held by the proprietor for the time being on trust for the person who, by virtue of the said Acts, has acquired title against any proprietor, but without prejudice to the estates and interests of any other person interested in the land whose estate or interest is not extinguished by those Acts.
>
> (2) Any person claiming to have acquired a title under the Limitation Acts to a registered estate in the land may apply to be registered as proprietor thereof.

The reason for the imposition of a trust was that, while the person whose title is barred remains the registered proprietor, he retained title to the land, and although normally the effect of adverse possession is to extinguish the title, this cannot happen until the register has been altered. Nevertheless, the registered proprietor is no longer entitled to the land and the solution to this paradox was to impose a trust upon him, thereby depriving him of the beneficial title.[229]

Although, in the *Fairweather* case, Lord Denning expressed the view that the imposition of the trust was a mere matter of machinery which 'does not alter the substantive law very much',[230] Lord Radcliffe was more cautious. He considered that the meaning of the section 'was not at all easy to discover'[231] and that he was 'not at all satisfied that section 75(1) does create a trust interest in the squatter of the kind that one would expect from the words used'.[232] It has now become apparent that the effect of s. 75 was not merely mechanical but caused there to be substantive differences between registered and unregistered land when considering the effect of adverse possession, in particular when adverse possession occurred against a tenant.

6.7.2.1 **The effect of registration**

Where the title is leasehold, upon the expiration of the limitation period, the leasehold estate was held upon trust for the squatter. There were difficulties caused by this, these difficulties first being explored in *Spectrum Investment Co. v. Holmes*.[233] The defendant had established a possessory title against a tenant. Sometime later she applied for registration. The Land Registry contacted the tenant but received no reply, whereupon the defendant was registered as a leasehold proprietor with a possessory title and the title under which the original tenant had been registered was closed. The plaintiff company, who had originally been registered with a possessory freehold title, was subsequently registered with an absolute title to the freehold. The position with regard to the defendant then being discovered, the original tenant then purported to surrender the lease to the company who,

---

[228] The date of entry into force of the LRA 2002. If twelve years of adverse possession has not been completed by that date, the claim is instead governed by the 2002 Act.

[229] See E.J. Cooke [1999] Conv. 136 at 142. For a penetrating analysis of the effect of adverse possession in registered land, see D. Cooke (1994) 14 L.S. 1. See also G. Battersby, in Bright and Dewar (eds), *Land Law: Themes and Perspectives* (Oxford, Oxford University Press, 1998), 487 at 490–4.

[230] [1963] A.C. 510 at 548.   [231] Ibid. at 541.

[232] Ibid. at 542–3.   [233] [1981] 1 W.L.R. 221.

thereupon, sought possession. Browne-Wilkinson J., distinguishing *Fairweather*, which he accepted was factually indistinguishable from the present case,[234] held in favour of the defendant.

The reason why a different conclusion was reached related to s. 75 of the 1925 Act. While noting that the section provides that the Limitation Acts are to apply to registered land to the same extent as they do to land which is unregistered, Browne-Wilkinson J. also observed that s. 17 of the Limitation Act 1980 operated expressly subject to s. 75 of the LRA 1925. Section 75(2) of the Act entitles the squatter who claims to be entitled to have acquired a title to a registered estate to apply for registration thereof. The word 'thereof'[235] was regarded as significant, as it referred back to s. 75(1). The effect of this was that the registration of the defendant with a possessory leasehold title operated to vest in her the estate held by the original tenant. In other words, the registration operated as a form of parliamentary conveyance of the tenant's estate to the squatter. The consequence of this is that the tenant had nothing to surrender to the landlord, and so a different result was arrived at because title was registered than would have been the case had title been unregistered.

6.7.2.2 The impact of the trust

In *Spectrum Investment Co. Ltd v. Holmes*, the squatter had applied for registration, and been registered as proprietor, prior to the purported surrender of the lease. The position was expressly left open as to what the result would have been had the surrender occurred after the squatter had established twelve years' adverse possession against a person registered with a leasehold title but before any application had been made for registration by the squatter.[236] This issue fell to be decided in *Central London Commercial Estates Ltd v. Kato Kagaku Co. Ltd*,[237] where it was held that the freeholder still took subject to the squatter's possessory title.

In reaching this conclusion Sedley J. was aware that a squatter, when in adverse possession of land, is, in accordance with general principle, occupying the property as a fee simple owner. The effect of s. 75, however, was that when the requisite statutory period had expired, a trust was imposed upon the leasehold estate and so he becomes the owner of that.[238] Even if the tenant then surrenders the lease to the landlord, the equitable lease which arose in the squatter's favour takes effect as an overriding interest which is, therefore, binding upon the landlord who will not be able to obtain possession of the land until the lease is determined: the opposite result to that which occurs when title is unregistered.

6.7.2.3 The transitional provisions under the LRA 2002

Schedule 12 of the LRA 2002 preserves the right conferred on the adverse possessor in s. 75(2) of the LRA 1925 to be registered as proprietor, but all trusts held under s. 75(1) are removed with the repeal of the LRA 1925 and the coming into force of the LRA 2002 on 13 October 2003. If a claimant had completed twelve years of adverse possession immediately before that date, and therefore a trust had arisen under the LRA 1925, then 'he is entitled to be registered as the proprietor of the estate'.[239] This means that, though the concept of the trust is no longer employed, the effect is the same by virtue of the statutory transfer that takes place, and so the decision in *Central London Commercial Estates Ltd v. Kato Kagaku Co. Ltd*[240] would also be reached under Sched. 12. If the land over which

---

[234] Ibid. at 225.

[235] This word is emphasized by Browne-Wilkinson J. in the judgment at [1981] 1 All E.R. 6 at 14 but the emphasis does not appear at [1981] 1 W.L.R. 222 at 230.

[236] [1981] 1 W.L.R. at 231.   [237] [1998] 4 All E.R. 948. See E.J. Cooke [1999] Conv. 136.

[238] [1998] 4 All E.R. 948 at 955.

[239] LRA 2002, Sched. 12, para. 18(1). See *Dyer v. Terry* (2013) EWHC 209 (Ch).

[240] [1998] 4 All E.R. 948.

the entitlement to register exists is sold, then the entitlement will be enforceable against the purchaser under the ordinary rules on overriding interests found in Sched. 3, para. 2, LRA 2002.[241]

6.7.3 Adverse possession in registered land under the LRA 2002

The ability of a squatter to acquire title to another person's property has always attracted controversy. When title to the land is unregistered, there are strong arguments in favour of such a state of affairs. The existence of adverse possession enables defective titles to be cured and so adds to the security of conveyancing. Where title is registered, however, the converse is true, in that the existence of possessory titles reduces the reliability of the register of title.[242] It was this latter consideration in particular that led the Law Commission and Land Registry[243] to propose radical changes to the law insofar as registered land is concerned and these proposals have been implemented in the LRA 2002. Before considering the new regime, which substantially reduces the ability of a squatter to acquire title to another person's land, it is convenient first to consider the necessary transitional arrangements.

6.7.3.1 Transitional arrangements: unregistered land

The changes effected by the 2002 Act apply where title is registered. Where title is unregistered, the rules of adverse possession will apply as they have always done. What must be considered is the position where the paper owner conveys the land to a purchaser, who is then registered with an absolute title. Under the 1925 Act, the registered proprietor would take subject to the squatter's possessory title as this interest was included within the list of overriding interests.[244] For three years after the Act came into force, this remained the case.[245] Now that this period of grace has expired, the possessory title will only override first registration if either the squatter is in actual occupation of the land,[246] or the proprietor has notice of the possessory right.[247]

6.7.3.2 Transitional arrangements: registered land

If before the 2002 Act came into force, a squatter had established adverse possession against a registered proprietor, the proprietor would hold the estate on trust for the squatter.[248] If the registered proprietor transferred the land, then, for a period of three years after the 2002 Act came into force, the squatter's beneficial interest would override the registered disposition.[249] The three-year period having elapsed, the squatter's beneficial interest will now only bind a registered proprietor if the squatter is in actual occupation of the land and that occupation would be obvious on a reasonably careful inspection of the land.[250] In the case of registered dispositions, there is no separate provision in respect of squatters' rights of which the transferee has notice.

6.7.3.3 The new limitation regime

The 2002 Act has made fundamental changes to the operation of limitation in respect of registered titles. These changes apply only to registered land and do not affect the rights of squatters who have achieved the requisite period of adverse possession prior to the Act

---

[241] In other words, if the adverse possessor is in actual occupation of a discoverable kind, or the purchaser knows of their entitlement.

[242] See 6.7.1.1.   [243] (2001) Law Com. No. 271, paras 2.69–2.74.

[244] LRA 1925, s. 70(1)(g).   [245] LRA 2002, Sched. 12, para. 7.

[246] Ibid., s. 11(4)(b), Sched. 1, para. 2.   [247] Ibid., s. 11(4)(c).   [248] LRA 1925, s. 75(1).

[249] LRA 2002, s. 29, Sched. 12, paras 11 and 18, inserting para. 15 into Sched. 3.

[250] Ibid., s. 29, Sched. 3, para. 2(c).

coming into force. For the future, therefore, the establishment of when the limitation period expired may be a crucial issue in disputes.

6.7.3.4 **The end of automatic possessory titles**

Under the old regime, if a squatter had been in adverse possession of land for at least twelve years then, as has been seen, the effect in unregistered land is that the title of the paper owner is extinguished. In the case of registered land, the land would be held on trust for the squatter who would, therefore, by virtue of his adverse possession of the land, have acquired an interest in it.[251] This is no longer the case. Under s. 96 of the 2002 Act, no period of limitation under s. 15 of the Limitation Act 1980 shall run against any person, other than a registered chargee, in respect of an estate in land or rentcharge the title to which is registered. As a consequence of this, the title of any person, other than a registered chargee, is not extinguished as a consequence of limitation.[252] The immediate effect of this is that there is no question of any trust arising in favour of a squatter by reason only of his prolonged occupation of another person's land. He acquires no interest as a result of that occupation.

6.7.3.5 **Registration of adverse possession**

The 2002 Act does not abolish adverse possession. As explained above, it prevents the automatic acquisition of a possessory title. A person may still apply for registration in respect of his adverse possession of land under s. 97 of the Act, in which case the provisions of Sched. 6 take effect. Similarly, if a person is in adverse possession of land, he can also rely, by way of defence to a possession action brought against him, on the provisions contained in that Schedule.[253] The way that the Act operates is to make it far more difficult for a squatter to obtain a possessory title. It achieves this not by changing the substantive law. Rather, it operates to introduce stringent new procedural safeguards to enable a registered proprietor to defeat a claim to a possessory title which, before the Act, would have succeeded. What constitutes adverse possession remains unaltered however. This is made clear by of Sched. 6, para. 11(1) to the Act, which provides that a person is in adverse possession of an estate in land for the purposes of this Schedule if, but for s. 96, a period of limitation under s. 15 of the Limitation Act 1980 would run in his favour in relation to the estate.

Under para. 1(1) of the Schedule, a person may apply to be registered as the proprietor of a registered estate if he has been in adverse possession of the estate for a period of ten years ending on the date of the application. He may also apply for registration under para. 1(2) if he has in the period of six months ending on the date of the application ceased to be in adverse possession because he has been evicted other than by a court order, and on the day before his eviction, he would otherwise have been entitled to make an application and the eviction was not as a result of a court order. He may not make an application for registration if either he is a defendant in a possession action or if a judgment for possession has been given against him in the last two years.[254]

Before looking at the operation of the new system, some preliminary points can be made.

Time

The first, fairly obvious, point to make is that the limitation period is reduced from twelve years to ten years. Second, the period of adverse possession has to be proximate to the application for registration or the bringing of a possession action. In the past, if a person had established adverse possession for the requisite twelve-year period, he would acquire a possessory title. That title would not be lost if he ceased to be in possession of the land.

---

[251] See 6.7.2.   [252] LRA 2002, s. 96(3).   [253] LRA 2002, s. 98.   [254] Ibid., Sched. 6, para. 1(3).

Under the 2002 Act, unless the reason for the person not being in possession is that he has been evicted other than by a court order, he will not have any rights under the Act, however long he had previously been in adverse possession of the land. A third point, which arises as a consequence of para. 11, concerns successive squatters.

Successive squatters

Under the old law, the periods of adverse possession of successive squatters could be aggregated, so that if A was in adverse possession of O's land for four years, and A was then dispossessed by B, who remained in adverse possession for a further eight years, O's title would be barred. A would have four years in which to bring possession proceedings against B, but B would have established a possessory title against O.[255] The position with regard to successive squatters has been modified by of Sched. 6, para. 11 to the 2002 Act. A person is to be regarded as having been in adverse possession for the requisite period if either he is the successor in title to an estate in land, during any period of adverse possession by a predecessor in title to that estate, or during any period of adverse possession by any other person which comes between, and is continuous with, periods of adverse possession of his own. The meaning of the provisions is best explained by examples.

1. **is the registered proprietor of land**. A goes into adverse possession and, after six years, dies. B, who is entitled under A's will or upon his intestacy, goes into possession and remains there for a further four years. B is A's successor in title and the two periods of adverse possession can be aggregated to make up the requisite ten years of adverse possession.

2. **is the registered proprietor of land**. He is dispossessed by C, who occupies the land for six years and is then dispossessed by D. D occupies the land for two years and is then dispossessed by C, who occupies the land for a further two years. Although C has not been in adverse possession himself for the full ten years, as he is in possession at the relevant time, the period of D's adverse possession can be aggregated to his own to make up the full ten-year period.

3. **is the registered proprietor of land**. He is dispossessed by E, who occupies the property for six years. E is then dispossessed by F, who occupies the land for a further four years. F is not a successor in title to E and, therefore, has not established the requisite period of adverse possession and cannot apply for registration.

6.7.3.6 Applications for registration

A person who has been in adverse possession for a period of ten years may apply for registration. When such an application is made, the registrar is required under Sched. 6, para. 2 to give notice of the application to the following people:

(a) the proprietor of the estate to which the application relates;

(b) the proprietor of any registered charge on the estate;

(c) where the estate is leasehold, the proprietor of any superior registered estate;

(d) any person who is registered in accordance with rules as a person to be notified under this paragraph; and

(e) such other person as rules may provide.

The notice given under this paragraph must include notice of the effect of para. 4.

---

[255] *Asher v. Whitlock* (1865) L.R. 1 Q.B. 1; *Sze To Chun Keung v. Kung Kwok Wai David* [1997] 1 W.L.R. 1232. See 6.7.1.2.

The effect of this notice is that the people upon whom it is served have a period of sixty-five business days[256] in which to respond to the application. If there is no response, then the applicant is entitled to be registered as the new proprietor of the estate. If that has happened, however, it will still be open to the former registered proprietor to argue that the requirements to establish a possessory title had not been met and, if successful, can then seek alteration of the register to restore the title to him.[257] If the person on whom the notice is served does respond, he may then require that the squatter's application be dealt with under para. 5. If this requirement is not made, then the effect of para. 4, to which the attention of the recipient of the notice is required to be drawn, is that the applicant must be registered as the new proprietor of the estate. Accordingly, if one of the people on whom the para. 2 notice has been served wishes to prevent the applicant from being registered as the new proprietor of the estate, he must require the application to be dealt with under para. 5.

6.7.3.7 Restricted scope of adverse possession

Once an application for registration has been made and the registered proprietor, upon whom notice has been served of the application, requires the application to be dealt with under para. 5, then the applicant is only entitled to be registered as the new proprietor if one of three alternative conditions has been met. In every other case, the application for regis tration must be rejected. Similarly, if the boot is on the other foot and the registered propri- etor seeks possession as against the squatter, a person only has a defence to such an action by virtue of his possession as a squatter[258] if he would have been entitled to make an ap- plication for registration under Sched. 6, para. 1 and, had he made such an application the condition in para. 5(4) would have been satisfied.[259] These conditions must be considered.

Estoppel

The first condition laid down in para. 5 is that it would be unconscionable because of an equity by estoppel for the registered proprietor to seek to dispossess the applicant and the circumstances are such that the applicant ought to be registered as the proprietor. This is a curious exception and one which is apt to mislead. It envisages a situation where a person has gone into possession of another person's property, pursuant to some informal agreement, in circumstances where it would be unconscionable for the proprietor, subse- quently, to object to the occupier's claim to the property. While this seems not unreason- able, the difficulty is that the person in occupation of the land is unlikely to be regarded as being in adverse possession at all, because his initial entry on to the land was almost certainly permissive. Moreover, if the dispute between the proprietor and the occupier occurs before there has been occupation of the land for ten years, the occupier will still be able to assert estoppel rights in the property although, in fairness, it should be recognized that this is most likely to occur when the proprietor seeks possession, and estoppel is used as a defence to that action, rather than when it is the occupier who seeks registration.[260]

Entitlement to registration

The second condition is that, for some other reason, the applicant is entitled to be reg- istered as the proprietor of the estate. This would cover a case such as *Bridges v. Mees*,[261]

---

[256] Land Registration Rules 2003, r. 189.

[257] *Baxter v. Mannion* [2010] EWCA Civ. 120.

[258] He may, of course, rely on any other defences which were open to him: LRA 2002, s. 98(6).

[259] In respect of the other conditions set out in para. 5, he would, independently of his possession as a squatter, have the right to defend possession proceedings and, therefore, come within s. 98(6).

[260] See S. Nield [2004] Conv. 137.   [261] [1957] Ch. 575.

where a purchaser of land paid the purchase price in full and went into possession but the land was never conveyed to him. This seems unexceptional.

Boundary disputes

The third condition provides a means of avoiding expensive boundary disputes and reflects the fact that, in the case of most registered titles, the precise boundaries are not fixed.[262] The condition is that:

(a) the land to which the application relates is adjacent to land belonging to the applicant;

(b) the exact line of the boundary between the two has not been determined under rules under s. 60;

(c) for at least ten years of the period of adverse possession ending on the date of application, the applicant (or any predecessor in title) reasonably believed that the land to which the application relates belonged to him; and

(d) the estate to which the application relates was registered more than one year prior to the date of the application.

The third requirement merits some discussion. If a person deliberately moves a fence so as to enclose some of his neighbour's land, he will not be able to rely on this condition to enable his application to be successful, or to resist a possession action brought by his neighbour, because he will not reasonably believe that the land belongs to him. If, however, although the fence was originally moved deliberately by a person, and that person's successor in title was unaware of this, he will, if he establishes the requisite period of occupation, come within this exception. Less obvious, however, is the position when the squatter, originally, had a reasonable belief that he owned the relevant land but, later, circumstances change so that the belief, if still held, is no longer reasonable.

This issue was raised in *Zarb v. Parry*.[263] A disputed strip of land was situated between the land owned by two neighbours. The strip was enclosed by a hedge, which was not situated on the correct boundary between the two properties, so that it had, wrongly, been enclosed by owners of the northern plot. When a dispute erupted between the owners of the northern and southern plots, a surveyor was engaged, and he determined, wrongly, that the hedge marked the correct boundary between the two properties. As the dispute became prolonged and was being litigated, a second survey was ordered, and this determined that the hedge had been wrongly located and that, as a result, the strip had been wrongly enclosed. The Court of Appeal held that the owners of the northern plot had established adverse possession of the plot for the requisite period of time, and were, therefore, entitled to be registered with a possessory title.

One of the issues in the case was whether the owners of the northern plot reasonably believed that they owned the strip. When they acquired the land in the first place, it was clear that they did. Subsequently, however, as the dispute erupted, the question arose as to whether their continued belief was a reasonable one. It was held that it was. Although it was clear that the ownership of the strip had become a matter of dispute that, in itself, would not prevent the belief being reasonable. As the initial survey supported their view as to the true position, the belief continued to be reasonable. Had that not been the case, however, then the belief would not have been reasonable with the result that reliance could no longer have been placed upon para. (c). The moral then would have been to have applied for registration immediately on doubt being cast on their ownership of the disputed

---

[262] See 5.1.4.1.   [263] [2011] EWCA Civ. 1306.

strip, in which case they would still have had the requisite ten-year period prior to the bringing of proceedings when they reasonably believed the land to belong to them.[264]

6.7.3.8 Restrictions on applications

Under the old law, provision was made with respect to people suffering from a disability, this relating to minors and people of unsound mind. The 2002 Act extends this protection. Under para. 8, no one may apply under Sched. 6 to be registered as the proprietor of an estate in land during any period in which the existing registered proprietor is:

(a) unable because of mental disability to make decisions about issues of the kind to which such an application would give rise or

(b) unable to communicate such decisions because of mental disability or physical impairment.

Under the new procedures, it may well happen that a squatter applies to be registered, and a notice is sent by the registrar to the registered proprietor and no response is received, with the result that the applicant will be registered as the new proprietor of the estate. The reason why there was no response, however, is that unbeknown to either the applicant or the registrar,[265] the registered proprietor comes within one of the two above paragraphs. If this occurred, the former registered proprietor would need to seek alteration of the register.

6.7.3.9 Repeated applications

It used to be the case that the period of limitation in respect of land was twelve years. Under the 2002 Act, the relevant period has been reduced to ten years. Twelve years may still become a relevant period owing to Sched. 6, paras 6 and 7. Under para. 6(1), a person whose application for registration under para. 1 was rejected may apply again to be registered as proprietor of the estate. He may do this if he is in adverse possession of the estate from the date of the application until the last day of the period from the date of its rejection. Paragraph 6(2) provides, however, that he may not apply under this paragraph if either he is a defendant in proceedings which involve asserting a right to possession of land, judgment in possession of the land has been given against him in the last two years,[266] or he has been evicted from the land pursuant to a judgment for possession.[267] If a person makes an application under para. 6, para. 7 provides that he is entitled to be registered as the new proprietor of the estate.

These provisions are designed to prevent a registered proprietor from sleeping on his rights. If a squatter has applied to be registered as proprietor and, because he cannot satisfy any of the conditions set out in para. 5, fails in his application, the registered proprietor cannot then afford to do nothing and allow matters to rest. Unless he seeks to remove the squatter from possession by obtaining a possession order then, two years later, the squatter, provided he has remained in adverse possession of the land, can apply again and, this time, his application cannot be resisted by the registered proprietor.

6.7.3.10 The effect of registration

Under the old law, the effect of adverse possession, as it affected unregistered land, was to operate negatively. The title of the paper owner was extinguished and the squatter had an

---

[264] Ibid. at [17] *per* Arden L.J.

[265] If it appears to the registrar that either of these paragraphs might apply in relation to an estate in land, he may include a note to that effect in the register: LRA 2002, Sched. 6, para. 8(4).

[266] A judgment for possession of land ceases to be enforceable at the end of two years from the date of the judgment: ibid., s. 98(2).

[267] Presumably in this situation, the applicant would not qualify under para. 6(1).

independent fee simple in the land. This was modified in the case of registered land by the imposition of a trust, whereby the registered proprietor would hold his estate on trust for the squatter.[268] The 2002 Act operates in a very different way.

If the squatter's application for registration is successful, then his name is substituted for that of the former proprietor. The effect is to transfer the estate to him. So if, as was likely to be the case, the person who was the registered proprietor had an absolute title, then this is the title with which the squatter will be registered. If the previous proprietor was a tenant, then the squatter will be registered as the proprietor of that lease and, therefore, unlike the position when title is unregistered, be directly liable on the covenants in the lease.[269] As a corollary to this, the fee simple estate which the squatter had by virtue of his occupation of the land is extinguished.[270] Again as one would anticipate, but subject to one important exception, the squatter, as the successor in title to the person who was previously the proprietor, will take subject to any interests which bound the former owner of the land.[271]

The exception to this latter point concerns registered charges. If a squatter applies to be registered as proprietor, this application may succeed for one of two reasons. These are that there was no objection to the application or that the squatter satisfied one of the conditions set out in para. 5. In the former situation, the squatter, when registered as proprietor, will not be bound by any registered charge affecting the estate immediately before his registration.[272] This does not occasion hardship to the chargee, as such a person must be notified by the registrar of the application for registration and can, therefore, serve a notice objecting to the registration.[273] Where the application for registration is contested, but eventually successful, the squatter, as the new registered proprietor, will take subject to the registered charge.[274]

6.8 Conclusion

The changes made to the law of limitation by the LRA 2002 are profound. While the old law relating to adverse possession has not been entirely swept away, its scope has been reduced considerably. This is to be welcomed. Provision is made for situations where a person has, effectively, abandoned land, thereby making it possible for it to be dealt with in the future. This is likely to be the situation when no objection is made to an application by a squatter to be registered as proprietor. Moreover, the new law enhances the reliability of the register, which is also to be welcomed. Finally, it makes it far less likely that a person will be deprived of their ownership of land without compensation; an aspect of the law of adverse possession which many people have always found to be objectionable. All in all, it can be said that the new law is a considerable improvement on the old and also, in a number of ways, puts it on a more secure and rational footing. This does not mean that the law of adverse possession is settled, however; wider social views about its acceptability, or morality, will continue to threaten its very existence. Much will depend on how the property-based human rights laws in Art. 1 Protocol 1 and Art. 8 of the European Convention on Human Rights are developed over the next few years, and how the criminal offence of squatting is interpreted by our higher courts.

---

[268] See 6.7.2.   [269] See *Tichborne v. Weir* (1892) 67 L.T. 735.   [270] LRA 2002, Sched. 6, para. 9(1).
[271] Ibid., para. 9(2).   [272] Ibid., para. 9(3).   [273] Ibid., para. 2(1)(b).   [274] Ibid., para. 9(4).

7

Consecutive and Concurrent Interests in Land

A central feature of the doctrine of estates is that a number of estates can exist simultaneously with regard to the same piece of land. Land could be settled upon A for life, remainder to B in fee tail,[1] remainder to C in fee simple. To reiterate a point made earlier, the estates are all the subject of present ownership. What the doctrine of estates facilitates is the division of various rights of ownership between the different parties. One of the most important rights, the right physically to possess the land, is granted to A. B, as yet, has no right to possess the land, this right being acquired on A's death. Similarly, C, or more likely his heirs, will not have the right to possess the land until both A's and B's estates have come to an end.[2] Because the right to possess the land is such an important right, the interests of B and C are termed future interests and are regarded as consecutive interests in the land.

As well as consecutive interests existing with regard to the same land, people can have concurrent interests in the land. A typical example would be where H and W jointly own a house together. This chapter deals with the methods by which the law accommodates both consecutive and concurrent interests, focusing, first, on successive interests. Succeeding chapters will then discuss the law relating to co-ownership of land, considering how one becomes a co-owner, the structure of co-ownership, and the respective rights of the co-owners.

7.1 Successive interests

Prior to 1925, a life estate, a fee tail, and an interest in remainder were all capable of existing as legal estates. Because of the operation of s. 1 of the Law of Property Act (LPA) 1925, these estates are no longer legal and can only be equitable. As the fee simple absolute in possession was to be the focal point of land ownership, steps had to be taken to ensure that a person was identified who was empowered to deal with this estate free from the family interests which existed under the settlement. For many years, two devices were employed to deal with this type of situation: the strict settlement and the trust for sale. Since 1997, a new regime designed to replace both of the previous legal devices has been introduced by the Trusts of Land and Appointment of Trustees Act (TOLATA) 1996. For a number of reasons, however, it remains necessary to have regard to the old law. First, existing settlements are not affected by the new legislation, so that settlements created between 1925 and 1997 continue to be governed by the old statutory regime. These settlements under the old regime retain the potential to trigger a legal claim, as demonstrated

---

[1] It is no longer possible to create a fee tail: Trusts of Land and Appointment of Trustees Act (TOLATA) 1996, Sched. 1, para. 5.

[2] This assumes that B has not enlarged his interest into a fee simple by barring the entail. See 2.6.4.

by the recent Court of Appeal judgment in *Howard v. Howard-Lawson*[3] and the even more recent High Court decision in *Pemberton v. Pemberton*.[4] Second, the new law is, to a considerable extent, coloured by the law it was designed to replace, so that it is difficult to understand the content of the new, and the reasons why it was introduced, without some reference to the old.

7.2 Settled land

One of the two ways in which the law sought to deal with successive interests in land was through the device of the strict settlement, whereby the intention of the settlor was to prevent the land being disposed of in the future.[5] The definition of a settlement is provided by s. 1 of the Settled Land Act (SLA) 1925. The essence of the definition is that any deed, will, agreement for a settlement, or other agreement under which land stands limited in trust for any person by way of succession is, for the purposes of the Act, a settlement.[6] The Act goes on to give four specific examples of when land is to be a settlement. The first three of these are, strictly speaking, not necessary, as all of them come within the general definition given above. The fourth example does not, it being provided that land limited in trust for a person being an infant, for an estate in fee simple or for a term of years absolute, is also a settlement within the meaning of the Act.[7]

The theme that runs through the definition is that the estates in question must, because of the legislation, exist only in equity. Apart from the lease, the only legal estate now known to the law is the fee simple absolute in possession.[8] If one considers the example of a settlement given earlier, to A for life, remainder to B in fee tail, remainder to C in fee simple, the effect of s. 1, LPA 1925 is that none of A, B, or C would have a legal estate in land. Neither A nor B have a fee simple at all. C does have a fee simple but it is in remainder and not in possession. Because the estates are equitable, it follows that the land must be limited in trust by way of succession. Where land is purported to be conveyed to a minor, because such a person lacks capacity to own a legal estate,[9] that estate can also only be equitable, although, on this occasion, the trust is not limited by way of succession.

7.2.1 The object of the Settled Land Act 1925

Where land was subject to a settlement, without some legislative reform, it would not be possible to deal safely with it. As no one person held the fee simple in the land, then, unless all the people with various interests in it were prepared to co-operate, that estate could not be sold to a purchaser. As the land was not readily sellable, people with limited interests in it would be less inclined to spend money on improvements to it. When land was settled, it was also common to create charges on it, normally by the creation of a rentcharge. The purpose of this was financial provision for other members of the settlor's family.[10] The result of doing this, however, was that land which was subject to a settlement tended to

---

[3] [2013] EWCA Civ. 654.   [4] [2016] EWHC 2345 (Ch).
[5] See Harvey, *Settlements of Land* (London, Sweet & Maxwell, 1973), 6–26; Smith, *Plural Ownership* (Oxford, Oxford University Press, 2005), Chapter 2.
[6] Expressly excluded from the settlement is land held on trust for sale: SLA 1925, s. 1(7).
[7] Ibid., s. 1(1)(ii)(d). See now TOLATA 1996, s. 2; Sched. 1, para. 1(1) and *Hammersmith London Borough Council v. Alexander-David* [2009] 3 All E.R. 1039.
[8] LPA 1925, s. 1(1)(a).   [9] LPA 1925, s. 1(6).
[10] Such charges were generally known as jointures or portions. The former is an annuity in favour of a widow, and the latter a lump sum paid to children who were not given a direct interest under the settlement.

become burdened with debt. As the social and economic conditions in England changed, and it was considered to be less desirable than was once the case for land to be subject to family settlements of this type, pressure grew to allow the casting off of the fetters imposed by them.[11] Building on the reforms brought in by the SLA 1882, the 1925 Act sought to arrive at a solution whereby such land became readily marketable.

The central plank in the scheme devised by the Act was to vest the legal fee simple in the hands of one person, the tenant for life, and then to give that person extensive powers to deal with that estate. As the person who is given that estate has only a limited beneficial interest in the property, it was also necessary to safeguard the interests of other people with interests in the land, to ensure that the tenant for life could not exercise the powers given to him by the statute to the detriment of those other people. To prevent this from occurring, the Act provides for the appointment of trustees of the settlement who, unusually for trustees, do not hold the legal title to the land, which is vested in the tenant for life. As will be seen, their role is, essentially, to act as watchdogs of the settlement.

7.2.2 The tenant for life

The central character when land is the subject of a settlement is the tenant for life. Section 4(2) of the Act requires that the land shall be conveyed by a vesting deed to the tenant for life or, if there is more than one such person, to them as joint tenants. Where the legal title is already vested in the person who is the tenant for life, as would be the case when a person who owned the fee simple settled the land upon himself for life, remainder to his son in fee simple, it is sufficient if the vesting deed simply declares that the land is vested in him for that estate.

Various issues arise. First, the person who is the tenant for life must be identified. Second, the powers of the tenant for life must be considered, a task which entails considering the purpose of the vesting deed. Finally, the role of the trustees of the settlement and the process of overreaching must also be addressed.

7.2.2.1 Who is the tenant for life?

Section 19(1) of the Act defines the tenant for life as the person being of full age who is for the time being beneficially entitled to an estate or interest in possession.[12] If there are two or more such persons then, together, they constitute the tenant for life.[13] If, for example, land is settled on A for life, to B in fee tail, remainder to C in fee simple, then A, as the person beneficially entitled in possession, is the tenant for life. On A's death, B, or his lineal heir, will then become the tenant for life and, on the termination of the fee tail, C, or, more likely, his heirs, will be entitled to the land, which will cease to be settled, and the land will simply be conveyed to him.

There are two situations where there is nobody who falls within the definition of a tenant for life. One is where there is no person who is entitled in possession to the land, for example, if a discretionary trust has been created,[14] and the other is where the person so entitled is a minor. In such cases, the person who dons the mantle of the tenant for life is termed the statutory owner.

---

[11] See *Re Mundy and Roper's Contract* [1895] 1 Ch. 275 at 278 *per* Chitty J.; Harvey, *Settlements of Land*, 1–5.

[12] For the more elaborate definition in the case of other limited owners, see SLA 1925, s. 20.

[13] Ibid., s. 19(2).

[14] *Re Galenga's Will Trusts* [1938] 1 All E.R. 106. See also *Re Frewen* [1926] Ch. 580. A discretionary trust occurs when the settlor nominates a class of people as the beneficiaries but leaves it to the trustees to decide which members of that class, and in what proportions, will benefit from the trust.

7.2.2.2 The statutory owner

If the person entitled in possession is a minor, provision is made that, during his minority, if the settled land is vested in a personal representative, then, until a principal vesting deed has been executed, the personal representative shall have the powers of the tenant for life and, in all other cases, the powers shall vest in the trustees of the settlement.[15] In other cases where there is no tenant for life, then the person who can exercise those powers is either the person of full age on whom such powers are expressly conferred or, if there is no such person, upon the trustees of the settlement.[16]

7.3 The powers of the tenant for life

Although the legal estate is vested in the tenant for life, he is not given unfettered power to deal with the land. The constraints come from two sources. First, while he is given the legal estate by the statute, that estate is held upon trust, the beneficial interests under that trust being those carved out by the settlement. Certain proposed transactions may be prevented by others interested in the land if those transactions are in some way improper. The second constraint upon his actions is that, although he, as tenant for life, is endowed with the legal estate, the Act does not simply confer upon him the normal powers incident upon the ownership of a fee simple. Instead, his powers to deal with the estate are elaborated by the Act. As will be seen, difficulties can arise if the tenant for life purports to deal with the land in a way which is not authorized by the Act.

7.3.1 Trusteeship

The tenant for life holds the legal estate on trust and, consequently, is subject to the normal fiduciary obligations imposed upon a trustee in respect of his dealing with trust property. In making such transactions, the tenant for life is obliged to consider the financial interests of the other beneficiaries and so cannot favour his own political or moral preferences where these would conflict with the interests of the beneficiaries.[17] In *Re Somers*,[18] the tenant for life, who was a confirmed teetotaller, sought to grant a lease of a hotel, the lease to contain a covenant prohibiting the sale of alcohol. As this was not in the best financial interests of the other beneficiaries, the trustees of the settlement obtained a declaration that she was not entitled to do this.

7.3.2 Statutory powers

The powers of the tenant for life to deal with the legal estate are conferred upon him by Part II of the SLA 1925. The statutory powers can be increased by the settlement but attempts to restrict them are rendered void.[19] Included within the powers of the tenant for life is the power to sell the land, to grant certain leases, and to mortgage the property for certain specified purposes. Before exercising these powers, the tenant for life is required to serve a written notice on the trustees not less than one month before the proposed transaction.[20] This imposition is not, however, particularly onerous, as it is sufficient if the tenant

---

[15] SLA 1925, s. 26.   [16] Ibid., s. 26.

[17] For the general position of trustees, see *Cowan v. Scargill* [1985] Ch. 270; *Harries v. Church Commissioners for England* [1992] 1 W.L.R. 1241.

[18] (1893) 11 T.L.R. 567. See also *Wheelwright v. Walker (No. 2)* (1883) W.N. 154; *Middlemas v. Stevens* [1901] 1 Ch. 574.

[19] SLA 1925, s. 106.   [20] Ibid., s. 101(1).

for life simply gives a general notice of his intention from time to time to exercise his powers under the Act,[21] and a purchaser, provided that he is in good faith, is not concerned to see that this requirement has been met.[22]

7.3.3 **Unauthorized dispositions**

Problems can arise if a tenant for life purports to make a disposition which the Act does not authorize him to do. In such situations, one must distinguish between cases where what has sought to be done is totally unauthorized by the Act, and cases where the transaction is one which is authorized but where there is some irregularity in the exercise of the power.

7.3.3.1 **Void transactions**

Section 18 of the Act provides that:

> Where land is the subject of a vesting instrument, and the trustees of the settlement have not been discharged under the Act, then—
> (a) any disposition by the tenant for life . . . other than a disposition authorised by this Act . . . shall be void, except for the purpose of conveying or creating such equitable interests as he has power, in right of his equitable interests and powers under the trust instrument, to convey or create.

The effect of this section was considered in the leading case of *Weston v. Henshaw*.[23] G sold property to his son, F, who later resold the land to his father. Sometime later, the father settled the land on F for life, remainder to F's sons. F then mortgaged the property for his own benefit, a transaction which is not authorized under the Act. To prove title to the mortgagee, F showed the conveyance to him by his father but suppressed the later documents, so that there was no way that the mortgagee could have known that the land was actually the subject of a vesting deed and that the transaction was being effected by a tenant for life. The issue subsequently arose as to whether the mortgage was valid and Danckwerts J. held that it was not.

In reaching this conclusion, the judge simply applied s. 18 of the Act, which does, indeed, suggest that this is the correct result. He also, however, rejected an argument based upon s. 110 of the Act. This section, which is designed to protect purchasers, provides that:

> On a sale, exchange, lease, mortgage, charge, or other disposition, a purchaser dealing in good faith with a tenant for life . . . shall, as against all parties entitled under the settlement, be conclusively taken to have given the best price . . . that could be reasonably obtained . . . and to have complied with all the requirements of the Act.

The mortgagee, who undoubtedly was in good faith, argued that he was protected by this section and that, consequently, the mortgage was valid. This argument was rejected on the somewhat curious ground that the section only applied to protect a purchaser if the purchaser knew that he was dealing with a tenant for life which, in the instant case, he manifestly did not.

7.3.3.2 **Irregularities**

The interpretation given to s. 110 in *Weston v. Henshaw* was doubted in *Re Morgan's Lease*.[24] In this case, the principal objection to a lease granted by the tenant for life was that the rent that had been obtained was not the best rent reasonably obtainable. So far

---

[21] Ibid., s. 101(2).   [22] Ibid., s. 101(5).   [23] [1950] Ch. 510.   [24] [1972] Ch. 1.

as the tenants were concerned, however, it was held that the lease was not liable to be set aside. They had acted in good faith and were therefore protected by s. 110 of the Act. The criticism of *Weston v. Henshaw* was, therefore, *obiter*. It is also, it is suggested, misplaced.

The fundamental difference between the two cases is that in the former case the person who was actually the tenant for life was purporting to engage in a transaction which was not authorized by the Act. It was *ultra vires*. In *Re Morgan's Lease*, on the other hand, the transaction was one which was permitted by the Act. The problem with the transaction related to the rent which was payable, a matter which is within the scope of s. 110.

The conclusion which should follow in cases such as these is that, if the purported transaction is one which is not authorized by the Act, then it is beyond the powers of the tenant for life and, in principle, should be void so far as the creation of a legal estate is concerned.[25] If the problem relates to technical matters relating to an authorized, and therefore intrinsically valid, transaction then, provided that the purchaser has acted in good faith, he will be able to rely upon s. 110 of the Act and will have a good title.

The effect of s. 18 can be hard on a purchaser who may find, through no fault of his own, that the transaction he has engaged in is void. This result is, however, a direct consequence of the scheme adopted by the Act. Instead of simply giving the tenant for life the legal fee simple, and the powers of dealing inherent with the ownership of that estate, the Act, instead, gives him the estate but limits his powers of dealing with it to those specified in the Act. The consequence of this is to leave an innocent purchaser exposed to the kind of fraud which occurred in *Weston v. Henshaw*.

The real source of the problem in a case such as *Weston v. Henshaw* is that, because title was unregistered, the fraudster could conceal the fact that he was actually a tenant for life rather than, as he presented himself to be, a straightforward owner of a fee simple. This situation is far less likely to occur when title is registered, as a purchaser will see, from searching the register of title, whether or not the registered proprietor is a limited owner and be able to deal with him accordingly. When title is registered, the only time when a purchaser may be at risk is where the transaction is not, itself, completed by registration, as is the case for a lease of less than seven years, when the prospective tenant may proceed with the transaction without searching the register in order to establish the nature of the freeholder's title.[26]

7.3.4 Attempts to fetter the powers of the tenant for life

Central to the operation of the Act is to allow settled land to be bought and sold and not to allow the succession of interests to prevent the land being sellable. To this end, the legal fee simple is vested in the tenant for life, who is then given powers of dealing with that estate. To ensure that this policy is not frustrated by the creator of the settlement, provision is made to prevent the powers of the tenant for life from being cut down.

Section 106 of the SLA 1925 provides that any provision in a settlement which purports, or tends or is intended to have, or would have the effect of either forbidding the tenant for life from exercising his statutory powers or inducing him not to do so will be void. Attempts to discourage a tenant for life from exercising his powers may not always be blatant. In some cases a fund is made available for the tenant for life and it is not always clear whether the existence of this fund is to act as an inducement to him not to exercise his statutory powers or if it is a genuine attempt to provide funds for the upkeep of the property. In the former situation, the clause will be void under the Act,[27] so that the tenant

---

[25] See also *Bevan v. Johnston* [1990] 2 E.G.L.R. 33, a decision adopting this view.
[26] Ibid.　　　[27] See *Re Ames* [1893] 2 Ch. 479.

for life can retain the money despite exercising his powers, whereas in the latter situation the clause is valid and the tenant for life's entitlement to the fund will cease when he no longer holds that position.[28]

The operation of s. 106 has arisen a number of times in the context of residence clauses, whereby a person is given a life interest determinable on their ceasing to reside at the property. If the reason why the person has ceased to reside at the property is that he has sold the property, then his interest will not be determined by the residence clause, as its effect is to seek to discourage him from the exercise of his powers.[29] If, however, the reason that the tenant for life ceases to reside in the settled property is simply a matter of choice, then the clause has not operated to discourage him from exercising his powers and is valid, with the result that his beneficial interest will determine on his ceasing to reside at the property.[30]

7.4 The structure of settlements

Having looked at the essential definition of a settlement and the role of the tenant for life, it is necessary now to turn to the mechanics of the settlement; how it is created and how the Act operates to enable settled land to be sold. A feature of the system introduced is that it adopts a two-document structure, the documents being the vesting deed and the trust instrument,[31] the purpose of this structure being to allow the land to be sold without the necessity of a purchaser having to investigate the beneficial interests existing behind the settlement.

7.4.1 The vesting deed

When a settlement is created, it is necessary for the legal estate to be vested in the tenant for life or, if it is already vested in him, to indicate that the capacity in which he holds that estate has changed. This task is performed by the vesting deed. The vesting deed contains the following information:

(i) it describes the settled land;

(ii) it declares that the settled land is vested in the person or persons to whom it was conveyed or in whom it is declared to be vested upon trusts from time affecting the settled land;

(iii) it states the names of the trustees of the settlement;

(iv) it states the names of any persons empowered to appoint new trustees of the settlement; and

(v) it states any additional powers conferred upon the tenant for life by the trust instrument.[32]

The role of the trust instrument will be considered shortly. First, the consequence of a failure to execute a vesting deed will be addressed.

7.4.2 Failure to execute a vesting deed

The sanction for failing to execute a vesting deed when a settlement has been created is provided by s. 13 of the Act. Under this section, where a person is entitled to have a

---

[28] See the different views expressed in *Re Aberconway's Settlement Trusts* [1953] Ch. 647. See also *Re Patten* [1929] 2 Ch. 276.

[29] See *Re Paget's S.E.* (1895) 30 Ch.D. 161; *Re Orlebar* [1936] Ch. 147.

[30] See *Re Haynes* (1887) 37 Ch.D. 306. [31] SLA 1925, s. 4(1). [32] SLA 1925, s. 5.

vesting deed executed in his favour, and this has not occurred, then any purported disposition of the land will not take effect except as a contract to carry out the purported
disposition after the vesting deed has been executed. An exception is provided in favour
of a purchaser of a legal estate without notice of the tenant for life who is entitled to have
a vesting deed executed in his favour.[33] The protection afforded to a purchaser in this
situation contrasts markedly with the effect of s. 18 of the Act. An example will illustrate
this.

S, who holds a legal estate in land, settles the land upon himself for life, remainder to
X but does not, as he should, execute a vesting deed indicating the change of capacity in
which he now holds the legal estate. He then mortgages the property for his own benefit: a
transaction which is not authorized by the Act. Assuming that the mortgagee has acted in
good faith, the effect of s. 13 is to protect him and the mortgage will be valid. If, however,
S did execute a vesting deed but, when mortgaging the property, suppressed that deed,
thereby concealing the fact that a settlement is in existence, the effect of s. 18 is to make
this transaction void.[34] Yet, the purchaser is as innocent in the second situation as he is
in the first. The disparity between the two situations is indefensible but is an inevitable
consequence of the different wording of the two sections.

7.4.3 **The trust instrument**

The second document essential to the creation of the settlement is the trust instrument,
which, as its name suggests, deals with the beneficial interests created by the settlement.
The trust instrument contains the following:

    (i) it declares the trusts of the settlement;

    (ii) it appoints the trustees of the settlement;

    (iii) it contains the power, if any, to appoint new trustees;

    (iv) it sets out any extended powers given to the tenant for life; and

    (v) it bears any *ad valorum* stamp duty which might be payable.[35]

When a settlement is created by will, the personal representatives of the deceased will vest
the legal estate in the tenant for life by means of a vesting assent and the will, under which
the settlement was created, will operate as the trust instrument.[36]

It will be observed that some of the information contained in the two documents is
common to both. The major difference between the contents of the two is that the trust instrument sets out the beneficial interests existing under the settlement, a matter on which
the vesting deed is silent. The reason for this strict demarcation is the curtain principle, a
principle which is central to the scheme of the Act and to the operation of the overreaching provisions.

7.4.4 **The curtain principle**

The purpose of the system of having two documents, one dealing with the legal estate
and the other detailing the beneficial interests existing under the settlement, is to free the
purchaser from the task of having to investigate the beneficial interests existing behind the
settlement. The object of the Act is that, if the correct procedure is adopted, those interests will be overreached and will take effect against the purchase money generated by the

---

[33] Conversely, if the purchaser does have notice, the conveyance should be void with regard to the transfer
of the legal estate. Cf. *Binions v. Evans* [1972] Ch. 359, where this point was overlooked.
    [34] *Weston v. Henshaw* [1950] Ch. 510.   [35] SLA 1925, s. 4(3).   [36] Ibid., s. 6.

sale of the land. As the purchaser will not be bound by these interests, he does not need to know what they are. The Act takes this policy to its logical conclusion. Not only is the purchaser discouraged from investigating the beneficial interests behind the settlement, he is actually precluded from doing so. Section 110(2) of the Act provides that a purchaser of a legal estate in settled land is not, save for four situations of varying importance, entitled to call for the production of the trust instrument and he is bound to assume that the particulars contained in the vesting deed are correct. The curtain principle operates, also, where title is registered. In this situation, the tenant for life is registered as the proprietor of the land and a restriction is entered upon the register that no disposition is to be registered unless capital money is paid to the trustees of the settlement. The effect of this procedure is that the beneficial interests are kept off the register.

Although the Act requires a purchaser to assume that the particulars contained in the vesting deed are correct, it does not deal with the situation where this is not the case. This may occur when title is unregistered. The Act provides no clear solution to the problem, which must be resolved by the application of first principles. To illustrate this potential problem: land is settled upon A for life, or until she remarries, remainder to B. A vesting deed has been executed in favour of A who then remarries, thereby causing the settlement to terminate. She then, although not entitled to do so, purports to exercise the powers of a tenant for life.

Assuming that the trustees of the settlement, to whom the purchase money will have to be paid, are not alive to the problem to prevent the transaction from taking place, it is thought that the purchaser would get a good title. A, because of the vesting deed, would still have the legal title vested in her and the conveyance would seem to operate to transfer the legal estate to the purchaser. As the purchaser would not have notice of the interests behind the settlement, then, as a purchaser without notice, he should, in principle, take free from those interests.[37]

This problem cannot occur when title is registered. This is because the tenant for life will be registered as the proprietor of the land subject to a restriction on his power to deal with the property. That restriction will relate to the payment of capital money having been made to the trustees of the settlement. Provided that the purchase money is paid in accordance with the terms of the restriction, then the purchaser will take free from any interests under the settlement.

7.4.5 **Settlements and overreaching**

The scheme of overreaching operates on a conveyance by the tenant for life and the payment of capital money to, or at the direction of, the trustees of the settlement.[38] On a conveyance by the tenant for life, s. 72 of the Act provides that a purchaser can take the land conveyed free from the interests under the settlement but subject to:

(i) all legal estates and charges by way of legal charges having priority to the settlement;

(ii) all legal estates and charges by way of legal mortgage which have been conveyed or created for securing money actually raised at the date of the deed; and

(iii) all leases and grants of other rights (except annuities, limited owner's charges, and general equitable charges) which at the date of the deed are:

(a) binding upon the successors in title of the tenant for life; and

(b) protected by registration, if capable of registration.

---

[37] See P.A. Stone [1984] Conv. 354. Cf. R. Warrington [1985] Conv. 377.
[38] SLA 1925, s. 75.

These provisions are, perhaps, not as clear as they might be. First, except where the Act provides expressly to the contrary, any right created prior to the creation of the settlement cannot be overreached by a conveyance by the tenant for life. The reference to legal estates and mortgages having priority to the settlement is unnecessary. The Act then makes reference to interests created by the tenant for life, such as a mortgage. Such interests are commercial interests in land which the tenant for life is authorized to make and so, although created under the settlement, cannot be overreached by a subsequent conveyance of the property. An example may assist.

In 1970, land was settled on A for life, remainder to B in fee simple. Prior to the creation of the settlement, a restrictive covenant affecting the land had been created and had been duly registered as a land charge. In 1980, to raise money to improve the land, a legal mortgage was created[39] and in 2017, A conveyed the land to P and the capital money was paid to the trustees of the settlement. The purchaser will take free from A's life interest and B's fee simple in remainder. He will be bound, however, by the prior restrictive covenant and by the authorized mortgage unless, as is very likely to be the case, the purchaser insisted upon its discharge prior to the transfer. When the purchase money is received by the trustees of the settlement, they will, in accordance with the directions of the tenant for life, invest it. The interest, which represents A's life interest, is paid to A and, on A's death, the capital sum is paid to B representing B's fee simple in remainder, which has fallen into possession.

7.4.6 Problems with the Settled Land Act

This thumbnail sketch of the working of the Act is intended to show the essentials of how the legislation was intended to deal with successive interests affecting land and how the law sought, by utilizing the concept of overreaching, to make such land marketable. There are, however, problems with the statutory regime. As has been seen, one problem is that it can throw the risk of fraudulent conduct onto the purchaser, a feature which is inconsistent with the general policy of the 1925 legislation. An additional problem is that the two-document procedure, while providing an effective curtain behind which to shield the equitable rights existing under the settlement, also creates somewhat complex and cumbersome machinery. Taking the settlement out of the ambit of the SLA 1925 in order to resettle the 300-year old family estate on new discretionary trusts with modern administrative powers was, in part, the reason for the successful variation of trust application in *Pemberton v. Pemberton*.[40]

7.4.7 Complexity

Integral to the strategy of the SLA 1925 is the system of basing it upon the existence of two documents and the vesting of the legal title in the tenant for life. A consequence of this is that when changes occur behind the curtain, new documents will need to be executed to reflect these changes, thereby ensuring that the legal estate is vested in the person currently entitled to be the tenant for life. A good illustration of the need for this is provided by the occasion of the death of a tenant for life, where the settlement continues in being. If land is settled upon A for life, remainder to B in fee tail, remainder to C in fee simple then, upon A's death, the land remains settled land.

In this situation, the settled land must be dealt with separately from the rest of A's estate. The part of his estate which is not subject to the settlement will devolve upon his personal representatives in the normal way. The land, however, will vest in the trustees of the

---

[39] SLA 1925, s. 71.   [40] [2016] EWHC 2345 (Ch).

settlement as his special personal representatives.[41] They will then vest the settled land in B by way of a vesting assent.[42] The upshot is that different people will be involved in the administration of the deceased's estate; a factor which increases the cost and complexity of dealing with the estate.

7.4.7.1 Accidental settlements

The desire to create settlements of any complexity is less strong than was once the case, as the wish to create dynastic settlements is much less prevalent than was true in the past,[43] this tendency being reflected by the prevention of the creation of any new fees tail.[44] As people have been less inclined, deliberately, to create settlements governed by the SLA 1925, there has been a tendency for this result to occur accidentally, sometimes as the result of a 'home-made' will, whereby a testator dies leaving his house to his widow, thereafter to their children. Such a testamentary statement brought into play the full structure imposed by the Act. Such a consequence could also ensue as a result of an informal arrangement between people with respect to land, it widely being perceived to be inappropriate that the Act should apply to such situations.

This issue arose in *Binions v. Evans*.[45] Tredegar Estate owned land upon which was a cottage occupied by Mr and Mrs Evans. Mr Evans, like his father and grandfather before him, had been employed by the Estate for a long time and, on his death, the Estate agreed with Mrs Evans that, if she kept the cottage and the garden in good order, she could remain in the cottage for the rest of her life. The cottage was then sold, expressly subject to this agreement, to Mr and Mrs Binions who, on account of this agreement, paid a reduced price for it. They then sought to evict her from the cottage. The majority of the Court of Appeal, Lord Denning M.R. dissenting on this point,[46] held that, on the proper construction of the agreement, and applying the earlier decision in *Bannister v. Bannister*,[47] she had a life interest in the property and, accordingly, was the tenant for life within the meaning of the SLA 1925.[48]

The result of this case was that Mrs Evans was entitled to have a vesting deed executed in her favour. After trustees of the settlement had been appointed, she would then be able to exercise all the powers conferred upon her by the Act including, should she so wish, that of selling the property. It is principally this latter consideration which led to Lord Denning's dissent on this aspect of the case and to academic disquiet.[49] It is, quite simply, regarded as inappropriate that a person in the position of Mrs Evans should be endowed with all the powers conferred by the Act as a result of an act of generosity towards her.

This concern has led to the courts, on subsequent occasions, to seek to craft solutions in similar situations, where it is sought to protect the occupation rights of persons without becoming involved with the complications of the SLA 1925.[50] In other cases, however, the courts have felt constrained to arrive at the conclusion that the parties' informal arrangement has created a life interest, with the consequence that the Act is applicable.[51]

---

[41] SLA 1925, s. 7; Administration of Estates Act 1925, s. 22.

[42] If title is unregistered, this will trigger the need for first registration of title: Land Registration Act (LRA) 2002, s. 4(1)(ii).

[43] For an example of a long-standing dynastic settlement giving rise to modern-day problems, see *Hambro v. Duke of Marlborough* [1995] Ch. 158 discussed by E. Cooke [1994] Conv. 492.

[44] TOLATA 1996, Sched. 1, para. 5. [45] [1972] Ch. 359. The case is discussed further, see 15.3.2.2.

[46] He did not, however, dissent from the result, whereby Mrs Evans was permitted to remain in the cottage. See 15.3.2.2.

[47] [1948] 2 All E.R. 133. [48] Cf. *Morrs v. Morrs* [1972] Fam. 204.

[49] See, e.g., J.A. Hornby (1977) 93 L.Q.R. 561.

[50] See, e.g., *Dodsworth v. Dodsworth* [1973] E.G.D. 233; *Griffiths v. Williams* [1978] E.G.D. 919.

[51] See *Ungarian v. Lessnoff* [1990] Ch. 206; *Costello v. Costello* (1994) 27 H.L.R. 12. Cf. *Dent v. Dent* [1996] 1 W.L.R. 683.

The cases dealing with this type of issue are not easily reconcilable and one can understand why concern is felt in some quarters about the application of the SLA to informal arrangements of this type. The consequences of the Act being applicable stem, however, from the long-standing policy of seeking to prevent land being made unsellable for a prolonged period. If in the above instances the court had been able to fashion a solution which secured the right of indefinite occupation of the person in occupation but without giving that person the statutory powers, this policy would be undermined. This, in modern times, may not necessarily be a bad thing[52] and, under the new law can now be achieved.[53] It can be conceded, however, that the complication that the Act involved did seem a cumbersome way of dealing with such cases and that the new trust of land copes better with such a situation.

7.5 Trusts for sale

The second legal device which was available as a means of creating settlements was the trust for sale. If land was the subject of a trust for sale, then it was not subject to the provisions of the SLA 1925.[54] Although the trust for sale has effectively been superseded by the trust of land, it remains necessary to consider it as a legal device, in that much of the new law derives from its antecedents. In doing this, one must consider the meaning of the term 'trust for sale' and when such a trust would be implied by law. One can then examine the respective positions of the trustees and the beneficiaries and the operation of overreaching.

7.5.1 The trust for sale

A trust for sale was defined by s. 205(1)(xxix), LPA 1925 as being an immediate binding trust for sale with or without a power at discretion to postpone the sale. The legal estate is held by the trustees for sale. There are various aspects of this definition which require elaboration.

7.5.1.1 Duty to sell

For a trust for sale to arise, the trust must impose a duty upon the trustees to sell the property. If a settlement provided that land was to be held by trustees for various persons in succession, with power for the trustees to sell the land, the trust did not impose a duty upon them to sell the land. The trust was not, therefore, a trust for sale. Instead, a strict settlement would have been created. An important consequence of this was that the legal title should then be vested in the tenant for life rather than, as directed, the trustees. Problems were at one time also caused by settlements which gave the trustees power to sell or retain the land. Such problems were resolved, however, as such provisions were to be construed as creating a trust to sell the property with power to postpone the sale.[55]

7.5.1.2 Immediate

For land to be held upon a trust for sale, the duty imposed upon the trustees to sell the property had to be immediate. This never meant that the land had actually to be sold forthwith; it meant merely that the duty to sell was an immediate one. That duty to sell was normally modified by the existence of a correlative power to postpone the sale. Such a power to postpone the performance of the duty to sell the property could be express but

[52] See M.P. Thompson [1994] Conv. 391 at 394–5.   [53] TOLATA 1996, s. 8.
[54] SLA 1925, s. 1(7).   [55] LPA 1925, s. 25(4).

need not be, as unless the contrary intention was expressed in the trust,[56] a power for the trustees to postpone the sale would be implied by statute.[57] The fact that the overriding duty on the trustees was to sell the property did have an important effect, however, when the trustees were not unanimous as to whether to exercise the power to postpone the sale, one wishing to sell the property and the other being opposed to a sale. Such disputes are now decided by applying the criteria laid out in s. 15, TOLATA 1996, although the express creation of a trust for sale may still be an important factor in the resolution of such a dispute.[58]

7.5.1.3 Consents

The sale of the property could be made subject to the consent of a given person. In some cases, the need for that consent may be implicit, as where a house was to be held upon trust for sale with a proviso that G was to have permission to reside in it for life or for as long as she desired. It was held that this was a trust for sale subject to G's consent being obtained before any sale took place.[59] Alternatively, the consent of a named individual could be made a prerequisite to the trustees selling the property. Paradoxically, the requirement of a consent to a sale could be used as a device to prevent the land being sold, this being done by requiring the consent of a person who was unlikely to agree.[60] Even this would not, necessarily, be successful to prevent a sale, however, as if that consent was not forthcoming, the court could be petitioned to order a sale, notwithstanding the refusal to give consent.[61]

7.5.2 Implied trusts for sale

The preceding account related to the creation of an express trust for sale. In certain situations, the law would also imply a trust for sale, the most important occasion being in cases of beneficial co-ownership of land. Where land was conveyed to persons as either joint tenants or tenants in common, specific provision was made that the land would be held upon an implied trust for sale.[62] Express provision was not made, however, for the increasingly common situation where land was conveyed to one person alone, but another person had, through contributing to its purchase, acquired an equitable interest in it.[63] This gap was filled in *Bull v. Bull*,[64] where a house had been conveyed to a son but his mother was a beneficial co-owner of it. The effect of this was held by the Court of Appeal to give rise to an implied trust for sale. The reasoning relied upon s. 36(4), SLA 1925, which provided that an undivided share in land, which was the interest held by the mother, should not be capable of being created except under a trust instrument or under the LPA 1925 and should then only take effect behind a trust for sale.

The conclusion that the interrelation of the statutory provisions had the effect that an implied trust for sale was created was subject to criticism.[65] It did, however, provide a convenient solution to a problem which may not have been foreseen by the drafters of the 1925 legislation, and has the express approval of the House of Lords.[66] The upshot was that, unless land was settled land within the meaning of the SLA 1925, all land which was the subject of co-ownership was subject to a trust for sale; a matter which remains significant under the new statutory regime.

---

[56] See *Re Rooke* [1953] Ch. 716. [57] LPA 1925, s. 25(1). [58] See 9.8.2.
[59] *Re Herklots' Will Trusts* [1964] 1 W.L.R. 583. Cf. *Re Hanson* [1928] Ch. 96.
[60] See *Re Inns* [1947] 1 Ch. 576.
[61] LPA 1925, s. 30; *Re Beale's Settlement Trusts* [1932] 2 Ch. 15.
[62] LPA 1925, ss 34, 36. For joint tenancies and tenancies in common, see Chapter 10.
[63] See Chapter 8. [64] [1955] 1 Q.B. 234.
[65] B. Rudden (1963) 17 Conv. (N.S.) 51; W. Swadling [1986] Conv. 379; [1987] Conv. 451 at 454–7.
[66] *Williams & Glyn's Bank Ltd v. Boland* [1981] A.C. 487 at 507 *per* Lord Wilberforce.

7.5.3 **The trustees for sale**

A crucial difference between the strict settlement and the trust for sale was the location of the legal estate. In the case of a strict settlement, the legal estate is vested in the tenant for life or the statutory owner. The role of the trustees of the settlement is to act as a watchdog of the settlement and to receive capital money when a transaction has taken place. In contrast to this, when land was held upon a trust for sale, the legal estate was held by the trustees for sale on trust for the beneficiaries. The trustees were then endowed with all the powers of both the tenant for life and the trustees of the settlement.[67] Although, in the case of settled land, it was expressly provided that the powers of the tenant for life could not be cut down,[68] no provision dealt with this issue in the case of trusts for sale. This point is now academic as the issue is addressed squarely by TOLATA 1996.[69] Conversely, if the trustees for sale refused to exercise their powers, then any person interested could apply to the court, which could make such order as it saw fit.[70]

When land was held upon trust for sale, the managerial role with respect to the land rested with the trustees. The person entitled to the income from the land occupied a far less important role than his counterpart when the land is settled. He is not, however, without rights. Certain rights of management of the property, albeit not the power of sale, could be delegated to him.[71] Second, his consent may be a prerequisite to a sale by the trustees. Third, the trustees may be under a duty to consult the beneficiaries, such a duty being imposed when the trust for sale was imposed by statute. That duty was not a particularly strong safeguard for the beneficiaries, however, as the right to be consulted does not carry with it a power of veto and a purchaser was, in any event, not concerned to see that this obligation had been complied with.[72] Finally, depending upon the circumstances surrounding the trust, the beneficiaries, if in occupation, may also have had the right not to be evicted from the property.[73] Ascertaining the rights of the beneficiaries was, however, approached in a somewhat piecemeal fashion and the new legislation has sought to formalize the position.

7.5.4 **Conversion**

The maxim that equity looks on that which ought to be done as already having been done is one of general application. The trust upon which the land was held was a trust for sale, the duty of the trustees being to sell the property. The application of this maxim in the present context led to the view that, regarding the property as already having been sold, the interests of the beneficiaries were in the proceeds of sale, rather than in the land itself, an approach known as the doctrine of conversion.[74]

This doctrine is a technical one and, although judicially endorsed,[75] its application tended to be pragmatic. In the context of succession, it was applied so that if a testator left his real property to A and his personal property to B, then his beneficial interest under a trust for sale would be classed as personal property and would pass to B.[76] In other contexts, however, the application of the principle was less predictable. While a contract to

---

[67] LPA 1925, s. 28.   [68] Settlement Land Act 1925, s. 106.

[69] TOLATA 1996, s. 8. Under the old law, it was probably the case that the powers could not be cut down. See Thompson, *Co-ownership* (London, Sweet & Maxwell, 1988), 7.

[70] LPA 1925, s. 30.   [71] Ibid., s. 29.   [72] Ibid., s. 26(3).

[73] See *Re Bagot's Settlement* [1894] 1 Ch. 177; G.A. Forrest (1956) 19 M.L.R. 312.

[74] For a penetrating historical analysis of this doctrine, which concludes that its general applicability was overstated, see S. Anderson [1984] (III) L.C.R. 40. See also H. Forrest [1978] Conv. 194; J. Warburton [1986] Conv. 415.

[75] See *City of London Building Society v. Flegg* [1988] A.C. 52 at 82–3 *per* Lord Oliver.

[76] *Re Kempthorne* [1930] 1 Ch. 268.

sell a beneficial interest behind a trust for sale was, for the formal requirements necessary for such contracts, regarded as a contract for the sale of land,[77] this was not the view taken with regard to other situations.[78] The doctrine was unpredictable in its application and its abolition[79] has effected a simplification of the law.

7.5.5 **Trusts for sale and overreaching**

As is the case when land is the subject of a strict settlement, when land was held upon a trust for sale, machinery exists whereby the beneficial interests are overreached. Although it was thought by some that the existence of the doctrine of conversion was, of itself, sufficient to achieve this end, in that as the beneficial interests took effect in the notional proceeds of sale, overreaching in the strict sense did not occur,[80] this view has been refuted.[81] The conveyance by the trustees of sale would convert the interests of the beneficiaries into the actual proceeds of sale, itself a form of overreaching, provided that the transaction was one that the trustees were empowered to make.[82]

The leading case is *City of London Building Society v. Flegg*.[83] Mr and Mrs Maxwell-Brown were the registered proprietors of a house which, by a happy coincidence, was called 'Bleak House', which they held on trust for themselves and for the Fleggs, who were the parents of Mrs Maxwell-Brown. Without informing the Fleggs, they executed a number of mortgages over the property until, finally, they mortgaged the property to the plaintiffs, the money being used to discharge the previous mortgages. When the Maxwell-Browns defaulted on the mortgage, the plaintiffs sought possession and the Fleggs resisted the action. They argued that, as beneficial co-owners of the property in actual occupation of the land, their interests took effect as overriding interests binding on the plaintiffs, in the same way as did Mrs Boland's in *Williams & Glyn's Bank Ltd v. Boland*.[84]

The defence failed. The fact that the Fleggs were in actual occupation of the land was irrelevant. This was because the effect of the mortgage was to overreach their interests. The effect of overreaching in this context was that the legal interest of the society under the mortgage had priority over that of Mr and Mrs Flegg, who did not, therefore, have an interest capable of binding the mortgagee. As the transaction was effected by two trustees for sale, which is the appropriate method of overreaching the interests of equitable co-owners in cases where land is subject to co-ownership, it was irrelevant whether there were four or forty-four beneficial co-owners with interests behind the trust. The result was that, pending a sale of the property, the interest of the Fleggs was in the value of the land subject to the rights of the mortgagee.[85]

7.5.5.1 **Inherent power of overreaching**

This result might have been thought to have been dictated by the overreaching provision contained in the LPA 1925. Section 2 provides that, provided that the provisions of s. 27 of the Act respecting the payment of capital money are complied with, then a conveyance

---

[77] *Cooper v. Critchley* [1955] Ch. 431; *Steadman v. Steadman* [1976] A.C. 536. See also the original Law of Property (Miscellaneous Provisions) Act 1989, s. 2(6), now repealed by TOLATA 1996, s. 25(2), Sched. 4.

[78] *Irani Finance Ltd v. Singh* [1971] Ch. 59, where it was held that a charging order (a form of security in respect of a judgment debt) against land could not be made against the interest of a beneficiary behind a trust of sale; a decision necessitating Charging Orders Act 1979, s. 2.

[79] TOLATA 1996, s. 3.   [80] See, e.g., J.M. Lightwood [1929] C.L.J. 59 at 65.

[81] See the seminal article by C. Harpum [1980] C.L.J. 277 at 278.   [82] Ibid.

[83] [1988] A.C. 54. Astonishingly, this case, although directly in point, was not cited in *AIB Group Plc v. Turner* [2015] EWHC 3994 (Ch).

[84] [1981] A.C. 487.

[85] That interest is termed the equity of redemption. See 11.3.3.

made by trustees for sale shall overreach the equitable interests existing behind the trust. Section 27 provides that a purchaser of a legal estate from trustees for sale is not to be concerned with the trusts affecting the land if the proceeds of sale or capital money are paid to no fewer than two trustees for sale.[86] The true position, however, is that these sections did not confer new powers upon the trustees for sale, whose ability to overreach these interests derives from the powers that they have as trustees.[87]

This point is illustrated by *State Bank of India v. Sood*.[88] Trustees for sale created a mortgage to secure future borrowing. Beneficiaries under the trust for sale argued that their interests had not been overreached because, for that to happen, the capital money had to be paid to or at the direction of the trustees. As, in the instant case, no capital money had arisen at the time of the mortgage, it was argued that no overreaching had occurred. This argument was rejected, the essential reason being that the provisions governing the payment of capital money are relevant only when capital money arises. This will not be the case where the transaction in question is a lease, where no premium is paid, or an exchange of land, or, as here, where the land is mortgaged but no capital money has arisen. The point then is whether or not the transaction is *intra vires* the powers of the trustees. If it is, the beneficial interests will be overreached.

7.5.6 **One trustee**

A vital feature of both *Flegg* and *Sood* was that the mortgages were created by two trustees. In *Williams & Glyn's Bank Ltd v. Boland*,[89] a mortgage was created by the sole registered proprietor, who held the legal title on an implied trust for sale for himself and his wife, who was a beneficial co-owner of the house. It was held that the wife, who was in actual occupation of the house at all material times, had an overriding interest binding upon the bank. An argument, based upon the doctrine of conversion, that she could not have such an interest because her interest was in the proceeds of sale, was considered to be 'just a little unreal'.[90] Because there was only one trustee for sale, he lacked the power to overreach the beneficial interest existing behind the trust and this interest is, therefore, potentially binding upon a purchaser.[91]

There has been the suggestion, in *Shami v. Shami*,[92] that where there is a sale by a single owner but no capital monies are payable, s. 27, LPA 1925 does not apply, with the effect that the statutory requirements on overreaching do not apply. That argument stems from the dicta of Peter Gibson L.J. in *Sood*, where it was said that, 'on its true construction section 2(1)(ii) only requires compliance with the statutory requirements respecting the payment of capital money if capital money arises'.[93] While it might be a logical extension of that remark to think that the statutory requirements, including that of two trustees, do not apply where no capital money arises, this is to view the scope of *Sood* far too widely. There were two trustees in *Sood*, and the Court of Appeal clearly had not directed their minds to a single trustee case. It is also important to keep in mind that s. 2(1)(ii), LPA 1925 requires a conveyance to be made by 'trustees of land', which would seem to preclude the possibility of the overreaching machinery applying in a conveyance to a single trustee, regardless of whether capital monies were payable or not.

---

[86] See also Trustee Delegation Act 1999, s. 2. The 1925 Act, as amended, now refers to trusts of land rather than trusts for sale, a point which is, for present purposes, immaterial.

[87] See Harpum [1980] C.L.J. 277 at 293–4.   [88] [1997] Ch. 276. See M.P. Thompson [1997] Conv. 134.

[89] [1981] A.C. 487.   [90] Ibid, at 507 per Lord Wilberforce.

[91] For an interesting historical critique of both *Flegg* and *Boland*, see N. Jackson (2006) 69 M.L.R. 214.

[92] [2012] EWHC 664 (Ch), at [63] per Judge David Donaldson Q.C.

[93] [1997] Ch. 276, at 288.

7.6 Trusts of land

The strict settlement and the trust for sale had different origins and different effects. Most particularly, the decisions as to such key matters as whether the land should be sold or mortgaged was vested in different people; in the case of the former, in the tenant for life, in the case of the latter, in the trustees for sale. This, of course, was an important difference and made distinguishing between the two forms of settlement crucial, something which, unfortunately, was not always easy. More fundamentally, however, the question arose whether it was really necessary or desirable to have in place two systems of settlement.

If the preferred view was simply to allow one form of settlement to be retained, then there is little doubt that, of the two systems, the trust for sale was both simpler and more efficient. A principal reason why this was so was the different documentation required to set up either mechanism. Because, under a strict settlement, the legal estate is vested in the tenant for life, every change which occurs behind the curtain which causes a change in the identity of the tenant for life means that a new vesting deed must be executed to effect the necessary change. This can be a cumbersome and expensive business. With a trust for sale, on the other hand, because the legal estate is vested in the trustees, what occurs behind the curtain is of no concern to a purchaser. When one considers also, that the trust for sale could accommodate both successive and concurrent interests in property and, by the process of requiring consents to the sale of property, could be used more effectively than a settlement to ensure that the property was retained, where that was desired, it was manifest that, of the two legal devices, the trust for sale was the preferable of the two.

If, in reforming the law, the choice was simply between abolishing one form of land-holding and retaining the other, then the most sensible option would have been to abolish the strict settlement and to retain the trust for sale.[94] The Law Commission[95] did not, however, adopt this course. Mindful of the artificiality of the concept of a trust for sale and the concomitant doctrine of conversion, the preferred option was to create a new form of trust, ultimately to replace both of the previous forms of landholding. This recommendation has substantially been implemented by TOLATA 1996,[96] although the new trust which has been created bears close similarities to the effect of the trust for sale.

7.6.1 The trust of land

Part I of the 1996 Act contains the provisions relevant to the creation of the new trust of land. Its general scheme is, first, to define the trust of land and then to provide when such a trust will exist. The powers and duties of the trustees are then detailed, together with the rights of the beneficiaries, the position of purchasers, and the procedure and criteria to be applied in the resolution of disputes.

7.6.1.1 Definition

A trust of land is defined by s. 1(1) of the Act as being any trust of property which consists of or includes land, and trustees of land means the trustees of a trust of land. Section 1(2) elaborates this definition, to make clear that the reference to a trust includes all trusts (whether express, implied, resulting, or constructive), including a trust for sale and a bare trust. It is then further provided that, subject to certain exceptions, the Act is retrospective; that is land which was held on trust for sale prior to the Act coming into force is

---

[94] See G.A. Grove (1961) 24 M.L.R. 123.   [95] (1989) Law Com. No. 181.
[96] See N. Hopkins [1996] Conv. 411.

now subject to a trust of land. As a consequence of this, there was a myriad of legislative changes, so that references previously been made in statute have been amended to refer instead to trusts of land.[97]

7.6.1.2 Settlements

Although the intention of the Act is to replace the previous dichotomy of strict settlement and trust for sale with the single new device of the trust of land, this could not be done retrospectively for all settlements. Whereas converting what was a trust for sale into a trust of land would not involve any action on the part of anybody, this is not the case when land is subject to a settlement. In the former case, the legal title was vested in the trustees, whereas, when land was settled the legal title was vested in the tenant for life. It would not be realistic to expect, in all cases, the legal title to be transferred from the tenant for life to the trustees of the trust and, consequently, existing settlements remain subject to the regime imposed by the SLA 1925.[98]

In the case of new settlements, s. 2(1) prohibits the creation of any new settlements for the purposes of the SLA 1925. If, therefore, after 1997, a settlement is created to A for life, remainder to B, it will take effect as a trust of land. Where a settlement would arise because a conveyance purports to convey land to a minor, the conveyance is inoperative for the purpose of conveying a legal estate but will, instead, operate as a declaration of trust in favour of the minor.[99] There are limited exceptions to the embargo upon the creation of new settlements. These relate to alterations to interests deriving from settlements in existence prior to the commencement of the Act.[100]

7.6.1.3 Imposition of the trust

After 1997, all new settlements take effect as trusts of land; with respect to other trusts involving land, the new trust is imposed retrospectively. For trusts created after 1997, the position is governed by ss 4 and 5 of the Act. Section 4 is concerned with the creation of an express trust for sale. This is not prohibited, but such a trust, nevertheless, comes within the definition of a trust of land supplied by s. 1. Moreover, if such a trust is created, then, despite any provision to the contrary made by the disposition, the trustees are given the power, at their absolute discretion, to postpone the sale of the land. If an express trust for sale is created, the only potential significance of doing so would appear to be that it might affect how the court might determine a dispute between interested parties as to whether the land should actually be sold.[101]

Section 5 of the Act is concerned with implied trusts of land. Under the old law, a trust for sale was implied by law in certain situations, notably when land was conveyed to joint tenants or to tenants in common.[102] Section 5 of and Sched. 2 to the Act impose a trust of land in the situations where previously a trust for sale would have been implied.

7.6.1.4 The nature of the trust

Under the old law, the trust was a trust for sale; the duty of the trustees was, subject to their power to postpone the sale, to sell the property. Under the new law, there is no such duty imposed upon the trustees. Instead, s. 6 of the Act operates to vest in the trustees all the powers of an absolute owner and, of course, one of the powers of an absolute owner is to sell the property.

---

[97] TOLATA 1996, Sched. 3.
[98] Ibid. s. 1(3). Also exempt from the Act is land held under the University and College Estates Act 1925.
[99] TOLATA 1996, s. 2(6), Sched. 1.   [100] Ibid., s. 2(3).   [101] Ibid., ss 14, 15. See 9.8.
[102] LPA 1925, ss 34, 36.

7.6.1.5 Abolition of conversion

Because the trustees are no longer under a duty to sell the property, a logical consequence is that the doctrine of conversion whereby, at least for some purposes, the interests of the beneficiaries were regarded as being in the proceeds of sale should no longer be applicable. This logical conclusion is spelled out explicitly by s. 3 of the Act, a provision that can now apply only to an express trust for sale, which provides that where land is held by trustees subject to a trust for sale, the land is not to be regarded as personal property. The reverse position is also catered for. If personal property is subject to a trust for sale in order that the trustees may acquire land, the personal property is not to be regarded as land.

7.6.1.6 Powers of the trustees

As stated above, s. 6 of the Act confers upon the trustees all the powers of an absolute owner. In contrast to the previous law, there is no prohibition on the restriction of the trustees' powers, it being provided by s. 8 that s. 6 does not apply in the case of a trust of land being created by a disposition which excludes its effect. It would seem, therefore, that the power of sale can be excluded, although if that is done, it would still be open to any person interested to petition the court for a sale of the property, although the exclusion of the power of sale would be a factor to which the court would presumably have regard in the exercise of its discretion.[103]

A new power given to trustees is a power, when land is subject to a trust of land and each of the beneficiaries is of full age, to convey the land to the beneficiaries even if they have not required the trustees to do so. If the trustees do convey the land to the beneficiaries, they are required to do what is necessary to secure that the legal title vests in them, which means applying to be registered as proprietors of the land. If the beneficiaries fail to do so a court may make an order requiring them to do so.[104] As an alternative to conveying the land to the beneficiaries, the trustees may, by power of attorney, delegate their powers to a beneficiary of full age, who is entitled to an interest in possession.[105]

7.6.1.7 Purchasing land

It was previously the case that difficulties arose as to whether trustees for sale, having sold the land which was subject to the trust, could use the proceeds of sale to purchase other land.[106] This doubt as to the ability of trustees to do this has now been removed by s. 6(3),[107] which empowers the trustees to purchase a legal estate in land in England and Wales for the purpose of investment, for occupation by any beneficiary, or for any other reason.

7.6.1.8 Misuse of powers

The conferment of powers on the trustees is done in a much simpler way than was previously the case by simply conferring upon them the powers of an absolute owner. It is then provided by s. 6(6) of the Act that these powers shall not be exercised in contravention of any other enactment or any rule of law or equity. The consequence of trustees exercising their powers wrongfully is controversial and will be considered in the section on overreaching.

---

[103] TOLATA 1996, ss 14, 15.   [104] Ibid., s. 6(2).

[105] Ibid., s. 9. The powers of delegation are much wider than was previously the case.

[106] *Re Wakeman* [1945] Ch. 177. Cf. *Re Wellstead's Will Trusts* [1949] 1 Ch. 296 at 319 *per* Cohen L.J. See D. Pollock (1953) Conv. (N.S.) 134 at 137.

[107] As amended by the Trustee Act 2000, s. 8.

7.7 **The rights of beneficiaries**

The Act, having conferred extensive powers to deal with the land upon the trustees, also confers rights upon the beneficiaries to which the trustees, perhaps somewhat unnecessarily, are required to have regard when exercising their powers.[108]

7.7.1 **Consultation and consents**

7.7.1.1 Consultation

As was the case when land was held upon trust for sale, the trustees are obliged to consult the beneficiaries prior to the exercise of any function relating to land subject to the trust. The duty to consult is imposed by s. 11 of the Act. The trustees are required, so far as is practicable, to consult the beneficiaries of full age and beneficially entitled to the land and, so far as is consistent with the general interest of the trust, give effect to the wishes of those beneficiaries or (having regard to the respective sizes of the beneficial interests) to the majority of the beneficiaries.

The duty to consult does not carry with it an obligation to carry out the wishes of the beneficiaries or the majority of them if, in the opinion of the trustees, the action proposed is not consistent with the general interests of the trust. Where there is such disagreement, application can be made to the court under s. 14 of the Act. The orders which the court can make and the criteria to be applied in determining disputes of this nature will be considered fully in a later chapter.[109]

7.7.1.2 Consents

Provision is made for the exercise of the trustees' powers to be made subject to the obtaining of consents. Section 8(2) of the Act provides that, if the disposition creating a trust of land requires any consent to be obtained to the exercise of any power conferred by s. 6 or 7, the power may not be exercised without that consent, thereby giving to that person or persons a power of veto over the exercise of the trustees' powers. If the consent of more than two persons is required then the consent of any two of them to the exercise of the function is sufficient in favour of a purchaser.

The position of the purchaser if the trustees do not comply with these provisions will be considered shortly.

7.7.1.3 Occupation

Most land which is held on a trust of land is the subject of co-ownership and an important aspect of the rights of co-owners relates to the occupation of the property and the regulation of rights of occupation. Detailed provision is made with respect to these issues by ss 12 and 13 of the Act and will be considered in the context of co-ownership of land.[110]

7.8 **Overreaching**

It was established by the House of Lords in *City of London Building Society v. Flegg*[111] that when land was held upon a trust for sale, a conveyance executed by the trustees for sale would overreach the interests of the beneficiaries, regardless of whether or not those beneficiaries were in actual occupation of the land. Although in a separate report from that dealing with trusts of land generally, the Law Commission recommended that Flegg be

---

[108] TOLATA 1996, s. 6(5).   [109] See Chapter 9.   [110] Ibid.   [111] [1988] A.C. 54.

reversed by legislation, it is not readily apparent that the Act either did, or was intended to, have this effect. Nevertheless, it has been argued[112] that, in the case of registered land, the Act has had this effect, and so this issue must be addressed, considering first the position where title is unregistered.

7.8.1 **Unregistered land**

Where title is unregistered, the first point to note is that the trustees are, by s. 6 of the Act, given all the powers of an absolute owner. However, s. 6(6) provides that the powers conferred in this section shall not be exercised in contravention of any rule of law or equity. The restrictions that would seem to be relevant would appear to be contained in various provisions, such as s. 6(5), which requires the trustees, in exercising their powers, to have regard to the rights of the beneficiaries;[113] s. 8, which provides that where a consent is required for any disposition, the trustees shall not make such a disposition without obtaining the requisite consent; and s. 11(1), which requires the trustees in the exercise of any function to consult the beneficiaries of full age entitled to possession.

The essential argument put forward is that these restrictions on the exercise of the powers of the trustees limit their powers of dealing with the trust property and, ordinarily, this would therefore invalidate the disposition by the trustees. This is not the case, however, with respect to unregistered land because of the protection afforded by s. 16 of the Act. Section 16(1) of the Act provides that:

> A purchaser of land which is or has been subject to a trust need not be concerned to see that any requirement imposed on the trustees by section 6(5), 7(3) or 11(1) has been complied with.

The section then goes on to afford further protection to a purchaser by stipulating that, where trustees of land conveying land contravene s. 6(6) or 6(8) of the Act, the conveyance shall not be invalidated unless the purchaser has actual notice of the contravention; and a similar provision is made in respect of a conveyance made in excess of any limitation imposed by s. 8.[114]

It is clear, therefore, that the purchaser of unregistered land will not be bound by beneficial interests existing behind a trust of land provided that the purchase money is paid to or at the direction of the trustees, unless he has actual notice that the disposition is a breach of trust. The argument that a purchaser of registered land will not be so protected is based upon s. 16(7) which provides, simply, that this section does not apply to registered land.

7.8.2 **Registered land**

The argument that the decision in *Flegg* has been overruled in respect of registered land rests principally on the fact that the protection afforded to purchasers of unregistered land by s. 16 is expressly made not to apply to registered land.[115] Accordingly, it is argued that if

---

[112] G. Ferris and G. Battersby [1998] Conv. 168. For a similar argument advanced some years previously, see S. Clayton [1981] Conv. 18. That article, however, relied heavily on the restrictions imposed upon trustees for sale by LPA 1925, s. 28, which has now been repealed.

[113] This is a curious provision, as a basic duty of trustees is to have regard to the interests of the beneficiaries. For an interesting discussion which links this duty to the criteria listed in s. 15, see G. Ferris and G. Battersby [2009] Conv. 39.

[114] TOLATA 1996, s. 16(2)(3). Cf. similar provisions in respect of the wrongful exercise of a mortgagee's power of sale: LPA 1925, s. 104(2).

[115] For the argument that overreaching overly favours the purchasers in registered land at the expense of beneficiaries behind a trust of land, see G. Owen and D. Cahill [2017] Conv. 26.

trustees contravene any of the limitations imposed by the 1996 Act, then a purchaser will not get a good title and will be bound by the rights of the beneficiaries.[116]

As an initial observation, one would anticipate that, were such a conclusion to be intended, then such a change in the law would be signposted in a rather less cryptic way than this. Nevertheless, if one looks at the arguments on the merits, they do not entirely convince. In the case of registered land, the proprietor, by virtue of s. 18 of the Land Registration Act (LRA) 1925, may, subject to any entry on the register, transfer the fee simple in possession. Accordingly, it has been said to be fundamental that:

> In order to deprive registered proprietors of full powers of mortgaging or leasing, for example, there would have to be a restriction on the register expressly preventing them from exercising those powers.[117]

In other words, the view is that the protection provided by s. 16 in the case of unregistered land is, quite simply, unnecessary in the case of registered land because any restrictions on the rights of the trustees to deal with the land must be entered on the register of title. This conclusion is reinforced by the amendment made to s. 94, LRA 1925 by the 1996 Act.[118] Section 94(1) requires that, when there is a trust of land, the land shall be registered in the names of the trustees. It is further provided by s. 94(4) that there shall be entered on the register such restrictions as may be prescribed, or are expedient, for the protection of the rights of persons beneficially entitled to the land. The clear implication is that, unless the beneficial rights are protected by the entry of a restriction, the purchaser shall not be concerned with them.

7.8.2.1 *Ultra vires* dispositions?

A final matter is that the argument that *Flegg* has been overruled rests upon the premise that dispositions made by the trustees in contravention of the limitations imposed by the Act have the effect of making such disposition *ultra vires* and, therefore, ineffective to overreach the beneficial interests behind the trust. It is not at all clear, however, that this is the case; it is quite feasible that the limitations on the powers of the trustees are designed to affect the position of the trustees *vis-à-vis* the beneficiaries rather than a purchaser so that if, for example, the trustees sell the land without consulting the beneficiaries this may make them liable to the beneficiaries for breach of trust but not affect the purchaser.[119] Indeed, given that the trustees are not obliged to follow the views expressed by the beneficiaries after consultation if they consider that such views are not in the best interests of the trust,[120] one would expect this conclusion to follow. It can hardly be the case that a mortgage or conveyance by trustees contrary to the wishes of beneficiaries, who have been consulted, will overreach those interests, whereas the same transactions carried out, without consulting them at all, will not. Consequently, it is submitted that although, to date, judicial views on this matter are inconclusive,[121] if and when the issue is squarely

---

[116] Ferris and Battersby [1998] Conv. 168 at 179–80. For a refutation of this analysis, see N. Jackson [2007] Conv. 120.

[117] Ruoff and Roper, *The Law and Practice of Registered Conveyancing* (London, Sweet & Maxwell, looseleaf), para. 32.05.

[118] TOLATA 1996, Sched. 3, para. 5.

[119] See M. Dixon [2000] Conv. 267. But see the reply by G. Ferris and G. Battersby [2001] Conv. 221.

[120] See 7.7.1.1

[121] See *State Bank of India v. Sood* [1997] Ch. 276 at 290 *per* Peter Gibson L.J., where this point was assumed without argument; and *Birmingham Midshires Mortgage Services Ltd v. Sabherwal* (2000) 80 P. & C.R. 256.

raised, the conclusion will be reached that a conveyance or mortgage of registered land[122] will overreach the beneficial interests existing behind the trust for sale, provided that the purchase money is paid to two trustees, and that the decision in *Flegg* remains good law.

7.8.2.2 Land Registration Act 2002

Although this issue is not explicitly dealt with in the LRA 2002, it would seem that the matter is put beyond doubt by a combination of ss 23, 24, and 26. Sections 23 and 24 confer owner's powers on the registered proprietor. Section 26(1) then provides that, subject to subsection (2), a person's right to exercise owner's powers in relation to an estate or charge is to be taken free from any limitation affecting the validity of the disposition. Section 26(2) provides that s. 26(1) does not apply to a limitation reflected by an entry on the register or imposed by, or under, the Act. Unless, therefore, the right of beneficiaries to be consulted is protected by the entry of a restriction, a purchaser will not be affected by failure of the trustees to do so.[123]

---

[122] The High Court in *Baker v. Craggs* [2016] EWHC 3250 (Ch) had held that a conveyance of an easement had overreaching effect, on the basis that a right of way is a 'legal estate' for the purposes of s. 2(1), LPA 1925. This was incorrect as a matter of principle; not only does it misread the universal interpretation of s. 2(1) to encompass only a conveyance of a freehold or leasehold estate, the approach is inimical to the concept of overreaching itself. The Court of Appeal in *Baker v. Craggs* [2018] EWCA Civ. 1126 has confirmed that the High Court was wrong; the conveyance of an easement cannot have overreaching effect.

[123] See also E. Cooke [2002] Conv. 11 at 23–5.

8

Acquisition of Interests in the Home

There are a number of situations where co-ownership may be encountered.[1] Perhaps the most usual is where a house is bought together by a husband and wife as the matrimonial home. There is also an increasingly common arrangement whereby a couple live together in a loving relationship but either out of choice,[2] or because they are legally unable to do so,[3] they do not marry. People can, of course, share the ownership of property without there being any romantic attachment between them. They could be siblings, or other relations, or simply friends. Co-ownership can also arise when the relationship between the co-owners is a commercial one, as where partners together buy land from which to operate a business.

Co-ownership of land can, therefore, involve a number of quite different relationships. It was, indeed, this considerable variety in the types of relationship that caused the Law Commission, in its long-awaited Report on Sharing Homes, to abandon the task of trying 'to devise a statutory scheme for the determination of shares in the shared home which can operate fairly and evenly across all the diverse circumstances which are now to be encountered'.[4] The type of relationship which has caused the most anxiety, however, is that between cohabiting couples who are in an intimate relationship. Between 1996 and 2017, cohabiting couple families were the fastest growing family type according to the Office for National Statistics,[5] more than doubling from 1.5 million families to 3.3 million families. The law governing this type of relationship has been stigmatized as being 'uncertain, difficult to apply and can lead to serious injustice'.[6] Perhaps for this reason, in the aftermath of the Report on Sharing Homes, the government referred the matter back to the Law Commission to consider only this type of relationship. The ensuing Report[7] will be considered at the end of this chapter.

The essential legal framework imposed whenever there is co-ownership of land is the same, regardless of the nature of the relationship. In all cases, there will be in existence a trust of land. Issues which can also arise will be to determine the respective beneficial rights of each co-owner in the property and the resolution of disputes between the co-owners; in particular, disputes as to occupation and as to when the property should be sold. It is with these latter issues, in particular, that the different types of relationship involved between the co-owners will become material. Before considering the legal framework of co-ownership and the respective rights of the co-owners, which is the subject matter of Chapter 10, the prior issue arises as to whether co-ownership actually exists.

---

[1] See, generally, Mee, *Property Rights of Cohabitees* (Oxford and Portland, OR, Hart Publishing, 1999).
[2] For the various reasons for this, see S. Duncan, A. Barlow, and G. James (2005) 17 C.F.L.Q. 383.
[3] See, e.g., *Churchill v. Roach* [2004] 2 F.L.R. 989.
[4] (2002) Law Com. No. 278, *Sharing Homes: A Discussion Paper*.
[5] Office for National Statistics, *Families and Households in the UK: 2017* (8 November 2017).
[6] (1995) Law Com. No. 234 at para. 34.
[7] (2007) Law Com. No. 307.

8.1 **The creation of co-ownership**

There are a number of situations where it may become necessary to establish the actual beneficial ownership of land. When the relationship between two people breaks down, the question will arise as to who owns what or, on the death of one of them, who owned what.[8] This question can also arise when a third party is involved, when it is argued that an occupier of a property has a beneficial interest in it which is binding upon a mortgagee.[9]

'Who owns what?' is a beguilingly simple question to ask, but English law has historically resisted providing a clear framework that will yield an equally simple answer. As the Law Commission put it, 'in a short time the enquirer will find themselves immersed in the off-putting, and sometimes obscure, terminology of the law of trusts and estoppel'.[10] Similar sentiments were expressed at greater length, and with more rhetorical flourish, in *Stack v. Dowden*,[11] where Carnwath L.J. said of this area of law:

> To the detached observer, the result may seem like a witches' brew, into which various esoteric ingredients have been stirred over the years, and in which different ideas bubble to the surface at different times. They include implied trust, constructive trust, resulting trust, presumption of advancement, proprietary estoppel, unjust enrichment and so on. These ideas are likely to mean nothing to a layman, and often little more to the lawyers who use them.

This chapter seeks to separate out some of these various ingredients, in order to elucidate the applicable principles, and then to assess how satisfactory their application is to disputes of this type.

8.1.1 **Divorce jurisdiction**

Section 24 of the Matrimonial Causes Act 1973 gives the courts, on granting a decree of divorce, nullity, or judicial separation, the power to order one party to the marriage to transfer to the other party, or to any child of the family, property to which he is entitled, either in possession or reversion.[12] After 5 December 2005, when the Civil Partnership Act 2004 came into force, this jurisdiction to reallocate property has been extended to the dissolution of a civil partnership.[13] A civil partnership can be entered into between same-sex couples,[14] and enables such people to register their partnership.[15] Most of the legal incidents of marriage are then conferred on the couple, including that of reallocation of property on the dissolution of the relationship. As of 2014, same-sex couples can choose to enter a marriage instead of a civil partnership.[16] It should be stressed, however, that there is no jurisdiction to reallocate property on the breakdown of a *non*-marital relationship. This point deserves emphasis because it is widely, although erroneously, believed that cohabitation for a period of time confers upon the parties the same legal rights as if they were married.[17] This is not so.[18]

---

[8] See, e.g., *Bindra v. Mawji* [2008] EWHC 1715 (Ch).   [9] See 11.6.8.

[10] (2002) Law Com. No. 288, para. 1.12.

[11] [2005] EWCA Civ. 857 at [75]; affmd for different reasons at [2007] 2 A.C. 929. See E. Cooke [2005] Conv. 555.

[12] For an analysis of the development of the law relating to matrimonial property, see the fifth edition of this work, 302–4.

[13] Civil Partnership Act 2004, s. 72, Sched. 5.   [14] Ibid, s. 1.   [15] Ibid., s. 2.

[16] Marriage (Same Sex Couples) Act 2013.

[17] See A. Barlow, C. Burgoyne, E. Clery, and J. Smithson in A. Park, *et al.*, *British Social Attitudes: The 24th Report* (London, Sage, 2008), 12. See also *Churchill v. Roach* [2004] 2 F.L.R. 989, where it appeared that a university teacher thought that cohabitation for seven days a week over six months would lead the law to consider his partner to be his wife: see at 991 *per* Judge Norris.

[18] For an account of how this myth has developed, see R. Probert [2011] Fam Law 283.

The statutory jurisdiction to adjust property rights on divorce or civil partnership dissolution has transformed the approach to be taken to property disputes between spouses, and civil partners, on the breakdown of the marriage or civil partnership. In making orders under the Matrimonial Causes Act, the court is not constrained by the ownership rights in the property prior to the order being made. Consequently, in such cases it is not of great importance to determine who owned what. This question will, however, be important if the dispute as to the ownership of property occurs outside the context of divorce or dissolution. This might occur if, for religious reasons, there are objections to divorce,[19] or if the dispute occurs after the death of one of the parties.[20] Much more important than this is the not uncommon situation where one party is seeking to assert rights against a mortgagee,[21] or, indeed, other creditors.[22] In such cases, the person who is asserting the claim will first have to establish that she actually has a right in the property,[23] and this is done by the application of equitable principles, which are principally those underlying the law of trusts.

8.2 Express declarations of ownership

By far the easiest way for the parties to avoid disputes in the future is to state, expressly and in writing, what the beneficial interests are in the house when it is being acquired. If the parties make an express declaration as to the beneficial interests[24] in the property, that declaration will be decisive.[25] It will cease to be decisive only if one of the parties can secure rectification of the document setting out the equitable interests. An example of this occurred in *Thames Guarantee Ltd v. Campbell*,[26] where a wife had provided the whole purchase price of the property but, out of courtesy to the husband, the solicitors were instructed to convey the property into their joint names. Although it was intended that she should be the sole beneficial owner in equity, by mistake they were described as being joint tenants in law and in equity. The intention having been proved, she succeeded in having the document rectified to delete the words 'in equity'. The onus of proof to secure rectification is, however, a heavy one.

Subject to any claim to rectification, however, the express statement of the beneficial interests in the property will be conclusive as to those interests at the time that the property was acquired, although those interests may later be varied as a consequence of subsequent events.[27] As such, it is clearly good practice when a house is being acquired by a couple for their intentions with regard to the beneficial ownership to be ascertained and reflected in a document signed by both parties.[28] Much time and expense can be avoided by an express declaration of the beneficial entitlements and judicial exhortations for advisers to

---

[19] See, e.g., *Shinh v. Shinh* [1977] 1 All E.R. 97.

[20] See, e.g., *Re Draper's Conveyance* [1969] 1 Ch. 486; and 9.6.2.1.

[21] See *Williams & Glyn's Bank Ltd v. Boland* [1981] A.C. 487.

[22] See *Hosking v. Michaelides* [2004] All E.R. (D.) 147.

[23] See *Lloyds Bank plc v. Rosset* [1991] 1 A.C. 107.

[24] The declaration of the beneficial ownership itself need not be in writing, as long as it is 'manifested and proved by some writing' so as to satisfy LPA 1925, s. 53(1)(b).

[25] *Goodman v. Gallant* [1986] Fam. 106; *Turton v. Turton* [1988] Ch. 542; *The Anglo Eastern Trust Ltd v Kermanshahchi (No. 3)* [2003] EWHC 1939 (Ch). A statement that the survivor may give a valid receipt for the capital money arising on a disposition of the land does not, of itself, amount to a declaration of a joint tenancy: *Harwood v. Harwood* [1991] 2 F.L.R. 274; *Huntingford v. Hobbs* [1993] 1 F.L.R. 376; *Stack v. Dowden, supra*, at [51] per Baroness Hale.

[26] [1985] Q.B. 510. See also *Wilson v. Wilson* [1969] 3 All E.R. 345.

[27] See *Jones v. Kernott* [2011] UKSC 53.

[28] See *Robinson v. Robinson* (1977) 241 E.G. 153. Cf. *Pink v. Lawrence* (1977) 36 P. & C.R. 37.

make sure that this is done are not hard to find. The latest *cri de coeur* with regard to this emanated from Ward L.J., who said:

> Perhaps conveyancers do not read the law reports. I will try one more time: *always try to agree on and then record how the beneficial interest is to be held.* It is not very difficult to do.[29]

A failure to perform this task may leave a legal adviser open to a claim in negligence.[30]

8.2.1 Land registration form

Since 1998, when title is being registered in joint names, the application form for transfers to joint proprietors, which must be completed to enable registration to occur, enables the applicants to tick one of three boxes.[31] The alternatives are that the applicants are holding for themselves as joint tenants; that they are holding for themselves as tenants in common in equal shares; or that they are holding the property on trust.[32] Unfortunately, it is not mandatory to tick any of the boxes,[33] and despite the strong exhortation by Lady Hale in *Stack v. Dowden*[34] that the rules should be changed to ensure that this is done, there has been no change to that part of the form.[35]

This is to be regretted. The policy decision to keep completion of the tick-boxes optional, rather than making it compulsory, is an attempt to shelter micro-businesses from the perceived pernicious effect of bureaucracy. A good deal of property which is purchased in joint names is bought to set up a small business, and the completion of this form is seen as an example of red tape which the government is committed to reduce.[36] As has been aptly commented, while 'it is always good to see bathwater sloshing down the drain, . . . are we seeing the baby disappearing with it?'[37] Had such a change occurred, disputes as to the beneficial ownership of houses transferred to joint proprietors would have all but disappeared, with the resulting saving of large amounts of money, and a good deal of angst, currently spent in contesting these cases.

8.3 Resulting, implied, and constructive trusts

Where the parties have failed to state what the beneficial interests in the property are to be, in a subsequent dispute this issue will fall to be decided principally by the application of the law of implied trusts. Section 53(1)(b) of the LPA 1925, requiring trusts of land to be proved by writing, does not affect or apply to the creation or operation of resulting, implied, or constructive trusts by virtue of s. 53(2). It is with resulting and constructive trusts that we are concerned, the usual scenario being a situation where the legal title to the house is in the name of one person, usually the male partner, and the other claims subsequently to have a beneficial interest in it. The resolution of problems concerning this

---

[29] *Carlton v. Goodman* [2002] 2 F.L.R. 259 at 273, Ward L.J.'s emphasis.

[30] See *Walker v. Hall* [1984] F.L.R. 126 at 129 *per* Dillon L.J.

[31] Empirical evidence, however, shows that the actual parties may not understand the import of the effect of this. See G. Douglas, J. Pearce, and H. Woodward [2008] Conv. 365 at 372–5.

[32] For the meaning of these terms, see Chapter 9. The beneficial interests of the parties are not revealed on the register of title.

[33] See the discussion at [2007] Conv. 364.   [34] [2007] 2 A.C. 432 at [52].

[35] The Land Registration Rules 2003 are periodically amended and updated. The last major amendment was through the Land Registration (Amendment) Rules 2008, and the last alterations to the TR1 and FR1 forms occurred in 2009. For critical comment on the 2008 amendments, see M.J. Dixon [2008] Conv. 355.

[36] See E. Cooke [2011] Fam Law 1142 at 1143.   [37] Ibid. at 1144.

type of situation necessitates one 'to climb again the familiar ground that slopes down from the twin peaks of *Pettitt v. Pettitt* and *Gissing v. Gissing*'.[38]

These two decisions of the House of Lords, decided within a short time of each other, formed the theoretical underpinning of this area of law. Since then, much litigation has ensued, including two further decisions of the House of Lords in *Lloyds Bank plc v. Rosset*,[39] and *Stack v. Dowden*,[40] and a decision of the Supreme Court in *Jones v. Kernott*.[41] Although this chapter will attempt to guide a path through this extensively litigated area of law, it is as well to note, at the outset, that 'as is notorious, it is not easy to reconcile every judicial utterance on this well-travelled area of law'.[42] Moreover, *Stack v. Dowden* has been criticized on the basis that it has failed to provide theoretical clarity to the law,[43] and it has been said, with a degree of understatement, that 'There is some debate about the principles underlying the decision of the majority in that case'.[44] That the conceptual debate may not be over was, somewhat depressingly, recognized in *Jones v. Kernott* itself, as Lord Collins, while expressing the hope that the correctness of the decision in *Stack v. Dowden* would not need to be revisited said that 'should it be necessary, the court (no doubt with a panel of seven or nine) would need much fuller argument (together with citation of the enormous critical literature which the decision has spawned) than was presented to the court on this appeal'.[45]

With that caveat in place, the structure of this chapter attempts to reflect the two broad factual matrices as encountered by the courts. First, cases where the legal title to the land in question is jointly owned, but there has been no express declaration to apportion the parties' beneficial shares. Second, cases where there is sole ownership of the legal title, and the non-owning claimant argues for a share in the beneficial title. As we shall see, the courts are guided by the principle that equity follows the law. If the legal title is jointly owned, therefore, the presumption is that the equitable title is jointly owned as well, which will result in equal shares (50 per cent each) when the relationship between the parties breaks down. One joint owner may argue that the shares should be unequal, however, and a constructive or resulting trust must be employed to achieve an *un*equal quantification of the beneficial interest.

Where the legal title is instead owned by one person, equity assumes that they are the sole beneficial owner. In order for someone else to claim any share of the equity, they will first need to acquire an interest through a resulting or constructive trust. If they succeed in that argument, their interest or share will be quantified by the court. Depending on the facts at play, a case can therefore involve simply a question as to the quantification of an equitable co-owner's interest, or the prior question of whether an interest in the equity has been acquired at all.

8.4 Joint ownership of the legal title

In *Pettitt v Pettitt*,[46] it was stated that the starting point in determining the beneficial ownership of the home is to look first at the position at law. If the legal title was in joint names, there was a presumption that it was intended to share the beneficial ownership.

---

[38] *Grant v. Edwards* [1986] Ch. 638 at 646 *per* Nourse L.J.

[39] [1991] 1 A.C. 107.   [40] [2007] 2 A.C. 432.   [41] [2011] UKSC 53.

[42] *Drake v. Whipp* [1996] 1 F.L.R. 826 at 827 *per* Peter Gibson L.J.

[43] See M.J. Dixon [2007] Conv. 352; W. Swadling (2007) 123 L.Q.R. 511 at 518. For a more favourable reaction, see N. Hopkins (2009) 125 L.Q.R. 310.

[44] *Bindra v. Mawji* [2008] EWHC 1715 (Ch) at [86] *per* Etherton J.   [45] [2011] UKSC 53 at [58].

[46] [1970] A.C. 777 at 813–14 *per* Lord Upjohn, who also said that it is seldom that this is determinative, a point ignored in *Stack v. Dowden*. The decision in *Pettitt* was described as 'being more Delphic than the Oracle which at least had the advantage that her ambiguities were uttered in only one voice': J. Tiley [1969] C.L.J. 191 at 196. See also the observations in *Jones v. Kernott* [2011] UKSC 53 at [28] *per* Lord Walker and Lady Hale.

Conversely, if there was sole ownership at law, the presumption was that this was also the position in equity. The presumptions were relatively easy to rebut, however, and, in cases of joint ownership of the legal estate, the fact that the parties had contributed unequally to the purchase price would tend to the conclusion that the parties intended the beneficial ownership to be shared unequally.[47] The House of Lords in *Stack v. Dowden*[48] has, however, strengthened considerably the force of the presumption, particularly with regard to the position when there is joint ownership at law.

Barry Stack and Dehra Dowden, who were in a relationship for twenty-seven years, had cohabited for a total of nineteen years, during which time they had four children. In 1983, when they first started living together, the house was in her sole name. This house was sold in 1993, and another house was bought, title to which was in their joint names. The purchase price was £190,000. Just over £128,000 came from her building society, and the balance from a bank loan to them jointly. This was secured by a mortgage and two endowment policies, one of which was in their joint names, and the other in her name alone. The interest payments on the mortgage and the joint endowment payments were made by Mr Stack, and the capital sum borrowed was repaid by a series of lump sum payments, of which he contributed £27,000, and she just over £38,000. The utility bills were in her name, although he claimed to have paid some of them. Throughout the period of their cohabitation they maintained separate bank accounts, and made a series of separate investments. When they separated in 2002, she remained in possession of the house with the children and litigation ensued as to the beneficial ownership of it. The House of Lords, unanimously—although Lord Neuberger dissented as to the reasoning—held that the beneficial ownership was divided between them in the proportion 65 per cent to 35 per cent in her favour.

8.4.1 **Presumption of joint beneficial ownership**

The leading speech was given by Lady Hale. She accepted that the task for the court is to determine what the parties intended.[49] In so doing, however, she stressed that:

> Just as the starting point where there is sole legal ownership is sole beneficial ownership, the starting point where there is joint legal ownership is joint beneficial ownership. The onus is on the person seeking to show that the beneficial ownership is different from the legal ownership. So, in sole ownership cases it is upon the non-owner to show that he has any interest at all. In joint ownership cases, it is upon the joint owner who claims to have other than a joint beneficial interest.[50]

Subsequently, she made it clear that it would be unusual for the courts to find that the common intention of the parties was that the beneficial interests in the house should be different from that which pertained at law.[51] This position was stressed in *Jones v. Kernott*,[52] where Lord Walker and Lady Hale, in a joint judgment, made it clear that, when the property is transferred to the parties in joint names, the default position is that the position in law is mirrored by that in equity.

The idea, according to Lady Hale, that it would be 'unusual' for the presumption of joint beneficial ownership to be rebutted by finding a common intention to share the equity in some unequal proportion raises an obvious question: what facts qualify as sufficiently

---

[47] See *Stack v. Dowden* [2005] EWCA Civ. 857 at [17] *per* Chadwick L.J; affmd on different grounds at [2007] 2 A.C. 432.

[48] [2007] 2 A.C. 432.   [49] Ibid. at [61].   [50] Ibid. at [56].   [51] Ibid. at [69].

[52] [2011] UKSC 53 at [15].

unusual? Before considering why the presumption was rebutted in *Stack v. Dowden* itself, and what might make other cases fall into the same category, an initial issue about the nature of the beneficial joint ownership when the presumption is applicable must first be addressed.

8.4.2 Joint tenancy or tenancy in common?

While it is clear that, as a result of *Stack v. Dowden*, the existence of joint legal ownership carries with it a strong presumption of joint beneficial ownership, it was not made as clear as it should have been whether this is as a joint tenancy or as a tenancy in common in equal shares. At law, it is only possible for there to be a joint tenancy,[53] whereas, in equity, co-ownership can take the form of either a joint tenancy or a tenancy in common. The distinction between the two will be considered in more detail in the next chapter, but, for present purposes, the main distinction between the two is what happens in the event of the death of one of the co-owners. If there is a beneficial joint tenancy, then the survivor becomes the sole owner of the property. If, on the other hand, there is a tenancy in common then, on the death of one of them, that person's share in the property will pass by will or upon intestacy. Lady Hale, who emphasized that equity followed the law, said that 'at least in the domestic context, a conveyance into joint names indicates both legal and beneficial joint tenancy unless and until the contrary is proved'.[54] While this is clear, earlier in the same paragraph she said that the issue was whether a conveyance into joint names established a *prima facie* case of joint and equal beneficial shares unless the contrary is established, a statement which indicates that the co-owners hold as equitable tenants in common in equal shares. On balance, the passage quoted supports the view that an equitable joint tenancy had been created, although the alternative view has been assumed to be the case by some commentators.[55] That assumption was supported by Lord Hope who said that, in the present context, 'joint beneficial ownership means that the shares are presumed to be divided equally',[56] a statement indicative of a tenancy in common. A similar lack of precision was exhibited in *Fowler v. Barron*,[57] where Arden L.J. said of the effect of the presumption that:

> It provides a default rule that, unless and until the contrary is proved, joint tenants in this context are treated as joint legal and beneficial owners. If the contrary were not proved, the mere fact that the property was transferred into their joint names would be enough to give both parties *an equal beneficial share.*

The first sentence is consistent with the existence of a beneficial joint tenancy, and the second with a tenancy in common.

While it is disappointing that this important issue should have been left unclear, and such a lack of clarity had the potential to lead to further litigation,[58] this point was finally settled by *Jones v. Kernott*,[59] where Lord Walker and Lady Hale said that when the property is in joint names, the starting point is that 'equity follows the law and they are joint tenants both in law and in equity'. This means that, when the relationship breaks down, the

---

[53] LPA 1925, s. 1(6).   [54] [2007] 2 A.C. 432 at [58].

[55] See G. Douglas, J. Pearce, and H. Woodward [2008] Conv. 365, 'the presumption is that equity follows the law so that the beneficial interests are held in equal shares'.

[56] [2007] 2 A.C. 432 at [4].

[57] [2008] EWCA Civ. 377 at [34], emphasis supplied. See also the comment by N. Piska [2008] Conv. 452 at 457.

[58] Cf. *Bindra v. Mawji* [2008] EWHC 1715 (Ch).   [59] [2011] UKSC 53 at [51].

equitable joint tenancy can be severed and both parties would then be entitled to 50 per cent of the equitable ownership.[60]

8.4.3 **Rebutting the presumption of joint ownership**

Prior to *Stack v. Dowden*, the fact that the legal title to a house was in joint names was rarely decisive as to the size of the beneficial shares each party had in the property. While there was certainly a presumption of beneficial co-ownership, the courts would look carefully at the respective contributions to the purchase of the property to determine the quantum of each party's beneficial interest in it.[61] This resulting trust approach to the problem, which was consistent with the reasoning in both *Pettitt v. Pettitt* and *Gissing v. Gissing*,[62] was abandoned in the domestic context.[63] Instead, while the question of the beneficial owner-ship is to be decided on the basis of what the parties intended,[64] the starting point is, em-phatically, to start from the basis that the house is to be jointly owned. This was stressed by Lord Walker, who considered there to be a heavy burden on a party who sought to argue that the ownership should be other than joint.[65] In similar vein, Lady Hale remarked that it 'cannot be the case that all of the hundreds of thousands, if not millions, of transfers into joint names using the old forms are vulnerable to challenge in the courts simply because it is likely that the owners contributed unequally to the purchase price'.[66]

It is evident that the reason why the majority held that a transfer into joint names leads to a strong presumption of an intention to share the beneficial ownership equally is to seek to avoid the torrent of litigation that can ensue to establish who owns what. This process can lead to the expenditure of far more money in legal costs than the value of the property warrants,[67] and result in a 'detailed examination of the parties' relationship and finances'.[68] Nevertheless, it is clear that the presumption of a beneficial joint tenancy is not irrebut-table, and attention can now be turned to the situations where such a presumption can be rebutted, as indeed was the case in *Stack v. Dowden* itself.

Stack v. Dowden was considered by Lady Hale to be 'a very unusual case'.[69] What ap-peared to make it so was that Ms Dowden had contributed far more than Mr Stack had done to the acquisition of the house, and it was not a case where they pooled their re-sources even notionally.[70] In Lady Hale's view, 'there cannot be many unmarried couples who have lived together for as long as this, who have had four children together, and whose affairs have been kept as rigidly separate as this couple's affairs were kept'.[71] The only item of property which was in their joint names was the house. This, quite reasonably, led to the conclusion that it was their intention that it was to be jointly owned, although as they were quite meticulous as to separate ownership of other assets, why the fact they did put the house into joint names led to the conclusion that they intended to have unequal shares in it is not entirely clear.[72] Nevertheless, the fact this was found to be their intention led to the difficult question of the quantification of their beneficial shares, an issue which will be returned to later in the chapter.

---

[60] For the rules relating to joint tenancies, tenancies in common, and severance, see Chapter 9.

[61] See *Walker v. Hall* [1984] 1 F.L.R. 126; *Springette v. Defoe* [1992] 2 F.L.R. 511; *Huntingford v. Hobbs* [1993] 1 F.L.R. 376, all of which were disapproved in *Stack v. Dowden, supra*, at [65] *per* Lady Hale.

[62] [1971] A.C. 886.

[63] It was this abandonment of the application of orthodox principles which led Lord Neuberger to dissent as to the reasoning, if not the result. For comment on the somewhat cavalier approach to precedent, see W. Swadling (2007) 123 L.Q.R. 511 at 517.

[64] How that intention is discerned is a contentious issue. See 8.5.3.1.

[65] [2007] 2 A.C. 42 at [33].   [66] Ibid. at [68].   [67] Ibid.   [68] Ibid. at [33] *per* Lord Walker.

[69] Ibid. at [92]. Lord Walker regarded it as an 'exceptional case': ibid. at [33].

[70] Ibid. at [87] and [90].   [71] Ibid. at [92].

[72] See also Lord Neuberger in the (2008) Chancery Bar Association Lecture, para. 16.

8.4.3.1 Relevant criteria for unequal ownership

It is arguable that the facts relied upon to rebut the inference of joint beneficial ownership are not that unusual. Lady Hale gave further criteria which may help to divine the
intentions of the parties with regard to the beneficial ownership of the home. Pointing
out that, in law, context is everything, and that every case will turn on its own facts, she
indicated what factors other than the financial may cast light upon their intentions. This
list, which she also pointed out was not intended to be exhaustive,[73] included any advice
or discussions at the time of the transfer; the reasons why the home was put into joint
names; the reason why (if that was the case) the survivor was authorized to give a receipt
for capital monies; the purpose for which the house was acquired; and whether they
had children for whom they had responsibility to provide a home. She also considered
that the individual characteristics of the parties may also be relevant in deciding where
their true intentions lay, and it may well be the case that, in the context of cohabitation,
mercenary considerations may be more to the fore than they would be in a marriage,
but it should not be assumed that they always take pride of place over natural love and
affection.

Lady Hale then turned to relevant financial matters. She drew attention to the issue of
how the purchase was financed, whether separately or together or a bit of both; how they
discharged the outgoings on the property and their other household expenses. She then
said that when a couple are joint owners of the house and jointly liable for the mortgage,
the inferences to be drawn are very different from the inferences to be drawn when only
one is the owner of the house. In such cases, she thought that the arithmetical calculation
of how much was paid by each is likely to be less important, and it will be easier to draw the
inference that each should contribute as much to the household as they reasonably could
and that they would share the eventual benefit or burden equally. Finally, she pointed out
that, whatever the intentions of the parties may have been at the outset, these may have
changed, an example being where one of the parties has paid for (or constructed himself)
a substantial improvement to the property.[74] A second situation where such a change of
intention may be found is when there is a significant variation in the manner of purchasing behaviour, a feature of the Supreme Court decision in *Jones v. Kernott*,[75] a decision to
be considered shortly.

Despite having listed these various criteria as being examples of matters which may
throw light on the parties' intentions, and presumably, therefore, being matters which
may rebut the presumption that where there is joint ownership of the legal estate there
will also be equal beneficial ownership, Lady Hale somewhat surprisingly concluded
that cases where there would not be joint beneficial ownership would be very unusual.[76] Hence, although one might have a great deal of sympathy with the hope that
there will be a diminishing number of future cases where it is necessary to embark on
a detailed examination of the parties' behaviour and expenditure, it is difficult to disagree with the view that 'it is hard to judge whether any given case is exceptional or not
until the evidence is heard'.[77] This consideration has led to the justified criticism that
'the judgments of the majority in *Stack* do not disclose any domestic arrangement so
exceptional as to suggest why a departure from the principle of equality was appropriate. The main result of the case may simply be to generate discussion of what exactly
its implications are'.[78]

---

[73] [2007] 2 A.C. 42 at [69].   [74] Ibid. at [69]–[70]. For improvements, see 8.6.1.4.

[75] [2011] UKSC 53,   [76] [2007] 2 A.C. 42 at [69].

[77] R. Probert [2007] Fam. Law 924 at 927.

[78] Ibid. at 929. See also the extra-judicial observations of Lord Neuberger in (2008) Chancery Bar
Association lecture at para. 17.

8.4.3.2 Unequal contributions

Prior to *Stack v. Dowden*, even when a house was transferred into joint names, the fact that the two parties made unequal financial contributions to its acquisition would normally give rise, through resulting trust principles, to a beneficial share proportionate to the size of the contribution. This was rejected in *Stack* and, instead it was held that there was a strong presumption of joint beneficial ownership. This was reiterated in *Jones v. Kernott*, where it was said that it was 'not possible at one and the same time to have a presumption or starting point of joint beneficial interests and a presumption (let alone a rule) that the parties' beneficial interests are in proportion to their respective financial contributions'.[79] While that must be the case, as the presumption of joint ownership can be rebutted, the issue of unequal contributions may still be relevant.

The matter was revisited in *Fowler v. Barron*.[80] A twenty-three-year relationship ended in 2005. When it started, she was seventeen and he was forty-seven. A house was bought in 1988, and it was deliberately put into joint names. He paid the initial deposit and, although the mortgage was in their joint names, it was paid for entirely out of his pension, he having retired early from the fire service. The balance of the purchase price was provided from the proceeds of sale of his flat. He also paid the council tax and utility bills. They had a daughter in 1994, having previously had a son. She continued to work, while he stayed at home to look after the children. Her wages were spent on herself and the children, miscellaneous items of food, school trips, seasonal gifts, personal clothing, and holidays. At first instance, it was held that she had no interest in the property but, on appeal, it was held that she was entitled to a half share of the beneficial interest.

At first blush, it does not seem easy to distinguish this case from *Stack v. Dowden*. In both cases there had been long-term cohabitation, the existence of children, and a failure to pool their resources. Yet *Stack* was seen as being an exceptional case, and this was not. The key to the distinction would seem to lie in the huge disparity between the size of the contribution in the present case as compared with the position in *Stack*, and the large difference in their ages. In the present case, there was a thirty-year age difference between them, and it was a conscious decision to put the house into their joint names. The reason for this, as found by the judge, was that he wanted to ensure that she would benefit in the event of his prior death. This, coupled with evidence that they had made mutual wills, was indicative of an intention that she should have some share in the property, although what that share should be was not discussed. From this, the inference was drawn 'that the parties simply did not care about the respective size of each other's share'.[81] Thus, it is a short step to infer an intention that the share should not be commensurate with the size of her contribution: were it to be otherwise, as her contribution could best be described as minimal, she would acquire virtually no share in the property, which was not what was intended. On the facts, therefore, it is not unreasonable to apply the presumption and hold that they shared the beneficial interest equally. The main problem with the decision is that, if she had made no contribution to the acquisition of the house, a not unreasonable finding on the facts, it is difficult to see why any sort of trust should have arisen because, it will be recalled, the basic rule is that a trust of land must be evidenced in writing.[82] If he had said to her that he held the house on trust for her and himself in equal shares, alone this would not create an enforceable trust, and an unarticulated intention to that effect should not do so either, unless there was material on which one could base the imposition

---

[79] [2011] UKSC 53 at [23] *per* Lord Walker and Lady Hale.

[80] [2008] EWCA Civ. 377. See N. Piska [2008] Conv. 451.

[81] *Fowler v. Barron, supra*, at [41] *per* Arden L.J. See also *Holman v. Homes* [2007] EWCA Civ. 877 at [16] *per* Lloyd L.J.

[82] LPA 1925, s. 53(1)(b).

of either a resulting or a constructive trust.[83] On the facts, it is not obvious as to why either trust should have arisen.

8.4.3.3 Inference as to intention

Leaving this aside, the issue of unequal contributions was dealt with by Arden L.J. She recognized that, in at least some instances, this fact may lead to the inference that the parties intended their beneficial interests in the house to reflect the respective size of those contributions. She said:

> In a case where the parties have made unequal contributions to the cost of acquiring their home, it is obvious that in some cases there may be a thin dividing line between the case where the parties' shared intention is properly to be inferred to be ownership of the home in equal shares and the case where the parties' shared intention is properly inferred to be that the party who contributed less should have a smaller interest than the other. The resolution of such cases must however all depend on the facts.[84]

This, of course, does not help to identify where the line is to be drawn. Clearly, however, it is envisaged that in some cases where the main feature of the case is the inequality of contribution, that fact alone can lead to an unequal sharing of the beneficial interest. The suggestions which follow must necessarily be speculative.

8.4.3.4 Disparity in size of contribution

In *Fowler v. Barron* virtually the entire contribution to the purchase price was made by Mr Barron, and yet the house was put into joint names. This must be indicative of an intention to share the beneficial ownership; otherwise there is no reason for joint ownership at law. If the intention is not to share the beneficial ownership equally, but for the shares to reflect the amount of the contribution, then one of the parties will acquire only a very small share in the property, which is at odds with putting the house into joint names in the first place. So, perhaps counter-intuitively, the fact that when the house is put into joint names, and there is a very wide disparity in the size of the respective contributions to the acquisition, may mean that it is more likely to be held to be the case that the presumption of joint ownership of the beneficial interest will apply. Conversely, where there is a significant difference in the size of the contribution, but, as in *Stack*, the contribution of both is substantial, then the presumption of joint beneficial ownership may more easily be rebutted.

8.4.3.5 Pooling of resources and nature of contribution

Although it has been argued that, in trying to pin down the exceptional nature of *Stack v. Dowden*, one is driven to conclude that what influenced each member of the House was the fact of unequal contributions to the acquisition of the property,[85] there must be more to it than that. If the position were otherwise, the decision becomes effectively broken-backed, in that virtually every case would become unusual. Another significant factor in *Stack* was that the couple kept their finances entirely separate. Although this may well not be that unusual, it could be taken to amount to an intention that each should get what they paid for.[86] If, on the other hand, the parties effectively pool their resources then, even if one of the parties brings in more money than the other, the very fact of sharing resources

---

[83] Ibid., s. 33(2).　　　[84] [2000] EWCA Civ 227 at [45].

[85] R. Probert (2007) 15 Fem. Leg. Stud. 341 at 348. See also Lord Neuberger (2008) Chancery Bar Association Annual Lecture, at paras 15–17.

[86] Although see 8.6.2.2, as to the importance of contributions to household expenditure.

would seem to indicate that the presumption of shared ownership of the house would be applicable.[87]

A further feature of *Stack* which may be relevant is that, in the purchase of the house, large lump sum payments were made. These were over and above the initial capital contribution to the purchase, and were the principal means by which the mortgage was repaid. This is an unusual method of repayment, and, in such circumstances may add weight to the inference that the parties intended their interests in the house to be commensurate with the size of their financial contributions, rather than sharing the beneficial interest equally.

All that said, *Stack v. Dowden* must be seen as representing a missed opportunity to bring clarity to an important area of law. The upshot of it is that it establishes different presumptions depending upon the relationship of the parties, and a distinct lack of clarity as to when the presumption of equality will be rebutted. The Supreme Court in *Jones v. Kernott* has done little to assuage those concerns.

8.4.4 **When does the presumption of joint beneficial ownership apply?**

Jones v. Kernott makes clear that the default presumption of joint beneficial ownership applies where a property is purchased 'in joint names for joint occupation by a married or unmarried couple, where both are responsible for any mortgage',[88] a narrower construction than the 'domestic consumer context' set out by Lady Hale in *Stack v. Dowden*.[89] That the difference is an important one, rather than a mere tweak of terminology, can be demonstrated by *Adekunle v. Ritchie*.[90] The right to buy a council house was exercised and it was transferred into the joint names of a mother, who was the council tenant, and her son. She contributed significantly more to the acquisition of the property than he did. Judge Behrens considered that, although the presumption of equal ownership articulated in *Stack v. Dowden* was applied to a cohabiting couple who were in a romantic relationship, it also applied to a 'domestic relationship' such as this.

Adekunle v. Ritchie should now be regarded as incorrect following the decision in *Jones v. Kernott*. The joint legal owners must be a 'couple' for the presumption of joint beneficial ownership to apply, and that must be right. The dynamic of various family relationships cannot be artificially homogenized for the convenience of the law, and the justifications laid out by the Court in *Kernott* for the applicability of the presumption—the discrimination between men and women and married and unmarried couples[91]—have no obvious relevance to the relationship between a parent and their child.

In all cases which fall outside the scope of the law laid out in *Stack* and *Kernott*, the presumption of a resulting trust as advocated by Lord Upjohn in *Pettitt v. Pettitt* should continue to operate. If correct, this means that the parties will receive an interest equivalent to their unequal contributions to the purchase price. The presumption of joint beneficial ownership will not hold sway. Most obviously, this will be true where a property is not bought for joint occupation, but instead serves as a business investment. In *Laskar v. Laskar*,[92] a mother was a council tenant who exercised her right to buy, the purchase price being reduced as she, as a sitting tenant, was entitled to a discount.[93] The purchase price was made up in part by money borrowed by way of mortgage for which the mother and her daughter were jointly liable, and the balance provided by the payment of cash sums by both of them. The house was transferred to them jointly, with no declaration of trust. As was always intended, soon after the transaction had been completed, the mother

---

[87] See *Stack v. Dowden* [2007] 2 A.C. 432 at [69] *per* Lady Hale. See also *Abbott v. Abbott* [2007] UKPC 55.
[88] [2011] UKSC 53 at [25].   [89] [2007] 2 A.C. 432, at [58].   [90] [2007] B.P.I.R. 1177.
[91] [2011] UKSC 53 at [24].   [92] [2008] EWCA Civ. 347.   [93] See 8.6.1.1.

moved out to live with another daughter, and the property was rented out. In short, it had been bought principally as an investment. When the pair fell out, there was a dispute as to the beneficial ownership. It was held that they had shares of two-thirds and one-third. According to Neuberger L.J., the presumption of a beneficial joint tenancy did not apply to a case such as this. The reason was that:

> although the parties were mother and daughter and not in that sense in an arm's length rela-
> tionship, they had independent lives, and . . . the purchase of the property was not really for
> the purpose of providing a home for them. . . . The property was purchased primarily as an
> investment.[94]

Laskar v. Laskar was handed down prior to the decision in *Jones v. Kernott*, and, like *Adekunle v. Ritchie*, it is probably true to say that the case would not now fall within the scope of the presumption simply because the joint owners' relationship was a mother and daughter. On that view, the purpose of their joint purchase is irrelevant, as it is the rela-tionship between the parties that drives the application of the presumption of joint ben-eficial ownership. Where, however, does this leave a couple who purchase a house as a commercial investment, rather than as a home? In *Erlam v. Rahman*,[95] a wife applied for a declaration that she had a beneficial interest in a property co-owned with her husband, which had been bought as a buy-to-let investment. The High Court held that 'the *Stack v Dowden* approach to the purchase of a domestic property as a home by married or co-habiting couples will not apply if the joint intention at the date purchase of [the house] was to acquire it for letting. There is no reason to apply the special approach to the acquisition of homes to an acquisition of property as a business proposition.'[96] Resulting trust prin-ciples therefore applied, and the wife failed to demonstrate on the balance of probabilities that she had made any contribution to the purchase of the house, with the result that the husband took 100 per cent of the beneficial interest.

The judge cited *Laskar v. Laskar* as authority, and noted that it 'appears to be a some-what neglected decision'.[97] This is arguably correct; *Laskar* was not mentioned in *Jones v. Kernott*, nor has it been cited in subsequent cases bearing on similar issues.[98] For the mo-ment, at least, it seems clear that the presumption of joint beneficial ownership will only apply where the joint legal owners are in an intimate relationship, *and* the purchase is for their joint occupation as a home. That view is supported by the recent decision in *Wodzicki v. Wodzicki*,[99] where the Court of Appeal found that it was 'not appropriate'[100] to apply the reasoning in *Jones v. Kernott* to a daughter who argued for sole beneficial ownership of a house jointly owned by her deceased father and his second wife. Instead, it was held that the daughter and second wife jointly owned the house in proportion to the contributions they had made to the purchase, outgoings, and maintenance under a resulting trust.[101]

8.4.4.1 The Privy Council decision in *Marr v. Collie*

There is a significant caveat to the analysis above on when the presumption of joint ben-eficial ownership should apply, and that caveat takes the form of the recent decision by the Privy Council in *Marr v. Collie*.[102] Terry Marr and Bryant Collie were in an intimate rela-tionship for about fifteen years. Several properties were purchased during that time, some for domestic purposes and others for commercial reasons, and all but one was conveyed

---

[94] [2008] EWCA Civ. at [15]. See also *Parrott v. Parkin* [2007] EWHC 210 (Admlty) (purchase of a yacht).
[95] [2016] EWHC 111 (Ch).   [96] Ibid. at [41] *per* Chief Master Marsh.   [97] Ibid. at [42].
[98] Most notably *Re Ali* [2012] EWHC 2302 (Admin); *Capehorn v. Harris* [2015] EWCA Civ. 955.
[99] [2017] EWCA Civ. 95.   [100] Ibid. at [25] *per* David Richards L.J.
[101] See also *Culliford v. Thorpe* [2018] EWHC 426 (Ch).
[102] [2017] UKPC 17. See M. George and B. Sloan [2017] Conv. 302.

into joint names. When the relationship broke down, Mr Marr sought a declaration that he was the sole beneficial owner of all of the properties because he had provided all of the purchase money. The case came from the Bahamas, which is why the appeal was heard by the Privy Council.

Lord Kerr gave the judgment on behalf of the Board, and he declared that 'it is the Board's view that to consign the reasoning in *Stack* to the purely domestic setting would be wrong'.[103] As for what Lady Hale had said in *Stack*, Lord Kerr went on to say that 'there is no reason to doubt its possible applicability to property purchased by a couple in an enterprise reflecting their joint commercial, as well as their personal, commitment' and 'it is clear that she [Lady Hale] did not intend that the principle should be confined exclusively to the domestic setting'.[104] The Board recognized the possible conflict between the *Stack/Kernott* joint presumption and the presumption of a resulting trust, noting that a 'simplistic' solution might be to say that if property is bought in a domestic situation the joint beneficial presumption applies, but if bought in a wholly non-domestic situation it does not and instead a resulting trust does.[105] This solution was rejected by Lord Kerr, who emphasized that the 'answer is not to be provided by the triumph of one presumption over another',[106] and instead the search must be for whether there was a common intention between the parties that purchasing in joint legal ownership was a reflection of their joint beneficial ownership. If there was no such intention, or they had not directed their thoughts to the possible consequences of purchasing in joint names, then 'the resulting trust solution may provide the answer'.[107]

One problem with the decision in *Marr v. Collie* is that it goes against the line of authority from *Stack* to *Kernott* to *Laskar*, where there was a clear consensus that the commercial/domestic dichotomy held sway, and yet *Marr* does not purport to overrule any previous judgment. There is also a flaw in the idea that the parties' common intention should be analysed *prior* to the application of any presumption, because it is inherent in the operation of a purchase money resulting trust that it is unnecessary to have regard to the actual intentions of the parties in order for the contributor to acquire an interest. As George and Sloan argue:

> While it is true that some basic reference to the parties' intentions in relation to the property is necessary in order to decide whether the case is domestic or commercial, their purpose in buying it can be distinguished from their intended ownership, and the factual inquiry for the former is likely to be more straightforward, broader brush and less realistically the subject of a dispute. For the latter, the essential problem is that while both the resulting trust and the *Stack* presumption could be *rebutted* by evidence of some contrary common intention about their ownership, their very purpose is to provide a starting point where such evidence might be insufficiently clear. If both presumptions depend on an analysis of the parties' common intention *before they arise in the first place*, even after a case has been categorised, that function is lost. That leads to a logical flaw in the interaction between the two types of trust, as the presumption of a resulting trust can be displaced by the existence of an agreement which gives rise to a constructive trust. How can that displacement happen if the presumption of a resulting trust is not applied by default to any purchase in joint names where they have contributed unequally to the purchase price, prior to adducing evidence regarding the parties' intentions?[108]

It should also be remembered that the stated rationale for the strong and simple presumption in domestic cases, espoused by Lady Hale in *Stack*, that equity should follow the law

---

[103] Ibid. at [39].   [104] Ibid. at [40].   [105] Ibid. at [53].   [106] Ibid. at [54].
[107] Ibid. at [59].   [108] M. George and B. Sloan [2017] Conv. 302 at 306.

was because 'strong feelings are aroused when couples split up', which leads 'people to spend far more on the legal battle than is warranted by the sums actually at stake'.[109] The view in *Marr v. Collie* that one should ascertain whether the parties have a 'mutual wish' prior to any presumption undermines that rationale, because it can only be answered by a court. The better view is that the commercial/domestic dichotomy reduces the threat of litigation, and thus should be preferred. Commercial partners almost invariably do not expect survivorship to apply to their relationship, and that means the presumption of joint beneficial ownership is not appropriate. Cohabiting couples, by contrast, 'have a much more complex attachment to their property and to each other, and the presumption of joint ownership together with the non-exhaustive factors listed in Stack to rebut that presumption provides a nuanced and discretionary (if sometimes difficult) approach'.[110]

What is less than clear is what the effect of *Marr v. Collie* will be on English law going forward. As a decision of the Privy Council, it is of great weight and persuasive value, but it is not binding upon an English court.[111] It arguably conflicts with the near-universal view of *Stack* and *Kernott* and *Laskar*, and it is also difficult to align with the decisions in *Wodzicki v. Wodzicki* and *Erlam v. Rahman* noted above. Subsequent judgments of the High Court in *Gaspar v. Zaleski*,[112] *Culliford v. Thorpe* [113] and *Wall v. Munday*,[114] and of the Family Court in *HRH Tessy Princess of Luxembourg v. HRH Louis Xavier Marie Guillame*,[115] suggest that the commercial/domestic dichotomy remains the preferred approach for the English judiciary. *Marr v. Collie* was not cited in any of those cases, and even in the rare instances it has been mentioned,[116] it does not seem to have affected the reasoning to any great degree. It therefore remains to be seen what impact it will have on the presumption of joint beneficial ownership. It is suggested that, for now at least, it should be treated with considerable caution.

8.5 Sole ownership of the legal title

Of the cases concerning the ownership of the family home, *Stack v. Dowden* and *Jones v. Kernott* are the only ones to reach either the House of Lords or the Supreme Court where the legal title was in the joint names of the parties. A much more common area of dispute is where the legal title is in the name of one person, usually the man's, and on the breakdown of the relationship, his partner claims to have an interest in the house.[117] This scenario is of considerable practical importance; a survey in 2001 revealed that only 30 per cent of cohabitants live in accommodation that is in joint names.[118] Unlike the position when the house is in joint names and there is then a presumption of joint beneficial ownership, in this situation the person whose name is not on the title has the burden of establishing that they have any interest in the property at all.[119] A person seeking to establish an interest in the home must rely on the principles of trusts and estoppel. The difficulty in sole ownership cases is that, where another person makes a direct financial contribution to the purchase, it is far from clear how the law of trusts should now approach the question of

---

[109] *Stack v. Dowden* [2007] UKHL 17 at [68].   [110] M. George and B. Sloan [2017] Conv. 302 at 307.
[111] As per *Willers v. Joyce (No.2)* [2016] UKSC 44.
[112] [2017] EWHC 1770 (Ch), though the lack of any mention of *Marr v. Collie* here may well be because it was handed down after the hearing dates.
[113] [2018] EWHC 426 (Ch).   [114] [2018] EWHC 879 (Ch).   [115] [2018] EWFC 77.
[116] *Bhusate v. Patel & Ors* [2018] EWHC 2362 (Ch); *NN v. AS* [2018] EWHC 2973 (Fam).
[117] On sole ownership cases, see R. Sloan (2015) 35 L.S. 226.
[118] J. Huskey (2001) Population Trends 103, cited by R. Probert (2007) 15 Fem. Leg. Stud. 341 at 350. The Land Registry does not record statistics on the percentage of jointly owned registered titles.
[119] *Jones v. Kernott* [2011] UKSC 53 at [17] *per* Lord Walker and Lady Hale.

whether the presumption of sole beneficial ownership is rebutted. Either the constructive trust is the only means by which that other person can acquire a beneficial interest in the house, something which entails searching for the common intention of the parties, or a role remains for the classic presumption of a resulting trust, which will confer an interest on the beneficiary which mirrors their financial contributions. It is unfortunate that this choice, between the imposition of a constructive trust or a resulting trust, has not been resolved by the courts since the judgments on joint ownership in *Stack* and *Kernott*. In the light of *obiter* comments made by the majority in both *Stack* and *Kernott* expressing disapproval of the presumption of a resulting trust,[120] the current tendency is to ignore or forget it in sole ownership cases, and instead focus entirely on the common intention constructive trust. This is unwise because, as will be seen, the two doctrines are much closer together than might at first appear, and courts have often confused one with the other.

8.5.1 Resulting trusts v. constructive trusts

In *Pettitt v. Pettitt*,[121] the speech of Lord Upjohn sought to employ traditional resulting trust principles to this area of law, and placed the focus very much on ascertaining what the parties intended when the property was acquired. This approach was also taken by Lords Morris and Hodson, who both stressed the need to find an agreement between the parties as to what the beneficial interests in the land were intended to be.[122] Lords Reid and Diplock, although concurring in the result, effectively dissented from the reasoning. Whereas the majority insisted that the task of the court was to infer from the conduct of the parties what they had agreed upon, the minority took what, at first sight, might appear to have been a more discretionary approach. According to Lord Diplock, this meant that, if the courts were able to infer that the parties had come to an agreement with regard to the beneficial ownership of the property, then effect should be given to that agreement; if not, however, then an intention should be imputed to them on the basis of what reasonable people would have intended.[123]

The emphasis placed upon the need to infer the intentions of the parties with regard to the beneficial ownership of the home, at the time when it was acquired, has been the source of a considerable amount of difficulty in relation to this branch of the law. The first difficulty relates to the issue of intention itself, for it is here that two quite different things are being confused. In the first type of case, the courts are prepared to draw inferences as to the intentions of the parties from their behaviour with regard to the acquisition of the property. The evidence does not support the conclusion that the parties have actually considered, consciously, the question of the beneficial ownership of the house. This, traditionally, was the domain of the resulting trust. The second type of case involves situations where the parties have engaged in what has been termed 'title talk'.[124] This is where the evidence shows that the parties have come to an actual agreement as to the beneficial ownership of the home, but where that agreement does not comply with the formalities required for the creation of an express trust.[125] In these quite different cases, the issue is whether the circumstances are such as to justify the imposition of a constructive trust to implement the actual agreement.

---

[120] See, for example, the comment by Lord Walker at para. [31] of *Stack*: 'In a case about beneficial ownership of a matrimonial or quasi-matrimonial home (whether registered in the names of one or two legal owners) the resulting trust should not in my opinion operate as a legal presumption, although it may (in an updated form which takes account of all significant contributions, direct or indirect, in cash or in kind) happen to be reflected in the parties' common intention.'

[121] [1970] A.C. 77.   [122] Ibid. at 804–5 and 810, respectively.

[123] Ibid. at 822–3. See also at 796 *per* Lord Reid.

[124] J.W. Harris in Jackson and Wilde, *Contemporary Property Law* (Aldershot, Ashgate, 1999), 97.

[125] LPA 1925, s. 53(1)(b). See also *Gissing v. Gissing* [1971] A.C. 886 at 905 *per* Lord Diplock.

This point is very clearly made in *Drake v. Whipp*,[126] where Peter Gibson L.J. said that:

> A potent source of confusion, to my mind, has been suggestions that it matters not whether the terminology used is that of the constructive trust, to which the intention, actual or imputed, of the parties is crucial, or that of the resulting trust which operates on a presumed intention of the contributing party in the absence of rebutting evidence of actual intention.

The modern tendency is to conflate the resulting and constructive trust, and to treat the latter concept as the more appropriate analysis in most matrimonial cases;[127] an analysis which has led to a considerable loss of clarity.

A second difficulty is the focus on the actual time of the acquisition of the property. It is a commonplace that most houses are bought with the aid of a mortgage from either a bank or a building society. The repayment of the mortgage occurs over a prolonged period. To consider the matter solely at the time of the actual purchase of the house is unrealistic, and would ignore entirely the not uncommon situation when a person moves into a house of which another person is already the legal owner. This point was made explicitly in *Gissing v. Gissing*,[128] where Lord Diplock said:

> But it would in my view be unreasonably legalistic to treat the relevant transaction involved in the acquisition of the matrimonial home as restricted to the actual conveyance of the fee simple into the name of the other spouse. . . . The conduct of the spouses in relation to the payment of the mortgage instalments may be no less relevant to their common intention as the beneficial interests in a matrimonial home acquired in this way than their conduct in relation to the payment of a cash deposit.

A failure always to bear these comments in mind has led to problems which will be considered below, and it is now clear that, in assessing the question of beneficial ownership, conduct occurring after the acquisition of the legal title can be highly relevant.[129]

8.5.2 **Intention at acquisition**

Subject to the above comments made by Lord Diplock, the emphasis placed by the House of Lords in *Pettitt* on the need to infer the actual intentions of the parties at the time when the house was acquired was repeated shortly afterwards in *Gissing v. Gissing*. In this case, a wife made an unsuccessful claim to an interest in the matrimonial home, the basis of that claim having been the expenditure of some £220 on furnishings and laying a lawn, the purchase of some clothes for herself and her son, and some extras around the house. Her husband paid all the mortgage instalments and had supplied the initial down payment on the house.

In unanimously rejecting her claim, all members of the House agreed that, for her to succeed, she had to establish an interest behind either a resulting or a constructive trust. To establish such a trust, it was again emphasized that it must be possible for the court to be able to infer an agreement that she should have a beneficial share in it. An intention could not be imputed to the parties which they had never had but, as reasonable people, they ought to have had.[130] Such an intention could only be inferred from the fact that a

---

[126] [1996] 1 F.L.R. 826 at 827.   [127] *Abbott v. Abbott* [2007] UKPC 55 at [3] *per* Lady Hale.
[128] [1971] A.C. 886 at 906. See also at 903 *per* Lord Pearson. See also *Stack v. Dowden* [2007] 2 A.C. 432 at [57] *per* Lady Hale.
[129] *Stack v. Dowden* [2007] 2 A.C. 432; *Jones v. Kernott* [2011] UKSC 53.
[130] *Gissing v. Gissing* [1971] A.C. 886 at 904 *per* Lord Diplock, who expressly recognized that his previously stated view to the contrary in *Pettitt* did not represent the law. Cf. the speech of Lord Reid, who adhered to the minority view that he had expressed in that case.

financial contribution had been made to the acquisition of the property, which was not so in the instant case.

The debate between whether one inferred what the parties intended with regard to the beneficial ownership of the property or whether, instead, one could impute intentions to parties which, as reasonable people, they ought to have formed was, in truth, something of an arid one, although it is one which has recently been rekindled.[131] Its principal relevance, however, was to the operation of resulting trusts; what the decision in *Gissing* did do was, perhaps surprisingly, to promote the potential importance of constructive trusts. This was due to an influential dictum of Lord Diplock.

When analysing the principles to be applied in cases of this type, Lord Diplock, in an oft-quoted dictum, said:

> A resulting, implied or constructive trust—and it is unnecessary for present purposes to distinguish between these three classes of trust—is created by a transaction between the trustee and the *cestui que trust*[132] in connection with the acquisition by the trustee of a legal estate in land, whenever the trustee has so conducted himself that it would be inequitable . . . to deny the *cestui que trust* a beneficial interest in the land acquired. And he will be held so to have conducted himself if by his words or conduct he has induced the *cestui que trust* to act to his own detriment in the reasonable belief that by so acting he was acquiring a beneficial interest in the property.[133]

Although influential, there are problems with this passage. The main difficulty is that it runs together conceptually different types of trust, a running together which has become the source of considerable confusion thereafter. A second problem was that it focused exclusively on the law of trusts as being the only method by which disputes of this nature could be resolved. More recently, estoppel has been seen to have a role to play.

8.5.3 Intention and resulting trusts

Despite the running together of resulting and constructive trusts, the development of the law has, until quite recently, shown a clear distinction between the two types of trust and, in particular, demonstrates the somewhat arid nature of the debate concerning the role of intention with regard to resulting trusts.

The role of resulting trusts in this context derives from at least 1788, when in *Dyer v. Dyer*,[134] it was said that:

> The clear result of all the cases, without a single exception is, that the trust of a legal estate . . . whether taken in the names of the purchasers and others jointly, or in the names of others without that of the purchaser; whether in one name or several; whether jointly or successive, results to the man who advanced the purchase money. This is a general proposition supported by all the cases . . . It is the established doctrine of a Court of equity, that this resulting trust may be rebutted by circumstances in evidence.

8.5.3.1 Presumed intention

The point about this is that the law is prepared to assume that if A and B, together, put up the purchase price for a particular item, and the legal title to that item is put into the name of A alone, then B will have an equitable interest in that property proportionate to the size

---

[131] See 8.8.2.3—Consistency with resulting trusts.   [132] Another term for the equitable owner.
[133] [1971] A.C. 886 at 905.
[134] (1788) 2 Cox. 92 at 93 *per* Eyre L.C.B. See Chambers, *Resulting Trusts* (Oxford, Oxford University Press, 1997), 12–39.

of his financial contribution,[135] this conclusion being said to rest upon 'the solid tug of money'.[136] This is so, unless there is evidence that this is not what was actually intended.[137] So if, for example, B has advanced money to A by means of a loan, then B will not acquire a beneficial interest in the property which has been purchased; the presumption of a resulting trust is rebutted by evidence of what was actually intended and B's right will merely be to have the loan repaid.[138]

It is integral to cases of this type that it is unnecessary, in order for a resulting trust to arise, to have regard to the actual intention of the parties in order for the contributor to acquire an interest in the property under a resulting trust. Where a person makes a contribution to the purchase price, the law does not look to see if there was a meeting of minds between the two parties; it is assumed, unless there is actual evidence to the contrary, that the contributor will acquire an interest in the property proportionate to the size of the contribution.[139] The role of this presumption is illustrated by cases where property is put into the name of another to facilitate the implementation of an unlawful purpose, such as the aim of defeating creditors. The presumption of resulting trust may still be relied upon because the person with the unlawful intention need not rely upon his own illegality to show his intention to remain the beneficial owner of the property; he relies upon the presumption which the law will make in any case that this is what was intended.[140]

Although this principle of a contribution to the purchase price of an item giving rise to the presumption of a resulting trust in favour of the contributor is relatively simple to state, in the context of the purchase of a house it is frequently not easy to apply. The main reason for this is that, unlike many items of personal property which can be bought outright, this is not the usual way in which a house is purchased. The normal method of house buying is to make a down payment and to borrow the remainder of the purchase price by way of a mortgage. That mortgage is then repaid over an extended period of time. It can, in such situations, be more difficult than when the purchase is outright to determine whether or not a person claiming to have an interest in the home actually has made a contribution to its purchase. Nevertheless, the task of the court when seeking to apply resulting trust principles is to ascertain whether such a contribution has been made.

Although the courts have stressed that the task is to determine what the parties intended with regard to the beneficial interest of the house, in many cases the real answer is that the parties have not given the matter any thought at all and so the task of ascertaining that intention has, aptly, been described as being 'simply unreal'.[141] Instead, the task with

---

[135] A new expression coined for this type of resulting trust is a 'money-down resulting trust interest': J.W. Harris in Jackson and Wilde, *Contemporary Property Law*, 97. For an unusual instance where one party provided the entirety of the purchase price but the title was put in the sole name of his girlfriend, see *Re Share* [2002] 2 F.L.R. 88, where the Court of Appeal held that she held the house on trust for him.

[136] *Hofman v. Hofman* [1965] N.Z.L.R. 795 at 800 *per* Woodhouse J.

[137] For a bizarre finding of a contrary intention, where a judge found that an older woman had advanced money towards the purchase of a house in the name of a younger man as being in the nature of risk capital advanced to seduce that younger man, see *Pettkus v. Becker* (1981) 117 D.L.R. (3d) 257 at 265 *per* Richie J., who described it as 'gratuitously insulting'. Cf. at 272 *per* Dickson J. For a valuable discussion of this influential Canadian decision, see M. Welstead (1987) 2 Denning L.J. 151.

[138] See *Re Sharpe* [1980] 1 W.L.R. 219. Cf. *Risch v. McPhee* (1990) 61 P. & C.R. 42, where an arrangement which was originally a loan became, as circumstances changed, a contribution to the acquisition of the house.

[139] See *Gissing v. Gissing* [1971] A.C. 886 at 902 *per* Lord Pearson; *Grant v. Edwards* [1986] Ch. 638 at 647 *per* Nourse L.J. See H.K. Bevan and F.W. Taylor (1966) 30 Conv. (N.S.) 354, 438 at 442–3; F. Webb (1976) 92 L.Q.R. 489.

[140] *Tinsley v. Milligan* [1994] A.C. 330; *Lowson v. Coombes* [1999] Ch. 373; *Barrett v. Barrett* [2008] EWHC 1061 (Ch). See M.P. Thompson [1999] Conv. 242.

[141] M.M. Helsham (1979) 9 Sydney L.R. 571 at 575. See also the reference in *Rathwell v. Rathwell* (1978) 83 D.L.R. (3d) 289 at 297 to the 'meaningless ritual of searching for a phantom intent' *per* Dickson J., and the comment in *Kerr v. Baranow* (2011) 328 D.L.R. (4th) 577 at [26] *per* Cromwell J.

which the courts are faced is to decide whether or not a person has actually made a contribution to the purchase of the house. This point is reinforced by the fact that although there was an acute division of opinion in *Pettitt v. Pettitt* as to whether the judicial function is to infer what the parties actually intended or to impute intentions to them which, as reasonable people, they should have formed, this is a fairly barren distinction, given that the House of Lords was unanimous that no interest in the house had been acquired. An intention would neither be inferred by the majority nor imputed by the minority unless the claimant had contributed to the acquisition of the house. In this context, it is really a matter of semantics as to which terminology is to be preferred.

This semantic dispute was revived in *Stack v. Dowden* when,[142] seemingly of his own volition,[143] Lord Walker expressed the view that it would have been better had the House of Lords in *Gissing* openly departed from the earlier decision in *Pettitt*, and, in essence, allowed the courts to impute intentions to parties which they had never had.[144] This seems to misunderstand the operation of the resulting trust, where intentions are ascribed to parties on the basis of their purchasing behaviour in circumstances when it is clear that no actual thought has been given to the question of the beneficial ownership; it really makes no practical difference as to whether one talks of inferring the intentions of the parties, or one talks of imputing intentions to them. What will be important is a consideration of what elements of the parties' behaviour are relevant to the performance of this task.[145]

8.5.4 Constructive trusts

In many cases, when a court is faced with the task of determining the beneficial ownership of a home, the real focus for the decision is whether what the claimant relies upon will amount to what the law regards as a contribution to the acquisition of the property. In such cases a search for the actual intention of the parties will frequently be a futile exercise. Deciding what amounts to such a contribution is a difficult task and will be considered shortly. In some situations, however, there is evidence that the parties have actually agreed as to what the beneficial interests in the home should be, and it is this type of case which can give rise to the conceptually different constructive trust.

8.5.4.1 Actual agreement

Where personal property is concerned, no formalities are necessary to create a trust. It is sufficient if there is a manifestation of a sufficient intention to create a trust and this intention can, on occasion, be established on the basis of fairly casual statements.[146] Where land is concerned, however, to establish a trust it is necessary that the provisions of s. 53(1)(b), LPA 1925 are satisfied: the declaration of trust must be proved by some writing. Alone, a statement by one person to the other that he regards the house as being as much hers as it is his is not sufficient to create a trust.[147] If, however, in reliance on what has been said, she contributes to the purchase of the property, then it would be fraudulent for him to plead the lack of writing to deny that she has a beneficial interest in the property. To do so would

---

[142] [2007] 2 A.C. 432 at [21].

[143] No trace of such an argument is apparent from the reports of the arguments of counsel.

[144] Contrast Lord Neuberger (2008) Chancery Bar Association Annual Lecture at para. 19, where the notion of imputed intention is described as 'heretical'.

[145] See *Jones v. Kernott* [2011] UKSC 53 at [67] *per* Lord Kerr, commenting on the different conceptual approaches to this issue taken by Lord Walker and Lady Hale, on the one hand, and Lord Wilson on the other.

[146] See *Paul v. Constance* [1977] 1 W.L.R. 527; *Rowe v. Prance* [1999] 2 F.L.R. 787. For criticism of the latter decision, see S. Baughen [2000] Conv. 58.

[147] *Austin v. Keele* (1987) 72 A.L.R. 579 at 587 *per* Lord Oliver; *Lloyds Bank plc v. Rosset* [1991] A.C. 107 at 129 *per* Lord Bridge.

entail him being unjustly enriched at her expense. To prevent this, a constructive trust is imposed to enforce the informal statement.

This principle, which is based upon the nineteenth-century decision in *Rochefoucauld v. Boustead*,[148] was illustrated excellently in *Re Densham*.[149] It was found as a fact that it had been orally agreed between a husband and wife that the matrimonial home was to be owned equally. The title was, however, put into his name alone. It was further found that she had made a financial contribution to the purchase price amounting to one-ninth. Goff J. held that, had the dispute been between the husband and wife as to the ownership of the matrimonial home, she would have been entitled to one-half of the beneficial interest. A constructive trust would have been imposed to give effect to the actual agreement between them.[150]

In this case, however, the husband was bankrupt and so the issue was the size of the beneficial share to which the trustee in bankruptcy was entitled. It was held that, had there been no antecedent agreement regarding the beneficial interest in the home, she would have been entitled to a share of one-ninth under a resulting trust. On the basis of her financial contribution to the property, the court would have presumed that it was intended that she would acquire a proportionate equitable share in the property and a resulting trust would arise to achieve this result. In the instant case, because there was an actual agreement to share the beneficial interest in the house equally, and she had contributed to the purchase of the house, a constructive trust was imposed to give effect to the actual agreement. As against the trustee in bankruptcy, however, the difference between one-half and one-ninth was regarded as being a voluntary settlement and, as against him, was set aside on that basis.[151]

This decision provides an extremely clear distinction between resulting trusts and constructive trusts.[152] In the case of the former category of trust, the task is to ascertain if the claimant has contributed to the purchase price and, if so, to quantify that contribution and decide that a corresponding equitable share in the property has been obtained.[153] In the latter, the key issue is what the parties have agreed. When there is a specific agreement as to what interest[154] each party is to have in the property then, provided that there has been an appropriate response,[155] it is the actual agreement which is enforced by the imposition of a constructive trust.[156] The quantum of the share is governed by the express, inferred, or imputed agreement, and not by the size of the contribution.[157]

---

[148] [1897] 1 Ch. 196. See also *De Bruyne v. De Bruyne* [2010] EWCA Civ. 519 at [51] *per* Patten L.J.; M.A. Neave (1978) 11 Melbourne U.L.R. 343 at 348; M.P. Thompson (1985) 36 N.I.L.Q. 343 at 348. Cf. Mee, *Property Rights of Cohabitees*, 156–64. For an interesting and unusual example of this in the commercial context, see *Banner Homes Holdings Ltd v. Luff* [2000] Ch. 372; M.P. Thompson [2001] Conv. 249; N. Hopkins [2002] Conv. 35; *Cox v. Jones* [2004] 2 F.L.R. 1010 at 1035–7 *per* Mann J. See R. Probert [2005] Conv. 168.

[149] [1975] 1 W.L.R. 1519; J. Mee [2007] Conv. 14.

[150] The distinction between 'money consensus' and 'interest consensus' drawn in *Cowcher v. Cowcher* [1972] 1 W.L.R. 425 at 436 *per* Bagnall J., which had been refuted by A.A.S. Zuckerman (1978) 94 L.Q.R. 26 at 45, was rejected: [1975] 1 W.L.R. 1519 at 1525 *per* Goff J. Contrast Mee, *Property Rights of Cohabitees*, 52–8.

[151] Bankruptcy Act 1914, s. 42. See now, Insolvency Act 1986, s. 339.

[152] See also *Grant v. Edwards* [1986] Ch. 635 at 637 *per* Nourse L.J.; *Midland Bank plc v. Dobson* [1986] 1 F.L.R. 171 at 177 *per* Dillon L.J.; *Lloyds Bank plc v. Rosset* [1991] A.C. 107 at 133 *per* Lord Bridge.

[153] See *Arogundade v. Arogundade* [2005] EWHC 1766 (Ch).

[154] The agreement may relate to a life interest as opposed to a concurrent interest. See *Ungarian v. Lessnoff* [1990] Ch. 206; *Buggs v. Buggs* [2003] EWHC 1538 (Ch).

[155] See 8 8 3.

[156] See *Chan v. Leung* [2003] 1 F.L.R. 23 (51%–49%); *Hyett v. Stanley* [2004] 1 F.L.R. 394, especially at 403–4 *per* Sir Martin Nourse.

[157] See *Wright v. Johnson* [2002] 1 P. & C.R. 15 at para. 17 *per* Sir Martin Nourse.

8.6 **The value of contributions**

The essence of the approach taken by the House of Lords in both *Pettitt v. Pettitt* and *Gissing v. Gissing* was that one had to determine the beneficial shares in the property by reference to the inferred intentions of the parties at the time when the house was acquired. The reference to inferring what the parties intended is misleading, in that in many cases it is evident that the parties never gave any thought at all to the question of who owned the house. What was meant, however, was that a court would be prepared to make the necessary inference if the claimant could establish that she had made what was considered to be a contribution to the acquisition of the property. The determination of what amounted to a qualifying contribution was not, however, always an easy task.[158]

8.6.1 **Direct contributions**

The easiest type of case to resolve is where the claimant makes a direct cash contribution to the purchase of the house. In the unusual case where a house is being bought outright, and one pays 30 per cent of the price and the other the remaining 70 per cent, the property will be shared in those proportions.[159] A more usual situation is where the property is bought with the aid of a mortgage.[160] In *Re Roger's Question*,[161] a house was bought for £1,000, the wife supplying the initial payment of £100 and her husband being solely responsible for the payments on the mortgage. This was regarded in the same way as if the property had been bought outright, so that the beneficial ownership was shared in proportion to their contributions, that is in a proportion of 9:1 in favour of the husband.

8.6.1.1 **Council house discounts**

When a house is bought with the aid of a mortgage, the position is quite straightforward if the claimant makes a direct cash contribution to the initial payment.[162] Slightly more problematic is the situation where the property is a council house which is bought by the tenant under the right to buy provisions contained in Part V of the Housing Act 1985.[163] Under this scheme, depending upon the length of residence, the council tenant is entitled to a discount on the value of the property, up to a maximum of 60 per cent. The question is then whether this discount is to be treated as a contribution to the purchase price. The answer to this is that, in general terms, the courts, although aware that a discount is not the same as cash,[164] are prepared, in effect, to treat it in this way. The normal result is that, if the house is being bought by the tenant with financial assistance from another, usually, but not always,[165] the tenant's children, then the beneficial ownership of the house will be shared. The size of the percentage discount will then determine the size of the tenant's beneficial share in the house.[166] As indeed is the case with a direct contribution, it is only a presumption that a discount is to be regarded as entitling the claimant to an equivalent beneficial share in the property.[167] It may be that the actual intention is to make a gift.[168]

---

[158] See the comments in *Bernard v. Josephs* [1982] Ch. 391 at 402 *per* Griffiths L.J.

[159] *Arogundade v. Arogundade* [2005] EWHC 1766 (Ch).

[160] See P. Sparkes (1991) 11 O.J.L.S. 39.   [161] [1948] 1 All E.R. 328.

[162] This may be satisfied by a wedding gift by the parents of one of the parties. See *Midland Bank plc v. Cooke* [1995] 4 All E.R. 562.

[163] Replacing the Housing Act 1980, Part 1.

[164] See *Evans v. Hayward* [1995] 2 F.L.R. 511 at 516 *per* Staughton L.J.

[165] See *Oxley v. Hiscock* [2005] Fam. 211.

[166] *Marsh v. Von Sternberg* [1986] 1 F.L.R. 26; *Springette v. Defoe* [1992] 2 F.L.R. 511; *Day v. Day* (2005) Case No. HC 04C00445.

[167] *Evans v. Hayward, supra.*   [168] See *Ashe v. Mumford* (2000) 33 H.L.R. 67.

Perhaps, more commonly, when the property is bought by a combination of the tenant's discount, together with the balance of the purchase price being provided by that person's children, an agreement may be made that the tenant can occupy the house for the rest of his life, and, after his death, to go to the children who provided the balance of the purchase money. In such a case, a constructive trust will be imposed, with the result that there will exist consecutive ownership, rather than the concurrent interests which would have arisen under a resulting trust.[169] In the absence of a contrary intention, however, it now seems settled that the discount will be regarded as a direct financial contribution to the purchase of the house.[170]

8.6.1.2 Mortgage payments

There are, potentially at least, theoretical difficulties when a person makes a claim to a beneficial share in the property on the basis of having made contributions to the payment of mortgage instalments.[171] The main problem is that, if the interests under a resulting trust are to be taken to have crystallized at the time when the property is acquired, a later payment of mortgage instalments occurs after that time and, so, it may be argued, this precludes the acquisition of an interest under a resulting trust. Second, the argument can be put that the payment of instalments does not actually contribute to the purchase of the house, which has already been bought. Until recently, judicially at least,[172] it was assumed that such a person would acquire an interest. In *Curley v. Parkes*[173] a different view was taken.

Andrew Curley and Nicola Parkes cohabited, first in a house in Richmond, and, subsequently, in a house in Luton. Although the subject matter of the dispute was the ownership of the Luton property, central to its resolution was the ownership of the first house, the proceeds of sale of which had helped to finance the second purchase. With regard to the house in Richmond, Ms Parkes was the sole registered proprietor and the mortgage was in her name.[174] When they moved into that house, they set up a joint bank account, into which they paid roughly equal amounts. Out of that account came all of the household expenditure, including the mortgage payments. Nevertheless, the Court of Appeal held that he acquired no interest in that house.

In arriving at what seems a quite remarkable conclusion, Peter Gibson L.J., with whom Sir William Aldous agreed, reasoned as follows:

> The relevant principle is that the resulting trust of a property purchased in the name of another, in the absence of a contrary intention, arises once and for all at the date on which the property is acquired. Because of the liability assumed by the mortgagor in a case where monies are borrowed by the mortgagor to be used on the purchase, the mortgagor is treated as having provided the proportion of the purchase price attributable to the monies so borrowed. Subsequent payments of the mortgage instalments are not part of the purchase price already paid to the vendor, but are sums paid for discharging the mortgagor's obligations under the mortgage.[175]

---

[169] See *Buggs v. Buggs* [2003] EWHC 153 (Ch); M.P. Thompson [2003] Conv. 411.

[170] See *Laskar v. Laskar* [2008] EWCA Civ. 347 at [22]–[26] *per* Neuberger L.J.

[171] See the inconclusive discussion of this issue in *Stack v. Dowden* [2007] 2 A.C. 432 at [120] *per* Lord Neuberger.

[172] For a detailed analysis of the problems, see Mee, *Property Rights of Cohabitees*, Chapter 3. See also P. Sparkes (1991) 11 O.J.L.S. 39.

[173] [2004] EWCA Civ. 1515.

[174] There was evidence that, because of financial problems emanating from his student days, he would not have been considered to be a suitable borrower by a mortgagee; ibid, at para. 7 *per* Peter Gibson L.J.

[175] Ibid. at para. 14. In reaching this conclusion considerable reliance was placed on the treatment of this topic in Underhill and Hayton, *Law of Trusts and Trustees* (16th edn) (London, Butterworths LexisNexis, 2003), 351–2.

Because in the instant case there had been found not to have been any actual agreement reached with regard to the beneficial ownership of the house, this precluded the imposition of a constructive trust. This meant that, despite Mr Curley's contributions to the payment of the mortgage, he acquired no interest in the house.

Disregard of authority

This treatment of an important issue prompts a number of observations. First, and quite remarkably, there is no mention at all of any of the numerous dicta, admittedly *obiter*, but of the highest authority, which point directly to the opposite conclusion. To the comment of Lord Diplock in *Gissing v. Gissing*, that:

> The conduct of the spouses in relation to the payment of the mortgage instalments may be no less relevant to their common intention as to the beneficial interest in the matrimonial home acquired in this way than their conduct in relation to the payment of the cash deposit.[176]

may be added those to similar effect by Viscount Dilhorne and Lord Pearson in the same case.[177] In *Lloyds Bank plc v. Rosset*,[178] Lord Bridge was equally explicit. He said that, 'direct contributions to the purchase price by the partner, who is not the legal owner, whether initially *or by payment of mortgage instalments*, will readily justify the inference necessary for the creation of a constructive trust'. Again, in *Stack v. Dowden*,[179] there is the unequivocal statement by Lady Hale 'that the payment of mortgage instalments is the equivalent of the payment of purchase price'. In addition to these dicta, there is a line of authority, considered later in this chapter,[180] where one party makes indirect contributions to the purchase of the property, in the sense of facilitating the other to be able to pay the mortgage instalments, and being held, as a result, to have acquired an interest in the home. The decision in *Curley v. Parkes* is not consistent with this line of authority. Even more crucially, Neuberger L.J.'s carefully reasoned judgment in *Laskar v. Laskar* was predicated on the basis that the £43,000 mortgage taken out in joint names amounted to a £21,500 contribution to the purchase price for the respondent.[181] No reference is made to *Curley v. Parkes* in *Laskar v. Laskar*, but the two decisions cannot stand alongside one another.

In addition to being at odds with the overwhelming judicial consensus, the decision fails to convince on its own terms. Peter Gibson L.J. was prepared to hold that a person who takes on responsibility for paying the mortgage is treated as having made a financial contribution to its purchase and so acquires a corresponding proportionate share.[182] It is not clear, however, why being legally responsible for the mortgage payments should make such a big difference. If the person who pays all or part of the instalments is seen as only discharging the mortgagor's liability under the mortgage, the house having been

---

[176] [1971] A.C. 886 at 906.

[177] Ibid. at 900 and 903, respectively. The payment of isolated instalments would not give rise to a resulting trust: ibid. at 900 *per* Viscount Dilhorne. For discussion of the position with regard to endowment mortgages, see Thompson, *Co-ownership* (London, Sweet & Maxwell, 1988), 52.

[178] [1991] 1 A.C. 107 at 132–3. Emphasis supplied. Query whether this should refer to a resulting trust. See also *Oxley v. Hiscock* [2005] Fam. 211 at 220 *per* Chadwick L.J., where the payment of mortgage instalments was regarded as a contribution to the purchase of a house. The case was disapproved, without reference to this issue, in *Stack v. Dowden* [2007] 2 A.C. 432 at [61] *per* Lady Hale.

[179] *Stack v. Dowden* at [57]. The statement by David Richards J. in *Barrett v. Barrett* [2008] EWHC 1061 (Ch) at [7] that there is nothing in the speeches in *Stack v. Dowden* to support the notion that the payment of mortgage instalments should be treated as contributions to the purchase price is clearly wrong.

[180] See 8.6.2.   [181] [2008] EWCA Civ. 347 at [28].

[182] This is supported by *Re Roger's Question* [1948] 1 All E.R. 328. See also the comments in *Ulrich v. Ulrich* [1968] 1 W.L.R. 180 at 186 *per* Lord Denning M.R., and at 289 *per* Diplock L.J., and in *Pettitt v. Pettitt* [1970] A.C. 777 at 816 *per* Lord Upjohn.

purchased with the money which was borrowed from the mortgagee, the same analysis should apply to a person who has made himself legally responsible to pay the loan.

Practical consequences

A potentially more difficult problem is where a house is in the name of one party, and another person then moves into the house and contributes to the mortgage payments. If, as has frequently been stressed, one acquires an interest under a resulting trust by reference to the intentions of the parties when the house was acquired, then, even if one accepts that the payment of mortgage instalments is potentially effective to enable an interest in the house to be obtained, there is an obvious problem. This is that, when the house was acquired, the only intention was that there should be sole ownership. In such cases, it is quite likely that the parties will come to actual agreement as to the ownership of the house, so as to bring a constructive trust into play. Even if that is not the case, it should still be possible for a resulting trust to arise. An analogy can be drawn with a position where A is buying a car on a hire-purchase agreement and, sometime later, B starts to pay half of the instalments. B has clearly contributed to the acquisition of the car and, in principle, should acquire an interest in it under a resulting trust.

Although the repayment of a mortgage is different in nature from a hire-purchase agreement, it is thought that the analogy is not inappropriate and the same should happen in the context of the purchase of a house. The essential difference between the operation of a resulting trust here and that envisaged in *Gissing* is that, in this situation, the resulting trust would operate to vary the initial beneficial interests in the property, rather than to determine from the outset what those beneficial interests are. In other words, there is no compelling reason to hold that the beneficial interests in a house are definitively fixed at the date when it is transferred to one person. There is no reason, in principle, why these interests cannot subsequently be varied by the creation of either a resulting or constructive trust. As against this, in *James v. Thomas*,[183] Sir John Chadwick expressed the view that 'a court will be very slow to infer from conduct alone that parties intended to vary existing beneficial interests established at the time of acquisition'. This should not, it is suggested, preclude the establishment of a beneficial share in the property when a person has moved into a house in sole legal ownership and made a regular contribution to the mortgage repayments. This is illustrated by the Supreme Court decision in *Jones v. Kernott*.[184]

In this case, Ms Jones bought a mobile home in 1981, and Mr Kernott moved in with her in 1983, and their first child was born in 1984. In 1985, this property was sold and another one, 39 Badger Hall Avenue, was acquired, and put into joint names. The purchase price of £30,000 was made up of £6,000 from the sale of the mobile home, and the balance by an endowment mortgage which was taken out in joint names. They had a second child in 1986. In that year they took out a further joint loan of £2,000 to finance the building of an extension. After nearly eight-and-a-half years of cohabitation, he left the house in 1993. Thereafter she continued to live in Badger Hall Avenue and met all of the outgoings on the house, including the mortgage. This situation continued for the next fourteen and a half years during which time he paid nothing towards the mortgage on the house, and very little towards the maintenance of their children. During this time, he had purchased another house. To finance this, a joint life insurance policy was cashed in, and the proceeds divided between them. He used his share to put down a deposit and took out a mortgage in respect of the balance. He could not have afforded to have done this if he was paying anything towards the mortgage on Badger Hall Avenue. Restoring the first instance decision,[185] and

---

[183] [2007] EWCA Civ. 1212 at [24]. See also *Morris v. Morris* [2008] EWCA Civ. 257 at [36] *per* May L.J.
[184] [2011] UKSC 53.   [185] [2009] EWHC 1713 (Ch).

reversing that of the Court of Appeal,[186] the Supreme Court held that the beneficial shares in Badger Hall Avenue were 90 per cent to her, and 10 per cent to him.

In reaching this conclusion, it was first accepted that, had the property been sold when the couple separated, the shares in it would have been equal. This followed from the property being in joint names, and there being insufficient evidence that the parties intended, at that stage, an outcome different from that which the law presumes: that joint ownership at law leads to the same position in equity. The Court of Appeal held that, because there had been no actual agreement to vary the beneficial ownership of the house, the original position of joint ownership remained. The Supreme Court, however, held that under a common intention constructive trust, the shares had been altered.

The Court was prepared to accept an earlier finding that the parties had actually agreed, when the insurance policy was cashed in, thereby enabling him to purchase a property on his own, to vary their shares in Badger Hall Avenue, thereby making it unnecessary to infer an agreement between them.[187] Even had that not been so, however, the same result would have been reached. This, on the facts, seems an eminently sensible conclusion and, in reality, reflected the purchasing behaviour of the parties. So, although the Supreme Court chose to eschew a resulting trust analysis of the facts, preferring instead to develop the law of constructive trusts, the outcome is consistent with an analysis based upon resulting trusts. This is if one applies, as one should, an approach to the entire purchasing behaviour of the property and does not confine one's attention to the acquisition of the legal title.

8.6.1.3 Improvements

A perceived problem with the decision in *Pettitt v. Pettitt* was that it could be taken as precluding a person from obtaining an interest in the home as a result of having spent money on improving it. The reason for this concern was that the general position is that, if a person spends money on another person's property, no interest in that property is acquired as a result. This, however, is subject to the important qualification that if the owner of the property encourages this expenditure, as is likely to be the case, then rights can be acquired through estoppel.[188]

8.6.1.4 Matrimonial Proceedings and Property Act 1970

Insofar as married couples are concerned, the position has been regulated by legislation.[189] Section 37 of the Matrimonial Proceedings and Property Act 1970 provides that where a husband or wife contributes in money or money's worth to the improvement of real or personal property then, if the improvement is substantial and, subject to any agreement to the contrary, the husband and wife shall be treated as having acquired by virtue of his or her contribution either to a share or an enhanced share in the property to such an extent as may have been agreed or may seem in all the circumstances just.

Although the legislation applies only to either married couples, couples who have registered a civil partnership, or an engaged couple whose agreement to marry has terminated,[190] it is declaratory in nature, which suggests strongly that it is restating the existing law;[191] a consideration which would seem to indicate that the principle enshrined in the

---

[186] [2010] EWCA Civ. 578.   [187] [2011] UKSC 53 at [48] *per* Lord Walker and Lady Hale.

[188] Ibid. at 818 *per* Lord Upjohn.

[189] An identical provision applies also to people who have registered a civil partnership. See Civil Partnership Act 2004, s. 65.

[190] Law Reform (Miscellaneous Provisions) Act 1970, s. 2.

[191] This point was stressed in *Davis v. Vale* [1971] 1 W.L.R. 1022 at 1026 *per* Lord Denning M.R. See also *Dibble v. Pfluger* [2010] EWCA Civ. 1005 at [25] *per* Ward L.J.

section is applicable also to couples who are neither married nor in a civil partnership.[192] This impression is reinforced by the comment by Lady Hale in *Stack v. Dowden*[193] that the initial beneficial shares in the property may be varied as a result of one of the parties financing or constructing a substantial improvement to the property.

Detailed consideration was given to the approach to be taken to the section in *Re Nicholson*.[194] A wife had spent money installing central heating into the matrimonial home. The approach taken was to assess the beneficial share that each party had in the house prior to the improvement and then ascertain the additional value of the house after the central heating had been installed, and to credit her with that gain. On this basis, her share increased from one half to 21/41ths of the house. Although this seems to be a principled approach to this issue, and one of general application, a different process was suggested in *Griffiths v. Griffiths*.[195] Arnold J. accepted that the valuation of the improvement was largely a matter of guesswork on the facts,[196] but also expressed the view that one should assess the value of the improvements at the time when the house was realized, rather than when they were made. The better view would seem to be that articulated in *Re Nicholson*, in that increases in value to a property over a time is, normally, a matter of house inflation and should not affect the size of the shares of the respective parties.

Substantial improvement

What is clear is that to qualify as a relevant improvement, the improvement has to be substantial. So, in *Re Nicholson*, relatively small sums spent on the installation of two gas fires and a cooker were discounted.[197] Rather more surprisingly, in *Hosking v. Michaelides*,[198] a wife who had contributed £20,000 to the cost of installing a swimming pool, the total cost being £29,000, was held not to have shown that she had made a substantial improvement to the property. The reason for this is that evidence had not been adduced to show that the construction of a swimming pool had added any value to the property and, for this reason, the judge declined to decide between the different approaches to valuation adopted in *Re Nicholson* and *Griffiths v. Griffiths*. This case, although somewhat dubious on the facts, does show the need for a claimant to provide valuation evidence of the significance of the improvement.

8.6.2 Indirect contributions

A problem which was also addressed, albeit briefly, in *Gissing v. Gissing* was the issue of indirect contributions to the acquisition of the house. It may be that a cohabiting couple arrange their finances so that one person's salary is devoted principally to paying the mortgage and the other's goes towards meeting the remainder of the household expenditure. In such a situation, the contribution of the latter does not go directly towards the acquisition of the house but it may, nevertheless, be sufficient in order for her to acquire an interest in it, although the circumstances when that would be the case were narrowly circumscribed. For the courts, in circumstances such as these, to be able to infer an agreement that the beneficial ownership in the house be shared, it was considered to be essential for the financial contribution of the claimant to be such that the other person could not have met the mortgage payments without that contribution.[199]

---

[192] Although see the comments in *Samuels (W.A.)'s Trustee v. Samuels* (1973) 233 E.G. 149 at 151 *per* Walton J.
[193] [2002] 2 A.C. 432 at [70].   [194] [1974] 1 W.L.R. 476.
[195] [1973] 1 W.L.R. 1454.   [196] Ibid. at 1456.
[197] [1974] 1 W.L.R. 476 at 483 *per* Sir John Pennycuick V.-C. See also *Bindra v. Mawji* [2008] EWHC 1715 (Ch), where a contribution of £2,500 over a nine-year period in respect of a house bought for £231,000 rising in value £400,000 was discounted
[198] [2004] All E.R. (D.) 147.
[199] *Gissing v. Gissing* [1971] A.C. 886 at 903 *per* Lord Pearson, at 909 *per* Lord Diplock. See also *Richards v. Dove* [1974] 1 All E.R. 888; *Burns v. Burns* [1984] Ch. 317 at 330 *per* Fox L.J.

8.6.2.1 Assistance in business

The strictness of these criteria became highly contentious. Before considering them more fully, one type of indirect contribution to the purchase of property can be considered, that of assistance in a business. Situations may arise where a man acquires a business, the profits of which are used to finance the purchase of a house where he lives with the claimant. The claimant works unpaid, or at a much reduced rate, in the business, thereby contributing to its profitability. In such circumstances, the courts will regard this form of contribution as being indistinguishable from a situation where both parties are in paid employment and their salaries are pooled together and used to buy the house, and she will acquire an interest in it.[200] None of these cases was cited, however, in *James v. Thomas*.[201] Sarah James moved into a house which was legally and beneficially owned by Peter Thomas. He was a building and drainage contractor, and from 1990 until they separated in 2004, she worked in the business for no pay, this work consisting of driving a tipper, digging trenches, laying concrete and gravel, and, along with her partner, the manual work associated with this business.[202] Although the proceeds of the business were used to service the mortgage, somewhat surprisingly, a claim under a resulting trust was abandoned[203] and it was held that she had acquired no interest in the house. It is submitted that this case is wrongly decided.

It should be appreciated that all of these authorities, except *James v. Thomas*, concerning the ability of a claimant to acquire an interest in a house by means of indirect contributions to its purchase are irreconcilable with the decision in *Curley v. Parkes*[204] concerning the payment of mortgage instalments. This consideration reinforces the view that that case was wrongly decided.[205]

8.6.2.2 Household contributions

The emphasis in resulting trust cases has always been on the need to make a financial contribution to the purchase of the property in question before one will acquire a beneficial interest in it. An attempt was made, however, to liberalize the judicial approach to this issue and thereby enable the courts to have regard to factors other than purely financial considerations. To do this, reference was made to the dictum of Lord Diplock in *Gissing*[206] cited earlier, where he referred to resulting, implied, and constructive trusts together in an attempt to construct a new form of trust to be imposed on the basis of broad principles of justice.

In *Hussey v. Palmer*,[207] the issue was whether an elderly lady who had advanced money to her daughter and son-in-law to build an additional bedroom to their house in which she could sleep was entitled to an interest in it. In upholding her claim,[208] Lord Denning M.R. considered whether she was entitled to an interest under either a resulting or a

---

[200] See *Nixon v. Nixon* [1969] 1 W.L.R. 1676; *Muetzel v. Muetzel* [1970] 1 W.L.R. 188; *Re Cummins* [1972] Ch. 62; *Bothe v. Amos* [1976] Fam. 47. Cf. *Ivin v. Blake* [1995] 1 F.L.R. 70, criticized by A. Lawson [1996] Conv. 462. Contrast, also, *Hosking v. Michaelides* [2004] All E.R. (D.) 147, where, although a wife was a director in the family company, she played no active part in its affairs.

[201] [2007] EWCA Civ. 1212. Contrast the not dissimilar Canadian case of *Sorochan v. Sorochan* (1986) D.L.R. (4th) 1.

[202] [2007] EWCA Civ. 1212 at [4] *per* Sir John Chadwick.

[203] Ibid. at [10].   [204] [2004] EWCA Civ. 1515.

[205] See 8.6.1.2—Practical consequences.

[206] [1971] A.C. 886 at 905. See 8.5.2.

[207] [1972] 1 W.L.R. 1286.

[208] Cairns L.J. dissented on the basis that the money had been advanced as a loan.

constructive trust and held that she was. He was unconcerned, however, as to which trust was appropriate. In his view:

> this is a matter of words more than anything else. The two run together. By whatever name it is described, it is a trust imposed whenever justice and good conscience require it. It is a liberal process founded upon large principles of equity, . . . to be applied in cases where the legal owner cannot conscientiously keep the property for himself alone, but ought to allow another to have the benefit of it or a share in it.[209]

8.7 The development of the common intention constructive trust

This post-*Gissing* line of cases sought to introduce a new method to the resolution of disputes of this kind, effectively amalgamating the resulting and constructive trust and declining to take a narrow financial view of what, in law, amounted to a contribution to the acquisition of a home. Not surprisingly, it was also highly controversial, both in England[210] and overseas.[211] The reasons for this controversy are not difficult to see. First, the adoption of a discretionary, justice-based approach is difficult to reconcile with the reasoning of the House of Lords.[212] From a substantive point of view, it was also criticized as being unpredictable. To critics of Lord Denning's approach, 'His Lordship's inspiration is a notion of justice, dim and ever-changing, to the eye of the spectator, but to him clear and compulsive of fervent and evangelical adherence.'[213]

It is perhaps no surprise that this approach failed to prosper, and could be seen as being ahead of its time. The focus of Lord Denning was more on the nature of the relationship, rather than the cold calculus of financial contributions to the purchase of the home. In more recent years, some moves have been made to decide the beneficial ownership of the home on the basis of what was perceived to be fair.[214] The task facing a claimant is: first, to establish that she has any interest in the property at all, and having done that, the issue becomes one of quantifying that interest. With regard to the first of these matters, the question of acquisition, the more liberal attitude of Lord Denning did not survive his retirement, though there are signs that elements of it are entering popular judicial thought once more.

8.7.1 The return to orthodoxy

In *Burns v. Burns*,[215] an unmarried couple began to cohabit in rented accommodation in 1961, where their first child was born. In 1963, when a second child was expected, they moved into another house which was conveyed into the man's name. He provided the initial finance and paid the mortgage instalments. The woman remained at home looking after the children until 1975, when she got a job as a driving instructor, her wages being

---

[209] [1972] 1 W.L.R. 1286 at 1289–90.   [210] See A.J. Oakley [1973] C.L.P. 17.

[211] See *Allen v. Snyder* [1977] 2 N.S.W.L.R. 685 at 700–1 *per* Samuels J.A.

[212] See *Grant v. Edwards* [1976] Ch. 638 at 654 *per* Sir Nicolas Browne-Wilkinson; D.J. Hayton in Jowell and McAuslan (eds), *Lord Denning: The Judge and the Law* (London, Sweet & Maxwell, 1984), 79 at 83–8.

[213] Meagher, Gummow, and Lehane, *Equity: Doctrines and Remedies* (3rd edn) (Sydney, Butterworths, 1992), para. 306.

[214] See *Oxley v. Hiscock* [2005] Fam. 211 at 247.

[215] [1984] Ch. 317. For rather different reactions to the decision, see N.V. Lowe and A. Smith (1984) 47 M.L.R. 341 and J. Dewar, ibid. at 735. This decision was cited in *Stack v. Dowden*, but was not referred to in any of the speeches.

used to pay the rates, telephone bills, and various items for the house. She also redecorated the interior of the house. In 1980, the relationship ended and she brought proceedings claiming a beneficial interest in the house. The Court of Appeal unanimously[216] rejected her claim. Despite her having cohabited with him for over nineteen years in total and seventeen years in the house which he had bought, during which time she looked after both the house and the family, she had acquired no interest in it.[217]

The reason that her claim failed was because the court, reverting to the principles laid down by the House of Lords in *Gissing*, held that they could not infer a common intention for her to have an interest in the property because there was no 'evidence of a payment or payments . . . which it can be inferred was referable to the acquisition of the house'.[218] Dicta, such as those in *Hall v. Hall*, which allowed a court to adopt a broader perspective as to contributions to the household in assessing whether a person should be regarded as having an interest in the home, were regarded as wrong.[219]

8.7.2 **Purchasing behaviour**

The decision in *Burns* marked a return to orthodoxy with regard to the role of the resulting trust; that orthodoxy being, in essence, that one gets what one pays for. This view was confirmed by the House of Lords in *Lloyds Bank plc v. Rosset*.[220] The facts were unusual. The entire purchase price to buy a semi-derelict farmhouse was provided from a Swiss trust fund held for Mr Rosset and, at the insistence of the trustees, the house was registered in his sole name. Unknown to his wife, he also took out a mortgage against the property to secure his overdraft. The bank manager accepted his story that his wife and children would not be living in the house. When he subsequently defaulted on the mortgage, the bank sought possession and Mrs Rosset argued that she had an overriding interest on the basis that she had a beneficial interest in the house and was in actual occupation of it at the relevant time. Reversing the decision of the Court of Appeal,[221] the House of Lords decided in favour of the bank on the basis that she had no beneficial interest in the house and could not, therefore, have an overriding interest in it.

The basis of her claim to an interest in the house was that she and her husband had agreed that the acquisition of the house was to be a joint venture. Relying on this, she asserted not that she had made a financial contribution to the purchase price but that she had carried out physical work in renovating the property, thereby entitling her to an interest under a common intention[222] constructive trust.

8.7.3 **The express agreement constructive trust**

Giving the only reasoned speech, Lord Bridge recognized that there were two methods by which one could acquire a beneficial interest in the house. The first method, which was argued to be applicable in the present case, was that there was an actual agreement to share the beneficial interest in the home and, in reliance on that agreement, the claimant has altered her position or acted to her detriment so as to give rise to a constructive trust or to rights in estoppel.[223]

---

[216] This decision was reached reluctantly by Waller L.J. See [1984] Ch. 317 at 326.

[217] An editorial comment on this decision remarked that 'even the most lukewarm feminist can see the injustice of [it]': [1984] Fam. Law 4.

[218] [1984] Ch. 317 at 328 *per* Fox L.J.   [219] [1984] Ch. 317 at 331.

[220] [1991] A.C. 107.   [221] [1989] Ch. 350.

[222] For a somewhat hyperbolic criticism of this term, see Mee, *Property Rights of Cohabitees*, 117. See also N. Glover and P. Todd (1996) 16 L.S. 325.

[223] [1991] 1 A.C. 107 at 129.

In what can be regarded as the first type of case, Lord Bridge said:

> The first and fundamental question which must always be resolved is whether, independently of any inference to be drawn from the conduct of the parties in the course of sharing the house as their home and managing their joint affairs, there has at any time prior to acquisition, or exceptionally at some later date, been any agreement, arrangement, or understanding reached between them that the property is to be shared beneficially. The finding of an agreement or arrangement to share can only, I think, be based upon evidence of express discussions between the partners, however imperfectly remembered and however imprecise their terms may have been. Once a finding to this effect is made it will only be necessary for the person asserting a claim to a beneficial interest against the partner entitled to the legal estate to show that he or she has acted to his or her detriment or significantly altered his or her position in reliance on the agreement in order to give rise to a constructive trust or a proprietary estoppel.[224]

8.7.3.1 Joint ventures

This is a description of the classical constructive trust, and it was contended that this should apply to Mrs Rosset. This argument was rejected. First, while the view was taken that the Rossets were buying the house as a joint venture, it was not accepted that this was the same thing as agreeing to share the beneficial ownership in it.[225] This, however, is an extremely fine distinction.[226] While it may have been justified on the particular facts, it should be treated with considerable caution. The money to purchase the house was only released from the trust on the explicit understanding that it was to be in his sole name. In these circumstances, for the Rossets to have agreed to share the beneficial ownership of it was regarded as a form of subterfuge to circumvent the intention of the trustee. Clearer evidence than that which is normally required to establish an intention to share the beneficial ownership in the property was, therefore, required, and the evidence presented in the case did not do this.[227] This finding, together with Lord Bridge's view that the work relied upon by Mrs Rosset to establish an interest under a constructive trust was 'almost de minimis'[228] meant that her claim failed. The facts were clearly unusual and should not lead to judges, in more usual contexts, to distinguish cases when the parties have agreed to buy a house as a joint venture from those when there has been a discussion as to beneficial ownership.[229] In either case, the position should be seen as being one where the parties have agreed to share[230] the ownership of the house.

8.7.3.2 'Express discussions'

The starting point in cases such as this is to find an agreement or arrangement between the parties with regard to the ownership of the house, through evidence of express discussions. An example of this occurred in *Eves v. Eves*.[231] A couple, Stuart and Janet, wished to acquire a house together but he told her that, because she was not yet twenty-one, the legal title could not be in their joint names.[232] She accepted this, and assumed that this

---

[224] Ibid. at 132.   [225] Ibid. at 130.   [226] See M.P. Thompson [1990] Conv. 314 at 315.

[227] [1991] A.C. 107 at 128.   [228] Ibid. at 131.

[229] This, unfortunately, is what was done in *Buggs v. Buggs* [2003] EWHC 1538 (Ch), criticized by M.P. Thompson [2003] Conv. 411 at 420–1.

[230] There must, in this type of case, be an express or inferred agreement. See, e.g., *Akhtar v. Arif* [2006] EWHC 2726 (Ch).

[231] [1975] 1 W.L.R. 1338. See also *Williamson v. Sheikh* [2008] EWCA Civ. 990.

[232] At the time this was said, it may well have been true, as the age of majority was reduced to eighteen in 1969, the year in which the house was bought. See Family Law Reform Act 1969, s. 1.

was merely an excuse, but he was determined, throughout, that the house should be in his name alone. The purchase was completed after she had attained majority but the house was still conveyed into his name alone. He provided the finance but she did a considerable amount of physical work on the property, which was previously in a dirty and dilapidated state. When they separated, the issue arose as to the beneficial ownership of the house. The Court of Appeal held her to be entitled to a quarter share.

Lord Denning M.R. decided the case on a broad view of constructive trusts and considered this quantum share to be appropriate. Brightman J., with whom Browne L.J. agreed, took a more principled route to this conclusion. In his view, the statement as to why the house was not to be in their joint names led her to believe that this was a mere technicality and that she would, nevertheless, be a co-owner of it. Such an oral understanding would not, of itself, have been sufficient for her to have acquired a beneficial interest in the house, however, because there was no written evidence of this statement as is required by s. 53(1)(b), LPA 1925. As there was a link between her conduct and the acquisition of the property, however, the court could impose a constructive trust to give effect to their agreement and he concurred with the outcome that she be entitled to a one-quarter share in the house.

8.7.3.3 Pretexts

Eves v. Eves is now accepted as being one of a line of cases where a constructive trust is imposed in order to enforce an anterior agreement, or common intention, to share the beneficial ownership of the property.[233] A common theme of these cases is that the legal owner gives the other person a pretext as to why the property is not being put into joint names. In *Eves*, the reason given was that she was too young. In other cases, the reasons have included possible complications in impending divorce proceedings,[234] or alleged tax advantages.[235] The fact that the legal owner has given some excuse or pretext to the other party for the legal title not being in joint names has led to criticism that there is, in fact, no common intention to share the beneficial ownership of the house at all.[236] The party giving the pretext may never actually intend to share the ownership: 'Excuses are usually made to hide bad intentions, not good ones.'[237]

8.7.3.4 Objective determination

From the point of view of a subjective enquiry into the actual intentions of the parties, there is obvious force in these criticisms, and, to that extent, the expression 'common intention' may be inapposite. Nevertheless, the better view is that the very fact that a pretext is given as to why the property is not to be in joint names is, itself, indicative of the fact that the person to whom the pretext is given expects to have an interest in the property and the other party knows this. So, while there may not be an actual agreement, in the sense of a bargain, the statement made should be taken, objectively, as a sufficient indication of an intention to share the beneficial ownership.

This argument was accepted in the leading case of *Grant v. Edwards*.[238] Ms Grant and Mr Edwards were involved in a relationship and were looking to buy a house together. The house was conveyed into the names of Mr Edwards and his brother, Mr Edwards having told Ms Grant that it would be inadvisable for her name to be on the title as this might

---

[233] See *Lloyds Bank plc v. Rosset* [1991] 1 A.C. 107 at 133 *per* Lord Bridge.

[234] *Grant v. Edwards* [1986] Ch. 638; *Oxley v. Hiscock* [2005] Fam. 111.

[235] *Hammond v. Mitchell* [1992] 2 All E.R. 109. In *Abbott v. Abbott* [2007] UKPC 53, Mrs Abbott, as a Canadian, would have needed a licence to be the legal owner of land in Antigua.

[236] See S. Gardner (1993) 109 L.Q.R. 263 at 264–5, 281–2; L. Clarke and R. Edmonds [1992] Fam. 523; C. Rotherham [2004] Conv. 268 at 277. See also *Van Laetham v. Brooker* [2005] EWHC 1478 (Ch) at [67] *per* Lawrence Collins J.

[237] U. Rinker [1998] Conv. 202 at 207.   [238] [1986] Ch. 638.

cause her prejudice in divorce proceedings in which she was involved. It was found that she contributed to the acquisition of the house and on this basis was awarded a half share in the house. With regard to the finding of a common intention, Mustill L.J. dealt head on with the problem of the giver of the pretext never intending to share the ownership of the property. He said:

> The reason given for placing the brother's name on the title was simply an untruthful excuse for not doing at once what he never intended to do at all.
>
> That however is not fatal to the claim. Whatever the defendant's actual intention, the nature of the excuse which he gave must have led the plaintiff to believe that she would in the future have her name on the title, and this in turn would justify her in concluding that she had from the outset some kind of right to the house.[239]

This belief, because it has been induced by the defendant, is sufficient to establish the common intention necessary to give rise to the imposition of a constructive trust.

Outside the context of the pretexts or excuses found in *Eves v. Eves* and *Grant v. Edwards*, finding agreement to share the beneficial ownership on the basis of express discussions is likely to be a futile exercise in the vast majority of cases. As Lord Hodson pointed out in *Pettitt v. Pettitt*, '[t]he conception of a normal married couple spending the long winter evenings hammering out agreements about their possessions appears grotesque'.[240] Put another way, it simply does not reflect the way people live their lives, which means the far more important route to finding an agreement to share the beneficial ownership is by inferring it from their conduct.

8.7.4 **The inferred agreement constructive trust**

Having analysed the first method by which a person may establish a beneficial share in a family home, Lord Bridge turned to the second:

> In sharp contrast with [a situation involving actual agreement] is the very different one where there is no evidence to support a finding of an agreement or arrangement to share, however reasonable it might have been for the parties to reach such an arrangement if they had applied their minds to the question, and where the courts must rely entirely on the conduct of the parties both as the basis from which to infer a common intention to share the property beneficially and as the conduct relied on to give rise to a constructive trust. In this situation direct contributions to the purchase price by the partner who is not the legal owner, whether initially or by payment of mortgage instalments will readily justify the inference necessary to the creation of a constructive trust. But as I read the authorities, it is at least extremely doubtful whether anything less will do.[241]

8.7.4.1 **Terminology**

A number of points can be made about this significant, albeit misleading, passage. The first concerns terminology. Although Lord Bridge, when referring to the second scenario, spoke of the creation of a constructive trust, this could have been regarded as being a slip, in that what is being described is a classic resulting trust. There is no evidence of an actual agreement between the parties, but, instead, one infers their intentions with regard to the beneficial ownership of the property from the fact that they have both contributed to the purchase of it. The supposition that this was a slip is strengthened by the fact he regarded

---

[239] Ibid. at 653.   [240] [1971] A.C. 777 at [810].   [241] [1991] A.C. 107 at 132–3.

Pettitt v. Pettitt[242] and *Gissing v. Gissing*,[243] both of which are authorities on the application of resulting trust principles to this area, as being leading cases which fell into the category of case which he had just described. Since then, however, except where the house has not been bought for the purposes of sharing,[244] the courts have repeatedly stressed that the trust which arises in this type of case is a constructive trust;[245] although, as will be seen, in its application, this constructive trust owes much to the principles underlying resulting trusts.

8.7.4.2 Indirect contributions in inferred agreement constructive trusts

A second point to make about this passage is that it appears to draw the ambit of what constitutes a contribution to the purchase price too narrowly, and in a way which was not warranted by previous authority.[246] In *Gissing*,[247] Lord Diplock was prepared to accept that indirect contributions to the purchase price would suffice in order to enable an interest to be acquired; instancing as an example a situation where one party's income goes to the meeting of household expenses, the effect of which is to enable the other to meet the mortgage repayments. Similarly, if one person has worked without payment in a business, the profits of which are used to purchase a house, then an interest in that house will be acquired as a result of the indirect contribution.[248] At first sight, Lord Bridge's formulation appears, implicitly, to overrule these authorities, although it is doubtful whether in this short passage, and without reference to them, he intended to do so.

That the law has not been narrowed in this way has since become clear. In *Le Foe v. Le Foe*,[249] the judge said:

> Although I am sure that H earned more than W . . . I have no doubt that the family economy depended for its function on W's earnings. It was an arbitrary allocation of responsibility that H paid the mortgage, service charge and outgoings, whereas W paid for day-to-day domestic expenditure. I have clearly concluded that W contributed indirectly to the mortgage repayments, the principal of which furnished part of the consideration of the initial purchase price.

On this basis, notwithstanding what was said in *Rosset*, it was held that W had established a beneficial interest in the house.

That the passage in Lord Bridge's speech was too restrictive[250] as to what would constitute a contribution to the purchase of a house has since been confirmed by the House of Lords in *Stack v. Dowden*, and by the Privy Council in *Abbott v. Abbott*, thus evidencing a trend not to deal with relevant authority on its merits. So, in the former case, it was said that the comments by Lord Bridge were *obiter* and had set the hurdle too high in certain respects,[251] and, in the latter, that the law had moved on since this had been said.[252] Somewhat remarkably, the Supreme Court in *Jones v. Kernott*[253] did not refer to *Rosset* at all.

---

[242] [1970] A.C. 777.   [243] [1971] A.C. 886.

[244] See *Laskar v. Laskar* [2008] EWCA Civ. 347 at [21] *per* Lord Neuberger, citing *Stack v. Dowden* [2007] 2 A.C. 423 at [11] *per* Lord Hope.

[245] See *Ledger-Bendell v. Ledger-Bendell* [2006] EWHC 2940 at [247] *per* Mr Nicholas Strauss Q.C.; *Abbott v. Abbott* [2007] UKPC 53.

[246] See M.P. Thompson [1990] Conv. 314 at 317; P. Ferguson (1993) 109 L.Q.R. 114 at 116.

[247] [1971] A.C. 107 at 132.   [248] See 8.6.2.

[249] [2001] 2 F.L.R. 970 at 973. See M.P. Thompson [2002] Conv. 273.

[250] For an argument that the perceived effect of Lord Bridge's dicta in *Rosset* 'embedded a deeply conservative vision of property', see L. Fox O'Mahony (2014) CLP 409 at 430.

[251] [2007] 2 A.C. 423 at [61] *per* Lady Hale. See also at [26] *per* Lord Walker.

[252] [2007] UKPC 53 at [3] *per* Lady Hale.   [253] [2011] UKSC 53.

That said, the third point which should be made about *Rosset* is that, although the statement that only direct contributions to the purchase price would suffice is too narrow, it was nevertheless clear that, in order to obtain an interest under a trust, where there is no evidence of an anterior agreement to share the beneficial ownership of the house, the conduct relied upon must be of a purchasing nature. The point made in *Burns v. Burns* of the need to establish a direct link between the conduct relied upon to establish an interest in the property and the acquisition of that property was accepted. Unless the claimant is contributing in money, or money's worth,[254] she will not acquire an interest in it. Subsequent developments in the House of Lords and the Supreme Court do not formally undermine this, because in both *Stack v. Dowden* and *Jones v. Kernott*, the starting position was co-ownership at law, with the corresponding presumption of joint beneficial ownership.[255]

There are, however, increasing calls[256] for the broad range of circumstances identified in *Stack v. Dowden*[257] as capable of rebutting the joint ownership presumption to be transplanted into sole ownership cases, in order to infer an agreement to share the beneficial ownership—to acquire the interest itself, in other words. This would have a significant effect on cases such as *Burns v. Burns*, and would allow for the possibility that non-purchasing conduct, including and especially domestic work and childcare, could amount to a contribution from which the courts can infer a common intention constructive trust. The desire to see activities of that kind, the exclusion of which have a disproportionate effect on women in society, brought into the category of qualifying behaviour may result in a further liberalization of the 'common intention' in a constructive trust in the near future. The Court of Appeal's decision in *Geary v. Rankine*[258] has been seen by some[259] as confirmation that the *Stack/Kernott* principles apply at the acquisition stage in sole name cases, but this should be treated with caution: the court did not need to invoke the restriction to financial contributions found in *Rosset* because, in the event, no common intention at all in relation to the house in question could be found. For now, the better view is that it remains the case that, when the legal title is in the sole name of one of the parties, to overcome the hurdle of establishing any sort of interest in the first place, the facts must fit into one of the broad categories set out in *Rosset*.

8.8 Quantification of the interest

The issue of quantification can arise primarily in two ways before a court. First, in joint legal ownership cases, where the presumption of joint beneficial ownership has been rebutted in order to acquire an unequal share. Second, in sole legal ownership cases, where an express or inferred common intention constructive trust has enabled another person to acquire a beneficial interest. In both circumstances, the question remains: what is the size of the interest that has been acquired?

8.8.1 Quantifying express agreement constructive trusts

The theory underlying the imposition of the constructive trust is that the trust is imposed to give effect to the common intention of the parties. Where, as in *Re Densham*, that

---

[254] This will include physical labour improving the house: *Eves v. Eves* [1975] 1 W.L.R. 1338.

[255] Neither does the suggestion in *Abbott v. Abbott* [2007] UKPC 53 at [20] that 'the whole course of conduct in relation to the property must be taken into account in determining their shared intentions as to the ownership' overrule the House in *Rosset*. *Abbott*, as a decision of the Privy Council, is not binding on the English courts, and the discussion of acquisition on the facts was obiter.

[256] Most notably by S. Gardner and K. Davidson (2011) 127 L.Q.R. 13; S. Gardner (2013) 72 C.L.J. 307.

[257] At [69]. See 8.4.3.   [258] [2012] EWCA Civ. 555.   [259] K. Lees [2012] Conv. 412.

intention is stated expressly, the result is that the courts should give effect to that intention.[260] In *Eves*, however, the claimant was awarded a one-quarter share. This aspect of the decision was regarded by Brightman J. as being the hardest part of the case[261] and is, it is suggested, also the least satisfactory part of it, there being no evidence at all that the parties had agreed that she should have a share of this magnitude.

In cases where some reason is given for the legal title not being shared, so that the reasonable supposition is that the person to whom the excuse is given is to have an interest in the property, the normal starting point should be one-half; a natural inference being that, if the house was in joint names, then it would be owned equally. Similarly, if the person giving the pretext at the time owns only a share in the relevant property, then the claimant would expect to own a half of that share.[262] The point is that the role of the court is to enforce what it is that the parties actually agreed.

A good example of this occurred in *Willliamson v. Sheikh*.[263] A couple met through the Internet in 2002, when she was fifteen and he was in his thirties. They bought a house together in 2004. She advanced a capital sum towards the purchase, that sum having been inherited from her grandfather. The house was, necessarily, put into his sole name, and he paid the mortgage repayments. A trust deed was prepared to set out their respective entitlements in the house, although this was not signed. The reason for this was that he assured her that there was no need to do this, and that he would see her all right. When the couple separated, it was held that he held the house on trust for her in the proportions set out in the unsigned trust document. She having contributed to the purchase price on the basis of their agreement, a constructive trust was imposed to give effect to the actual intention of the parties.

Where, however, the express agreement is subject to a condition that is not fulfilled by one of the parties, the courts may decline to give effect to it. In *Gallarotti v. Sebastianelli*,[264] two business associates bought a flat, registered in Mr Sebastianelli's name. They each paid a cash deposit, though Mr Sebastianelli contributed the larger amount, and they covered the remainder with a mortgage. There was an express agreement that the interests would be 50 per cent each on the condition that Mr Gallarotti would make larger payments to the mortgage, which he never did. After they fell out, Mr Gallorotti brought an action for a 50 per cent share in the flat. Arden L.J. held that the express agreement came to an end when Mr Gallarotti failed to make larger mortgage payments. The parties had foreseen some imbalance in their contributions, but not in the magnitude that had in fact occurred. As a result, 'it was wholly implausible that Mr Sebastianelli should make a substantial gift to Mr Gallarotti',[265] and the beneficial interest was split 75 per cent to 25 per cent respectively.

8.8.2 Quantifying inferred agreement constructive trusts

Where there is an actual agreement to share the beneficial interest in the property then, provided that the claimant has made a contribution to the purchase of the property, the task of the court is straightforward: it is to enforce what has been agreed. Where there is no such agreement, the task is to draw inferences as to what the parties intended, such inferences being drawn from their conduct. This latter situation was traditionally the area of operation of the resulting trust, with the size of the share reflecting the size of the

---

[260] See also *Stack v. Dowden* [2007] 2 A.C. 432 at [37] *per* Lord Walker; *Q v. Q* [2008] EWHC 1874 (Fam.) at [113] *per* Black J.

[261] [1975] 1 W.L.R. 1338 at 1345.

[262] See *Stokes v. Anderson* [1991] 1 F.L.R. 391; *Chan Pui Chun v. Leung Kam Ho* [2002] EWCA Civ. 1075. See also *Hapeshi v. Allnatt* [2010] EWHC 392 (Ch). Contrast *Ungarian v. Lessnoff* [1990] Ch. 206 (a life interest).

[263] [2008] EWCA Civ. 990.   [264] [2012] EWCA Civ. 865.   [265] Ibid. at [26] per Arden L.J.

contribution. The reclassification of this form of trust as an inferred constructive trust, as occurred in *Lloyd's Bank plc v. Rosset*,[266] has led to a blurring of the distinction between enforcing an agreement which the parties actually made and inferring intentions from the conduct of the parties, which runs the risk of constructing agreements for people which they never had. This risk has been exacerbated by the decision in *Jones v. Kernott* which, as we shall see, conceives of the possibility of imputing a common intention to the parties in circumstances where it cannot be inferred in order to quantify their respective shares.

8.8.2.1 The role of fairness

In the influential case of *Oxley v. Hiscock*,[267] Mr Hiscock and Mrs Oxley had been in a relationship for many years and had lived together in various houses. The house that was the subject matter of the litigation was put into his sole name, the reason for this being to prevent a claim to it being made by her former husband. It was found as a fact that, although they had agreed to share the beneficial ownership of the house, there was no agreement as to what those actual shares should be.[268] The purchase price was derived from a variety of sources, including the proceeds of sale of a house which they had previously owned. Despite it being clear that she was making a sizeable financial contribution to the purchase of the house, she, very unwisely, turned down advice from her solicitor that the beneficial interests should be stated at the outset, her reason being that she trusted him.[269] At first instance, it was held that the house was owned beneficially in equal shares. On appeal, the Court of Appeal held that the property was shared in proportion 60 per cent to 40 per cent in his favour.

In reaching this conclusion, Chadwick L.J., accepted that a beneficial interest in a house could be acquired in one of the two situations referred to in *Rosset*. These situations were when there was an actual agreement as to the respective shares which each party was to have in the property, and those when there was not. In the latter situation, the relevant intention to share the beneficial ownership is derived from the contributions made to its purchase. The present case did not fall neatly into either category. This was because, although there was an actual agreement to share the beneficial ownership of the house, the two of them had agreed that the shares would not be equal[270] but had not come to an agreement as to what those shares should be. Consequently, the case was decided on the basis that it fell into the second of the categories laid down by Lord Bridge in *Rosset*. This then led to the issue of the quantification of the beneficial interest, in cases of this type and, in particular, the principles upon which such quantification is to be carried.

The principal argument of Mr Hiscock was that the size of Mrs Oxley's beneficial share in the property should be determined by the size of her contribution to the purchase price. On this basis, it was argued, her share should have been in the region of 22 per cent, that being the assessment of her contribution at first instance. This analysis was rejected.[271] In cases where the parties have not come to an agreement as to the proportions in which they are to share the ownership of the property, a court may infer the requisite intention to share ownership from the fact that the person who is not on the legal title has made direct contributions to its purchase. That is not determinative of the size of the proportionate share. This was stated in terms by Chadwick L.J., who said, 'Direct contributions to the purchase price may lead to an inference that each party should have some beneficial

---

[266] [1991] A.C. 107.

[267] [2005] Fam. 211. See S. Gardner (2004) 120 L.Q.R. 541; M.P. Thompson [2004] Conv. 496; M. Dixon [2003] Conv. 79.

[268] [2005] Fam. 211 at 217–18 *per* Chadwick L.J.   [269] Ibid. at 215–16 *per* Chadwick L.J.

[270] Ibid. at 218 and 248 *per* Chadwick L.J.

[271] It was based, principally, on *Springette v. Defoe* [1992] 1 F.L.R. 388.

interest without, necessarily, leading to the further inference that their respective shares should be proportionate to the amount of their direct contributions.'[272]

8.8.2.2 Fairness

This, of course, leaves unresolved how one does determine what those shares should be. The correct approach was said to be that:

> if it were their common intention that each should have some beneficial interest in the property—which is the hypothesis upon which it becomes necessary to answer the second question [sc. the size of that share]—then, in the absence of evidence that they gave any thought to the amount of their respective shares, the necessary inference is that they must have intended that question would be answered on the basis of what was seen to be fair.[273]

This approach is open to the standard objection that, except in cases where the parties have actually considered the question of the ownership of the house, it perpetuates the myth that what the courts are doing is to gauge what the parties intended when no real thought had been given to the matter at all.[274] It has also met with fierce criticism, on the basis that it gives to the judiciary an unfettered discretion to decide on the beneficial ownership of a family home and leads to 'palm-tree justice'.[275] A good deal of the sting goes out of this criticism, however, when regard is had to how the court determined what was fair.

8.8.2.3 A wider view of financial contributions

With regard to this issue, it was clear that what was relevant to the court were financial contributions. What emerges is a wider, and more welcome, view of what constitutes a financial contribution than had been previously articulated. This is evident in the following important passage:

> It must now be accepted that (at least as far as this court and below) the answer is that each is entitled to that share which the court considers fair having regard to the whole course of dealing between them *in relation to the property*. And in that context, 'the whole course of dealing between them in relation to the property' includes the arrangements which they make from time to time to meet the outgoings (for example, mortgage contributions, council tax and utilities, repairs insurance and housekeeping) which have to be met if they are to live in their property as their home.[276]

On the basis of this, Mrs Oxley was held to have a 40 per cent share. This was arrived at by first assessing the size of their respective initial contributions to the purchase, his contribution being considerably in excess to that provided by her. Regard was then had to the subsequent pooling of their resources and the consequent expenditure related to the house and, in particular, that they contributed equally to the repayment of the debt incurred to finance the purchase of the home.[277] Her share in the house was, therefore, larger than it would have been had attention been confined solely to her initial contribution.

Consistency with resulting trusts

Although the language used in *Oxley v. Hiscock* is that of constructive trust and fairness, the result of the case is entirely consistent with that which would have been arrived at

---

[272] [2005] Fam. 211 at 231.   [273] Ibid. at 247.   [274] See 8.5.3.1.
[275] See G. Battersby (2005) 17 C.F.L.Q. 259 at 263.
[276] [2005] Fam. 211 at 246 *per* Chadwick L.J. Emphasis supplied.
[277] Ibid. at 220 *per* Chadwick L.J.

on the application of resulting trust principles. The share she was held to be entitled to was commensurate with what she had paid.[278] The case does, however, represent a welcome development in the law, in that credit is given for financial contributions made after the date of the actual transfer of the house. This seems an entirely realistic way to view the purchase of a house, which in most cases is a process occupying over twenty years. Moreover, it also pays regard to payments associated with the purchase, such as the payment of council tax. It may be purely a matter of convenience which person's salary goes towards the payment of the mortgage instalments, and which goes to the other expenditure associated with house ownership and it is undesirable that major differences in outcome should depend on such a distinction.[279] Nevertheless, despite protestations to the contrary, the principles applicable to the resolution of this type of dispute do seem to be those underlying resulting trusts, and the size of the share is governed by the size of the financial contribution, albeit what counts as financial contribution is viewed more widely than was once the case.

The return to inferred common intention

In *Stack v. Dowden*, Lady Hale disapproved of the statement in *Oxley v. Hiscock* that the task of the court is to determine the size of each person's beneficial interest in the property on the basis of what was fair.[280] She also disapproved of cases which appeared to adopt an arithmetical approach to the calculation of those interests.[281] When turning to the facts of the case itself, however, she was also critical of the approach of the trial judge, in that 'he had looked at their relationship rather than the matters which were relevant to their intentions about this property'.[282] This then leaves the question as to how those intentions are to be discerned. The answer would seem to be that one looks at the whole course of dealings between the parties, and the broad range of non-exhaustive factors taken into account when rebutting the presumption of joint beneficial ownership. Lady Hale stressed that 'many more factors than financial contributions may be relevant to divining the parties' true intentions'.[283] Whilst this may be correct in principle, whether it really makes any difference in practice is another matter. At first blush, it was the financial contributions that each party made which led Lady Hale to conclude that shares of 64 per cent to 36 per cent would have been appropriate, and she was content to accept the reasoning of the Court of Appeal who, by calculating the shares on the basis of contribution, had arrived at proportions of 65 per cent to 35 per cent.[284] This is also the case in *Jones v. Kernott*,[285] where Lord Walker and Lady Hale, despite favouring the notion of inferred intentions, concluded that the division of the beneficial interests in the proportion of 90 per cent to 10 per cent was, in fact, consistent with their respective financial contributions. It would be trite to observe that, in both *Stack* and *Kernott*, the actual result is consistent with resulting trust principles, raising the question whether there is ultimately a substantial difference between the two forms of trust in the way they are applied in the context of the family home.

---

[278] See also *Pinfield v. Eagles* [2005] EWHC 577 (Ch) at [39], where the adjudication of what was a fair share was based explicitly on the size of the financial contribution, and *Stack v. Dowden* [2005] EWCA Civ. 857 (in the Court of Appeal), and at [2007] 2 A.C. 432 at [107] *per* Lord Neuberger. See also S. Gardner (2004) 120 L.Q.R. 541 at 544; M.P. Thompson [2004] Conv. 496 at 502.

[279] See *Pettitt v. Pettitt* [1970] A.C. 777 at 794 *per* Lord Reid.   [280] Ibid. at [61].

[281] Ibid. at [65], disapproving *Walker v. Hall* [1984] F.L.R. 126; *Springette v. Defoe* [1992] 2 F.L.R. 511 and *Huntingford v. Hobbs* [1993] 1 F.L.R. 376.

[282] Ibid. at [86].   [283] [2007] UKHL 17 at [69].

[284] Ibid. at [88] and [92]. Lord Neuberger would have put the proportions at 70 per cent and 30 per cent, but, as Ms Dowden had conceded that Mr Stack was entitled to a 35 per cent share, was prepared to leave it at that: see at [122].

[285] [2011] UKSC 53.

Imputed intention

At its core, an inferred intention is deduced from the subjective intentions of the parties through their conduct. An imputed intention, on the other hand, is one which is attributed to the parties, even though their actual intention cannot be deduced. As Lord Neuberger has put it, '[i]mputation involves concluding what the parties would have intended, whereas inference involves concluding what they did intend'.[286]

Lord Walker and Lady Hale in *Jones v. Kernott* stated that, where it is not possible by direct evidence or by inference to determine what the parties' 'actual intention was as to the shares in which they would own the property'[287] the matter is resolved by reference to Chadwick L.J.'s dictum in *Oxley v. Hiscock*: 'the answer is that each is entitled to that share which the court considers fair having regard to the whole course of dealing between them in relation to the property'.[288]

This reference back to the concept of fairness espoused by the court in *Oxley* is strange, because Lady Hale had been clear in *Stack* that 'for the court to impose its own view of what is fair upon the situation in which the parties find themselves would be to return to the days before *Pettitt v Pettitt*'.[289] Lord Neuberger, in his dissenting judgment in *Stack*, made several forceful points about imputing an intention, and its relationship with the concept of fairness:

> To impute an intention would not only be wrong in principle and a departure from two decisions of your Lordships' House in this very area, but it also would involve a judge in an exercise which was difficult, subjective and uncertain. (Hence the advantage of the resulting trust presumption). It would be difficult because the judge would be constructing an intention where none existed at the time, and where the parties may well not have been able to agree. It would be subjective for obvious reasons. It would be uncertain because it is unclear whether one considers a hypothetical negotiation between the actual parties, or what reasonable parties would have agreed. The former is more logical, but would redound to the advantage of an unreasonable party. The latter is more attractive, but is inconsistent with the principle, identified by Baroness Hale at paragraph 61, that the court's view of fairness is not the correct yardstick for determining the parties' shares.[290]

Although Lord Neuberger's remarks were never taken up by the majority in *Stack*, Lord Wilson in *Kernott* again raised the logical flaw in allowing imputation of an intention but denying fairness: 'where equity is driven to impute the common intention, how can it do so other than by search for the result which the court itself considers fair?'[291] The response by Lord Walker and Lady Hale simply seems to be that the difference between inferring and imputing a common intention to the parties may not be great in practice. That seems an unsatisfactory place to leave the issue. If courts can now impute an intention to share the beneficial ownership in order to quantify the interests at stake, on what basis can they decide to do so? Somewhat inevitably, this question has fallen on lower courts since *Kernott*, and it is understandable that the answers which have emerged thus far are not particularly clear.

Imputation, contributions, and fairness

The first decision after *Jones v. Kernott* to wrestle with the idea of imputing an intention in order to quantify the beneficial interests was *Aspden v. Elvy*.[292] Mr Aspden claimed

---

[286] *Stack v. Dowden* [2007] UKHL 17 at [126].   [287] [2011] UKSC 53 at [51].
[288] [2004] EWCA Civ. 546 at [69].   [289] [2007] UKHL 17 at [61].
[290] [2007] UKHL 17 at [127].   [291] [2011] UKSC 53 at [87].
[292] [2012] EWHC 1387 (Ch); noted J. Lee [2012] Conv. 421. See also *Thompson v. Hurst* [2012] EWCA Civ. 1752.

a share of the beneficial interest in a barn, owned by Ms Elvy, that he had substantially contributed to, both financially and physically, in order to convert into a home. His contention was that his contributions were on the basis of a common intention that he and Ms Elvy would move back in together, with their children, and marry. Her contention was that his contributions were intended as gifts, in recognition of her work in their previous relationship and her care for the children. Judge Behrens quickly concluded that there was a common intention to share the beneficial ownership, thus displacing the presumption of sole legal and equitable ownership for Ms Elvy, on the basis of Mr Aspden's substantial contributions and his hope that he was to live in the converted barn, which Ms Elvy knew. To quantify the share acquired by Mr Aspden, the judge conceded that the exercise was 'difficult'.[293] No express common intention could be found, so the judge was driven to impute an intention. Mr Aspden received 25 per cent, on the basis that this was a 'fair return for the investment of £65,000–£70,000 and the work carried out by Mr Aspden in a property now worth £400,000'.[294] Judge Behrens apologized that the award was 'somewhat arbitrary', but it was the best he could do with the available material. That final remark reveals, perhaps, a sense of frustration that the court in *Kernott* had not given clearer guidance on the approach to imputation.

One criticism of the judgment in *Aspden* is that a key step in the exercise of quantification was missed. If there are no express agreements to be found, the court must decide whether it is possible to infer a common intention from the parties' conduct. Only if that is not an option is it then open to a court to impute an intention, and 'ask what their intentions as reasonable and just people would have been had they thought about it at the time'.[295] Judge Behrens never probed the second of those steps: inferring an intention. This might well be because the parties' common intention had already been inferred for the acquisition of Mr Aspden's constructive trust interest, and the judge did not think to direct his mind to that question again for the purposes of quantification. Curiously, the same oversight plagued the trial judge in *Barnes v. Phillips*.[296]

As to imputing their intention, it came down to the respective contributions, overwhelmingly financial, of Mr Aspden and Ms Elvy. The broad list of factors identified in *Stack* was ignored. This is unsurprising; Judge Behrens was evidently uncomfortable in producing a result he deemed arbitrary, and it therefore made sense to base his judgement on what was fair in the relatively certain mathematics of financial contributions. This was also the approach taken in *Thompson v. Hurst*.[297]

While it is unnecessary to rehearse the facts, the judgment of Mostyn J. in *Bhura v. Bhura*[298] is conspicuous for two reasons: first, he notes that resulting trusts may still be applicable to cases which bear upon *Stack* and *Kernott*. This has the ring of truth about it, given that the vast majority of inferred and imputed common intention constructive trust cases have arrived at the same result as a resulting trust analysis would have led them to; yet this is thinking that has been expressly denied by *Kernott*. Second, Mostyn J. elided the separate stages of acquisition and quantification with the idea that a judge should ask, 'what is fair and reasonable in the circumstances?' While it might be attractively simple to apply imputation at the acquisition stage, it would destroy any credibility left to the idea of searching for a 'common intention'. If the intention of the parties could be drawn up

---

[293] [2012] EWHC 1387 (Ch) at [127].   [294] Ibid. at [128].

[295] *Jones v. Kernott* [2012] UKSC 53 at [47] *per* Lord Walker and Lady Hale. Somewhat ironically, Judge Behrens in *Aspden v. Elvy* found both parties to be unreasonable, with selfish intentions. How can one impute an intention to the parties on the basis they are reasonable and just people if they have been expressly found to be unreasonable?

[296] [2015] EWCA Civ. 1056; noted A. Hayward [2016] Conv. 233.   [297] [2012] EWCA Civ. 1752.

[298] [2014] EWHC 727 (Fam); noted S. Gardner [2015] Conv. 332.

on the basis of what reasonable people might have intended so as to acquire a beneficial interest over property, it artificially manufactures the unconscionability that operates at the heart of a trust.

That it is impermissible to impute an intention to the parties at the acquisition stage has since been reiterated by the Court of Appeal. In *Capehorn v. Harris*,[299] the trial judge had imputed an intention to share the beneficial ownership in a house solely registered to Mrs Capehorn on the basis of Mr Harris' contribution to their frozen food business, awarding him 25 per cent. The Court of Appeal found that the judge had erroneously elided the questions of acquisition and quantification in imputing an intention to acquire an interest in the house. On the facts, the express discussions showed that no agreement had been reached, and as such it was impossible 'in the circumstances of this case to infer that nonetheless (unbeknown to themselves) the parties did in fact make an agreement by their conduct'.[300] As a result, Mr Harris' claim to have an interest in the house by way of constructive trust failed. This is a welcome clarification that imputing an intention has no relevance to the first question—has the claimant acquired an interest?—in sole name cases. That principle was confirmed again by the Court of Appeal in *Barnes v. Phillips*.[301] In *S v. J and others*,[302] Roberts J. found a common intention to share the beneficial ownership for the respondent because of his contribution to the purchase price, and inferred from what they said and did at the time of the acquisition that their intention was for the shares to be exactly proportionate to the financial amount they contributed: 82 per cent to her, 18 per cent to him.[303] Interestingly, Roberts J. also said the result would be the same whether their intent was imputed, *or* if she had to decide on the basis of what was fair. This suggests she considered imputation and fairness as separate stages, but it is not clear from the judgment how she would impute their intent without considering what was fair. In *Graham-York v. York*,[304] Miss Graham-York claimed a beneficial interest in the house she had shared with her deceased partner, which had been registered in his sole name. The court found an intention to share the equity, but no evidence from which express agreements could be found or inferences drawn from conduct in order to quantify Miss Graham-York's share. Her argument was that only equal shares would be fair, but on the basis of her 'contribution, financial and non-financial, to the enterprise of acquiring and living at the property', the Court of Appeal agreed with the trial judge's assessment that 25 per cent would be a fair result. *Graham-York* seems wider than other post-*Kernott* cases in allowing non-financial contributions to form part of the fairness equation, but it is not at all obvious what those non-financial considerations might have been.[305] The relationship was 'abusive in every sense of that word', and yet Tomlinson L.J. stressed that this was not relevant to the question of what was fair:

> It is essential, in my judgment, to bear in mind that, in deciding in such a case what shares are fair, the court is not concerned with some form of redistributive justice. Thus it is irrelevant that it may be thought a 'fair' outcome for a woman who has endured years of abusive conduct by her partner to be allotted a substantial interest in his property on his death. The plight of Miss Graham-York attracts sympathy, but it does not enable the court to redistribute property interests in a manner which right-minded people might think amounts to appropriate compensation.[306]

---

[299] [2015] EWCA Civ. 955.   [300] Ibid. at [23] per Sales L.J.   [301] [2015] EWCA Civ. 1056.
[302] [2016] EWHC 586 (Fam).   [303] See the remarks at [123]–[125].
[304] [2015] EWCA Civ. 72; noted S. Gardner (2016) 123 L.Q.R. 373.
[305] See also *Curran v. Collins* [2015] EWCA Civ. 404.
[306] [2015] EWCA Civ. 72, at [22].

While this must be correct, it leaves unanswered how the court imputed a 25 per cent share for Miss Graham-York, given that she had contributed a total of £4,000 to the mortgage on a house conservatively worth between £1.2 million and £1.75 million.

In *Sandhu v. Sandhu*,[307] a house was registered in the son's name, but the father had provided a substantial amount of the price on completion, and met the mortgage repayments and other outgoings for many years. The father suffered a stroke while away in India, and the son rented the property out, making the father homeless on his return. The question was whether the father had a beneficial interest in the house. At first instance, the judge had found the evidence of both parties unreliable for different reasons, but nevertheless found a constructive trust interest for the father owing to his direct contribution to the purchase price (as per *Rosset*). To quantify the father's interest, the lack of evidence meant their intentions would have to be imputed. The judge calculated his contribution to the purchase price as between £87,500 and £100,000 of the £139,000 purchase price, and on the basis of that financial contribution she held that a 70 per cent share would be fair. The other payments by the father did not substantially alter that result.

In the Court of Appeal, the son contended that the completion statement had been misread by the trial judge, and in fact the father's contribution was approximately £61,000 (or 43 per cent of the purchase price). Floyd L.J. accepted that the judge had made a mistake in interpreting the completion statement, and indeed the father had contributed that lower amount, but the mortgage payments made by the father meant that the 70 per cent share the judge had calculated in error was nevertheless correct. This is remarkable. The judge at first instance had expressly taken into account the mortgage payments in deciding that the 70 per cent share was a fair one; it had formed part of the whole course of dealing from which their intention was imputed. It makes no sense for the Court of Appeal to accept that the initial contribution was significantly lower than had been decided previously, but then make up the gap in equitable interest by reference to contributions that were already part of the trial judge's overall calculations. Although Floyd L.J stressed that the exercise was not a 'rigidly arithmetical one',[308] it is extremely difficult to see how the same quantification of the father's share could have been adduced after finding that the initial contribution was far lower than the trial judge had held it to be. It reinforces the concern voiced by Judge Behrens in *Aspden v. Elvy* that the result when imputing an intention can be 'somewhat arbitrary'.

Some general observations can be made about these cases. First, several have highlighted a tendency in the judiciary to collapse, inadvertently, the distinction between acquisition and quantification, either by failing to ask whether an intention could be inferred or assuming that an intention could be imputed at the acquisition stage. Second, despite their collective efforts, we are no closer to knowing how a court should approach the imputation of an intention, or how the concept of fairness might be constructed.[309] Third, though the courts are mostly careful to cite *Stack* and *Kernott*, and the contextual factors that are to be taken into account in the whole course of dealing, the outcomes in virtually all of the cases have been based squarely on the parties' financial contributions. Do imputed intention constructive trusts and resulting trusts habitually arrive at the same conclusion? It would certainly appear so. Fourth, the courts have applied *Stack/Kernott* constructive trust reasoning to disputes involving a domestic property, but have done so

---

[307] [2016] EWCA Civ. 1050.   [308] Ibid. at [12].

[309] It has been suggested that the imputation of an intention should be made on the basis that, where there has been a pooling of resources sufficient to view the parties' relationship as 'materially communal', they should receive equal shares. Where this communality does not exist, the beneficial ownership can be adjusted to correct the unjust enrichment of one party by the other's contributions. See S. Gardner (2008) 124 L.Q.R. 422 at 431–3.

without regard to whether the parties were a couple; family-controlled business empires[310] and disputes between parents and children[311] have been decided on constructive trust principles. That cannot be right.[312]

Unjust enrichment

It has been argued that *Stack v. Dowden* is moving the law forward by using the constructive trust as a form of proprietary relief for unjust enrichment.[313] It is difficult, however, to see the force of this, because the nature of the unjust enrichment seems simply to be that she contributed more to the acquisition of the house than he did, and for them to share the beneficial ownership equally would amount to his unjust enrichment at her expense.[314] This is, in essence, what the resulting trust is designed to avoid. Consequently, despite protestations to the contrary, it is difficult to see *Stack v. Dowden* as being more than 'an "updated" resulting trust which takes account of all significant contributions to the family home, whether direct or indirect, in cash or in kind'.[315] The insistence on stressing the role of the constructive trust may be because of the perception that a resulting trust arises when the property is acquired, and that conduct subsequent to that is not relevant. Whether this is the case, unfortunately, neither *Stack v. Dowden* nor *Jones v. Kernott* do much to clarify the conceptual basis underlying this area of law, as the plethora of cases since *Kernott* was handed down demonstrates. Nor do they give much guidance as to when the presumption of joint ownership is to be rebutted, or how shares in the property are to be quantified when it is.

8.8.3 **The nature of reliance**

It is quite clear that a mere statement by one party to another that the ownership in the house is to be shared is, on its own, insufficient to generate an equitable interest in the property. It must be relied upon. The question which then arises concerns the nature of the reliance necessary for a constructive trust to be imposed.

The theoretical root of the imposition of the constructive trust in situations of this type is the decision in *Rochefoucauld v. Boustead*,[316] where an oral agreement to hold property on trust was denied despite the purchase price reflecting this oral agreement. A constructive trust was imposed to give effect to that agreement. The underlying basis of the doctrine would appear to be that the trust is imposed to prevent unjust enrichment; were a trust not to be imposed, the purchaser would have retained the whole beneficial interest in the property, having paid less than its worth because of the agreement to hold the property on trust. One would anticipate, therefore, that the nature of the reliance for a trust to arise would be of a type which is contributory in nature, that is that the claimant has contributed to the acquisition of the property, so that, if the legal owner were allowed to deny the oral agreement to share the beneficial ownership, he would be enriched at the claimant's expense. The courts, in the current context, appear to view reliance more broadly than this.

In *Grant v. Edwards*, the reliance by the claimant on what had been said to her was in the nature of indirect contributions to the mortgage and, had there not been this prior statement, it is not clear that she would have succeeded under a resulting trust,[317] although as it

---

[310] See *Singh v. Singh* [2014] EWHC 1060 (Ch) at [117], in which Blackburne J. assumed that the principles in *Stack v. Dowden* and *Jones v. Kernott* did apply to the 'family-controlled business empire'.

[311] *Sandhu v. Sandhu* [2016] EWCA Civ. 1050 is one example.

[312] See 8.4.4.   [313] T. Etherton [2008] C.L.J. 266.   [314] Ibid. at 280–1.

[315] N. Piska (2008) 71 M.L.R. 120 at 129.

[316] [1897] 1 Ch. 196. See also *Bannister v. Bannister* [1948] 2 All E.R. 133.

[317] [1996] Ch. 638 at 650 *per* Nourse L.J.

had been found that the defendant would almost certainly not have been able to meet the mortgage payments without the plaintiff's indirect financial contributions, it is probable that she would.[318] Nevertheless, the nature of the necessary reliance was not confined to contributions to the acquisition of the house but was put more widely, as being 'conduct on which the woman could not reasonably have been expected to embark unless she was to have an interest in the house'.[319]

It has been asked whether detrimental reliance is still a requirement given that it was not mentioned by the Supreme Court in *Jones v. Kernott*, and the resounding answer must be yes. In *Curran v. Collins*,[320] counsel for the appellant argued that 'the need for detrimental reliance had been abolished by *Stack v Dowden* and *Jones v Kernott*'. Lewison L.J. commented that counsel had 'rightly abandoned that argument in the course of her oral address', and the appellant's failure to act to her detriment in reliance was 'fatal' to her claim.[321]

8.8.3.1 Relationship with estoppel

The focus on the expectation of having an interest in the home, rather than concentrating on the need to contribute to its acquisition has led to parallels being drawn between the operation of the constructive trusts in this area and the operation of proprietary estoppel.[322] Owing, perhaps, to the attempt to assimilate the role of the constructive trust with that of proprietary estoppel in the context of agreements relating to the sale of land which do not satisfy the formal requirements imposed by s. 2 of the Law of Property (Miscellaneous Provisions) Act 1989,[323] these parallels have been stressed. Thus, in *Oxley v. Hiscock*,[324] Chadwick L.J. said that: 'I think that the time has come to accept that there is no difference, in cases of this nature, whether the true analysis lies in constructive trust or in proprietary estoppel.' Equally explicit, however, and to directly opposite effect, in *Hyett v. Stanley*,[325] Sir Martin Nourse said that: 'Although it has been suggested more than once . . . that the principles underlying the law of proprietary estoppel might provide useful guidance both in regard to the conduct necessary to constitute an acting upon the common intention of the claimant and in regard to the quantification of his or her beneficial interest in the property, the two doctrines have not been assimilated.' Some attempt to clarify this issue, therefore, seems to be appropriate.

Proprietary estoppel, which will be considered in detail in Chapter 14, is a flexible doctrine, whereby rights can be acquired in another person's land. The essence of the doctrine is that one person relies upon an expectation that he either has, or will, acquire rights in that other person's land in circumstances when it is unconscionable to deny some effect to that expectation. The claimant who has acted upon this expectation acquires rights in equity, and it is for the court to determine what is the appropriate remedy to satisfy the equity which has arisen.

8.8.3.2 Differences between the concepts

From this outline of proprietary estoppel, it is evident that there are close similarities between it and the constructive trust. It is not the case, however, that the two doctrines

---

[318] [1996] Ch. 638 at 649.   [319] Ibid. at 648 *per* Nourse L.J.
[320] [2015] EWCA Civ. 404 at [78].   [321] Ibid.
[322] Ibid. at 656–7 *per* Sir Nicolas Browne-Wilkinson V.-C. See also *Lloyds Bank plc v. Rosset* [1991] 1 A.C. 107 at 132–3 *per* Lord Bridge.
[323] See *Yaxley v. Gotts* [2000] 1 All E.R. 711 at 721 *per* Robert Walker L.J. For criticism of this, see Chapter 14.
[324] [2005] Fam. 211 at 247. See also *Van Laetham v. Brooker* [2005] EWHC 1478 (Ch) at para. 77 *per* Lawrence Collins J.
[325] [2004] 1 F.L.R. 394 at 404.

are identical.[326] The basis of the constructive trust is that there is an agreement that the beneficial ownership of the house will be shared, or at least a statement from which it can reasonably be inferred that this is what was intended. Estoppel is wider than this. It can be relevant in situations when there has been no statement at all, but where both parties are mistaken as to what the true legal position is.[327] More importantly, in constructive trust cases, the agreement is to share the ownership of property; in estoppel cases, the expectation can be that, at some time in the future, property will be transferred to the claimant.[328] It may also occur that, in an estoppel case, there is no expectation of gaining a share in the property at all; rather the expectation may be limited to a right of secure accommodation.[329]

Just as the nature of the expectation can be different in cases of constructive trust and estoppel, what can amount to reliance may also differ. Although in recent times the requirements of reliance in the case of a constructive trust have been relaxed, there do not appear to be any examples of a constructive trust being imposed when the reliance has not been in some way related to the acquisition of the house.[330] In estoppel cases, on the other hand, reliance can take many different forms, and can include the giving up of career prospects in reliance on the expectation of obtaining property in the future.[331]

A further, important, distinction exists between cases of constructive trust and proprietary estoppel. In cases of constructive trust, there is an agreement between the parties as to the beneficial ownership of the house. Provided that there has been sufficient reliance, then the role of the court is to enforce that agreement.[332] This may well result in a beneficial share in the property being obtained which is considerably larger than the size of the contribution to its purchase.[333] In estoppel cases, on the other hand, once an equity has arisen, the court has a considerable discretion as to how that equity should be satisfied. The court will have regard to both the nature of the expectation and the extent of the detrimental reliance and, in determining the appropriate remedy, will be concerned that there is proportionality between the expectation and the reliance.[334] In an estoppel case, therefore, the claimant may well end up with some award which is less than the full satisfaction of the expectation.[335] In *Aspden v. Elvy*,[336] considered above, Mr Aspden made an alternative argument that he had an interest in the house through proprietary estoppel. The court did not give it their full attention because 25 per cent was found through a constructive trust, but Judge Behrens thought the result would, in any event, be the same in a claim based on proprietary estoppel.[337]

---

[326] See P. Ferguson (1993) 109 L.Q.R. 114 arguing persuasively against an attempt to treat the two doctrines as being coterminous: see D. Hayton [1990] Conv. 370. For support for the former view, see also S. Gardner (2004) 120 L.Q.R. 541 at 546.

[327] See, e.g., *E.R. Ives Investment Ltd v. High* [1967] 2 Q.B. 379; *Taylors Fashions Ltd v. Liverpool Victoria Trustees Ltd* [1982] 1 Q.B. 133n.

[328] See, e.g., *Gillett v. Holt* [2000] 2 All E.R. 289; *Ottey v. Grundy* [2003] EWCA Civ. 1176.

[329] See *Maharaj v. Chand* [1986] A.C. 898; *H. v. M. (Property Occupied by H's Parents)* [2004] 2 F.L.R. 16.

[330] See *Van Laetham v. Brooker* [2005] EWHC 1478 (Ch) at para. 71 *per* Lawrence Collins J.

[331] See *Gillet v. Holt* [2000] 2 All E.R. 289; *Ottey v. Grundy* [2003] EWCA Civ. 1176. Cf. *Lissimore v. Downing* [2003] 2 F.L.R. 308.

[332] See *Gissing v. Gissing* [1971] A.C. 886 at 905 *per* Lord Diplock; *Grant v. Edwards* [1986] Ch. 638 at 657 *per* Sir Nicolas Browne-Wilkinson V.-C.; *Hyett v. Stanley* [2004] 1 F.L.R. 394 at 404 *per* Sir Martin Nourse.

[333] See *Re Densham* [1975] 1 W.L.R. 1519; *Wright v. Johnson* [2002] 1 P. & C.R. 15 at para. 17 *per* Sir Martin Nourse.

[334] *Jennings v. Rice* [2003] 1 P. & C.R. 8 at para. 36 *per* Aldous L.J.

[335] See, in particular, the comments in *Q v. Q* [2008] EWHC 1874 (Fam.) at [113] *per* Black J; *Arif v. Anwar* [2015] EWHC 124 (Fam).

[336] [2012] EWHC 1387 (Ch).   [337] Ibid. at [129].

8.9 Reform

It has long been accepted that this area of the law is unsatisfactory. In 1995, the Law Commission published its Sixth Programme of Law Reform, and identified the law relating to home-sharers as one of the areas in which it wanted to work, being of the view that, 'The present rules are uncertain, difficult to apply and can lead to serious injustice.'[338] Seven years on, however, perhaps as a consequence of being unable to devise a scheme which could apply to all types of home-sharers, it had changed its mind. It had, apparently, 'become clear that the current law offers a degree of flexibility which is positively desirable in that it can respond with sophistication to different factual circumstances and to different personal relationships.'[339] Matters were not allowed to rest there, however, and the government referred back to the Commission the narrower issue of the position of cohabitants who are in a non-marital, intimate relationship, and a Report has now been published which advocates legislative reform.[340]

The types of person to whom the proposed legislation would be relevant would be persons who are living together in a joint household and are neither married to each other nor civil partners.[341] No attempt to define this concept was made, the Commission being content to adopt the 'six signposts' currently used in social security law to identify such couples.[342] Thereafter, there would also be eligibility criteria to satisfy before there would be jurisdiction to make a property order. Before a cohabitant could apply for financial relief under the proposed legislation, the couple must either have had children,[343] or, to avoid frivolous applications, the couple must have cohabited for a specified period of time. The time factor was left for Parliament to decide, the suggested range being between two and five years.[344]

The meeting of the eligibility criteria would not, of itself, enable a cohabitant to apply for financial relief. The notion of simply applying the jurisdiction to reallocate property on a divorce or dissolution of a civil partnership to non-married couples was rejected.[345] Instead, the claimant would need to prove that the respondent had a retained benefit from the cohabitation or that she had suffered an economic disadvantage.[346] The former would include non-financial contributions, such as the care of children, and the latter would encompass factors such as loss of earnings, something that is a likely consequence of giving up employment to look after children, but could also include the giving up of secure accommodation to move in with the respondent. Should these criteria be satisfied, it is then proposed that the courts would have jurisdiction to make a range of property orders, including lump sum payments, property transfers, and pension sharing, subject to the guidelines as to the exercise of its discretion.[347]

These proposals which, if implemented, are intended to replace the current legal regime of implied trust, estoppel, and contract,[348] are, no doubt, contentious. Some would see such reforms as dealing 'with the problems of past generations and not the position of the modern woman.'[349] Others might object on the basis that, if a couple choose not to marry or enter into a civil partnership, they should not have law imposed upon them, although it has been said, with much force, by one of the framers of these proposals that, 'pushed

---

[338] (1995) Law Com. No. 234, para. 34.   [339] (2002) Law Com. No. 278, para. 1.3.
[340] (2007) Law Com. No. 307. See D. Hughes, M. Davis, and L. Jacklin [2008] Conv. 197. For examples of Commonwealth legislation dealing with this issue, see, e.g., De Facto Relations Act 1964 (New South Wales), Property Law (Amendment) Act 1987 (Victoria).
[341] Law Com. No. 307 at 3.14.   [342] Ibid. at 3.19.
[343] The existing jurisdiction to make orders under Sched. 1 to the Children Act 1989 was not considered to be adequate to meet the needs of the situation: ibid. at 2.66–2.74.
[344] Ibid. at 3.63.   [345] Ibid. at 4.5–4.10.   [346] Ibid. at 4.33.   [347] Ibid. at 4.34–4.105.
[348] Ibid. at 4.42.   [349] R. Probert (2001) 13 C.L.F.Q. 275 at 286.

too far, the autonomy argument may leave the vulnerable facing unjustified hardship on separation'.[350] Pending any legislative reform, however, one way forward is for the courts to develop the scope of estoppel in the resolution of disputes of this nature.[351] For such arguments to succeed, the courts will need to proceed on the basis of reasonable expectations with regard to security of accommodation,[352] which have been relied upon. In terms of what constitutes reliance, the focus should include a consideration of what the claimant has given up, in terms of career opportunities and secure accommodation, prior to the commencement of the cohabitation:[353] a criterion similar to that proposed by the Law Commission of economic disadvantage. This, it is suggested, is a better avenue to explore than the law of trusts, with its necessary focus on financial contributions to the purchase of the house, particularly as there appears to be little prospect of the Law Commission's proposals being implemented within the foreseeable future.

[350] S. Bridge [2007] Fam. Law 911 at 912.

[351] See M.P. Thompson in Jackson and Wilde (eds), *Contemporary Issues in Property Law* (Aldershot, Ashgate, 1999), 135–7. See 14.3.8.

[352] See C. Rotherham [2004] Conv. 268 at 284.

[353] See the observations in *Grant v. Edwards* [1986] Ch. 638 at 648 *per* Nourse L.J.; at 657 *per* Sir Nicolas Browne-Wilkinson V.-C.

9

The Legal Framework of Co-ownership

Whenever land is the subject of co-ownership, a trust is imposed.[1] The previous chapter identified the circumstances in which co-ownership of land exists, or will be presumed to exist. But, just as relationships between people change throughout their lives, it is in the nature of things that the co-ownership of land may also evolve and the law must provide an answer as to what will happen when, for example, a co-owner wishes to sell his or her share in the land, or when a co-owner dies. The legal framework upon which co-ownership of land rests means that, because it takes place behind a trust, the rights and duties of co owners are governed by the rules at law and in equity.[2]

There are, for all practical purposes in modern land law, two forms of co-ownership: the joint tenancy, and the tenancy in common.

9.1 Joint tenancies

The essential nature of the joint tenancy is that the co-owners are, as a group, regarded as a single entity. Collectively, they own the entire interest in the property but, individually, they own nothing.[3] The significance of this is seen when one joint tenant dies. Because the deceased did not, prior to his death, own a specific share in the land, he has nothing to leave either by will, or upon intestacy. The consequence of this is the *ius accrescendi*: the right of survivorship.

9.1.1 The right of survivorship

The right of survivorship is the most significant feature of the joint tenancy. If A, B, and C are joint tenants, and A dies, the effect of the doctrine of survivorship is that the ownership of the land devolves automatically upon B and C. A simply drops out of the picture. In this situation, the surviving joint tenant is not regarded as having acquired an enhanced share in the property by succession; it is an automatic process.[4] It is quite immaterial that A has purported to leave what he might perceive to be his share in the property to another person, D. A did not have a share in the property and, therefore, had nothing on which the will could operate. If B then dies, the same process of survivorship will take place and C

---

[1] Originally this was a trust for sale, but it is now simply a trust of land.

[2] For a valuable discussion, see L. Tee in Tee (ed.), *Land Law Issues, Debates, Policy* (Willan Publishing, 2002), Chapter 5.

[3] It has recently been said that 'this esoteric concept is remote from the realities of life. It should be handled with care and treated with caution': *Burton v. Camden Borough Council* [2000] 1 All E.R. 943 at 947 *per* Lord Nicholls.

[4] See *Solihull Metropolitan District Council v. Hickin* [2012] UKSC 39.

will remain as the sole owner of the land. It is because of this process of survivorship that it has been said of each joint tenant that they 'each hold nothing and yet holds the whole'.[5] The last survivor will hold the land absolutely, for his own benefit; the joint tenants who pre-deceased him will have left nothing to their heirs.

The right of survivorship can, as was recognized in *Solihull Metropolitan Borough Council v. Hickin,*[6] give rise to anomalous results in the context of succession to secure tenancies under the Housing Act 1985,[7] although it was also recognized that to hold that the Act had changed the substantive law relating to joint tenants could cause quite different anomalies: a position which militates against arguments that significant changes should be made to the substantive law in individual cases where there is a perceived incompatibility with the Human Rights Act 1998.

9.1.1.1 Contemporaneous deaths

Because of the right of survivorship, it is important to know which of the joint tenants died first. When they die together, for example in a car accident, that may well be impossible to determine as a matter of fact. At common law, this difficulty was resolved by holding that the property remained in joint tenancy in their respective heirs.[8] The matter is now regulated by statute, s. 184 of the Law of Property Act (LPA) 1925 providing that in these circumstances, the older is deemed to have died first, so that the property will devolve with the younger's estate.[9]

9.1.2 The four unities

Joint tenants are viewed by the law as being, collectively, one entity. For such a relationship to be created, it is necessary that what are known as the four unities are present. If the any of these unities are missing a tenancy in common will arise.[10] The four unities are the unities of possession, interest, title, and time.

9.1.2.1 Possession

A feature common to co-ownership is that the co-owners, being simultaneously entitled to the land, each has the right to possess it. It can happen, however, that one joint tenant forcibly excludes the other from the property. In such circumstances, the tenant in occupation can be ordered to pay an occupation rent to the one who has been excluded from the property.[11]

9.1.2.2 Interest

As it is the nature of a joint tenancy that none of the joint tenants have specific interests in the property, it follows that one cannot have a larger interest than the other. Thus, if one co-owner has a life interest and the other an entailed interest, they cannot be joint tenants.[12] If there is an element of succession involved, however, then the co-owners can be joint tenants. So, if property is left to A and B for life, remainder to B, then A and B can be joint tenants of the life interest, despite the fact that B also has a fee simple in remainder.[13]

---

[5] *Murray v. Hall* (1840) 7 C.B. 441 at 455.   [6] [2012] UKSC 39.

[7] For a more general discussion of some of these issues, see S. Goulding [2016] Conv. 90.

[8] *Bradshaw v. Tolmin* (1784) Dick. 633.

[9] This rule does not apply in the case of a husband and wife who die intestate: Administration of Estates Act 1925, s. 46(3) as inserted into the Act by Intestates' Estates Act 1952, s. 1(4).

[10] Though, as noted in 9.2, the unity of possession is also required under a tenancy in common.

[11] See *Dennis v. McDonald* [1982] Fam. 63; *Re Pavlou* [1993] 1 W.L.R. 1046.

[12] See Harpum, Bridge, and Dixon, *Megarry and Wade's Law of Real Property* (8th edn) (London, Sweet & Maxwell, 2012), 13–008.

[13] *Wiscot's Case* (1599) 2 Co. Rep. 60b.

As the joint tenants hold the title together, they must act together with respect to trans-actions affecting the legal title. This creates some difficulties with regard to leasehold prop-erty.[14] If there is a break clause in the lease, whereby the tenants can bring the lease to a premature end, then, to be effective, the clause must be exercised by all the joint tenants.[15] Similarly, a purported surrender of the lease by only one of two joint tenants is ineffec-tive.[16] The situation where a notice to quit is exercised may appear, at first sight, to be at odds with this principle, but is in fact consistent with it.

Notices to quit

In *Doe d. Aslin v. Summersett*,[17] one joint landlord served a notice to quit on a periodic tenant and this was held to be effective to terminate the lease, despite the other joint land-lord not being a party to the notice. The reason for this is that, where there is a periodic tenancy,[18] each successive period operates as a renewal of the lease. For this to happen, each of the joint landlords must agree and, if one of them serves a notice to quit, this indi-cates that he does not do so.

The same reasoning has been applied in the case of the service of a notice to quit by one joint tenant. If one joint tenant serves a notice to quit on the landlord, then this is effec-tive to end the tenancy despite the other joint tenants being opposed to this being done.[19] Such a course of action was taken in *Harrow London Borough Council v. Johnstone*.[20] Mr and Mrs Johnstone were joint tenants of a council house. He had obtained an injunction restraining her from using or threatening violence against him or to exclude or attempt to exclude him from the house. She then served a notice to quit on the council, who brought possession proceedings against him. The claim to possession succeeded in the House of Lords. The role of the injunction was to protect the husband's rights under the existing tenancy; it did not relate to its continued existence.

This result seems inevitable but can, nevertheless, cause hardship to the tenant who wishes to remain. Although it has been suggested that the tenant whose right to remain in occupation has been defeated in this way might have some remedy against the other joint tenant,[21] this view was rejected by the Court of Appeal in *Notting Hill Housing Trust v. Brackley*.[22] Any such remedy might, in any event, be of little consolation for the tenant and one suggestion which has been made to deal with this issue is for legislation to be enacted allowing the occupying tenant to take over the tenancy in a situation such as this.[23] Failing that, in cases of matrimonial disharmony, which is where this problem tends to occur, an undertaking can be sought from the spouse who might by a unilateral action terminate the tenancy not to do so. That undertaking can be served on the landlord, or, if such an under-taking cannot be obtained, application can be made for an injunction to this effect.[24] Once

---

[14] See J. Martin [1978] Conv. 436.

[15] *Re Viola's Indenture of Lease* [1909] 1 Ch. 244. See also *Meyer v. Riddick* (1989) 60 P. & C.R. 50.

[16] *Leek and Moreland Building Society v. Clark* [1952] Q.B. 788. If the lease contains an option to renew, this option must also be exercised by all the joint tenants: ibid. at 793 *per* Somervell L.J.

[17] (1830) 1 B. & Ad. 135; *Parsons v. Parsons* [1983] 1 W.L.R. 1390.

[18] See 10.4.2.

[19] *Hammersmith and Fulham London Borough Council v. Monk* [1992] 1 A.C. 478; *Greenwich London Borough Council v. McGrady* (1983) 46 P. & C.R. 223. The doubt as to this expressed in *Howson v. Buxton* (1928) 97 L.J.K.B. 749 at 752 *per* Scrutton L.J. is unfounded, although supported by F. Webb [1983] Conv. 183.

[20] [1997] 1 W.L.R. 459. See M.P. Thompson [1997] Conv. 288.

[21] See *Parsons v. Parsons* [1983] 1 W.L.R. 1390 at 1400 *per* Mr Donald Rattee Q.C., but see the strong doubts expressed as to this in *Hammersmith and London Borough Council v. Monk* [1992] 1 A.C. 478, *per* Lord Browne-Wilkinson.

[22] [2002] H.L.R. 276.   [23] L. Tee [1992] C.L.J. 218 at 220.

[24] *Bater v. Bater, Greenwich London Borough Council v. Bater* [1999] 4 All E.R. 944 at 952–3 *per* Thorpe L.J.

the joint tenancy has been determined by the unilateral act of one party, however, this is not a disposition which a court can later set aside under s. 37(2) of the Matrimonial Causes Act 1973,[25] so any injunctive relief must be sought before the notice to quit is served, because 'the stable door can be bolted if, but only if, the bolt is thrown before the horse has gone'.[26]

Human rights

The cases where one joint tenant has terminated a tenancy by the unilateral service of a notice to quit have involved public sector housing.[27] The sub-text in these cases is that the property is a family home. On the breakdown of a relationship, a situation which commonly has arisen is that the mother vacates the property, taking any children with her, leaving the father remaining alone in accommodation which is suitable for occupation by a family. The local authority is prepared to provide accommodation for the mother and children, but also wishes to recover possession of the tenanted property from the individual occupier, who is now occupying a property which is too large for his needs.[28] The departing tenant is then sometimes advised by the council to serve a notice to quit, the effect of this being to end the tenancy and results, as a matter of property law, in the council having an absolute right to possession.

The scenario featured in a number of the cases which dealt with the question as to whether, if a public authority had an absolute right to possession, the occupier could, nevertheless present an argument that her Art 8 rights had been infringed: to argue that the making of a possession order was disproportionate. That debate has now been settled by the Supreme Court decision in *Manchester City Council v. Pinnock*,[29] where it was decided that such a defence was available. It has been argued, however, that the substantive law which allows one joint tenant to terminate a periodic tenancy without the other's consent is, itself, in breach of Art. 8. The essence of this argument is that this principle is not compliant in that 'it enables a person's interest in his or her home to be brought to an end without his or her knowledge and without recourse to an independent adjudicatory tribunal to seek due process of law'.[30] This, it is suggested, goes much too far.

In the first place, such a finding would apply not only to the public sector. The substantive law does not alter depending upon the identity of the parties to litigation,[31] and so a finding that one joint periodic tenant in the public sector could not effectively end the tenancy by the service of a notice to quit would apply equally to tenants in the private sector. This, as was pointed out in *London Borough of Wandsworth v. Dixon*,[32] would have various repercussions. A change of this nature would mean that the departing tenant would continue to be jointly and severally liable for the rent, despite no longer wishing to live in the property. Alternatively, the remaining tenant would be liable for the whole rent, which would mean the substitution of a joint periodic tenancy for a sole tenancy in favour of the remaining tenant. There is nothing to suggest that the European Convention would justify the re-writing of legal agreements in this way, and the recent Supreme Court judgment in

---

[25] *Newlon Housing Trust v. Alsulaimen* [1999] 1 A.C. 313. An objection that this provision was incompatible with Art. 8 of the Convention was rejected in *Muema v. Muema* [2013] EWHC 3864 (Fam).

[26] *Bater v. Bater* [1999] 4 All E.R. 944 at 953 *per* Thorpe L.J.

[27] For a general discussion of this area, see M. Davis and D. Hughes [2004] Conv. 19.

[28] This was not actually so in the leading case of *Harrow London Borough Council v. Qazi* [2004] 1 A.C. 983, where another woman and her children had moved into the original property.

[29] [2010] UKSC 45. For a full discussion of this debate, see Chapter 3.

[30] M. Davis and D. Hughes [2010] Conv. 57 at 72. See also I. Loveland (2011) 2 E.H.L.R. 151 at 158.

[31] See M.P. Thompson [2011] Conv. 421 at 436–9.

[32] [2009] EWHC 27 (Admin) at [35]–[36] *per* H.H.J. Bidder.

Sims v. Dacorum Borough Council[33] confirms that the common law rule that a periodic tenancy is brought to an end by the unilateral act of the service of a notice to quit does not infringe Art. 8.

9.1.2.3 Title

It follows rationally from the theoretical basis of the joint tenancy of no one joint tenant having an individual interest to call his own that they all acquired their collective interest in the same way; they must derive their title from the same act or document. This will include a conveyance, an assent, or a joint act of adverse possession.[34]

9.1.2.4 Time

Again, it follows from the nature of a joint tenancy that every joint tenant should acquire their interest in the property simultaneously. In other words, their interests should vest at the same time.

9.2 Tenancies in common

The tenancy in common differs crucially from the joint tenancy. Each tenant in common owns a separate share in the property. That share is not physically demarcated and that is why a tenancy in common is often referred to as an undivided share in the property. It is perfectly possible and, indeed, not unusual, for these shares to be of different proportions. If A and B hold land as tenants in common, it may be the case that A has a one-quarter share and B a three-quarter share. Because each tenant in common holds an undivided share in the property, there is no right of survivorship. On the death of one tenant in common, his share does not devolve automatically on the surviving tenants in common. Instead, it will pass either under the deceased's will or upon his intestacy.

Each tenant in common is described as having an undivided share in the property. Unless it is physically partitioned, each tenant in common has the right to occupy the property; one tenant in common does not have the right to exclude the others. The unity of possession is, therefore, the only unity necessary for a tenancy in common.

9.3 Co-ownership after 1925

From a conveyancing point of view, there is no doubt that the joint tenancy is far more convenient than the tenancy in common. The reason for this is that the existence of a tenancy in common can lead to the fragmentation of ownership and the proliferation of the number of people interested in the land. If, for example, A and B held land as tenants in common and A died leaving his share to C and D and then C died leaving his share to E and F then, to deal with the legal title, B, D, E, and F would all have to be parties to the conveyance. This would be the case although E and F held only one-eighth shares in the property.[35] Had A and B been joint tenants then, on A's death, B would have been left as the sole owner of the property.

While, from a conveyancing point of view, there are distinct advantages to the property being held on a joint tenancy, from the point of view of the joint tenants themselves, the

[33] [2014] UKSC 63. For a discussion of the case, see 3.7.24.
[34] *Ward v. Ward* (1871) 9 Ch. App. 789.
[35] See *Higgs v. Leshel Maryas Investment Co. Ltd* [2009] UKPC 47 at [10], where it was found that one legal co-owner of land in the Bahamas, where this legislation does not apply, held a 1/84th share in the property.

doctrine of survivorship may produce results which are unfair or inopportune. Who survives the longest is a matter of chance. If A and B are joint tenants, A may not want on his death for his 'share' of the property to go to B, his preference being to leave it to his own family. One is left with the position that convenience favours the joint tenancy and fairness the tenancy in common. The 1925 legislation sought to accommodate both aspirations and, in doing so, made it absolutely essential to distinguish between the position at law and in equity.

9.3.1 Legal joint tenancies

In what has been described as 'the greatest boon that the . . . statutes could confer',[36] the 1925 legislation abolished the legal tenancy in common. It is provided by s. 1(6), LPA 1925 that, 'A legal estate is not capable of subsisting or of being created in an undivided share'. In addition to this reform, it was further provided that the maximum number of legal owners of land is four. If land is conveyed to more than four people, then the conveyance will operate to vest the land in the first four people named.[37] The effect of these provisions is that when land is conveyed to more than one person, they must hold the legal title as joint tenants. A legal tenancy in common is not possible.

9.3.2 Imposition of a trust

When land is subject to co-ownership then, at law, the co-owners must hold as joint tenants. In equity, however, the co-owners can be either joint tenants or tenants in common. The scheme of the legislation was in all cases of legal co-ownership to impose a trust on the land, so that if land was conveyed to A and B, they would, at law, be joint tenants. They would then hold the land on trust, the beneficiaries being either themselves or others.

Until the enactment of the Trusts of Land and Appointment of Trustees Act (TOLATA) 1996, provision was made for the imposition of a trust for sale in certain cases of co-ownership. The position is now that, in those situations, a trust of land will be implied. The position where there is co-ownership of the legal estate is dealt with separately.[38]

9.3.2.1 Conveyance to tenants in common

If land is conveyed to tenants in common, the position is governed by s. 34(2), LPA 1925, which provides for the legal estate to be held by the persons named in the conveyance as joint tenants in trust for the persons interested in the land. If land is conveyed to A and B as tenants in common, the effect of this is that A and B hold the legal estate as joint tenants subject to a trust of land for themselves as tenants in common. This may be represented as shown in Figure 9.1.

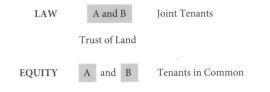

Fig. **9.1** Conveyance to tenants in common

[36] A.H. Cosway (1929) 15 Conv. (O.S.) 82.
[37] Trustee Act 1925, s. 34(2). For suggested reform of this in the case of residential tena
[38] Where there is sole ownership at law and co-ownership in equity, see Chapter 7.

9.3.2.2 Devise to tenants in common

Where land is left by will to A and B as tenants in common, again the land is held upon trust but there is a difference in the identity of the trustees. In this case, the land vests in the testator's personal representatives, X and Y, who hold the land as trustees.[39] The position is as shown in Figure 9.2.

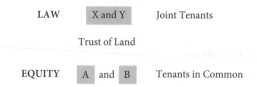

Fig. 9.2 Devise to tenants in common

9.3.2.3 Conveyance to joint tenants

If property is conveyed to A and B as joint tenants, the land is, again, made subject to a trust of land but the manner in which this is done is somewhat tortuous. By s. 36(1) of the Act the effect of the conveyance is to vest the legal estate in A and B on trust in like manner as if the land had been conveyed to them as tenants in common but not so as to sever their joint tenancy in equity, that is to change the position in equity from a joint tenancy into a tenancy in common. The outcome of this convoluted section is as shown in Figure 9.3. This position looks curious because the position at law and in equity is identical. What is the purpose of a trust of land in a situation such as this? The main answer to this is that, although at the outset the position at law and in equity is identical, this may not remain the case. The equitable joint tenancy may, in the future, be converted into a tenancy in common. A purchaser, however, neither knows of this nor needs to know of it. Provided that he pays the purchase money to two trustees, he will overreach the beneficial interests existing behind the trust[40] and so, as far as he is concerned, it does not matter if there has been fragmentation of ownership in equity. The task of dividing the proceeds of sale between the beneficiaries is the task of the trustees; provided that the money is paid to the trustees, the beneficial interests which exist behind the trust are of no concern to the purchaser.

	LAW	A and B	Joint Tenants
		Trust of Land	
EQUITY		A and B	Joint Tenants

Fig. 9.3 Conveyance to joint tenants

9.4 Severance

As has been seen, the framework of co-ownership is that the legal title is held by joint tenants who hold the land on trust. In equity, the beneficiaries can be either joint tenants or tenants in common. This section is concerned with how one determines which form of tenancy has been created from the outset and then how one converts an equitable joint tenancy into a tenancy in common.

PA 1925, s. 34(3).   [40] *City of London Building Society v. Flegg* [1988] A.C. 54. See 7.5.5.

9.4.1 **Words of severance**

The simplest method of establishing beyond doubt whether the initial holding is as a joint tenancy or a tenancy in common is for there to be an express declaration to that effect. If, at the outset, it is stated that the co-owners are to hold as tenants in common, then this will avoid disputes on the death of one of them as to whether the doctrine of survivorship applies. If the property is being sold by the surviving legal joint tenant, then a purchaser will be alerted that co-ownership may continue to subsist in equity and that it is necessary to appoint an additional trustee.[41]

While it is desirable, if it is intended to create a tenancy in common, to make this clear beyond argument by using these words, it is not essential to do so. Other expressions, these being termed words of severance, contained in a conveyance or a will have been held to have this effect. The following are examples of words sufficient to display an intention to create a tenancy in common:

> 'in equal shares';[42]
> 'share and share alike';[43]
> 'equally';[44]
> 'to be divided between'.[45]

These are examples of particular expressions which have been construed as giving rise to a tenancy in common. There is no particular magic in these words. Even if an expression such as one of those given above is used, a tenancy in common will not necessarily arise if it is evident from the rest of the document that this is not what was intended,[46] although the presumption in favour of a tenancy in common will be very strong.

The converse is also true; it is not essential to use words that have previously been held to have effected the creation of a tenancy in common in order to achieve this result. The task is to determine from the words of the document whether the general intention is to create a tenancy in common. In construing the documents, there is a judicial tendency to favour the finding of a tenancy in common,[47] so that if, for example, a will envisages only limited rights of survivorship between the co-owners,[48] or in the slightest degree indicates an intention that the co-owners should have shares in the property,[49] a tenancy in common will be created. Examples of this are where trustees are given power to apply income derived from the property for the maintenance of the beneficiaries,[50] or to advance capital to them,[51] in each case this being indicative that the beneficiaries have individual shares behind the trust.

9.4.1.1 **Contradictory statements**

It can happen, by inept draftsmanship, that a conveyance or will uses mutually contradictory expressions, such as to A and B as joint tenants in common in equal shares.[52] The traditional means of construction in cases like this was to apply the rule in *Slingsby's*

---

[41] See 9.6.5.   [42] *Payne v. Webb* (1874) L.R. 19 Eq. 26.

[43] *Heathe v. Heathe* (1740) 2 A. & R. 121.

[44] *Lewen v. Dodd* (1595) Cro. Eli. 443; see also *Re Kilvert* [1957] Ch. 388.

[45] *Fisher v. Wigg* (1700) 1 P. Wms. 14.

[46] *Frewen v. Relfe* (1787) 2 Bro. C.C. 220 at 224 *per* Lord Thurlow L.C.

[47] *Re Woolley* [1903] 2 Ch. 206 at 211 *per* Joyce J.

[48] *Ryves v. Ryves* (1871) 11 Eq. 539.

[49] *Robertshaw v. Fraser* (1871) 6 Ch. App. 696 at 699 *per* Lord Hatherley L.C. See also *Surtees v. Surtees* (1871) 12 Eq. 400.

[50] *Re Ward* [1920] 1 Ch. 334.

[51] *L'Estrange v. L'Estrange* [1902] 1 I.R. 467; *Re Dunn* [1916] 1 Ch. 97.

[52] Described as 'a meaningless jumble of words': *Martin v. Martin* (1987) 54 P. & C.R. 238 at 240 *per* Millett J.

Case,[53] whereby, in such cases, the first words would prevail in a deed but the last in a will. Although this rule of construction has been employed in modern times to resolve a dispute of this nature,[54] it seems unlikely to be taken as a reliable guide today,[55] so that in cases of ambiguity or contradictory statements,[56] it is likely that a tenancy in common will be held to have been created.[57]

9.5 Implied severance

The potential consequence of the creation of a tenancy in common is the fragmentation of ownership. This was never favoured at law; 'joint tenancies were favoured for the law loves not fractions of estates, nor to divide and multiply tenures'.[58] Equity, on the other hand, took a different view, principally because it sees the right of survivorship, or *ius accrescendi,* as being potentially unfair. Accordingly, the traditional approach of equity is, where there is any doubt, to lean in favour of a tenancy in common.[59] In particular, there are a number of situations where equity will presume that a tenancy in common has been created.

9.5.1 Commercial purchasers and unequal contributions

When two people buy land together as a commercial investment, it is highly improbable that they intend the doctrine of survivorship to operate, so that the survivor of them would end up as the absolute owner. They would wish their shares to devolve upon their own families. Equity recognizes this by presuming that they originally took the property as tenants in common. A joint tenancy is seen as being inappropriate between merchants, so that land acquired for business purposes is presumed to be held on a tenancy in common. If, however, business partners acquire land for purposes unconnected with commerce, there is no presumption that they hold that land as tenants in common.[60] For this presumption to arise, it is not necessary that there is a formal partnership in existence. In *Malayan Credit Ltd v. Jack Chia-Mph Ltd,*[61] two businessmen together took a lease of commercial property. The areas which they occupied were of different sizes and, to reflect this, they paid different amounts in rent. The Privy Council held that they held the lease on a presumed tenancy in common rather than as joint tenants.

9.5.2 Mortgages

For the same reason that business partners are presumed to take as tenants in common, there is a strong presumption that lenders of money take their mortgage security as tenants in common.[62] Although it has been said that this presumption can be

---

[53] (1587) 5 Co. Rep. 186.   [54] *Joyce v. Barker Bros (Builders) Ltd* (1980) 40 P. & C.R. 512.

[55] 'The nonsense of one man cannot be a guide for that of another': *Smith v. Coffin* (1795) 2 Hy. Bl. 444 at 450 *per* Buller J., cited in *Martin v. Martin* (1987) 54 P. & C.R. 238 at 242 *per* Millett J. See also *Slater v. Simm* [2007] EWHC 951 (Ch) at [14] *per* Peter Smith J.

[56] For an unusual case where the parties agreed on a beneficial joint tenancy while a house was unsold, but a tenancy in common thereafter, see *Chopra v. Bindra* [2009] EWCA Civ. 203.

[57] *Slater v. Simm* [2007] EWHC 951 (Ch). See also *Carr v. Isard* [2006] EWHC 2095 (Ch), where the headnote refers to the parties as being joint tenants in equal shares. In the judgment, they are referred to as beneficial joint tenants.

[58] *Fisher v. Wigg* (1700) 1 Salk 391 at 392 *per* Holt C.J. (dissenting).

[59] *Burgess v. Rawnsley* [1975] Ch. 429 at 438 *per* Lord Denning M.R.

[60] *Lake v. Craddock* (1732) 3 P. Wms. 157; *Jackson v. Dulland* (1702) 1 Ves. Jnn. 432; *Darby v. Darby* (1856) 3 Drew. 495.

[61] [1986] A.C. 549.

[62] *Petty v. Styward* (1632) 1 Ch. Rep. 57; *Vickers v. Cowell* (1839) 1 Beav. 529.

rebutted,[63] a joint account clause in the mortgage does not have this effect, it being held that the purpose of the clause was to protect the purchaser rather than to indicate an intention to create a joint tenancy.[64]

9.5.3 **Unequal contributions**

A beneficial interest in land can be acquired by a contribution to its purchase. Where an interest is acquired under a resulting trust, then it is presumed that the respective size of each party's share will be commensurate to the size of their contribution and, if they contribute unequally, they will have unequal beneficial shares in the property and, consequently, take as tenants in common. If, however, the property is bought as a shared home, and that property is put into joint names, the presumption now is 'that the parties intended a joint tenancy both in law and in equity'.[65] If the parties contribute equally to the purchase of the property, the presumption is that they take as joint tenants.[66] Prior to the Privy Council's decision in *Marr v. Collie*, it was thought that joint purchases of homes by people not in an intimate relationship would not be governed by the same strong presumption of a joint tenancy as now exists for couples following *Stack v. Dowden* and *Jones v. Kernott*. On that basis, unequal contributions would quite easily rebut the starting presumption of an equitable joint tenant under resulting trust principles, so that a tenancy in common instead was created. This logic has possibly been undermined by the decision in *Marr v. Collie*, and instead the question might be what (if any) common intention the parties may have before any presumption on the basis of unequal contributions might be relevant. *Marr v. Collie* is considered fully at 8.4.4.1.

9.5.4 **Rebutting the presumption by express statements**

In each of the above situations, it should be remembered that there is only a presumption that there is a beneficial tenancy in common and, like all presumptions, it is capable of being rebutted. The most straightforward way of rebutting this presumption is if there is a statement in the conveyance or the will that a joint tenancy is intended.[67] So, in *Barton v. Morris*,[68] a cohabiting couple bought a cottage in their joint names, the purpose being to use it for commercial purposes as a guest house. As the conveyance declared that they held the property as joint tenants, the normal presumption of a tenancy in common was displaced. Similarly, in *Goodman v. Gallant*,[69] a couple had contributed unequally to the purchase price of a house but, because the conveyance declared that they were to hold as joint tenants, this statement was effective to rebut the presumption of a tenancy in common, which would otherwise have arisen.

In the absence of a claim to rectification,[70] a declaration by the parties that they are to hold the property as beneficial joint tenants is conclusive. A somewhat unfortunate

[63] *Steeds v. Steeds* (1889) 22 Q.B.D. 537 at 541 *per* Willes J., instancing trustees, an example which relates to severance at law, which is no longer possible.

[64] *Powell v. Broadhurst* [1901] 2 Ch. 160; *Re Jackson* (1887) 34 Ch.D. 732.

[65] *Jones v. Kernott* [2011] UKSC 53 at [25] per Lord Walker and Lady Hale. Contrast *Laskar v. Laskar* [2008] EWCA Civ. 347. See 8.4.1.

[66] *Lake v. Gibson* (1729) 1 Eq. Cas. Ab. 391; *Chandler v. Clark* [2003] 1 P. & C.R. 15.

[67] See *Morris v. Barrett* (1829) 3 Y. & J. 384. See, also, *Ward v. Ward* (1871) 9 Ch. App. 789 (joint adverse possession of a farm, held that they took as joint tenants).

[68] [1995] 1 W.L.R. 1257.

[69] [1986] Fam. 106. See also *Pink v. Lawrence* (1977) 36 P. & C.R. 98; *The Anglo Eastern Trust Ltd v. Kermanshahchi* [2003] EWHC 1939 (Ch).

[70] See *Thames Guarantee Ltd v. Campbell* [1985] Q.B. 210. For the possible impact of undue influence, see *Knott v. Day* [2004] EWHC 484 (Ch).

distinction is made, however, if the parties make a declaration that the survivor of them is able to give a valid receipt for capital moneys. Such a declaration is apt to indicate to a purchaser that the property has been conveyed to joint tenants but, as between the parties themselves, is not conclusive in this respect.[71] Where two parties are applying to be registered as joint proprietors, the current form which has to be completed to make such an application is drafted in such a way as to make the intentions of the parties clear,[72] and so this issue may not reappear.

9.6 Acts of severance

If a beneficial joint tenancy is created at the outset, it is open to the parties, subsequently, to convert that joint tenancy into a tenancy in common. This process is termed severance. The ability to sever a joint tenancy and to create a tenancy in common exists, so it is said, so that if one joint tenant has an 'ill opinion of his own life', he can sever the joint tenancy to ensure that survivorship does not work any hardship.[73]

For severance to take place, it is essential that the process occurs during the lifetime of the joint tenancy. A joint tenancy cannot be severed by will.[74] This latter point is illustrated by *Carr-Glynn v. Frearsons (A Firm)*.[75] A testatrix instructed solicitors to leave her 'share' in a house to her niece. She held the house on a beneficial joint tenancy with her nephew. On her death, it was discovered that the joint tenancy had not been severed with the result that her nephew became solely entitled to the house by survivorship. The solicitors were held liable in negligence to the niece for failing to ensure that severance had occurred prior to the testatrix's death, action which was necessary to ensure that she had a share in the house to leave.

9.6.1 Methods of severance

The process of severance is governed by s. 36(2), LPA 1925, which first provides that no severance of a joint tenancy of a legal estate so as to create a tenancy in common shall be permissible but that this subsection does not affect the right of a joint tenant to sever his equitable interest whether or not the legal estate is vested in the joint tenants. The means of severance are then detailed as follows:

> Provided that, where a legal estate (not being settled land) is vested in joint tenants beneficially, and any tenant desires to sever the joint tenancy in equity, he shall give to the other joint tenants a notice in writing of such desire or do such other acts or things as would, in the case of personal estate, have been effectual to sever the tenancy in equity, and thereupon the land shall be held in trust on terms which would have been requisite for giving effect to the beneficial interests if there had been an actual severance.

It is proposed, first, to deal with the statutory method of severance, and then with the methods of severance at common law which have been preserved by the Act.

---

[71] See *Harwood v. Harwood* [1991] 2 F.L.R. 274; *Huntingford v. Hobbs* [1993] 1 F.L.R. 376; *Stack v. Dowden* [2007] 2 A.C. 432.

[72] See 8.2.   [73] *Cray v. Willis* (1729) 2 P. Wms 529

[74] See, e.g., *Re Caines (dec'd)* [1978] 1 W.L.R. 540 at 545 *per* Sir Robert Megarry V.-C.

[75] [1999] Ch. 326.

9.6.2 **Statutory severance**

The statutory form of severance makes reference to a situation where the legal estate is 'vested in joint tenants beneficially' which, it has been argued, on a strict construction could be interpreted to mean that the legal and beneficial interests are the same. If this view is correct, it would lead to the result that, if A and B hold on trust for A, B, and C or for A, B, and Y, then the beneficial joint tenants would not be empowered to sever the joint tenancy by this method,[76] a result which would be unfortunate. It is suggested that such a conclusion can be avoided, however, when regard is had to the opening words of the subsection, which provide that 'this subsection does not affect the right of a joint tenant . . . to sever a joint tenancy in an equitable interest whether or not the legal estate is vested in the joint tenants'. So it is thought that, except for situations specifically excepted, equitable joint tenants can use this method to sever the joint tenancy by use of the statutory method, regardless of the ownership of the legal estate.[77]

9.6.2.1 **Form of notice**

To effect severance using the statutory notice, it is necessary that the notice be served upon all of the joint tenants but it is not essential that it complies with any particular form. What is required is the statement of an unequivocal intention to sever.[78] In *Re Draper's Conveyance*,[79] an affidavit in support of a divorce petition asked for the property to be sold and that the proceeds of sale be divided equally. This was held to be sufficient to effect a severance of the beneficial joint tenancy. In contrast, in *Harris v. Goddard*,[80] a married couple held their house as beneficial joint tenants. When their marriage was foundering, a divorce petition was submitted which sought relief in the terms of s. 24 of the Matrimonial Causes Act 1973 asking that such order may be made by way of transfer of property in respect of the matrimonial home as may be considered just. Shortly before the date of the hearing, the husband died and the issue was whether or not the beneficial joint tenancy had been severed prior to his death. If not, the doctrine of survivorship would operate. It was held that as the petition did not assert a present claim to a share of the property,[81] no severance had occurred, with the result that the wife became solely entitled to the property. Conversely, if a notice asserts the ownership of a half share in the property, but is content for that share to be realized by a later disposal of it, this document will suffice to effect a severance.[82]

9.6.2.2 **Husband and wife**

An additional feature of the dispute in *Harris v. Goddard* was the express acceptance of the proposition that there was no restriction on the ability of a husband and wife to sever a joint tenancy. Somewhat surprisingly, this had previously been uncertain owing to a

---

[76] Harpum, Bridge, and Dixon, *Megarry and Wade's Law of Real Property*, 13–044.

[77] Severance can also be effected using this method even if the statutory notice does not comply with a condition as to severance appearing on the conveyance: *Grindal v. Hooper* [1999] E.G.C.S. 150. See N.P. Gravells [2000] Conv. 461.

[78] For an example of an equivocal and, therefore, ineffective notice, see *Gore and Snell v. Carpenter* (1990) 60 P. & C.R. 456 at 462 *per* Judge Blackett-Ord.

[79] [1969] 1 Ch. 486. The doubts expressed as to the correctness of this decision in *Nielson-Jones v. Fedden* [1975] Ch. 222 at 236 *per* Walton J. were themselves disapproved in *Harris v. Goddard* [1983] 1 W.L.R. 1203 at 1210 *per* Lawton L.J.

[80] [1983] 1 W.L.R. 1203. See S. Coneys [1984] Conv. 148.

[81] See also *Hunter v. Babbage* [1994] 2 F.L.R. 806; *Edwards v. Hastings* [1996] N.P.C. 87; *Chandler v. Clark* [2003] 1 P. & C.R. 15.

[82] *Wallbank v. Price* [2007] EWHC 3001(Ch). See also *Quigley v. Masterson* [2011] EWHC 2529 (Ch) (Application to the Court of Protection).

dictum of Lord Denning M.R. in *Bedson v. Bedson*[83] that, if a matrimonial home is used as a dwelling, this was not possible. Although this view was described, perhaps without the usual judicial courtesy, as being 'without the slightest foundation in law or in equity',[84] it was repeated six years later.[85] This caused some difficulty, as the opposite, and orthodox, view was consistently preferred at first instance[86] and so the authoritative endorsement in *Harris v. Goddard*[87] of the proposition that there is no theoretical difficulty in either a husband or wife severing a joint tenancy is to be welcomed.[88] It is also logical, as there is no impediment to a husband and wife being beneficial tenants in common in the first place.

9.6.2.3 Service by post

A statutory notice of severance can be sent by post. If it is sent by registered or recorded delivery, it is regarded as being sufficiently served if it is addressed to the person on whom it should be served and has not been returned as undelivered to the Post Office.[89] Even if it is not sent by recorded delivery, it is regarded as being sufficiently served if the letter is delivered to the address of the recipient, or his last known place of business, this latter expression, for no obvious reason, having been held not to include a person's work address.[90] It does not matter if the letter is not received, even if the sender, upon delivery at the recipient's address manages to intercept and destroy it,[91] although, if it is intercepted prior to delivery, it would seem that there has not been an effective delivery.

9.6.3 Severance at common law

In addition to introducing a new method of severing a joint tenancy by a unilateral notice of severance, s. 36(2), LPA 1925 expressly preserved as a means of severing a joint tenancy such things as would, prior to the Act, have been sufficient to sever a joint tenancy in personal property. The classic statement of the means of effecting a severance at common law was given by Sir William Page-Wood V.-C. in *Williams v. Hensman*.[92] He said:

> A joint tenancy may be severed in three ways: in the first place, an act of any one of the persons interested operating on his own share may create a severance as to that share. The right of each joint-tenant is a right by survivorship only in the event of no severance having taken place of the share which is claimed under the *jus accrescendi*. Each one is at liberty to dispose of his own interest in such manner as to sever it from the joint fund—losing, of course at the same time, his own right of survivorship. Secondly, a joint tenancy may be severed by mutual agreement. And, in the third place, there may be a severance by any course of dealing sufficient to intimate that the interests of all were mutually treated as constituting a tenancy in common. When the severance depends upon an inference of this kind without any express act of severance, it will not suffice to rely on an intention, with respect to the particular share, declared only behind the backs of the other persons interested.

---

[83] [1965] 2 Q.B. 666 at 678. For the expression of the opposite view, see *Smith v. Smith* [1945] 1 All E.R. 584 at 586 *per* Denning J. For devastating criticism of Lord Denning's later opinion, see R.E.M. (1966) 82 L.Q.R. 29.

[84] [1965] 2 Q.B. 666 at 690 *per* Russell L.J.

[85] *Jackson v. Jackson* [1971] 1 W.L.R. 1539 at 1542 *per* Lord Denning M.R.

[86] *Radziej v. Radziej* [1968] 1 W.L.R. 1928; *Re Draper's Conveyance* [1969] 1 W.L.R. 486; *Cowcher v. Cowcher* [1972] 1 W.L.R. 425.

[87] [1983] 1 W.L.R. 1203 at 1208 *per* Lawton L.J.

[88] If there is an actual agreement not to sever the joint tenancy then, somewhat surprisingly, a notice which purports to effect a severance is ineffective: *White v. White* [2001] EWCA Civ. 955 at [38] *per* Robert Walker L.J.

[89] LPA 1925, s. 196(4); *Re 88 Berkeley Road, N.W. 9* [1971] Ch. 648.

[90] *Quigley v. Masterson* [2011] EWHC 2529 (Ch).

[91] *Kinch v. Bullard* [1999] 1 W.L.R. 423. See also *Wandsworth London Borough Council v. Attwell* [1996] 1 E.G.L.R. 57; *Blundell v. Frogmore Investments Ltd* [2002] EWCA Civ. 573.

[92] (1861) 1 J. & H. 546 at 557–8.

The three methods of severance described in *Williams v. Hensman* will be considered in turn, together with a fourth method of severance: homicide.

9.6.3.1 Operating on one's own share

The most clear-cut method of severance is to alienate one's own interest in the property.[93] Such an alienation must be during the lifetime of the joint tenant and cannot be by will.[94] Such alienation may be involuntary as on bankruptcy, the effect of which is that the joint tenancy will be severed in equity, it not being possible for this to occur at law, and the share of the bankrupt will vest in the trustee in bankruptcy.[95] To constitute an act whereby one operates on one's own share, it is not essential that a formal alienation occurs. If one joint tenant contracts to sell his interest, this will effect a severance of the joint tenancy,[96] and this includes contracts to settle after-acquired property,[97] that is property which a person does not yet own but anticipates receiving in the future.

Severance by one joint tenant deliberately purporting to deal with his own share in the property is rare. Severance under this head can occur, however, when one joint tenant purports to deal with the legal estate, as when one legal co-owner purports to grant a lease, such a lease being binding upon his own interest.[98] Such a transaction is unusual. Hopefully also unusual is the situation where one joint tenant procures the forgery of the other joint tenant's signature to a mortgage. The effect of this is that the beneficial joint tenancy is severed and the mortgage takes effect only against the forger's beneficial share in the property.[99]

One matter on which there is some uncertainty is whether an oral statement by one joint tenant to the other of a desire to sever is sufficient for this purpose. Although there is support for the view that this would be effective,[100] the better view is that it would not be. It would make little sense to introduce, by statute, a new method of severance by the service of a written notice of severance, if this could already be done orally.[101]

9.6.3.2 Mutual agreement and course of dealings

Although these are separate methods of severance[102] they are closely related and it is convenient to treat them together. To sever a joint tenancy by mutual agreement, it is not necessary that a binding agreement has been entered into. In the leading case of *Burgess v.*

---

[93] See *Goddard v. Lewis* (1909) 101 L.T. 528, where many of the authorities are collected.

[94] It is arguable that if one joint tenant shows the other joint tenant his will, whereby he purports to leave his 'share' of the property to another, this may amount to the service of a statutory notice of severance because, although one cannot sever a joint tenancy by a will which operates on death, the will is itself a written document whereby the testator is asserting an entitlement to an immediate share in the property. Cf., however, *Carr v. Isard* [2006] EWHC 2095 (Ch).

[95] Insolvency Act 1986, s. 306. See *Morgan v. Marquis* (1853) 9 Exch. 145.

[96] *Brown v. Randle* (1796) 3 Ves. 256. If they all agree to sell the property this, apparently, will not of itself constitute severance: *Re Hayes' Estate* [1920] I.R. 207. In such circumstances it would be normal, however, to find an intention to divide up the proceeds of sale and this agreement should amount to severance: *Morris v. Barrett* (1829) 3 Y. & J. 384.

[97] *Re Hewett* [1894] 1 Ch. 363.

[98] See *Cantanzarati v. Whitehouse* (1981) 55 F.L.R. 426. See L. Fox [2000] Conv. 208.

[99] *First National Securities Ltd v. Hegarty* [1985] Q.B. 850. See also *Re Ng* [1998] 2 F.L.R. 386 *Mortgage Corpn v. Shaire* [2001] Ch. 743. See S. Nield [2001] Conv. 462.

[100] *Hawkesley v. May* [1956] 1 Q.B. 304 at 311 *per* Havers J.

[101] *Nielson-Jones v. Fedden* [1975] Ch. 222 at 236–7 *per* Walton J. Although the actual decision in this case has been disapproved, this aspect of the judgment seems to be right; *Burgess v. Rawnsley* [1975] Ch. 429 at 448 *per* Sir John Pennycuick.

[102] [1975] Ch. 429 at 447; *Hunter v. Babbage* [1994] 2 F.L.R. 806 at 812 *per* Mr John McDonnell Q.C., sitting as a Deputy High Court judge. See also H. Conway [2009] Conv. 67 commenting on the Australian decision in *Saleeba v. Wilke* [2007] QSC 298.

Rawnsley,[103] an oral contract between two beneficial joint tenants was entered into for one to buy the other's share in the house. Despite the contract being unenforceable, because it did not comply with the then existing formalities governing contracts for the sale of land or interests in land,[104] this contract was held to have severed the beneficial joint tenancy.

In cases where there is a completed agreement, such as where the joint tenants deal with the property in question by the making of mutual wills,[105] there is little difficulty in finding a mutual agreement to sever. The position is less clear when final agreement is lacking. Certainly, it would not appear to be necessary for the parties actually to form a contract, because 'the significance of an agreement is not that it binds the parties; but it serves as an indication of a common intention to sever'.[106] If the facts of *Burgess v. Rawnsley* were to occur today, the lack of writing would not have resulted in the formation of a valid, but unenforceable contract; there would be no contract at all.[107] Yet, it would seem from the fact that there was a concluded agreement that it would still be held that severance had occurred. If the negotiations have not been concluded, however, the position is uncertain.

In *Burgess v. Rawnsley*, Sir John Pennycuick made it clear that, in his view, 'negotiations which, although not otherwise resulting in an agreement, [may] indicate a common intention that the joint tenancy should be regarded as severed'.[108] He also said, however, that one 'could not ascribe to joint tenants an intention to sever merely because one offers to buy out the other for £X and the other makes a counter-offer of £Y'.[109] The problem with this latter view, which is difficult to reconcile with his earlier comment, is that it is difficult to see why not. If the two joint tenants are bargaining over the price of the share in the property then, for their conversation to have any meaning, each must regard the other as having a share which is capable of being sold and this should, it is thought, be sufficient evidence of a mutual intention to have separate shares in the property. The decision in *Gore and Snell v. Carpenter*,[110] where abortive negotiations were held not to effect severance does, at first sight, appear to go against this view but the facts were unusual, in that the co-owners were joint tenants of two houses and the negotiations concerned whether, on their separation, each party should become the sole owner of one house each. The negotiations were not, therefore, related to each other's share in the property; had they been so, then it is thought that the better view is that these negotiations should have caused severance to occur.[111] This is particularly the case when the trend of recent authority supports the policy that a court should lean in favour of severance when it properly can.[112]

9.6.3.3 Inferred agreements

Where the parties have not concluded an express agreement to sever the joint tenancy, such an agreement can be inferred from the conduct of the parties. For this to occur, each party must have capacity to enter an agreement.[113] Despite the judicial tendency to lean in favour of finding a tenancy in common,[114] the onus of proof is on the person arguing

---

[103] [1975] Ch. 429. See also *Hunter v. Babbage* [1994] 2 F.L.R. 806, where severance occurred by mutual agreement despite specific performance not necessarily being available.

[104] LPA 1925, s. 40(1).   [105] *Re Wilford's Estate* (1879) 1 Ch.D. 267; *Re Heys* [1914] P. 192.

[106] *Burgess v. Rawnsley*, [1975] Ch. 429 at 446 *per* Sir John Pennycuick.

[107] Law of Property (Miscellaneous Provisions) Act 1989, s. 2.   [108] [1975] Ch. 429 at 447.

[109] Ibid.

[110] (1990) 60 P. & C.R. 456. See also *McDowell v. Hirschfield Lipson and Rumney* [1992] 2 F.L.R. 126, where the negotiations in the run up to a divorce were regarded as similar, on the facts, to *Harris v. Goddard* [1983] 1 W.L.R. 1203.

[111] See *Davis v. Smith* [2011] EWCA Civ. 1603.

[112] *Quigley v. Masterson* [2011] EWHC 2529 (Ch) at [35] *per* Henderson J.

[113] *Re Wilks* [1891] 3 Ch. 59 at 61–2 *per* Stirling J.

[114] See *Burgess v. Rawnsley* [1975] Ch. 429 at 438 *per* Lord Denning M.R.

that severance has occurred[115] and to establish the requisite intention the evidence will be sifted carefully and it may transpire that acts which appear to be acts of severance were not carried out with the requisite intention. So, in *Greenfield v. Greenfield*, the property was physically partitioned but severance was held not to have occurred because it appeared that the parties were happy for the doctrine of survivorship to continue to operate. Perhaps, more controversially, in *Barton v. Morris*,[116] joint tenants of a guest house put the proceeds from the business into their separate names and it was, nevertheless, held that the joint tenancy had not been severed. The reason for the decision was that this manner of dealing with the money was employed for tax reasons, although it is questionable whether such evidence should have been admissible to rebut the normal inference which would have been drawn from dealing with the money in this way.[117]

An interesting decision in the context of severance occurred in *Carr v. Isard*.[118] A married couple were beneficial joint tenants of a house. On the same day in 1967 they, separately, saw a solicitor to make their wills, in each case purporting to deal with their interest in the house. The wills were similar but not identical, and it was accepted that there was insufficient evidence to establish an intention to make mutual wills.[119] Neither was there any evidence that they had given their respective instructions in each other's presence. On these facts Mr Michael Furniss Q.C. held that there had been no evidence of an agreement between the parties to sever the joint tenancy,[120] and so, on the death of the husband, his widow was held to be entitled, by survivorship, to the entire beneficial ownership of the house. This seems unfortunate, in that both parties seemed clearly to be acting in the belief that they had separate interests in the property, and it does little credit to the law that their perceptions are thwarted by an overly legalistic attitude to an area of law which affects many people, but where its intricacies are not really appreciated.

Imputed agreements

None of the authorities on the severance of a joint tenancy were cited in *Jones v. Kernott*.[121] A couple originally owned their house, Badger Hall Avenue, as legal and beneficial joint tenants. When they separated, the house was originally put up for sale, but did not sell. Thereafter, they cashed in a joint life insurance policy, the proceeds of which were used for him to put down a deposit on a house which was transferred into his sole name. She remained in Badger Hall Avenue, which remained in joint names, for the next fifteen years, and she paid all the mortgage payments during that period. The Supreme Court held that the beneficial ownership of Badger Hall Avenue was shared in proportion of 90 per cent to her and 10 per cent to him.[122] Although there was no express agreement between them as to the position with regard to Badger Hall Avenue, the Supreme Court held that a logical inference from their behaviour was that his interest in the property should crystallize at the time when their new plan was formed.[123] This inferred, or imputed, agreement was, therefore, sufficient to sever the joint tenancy, leaving the ultimate shares in the property to be determined in the light of their conduct over the forthcoming years. While it is to be regretted that there was no discussion of the issue of severance, it may be indicative

---

[115] *Re Denny* [1947] L.J.R. 1029; *Greenfield v. Greenfield* (1970) 38 P. & C.R. 570.

[116] [1985] 1 W.L.R. 1257.

[117] See P.J. Clarke [1985] All E. Rev. 187 at 198. See also, in a related context, *Tinsley v. Milligan* [1994] 1 A.C. 340.

[118] [2006] EWHC 2095 (Ch).   [119] Ibid. at [10] *per* Mr Michael Furniss Q.C.

[120] Surely it could have been inferred that the couple had discussed the disposition of the house, which should have amounted to a severance.

[121] [2011] UKSC 53.   [122] This aspect of the decision is discussed fully at 8.6.1.2.

[123] [2011] UKSC 53 at [48] *per* Lord Walker and Lady Hale.

of a more relaxed approach to finding that this has occurred; it enables judges to find that abortive negotiations between the joint tenants for one to buy the other out should be regarded as sufficient to effect a severance. The fact that cases on severance were not discussed at all, however, means that the impact of the decision on severance is unclear.

9.6.3.4 Homicide

A final method of severance not referred to in *Williams v. Hensman* where severance will occur is where one joint tenant kills another. The normal rule at common law is that a person who kills another is not permitted to benefit from that person's death. In the case of a murderer who stands to inherit under the will of his victim, to prevent him from profiting in this way, the killer will hold the legacy on a constructive trust.[124] This principle, known as the forfeiture principle, has, except for the case of murder, been modified by legislation, so that, in appropriate cases, the court may give relief against forfeiture under s. 2(5) of the Forfeiture Act 1982.

A number of difficulties arose in relation to the forfeiture rule. The first reflected the fact that the moral culpability involved in the involvement of another's death can vary considerably, from premeditated murder to an accidental killing. One of the problems was to determine when the rule operated in the first place and, in particular, in cases where the killer was not considered to be deserving of serious punishment, whether the forfeiture rule still operated.[125] Because the courts now have the jurisdiction to grant relief from the operation of the rule, in most cases any potential injustice caused by a blanket application of the forfeiture rule will be avoided. In the exercise of the jurisdiction under the Act, the courts will have regard principally to the culpability of the offender.[126]

That said, difficult decisions still sometimes have to be made on the facts of cases. In *Chadwick v. Collinson*,[127] relief against forfeiture was denied to a man found guilty of the manslaughter, on the grounds of diminished responsibility, of his partner and their child. He had suffered a severe psychotic episode, and was subsequently sectioned under the Mental Health Act 1983. The judge held that the forfeiture rule nevertheless applied because the claimant was sufficiently aware of his actions at the time; relief was denied because of his resulting culpability, as well as his conduct during the offence and the broader financial position, although this latter consideration seems to be more relevant to the exercise of discretion rather than to whether the rule was applicable in the first place. In *Re K (deceased)*,[128] relief against forfeiture was granted to a wife found guilty of the manslaughter of her husband. She had suffered domestic abuse for some years before threatening her husband with a gun, which she unintentionally fired, the shot resulting in his death. Although the joint tenancy had therefore been severed between them, the court allowed the wife to take under the husband's will. The absence of a bright-line rule to establish the precise circumstances in which relief against forfeiture will be granted means that cases such as *Chadwick v. Collinson* and *Re K (deceased)* will necessarily be decided according to their particular facts. It makes it far more difficult to predict when a court may grant relief, but arguably it is the only way of ensuring that, in the words of s. 2(2) of the Forfeiture Act 1982, 'the justice of the case requires the effect of the rule to be so modified'.

A second difficulty relates to the effect of the forfeiture rule. If one joint tenant kills another, in circumstances when the rule applies, in the Commonwealth, it has long been

---

[124] See, e.g., *Re Crippen* [1911] P. 108. For valuable discussions of this area of the law, see T.G. Youdan (1973) 89 L.Q.R. 235; T.K. Earnshaw and P.J. Pace (1974) 37 M.L.R. 481.

[125] See *R. v. National Insurance Commissioner, ex parte Connor* [1981] Q.B. 758.

[126] *Dunbar v. Plant* [1998] Ch. 412 (suicide pact). *Cas M.H. Thompson* [1997] Conv. 45. See also *Henderson v. Wilcox* [2015] EWHC 3469 *per* HHJ. Cooke.

[127] [2014] EWHC 3055 (Ch).   [128] [1986] Fam. 180.

accepted that the survivor cannot benefit by taking the whole interest by survivorship but will hold subject to a constructive trust, with the result that the estate of the deceased is entitled to a half share.[129] The homicide does not automatically cause the beneficial joint tenancy to be severed. Instead, the doctrine of survivorship operates in the normal way and a constructive trust is imposed to deprive the killer of the gain which he would otherwise have made from the killing.[130] By contrast, English law interprets the provisions of the Forfeiture Act to mean that a joint tenancy is automatically severed where an unlawful killing occurs, with the potential for relief against forfeiture so that the killer may take under the deceased's will.

The approach taken in English law is perhaps to be regretted in that it can work unfairly in situations where there are more than two beneficial joint tenants. If A, B, and C are beneficial joint tenants and A kills B, under the Commonwealth approach, survivorship would operate, so that the beneficial ownership would devolve upon A and C. A constructive trust would then be imposed upon A, which would then sever the joint tenancy between him and C, leaving C with a half share in the property. Under the English approach, however, if the killing itself occasioned the forfeiture, then C would have only a one-third share in the property. To avoid this result, which seems to be unfair to C, it is suggested that the better approach to this issue is that followed elsewhere in the Commonwealth, where homicide is not regarded as a means of severing a joint tenancy and the problem of unjust enrichment is resolved by the imposition of a constructive trust.

9.6.4 **The effect of severance**

Before a beneficial joint tenancy is severed, none of the joint tenants have quantifiable interests in the property. Between them, they own the whole interest and the law regards them as together constituting one person. If severance occurs, then, in principle, the joint tenants should have equal interests in the property. At one time, there was doubt as to this because of dicta in *Benson v. Benson*,[131] which envisaged ownership in unequal shares after severance had occurred. This was contrary to principle and was repudiated in *Goodman v. Gallant*,[132] where it was held, first, that in the absence of a claim to rectification,[133] an express declaration of a beneficial joint tenancy is conclusive and, second, that upon severance the joint tenants will then hold the property as tenants in common in equal shares, regardless of the sizes of their initial contributions to the purchase of the property. This seemed like a settled point of law, but the judgments in *Stack v. Dowden* and *Jones v. Kernott* have thrown fresh doubt on its application. In both cases, the parties initially held under a joint tenancy, but the ambulatory nature of their intentions meant that the court decided to award a 65 per cent to 35 per cent split of the beneficial interest for Ms Dowden and Mr Stack respectively, and a 90 per cent to 10 per cent split to Ms Jones and Mr Kernott. Not only was the basis of severance not discussed in either case, it is also unclear why or how severance in unequal shares was possible, as it seems to fly in the face of *Goodman v. Gallant*. Any variation on severance in equal shares should, in theory, require a disposition of the equitable interest from one co-owner to the other under s. 53(1)(c), LPA 1925, which says it must be in writing. It has been argued that if the transfer of the beneficial interest takes place inside the constructive trust between the parties, it should be

---

[129] *Schobelt v. Barber* (1967) 60 D.L.R. (2d) 519; *Re Pechar* [1969] N.Z.L.R. 574; *Rasmanis v. Jurewitsch* [1968] 2 N.S.W.R. 166.

[130] See Youdan (1973) 89 L.Q.R. 235, 254–5; Earnshaw and Pace (1974) 37 M.L.R. 481, 488–92.

[131] [1965] 2 Q.B. 666 at 681–2 *per* Lord Denning M.R.; at 685 *per* Davies L.J.

[132] [1986] Fam. 106.

[133] See *Thames Guarantee Ltd v. Campbell* [1985] Q.B. 210 at 227–9 *per* Slade L.J.

exempt from the requirements in s. 53(1)(c) by virtue of s. 53(2).[134] This may be a work-able solution, but it remains unfortunate that our most senior appellate court has twice had the opportunity to clarify the basis and effect of severance in cases where a construc-tive trust exists, and has failed to do so.[135]

It is open to the co-owners to agree explicitly on an unequal division of the equitable estate. In *Singla v. Brown*,[136] a notice of severance was served, which stated that the property would thereafter be held as tenants in common in unequal shares, 99 per cent for her and 1 per cent for him; this reflecting the fact that he had contributed virtually nothing to the pur-chase of the property, which had been put into joint names in the first place at the insistence of the mortgage company.[137] He agreed to this, and this division of the equitable interest was upheld. In the absence of any such agreement, or a successful claim to rectification, however, the general rule should apply and the parties will share the beneficial interest equally.[138]

If there are only two joint tenants, then severance by one necessarily effects total sever-ance of the joint tenancy. Where there are more than two joint tenants, however, this result does not automatically follow. Suppose a situation where A, B, C, and D hold the legal title on trust for themselves as beneficial joint tenants. A then serves a notice of severance on the other three. This will not affect the position at law, but will operate to sever the benefi-cial joint tenancy between A and the others. It will not affect the position as between B, C, and D, who will remain, as between themselves, joint tenants. A will have a one-quarter share, and B, C, and D will, collectively, own a three-quarter share. The position is illus-trated in Figure 9.4.

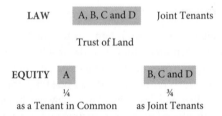

Fig. 9.4 Example of severance where there are more than two joint tenants

If A then dies leaving his property to E, as there can be no severance of the legal joint tenancy, the doctrine of survivorship will operate. As he has severed in equity, his one-quarter share can now pass under his will. The position would be as shown in Figure 9.5.

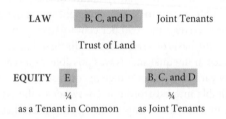

Fig. 9.5 Position on death of A

---

[134] M. Pawlowski and J. Brown, (2013) 27 Tru LI 59.

[135] For further discussion, see J. Mee (2012) 128 L.Q.R. 500, and S. Gardner [2015] Conv. 199.

[136] [2007] EWHC 405 (Ch).

[137] Owing to the high standard of proof required although still somewhat surprisingly, no claim to rectification was pursued: ibid. at [23]–[26] *per* Mr Thomas Ivory Q.C.

[138] See also *Hunter v. Babbage* [1994] 2 F.L.R. 806.

9.6.5 **Procedure on death**

A legal joint tenancy can never be severed but an equitable joint tenancy can be. Suppose a situation where A and B together bought a home in 1980 and that home was conveyed to them as beneficial joint tenants. In 2017, B died. The effect of this, at law, is that A would, by survivorship, be the sole legal owner. What a purchaser could not know, however, was the position in equity. Prior to B's death, the beneficial joint tenancy might have been severed and his share in the house passed to C. The situation then is that, although A is the sole owner at law, there remains co-ownership in equity and A, acting alone, could not give a good title. On the other hand, however, if severance had not occurred, then A would be the sole owner at law and in equity and perfectly entitled to deal with the property. The difficulty is that, in the nature of things, it is difficult to prove a negative: that severance did not occur. As severance might have occurred, with the result that co-ownership continued to exist in equity, as a counsel of prudence, a purchaser would insist upon the appointment of a second trustee[139] to ensure that, if beneficial co-ownership continued, any beneficial interests would be overreached by a conveyance by two trustees, this procedure being necessary whether or not severance had actually occurred. To obviate this complexity, reform was introduced, that reform being relevant only to unregistered land.

9.6.5.1 Unregistered land

The Law of Property (Joint Tenants) Act 1964, which applies only to unregistered land, and operates retrospectively,[140] provides by s. 1 that, for the purposes of s. 36(2), LPA 1925, the survivor of two or more joint tenants shall, in favour of a purchaser, be deemed to be solely and beneficially interested if he conveys as beneficial owner, or the conveyance contains a statement that he is so interested. A purchaser need not, therefore, insist upon the appointment of a second trustee in the circumstances described above, provided that:

(a) a memorandum of severance has not been endorsed on or annexed to the conveyance by virtue of which the legal estate was vested in the joint tenants; or

(b) a receiving order in bankruptcy, or a petition for such an order, has not been registered against any of the joint tenants under the Land Charges Act 1972.

One uncertainty as to the operation of the Act relates to the position where there was no memorandum of severance attached to the conveyance but the purchaser was aware that severance had, in fact, occurred.[141] One argument was that the deeming provision in s. 1 was sufficiently strong to ensure that the purchaser would, in these circumstances, still obtain a good title.[142] This uncertainty, however, was resolved in *Grindal v. Hooper*,[143] where it was held that a purchaser with actual notice of severance having occurred would be bound by the interest of a beneficial co-owner despite there being no memorandum of severance on the conveyance to indicate that the surviving joint tenant was not the sole beneficial owner.

---

[139] This does not seem to offend against the principle that, as between joint tenants, there must be unity of title and time. This is because the title of both A and the new trustee derives from the deed of appointment and so these unities exist. For the opposite view, see D.G. Barnsley [1998] C.L.J. 123 at 127, n. 18.

[140] Law of Property (Joint Tenants) Act 1964, ss 2, 3.

[141] See P. Jackson (1966) 30 Conv. (N.S.) 27.

[142] Thompson [1997] Conv. 45, 25, an analogy being drawn with *Midland Bank Trust Co. Ltd v. Green* [1981] A.C. 513.

[143] [1999] E.G.C.S. 150. See N.P. Gravells [2000] Conv. 461.

9.6.5.2 Registered land

The 1964 Act does not apply to registered land. The reason for this is that the existence of a beneficial tenancy in common is intended to be revealed by a restriction, that restriction being to the effect that the surviving co-owner cannot give a valid receipt for capital money. If there is no such restriction, a purchaser from a surviving joint tenant will normally acquire a good title. A potential problem may arise, however, if beneficial co-ownership continues after the death of one of the legal co-owners. Suppose A and B are registered as proprietors of a house and there is no restriction entered on the register of title. B then marries C, who moves into the house and B then severs the joint tenancy but no restriction is entered on the register. B then dies, leaving his share in the property to C. On a transfer of the house by A, C, as a beneficial co-owner in actual occupation of the property, would appear to have an interest which would override the registered disposition.[144]

9.6.6 The need for beneficial joint tenancies

The abolition of legal tenancies in common has without doubt simplified the structure of co-ownership by preventing the fragmentation of the legal title amongst, potentially, a large number of people; the doctrine of survivorship works well with respect to the legal title. A question which can be asked, however, is whether the existence of an equitable joint tenancy is as welcome.[145]

One of the drawbacks of the joint tenancy is the doctrine of survivorship. If one considers some of the cases on severance discussed above, a number of points may be made. First, this litigation is expensive and would not have been necessary had there been a tenancy in common in the first place. Second, a finding that severance had not occurred will result in the property, on death, going to a person whom the deceased would not have intended to benefit on his death, their relationship having broken down: a consequence of what has aptly been described as 'the survivorship wheel of fortune'.[146] Had they been tenants in common from the outset, and the couple had not been married, then for one tenant in common to leave his property to the other would have required the making of a will. If this was the case then, if the testamentary intention subsequently changed, it would be known that a new will would have to be made. A related point, and one which may not be known to the parties, is that while a joint tenancy subsists neither joint tenant has any share in the property to leave by will. So, if A and B are beneficial joint tenants, and A makes a will leaving 'his share' in the property to C then, unless there had been some act of severance, A will have no share to leave and the will would be ineffective. This is borne out by two recent decisions, where a joint tenant had sought to make a testamentary disposition in relation to the beneficial interest, and in each case, the intended will was ineffective, as there had not been a severance of the joint tenancy,[147] although one does wonder why the solicitors acting in these situations had not ensured that this had been done.[148]

---

[144] Land Registration Act 2002, Sched. 3, para. 2. See E.J. Cooke [2003] Conv. 41.

[145] See S.M. Bandali (1977) 41 Conv. (N.S.) 243; M.P. Thompson [1987] Conv. 29, 375 arguing for abolition and A.M. Prichard [1987] Conv. 272 arguing for the opposite point of view. See also the discussion by Tee, *Land Law Issues, Debates, Policy*, 142–6, which is sympathetic to the abolitionist approach, and N. Piska [2008] Conv. 452 at 457. For a thoughtful discussion, prompted by the Thompson/Prichard debate which comes out against abolition, see Smith, *Plural Ownership* (Oxford, Oxford University Press, 2005), Chapter 5.

[146] S. Nield [2001] Conv. 462 at 463.

[147] See *Campbell v. Griffin* [2001] EWCA Civ 1176 discussed by M.P. Thompson [2003] Conv. 157 at 159–60, and *Carr v. Issard* [2006] EWHC 2095 (Ch).

[148] Although see *Carr-Glynn v. Frearsons (A Firm)* [1999] Ch. 326.

A final point is that the effect of the severance of a joint tenancy may not be fully appreciated and, in particular, that each tenant in common will, subject to what was said above, receive a half share in the property regardless of each person's initial contribution to the purchase. This may come as an unpleasant surprise if a couple split up shortly after buying a house together as beneficial joint tenants and where one of them has contributed substantially more to the purchase of the property than the other.[149]

As against this, it remains the case that the beneficial joint tenancy remains popular,[150] although whether all the consequences of the property being held in this way are fully explained is perhaps doubtful. When a solicitor is told by a couple buying a house that, on death, they would like their 'share' in it to go to the other, a joint tenancy may then be employed as an alternative to making a will.[151] In any event, any legislative change to the existing position seems unlikely, so one is left to hope that the full pros and cons of this type of beneficial holding are, at the outset, fully explained to the parties by their legal adviser.[152] This may be a pious hope, for, as Ward L.J. lamented in *Carlton v Goodman*:

> I ask in despair how often this court has to remind conveyancers that they would save their clients a good deal of later difficulty if only they would sit the purchasers down, explain the difference between a joint tenancy and a tenancy in common and then expressly declare in the conveyance or transfer how the beneficial interest is to be held because that will be conclusive and save all argument.[153]

9.7 Disputes between co-owners

When land is acquired by co-owners, then, at the outset, the relationship between them is likely to be harmonious. Disputes can arise subsequently, such disputes generally involving the related areas of occupation and sale. This section considers these matters.

9.7.1 Occupation

The law relating to the rights of occupation of beneficial co-owners prior to the enactment of TOLATA 1996 was quite complex.[154] It was coloured to a considerable extent by the doctrine of conversion. Under this doctrine, for some purposes at least, the interests of the beneficiaries were regarded as being in the proceeds of sale, a proposition which would, *prima facie*, militate against them having the right to occupy the land. This position was, however, modified by reference to the pre-1926 law.

If there was legal co-ownership of the land, either by way of joint tenancy or tenancy in common, then each of the legal co-owners would have the right to possess the land, this

---

[149] For empirical research which supports the view that the parties may be unaware of this consequence, see G. Douglas, J. Pearce, and H. Woodward [2008] Conv. 365 at 372–5. See also *Singla v. Brown* [2007] EWHC 405 (Ch) at [38] *per* Mr Thomas Ivory Q.C.

[150] See the remarkable case of *Bindra v. Mawji* [2008] EWHC 1715 (Ch), where the parties intended to create a tenancy in common during their lives, to change to a joint tenancy on the death of either: see at [44] *per* Etherton J.

[151] As, if the couple are unmarried, they will certainly need to make a will in respect of their other property, this is, perhaps, a false economy.

[152] Purchasers of land are asked to specify how they intend to hold the property in the Land Registry's transfer forms, with associated guidance available under *Practice Guide 24: private trusts of land (updated October 2018)*. The government's summary is available at: https://www.gov.uk/joint-property-ownership.

[153] *Carlton v. Goodman* [2002] 2 F.L.R. 259 at 273.

[154] On occupation generally, see D.G. Barnsley [1998] C.L.J. 123. See also J.G. Ross Martyn [1997] Conv. 237.

right stemming from the unity of possession inherent in co-ownership. This, subject to the abolition of a legal tenancy in common, remains true after 1926. What was regarded as being more problematic was the situation where the beneficiary asserting a right of occupation was not a legal co-owner of the land. This problem occurred in *Bull v. Bull*,[155] where a mother and son had bought a house for their joint occupation but the house was in the sole name of the son. He subsequently sought possession of the property as against her and this action failed.

In reaching this conclusion, Denning L.J. equated the position of the mother, who was a beneficial tenant in common, with that of a legal tenant in common prior to 1926. The importance of this was that a legal tenant in common had, at that time, the right to go into occupation. A legal joint tenancy in common is now no longer possible, this being prevented by statutory provisions.[156] Those provisions are in Part I of the LPA 1925, provided by s. 14:

> This Part of this Act shall not prejudicially affect the interest of any person in actual occupation of the land to which he may be entitled in right of such possession or occupation.

Because the mother was in actual occupation, her rights were regarded as being the equivalent of the rights of a legal tenant in common prior to 1926 and so she could not be evicted by her son.[157]

9.7.1.1 Limits on right

An integral part of the reasoning was the role of s. 14 of the Act, which affords protection to people in actual occupation. Accordingly, if a beneficial tenant in common was not in actual occupation, it would not seem that he had the right to insist upon taking possession.[158] In addition, the occupation rights of the beneficiaries appeared to depend upon the underlying purpose of the trust. If, as in *Bull v. Bull*, the property, while held upon a trust for sale, was acquired for the purpose of providing a joint home, then, pending a sale of the property, the beneficiary would have the right to continue in occupation of the land.[159]

This point emerged clearly in *Barclay v. Barclay*,[160] where a bungalow was devised with a direction that it be sold and the proceeds divided between five beneficiaries. One of the five had lived with the testator prior to his death and had continued in possession thereafter. The plaintiff acquired the legal title and brought an action for possession which succeeded in the Court of Appeal. *Bull v. Bull* was distinguished on the basis that, in the present case, 'the prime purpose of the trust was that the bungalow should be sold'.[161] Although the beneficiary was in occupation of the land, because the purpose of the trust was not to provide a home for the beneficiaries, he had no right, as against the owner of the legal title, to remain in the bungalow.

9.7.2 The statutory regime

The Trusts of Land and Appointment of Trustees Act 1996 seeks to set out a comprehensive account of the new law relating to the rights of beneficiaries to occupy the property. It

---

[155] [1955] 1 Q.B. 234.   [156] LPA 1925, ss 1(6), 36(2).
[157] This was expressly approved in *Williams & Glyn's Bank Ltd v. Boland* [1981] A.C. 487 at 507 *per* Lord Wilberforce. See also *Ramroop v. Ishmael* [2010] UKPC 14 at [14] *per* Lord Walker.
[158] See *Re Bagot's Settlement* [1894] 1 Ch. 177; G.A. Forrest (1956) 19 M.L.R. 312.
[159] See *City of London Building Society v. Flegg* [1988] A.C. 54 at 81 *per* Lord Oliver.
[160] [1970] 2 Q.B. 677.
[161] Ibid. at 684 *per* Lord Denning M.R. For a discussion of this distinction, see M.J. Prichard (1971) 29 C.L.J. 44 at 46; S.M. Cretney (1971) 44 M.L.R. 441 at 443; and A.E. Boyle [1981] Conv. 108.

operates by first conferring rights of occupation on the beneficiaries and then by stipulating the circumstances in which the right can be modified or excluded. These sections, it should be added, are directed at the situation where the beneficiary is not a legal co-owner, in which case there is no problem in that that person, as an incident of the legal joint tenancy, has the right of occupation. The right of occupation in respect of beneficial co-owners of the land is conferred by s. 12, which provides that:

> 12–(1) A beneficiary who is beneficially entitled to an interest in possession in land subject to a trust of land is entitled by reason of his interest to occupy the land at any time if at that time—
>
> (a) the purpose of the trust includes making the land available for his occupation (or for the occupation of beneficiaries of a class of which he is a member or of beneficiaries in general), or
>
> (b) the land is held by trustees to be so available.
>
> (2) Subsection (1) does not confer on a beneficiary a right to occupy land if it is either unavailable or unsuitable for occupation by him.
>
> (3) This section is subject to section 13.

9.7.2.1 Time at which purpose is assessed

A number of points call for elaboration. The first point is that it would appear from the wording of this subsection that one has regard to the purpose of the trust at the time when a beneficiary seeks to exercise his right to possession and not the time when the trust was created. This purpose may change over time. Suppose, for example, two sisters, A and B, are beneficial tenants in common of a house. B makes a will leaving her share in the property to her nephew, who is shortly to marry, so that, on her death, the nephew and his wife can live in the property. In this situation, subject to s. 13 of the Act, it would seem that, on the death of his aunt, the nephew would, under s. 12 of the Act, have the right of occupation. This would appear to be the case, unless the unhappily drafted subsection (2) is applicable, in that, if the nephew and A do not get on, it is perhaps the case that the property is not suitable for him.

Subsection (2) denies the beneficiary a right of occupation if the land subject to the trust is unavailable or unsuitable for occupation by him. The former criterion would seem to envisage a situation where the property in question is subject to a tenancy so that the trustees cannot grant others the right of possession. It is the second criterion which may cause difficulty, that is determining whether the property is unsuitable for his occupation.[162] In assessing whether the property is suitable for a person's occupation, regard should be had to the general physical characteristics of the particular property, and also a consideration of the personal characteristics and circumstances of that person;[163] a common example of unsuitability being, apparently, when a farm is bequeathed to a non-farmer beneficiary.[164] If there is some personality clash between the beneficiary and the other occupiers, this may make the property unsuitable for his occupation.[165]

9.7.2.2 Restrictions

Section 13(1) of the Act enables the trustees to restrict the right of occupation. If there are two or more beneficiaries, the trustees may restrict or exclude the entitlement of any one or more of the beneficiaries, but not all of them, to occupy the property. In exercising this

---

[162] See R. Martyn [1997] Conv. 237, 260.
[163] *Chan v. Leung* [2003] 1 F.L.R. 23 at 48 *per* Jonathan Parker L.J.
[164] See R. Smith [1989] Conv. 12 at 19.
[165] For a critical discussion of TOLATA, s. 12, see S. Pascoe [2006] Conv. 54.

power, the trustees may not act unreasonably,[166] and are also entitled under s. 13(3) of the Act to impose reasonable conditions on any beneficiaries in relation to their occupation. It is possible under this provision for the court to sanction a physical partition of the property, with each beneficial owner entitled to occupy one part and be excluded from the other,[167] although such an outcome is likely to be rare.

In the exercise of their power to restrict the right of occupation then, as with the position generally with regard to the exercise of a discretion by trustees, they must act unanimously. This is why a beneficiary, who is also a legal owner of the property, cannot be excluded, against his will, from occupation of the trust property by the other trustees because, in such a case, there is obviously no unanimity amongst the trustees.

9.7.2.3 Reasonableness

With regard to the issue of reasonableness, certain criteria to which the trustees are to have regard are listed by s. 13(4) of the Act. They are:

(a) the intentions of the person who created the trust;

(b) the purpose for which the land is held; and

(c) the circumstances and wishes of each of the beneficiaries entitled to occupy the land under s. 12.

In having regard to these criteria, there may be some conflict between (a) and (b). The former relates to the purpose of the trust at the time of its creation and the latter to the current position, so that in the example given above, the nephew who inherits the interest of his aunt might be able to be excluded under paragraph (a) as someone not within the contemplation of the persons creating the trust at the time of its creation, whereas the second criterion would appear to apply to the current purpose of the trust, which is to provide him with a home. It remains to be seen what weight the courts will give to these different criteria.

9.7.2.4 Conditional occupation

Section 13 of the Act envisages that a beneficiary may be allowed to exercise his right of occupation on various conditions or be excluded from the property. Any conditions imposed upon occupation must be reasonable and can include a condition requiring him to pay any outgoings and expenses in respect of the land, or to assume any other obligation in relation to the land or to any activity which is or proposed to be conducted there.[168] If a beneficiary is excluded from the land, then conditions may be imposed upon those beneficiaries who are in occupation and this may include a requirement to make payments to the beneficiary as compensation for being excluded.[169]

9.7.2.5 Occupiers of land

The Act draws a distinction between beneficiaries who are not in occupation and who wish to go into occupation and people who are in occupation of land held under a trust of land. Under s. 13(7) of the Act, the powers of the trustees to either exclude a beneficiary or to impose conditions on him shall not be exercised so as to prevent any person who is in occupation of land (whether or not by reason of an entitlement to occupy it) from continuing to occupy the land unless either that person consents or a court has given its

---

[166] TOLATA 1996, s. 13(2).

[167] *Rodway v. Landy* [2001] Ch. 703. A jointly owned surgery which could be divided, with each doctor occupying a separate part of the premises.

[168] TOLATA 1996, s. 13(5).   [169] Ibid., s. 13(6). See 9.8.4.

approval. The court, in determining whether to approve a possession order, has regard to the criteria listed above.[170]

One point which should be noted about this provision is that the person in occupation of the land need not actually be a beneficiary under the trust. It could be the spouse or cohabitant of one of the co-owners of the property.

9.8 Disputes as to sale

When the beneficial owners under a trust of land are in dispute as to the occupation rights, a factor which is likely to be considered is whether or not the land should be sold and its capital value distributed amongst them. Disputes of this nature are not uncommon; one co-owner wants the house to be sold, while another wants it to be retained for residential purposes. The 1996 Act makes provision for this situation and provides, also, a list of issues to which the court should have regard when faced with such disputes. These matters derive to a considerable extent from the previous case law which will continue to provide a guide to the approach to be taken in such matters, although, as will be seen, the Act has enabled different results to be achieved in some situations than would previously have been the case.

9.8.1 The statutory criteria

Under s. 14, TOLATA 1996, any person who is a trustee of land or has an interest in property subject to a trust of land may make an application to the court for an order under the section. The court may then make any such order relating to the exercise by the trustees of any of their functions or declare the nature or extent of a person's interest in the property subject to the trust as it sees fit. In making such orders, the court is required to have regard to the following matters, which are listed in s. 15.[171] These are:

(a) the intentions of the person or persons who created the trust;

(b) the purposes for which the property subject to the trust is held;

(c) the welfare of any minor who occupies or might reasonably be expected to occupy any land subject to the trust as his home; and

(d) the interests of any secured creditor of any beneficiary.

In the case of an application relating to the exercise of powers under s. 13, the matters to which the court should have regard include the circumstances and wishes of the beneficiaries entitled to occupy the land, and in respect of any other application the court shall have regard to the circumstances and wishes of the beneficiaries or the majority of them, having regard to the size of their interests.[172]

9.8.2 Intention and purpose

Matters to which the court is to have regard when making an order include the intention of the person or persons who created the trust and the purposes for which the property subject to the trust is held. These criteria reflect the case law which had developed under the previous legal regime governing co-ownership.

---

[170] Ibid., s. 13(8).

[171] For a useful account of the case law developed under TOLATA 1996, s. 14, see M. Dixon (2011) 70 C.L.J. 579.

[172] TOLATA 1996, s. 15(2)(3). See *Dear v. Robinson* [2001] EWCA Civ. 1543.

When land was held upon a trust for sale, disputes as to whether or not the property should be sold were determined on applications to the court under s. 30, LPA 1925. The starting point in such cases was that, as the trust was a trust for sale, the prime duty of the trustees, subject to their power to postpone the sale, was to sell the property. If they were not unanimous in exercising their power to postpone the sale, then, *prima facie*, the property should be sold.[173] This proposition was, however, subject to a qualification. Where, prior to the acquisition of the land, there was an agreement between the co-owners that the property should not be sold unless all the co-owners agreed to this, then the court would not order a sale where such agreement was lacking.[174]

Cases where there is a prior agreement with respect to how the property is to be used are now expressly catered for by the Act. In *Charlton v. Lester*,[175] a sitting, protected, tenant bought a house with her son and daughter-in-law on the clear understanding that she could always remain in the house as her home. Despite the couple having moved out, it was held that, because of the anterior understanding, the house should not be sold; a conclusion which, without reference to this decision, has been arrived at under the Act. In *Finch v. Hall*,[176] a house was owned by four siblings as tenants in common in equal shares. The original trust deed provided that all decisions about selling the property would be made on the basis of shares constituting a majority interest in the property or, put another way, if three of the four co-owners agreed. Subsequently, when the house was put on the market with estate agents, it was expressly agreed that for any sale to be agreed, all four co-owners needed to agree. It was held that this later agreement gave an unwilling co-owner a power of veto, during the subsistence of the agreement with the estate agent. The court would, unless circumstances changed in a material way, give effect to what had been agreed at the time of the creation of the trust, or as later agreed between the beneficial owners.[177]

Such cases afford examples where the initial agreement between the co-owners was that the house should not be sold. Conversely, it may be the case that the real purpose of the trust was precisely that the house should be sold and the proceeds of sale divided between the beneficiaries.[178] Today, if an express trust for sale is created, this would indicate this intention and, in the event of a dispute between the co-owners, a sale would be likely to be ordered.

9.8.2.1 Underlying purpose

The cases where there was an actual agreement with respect to the circumstances in which the house should be sold were developed by the courts. While recognizing that the co-owned property was to be held upon a trust for sale, regard was also had to the underlying purpose of the trust which, at the outset, may well have been to provide a home. A consideration of an underlying purpose may lead to the conclusion that, when a dispute emerges, the result should be that the house be sold. If a house was bought for the purpose of being a 'quasi-matrimonial' home and the couple has split up, then that purpose no longer exists, with the consequence that it is likely that a sale will be ordered.[179] Where the house has been bought for joint occupation and one of the co-owners leaves, then it is likely, subject to the occupying tenant in common being given an opportunity to buy out

---

[173] *Re Mayo* [1943] Ch. 302.

[174] *Re Buchanan-Wollaston's Conveyance* [1939] Ch. 738. See also *Re Hyde's Conveyance* (1952) 102 L.J. 58.

[175] [1976] 1 E.G.L.R. 131. See also *Jones v. Jones* [1977] 1 W.L.R. 438; *Chan v. Leung* [2003] 1 F.L.R. 23.

[176] [2013] EWHC 4360 (Ch).

[177] Ibid. at [24] *per* Mr David Donaldson Q.C., sitting as a Deputy High Court judge.

[178] See *Barclay v. Barclay* [1970] 2 Q.B. 677.

[179] See [1961] 1 Q.B. 176. *Van Bank of Ireland Home Mortgages Ltd v. Bell* [2001] 2 F.L.R. 809 at 815 *per* Peter Gibson L.J. See also *Smith v. Smith and Smith* (1976) 120 S.J. 100, where the house was initially to be used as a joint home for the plaintiff, her brother, and her sister-in-law.

the other,[180] that the court would order a sale of the property. A good example of this was seen in *Bagum v. Hafiz.*[181] A house was held on a trust of land under which a mother and her two sons held the property in equal shares. One of the sons moved out and a dispute arose as to how the property should be sold. The Court of Appeal held, first, that there was no jurisdiction under the Act to order that the son who had left the property should sell his beneficial interest directly to his brother. It upheld the order at first instance, however, that the house should be put on the market at a price agreed by an independent valuer, with the son wishing to acquire his sibling's interest in the house being given a right of pre-emption for a limited period of time to purchase the property at that price.

Where the concept of the underlying purpose was developed further, in order to prevent an immediate sale, was where there were children involved. The idea was that, when the house was acquired, the underlying purpose of the trust was to provide a home not just for the co-owners but also for their children.

9.8.3 **Welfare of minors**

When a house was subject to co-ownership and was used as a family home, the position of children was a matter to which the courts were used to paying regard.[182] Initially, their existence was regarded as merely an incidental matter in considering whether or not to order a sale.[183] Latterly, however, the prevalent view came to be that the interests of children should be accorded priority and, in so doing, it became apparent that the courts would arrive at solutions similar to those which would result if the case involved a married couple and the property dispute was being resolved under the provisions of the Matrimonial Causes Act 1973.[184]

The approach to be taken in cases where there were children was laid down in *Rawlings v. Rawlings,*[185] by Salmon L.J. who, although ordering a sale on the facts of the case itself, said: 'if there were young children, the position would be different. One of the purposes of the trust would no doubt have been to provide a home for them, and whilst that purpose still existed, a sale would not generally be ordered.' These sentiments were applied in *Re Evers' Trust.*[186] A couple had been cohabiting in a house with three children, two of whom were hers from an earlier marriage and the third was a child of them both. The parties, who were joint tenants, separated and he petitioned the court for an order that the house, where she continued to live with the children, should be sold. The Court of Appeal refused to make such an order, but instead postponed the sale indefinitely, with liberty to either party to apply for a sale at some time in the future.

The decision to postpone the sale was based upon the view being taken that the underlying purpose of the trust was to provide a home for the family and that this purpose continued to exist. Such reasoning should, however, only be apposite where a family was envisaged, it being quite possible that a couple could begin cohabitation without any intention to have a family, in which case to argue that this was an underlying purpose of the trust would be artificial. The purpose should, however, end in any case when the youngest child no longer needs the house as a residence, which would normally be when he reached

---

[180] See *Ali v. Hussein* (1974) 231 E.G. 372; *Pariser v. Wilson* (1973) 229 E.G. 786.

[181] [2015] EWCA Civ. 801.

[182] See generally Fox, *Conceptualising Home* (Oxford, Hart Publishing, 2007), Chapter 9.

[183] See *Burke v. Burke* [1974] 1 W.L.R. 1063.

[184] See R. Schuz (1982) 12 Fam. Law 108; M. Hayes and G. Battersby [1981] Conv. 404; M.P. Thompson [1984] Conv. 103.

[185] [1964] P. 398 at 419.   [186] [1980] 1 W.L.R. 1327.

a certain specified age. Under the statutory provisions, the first point becomes academic but the second remains relevant.

Under s. 15(1)(c), TOLATA 1996, one of the matters to which the court is required to have regard is the welfare of any minor who occupies or might reasonably be expected to occupy the land which is subject to the trust as his home. There would be no difficulty, therefore, in refusing to order a sale to take account of the interests of children, but equally s. 15(1)(c) does not mean that a sale will never be allowed when children are in occupation. In *White v. White*,[187] the interests of the children in remaining in the family home were outweighed by Mrs White's need for realization of her only capital in order to acquire a house following her separation from Mr White, and so the order of sale was confirmed.

When the children have reached eighteen, they cease to be minors and so their welfare ceases to be a relevant consideration when considering what order to make.[188] It is also the case that the closer the children come to achieving majority, the less weight will be given to considerations of their welfare.[189]

9.8.4 Rent

Cases where there is a dispute between co-owners as to whether the property should be sold or retained frequently occur in a family context and the court, in resolving the dispute, will have regard to family considerations and, in particular, the interests of any children. The consequence of doing this is that the house may remain unsold for a considerable period with one co-owner deriving no benefit from it and being unable to realize its capital value. To mitigate the hardship that this might cause to the non-occupying co-owner, the courts have been able to combine the postponement of a sale with an order that the occupier pay rent to the other.[190]

Under the old law, although it was sometimes said that the court could simply order one co-owner to pay rent to the other on the basis that this was fair,[191] it was not clear that the courts did have this general power. Rather, the true position was thought to be that a court had jurisdiction to order one co-owner to pay rent to the other only when the former had, effectively, ousted the latter from the property.[192] If one co-owner simply chose not to remain in the property, the one remaining in occupation was not liable to pay rent to the other.[193] This problem was more apparent than real, however, as it was always open to the court, in an appropriate case,[194] to achieve indirectly what could not be achieved directly; the person seeking to resist an order of sale could be told that, unless she undertook to pay an occupation rent, then a sale would be ordered.[195] This dispute, such as it was, appeared to have been resolved as the courts have since asserted a general right to order the payment of rent where this is necessary to do equity between the parties,[196] and this jurisdiction exists alongside the statutory provisions whereby the payment of rent can be ordered.[197]

---

[187] [2004] 2 F.L.R. 321.   [188] See *TSB Bank plc v. Marshall* [1998] 3 E.G.L.R. 100.

[189] *Bank of Ireland Home Mortgages Ltd v. Bell* [2001] 2 F.L.R. 809 at 816 *per* Peter Gibson L.J.

[190] See S. Bright [2009] Conv. 378.

[191] *Chhokar v. Chhokar* [1984] F.L.R. 313 at 332 *per* Cumming-Bruce L.J. See also *Cousins v. Dzosens* (1984) 81 L.S.G. 2855.

[192] See *Dennis v. McDonald* [1981] 1 W.L.R. 810, affirmed in principle: [1982] Fam. 63.

[193] See *McMahon v. Burchill* (1846) 5 Hare 322 and R.E. Annand (1982) 132 N.L.J. 526.

[194] Such a solution should not be seen as a universal panacea to all cohabitation cases. See *Stott v. Rafcliffe* (1982) 79 L.S.G. 643; *Chan v. Leung* [2003] 1 F.L.R. 23.

[195] See M.P. Thompson [1984] Conv. 103 at 110.

[196] *Re Pavlou* [1993] 1 W.L.R. 1046; *Byford v. Butler* [2004] 1 F.L.R. 56; *Murphy v. Gooch* [2007] EWCA Civ 603.

[197] *French v. Barcham* [2008] EWHC 1505 (Ch).

In most cases the court will now proceed to assess this matter under the 1996 Act, as if a court has excluded a beneficiary's right of occupation, such exclusion can be on terms that payment by way of compensation be made to that person[198] and such compensation would include the payment of rent.

In *Stack v. Dowden*,[199] although the main issue was the quantification of the beneficial interests in the home, a subsidiary matter was whether, pending the sale of the property, Ms Dowden, who was living in the property with the children, should be required to pay an occupation rent to Mr Stack, who was in alternative accommodation. At first instance, she was ordered to pay him £900 per month but, on appeal, this was set aside, and the House of Lords, Lord Neuberger dissenting, confirmed that no rent should be paid. The difficulty is in establishing the reason why.

Lady Hale dealt with this matter very briefly. She criticized the trial judge for not having regard to the criteria listed in s. 15 of the Act. She then briefly referred to the obligation to maintain the children and the respective outgoings on the properties before concluding that, although she could see that there was a case for him to receive compensation, it should be borne in mind that in earlier proceedings under the Family Law Act 1996 he had agreed to leave the house. That, coupled with the fact that the house was to be sold as soon as possible, mitigated against an order to pay rent. Neither of these reasons is convincing. As Lord Neuberger subsequently pointed out, if the fact that he agreed to leave the house militated against ordering that a rent be paid to him, then this 'appears to reward intransigence and to penalise reasonableness'.[200] He also said, in a convincing dissenting opinion which did relate the facts of the case to the criteria contained in s. 15,[201] the fact that it is intended that the house should be sold quickly is irrelevant to the issue as to whether the occupier of it should pay rent to the co-owner who is not in occupation; a consideration which carries greater credence when the housing market is depressed and it is difficult to sell properties.

Because the issue of the payment of an occupation rent was treated in such a cursory manner in *Stack v. Dowden*, it is difficult to see the decision as laying down any principles of general application save that a judge must, in deciding both whether the house should be sold, and whether, pending a sale, the occupier should pay an occupation rent to the party out of occupation, have regard to the criteria laid down in s. 15. Once that has been done, one would envisage that the normal outcome would be that a rent should be paid, and such an order was made in *Murphy v. Gooch*,[202] this being considered by the Court of Appeal to be almost a matter of course. In quantifying the rent, however, regard is had to how the outgoings are paid on the co-owned house, so that if the person in occupation is paying the mortgage on that house, credit should be given for this.[203] The beneficial interests of the parties are also a relevant consideration in the determination of the appropriate rent. So, in *Akhtar v. Hussain*,[204] the Court of Appeal reduced the rent of £350 per calendar month to £175 to reflect the fact that the non-occupier had a 50 per cent beneficial share in the house and this had not been taken into account when the original order had been made.

9.8.5 **Insolvency**

The above section was concerned with disputes between the co-owners as to whether the property should be sold. This issue may also arise in a rather different context, when one

---

[198] TOLATA 1996, s. 13(6)(a).   [199] [2007] 2 A.C. 432.
[200] (2008) Chancery Bar Association Annual Lecture, para. 21, where he also expressed his mystification as to why the majority had refused to order that an occupation rent be paid.
[201] [2007] 2 A.C. 432 at [153]–[156].   [202] [2007] EWCA Civ. 608 at [22] *per* Lightman J.
[203] Ibid. at [23]–[25].   [204] [2012] EWCA Civ. 1762.

of the co-owners has financial problems and the pressure for the house to be sold comes from the creditors.[205] In this situation, rather different considerations arise in the exercise of the court's discretion.

9.8.5.1 Bankruptcy

When one of the co-owners has been declared bankrupt, the effect of the bankruptcy is that the bankrupt's beneficial share in the property will vest in the trustee in bankruptcy. The trustee would then petition the court for a sale of the property, such petitions being made, first, under s. 30, LPA 1925, and now under s. 14, TOLATA 1996. The trustee must lodge such a petition within three years of the bankruptcy, because after that period the bankrupt's interest in the home will re-vest in him.[206] A petition may also be lodged, even if the house has been the subject of a matrimonial order to the effect that it should not be sold unless one of a number of events has occurred.[207]

The common law approach

The judicial tone to how such applications should be approached was set in *Re Solomon*.[208] A married couple had held their home as joint tenants. In matrimonial proceedings, she had obtained an undertaking from him not to dispose of the property. He was then adjudicated bankrupt and the trustee petitioned the court for a sale of the matrimonial home. Goff J. held that the contest here was not simply between husband and wife but also between the wife and the husband's creditors. In the case of such a contest, he was of the view that the voice of the trustee in bankruptcy should prevail. The house was ordered to be sold, the wife being given a short time in which to order her affairs.

The approach, which favours the order of a sale, has been consistently followed. Although the court has a discretion, that discretion has, almost without fail, been exercised in favour of the trustee. The judicial attitude is that, 'One's debts must be paid, and paid promptly, and if they cannot be paid promptly, then the trustee in bankruptcy must prevail.'[209]

It became abundantly clear that, for a sale to be refused to the trustee in bankruptcy, exceptional circumstances must exist. It has been argued on more than one occasion that, if the effect of a sale being ordered was that the bankrupt's spouse and children would as a consequence lose their home, then a sale should not be ordered. Such an argument has been consistently rejected, this consequence not being seen as exceptional but as being a normal outcome of bankruptcy.[210] Typical of the judicial response is to say that the resulting problems caused to the bankrupt's family are 'yet another case where the sins of the father have to be visited upon the children, but that is the way in which the world is constructed, and one must be just before one can be generous'.[211] In similar vein, they are said to be 'the melancholy consequences of debt and improvidence'.[212]

---

[205] For critical accounts of the jurisprudence relating to this area, see Fox, *Conceptualising Home*, Chapter 3; R. Probert in Dixon and Griffiths (eds), *Contemporary Perspectives on Property, Equity and Trusts Law* (Oxford, Oxford University Press, 2007), Chapter 4.

[206] Insolvency Act 1986, s. 283A, a provision inserted by the Enterprise Act 2002, s. 261.

[207] *Avis v. Avis* [2007] EWCA Civ. 748.

[208] [1967] Ch. 573. For criticism, see C. Palley (1969) 20 N.I.L.Q. 132.

[209] *Re Bailey* [1977] 1 W.L.R. 278 at 283 *per* Walton J. See also *Re Densham* [1975] 1 W.L.R. 1519 at 1531 *per* Goff J.

[210] *Re Lowrie* [1981] 3 All E.R. 353.   [211] *Re Bailey* [1977] 1 W.L.R. 278 at 284 *per* Walton J.

[212] *Re Citro* [1991] Ch. 142 at 157 *per* Nourse L.J. For a very different approach, which did not actually involve the trustee in bankruptcy, see *Abbey National plc v. Moss* (1994) 29 H.L.R. 249, discussed by D.H. Clarke [1994] Conv. 331.

Until quite recently, there appeared to be only one case where the trustee in bankruptcy was refused a sale of the property as a result of objections by a co-owner. In *Re Holliday*,[213] a matrimonial home was in the joint names of husband and wife. The wife obtained a decree nisi and was seeking ancillary relief, whereupon the husband lodged his own petition for bankruptcy. After the bankruptcy order was made, the trustee petitioned for a sale of the house. Owing to the needs of the wife and their three children, the Court of Appeal postponed a sale of the property for a period of five years.

The case was clearly highly unusual. The creditors, who were essentially the husband's solicitor and a bank, were not pressing for payment and the bankruptcy petition was, in reality, a device to seek to avoid a property adjustment order being made against him. Moreover, the level of indebtedness was such that it was probable that the creditors would be paid at 100 pence on the £1, itself a highly unusual occurrence. The upshot was that it was highly unlikely that the creditors would suffer any hardship because of a postponement of a sale.[214] As such, the case has not subsequently been regarded as providing much guidance as to when a sale of the property should be refused to protect the interests of a co-owner.[215] The usual approach, albeit one at times applied reluctantly,[216] was that there was a strong presumption that, if a sale was sought by the trustee in bankruptcy, a sale would be ordered.

9.8.5.2 Insolvency Act

The case law which developed in relation to this issue did so in the context of petitions for sale by the trustee in bankruptcy and represented a consistent judicial approach to the exercise of discretion. The ethos underlying the case law received statutory recognition in the Insolvency Act 1986. Section 335A provides that:

> (1) Any application by a trustee in bankrupt's estate under section 14 of the Trusts of Land and Appointment of Trustees Act 1996 . . . for an order under that section shall be made to the court having jurisdiction in relation to the bankruptcy.
>
> (2) On such an application the court shall make such order as it thinks just and reasonable having regard to—
>
>> (a) the interests of the bankrupt's creditors;
>>
>> (b) where the application is made in respect of land which includes a dwelling house which is or has been the home of the bankrupt or the bankrupt's spouse or former spouse—
>>
>>> (i) the conduct of the spouse or former spouse, so far as contributing to the bankruptcy,
>>>
>>> (ii) the needs and financial resources of the spouse or former spouse, and
>>>
>>> (iii) the needs of any children; and
>>
>> (c) all the circumstances of the case other than the needs of the bankrupt.
>
> (3) Where such an application is made after the end of the period of one year beginning with the first vesting . . . of the bankrupt's estate in a trustee, the court shall assume, unless the circumstances of the case are exceptional, that the interests of the creditors outweigh all other considerations.[217]

---

[213] [1981] Ch. 405.   [214] *Re Citro* [1991] Ch. 132 at 157 *per* Nourse L.J.
[215] See *Re Lowrie* [1981] 3 All E.R. 353 at 356 *per* Walton L.J.; *Harman v. Glencross* [1986] Fam. 81 at 95 *per* Balcombe L.J.
[216] *Re Citro* [1991] at 161 *per* Bingham L.J.
[217] Section inserted by TOLATA 1996, s. 25(1), Sched. 3, para. 23.

Section 15(4), TOLATA 1996 provides that, if s. 335A of the Insolvency Act 1986 applies, then the criteria to which the court will normally have regard, contained in s. 15, do not apply. In other words, if, a year after the bankruptcy, the trustee petitions for a sale of the bankrupt's home, the interests of the creditors will, unless the circumstances are exceptional, prevail, and an order for sale will be made. [218]

Human rights

It had been suggested that this section may be incompatible with Art. 8 of the European Convention on Human Rights,[219] although the opposite view had also been asserted.[220] Although it is clear that the trustee in bankruptcy is a public body and, as a consequence, a court must be able to determine whether the making of a possession order is proportionate, the far more convincing argument is that Art. 8 is satisfied because the Act expressly makes provision for the personal circumstances of an occupier to be taken into account. While it is true that the family dislocation inherent in a forced sale is seen as the default position, and is regarded as being one of 'the melancholy consequences of debt and improvidence',[221] it is clear that an order for possession is not an inevitable conclusion in such cases. While one might argue that the balance struck by English law is too favourable to the trustee, acting on behalf of creditors, and insufficiently sympathetic to the problems of occupiers, such an argument should not lead to the conclusion that the approach taken under English law is outside the margin of appreciation afforded to individual states. In *Ford v. Alexander*,[222] the High Court gave a clear answer to the question of whether Art. 8 required a proportionality test to be read into s. 335A following the Supreme Court's decision in *Manchester City Council v. Pinnock*.[223] Peter Smith J. held that the requirements of s. 335A 'provide a necessary balance as between the rights of creditors and the respect for privacy and the home of the debtor. That balance serves the legitimate aim of protecting the rights and freedoms of others.' As a result, they 'satisfy the test of being necessary in a democratic society and are thus proportionate'. Until and unless a new argument is brought on this point,[224] it is now safe to assume that Art. 8 of the European Convention on Human Rights, just as it is not incompatible with the mortgagee's right to obtain possession,[225] does not impinge on a petition for sale by a trustee in bankruptcy, and the rules laid down in s. 335A.

9.8.5.3 Exceptional circumstances

Because the criteria listed by s. 15 of the 1996 Act do not apply to applications for a sale made by the trustee in bankruptcy, it is evident that the previous case law remains a reliable guide to the exercise of the court's discretion in such cases. The onus is therefore very much on the person seeking to obtain a postponement of the sale to establish that the circumstances are exceptional.

---

[218] For an example of an exceptional circumstances, see *Everitt v. Budhram* [2010] Ch 170, where sale was postponed owing to the claimant's physical and mental needs flowing from a history of ill health.

[219] *Jackson v. Bell* [2001] EWCA Civ. 387 at [24] *per* Sir Andrew Morritt V.-C.; *Barca v. Mears* [2004] EWHC 2170 (Ch) at [39] *per* Mr Nicholas Strauss Q.C. See M. Dixon [2005] Conv. 161 at 165–7; A. Barker [2010] Conv. 352.

[220] *Hoskings v. Michaelides* [2004] All E.R. (D.) 147 [70], Mr Paul Morgan Q.C. See also *Nicholls v. Lan* [2006] EWHC 1255 (Ch) at [42]–[44] *per* Mr Paul Morgan Q.C.

[221] *Re Citro* [1991] Ch. 142 at 147 *per* Nourse L.J.   [222] [2012] EWHC 266 (Ch).

[223] [2011] 2 AC 104. See Chapter 3 for a discussion of *Pinnock* and, in particular, 3.7.12.

[224] Peter Smith J. in *Ford v. Alexander* refused permission to appeal his judgment, which means his decision is technically non-binding on future cases of this kind.

[225] *Wood v. United Kingdom* (1997) 24 E.H.R.R. C.D. 69.

In determining what are exceptional circumstances, the courts have wisely refused to lay down general guidelines as to what these might be, preferring to treat each case on its merits.[226] But it remains the case that the family disruption, which is the normal result of a forced sale of a family property, will not be so regarded, even in situations where, given the size of the bankrupt's share in the house, little will be generated for the creditors by the sale, the proceeds of which being sufficient only to meet the costs of the trustee in bankruptcy.[227] What can change the courts' perspective is illness.

The illness or disability of the bankrupt's spouse or children may disincline the court to order a sale, one example which has been given being where the house is specially adapted to meet the physical needs of a disabled child, in which case the court would hesitate long before ordering an immediate sale.[228] In another case, the sale of a house was postponed for a year when the bankrupt's wife suffered from paranoid schizophrenia, a condition which made the impact upon her of adverse events, such as having to leave her home, particularly distressing.[229] Although the circumstances of the bankrupt personally are not a relevant consideration, they may become so indirectly, so that in *Re Bremner*,[230] the bankrupt had terminal cancer and a life expectancy of six months and the court postponed a sale of the matrimonial home until three months after his death, the exceptional circumstance being the wish of his wife to care for him during the latter stages of his life. It is evident, however, that it will require something out of the ordinary for the court to refuse a sale on the petition of the trustee in bankruptcy, and also that an indefinite delay is unlikely to be acceptable. In *Pickard v. Constable*,[231] Mrs Constable had been declared bankrupt and the trustees in bankruptcy applied for an order for the sale of the home she owned jointly with her husband. Mr Constable suffered from a debilitating disease, and also lacked the money to purchase or rent alternative accommodation. The district judge who heard the application at first instance postponed the sale until either Mr Constable died or had means of vacating the home and finding somewhere else to live. On appeal, Warren J. held that it was not open to a court to indefinitely postpone an order for sale, because of the paramount interests of the creditors, and existing authority indicated that the maximum postponement allowable would be twelve months. Warren J., therefore, allowed the trustees' appeal and reduced the postponement of the sale to twelve months, with permission for Mr Constable to apply for further postponement if the local authority was not able to find suitable housing in performance of their statutory duty.

9.8.5.4 Secured creditors

Prior to the enactment of TOLATA 1996, the courts used to adopt the same approach to petitions for sale brought by a secured creditor as they did if it had been brought by a trustee in bankruptcy,[232] an approach which meant that a sale of the property would normally be ordered.[233] Section 15 of the Act, however, simply includes the interest of any

---

[226] See *Claughton v. Charalambous* [1999] 1 F.L.R. 740 at 744, 745 *per* Jonathan Parker J.

[227] *Trustee of the Estate of Bowe v. Bowe* [1998] 2 F.L.R. 439; *Harrington v. Bennett* [2000] E.G.C.S. 41.

[228] *Re Bailey* [1977] 1 W.L.R. 278 at 284 *per* Walton J.

[229] *Re Raval* [1998] 2 F.L.R. 718. See also *Claughton v. Charalambous* [1999] 1 F.L.R. 740, where an indefinite postponement was ordered on account of the bankrupt's wife suffering from renal failure and arthritis, although, on the facts, a sale of the property would not have benefited the creditors; *Judd v. Barr* [1988] 2 F.L.R. 368 (cancer), reversed with respect to the non-matrimonial property: [1999] 1 F.L.R. 1191. *Hoskings v. Michaelides* [2004] All E.R. (D.) 147; *Nicholls v. Lan* [2006] EWHC 1255 (Ch) (mental health).

[230] [1999] 1 F.L.R. 912.

[231] [2017] EWHC 2475 (Ch). See also *Grant v. Baker* [2017] 2 FLR 646.

[232] *Lloyds Bank plc v. Byrne* [1993] 1 F.L.R. 369; *Barclays Bank plc v. Hendricks* [1996] 1 F.L.R. 258. See N.S. Price [1996] Conv. 464.

[233] But see *Abbey National plc v. Moss* (1993) 26 H.L.R. 249, a decision which was out of line with the rest of the authorities.

secured creditor of any beneficiary as one factor to be considered when deciding whether to order a sale. The interests of a secured creditor would no longer seem, therefore, to be a decisive consideration, a view confirmed in *Mortgage Corporation Ltd v. Shaire*.[234] Nevertheless, the voice of the creditor will be a powerful one, particularly, as was the case in *Bank of Ireland Home Mortgages Ltd v. Bell*,[235] if there is little, if any, equity in the house and no prospect of any payments being made to reduce the debt. It should also be remembered that, if the court refuses to order a sale at the behest of a secured creditor, that creditor can then petition for the debtor's bankruptcy and, if the debtor is declared bankrupt, the trustee in bankruptcy will petition the court for a sale of the property and, unless there are exceptional circumstances, the court will, a year after the bankrupt's property has vested in him, order that the property be sold.[236]

---

[234] [2000] 2 F.L.R. 222. Although criticized by S. Pascoe [2000] Conv. 315, the actual wording of the section does lead to this conclusion. See M.P. Thompson [2000] Conv. 329; L. Tee, *Land Law Issues, Debates, Policy*, 152.

[235] [2001] F.L.R. 809. See also *First National Bank plc v. Achampong* [2004] 1 F.L.R. 18 and M.P. Thompson [2003] Conv. 314 at 320–3.

[236] See *Zandfarid v. BCCI International S.A.* [1996] 1 W.L.R. 1420; *Re Ng* [1998] 2 F.L.R. 386; *Judd v. Brown* [1999] 1 F.L.R. 1191.

10

Leasehold Estates

While the lease is now a familiar part of landholding, it was not originally seen as being within land law at all. Leases were principally a commercial relationship, while the doctrine of tenure, which dominated the development of early land law, was concerned with a person's status in society. The impact of this early classification is essentially historical, it having long been recognized that a lease is both an estate in land and a contract. This has at times, led to some tension as to whether the relationship between landlord and tenant should be regarded as incidents of that estate, or should be governed by normal contractual principles.

The three main areas where leases are used are residential, commercial, and agricultural property. Within the residential context, the type of lease can vary considerably. One obvious divide is between the private and the public sector. Even within the private sector, however, there is variation as to the type of lease involved. One can have a short-term let, where a person takes a lease of a property for a term of six months. Alternatively, a very long lease of, say, 999 years can be created, the object of which is, effectively, to give the leaseholder the rights of a freeholder. The lease is employed instead of a freehold estate so as to make it possible for the burden of certain covenants to attach to the land in question, this being difficult to do if the property is actually freehold. This is the key reason why the transfer of flats is normally done by the employment of long leases rather than by a sale of the freehold.[1]

The lease is therefore used for many different purposes. It is also an area of law where there has been extensive statutory regulation, different statutory codes applying to different types of lease. A consequence of this is that the law of landlord and tenant has become an increasingly specialized area. This specialization has extended not only to the comprehensive coverage of the topic but also to extensive treatments of different areas of statutory regulation. In a work of this nature, it is not possible to attempt a proper coverage of the different statutory regimes which exist in the leasehold sector; rather, this chapter will seek to explain the general principles underlying the subject.

10.1 Terminology

Before examining the essentials of a lease, it is helpful to explain some of the terminology. The term 'demise' is often used instead of the word lease. Similarly, the expressions 'term of years', 'tenancy', and 'lease' are frequently used interchangeably. They mean the same thing.

The person who grants the lease is called the lessor or the landlord. The landlord carves the leasehold estate out of his freehold interest, which he retains. While the landlord, as the person in receipt of rents and profits, is legally regarded as being in possession,[2] physically

---

[1] A new system of landholding termed commonhold has, with extremely limited success, been introduced to seek to deal with this issue. See Chapter 11.

[2] Law of Property Act (LPA) 1925, s. 205(1)(xix).

he does not have the right to possess the property. The landlord's interest is called the reversion. This estate can be assigned, the person to whom it is assigned being termed the assignee of the reversion.

The tenant also has an estate in the land. This, too, can be assigned to an assignee. Because leases were not originally regarded as land, the statute Quia Emptores 1290 and its prohibition on subinfeudation[3] did not apply and so, instead of transferring his entire estate as is the case with freehold property, the tenant can create a smaller lease out of it. If a tenant holds a ninety-nine-year lease of property, he can carve out of that tenancy a sub-lease of, say, fifty years. The person to whom the sub-lease is granted is called the sub-tenant and the lease out of which the sub-tenancy was created is called the head lease. The head tenant occupies a dual role; under the head lease he is the tenant but, with regard to the sub-lease, he is the sub-landlord. Diagrammatically, this can be represented as shown in Figure 10.1.

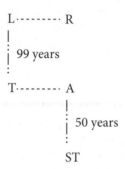

Fig. 10.1 Freehold estate, lease, and sub-lease

The original lease is a ninety-nine-year lease between L and T. L has assigned his reversion to R. T has assigned his interest to A, who has, in turn, created a fifty-year sub-lease in favour of ST.

10.2 The context of leases

Leases are particularly important in the residential context where, since 1915, there has been in existence protective legislation affecting the relationship between landlord and tenant in the private sector, this legislation being known, collectively, as the Rent Acts.[4] This legislation was designed to improve the position of tenants *vis-à-vis* their landlords. It did this by focusing on two central elements—the rent which could be charged, and the security of the tenant.

One key element in the strategy adopted by the Rent Acts was to control the rent which had to be paid by the tenant. Whatever the contractually agreed rent might have been, if the tenant was protected under the Acts he could refer the rent to a rent officer, who would then assess and register a fair rent for the property.[5] The consequence of the registration of a fair rent, which was almost invariably lower than the rent specified in the lease, was that the landlord was precluded from collecting more than that sum from the tenant.

---

[3] See 1.1

[4] The first such Act was the Rent and Mortgage Interest (War Restrictions) Act 1915.

[5] Rent Act 1977, s. 67.

The second main form of protection afforded by the Acts was to confer upon the tenant security of tenure. This meant that additional hurdles were placed in the way of a landlord seeking to recover possession of the property from the tenant upon whom was conferred what has been described as a 'status of irremovability'.[6] The security conferred upon tenants was such that, in many cases, it would be nigh on impossible for the landlord to regain possession of the property, notwithstanding that the original lease had expired many years previously. Moreover, as well as conferring security on the original tenant, the legislation enabled members of the tenant's family to succeed to that tenancy, and this could occur on two occasions. The upshot was that if a tenancy was created to last for an original period of six months, the landlord could be prevented from regaining possession of the property for two generations and, during that period, be precluded from charging more than an independently established fair rent for that period.

The impact of the Rent Acts upon landlords was considerable and affected significantly the capital value of that property. If a house was subject to a protected tenancy, it would be difficult to sell the freehold to anyone else, as any purchaser would also be precluded from obtaining a commercial return on the property. Consequently, many owners of property sought to enter contractual relationships affecting the property without creating a tenancy which would attract the protection of the Rent Acts and considerable ingenuity was expended towards the achievement of this aim.[7]

The desire to avoid the Rent Acts is *the leitmotif* running through many of the cases involving the distinction between a lease and a licence, including *Street v. Mountford*. Since the enactment of the Housing Act 1988, however, the degree of protection afforded to private sector tenants has diminished substantially.[8] As a result, there have been far fewer attempts to create residential occupancy agreements which are not tenancies. The cases which have involved such attempts can only properly be understood, however, if one appreciates some of the motivation on the part of landowners.

10.3 **The essentials of a lease**

There are two estates which are capable of existing at law—the fee simple absolute in possession (a freehold) and the term of years absolute (a lease).[9] Section 205 of the LPA 1925 defines a 'Term of years absolute' as a:

> term of years (taking effect either in possession or in reversion whether or not at a rent) . . . either certain or liable to determination by notice, re-entry, operation of law, or by a provision for cesser on redemption . . . and in this definition the expression "term of years" includes a term for less than a year, or for a year or years and a fraction of a year or from year to year.

This definition sets out how a lease can be brought to an end ('determined') by notice, re-entry, operation of law, or by a provision for cesser on redemption. While s. 205, LPA 1925 clearly sets out the need for certainty of term, it does not require rent.

For a lease to exist, there must be an intention to create legal relations. This may be missing if the arrangement is made to offer charity or a service occupancy.[10] As Lord

---

[6] *Jessamine Investments Co. v. Schwartz* [1978] Q.B. 264 at 277 *per* Stephenson L.J.

[7] For a penetrating discussion, see S. Bright [2002] C.L.J. 146.

[8] The 1977 Act continues to govern leases created prior to 1988. For a recent example involving rent control affecting a lease created in 1983, see *Bacon v. Mountview Estates Ltd* [2015] UKUT 0588 (LC).

[9] LPA 1925, s. 1(1).   [10] See below, 10.3.3.2

Templeman held in *Street v. Mountford*, this depends on the intention of the parties, not any labels attached to the agreement:

> If the agreement satisfied all the requirements of a tenancy, then the agreement produced a tenancy and the parties cannot alter the effect of the agreement by insisting that they only created a licence. The manufacture of a five-pronged implement for manual digging results in a fork even if the manufacturer, unfamiliar with the English language, insists that he intended to make and has made a spade.

As the Court of Appeal confirmed in *Watts v. Stewart*, where they held that there was no lease, in part since the relationship was one of charity, this question is about the substance of the arrangement, rather than the form, of the arrangement: it 'turns on the intention of the parties having regard to all the admissible evidence'.[11]

10.3.1 Term

A key element of the definition of a lease is that it is either for a term certain or that it is clear how the arrangement can be brought to a premature end. This can occur if the lease is expressly made determinable upon the occurrence of a specified event. Alternatively, in a long lease either side may be given the right to terminate the lease on specified occasions. Such clauses are called break clauses. What may also occur is that a periodic tenancy is created. In such cases, the original period is agreed, and that period will recur until either of the parties to the lease brings it to an end.[12] The essential idea remains, however, that the parties have agreed upon the term of the lease. If the period of time agreed upon is uncertain, then the intended lease will be void.

This principle underpins the decision in *Lace v. Chantler*.[13] Here, there was 'ordinary weekly tenancy, duly determinable by a week's notice'.[14] However, in the rent book the parties also agreed that the dwelling-house would be 'furnished for duration', which the Court of Appeal held 'must mean the duration of the war'.[15] As a result, the lease must fail for uncertainty: 'A term created by a leasehold tenancy agreement must be expressed either with certainty and specifically or by reference to something which can, at the time when the lease takes effect, be looked to as a certain ascertainment of what the term is meant to be. In the present case, when this tenancy agreement took effect, the term was completely uncertain. It was impossible to say how long the tenancy would last.'[16] Such wartime leases were, it seems, quite common and were subsequently rescued by statute by being converted into ten-year leases determinable by either party giving one month's notice to the other to determine the lease upon the end of hostilities.[17] This legislative work-around created a lease where there was a certain term, in the sense of there being a maximum period agreed upon at the outset, but where the lease could be brought to a premature end once the war had ended. The general principle confirmed in *Lace v. Chantler* continued: to be a valid lease one must know at the outset what the period of it is. Consistent with this, if, although the length of the term is agreed, there is no agreed starting date for it, then the purported lease will be void.[18]

---

[11] [2016] EWCA Civ. 1247 at [38]. See 10.3.4.1   [12] See 10.4.2.
[13] [1944] K.B. 368.   [14] Ibid. at 370   [15] Ibid.
[16] Ibid. Per Lord Greene M.R.   [17] Validation of Wartime Leases Act 1944, s. 1.
[18] *Harvey v. Pratt* [1965] 1 W.L.R. 1025. Cf *Canada Square Corp. Ltd v. Versafood Services Ltd* (1980) 101 D.L.R. (3d) 743. A lease to start on the substantial completion of a rooftop restaurant was regarded as having a sufficiently certain starting date. See also *Liverpool City Council v. Walton Group plc* [2002] 1 E.G.L.R. 149; *Ahmed v. Wingrove* [2007] EWHC 1918 (Ch) at [16]–[17] *per* Mr Michael Toulson Q.C.

This principle of certainty of term was challenged in *Prudential Assurance Co. Ltd v. London Residuary Body*.[19] In 1930, the then owner of a strip of land fronting a highway sold it to the council and took a lease back of it, that lease being expressed to continue until the land was required by the council for the purpose of widening the highway. The council abandoned its road-widening plan and the reversion passed to the defendant with the lease was assigned to the plaintiff. The defendant purported to terminate the tenancy by the service of a notice to quit and the plaintiff sought a declaration that the lease could only be terminated when the highway was widened. The declaration was refused. The House of Lords held that the purported lease was void for uncertainty. That being the case, the position was that, as the person to whom the grant was made had gone into possession and paid rent, a yearly tenancy arose by implication and the landlord could terminate this lease by serving an appropriate notice to quit.[20] Lord Templeman considered that 'the principle in *Lace v. Chantler*, reaffirming 500 years of judicial acceptance of the requirement that a term must be certain, applies to all leases and tenancy agreements'.[21] As the widening of the road was an uncertain event which may, indeed, never happen, a lease calculated by reference to such a contingency was void for uncertainty.

This result was reached with reluctance by some members of the House. Lord Browne-Wilkinson, with whom Lords Griffiths and Mustill agreed, described the result as 'bizarre' and 'resulting from the application of an ancient and technical rule which requires the maximum duration of a lease to be ascertainable from the outset'. He went on to say that: 'No one has produced any satisfactory rationale for the genesis of this rule. No one has been able to point to any useful purpose that it serves at the present day'.[22] These critical comments, have unsurprisingly, generated a debate with arguments in favour of both for and against the rule of certainty of term.[23] However, in *Prudential* a way was found around the harshness of the rule. For even though there could be no fixed-term tenancy (because the road could no longer be widened as anticipated), a yearly periodic tenancy had been created instead. For although the agreement failed to grant an estate in the land, when the tenant entered into possession and paid the £30 yearly rent, a periodic tenancy was created. Since six months' notice had been given, the court deemed this sufficient to end the periodic tenancy.[24] Yet, the House of Lords confirmed the principle that a periodic tenancy can arise through possession and the payment of the periodic rent, even though there is no certain fixed term.

10.3.1.1 *Berrisford v. Mexfield Housing Co-operative*

The Supreme Court in *Berrisford v. Mexfield Housing Co-operative Ltd*[25] found another way around the harshness of the fixed-term rule. Here, Mexfield was a housing co-opera-tive body which effected mortgage rescues. To do this, it bought property from borrowers who were in financial difficulties, and then let them back to them. In 1993 it entered such an arrangement with Ms Berrisford. She signed an Occupancy Agreement that continued from month to month until determined as provided by the Agreement. The Agreement provided by Clause 5 that Ms Berrisford could determine the tenancy by giving one month's notice to quit. Mexfield, on the other hand, could by Clause 6 only determine the lease on one of four grounds, of which mention need only be made to the first two: that

---

[19] [1992] 2 A.C. 386.   [20] [1992] 2 A.C. 386 at 392 *per* Lord Templeman. See 10.4.2.

[21] [1992] 2 A.C. 386 at 394.

[22] Ibid. at 396. For a spirited critique of this decision, see J. Roche [2011] Conv. 444.

[23] See P. Sparkes (1993) 109 L.Q.R. 103, supporting the rule, and S. Bright (1993) 13 L.S. 38, opposing it.

[24] [1992] 2 A.C. 386 at 392.

[25] [2011] UKSC 52. This was an important test case as a considerable number of identical agreements had been entered into.

there were rent arrears; or that she had neglected to perform any terms of the agreement. Neither condition was applicable. Nevertheless, Mexfield sought to terminate the lease by the service of a notice to quit. The argument was that the original agreement was ineffective to create a lease because its duration was, from the landlord's perspective, uncertain; it was unclear as to when, if ever, the landlord would be able to terminate the lease. As Ms Berrisford was in possession paying rent, it was argued that there was an implied periodic tenancy, which could be ended by an appropriate notice to quit (as in *Prudential*), despite the Agreement precluding it from doing so. The Supreme Court rejected this argument on the basis that 'the parties did in fact intend a lease for life determinable earlier by the tenant on one month's notice and by the landlords on the happening of certain specified events'.[26]

Although the members of the Court were highly critical of the certainty rule as reaffirmed in *Prudential*, they declined to overrule it. This meant that that the lease, as set out in the contract, could not take effect.[27] Nevertheless, this was not considered to be determinative of the matter. The argument was advanced that, prior to 1925, a lease for an individual for an uncertain term took effect as a lease for life, and this was accepted as being correct in court (although the conclusion has been criticized by legal historians).[28]

Since the LPA 1925 a life interest cannot take effect at law[29] and if not overreached is converted by s. 149(6), LPA 1925 to a ninety-year term, determinable upon death. This statutory solution overcomes the difficulty that otherwise such a lease would be void for uncertainty. So, In the present case, Ms Berrisford was held to have a legal ninety-year lease, determinable either upon her death, or the service of one month's notice to quit by her, or a notice served by Mexfield in accordance with the terms of the Agreement. While legal historians have argued that the creation of a tenancy for life in this case was simply mistaken, Lord Neuberger, asking why the same analysis, reliant on s. 149(6) was not raised in *Lace v. Chantler* concluded instead that the reason this conclusion was not reached in *Lace v. Chantler* was because the argument was never raised and had not been prior to it being successfully argued in the present case.[30]

Since then, however, in *Southward Housing Co-operative v. Walker*,[31] *Mexfield* has been distinguished on the basis that such an outcome was not intended by the parties. *Walker* concerned a dispute between a fully mutual co-operative housing association and tenants who had fallen behind with the rent under a tenancy that had (the court held) an uncertain term. Rather than finding a tenancy for life, and the translation into a ninety-year term under s. 149(6) LPA 1925, which the court held the parties had not intended, Hildyard J. concluded that the outcome in *Mexfield* should be confined to situations where there was uncertainty of term *and* the intention of the parties could be said to support the finding of a tenancy for life:

> the origin of the 'rule' must have been intended to save agreements that would otherwise fail, in accordance with the maxim '*ut res magis valeat quam pereat*', not to destroy the essence of their bargain and foist on them a long term relationship against their will and which one of them may not be able to terminate.[32]

---

[26] UKSC ref—at 982 in AC.   [27] See ibid. at [23]–[37] *per* Lord Neuberger.

[28] Ibid. at [42] *per* Lord Neuberger. See also at [116] *per* Lord Dyson, citing Williams, *Law of Real Property* (23rd edn) (London, Sweet & Maxwell, 1920), 135. For critique see, for example, Juanita Roche 'Legal history in court: lessons from Mexfield and Southward' (2016) The Conveyancer and Property Lawyer 206–302 and Kelvin Low, 'Certainty of Terms and Leases: Curiouser and Curiouser' 75 Mod L Rev 401 (2012).

[29] LPA 1925, s. 1.   [30] [2011] UKSC 52 at [53].

[31] [2015] EWHC 1615 (Ch). See also *Secretary of State for Transport v Blake* [2013] EWHC 2945 (Ch) (Ch D)

[32] [2015] EWHC 1615 (Ch) at [92].

Certainly, *Southward Housing Co-operative v. Walker* has been criticized[33] and it is true that the reasoning in *Mexfield* did not necessarily justify the outcome according to the intentions of the parties.[34] However, if the consequence of *Mexfield* is that regardless of the intention of the parties, courts will 'inexorably' find a tenancy for life when there is a tenancy of uncertain duration as a consequence of a fetter of uncertain duration, then this has profound consequences for all landlords, not just housing co-operatives as in *Mexfield*.[35] In particular, as Susan Pascoe argues: 'The dual transmogrification process applied in *Mexfield* would be antithetical to the core essence of a periodic tenancy.'[36] For these reasons, as well as the doubts as to the interpretations of the legal history in *Mexfield*, the result in *Walker* deserves consideration.

10.3.1.2 Contractual licence

Although the argument concerning a life tenancy was accepted in *Berrisford*, and this was enough to determine the outcome of the appeal, the Supreme Court also considered a second argument. This was that, even if the original tenancy had been void for uncertainty, there would still be in existence an enforceable contractual licence between the parties, and Mexfield could have been prevented by equitable relief from breaking that contract. Such an argument had been raised, but rejected, in *Lace v. Chantler*,[37] where Lord Greene M.R. thought it impossible to construe the agreement in this way. In his view, if the parties intended to create a lease, and the law says that it is bad as a tenancy, it cannot be construed as a licence. In *Berrisford*,[38] however, Lord Neuberger did not think that these observations could withstand principled analysis. Instead, he thought the true position to be that, 'If the Agreement is incapable of giving rise to a tenancy for some old and technical rule or property law, I do not see why, as a matter of principle, that should render the Agreement invalid as matter of contract.'

On this analysis, if an intended lease fails for uncertainty, then that same agreement will take effect as a contractual licence. This was the outcome in *Southward Housing Co-operative v. Walker*.[39] As between the parties themselves this may not be that important and, in particular, the landlord will be unable to terminate the occupancy in a way that is not envisaged by the contract. Unlike a lease, however, this licence does not create an interest in land. As was explained in *Berrisford*:

> If the Agreement does not create a tenancy for technical reasons, namely because it purports to create an uncertain term, it is hard to see why, as a matter of principle, it should not be capable of taking effect as a contract, enforceable as between the parties personally, *albeit not capable of binding their respective successors, as no interest in land or other proprietary interest would subsist.*[40]

The finding of a contractual licence to exist when an intended lease fails for uncertainty will affect companies rather than human tenants. This is because a company is not capable of holding a life interest in property, and so the argument that an uncertain lease can take

---

[33] See the 6th edition of this book, at 378.

[34] For slightly different perspectives on the relevance of the intentions of the parties, see Lord Neuberger at [44], Lady Hale at [94], and Lord Dyson at [117].

[35] This is the word that Hildyard J. uses to convey his concern, [2015] EWHC 1615 (Ch) at [94].

[36] Susan Pascoe, 'Periodic tenancies subject to a fetter on the tenant—doctrinal dilemmas?' Conveyancer and Property Lawyer (2018) 119–32 at 124 citing Kelvin Low's use of the word 'transmogrification' in Kelvin Low, 'Certainty of Terms and Leases: Curiouser and Curiouser' 75 Mod. L. Rev. 401 (2012).

[37] [1944] K.B. 368 at 372.

[38] [2011] UKSC 52 at [62]. See also *Southward Housing Co-operative v. Walker*, *supra*, at [95] *per* Hildyard J.

[39] [2015] EWHC 1615 (Ch).   [40] [2011] UKSC 52 at [60]. Emphasis supplied

effect as a lease for life, which is then converted by s. 149(6), LPA 1925 into a determinable ninety-year lease is not tenable. That this is the result of the refusal to overrule *Prudential* was recognized in terms by Lord Collins, who considered it to be a mystery as to why, in 2011, the position of a tenant who is a human being and a tenant that is a company should, in this respect, be different.[41] It is easy to sympathize with this view, and it would seem that this area of law is one, as all the Supreme Court justices recognized, would benefit from an examination by the Law Commission, with a view to changing a rule that appears to have outlived its usefulness.

10.3.2 Rent

Section 205 of the LPA 1925 includes no requirement for rent in its definition of a lease ('a term of years absolute . . . whether or not for a rent'),[42] a conclusion that is also supported in case law.[43] Yet, in practice, few landlords will let their property without some form of payment in return. In *Street v. Mountford*, Lord Templeman did include rent as part of his definition of a tenancy,[44] holding that s. 205 had translated the requirements from the common law and it is widely accepted that where there is no requirement for rent there *may* be a lack of legal intention to create a lease, the arrangement may be one of charity, for example.

On the other hand, the fact that money is paid in respect of occupation does not necessarily mean that this payment constitutes rent, or that there is necessarily an intention to create legal relations. In *Leadenhall Residential 2 Ltd v. Stirling*,[45] a possession order was made against a tenant on the ground of non-payment of rent. Pending the actual delivering up of possession, liberty had been given to the landlord to accept some £411.66 per month as mesne profits until possession was given. The tenant was allowed to continue in occupation and paid this sum, together with £100 per month in respect of the accumulated arrears. The Court of Appeal held that there was no payment of rent. The landlord had allowed the tenant to remain in the property as an act of kindness and there was no intention to create legal relations.[46] The monetary payment was in lieu of damages for trespass.

10.3.3 Exclusive possession

Section 1 of the Rent Act 1977 provides that:

> Subject to this Part of this Act a tenancy under which a dwelling-house (which may be a house or a part of a house) is let as a separate dwelling is a protected tenancy for the purposes of this Act.

Central to the definition is that the dwelling-house is '*let*'. To avoid the occupancy agreement, to use a neutral term, attracting the protection afforded by the Act, attempts were made to create such agreements without creating a lease, the aim instead being to create a licence. A key element in the distinction between a lease and a licence is the concept of exclusive possession. As a lease is an estate in land, the tenant, as the holder of that estate, has the right to exclude everyone else, including the landlord, from the property: the right

---

[41] Ibid. at [105].   [42] Section 205 (xxvii), LPA 1925.
[43] *Ashburn Anstalt v. Arnold* [1989] Ch. 1 at 9–10 *per* Fox L.J. This aspect of the case is not affected by the overruling of the decision in *Prudential Assurance Co Ltd v. London Residuary Body* [1992] 2 A.C. 386.
[44] [1985] 1 AC 809 at 814E.   [45] [2002] 1 W.L.R. 499.
[46] The relevant intention is to create legal relations, not an intention to create a lease, contrary to what was said in *Vesely v. Hart* [2007] EWCA Civ. 367 at [49] *per* Mummery L.J.

to exclude being a central component of the concept of a right of ownership.[47] Whether or not exclusive possession was granted became, therefore, a central feature in determining whether a lease had been created, although the true meaning and importance of this concept came to be somewhat obscured.

10.3.3.1 **Single occupancy**

In considering the question as to whether a particular transaction created a lease or a licence, it is necessary to distinguish between cases where the property is occupied by one person and cases where there is more than one occupier, because different considerations arise.

At first, the presence of exclusive possession was regarded as being conclusive as to whether or not there was a lease.[48] Subsequently, however, its importance seemed to be downplayed. In *Marchant v. Charters*,[49] a single man occupied a room in a large house, that house having been converted into bedsits. There was a gas ring for cooking in the room, and the toilet and bathroom were shared with other occupants. A housekeeper cleaned the room on a daily basis and the linen was changed once a week. The occupier applied to the rent officer for the registration of a fair rent and the owner of the house responded by serving on him a notice to quit. Central to the case was whether the occupier was a tenant or a licensee. The Court of Appeal unanimously held him to be a licensee.

Lord Denning M.R. sought to explain how one decides these matters. He said:

> What is the test to see whether the occupier of one room in a house is a tenant or a licensee? It does not depend on whether he has exclusive possession or not. It does not depend on whether the room is furnished or not. It does not depend on whether the occupation is permanent or temporary. It does not depend on the label which the parties put on it. All these are factors which may influence the decision but none of them is conclusive. All the circumstances have to be worked out. Eventually the answer depends upon the nature and quality of the occupancy. Was it intended that the occupier should have a stake in the room or did he have only permission for himself personally to occupy the room, whether under a contract or not? In which case he is a licensee.[50]

10.3.3.2 **Exclusive possession or exclusive occupation**

The decision in *Marchant v. Charters* was undoubtedly correct yet appeared to understand the grant of exclusive possession as being only one factor in the determination of whether a lease or a licence was created. It is quite possible that Lord Denning was using the term 'exclusive possession' loosely, to mean exclusive occupation: a factual description of the situation where a room is not actually shared.[51] Historically, 'exclusive occupation' is not an expression that answers the question whether the occupier has the right to exclude all others: it was a legal and not a factual issue.[52] *Marchant v. Charters* did, however, give weight to the stated intention of the parties not to create an interest in land,[53] an outcome that has been criticized.[54] This treads a difficult line, since it is clear from the case law on shams and pretences that parties may not convert a lease into a licence simply by attaching

---

[47] See 1.1.3.   [48] See *Lynes v. Snaith* [1899] 1 Q.B. 466.   [49] [1977] 1 W.L.R. 1181.

[50] Ibid. at 1185. For an unwelcome echo of this approach, see *Mehta v. Royal Bank of Scotland* [1999] 3 E.G.L.R. 153 at 156 *per* Mr Richard Southwell Q.C.

[51] For a more recent example of this, see *Vesely v. Levy* [2007] EWCA Civ. 367 at [43] *per* Mummery L.J.

[52] For a valuable discussion of this matter, see M.C. Cullity (1965) 28 Conv. (N.S.) 336.

[53] For a general discussion of the role of intention in the creation of interests in land, see M. Howard and J. Hill (1995) 15 L.S. 356.

[54] See the 6th edition of this book, 382.

that title to the relevant document and it would be counter-intuitive if the parties, particularly the landlord, could achieve the same result by the statement of an intention to create only a personal interest in the property.

This debate resurfaced in *Watts v. Stewart*[55] where a charity was held to have granted only a licence to Mrs Watts, given the nature of their arrangement. In distinguishing exclusive occupation from exclusive possession, Etherton L.J. held that:

> there is a distinction between legal exclusive possession or a legal right of exclusive possession, on the one hand, and a personal right of exclusive occupation, on the other hand . . . Legal exclusive possession entitles the occupier to exclude all others, including the legal owner, from the property. Exclusive occupation may, or may not, amount to legal possession. If it does, the occupier is a tenant. If it does not, the occupier is not a tenant and occupies in some different capacity.[56]

This was a question of fact to be determined by the court. Since there was 'no question of the Trustees trying artificially to colour the Appointment Letter as licence rather than a tenancy in order to disguise the true nature of the relationship',[57] this was a licence and not a lease, as Mrs Watts had only been granted exclusive occupation and not exclusive possession.[58]

10.3.3.3 The primacy of exclusive possession

Whatever the correct reading of this passage, greater clarity was restored by the House of Lords in the leading case of *Street v. Mountford*,[59] a decision which re-established the primacy of exclusive possession and downplayed the stated intentions of the parties. Mrs Mountford[60] signed a document, termed a licence agreement, whereby she was given the right to occupy two rooms for a weekly licence fee of £37. At the foot of the document was a statement, signed by her, which read: 'I understand and accept that a licence in the above form does not and is not intended to give me a tenancy protected under the Rent Acts.' She then sought to have a fair rent registered, whereupon the owner of the house sought a declaration that she was a licensee and not a tenant. The House of Lords held her to be a tenant.

A key concession was made. It was conceded that the agreement gave Mrs Mountford exclusive possession of the rooms. Nevertheless, it was argued that, because there was no intention to create a lease, the agreement operated only to create a contractual licence. This argument was rejected. Lord Templeman, who gave the only speech, was at pains to re-assert the role of exclusive possession. He said:

> the court must decide whether upon its true construction, the agreement confers upon the occupier exclusive possession. If exclusive possession at a rent for a term[61] does not constitute a tenancy then the distinction between a contractual tenancy and a contractual licence of land becomes wholly illusory.[62]

---

[55] [2016] EWCA Civ. 1247.

[56] At [31] citing Windeyer J. in *Radaich v. Smith* (1959) 101 C.L.R. 209 at 222 as approved by Lord Templeman in *Street v. Mountford* at 827 as well as *Allan v. The Overseers of Liverpool* (1873–74) L.R. 9 Q.B. 180 and *Errington v. Errington* [1952] 1 K.B. 291.

[57] [2016] EWCA Civ. 1247 at [40].   [58] Ibid. at [46] and [50].

[59] [1985] A.C. 809. See S. Anderson (1985) 48 M.L.R. 712; D.N. Clarke [1986] Conv. 39. For a critical reaction by the draftsman of the document, and the loser in the litigation, see R. Street [1985] Conv. 328. For a valuable retrospective, see S. Bridge in Gravells (ed.), *Landmark Cases in Land Law* (Oxford, Hart Publishing, 2013), Chapter 11.

[60] The headnote refers to her husband occupying the rooms but no mention of him appears in the speech of Lord Templeman and the case is treated throughout as a single occupancy agreement.

[61] For the need for a certain term, see *Berrisford v. Mansfield Housing Co operative* [2011] UKSC 52, and see 10.3.1.

[62] [1985] A.C. 809 at 825.

As it had been conceded that Mrs Mountford had exclusive possession for a term at a rent, it followed that she was a tenant. The fact that the parties had stated that their intention was to create a licence was irrelevant. Intention is relevant only insofar as it indicates an intent to grant exclusive possession. Once an agreement has been made, the consequences of that agreement have to be determined as a matter of law.[63]

10.3.4 **The lease/licence distinction**

In his analysis of the previous case law, Lord Templeman shifted the focus from the intention of the parties with regard to what it was that the agreement created, to the central issue of whether or not the agreement conferred exclusive possession in the sense of the right to exclude all others from the property. In determining whether or not exclusive possession had been granted, he distinguished between a lease and lodgings. He said:

> In the case of residential accommodation there is no difficulty in deciding whether the grant confers exclusive accommodation. An occupier of residential accommodation at a rent for a term is either a lodger or a tenant. The occupier is a lodger if the landlord provides attendance or services *which require the landlord or his servants to exercise unrestricted access to and use of the premises.* A lodger is entitled to live in the premises but cannot call the place his own.[64]

This passage explains why the decision in a case like *Marchant v. Charters* is correct, although the language used in it is not. In that case, the occupant's room was cleaned on a daily basis and fresh linen supplied weekly. The real reason why this was not a tenancy was that the occupier did not have exclusive possession; the provision of services was such that the landlady's employee required unrestricted access to the property and so, in Lord Templeman's terminology, the occupier was a lodger.

In the residential context,[65] it should be fairly straightforward to determine whether the agreement confers exclusive possession on the occupier. The level of access necessary for the provision of services is a decisive factor and means that, although a student in a hall of residence or an occupant in a hotel has exclusive occupation in the sense that they do not share a room, they do not have exclusive possession of that room.[66] What can present rather more difficulty is where it is not clear that the terms of the agreement represent the reality of the situation due to the inclusion of arguably unrealistic clauses into the agreement. An example of this is a rent review clause enabling the landlord to raise the rent paid by tenants on housing benefit from £4,690 per annum to £25,000 per annum,[67] designed, in this case unsuccessfully, to deprive tenants of their statutory protection.

10.3.4.1 **Shams**

In *Crancour Ltd v. Da Silvaesa*,[68] one of the terms of a 'licence' agreement required the occupants to vacate their rooms between 10.30 a.m. and noon on each day to enable cleaning to take place. Such a term was, in the context of the case, regarded with suspicion and was arguably a sham, so that a summary order for possession was not regarded as appropriate.

---

[63] Ibid. at 819 *per* Lord Templeman. See also *Addiscombe Garden Estates Ltd v. Crabbe* [1958] 1 Q.B. 513 at 533 *per* Jenkins L.J.

[64] [1985] A.C. 809 at 817–18, emphasis supplied.

[65] For more problematic cases in the commercial sector, see *Addiscombe Garden Estates Ltd v. Crabbe* [1958] 1 Q.B. 513; *Shell-Mex and B.P. Ltd v. Manchester Garages Ltd* [1971] 1 W.L.R. 612.

[66] See *Isaac v. Hotel de Paris Ltd* [1960] 1 W.L.R. 238; *Abbeyfield (Harpenden) Society Ltd v. Woods* [1968] 1 W.L.R. 374.

[67] *Bankway Properties Ltd v. Pensfold-Dunsford* [2001] 1 W.L.R. 1369.

[68] (1986) 18 H.L.R. 265.

The agreements also provided for the provision of extensive services, although it was not clear that these were actually provided. In the circumstances, it was not clear whether the written agreement reflected the actuality and so, before deciding whether the agreement was for a lease or lodgings, further factual investigation was necessary.

When the agreement envisages the provision of services which require the landlord to be able to go in and out of the lodger's rooms at his convenience,[69] a question arises as to what the position is if such services are not provided. If they are provided at the outset but their provision subsequently drops off, then the case is still likely to be regarded as involving lodgings, with the lodger having the right to insist upon their resumption.[70] Where the services are never provided, although under the agreement the occupier could presumably insist upon them, another way of looking at the situation is to regard the clause as being inserted solely to seek to prevent the creation of the tenancy and not reflecting the reality of the situation. In such a case a tenancy is likely to be the result of the agreement.[71]

10.3.4.2 Access and the provision of services

The key issue in such cases is whether the clause in the contract relating to access is genuine. The matter was explained thus, by Peter Gibson L.J., in *Uratemp Ventures Ltd v. Collins*:[72]

> The crucial matter is whether the occupier has exclusive possession. If the owner of the building is contractually obliged to provide attendance or services that require entry into the room, then the retention of a key for that purpose is a strong indication that the occupier of the room is only a lodger under a licence, without exclusive possession. The fact that an occupier chooses not to avail himself of the attendance or services to which he is entitled cannot convert a licence into a tenancy.

The point here is choice. If it is never envisaged that the services will be provided, then the arrangement will be a tenancy. If the occupier genuinely declines to accept the services to which he is entitled, the occupancy will be as a lodger.

The extent of the degree of access can be important. One of the issues which arose in *Mehta v. Royal Bank of Scotland*[73] was the status of a long-term resident of a hotel, who had been wrongly evicted from his room. Under the terms of the agreement, the occupier was entitled to have his linen changed and his room cleaned every fortnight. In approaching the question as to whether the plaintiff was a tenant or a licensee, Mr Richard Southwell Q.C., sitting as a Deputy High Court judge, said:

> Like Lord Templeman, I have concerns as to how contractual tenancies and licences are, in general, to be distinguished but, in my judgment, there is no simple all-embracing test for such a distinction. The search for such a test would be a chimera. What each court, faced with the need to make the distinction, has to do is to weigh all the relevant and significant factors and decide in the light of them on which side of the line the particular case falls.[74]

Applying this, seemingly intuitive, process, the judge concluded that the claimant was a licensee.[75]

---

[69] Ibid. at 273 *per* Ralph Gibson L.J.   [70] See *Huwyler v. Ruddy* (1995) 28 H.L.R. 550.

[71] See *Crancour Ltd v. Da Silvaesa* (1986) 18 H.L.R. 265 at 278 *per* Ralph Gibson L.J.; *Grimsby College Enterprises Ltd v. HMRC* [2010] UKUT at [22]–[23] *per* Briggs J.

[72] [2000] 1 E.G.L.R. 156 at 157 reversed without reference to this issue: [2002] A.C. 301.

[73] [1999] 3 E.G.L.R. 153.   [74] Ibid. at 156.

[75] Reliance was placed on *Luganda v. Service Hotels* [1969] 2 Ch. 209 and *Marchant v. Charters* [1977] 1 W.L.R. 1181, both of which have to be read in the light of Lord Templeman's speech in *Street v. Mountford*.

It is suggested that this approach to the problem is entirely misconceived and flies in the face of *Street v. Mountford*. The issue in the case should have been whether the plaintiff actually had exclusive possession. This, in turn, should have depended upon whether the degree of access necessary for the provision of attendance meant that, in Lord Templeman's terms, the occupier was a lodger. In *Mehta*, the degree of access was regarded by the judge as being 'almost minimal'.[76] If that truly was the case, then the occupier should have been regarded as being a tenant: if not, a licensee. It is to be hoped that this decision does not mark a return to the uncertainties which bedevilled this branch of the law prior to the landmark decision in *Street v. Mountford*.

10.3.4.3 New occupiers

Subject to what has just been said, in the context of residential property, the easiest way of distinguishing between a lease and a licence is the provision of services and the resulting need of access by the landlord or his representatives. Another method which has been employed in an attempt to create a licence is to seek to insist upon the right to introduce new occupiers into the property or to be able to move the occupier into alternative accommodation. In the private sector, such a clause is unlikely to be successful as a means of preventing the creation of a tenancy. In *Aslan v. Murphy*,[77] an occupier of a basement measuring 4'3" by 12'6" was required by the document he had signed to share the accommodation with another occupier and to vacate the property for one hour and thirty minutes each day. Both clauses were regarded as being 'wholly unrealistic and were clearly pretences'.[78] They were disregarded and the occupier was held to be a tenant. In the public sector, on the other hand, clauses requiring occupiers to share rooms with others and to move to a different room when required to do so were regarded by the House of Lords in *Westminster City Council v. Jones*,[79] in the context of the provision of shelter for homeless men, as being quite genuine with the result that exclusive possession had not been granted and such agreements were regarded as licences.

10.3.4.4 Other relationships

Although Lord Templeman, in *Street v. Mountford*, accepted that the grant of exclusive possession was one of the hallmarks of a lease, he accepted also that situations could exist where exclusive possession had been granted but a lease had not been created. Examples of this were given as including an owner in fee simple, a trespasser, a mortgagee in possession, an object of charity, or a service occupier.[80]

Of these examples, some, such as the owner in fee simple, obviously do not involve the relationship of landlord and tenant but others seem to misuse the term 'exclusive possession' in that the nature of the relationship is such that the occupier does not have the right to exclude others from the property. Thus, for example, a trespasser has the right to exclude all others but the actual owner from the property and the issue which can then arise is whether the acceptance of payment in respect of the occupation will give rise to a tenancy.[81]

---

[76] [1999] 3 E.G.L.R. 153 at 155.   [77] [1990] 1 W.L.R. 766.

[78] Ibid. at 773 *per* Lord Donaldson M.R.   [79] [1992] 2 A.C. 288.

[80] [1985] A.C. 809 at 818; *Ramnarace v. Lutchman* [2001] 1 W.L.R. 1651 at 1656 *per* Lord Millett. That the landlord is fulfilling a social function in providing accommodation for the homeless or lacks title to grant a tenancy are not special considerations preventing the formation of a lease: *Bruton v. London and Quadrant Housing Trust* [2000] 1 A.C. 406.

[81] Cf. *Westminster City Council v. Basson* (1990) 62 P. & C.R. 57 and *Tower Hamlets London Borough v. Ayinde* (1994) 26 H.L.R. 631.

Charity

There have been a number of cases where a person has been allowed exclusive use of property but no tenancy has been created, the reason being that the arrangement was based upon an act of charity. In *Booker v. Palmer*,[82] the owner of a cottage allowed a person who had been bombed out of her own home to occupy the cottage for the duration of the war. It was held that a licence had been created, the reason being that there was no intention to enter into legal relations or, put another way, there was no contractual relationship between the parties at all.[83]

Such cases are, by their nature, unusual and are very unlikely to occur when the parties are, at the outset, dealing with each other at arm's length.[84] Even in cases where the parties are related, this does not preclude a contractual relationship being created.[85] The type of case where a licence is found is where 'there has been something in the circumstances, such as a family arrangement, an act of friendship or generosity, or such like, to negative any intention to create a tenancy'.[86] In such cases, the occupier, as a gratuitous licensee, does not have exclusive possession at all, as he can be evicted by the owner on the giving of reasonable notice. In *Watts v. Stewart*,[87] a charity, which provided almshouse accommodation, claimed that Mrs Watts was a licensee rather than a tenant given the nature of their arrangement. The Court of Appeal held that the letter of appointment confirming their relationship was not a sham. Etherton L.J. confirmed that the charity's Trustees 'could only properly discharge the trusts of the Charity, which limited its objects to those in need, hardship or distress, if a personal revocable licence was granted'.[88] The nature of the relationship was such that there was no intention to create a lease.

Service occupancy

An occupier will not be a tenant if he is required to live in particular accommodation for the better performance of his employment.[89] An example of such a relationship would be a farm worker living in a tied cottage and, perhaps less obviously, a university vice-chancellor who, not infrequently, may be required as part of the contract of employment to live in a house owned by the university.

Purchasers

In *Street v. Mountford*,[90] Lord Templeman accepted that a purchaser who entered into possession after the entry into a contract to buy the property would occupy as a licensee. To come within this exception the occupation must be under the contract and not in contemplation of the making of such a contract in the future.[91]

10.3.4.5 Multiple occupancy

In most cases of single occupancy, the test of whether the occupier has exclusive possession relates to whether the provision of services requires the landlord to have unrestricted access to the property; the distinction is between leases and lodgings. In cases of multiple occupancy, the issue of whether or not exclusive possession does not rest on the degree of access required by the landlord to provide services. Rather, it is the relationship between the occupiers that can determine whether they are tenants or licensees.

---

[82] [1942] 2 All E.R. 674. See also *Heslop v. Burns* [1974] 1 W.L.R. 1241.
[83] See also *Marcroft Wagons Ltd v. Smith* [1951] 2 K.B. 496.
[84] See *Facchini v. Bryson* [1952] 1 T.L.R. 1386.   [85] See *Nunn v. Dalrymple* (1989) 21 H.L.R. 569.
[86] *Facchini v. Bryson* [1952] 1 T.L.R. 1386 at 1389–90 *per* Denning L.J. See also *Holt v. Wellington* (1996) 71 P. & C.R. D. 40.
[87] [2016] EWCA Civ 1047.   [88] *Ibid.* at [10].
[89] *Glasgow Corporation v. Johnstone* [1965] A.C. 609; *Wragg v. Surrey County Council* [2008] H.L.R. 30.
[90] [1985] A.C. 809 at 827.   [91] *Bretherton v. Paton* (1986) 18 H.L.R. 257.

In *Somma v. Hazelhurst*,[92] a cohabiting couple agreed to take a one-room bedsit, which contained two single beds. They signed separate agreements under which each of them agreed to pay a specified sum of money by weekly instalments. The agreements, entitled licences, which they each signed, were identical. Under the terms of the licences, each licensee was required to share the room with the licensor and such other licensees as the licensor should permit to occupy it. The question arose as to their status and the Court of Appeal rejected the argument that they were joint tenants and, instead, held that they were licensees.

Liability to pay rent

The crucial aspects of the reasoning related to the reservation of the right by the licensor to move into the room with the couple, this not being regarded as being contrary to public policy, and the provisions regarding the payment for the room. If the couple were joint tenants, then each, as an incident of the joint tenancy, would be jointly and severally liable for the rent; either of them could be pursued by the landlady for the entire rent payable for the room. In the present case, however, each was only liable to pay a specified sum, that amounting to half of the total consideration payable. As they were not jointly and severally liable, this was considered to be fatal to the claim that they were joint tenants. As they were not joint tenants, the result was that they did not form one legal entity enjoying exclusive possession;[93] neither did they, as individuals, enjoy exclusive possession, as each was required to share with the other. The result was that they were licensees.

The effect of this decision was potentially very wide-ranging as it enabled landlords in cases of multiple occupancy arrangements to avoid creating tenancies by the simple expedient of entering into separate agreements with each of the occupiers.[94] As such, it meant that it was facile for the Rent Acts to be neatly avoided in this type of situation. For this reason, there was some relief when *Somma* was overruled in *Street v. Mountford*. Unfortunately, however, when overruling this decision, Lord Templeman did not address the reasoning employed in the case. Instead, he based his disapproval of the decision on his view of the separate licences being a sham. He regarded the couple as being joint tenants. As to the notion that, realistically, the couple could be expected to share the room with such other person as the landlady might nominate, he was scathing. In his view:

> The sham nature of this obligation would have only been slightly more obvious if H and S had been married or if the room had been furnished with a double bed instead of two single beds.[95]

As the documents signed separately by the couple bore no relation to the reality of the situation, the situation was analysed as being a straightforward case of a joint tenancy.

10.3.5 Genuine sharing arrangements

This view of *Somma v. Hazelhurst* was entirely understandable. What was unfortunate was that the reasoning provided no assistance in cases where such agreements were, at

---

[92] [1978] 1 W.L.R. 1014.

[93] For an argument that they could have been regarded as joint tenants at law, but tenancies in common in equity, see Thompson, *Co-Ownership* (London, Sweet & Maxwell, 1988), 63–4.

[94] For attempts to do this which failed on the facts, see *Demuren v. Seal Estates Ltd* (1978) 249 E.G. 440; *O'Malley v. Seymour* (1978) 250 E.G. 1083, which, for different reasons, were considered to be shams. For successful attempts, see *Aldrington Garages Ltd v. Fielder* (1978) 248 E.G. 557; *Sturulson & Co. v. Weniz* (1984) 17 H.L.R. 740.

[95] [1985] A.C. 809 at 825.

least arguably, genuine. A number of cases such as this occurred subsequent to *Street v. Mountford* and it was found that the simple disapproval of *Somma* on the basis that it was a sham provided little assistance.[96] In sharing cases, one could not determine whether or not a lease had been created simply by distinguishing between leases and lodgings. In *Hadjiloucas v. Crean*,[97] two friends agreed to rent an unfurnished two-roomed flat. Each signed separate, but identical, licence agreements which required each of them to share the flat with one other licensee. After one of the licensees had left, the question arose as to the status of the other and whether a tenancy or a licence had originally been created.

The Court of Appeal remitted the case for a retrial so that the actual facts of the case could be more clearly established. It was considered, however, that Lord Templeman's speech should be read principally in the context of single occupation where exclusive possession was conceded,[98] and that cases such as the present one needed a more careful factual analysis. Mustill L.J. considered that, in cases of this type, there were three possibilities. These were that the occupiers were licensees or that one of two forms of tenancy had been created. The first involved all the occupiers being joint tenants and the second involved each occupier having a separate tenancy of part of the house—that is, their own room—with the landlord.[99]

The matter was revisited by the House of Lords in the conjoined appeals in *A.G. Securities Ltd v. Vaughan* and *Antoniades v. Villiers*.[100] The facts of the two cases were very different. In *Vaughan*, the property in question was a furnished four-bedroom flat. Individual agreements were entered into with each occupier. Under these agreements, the rent payable by each occupier was different from that paid by the others and, in some cases, the period of occupation also differed. When one occupant left, he was replaced by another who entered into a new, and separate, agreement with the freeholder. In *Villiers*, the facts were virtually identical to those of *Somma v. Hazelhurst* and it was clear that the agreements signed by the occupants were modelled on those used in *Somma*. Each licence agreement gave the 'licensor' the right to introduce a third occupier into the flat. The only distinction between this case and *Somma* was that here there were two bedrooms, so that the possibility of introducing a third person into the flat was rather more feasible than was the case in *Somma*. The House of Lords, in each case reversing decisions of the Court of Appeal, held that in *Vaughan* the occupiers were licensees and in *Villiers* they were joint tenants.

10.3.5.1 Independent and interdependent agreements

The difference between the two cases was that in *Vaughan*, the documents reflected the reality of the situation, whereas in *Villiers* they did not. In *Vaughan*, the reality of the situation was that these were genuinely independent agreements to cater for a fluctuating body of people occupying the same household.[101] While it was accepted that there could have been separate tenancies of a part of the house,[102] this did not occur in the present case, perhaps because the practice was that, when one of the occupants left, the remaining occupants chose whether they wished to move into the vacated room. Neither could they, collectively, be seen as joint tenants, as there was no unity of time, title, or interest between them. In *Villiers*, on the other hand, the view was taken that 'the two agreements were interdependent. Both would have signed or neither. The two agreements must therefore be read together.'[103] Reading them together, the effect was that the couple were joint tenants,

[96] See *Stribling v. Wickham* [1989] 2 E.G.L.R. 35; *Brooker Estates Ltd v. Ayres* (1986) 19 H.L.R. 1375.
[97] [1988] 1 W.L.R. 1006   [98] Ibid. at 1013 *per* Purchas L.J.   [99] Ibid. at 1023.
[100] [1990] 1 A.C. 417.   [101] See also *UHU Property Trust v. Lincoln City Council* [2000] R. A. 419
[102] [2000] R.A. 419 at 460 *per* Lord Templeman.   [103] Ibid.

each being jointly and severally liable for the rent. The provision in the agreements to introduce a third person into the property was seen as being quite unrealistic and, in any event, as the original agreement had been held to create a joint tenancy, the introduction of a third person was not something which the landlord could do. To do this would have involved the termination of the original lease and the creation of a new licence and this is not permitted by the Rent Act 1977.[104]

In a case such as *Villiers*, where the couple are in a marriage-like relationship, it is relatively easy to conclude that the agreements are interdependent and should be read together as a composite whole. Other sharing arrangements may occur, however, where the occupants of the property are not linked together in this way, a good example being where a group of students rent a house together and are made to sign separate documents. It may then be difficult, on the facts, to determine whether the agreements should be regarded as genuinely independent or interdependent.[105] Perhaps ironically, it is now more in the landlord's interest to ensure that the occupiers are, in fact, joint tenants. This is because the statutory regime now in operation is far less onerous to landlords and the desire to avoid the creation of a tenancy is far less strong than was previously the case. A joint tenancy is now preferable because, if one of the occupiers leaves before the end of the term, the landlord can, if the group were joint tenants, look to the remaining occupants for the rent on the property and not have to pursue the person who left prematurely for the money he had agreed to pay. It is noticeable that with the reduction in the protection afforded to residential tenants, cases involving the lease/licence distinction have become far less common than was previously the case.

10.3.6 **Reform**

As indicated previously, the backcloth against which much of this litigation took place was that of a high degree of regulation of the rental sector. Landlords were very keen to avoid creating agreements which conferred the protection of the Rent Acts on residential occupiers and, to this end, expended considerable ingenuity in seeking to craft agreements which fell outside the terms of the legislation. A favourite device employed to achieve this aim was to attempt to create a contractual occupancy licence, as opposed to a lease. Since the changes introduced by the Housing Act 1988, much of the heat has been removed from this area with the result that, as between the parties to the agreement, the significance of the agreement being a lease, as opposed to a licence, has declined significantly. In recognition of this, the Law Commission has proposed that this once fundamental divide be to a large extent abrogated.

What was proposed is that, in the residential sector,[106] the rights and obligations of the parties would be governed by the residential contract which they enter into. As between the parties themselves,[107] it would be immaterial whether the contract created a lease or a licence. It is the contract itself which would govern the relationship between the parties. The contents of those contracts would then be regulated by a consumer approach, so

---

[104] Ibid. at 462 *per* Lord Templeman. See also *Duke v. Wynne* [1990] 1 W.L.R. 766 at 775–6 *per* Lord Donaldson M.R.

[105] See *Mikeover v. Brady* (1989) 21 H.L.R. 513 (an unfortunate decision on the facts).

[106] Agreements such as business tenancies or agricultural tenancies will be excluded from the new scheme, as will certain types of agreement excluded on social grounds. See (2003) Law Com. No. 284, paras 3.15 and 6.26–6.29.

[107] As is recognized in the Report itself, this distinction will remain important insofar as third parties are concerned: ibid. at para. 6.20. See also *Berrisfield v. Mexfield Housing Co-operative Ltd* [2011] UKSC 52. See 10.3.1.2.

that respective rights and obligations of the parties to it would be substantially the same as those which exist already with regard to residential tenancies.[108] Given the substantial deregulation of the residential leasehold sector, this reform may now be seen as being unnecessary, and what at one time seemed to be a perennial source of litigation, whether an agreement created a lease or a licence, has largely dried up. Although the Welsh Assembly has implemented this change to the law,[109] there appears to be little sign of its implementation in England.

10.3.7 **Contracting parties**

Under the existing law, because a lease creates a legal estate in land, a minor lacks the capacity to become a legal tenant.[110] It is now proposed that residential contracts can be entered into by people aged sixteen and seventeen.[111] The reason given for this proposal is that the present law presents problems, in particular for social landlords who want to provide secure accommodation for people in this age group.[112] To this reason can be added a second, that people of this age do have the capacity to marry but, under the existing law, lack capacity to own a legal estate in their matrimonial home.

10.3.7.1 **Minors**

The potential problems inherent in this area were highlighted in *Hammersmith and Fulham London Borough Council v. Alexander-David*[113] A local authority granted a tenancy to a homeless sixteen-year-old girl, who had a priority need. A year later, following various complaints concerning her conduct, the authority served a notice to quit. This was held to be invalid. The reason was that, because the lease purported to be granted to a minor, under para. 1(1) of Sched. 1, TOLATA 1996 this was ineffective to pass a legal estate, and, instead, took effect as a declaration of trust in favour of the minor. Because the authority was a trustee, it was not open to it to serve a notice to quit, thereby terminating the beneficial interest which had been created. Pending any change in the law relating to minors, the solution to this practical problem would appear to be for the local authority to provide sufficient services to the minor so as to create a licence as opposed to a lease, such an arrangement not creating a trust.[114]

10.3.7.2 **Number of tenants**

Under the current law, the maximum number of people who can own a legal estate is four.[115] The Law Commission sees this restriction on estate ownership as being irrelevant to housing law, and recommends that, subject to the statutory rules on overcrowding, this restriction should be lifted, so that any number of people can be party to an occupation agreement. Again, this seems sensible. It is commonplace for more than four students to take a tenancy of a house, little realizing that, under the existing law, only the first four named in the agreement are actually legal tenants of the property, holding on trust for their fellow occupants.[116]

---

[108] (2003) Law Com. No. 284, Part VIII.
[109] Renting Homes (Wales) Act 2016, s.7.   [110] LPA 1925, s. 1(6).
[111] (2003) Law Com. No. 284, para. 3.18.
[112] See J. Morgan in Cooke (ed.), *Modern Studies in Property Law, Volume 2* (Oxford, Hart Publishing, 2002), Chapter 13.
[113] [2009] 3 All E.R. 1098.
[114] Ibid. at [37] *per* Sullivan L.J. For strong, and convincing, criticism of the use of a trust to accommodate an equitable tenancy see L. Tolani-Taylor in Hopkins (ed.), *Modern Studies in Property Law (Vol. 7)* (Oxford, Hart Publishing, 2013) Chapter 6.
[115] LPA 1925, s. 34(2).   [116] Ibid.

10.4 Types of tenancy

There are a number of different types of tenancy which can be created, which will be considered in turn.

10.4.1 Fixed-term tenancy

As the name suggests, this form of tenancy occurs when the start and finish of the lease is set out in advance. A fixed-term tenancy can be of any length. As a term of years is defined to include terms of less than a year,[117] a fixed-term tenancy of a week is a perfectly valid, if unusual, concept. At the other extreme, one can have a fixed-term tenancy of 2,000 years. The parties are free to choose whatever length of term they please.

Once a fixed term tenancy has been created, unless there is a break clause, it is not open to one party, unilaterally, to determine it. It is not open for the tenant to seek simply to abandon the tenancy. If he purports to do so, the landlord is not under any obligation in order to mitigate his loss to forfeit the lease for non-payment of rent,[118] and it is, in any event, unclear whether a landlord who adopted this course could sue for the future rent.[119] In the case of long leases at a rent, the rent originally reserved by the lease will, in time, cease to reflect the prevailing economic conditions. For this reason, it is usual for commercial leases to contain rent review clauses to provide a mechanism whereby the rent can be recalculated periodically during the duration of the lease.

A lease need not take effect in possession. A lease created in 2017 may take effect in 2018. Such a lease is termed a reversionary lease. Such a lease, if granted at a rent or in consideration of a fine, must take effect in possession not more than twenty-one years from the date of the grant and otherwise will be void. Similarly, a contract to create such a lease will also be void.[120] A lease granted in 2017 to take effect in possession in 2039 is therefore void, as is a contract in 2017 to create a lease in 2018 to take effect in possession in 2040. Perhaps somewhat oddly, a contract in 2017 to create a lease to take effect in possession in 2038 is not void as the lease to be created at that date is not a reversionary lease.[121]

10.4.2 Periodic tenancies

A periodic tenancy is a tenancy created initially for a given period but that period will recur until the lease is brought to an end. Thus, if a yearly tenancy is created, then at the end of the first year, a new period of a year will automatically be created and this process will be repeated at the end of the second year, and so on. A periodic tenancy can, therefore, in theory run indefinitely.

An obvious objection to such a lease is the requirement that, to be valid, a lease must be for a term certain. At the start of a periodic tenancy, one cannot know in advance for how long the landlord and tenant relationship will continue.[122] The answer is that the original uncertainty can be made certain by the act of either of the parties; the periodic tenancy will continue to recur until either party brings it to an end by the service of a notice to quit. It is not dependent upon the occurrence of some external event, the happening of which is not necessarily in the control of either party. For this reason, the courts have had

---

[117] LPA 1925, s. 205(1)(xxvii).

[118] *Reichman v. Beveridge* [2006] EWCA Civ. 1659. For forfeiture, see 10.10.3

[119] *Reichman v. Beveridge, supra*, at [22]–[28] *per* Thomas L.J.   [120] LPA 1925, s. 149(3).

[121] *Re Strand and Savoy Properties Ltd* [1960] Ch. 582.

[122] See *Berrisford v. Mexfield Housing Co-operative Ltd* [2011] UKSC 52 at [87]–[88] *per* Lady Hale, who described the rules as having an 'Alice in Wonderland quality'.

difficulties with agreements which have the effect of fettering the power of one of them, normally the landlord, to end the periodic tenancy by the service of a notice to quit.

10.4.2.1 Restricting service of notice to quit

The ability of either side to end a periodic tenancy by the service of a notice to quit was seen as a vital element in such a tenancy being considered to be sufficiently certain so as to constitute a valid lease. As Lord Templeman put it in *Prudential Assurance Co. Ltd v. London Residuary Body*:[123]

> A term must be either certain or uncertain. It cannot be partly certain because the tenant can determine it at any time and partly uncertain because the landlord cannot determine it for an uncertain period. If a landlord does not grant and the tenant does not take a certain term the grant does not create a lease.

On the basis of this reasoning, a restriction on the ability of either side to serve a valid notice to quit would cause the lease to fail.[124] In *Berrisford v. Mexfield Housing Co-operative Ltd*,[125] however, the Supreme Court modified this principle considerably but, although out of sympathy with the underlying reasoning, declined to overrule the earlier House of Lords decision in *Prudential*.

In approaching this issue, it was first noted that a periodic tenancy with a fetter on the service of a notice to quit for a specified period was valid. In *Breams Property Investment Co. Ltd v. Stroulger*[126] it was agreed that there should be a quarterly tenancy, but that the landlord would be restrained from serving a notice to quit for the first three years unless the premises were required by the landlord for its own occupation. This was upheld as a valid lease, it being explained as being a fixed three-year term terminable by notice served by the tenant, to be followed by a normal quarterly tenancy.[127] If the fetter was for an indeterminate period, however, this reasoning could not apply. The solution, therefore, was to hold that such an agreement was effective to create a lease for life. This, in turn, was converted by s. 149(6), LPA 1925 into a ninety-year term determinable on either the death of the tenant, or an appropriately served notice to quit.

10.4.2.2 Corporate tenants

This reasoning is applicable only to human tenants, it being accepted that a company, albeit an entity with legal personality, cannot possess a lease for life. In the case of such an agreement, however, the Supreme Court accepted that, despite the agreement not being a lease, the parties would, as a matter of contract law, be bound by what had been agreed. The effect of this is that the freeholder will be precluded from terminating the licence except on the terms set out in the agreement. The licensee will be vulnerable, however, if the freeholder sells the land to a purchaser, who will not be bound by the licence.[128]

10.4.2.3 Express or implied periodic tenancies

A periodic tenancy may arise either expressly or by implication.

---

[123] [1992] A.C. 386 at 395.
[124] *Cheshire Lines Committee v. Lewis & Co.* (1880) 50 L.J.Q.B. 121; *Centaploy Ltd v. Matlodge Ltd* [1974] Ch.1; *Re Midland Railway Co.'s Agreement* [1971] Ch. 725 and *Ashburn Anstalt v. Arnold* [1989] Ch. 1 to the contrary were all overruled in the *Prudential Case* [1992] A.C. 386 at 395 *per* Lord Templeman.
[125] [2011] UKSC 52.   [126] [1948] 2 K.B. 1.
[127] [2011] UKSC 52 at [88] *per* Lady Hale. See also *Leeds City Council v. Broadley* [2016] EWCA Civ. 1213 at [18] *per* McCombe L.J.
[128] See 10.3.1.2.

Express periodic tenancies

An express periodic tenancy would arise by a statement such as the tenancy to be granted is a yearly tenancy or a tenancy from year to year and the earliest date on which a notice to quit can be given is at the end of the first period, that is one year from the creation of the tenancy. If, however, the grant is for a year and then from year to year, this takes effect as a fixed term tenancy of one year, followed by a yearly periodic tenancy and, so notice to quit can only be served two years from the commencement of the term.[129]

Implied periodic tenancies

When a person goes into possession and pays rent to the freeholder, the law will imply a periodic tenancy.[130] This situation can occur in more than one situation. First, there is a situation where there is no actual agreement between the parties and a periodic tenancy is implied. Second, the purported lease may, for some reason, be void. This occurred in *Prudential Assurance Co. Ltd v. London Residuary Body*,[131] where the purported lease was held to be void for uncertainty but the tenant had gone into possession and had paid rent. 'The tenant entering under a void lease became by virtue of possession and the payment of a yearly rent, a yearly tenant holding on the terms of the agreement so far as those terms were consistent with the yearly tenancy.'[132] As the tenancy was a periodic tenancy, it could be terminated upon the service by the landlord of an appropriate notice to quit. In the light of the decision in *Berrisford*, however, such a situation will now be rare.

Statutory periodic tenancies

A periodic tenancy can also be imposed by statute. Under s. 5 of the Housing Act 1988, on the expiry of an assured shorthold tenancy, which is a fixed-term lease of at least six months' duration,[133] a statutory periodic tenancy will arise. Such a tenancy can then be terminated by the service of a notice to quit, the period of that notice being two months. The introduction of this type of tenancy, originally under the Housing Act 1980, severely reduced security of tenure for private sector tenants created after that legislation came into force.

10.4.2.4 The period

The way that the period on which the periodic tenancy is based is arrived at by having regard to the method by which the rent is quantified. If the rent is £104 per annum, paid at £2.00 per week, then the tenancy is a yearly tenancy because the rent is measured by the year. If, however, the rent is simply £2.00 per week, then a weekly tenancy is created.[134] The length of the period is important as it is determinative of the length of the notice to quit which must be given to terminate the lease.

10.4.3 Tenancy with an option to renew

What, at first sight, may appear to be similar to a periodic tenancy is a tenancy which contains an option for the tenant to renew the lease. Such a position is, in fact, the opposite of a periodic tenancy in that, whereas a periodic tenancy will continue in being until either party brings it to an end by the service of a notice to quit, a lease with an

---

[129] *Re Searle* [1912] 1 Ch. 610.   [130] *Doe d. Rigg v. Bell* (1793) 5 Durn. & E. 471.
[131] [1992] 2 A.C. 386.   [132] Ibid. at 392 *per* Lord Templeman.
[133] Housing Act 1988, s. 20.
[134] See *Ladies' Hosiery and Knitwear Ltd v. Parker* [1930] 1 Ch. 304 at 328–9 *per* Maugham J.; *Adler v. Blackman* [1953] 1 Q.B. 146.

option to renew will end naturally, unless the tenant exercises the option.[135] Care must be taken when drafting such an option. In particular, the option should not be worded so as to state that the new lease which will be created by the exercise of the option will be on the same terms as the original lease. The effect of such a clause is that the lease created on the exercise of the option will, itself, confer upon the tenant an option to renew, again on the same terms as the original lease. Such a lease is regarded as being perpetually renewable,[136] and such leases are converted by statute into a 2,000-year fixed-term lease;[137] potentially a disastrous outcome for the landlord. It has been said, with justice, that this is 'an area of law where the courts have manoeuvred themselves into an unhappy position'.[138]

10.4.4 Tenancies at will

A tenancy at will involves a situation where a person is let into possession of property as a tenant but the agreement is such that the tenancy can be determined by either side, at will. The normal situation where such a tenancy will arise is where a person who is minded to purchase the property is allowed into possession.[139] If rent is paid by the tenant after entry, a periodic tenancy will be implied,[140] unless it is clear that both parties intend the relationship to remain as a tenancy at will.[141]

The tenancy at will is a personal relationship between the parties.[142] As such, it cannot be assigned or pass on death. If the tenant at will purports to assign the tenancy this will, on giving notice to the landlord, terminate the tenancy.[143]

10.4.5 Tenancy at sufferance

This term is used to describe what is not really a tenancy at all. A tenancy at sufferance arises when a tenant holds over after the lease has expired with neither the landlord's assent nor dissent. The only difference between him and a trespasser is that the initial occupation of the land was lawful. If the holding over follows the service by the tenant of a notice to quit then, under ancient legislation, he is liable to pay double rent for the period of the holding over after the notice has expired.[144]

In cases of tenancies at sufferance, the normal position is that, if the relationship becomes consensual, a new tenancy will arise.[145] In the public sector, however, when a local authority, having obtained a possession order against a tenant, nevertheless allows the tenant to remain in the property, and accepts payment, the former tenant used to be described as being a 'tolerated trespasser'.[146] This was a strange and anomalous relationship, the

---

[135] Where title is unregistered, such an option will only bind a purchaser of the reversion if it has been registered as a land charge: *Phillips v. Mobil Oil Co. Ltd* [1980] 1 W.L.R. 888. If title is registered and the tenant is in actual occupation of the land, then the option will take effect under Land Registration Act 2002, Sched. 3, para. 2 as an interest overriding a registered disposition: *Webb v. Pollmount* [1966] Ch. 584.

[136] *Parkus v. Greenwood* [1950] Ch. 33; *Caerphilly Concrete Products Ltd v. Owen* [1972] 1 W.L.R. 372.

[137] LPA 1922, s. 145, Sched. 15.

[138] *Caerphilly Concrete Products Ltd v. Owen* [1972] 1 W.L.R. 372 at 376 *per* Sachs L.J.

[139] See *Ramnarace v. Lutchman* [2001] 1 W.L.R. 1651.

[140] *Walji v. Mount Cook Land Ltd* [2002] 1 P. & C.R. 13.

[141] See *Javad v. Aqil* [1991] 1 W.L.R. 1007.

[142] See *Wheeler v. Mercer* [1957] A.C. 426 at 427–8 *per* Lord Morton.

[143] *Pinhorn v. Souster* (1853) 8 Exch. 763 at 772–3 *per* Parke B.

[144] Distress for Rent Act 1737, s. 18

[145] See *Dougal v. McCarthy* [1892] 1 Q.B. 736.

[146] See *Burrows v. Brent London Borough Council* [1996] 1 W.L.R. 1448.

consequences of which were never fully worked out,[147] and its abolition by the Supreme Court in *Austin v. Southwark London Borough Council*[148] is welcome.

10.4.6 **Tenancies by estoppel**

On the grant of a tenancy, both landlord and tenant are mutually estopped from denying the validity of the transaction. It is no defence for a tenant, sued by the landlord, to argue that the landlord had no title to grant a lease.[149] As between the parties to the agreement, the lease is perfectly binding and the tenancy is referred to as a tenancy by estoppel.[150] It is not entirely clear, however, what the value is in describing the lease in these terms.

10.5 **The *Bruton* tenancy**

In *Bruton v. London and Quadrant Housing Trust*,[151] a local authority had compulsorily acquired a block of flats with a view to demolishing them and redeveloping the land. Pending this, the council granted a licence to the Trust, which was a charitable organization, to use the property for the purposes of housing the homeless. The licence did not purport to grant the Trust any proprietary interest in the flats, something which the council did not have the power to do.[152] The Trust then entered into an agreement with Mr Bruton, termed a licence, whereby he gained the occupancy of a flat in return for a weekly payment. The issue in the case was whether the Trust was liable for certain repairs under s. 11 of the Landlord and Tenant Act 1985, which would only be the case if a tenancy had been created.[153] The argument for the Trust was that, as both parties knew that it did not own the land, and therefore lacked the power to create tenancies, the agreement could not take effect as a lease. While plausible, this was rejected by the House of Lords, who held that Mr Bruton was a tenant.

The central reason was that the agreement between the Trust and Mr Bruton conferred upon him exclusive possession for a term at a rent, a finding which, unless there are exceptional circumstances, leads to the conclusion that, whatever the parties may choose to call the agreement, a lease has been created. According to Lord Hoffmann:

> the term 'lease' or 'tenancy' describes a relationship between two parties who are designated landlord and tenant. It is not concerned with the question of whether the agreement creates an estate or other proprietary interest which may be binding upon third parties. A lease may, and usually does, create a proprietary interest called a leasehold estate, or more technically, a 'term of years absolute'. This will depend upon whether the landlord had an estate out of which he could grant it.[154]

---

[147] See the valuable analysis by S. Bright (2003) 119 L.Q.R. 495, where it is also pointed out that this concept applies only in the public sector: ibid., at 496. See also I. Loveland (2007) 123 L.Q.R. 455.

[148] [2010] UKSC 28 at [43] *per* Lord Walker and at [45] *per* Lady Hale.

[149] See *Cuthbertson v. Irvine* (1859) 4 H. & N. 742 at 754–5 *per* Martin B.

[150] For a helpful account of this, see *Mitchell v. Watkinson* [2013] EWCA Civ. 1471 at [33]–[38] *per* Barling J., giving the judgment of the Court.

[151] [2000] 1 A.C. 406. See D. Rook [1999] Conv. 517; P. Routley (2000) 63 M.L.R. 424, where some of the reasoning but not the result is criticized. See also J.P. Hinojosa [2005] Conv. 114; M. Lower [2010] Conv. 38.

[152] Housing Act 1985, s. 32. If a statutory body lacks the power to grant a lease, estoppel principles cannot confer validity on something which the body has no power to do. See *Rhyl Urban District Council v. Rhyl Amusements Ltd* [1959] 1 W.L.R. 465.

[153] For these obligations, see 10.8.7.   [154] [2000] 1 A.C. 406 at 415.

10.5.1 The *Bruton* tenancy as an estate

The conclusion that Mr Bruton held a tenancy in the land rests upon the essential relativity of title upon which land law is based, and seems to be entirely correct.[155] The difficulty with this passage, however, is the comment that the lease might not create a proprietary interest in the land. This is wrong. The lease which was created in *Bruton* was proprietary in the sense that it would be binding on certain people. Unlike the situation where the landlord held the legal title to the freehold, it would not be binding upon everyone. It would, however, have a proprietary effect on people who derived title from the landlord.

If a squatter goes into possession of freehold land, he occupies the land as the holder of an estate in fee simple. His title is good as against anyone except a person with a better title.[156] It is open to him to convey his possessory title to anyone else, in which case that person's title will be as good as that of the squatter. That is, his right to possession is only liable to be defeated by the owner of the paper title to the land. If, instead of conveying the land to a purchaser, the squatter purports to grant a lease of it, then similar reasoning should apply. As between the squatter and the tenant, the lease is perfectly valid, and the tenant's right of occupation can only be upset by title paramount: that is an action brought by the true owner of the land.[157] Whether or not the parties to the original lease knew that the landlord had no title to the land should be quite irrelevant. If the squatter transfers his title to a purchaser then, as a person deriving title from the squatter, the purchaser will be in no better position than the squatter and so the tenancy will be binding on him.[158] On this analysis, it should make no difference if the person purporting to create a licence is himself a licensee rather than a squatter. In both cases, one should look to the agreement between the parties to see if it is consistent with a lease or a licence.

In this sense, *pace*, Lord Hoffmann, the lease created by the squatter does create an interest in land: it is an estate, however, that is vulnerable in that it can be defeated by a better title to that land. The vulnerability of the tenant's position when a *Bruton* tenancy has been created has since been demonstrated in *London Borough Council of Islington v. Green*.[159] Islington Council granted Patchwork Community Housing Association a licence to use its property as temporary accommodation. In the same way as occurred in *Bruton*, the Association purported to create a licence to occupy the property to Ms Green and Mr O'shea. When the council terminated the licence given to the Association, Mr O'shea had no defence to a possession action brought by the council. Although the agreement between the Association and Ms Green, who had since left the property, and Mr O'shea created a tenancy, this tenancy was not binding on the council, who were not transferees of the Association's interest and were not parties to the agreement. Accordingly, the case succeeded on the basis of title paramount.

The same point has since been made by Lord Neuberger in *Berrisford v. Mexfield Housing Co-operative Ltd.*[160] Commenting on the *Bruton* case, he said:

> The point being made by Lord Hoffmann was that the fact that the trust was only a licensee, and therefore could not grant a tenancy binding on its licensor, did not prevent the agreement with Mr Bruton amounting to a tenancy as between him and the trust. The tenancy would thus have been binding as such not only on Mr Bruton and the trust, *but also on any assignee of Mr Bruton or the trust*.

---

[155] See also *Berrisford v. Mexfield Housing Co-operative Ltd* [2011] UKSC 53 at [65] *per* Lord Neuberger.
[156] See 10.6.2.3.
[157] See *Kay v. London Borough of Lambeth* [2006] UKHL 10 at para. 144 *per* Lord Scott.
[158] Contrast M. Dixon [2000] C.L.J. 25 at 26.
[159] [2005] EWCA Civ. 56. See also *Kay v. Lambeth London Borough Council, supra*.
[160] [2011] UKSC 52 at [65]. Emphasis added.

In other words, the real unorthodoxy in Lord Hoffmann's remarks is to deny that the agreement created an estate. In all aspects it resembles a tenancy by estoppel. Such tenancies are binding between the parties to it, and on those who derive title from them. It is not binding on a person with a better title to the land than the person purporting to create the lease. The tenancy by estoppel, while it remains in existence, is subject to the same statutory regime as is the case with more orthodox tenancies.

10.6 Formalities and parol leases

10.6.1 Deed

A lease is a legal estate in land and s. 52, LPA 1925 requires a deed to create a legal lease,[161] unless the lease is a parol lease, in which case an oral or written agreement is sufficient.

10.6.2 Parol leases

Parol leases are an exception to the rule that a deed is required to create a legal lease. They are governed by s. 52(2)(d), LPA 1925, which refers to those leases or tenancies not required by law to be in writing. Parol leases are leases taking effect in possession for a term not exceeding three years (whether or not the lessee is given power to extend the term) at the best rent which can be reasonably obtained without taking a fine. A contract to create such a lease is also exempt from the normal requirements of formality imposed upon land contracts.[162]

Some comments can be made as to s. 54(2), LPA 1925 and parol leases.

10.6.2.1 Term

First, the LPA 1925 itself provides that a lease which the tenant has power to extend beyond three years need not be by deed. This would cover the situation where there is a two-year lease which confers on the tenant the option to renew it for a further two years. The Act makes no mention of periodic tenancies, which will last for considerably longer than three years if neither side serves a notice to quit. Such tenancies are not required to be made by deed. The reason for this is that the original term is that specified in the grant, so that a yearly tenancy is seen as an initial grant of one year and so need not be made by deed.

10.6.2.2 Rent

The lease must be for the best rent which can be reasonably obtained without taking a fine. A fine is a lump sum or premium and it is very unusual for such a payment to be sought on the grant of a short lease.

10.6.2.3 In possession

To be exempt from the requirement that a deed is necessary to create a legal lease, the lease must take effect in possession. This is an extremely unfortunate requirement. It was held in *Long v. Tower Hamlets London Borough Council*[163] that a quarterly tenancy created at the

---

[161] Law of Property Act 1925, s. 52(1).
[162] Law of Property (Miscellaneous Provisions) Act (LP(MP)A) 1989, s. 2(5)(a).
[163] [1998] Ch. 197.

start of September to begin later in the month did not take effect in possession and to be legal must, therefore, be created by deed, which was not the case. This result seems to be an inevitable consequence of the wording of the Act but is extremely inconvenient.[164] Many short leases are created without using a deed. If possession is not granted from the date of the lease, then a deed is necessary. Many students rent accommodation in the private sector and sign agreements at the beginning of the summer under which the term will begin in September. These agreements are highly unlikely to be contained in deeds and, because the leases which they purport to create do not take effect in possession, they will be ineffective to create legal tenancies. The removal of the requirement in s. 54(2) of the Act that the lease take effect in possession would be desirable.

10.7 Equitable leases

If a person fails to use a deed to create a lease when one is required, the position is looked at differently by law and equity. At law, if, as is likely, the tenant takes possession of the property and pays rent, there will be an implication that he holds under a periodic tenancy, the period being calculated by reference to how the rent is measured. Equity, however, takes a quite different view of the matter.

If the landlord purports to grant the tenant a seven-year lease, but does not execute a deed, then there can be no seven-year lease at law. By means of a fiction, however, the ineffective attempt to create the legal tenancy is viewed as a contract to create one.[165] That this is a fiction should be manifest. The landlord has purported to grant a lease; he has not promised to create one in the future. Nevertheless, the fiction is well established. Starting from the fictitious premise that the attempt to grant a lease takes effect as a contract to create a lease, the next step in the reasoning process is that such a contract is one that a court would normally enforce by a decree of specific performance. Applying the maxim that equity looks upon that which ought to be done as already having been done, the consequence is that, in equity, there is a valid seven-year lease.

The leading case is *Walsh v. Lonsdale*.[166] Here the landlord, by a document in writing, purported to grant a seven-year lease of a mill to the tenant. It was a term of the lease that the tenant should pay a year's rent in advance. The tenant went into possession and paid rent on a quarterly basis for a year and a quarter, whereupon the landlord insisted that he pay a year's rent in advance as had been agreed. The tenant refused to pay and the landlord responded by seizing the tenant's goods in lieu of such payment and the tenant sued him in trespass. The tenant's argument was that the remedy of distress, the seizing of goods for non-payment of rent, is a legal remedy. At law, because he had gone into possession and paid rent, he was a yearly tenant. As such, he could terminate the lease by giving six months' notice to quit.[167] The obligation to pay a year's rent in advance was inconsistent with his ability to end the lease by giving the requisite notice to quit and it therefore followed that what the landlord had done was unlawful.

As a statement of the effect of what had happened at law, this was perfectly accurate. It ignored, however, the view which equity took of the situation. There was not a legal seven-year lease but, in the view of equity, there was a perfectly valid contract to create such a lease and specific performance would be granted to enforce that contract. Taking the view

---

[164] See S. Bright [1998] Conv. 229, who accepts the reasoning as correct, but points to the serious consequences which may arise because of it.

[165] *Parker v. Taswell* (1858) 2 De G, & J, 559.

[166] (1882) 21 Ch.D. 9. See also the elucidation of this principle in *R. v. Tower Hamlets London Borough Council, ex p. Goetz* [1999] Q.B. 1019 at 1024 *per* Mummery L.J.   [167] See 10.10.2.

that what ought to be done should be regarded as having been done, in equity there was a seven-year lease in existence and, under the terms of that lease, what L had done was perfectly lawful. The tenant's claim, therefore, failed.

Although the actual decision is controversial, in the sense that it is not clear that distress, as a remedy, was available in equity,[168] the case presents an excellent example of the role of equity when the formal requirements at law have not been complied with. From this, it might be seen that an equitable lease is as good as a legal lease. For a number of reasons, this is not so.

10.7.1 **Contract**

The starting point in the evolution of the equitable tenancy is that the informal grant of a lease is viewed as being a contract to create a lease and, unless s. 2 of the Law of Property (Miscellaneous Provisions) Act (LP(MP)A) 1989 is complied with there will be no contract to create a lease and the basis of the equitable lease will be gone.[169] If the tenant goes into possession of the property and pays rent, then a court may seek to fashion such remedy as seems appropriate, using estoppel principles.[170] Alternatively, it might regard the relationship as being governed by law, which would imply a periodic tenancy in these circumstances. It is perhaps as well that this problem is unlikely to occur because, whereas the parties may neglect to use a deed, it is normal for a lease of this length at least to be in writing and signed by both landlord and tenant so that the requirements of s. 2 will be met. When Part 8 of the LRA 2002, which will make compulsory electronic conveyancing, is brought into force, however, this issue will become very much a live one. This will be considered after other aspects of equitable tenancies have been dealt with.[171]

10.7.2 **Specific performance**

For an equitable lease to be created, it is necessary for there not only to be a contract to create a lease but that contract needs to be specifically enforceable. If the contract is to create a sub-tenancy and there is a covenant in the head lease which prohibits the granting of sub-tenancies, then specific performance will not be granted of the contract and an equitable sub-tenancy will not arise.[172] The case of *Bell Street Investments Ltd v. Wood*[173] is instructive. A landlord had purported to grant a seven-year lease of a yard but had not used a deed. The yard was in a dilapidated condition owing, in part, to various breaches of covenant by the tenant. In possession proceedings brought by the landlord, one of the issues to be determined was the status of the tenant. Because there was no deed, there was no legal seven-year lease. Because the landlord had behaved inequitably himself, specific performance was not available. As a result, there was no equitable seven-year lease. The tenant had gone into possession and paid rent, however, thus giving rise to an implied periodic tenancy at law. As there was now no conflict between law and equity, his position was governed by the incidents of that periodic tenancy.

---

[168] See Harpum, Bridge, and Dixon, *Megarry and Wade's Law of Real Property* (8th edn) (London, Sweet & Maxwell, 2012), 17–053. The ancient common law remedy of distress has, in respect of residential property, now been abolished: Tribunals, Courts and Enforcement Act 2007, s. 71. A new system in respect of commercial property has been introduced: ibid., s. 72.

[169] See in the context of equitable mortgages, where the same argument was used, *United Bank of Kuwait plc v. Sahib* [1997] Ch. 107.

[170] See *Yaxley v. Gotts* [2000] 1 All E.R. 711. Contrast *Yeoman's Row Management Ltd v. Cobbe* [2008] UKHL 55, discussed in Chapter 14.

[171] See Chapter 5.   [172] *Warmington v. Miller* [1973] 2 All E.R. 372.   [173] [1970] E.G.D. 812.

10.7.3 **Third parties**

In common with all equitable rights, the equitable lease is vulnerable to being defeated if the property gets into the hands of a bona fide purchaser, although one must distinguish between unregistered and registered land.

10.7.3.1 Unregistered land

Where title is unregistered, an equitable lease is registrable as a land charge. As a contract to create a legal estate, the lease, it is registrable as a Class C(iv) land charge. This will be void for non-registration against a purchaser for value of the reversion.[174] If the tenant has gone into possession and has paid rent, the equitable lease will still be void for non-registration,[175] but there will now be in existence an implied legal periodic tenancy which will be binding upon the purchaser.

10.7.3.2 Registered land

An equitable lease is an interest affecting registered land and, as such should be protected by the entry of a notice. Although most leases granted for a term of less than seven years are interests which will override a registered disposition,[176] this definition does not include an equitable lease because, as there is no deed, there is no grant.[177] If, however, as is likely to be the case, the tenant has gone into possession, then the equitable lease will override a registered disposition under Sched. 3, para. 2, LRA 2002, a further example of the superior protection afforded to the rights of occupiers where title is registered than when it is not.

10.7.4 **Easements**

On a conveyance of land, easements will, in certain situations, be implied into the conveyance. Because the creation of an equitable lease does not involve a conveyance, there is no such statutory implication in the case of equitable tenancies, although some easements may be acquired under the common law rules.[178]

10.7.5 **Covenants**

In the case of leases created before 1995, on the assignment of the lease or the reversion, certain covenants would run with that estate, so that the assignee could sue and be sued upon them. For this to occur there had to exist privity of estate between the parties to the action, and this did not occur in the case of equitable tenancies. With the enactment of the Landlord and Tenant (Covenants) Act 1995, this distinction has now been removed, so that covenants in a legal lease and in an equitable lease will run on the same basis.[179]

10.7.6 **Electronic conveyancing**

If Part 8 of the LRA 2002 is brought into force, electronic conveyancing will become compulsory. Crucially, s. 93(2) provides that contracts to make dispositions to which the section applies will only have effect if made in a document in electronic form and, if when

---

[174] Land Charges Act 1972, s. 4(6).   [175] See *Lloyds Bank plc v. Carrick* [1996] 4 All E.R. 630.
[176] LRA 2002, Sched. 3, para. 1.   [177] *City Permanent Building Society v. Miller* [1952] Ch. 840.
[178] See *Borman v. Griffith* [1930] Ch. 493. See 12.4.4.3.   [179] See 10.9.2.

the document purports to take effect it is electronically communicated to the registrar and the relevant registration requirements are met. In the present context, this means that the section will apply to the assignment of leases which are already registered and the grant of certain leases which, principally, refers to leases of more than seven years, will trigger the requirement of registration. The potential effect of this on 'the rather quaint, if well established, doctrine in *Walsh v. Lonsdale*'[180] must now be considered.

The key point is that in the case of leases for more than seven years, a necessary consequence of s. 93(2) of the Act is that there can be no contract to create the lease and, therefore, the doctrine of *Walsh v. Lonsdale* will be abolished. If the purported tenant goes into possession and pays rent, there seems to be no reason in principle why a legal periodic tenancy should not be implied. As to whether any greater rights will be acquired, this will depend on the willingness of the courts to apply estoppel principles: the basis of this argument being that parties who have acted on the faith of their belief that there was in existence a lease of more than seven years should have rather greater rights than would be the case if there was in existence merely a periodic tenancy. A similar issue arose in *Liverpool City Council v. Walton*.[181] In this case, it was argued that a contract to create a 999-year lease was void for uncertainty. Although this argument failed, Neuberger J. considered what the position would have been had that not been the case. The prospective tenant had, in reliance on the agreement, spent some £1 million in circumstances where it would have been inequitable for the landlord to deny him some effect to his expectation. In these circumstances the judge expressed the view that, to satisfy the equity which had arisen, he would have ordered the grant of the agreed lease, but he also made it clear that this would not be the appropriate remedy in all cases.[182] This is an area where uncertainty is likely to prevail.

10.7.7 **Reversionary leases**

If Part 8 of the 2002 Act is brought into force, it is likely that, in the vast majority of cases, problems of non-compliance will not arise; a lease of more than seven years is a commercial transaction and advice is likely to be taken and the formal requirements will be met. Where one can envisage problems is with regard to certain reversionary leases. Any lease to take effect in possession more than three months after the date of the grant is required to be registered. A purported let to a group of students granted in March, to take effect in September, will require registration. When s. 93 of the Act is in force, unless this transaction is effected electronically and communicated in that form to the registrar, it will have no effect at all. One suspects that non-compliance in these circumstances will not be uncommon. A useful reform in this area might be to exempt reversionary leases of less than three years from compulsory registration.

10.8 **Rights and duties under a lease**

A lease is an estate in land. It is, however, also a contractual relationship and, as such, the parties are free to include in the lease such contractual terms, or covenants, as they see fit. In addition to the terms which the parties actually agree upon, certain obligations are implied into the agreement, sometimes by statute and sometimes by the common law. This section deals with the covenants or obligations commonly found in leases.

---

[180] *Liverpool City Council v. Walton* [2002] 1 E.G.L.R. 149 at 154 *per* Neuberger J.
[181] [2002] 1 E.G.L.R. 149.   [182] Ibid. at 156.

10.8.1 **Quiet enjoyment**

There is implied into every lease a covenant by the landlord that the tenant shall enjoy quiet enjoyment of the property.[183] The scope of this covenant involves the actions of the landlord and the lawful acts of his other tenants. The landlord, unless he expressly covenants to prevent acts of nuisance committed by his other tenants, will not be liable for such acts.[184] Neither will acts of third parties come within the terms of the covenant, so if the tenant is evicted by title paramount, the tenant will have no remedy for breach of the covenant for quiet enjoyment.[185]

It was at one time thought that the covenant for quiet enjoyment extended only to some physical interference with the tenant's enjoyment of the property. This matter was considered by the House of Lords in *Southwark London Borough Council v. Mills*.[186] The tenants lived in a block of flats which had been constructed in 1919. The tenants complained that the sound insulation between the flats was inadequate, so that noise generated by the normal activity of tenants in adjoining flats could clearly be heard. This argument that this amounted to a breach of covenant was rejected.

Lord Hoffmann observed that the covenant could not be read literally. In the instant case 'the flat is not quiet and the tenant is not enjoying it'.[187] While it was accepted that excessive noise could, in principle, amount to a breach of the covenant,[188] it did not do so, however, in the present case. The level of noise did not amount to a nuisance, because the ordinary use of residential premises is not being capable of amounting to a nuisance.[189] More importantly, however, the problem was caused by the way that the property was initially built. The landlord had not done anything after the initial grant of the lease to make the position worse.[190] As there is no implied condition that the property is fit for the purpose for which it is let,[191] the covenant did not extend to interference with the tenant's enjoyment of the property which resulted from the condition of the property before the grant was made. For the same reason, neither did the covenant extend to the use of parts of the building let by the landlord, which the parties must have contemplated before the lease was granted. As it was clear that the other flats in the building would also be let, the tenant could not complain in respect of normal activity of the other tenants which took place in those other flats.

This remains subject to the qualification of reasonableness. In *Timothy Taylor Ltd v. Mayfair House Corp*,[192] a tenant had been granted a twenty-year lease of ground floor and basement premises of a five-storey building in Mayfair, the purpose of the lease being to operate a fine art gallery. In addition to a covenant for quiet enjoyment by the landlord, the lease also reserved the right to develop the other floors of the building. When this right was exercised, the effect on the tenant's business was substantial and amounted to a breach

---

[183] *Budd-Scott v. Daniel* [1902] 2 K.B. 351.

[184] *Baxter v. Camden London Borough Council* [1999] 2 W.L.R. 566. See also *Smith v. Scott* [1973] Ch. 314.

[185] *Jones v. Lavington* [1903] 1 K.B. 523. In the case of leases granted after 1995, when a full title guarantee is given, the landlord will be liable on the covenants for title if the tenant is evicted for this reason: LP(MP)A 1994, s. 1(1).

[186] [2001] A.C. 1.   [187] Ibid. at 10.

[188] Cf. *Jenkins v. Jackson* (1888) 40 Ch.D. 71 at 74 *per* Kekewich J.

[189] *Baxter v. Camden London Borough Council* [1999] 2 W.L.R. 566 at 574 *per* Tuckey L.J.

[190] See also *Long v. Southwark London Borough Council* [2002] EWCA Civ. 403 at paras 60–4 *per* Arden L. Cf. *Sampson v. Hodson-Presinger* [1981] 3 All E.R. 710, where a subsequent conversion of the property exacerbated the noise problem.

[191] See *Hart v. Windsor* (1844) 12 M. & W. 68 at 77–8 *per* Parke B.; *Edler v. Auerbach* [1950] 1 K.B. 359 at 374 *per* Devlin J.

[192] [2016] EWHC 1075 (Ch).

of covenant. Although development was permitted, what was being done amounted to an unreasonable interference with the tenant's use of the property as a gallery.

Although the covenant for quiet enjoyment can be broken by acts other than an act of physical interference with the tenant's enjoyment of the property, most acts which have been held to amount to a breach have involved such behaviour. Acts which have been held to amount to breaches of the covenant for quiet enjoyment include subsidence caused by mining,[193] the removal of the tenant's door,[194] and general intimidation to persuade the tenant to leave.[195]

10.8.1.1 Remedies

If the landlord is committing a breach of the covenant for quiet enjoyment, then the tenant may obtain an injunction to restrain his behaviour. He may also claim damages. These are assessed on the principles governing the award of damages in the law of contract and, as such, do not include the possibility of the award of exemplary damages. Such a limitation on the award of damages could act as an inducement to unscrupulous landlords to bully tenants who enjoy statutory protection into leaving the property, it being impossible, or at least very difficult, to evict such tenants lawfully. This unacceptable practice, known after its most famous practitioner, was termed 'Rachmanism'.

Exemplary damages, to punish the wrongdoer, can, however, be awarded in tort, one of the circumstances being when a tortfeasor calculates that he stands to make more money out of committing the tort than he would be liable to pay in damages.[196] That this could apply in the present context was made clear by Lord Hailsham L.C., who, when discussing the principles upon which exemplary damages are awarded, said:

> How, it may be asked, about the late Mr Rachman, who is alleged to have hired bullies to intimidate statutory tenants by violence or threats of violence into giving vacant possession of their premises and so placing a valuable asset in the hands of the landlord? The answer must be that if this is not a cynical calculation of profit and cold-blooded disregard of a plaintiffs' rights, I do not know what is.[197]

Following this very clear steer, in *Drane v. Evangelou*,[198] a landlord was held liable to pay exemplary damages to a tenant, who, when he was out, returned to find that his belongings had been thrown into the street and his access to the house blocked by a large man standing in the doorway. In addition to a breach of the covenant, the landlord had also committed the tort of trespass and, for this, exemplary damages were available.

10.8.1.2 Statutory liability

In any claim for exemplary damages, the tenant must show that the landlord has calculated that he will stand to gain more from unlawfully evicting the tenant than he would have to pay him in damages. This may prove to be difficult. A tenant is more likely now to use the civil remedy contained in s. 27 of the Housing Act 1988.

This section provides for the civil liability of the landlord in tort if he, or any person acting on his behalf, unlawfully deprives the residential occupier of any premises of his occupation of the whole or part of the premises. He is also liable if he attempts unlawfully

---

[193] *Markham v. Paget* [1908] Ch. 697.   [194] *Lavender v. Betts* [1942] 2 All E.R. 72.

[195] *Kenny v. Preen* [1963] 1 Q.B. 499.

[196] *Cassell & Co. Ltd v. Broome* [1972] A.C. 1027 (a libel case involving a book written by David Irving).

[197] [1972] A.C. 1027 at 1074.

[198] [1978] 1 W.L.R. 455. See also *Guppy's (Bridport) Ltd v. Brookling* (1983) 14 H.L.R. 1; *Mehta v. Royal Bank of Scotland* [1999] 3 E.G.L.R. 153.

to deprive the residential occupier of any premises of his occupation of the whole or part of the premises or, knowing or having reason to believe that the conduct is likely to cause the occupier to give up the premises in whole or in part, or to refrain from exercising any right or pursuing any right or pursuing any remedy in respect of the premises, does acts likely to interfere with the peace and comfort of the residential occupier or members of his household, or persistently withdraws or withholds services reasonably required for the occupation of the premises as a residence and as a result the occupier gives up his occupation of the premises as a residence.[199] It should be noted, however, that damages are only payable if the occupier gives up occupation. If he resists the acts of the landlord and remains in occupation, there is no civil liability under the statute and the tenant's remedies would appear to lie in an action on the covenant for quiet enjoyment and, possibly, trespass.

10.8.1.3 Criminal liability

In addition to the imposition of civil liability in respect of unlawful eviction, criminal sanctions are also imposed in respect of harassment committed by the landlord. Separate criminal offences are created by s. 1 of the Protection of Eviction Act 1977[200] in respect of unlawful eviction and harassment of a residential occupier. It is also unlawful for the owner of property which has been subject to a tenancy which has come to an end, but where the occupier continues to occupy the premises as a residence, to seek to enforce his right to possession otherwise than by court proceedings.[201]

10.8.2 Derogation from grant

What at one time was thought to be a separate obligation from the covenant for quiet enjoyment implied upon the landlord was the obligation not to derogate from his grant.[202] The essential idea is that, if the property has been let for a particular purpose, then the landlord may not do acts which interfere with that purpose. A reason for seeing the two obligations as being separate was that, originally, the former obligation was seen as being confined to physical acts interfering with the tenant's enjoyment of the property. The present view, however, is that 'The principle is the same in both cases: a man must not give with one hand and take away with the other'.[203]

The essence of the doctrine is the purpose of the letting. In *North Eastern Railway Co. v. Elliot*,[204] the principle was expressed as being:

> If a landowner conveys one of two closes to another, he cannot afterwards do anything to derogate from his own grant; and if the conveyance is made for the express purpose of having buildings erected upon the land so granted, a contract is implied on the part of the grantor to do nothing to prevent the land being used for the purpose for which to the knowledge of the grantor the conveyance was made.

This principle has been applied to situations where land has been let for the purpose of a particular business and the proposed use by the landlord of his other property would interfere with the tenant's use of his land. In one case, land was let for the purpose of use as a timber merchant and the landlord was restrained from building so as to obstruct the flow

---

[199] Housing Act 1988, s. 27(1)(2).   [200] As amended by Housing Act 1988. ss 27, 28.
[201] Protection from Eviction Act 1977, s. 3.   [202] See, generally, D.W. Elliott (1964) 80 L.Q.R. 244.
[203] *Southwark London Borough Council v. Mills* [2001] 1 A.C. 1 at 23 *per* Lord Millett. For a fuller statement, see *Platt v. London Underground Ltd* [2001] 2 E.G.L.R. 121 at 122 *per* Neuberger J. See also *Century Projects Ltd v. Almacantar (Centre Point) Ltd* [2014] EWHC 394 (Ch).
[204] (1860) 1 J. & H. 145 at 153 *per* Sir William Page Wood V.-C.

of air to the sheds used for the drying of timber.[205] Again, in *Owen v. Gadd*,[206] premises were let for business purposes. The landlord then erected scaffolding, the effect of which was to make it difficult for customers to access the property and this was held to amount to a breach of the covenant for quiet enjoyment.

By way of contrast, however, in *Browne v. Flower*,[207] a case concerning the residential as opposed to the commercial sector, the plaintiff was the tenant of a flat and the landlord then built an outside staircase, this having the effect that, whenever the landlord used it, he could see into the tenant's living room. This was held not to be a breach of the covenant of quiet enjoyment, the act of the landlord not being considered to make the premises materially less fit for the purpose for which they were let. Given the greater importance attached to privacy today, such a case may well be viewed differently now.

What is clear from the case law, however, is that for the landlord to be liable he must do some act after the commencement of the lease which affects the tenant's enjoyment of the land. This obligation will not operate to prevent the landlord from competing with the tenant's business,[208] although, if the property is let as part of a specifically designed commercial operation, such as a shopping mall, if the landlord permits activity inconsistent with that design, he may be found to have derogated from his grant.[209] The fact that, from the outset, the land was not fully fit for the purpose for which it was let will not be sufficient to afford the tenant any remedy.

10.8.3 Rent

Although, strictly speaking, it is not necessary for the creation of a lease that a rent be reserved, it is almost universally the case that this will happen. While a lease is clearly a contractual relationship, it is also an estate in land. Because of this, it was considered to be doubtful if the lease could be ended only by methods appropriate to the termination of that estate, or whether the normal contractual rules are applicable to the ending of the relationship.

10.8.4 Frustration

For quite some time, it was uncertain whether, like other contracts, a lease could be frustrated. The House of Lords in *Cricklewood Property and Investment Trustee Ltd v. Leighton's Investment Trust Ltd*,[210] divided evenly on the issue of principle, with two saying yes, two saying no, and the fifth member of the Appellate Committee reserving his opinion. As a matter of principle, this matter was resolved in *National Carriers Ltd v. Panalpina (Northern) Ltd*,[211] it being considered that, in rare cases, a lease could be frustrated. The doctrine was not applied in the case itself, however, where the inaccessibility of a warehouse for twenty months of a ten-year lease did not amount to frustration. It would seem that some truly cataclysmic event, such as the destruction of a flat in a block caused by landslip[212] or the

---

[205] *Aldin v. Latimer, Clark, Muirhead & Co.* [1894] 2 Ch. 437. See also *Harmer v. Jumbil (Nigeria) Tin Areas Ltd* [1921] 1 Ch. 20; *Chartered Trust plc v. Davies* (1997) 76 P. & C.R. 396; and *Carter v. Cole* [2009] EWCA Civ. 410 (a case concerning an easement).

[206] [1956] 2 Q.B. 99. See also *Timothy Taylor Ltd v. Mayfair House Corp* [2016] EWHC 394 (Ch).

[207] [1911] 2 Ch. 219.

[208] *Romulus Trading Co. Ltd v. Comet Properties Ltd* [1996] 2 E.G.L.R. 70.

[209] See *Petra Investments Ltd v. Jeffrey Rogers plc* [2000] 3 E.G.L.R. 120, where this argument failed on the facts.

[210] [1945] A.C. 221.   [211] [1981] A.C. 675.

[212] See *Wong Lai Ying v. Chinachem Investment Co. Ltd* (1979) 13 B.L.R. 81.

falling of a hotel into the sea caused by coastal erosion[213] would be necessary before a lease of any length would be held to be frustrated.

In 2019, the European Medicines Agency, which moved from London to Amsterdam in 2019 as a response to the outcome of the 2016 Brexit referendum, argued that it was entitled to end its lease of a building in Canary Wharf in London as a result of frustration. This was held not to be a frustrating event, not least for the reason that the European Medicine Agency's purpose in agreeing the lease did not coincide with Canary Wharf's, there was no common purpose, as the former sought flexibility and low rent while the latter sought to protect its long-term cash flow.[214]

10.8.5 Repudiation

As a normal incident of a contractual relationship, if one party commits a sufficiently serious breach of the contract, it is open to the other to terminate the contract, he being discharged from his own obligations by the repudiatory breach of the other. It was first accepted, at county court level, that it was open to the tenant to regard the lease as being repudiated by the landlord's breach of his own obligations[215] and, independently of this decision, the same conclusion has been accepted by the Court of Appeal.[216] It will not be every breach of covenant by the landlord which will have this effect, however; it would seem to be necessary for the breach to deprive the tenant, substantially, of the whole benefit of the lease.[217] Whether the landlord can adopt this course is unclear[218] but it seems unlikely given the statutory procedures which are normally required to be followed in respect of termination of a lease in the event of breaches of covenant by the tenant.[219]

10.8.6 Repair

Obligations to repair can be express or implied and can also, in the case of some tenancies, be imposed by statute.

10.8.6.1 Express covenants

As a general proposition, the parties are free to deal with the question of liability for repairs to the property as they choose. Where the matter is not regulated by statute, the main difficulty relates to the ambit of the covenant which, in turn, can relate to matters of construction.

As a general matter of construction, if the covenant requires the tenant to keep the property in good repair, this carries an obligation to put the property in good repair if that is not currently the case.[220] The actual words used do not, however, materially affect the content of the covenant, so that expressing the obligation as being to put the property in good repair, or tenantable repair, or even perfect repair, does not affect what is expected of the tenant. What constitutes such a state of repair is judged, however, by the condition of the property and its environs at the date of the lease and not the date of the dispute, so

[213] Cf. *Holbeck Hall Hotel Ltd v. Scarborough Borough Council* [2000] 2 All E.R. 705, where the point was not argued.
[214] *Canary Wharf v. European Medicines Agency* [2019] EWHC 335 (Ch).
[215] *Hussein v. Mehlman* [1992] 2 E.G.L.R. 87 (covenant to repair).
[216] *Chartered Trust plc v. Davies* (1997) 76 P. & C.R. 396 (derogation from grant).
[217] See *Nynehead Developments Ltd v. R.H. Fireboard Containers Ltd* [1999] 02 E.G. 139 discussed by M. Pawlowski and J. Brown [1999] Conv. 150.
[218] The point was left open in *Reichman v. Beveridge* [2006] EWCA Civ. 1659 at [10] *per* Lloyd L.J.
[219] See 10.10.3.
[220] *Proudfoot v. Hart* (1890) 25 Q.B.D. 92.

if surrounding property has deteriorated since then, this does not reduce the obligation placed upon the tenant.[221]

10.8.6.2 Repair or improvement?

The main bone of contention in determining whether a particular item comes within the ambit of a covenant to repair is whether the work in question amounts to a repair or an improvement. This distinction may be easier to state than to apply as, frequently, a repair will also involve the improvement of the property. In deciding this issue, a broad rule of thumb may be taken to be that the replacement of an item which is defective is a repair, while the installation of something new is an improvement. On this basis, the installation of a damp course in a building which does not have one is likely to be seen as an improvement, and, consequently, outside the scope of a covenant to repair,[222] whereas the replacement of an existing course which has broken down would be a repair, even though what would now be installed would be an improvement on the original.[223] In similar vein, the fact that a steep flight of steps is a hazard because there is no handrail does not mean that the property is in disrepair. This is because there is no obligation on the landlord to provide one in the first place.[224] Neither is it the case that the fact that part of a building does not perform its principal task mean that it is necessarily in disrepair. So, for example, in *Post Office v. Aquarius Property Ltd*,[225] the basement of an office was built of porous cement so that, whenever the water table rose, the basement became ankle-deep in water. No damage was caused by the incursion of water, however, and the Court of Appeal held that the tenant's covenant to repair did not extend to the correction of design faults in the building, as originally constructed.

Two issues arise from this case. First, the notion of disrepair involves some element of damage. In *Quick v. Taff-Ely Borough Council*,[226] the lack of insulation around single-glazed windows caused serious condensation. Although the problems caused by this were so serious that the house was uninhabitable at various times of year, little actual damage to the house occurred as a result of it. The fact that the design of the windows was totally inadequate did not mean that they were in a state of disrepair and so within the ambit of the landlord's covenant to repair. This would only have been the case if the design fault had led to actual physical damage.[227] The second point is that the damage can be the result of an inherent flaw in the building and so, to repair the damage, correction of this flaw will result in an improvement of the property. Such correction will then amount to a repair.

Although it has been said that the covenant to repair extends to the restoration of a house to its previous condition and does not entail making it better than it previously was,[228] a repair, properly called, may have this effect. In *Ravenseft Properties Ltd v. Davstone (Holdings) Ltd*,[229] a block of flats was built and stone cladding had been attached. When

---

[221] See *Anstruther-Gough-Calthorpe v. McOscar* [1928] 1 K.B. 726.

[222] *Wainwright v. Leeds City Council* (1984) 82 L.G.R. 657; *Eyre v. McCracken* (2000) 80 P. & C.R. 220.

[223] *Pembury v. Lamdin* [1940] 2 All E.R. 434; *Elmcroft Developments Ltd v. Tankersley-Sawyer* [1984] 1 E.G.L.R. 47; *Uddin v. London Borough of Islington* [2015] EWCA Civ. 369. See also *Creska Ltd v. Hammersmith London Borough Council* [1998] 3 E.G.L.R. 35 (underfloor heating).

[224] *Sternbaum v. Dhesi* [2016] EWCA Civ. 155 at [29]–[30] *per* Hallett L.J.

[225] [1987] 1 All E.R. 1055.

[226] [1986] Q.B. 821. See also *Mullaney v. Maybourne Grange (Croydon) Management Co. Ltd* [1986] 1 E.G.L.R. 70; *McErney v. Lambeth London Borough Council* (1988) 21 H.L.R. 188.

[227] See *Stent v. Monmouth District Council* (1987) 54 P. & C.R. 193; *Staves and Staves v. Leeds City Council* (1990) 23 H.L.R. 107.

[228] See *Quick v. Taff-Ely Borough Council* [1986] Q.B. 809 at 821 *per* Lawton L.J.; *Southwark London Borough Council v. Mills* [2001] 1 A.C. 1 at 8 *per* Lord Hoffmann.

[229] [1980] Q.B. 12. See also *Brew Brothers Ltd v. Snax (Ross) Ltd* [1970] 1 Q.B. 12.

the flats were built, expansion joints had not been fitted, the result of this deficiency being that the stones were in danger of falling off the building and, in the interest of safety, this defect had to be remedied. The issue was who had to pay for this work, and this depended upon whether such work was within the scope of the tenant's covenant to repair. It was held that it was. In deciding whether a particular matter constitutes a repair or an improvement,

> The true test is . . . that it is always a question of degree whether that which the tenant is being asked to do can properly be described as repair, or whether on the contrary it would involve giving back to the landlord a wholly different thing from that which he demised.[230]

One factor which is then relevant is the cost and the physical scale of what is necessary,[231] so that, in *Ravenseft*, the fact that the cost of the work was in the region of £55,000, when set against a rebuilding cost of £3 million tended to the conclusion that what was involved was a repair. The fact that the problem stemmed from an inherent fault in the building did not alter this conclusion.

10.8.6.3 Implied terms

As stated previously, it is normally the case that the parties are free to negotiate as to who should bear the burden of repairs. In certain situations, however, there are obligations implied as to this matter, either at common law or by statute.

Common law

The common law has traditionally been loath to imply terms relating to the physical quality of the property in to a lease, the standard position being that:

> A landlord who lets a house in a dangerous state is not liable to the tenant's customers or guests for accidents happening during the term; for fraud apart, there is no law against letting a tumble-down house; and the tenant's remedy is upon his contract, if any.[232]

The only general modification to this at common law is that, if the letting is of a furnished house, then there is an obligation on the landlord that the house is, at the outset of the tenancy, fit for human habitation.[233] Even this somewhat limited obligation is construed narrowly, there being no implied obligation that the property remains fit for human habitation throughout the lease.[234]

The other source of liability is where a court will imply a term as to liability for repair if to do so it is necessary to give business efficacy to the contract. In *Liverpool City Council v. Irwin*,[235] the council was the landlord of a block of flats, the tenants being subject to various obligations imposed by their agreements. To interpret the lease, the House of Lords held that, by necessary implication, the landlord was under an obligation to take reasonable care to keep the common parts of the building, including the lift, in a state of repair. It

---

[230] *Ravenseft Properties Ltd v. Davstone (Holdings) Ltd, supra,* at 21 *per* Forbes J.

[231] Cf. *Lurcott v. Wakely* [1911] 1 K.B. 905 (rebuilding a wall held to be a repair) with *Sotheby v. Grundy* [1947] 2 All E.R. 761 (house condemned, rebuilding of it on proper foundations not a repair).

[232] *Robbins v. Jones* (1863) 15 C.B. (N.S.) 221 at 240 *per* Erle C.J. See also *Carstairs v. Taylor* (1871) L.R. 6 Exch. 217 at 222 *per* Martin B. See now Defective Premises Act 1972, s. 4.

[233] *Smith v. Marrable* (1843) 11 M. & W. 5 (bug infestation). See also *Summers v. Salford Corporation* [1943] A.C. 283 where the effect of a broken window sash meant that a window could not be opened or closed without the risk of physical injury. This meant that the house was unfit for habitation.

[234] *Sarson v. Roberts* [1895] 2 Q.B. 395 (outbreak of scarlet fever).   [235] [1977] A.C. 239.

was not open to the courts to imply terms on the basis that it was reasonable to do so; the test is one of necessity, a finding which is more likely to be achieved when the term to be implied is correlative to an obligation accepted by the tenant.[236]

10.8.7 **Statutory obligations**

In respect of certain residential leases, certain statutory obligations are imposed upon the landlord.

10.8.7.1 **Homes (Fitness for Human Habitation) Act 2018**

In the case of a house which is let for a period of not more than three years, s. 8 of the Landlord and Tenant Act 1985 imposed an obligation on the landlord by that the house will, at the time of the letting and thereafter, be fit for human habitation.[237] The problem with this provision was that it applied only to tenancies where the annual rent is no more than £52.00 per annum outside London and no more than £80.00 per annum in London. While it has long been clear that this requirement is unrealistic[238] and there were frequent pleas for the rent ceilings to be raised from the levels first set in 1957[239], the levels were not updated, with judges concluding that greater protection for tenants was a question for Parliament, not the courts.[240]

Now, the Homes (Fitness for Human Habitation) Act 2018[241] has introduced s. 9A of the Landlord and Tenant Act 1985 requiring landlords to ensure that the properties they rent out are free of potentially harmful hazards. Section 9A[242] introduces an implied covenant by the landlord into a lease for the dwelling that the dwelling '(a) is fit for human habitation at the time the lease was granted; and (b) will be kept fit for human habitation during the term of the lease'. This will apply to leases of less than seven years with only minimal exceptions.[243]

To avoid re-negotiations or retaliatory evictions, s. 9A(4) states that any provision of a lease or any agreement relating to a lease is void where that provision attempts to '(a) exclude or limit the obligations of the landlord under the implied covenant; or (b) authorises any forfeiture or imposes on the tenant any penalty, disability or obligation in the event of the tenant enforcing their rights under the implied covenant introduced through this section'. The restriction on forfeiture or additional penalties is particularly important as it underscores the tenant's right to bring an action if the implied covenant for fitness for human habitation is breached. Before the 2018 Act came into force, unless there was an express covenant for fitness for human habitation in the lease, the landlord would only be committing an offence where they failed to comply with a local authority's enforcement notice under the Housing Act 2004. This put the burden of enforcing these leasehold covenants on local authorities, excluding the tenant. Under the 2018 Act, tenants can now bring breaches of this implied covenant to court directly, seeking specific performance.[244]

---

[236] Ibid. at 254 *per* Lord Wilberforce. See also *Barrett v. Lounava (1982) Ltd* [1990] 1 Q.B. 348, but contrast *Demetriou v. Poolaction Ltd* [1981] 1 E.G.L.R. 100.

[237] For a list of the criteria to be applied in determining this issue, see Landlord and Tenant Act 1985, s. 10.

[238] The provision has been described as 'completely dead letters': *Issa v. Hackney London Borough Council* [1997] 1 W.L.R. 956 at 964 *per* Brooke L.J.

[239] Housing Act 1957, s. 6. For a plea for change, see, e.g., [1986] Q.B. 809 at 821 *per* Lawton L.J.

[240] *McErney v. Lambeth London Borough Council*, (1988) 21 H.L.R. 188 at 194.

[241] This entered into force in March 2019.

[242] Of the Landlord and Tenant Act 1985, inserted by the Homes (Fitness for Human Habitation Act) 2018, s. 1(3)

[243] Section 9B.   [244] Section 9A(5).

As Karen Buck MP, who brought the Bill to Parliament, has said:

> Living in a cold, damp or unsafe home is hell. It damages people's physical and mental wellbe-
> ing, erodes the income of the poorest households and impacts on children's education. The
> most vulnerable tenants are those most at risk of being trapped in substandard accommoda-
> tion, and they are often the least able to withstand the damage such conditions do, or to fight
> their corner unaided.[245]

The introduction of the Homes (Fitness for Human Habitation) Act 2018 brings some hope now that if courts regularly enforce the implied covenant for human habitation, then the thousands of tenants living in properties judged unfit for human habitation will have a legal means of redress.[246]

In Wales, the 2016 Renting Homes (Wales) Act 2016 has already imposed an obligation on landlords that the properties they let should be, and remain, fit for habitation.[247]

10.8.7.2 Liability to repair

Section 11 of the Landlord and Tenant Act 1985 was long considered more useful than the financially outdated s. 8. Section 11 applies to a lease of a dwelling-house, granted after 24 October 1961, of not more than seven years.[248] Any attempt to exclude, or vary, the liability imposed is void unless such a term has been approved by the county court.[249] Under s. 11, there is an implied covenant by the lessor—

(a) to keep in repair the structure and exterior of the dwelling-house (including drains, gutters and external pipes);

(b) to keep in repair and proper working order the installations in the dwelling-house for the supply of water, gas and electricity and for sanitation (including basins, sinks, baths and sanitary conveniences, but not other fixtures, fittings and appliances for making use of the supply of water gas and electricity); and

(c) to keep in repair and proper working order the installations in the dwelling-house for space heating and heating water.

A number of points can be made concerning this provision. First, the landlord is only liable under the covenant if he is given notice by the tenant of the defect in question.[250] Second, the covenant is qualified by the obligation, which is in any event imposed upon a periodic tenant, to use the property in a tenant-like manner.[251] The ambit of this duty is to perform routine acts of maintenance around the house, doing all the jobs, such as unblocking the sink and taking precautions against freezing pipes in winter, that a reasonable tenant would do.[252] Third, the obligation relates to the keeping in repair of various services and installations. This would not appear to impose any liability for a failure to supply them, so that, if a house has no central heating in the first place, the landlord would be under no duty to install it. Much the same point was accepted in *Sternbaum v. Dhesi*,[253]

---

[245] House of Commons Hansard, (2018) Vol. 648, Col. 536.

[246] For a background on conditions see Wendy Wilson (2018) Briefing Paper No. CBP08185, House of Commons Library. Homes (Fitness for Human Habitation) Bill 2017–19.

[247] Section 91.   [248] Landlord and Tenant Act 1985, s. 13.

[249] Landlord and Tenant Act 1985, s. 12.

[250] *O'Brien v. Robinson* [1973] A.C. 912. If such notice is given, a retaliatory notice to quit served by the landlord is invalid for a period of six months: Deregulation Act 2015, s. 33.

[251] Landlord and Tenant Act 1985, s. 11(2)(a).

[252] See *Warren v. Keen* [1954] 1 Q.B. 15 at 22 per Denning L.J. Cf. *Wycombe Health Authority v. Barnett* (1982) 47 P. & C.R. 392, criticized by M.P. Thompson (1984) 81 L.S.G. 3408.

[253] [2016] EWCA Civ. 155.

where it was held that a steep staircase which was hazardous because there was no handrail was not in disrepair. The landlord was under no duty to supply this safety measure and the fact that a building is unsafe does not mean it is in a state of disrepair.[254]

The ambit of the landlord's covenant in respect of services and installations was recently considered in *O'Connor v. Old Etonian Housing Association Ltd*,[255] a case concerning an express covenant but one to the same effect as the statutory obligation. The problem was that the pipes were too narrow in diameter to enable the proper circulation of water for the heating system to work adequately for tenants in upper-storey flats. The first point which was made was that the obligation is to keep the installations in proper working order. This means that, if the system is not working because of some design defect, it is not in proper working order and it is the landlord's responsibility to rectify the problem.[256] The next issue is the effect of changes to the supply of water, gas, or electricity. The view was taken that the installations would be in proper working order if they were able to function under those conditions of supply that it would be reasonable to foresee would prevail during the subsistence of the lease. If there was a change in the manner of supply then, if this was the result of a deliberate change due to technological advances or business efficacy—for example, the change from coal gas to natural gas, or a change in the voltage supply—the responsibility would rest on the landlord to ensure that the installation would be able to work properly in the new conditions. If there were unplanned changes to the supply, then, whether or not the landlord has to do anything to the installations will depend upon the nature of the change and, in particular, its likely duration. If, for example, there was a fall in the water pressure as a result of the collapse of a reservoir or a drought, it may not be necessary for the landlord to have to make expensive alterations to the installations.[257]

Structure and exterior

As a matter of construction, the issue which can give rise to difficulty is to ascertain what is meant by the structure and exterior of the dwelling-house. Useful guidance was provided in *Re Irvine's Estate v. Moran*,[258] where the view was expressed that structure is not confined to load-bearing parts. It must, however, be a material or significant element of the property. The focus, it will be observed, is on the structure of the property itself and, in *Edwards v. Kumarasamy*,[259] it was held that this does not extend to liability in respect of a path leading to the property. Although windows, window frames, and sashes are part of the structure, the internal plastering was considered not to be, this being regarded in *Moran* as being in the nature of a decorative finish. This aspect of the decision was not followed, however, in *Grand v. Gill*,[260] where the landlord was held liable in respect of damage caused to the plasterwork by damp, this being contributed to by a lack of adequate heating as a result of a defective boiler. As to matters decorative, depending on the length of the lease, the obligation to decorate could be placed upon the tenant.

With regard to the outside, however, because external decoration provides a protective function against rot being caused by the weather, this would come within the implied covenant by the landlord.[261] A further matter relating to the exterior of the property

---

[254] See *Asker v. Collingwood Housing Association* [2007] 1 W.L.R. 2230.

[255] [2002] 2 All E.R. 1015. See also *Niazi Services Ltd v. van der Loo* [2004] 1 W.L.R. 1254; M.P. Thompson [2003] Conv. 80.

[256] [2002] 2 All E.R. 1015 at 1019 *per* Lord Phillips M.R., who pointed out at 1020 that there is a difference between keeping something in repair and keeping it in working order.

[257] Ibid. at 1023.

[258] (1992) 24 M.L.R. 1. See also *Ibrahim v. Dovecom Reversions Ltd* [2001] 30 E.G. 116; *Marlborough Park Services Ltd v. Rowe* [2006] H.L.R. 30.

[259] [2016] UKSC 40.   [260] [2011] EWCA Civ. 354.

[261] This would seem to be a better explanation of *Barrett v. Lounava (1982) Ltd* [1990] 1 Q.B. 348.

was clarified by an amendment to the legislation to make clear that, if the dwelling-house forms part of a building, and the landlord either owns or has an interest in the other part, then the implied covenant extends to that part of the building also.[262]

Although the Act provides welcome protection for tenants of residential property held on short leases, it is not all embracing and has its limitations. In particular, it must be stressed that the structure of the house must be in disrepair. While it may be surprising that a door which cannot perform its primary function of keeping out the rain is not, for that reason alone, in a state of disrepair,[263] the position is that, unless the ingress of water occasions damage to relevant parts of the property, the tenant has no remedy under the section.[264] This position was recently reviewed in *Lee v. Leeds City Council*.[265] The case involved two appeals raising the same issue. In each case, owing to a design fault, the interiors of both houses, which were let by local authorities, suffered severe condensation leading to mould. The effect of this problem was that the houses were unfit for human habitation and a danger to health. The tenants brought proceedings against the local authorities, which failed. The statutory obligation with respect to fitness for human habitation imposed by s. 8 of the Landlord and Tenant Act 1985[266] was inapplicable as the rent paid exceeded the statutory limits. The main issue was whether the condensation and mould amounted to a breach of the obligation under s. 11 of the Act. The Court of Appeal held that it did not. Following the earlier decision in *Quick v. Taff-Ely Borough Council*,[267] Chadwick L.J. explained the position in the following terms:

> The cases show that, where there is a need to repair damage to the structure, the due performance of the obligation to repair may require the landlord to remedy the design defect which is the cause of the damage. They do not support the proposition that the obligation to repair will require the landlord to remedy a design defect which has not been a cause of damage to the structure; notwithstanding that the defect may make the premises unsuitable for accommodation or unfit for human habitation.[268]

Personal injury

The imposition of liability upon the landlord in respect of certain repairs impacts also on his liability to all persons who might reasonably be expected to be affected by defects in the property. Under s. 4(1) of the Defective Premises Act 1972, the landlord is liable to such people in respect of personal injury or damage to their property if he fails in his duty to take reasonable care to see that the premises are reasonably safe from such damage. Under s. 4(3), however, this liability is limited to matters which come within the landlord's obligation to repair so, unless it does so, the landlord will not be liable in respect of injury caused by a safety hazard such as the lack of a handrail on a steep staircase.[269] The duty is owed when the landlord knew, or ought to have known, of the relevant defect or has a right to enter the premises to carry out repairs.[270] Under s. 11(6) of the Landlord and Tenant Act 1985, the landlord has a right at reasonable times in the day and, on giving twenty-four

---

[262] Landlord and Tenant Act 1985, s. 1A inserted by Housing Act 1988, s. 116. The problem may, however, be caused by a defective roof or guttering in which the landlord does not have an interest: see *Grand v. Gill* [2011] EWCA Civ. 354.

[263] See *Stent v. Monmouth District Council* (1987) 54 P. & C.R. 193 at 209 *per* Stocker L.J.

[264] *Quick v. Taff-Ely Borough Council* [1986] Q.B. 809.

[265] [2002] 1 W.L.R. 1488. See M.P. Thompson [2003] Conv. 80; P.F. Smith [2003] Conv. 112.

[266] For an account of the history of this provision from its origin in the Housing of the Working Classes Act 1885, or 12, see [2002] 1 W.L.R. 1488 at 1492–3 *per* Chadwick L.J.

[267] [1986] Q.B. 809.   [268] [2002] 1 W.L.R. 1488 at 1496.

[269] See *Sternbaum v. Dhesi* [2016] EWCA Civ. 155.   [270] Defective Premises Act 1972, s. 4(2)(4)

hours' notice in writing, to enter the property for the purpose of viewing their condition and state of repair.

10.8.7.3 Remedies

It may be the case that the disrepair is sufficiently serious to allow either party to terminate the lease, the landlord by forfeiture or the tenant by accepting that the landlord's breach of covenant is sufficiently serious to amount to a repudiatory breach of the lease.[271] There are other, less extreme, remedies.

Damages

The recovery of damages by the landlord is regulated by statute. The landlord is not able to recover more in damages than the diminution of the value of the reversion caused by the lack of repair and, if it is proposed to demolish the buildings at the end of the lease, then no damages are recoverable.[272] For leases granted initially for more than seven years, of which there are more than three years to run, then the landlord's ability to enforce repairing covenants is regulated by the Leasehold Property (Repairs Act) 1938, which relates to issues of forfeiture of the lease.

The tenant may also, of course, claim damages for breach of the landlord's covenant to repair and such a claim may, depending upon the seriousness of the breach, include the cost of alternative accommodation.[273]

Specific performance

Although specific performance is generally available to enforce a contract to create a lease, it does not follow that this remedy will be available in respect of particular covenants in leases. For example, in *Co-operative Insurance Society Ltd v. Argyll Stores (Holdings) Ltd*,[274] the House of Lords refused to grant specific performance of a covenant by a tenant to keep open a store during the currency of the lease, the main reason for this being the reluctance to grant this remedy when its performance would require constant supervision by the courts.[275] In the context of repairing covenants, the courts have, in the case of express covenants, specifically enforced covenants by the landlord[276] and, in the case of repairing covenants implied under the Landlord and Tenant Act 1985, it is provided specifically that specific performance may be ordered, notwithstanding any equitable rule restricting the scope of the remedy as against the tenant.[277] It has recently been held that this remedy is also, in principle, available to landlords[278] but the facts of the case were unusual and it is unlikely to be a remedy of general application.

Self-help

Although specific performance is available in respect of the landlord's repairing obligations, this may not be the ideal remedy for the tenant. If a tenant, particularly one holding on a short lease, complains that the house is in disrepair, perhaps as a result of storm damage finding that the roof has been damaged and is leaking, he may find that the landlord is dilatory in effecting the repair. As an alternative to bringing an action for specific

---

[271] See 10.10.3 Forfeiture and 10.8.5 Repudiation. [272] Landlord and Tenant Act 1927, s. 18.
[273] See *McGreal v. Wake* [1984] 1 E.G.L.R. 42.
[274] [1998] A.C. 1. Contrast *Capita Trust Co. (Channel Islands) Ltd v. Chatham Maritime J3 Developments Ltd* [2006] EWHC 2956 (Ch) at [27] *per* Pumfrey J.
[275] For cogent criticism, see A. Tettenborn [1998] Conv. 23.
[276] *Jeune v. Queen's Cross Properties Ltd* [1974] Ch. 97; *Gordon v. Selico Co. Ltd* [1985] 2 E.G.L.R. 79.
[277] Landlord and Tenant Act 1985, s. 17.
[278] *Rainbow Estates Ltd v. Tokenhold Ltd* [1999] Ch. 64. See M. Pawlowski and J. Brown [1998] Conv. 495.

performance, which will obviously take time, one possible course of action, in these circumstances, is for the tenant to do, or pay for, the work himself and then deduct the cost of the work from future payments of rent.[279] Before this course of action is taken, however, it is necessary to notify the landlord that this will be done.[280]

10.8.8 Assignment and sub-letting

As a general proposition, a tenant, as the holder of an estate in land, is perfectly free either to assign it or to create sub-tenancies if he so chooses. It is common, however, for the landlord, by the insertion of a covenant in the lease, to curtail the tenant's right to do this. The most complete form of covenant will be a covenant restricting the tenant from assigning, underletting, or parting with possession of the property. If the covenant is more limited to prohibit only assignment, it may become a matter of law whether a particular transaction operates in this way. For example, a purported sub-tenancy which is longer than the existing lease will take effect as an assignment[281] and so, somewhat surprisingly, is a release by one joint tenant to the other of his interest under the lease.[282]

10.8.8.1 Absolute and qualified covenants

A covenant against assignment, to use this as shorthand for the full covenant, may be absolute or qualified. An absolute covenant, as its name suggests, prohibits the tenant from assigning the lease at all. Should he, nevertheless, assign, the assignment is effective to transfer the estate,[283] but is automatically a breach of covenant. It is unusual to find an absolute prohibition of this type in a commercial lease.

It is more common to find that the covenant is qualified, that qualification being that the lease should not be assigned without the landlord's consent. In such cases, it is provided by s. 19 of the Landlord and Tenant Act 1927 that such consent shall not be unreasonably withheld.[284] Even though the landlord must not unreasonably withhold consent, it is nevertheless a breach of covenant to assign without first seeking it.[285]

The obtaining of such consent became, in practice, a considerable problem, and the delays involved in obtaining such consents were a considerable source of frustration.[286] To alleviate this problem, pursuant to the recommendation of the Law Commission,[287] what has been described as 'this curious little Act',[288] the Landlord and Tenant Act 1988, was enacted.

Under s. 1(3) of the Act, the landlord, upon receipt of a written request for consent to assignment is under a duty, within a reasonable time, to give consent, unless it is reasonable not to give that consent. If consent is withheld, written notice must be served on the tenant as to the reasons,[289] and, if the consent is made subject to any conditions, those

---

[279] *Lee-Parker v. Izzet* [1971] 1 W.L.R. 1688; *Asco Developments Ltd v. Gordon* [1978] E.G.D. 376.

[280] See, generally, A. Waite [1981] Conv. 199.

[281] See *Milmo v. Carreras* [1946] K.B. 306.

[282] *Burton v. Camden London Borough Council* [2000] 1 All E.R. 943, criticized by S. Bridge [2000] Conv. 474.

[283] See *Old Grovebury Manor Farm Ltd v. W. Seymour Plant Sales and Hire Ltd (No. 2)* [1979] 1 W.L.R. 1397.

[284] This qualification does not apply to a covenant to offer to surrender the lease to the landlord prior to any assignment: see *Bocardo S.A. v. S. & M. Hotels Ltd* [1980] 1 W.L.R. 17.

[285] *Eastern Telegraph Co. Ltd v. Dent* [1899] 1 Q.B. 835.

[286] See the observations in *29 Equities Ltd v. Bank Leumi (U.K.) Ltd* [1987] 1 All E.R. 108 at 114 *per* Dillon L.J.

[287] (1987) Law Com. No. 261.

[288] *Venetian Glass Gallery Ltd v. Next Properties Ltd* [1989] 2 E.G.L.R. 42 at 46 *per* Harman J.

[289] This is not satisfied by giving oral reasons: *Footwear Corp. Ltd v. Amplight Properties Ltd* [1999] 1 W.L.R. 551.

conditions must themselves be reasonable.[290] A failure to comply with the obligations imposed by the Act leads to liability in tort for breach of statutory duty.[291] This may lead to an award of exemplary damages if the landlord seeks to profit by an unreasonable refusal to give his consent to an assignment.[292]

There is no definition of what is a reasonable time. The starting point in the assessment of what is reasonable is the date on which the tenant serves his request. That does not mean, however, that one can determine conclusively what would be a reasonable time from the date when the application is made. Regard must be had to all the circumstances of an individual case, including negotiations between the landlord and tenant prior to the landlord giving his decision.[293] The onus of proof is on the landlord to establish both that the time taken to reply, and the grounds for a refusal of consent, are reasonable.[294] If the landlord seeks to argue that his refusal of consent is reasonable, he can rely only on those grounds which existed at the end of the reasonable period of time from the making of the request,[295] and he is also limited to the reasons actually given.[296]

10.8.8.2 Reasonableness

As to what is reasonable, much will depend on the facts of a given case, and the authorities dealing with this issue are generally only of illustrative value,[297] although, if the landlord reasonably suspects that the proposed assignee will breach the user conditions in the lease, a refusal to consent will be reasonable.[298] The essential test which the courts will apply is that 'a landlord is not entitled to refuse his consent on grounds which have nothing to do with the relationship of landlord and tenant in regard to the subject matter of the lease',[299] and it is not reasonable to refuse consent to an assignment on terms which will give the landlord greater rights than he enjoyed under the original lease.[300] Ultimately, in determining whether a refusal of consent is reasonable, that expression should be 'given a broad common sense meaning',[301] although under the Landlord and Tenant (Covenants) Act 1995, the landlord is entitled to stipulate in advance that his consent is subject to undertakings relevant to the operation of that Act.[302] Where the reasonableness of the refusal is in issue, the safest course for the tenant to take is to refer the matter to the court for a declaration. If the refusal was unreasonable, the assignment will not amount to a breach of covenant, but a breach will have occurred if the refusal was reasonable.

10.9 **The enforceability of covenants**

An important issue, particularly in the case of long leases, is the matter of who can enforce the covenants contained in a lease and against whom. In determining this matter it is necessary to consider the position of the original parties to the lease and, also, the position

---

[290] Landlord and Tenant Act 1988, s. 1(3).   [291] Ibid., s. 4.

[292] *Design Progression Ltd v. Thurloe Properties Ltd* [2004] EWHC 324 (Ch).

[293] See *Go West Ltd v. Spigarolo* [2003] 2 All E.R. 141 at 149–51 *per* Mumby J.

[294] Landlord and Tenant Act 1988, s. 1(4)(c).

[295] *Norwich Union Life Insurance Co. Ltd v. Shopmoor Ltd* [1991] 1 W.L.R. 531 at 545 *per* Sir Richard Scott V.-C.; *Go West Ltd v. Spigarolo, supra.*

[296] *Southern Depot Co. Ltd v. British Railway Board* [1990] 2 E.G.L.R. 39 at 44 *per* Morritt L.J.

[297] *Ashworth Frazer Ltd v. Gloucester City Council* [2001] 1 W.L.R. 2180 at 2183 *per* Lord Bingham.

[298] Ibid., overruling *Killick v. Second Covent Garden Property Co. Ltd* [1973] 1 W.L.R. 658.

[299] *International Drilling Fluids Ltd v. Louisville Investments (Uxbridge) Ltd* [1986] Ch. 513 at 520 *per* Balcombe L.J. See also *Houlder Bros & Co. Ltd v. Gibbs* [1925] Ch. 575 at 587 *per* Sargent J.

[300] *Mount Eden Land Ltd v. Straudley Investments Ltd* (1996) 74 P. & C.R. 306; *Landlord Protect Ltd v. St Anselm Development Co. Ltd* [2009] EWCA Civ. 99.

[301] *Ashworth Frazer Ltd v. Gloucester City Council* [2001] 1 W.L.R. 2180 at 2183 *per* Lord Bingham.

[302] See 10.9.2.2.

of assignees of either the lease or the reversion. It is also essential to distinguish between leases created before 1996 and those created after that date.

10.9.1 **Pre-1996 leases**

The liability of various parties with respect to leases created prior to 1 January 1996 was dependent upon an amalgam of common law and statute. Attention will be given, first, to the position of the original parties to the lease and then to the position of assignees and sub-tenants.

10.9.1.1 **Original parties**

At common law, the liability of the original parties to the lease was governed by the principles of contract law. Quite simply, this meant that, as signatories to the original tenancy, each remained liable to the other for the duration of the term, notwithstanding that their interests had subsequently been assigned. This presented considerable problems for the tenants of commercial properties.[303] Even after the tenant had assigned the lease, he remained liable to the original landlord in respect of the rent for the remainder of the term,[304] so that, if the assignee became insolvent, the landlord could look to the original tenant, maybe some years after the lease had been assigned, for payment[305] and this liability would extend to rent increased pursuant to a rent review clause in the lease.[306] For one large company, this potential liability was estimated as being in the region of £50 million.[307] This aspect of the law was considered to represent a considerable trap and to be unfair. Reforms have been implemented, although not in the form originally proposed.

10.9.1.2 **Assignments and sub-letting**

The mutual liability of the original parties to a lease stems from privity of contract. When either the lease or the reversion has been assigned, the question which then arises is as to the liability of the assignees. The basis of liability, derived from *Spencer's Case*,[308] depended upon two issues: privity of estate and whether or not the covenant in question touched and concerned the land. If both conditions were satisfied, then there would be mutual liability between the parties. The covenants are said to run with the lease.

Privity of estate

What is meant by privity of estate is that a direct relationship of landlord and tenant exists between the two parties. If one starts with a lease between L and T, there exists both privity of contract and privity of estate between the two, the latter meaning that the relationship of landlord and tenant exists between them. If T assigns the lease to A, then, as between L and A, there is no privity of contract but there is privity of estate; L is A's landlord. Similarly, if it was L who assigned the reversion to R, then there would now exist privity of estate between R and A, there being a direct landlord and tenant relationship between them. If, subsequently, A assigns the lease to A2, there is now privity of estate between R and A2 but, as between R and A, there is no relationship at all. There never was privity of

---

[303] See K. Reynolds and S. Fogel (1984) 81 L.S.G. 2214.

[304] He would not be liable in respect of a statutory extension of that term. See *City of London Corp. v. Fell* [1994] 1 A.C. 458.

[305] See *Hindcastle Ltd v. Barbara Attenborough Associates Ltd* [1997] A.C. 70.

[306] See *Centrovincial Estates plc v. Bulk Storage Ltd* (1983) 46 P. & C.R. 393; *Selous Street Properties Ltd v. Oronel Fabrics Ltd* [1984] 1 E.G.L.R. 50. Where the terms of the lease are subsequently varied, the liability of the original tenant depended upon whether the variation was so substantial as to amount to a surrender and re grant of a new lease. See *Friends Provident Life Office v. British Railways Board* [1996] 1 All E.R. 336. See S Bright in Jackson and Wilde (eds), *The Reform of Property Law* (Aldershot, Ashgate, 1997), Chapter 5.

[307] (1988) Law Com. No. 174, 15.   [308] (1583) 5 Co. Rep. 16a.

contract and there is no longer privity of estate as R is not A's landlord. A is not, therefore, liable to R in respect of breaches of covenant committed after he assigned the lease.

If the original lease is between L and T and, this time, instead of assigning the lease, T created a sub-tenancy in favour of ST then, as between L and ST, there is neither privity of contract nor privity of estate. ST's landlord is T and not L. Unless the covenant in question is negative in nature and enforceable by other means, the lack of either privity of contract or of estate between L and ST means that L cannot sue ST directly in respect of any breach of covenant. In practice, this did not cause difficulties because T would be liable to L in respect of any breaches of covenant, albeit committed by ST, contained in the head lease and so it would be in T's own interest to ensure that the covenants contained in the sub-lease were at least as stringent as those which were in the head lease, in order to avoid liability in respect of ST's actions.

Touching and concerning the land

Parties to a lease are, as a general proposition, free to include within it such terms as they please. For the rights and obligations created by these covenants to run with the lease, however, it is necessary that these obligations are not regarded as being merely personal. For them to run due to the existence of privity of estate, it is necessary that those covenants touch and concern the land or, to put the matter into modern parlance, affect the landlord in his capacity as landlord and the tenant in his capacity as tenant.[309] What this means was elaborated by the House of Lords in *P. & A. Swift Investments v. Combined English Stores Group*.[310] A covenant by a tenant will touch and concern the land if (i) it is beneficial to the reversioner only for the time being; (ii) it affects the nature, quality, mode of user, or value of the reversioner's land; and (iii) it is not expressed to be merely personal in nature. A similar test is imposed concerning covenants by the landlord.

Despite the articulation of these criteria to determine whether a covenant touched and concerned the land, it is widely accepted that the distinction between those which do and those which do not is largely arbitrary and has been described as being 'quite illogical'.[311] The removal of this criterion[312] to determine whether or not covenants will run with the lease is therefore welcome.

10.9.1.3 Assignment of the lease

The rules concerning the running of covenants on the assignment of a lease derive from *Spencer's Case* and, as a common law rule, certain consequences followed. First, the lease had to be a legal lease. The doctrine of privity of estates does not apply to equitable tenancies.[313] Second, the basis of the common law rule was that of privity of estate. This explains why a sub-tenant is not liable under the common law rules, in that there is no privity between him and the landlord of the head lease. For the same reason, the lack of privity of estate, a squatter who acquires a possessory title against a tenant is not liable to the landlord in respect of covenants in the lease.[314]

10.9.1.4 Assignment of the reversion

When the landlord assigns the reversion, the original position at common law was that, subject to certain limited exceptions, the assignee could neither sue nor be sued on the obligations contained in the lease. This position was modified by statute, the position now

---

[309] *Breams Property Investment Ltd v. Stroulger* [1948] 2 K.B. 1.
[310] [1989] A.C. 632 at 642 *per* Lord Oliver.
[311] *Grant v. Edmondson* [1931] 1 Ch. 1 at 29 *per* Romer L.J.
[312] Landlord and Tenant (Covenants) Act 1995, s. 2.   [313] *Elliott v. Johnson* (1866) L.R. 2 Q.B. 120.
[314] *Tichborne v. Weir* (1892) 67 L.T. 735.

being governed by ss 141 and 142, LPA 1925. The position is, *mutatis mutandis*, essentially the same as that arrived at when it is the lease which has been assigned, but there are some differences.

Section 154 of the Landlord and Tenant (Covenants) Act 1995 provides that the Part of the Act which includes ss 141 and 142 applies to leases created before or after the commencement of the Act and includes an under-lease or other tenancy. This latter expression would seem to be sufficiently wide to include an equitable tenancy so that, on the assignment of the freehold reversion of an equitable lease, the benefit and burden of the covenants contained in the lease will run.

A second point concerns remedies for breaches of covenant occurring prior to the assignment. On an assignment of the reversion, the assignee acquires the benefit of all covenants. This means that the assignee acquires the right to sue for breaches of any covenant made by the tenant. Even after assignment, however, the landlord remains liable to the original tenant for breaches of covenant committed while he was in possession of the land.[315]

10.9.2 Post-1996 tenancies

The subject of covenants in leases was subject to review by the Law Commission, who proposed wide-ranging reform.[316] After considerable consultation, the central thrust of these proposals, subject to considerable alteration,[317] was implemented by the Landlord and Tenant (Covenants) Act 1995.[318] For present purposes, the principal changes introduced by the Act relate to the continuing liability of the tenant through the operation of privity of contract and the nature of covenants which will run with the lease.

10.9.2.1 Liability of tenant

One of the principal objections to the old law was that the original tenant would continue to be liable to the original landlord on the covenants contained in the lease throughout the agreed term. Under the Act, which is not retrospective, when a tenant assigns the entire property comprised in the lease, he is released from the tenant's covenants contained in the lease and ceases to be entitled to the benefit of the landlord's covenants. Upon assignment of part of the property the release operates with respect to the part contained in the assignment.[319] This release does not, however, absolve him from liability in respect of breaches of covenant committed prior to the assignment.[320]

10.9.2.2 Consent to assignment

Although it is not possible to contract out of the Act,[321] as a major concession to commercial landlords, provision was made to safeguard their position on an assignment of a post-1996 lease. Under s. 16 of the Act, the landlord is not precluded from obtaining from the tenant, when assigning the lease, a guarantee of the performance of the covenants in the lease. For such a guarantee to be valid, the lease must contain a qualified covenant against assignment and the condition imposed for consent to be given is that the tenant enters into an agreement guaranteeing the performance of the covenants by the assignee.

---

[315] See *City and Metropolitan Properties Ltd v. Greycroft Ltd* [1987] 1 W.L.R. 1085.

[316] (1988) Law Com. No. 174.

[317] For an interesting discussion by one of the responsible Law Commissioners of the process of the implementation of these proposals, see T.M. Aldridge in Jackson and Wilde, *The Reform of Property Law*, Chapter 2.

[318] For excellent discussions of the background and the changes introduced by the Act, see S. Bridge [1996] C.L.J. 313; M. Davey (1996) 59 M.L.R. 78.

[319] Landlord and Tenant (Covenants) Act 1995, s. 5.   [320] Ibid., s. 24.   [321] Ibid., s. 25.

Section 22 of the Act then amended s. 19 of the Landlord and Tenant Act 1927 to provide that, if a landlord refuses consent to an assignment on the ground that the tenant will not give such a guarantee, then that refusal is reasonable.

10.9.2.3 Overriding leases

The ability of the landlord to seek a guarantee from the tenant that the assignee will perform the covenants in the lease means, in effect, that, just as was the case before the introduction of the Act. If such a guarantee is imposed the tenant will continue to be liable under the covenants contained in the lease for the duration of the term. To meet both these situations, the tenant is given the right to have granted to him what is termed an overriding lease. Under s. 19 of the Act, when a tenant has met in full payment that he has been required to make under either the original lease, when such a lease was created before the implementation of the Act, or under a guarantee covenant,[322] he is entitled to have the landlord grant him an overriding lease. This lease is a tenancy of the reversion expectant on the tenancy, the meaning of which is that the tenant becomes, directly, the landlord of the assignee. This lease is subject to the same covenants as the original lease. The point of this is that, if, in the future, the assignee commits further breaches of covenant, the original tenant is now the landlord of the assignee and can pursue remedies against him including, where appropriate, forfeiture of the lease.

10.9.2.4 Liability of landlords

While the Act operates to release the tenant from liability under the covenants in the lease after it has been assigned, it does not work in the same way insofar as the landlord is concerned upon an assignment of the reversion. He will remain liable on the covenants unless he is released from them. To obtain a release, he must, within four weeks of the assignment, serve a notice on the tenant informing him of the assignment and seeking a release from the covenants. If the tenant does not respond within four weeks of the service of the notice, the landlord will be released from his covenants. If the tenant does object, the matter can be referred to the court to determine if such a refusal is reasonable.[323]

10.9.2.5 Landlord and tenant covenants

For centuries, a key factor in determining whether a particular covenant ran with a lease was if it touched and concerned the land. Now, the position is that, unless covenants are expressed to be personal to the parties,[324] the benefit and burden of all landlord and tenant covenants will pass on assignment, whether or not such covenants have reference to the subject matter of the tenancy.[325]

10.10 Termination of tenancies

There are a number of ways in which a lease can be determined. This section deals with the most important of them. What should be stressed is that this section deals with the termination of tenancies under the general law. In many instances, the tenant will continue to enjoy security of tenure under various statutory provisions. Unless the lease has come to an end under the general law, these provisions will not come into play. In other words, the various provisions conferring security of tenure upon tenants represent additional hurdles for a landlord to surmount before he is enabled, physically, to regain possession of the land.

[322] Ibid., s. 17.   [323] Ibid., ss 7, 8.
[324] Ibid., s. 3(3). See *BHP Petroleum Great Britain Ltd v. Chesterfield Properties Ltd* [2000] Ch. 234.
[325] Landlord and Tenant (Covenants) Act 1995, ss 7, 8.

10.10.1 **Effluxion of time**

When a fixed-term tenancy has been created, then the lease will end at the term date. This is termed effluxion of time. In the case of such tenancies, unless the lease contains a break clause, neither side has the right, unilaterally, to bring the tenancy to a premature conclusion.

10.10.2 **Notice to quit**

The nature of a periodic tenancy is that an original period is agreed between the parties and this period will continue to recur until either side puts an end to this process by the service of a notice to quit.

In the case of a yearly tenancy, the period of notice is at least half a year, expiring upon the end of a completed year of the tenancy. With respect to other periodic tenancies, such as a monthly or weekly tenancy, the period of notice is one full period, expiring at the date of the completion of a period. In the case of residential tenancies, however, a minimum of four weeks' notice in writing must be given.[326]

In the case of either joint landlords or joint tenants, a notice to quit served by one of the joint owners will be sufficient to determine the tenancy.[327] To obviate some of the problems caused by this, the Law Commission has proposed that, where one joint tenant serves notice to quit, this should terminate the interest of that person alone, and not the other.[328] This proposal has not been implemented.

10.10.3 **Forfeiture**

It is normally the case that a lease contains a number of covenants by the tenant. If the tenant breaches any of these covenants then, subject to the very limited possibility of specific performance being available,[329] the landlord's remedy will lie in damages. He is limited to that remedy, however, unless, as is normally the case, the lease contains a clause, termed a forfeiture clause, which enables the landlord to terminate the lease. A forfeiture clause reserves to the landlord the right to re-enter the property upon a breach of covenant and to determine the lease. Alternatively, but less commonly, the lease may be made conditional upon the tenant adhering to the covenants in the lease, in which case, if the tenant is in breach of covenant, the lease becomes voidable at the instance of the landlord.[330]

Termination of a lease, either by forfeiture or by peaceable re-entry, is an area of the law which is dogged by complexity and is an amalgam of statutory regulation and judicial development. The result is that it is necessary to consider, first, the circumstances when a landlord may lose the right to forfeit the lease and then the procedures to be adopted upon the breach of different covenants. Finally, the jurisdiction of the courts to grant relief against forfeiture must be examined.

10.10.3.1 **Waiver**

The landlord will lose his right to forfeit the lease if he has waived the breach of the covenant complained of. A waiver may be express but, more usually, is implied. An implied waiver of the breach will occur when the landlord, with knowledge of the breach, does some act which, unequivocally, recognizes the continuing existence of the lease.[331]

---

[326] Protection from Eviction Act 1977, ss 3A, 5; Housing Act 1988, ss 31, 32.
[327] See 10.10.2.   [328] (2003) Law Com No. 284, para. 11.27.
[329] See 10.7.2.   [330] See *Doe d. Lockwood v. Clarke* (1807) 8 East 185.
[331] *Matthews v. Smallwood* [1910] 1 Ch. 777 at 786 *per* Parker J.

There are, therefore, two aspects of waiver which must both be present. First, the landlord or his agent[332] must know of the breach. Mere suspicion that there has been a breach of covenant is said not to be enough to constitute knowledge.[333] Yet, in *Van Haarlem v. Kasner*,[334] a landlord was considered to have knowledge of a tenant's breach of a covenant not to use the property for illegal or immoral purposes on the basis that he knew that the tenant had been arrested upon suspicion of spying; a decision which seems to be unduly harsh upon the landlord.

Mere knowledge that the tenant has committed a breach of covenant is, obviously, not of itself sufficient to amount to a waiver of that breach by the landlord. He must also do some act which unequivocally recognizes the continued existence of the lease. The clearest, and most usual, act which is regarded as constituting waiver is a demand or acceptance of rent after the landlord has notice of the breach, and in *Greenwood Reservations Ltd v. World Environment Ltd*,[335] Thomas L.J. was prepared to assume, without necessarily deciding, that an unqualified demand for future rent would always operate as a waiver. Even if a demand is made as a result of clerical error by the landlord's agent, this will amount to a waiver.[336] In the case of negotiations between the landlord and tenant, difficulties may also arise. Such negotiations are themselves capable of amounting to waiver but will not do so if they are conducted against a background of threatened forfeiture proceedings.[337] It is an area where the landlord must tread very carefully if he is not to lose the right to forfeit the lease.

The doctrine of waiver relates principally to the right to forfeit the lease. While it is possible for the conduct of the landlord to preclude him from obtaining any remedy at all,[338] this will only occur in cases where there is a very clear representation to this effect. The normal impact of waiver is that it relates only to the right of forfeiture; the landlord will still be able to recover damages in respect of the breach.[339] Second, waiver operates only in respect of existing breaches of covenant. In the case of a continuing breach, or a subsequent breach of covenant, the landlord will not be prevented by a previous waiver from instituting forfeiture proceedings.

10.10.3.2 Forfeiture proceedings

To forfeit a lease, the landlord will normally issue a writ seeking possession of the property. It is also possible to terminate the lease by effecting a peaceable re-entry of the property. Except in the case of non-payment of rent, notice must first be served upon a tenant of the intention to re-enter.[340] In the case of residential property, it is very unwise for a landlord to seek to terminate a lease by re-entry as, if he does, he runs the considerable risk of committing a criminal offence.[341] In the case of forfeiture actions, generally, the landlord must follow a statutory procedure laid down by s. 146(1), LPA 1925. This procedure does not apply, however, in the case of forfeiture for non-payment of rent,[342] to which different rules apply.

---

[332] See *Metropolitan Properties Co. Ltd v. Cordery* (1979) 39 P. & C.R. 10.

[333] *Chrisdell Ltd v. Johnson* (1987) 54 P. & C.R. 257.

[334] [1992] 2 E.G.L.R. 257.   [335] [2008] H.L.R. 31 at [27].

[336] *Central Estates (Belgravia) Ltd v. Woolgar (No. 2)* [1972] 1 W.L.R. 1048. A demand for the payment of insurance will not have this effect: *Yorkshire Metropolitan Properties Ltd v. Co-operative Retail Services Ltd* [2001] L. & T.R. 26.

[337] *Expert Clothing Services & Sales Ltd v. Hillgate House Ltd* [1986] Ch. 340.

[338] See, e.g., *Brikom Investments Ltd v. Carr* [1979] 1 Q.B. 497 (estoppel).

[339] See *Greenwich London Borough Council v. Discreet Selling Estates Ltd* (1990) 61 P. & C.R. 405.

[340] LPA 1925, s. 146(1).   [341] Criminal Law Act 1977, s. 6.

[342] LPA 1925, s. 146(11).

10.10.3.3 Non-payment of rent

When a landlord seeks to forfeit a lease for non-payment of rent, he must first make a formal demand for payment. The nature of a formal demand is that the landlord must demand the exact sum due, on the day it falls due, at such convenient time before sunset as to allow the tenant to count out the exact sum due before sunset. To avoid having to comply with this arcane procedure, it is normal for the lease to stipulate that the landlord may forfeit the lease for non-payment of rent, whether the rent has been lawfully demanded or not. This wording is unfortunate, in that it may give the tenant a rather misleading impression of what rent the landlord is entitled to demand, rather than relating, as it does, to the formal requirements of how the demand is made. If half a year's rent is in arrears and no goods are available to the landlord to sell in order to clear off those arrears, then under s. 210 of the Common Law Procedure Act 1852, the landlord need not make a formal demand for rent before forfeiting the lease.

Once the landlord has instituted forfeiture proceedings for non-payment of rent, the tenant may seek relief against forfeiture. If, before the trial, the tenant pays off all the arrears and costs, the possession proceedings must be stayed.[343] If a possession order has been made, the tenant may, within six months of the order, apply for relief against forfeiture,[344] at the end of which time the tenant loses his right to relief.[345] In deciding whether to relieve against forfeiture, the court will have regard to whether the arrears have been repaid, if the landlord has been compensated for any expenses he has incurred, and whether it is just and equitable to grant relief.

10.10.3.4 Breaches of other covenants

In the case of covenants other than the covenant to pay rent, the landlord, to forfeit the lease, must follow the procedure laid down by s. 146(1), LPA 1925.[346] Under this section a right of re-entry or forfeiture shall not be enforceable unless the landlord has served on the tenant a notice:

(a) specifying the particular breach complained of; and

(b) if the breach is capable of remedy, requiring the lessee to remedy the breach; and

(c) in any case, requiring the lessee to make compensation in money for the breach;

and the lessee fails, within a reasonable time thereafter, to remedy the breach, if it is capable of remedy, and to make reasonable compensation in money, to the satisfaction of the lessor, for the breach.

10.10.3.5 Negative covenants

The principal difficulty with complying with the requirements of the section has concerned the question of whether or not a particular breach of covenant is capable of remedy, as, if it is not, then it is not necessary for the notice to require the tenant to remedy it. One view is that if the covenant is negative in terms then, if the tenant has done what he has covenanted not to do, the breach is incapable of remedy.[347] With the apparent exception

---

[343] Common Law Procedure Act 1852, s. 212. See *Thomas v. Ken Thomas Ltd* [2006] EWCA Civ. 1504 at [53]–[59] *per* Neuberger L.J.

[344] Common Law Procedure Act 1852, s. 210; County Courts Act 1984, s. 138.

[345] *U.D.T. Ltd v. Shellpoint Trustees Ltd* [1993] 4 All E.R. 310.

[346] There are five specified cases where the landlord need not comply with this procedure. See LPA 1925, s. 146(9).

[347] See *Rugby School (Governors) Ltd v. Tannahill* [1934] 1 K.B. 695 at 701 *per* Mackinnon J.

of a covenant against assignment,[348] this view is seen as being too extreme[349] and it is possible that what has been done can be undone so that if, in breach of covenant, the tenant creates a sub-lease, this can be undone by securing the surrender of that sub-tenancy.[350]

In some situations, however, the courts will consider that the breach of a negative covenant cannot be remedied, for example if, in breach of a covenant not to use the premises for illegal or immoral purposes, the property has been used for the purposes of prostitution, a stigma may attach to the property with the result that the breach may be regarded as irremediable by the tenant.[351] If by taking prompt action to stop the prohibited use of the property, the tenant succeeds in removing the stigma which would otherwise attach to the property, then the breach may be regarded as being remediable.[352] If there is any doubt as to this matter, then much the safest course of action for the landlord to take is to require the tenant to remedy the breach 'if it is capable of remedy'.[353]

10.10.3.6 Time

Section 146(1), LPA 1925 requires the landlord's notice to give the tenant a reasonable time in which to remedy the breach. What is reasonable will depend upon the facts of the case and the nature of the breach in question. If the breach is not capable of being remedied, it might be thought that no time need be given, but it has been held that, even then, the tenant should be given some time in which to consider his position.[354] The time given can, however, be as little as fourteen days.[355]

10.10.3.7 Compensation

Although the wording of the section is mandatory, requiring the tenant to compensate the landlord, a s. 146 notice is not defective if a claim for compensation is omitted.[356]

10.10.3.8 Repairing covenants

The position with regard to repairing covenants is regulated by the Leasehold Property (Repairs) Act 1938. The Act applies to non-agricultural leases of seven years or more which have more than three years left to run.[357] The aim of the Act is to prevent people from buying the reversion of such leases and then forfeiting the lease due to breach of a repairing covenant and, in the process, making a considerable profit. The Act provides that if a s. 146 notice is served upon a tenant in respect of a repairing covenant, then that notice must inform the tenant of his right to serve a counter-notice under the Act. The tenant then has twenty-eight days in which to serve a counter-notice on the landlord[358] and, if he does so, the landlord is precluded by s. 1(3) of the Act from pursuing the action for forfeiture, re-entry, or damages without the leave of the court. A number of criteria are then set

---

[348] *Scala House & District Property Co. Ltd v. Forbes* [1974] Q.B. 575. This may now need to be reconsidered in the light of *Freifield v. West Kensington Court Ltd* [2016] EWCA Civ. 801.

[349] *Rugby School (Governors) Ltd v. Tannahill* [1935] 1 K.B. 87. See also *Savva v. Hussein* (1996) 64 P. & C.R. 214; *Akici v. L.R. Butlin Ltd* [2005] EWCA Civ. 1296 at paras 62–71 *per* Neuberger L.J.

[350] See *Freifeld v. West Kensington Court Ltd* [2016] EWCA Civ. 806.

[351] *Rugby School (Governors) Ltd v. Tannahill* [1935] 1 K.B. 87; *British Petroleum Pension Trust Ltd v. Behrendt* (1985) 52 P. & C.R. 117. See also *Van Haarlem v. Kasner* [1992] 2 E.G.L.R. 59 (spying).

[352] *Glass v. Kencakes Ltd* [1966] 1 Q.B. 611. See also *Patel v. K. &. J. Restaurants Ltd* [2010] EWCA Civ. 211.

[353] *Glass v. Kencakes Ltd, supra*, at 629 *per* Paull J. See also *Expert Clothing Service & Sales Ltd v. Highgate House Ltd* [1986] Ch. 340.

[354] *Horsey Estate Ltd v. Steiger* [1899] 2 Q.B. 79.

[355] *Scala House & District Land Property Co. v. Forbes* [1974] Q.B. 575. Contrast *Courtney Lodge Management Ltd v. Blake* [2004] EWCA Civ. 975 (four working days was too short).

[356] *Rugby School (Governors) Ltd v. Tannahill* [1935] 1 K.B. 87.

[357] Leasehold Property (Repairs) Act 1938, ss 1(1), 7.   [358] Ibid., s. 1(2).

out in s. 1(5) of the Act, one of which must be established by the landlord if leave is to be given.[359] The general theme of the criteria is that the property is in urgent need of repair.

10.10.3.9 Relief against forfeiture

After a reasonable time has elapsed after the s. 146 notice has been served, the landlord may proceed to enforce the forfeiture. While the landlord is proceeding to enforce a right of re-entry or forfeiture, the tenant may apply to the court for relief against forfeiture.[360] It is then a matter for the court's discretion as to how this jurisdiction is to be exercised and a relevant factor will be the seriousness of the breach and the circumstances of the parties.[361] Another relevant factor will be the value of the property. In *Van Haarlam v. Kasner,*[362] a tenant was in breach of a covenant not to use the property for illegal or immoral purposes, he having been convicted of spying and sentenced to ten years' imprisonment with an order that he be deported upon his release. Harman J. would, nevertheless, have granted him relief against forfeiture. The reason was that the lease was for eighty years and had been bought by the tenant some four or five years previously for £36,000. To have refused relief against forfeiture would have deprived the tenant of a valuable asset, a consequence which the judge considered would have amounted to a double punishment. In the case of commercial property, this issue is likely to be relevant although, on its own, it is not decisive, particularly if the breach of covenant was flagrant and deliberate.[363] At the end of the day, the central question is whether the grant of relief will put the landlord into the position he would have been in had there been no breaches of covenant[364] and, to this end, relief may be granted on terms. In *Freifeld v. West Kensington Court Ltd,*[365] the value of the lease was in the region of £1–2 million. Relief was granted on terms that the tenant sold and assigned the lease within a six-month period to a new tenant acceptable to the landlord, the behaviour of the tenant having been such that it was no longer reasonable to expect the landlord to continue the legal relationship with the original tenant.

The statutory jurisdiction to grant relief against forfeiture is conferred by the Act when the landlord 'is proceeding . . . to enforce . . . a right of re-entry or forfeiture'. This raised the question of whether a court could grant relief when the landlord had already forfeited the lease by effecting a peaceable re-entry of the property. The House of Lords, in *Billson v. Residential Properties Ltd,*[366] construed the words 'is proceeding' to mean also 'has proceeded' and so, in these circumstances had jurisdiction under the Act to grant relief. Where, however, the court has made a forfeiture order and the landlord has taken possession, then the tenant can no longer seek relief.

10.10.3.10 Parties

When a landlord is seeking to forfeit a lease, it is not only the immediate tenant who may be affected by this action. Other people, such as a sub-tenant or a mortgagee, may have derivative interests in the property. If the lease is forfeited, then their interests, which

---

[359] See *Associated British Ports v. C.H. Bailey plc* [1990] 2 A.C. 703.

[360] LPA 1925, s. 146(2). Relief may be granted in respect of a part of a building where there is a physical division. See *G.M.S. Syndicate Ltd v. Gary Elliott Ltd* [1982] Ch. 1.

[361] See *Central Estates (Belgravia) Ltd v. Woolgar (No. 2)* [1972] 1 W.L.R. 1048. Cf. *Bathurst (Earl) v. Fine* [1974] 1 W.L.R. 905.

[362] [1992] 2 E.G.L.R. 59. See also *Ropemaker Properties Ltd v. Noonhaven Ltd* [1989] 2 E.G.L.R. 50. This is, however, only one factor to be considered: see *Greenwood Reservations Ltd v. World Environment Ltd* [2008] H.L.R. 31 at [33]–[38] *per* Thomas L.J.

[363] See *Freifeld v. West Kensington Court Ltd* [2016] EWCA Civ. 806 at [69] *per* Briggs L.J.

[364] See *Magnic Ltd v. Ul-Hussan* [2015] EWCA Civ. 224 at [53] *per* Patten L.J.

[365] [2016] EWCA Civ. 806.   [366] [1992] 2 A.C. 494.

derive from the lease, will be destroyed. Consequently, such parties may seek relief against forfeiture.[367]

10.10.3.11 Recommended reform

Few could deny that the current law relating to forfeiture of leases is unnecessarily complicated. The Law Commission has recommended wide-ranging reform, which would simplify considerably the existing law.[368] No distinction would be made between covenants relating to rent and other covenants and the existing procedure would be considerably simplified and the law on waiver would be reformed, so that a mere acceptance of rent would no longer prevent the landlord from forfeiting a lease. The court could make an absolute or remedial termination order, the latter being designed to allow the tenant to remedy the breach complained of. It is unfortunate that these proposed reforms have yet to be enacted.

10.10.4 Surrender

In the absence of a break clause neither party to the lease has the right, unilaterally, to end a fixed-term tenancy prior to the term date. Surrender involves the tenant giving up the lease to the landlord, who accepts this action. A surrender should be by deed, but a contract to surrender should have the same effect in equity.[369] If, however, the tenant gives up possession, and this is accepted by the landlord, then each party will be estopped from denying that a surrender has taken place.[370]

10.10.5 Merger

Merger is, in effect, the opposite of surrender. Merger will occur when the tenant acquires the landlord's reversion. As the tenant cannot be his own landlord, the lease is said to merge in the reversion.

---

[367] LPA 1925, s. 146(5).

[368] (1985) Law Com. No. 142; (1994) Law Com. No. 221. See P.F. Smith [1986] Conv. 165; H.W. Wilkinson [1994] Conv. 177. See also (2006) Law Com. No. 303.

[369] Such a contract would need to comply with the LP(MP)A 1989, s. 2.

[370] See *Oastler v. Henderson* (1877) 2 Q.B.D. 575.

11

Mortgages

A mortgage is a form of security for a loan. The purpose of the loan is often to finance the purchase of a house, in which case it is called an acquisition mortgage. Alternatively, the house can be used as security for other borrowing, for example to pay for an extension to a house or to act as security for the provision of finance for a small business, in which case it is a non-acquisition (or post-acquisition) mortgage. Non-acquisition mortgages are normally second, or even third, mortgages. Although property other than land can be mortgaged, the main context of mortgages is as a security over land.

The person who creates the mortgage (the borrower) is called the mortgagor and the person in whose favour it is created (the lender) is called the mortgagee. The mortgagee is a secured creditor and the interest which is acquired is a proprietary right over the land. As it is an interest in land, the mortgagee can transfer the mortgage to another person. If the mortgagor sells the land to a purchaser, then, unless the mortgage is redeemed by repaying the loan, the purchaser will, generally speaking, take the land subject to that mortgage.

The concept of security for a loan is quite straightforward. If the borrower cannot repay the loan, then the creditor may sell the property in question in order to recover what he is owed. The secured creditor is then entitled to recover his debt from the proceeds of sale. He is entitled to be paid in full before any of the proceeds are made available to either unsecured creditors or other secured creditors over whose securities he has priority.

11.1 The role of mortgages

The nature of home ownership has changed considerably over the course of the twentieth and twenty-first centuries. At the outset of the twentieth century, the majority of the population lived in rented accommodation. This changed markedly during that century so that by 2003 71 per cent of households were owner-occupiers. Although this proportion has decreased since then, in part because it has become more difficult to get onto the 'housing ladder', nevertheless by 2017 63 per cent of the estimated 23.1 million households in England were owner-occupiers.[1] This increase in home ownership since the start of the twentieth century is due to a number of reasons. First was the rise of the building society movement, a principal purpose of which was to make funds available for the purpose of house buying. Second, central government provided active encouragement for people to buy homes. Such encouragement has, over the years, taken a number of forms including, until comparatively recently, tax relief on interest payments under the mortgage and the introduction of the right of certain council tenants to buy their homes at a discount. This right to buy, which was introduced by the Housing Act 1980,[2] led to the shift from occupiers of homes being tenants to their being owners of the property.

[1] (2018) English Housing Survey: Headline Report, 2016–17, 1 https://www.gov.uk/government/statistics/english-housing-survey-2016-to-2017-headline-report

[2] The provisions are now contained in the Housing Act 1985, Part V.

The money to finance the purchase of most homes comes, principally, from borrowing the money from a bank or a building society. It is agreed that the money will be repaid, with interest, to the mortgagee over a prolonged period of time. The loan is then secured by the creation of a mortgage over the property. The mortgage operates to secure the amount, with interest, that has been borrowed. The mortgagee does not get a proportionate share in the property so that, if the value of the house increases, the mortgagee derives no direct benefit from this; the rise in value accrues for the benefit of the mortgagor. This means that, over time, despite being already mortgaged, the house may provide good security for further borrowing. In those circumstances, the borrowing is not for the purpose of acquiring the house but to raise money for other purposes (such a mortgage is called a non-acquisition mortgage).

11.1.1 **The credit crunch**

A major activity of banks is to lend money to enable people to buy houses. Unfortunately, the practices adopted led to a major banking crisis in 2008/9. In the USA, banks lent vast amounts of money in what has been termed the 'sub-prime' market. What this meant was that the banks were lending money to people whose income was not sufficient to service the loan. Similarly, on this side of the Atlantic, as a response to the boom in the housing market, loans were made to people of amounts which were many times their annual incomes, those incomes frequently being self-certificated as opposed to being objectively verified. These practices meant that widespread failures to meet the payments became a very real possibility. An additional factor contributing to the crisis was the willingness of banks to lend more than the properties were worth, a loan of 125 per cent of the value of the property not being uncommon. Underlying these practices was the mistaken belief that the securities would be safe as the prices of houses would continue on an ever-upwards curve.

This form of lending carried considerable risks for the lending institutions. This led to many banks being exposed to the risk of a collapsing housing market. This collapse duly occurred, first in the USA, and then in the UK. A direct consequence of this was that major banks found that they had very large loans on their account books, and inadequate security to underpin them. Because of the complexity of some of the financial instruments used to bundle up the various loans made by the banks, a crisis of confidence ensued. Banks, concerned about the financial soundness of each other's positions, became reluctant to lend to each other. This led to the so-called credit crunch, and a resultant financial crisis. Deep concern came to be felt about the liquidity and, indeed, solvency of major financial institutions. These concerns were made worse by the actions of speculators trading in the shares of these institutions. To avoid the collapse of the financial sector, the government took powers under s. 3 of the Banking (Special Provisions) Act 2008 to nationalize authorized UK deposit takers, and two institutions, Northern Rock and Bradford and Bingley, were taken into public ownership. Moreover, the government also felt it necessary to invest large amounts of capital in other major banks in return for a major share in those companies, a practice which has been adopted overseas, where this crisis has also been felt. The effects of the financial crisis brought about principally by the practices in relation to mortgage lending will be felt globally for years to come.

11.1.2 **Repossessions**

Banks may enforce their security; debts must be repaid. Mortgagees can realize their securities by taking possession of the properties in question and then selling them. The problem is a serious one, although the recent evidence published on the Ministry of

Justice website[3] reveals that the number of possession actions brought by lenders, having increased every year from 2002 to 2009, has since fallen back considerably.

This fall in the number of possession actions is attributed both to low interest rates and to the introduction of the Mortgage Arrears Pre-Action Protocol, which came into effect in November 2008. The Pre-Action Protocol does not change the law but requires lenders who abide by it to make initial contact with the borrower and provide specified information (para. 5); postpone the start of a possession claim in specified circumstances where it is likely that the borrower will be able to repay (para. 6); and to be reasonable wherever possible, so that '[s]tarting a possession claim should be a last resort and must not normally be started unless all other reasonable attempts to resolve the situation have failed' (para. 7).[4]

Further support came from the 2008 agreement reached between some banks and the then government, whereby householders who had experienced a significant loss of income, as a result of redundancy or as a consequence of the financial downturn, were permitted to defer payment of interest for up to two years, with the government providing a guarantee to the banks against any loss which they might suffer as a consequence of this agreement.

This phenomenon of mortgage repossessions has brought in its wake a significant increase in the amount of litigation relating to this issue. This litigation has focused on the protection of the mortgagor when faced with an action which will result in the loss of his home as well as, increasingly, the rights of other persons who live in the property and claim to have an interest in it. The action for possession, and the related issue of the sale of mortgaged property, has become the dominant theme in the modern law of mortgages and this chapter will concentrate on these matters.

Other issues also arise, however, in the context of mortgages; most notably, how the law has regulated the mortgage relationship itself. To understand how the law has developed, it is necessary to grasp the theoretical basis of the mortgage, which cannot be done without regard to its development over history. Before considering this, however, it may be helpful to consider briefly the types of mortgage most commonly encountered in modern times. For while the concept of security is straightforward, it is unfortunately the case that the modern law of mortgages, in appearance at least, disguises its real nature; so much so that it has famously been said that 'No one by the light of nature ever understood an English mortgage of real estate'.[5] Although it is always desirable for the legal form to accord with the reality of a transaction, this is particularly so here. A mortgage is one of the most important commercial transactions with which most people will be involved, and it is much to be regretted that the form of the transaction is mystifying, and, at times, positively misleading to those who enter into it. The reasons for this obfuscation are largely historical, as the next section will explain.

11.2 Types of mortgage

When land is mortgaged, this is usually done for one of two reasons and the purpose of the loan may affect the type of mortgage created.

---

[3] Mortgage and Landlord Possession Statistics in England and Wales, July to September 2018 (Provisional) available at https://assets.publishing.service.gov.uk/government/uploads/system/uploads/attachment_data/file/754480/Mortgage_and_Landlord_Possession_Statistics_Jul-Sep_18.pdf

[4] Pre-Action Protocol for Possession Claims based on Mortgage or Home Purchase Plan Arrears in Respect of Residential Property available at https://www.justice.gov.uk/courts/procedure-rules/civil/protocol/prot_mha

[5] *Samuel v. Jarrah Timber and Wood Paving Corp. Ltd* [1904] A.C. 323 at 326 per Lord Macnaghten. For recommendations for reform, see (1991) Law Com. No. 204.

11.2.1 **Acquisition mortgages**

An acquisition mortgage is a loan to acquire a property. It is very common for the purchase price of the home to be raised by a combination of a down payment of, say, 10 per cent of the purchase price being provided by the purchaser and the balance by the mortgagee. This loan, together with interest, is then repaid over a prolonged period such as twenty-five years. Although there is now a vast variety of mortgage products available on the market, the traditional mortgage tends to fall into one of two basic types: repayment mortgages and endowment mortgages.

11.2.1.1 **Repayment mortgage**

Under a repayment mortgage, a sum of money is borrowed which, it is agreed, will be repaid over a substantial period of time, a term of twenty-five years being quite common. The total interest to be paid on the loan over that period is calculated and a schedule of payments is then worked out which, by monthly instalments, will be sufficient to repay the loan plus interest over the entire period. At the outset, the monthly instalments will consist almost entirely of payments of interest, so that there is very little reduction in the capital indebtedness. As time goes on, the amount of capital repayments will increase steadily and, towards the end of the loan, the instalments will consist very largely of capital repayments. When tax relief was granted to mortgage repayments, this was granted in respect of payments of interest, so that a mortgagor got most tax relief at the early stages of the mortgage. Now that there is no longer tax relief granted on mortgages, this is no longer an issue.

11.2.1.2 **Endowment mortgages**

The main alternative to the repayment mortgage is the endowment mortgage. Under this scheme, there is no repayment of any capital until the end of the agreed mortgage period. The only payment made to the mortgagee during the subsistence of the mortgage is in respect of interest payments. The mortgagor is also required to take out an endowment policy, which is assigned to the mortgagee. This policy is scheduled to mature at the end of the mortgage period thereby producing a lump sum sufficient to pay off the capital sum that has been borrowed. In some cases, the lump sum envisaged to be payable on the maturation of policy would be calculated to exceed the sum borrowed, the balance being paid to the mortgagor. Such a policy is known as a 'with profits' policy. As part of the policy, there would also be a life assurance policy, so that, if the mortgagor died during the subsistence of the mortgage, the capital amount borrowed would become payable under the terms of the policy.

Such mortgages are now less popular than they once were. One reason for their initial popularity was that, because the borrower was paying only interest to the mortgagee throughout the mortgage, this maximized his tax relief. This reason no longer exists. A second reason why this type of mortgage has declined in popularity is that everything depended upon the return on the endowment policy producing a sufficient lump sum to pay off the mortgage. This was not guaranteed. Whether it would do so depended on the success of the investment policy of the company with whom the policy was held. Endowment mortgages, therefore, carry an element of risk, and in recent times a considerable number of people have had to face up to the prospect that there will still be money owing on the mortgage after the endowment policy has matured. This, in turn, has led to allegations of malpractice against companies selling such policies. For these reasons, endowment mortgages are less popular today than once was the case.

11.2.2 **Non-acquisition mortgages**

A mortgage can also be raised on a property after the house has been acquired either, for example, to spend money on maintenance or home improvement, or, alternatively, to raise funds for a separate venture; for example, to invest in a business. When a house is used as security for borrowing after the house has been acquired, then in principle, either of the two forms of mortgage considered above can be used; an original mortgage can be extended, or a new mortgage can be created. The terms governing repayment may differ, however, from those normally encountered in an acquisition mortgage. If a property is used as security for a bank overdraft, it may be the case that it is envisaged that the loan will be repayable upon demand. Such an arrangement may affect significantly the ability of the mortgagor to resist a possession action if he defaults on the mortgage.

11.3 The nature of mortgages

The modern form of the mortgage, and certain of its characteristics, derives from its historical development,[6] which, initially at least, was a device to avoid the usury laws which prevented the creation of loans at a fixed rate of interest. To avoid this, the mortgagor, originally in consideration of a loan, granted a lease of the property to the mortgagee. If the income from the land was used to discharge the loan, the transaction was termed a *vivum vadium*, or living pledge. Alternatively, the mortgagee could retain the income, leaving the loan outstanding. This was known as a *mortuum vadium* or dead pledge, from which the term 'mortgage' derives. In both cases, if the loan was not repaid by the time agreed, the mortgagee would have the right to have the leasehold interest enlarged into a freehold.

11.3.1 Conveyance

By around the fifteenth century, the method of mortgaging land by granting a lease of it to the mortgagee had changed. What happened instead was that, in return for the loan, the mortgagor would convey the land to the mortgagee who, as a result, had security for the money which had been lent. A date would be set by the mortgage agreement for the repayment of that loan. If the mortgagor was not able to repay it upon the agreed date, then he lost his right to have the land conveyed back to him. Still worse, he remained liable to repay what he had borrowed, the upshot being that the mortgagor had lost his land to the mortgagee and remained liable on the debt. This outcome seems manifestly unjust and, as was to be expected, equity intervened to temper the harshness of the common law.

11.3.2 The mortgagor's equitable right to redeem

By way of contrast to the common law position, equity took a different view of the mortgage. In the eye of equity, the reality of the position was that the mortgagee had security for a loan. If the money had not been repaid by the date agreed, then his security remained good; generally speaking, his position had not been prejudiced. Equity, therefore, was prepared to allow the mortgagor to repay the loan after the contractual date for repayment had passed. This right, which arises only once the contractual date for redemption has passed, is termed the equitable right to redeem.

This right remains relevant today and is relied upon when, not uncommonly, the mortgage agreement stipulates that the mortgagor will repay the loan within six months of that loan having been granted. The reason why such an unrealistic clause is inserted into a modern mortgage agreement will be explained later in the chapter.[7] From that date, however, the right of the mortgagor to redeem the mortgage exists in equity.

---

[6] For a fuller account, see Harpum, Bridge, and Dixon, *Megarry and Wade's Law of Real Property* (8th edn) (London, Sweet & Maxwell, 2012), 24-000-14-818.

[7] See 11.6.5.1.

11.3.3 **The equity of redemption**

Historically, when mortgages were still predicated on conveyance, the owner of mortgaged property at common law was the mortgagee. Equity, however, looked to the substance of the transaction, which was that the mortgagee was simply a secured creditor. Consistent with this view, equity considered that, subject to the rights of the mortgagee as a secured creditor, the true owner of the property was the mortgagor.[8] To reflect that view, the sum total of the rights of the mortgagor, which consist of the rights of the mortgagor as beneficial owner of the property, minus the rights of the mortgagee as a secured creditor, is termed the equity of redemption. The equity of redemption, which includes the equitable right to redeem, comes into existence from the moment that the mortgage is created; the equitable right to redeem, which is, admittedly, one of the more important rights owned by the mortgagor, comes into being only when the date of redemption has passed.

The equity of redemption, which is commonly referred to in its abbreviated form as 'the equity', is a valuable asset. 'It constitutes an interest in the mortgaged property and, in terms of value, is the principal element of that which the mortgagor retains after the grant of the mortgage. Thus when a house owner describes himself as having an equity of £300,000 in a property which is worth £500,000 and is mortgaged to secure a debt of £200,000, it is strictly the equity of redemption to which the owner refers.'[9] A further mortgage can then be created against the security of the equity of redemption, a process which has been termed asset mobilization.[10]

The equity of redemption can increase in value in one of two ways. First, under a repayment mortgage, the payment of the mortgage instalments will, over time, reduce the level of indebtedness and cause a corresponding rise in the value of the equity. More importantly, the house can simply increase in value. If the house was originally bought for £500,000 with the help of a £200,000 mortgage, the original value of the equity was £300,000. If the value of the house doubles to £1 million, there is also an increase in the value of the equity to £800,000. If, on the other hand, property prices fall, the position may be arrived at where the size of the mortgage exceeds the value of the house. If, to change the facts of the example given above, the value of the house had fallen to £150,000 then the position is that the mortgagor has what is known as negative equity, in this case £50,000. The existence of negative equity, which is a fairly recent phenomenon, is a considerable social and economic problem.[11] In the aftermath of the financial crisis affecting banks, and the resultant collapse of the housing market, it made an unwelcome return. A major consequence of it was that it became extremely difficult for people in this position to be able to sell their houses because the purchase price would not be sufficient to discharge the mortgage. This, coupled with considerable regional variation in house prices, has significant consequences for geographical mobility.

Scholars have argued that, in registered land, where mortgages are by way of legal charge,[12] there is little sense in retaining the equity of redemption. Once a mortgage no longer consists of a conveyance and re-conveyance, the land is not 'redeemed' and there is no 'redemption'. A mortgage by way of legal charge is an interest in land[13] and is discharged from the land once the debt is repaid.[14] So far, however, no legislative change has come.

---

   [8] See, e.g., *Re Sir Thomas Spencer Wells* [1933] Ch. 29.

   [9] *Horsham Properties Group Ltd v. Clark* [2009] 1 W.L.R. 1255 at [22] *per* Briggs J.

   [10] See M. Oldham in Tee (ed.), *Land Law: Issues, Debates, Policy* (Cullompton, Willan Publishing, 2002), 169–70.

   [11] See Dorling, Gentle, and Cornford, *Housing Crisis: Disaster or Opportunity* (1992), University of Newcastle upon Tyne, C.U.R.D.S., Discussion Paper No. 96.

   [12] LRA 2002, s.23(1)(a).   [13] LPA 1925, s.1(2)(c).

   [14] G. Watt 'The Lie of the Land: Mortgage Law as Legal Fiction' in E. Cooke (ed.) *Modern Studies in Property Law*, vol. 4 (Oxford, Hart Publishing, 2007), 87.

11.4 The creation of mortgages

The pre-1925 method of mortgaging land was manifestly artificial, the artificiality of the position being accentuated by the approach of equity to the subject. The pre-1925 position, where the legal owner of the land was the mortgagee but the equitable owner was the mortgagor, was abandoned by the 1925 legislation to enable the legal position to reflect more accurately the reality of the situation.

11.4.1 Legal mortgages

After 1925, it was no longer possible to create a legal mortgage of land by conveying the estate to the mortgagee. In the case of freehold, unregistered land, a legal mortgage can now only be created in one of two ways. Under s. 85 of the Law of Property Act (LPA) 1925, a mortgage of an estate in fee simple can only be created by:

(i)   a demise for a term of years absolute, subject to a provision for cessor on redemption;[15] and

(ii)   a charge by deed expressed to be by way of legal mortgage.

It is further provided by s. 85(2) of the Act that any purported conveyance of the fee simple by way of mortgage shall operate to create a 3,000-year lease subject to cessor on redemption.

In the case of a mortgage of leasehold property, similar provisions exist, so that the method of creating a mortgage is either to create a sub-lease in favour of the mortgagee of a period not less than one day shorter than the head lease or, alternatively, to execute a deed expressed to be a charge by way of legal mortgage.[16] If, instead of using one of these methods, the mortgagor purports to mortgage the lease by assigning it to the mortgagee, then the assignment will not be effective as such, but will, instead, operate to create a sub-lease ten days shorter than the lease which was purported to be assigned.[17]

11.4.1.1 Charge by way of legal mortgage

The charge by way of legal mortgage was a new method of mortgaging land created in 1925. Its effect is defined by the Act as being that, in the case of a mortgage of freehold land, the mortgagee is given the same rights and powers as if he had been granted a 3,000-year lease and, in the case of leasehold land, as if he had been granted a sub-lease, one day less than the lease which was mortgaged.[18]

11.4.1.2 Mortgage by lease

It is now the case that, whenever a legal mortgage is created, then either the freehold or leasehold estate or remains vested in the mortgagor. In unregistered land, where mortgages by leases are still permitted,[19] the legal position continues to give a misleading picture of the reality of the situation. The actual position, at law, is that the mortgagor of freehold land holds the reversion on a 3,000-year lease, that lease being one which will determine when the loan is repaid and the mortgage is redeemed. Ordinarily, such a reversionary lease would be of little intrinsic value (since the lease is so long), but it remains true to say that the mortgagor continues to hold a valuable interest in the property. The true value of

---

[15] This means that the lease will determine when the mortgage is redeemed.
[16] LPA 1925, s. 86(1).
[17] Ibid., s. 86(2). See *Grangeside Properties Ltd v. Collingwood Securities Ltd* [1964] 1 W.L.R. 139.
[18] LPA 1925, s. 87(1).
[19] Under LPA 1925, s. 85, since LRA 2002, s. 23 does not apply.

the interest held by the mortgagor reflects the position taken by equity and is the value of his equity of redemption. The equity of redemption continues to exist despite the original reason for its creation, that the legal fee simple had been conveyed to the mortgagee, does not. The reality of the position is that, 'The owner of property entering into a mortgage does not by entering into that mortgage cease to be the owner of the property any further than is necessary to give effect to the security he has created.'[20]

11.4.2 Registered land

When mortgaging property, it became far more common for it to be done by the creation of a charge by way of legal mortgage than by the creation of a long lease. The reason for this is essentially pragmatic, it being rather easier to explain to a purchaser of a house that a legal charge is being created in favour of a building society rather than a long lease. Where title to land is registered, the reality of the situation is recognized and s. 23(1)(a) of the Land Registration Act (LRA) 2002 provides that it is no longer possible to create a mortgage by either a demise or a sub-demise. The only way to mortgage registered land is now to do so by legal charge. This legal charge is an interest in land[21] as well as a registrable disposition.[22]

11.4.3 Purchaser of a legal estate for value

Since the effect of the creation of a charge by way of legal mortgage is that the mortgagee is treated as if a 3,000-year lease had been created in his favour,[23] he is a purchaser of a legal estate for value. This means that the mortgagee will take free of prior equitable interests, unless either, in registered land, such interests have been protected by registration or it is an interest which overrides a registered disposition, or in unregistered land, unless the interest is binding on the mortgagee under the doctrine of notice.

11.4.4 Equitable mortgages

Traditionally, and still in unregistered land, an equitable mortgage could be created in one of two ways: (1) by mortgaging an equitable interest; or (2) by mortgaging a legal interest by the deposit of title deeds. In registered land a mortgage by way of legal charge will not operate at law (and so be limited to equity) if it is not registered as a registrable disposition under s. 27, LRA 2002 and so an equitable mortgage may be inadvertently created through a failure to register the mortgage.[24]

11.4.4.1 Equitable interest

If a person has only an equitable interest in land, then he can only create an equitable mortgage over that interest. If land is held upon a trust for a person, that person can mortgage his beneficial interest in the land by using the pre-1925 method of mortgaging land: that is, he can assign his interest to the mortgagee, with provision for it to be re-assigned upon the repayment of a loan. To be effective, a mortgage of this type need not be created by deed; the assignment must, however, be in writing and signed by the mortgagor or his agent.[25]

A second way in which a mortgage of an equitable interest can occur is in the event of forgery. In *First National Securities Ltd v. Hegerty*,[26] a legal co-owner of a house got someone to impersonate his wife, who was the other co-owner, and she forged the wife's signature on the mortgage. The forged document did not create a legal mortgage but operated

---

[20] *Downsview Nominees Ltd v. First City Corporation Ltd* [1993] A.C. 295 at 311 *per* Lord Templeman.
[21] LPA 1925, s.1(2)(c).   [22] LRA 2002, s. 27(2)(f).   [23] LPA 1925, s. 87.
[24] LRA 2002, s. 27(2)(f).   [25] LPA 1925, s. 53(1)(c).   [26] [1985] Q.B. 850.

to sever the equitable joint tenancy and the mortgage took effect against his equitable half share in the property. When title is registered, the position is slightly more complex. If the mortgage is registered on the title of the joint proprietors then, despite the mortgage having been forged, the borrower would appear to have a legal mortgage. The innocent co-owner should then seek alteration of the register.[27] The effect of this is that the mortgage would be removed from the register of title and the forged mortgage would then operate as a charge against the forger's beneficial interest in the property.[28]

11.4.4.2 Deposit of title deeds

A second, and quite common, method of creating an equitable mortgage in order to secure a loan was, before 1989, to deposit the title deeds with the creditor.[29] The theoretical basis of this type of transaction being recognized as an equitable mortgage[30] was that it was seen as a contract to create a mortgage and that the deposit of title deeds was seen as a mutual act of part performance by the lender and the borrower. As there existed a specifically enforceable contract to create a mortgage, then equity, looking on that which ought to be done as already having been done, considered that an equitable mortgage had been created.

This changed with the introduction of s. 2 of the Law of Property (Miscellaneous Provisions) Act 1989. Since s. 2, there can be no such thing as an oral contract to create a legal mortgage and, as a consequence, there is no room for the doctrine of part performance. Accordingly, in *United Bank of Kuwait v. Sahib*,[31] the Court of Appeal held that to create an equitable mortgage in this way, the provisions of s. 2 must be complied with. A deposit of title deeds with the intention of providing security for a loan will no longer give rise to an equitable mortgage although, as between the parties themselves, it may give rise to rights arising out of estoppel.[32]

11.4.4.3 Registered land

A mortgage of registered land is effected by a registered charge. Such a charge will not operate at law until registered.[33] Until the charge is registered, the charge will only be effective in equity and would, therefore, need to be protected by the registration of a notice.[34] When electronic conveyancing is made compulsory, this will cease to be an issue as the creation of the charge and the notification of the registrar will be simultaneous.[35]

11.5 Rights of the mortgagor

This and the following sections deal with the respective rights of the parties to the mortgage. They do not purport to be an exhaustive account; they focus on the more important issues of contemporary relevance, starting, first, with the rights of the mortgagor. These rights are associated with the equity of redemption but it is strongly arguable that when

---

[27] This was overlooked in *Mortgage Corporation v. Shaire* [2001] 1 F.L.R. 273. See M.P. Thompson [2000] Conv. 329 at 331.

[28] See *Bank of Ireland Home Mortgages Ltd v. Bell* [2001] 2 F.L.R. 809.

[29] See *Re Wallis & Simmonds (Builders) Ltd* [1974] 1 W.L.R. 391.

[30] This method of creating an equitable mortgage had been recognized for centuries: see, e.g., *Russel v. Russel* (1793) 1 Bro. C.C. 269.

[31] [1997] Ch. 107.

[32] See M.P. Thompson [1994] Conv. 465 at 468–9; P. Critchley [1998] Conv. 502.

[33] LRA 2002, s. 27; *Grace Rymer Investments Ltd v. Waite* [1958] Ch. 831. See also *Barclays Bank plc v. Zaroovabli* [1997] Ch. 321.

[34] Although if the mortgage is not registered in compliance with LRA 2002, s. 27(2)(f), it is somewhat unlikely that the mortgage will be protected by entering a notice.

[35] LRA 2002, s. 93(1)(2).

the mortgage is created by legal charge (as all mortgages on registered land are now required to be) that there is no scope for the rules on the equity of redemption to apply. So far, however, legislation has not confirmed this and courts have not clarified the point. It is striking, however, that today equity of redemption is rarely referred to in litigation about mortgages secured on land. Indeed, there are good reasons to argue that these rules simply no longer apply to mortgages created by legal charge, which are an interest in the land rather than predicated on a conveyance from the mortgagor to the mortgagee (where equity might be expected to intervene).

11.5.1 **No clogs on the equity of redemption**

The equity of redemption was introduced essentially for two reasons. First, equity was giving recognition to the reality of the transaction. While at law the transaction took the form of a conveyance of the property to the mortgagee, the substance of the arrangement was that the mortgagee was to have security for his loan. Recognizing this, equity viewed the true owner of the property as being the mortgagor, that ownership being subject to the secured rights of the mortgagee. A related reason was that equity saw the mortgage transaction as being, potentially, an instrument of oppression. The most obvious aspect of this was that, if the loan was not repaid on time, the mortgagor would lose his land and still be liable to repay the loan. This was prevented by the introduction of the equitable right to redeem. Other aspects of the mortgage transaction were also potentially onerous to the mortgagor, however, and equity intervened to afford him protection, that protection being embraced compendiously within the doctrine that there should be no clogs on the equity of redemption.

In approaching this area of law, it is as well to point out at the outset that a number of the cases are not easy to reconcile with each other. The reason for this is that there are two competing pressures at work, each of which has been afforded different priority at different stages of history. The first pressure is a paternalist approach taken towards the mortgagor to protect him from oppressive terms in the mortgage. The second is the general policy of freedom of contract, where the courts give effect to what the parties have agreed. In modern times, rather greater priority, in this area at least, is afforded to the latter policy and it is arguable that the doctrine of clogs and fetters has now outlived its usefulness.

Broadly speaking, there are three types of clause in a mortgage that are open to attack as being a clog on the equity of redemption. These are attempts to restrict the mortgagor's right to redeem the mortgage; clauses giving the mortgagee the right to acquire the mortgaged property, and collateral advantages afforded to the mortgagee by the mortgage. These will be considered in turn.

11.5.1.1 **Restricting the right to redeem**

The first problem area concerns attempts by the mortgagee to restrict the mortgagor's right to redeem the mortgage.[36] A relatively modern example is provided by *Fairclough v. Swan Brewery Ltd.*[37] The mortgaged property was held on a twenty-year lease. It was a term of the mortgage agreement that the mortgagor could not redeem the mortgage until a date six weeks prior to the end of the lease. Despite this clause, the mortgagor was permitted to redeem the mortgage at an earlier date, the reason being that:

> equity will not permit any device or contrivance being part of the mortgage transaction or contemporaneous with it to prevent or impede redemption . . . [A] mortgage cannot be made irredeemable.[38]

---

[36] For a very early example, see *Howard v. Harris* (1681) 1 Vern. 33.   [37] [1912] A.C. 565.

[38] Ibid. at 570 *per* Lord Macnaghten. See also *Re Wells* [1933] Ch. 29 at 52 *per* Lawrence L.J.

This case does not decide that a postponement of the right to redeem will always be regarded as being a clog and, therefore, liable to be struck out. In *Knightsbridge Estates Ltd v.
Byrne*,[39] a company had created a mortgage over freehold property and it was agreed that
the loan would be paid by eighty-six monthly instalments; in other words, the mortgage
could not be redeemed for forty years. The mortgagor wished to redeem the mortgage
earlier, so that he could create a new mortgage at a lower rate of interest than that which
he was obliged to pay under the existing mortgage. It was held that he could not do so.
The clause postponing the right to redeem was not a clog on the equity of redemption
and, instead, the court upheld the terms of a freely negotiated commercial bargain. What
distinguished the case from *Fairclough* was that the right to redeem had not been rendered
illusory. The property was freehold and not leasehold. Second, the term was not unconscionable. The decision is also representative of the emerging trend for the court to give
effect to the policy of freedom of contract and a resulting unwillingness to set aside terms
which the parties have freely agreed.

Penalties

In the residential sector, one is unlikely to encounter terms in the mortgage that bluntly
postpone the mortgagor's ability to redeem at all. More common is the situation where a
financial penalty is imposed upon the mortgagor should he seek to redeem the mortgage
within a certain period from the date of the mortgage. Such clauses are usually found
when the payments for an agreed number of years are at a fixed rate of interest, such offers being common and are intended to act as an inducement to a potential borrower to
take this particular form of mortgage, safe in the knowledge that he will be sheltered from
the consequences of a general rise in interest rates. Although such penalty clauses do give
rise to complaints, none has yet featured in litigation. It is thought that such a clause is
unlikely to be considered to be a clog, unless the period specified upon which a penalty
can be levied is regarded as unconscionable, or is made to extend for the entire period of
the mortgage. In the cases of mortgages created after 2004, matters such as this will fall to
be dealt with under the regulatory scheme introduced under the Financial Services and
Marketing Act 2000.

11.5.1.2 Options to purchase

A second type of clog on the equity of redemption is the grant to the mortgagee of an option to purchase the mortgaged property. Such a clause was struck out with a marked lack of
enthusiasm by the House of Lords in *Samuel v. Jarrah Timber and Wood Paving Corporation
Ltd*.[40] A mortgage of certain stock gave the mortgagee the option to purchase that stock at
any time within twelve months of the date of the mortgage. Even though this term was in
no way oppressive, it was held to be a clog on the equity of redemption. This was because
it was a term contained in a mortgage which enabled the mortgagee to buy the mortgaged
property; it was a right which, if exercised, would prevent the mortgagor from redeeming
the mortgage. It was, therefore, struck out as being, in the words of the Earl of Halsbury,
'contrary to a principle of equity the sense or reason of which I am unable to understand'.[41]

Separate agreements

A distinction is drawn if the option to buy the mortgaged property is not contained in the
actual mortgage but is part of a separate agreement. Thus, in *Reeve v. Lisle*,[42] a ship had

---

[39] [1939] Ch. 441, affirmed on other grounds at [1940] A.C. 613.
[40] [1904] A.C. 323. For contemporary criticism of a decision to the same effect of the Court of Appeal,
[1903] 2 Ch. 1, see F. Pollock (1903) 19 L.Q.R. 359, describing the doctrine as 'anachronistic'.
[41] [1904] A.C. 323 at 325.   [42] [1902] A.C. 461.

been mortgaged and, twelve days after the creation of the mortgage, the mortgagee was granted an option to purchase it. Because this option was not contained in the mortgage agreement itself, but was separate from it, the option was upheld. The essential aspect of the rule remains in force, however, so that if the mortgage gives the mortgagee the option to purchase the mortgaged property, this will be struck out as a clog on the equity of redemption.[43]

This rule has nothing to do with the fairness, or otherwise, of the particular clause, as can be seen from the case of *Jones v. Morgan*.[44] Three years after a mortgage was created, a second agreement was entered into between the parties. Under the terms of that agreement, the mortgagee acquired the right to purchase some of the mortgaged land. Although the Court of Appeal was unanimous that this clause should not be struck out on the basis that it was either an unconscionable bargain or had been secured by duress, the majority held the clause to be void as constituting a clog of the equity of redemption. This was because the second agreement was seen as being a variation of the mortgage, a view that on the facts appeared to be correct, rather than a separate, independent contract. As such, because it gave the mortgagee the right to purchase the mortgaged property, it was automatically void, regardless of the fairness or otherwise of the agreement.

The origin of the rules on clogs lay in the inequality of the bargaining positions of the mortgagor and the mortgagee, the result being that unconscionable terms could be imposed upon the former by the latter, an example of such a term being that the mortgagee should have the right to purchase the mortgaged property. Because such a clause is, technically, a clog, it will be struck out regardless of the lack of any oppression and is an unfortunate relic of a doctrine of equity which has now a propensity to upset unexceptional contracts.

11.5.1.3 Collateral advantages

Typically, a mortgagee will seek more than security for a loan. A mortgage is, of course, a business transaction and the lender will charge interest on the loan. During the development of the law of mortgages, the mortgagee would frequently seek to recover more than interest on the loan. Quite commonly, the mortgagee was a brewery who, as part of the mortgage transaction, would seek to tie the mortgagor to buying its product, such a clause being known as a *solus* agreement. More recently, this issue has arisen with mortgages of garages, whereby the mortgagee seeks to tie the mortgagor to the purchase of its petroleum products. Traditionally, the efficacy of such clauses, and other provisions conferring collateral advantages on the mortgagee, was considered as part of the equitable doctrine of clogs and fetters. It is this area of the law of mortgages where there has been the greatest shift in the judicial attitude as to when to intervene to invalidate a particular clause in a mortgage.

Duration of advantage

The traditional approach was to distinguish between cases where the collateral advantage would continue for only as long as the mortgage was in being and those where the advantage was to endure for a longer period. In *Noakes v. Rice*,[45] the mortgagor of a public house agreed with the mortgagee that he would purchase the latter's beer for the duration of his lease of the property. This agreement was held to be invalid. The effect of this clause

---

[43] See *Lewis v. Frank Love Ltd* [1961] 1 W.L.R. 261; P.V. Baker (1961) 77 L.Q.R. 163.

[44] [2002] 1 E.G.L.R. 125; M.P. Thompson [2001] Conv. 502. Contrast *Warnborough Ltd v. Garmite Ltd* [2006] EWHC 10 (Ch), where the transaction in question was held not to be a mortgage. See also *Brighton & Hove City Council v. Audus* [2009] EWHC 340 (Ch).

[45] [1902] A.C. 24.

was that what was a free house prior to the mortgage would, on the redemption of the mortgage, remain as a tied house and this was held to be a clog on the equity of redemption. By way of contrast, in *Biggs v. Hoddinott*,[46] the mortgage agreement provided that the mortgage would not be redeemed for a period of five years and, during that period, the mortgagor would buy only the mortgagee's products. It having been held that the postponement of the right to redeem for five years was acceptable, the *solus* agreement limited to that period was also valid.

This essential distinction was upheld by a bare majority of the House of Lords in *Bradley v. Carritt*,[47] where, after redemption of a mortgage of shares, a clause requiring the mortgagor to employ the mortgagee as a broker was struck down as a clog on the equity of redemption. This may be seen as the high point of the doctrine as it is applied to the area of collateral advantages and the turning point in the judicial approach to this issue occurred in *Kreglinger v. New Patagonia Meat and Cold Storage Co. Ltd.*[48] Under the terms of a mortgage entered into by a wool company, the mortgagee was, for a period of five years, to have a right of pre-emption in respect of sheepskins produced by the mortgagor. It was argued that this provision could not be enforced once the mortgage had been redeemed, the redemption having occurred before the five-year period had elapsed. This argument was unanimously rejected by the House of Lords.

Although it is possible to find technical distinctions between *Bradley v. Carritt* and *Kreglinger*, it is quite evident that the House of Lords was keen to limit the scope of the equitable doctrine and, instead, to enforce a freely entered contractual agreement. This enthusiasm was marked by the speech of Lord Mersey, who likened the equitable doctrine to 'an unruly dog which, if not securely chained to its kennel is prone to wander into places where it ought not to be'.[49]

Kreglinger involved an entirely normal commercial contract, which the House of Lords was anxious to uphold. To that end, it was held that there was no rule of equity which prohibited the mortgagee from stipulating in a mortgage for a collateral advantage which will continue after the mortgage has been redeemed. Such a clause will be struck out only if it is unfair or unreasonable; if it operates in the nature of a penalty, clogging the equity of redemption; or it is inconsistent with or repugnant to the contractual or equitable right to redeem.

11.5.2 **Unconscionability**

Today, the test to decide whether a clause in a mortgage should be struck out is more stringent than the rules on collateral advantage, and is one of unconscionability. In *Cityland Holdings Ltd v. Dabrah*,[50] at a time when the base lending rate was 7 per cent, the annual rate of interest under the mortgage in question was 19 per cent and, if there was default in payment, the rate of interest would have been 57 per cent. This was considered to be a penal rate of interest and a rate of 7 per cent was substituted for that which had been agreed in the mortgage.

That the mortgagor was an individual had a bearing on this decision. In *Multiservice Bookbinding Co. Ltd v. Marden*,[51] a small company borrowed money by way of mortgage. Under the terms of the mortgage, the interest payable was index-linked to the Swiss franc, the result of which was that, when the value of the pound plummeted as against the Swiss currency, the amount of interest payable rose dramatically. The clause was, nevertheless,

---

[46] [1898] 2 Ch. 307.   [47] [1903] A.C. 307.
[48] [1914] A.C. 25. The speech of Lord Parker contains a valuable review of the law of clogs and fetters.
[49] Ibid. at 46.   [50] [1968] Ch. 166.   [51] [1979] Ch. 84.

upheld. Although it was a hard bargain, it was not unconscionable[52] and, for a collateral advantage contained in a mortgage to be struck out, it is not sufficient to show that it was unreasonable; the test is one of unconscionability.[53] To establish unconscionability, the relative strength of the bargaining position of the two parties is a relevant, if not necessarily decisive, factor. In the instant case, the parties had relative equality of bargaining position. As a result, the mortgagor was unable to establish that the objectionable term had been imposed in a morally reprehensible way so that the conscience of the mortgagee was affected, this being the test which had to be satisfied.[54]

11.5.3 The Consumer Credit Acts

Under s. 137 of the Consumer Credit Act 1974, the court is empowered to reopen certain extortionate credit arrangements, such arrangements being where the borrower is an individual. To judge whether or not a transaction is extortionate, the court is required to have regard to certain criteria laid down by s. 138 of the Act. These criteria include the prevailing level of interest rates when the loan was made, the age, experience, business capacity, and state of health of the debtor at the time of the loan, and also the degree of financial pressure he was under at the time and the nature of that pressure. From the creditor's point of view, the court must have regard, *inter alia*, to the degree of risk undertaken by him, having regard to the value of any security offered.

To date, the courts have not interfered in the case of mortgages, even in cases where the interest rate was over 40 per cent.[55] In both cases, however, the debtor had a poor record as a repayer of debts and the increased risk of default meant that arrangements of this type were normal for risks of this kind. Although there has not been intervention under the Act, the jurisdiction under it, and the criteria laid down, seem a preferable way of approaching issues of this nature rather than reliance on a general principle of equity developed many years ago.

Under the 1974 Act, the criterion that had to be satisfied for the court to intervene was that the credit arrangement was extortionate. Section 19 of the Consumer Credit Act 2006 has added a new s. 140A to the original Act, and the test is now that of an unfair relationship.[56]

In particular, clauses in mortgage agreements allowing the mortgagee to vary interest rates, where that variation is not governed by changes in the rates set by the Bank of England, have come under attack. Such clauses are not immune from challenge, but it will be only very rarely that such a challenge will be successful. In *Paragon Finance plc v. Nash*,[57] Dyson L.J. accepted that such a power was not completely unfettered.[58] A variation would only be liable to challenge, however, if the lender acted in a way that no reasonable lender, acting reasonably, would do. The fact that the rate which has been set may be regarded as being unreasonable is not a sufficient basis on which to invalidate the rate which has been set. The reason for this is that, although such a rate may be unreasonable from the borrower's point of view, it may be commercially necessary for the lender, and therefore reasonable from its point of view, to set such a rate.[59]

---

[52] Cf. *Macklin v. Dowsett* [2004] 2 E.G.L.R. 75, where what could certainly be seen as an unconscionable agreement but was not, however, part of a mortgage agreement, was successfully attacked on the basis of undue influence. See 11.5.7.

[53] Ibid. at 108 *per* Browne-Wilkinson J. [54] Ibid. at 110 *per* Browne-Wilkinson J.

[55] A. *Ketley Ltd v. Scott* [1980] C.C.L.R. 47, 41; *Woodstead Finance Ltd v. Petrou* [1986] C.C.L.R. 47.

[56] *Plevin v. Paragon Personal Finance Ltd* [2014] UKSC 61; *Pontearso v. Greenlands Trading Ltd* [2019] 1 WLUK 102.

[57] [2002] 1 W.L.R. 685. See also *Paragon Finance plc v. Pender* [2005] EWCA Civ. 760.

[58] *Paragon Finance plc v. Nash, supra.* [59] [2002] 1 W.L.R. 685 at 702.

11.5.4 **Restraint of trade**

The issue of *solus* agreements contained in mortgages was considered by the House of Lords in *Esso Petroleum Ltd v. Harper's Garage (Stourport) Ltd.*[60] Two mortgages were in issue, both of which sought to tie garage owners to the purchase of only the mortgagee's products. One of them concerned a *solus* agreement of five years; the other an agreement for twenty-one years. The first tie was upheld, but not the second. The decisions were made, however, on the basis of the common law doctrine of restraint of trade[61] and not by reference to the equitable principles of clogs and fetters on the equity of redemption. As Diplock L.J. put it in the Court of Appeal:

> I am not persuaded that mortgages of land are condemned today to linger in a jurisprudential cul-de-sac built by the Courts of Chancery before the Judicature Acts from which the robust doctrines of the common law are excluded.[62]

The use of the common law doctrine of restraint of trade seems a more apposite way of resolving disputes of this kind than having to apply the somewhat anachronistic equitable rules which were developed centuries ago.

11.5.5 **Regulating mortgages**

Until 2004, the only statutory regulation of terms in mortgages was that contained in the Consumer Credit Act 1974. In respect of regulated mortgages, the terms of mortgage agreements after 31 October 2004 are governed by a code of conduct promulgated by the Financial Services Authority acting under the terms of the Financial Services and Markets Act 2000.

One of the objectives of this Act is to provide protection for consumers.[63] In securing the appropriate degree of protection for consumers the Authority was empowered to make regulations,[64] and, in so doing, regard must be had to the different degrees of risk affecting the parties to the transaction, the different degrees of experience and expertise, and the need of consumers for advice and accurate information. This is, however, subject to the general principle that consumers should take responsibility for their actions.[65] The Financial Services Authority has published a handbook, *Mortgages: Conduct of Business* (MCOB), which relates to regulated mortgage agreements. Failure to comply with the Code of Practice does not invalidate the mortgage, but can lead to the imposition of sanctions against the mortgagee.[66]

Regulated mortgage agreements include most first mortgages, and the purpose of the Code of Practice is to ensure that borrowers are given adequate information concerning the content of mortgage agreements. This, coupled with the power to re-open extortionate credit bargains, is a much better way of regulating mortgage agreements than the use of the anachronistic doctrine of clogs and fetters. The clogs and fetters doctrine was recently described as 'an appendix to our law that no longer serves any useful purpose and would be better excised'.[67] Jonathan Parker L.J. developed this metaphor further:

> the unruly dog is still alive (although one might reasonably expect its venerable age to inhibit it from straying too far from its kennel); and that however desirable an appendectomy might be thought to be, no such relieving operation has as yet been carried out.[68]

---

[60] [1968] A.C. 269.

[61] For the possible impact of European Law on *solus* agreements, see T. Frazer [1994] Conv. 150.

[62] [1966] 2 Q.B. 514 at 577–8.   [63] Financial Services and Markets Act 2000, s. 2(2)(c).

[64] Ibid., s. 138.   [65] Ibid., s. 5.   [66] Ibid. Part XIV

[67] *Jones v. Morgan* [2002] 1 E.G.L.R. 125 at 136 *per* Lord Phillips.

[68] *Warborough Ltd v. Garmite Ltd* [2003] EWCA Civ. 1544 at para. 72.

In 2002 (before the entry into force of the LRA 2002), the doctrine of clogs and fetters was then thought to remain. Given the available methods of providing consumers with protection against unconscionable bargains, it is to be hoped that the doctrine is soon done away with. Its only remaining scope appears to be to upset transactions, otherwise regarded as unobjectionable, whereby a mortgagee acquires the right to purchase the mortgaged property.

11.5.6 **Power to lease**

The mortgagor is empowered by s. 99, LPA 1925 to grant certain leases that will be binding upon the mortgagee. This is, however, subject to that power not having been excluded by the mortgage agreement. It is almost universal practice for this power to be excluded. The effect on the mortgagee of leases granted by the mortgagor will be considered shortly when considering possession actions brought by the mortgagee.

11.5.7 **Undue influence**

When a transaction is impugned on the basis of undue influence, there are, in the present context, three separate yet related scenarios which can arise. They are:

(1) A transaction is entered into between A and B, which involves A either giving or selling property to B. Subsequently A seeks to set aside the transaction arguing that it was brought about as a result of undue influence practised on her by B.

(2) The position is the same as above, except that B has subsequently transferred the land for value to C. A now seeks to recover the land from C. In this situation, her ability to do so will depend upon whether, first, an equity to set aside the transaction has arisen in favour of A against B, and then, second, whether or not C has taken subject to that prior equity.[69]

(3) A and B are the co-owners of a house and they both sign a mortgage over it in favour of a bank, C. A then argues that the mortgage in favour of C should, as against her, be set aside because her signature to it was obtained as a result of undue influence exerted on her by B. It will not normally be the case that it is alleged that it is the actual creditor that has been the wrongdoer.[70] This, apart from the vitiating factor in the actual case being misrepresentation rather than undue influence, was the situation in *O'Brien* and in much of the subsequent case law, and is the main issue to be addressed in this section.

In all of these scenarios, undue influence is the central factor although the issues involved differ. The first involves a transaction between just two parties and is a straightforward case of determining whether A has been the victim of some malpractice by the other party to it, B. In the second situation, assuming that B has committed a wrong against A, the question is whether the equity to set aside the transaction is enforceable against a third party, C. This is an issue determined by the normal principles governing the enforceability of equities against purchasers. The third transaction is a contract between A and B on one side and C on the other and the issue is to determine the circumstances in which a wrong committed by B against A can affect the enforceability of the contract involving the two of them and C. It should be borne in mind that the main area of contention deriving from *O'Brien* and subsequent judicial developments relates to the resolution of the third

---

[69] See, e.g., *Mortgage Express v. Lambert* [2016] EWCA Civ. 555.
[70] Although see *Mahon v. FBN Bank (UK) Ltd* [2011] EWHC 1432 (Ch).

situation. A good deal of the difficulties in the development of the law, however, have stemmed from a tendency to conflate the various scenarios, a tendency which leads to considerable confusion as to what the appropriate applicable principles are.

11.5.7.1 *Barclays Bank v. O'Brien*

The House of Lords' decision in *Barclays Bank plc v. O'Brien*[71] sought to lay down a sound conceptual base for the law's intervention in this area and to provide principled guidelines to enable a proper balance to be struck between the competing interests of commercial lenders on the one hand and residential occupiers on the other. Unfortunately, the attempt to do this was far from being an unmitigated success. A torrent of litigation followed on from the decision and this led to the House of Lords, to a considerable extent, recasting the law in what is now the leading case of *Royal Bank of Scotland v. Etridge (No. 2)*.[72] To understand the issues which arose in *Etridge*, and how the House of Lords sought to re-solve them, it remains necessary to explain the basis of *O'Brien* and some of the resulting difficulties which emanated from it.

Mr and Mrs O'Brien were joint legal owners of their matrimonial home. He was closely involved in a company which had an overdraft facility with the bank. He agreed with the bank to stand as surety for the debts of the company and, in order to secure that guarantee, to create a mortgage over the matrimonial home. He told his wife that the proposed mort-gage was to secure a loan of £60,000 repayable within three weeks. When, sometime later, the mortgage was created the level of debt was £135,000 and the mortgage contained an 'all moneys clause': the mortgage secured unlimited liability, so that whatever the company owed was secured by the mortgage against the matrimonial home. At the time when the bank sought possession, the company's debt amounted to £154,000. When the mortgage was signed by Mrs O'Brien, the bank official did not follow the bank's policy. That policy entailed that a person in Mrs O'Brien's position should have had the nature and effect of the mortgage explained to her and been recommended to take independent legal advice. Instead, she simply signed the mortgage document and a side letter which acknowledged that she had understood it. This was not the case. She believed what her husband had misrepresented to her which was that the mortgage was to secure a short-term loan of £60,000 rather than, as was the case, open-ended liability. The House of Lords held that the mortgage was void against her.

In deciding in what circumstances a person could avoid liability under a mortgage which she had signed, giving the only speech, Lord Browne-Wilkinson adverted to a fa-miliar dilemma. One competing pressure stems from an instinctive sympathy for a wife who is threatened with the loss of her home at the suit of a rich bank which had been deal-ing, principally, with her husband. Set against that is a competing need that wealth locked up in a matrimonial home should not be made economically sterile. He recognized a need to strike a balance between these competing interests, it being in his view 'essential that a law designed to protect the vulnerable does not render the matrimonial home unaccept-able as security to financial institutions'.[73]

To determine where the balance between these competing interests should be struck, Lord Browne-Wilkinson sought to tackle the problem by the application of what he

---

[71] [1994] 1 A.C. 180. For the fullest accounts of the issues pertaining to this area of the law, see Fehlberg, *Sexually Transmitted Debt: Surety Experience in English Law* (Oxford, Clarendon Press, 1997); Pawlowski and Brown, *Undue Influence and the Family Home* (London, Cavendish Publishing Ltd, 2002); Enonchong, *Duress, Undue Influence and Unconscionable Dealing* (2nd edn) (London, Sweet & Maxwell, 2012), Chapters 6–12. See also M.P. Thompson in Cooke (ed.), *Modern Studies in Property Law, Volume 2* (Oxford, Hart Publishing, 2003), Chapter 7.

[72] [2001] 4 All E.R. 449.   [73] Ibid. at 188.

perceived to be first principles. At the outset, he rejected the argument which had succeeded in the Court of Appeal[74] that there was some special rule of equity that required a creditor, where a wife was standing as a surety for the debts of her husband, to ensure that she fully understood the transaction and had been separately advised prior to entering into it. Neither did he accept a previous line of authority which had sought to apply the principles of the law of agency whereby a person in the position of Mr O'Brien was regarded as being the agent of the mortgagee, so that any misconduct by him was regarded as being that of his principal. Actual cases of agency were, in this context, rightly considered to be very rare.[75] Instead, although appreciating that the present case concerned the effect of misrepresentation and not undue influence, an earlier argument based on the latter concept having been abandoned,[76] he chose to lay down how the principles of undue influence should operate in the present context. In his analysis of undue influence, Lord Browne-Wilkinson adopted the classification which had previously been employed by the Court of Appeal in *Bank of Credit and Commerce International SA v. Aboody*.[77] This categorization put cases of undue influence into either Class 1 or Class 2. Class 1 provides for actual undue influence and does not involve any form of presumption. It is not predicated upon the existence of any particular prior relationship[78] but occurs where A establishes as a fact that B has exerted undue influence on her. The establishment of this fact will, of itself, enable A to set aside the transaction between herself and B.[79] The other category is Class 2, or presumed undue influence, which was originally subdivided into Class 2(A) and Class 2(B). Cases which came within one of these categories gave rise to an evidential presumption of undue influence.

Class 2(A) presumed undue influence as a consequence of the type of relationship

The first category, which derives from the leading case of *Allcard v. Skinner*,[80] involves a situation where, because of the relationship between the two parties, the law will presume that, in certain circumstances, one of them has exerted undue influence over the other provided the transaction is not readily explicable on other grounds. The type of relationship which will cause this presumption to arise is where one party stands in a fiduciary position to the other. Relationships falling within this category include doctor and patient, solicitor and client,[81] and spiritual adviser and penitent. Where there is such a relationship and there has been a transaction between the parties to it, that alone will not mean that that transaction will be set aside. As well as proving the existence of such a relationship, the person seeking to set the transaction aside must show that there is something in that transaction which calls for an explanation. Otherwise, a small gift from one to the other, for example as a birthday or Christmas present, would be liable to be set aside: a conclusion which would be absurd.[82]

Class 2(B) presumed undue influence in a relationship of 'trust and confidence'

In Class 2(B) the initial relationship between the two parties was not one which, of itself, gave rise to any presumption of undue influence. Rather, what had to be established was the

---

[74] [1993] Q.B. 109. For criticism, see M.P. Thompson [1994] Conv. 433. The doctrine was based on *Yerkey v. Jones* (1939) 63 C.L.R. 649, an approach which has been continued in Australia: *Garcia v. National Australia Bank Ltd* (1998) 72 A.J.L.R. 1243. See P.J. Clarke [1998] All E. Rev. 271.

[75] [1994] 1 A.C. 180 at 195.   [76] Ibid. at 187.   [77] [1991] Q.B. 923 at 957 *per* Slade L.J.

[78] *Royal Bank of Scotland v. Etridge (No. 2), supra,* at [103] *per Lord Hobhouse.*

[79] The requirement laid down in *Aboody* that the complainant had also to show that the transaction was to her manifest disadvantage was overruled in *CIBC Mortgages Plc v. Pitt* [1994] 1 A.C. 200.

[80] (1887) 46 Ch.D. 145. The case concerned a nun who transferred her goods to the head of a convent.

[81] If the solicitor and client are also living together as 'domestic partners', this strengthens, rather than reduces, the presumption: see *Markham v. Karsten* [2007] EWHC 1509 (Ch) 1509 at [35] *per* Briggs J.

[82] See *Allcard v. Skinner, supra,* at 185 *per* Lindley L.J.; *Royal Bank of Scotland v. Etridge (No. 2), supra,* at [25] *per* Lord Nicholls.

de facto existence of a relationship whereby the complainant generally reposed trust and confidence in the wrongdoer.[83] Once that relationship had been established then, apparently, a presumption of undue influence arose and the onus of proof shifted to the alleged wrongdoer to show that undue influence had not occurred.[84] Lord Browne-Wilkinson said:

> In a Class 2(B) case, therefore, in the absence of evidence disproving undue influence, the complainant will succeed in setting aside the impugned transaction *merely by proof that the complainant reposed trust and confidence in the wrongdoer without having to prove that wrongdoer exerted actual undue influence or otherwise abused such trust and confidence in relation to the particular transaction impugned.*[85]

This is a question of fact, rarely overturned on appeal.[86] In *O'Brien*, Lord Browne-Wilkinson had accepted that a Class 2(B) relationship had been established on the facts between Mr and Mrs O'Brien. The mortgage was then held to be void against the bank because, as a result of the conduct of the bank official in obtaining her signature to the mortgage, it was fixed with constructive notice of the vitiating factor, in this case misrepresentation. Undue influence and misrepresentation, although different concepts, are both vitiating factors and either can be relevant to the type of situation being discussed because it is apparently the case, albeit no evidence was advanced for this assertion, that the informality of business dealings between spouses raises a substantial risk of the occurrence of misrepresentation.[87] References hereafter to undue influence should be taken to include misrepresentation.

Digressing, perhaps, herein may lie the genesis of the theoretical confusion which underpins the judgment in *O'Brien*. As a statement of law, it is wrong. In cases of category 2(A), it is not sufficient in order to raise the presumption of undue influence simply to establish a particular relationship such as solicitor/client. There must also be something in the nature of the transaction to call for an explanation. Were it otherwise, then a Christmas present from a client to a solicitor would be immediately suspect. This is not the case. Yet in *O'Brien*, Lord Browne-Wilkinson is saying that if A establishes, by actual evidence, the existence of a relationship of trust and confidence with B (a Class 2(B) case), then, without more, this places a burden upon B to disprove that a gift in his favour is not tainted by undue influence. This cannot be right.

11.5.7.2 The position of the mortgagee

In *O'Brien*, Mrs O'Brien was not relying on the existence of a vitiating factor to set aside a transaction with her husband, as would have been the case in Scenario 1 as described above. What she was arguing was that the effect of the vitiating factor was that a contract between her and her husband on one side and the bank on the other should be set aside: Scenario 3. Unfortunately, the reasoning employed in this case, which was a source of considerable confusion thereafter, was framed in terms of a Scenario 2, where A and B have entered into a transaction, which involves A either giving or selling property to B and B subsequently transfers the land for value to C. This confusion is apparent from Lord

---

[83] A *de facto* relationship may not be limited to trust and confidence but could arise out of a different basis for vulnerability, see *Malik v. Sheikh* [2018] EWHC 973, as well as intimidation, see *National Westminster Bank Plc v. Morgan* [1985] 1 A.C. 686 at 709 or 'ascendancy and dependence' in *Macklin v. Dowsett* [2004] EWCA Civ. 904.

[84] *Barclays Bank v. O'Brien* [1994] 1 A.C. 180 at 189 *per* Lord Browne-Wilkinson.

[85] Ibid. at 189–90. Emphasis supplied.

[86] Gloster L.J. in *Crossfield v. Jackson* [2014] EWCA Civ. 1548 at para. 21, though see *Malik v. Sheikh* [2018] EWHC 973.

[87] *Barclays Bank v. O'Brien* [1994] 1 A. C. 180 at 196 *per* Lord Browne-Wilkinson.

Browne-Wilkinson's analysis of the circumstances in which a mortgage was liable to be set aside. For him the central element in this was the doctrine of notice and, in particular, whether there was something in the nature of the transaction to alert the mortgagee that the consent to the mortgage had not been freely given. The importance of notice is clearly demonstrated by the decision of the House of Lords in *CIBC Mortgages plc v. Pitt*,[88] a decision given on the same day and by the same appellate panel as that in *O'Brien*.

In *Pitt*, a married couple were joint owners of their matrimonial home in which there was a very large equity. He was keen to borrow money against the security of the home to enable him to speculate on the stock market. She was very reluctant to do this but succumbed to significant pressure from him to sign the mortgage. When the application for the mortgage was made, the actual reason for the borrowing was not revealed. Instead, the purpose of the loan was said to be to pay off the small mortgage existing on the matrimonial home and to enable them to buy a holiday home. The company lent £150,000 to the Pitts, who executed a mortgage against their matrimonial home.[89] His investment policy proved to be disastrous and, when he defaulted on the mortgage, the bank sought possession. Mrs Pitt argued that the mortgage was void as against her because her signature had been secured by the use of undue influence and that the bank had neither explained the mortgage to her, nor urged her to seek independent legal advice prior to signing it.

While the House of Lords accepted that Mr Pitt had exerted undue influence on his wife, it nevertheless upheld the validity of the mortgage. The reason for this was that there was nothing in the transaction, *as it was presented to the bank*, to alert it to the fact that this was not a loan for the mutual benefit of them both. Because this appeared to be a joint venture, the mortgagee did not have constructive notice of the presence of a vitiating factor. That notice was a critical factor was stressed by Lord Browne-Wilkinson, who said:

> Even though, in my view, Mrs Pitt is entitled to set aside the transaction against Mr Pitt, she has to establish that in some way the plaintiff is affected by the wrongdoing of Mr Pitt so as to be entitled to set aside the legal charge as against the plaintiff.[90]

This had also been emphasized in *O'Brien*, where Lord Browne-Wilkinson said:

> A wife who has been influenced to stand surety for her husband's debts by his undue influence, misrepresentation or other wrong has an equity as against him to set aside that transaction. Under the ordinary principles of equity, her right to set aside that transaction will be enforceable against third parties (e.g. against a creditor) if either the husband was acting as the third party's agent or the third party had actual notice of the facts giving rise to her equity.[91]

Clearly, notice was a key issue with the mortgagee in *O'Brien* being held to have notice of an equity, whereas, in *Pitt*, it did not. The circumstances when a lender would be fixed with constructive notice were stated in *O'Brien* in the following terms:

> a creditor is put on inquiry when a wife offers to stand surety for her husband's debts by the combination of two factors: (a) the transaction is on its face not to the financial advantage of the wife; and (b) there is a substantial risk in transactions of this kind that, in procuring the wife to act as surety, the husband committed a legal or equitable wrong that entitles the wife to set aside the transaction.[92]

---

[88] [1994] 1 A.C. 200.

[89] Curiously the loan was not to be secured against the holiday home, a matter about which no comment was made: ibid. at 205.

[90] Ibid. at 210. [91] [1994] 1 A.C. 180 at 195. [92] Ibid. at 196.

The difference between the two cases was that, in *O'Brien*, the purpose of the loan was to provide finance for a company in which Mr O'Brien was heavily involved whereas, in *Pitt*, the stated purpose of the loan was to buy a holiday home, and therefore it appeared to be for their mutual benefit. In *O'Brien*, the bank was put on notice that undue influence may have been exercised so that, if a mortgage to which Mrs O'Brien was to be a party was granted then, for it to be enforceable against her, it was necessary for the bank to take precautions to ensure, so far as possible, that this had not occurred.[93] As there was nothing on the facts as presented to the bank in *Pitt*[94] to alert it to the possibility that undue influence might have been exerted on her, there was no need for the bank to take any special precautions before accepting Mrs Pitt's signature to the mortgage.

11.5.7.3 Precautions

In *O'Brien*, Lord Browne-Wilkinson set out requirements to be followed by mortgagees who were put on notice that one of the mortgagors may be subject to undue influence. In his view:

> a creditor will meet these requirements if it insists that the wife attend a prior meeting (in the absence of the husband) with a representative of the creditor at which she is told the extent of her liability as a creditor, warned of the risk she is running and urged to take legal advice.[95]

Following this decision came a veritable deluge of litigation at the heart of which was the question of whether the precautions taken by the bank had been adequate. Although this litigation was complicated by the fact that most of the transactions pre-dated *O'Brien* and Lord Browne-Wilkinson had stated that his guidelines were intended to apply to future transactions, it soon became clear that the courts were diluting them.[96] In particular, despite what had been said in *O'Brien*, in none of the subsequent litigation had an official of the bank conducted a private meeting with the wife. What became a central feature of the litigation was the independence of the legal advice and the quality of it.

11.5.7.4 Recasting undue influence in *Etridge*

While the decision in *O'Brien* was of major importance in resetting an important area of law, the manner in which it had done this was seriously flawed at both a theoretical and a practical level. The whole area was reconsidered in *Royal Bank of Scotland v. Etridge* (No.2),[97] where the House of Lords was given the opportunity to review both the appropriate principles to be applied to this area of law and also the practical issues facing lenders and legal advisers.

The decision in *Royal Bank of Scotland v. Etridge (No. 2)* involved eight conjoined appeals. In seven of them, wives who, along with their husbands, had been a party to a mortgage, argued that the mortgage should be held to be void as against them on the basis of undue influence. In the eighth, a wife was suing her solicitor in negligence, in respect of advice given to her before she signed the mortgage. In each case, the purpose of the mortgage was principally for the benefit of the husband. The stage was set for a major review of this area of law,[98] and, although a number of speeches were given, the leading speech was

---

[93] For what the bank should do, see 11.5.7.3.

[94] It is unfortunate that what the position would have been had the truth been told was not explored.

[95] *Barclays Bank plc v. O'Brien* [1994] 1 A.C. 180 at 196.

[96] See S. Wong [1998] Conv. 457 at 458. See also *Royal Bank of Scotland v. Etridge (No. 2)* [2002] 2 A.C. 773 at [113] *per* Lord Hobhouse.

[97] [2002] 2 A.C. 773.

[98] Unsurprisingly, the decision has generated considerable academic comment: see, e.g., R. Bigwood (2002) 65 M.L.R. 435; M. Haley (2002) 14 C.F.L.Q. 33, and (2010) 61 N.I.L.Q. 141; M. Oldham [2002] C.L.J. 29; M.P. Thompson [2002] Conv. 174 and in Cooke (ed.), *Modern Studies in Property Law* (Volume 2) (Oxford, Hart Publishing, 2003) Chapter 7; P. Watts (2002) 118 L.Q.R. 337.

that of Lord Nicholls and it was made clear by Lord Bingham that, whatever differences in nuance there might be between the various speeches, 'it is plain that the opinion of Lord Nicholls commands the unqualified support of the House'.[99]

Policy issues

The competing policy issues underlying this area of law were clearly articulated by Lord Nicholls. He pointed out that bank finance is the most important form of external finance for small businesses with less than ten employees. These enterprises make up about 95 per cent of businesses in this country and are responsible for nearly one-third of all employment. Finance raised by second mortgages on homes is an important source of capital for these businesses. It is important, therefore, that:

> If the freedom of home-owners to make economic use of their homes is not to be frustrated, a bank must be able to have confidence that a wife's signature of the necessary guarantee and charge will be as binding upon her as is the signature of anyone else on documents which he or she may sign. Otherwise banks will not be willing to lend money on the security of a jointly owned house or flat.[100]

As against this, it was recognized that the marriage relationship is normally characterized by a high degree of trust and confidence and that there is scope for that trust and confidence to be abused. In particular, a husband, anxious, or even desperate, for finance may misstate the financial position or mislead his wife and it was considered that the 'law would be seriously defective if it did not recognise these realities'.[101] The task, therefore, as had been the case in *O'Brien*, was to strike a balance between the desire to protect potentially vulnerable parties in respect of financial transactions affecting their homes while, at the same time, not making the degree of protection such that financial institutions were no longer prepared to advance finance against the security of a family home. As Lord Bingham put it:

> The law must afford both parties a measure of protection. It cannot prescribe a code which will be proof against error, misunderstanding or mishap. But it can indicate minimum standards which, if met, will reduce the risk of error, misunderstanding or mishap to an acceptable level. The paramount need in this important area is that these minimum requirements should be clear, simple and practically operable.[102]

The critical question in *Etridge* was whether the wife stood surety for *her husband's debts*. This is a much clearer situation than where a wife stands as surety for company debts in which both she and her husband hold shares, which may, or may not be, a joint loan.[103] In cases where money is advanced jointly to husband and wife, the lender is *not* put on enquiry unless it 'is aware that that the loan is being made for the husband's purposes, as distinct from their joint purposes'.[104]

11.5.7.5 Establishment of a wrong

Undue influence is dependent on a wrong. As Andrew Hochhauser Q.C. remarked in *Ennis v. Thompson*:

> It is trite law that not all influence is undue: it is usual for spouses to influence each other. Undue influence, by sharp contrast, is an equitable wrong.[105]

---

[99] [2001] 4 All E.R. 449 at [3] *per* Lord Bingham.   [100] Ibid. at [36] *per* Lord Nicholl.
[101] Ibid.   [102] [2001] 4 All E.R. 449 at [2].   [103] *Etridge*, at [49].
[104] Lord Nicholls, Etridge [48], noting that this was decided in *CIBC Mortgages plc v. Pitt* [1994] 1 A.C. 200.
[105] *Ennis Property Finance Ltd v. Thompson* [2018] EWHC 1929 (Ch) at [242] *per* Andrew Hochhauser Q.C.

Influence itself is unexceptional. This 'undue' part, can be either actual or presumed and in *Etridge*, Lord Nicholls distinguished the two forms of undue influence as follows:

> The first comprises overt acts of improper pressure or coercion such as unlawful threats . . . The second form arises out of a relationship between two persons where one has acquired over another a measure of Influence, or ascendancy, of which the ascendant person then takes unfair advantage.[106]

Etridge retains the broad distinction but shifts towards a question of evidential burden rather than one of rigid categorization.

11.5.7.6 Burden of proof

Normally, if someone wishes to set aside a transaction entered into between two parties on the basis of undue influence exerted by the wrongdoer, the burden of proof is on the complainant to establish that undue influence occurred. Proof that first there was a relationship of trust between the two, and then that the transaction is such that it calls for an explanation, is normally sufficient to discharge the onus of proof.

The relationship of trust and confidence is not limited to trust and confidence in financial affairs.[107] In the case of certain relationships, however, which it was accepted do not include husband and wife, the courts are prepared to assume that the relationship is one of trust and confidence. What must then be shown is a transaction between them that calls for an explanation. Once this has been done, there is a presumption of undue influence that it is then for the other party to rebut. If this cannot be done, the transaction is liable to be set aside. These cases, which almost invariably involve only two parties and were previously classified as belonging to Class 2(A), are unaffected by *Etridge*.

Once the burden has been shifted in this way, the onus then shifts to the alleged wrongdoer to show that undue influence has not taken place.[108] In cases of both actual and presumed undue influence, the complainant must prove the undue influence. However, while in actual undue influence cases the burden stays with the complainant throughout, in presumed undue influence cases, once the complainant can satisfy their burden by proving first, that there was a relationship of trust and confidence and second, that there was a transaction not readily to be accounted for by the ordinary motives of people in that relationship, then the burden shifts to the lender. This reframing of the approach in *Etridge* from the Class 2A and 2B distinction in *O'Brien* to one of evidential burden, moving beyond a rigid categorization is a key feature of the case.[109]

If the presumption of undue influence is rebutted the transaction can stand[110] but it is the person seeking to set aside a particular transaction who must establish the existence of a wrong.[111] If the presumption of undue influence is not rebutted, the transaction cannot stand. These are profoundly fact-sensitive decisions.[112]

---

[106] *Etridge*, at [8].

[107] See *Thompson v. Foy* [2009] EWHC 1076 (Ch) at [100] *per* Lewison J.

[108] *Royal Bank of Scotland (No. 2) v. Etridge* [2001] 4 All E.R. 449 at [459]. See also *Turkey v. Awadh* [2005] EWCA Civ. 382 at [38]–[39] *per* Chadwick L.J.

[109] See Lord Nicholls at para. 18, Lord Hobhouse at para. 107, and Lord Scott at para. 161

[110] See *Smith v. Cooper* [2010] EWCA Civ. 722 at [61] *per* Lloyd L.J.

[111] Ibid. at [87] *per* Lord Nicholls; at [107] *per* Lord Hobhouse; at [146] *per* Lord Scott. See also *Habib Bank Ltd v. Tufail* [2006] EWCA Civ. 374 at [11] *per* Lloyd L.J.).

[112] *Pesticcio v. Branbury* [2006] EWCA Civ. 1868; *Turkey v. Awadh* [2005] EWCA Civ. 382; *Thompson v. Foy* [2009] EWHC 1076; and *Ennis v. Thompson* [2018] EWHC 1929 (Ch).

11.5.7.7 The *Etridge* guidelines

One effect of *Etridge* was to lower the threshold as to when a mortgagee must take precautions to ensure that the potential complainant is protected from the possibilities of undue influence or misrepresentation being exercised. It is no longer necessary to demonstrate that a particular transaction is not to the complainant's financial advantage. It will suffice simply to show a non-commercial relationship and that the transaction is not for a mutual purpose. The opportunity was also taken in *Etridge* to review the precautions the bank must take when that threshold has been crossed.[113]

Private meeting

The House of Lords accepted that, despite what had been said in *O'Brien*, banks did not have a private meeting with the wife prior to her signing the mortgage. Provided that the mortgagee 'has taken reasonable steps to satisfy itself that the wife has had brought home to her in a meaningful way, the practical implications of the proposed transaction',[114] it will be protected and it is not essential that the mortgagee conduct this private meeting.

Independent legal advice

The clearest way to demonstrate that that the transaction was not procured by undue influence is to show that the claimant received independent legal advice. After *O'Brien*, provided a solicitor was prepared to certify that he had provided legal advice to the wife before she signed the mortgage, then, in virtually every case, the bank's interest would be protected. This was so, even if the solicitor was acting for the potential wrongdoer,[115] the company with which the wrongdoer was associated,[116] or even, so it seemed, for the mortgagee, itself.[117] The only exception to this appeared to be if the mortgagee was privy to information concerning the transaction which it does not communicate to the solicitor.[118] There may also occur exceptional cases where it is glaringly obvious that the wife is being grievously wronged.[119] In such a case, the proper course for the solicitor is to refuse to act for the wife. In *Etridge*, Lord Nicholls considered whether it was acceptable for the same solicitor to act for both parties to the transaction. He could see arguments both ways, contrasting the potential for a conflict of interest with the question of cost. Obviously, it would add to the expense of the transaction if, in every case, the bank, to protect its own interests, had to insist that a different solicitor represented both husband and wife. On balance, Lord Nicholls felt that the latter point outweighed the former and he considered it to be acceptable for the same solicitor to act for both parties. He stressed, however, that the solicitor must be clear that, when advising the wife, he is acting solely in her interests and that if he feels at any stage in that advice that there is a conflict of interest he must cease to act for her.[120]

---

[113] For an interesting discussion of the positive impact of *Etridge* on bank lending practice, see J. Wadsley [2003] L.M.C.L.Q. 341. The Guidelines are now incorporated in the Banks' Revised Voluntary Code of Practice (2013), paras 30.1–32.2.

[114] *Royal Bank of Scotland v. Etridge (No. 2)* [2002] 2 A.C. 773 at 467 *per* Lord Nicholls.

[115] *Midland Bank plc v. Serter* [1995] 1 F.L.R. 1034; *Ennis v. Thompson* [2018] EWHC 1929 (Ch).

[116] *Banco Exterior International v. Mann* [1995] 1 All E.R. 936, criticized by A. Dunn [1995] Conv. 325 at 330–2.

[117] *Halifax Building Society v. Stepsky* [1997] 1 All E.R. 46; *Barclays Bank plc v. Thomson* [1997] 4 All E.R. 816, criticized by M.P. Thompson [1997] Conv. 216.

[118] *Northern Rock Building Society v. Archer* (1998) 78 P. & C.R. 65; M.P. Thompson [1999] Conv. 510.

[119] *Royal Bank of Scotland v. Etridge (No. 2)* [2002] 2 A.C. 773 at [62] *per* Lord Nicholls. For an example, see *Credit Lyonnais Nederland N.V. v. Burch* [1997] 1 All E.R. 144.

[120] Ibid. at [74]. See also at [96] *per* Lord Clyde.

Provision of information

Lord Nicholls was aware that, although a certificate from a solicitor that he had advised the wife had been sufficient to protect the mortgagee, on many occasions the advice which had been given was of poor quality. This was something which he regarded as the most disturbing feature of some of the appeals he was considering,[121] and amounted to little more than what Sir Anthony Mason had described as the 'ritual reliance on the provision of legal advice'.[122] In an effort to make this advice more useful, he laid down a practice which the lending institutions should follow to protect their position. In so doing, he made it clear that these guidelines were to operate prospectively:[123]

> In respect of past transactions, the bank will ordinarily be regarded as having discharged its obligations if a solicitor who was acting for the wife in the transaction gave the bank confirmation to the effect that he had brought home to the wife the risks she was running by standing surety.[124]

When security is being sought from a wife in respect of her husband's debts, Lord Nicholls stressed that it is necessary for the bank to communicate directly with her.[125] In that communication, the mortgagee should make clear that it will require written confirmation from a solicitor, acting for her, that the transaction, its effects, and practical implications have been explained to her and that the effect of this confirmation will be that she will not be able, subsequently, to dispute the validity of the mortgage. She will be asked to nominate her solicitor, and that solicitor may be the same person who is acting for her husband. Until an appropriate response is received from her, the mortgagee should not go ahead with the transaction. This procedure would preclude the mortgagee from using its own legal department to advise the wife, and it is also inadequate for a bank to instruct a solicitor to attend to the formalities of the transaction on its behalf. The solicitor will then be seen as the agent of the bank and any deficiencies in the advice given will be attributed to the mortgagee.[126]

The duties of the mortgagee do not stop there. Once a solicitor has been nominated, the bank must furnish that person with sufficient information for him to be in a position to advise her fully. To this end, the bank must supply the solicitor with financial information concerning the husband and a copy of the mortgage application. This information is, as between the bank and the husband, confidential and the bank cannot release it without his consent. If that consent is not forthcoming, however, then the mortgagee should not proceed further with the proposed transaction.[127]

These precautions are designed to strike an acceptable balance between the interests of the mortgagee and the wife and would seem to do so. They are to be applied in normal cases of mortgage applications. Where the potential complainant is, to the knowledge of

---

[121] Ibid. at [68].   [122] Cited by Sir Peter Millett (1998) 114 L.Q.R. 214 at 220.

[123] It is unusual for judgments to operate in this way. The normal position is that they state what the law has always been. For a striking example, see *Kleinwort Benson Ltd v. Lincoln City Council* [1999] 2 A.C. 349. See M.P. Thompson [1999] Conv. 40. For a full discussion of prospective decisions, see *In re Spectrum Plus Ltd (in liquidation)* [2005] 2 A.C. 680.

[124] [2001] 2 A.C. 773 at [80]. See also *Bank of Scotland v. Hill* [2002] EWCA Civ. 1081; *First National Bank plc v. Achampong* [2003] EWCA Civ. 487. See M.P. Thompson [2003] Conv. 314.

[125] [2002] 2 A.C. 773 at [79]. See also *HSBC Bank plc v. Brown* [2015] EWHC 359 (Ch), where the Bank failed to do this.

[126] *National Westminster Bank plc v. Amin* [2002] 1 F.L.R. 735 at 741–2 *per* Lord Scott. See M. Haley [2002] Conv. 499.

[127] [2002] 2 A.C. 773 at [79].

the bank, particularly vulnerable, however, this should be made known to the solicitor acting for her, so that additional care may be taken in advising her.[128]

The role of the solicitor

Provided that the mortgagee follows the guidelines laid down by Lord Nicholls, and receives a certificate from the solicitor to the effect that the wife has been fully advised, the complainant will not be able to argue that the mortgage is liable to be set aside.[129] It may, however, be the case that there is a cause of action against the solicitor if, contrary to the certificate, this is not actually the case. Guidance was given by Lord Nicholls as to what the role of the solicitor is. He should see her separately from her husband and explain the transaction to her in non-technical language. He should explain the consequences which will follow if the mortgage payments are not met. He should also explore with her the financial position of her husband and the amount being borrowed and, above all, make it clear to her that she has a choice as to whether to proceed with the transaction. She should be asked if she is happy for the solicitor to confirm to the mortgagee that she has been fully advised and wishes to proceed, or whether she wishes the solicitor to negotiate on her behalf with the mortgagee. If she wishes to proceed, then the solicitor can go ahead and give the requisite confirmation to the bank.[130]

11.5.7.8 Obligation of candour

In *Etridge*, Lord Nicholls was clear that the real purpose of the guidelines being introduced was not to provide a test as to whether or not the mortgagee had notice of a prior wrongdoing: it was to seek to ensure, so far as one could, that no wrong was committed in the first place. This can be seen from his comments explaining why banks should take certain precautions. He said:

> The furthest a bank can be expected to go is to take reasonable steps to satisfy itself that the wife has had brought home to her, in a meaningful way, the practical implications of the proposed transaction. This does not wholly eliminate the risk of undue influence or misrepresentation. But it does mean that a wife enters into a transaction with her eyes open so far as the basic elements of the transaction are concerned.[131]

Here one sees a greater emphasis on the need for informed consent rather than that of notice of a wrong. This is possibly the best explanation of the odd decision in *Hewett v. First Plus Financial Group Ltd*.[132] A husband persuaded his wife to sign a mortgage over the matrimonial home, the purpose of that loan being to provide security for his credit card debts. There was no evidence that the nature of the transaction had been misrepresented to her or that he had exerted undue influence upon her. He did, however, fail to reveal to her that he was, at the time, having an affair. The Court of Appeal held that this non-disclosure amounted to a significant breach of trust and confidence. The mortgage in favour of the bank, which had not followed the procedures laid down in *Etridge*, was set aside.

This is hard to follow. Failure to disclose marital infidelity is not a legal wrong. While it is true that, had she known the truth, his wife would almost certainly not have signed the mortgage, that is not the relevant test. The questions are whether some legal wrong was

---

[128] See *National Westminster Bank plc v. Amin* [2002] 1 F.L.R. 735. Here, the parents of the mortgagor spoke no English. This is not a very good example, however, as surely this fact would have been obvious to the solicitor. See also *Burbank Securities Ltd v. Wong* [2008] EWHC 553 (Ch) where the complainant who was suffering from cerebral palsy had obvious problems of cognition.

[129] See also *Ennis Property Finance Ltd v. Thompson* [2018] EWHC 1929 (Ch) at [242].

[130] [2002] A.C. 773 at [62].   [131] [2002] 2 A.C. 773 at [54].   [132] [2010] EWCA Civ. 312.

done to her and did the mortgagee have notice of that wrong. As the answer to the first question would seem to be no, the second question should not have arisen. In this case, the best explanation of the case is that, it being apparent that the bank had taken no steps at all to establish that the wife had given informed consent to the mortgage, the court was reluctant to allow the mortgage to stand. This was despite it, first, being difficult to see that any legally relevant wrong had occurred between the husband and wife and, second, even had the bank followed the *Etridge* guidelines, it was highly unlikely that the true position would, prior to the mortgage, have come to light.

The current position, which bases the law on the existence of some vitiating factor, remains unsatisfactory. It really should not be open to lending institutions which have failed to follow clear guidelines laid down by the House of Lords and encapsulated within the voluntary Code of Practice to argue that this failure did not matter because, on the facts, no vitiating factor has been established. A better, and more straightforward, rule would be to be clear that, as a matter of the law of contract, in the circumstances when the *Etridge* guidelines are applicable and not followed, the contract should be regarded as voidable at the instance of the surety and it should not also be necessary to establish the existence of some legal wrong. Notwithstanding the comment by Lord Nicholls in Etridge that 'the decision in *O'Brien* is directed at a class of contracts which has special features of its own,[133] it is possibly too late for the law to accept the position that the focus should simply be on the formation of this type of contract without regard to the need to find the presence of some legal wrong.

11.5.7.9 Failure to comply with the guidelines

Lord Nicholls spelled out with considerable care the procedures which a lending institution should follow when lending against the security of the matrimonial home. Similarly, although this is a matter between the wife and the solicitor rather than the wife and the mortgagee, what is expected of the legal advisor was also laid down in some detail. The question as to what the position would be should the bank fail to comply with the *Etridge* guidelines would seem, therefore, to be an easy one to answer: the mortgage would be liable to be set aside at the behest of the complainant. This however, may not be the case. Lord Nicholls said that 'If the bank or other creditor does not take these steps, it is deemed to have notice of any claim that the guarantor may have that the transaction was procured by undue influence or misrepresentation on behalf of the debtor.'[134]

It will be observed that this, once again, uses the language of a mortgagee having notice of a wrong. Although notice is not being used in the same way as it was in *O'Brien*, where it was, wrongly, employed to decide whether a purchaser was bound by a pre-existing equity, it does play an important role. Its role appears to be that, if the mortgagee has notice of a wrong, then it cannot enforce the mortgage directly against the complainant; it is a matter which goes to the formation of the contract which underlies the mortgage. This does, however, leave open the logically anterior question of the establishment of an initial wrong and it is here that one finds that, on a theoretical level at least, there is an uneasy hybrid between principles of undue influence and the creation of contracts.

11.5.7.10 The effect of a vitiating factor

An important issue, particularly when the vitiating factor is misrepresentation rather than undue influence, is whether the effect of the misrepresentation is that the mortgage can be avoided entirely by the misrepresentee, or whether it will be upheld up to the limit of that person's understanding of the transaction. The point, which appeared to have been

---

[133] [2002] 2 A.C. 733 at [43]. [134] [2002] 2 A.C. 733 at [87].

decided in *O'Brien*, is now settled: the mortgage will be regarded as voidable.[135] If a mortgage is tainted by the existence of a vitiating factor then a second mortgage used to redeem the first will be similarly tainted.[136]

In *Santander UK Plc v. Fletcher*, where a son had fraudulently induced his mother to enter into a mortgage after transferring her property into their joint names, the bank acquired an enforceable equitable charge over his beneficial interest arising from the declaration of trust in the transfer deed, even though the mortgage was void for undue influence.[137]

11.6 The rights and remedies of the mortgagee

The mortgagee has actions available to him to recover the money owed. These actions can be divided into personal actions and proprietary actions; the former being the rights that the mortgagee has, personally, against the mortgagor, while the latter concern the rights and remedies exercisable against the mortgaged property.

11.6.1 The covenant to repay

A mortgage is granted to secure a loan. One option for a mortgagee is to sue the mortgagor, personally, for repayment of that loan. Ordinarily, the mortgagee does not do this, it being preferable to utilize his more favourable position as a secured creditor. There are two situations, however, where the mortgagee may wish to pursue his personal remedy against the mortgagor either in conjunction with his rights as a secured creditor or as an alternative to such rights.

The remedies of a mortgagee have always been regarded as being cumulative; that is, subject to the nature of the remedy which has been pursued, the mortgagee may avail himself of more than one remedy in order to secure the repayment of what is owed. So, if the mortgagee has secured a sale of the property and the proceeds of sale are insufficient to discharge the debt, the mortgagee can pursue a personal remedy against the mortgagor in respect of the balance.[138] In cases of negative equity, this is an additional option available to mortgagees if a sale of the property has failed to realize sufficient money to repay in full all that is owed.

A second situation where the availability of a personal action against the mortgagor will potentially be of value to the mortgagee is where he is unable to pursue his rights as a secured creditor. This may be because, as in *Williams & Glyn's Bank Ltd v. Boland*,[139] a third party has rights in the property with priority to the mortgagee.[140] The remedy open to the bank in this situation would be to sue Mr Boland on his personal covenant to repay the loan. If, as is probable, he would be unable to pay this sum, then a petition for bankruptcy could be lodged and, if granted, upon the adjudication of bankruptcy the trustee in bankruptcy would then petition the court for a sale of the property. Unless there were exceptional circumstances, this petition would almost certainly be granted a year after the date of the bankruptcy. While it is true that the wife would be entitled to her share of the

---

[135] *Bank Melli Iran v. Samadi-Rad* [1995] 2 F.L.R. 367; *TSB Bank plc v. Camfield* [1995] Conv. 325. See A. Dunn [1995] Conv. 325; P. Ferguson (1995) 111 L.Q.R. 555.

[136] *Yorkshire Bank plc v. Tinsley* [2004] 3 All E.R. 363. See M.P. Thompson [2004] Conv. 399.

[137] [2018] EWHC 2778 (Ch).

[138] *Rudge v. Richards* (1873) L.R. 8 C.P. 358; *Palk v. Mortgage Services Funding plc* [1993] Ch. 330 at 337 *per* Sir Donald Nicholls V.-C.

[139] [1981] A.C. 487.　　[140] See 5.1.5.3.

proceeds of sale first, the bank would still be able to recover a significant amount of that which was owed and in *Alliance &. Leicester plc v. Slayford*,[141] the Court of Appeal held that a mortgagee could do precisely this. Were this not to be the case, the mortgagee would be in a worse position as a secured creditor than would be the case if the loan had not been secured: a position which would be absurd.[142]

11.6.2 **Possession**

While the most usual way for a mortgagee to enforce his security is by procuring a sale of the property, the mortgagee will usually first obtain possession[143] as it is difficult to sell a property if it remains occupied by the mortgagor.

11.6.2.1 **The right to possession**

A mortgagee has an inherent right of possession. Although it is easy to see the taking of possession by the mortgagee as a remedy available to him as a secured creditor, juridically, this is not correct. It is a right and not a remedy. Harman J. put this in stark terms in an oft-quoted passage in *Four-Maids v. Dudley Marshall (Properties) Ltd*:

> the right of a mortgagee to possession in the absence of some contract has nothing to do with default on the part of the mortgagor. The mortgagee may go into possession before the ink is dry on the mortgage unless there is something in the mortgage, express or by implication, whereby he has contracted out of that right.[144]

At one time, the courts sought to modify the mortgagee's inherent right of possession by invoking its jurisdiction to adjourn possession proceedings so that, 'in proper cases the wind was tempered for the shorn lamb, time being given for payment and so forth'.[145] This claimed jurisdiction did not, however, command general assent, and the traditional perspective that the possession was a right and not a remedy was re-established in 1962 in *Birmingham Citizens Permanent Building Society v. Caunt*.[146]

The mortgagee's inherent right of possession caused potential difficulties for mortgagors since although in practice possession would only be sought if there was default, this was not necessarily required. The position of a mortgagor was then less favourable than that of a tenant who was in arrears with the rent where, if the landlord sought to forfeit the lease, the tenant had considerable scope on paying off the arrears to obtain relief against forfeiture.[147] As a consequence of the mortgagee's inherent right of possession, there was no such jurisdiction in the case of mortgage arrears. To rectify this anomaly, the 1969 Payne Committee[148] recommended legislation giving a court discretion to suspend or postpone possession proceedings if there appeared to be a realistic chance of the mortgagor being able, within a reasonable period of time, to pay off the arrears while continuing to service the mortgage payments.

---

[141] [2001] 1 All E.R. (Comm) 1. See M.P. Thompson [2002] Conv. 53. See also *First National Bank plc v. Achampong* [2003] EWCA Civ. 487.

[142] See *Cheltenham &. Gloucester Building Society v. Grattidge* (1993) 25 H.L.R. 454 at 457 *per* Hoffmann L.J.

[143] But not always, see *Horsham Properties Group Ltd v. Clark* [2009] 1 W.L.R. 1255.

[144] *Four-Maids Ltd v. Dudley Marshall (Properties) Ltd* [1957] Ch. 317 at 320. See, generally, M. Haley (1997) 17 L.S. 483.

[145] *Redditch Benefit Building Society v. Roberts* [1940] Ch. 415 at 420 *per* Clauson L.J.

[146] *Birmingham Citizens Permanent Building Society v. Caunt* [1962] Ch. 863. See R.E.M. (1962) 78 L.Q.R. 171.

[147] See 10.10.3.   [148] Enforcement of Judgment Debts (1969), Cmnd. 3909.

11.6.2.2 **The Administration of Justice Acts**

Under s. 36 of the Administration of Justice Act 1970,[149] where a mortgagee under a mortgage of land, which consists of or includes a dwelling-house,[150] brings an action for possession, the court is given the power to adjourn the proceedings or, on making an order for possession, stay or suspend execution of the order or postpone the date for delivery of possession for such period or periods as the court thinks reasonable.[151] These powers may be exercised if it appears to the court that the mortgagor is likely to be able, within a reasonable period of time, to pay any sums due under the mortgage or to remedy a default[152] consisting of any breach of any other obligation arising under or by virtue of the mortgage.

In *Ropaigealach v. Barclays Bank plc*,[153] the borrowers did not live in the property and the house was sold after peaceful possession had been taken. While this set of facts made it somewhat difficult to see how the AJA 1970 could apply retrospectively,[154] Chadwick L.J. held that in enacting the AJA 1970, Parliament cannot have meant that 'the mortgagee's common law right to take possession by virtue of his estate should only be exercisable with the assistance of the court'. This confirmed that despite the introduction of the AJA 1970, the mortgagee's common law right of possession remained. More recently, in *Goldhill Finance v. Berry*[155] it was held that the common law right to possession does not continue once the lender has made an application under the AJA 1970. H.H.J. Monty Q.C. concluded that: 'Once court proceedings have been started and once an order under section 36 has been made suspending the warrant, it is no longer open to the mortgagee to exercise its common law right to possession.'[156] The right to possession is consequently ended once an application for a possession order is made under the AJA 1970, particularly if, as in *Goldhill*, the court suspends the order to possession (otherwise the court's decision would be rendered irrelevant).

11.6.2.3 **'Any sums due'**

Although the aim of s. 36 of the AJA 1970 was tolerably clear—to allow a mortgagor who had got into arrears with the mortgage repayments a reasonable time to in which to clear those arrears—one potential problem was unforeseen. This was that certain mortgages included default clauses whereby, in the event that the mortgagor failed to pay one or two instalments, the whole sum borrowed would become payable immediately.[157] These clauses are not intended to be taken literally but are included in some mortgages as a means of ensuring that the statutory power of sale arises.[158] The question arose, however, as to the effect of such clauses on the judicial approach to s. 36. Did 'any sums due' mean the missed the whole sum that was no payable or just the arrears?

---

[149] For commentary, see M. Haley (1997) 17 L.S. 483; M. Dixon (1998) 18 L.S. 279.

[150] The date to determine whether the property consists of a dwelling-house is the date of the hearing: *Royal Bank of Scotland v. Miller* [2002] Q.B. 225.

[151] Even were the Human Rights Act relevant to an action between two private individuals, the existence of this discretion would make it unarguable that any order for possession could be disproportionate: see *Barclays Bank plc v. Alcorn* [2002] EWHC 498 (Ch) at [26] *per* Hart J.

[152] It has since been held that the court has jurisdiction under the Act even if the mortgagor is not in default: *Western Bank Ltd v. Schindler* [1977] Ch. 1.

[153] [1999] 4 All E.R. 235. See A. Dunn [1999] Conv. 263.

[154] See also *Horsham Properties Group Ltd v. Clark* [2009] 1 W.L.R. 1255.

[155] *Goldhill Finance Ltd v. Cynthia Berry* 2018 WL 05650000

[156] *Goldhill Finance Ltd v. Berry*, 2018 WL 05650000 (2018) at [71].

[157] If such an early payment is called for without default, this may be struck out as being inconsistent with the general terms of the mortgage which envisages payment over a prolonged period: *Alexander v. West Bromwich Building Society* [2016] EWCA Civ. 496.

[158] See 11.6.5.1.

In *Halifax Building Society v. Clark*,[159] the payment of two instalments had been missed leading to arrears of £72.97. The effect of the default clause was that the full some owing under the mortgage, some £1,420.58, became payable. It was held that the sum due under the mortgage was the larger of the two amounts. To make matters worse, it was further held that there was no prospect of this being paid within a reasonable period of time, taken to be a matter of months,[160] and there was no jurisdiction to postpone possession.

This decision threatened to stultify the purpose of the Act[161] and led directly to the passing of s. 8 of the Administration of Justice Act 1973, which provides that:

> Where [a] mortgagor is entitled or is to be permitted to pay the principal sum secured by instalments or otherwise to defer payment of it in whole or in part, but provision is also made for earlier payment in the event of any default by the mortgagor or of a demand by the mortgagee or otherwise, the, for the purposes of section 36 of the Administration of Justice Act 1970 ... a court may treat as due under the mortgage on account of the principal sum secured and of interest on it only such amounts as the mortgagor would have expected to be required to pay if there had been no such provision for earlier payment.

Section 8(2) then makes clear that the court shall not exercise its powers under the 1970 Act unless, in addition to paying off within a reasonable time the arrears which have accumulated, the mortgagor is also able to meet the payments which he would ordinarily have expected to make under the mortgage. In other words, the payments schedule must be such as will meet the normal repayments had there been no default and such as is necessary to clear the arrears within a reasonable time.

11.6.2.4 Mortgages to which the Administration of Justice Acts apply

For a second time, although the objective of the section is clear, the meaning of the words used was not. In particular, it is far from obvious what is meant by the expression 'being permitted to defer payment'. In *Habib Bank Ltd v. Tailor*,[162] Mr Tailor had a bank overdraft secured by a mortgage against his house. It was a term of the mortgage that the loan was repayable on demand. After he exceeded his overdraft limit, the bank called in the whole loan. He argued that s. 8 was applicable and that he should be allowed a reasonable period within which to repay the amount by which he had exceeded his overdraft. This was rejected. The Court of Appeal held that he was not entitled to defer payment and so the calling in of the entire loan did not, in effect, operate as a default clause. The money only became due when the bank required payment and, therefore, this did not amount to a demand for earlier payment.

While, on the facts, this seems eminently sensible, the reasoning was thought to create a problem with respect to endowment mortgages. In the case of such mortgages, the capital sum is not repayable until the end of the agreed mortgage term. Thereafter, there is no provision for any deferment of payment. If, because the mortgagor defaulted on the payment of either interest or the endowment policy, the capital sum borrowed became payable, it was arguable that s. 8 did not apply at all because the mortgage was not one whereby the mortgagor had been permitted to defer payment. Faced with this argument, in *Bank of*

---

[159] [1973] 2 All E.R. 33.

[160] For a more sensible interpretation which would have avoided this problem by taking as a reasonable period the anticipated length of the mortgage, see *First Middlesbrough Trading and Mortgage Co. Ltd v. Cunningham* (1974) 28 P. & C.R. 29. See 11.6.2.5.

[161] See H.L. Deb., vol. 338, col. 398 *per* Lord Hailsham L.C. This debate contains some unusual and touching expressions of ignorance by senior lawyers.

[162] [1982] 1 W.L.R. 1218. For a penetrating discussion of the problems caused by these statutory provisions, see S. Tromans [1984] Conv. 91.

Scotland v. Grimes,[163] the Court of Appeal, first, accepted that *Tailor* was correctly decided. Although unable to come to any conclusion as to the meaning of the words 'permitted to defer payment',[164] the court adopted a purposive construction to the interpretation of a section and distinguished *Tailor*. It was held that where it was envisaged that the mortgage would not be repaid for twenty-five years, the mortgagor was permitted to defer payment. A sensible distinction has been drawn between mortgages to be repaid either by instalments or through an endowment policy over a prolonged period, and mortgages where the reality of the transaction is that the amount borrowed is repayable on demand. In other words, the Administration of Justice Acts will apply to all mortgages commonly used to finance the purchase of a home.

11.6.2.5 The exercise of discretion under the 1970 Act

How the court will exercise its discretion will, to a considerable extent, depend upon the facts of individual cases which may, themselves, be influenced by the different practices of lending institutions, who display quite varied reactions to instances of mortgage default in terms of how readily they will seek to enforce their rights as secured creditors,[165] although the position has been improved by the introduction of the Pre-Action Protocol for Possession Claims based on Mortgage or Home Purchase Plan Arrears in Respect of Residential Property[166] promulgated in November 2008. The Protocol describes the behaviour that the court will normally expect of the parties prior to the start of a possession action, although its existence does not alter the parties' rights and obligations.[167] The overall aims of the Protocol are to ensure that the lender and borrower act fairly towards one another, and to encourage more pre-action contact between the parties.[168] In particular, the lender should then provide the borrower with information pertaining to the mortgage arrears, and be prepared to consider proposals from the borrower in respect of changes to manner of repayments.[169]

For the court to have any discretion at all under the Acts, the mortgagor must show the ability to pay off the arrears within a reasonable time. This is a jurisdictional issue.[170] Once that hurdle has been cleared, the issue becomes one of discretion. Although much will depend on the facts of individual cases, some general principles have emerged. First, the court should not grant an open-ended postponement of a possession order; a finite period must be stipulated by the end of which the arrears should be paid off, together with the payments which would normally be expected under the mortgage.[171] Second, any counterclaim that the mortgagor might have against the mortgagee is to be disregarded: the two actions are seen as independent of each other,[172] and it has been said recently that the position is clearly established that a mortgagor has no right to rely upon cross-claims and equitable set off in answer to a mortgagee's reliance upon a legal charge.[173] This is the

---

[163] [1985] Q.B. 1179.

[164] Ibid. at 1188 *per* Sir John Arnold P. See also *Royal Bank of Scotland v. Miller* [2002] Q.B. 225.

[165] See L. Whitehouse in Jackson and Wilde (eds), *The Reform of Property Law* (Dartmouth, Ashgate, 1997), Chapter 9 and in Bright and Dewar (eds), *Land Law: Themes and Perspectives* (Oxford, Oxford University Press, 1998), Chapter 7.

[166] 48th update to the Civil Procedure Rules.   [167] Ibid., paras 1.1–1.2.

[168] Ibid., para. 2.1.   [169] Ibid., para. 5.

[170] See *Jameer v. Paratus AMC* [2012] EWCA Civ. 1924 at [11] *per* Lewison L.J. See also *Zinda v. Bank of Scotland* [2011] EWCA Civ. 706.

[171] *Royal Trust Co. of Canada v. Markham* [1975] 1 W.L.R. 1416.

[172] *Citibank Trust Ltd v. Ayivor* [1987] 1 W.L.R. 1157; *National Westminster Bank plc v. Skelton* [1993] 1 W.L.R. 72n. Cf. *Ashley Guarantee plc v. Zacaria* [1993] 1 All E.R. 254 and *Banfield v. Leeds Building Society* [2007] EWCA Civ. 1369 at [66] *per* Lawrence Collins L.J.

[173] *Day v. Tiuta International Ltd* [2014] EWHC 4583 (Ch) at [19] *per* Sales J. See also *Dunbar Assets plc v. Dookas Holdings Ltd* [2013] EWCA Civ. 864 at [22] *per* Briggs L.J.

case even if the counterclaim is based upon an alleged breach of the Mortgage Conduct of Business Rules.[174] A third point is that the court should look realistically at the mortgagor's financial situation. In particular, it should not sanction the postponement of a possession order that is not based upon a realistic assessment of the situation. It is improper either for the court to make an order for payments which, while it would clear the arrears and meet the ongoing payments, is one which the mortgagor cannot afford, or, alternatively, make an order which the mortgagor could afford but would not, within a reasonable period of time, enable the arrears to be cleared while also servicing the normal mortgage repayments.[175] In assessing the financial situation of the mortgagor, regard should not be had to speculative windfalls, such as winning the pools (or, nowadays, the lottery) or receiving a large legacy,[176] or the hope, at some time in the future, of securing highly paid employment.[177]

Reasonable period

A key issue in the exercise of discretion under the Act was the period of time that a court was prepared to accept as being reasonable in which to pay off the accumulated arrears. Although in one case,[178] the Court of Appeal accepted that this was essentially a matter for the judgment of county court judges and that their exercise of discretion would not be interfered with unless it was clearly wrong, in the leading case of *Cheltenham and Gloucester Building Society v. Norgan*[179] clear guidelines were laid down as to how this discretion should be exercised. This is far preferable to the earlier approach of allowing trial judges a wide general discretion, the consequence of which would be to lead to different results being reached in essentially similar cases.

In *Cheltenham and Gloucester Building Society v. Norgan*, Mrs Norgan had experienced constant difficulty in meeting the mortgage payments and, on several occasions, actions for possession had been brought and orders had been made but, in the exercise of the statutory discretion, postponed. Finally, although the amount of the arrears was disputed, another action for possession was brought and this time was granted. Mrs Norgan appealed.

Whole term

It was recognized that a practice had developed whereby a period of two to four years had been accepted as being the maximum which would be allowed to the mortgagor to pay off the arrears.[180] The opportunity was taken to introduce a new policy. It was accepted that, in assessing what is a reasonable period by which to postpone a possession order to enable arrears to be paid off, the starting point should be the agreed length of the mortgage term, that being the period when the mortgagee would expect to be paid, in full, the capital sum with interest. To obtain relief, the mortgagor should present a detailed financial plan,[181] which, if implemented, would result in the loan itself, including the arrears, being paid off

---

[174] *Thakker v. Northern Rock plc* [2014] EWHC 2107 (Ch).

[175] *First National Bank plc v. Syed* [1991] 2 All E.R. 250 at 255 *per* Dillon L.J.

[176] *Hastings & Thanet Building Sociey v. Goddard* [1970] 1 W.L.R. 1544 at 1548 *per* Russell L.J.

[177] *Town & Country Building Society v. Julien* (1991) 24 H.L.R. 261. Cf. *Cheltenham and Gloucester Building Society v. Grant* (1993) 24 H.L.R. 48.

[178] *Cheltenham and Gloucester Building Society v. Grant* (1993) 24 H.L.R. 48, criticized by M.P. Thompson [1995] Conv. 51.

[179] [1996] 1 All E.R. 499. See M.P. Thompson [1996] Conv. 118.

[180] [1996] 1 All E.R. 449 at 456 *per* Waite L.J. See also Judge Parmiter (1992) 16 L.S.G 17 referring to a Judicial Studies Board 'recommendation' of two years. Cf. *Clyddesk Trust v. Aylwor* [1987] 1 W.L.R. 1157 at 1164 *per* McWilliam-T?dhon L.J., who considered eighteen months to be an appropriate period. This must now be considered to be unduly restrictive.

[181] See *Jameer v. Paratus AMC* [2012] EWCA Civ. 1924 at [12] *per* Lewison L.J.

by the term date of the mortgage.[182] Because, in the instant case, the judge had not considered the prospects of Mrs Norgan being able to achieve this in the remaining thirteen years of the mortgage, the matter was remitted for it to be determined, there being insufficient evidence before the Court of Appeal for a final decision to be made.

The decision in *Norgan* is to be welcomed.[183] First, authoritative guidelines were laid down, which should lead to a greater consistency of approach at county court level to an important issue. Second, it would seem to give adequate protection to the mortgagee,[184] while offering greater prospects for the mortgagor to be able to remain in the home, in that, financially, it will clearly be easier to meet the additional payments necessary to clear the arrears and meet the ongoing payments if such payments are spread out over the whole period of the loan rather than having to be made within a set, and somewhat arbitrary, period.

One reason for the court taking as a reasonable period the entire length of the mortgage was that, as this was the most favourable view so far as the mortgagor was concerned, further litigation could be avoided.[185] If a possession order has been postponed once, on the basis of the mortgagor's financial plan being considered to be acceptable, and the mortgagor fails to comply with the terms of that plan thereby falling into arrears again, then it was said that there would be a presumption, if a further possession action was brought, against there being any further postponement. This is because one of the aims of introducing the new guidelines was to avoid serial litigation relating to possession actions,[186] such a multiplicity of actions being a feature of *Norgan* itself.

Sale

The decision in *Norgan* is of relevance to a situation where a mortgagor is in a financial position to make payments additional to those which he would have been expected to make had default not occurred. He must make the normal payments together with such additional amount as would, over the life of the mortgage, also pay off the accumulated arrears. If the mortgagor cannot do this, an alternative position for him to take is to seek to argue that possession should be postponed to allow him to sell the property in order to discharge the debt. The question which will then arise, in these circumstances, is as to how long a postponement a court will countenance.

The normal judicial position in cases such as this is that any postponement of the sale will be only for a relatively short time and the court will require quite strong evidence that an early sale of the property is likely.[187] The mere fact that the mortgagor has put the property in the hands of estate agents will not, of itself, be convincing evidence that a sale is imminent, even if the agent is quite bullish as to the prospects of a quick sale. The reason for this is that such optimism might be misplaced, it having been said that 'the estate agency profession would win by a distance any competition between members of different professions for optimism'.[188]

---

[182] Had this approach been established when the 1970 Act was passed, there would have been no need for the amendment brought in by the Administration of Justice Act 1973, s. 8.

[183] For an account of the more hostile reaction to the decision in Northern Ireland, see L. McMurtry (2007) 58 N.I.L.Q. 194.

[184] For the importance of the position of the mortgagee being safeguarded, see *Realkredit Danmark v. Brookfield House* (1999), unreported.

[185] [1996] 1 All E.R. 449 at 459–60 *per* Waite L.J.

[186] Although contrast the seemingly very benevolent approach taken in *LBI HF v. Stanford* [2015] EWHC 3130 (Ch), where no authorities were cited.

[187] *Royal Trust Co. of Canada v. Markham* [1975] 1 All E.R. 433; *National and Provincial Building Society v. Lloyd* [1996] 1 All E.R. 630.

[188] *Target Home Loans Ltd v. Clothier* (1992) 25 H.L.R. 48 at 53 *per* Nolan L.J.

The reluctance of the courts to grant a prolonged possession order to a mortgagor in order to allow him to sell the property and repay what is owed is understandable, particularly if the level of indebtedness is continuing to rise as the mortgagor is unable to meet the ongoing mortgage repayments. A more interesting problem occurred in *Bristol and West Building Society v. Ellis*.[189] Arrears of some £16,000 had accrued on an initial loan of £60,000, amounting to a total indebtedness of £76,000. The mortgagor, Mrs Ellis, was in a position to pay the mortgagee a lump sum of £5,000 and meet the normal repayments and also to pay £10 per month towards clearing off the arrears. On these facts alone, she would have succeeded in paying off the arrears in ninety-eight years, which nobody argued was a reasonable period within the meaning of the Act. She argued, however, that the position was that the debt was stabilized. She then proposed that the sale of the property should be postponed for a period of five years to allow her son to finish his education and that, when the house was sold in five years' time, enough would be realized on the sale to discharge, in full, her debt to the mortgagee. The Court of Appeal rejected her argument and awarded the mortgagee possession.

Although possession was ordered, the Court of Appeal did not accept that there was a rule that the mortgagor must necessarily show, in cases of this type, that a sale would take place imminently, or even within a short space of time. Regard must be had to two criteria. In a case such as this, Auld L.J. stressed that:

> the critical matters are the adequacy of the security for the debt and the length of the period necessary to achieve a sale. There should be evidence, or at least some informal material . . . before the court of the likelihood of a sale the proceeds of which will discharge the debt and of the period in which such a sale is likely to be achieved.[190]

While it is true that the second criterion, the likelihood of a sale, points to a sale in the near future, this may be coloured by the adequacy of the security. In *Ellis*, the value of the property was disputed and the equity in the house was small. To postpone a sale for a five-year period, even though the arrears were not increasing, might prejudice a mortgagee if house prices started to fall, the result of that being that there might no longer be full security for the loan. In cases such as *Ellis*, however, where there is a larger equity in the house, the postponement of possession to allow a sale in a few years' time may be an attractive solution, protecting to an extent the mortgagor's use of the property as a home without endangering unduly the position of the mortgagee.

Who sells the property?

The previous section was concerned with arguments put by the mortgagor that the arrears can be cleared by means of a sale of the property at some time in the future. A further argument relating to the sale of the property has emerged, except on this occasion, the argument being put is that the mortgagor wishes the property to be sold against the wishes of the mortgagee, this situation usually occurring in cases of negative equity. In such cases, applications have been made under s. 91(2) of the LPA 1925 for a sale to be conducted by the mortgagor against the wishes of the mortgagee.

In *Palk v. Mortgage Services Funding plc*,[191] the mortgagee brought a possession action in respect of a house in which there was a negative equity. Its purpose in obtaining possession was not, however, as a prelude to the exercise of its power of sale. Instead, it intended to rent out the property with a view to selling it some years later, by which time it was confident that the value of the house would have risen sufficiently to enable the mortgagors'

---

[189] (1996) 73 P. & C.R. 158. See M.P. Thompson [1998] Conv. 125.
[190] (1996) 73 P. & C.R. 158 at 162.   [191] [1993] Ch. 330.

debt to be recouped in full. The mortgagors argued that the house should be sold straight away as, under the mortgagee's scheme, their indebtedness would increase progressively as the projected rental income was less than they would be expected to pay each month under the mortgage. The Court of Appeal accepted this argument and directed a sale of the property.

Negative equity

The facts of the case were unusual, in that the mortgagee was seeking to speculate on the recovery of the property market. This was at the risk of the mortgagors, who would remain liable on the personal covenant to repay if, subsequently, the house could not be sold at a price sufficient to recoup what was owed. Moreover, the level of indebtedness of the mortgagors would continue to increase while, if possession was granted, they would be unable actually to occupy the property, a result which, potentially, would cause them considerable hardship. The unusual nature of the facts in *Palk* was stressed in *Cheltenham and Gloucester plc v. Krausz*,[192] where, again, a mortgagor sought an order for the sale of a mortgaged property, on this occasion when the mortgagee had obtained a warrant for possession and had yet to execute that warrant. The proposed sale price would not have produced sufficient funds to pay off what was owed. The Court of Appeal refused to order a sale and instead allowed the warrant for possession to be enforced.

As a matter of principle, it was held that the normal position was that possession should be granted and the mortgagor not allowed to conduct the sale.[193] To do otherwise would create a state of affairs whereby a mortgagor, understandably reluctant to lose his home, could conduct the sale in such a way as to allow him to spin matters out and delay the conclusion of any sale; something that is potentially unfair to the mortgagee.[194]

11.6.2.6 Duty on taking possession

The mortgagee will normally only seek possession of the mortgaged property in order to be able to sell the property. Ordinarily, the mortgagee will not wish to take possession as an end in itself because of the potential liability imposed by equity. In equity, the mortgagee is under a liability to account strictly in respect of any profits, such liability being on the basis of wilful default.[195] In cases where the mortgaged property is used for commercial purposes, it is likely, if possession is being sought, that that business is in difficulty. In such circumstances, a mortgagee who has taken possession should seek either to sell the property as expeditiously as possible or, alternatively, not run that business himself but appoint a receiver to do so.[196] The decision in *McDonald v. McDonald* also confirmed that as the Human Rights Act 1998 does not directly impinge upon actions brought between private bodies, a person who has been peacefully dispossessed by a mortgagee cannot claim that his human rights have been infringed.[197] This approach was confirmed at first instance in *Southern Pacific Mortgage v. Green*,[198] where an attempt to raise equality concerns in the

[192] [1997] 1 All E.R. 21. See also *Cheltenham and Gloucester plc v. Booker* (1997) 29 H.L.R. 634; A. Kenny [1998] Conv. 223, and *Toor v. State Bank of India* [2010] EWHC 1097 (Ch) and *The Mortgage Business plc v. Green* [2013] EWHC 4243 (Ch) at [58]–[61] *per* Morgan J.

[193] But see *Polonski v. Lloyds Bank Mortgages Ltd* [1998] 1 F.L.R. 896, where *Krausz* was not cited and is, it is submitted, wrongly decided. See also M.P. Thompson [1998] Conv. 125 at 130–2. *Polonski* was regarded as being an atypical case in *Toor v. State Bank of India* [2010] EWHC 1097 (Ch) at [23]–[24] *per* H.H.J. Cooke.

[194] [1997] 1 All E.R. 21 at 27 *per* Phillips L.J. *Barrett v. Halifax Building Society* (1995) 28 H.L.R. 634, which seemed to adopt this course, was strongly doubted: at 31 *per* Millett L.J.

[195] See *White v. City of London Building Society* (1889) 42 Ch.D. 237.

[196] Cf. *AIB Finance Ltd v. Debtors* [1998] 2 All E.R. 929; M.P. Thompson [1998] Conv. 391 at 395.

[197] See *McDonald v. McDonald* [2016] UKSC 28 at [42] *per* Lord Neuberger and Lady Hale referring directly to this issue. See also *Horsham Properties Group Ltd v. Clark* [2009] 1 W.L.R. 1255.

[198] [2015] 11 WLUK 495.

Court of Appeal also failed.[199] Where, as is not uncommon, a mortgagor in arrears has simply left the property and returned the keys to the mortgagee, the fact that formal possession proceedings need not be brought is, in truth, a benefit for him as it reduces cost. Of course, if the mortgagor is in possession, then formal proceedings must be brought.

11.6.3 **Appointment of a receiver**

The mortgagee may appoint a receiver provided that his power of sale has become exercisable.[200] If the criteria, to be considered shortly, enabling the power to be exercised are satisfied, then an appointment of a receiver must be in writing. The advantage of appointing a receiver is that, by s. 109(2), LPA 1925, the receiver is deemed to be the agent of the mortgagor. This means that, although the receiver will collect money derived from the property and use that money to pay the interest due under the mortgage, the mortgagee will escape the strict liability which would be imposed upon him had he taken possession of the property himself.[201] A further advantage is that, if the income takes the form of the payment of rent by an occupying tenant, receipt of the rent by a receiver will not, of itself, amount to the adoption of the tenancy by the mortgagee. If the mortgagee receives rent directly from the tenant, then that tenancy will be adopted, with the result that, assuming the creation of that tenancy was unauthorized, the mortgagee will be bound by the tenancy and may not be able, subsequently, to obtain possession from the tenant, whereas previously he would have been able to do so.

11.6.4 **Foreclosure**

The right of the mortgagor to redeem the mortgage after the contractual date of redemption has passed is a right conferred by equity; it is the equitable right to redeem. What equity has given, equity can also take away. The removal of the equitable right to redeem is effected by foreclosure. Under s. 91, LPA 1925, the court may, at the instance of the mortgagee or any person interested, order a sale of the property rather than grant a foreclosure order. As the effect of foreclosure may well be to overcompensate the mortgagee by vesting in him property worth more than the debt, 'foreclosure actions are almost unheard of today and have been so for many years. [Mortgagees] usually appoint a receiver or exercise their powers of sale.'[202] If a foreclosure action is actually brought, it would be anticipated that the mortgagor would petition for the property to be sold.

11.6.5 **Sale**

The most potent remedy available to the mortgagee is to sell the property. With respect to sales of the property, various issues arise. These concern the question of when the property can be sold and the effect of the sale, the duties imposed upon the mortgagee when selling the property, and, finally, determining what is to happen to the proceeds of sale. This issue may be affected by the existence of more than one mortgage having being created over the property, when questions of priority may arise.

---

[199] *Green v. Southern Pacific Mortgage Ltd* [2018] EWCA Civ. 854. On discrimination, this case in the provision of *Support for Mortgage Benefit*, see [2017] EWCA Civ. 2123.

[200] LPA 1925, s. 109(1).

[201] The receiver may, however, be liable to the mortgagor if he fails to exercise reasonable care in the management of the property: *Medforth v. Blake* [1999] 3 All E.R. 97; A. Kenny [1999] Conv. 434. See *Purewal v. Countrywide Residential Lettings* [2015] EWCA Civ. 122 at [8]–[20] *per* Patten L.J.

[202] *Palk v. Mortgage Services Funding plc* [1993] Ch. 330 at 336 *per* Sir Donald Nicholls V.-C.

11.6.5.1 **Power of sale**

Since 1925, the legal fee simple remains vested in the mortgagor. When selling the mortgaged property, therefore, the transfer by the mortgagee will operate to transfer something which he does not actually own. For him to be able to do this, it is essential that the statutory power of sale has arisen. A further matter which then becomes relevant is whether the power of sale is exercisable. There is an important difference between the power arising and it becoming exercisable.

Power arising

For the mortgagee to have the power to sell the mortgaged property, the criteria set out in s. 101, LPA 1925[203] must be satisfied. These are:

(a) that the mortgage is made by deed; and

(b) that the mortgage money has become due.

In the case of legal mortgages, these must be created by deed and so the first condition will always be satisfied.[204] It is the second requirement, that the mortgage money has become due, that has caused mortgage deeds to convey a misleading impression. To ensure that the mortgage money is due, with the result that the power of sale arises, it is common for the mortgage deed to stipulate either that the whole sum borrowed will be repaid within six months of the creation of the mortgage, or to insert a clause that if there is a default in the payment of any instalment, the whole sum borrowed becomes payable.[205] It is unfortunate that the need to ensure that the statutory power of sale arises necessitates the insertion of clauses of this nature into mortgages, as both clauses are artificial and distort the apparent nature of the transaction.

The effect of a sale

On a sale of freehold property by a mortgagee exercising the power conferred by the Act, the purchaser will acquire the fee simple freed from all estates, rights, and interests, and rights to which the mortgagee has priority, but subject to all estates, interests, and rights which have priority to the mortgage.[206] This means that the purchaser will take subject to any third-party rights, including mortgages, which were binding upon the mortgagee, but free from all other rights including, most importantly, the mortgagor's equity of redemption which is overreached.

For overreaching to occur, the mortgagee must exercise the power conferred by the Act or by the terms of the mortgage contract. If the power of sale has not arisen, then all that the mortgagee can convey is his own interest in the property, that is, his own mortgage. So, if there is a £40,000 mortgage on a property and the mortgagee sells the property for its actual value, say £200,000, but the power of sale has not arisen, then all the purchaser will acquire is a mortgage worth £40,000. To avoid such a catastrophic result, it is therefore imperative that the purchaser satisfies himself that the power of sale has arisen. For this reason, the purchaser's task is easier if the mortgage stipulates that the money is repaid within six months of the creation of the mortgage, rather than if the mortgage contains a

---

[203] The provisions relating to the power of sale may be varied or excluded by the mortgage deed: LPA 1925, s. 101(3), (4).

[204] This may not always be the case for equitable mortgages and it is preferable that such mortgages are also created by deed.

[205] It would seem that this is unnecessary as, if there is default in the payment of an instalment, the courts are prepared to accept that the mortgage money is due: *Payne v. Cardiff Rural District Council* [1932] 1 K.B. 241. See H.P. (1932) 48 L.Q.R. 158.

[206] LPA 1925, s. 104(1).

default clause. One can easily tell if the contractual date for redemption has passed; it is less easy to be sure that the default clause has been activated.

Power becoming exercisable

For the power of sale to arise, the criteria laid down in s. 101, LPA 1925 must be satisfied. Once the power of sale has arisen, it only becomes exercisable if one of the criteria laid down in s. 103 are fulfilled. The power is not exercisable unless either:

(a) notice requiring payment of the mortgage money has been served on the mortgagor and default has been made in payment of the mortgage money, or of part thereof, for three months after service of such notice; or

(b) some interest under the mortgage is in arrears and unpaid for two months after becoming due; or

(c) there has been breach of some provision in the mortgage other than the payment of the mortgage money or interest.

There is a significant difference between the mortgagee purporting to exercise the power of sale when that power has not arisen and him selling the property when the power of sale is not exercisable. As has been seen, if the power of sale has not arisen then the mortgagee lacks capacity to transfer the fee simple and can transfer only his own mortgage. If the property is sold before the power of sale has become exercisable, the consequence is less drastic. It is provided by s. 104(2) of the Act that when a conveyance is made in exercise of the power of sale, the title of the purchaser shall not be impeachable on the ground that the power of sale is not exercisable and the purchaser is not concerned to make enquiries as to whether the power is exercisable. If the purchaser, however, is actually aware that the power of sale is not exercisable, then the sale will be set aside,[207] but such a situation is likely to be very rare, particularly as the purchaser is exonerated from making any enquiry as to this. The sanction for selling the property before the power of sale has become exercisable is that the mortgagee is liable to pay damages to any person who suffers loss by the improper exercise of the power of sale.[208]

11.6.5.2 Duties on sale

In practical terms, the exercise of the power of sale is the most fundamental remedy of the mortgagee and will, in most cases, bring to an end the relationship between the mortgagor and the mortgagee. Given the nature of the remedy, it has a considerable impact upon the mortgagor. In the residential sector, the effect will be, of course, that the mortgagor will lose his existing home and have to seek alternative accommodation. In addition, the mortgagor will retain a financial interest in the transaction. If there is equity in the house then, after the sale has occurred, the mortgagor will be entitled to the balance of the proceeds of sale after the debt to the mortgagee has been discharged. Conversely, if there is negative equity, the mortgagor will remain personally liable to the mortgagee for the shortfall after the property has been sold. The conduct of the sale is, therefore, a matter of considerable importance to the mortgagor and, as one would expect, certain duties are imposed upon the mortgagee with respect to the exercise of the power of sale.

Genuine sale

The first point to make is that the sale must be a genuine one. This means that the mortgagee cannot buy the property himself, or through an agent.[209] Where this principle has

---

[207] *Waring v. London and Manchester Assurance Co. Ltd* [1935] Ch. 310 at 318 *per* Crossman J. See also *Jenkins v. Jones* (1860) 2 Giff. 99.

[208] LPA 1925, s. 104(2).   [209] *Martinson v. Clowes* (1882) 21 Ch.D. 857 at 860 *per* North J.

been infringed, the mortgagor is entitled to set the transaction aside and does not have to prove that there was any fraud involved, as such a transaction is not really a sale at all.[210] Unless the sale is under the direction of the court,[211] or the mortgagee is expressly permitted by statute to buy the mortgaged property,[212] the rule prohibiting the mortgagee from buying the property appears to be absolute.[213]

Associated persons

While it is clear that the mortgagee cannot buy the mortgaged property himself the position with regard to a sale to an associated person is more flexible. There is no rule that such a sale cannot take place[214] but, depending on the circumstances, the sale may be liable to be set aside. In *Tse Kwok Lam v. Wong Chit Sen*,[215] the mortgagee sold the mortgaged property at an auction. The only bidder was the mortgagee's wife, whose bid matched exactly the reserve price. Subsequently the mortgagor sought to have the sale set aside. The Privy Council held that, while the close relationship between the seller and the buyer did not entitle the mortgagor automatically to set the sale aside, the existence of the relationship meant that the onus of proof was thrown onto the purchaser to show that the sale was in good faith and at the best price reasonably obtainable at the time.[216] On the facts, this onus was not discharged. Had it not been for the excessive delay on the part of the mortgagor in seeking to impugn the sale, the transaction would have been set aside.

Where, as in this case, the mortgagee is knowingly selling to a closely associated person, then the shifting of the normal burden of proof from the mortgagor to the parties to the sale seems entirely appropriate. If the mortgagee is unaware of the identity of the buyer, however, this will not be the case. In *Corbett v. Halifax plc*,[217] the Halifax was exercising its power of sale. It was the strict policy of the company that under no circumstances could staff of the Halifax group of companies or agents' staff or their families purchase a property in possession. Notwithstanding this policy, a Mr Deakin, who was employed by the Halifax and was aware of the policy, contrived a plan whereby his uncle bought the property and then re-sold it to him and his wife. As the Halifax was unaware of this deception, the sale was not challengeable by the mortgagor on the basis of the sale being to an associated person. Even had the Halifax been aware that the real buyer was Mr Deakin and his wife, however, it is thought that the sale would still have been unimpeachable. He had had nothing to do with the conduct of the sale, and derived no advantage from his association with the mortgagee.[218] An even clearer situation where a sale to an associated person would be free from subsequent challenge by the mortgagor is where the sale is conducted in accordance with instructions given by him.[219]

---

[210] *Farrar v. Farrars Ltd* (1888) 40 Ch.D. 395 at 409 *per* Lindley L.J.

[211] See *Palk v. Mortgage Services Funding plc* [1993] Ch. 330 at 340 *per* Sir Donald Nicholls V.-C.

[212] See Housing Act 1985, s. 452, Sched. 17, para. 1, as amended by the Housing and Planning Act 1986, which avoids the difficulty relating to this issue highlighted in *Williams v. Wellingborough B.C.* [1975] 1 W.L.R. 1327.

[213] For a very benevolent view of the facts to avoid holding that a sale fell foul of this rule, see *Alpstream AG v. PK Airfinance Sari* [2015] EWCA Civ. 1318 at [81] *per* Clarke L.J.

[214] *Newport Farm Ltd v. Damesh Holdings Ltd* [2003] UKPC 54 at para. 25 *per* Lord Scott.

[215] [1983] 1 W.L.R. 1349.

[216] See also *Alpstream AG v. PK Airfinance Sari, supra*, at [82] *per* Clarke L.J.

[217] [2003] 4 All E.R. 180; M.P. Thompson [2004] Conv. 49.

[218] See M.P. Thompson [2004] Conv. 49, at 59–60.

[219] *Newport Farm Ltd v. Damesh Holdings Ltd, supra*.

Conduct of the sale

Assuming that the sale is not open to objection on the basis of the identity of the purchaser, the next issue to consider is what duties are owed to the mortgagor by the mortgagee when exercising the power of sale.

It has long been accepted that the exercise of the power of sale was subject to some judicial control, although the extent, and indeed the juridical basis, of that control was less certain. In some cases, it was said that the mortgagee would only incur liability if the sale was not exercised in good faith.[220] In other decisions, however, the standard was pitched somewhat higher, it being said that the mortgagee owed a duty to the mortgagor to obtain the best price reasonably obtainable.[221] The conflict between these differing formulations was settled by the Court of Appeal in *Cuckmere Brick Co. Mutual Finance Ltd.*[222] In this case, after the property had been sold, the mortgagor sued the mortgagee alleging that the sale price achieved was too low, the result, it was said, of the extent of the planning permission attached to the land not being properly advertised.

Although the court was divided as to the application of the law to the facts of the case,[223] it was unanimous as to the standard of care to be expected of a mortgagee. It was agreed that the mortgagee was under a duty to take reasonable care to obtain the true market price for the property. This was explained on the basis that:

> The proximity between them could hardly be greater. Surely they are 'neighbours'. Given that the power of sale is for the benefit of the mortgagee and that he is entitled to choose the moment that suits him, it would be strange indeed if he were under no legal obligation to take reasonable care to obtain what I call the true market value at the date of the sale.[224]

Tort or equity?

The dichotomy of view as to whether the obligation imposed on the mortgagee was to act in good faith, or was the higher duty to take reasonable care to obtain the true market value of the property, was solved by holding that the mortgagee owes both duties to the mortgagor.[225] With regard to the former, this will add little to the higher duty of care imposed on the mortgagee. Provided that the power of sale is not exercised for reasons other than the recovery of the debt, it will not be considered to have been wrongly exercised.[226] It will, of course, be extremely difficult to establish this.[227]

The language used in *Cuckmere* in respect of the duty of care imposed upon the mortgagee is redolent of the application of tortious principles. Since then, however, the opportunity has been taken to stress that it is the province of equity and not tort to regulate the exercise of the mortgagee's power of sale.[228] As between the mortgagor and the mortgagee,

---

[220] See, e.g., *Kennedy v. De Trafford* [1897] A.C. 762; *Warner v. Jacob* (1882) 20 Ch.D. 220; *Reliance Permanent Building Society v. Harwood-Stamper* [1944] Ch. 362.

[221] See, e.g., *McHugh v. Union Bank of Canada* [1913] A.C. 299; *National Bank of Australia v. United Hand-in-Hand Band of Hope* (1879) 4 App. Cas. 391; *Farrar v. Farrars Ltd* (1888) 40 Ch.D. 395; *Colson v. Williams* (1889) 58 L.J. Ch. 539.

[222] [1971] Ch. 949.

[223] For a helpful discussion of this issue, see *Meah v. GE Money Home Finance Ltd* [2013] EWHC 20 (Ch).

[224] [1971] Ch. 949 at 966 *per* Salmon L.J.   [225] Ibid.

[226] See *Meretz Investments NV v. APC Ltd* [2006] EWHC 74 (Ch) at para. 314 *per* Lewison J.

[227] Although, in the context of an action for possession, see *Quennell v. Maltby* [1979] 1 W.L.R. 318.

[228] *Downsview Nominees Ltd v. First City Corporation Ltd* [1993] A.C. 295 at 315 *per* Lord Templeman; *Yorkshire Bank plc v. Hall* [1999] 1 W.L.R. 1713 at 1728 *per* Robert Walker L.J.

this is of little practical consequence as it is clear that the standard laid down in *Cuckmere* is also the appropriate standard to be imposed by equity.[229]

The main significance of the debate as to whether the source of the mortgagee's liability lay in tort or in equity related to whether or not the mortgagee could be liable in respect of the timing of the sale. For a long time, it has been established that the mortgagee need not wait until the market is favourable before exercising the power of sale.[230] Indeed, provided that power of sale is exercisable, the mortgagee could sell the property at the least advantageous time for the mortgagor.[231] In the aftermath of *Cuckmere*, it was thought to be arguable, on the supposition that the position was governed by the law of tort, that this position might need reconsideration, so that it might be the case that the mortgagee should exercise reasonable care as to when the property is put onto the market.[232] This argument was rejected, however, in *China and South Sea Bank Ltd v. Tan Soon Gin*,[233] where the Privy Council held that a mortgagee could not be liable for failing to exercise its power of sale when market conditions were more favourable than they subsequently became, as the timing of the sale was a matter entirely for the mortgagee.

The position was restated by the Court of Appeal in *Silven Properties Ltd v. Royal Bank of Scotland plc*.[234] Lightman J., giving the judgment of the court, said:

> When and if the mortgagee does exercise the power of sale, he comes under a duty in equity (and not tort) to the mortgagor (and all others interested in the equity of redemption) to take reasonable precautions to obtain 'the fair' or 'the true market' value of or 'the proper price' for the mortgaged property at the date of the sale and not . . . the date of the decision to sell. . . . The remedy for breach of this duty is not common law damages, but an order that the mortgagee account to the mortgagor and all others interested in the equity of redemption, not just for what he received but for what he should have received . . .

It will be observed that, in this passage, Lightman J. refers to the duty being owed to others interested in the equity of redemption. Thus, it has been held that the duty is owed to a surety of the loan,[235] and to a subsequent mortgagee,[236] but, perhaps surprisingly, not to an equitable co-owner of the property.[237]

11.6.5.3 Breach of duty

The question of whether a mortgagee is in breach of his duty to take reasonable care is essentially one of fact, and in determining whether the mortgagee has fallen below the requisite standard, the court will consider whether the sale was within a bracket of

---

[229] See *Medforth v. Blake* [2000] Ch. 86 at 102 *per* Sir Richard Scott V.-C.; *Glatt v. Sinclair* [2011] EWCA Civ. 1317 at [12] *per* Kitchin L.J. The duty was, in respect of building societies, for a long time statutory: see Building Societies Act 1986, Sched. 4, replacing earlier legislation. The position is now governed by the general law; Building Societies Act 1997, s. 2.

[230] See *Warner v. Jacob* (1882) 20 Ch.D. 220 at 224 *per* Kay J., *Bank of Cyprus (London) Ltd v. Gill* [1980] 2 Lloyd's Rep. 51.

[231] See *Duke v. Robson* [1973] 1 W.L.R. 267.

[232] *Standard Chartered Bank Ltd v. Walker* [1982] 1 W.L.R. 1410 at 1415 *per* Lord Denning M.R.

[233] [1991] 1 A.C. 531. See also *Silven Properties Ltd v. Royal Bank of Scotland plc* [2004] 4 All E.R. 484 at 491–2 *per* Lightman J., and *Alpstream AG v. PK Airfinance Sari, supra*, at [198] *per* Clarke L.J.

[234] At 492–3.

[235] *Standard Chartered Bank Ltd v. Walker* [1982] 1 W.L.R. 1410. 'Equity intervenes to protect a surety': *China and South Sea Bank Ltd v. Tan Soon Gin* [1991] 1 A.C. 536 at 544 *per* Lord Templeman.

[236] *Downsview Nominees Ltd v. First City Corporation Ltd* [1993] A.C. 295 at 311 *per* Lord Templeman. See also *Adamson v. Halifax plc* [2003] 4 All E.R. 423 at 425 *per* Sir Murray Stuart-Smith.

[237] *Parker-Tweedale v. Dunbar Bank* [1991] Ch. 12. For a review of the ambit of the duty, see *Alpstream v. PK Airfinance Sari, supra*, at [115]–[119] *per* Clarke L.J.

reasonableness.[238] In *Corbett v. Halifax plc*[239] the suggestion at first instance was made that a margin of error of 10 per cent was the right benchmark, and this was not commented upon in the Court of Appeal. That figure does seem to be quite generous and, more recently, in *Barclays Bank plc v. TSB & V Ltd*,[240] a case involving the related context of negligent property valuations, Dove J. expressed the view that the relevant margins of error should be 5 per cent for a standard residential property; 10 per cent for a one-off property; and 15 per cent for a property with exceptional features. These figures would seem to be appropriate in the present context. If the house is immediately re-sold for a considerable profit, this will provide strong evidence that the original sale was at an undervalue.[241]

When property is sold at an undervalue, the measure of damages is to reflect the diminution in value of the equity of redemption. In *Adamson v. Halifax Bank plc*,[242] a property was sold by a mortgagee at an undervalue of £6,000. A second bank was entitled to £5,000 from the proceeds of sale but opted neither to sue the first mortgagee for selling at an undervalue nor to pursue the mortgagor for what was owed. Had it done so, the mortgagor would have received £1,000. The mortgagor was held to be entitled to damages of £6,000, which was the loss of value of the equity of redemption. This was unaffected by the decisions made by the second bank.

An issue relevant to this is whether or not the mortgagee owes a duty to the mortgagor to gazump, to accept a higher offer than one which has previously been accepted, subject to contract. In *Corbett v. Halifax plc*,[243] it emerged that the policy of the Halifax, when selling mortgaged property, was not to entertain a higher offer, unless it exceeded a previous offer by more than 5 per cent. This was not commented on in the Court of Appeal, but in principle, it would seem that the mortgagee's duty to the mortgagor should override any considerations of commercial ethics.[244]

In assessing whether the mortgagee is in breach of its duty, some general principles have emerged. First, to escape liability it is not sufficient to show that the property has been put into the hands of a reputable agent. Any negligence on the part of the agent will be attributed to the mortgagee.[245] Second, when selling the property it must be properly exposed to the market, and whether or not that is the case will, of course, be evaluated in the light of all the circumstances.[246] If a lower price is obtained than would otherwise have been the case, because the property was sold on a 'crash sale' basis, the mortgagee will be liable to the mortgagor in respect of the shortfall.[247] On the same basis, as it is generally perceived that a lower price for a house can be obtained when it has been repossessed than would be the case if the sale were conducted in the normal way by the owners of it, the property should not, it is thought, be marketed on the basis that it is a forced sale.[248]

---

[238] *Michael v. Miller* [2004] 2 E.G.L.R. 151 at 160 *per* Jonathan Parker L.J.

[239] [2003] 4 All E.R. 180 at 187 *per* Pumphrey J. See M.P. Thompson [2004] Conv. 49 at 54.

[240] [2016] EWHC 2948 at [69]–[70].

[241] See *Glatt v. Sinclair* [2011] EWCA Civ. 1317 (re-sale at a 38 per cent uplift in price).

[242] [2003] 4 All E.R. 423.   [243] [2003] 4 All E.R. 180.

[244] See *Buttle v. Saunders* [1950] 2 All E.R. 193; M.P. Thompson [2004] Conv. 49, at 54–6.

[245] *Tomlin v. Luce* (1889) 43 Ch.D. 191 at 194 *per* Collins L.J.; *Cuckmere Brick Co. Ltd v. Mutual Finance Ltd* [1971] Ch. 949; *Francis v. Barclays Bank plc* [2004] EWHC 2787 (Ch) at para. 13 *per* Rattee J.; *Glatt v. Sinclair* [2011] EWCA Civ. 1317 at [52] *per* Kitchin L.J.

[246] *Meftah v. Lloyds TSB plc* [2001] All E.R. (Commercial) 741 at [9] *per* Lawrence Collins J.

[247] *Predeth v. Castle Phillips Ltd* [1986] 2 E.G.L.R. 141. See also *Skipton Building Society v. Stott* [2000] All E.R. 779; *Michael v. Miller* [2004] 2 E.G.L.R. 151 at 160.

[248] For an interesting account of the practice of agents in respect of the sale of mortgaged property, see *Meah v. GE Money Home Finance Ltd* [2013] EWHC 20 (Ch) at [10]–[23] *per* Mr Alan Steinfield Q.C., sitting as a Deputy High Court judge.

It is open to the mortgagee to exclude liability in respect of his duty on a sale of the property, although any exclusion clause will have to be very clearly drafted in order to be efficacious.[249]

11.6.6 Proceeds of sale

While the mortgagee is not a trustee of the power of sale,[250] he is a trustee of the proceeds of sale. When the property has been sold, the mortgagee is required by s. 105, LPA 1925 to apply the proceeds of sale in the following order:

(a) the discharge of any prior incumbrances free from which the property was sold;

(b) the payment of expenses properly incurred in the sale;

(c) the discharge of any money due under the mortgage; and

(d) payment of any balance to a subsequent mortgagee and, if there is none, to the mortgagor.

The existence of subsequent mortgages can be discovered by searching in the land charges register or the Land Registry, as appropriate. The mortgagee will have notice of subsequent mortgages if they are either registered as a land charge or protected by the entry of a notice on the register,[251] so the mortgagee exercising its power of sale should make the requisite searches. If the mortgagee sells the property, because he holds the balance of the proceeds of sale on trust for subsequent mortgagees, they have proprietary interests in that money. In *Buhr v. Barclays Bank plc*,[252] it was held that when the mortgagor sells the property to discharge the first mortgage, the interests of subsequent mortgagees in the balance of the proceeds of sale are also proprietary.

11.6.7 Third-party rights

In considering the rights of other occupiers of mortgaged property, the mortgagee is in general likely to be concerned with two sorts of occupier: tenants and co-owners. These types of occupier will be considered in turn.

11.6.7.1 Tenants

Whether or not a mortgagee will be bound by the interest of a tenant will depend to a large extent on when the tenancy was created: that is whether it came into being prior to the mortgage or subsequent to it. With regard to tenancies created before the mortgage and so, *prima facie*, binding upon the mortgagee, it may make a difference as to whether or not title is registered.

Lease prior to mortgage

In the case of leases granted prior to the creation of the mortgage, the principal issue when title is unregistered is whether the lease is legal or equitable. If it is a legal lease then, in accordance with general principles, that lease will be binding on the mortgagee, who will be unable to obtain possession as against the tenant. If the lease is equitable, then to be enforceable as against the mortgagee, it must be protected by the registration of a C(iv) land charge, an equitable lease being an estate contract: a contract to create a legal estate. If it has not been registered, it will be void against the mortgagee.[253] If, as is likely, the equitable

---

[249] See *Bishop v. Bonham* [1988] 1 W.L.R. 742.
[250] *Walker v. Jacob* (1882) 21 Ch.D. 220 at 224 *per* Kay J.   [251] LRA 2002, s. 54.
[252] [2001] EWCA Civ. 1223. See L. McMurtry [2002] Conv. 53.
[253] *Hollington Bros Ltd v. Rhodes* [1951] 2 T.L.R. 691.

tenant has gone into possession and paid rent, the equitable lease will still be void for non-registration, but a legal periodic tenancy will have arisen by implication and that tenancy will be binding upon the mortgagee.[254]

Registered land

Where title is registered, the issue is whether the lease has to be protected by registration or will take effect as an interest overriding a registered disposition. In the case of a lease granted for a term not exceeding seven years, this takes effect as an interest which over-rides a registered disposition.[255] The word 'granted' is important in this context as it pre-supposes that the lease is a legal lease and so an equitable tenancy of less than seven years will not automatically override a registered disposition.[256]

If, however, as is quite likely to be the case, the tenant is in actual occupation of the land then, under Sched. 3, para. 2, the equitable tenancy will override a registered disposition. A lease of more than seven years is not an interest which will override a registered disposition, and should be registered with an independent title and its existence protected by a notice on the register of the freehold title. Again, however, if the tenant is in actual occupation of the property it will override a registered disposition and so be binding on a mortgagee.

For the lease to be binding upon the mortgagee, it is important that it was created before the mortgage. Determining this matter is usually no problem, but can sometimes become an issue. The first potential problem arose from tenancies by estoppel.[257] In *Church of England Building Society v. Piskor*,[258] a purchaser of a house, who was financing its purchase with a mortgage, purported to grant a tenancy before the conveyance had taken place. As at the time when the purported grant took place the grantor did not have a legal title to the land, the grant operated to create a tenancy by estoppel, whereby both landlord and tenant are es-topped from denying the validity of the transaction. The conveyance and mortgage occurred subsequently. It was held that technically the conveyance which vested the legal title in the purchaser and the mortgage were two separate transactions, the conveyance, which vested the legal title in the purchaser preceding, albeit momentarily, the grant by the purchaser of the legal mortgage. The conveyance to the landlord vested in him the legal fee simple and, automatically, by a process termed feeding the estoppel, the effect of this was that the tenant's tenancy by estoppel became a legal lease. As this legal lease was created a split second prior to the creation of the legal mortgage, the mortgagee was bound by the tenancy.

While there is a logic to this reasoning, it was manifestly inconvenient in that it put the security of the mortgagee at risk in circumstances where it was difficult to see how he could protect its own position. For this reason, *Piskor* was overruled in *Abbey National Building Society v. Cann*,[259] so that, in this type of situation, the tenancy would not be regarded as having been created before the mortgage.

The matter was revisited by the Supreme Court in *Scott v. Southern Pacific Mortgages Ltd*,[260] a test case affecting potentially over a hundred similar disputes. The case involved a number of equity release schemes. A registered proprietor of a house agreed to sell it to a nominee of NEPB. The price was the market value of the property, although a signifi-cant part of the purchase price was then repaid to NEPB. The nominee would then, prior to the completion of the transactions, lease the property back to the former registered proprietors, who would then pay rent to the nominees.[261] To finance the purchase of the

---

[254] Cf. *Bell St Investments Ltd v. Wood* [1970] E.G.D. 812.   [255] LRA 2002, Sched. 1, para.3.
[256] *City Permanent Building Society v. Miller* [1952] Ch. 840.
[257] See 10.4.6.   [258] [1954] Ch. 553.   [259] [1991] 1 A C 56.
[260] [2014] UKSC 52. The earlier decision in *Redstone v. Welch & Jackson* [2009] E.G. 98 was not followed.
[261] This could not, on the facts, create a tenancy by estoppel because the vendors still held the legal title to the freehold and it is not possible for the same person to be both landlord and tenant of the same property: see *Rye v. Rye* [1962] A.C. 496.

properties, the nominees borrowed the money, and at the time of the transfers, mortgages were created in favour of the lenders. When the nominees defaulted on the mortgages, the mortgagees sought possession and were met with the defence that the leases were binding on them. This defence failed. Applying *Cann*, the Supreme Court held that the transfer and the mortgage were simultaneous transactions, so that the purchaser, in this case the nominee of NEPB, never acquired an unencumbered fee simple; what it acquired was, in substance, an equity of redemption. It was not, therefore, in a position to create an interest, in this case the leaseback to the vendor, which had priority over the mortgage.

Delayed registration

A rather different issue occurred in *Barclays Bank Plc v. Zaroovabli*.[262] A married couple were registered as joint proprietors of a house in April 1988. In May of that year they created a mortgage in favour of the bank, but for some inexplicable reason, the bank did not apply for registration of the mortgage until 1994. Without seeking the consent of the bank, the mortgagors had earlier let the property to the tenant who, at the time of the action, was still in occupation of the property enjoying the security of tenure conferred upon her by the Rent Act 1977, the original contractual tenancy having ended. When the bank sought possession of the property, the issue was whether it was bound by the tenancy. Sir Richard Scott V.-C. held that it was. The reason for this finding was that, because of the delay in applying for registration of the mortgage, the bank only acquired a legal charge from the date when it applied for registration. In law, therefore, the lease, admittedly created in contravention of the mortgage agreement, arose before the mortgage and took effect as an overriding interest with the result that the mortgagee was bound by it; a consequence of the bank's own fault in not applying for registration of the mortgage until some considerable time after its creation.

11.6.7.2 The effect of the tenancy

The general position is that a mortgagee will be bound by a tenancy created *before* the mortgage. What is also true is that a tenant cannot waive any statutory rights he may have. If the property was occupied by tenants who enjoyed security of tenure under the Rent Act 1977, these rights could not be waived in favour of an intending mortgagee who would, consequently, take subject to those rights.[263] This, for a time, was a potentially significant problem for lenders but, since the considerable reduction of the security rights of tenants since 1980, the problem has by and large disappeared.

11.6.7.3 Unauthorized leases

One of the rights of a mortgagor is to create leases of the mortgaged property. This power is subject, however, to the expression of a contrary intention in the mortgage deed or otherwise in writing.[264] If there is no contrary intention expressed, then any lease created by the mortgagor will be binding upon the mortgagee. In practice, however, it is normal for the mortgage to exclude the power of the mortgagor to create leases. The question then arises as to the position of the tenant when, notwithstanding such a clause in the mortgage, the mortgagor does let the mortgaged property.

The general position is that, while as between the mortgagor and the tenant the lease is entirely valid, the lease is not binding upon the mortgagee, who will, therefore, be able to obtain possession as against the tenant.[265] The tenant's position is not improved by the

---

[262] [1997] Ch. 321.   [263] See *Woolwich Building Society v. Dickman* [1996] 3 All E.R. 204.

[264] LPA 1925, s. 99(1)(13).

[265] See *Corbett v. Plowden* (1884) 25 Ch.D. 678 at 681 *per* Lord Selborne L.C.; *Dudley and District Building Society v. Emerson* [1949] Ch. 707.

statutory protection afforded to residential tenants. This point was considered in *Britannia Building Society v. Earl*,[266] where despite a clause in the mortgage excluding the mortgagor's power to create leases, the mortgagor did create a tenancy. When he defaulted on the mortgage, the mortgagee sought possession and this action was resisted by the tenants. Their principal argument was that, as they were protected by the Rent Act 1977, possession could be obtained only on one of the grounds stipulated in that Act. This was rejected. The lease was not binding upon the mortgagee and, consequently, the statutory code regulating possession actions was not relevant to the action brought by him.

11.6.7.4 Limits to right of possession

The decision in *Earl* demonstrates the vulnerable position of a tenant who, having entered into the lease in good faith and performed his obligations under the tenancy, may find himself being forced to leave property at the behest of the mortgagee, almost certainly as a result of default on the mortgage by his landlord. This result can appear harsh.[267] One's view as to the harshness of this should be tempered, however, by the consideration that the opposite result would be hard on a mortgagee, who would be unable to gain possession of property because of the creation of an interest which he had expressly tried to prevent from being created. The decision in favour of the mortgagee is consistent with principle and establishes the general right of the mortgagee to possession as against a tenant, whose lease was created by a mortgagor in contravention of the terms of the mortgage. The mortgagee's right is not unqualified, however, there being two situations where a possession action may fail.

Collusive actions

The first situation where a mortgagee may fail in an action for possession against a tenant is where such an action is seen as being essentially collusive. In *Quennell v. Maltby*,[268] a husband owned a property subject to a small mortgage in favour of a bank. The mortgage deed excluded the power to create leases. Nevertheless, he created a lease of the property. Later, he wished to sell the property but would have found it difficult to do so as it was occupied by tenants who were protected under the Rent Acts, and were unwilling to leave. To obtain possession, he approached the bank and sought to persuade it to bring possession proceedings, the tenancy not being binding upon it. The bank, however, taking the view that its security was safe, declined to do so. The mortgagor's wife then paid off the sum owing under the mortgage and the mortgage was then transferred to her. She then, standing in the shoes of the bank, sought to evict the tenants. The action failed. Although it was accepted that the bank could have obtained possession, on the facts of the case the wife was acting as her husband's agent. As he could not have obtained possession, neither could she. To have held otherwise would have opened the door to a facile means of evading the Rent Acts.

Adoption

Situations where the possession action is seen as collusive are probably not of general importance. Potentially, a more serious issue for mortgagees is where a lease is regarded as having been adopted. This occurred in *Stroud Building Society v. Delamont*.[269] A mortgagor created an unauthorized mortgage. Sometime later, he was declared bankrupt. Although the mortgagee served a notice to quit on the tenant, this was not complied with

---

[266] [1990] 1 W.L.R. 422.   [267] See P. Smith (1977) 41 Conv. (N.S.) 197.
[268] [1979] 1 W.L.R. 318.
[269] [1960] 1 W.L.R. 431. See also *Chatsworth Building Society v. Effion* [1971] 1 W.L.R. 144.

and, thereafter, rent was paid to the mortgagor's trustee in bankruptcy. A little later, the mortgagee appointed a receiver, who instructed the tenant to pay the rent to him. After that, the society, replying to a letter it had received, wrote to the tenant, informing her that she held on the same terms as she had previously. When a possession action was brought on behalf of the society against the tenant, it failed, it being held that the action of the society had caused the relationship of landlord and tenant to arise between it and the tenant.

It was accepted that the society could, at the outset, have treated the tenant as a trespasser on the basis that the lease was unauthorized and so not binding upon it. On the facts, however, it did not do so. If the society had done nothing, but simply allowed the tenant to remain in possession, this would not, of itself, have prevented it from seeking possession, because something more than mere knowledge of the tenancy is required if the mortgagee is to lose his right to evict the tenant.[270] In this case, the terms of the correspondence amounted to a consent to the tenancy, thereby creating the relationship of landlord and tenant between them. The basis of the decision is simply one of consent. It is not, as was assumed to have been the case in *Paratus AMC v. Persons Unknown*,[271] an instance of estoppel. To avoid such a consequence, the mortgagee should avoid taking rent directly from the tenant.

Appointing a receiver

The refusal of a mortgagee to accept rent from a tenant when the lease is unauthorized may, understandably, occasion some distress to the tenant when faced with a possession action arising as a consequence of default by his landlord. Yet the reluctance of the landlord to accept payment is, in his own interest, entirely understandable. One solution is to appoint a receiver. A receiver, when appointed, is the agent of the mortgagor,[272] and so his receipt of rent from the tenant, although paid to the mortgagee, will not amount to the adoption of the tenancy. A potential difficulty here, as pointed out by Cross J., is that 'the idea that a mortgagee can through the medium of receivership get the benefit of the rent while remaining at liberty to treat him as a trespasser is a highly artificial one which would not readily occur to a layman or even a good many lawyers'.[273] Accordingly, the conduct of the receiver towards the tenant may quite easily amount to an adoption of the tenancy.[274] If the mortgagee is willing to allow the tenant to retain possession, he should make it clear that the receipt of rent by a receiver is done without prejudice to his position. Alternatively, as the appointment of a receiver in respect of domestic property is uncommon, it is hoped that the courts would accept that the receipt of rent directly from the tenant, on the basis that that receipt is without prejudice, should not result in the tenancy being held to have been adopted as this would ensure that his right to possession is not prejudiced, while also ensuring that the tenant does not have to leave the property at short notice.

11.6.7.5 Statutory reform

If a tenancy was entered into after the mortgage and the lender has not accepted the tenancy, then unless a tenant might be faced with summary eviction from their home, through no fault of their own. To alleviate this position, under s. 1(4) of the Mortgage

---

[270] See *Nijar v. Mann* (1998) 30 H.L.R. 223 at 227 *per* Ward L.J.

[271] [2012] EWHC 3791 (Ch) at [26] and [31] *per* Ms Lesley Anderson Q.C., sitting as a Deputy High Court judge.

[272] LPA 1925, s. 109(2).

[273] *Stroud Building Society v. Delamont* [1960] 1 W.L.R. 431 at 435. In *Nijar v. Mann* (1998) 30 H.L.R. 223 at 228, Ward L.J. confessed 'with hardly a tinge of shame, that until I read the papers in this case I was also one of that merry ignorant band'.

[274] See *Nijar v. Mann* (1998) 30 H.L.R. 223.

Repossessions (Protection of Tenants etc) Act 2010, a court may stay or suspend a possession order against an unauthorized tenant for a period of up to two months. While not necessarily perfect from the point of view of the tenant, this legislative reform does afford him some time to find suitable alternative accommodation when faced with a possession action brought by a mortgagee.

11.6.8 Co-owners

Perhaps the most likely person to claim to have an interest in mortgaged property which has priority to that of the mortgagee is a co-owner of that property. This is an area of law that has seen considerable development over a comparatively short period of time. It has seen the courts seeking to strike a balance between two competing interests. On the one hand, one must consider the position of mortgagees. They lend money as part of a commercial enterprise. For them, the ability, in cases of default, to be able to realize their security by gaining possession and subsequently selling the property is paramount. On the other hand, one must consider the position of people other than the mortgagor, who use the property as their home and who have interests in that property. Their principal concern is not to lose their home as a result of the mortgagor using the house as security for a loan.[275] This is particularly the case if they were unaware of the existence of the loan in the first place, or if their consent to the loan was obtained in questionable circumstances. In the course of the judicial development of this aspect of the law of co-ownership and mortgages, various different situations have arisen. Put broadly, one must consider whether there was sole ownership or co-ownership at law, and the type of mortgage involved. As will be seen, it is particularly important to determine whether the purpose of the loan is for the acquisition of the house or, at least, for the mutual benefit of the co-owners, or whether the house is being used as security for loans for the sole or principal benefit of the mortgagor.

11.6.8.1 Sole legal ownership

In *Williams & Glyn's Bank Ltd v. Boland*,[276] a matrimonial home was in the sole name of Mr Boland, but it was conceded that Mrs Boland was a beneficial co-owner of it. He mortgaged the house to the bank which, when he defaulted on the mortgage, sought possession. It was held by the House of Lords that her equitable interest in the house, coupled with the fact that she was in actual occupation of it, meant that she had an overriding interest and that, as against her, the bank was not entitled to possession. *Boland* was a case concerning registered land. Where title is unregistered, the same result would also have occurred, it being clear that a mortgagee would, in circumstances such as those which occurred in *Boland*, be fixed with constructive notice of her right and, therefore, be bound by it.[277]

The upshot of this is that, although as a matter of law the husband, the borrower in default, has no defence to an action for possession, it is pointless for a mortgagee to seek to oust him from the property. This is because, as his wife has the right to remain in the property, vacant possession cannot be obtained, and so the house could not be sold. This led the Court of Appeal in *Albany Home Loans Ltd v. Massey*[278] to decline to order possession against the husband in these circumstances, not least because the effect of such an order

---

[275] See, generally, M.P. Thompson in Meisel and Cook (eds), *Property and Protection: Essays in Honour of Brian Harvey* (Oxford, Hart Publishing 2000), 177.

[276] [1981] A.C. 487. See D. Smith in Gravells (ed.), *Landmark Cases in Land Law* (Oxford, Hart Publishing, 2013), 125.

[277] See *Kingsnorth Trust Ltd v. Tizard* [1986] 1 W.L.R. 783.   [278] [1997] 2 All E.R. 609.

would be to prevent a husband from living with his wife, on pain of being in contempt of court should he flout such an order.[279] Understandably, this was not something that the court was prepared to do. As the house cannot be sold in these circumstances, it may be thought that the outcome would be that both of them could continue living in the house, presumably without making further payments on the mortgage. This is not so, because, as will be seen, the mortgagee will be able to pursue a personal action against the mortgagor, the end result of which is likely to be that the house is ultimately sold.[280]

Although, with the benefit of hindsight, the decision in *Boland* might appear to be un-controversial, it was not viewed in this way at the time.[281] The first objection was that to hold that such interests fell within the category of overriding interests was undesirable because it undermined the reliability of the register and, as a result, increased the need for conveyancers to make actual enquiries of occupants, thereby leading to an increase in cost. The principal concern of the lending institutions, however, was with one particu-lar situation. This was where a single person, normally a man, would approach a poten-tial mortgagee to agree a mortgage. Unbeknown to the lender, however, he was planning to cohabit and his partner would contribute to the initial down payment on the house, thereby acquiring a beneficial interest in it. For some reason she was not to be a legal co-owner of the property. The fear was that her interest in the house would be binding upon the mortgagee, this concern being exacerbated in the case of registered land because of the gap between the transfer of the property and the subsequent application for registration. In this period, it was thought that, if the equitable co-owner, as would be normal, went into actual occupation of the house, she would, at the time when the mortgage was regis-tered, be able to establish an overriding interest binding upon the mortgagee, who would have little opportunity to discover its existence.

Response to Boland

As will be seen, these fears have proved to be exaggerated but, at the time, were keenly felt. The matter was referred to the Law Commission, who recommended that the decision in *Boland* be reversed by legislation, so that the interest of a beneficial co-owner should only bind a purchaser including, of course, a mortgagee, if it was protected by registration.[282] The proposed legislative response was unfortunate. Under the provisions of the misguided Land Registration and Law of Property Bill 1985, the beneficial interest of a wife who was in actual occupation of the home would, unless she had consented to the mortgage, con-tinue to take effect as an overriding interest, whereas if the occupier was not married to the legal owner, the same interest would only bind a mortgagee if it was registered. Leaving aside the undesirability of discriminating against non-married cohabitees in this way, this solution, if implemented, would have made matters worse and would have necessitated an inquiry as to the marital status of occupiers of a home. If it transpired that the couple were married, a further inquiry would need to be addressed to the wife as to whether she had a beneficial interest in the house and, if so, whether she consented to the transaction. If they were not married, then no further inquiries would need to be made of the woman as her interest could only be binding if it had been registered. This would seem to be a convey-ancing absurdity.[283] Fortunately, the Bill was not enacted and the issues involved were left for resolution by the courts.

---

[279] Ibid. at 612 *per* Schiemann L.J. [280] See 11.6.1.

[281] For a hostile response, see S. Freeman (1980) 43 M.L.R. 692, but contrast the more measured reaction by J. Martin [1980] Conv. 361.

[282] (1982) Law Com. No. 115.

[283] See the critical comments on the need for enquiries such as this in *National Provincial Bank Ltd v. Ainsworth* [1965] A.C. 1175 at 1234 *per* Lord Upjohn.

In particular, the decision in *Boland* was underpinned by Lord Wilberforce's stress on conveyancing practice, emphasizing that lenders should make adequate enquiries of all those in the property and, particularly in the case of couples, that banks should ensure that both parties are either legal owners, consenting to the mortgage and so overreaching their beneficial interests,[284] or, if there is a sole owner, that banks should ensure that any beneficial owner who is also in occupation is given an opportunity to disclose their interest, so that if they fail to disclose their beneficial interest on inquiry, their interests will not override.[285] As with the law of undue influence, the effect of these practical conveyancing changes is to encourage banks to protect themselves. For as feminists have repeatedly noted, this emphasis on documentary evidence of consent and the workings of the overreaching machinery do more to protect the banks than vulnerable women.[286]

Limits on Boland

Subsequent case law has done much to clarify the position with regard to the rights of beneficial co-owners when the property has been mortgaged. The general impact of the decisions has been to limit the potential impact of *Boland*, albeit in a way that in most, albeit not all, cases seems to strike a fair balance between the competing interests of secured creditors on the one hand and residential occupiers on the other.

11.6.8.2 Acquisition mortgages

A principal concern of lending institutions is that, if they lend money to a single person to finance the purchase of a house, they could find that a person cohabiting with him has acquired a beneficial interest in the property which would be binding upon the lender; a matter which, in the case of subsequent mortgage default, would seriously affect their ability to realize their security by selling the house.

Imputed intention

This issue first arose in *Bristol and West Building Society v. Henning*.[287] A house was conveyed into the sole name of Mr Henning in circumstances where it was clear that, because of a financial contribution to the down payment on it, Mrs Henning[288] would acquire a beneficial interest in it. The balance of the purchase price was, to the knowledge of Mrs Henning, being borrowed from the building society who took a mortgage over the house. The society had no idea that the house was to be shared and did not address any questions to Mrs Henning, a person about whom it knew nothing. When he defaulted on the mortgage, the society sought possession and she argued that it was bound by her beneficial interest in the home. This defence failed. The Court of Appeal held that, because Mrs Henning knew that a mortgage was being created, and benefited from it in the important sense that the house could not have been acquired without it, the intention would be imputed to her that the interest of the society should take priority to hers.

The reasoning process, that of imputing an intention to a person on the basis of what that person might be taken to have intended had any thought been given to the matter, has long been seen as suspect. One reason for this is that, in the context in which this issue

---

[284] *City of London Building Society v. Flegg* [1987] UKHL 6.

[285] This exception for non-disclosure is now explicitly included in Sched. 3, para. 2(b) LRA 2002 as well as the cases discussed below.

[286] P. Baron, 'The Free Exercise of Her Will: Women and Emotionally Transmitted Debt', Law in Context 13 (1995), 23–56; B. Fehlberg, *Sexually Transmitted Debt: Surety Experience and English Law* (Clarendon Press, 1997) and M. Kaye, 'Equity's treatment of sexually transmitted debt', Feminist Legal Studies 5(1) (1997), 35–55.

[287] [1985] 1 WLR 778.

[288] The couple were not actually married. It is important to remember that, in cases of this nature, the marital status of the co-owners is immaterial.

normally arises, the determination of the beneficial ownership of a house, the normal judicial process is to seek to infer what the intentions of the parties were rather than imputing intentions to them that the court considers that they should have formed. Moreover, to decide a case on an intention which has never been formed but is imposed upon a party is, fairly transparently, a result-driven form of reasoning: it achieves an intended result based upon the fiction of what the law, apparently conclusively, takes to be a person's intention.

In circumstances such as those that occurred in *Henning*, and the case that immediately followed it, *Paddington Building Society v. Mendelsohn*,[289] it seems to be obviously wrong that a person in her position can claim to have a prior right to a mortgagee that is financing the purchase of a house in which she is going to live. The difficulty is to find an acceptable principle to achieve this end. Possibly because of the inherent problems in reasoning based on the notion of an imputed intention, some subsequent judicial discussions of this issue have tended to rely on an alternative basis for the decision, that being that a person in the position of Mrs Henning is estopped from asserting that her beneficial interest has priority over that of the mortgagee:[290] a more plausible, but also flawed, rationalization.

This focus on knowledge, or a similar principle, appeared to be endorsed by the House of Lords in *Abbey National Building Society v. Cann*,[291] although it should also be said at the outset that there was a much more convincing ground relied upon for the actual decision. In this case, George Cann was buying a house and his mother was making a sizeable contribution to the purchase price. It was clear that, once the house had been acquired, she would acquire an interest in it. The issue in the case was whether that interest would be binding on the bank who had lent money to George in order for him to finance its purchase. In deciding against her, the House considered, albeit briefly, the point as to what knowledge she had that her son was taking out a mortgage over the house in order for the house to be bought and the significance of such knowledge. Appraising her argument that she did not know that her son would be mortgaging the house to secure money to finance its purchase, Lord Oliver said:

> In the circumstances of his known lack of resources, however, this is fanciful and in my judgment the court was entitled to draw the inference that it did draw. If that is right, it follows that George Cann was permitted to raise money on the security of the property without any limitation on his authority being communicated to the society. She is not, therefore, in a position to complain, as against the lender, that too much was raised and even if, contrary to the view which I have formed, she had been able to establish an interest in the property which would otherwise prevail against the society, the circumstances to which I have alluded would preclude her from relying upon it as prevailing over the society's interest.[292]

Clearly, the context in which Lord Oliver made these remarks was to cover a situation where a person knew that a mortgage was being created *and that the purpose of that mortgage was to enable the house to be bought*. The only difference in this respect between *Cann* and *Henning*, which was not cited, was that in *Cann* the legal owner of the house borrowed considerably more than she had envisaged, whereas this was not an issue in *Henning*. That, however, is not a material difference. Unfortunately, however, Lord Oliver's comments were cited entirely out of context in the unfortunate decision in *Wishart v. Credit and Mercantile Plc*,[293] a case which exposes a serious weakness in the estoppel analysis.

---

[289] (1995) 50 P. &.C.R. 244. See M.P. Thompson (1986) 49 M.L.R. 57.

[290] *Skipton Building Society v. Clayton* (1993) 25 H.L.R. 596 at 602 *per* Slade L.J. See also *Thompson v. Foy* [2009] EWHC 1079 (Ch) at [142]–[143] *per* Lewison J., and the detailed analysis of this issue in *Bank of Scotland v. Hussain* [2010] EWHC 2812 (Ch) at [96]–[111] *per* Newey J.

[291] [1991] 1 A.C. 56.   [292] Ibid. at 94.

[293] [2015] EWCA Civ. 655. Also known as *Credit and Mercantile Plc v. Kaymuu Ltd.*

The land in question, Dalhanna, was purchased in May 2010 and transferred into the name of Kaymuu Ltd, which was registered as the proprietor. This company was owned by a person called Sami who was, at that time, a close friend of Mr Wishart who, it was accepted, was the beneficial owner of Dalhanna and was in actual occupation of it at all material times. The reason that the house was put into the name of the company appeared to be to avoid tax. The business affairs of both the main players were, however, somewhat muddy. Both Mr Wishart and Sami were fraudsters, Mr Wishart having served a prison term for financial offences. Sami got the company to borrow £500,000 from Credit and Mercantile against the security of Dalhanna and a charge was registered in its favour. He then lost that money gambling. The bank brought possession proceedings against Mr Wishart of whom it had made no inquiries prior to the creation of the mortgage. He argued that the bank took subject to his overriding interest. His defence failed and the Court of Appeal held that the bank was entitled to possession.

In *Wishart*, the Court of Appeal, in effect, held that a beneficial co-owner is estopped from asserting that interest against a purchaser because he or she has allowed another person to appear as the sole legal owner. There are a number of problems with this view. First, the normal concept of estoppel involves A making some kind of representation to B which B then relies upon. In a case such as *Wishart*, however, A allows B to be in a position to make a representation of unencumbered ownership to C, C being completely unaware of A's existence. This difference from the usual type of estoppel case may also explain why, in *Brocklesby* itself, before the court would be prepared to hold that A lost priority to C there must have been 'on the part of the person who trusts the other with the deeds either fraud, or, as it has been sometimes said, such negligence as to be evidence of fraud that the permitted possession of deeds of another will validate a security given without the authority of the owner of the deeds'.[294] There is no hint of such a stringent requirement in *Wishart*, and it is noticeable that in other cases where estoppel has been employed to defeat the priority claim of a beneficial owner of property some direct involvement of that owner has been significant: an important point of distinction with *Wishart*.

In *Midland Bank Ltd v. Farmpride Hatcheries Ltd*,[295] for example, a Mr Willey and his wife were the sole owners and directors of a company. A house was purchased and transferred into the name of that company. The company then granted him and his wife an occupancy right in respect of the house.[296] He then, on behalf of the company, negotiated a mortgage over the property. Following default by the company, he defended the possession action arguing that his equitable interest in the house was binding on the bank. Unsurprisingly this defence failed. Mr Willey was estopped from asserting his beneficial interest in the property. This was not, however, simply because he had allowed the company to appear to be the sole legal owner of the house. The estoppel arose because Mr Willey, having conducted the negotiations with the bank on behalf of the company, was clearly creating the impression that he would not personally be asserting on his own behalf any interest adverse to the bank with whom he had been negotiating.

Again, in *Thompson v. Foy*,[297] although Newey J. cited with approval the decision in *Brocklesby*, he went on to point out that on the facts Mrs Thompson, who was claiming to have an interest binding on the bank, knew from the outset that the house was to be

---

[294] *Brocklesby v. Temperance Permanent Building Society* [1895] A.C. 173 at 180 *per* Lord Herschell. This is the same test employed to determine if a prior legal mortgagee loses priority by parting with possession of the title deeds. See, e.g., *Perry-Herrick v. Attwood* (1857) 2 De G. &. J, 21 at 39 *per* Lord Cranworth L.C.

[295] [1981] 2 E.G.L.R. 142.

[296] Subsequently it has been established that the right in question was not a proprietary right. For present purposes, this point is immaterial.

[297] [2010] 1 P. &. C.R. 16 at [141]–[142].

mortgaged. She approved of this transaction, benefited from it, and executed a legal document to allow the transaction to take place.[298] As such, it is a far cry from the situation in *Wishart* where, at least on the facts as presented, there was no evidence that Mr Wishart was in any way complicit in the disputed mortgage or that he intended to allow Sami, through the medium of the company, to have *carte blanche* to mortgage the property in the future.

11.6.8.3 The registration gap

The real solution to the problem which arose in *Henning* derives from the solution arrived at by the House of Lords to defuse a closely related problem, that of the so-called registration gap. Registered conveyancing involves two stages pertinent to the transfer of the legal estate and the creation of a mortgage in favour of a bank which is partially funding the purchase. First, there is the execution of the transfer document by the vendor in favour of the purchaser and the creation of the mortgage document in favour of the bank. Applications are then made for the registration of the purchaser as the new proprietor and of the new legal charge by the bank.

Inevitably there exists a gap between the execution of the documents and their registration. Under s. 20, LRA 1925, the legal title passed on the date of registration. This is also the earliest time when the legal mortgage is created. This is what has been termed the registration gap. The perceived problem was that in this gap between the disposition and the subsequent registration, a person with a beneficial interest in the property could go into actual occupation of the property. As the time of registration was the time when the legal title passed, this, rather than the date of the transfer, was widely seen as being the relevant time for determining whether or not an overriding interest was in existence.[299] This argument led to the alarming scenario that someone who held a beneficial interest in the house, would acquire an overriding interest because at the date of registration she was in actual occupation of the property despite not being in actual occupation at the date of the transfer. This would be particularly tough on the mortgagee who would, in this scenario, end up being bound by an interest which it could not realistically expect to have discovered.

In *Abbey National Building Society v. Cann*,[300] the House of Lords, who considered such an outcome to be a conveyancing absurdity, managed by a purposive approach to the interpretation of s. 70(1)(g) of the LRA 1925 to conclude that the relevant date for the person claiming an overriding interest under this provision was the date of the transfer rather than the date of registration; a conclusion which is now confirmed under the LRA 2002.[301] Much more importantly, the House of Lords analysed the general legal position when land is purchased with the aid of a mortgage and a person claims to have an interest binding on the mortgagee.

11.6.8.4 Distinguishing acquisition and non-acquisition mortgages

The essential problem with an analysis of the type of problem exemplified in *Henning* is that it is unable to differentiate between two very different situations. The first is where the transfer is of the legal title of a house to A and a mortgage is created, that mortgage being an essential part of the financing of the purchase (this is an acquisition mortgage). B who, by contributing to the purchase price of that property will acquire an interest in it, then seeks to assert that right against the mortgagee. This is the *Henning/Mendelsohn*

---

[298] Ibid. at [143].   [299] For an argument to the contrary, see P. Sparkes [1986] Conv. 309.
[300] [1991] 1 A.C. 56. See S. Baughen [1991] Conv. 116; P.T. Evans [1991] Conv. 309.
[301] LRA 2002, Sched. 3, para. 2.

scenario where it is clear that B cannot assert that her interest has priority over that of the mortgagee. The second type of case is where A is the legal owner of a house and B has a beneficial interest in it (this is a non-acquisition mortgage). At some time subsequent to the acquisition of the property, A creates a mortgage and, when the mortgagee seeks to enforce its rights, B asserts that her beneficial interest is binding on the bank. These, essentially, are the facts of *Boland* where, of course, the bank lost. They are also, of course, the facts of *Wishart* where the bank prevailed. This must be wrong. Where the error lies, it is suggested, is in the wrongful acceptance of the notion that for a beneficial owner to allow another person to become the sole legal owner gives rise to a form of estoppel so that the beneficial owner is estopped from asserting rights against a mortgagee, or indeed any other purchaser, when that mortgage is created by the sole legal owner.

It is clear that, in the second scenario, prior to any further transaction entered into by A, A holds the property on trust for himself and B. B plainly has a beneficial interest in the property. If A then creates a mortgage and B is in actual occupation of the property, B's interest is binding on the mortgagee unless it makes inquiries of B and B then fails to disclose her interest in the property.[302] To hold that, absent any such inquiry, B is in some way estopped from asserting that right against the mortgagee is, effectively, making this source of overriding interest redundant. Consequently, there has to be a justification other than estoppel or some form of ostensible authority to justify the distinction between the two cases. This justification comes not from the alternative notion of imputed intention, but from an analysis of the mode of acquisition of interests in land.

11.6.8.5 Non-acquisition mortgages and overreaching

A mortgagee is most likely to be affected by the interest of a co-owner if the mortgage is created some time after the property has been acquired, that is when the house is used as security for further borrowing. When there is only one legal owner of the property, then the mortgagee must make enquiries of any adults[303] who are in actual occupation of the property. Where there is co-ownership at law, the position is different.

Legal co-ownership

In *City of London Building Society v. Flegg*,[304] a married couple were registered proprietors of a house which they held on trust for themselves and her parents. Without informing the parents, the legal owners created a number of mortgages over the house until, finally, they created a mortgage in favour of the plaintiffs, and the money borrowed[305] was used to redeem the existing mortgages. No enquiries were addressed to the parents who, when the mortgagee sought possession, argued that, as beneficial co-owners who were in actual occupation, they had an overriding interest binding upon the mortgagee. Reversing a highly controversial decision of the Court of Appeal[306] in favour of the parents, the House of Lords held in favour of the society and made an order for possession.[307]

---

[302] LRA 2002, Sched. 3.

[303] Persons under the age of eighteen are not regarded as being in actual occupation of the property and so, even if they have a beneficial interest in the property, will not have an overriding interest: *Hypo-Mortgage Services Ltd v. Robinson* [1997] 2 F.L.R. 422.

[304] [1988] A.C. 54. See M.P. Thompson [1988] Conv. 108; N. Hopkins in Gravells (ed.), *Landmark Cases in Land Law* (Oxford, Hart Publishing, 2013), Chapter 9.

[305] It is immaterial if the mortgage was created but no capital money was paid. *State Bank of India v. Sood* [1997] Ch. 276. See C. Harpum [1980] C.L.J. 277; M.P. Thompson [1997] Conv. 134.

[306] [1986] Ch. 605. For strong criticism, see [1] Harpum (1986) 136 N.L.J. 208. For a lone defence, see M.P. Thompson (1986) C.L.J. 140.

[307] Astonishingly, this decision, which was directly on point, was completely overlooked in *AIB Group (UK) Plc v. Turner* [2015] EWHC 3994 (Ch). For critique see M. Dixon [2016] Conv. 81.

This decision very much reflected orthodox opinion as to the effect of a mortgage executed by two legal owners, which was that it would operate to overreach the beneficial interests[308] which exist behind the trust.[309] It was also apparent that the House of Lords were strongly motivated by the perceived conveyancing implications of the case, and considered that a decision in favour of the occupiers would have the consequence that 'financial institutions [would] face hitherto unsuspected hazards';[310] a prospect which was not viewed with equanimity.

While one can appreciate the force of this argument, it is not necessarily compelling.[311] The rationale behind the decision in *Boland* is to prevent occupiers of property, who have a beneficial interest in it, from losing their homes as a result of the actions of the legal owner in mortgaging the property for his own financial purposes without consulting them. From the perspective of the occupier, it is doubtful if the significance of the mortgage being executed by two, as opposed to one, legal owner would be fully appreciated. When one considers that the type of mortgage in question involves a situation where a home is being used as security for future borrowing, a case can be made that it is not unreasonable to expect the lender to consult all the occupants of the house before lending the money by way of mortgage.

Such arguments found favour with the Law Commission who, in contrast to the view taken of the decision in *Boland*, recommended that the decision in *Flegg* be reversed by legislation.[312] This recommendation has not been implemented.[313] Although it has been argued that *Flegg* had been overruled by the provisions of the Trusts of Land (Appointment of Trustees) Act (TOLATA) 1996,[314] this argument, which has been considered earlier,[315] seems unlikely to prevail and the decision in *Flegg* will remain as the definitive determination of this issue. For dispositions occurring after the LRA 2002 came into force, this matter is made clear by s. 26. It provides that, insofar as a disponee is concerned, a person's right to exercise owner's powers in relation to a registered charge or estate is to be taken free from any limitations affecting the validity of the disposition thereby, *inter alia*, confirming the result in *Flegg*.

11.7 Priority of mortgages

The principal advantage of being a secured creditor is that, when the property is sold, the creditor is paid what is owed to him, in full, from the proceeds of sale. Where there is more than one secured creditor, then they do not share the proceeds of sale proportionately; they are paid on the basis of the priority of their securities.[316] Thus, if a house is mortgaged, first, to A for £60,000 and, second, to B for £50,000 and then sold for £100,000, A, assuming that his mortgage has priority, will receive £60,000 from the proceeds of sale. B will then receive £40,000 but will be an unsecured creditor in respect of the remaining

---

[308] This term also includes mere equities. See *Birmingham Midshires Mortgages Ltd v. Saberwal* (2000) 80 P. &.C.R. 256 at 262 *per* Robert Goff L.J.; *Mortgage Express v. Lambert* [2016] EWCA Civ. 555 at [18] *per* Lewison L.J.

[309] See, e.g., H. Forrest [1978] Conv. 194 at 199–201; M.D.A. Freeman (1981) Fam. Law 37 at 40; J. Martin [1980] Conv. 361; W.T. Murphy (1979) 42 M.L.R. 467. For an unsuccessful argument to the contrary, see M.P. Thompson (1986) 6 L.S. 140.

[310] [1988] A.C. 54 at 72 *per* Lord Oliver.   [311] See G. Owen and D. Cahill [2017] Conv. 26.

[312] (1989) Law Com. No. 188.

[313] See the comments in *State Bank of India v. Sood* [1987] Ch. 276 at 290 *per* Peter Gibson L.J. See also M.P. Thompson in Meisel and Cook, *Property and Protection*, 157 at 171–2.

[314] G. Ferris and G. Battersby [1998] Conv. 168.

[315] See Chapter 5.   [316] See, generally, R.E. Megarry (1940) 7 C.L.J. 243.

£10,000. If, as in the example just considered, the property is mortgaged for more than it is worth when it is actually sold, the issue of priority will become of central importance.

The law relating to this matter when title was unregistered was difficult and, in many respects, unsatisfactory. As it is only of very limited importance today, much of this can be regarded as being of historical interest[317] and attention confined to where title is registered.

11.7.1 **Unregistered land**

The law relating to this matter when title was unregistered was difficult and, in many respects, unsatisfactory. As it is only of very limited importance today, much of this can be regarded as being of historical interest[318] and attention confined to where title is registered.

11.7.2 **Registered land**

When title is registered, a mortgage is created by a registered charge. The priority of charges is governed by s. 48, LRA 2002,[319] which provides that the charges rank between themselves in the order on which they are shown on the register. Until a charge is registered it operates only in equity. If there are two such charges, the priority is the order in which they were created.[320] This can be illustrated by an example.

A charge over registered land is created in favour of A. Two weeks later another charge is created in favour of B. Neither has yet applied for registration of their charges. The priority order is A then B, the order of their creation. B then registers his charge. The effect of this is that A's charge, which has yet to be registered will be postponed to that of B,[321] so the priority order will now be B then A.

This result will occur unless the remedy of subrogation is available, as occurred in *Anfield (UK) Ltd v. Bank of Scotland Plc.*[322] In September 2000, a charge was registered in favour of the Halifax. A registered charge was created in June 2007 in favour of LSL and, in October of that year, a unilateral notice was registered in respect of a pending land action, and, in April 2008, an equitable charge was created, these two registrations being by Anfield. In April 2009 a charge was registered in favour of the Bank of Scotland. Ordinarily, the order of priorities would have been, first, LSL, second Anfield, and finally the Bank of Scotland. The 2009 charge was, however, registered in respect of a mortgage granted by the Bank in 2006, and the purpose of that mortgage was to pay off the mortgage in favour of the Halifax. It was held that the Bank of Scotland had priority over the other charges. This was because, as the purpose of the loan was to pay off that mortgage, it was subrogated to the rights of the Halifax, whose charge clearly had priority over the subsequent charges.

11.7.3 **Tacking**

The process of tacking involves a mortgagee granting a further loan to the mortgagor and adding that loan to the amount which is already secured by the existing mortgage. The ability to do this may, of course, impact upon the rights of subsequent mortgagees who may, as a result, find that their loans are no longer fully secured. Because of this, restrictions are imposed upon the right to tack and it is again necessary to distinguish between registered and unregistered land.

---

[317] See the fifth edition of this title, 532–5.   [318] See the fifth edition of this title, 532–5.
[319] For the position prior to the 2002 Act coming into force, see first edition of this title, 380–1.
[320] LRA 2002, s. 48.   [321] Ibid., s. 30.
[322] [2010] EWHC 2374 (Ch). See also *Cheltenham & Gloucester plc v. Appleyard* [2004] EWCA Civ. 291.

11.7.3.1 **Unregistered land**

The right to tack, where title is unregistered, is governed by s. 94, LPA 1925 and can be done in three situations.

Consent of intervening mortgagee

If property is mortgaged, first to A, and then to B, A may tack a loan to the existing mortgage if B consents to this being done. This is unsurprising as it is, in any event, open to mortgagees, to agree to change the normal order of priorities if they wish.[323]

No notice of intervening mortgage

A mortgagee may tack a further loan to an existing mortgage if he has no notice of an intervening mortgage. If the property is mortgaged first to A and then to B, A cannot tack if he has notice of B's mortgage. A will have notice of B's mortgage if B has registered the mortgage as a land charge. If the mortgage to A is to secure further advances, then A will not be deemed to have notice of B's mortgage merely because it has been registered as a land charge.[324] To avoid any difficulties, B should inform A of the existence of his mortgage.

Obligation to make further advances

If the first mortgagee is obliged, under the terms of the mortgage, to make further advances to the mortgagor, he is entitled to tack the loan to the original mortgage regardless of whether he has notice of a subsequent mortgage.

11.7.3.2 **Registered land**

The right to tack is governed by s. 49, LRA 2002, which reproduces the conditions contained in the 1925 Act and adds one further situation when tacking can occur. It also puts on to a statutory footing what had been the previous practice of lenders.

Under s. 49(1) of the Act, the proprietor of a registered charge may tack a further advance if he has not received from a subsequent chargee notice of the creation of a subsequent charge. This puts on a statutory footing the previous practice of lenders. Tacking may also occur if, under the charge, the proprietor is obliged to make further advances and this is noted on the register.[325] He may also tack if a subsequent chargee agrees.[326] These two provisions replicate the previous law.[327]

Under the LRA 2002, one new situation when tacking can occur has been introduced. Under s. 49(4), if the parties to a charge have agreed a maximum amount for which the charge is created, tacking can occur up to that limit. If A creates a charge in favour of B to secure borrowing of up to £100,000 and, at the time when the charge is created, only £50,000 has been lent, then further advances up to the £100,000 limit can be tacked to the charge. For this to happen, the agreement in relation to the maximum amount must be entered on the register.

---

[323] *Cheah Theam Swee v. Equitcorp Finance Group Ltd* [1992] A.C. 472.
[324] LPA 1925, s. 94(2).   [325] LRA 2002, s. 49(3).   [326] Ibid., s. 49(6).   [327] Ibid., s. 30.

12

Easements

The first part of this book had been concerned largely with ownership rights. The previous chapter on mortgages dealt with an important third-party right, although the origins of this right lay also in ownership of the property and it is still the case that a mortgagee is regarded as the purchaser of a legal estate in land. In the course of the consideration of the law relating to land ownership, the enforceability of third-party rights has been considered. The remainder of the book is concerned with the substance of those rights. This chapter is concerned with the form of third-party right categorized as an easement. The remaining chapters will deal with freehold covenants and licences.[1]

12.1 The nature of an easement

The essential nature of an easement is that it is a right over another person's land. These rights are so important it has been said that, '[w]ithout easements it may be very difficult if not impossible to enjoy the benefits of land ownership';[2] an observation attested to by the fact that at least 65 per cent of registered freehold titles are subject to at least one easement.[3] Classic examples of easements are rights of way and rights of light, but there are numerous others, including the right to use a washing line on a neighbour's land,[4] the right to use a neighbour's lavatory,[5] and the right to park a car on another person's land.[6] This, of course, is not an exhaustive list. These are simply examples of rights which have been afforded the status of easements. What is necessary is to identify the characteristics common to all easements.

The most authoritative exposition of the nature of easements was given by the Court of Appeal in *Re Ellenborough Park*[7] where, for the first time, the right of householders to walk freely in a nearby park was recognized as satisfying the requirements to qualify as an easement.

12.1.1 Dominant and servient tenement

For a right to exist as an easement, that right must affect two plots of land, or tenements. It is 'an essential element of an easement that it is annexed to land, and that no person can

---

[1] For reasons of space, neither rentcharges nor *profits à prendre*, which today are of relatively little importance, will be considered in any detail.

[2] *Wall v. Collins* [2008] 1 All E.R. 122 at [58] *per* Hooper L.J.

[3] (2008) Law Com. Consultation Paper No. 186, para. 1.3.

[4] *Drewell v. Towler* (1832) 3 B. & Ad. 735. See also *Mulvaney v. Gough* [2002] EWCA Civ. 1078.

[5] *Miller v. Emcer Products Ltd* [1956] Ch. 304.

[6] See *Patel v. W.H. Smith (Eziot) Ltd* [1987] 1 W.L.R. 853 at 859 *per* Balcombe L.J. See 12.1.4.7.

[7] [1956] Ch. 131 at 163 *per* Sir Raymond Evershed M.R., adopting a passage in Cheshire, *The Modern Law of Real Property* (7th edn) (London, Butterworths, 1954), 456. See also *Mulvaney v. Gough* [2002] EWCA Civ. 1078.

possess an easement otherwise than in respect of land and in amplification of his enjoyment of some estate or interest in a piece of land'.[8] If the easement in question is a right of way, then the person claiming the right over another plot of land does so in his capacity as the owner of a tenement. The land which enjoys the benefit of the right is termed the dominant tenement and the land over which the right is exercised is the servient tenement. If a person claiming to have a right to cross another person's land does not own land himself, then the right may be either a licence or even a public right of way, but it cannot be an easement. The easement must exist for the benefit of land or, putting the same point another way, an easement cannot exist in gross.[9]

The rule that an easement cannot exist in gross has been subject to criticism. It has been argued that, in a modern society, it should be possible to possess an easement without there having to be a dominant tenement.[10] On the other hand, a complementary requirement for an interest to be recognized as an easement is that, not only must there be a dominant tenement, but the right in question must also accommodate that tenement. To abandon the need for a dominant tenement may lead to a number of new rights being found to burden land, and this is not something the law has been keen to encourage.[11] The Law Commission, having explored the pros and cons of this issue, provisionally concluded that there should be no change in the existing law,[12] and this conclusion, which was supported after consultation,[13] seems sensible.

Once an easement has been created, it will run automatically with the dominant land and can be enjoyed by any occupier of that land. If there was no need for there to be a dominant tenement, the passing of the benefit of easements may present problems.

12.1.2 **The right must accommodate the dominant tenement**

An easement exists to benefit land. As such it is necessary, but not sufficient, that the person claiming the right in question must own land; it is also a requirement that the right claimed actually benefits his land or, again, putting the same point in a different way, the right must accommodate the dominant tenement. The right must benefit the owner of the land in that capacity and not simply confer a personal benefit on him incidental to his ownership of the land. The fact that the easement benefits one plot of land does not mean that the owner of that land can use the easement for the benefit of other plots of land which he owns but which do not have the benefit of that easement.[14] In general, with regard to this matter, two issues arise. These are the mutual proximity of the two plots and the nature of the advantage claimed.

12.1.2.1 **Proximity**

For a right over one tenement to confer a benefit on another, common sense would dictate that the two plots of land need to be reasonably close to each other. So, as was once famously commented, if the owner of an estate in Northumberland granted a right of way over that land to the owner of an estate in Kent, there would be no link between the two estates and

---

[8] *Alfred F. Beckett v. Lyons* [1967] Ch. 449 at 483 *per* Winn L.J., and includes an incorporeal interest such as a fishing right: *Hanbury v. Jenkins* [1901] 2 Ch. 401 at 422–3 *per* Buckley L.J.

[9] See *Hawkins v. Rutter* [1892] 1 Q.B. 668; *London and Blenheim Estates Ltd v. Ladbroke Retail Parks Ltd* [1994] 1 W.L.R. 31 at 36 *per* Peter Gibson L.J.

[10] See M.F. Sturley (1980) 96 L.Q.R. 557.

[11] See A. Lawson in Tee (ed.), *Land Law: Issues, Debates, Policy* (Cullompton, Willan Publishing, 2002), 64 at 69–74.

[12] (2008) Law Com. Consultation Paper No. 186, para. 3.18.

[13] (2011) Law Com. No. 327, para. 2.24.   [14] *Peacock v. Custins* [2001] 2 All E.R. 827.

so the right could not take effect as an easement.[15] This is not to say, however, that the two plots must necessarily be physically contiguous as a right may exist over land which is separated from the dominant plot by other land. So, for example, in *Re Ellenborough Park*,[16] it was held that the right to walk in a park could be enjoyed as an easement by the owners of property on an estate when those properties did not physically adjoin the park. There was sufficient connection between the right in question and the particular properties. Clearly, however, whether the two tenements are sufficiently proximate to each other so that the right really does benefit the dominant tenement is essentially one of fact and the greater the physical separation of the two plots in question, the more difficult it will be to establish that the right actually does accommodate the dominant tenement.

12.1.2.2 Nature of the claim

Leaving aside the question of physical proximity, the other main aspect of whether the right claimed accommodates the dominant tenement concerns the nature of the right claimed; whether it has some natural connection with the estate,[17] or whether it confers merely a personal advantage for the current owner of that estate. This, again, is essentially a question of fact and the essential test to determine this matter is whether the right makes the occupation or use of the dominant tenement more convenient.

Business use

If the dominant tenement is used for business purposes, a right which facilitates that business use can exist as an easement. In *Moody v. Steggles*,[18] the dominant tenement was a pub. The right to place a sign on neighbouring land in respect of that pub was accepted as accommodating the dominant tenement and recognized as being an easement. Conversely, in *Hill v. Tupper*,[19] the tenant of land on a canal bank had been given the exclusive right by the freeholder to put pleasure boats on the canal. The defendant put rival boats on the canal and so the tenant sued, his claim being based on the argument that the defendant was interfering with his easement to put the boats on the canal. The claim failed. It was held that this right did not amount to an easement because it did not accommodate the dominant tenement.

The difference between the cases, which both involved business use, would seem to be that, in the former, the right being claimed was supportive of the business use of the dominant tenement, whilst, in the latter, the right being claimed as an easement was the business itself. While the existence of the exclusive right to put boats onto the canal would have been an advantage to the owner of the land, it did not benefit the land itself. This argument gains support from the decision in *P. & S. Platt Ltd v. Crouch*,[20] where it was accepted, seemingly without argument to the contrary, that a right to moor boats on an island close to the dominant land which was used as an hotel accommodated the dominant tenement. The right to moor boats could be seen as an advantage to the existing use of the benefited land.

Recreational use

One of the key questions in *Re Ellenborough Park* itself was whether the right to enjoy the park was capable of accommodating the houses surrounding it. There is clear authority that, for a right to be an easement, it 'must be a right of utility and benefit, and not one of

---

[15] See *Bailey v. Stephens* (1862) 12 C.B. (N.S.) 91 at 115 *per* Byles J,
[16] [1956] Ch. 131. See also *Pugh v Savage* [1034] 1 Ch. 631.
[17] *Bailey v Stephens, supra.*
[18] (1879) 12 Ch.D. 261. See also *Wong v. Beaumont Property Trust Ltd* [1965] 1 Q.B. 173.
[19] (1863) 2 H. & C. 121.   [20] [2003] EWCA Civ. 1110.

mere recreation and amusement'.[21] Lord Evershed M.R. accepted that broad principle in *Re Ellenborough Park*, but also said that the right to use the park for exercise, rest, and taking out small children in their perambulators made it beneficial to the premises to which the park is attached.[22] He distinguished those activities from horse-racing[23] or playing games, which he considered would not accommodate the dominant land because they would be classed as mere recreation.[24]

This issue of recreational use arose again recently in *Regency Villas Title Ltd v. Diamond Resorts (Europe) Ltd.*[25] A transfer of land had purported to include the right of the time-share-owning occupiers of the villas to use the sporting and leisure facilities in the adjoining resort. At first instance, Judge Purle Q.C. held that *Re Ellenborough Park* is 'authority for the proposition that an easement permitting the dominant owner to walk over all parts of the servient tenement purely for pleasure can exist in law', and therefore 'it is a relatively small step to extend that to the enjoyment of sporting and other recreational facilities'.[26] He thought that the emphasis on the exclusion of 'mere recreation' should be in the word 'mere', in that the recreational right may not benefit dominant land at all.[27] As a result, 'rights of recreation can take effect as easements, so long as they accommodate dominant land, are not too wide and vague, do not amount to rights of joint occupation and do not deprive the servient owner of proprietorship or legal possession'.[28]

The Court of Appeal agreed with Purle J., and went further in declaring the perceived exclusion of rights of 'mere recreation of amusement' as neither useful in today's society nor binding upon them. Sir Geoffrey Vos said:[29]

> an easement should not in the modern world be held to be invalid on the ground that it was 'mere recreation or amusement' because the form of physical exercise it envisaged was a game or a sport. To be clear, we do not regard Baron Martin's *dictum* [in *Mounsey v. Ismay*] as binding on this court, and we would decline to follow it insofar as it suggests that an easement cannot be held to exist in respect of a right to engage in recreational physical activities on servient land.

The case was appealed to the Supreme Court, and they squarely agreed with the 'principled analysis' of the courts below. Lord Briggs, writing the majority judgment, concluded that, 'whatever may have been the attitude in the past to "mere recreation or amusement," recreational and sporting activity of the type exemplified [by the facts in this case] is so clearly a beneficial part of modern life that the common law should support structures which promote and encourage it, rather than treat it as devoid of practical utility or benefit'.[30] Following the decision in *Regency Villas*, it is now correct to say that there is, in and of itself, no rule against rights that amount to recreational use, as long as they satisfy the other requirements of *Re Ellenborough Park*.

12.1.3 **The tenements must be owned by different people**

An easement is a right over another person's land. The rule that the two tenements must be owned by different people is, therefore, at first sight at least, an almost self-evident proposition. So, if a person owns a house and a nearby field and uses the field as a convenient means of access to a main road, there is no easement. His use of the field is as the owner

---

[21] *Mounsey v. Ismay* (1865) 159 E.R. 621 *per* Hurlstone and Coltman JJ.
[22] [1956] Ch. 131 at 177–8.
[23] Horse-racing was the activity in *Mounsey v. Ismay* (1865) 159 E.R. 621.
[24] [1956] Ch. 131 at 178.   [25] [2018] UKSC 57.   [26] [2015] EWHC 3564 (Ch) at [54].
[27] Ibid. at [55].   [28] Ibid.   [29] [2017] EWCA Civ. 238 at [56].   [30] [2018] UKSC 57 at [81].

of it. The field is being used in a subordinate way to the house and, had the two tenements been separately owned, the right of way would exhibit the essential characteristics of an easement. In recognition of this, the use of the field in these circumstances is described as a quasi-easement. While the land is in common ownership, the existence of a quasi-easement is of little importance. It may become very important, however, if the land is subsequently sold off separately.[31]

Somewhat counter-intuitively, although persuasively, the Law Commission provisionally recommended, insofar as registered land is concerned, a relaxation of this rule to enable a person to create an easement in respect of land which he also owns. The situation that the Commission had in mind is one where a developer builds a housing estate and sells off individual houses. Then, it will be necessary to grant easements over the various plots but, as the law currently stands, he cannot do this while he still owns the relevant land. Consequently, it was provisionally proposed that, provided that the plots are registered with separate titles, a person should be able to create easements over land which he owns.[32] This proposal was described by one consultee as the single most important proposal in the Consultation Paper,[33] and met with general support. Consequently it has been recommended that, provided that title to the benefited and burdened land is registered, the fact that they are in common ownership and possession shall not prevent the creation or existence of easements or profits.[34]

12.1.3.1 Leasehold property

The rule that an easement cannot exist if the two tenements are owned by the same person admits of one important exception. If the one person owns the freehold of two properties and lets one of them, there is no objection to the tenant of that property owning an easement over his landlord's other property. Such an easement exists for the benefit of the leasehold estate and so will end on the termination of the lease.

12.1.4 The right must be capable of being the subject matter of a grant

An easement is capable of existing as a legal interest in land. As such, it is a prerequisite that it is capable of being granted by deed. This entails that there must be both a capable grantor and a capable grantee. In addition to this, the right claimed must be sufficiently definite. This requirement has defeated claims to an easement entitling a landowner to a good view,[35] a passage of air through an undefined channel,[36] and the right to drain water through an undefined channel.[37]

12.1.4.1 Recognition of new easements

In considering this final criterion for the recognition of easements, the need for the right claimed to have sufficient certainty to form the subject matter of a grant is not the only matter to which the courts will pay regard. Although it has been said that there was a tendency in the past to freeze the categories of easements, the decision in *Re Ellenborough Park*,[38] where the right to use a park for recreational purposes was recognized to be an

---

[31] See 12.4.3.2.

[32] See (2008) Law Com. Consultation Paper No. 186, paras 3.56–3.66. See also in respect of restrictive covenants, 13.5.8.

[33] (2011) Law Com. No. 327, para. 4.24.   [34] Ibid, para. 4.44.

[35] *William Aldred's Case* (1610) 9 Co. Rep. 57b.   [36] *Harris v. De Pinna* (1886) 33 Ch.D. 231.

[37] *Home Brewery plc v. William Davis & Co. (Loughborough) Ltd* [1987] Q.B. 339; *Palmer v. Bowman* [2000] 1 All E.R. 22. A right to the supply of water through a defined channel can be an easement. See *Rance v. Elvin* (1985) 50 P. & C.R. 9.

[38] [1956] Ch. 131.

easement for the first time, has been said to have been a defrosting operation,[39] so that the courts are prepared to accept new rights as being capable of being easements.[40] In so doing, the courts are prepared to accept that the law should be prepared to adapt to changing social conditions, hence the comparatively recent acceptance that the right to park a car anywhere in a defined area can exist as an easement.[41] A more recent example lies in *Coventry v. Lawrence (No. 2)*, where Lord Neuberger thought that 'the right to carry on an activity which results in noise, or the right to emit a noise, which would otherwise cause an actionable nuisance, is capable of being an easement.'[42] The noise, in other words, would be made on the dominant land, and the owner of the servient land would not be able to bring a claim (in nuisance) to stop it. This is difficult to see as properly belonging to the law of easements, because the right to make a noise is likely to fall foul of the rule that it must be sufficiently definite, unless the noise itself is clearly defined in terms of how loud and how frequent it will be.

As against this broad policy to adapt the class of rights capable of being easements as society develops, the courts have traditionally been wary of allowing novel rights to be attached to land because to allow this would place impediments on a person's subsequent ability to deal with the land.[43] As part of the resolution of these tensions, certain types of right are unlikely to be recognized as capable of being easements.

12.1.4.2 Negative rights

Subject to two well-established exceptions, it is highly unlikely that the courts will recognize as an easement a claim which restricts the use to which the owner of the servient land can put his land.[44] The exceptions to this general principle concern a right to light, the existence of which was recognized by statute in the nineteenth century,[45] and the right to the support of buildings.[46] In the case of the first easement, the effect of the existence of the easement is that the owner of the servient tenement is restricted as to how he can build upon his own land. In the case of the latter, the tenement owner cannot demolish structures on his own land if the effect of so doing would be to undermine buildings on the dominant land.

Other than that, negative easements will not be recognized. Hence, a right to privacy,[47] or to an interrupted flow of air over an undefined area[48] have been held not to be easements. More recently, it was argued in *Hunter v. Canary Wharf Ltd*[49] that there could be an easement in respect of the uninterrupted receipt of a television signal. Such a claim failed, however, on the basis that no such easement could exist.[50] Should it be sought to restrict the user of servient land, an easement is not the most apt means of so doing. Instead, this can be achieved by the use of an appropriately drafted restrictive covenant.[51]

---

[39] *Dowty Ltd v. Wolverhampton Corporation (No. 2)* [1976] Ch. 13 at 22 *per* Russell L.J. (right to use an airfield).

[40] See also *Dyce v. Hay* (1852) 1 Macq. 305 at 312 *per* Lord St Leonards L.C.

[41] See *Patel v. W.H. Smith (Eziot) Ltd* [1987] 1 W.L.R. 853 at 859 *per* Balcombe L.J.; *London and Blenheim Estates Ltd v. Ladbroke Retail Parks Ltd* [1992] 1 W.L.R. 1278 at 1287 *per* Judge Baker Q.C., see 12.1.4.7. See also *Horton v. Tidd* (1965) 196 E.G. 697 (right to retrieve cricket balls).

[42] [2014] UKSC 46, at [108]. Technically, Lord Neuberger's comments on the status of the right as an easement were made *obiter*.

[43] *Keppell v. Bailey* (1834) 2 My & K. 517 at 535 *per* Lord Brougham L.C.

[44] For an historical, and critical, approach to this issue, see I. Dawson and A. Dunn (1998) 18 L.S. 510.

[45] Prescription Act 1832, s. 3.   [46] See *Dalton v. Angus* (1881) 6 App. Cas. 740.

[47] *Browne v. Flower* [1911] 1 Ch. 219.   [48] *Bryant v. Lefever* (1879) 4 C.P.D. 172.

[49] [1997] A.C. 655.   [50] Ibid., *per* Lord Hoffmann.   [51] See Chapter 13.

12.1.4.3 **Expenditure of money**

The essential nature of an easement is that it enables the owner of the dominant tenement to do something on the servient tenement. A 'positive obligation on the owner of the servient tenement owner to do something is inconsistent with the existence of such an easement'.[52] A court is, therefore, unwilling to recognize as an easement a right which requires the owner of the servient tenement either to spend money or to do some positive act and, on this basis, has declined to accept that a claim to have one's property protected from the weather could exist as an easement.[53] Similarly, a claim to use a neighbour's swimming pool is unlikely to be recognized as an easement, because it would impose on the owner of the servient tenement an obligation to keep it filled.[54]

12.1.4.4 **Fencing of livestock**

An exception exists to this general rule, in what has been described as being 'in the nature of a spurious easement'.[55] This is the obligation to maintain fencing to keep in livestock.[56] This exception is limited to fences for the purpose of enclosing certain animals and does not apply to the erection of fences in general, so that an agreement between neighbours that one of them is responsible for maintaining a boundary fence is enforceable as between them but the burden of that obligation will not run with the land.[57] Recognizing the spurious nature of such easements, the Law Commission has recommended that it should not be possible to create an easement of fencing, and that any such obligation would need to be expressly created as a land obligation, a new legal right in land which it has proposed should be created.[58]

12.1.4.5 **Access to neighbouring land**

If there exists an easement, the owner of the servient tenement is under no obligation to do any repairs or maintenance to enable the dominant owner to enjoy the easement but the owner of the dominant land may enter the land to effect necessary repairs.[59] This is only a limited right of access and, together with the fact that there is no easement to protect one's property from the elements, this created problems for a person who needed to go onto his neighbour's land to effect repairs and maintenance to his own property. To meet this problem, the Access to Neighbouring Land Act 1992 was passed. Under s. 1, a landowner may apply to a court for an order to enable access to adjoining or adjacent land. Such an order will be made if the court is satisfied that a landowner needs to go onto that land to do work which is reasonably necessary for the protection of his own land and that the work can only be done, or would be substantially more difficult to do, without entering the servient land. This access order will be binding upon a purchaser of the servient land if protected by registration: in the case of unregistered land, by the registration of a writ or order affecting the land and, where title is registered, by the registration of a notice.[60]

---

[52] *Rance v. Elvin* (1985) 50 P. & C.R. 9 at 13 *per* Browne-Wilkinson L.J.; *William Old International Ltd v. Arya* [2009] EWHC 599 (Ch). See also *Jones v. Price* [1965] 2 Q.B. 618 at 644 *per* Winn L.J.

[53] *Phipps v. Pears* [1965] 1 Q.B. 76. Contrast *Sedgwick Forbes Bland Payne Group Ltd v. Regional Properties Ltd* (1979) 257 E.G. 64 at 70 *per* Oliver J. (property divided horizontally, i.e. flats, rather than vertically).

[54] *Moncrieff v. Jamieson* [2007] 1 W.L.R. 2620 at [47] *per* Lord Scott.

[55] *Lawrence v. Jenkins* (1873) L.R. 8 Q.B. 274 at 279 *per* Archibald J.

[56] *Bolus v. Hinstorke* (1670) 2 Keb. 686. See also *Crow v. Wood* [1971] 1 Q.B. 77.

[57] See *Jones v. Price* [1965] 2 Q.B. 618 at 637 *per* Willmer L.J. See also at 639 *per* Diplock L.J., where the existence of the easement in respect of livestock is described as 'anomalous'.

[58] (2011) Law Com. No. 327, para. 5.94. See Chapter 13.

[59] See *Jones v. Prichard* [1906] 1 Ch. 630 at 637–8 *per* Parker J. See also *Bond v. Nottingham Corporation* [1940] Ch. 429 at 438–9 *per* Sir Wilfrid Greene M.R.; *Carter v. Cole* [2006] EWCA Civ. 398.

[60] Access to Neighbouring Land Act 1992, ss 4, 5.

12.1.4.6 **Excessive claims**

A further ground on which it was thought that a claim to an easement could be defeated was if the claim amounted to an excessive user of the servient tenement.[61] Thus, in *Copeland v. Greenhalf,*[62] a person claimed to have an easement to store vehicles on adjoining land. Although a right to deposit trade goods on another person's land had previously been recognized as being an easement,[63] in the instant case the claimed failed because, on the facts, it was regarded as being too extensive a use of the servient land to amount to an easement.[64] On the other hand, in *Wright v. Macadam,*[65] not cited in *Copeland v. Greenhalf,* the right to store coal in a shed was held to be an easement. The cases were not easy to reconcile.[66] An attempt at reconciliation was made in *London and Blenheim Estates Ltd v. Ladbroke Retail Parks Ltd,*[67] where Judge Baker Q.C. concluded that the matter was one of degree and that the more extensive the use, the less likely it is that the claim would be upheld as being an easement.

Before exploring this issue further, one related matter can first be considered. In *Copeland v. Greenhalf,* the easement was claimed on the basis of prescription, that is long user,[68] and the judge thought that the claim should really have been based on adverse possession, whereas in *Wright v. Macadam,* the right of storage had been the subject of an express grant. It was thought that the courts might be more willing to recognize that extensive use of the servient land could be an easement if there was an express grant rather than a claim based on long user.[69] Any such distinction was rejected, however, in *Moncrieff v. Jamieson,*[70] where Lord Scott expressly stated that there was no difference between the characteristics of an easement created by prescription and one created expressly.

To return to the main issue, recent case law had accepted, as a general proposition, the notion that if a right amounted to an extensive use of the servient land, it could not be an easement. In *Mulvaney v. Gough,*[71] the Court of Appeal, while prepared to accept that the right to cultivate flower beds on adjoining land could be an easement, was concerned that this right was not focused on a particular part of the servient land. If it had been, then this would have been a claim to the exclusive use of part of the servient land which, it was felt, was inconsistent with the nature of an easement.[72] This consensus has, however, been cast aside by far-reaching dicta in *Moncrieff v. Jamieson.*[73]

12.1.4.7 **Car parking**

The question of excessive user has arisen on a number of occasions when consideration has been given to the question of whether the right to park a car can exist as an easement, an issue which has been described as being very important in practice.[74] Although the judicial

---

[61] See M. Haley and L. McMurtry (2007) 58 N.I.L.Q. 490; A. Hill-Smith [2007] Conv. 223.

[62] [1952] Ch. 488.

[63] *Dyce v. Hay* (1852) 1 Macq. 305. See also *Attorney-General of Southern Nigeria v. John Holt & Co. (Liverpool) Ltd* [1915] A.C. 599 at 617 *per* Lord Shaw.

[64] [1952] Ch. 488 at 498 *per* Upjohn J.

[65] [1949] 2 K.B. 744.

[66] See the general observations on the confused state of the authorities concerning easements in *McAdams Homes Ltd v. Robinson* [2004] 3 E.G.L.R. 93 at [1] *per* Neuberger J.

[67] [1992] 1 W.L.R. 1278 at 1285–6, affirmed at [1994] 2 K.B. 744.   [68] See 12.6.

[69] See J.R. Spencer [1973] C.L.J. 30 at 32.   [70] [2007] 1 W.L.R. 2620 at [59].

[71] [2002] EWCA Civ. 1078. See M.P. Thompson [2002] Conv. 571.

[72] See also *Grigsby v. Melville* [1972] 1 W.L.R. 1278 at 1285–6 *per* Brightman J., affirmed without reference to this point at [1974] 1 W.L.R. 80. Cf. J.R. Spencer [1973] C.L.J. 30 at 34, who considers *Copeland v. Greenhalf* to have been wrongly decided, although it was approved in *Hair v. Gillman* (2000) 80 P. & C.R. 108 at 113 *per* Chadwick L.J.

[73] [2007] 1 W.L.R. 2620.   [74] *Waterman v. Boyle* [2009] EWCA Civ. 115 at [24] *per* Arden L.J.

consensus appeared to favour the acceptance that it could,[75] it was initially considered to be important as to how the right was to be exercised. In *Batchelor v. Marlow*,[76] a claim to the exclusive right to park cars on a particular strip of land between 8.30 a.m. and 6.30 p.m. on Mondays to Fridays was considered to amount to too extensive a use of the servient land to be capable of being an easement, whereas in *Hair v. Gillman*,[77] the court held that a right to park one car on any part of a forecourt which could accommodate four cars could be an easement.

Recent cases have shown a willingness to apply the 'reasonable use' test from *Batchelor v. Marlow* in a broad and expansive way; in recognition, perhaps, of the fact that car parking is unique in the prevalence of real-world usage when compared with other forms of easement, and the law must find an approach that reflects that. In *Kettel v. Bloomfold*,[78] the respondent landlord was injuncted from building on the parking spaces on his land, which the appellants had a right to use. This did not leave the landlord with no reasonable use of his land, applying *Batchelor v. Marlow*, because he could still do anything a freehold owner could do, including repairing or cleaning the surface, laying pipes under it, or building over it.[79] Similarly, in *R Square Properties Ltd v. Nissan Motors (GB) Ltd*,[80] the judge held that the respondent's exclusive right to use eighty parking spaces on the servient land did not deprive the appellant of reasonable use, because he could still use the land for other purposes. The appellant's rights were not, therefore, illusory.[81]

Although the cases on car parking have considered the extensive nature of the use of the servient land to be an important criterion, this was not considered to be the case, however, by the House of Lords in *Moncrieff v. Jamieson*.[82] The case concerned whether a person who had a right of way over adjoining land also had an implied right to park on that land. Given the topology of the two plots of land, it was not possible to park on the dominant land, and it was held, applying *Jones v. Prichard*,[83] that the grant of an easement is, *prima facie*, also the grant of such ancillary rights as are reasonably necessary to its exercise and enjoyment. In this case, if there was no such right to park, the owners of the dominant tenement would have had to walk 150 yards in all weathers from where they parked their car to their own property,[84] and it was held that such a right was ancillary to the right of way. In so doing, the House confirmed that the right to park a car is capable of being an easement.[85] Of wider significance are the *obiter* remarks concerning the nature of easements.

12.1.4.8 Nature of use

Both Lord Scott and Lord Neuberger rejected as a test that one determined whether the use was too excessive as being one of fact and degree, and disapproved *Batchelor v. Marlow*.[86] Lord Scott, who was prepared to accept that *Copeland v. Greenhalf* was correctly

---

[75] *Newman v. Jones* (1982), unreported (a decision of Sir Robert Megarry V.-C.); *Patel v. W.H. Smith (Eziot) Ltd* [1987] 1 W.L.R. 853 at 859 *per* Balcombe L.J.; *London & Blenheim Estates Ltd v. Ladbroke Retail Parks Ltd* [1992] 1 W.L.R. 1278 at 1287 *per* Judge Baker Q.C. (affirmed at [1994] 1 W.L.R. 31). Cf. *Saeed v. Plustrade Ltd* [2002] P. & C.R. 19 at [22], where Sir Christopher Slade left this point open.

[76] (2001) 32 P. & C.R. 36.

[77] (2000) 80 P. & C.R. 108. See also *P. & S. Platt Ltd v. Crouch* [2003] EWCA Civ. 1110, where the right to moor boats in a specific place on an island was accepted as being an easement, this issue being considered to be one of fact and degree: ibid. at [45] *per* Peter Gibson L.J.

[78] [2012] EWHC 1422 (Ch).   [79] Ibid. at [23] *per* H.H.J. David Cooke.

[80] 13 March 2014, Chancery Division, unreported. See also *De Le Cuona v. Big Apple Marketing Ltd*, 12 April 2017, Chancery Division, unreported.

[81] See also *Begley v. Taylor* [2014] EWHC 1180 (Ch).   [82] [2007] 1 W.L.R. 2620.

[83] [1908] 1 Ch. 630 at 638 *per* Parker J.

[84] [2007] 1 W.L.R. 2620 at [34] *per* Lord Hope. Contrast the view of Lord Rodger at [83].

[85] Lord Hope reserved his opinion as to whether the right to park which is not ancillary to a right of way could be an easement: ibid. at [22]. No such doubts were expressed by other members of the panel.

[86] Ibid. at [60] and, more tentatively, at [143], respectively.

decided on the facts,[87] was minded 'to reject the test that asks whether the servient owner is left with any reasonable use of his land, and substitute for it a test which asks whether the servient owner retains possession of, and subject to the reasonable exercise of the right in question, control of the servient land'.[88]

It is envisaged that the application of this test will be difficult to apply. Lord Scott was prepared to say that sole user of a shed to store coal by the owner of the dominant tenement would not mean that the owner of the servient tenement had not retained possession of it, as he could use the shed for any other purpose which did not interfere with the storage right,[89] although he cast no light on what realistically this might entail. Lord Neuberger arguably went further, as he said that 'as at presently advised, I am not satisfied that a right is prevented from being a servitude or an easement simply because the right granted would involve the servient owner being effectively excluded from the property'.[90] One difficulty with this is that, where there is no express grant but the claim is based upon long user, it is difficult to distinguish between the type of use referred to and a claim for adverse possession. As the owner of land now has, effectively, a power of veto over claims to a possessory title,[91] the dicta in *Moncrieff* may now lead a person who would, in the past, be regarded as a squatter to argue that, provided that the period of use has been long enough, he has an easement.

A real problem with the dicta in *Moncrieff*, it is suggested, is that it makes it difficult to distinguish between a use which amounts to adverse possession and use to support a claim to an easement.[92] A further difficulty lies in distinguishing some forms of easements from a lease. In the light of Lord Scott's comments concerning an easement of storage, it is clear that a right to park a car in a garage can be an easement.[93] The difficulty here is that such a right would normally be granted by a lease.[94] If, in return for a lump sum, a document grants a person a right to park a car for a period of a year in a garage then, provided that the grantee has land nearby which would benefit, it is now very difficult to say whether this is an easement for a year, or a lease. If the former, it would be required to be registered; if the latter it would not.[95]

A further point which can now arise is the enforceability of easements against third parties. Prior to the coming into force of the Land Registration Act (LRA) 2002, easements were overriding interests.[96] Quite deliberately, the range of easements which were to be overriding was reduced by the 2002 Act to those easements created by implication or by prescription. An easement created by express grant or reservation is required to be registered.[97] Now that the House of Lords has accepted that an easement can exist whereby the owner of it can occupy the servient land, this raises the possibility that an expressly granted easement may override a registered disposition of the servient land, as a person in actual occupation of that land.[98] In *Chaudhary v. Yavuz*,[99] Mr Chaudhary contended that he was in actual occupation of land over which he also held an equitable easement, thereby satisfying Sched. 2, para. 2 of the LRA 2002. The Court of Appeal thought that a 'counter-intuitive' claim,[100] to say the least, though on the facts actual occupation could not be found, so the point did not need to be decided.

---

[87] Ibid. at [56].   [88] Ibid. at [59].   [89] Ibid. at [55].   [90] Ibid. at [139].

[91] See 6.7.3.3.   [92] For the difficulties, see 12.6.4.

[93] The view expressed by M. Haley and L. McMurtry (2007) 58 N.I.L.Q. 490 at 502–3 that an exclusive right to park in an allocated space cannot be an easement has now been overtaken by events, and does not represent the law.

[94] See, e.g., *Kling v. Keston Properties Ltd* (1989) 49 P. & C.R. 212.

[95] LRA 2002, ss 4(1)(c), 27(2)(d).   [96] LRA 1925, s. 70(1)(a).   [97] LRA 2002.

[98] Ibid., Sched. 3, para. 2. See M.P. Thompson [1986] Conv. 31 at 36.

[99] [2013] Ch. 249.   [100] Ibid. at [28].

While the decision in *Moncrieff* itself is to be welcomed in providing confirmation that a right to park a car is capable of being an easement, some of the wider dicta have, it is suggested, disturbed some quite well-settled principles underlying the law of easements, and may give rise to considerable difficulty in the future.

The Law Commission considered this matter and concluded that the law must continue to distinguish between arrangements which confer exclusive possession and those which do not. If exclusive possession is granted, then this should entail the grant of a freehold or a lease, but should not amount to an easement.[101] It went on to say, however, that the law should continue to recognize as an easement a use that stops short of exclusive possession, even if it deprives the owner of the servient land all reasonable use of it.[102] This seems regrettable, in that it will make the distinction between an easement and other legal concepts difficult, and recognize as a third-party interest in land a right which, to most intents and purposes, is exclusionary in nature and is something which goes beyond what has traditionally been recognized as an easement.[103]

12.2 Easements and related concepts

The essential nature of an easement is that it is a right to do something on or over another person's land. Rights of a similar nature can arise in other ways and it is useful, briefly, to consider some of those rights by way of comparison.

12.2.1 Natural rights

The law implies certain natural rights for landowners, the interference with which will make the neighbour liable in nuisance. There are two such rights: the right of support and the right to water.

12.2.1.1 Right of support

The right of support exists to protect the land itself but, not entirely logically, this right does not extend to any buildings on the land. In respect of support for the land itself the owner of the adjoining land is liable for his action which causes neighbouring land to subside.[104] So, if by excavation[105] or the removal of underground salt[106] damage is caused to neighbouring land, this is actionable.

The obligation with regard to support extends to acts of omission as well as to acts of commission. In *Holbeck Hall Hotel Ltd v. Scarborough Borough Council*,[107] the plaintiff owned a hotel which stood on a cliff overlooking the sea. The land between the hotel and the sea was owned by the defendant. After two minor slips caused by coastal erosion, there was a massive slip which caused the ground under the hotel's seaward wing to collapse and the issue arose as to the defendant's liability. It was held that the duty of support extended to omissions as well as to commissions. That duty is not, however, absolute. Liability will only arise in such cases if the landowner is aware, or should be aware, of the danger. Moreover, in cases of omission, regard must also be had to the extent of the duty

---

[101] (2011) Law Com. No. 327, para. 3.206.　　[102] Ibid. at 3.208.

[103] For the argument that while car parking rights have already moved beyond a test based on reasonable use, other forms of easement should not, see L. Xu [2012] Conv. 291.

[104] There is no cause of action unless the withdrawal of support causes damage: *Darley Main Colliery v. Mitchell* (1886) 11 App. Cas. 127. See, generally, T.H. Wu [2002] Conv. 237.

[105] *Redland Bricks Ltd v. Morris* [1970] A.C. 652.　　[106] *Lotus Ltd v. British Soda Co. Ltd* [1972] Ch. 123.

[107] [2000] 2 All E.R. 705; *Leakey v. National Trust* [1980] Q.B. 485. See M.P. Thompson [2001] Conv. 177.

and, in particular, whether it is fair and reasonable to impose potentially huge expense on a landowner in respect of geological problems which are not his fault.[108] In the instant case, while the authority was aware that there was a problem of erosion, it was not aware of the scale of the problem. Given the cost of any remedial work, it was considered, also, that the scope of its duty may have been limited to sharing its knowledge of the danger with affected parties.[109]

There is no natural right to the support of buildings, although such a right can be obtained as an easement.[110] If the damage to the buildings is caused by withdrawal of support for the land itself, however, then the loss caused by the damage to the building is also recoverable.

12.2.1.2 Water

There is a natural right to water which flows through a natural channel.[111] Where water does not flow through a defined channel but percolates naturally through the land, the owner of the lower land does not have the right to receive that water.[112] In the case of water which accumulates naturally on land, there is a natural right of drainage onto adjoining land,[113] so that the owner of the land on which the water accumulates is not liable for any flooding caused to the land onto which that water drains. Whether the owner of the lower land can take steps to prevent that drainage in order to protect his own land is unclear.[114] There is authority to favour this view,[115] which leads to the slightly odd proposition that the owner of the higher land has the right of drainage but the owner of the lower land is not under a duty to receive the water, but this nevertheless, seems reasonable.

12.2.2 **Public rights**

An easement is a private right which one landowner owns and which is enforced against another person's land. Some rights are exercisable by the public at large, the most common of those rights being a public right of way.[116] Such rights can be created expressly by statute, or under common law. The common law method is by a process known as dedication and acceptance. The essence of this method is long user, the general presumption being that a public right of way can be established after twenty years' uninterrupted use.[117]

12.2.3 *Profits à prendre*

A *profit à prendre*, or as it is more commonly known, a profit, is similar to an easement in that it gives a person the right to go onto another's land. The essential aspect of the profit, however, is the right to take something off that land, that something being either the natural produce of the land, such as crops, or the animals existing on it. The right to fish

---

[108] See also *Goldman v. Hargrave* [1967] 1 A.C. 645 at 663 *per* Lord Wilberforce.

[109] [2000] 2 All E.R. 705 at 726 *per* Stuart-Smith L.J. This reasoning from *Holbeck Hall* was applied recently by the Court of Appeal in *Ward v. Coope* [2015] EWCA Civ. 30.

[110] See *Dalton v. Angus & Co.* (1881) 6 App. Cas. 740.

[111] *Swindon Waterworks Co. Ltd v. Wilts and Berks Canal Navigation Co.* (1875) L.R. 7 H.L. 697.

[112] *Chasemore v. Richards* (1859) 7 H.L.C. 376.

[113] *Palmer v. Bowman* [2000] 1 All E.R. 22.

[114] The point was left open in *Palmer v. Bowman* [2000] 1 All E.R. 22 at 35 *per* Rattee J. (a Court of Appeal authority).

[115] *Home Brewery plc v. William Davis & Co. (Loughborough) Ltd* [1987] Q.B. 339 at 349 *per* Mr Piers Ashworth Q.C.

[116] For a major extension of public rights, see Countryside and Rights of Way Act 2000.

[117] Highways Act 1980, s. 31(1).

another's land, for example, known as a right of piscary,[118] can exist as a profit. A profit can be appurtenant to land; that is, exist for the benefit of a dominant tenement, or, unlike an easement, it can exist in gross; that is, it can be owned independently of land.

12.2.4 Restrictive covenants

As has been seen, the law is highly reluctant to recognize as an easement a claim which restricts the use of the servient tenement, such rights being limited effectively to rights of light and rights of support. This gap in the law is catered for by the law relating to restrictive covenants, an equitable development modelled closely on the law of easements. Whereas easements can be either legal or equitable, restrictive covenants are entirely an equitable construct. It is an important area of law which will be considered in Chapter 14.

12.2.5 Licences

The essence of a licence is that it makes lawful what would otherwise amount to a trespass. It is a permission to use another's land. A licence may display some, or indeed all, of the characteristics of an easement but nevertheless not qualify as one. If a person is given permission to cross another's land but does not own land himself, then this right of way cannot be an easement because there is no dominant tenement. The right can therefore only be a licence. If a landowner allows his neighbour to cross his land, then this does display the characteristics of an easement, but will not be one if all that was intended was to give that neighbour a personal permission to use the land in this way. Again, the right in question would be a licence. The law relating to licences is an area which has, in recent years, assumed considerable importance and forms the subject matter of Chapter 15.

12.3 Legal and equitable easements

An easement may be either legal or equitable. To be legal, an easement must come within the terms of s. 1(2), Law of Property Act (LPA) 1925. This means that it must exist for the equivalent of a fee simple absolute in possession or a term of years absolute. It follows from this that an easement for life must necessarily be equitable. In the case of easements for the equivalent of a term of years, this will normally arise when a tenant enjoys an easement, the duration of that easement, so far as the tenant is concerned, being coterminous with the lease. This is not necessarily the case, however, so that if the tenant acquires the title to the reversion, thereby causing the lease to merge with the freehold,[119] the easement will continue to exist for the time originally envisaged.[120]

12.3.1 Legal easements

A legal easement can be created in one of three ways: by statute, by deed, or by prescription. Easements created by statute are relatively unimportant and tend to involve local Acts of Parliament creating a particular right, such as a right of support. Legal easements created by deed or by prescription are important and will be discussed fully later in this chapter.

---

[118] For a rare case on the profit of piscary and in the Supreme Court no less, see *Loose v Lynn Shellfish Ltd* [2016] UKSC 14.

[119] See 10.10.5.   [120] *Wall v. Collins* [2008] 1 All E.R. 122.

12.3.2 **Equitable easements**

Equitable easements can arise in a number of ways. First, if the owner of the dominant land has only an equitable estate, which will be the case if he holds an equitable lease, then any easement will itself take effect only in equity. Second, if the easement does not come within the definition of legal easement provided by s. 1(2), LPA 1925, then it can only be equitable. Finally, where title is unregistered, if a purported grant of an easement is not by deed, then no legal easement can arise and any easement can only take effect in equity. In the case of registered land, the creation of a legal easement must be completed by registration. This means noting the benefit of the easement on the title of the dominant tenement and the burden on that of the servient tenement. If this is not done, the transaction will operate only in equity.[121]

If a deed is not used, the purported grant may not be entirely ineffectual. Provided that the purported grant complies with the formal requirements of s. 2 of the Law of Property (Miscellaneous Provisions) Act 1989, then it may take effect as a contract to create an easement. Provided, as will normally be the case, that this contract is specifically enforceable, then, on the principle that equity looks on that as done which ought to be done,[122] an equitable easement will arise.[123]

12.3.3 **The effect of easements**

If a legal easement is created, then, if title is unregistered, a purchaser will automatically take subject to it, precisely because it is a legal interest. In the case of registered land, the position was that legal easements would be binding on purchasers because they were overriding interests.[124] If an equitable easement is created, if title is unregistered, to bind a purchaser, it must be registered as a land charge.[125] If title was registered, provided that the equitable easement was exercised openly, it took effect as an overriding interest.[126] Under the LRA 2002, only legal easements will override a registered disposition.[127] Subject to transitional provisions, the intention is that only easements created by implication[128] or by prescription will override a registered disposition, and only then if it is either within the knowledge of the purchaser, or would have been obvious on a reasonably careful inspection of the land, save where the easement has been exercised within a year of the disposition.[129]

12.4 **The creation of easements**

Legal easements are commonly created by the parties themselves by an express act. To do this a deed is essential. The usual, although not invariable, occasion when this occurs is when a person is selling some of his land and retaining the rest. In this circumstance, it

---

[121] LRA 2002, s. 27.

[122] See, generally, *E.R. Ives Investment Ltd v. High* [1967] 2 Q.B. 379 at 397 *per* Danckwerts L.J.; at 403 *per* Winn L.J.; *R (on the application of Beresford) v. Sunderland City Council* [2004] 1 All E.R. 160 at 172 *per* Lord Scott.

[123] One other option, even where there is no written contract, is for an equitable easement to arise through the operation of proprietary estoppel. See, for example, *Chaudhary v. Yavuz* [2013] Ch. 249. The potential remedies in satisfying an estoppel claim are discussed in detail in Chapter 14.

[124] LRA 1925, s. 70(1)(a).　　　[125] Land Charges Act 1972, s. 2(2).

[126] *Celsteel Ltd v. Alton House Holdings Ltd* [1985] 1 W.L.R. 204 (reversed in part on another point [1986] 1 W.L.R. 31); *Thatcher v. Douglas* (1996) 146 N.L.J. 282.

[127] LRA 2002, Sched. 1, para. 3, and Sched. 3, para. 3.

[128] This includes easements created by the operation of the LPA 1925, s. 62. See 5.1.5.2.

[129] LRA 2002, s. 27, Sched. 3, para. 3. See 5.1.5.2.

is important to know whether the vendor has retained rights over the land which he has sold or, alternatively, given rights to the purchaser over the land which he has retained. The former process is known as reservation and the latter a grant. In either case, this may be express or implied.

12.4.1 Express reservation

If the vendor of land wishes to retain rights over property which he is selling, it is normally necessary for him to do so expressly. This is because the law is reluctant to imply rights in favour of a grantor who, if he wishes to retain such rights, should expressly stipulate them.[130] If A owns a house and a field, and sells the field to B, and he wishes to retain the right to cross that field as he had done when he owned both properties, then he must take care to ensure that this right is expressly reserved. If he fails to do so, it is very unlikely that the law will imply such a right in his favour.

In the example given above, the only person who has the right to grant an easement over the field is the purchaser of it, B. In a situation such as this, until 1926, B would have had formally to grant to A the requisite easement, which was inconvenient. To simplify matters, s. 65, LPA 1925 provides that the reservation of a right will operate as a regrant by the purchaser[131] without the need for him to execute the conveyance by a regrant. So, in the example being considered, if A conveyed the field to B and, in the conveyance, reserved the right to cross the field, this would be sufficient to create a legal easement in favour of A without the need for B to execute the conveyance. As an alternative method, if A conveys the field subject to a right of way over it, this will operate to create an easement in his favour.[132]

The effect of this provision is that the reservation operates as a regrant of an easement by the purchaser. Applying the *contra proferentem* principle, whereby, in cases of ambiguity, a document is construed against the grantor and in favour of the grantee, it has been held that any ambiguities should be resolved in favour of the vendor.[133] This has rightly been criticized because the reality is that the terms of the easement will have been drafted by the vendor and, consequently, any ambiguities should be construed against him.[134]

12.4.2 Implied reservation

As has already been observed, when one person transfers land to another, the law is very reluctant to imply rights over that land in favour of the grantor. In the present context, easements over land which has been transferred will, in the absence of an express reservation, arise in favour of the grantor in two situations, these being where the law is prepared to imply such a grant.

12.4.2.1 Necessity

It may happen that, when a person sells off part of his land and retains another plot, he has so arranged matters that he has not reserved to himself any access to or from the retained plot. The land has now become landlocked. When this occurs, the court will be prepared to imply an easement of necessity in favour of the grantor.[135] For an easement of necessity

---

[130] See *Ray v. Hazeldine* [1902] 2 Ch. 17 at 19 *per* Kekewich J.
[131] See *Johnstone v. Holdway* [1963] 1 All E.R. 432.
[132] LPA 1925, s. 65(2); *Wiles v. Banks* (1984) 50 P. & C.R. 80.
[133] *St Edmundsbury & Ipswich Diocesan Board of Finance v. Clark (No. 2)* [1975] 1 W.L.R. 468.
[134] (2008) Law Com. Consultation Paper No. 186, para. 4.31. The rule is unfortunate rather than, as the Law Commission thinks, illogical.
[135] See *Pinnington v. Galland* (1853) 9 Exch. 1. See L. Crabb [1981] Conv. 442.

to be implied, the case must really be one of necessity. The fact that the proposed right will form a much more convenient means of access will not be sufficient for an easement to be implied.[136] In *Titchmarsh v. Royston Water Co.*,[137] land had been sold and the only means of access to the retained land was by means of a road which was some twenty feet below the land itself. It was held that, while this means of access was undeniably inconvenient, it was not impossible and, consequently, no easement of necessity was implied. Similarly, in *Walby v. Walby*,[138] the court found that no easement of drainage had been impliedly reserved as an easement of necessity, because the test was a 'strict one' and it was 'not enough to show that the easement is necessary for the reasonable enjoyment of the land retained'.

The prerequisites for a claim to an easement of necessity to be successful were spelled out by the Privy Council in *Manjang v. Drameh*,[139] as being that:

> There has to be, first, a common owner of a legal estate in two plots of land. It has, secondly, to be established that access between one of those plots and the public highway can be obtained only over the other plot. Thirdly, there has to be found a disposition of one of those plots without any specific grant or reservation of a right of access.

If these criteria are met, the basis upon which the courts will imply an easement of necessity is that this is taken to be what the parties intended: it is not supposed that either party intended the grantor of the land to be left marooned on the retained land. If, however, it is clear that there was no intention to create an easement, then the courts will not invoke the doctrine of public policy, which is against land being sterilized in this way, to impose an easement of necessity against the will of the grantee.[140] While such a situation is likely to be very rare, it is nevertheless clear that a claim to an easement of necessity is extremely hard to establish.

Notwithstanding clear authority that indicates that easements of necessity are only to be implied very sparingly, in *Sweet v. Sommer*,[141] Hart J. felt able to imply a right of vehicular access as an easement of necessity. This seems to be wrong. To prevent the property being landlocked, a right of access by foot is all that is necessary, and to imply a greater right than this is not justified. The Court of Appeal, while upholding the decision on an alternative ground, declined to comment on this aspect of the case,[142] which, it is suggested, should be treated with considerable caution, it having been said more than 150 years ago that 'A grant, arising out of the implication of necessity, cannot be carried further than the necessity of the case requires'.[143]

12.4.2.2 Implied intention

Although the creation of easements is said to be based upon the intention of the parties,[144] there can also be an implied reservation of an easement if the court is satisfied that this was the mutual intention of the parties. Such an intention can be implied when there is no actual necessity but, again, the person arguing in favour of an implied reservation will face

---

[136] See *Peckham v. Ellison* (1998) 31 H.L.R. 1031 at 1036–7 *per* Cazalet J.

[137] (1900) 81 L.T. 673. For a more recent, if less extreme, example, see *M.R.A. Engineering Ltd v. Trimster Co. Ltd* (1987) 56 P. & C.R. 1.

[138] [2012] EWHC 3089 (Ch), at [32] *per* Morgan J.

[139] (1990) 61 P. & C.R. 194 at 197 *per* Lord Oliver.

[140] *Nickerson v. Barraclough* [1981] Ch. 426. See also *Adealon International Proprietary Ltd v. The Mayor and Burgesses of the London Borough of Merton* [2007] EWCA Civ. 362. One suggestion put forward by the Law Commission is that, subject to the expression of a contrary intention, public policy should favour the grant of an easement of necessity: (2008) Law Com. Consultation Paper No. 186, para. 4.133.

[141] [2004] EWHC 1504 (Ch). [142] [2005] EWCA Civ. 227.

[143] *Holmes v. Goring* (1824) 2 Bing. 76 at 84 *per* Best C.J.

[144] For strong, and justified, criticism of the process of discerning the intentions of the parties, see (2011) Law Com No. 327, para. 3.45.

a difficult task.[145] The most common situation where there will be an implied easement on the basis of mutual intention is where a person sells a house and retains a house next door. A mutual easement of support is then likely to be implied.[146]

With regard to other easements, the courts are reluctant to imply a reservation but the Court of Appeal was prepared to do so in the recent case of *Peckham v. Ellison.*[147] In this case, the facts were exceptional. All concerned thought at the relevant time that a right of way, which had been exercised in fact for a considerable number of years, actually existed in law and it was held that, had thought been given as to the need for a reservation of the right, both parties would have accepted that this should be done. It was made clear, however, that the onus that the person claiming an implied reservation must discharge is a heavy one.

The court does not approach the issue on the same basis that it would when the issue is what terms should be implied into a contract.[148] What is necessary to infer a common intention to reserve an easement across the land being transferred is 'that the facts are not reasonably consistent with any other explanation—it is not enough that they are simply consistent with such an explanation'.[149] So, the fact that the owner of the quasi-dominant plot exercised the right at the time of the conveyance is not sufficient for the court to imply a common intention to reserve an easement over the servient land;[150] neither is it sufficient that the use of the right is physically apparent.[151] In short, it will only be in the clearest cases that the court will feel able to imply a common intention that an easement is to be reserved over the land being transferred.[152] Somewhat surprisingly, the view of the Law Commission is that an implied reservation of an easement should occur on the same basis as an implied grant.[153] This would represent quite a shift as the law has consistently, and rightly, been very reluctant to imply rights in favour of a grantor. The proposed changes to the law will be considered later in the chapter.[154]

12.4.3 Express grant

Little need be said about the situation where one person expressly grants an easement to another. Care should be taken in drafting such a grant in order to avoid later disputes. So, if a right of way is being granted, it is preferable to stipulate whether this includes access by car or lorry as well as pedestrian use. Similarly, if the right in question is a right of light and more light is required than is necessary for domestic use, as might be the case where the dominant land is being used as a market garden, then this should also be stipulated in the grant.[155] What requires rather more consideration is the effect of s. 62, LPA 1925, the effect of which, paradoxically, can be to cause the express grant of an easement to occur when there is no actual mention of the right in the deed itself.

12.4.3.1 Section 62 of the LPA 1925

Until the enactment of the Conveyancing Act 1881, it was necessary, when conveying land, to include expressly all rights appurtenant to that land. So, if land had the benefit of an easement, for that right to pass, the conveyance had not only to convey the land but also expressly to transfer the benefit of that easement. With a view to shortening conveyances,

---

[145] See *Re Webb's Lease* [1951] Ch. 808.   [146] See *Jones v. Prichard* [1908] 1 Ch. 630 at 638 *per* Parker J.
[147] (1998) 31 H.L.R. 1031. See L. Fox [1999] Conv. 353.
[148] (1998) 31 H.L.R. 1031 at 1044 *per* Cazalet J.   [149] Ibid. at 1043 *per* Cazalet J.
[150] *Re Webb's Lease* [1952] 1 Ch.D. 808 at 828 *per* Jenkins L.J.
[151] *Wheeldon v. Burrows* (1879) 12 Ch.D. 31.
[152] See *Chaffe v. Kingsley* [2000] 1 E.G.L.R. 104. See also *Shrewsbury v. Adam* [2006] 1 P. & C.R. 27.
[153] (2011) Law Com. No. 32, para. 3.30.
[154] See 12.5.   [155] Cf. *Allen v. Greenwood* [1980] Ch. 119.

first, s. 6 of the 1881 Act and latterly s. 62, LPA 1925 made this unnecessary. Section 62 provides that:

> A conveyance of land shall be deemed to include and shall by virtue of this Act operate to convey, with the land, all . . . liberties, privileges, easements, rights, and advantages whatsoever, appertaining or reputed to appertain to the land, or any part thereof, or, at the time of the conveyance . . . enjoyed with, or reputed or known as part or parcel of or appurtenant to the land or any part thereof.

12.4.3.2 Precarious rights

So s. 62, which is subject to the expression of a contrary intention in the conveyance,[156] is obviously sufficient to pass the benefit of an existing easement. If A has been granted an easement over B's land and A then conveys his land to C, C will, by operation of s. 62, obtain the benefit of that easement notwithstanding that there is no mention of it in the conveyance. Rather less obviously, the effect of s. 62 can be to convert licences and certain quasi-easements into full legal easements. This was explained in *Campbell v. Banks*[157] by Mummery L.J., who said:

> On a conveyance by a vendor selling part of his land, the land conveyed may become a dominant tenement and the land retained by him, or sold by him to a different purchaser, may become a servient tenement. In this fashion a facility previously enjoyed over part of the vendor's land may be transformed into a legal easement for the benefit of dominant land now in different ownership.

A good illustration of this occurred in *International Tea Stores Co. Ltd v. Hobbs*.[158] A tenant was given permission by his landlord to use a roadway. Sometime later, the landlord sold the reversion of the tenancy to the tenant. It was held that what had previously been a licence to use the roadway on the landlord's land had now become a full legal easement. As the licence was a liberty or privilege existing at the time of the conveyance,[159] the effect of the section was to include in the conveyance of the property words to the effect that the premises were sold together with the right to use the roadway. In other words, the effect of the predecessor to s. 62 was to operate to create an easement by an express grant.

It should be appreciated that in this case, prior to the conveyance, the landlord would have been entirely free to have revoked the tenant's licence, so that his right to use the roadway was precarious. It has been argued that the section should have been construed in such a way as not to enlarge the licensor's right, so that if the right was revocable before the conveyance, it should remain revocable after it.[160] While there is force in this argument, this is not the approach the courts have taken, so that, provided certain conditions are met, if a licensor conveys land to a licensee, s. 62 will operate to upgrade a licence into an easement over land retained by the licensor.[161] The 'key to the operation of [s. 62] is enjoyment in fact, not title'.[162] As such, the section can operate as a trap for the unwary[163] and the conditions when the section will operate in this way must now be considered.

---

[156] LPA 1925, s. 62(4).   [157] [2011] EWCA Civ. 61 at [2].   [158] [1903] 1 Ch. 165.

[159] It is essential that the claimed right was being exercised at the time of the conveyance. See *Campbell v. Banks* [2011] EWCA Civ. 61.

[160] See L. Tee [1998] Conv. 115; C. Davis (2000) 20 L.S. 198 at 210.

[161] See, e.g., *Goldberg v. Edwards* [1950] Ch. 247; *Wright v. Macadam* [1949] 2 K.B. 744. See also *Graham v. Philcox* [1984] Ch. 747 (a case on the enlargement of an easement) noted by P. Todd [1985] Conv. 60.

[162] *Wall v. Collins* [2008] 1 All E.R. 122 at [15] *per* Carnwarth L.J.

[163] This is the view of the Law Commission, who recommend that this aspect of the law should be changed: (2011) Law Com. No. 327, para. 3.64. This view does not sit easily, however, with its proposals to change the law regarding the implication of easements. See 12.5.

Competent grantor

For the section to operate, the person who conveys the land must have the power to grant an easement: there must be a competent grantor.[164] This, seemingly obvious point, can sometimes be overlooked.[165] Where the section will be relevant is where a vendor owns land and sells off part of it to a purchaser. Any licence granted to the purchaser prior to the conveyance to him is then, potentially, liable to be upgraded into an easement. The essential point is that, prior to the conveyance, the two plots must have been in common ownership.[166]

Right capable of being an easement

For an easement to be created as a result of the operation of s. 62, the right in question must be capable of being an easement. It must satisfy the criteria laid down in *Re Ellenborough Park*.[167] In *Green v. Ascho Horticulturist Ltd*,[168] a tenant had been given a licence to use a passageway on his landlord's property whenever it was convenient to the landlord. The landlord then conveyed the reversion to the tenant and the issue arose as to whether the licence had become an easement. It was held not. The licence was of too intermittent a nature to be the subject matter of a grant and, consequently, s. 62 did not operate to convert it into an easement.

The rule in Long v. Gowlett

In *Long v. Gowlett*,[169] two plots of land had at one time been in common ownership. The owner of plot 1 used to go onto plot 2 to clear weeds from the river. The person who acquired plot 1 claimed to have an easement to go onto plot 2 to clear the weeds. The claim failed. According to Sargent J., before an easement can be acquired under s. 62 there must be a prior diversity of occupation of the dominant land prior to the conveyance. This means that there must have been a licensee or a tenant in occupation of the dominant land, owned by the owner of the servient land, prior to the dominant land being conveyed to him.

Quasi-easements

The existence of this rule was the subject of some debate.[170] The reason for this debate was the decision of the Court of Appeal in *Broomfield v. Williams*.[171] In this case, there was a quasi-easement of light and the vendor sold the quasi-dominant plot to a purchaser and it was held that he acquired, under the statutory predecessor to s. 62, a full legal easement of light. In this case there was not, prior to the conveyance, a diversity of occupation; both plots were occupied by the vendor. There was, however, in existence a quasi-easement and this was continuous and apparent: that is, one could see from an inspection of the two properties that the quasi-dominant plot enjoyed access to light over the quasi-servient plot. The result is that s. 62 operates to convert into easements either licences enjoyed prior to the conveyance, the situation where there is a prior diversity of occupation, or

---

[164] LPA 1925, s. 62(5).

[165] Cf. *M.R.A. Engineering Ltd v. Trimster Co. Ltd* (1987) 56 P. & C.R. 1 at 5 *per* Dillon L.J.; at 7 *per* Nourse L.J.

[166] See *Odey v. Barber* [2008] Ch. 175 *per* Silber J.

[167] [1956] Ch. 131.

[168] [1966] 1 W.L.R. 889. See also the discussion of this issue in *P. & S. Platt Ltd v. Crouch* [2003] EWCA Civ. 1110 at paras 43–6 *per* Peter Gibson L.J.

[169] [1932] 2 Ch. 177.

[170] P. Jackson [1966] 30 *Conv.* (N.S.) 340; P. Smith [1978] *Conv.* 449. For a convincing and instructive defence of the rule, see C. Harpum [1979] *Conv.* 113.

[171] [1897] 1 Ch. 602.

quasi-easements which are continuous and apparent. In short, there are two alternative aspects to the rule in *Long v. Gowlett*.

The primary aspect of the rule that prior to the conveyance there must be diversity of occupation was confirmed, *obiter*, by the House of Lords in *Sovmots v. Secretary of State for the Environment*,[172] where Lord Edmund-Davies said, 'the section cannot operate unless there has been some diversity of ownership or occupation of the quasi-dominant and quasi-servient tenements prior to the conveyance'.[173] This dictum is a little misleading, in that before the section can operate at all, the two plots of land must have been in common ownership. It does, however, confirm the main plank of the rule. *Broomfield v. Williams* was, misleadingly, disregarded simply on the basis that it concerned an easement of light, which was considered to involve different considerations.

It is wrong to seek to distinguish *Broomfield v. Williams* in this way. It overlooks that there are two limbs to the rule, which are that, for the section to operate, then prior to the conveyance there must have been either a diversity of occupation, or there was in existence a continuous and apparent quasi-easement. That this is so is illustrated by a number of decisions, not involving light, where the section was held to operate to convert a continuous and apparent quasi-easement into a full legal easement.[174] That s. 62 will operate to convert a quasi-easement into a full legal easement was made plain in *Alford v. Hannaford*,[175] where Patten L.J said:

> But where there has not been diversity of occupation prior to the sale, the generally held view is that s. 62 can only operate to grant easements over the land retained by the vendor when the exercise of the relevant rights has been continuous and apparent.

This approach has, once again, been recently confirmed by the Court of Appeal in *Wood v. Waddington*,[176] where Lewison L.J. expressly approved[177] Patten L.J.'s dicta above in *Alford v. Hanniford*. To sum up, s. 62 will apply in two primary situations. First, cases where there is prior diversity of occupation: where A owns two plots of land, and the second plot is occupied by B as a tenant or licensee, s. 62 will pass the benefit of any quasi-easement that exists for the benefit of the second (dominant) plot when it is conveyed to B (or someone else). Second, cases where there is no prior diversity of occupation but there is continuous and apparent use: where A owns and occupies two plots of land, and the second plot is conveyed to B, s. 62 will pass the benefit of any quasi-easement that is continuous and apparent.

Rationale of the rule

The underlying basis of the rule in *Long v. Gowlett* is to allow the section to operate in a way which might be supposed to accord with the implied intention of the parties: hence the section is not operative in the case of a compulsory purchase.[178] If a person is allowed into occupation of land prior to the conveyance, and is given a licence to use other land owned by the vendor, it is not unreasonable to suppose that he might be expecting to enjoy

---

[172] [1979] A.C. 144.   [173] Ibid. at 176.

[174] See *Watts v. Kelsen* (1870) 6 Ch. App. 166 (a case where general words were used in the conveyance); *Kay v. Oxlye* (1875) L.R. 10 Q.B. 360, especially at 365 *per* Blackburn J.; *Bayley v. G.W.R.* (1884) 26 Ch.D. 434. It is unfortunate that, in *Payne v. Inwood*, this point was not made as unambiguously as it could have been: (1996) 74 P. & C.R. 42 at 47 and at 51 *per* Roch L.J. See M.P. Thompson [1997] Conv. 453.

[175] [2011] EWCA Civ. 1099 at [36]. See also *P. & S. Platt v. Crouch* [2003] EWCA Civ. 1110 at [42] *per* Peter Gibson L.J., and *Campbell v. Banks* [2011] EWCA Civ. 61 at [4] *per* Mummery L.J.

[176] [2015] EWCA Civ. 538. Noted K. Lees [2015] Conv. 423; S. Gardner (2016) 132 L.Q.R. 192.

[177] [2015] EWCA Civ. 538 at [35].

[178] *Sovmots v. Secretary of State for the Environment* [1979] A.C. 144. The position is different in respect of leasehold enfranchisement: see *Kent v. Kavanagh* [2006] EWCA Civ. 162.

that right after the conveyance. Similarly, if it is evident from looking at the two properties that the quasi-servient land was used for the advantage of the quasi-dominant plot, it is not unreasonable to suppose that it was intended that the purchaser might acquire as a right that which had previously existed only as a quasi-easement. When neither of these factors is present, it would occur to neither party that the purchaser might acquire rights over land retained by the vendor. The rule in *Long v. Gowlett* operates to prevent s. 62 being more of a trap than it potentially already is.

Conveyance

Section 62 only operates if there has been a conveyance. A conveyance is a document which operates to transfer a legal estate or charge in land.[179] This includes an assent or a written lease of less than three years, a transaction which is not required to be created by deed.[180] Such a lease can, in fact, be created orally, but such a lease is not a conveyance.[181] Neither is a document which creates an equitable lease.[182] If there has been no conveyance, s. 62 will not apply, but the rule in *Wheeldon v. Burrows*, discussed fully at 12.4.4.3, might.

Contrary intention

Section 62 is subject to a contrary intention. If a vendor is selling part of his land and has let a purchaser into possession prior to the conveyance, he should take care to revoke any licences he has given prior to conveying the property. This is a matter which should, in any event, be dealt with in the contract of sale. It is the case, however, that the section operates to give effect to the intention of the parties, and if it is clear that both of them are aware that no such right is intended to be created, the section will not operate to create an easement.[183] There is, however, a heavy burden of proof on the vendor to establish that this is the case.[184]

12.4.4 Implied grants

There are three situations when the grant of an easement will be implied.

12.4.4.1 Necessity

The same principles apply in the context of an implied grant as in the case of an implied reservation.[185]

12.4.4.2 Mutual intention

Again, similar principles apply as in the case of reservations, save that the task of persuading the court that the grant of an easement was intended is a little easier than is the case when the grantor is seeking to establish an implied reservation. In *Wong v. Beaumont Property Trust Ltd*,[186] a property had been let as a restaurant. To comply with health regulations, it was necessary for there to be adequate ventilation. An easement to install a ventilation duct on the landlord's property was implied. Similarly, an easement was also impliedly granted in *Donovan v. Rana*,[187] on the basis that the inferred common intention of the parties was for the dwelling house sold to have access to the servient land in order to install and maintain the connection to the public utility services in the road.

---

[179] LPA 1925, s. 205(1)(ii).   [180] Ibid., s. 54. See *Wright v. Macadam* [1949] 2 K.B. 74.
[181] *Rye v. Rye* [1962] A.C. 496.   [182] *Borman v. Griffith* [1930] 1 Ch. 493.
[183] See *Birmingham, Dudley and District Banking Company v. Ross* (1888) 38 Ch.D. 295.
[184] See *P. & S. Platt Ltd v. Crouch* [2003] EWCA Civ. 1110.   [185] See 12.4.2.
[186] [1965] 1 Q.B. 173.   [187] [2014] EWCA Civ. 99.

12.4.4.3 The rule in *Wheeldon v. Burrows*

The rule in *Wheeldon v. Burrows*[188] is similar, but not identical, to the operation of s. 62, LPA 1925. In this case, the vendor owned two plots of land. On one plot, there was a shed which had three windows overlooking the other plot. There was a quasi-easement of light over that plot. In 1875, he sold the quasi-servient plot to the defendant and, a year later, sold the quasi-dominant plot to the plaintiff. When the defendant erected hoardings which blocked the light to the plaintiff's windows the issue arose as to whether the plaintiff had an easement of light. He did not. The reason was that it was the quasi-servient plot which had been sold first and there was no implied reservation of an easement.[189] Had it been the case that it was the quasi-dominant plot which had been sold first, then there would have been an implied grant. Of this, Thesiger L.J. said:

> on the grant by the owner of a tenement or part of that tenement as it is then used and enjoyed, there will pass to the grantee all those continuous and apparent easements (by which, of course, I mean *quasi*-easements), or, in other words, all those easements which are necessary for the reasonable enjoyment of the property granted, and which have been and are at the time of the grant used by the owners of the entirety for the benefit of the part granted.[190]

There are three aspects to the rule. The first is that this is an implied grant. It must be the quasi-dominant part of the land which is sold first. Second, the quasi-easement must be continuous and apparent. This means that there is some visible sign, such as a marked track, across the quasi-servient land,[191] and the finding in *Donaldson v. Smith*,[192] that to be continuous and apparent there needs be neither a made-up track, nor any discernible traces of the use on the quasi-servient land, appears to be clearly wrong. In the case of light, the fact that adjoining land is uncovered, so that the quasi-dominant plot enjoys an uninterrupted flow of light, means that this is continuous and apparent. The fact that the quasi-dominant plot enjoys access to light over the quasi-servient plot is visible by looking at the two plots of land.[193] Third, the right must be necessary for the reasonable enjoyment of the land.[194]

This last aspect of the rule is problematic. It does not mean that the right in question is essential for the enjoyment of the land, as is the case for an easement of necessity. On the other hand, it appears to mean more than that the right accommodates the dominant tenement.[195] This distinction was made by Mummery L.J. in *Campbell v. Banks*,[196] as being the difference between a right necessary for the reasonable enjoyment of the land, which can be created by implication, and those which are convenient and can be created by s. 62. This is hopelessly imprecise and, fortunately, now redundant. Any continuous and apparent quasi-easements pass on a conveyance of the quasi-dominant land due to the operation of s. 62, LPA 1925, as confirmed in *Alford v. Hanniford*[197] and *Wood v. Waddington*.[198] Under that section, there is no need to show that the right claimed is necessary for the reasonable enjoyment of the land; merely that the right in question satisfies the normal requirements of easements. This would leave the rule in *Wheeldon v. Burrows* scope to operate only in situations where there is no conveyance; for example, when there is a document which has created an equitable lease.[199]

---

[188] (1878) 12 Ch.D. 31. [189] See also *Ray v. Hazeldine* [1902] 2 Ch. 17. [190] Ibid. at 49.

[191] See the discussion of this in *Ward v. Kirkland* [1967] Ch. 194 at 224–6 *per* Ungoed-Thomas J.

[192] (2006), unreported, at [23] *per* Mr David Donaldson Q.C.

[193] See *Phillips v. Low* [1892] 1 Ch. 47.

[194] See *Millman v. Ellis* (1995) 71 P. & C.R. 158 at 162–3 *per* Sir Thomas Bingham M.R; *Wood v. Waddington* [2015] EWCA Civ. 538.

[195] See, generally, *Wheeler v. J.J. Saunders Ltd* [1996] Ch. 19, criticized by M.P. Thompson [1995] Conv. 239.

[196] [2011] EWCA Civ. 61 at [32]. [197] [2011] EWCA Civ. 1099. [198] [2015] EWCA Civ. 538.

[199] See *Borman v. Griffith* [193] 1 Ch. 493; *Donaldson v. Smith* (2006), unreported.

12.5 Law reform proposals

The Law Commission has made proposals which, if implemented, would change considerably the law relating to the implied acquisition of easements. The reform proposals also include easements currently created as a result of s. 62, LPA 1925. Although it was recognized that, strictly speaking, such easements are created by express grant, and not by implication, because the operation of the section overlaps to a considerable extent with the rule in *Wheeldon v. Burrows*, it was appropriate to consider this section as part of its work on the implied creation of easements,[200] an approach which seems sensible.

12.5.1 Reform of section 62

The Law Commission was impressed with the criticisms of the manner in which s. 62 can operate to upgrade precarious rights into full legal easements. It has, therefore, been proposed that the section shall no longer operate to transform precarious benefits into legal easements on a conveyance of land.[201] While many critics of the current law might welcome this proposal, if it and the complementary proposals with regard to the law relating to the implication of easements are enacted there may be, in fact, very little change in substance to the law.

12.5.2 Implication of easements

At the heart of the Law Commission's approach to this matter is the replacement of the current circumstances when an easement is created by implication with one unified test. This test is not to be based on any attempt to discern the intentions of the parties but is, instead, to be underpinned by an objective test based on what is necessary for the reasonable enjoyment of the land.[202] To this end, it is proposed 'that an easement should be implied as a term of a disposition where it is necessary for the reasonable use of the land at that date, bearing in mind:

(1) The use of the land at the time of the grant;

(2) The presence on the servient land of any relevant physical features;

(3) An intention for the future use of the land, known to both parties at the time of the grant;

(4) So far as relevant, the available routes for the easement sought; and

(5) The potential interference with the servient land or inconvenience to the servient owner.'[203]

12.5.3 Implied reservation

An initial point to make about this proposal is that the various criteria to which regard is to be had in determining whether an easement is to be implied appear to be alternatives, and this view is reinforced when regard is had to clause 20 of the draft LP Bill appended to the Report, which makes clear that the criteria to which regard is to be had in determining whether a particular easement is necessary for the reasonable enjoyment of the land includes the items listed above. The first two criteria quoted seem to indicate the current requirements that the right which is to be implied was, first, in use at the time of

---

[200] (2011) Law Com. No. 327, paras 3.67–3.84.   [201] Ibid., para. 3.64.
[202] Ibid., paras 3.39–3.43.   [203] Ibid., para. 3.45.

the disposition and, second, was continuous and apparent, or at least apparent, in current terminology. Under the existing law, both criteria had to be satisfied; under the proposal, they would seem to be alternatives.

A second important feature of this proposal is that it applies to all dispositions of land, and not, as is presently the case, to dispositions of the quasi-dominant tenement. This will enable easements to be implied in favour of a grantor on the same basis as is currently the case for a grantee. This is a significant change. As has been seen, the current position is that the law is highly reluctant to imply any rights in favour of the vendor of land, and will do so only in a case of necessity, which is narrowly defined, and where the implication is necessary to give effect to the implied intention of the parties. The rationale for this approach is that, if a vendor wishes to retain rights over land which he is selling, he should expressly reserve them.[204] Under this proposal the law would change, and one result would be that the actual decision in *Wheeldon v. Burrows* would now be different.

In that case, it will be recalled, there was a quasi-easement of light, and it was the quasi-servient land which was then sold first. It was held that no easement was implied in favour of the vendor, precisely because the law is reluctant to imply easements in favour of the grantor, and against the grantee; had it been the quasi-dominant plot which had been conveyed first, the law would have implied an easement in favour of the purchaser. Under the proposed new law, a right to light would be implied in favour of the vendor; it was in use at the time of the grant, and that use would have been apparent on an inspection of the servient land and also, it would seem, it was necessary for the reasonable enjoyment of the land. One would have anticipated rather more justification for such a major change than is present in the Report.

12.5.4 Repeal of section 62

The Law Commission, as has been seen, proposed to reform the current position whereby s. 62, LPA 1925 allows precarious rights to be upgraded into easements. Unfortunately, it seems to be overlooked that the new proposal on the implication of easements would, if enacted, reintroduce the substance of the existing law in another guise. In *International Tea Stores Co. Ltd v. Hobbs*,[205] a tenant had been given permission to use a roadway on the landlord's land. On the conveyance of the reversion to the tenant, this precarious licence, due to the operation of the statutory predecessor of s. 62,[206] was converted into a legal easement. Despite the recommendation of the Law Commission to prevent s. 62 from operating in this way, the proposal for the implication of easements would seem to produce the same result: as the right was exercised at the time of the disposition then, assuming that it was necessary for the reasonable enjoyment of the land, that fact would cause an implied easement to be created.

12.5.5 Necessary for the reasonable enjoyment of the land

The overarching criterion for the implication of easements is to be that the right in question is necessary for the reasonable enjoyment of land. This currently is a requirement for an easement to be implied under the rule in *Wheeldon v. Burrows*, but is not a separate requirement for the operation of s. 62. In that context, it is sufficient that the right claimed accommodates the dominant tenement. This additional requirement is one of some uncertainty, and its introduction as the guiding criterion is not to be welcomed.[207]

---

[204] See 12.4.1. [205] [1903] 1 Ch. 165. [206] Conveyancing Act 1881, s. 6.

[207] For a detailed discussion of s. 62 and the Law Commission's proposals, see S. Douglas [2015] 131 L.Q.R. 251; S. Douglas [2015] Conv. 13.

12.5.6 **Conclusion**

While the implementation of the Law Commission's proposal would appear to simplify the law, in that it would provide a unified test for the implication of easements, thereby doing away with the old law concerning easements of necessity and the position when an easement will be implied to give effect to the intentions of the parties, it does so at a price. In particular, it shifts the law a long way from the present, justifiable, state whereby the law is reluctant to imply rights in favour of a person who is disposing of part of his land. Second, while at first sight, the trap inherent in s. 62, LPA 1925 is removed, that is likely to prove to be illusory. Finally, the emphasis on the need for the right in question to be necessary for the reasonable enjoyment of land is likely to be the subject matter of litigation, it being unclear what, if anything, it adds to the requirement that the right in question accommodates the dominant tenement.

12.6 **Prescription**

The final method by which an easement can be acquired is by prescription. The basis of prescription is that a right has been enjoyed for a long period of time. Unlike the position with adverse possession, where the law operates negatively to extinguish the title of the paper owner of the land,[208] prescription works positively. It enables a person to make a positive claim to a right over another person's land, and it has been said that 'Any legal system must have rules of prescription which prevent the disturbance of long-established de facto enjoyment.'[209]

As one would expect, before any right can be acquired by prescription, it must display the general characteristics of an easement. A number of issues then arise. These relate to the nature of the user of the right and the length of time that the use has been enjoyed. Unfortunately, this latter issue is complicated by the fact that there are three separate forms of prescription, a matter which reflects little credit on the law.

12.6.1 **Nature of the use**

To establish a claim to an easement by prescription, the claimant must be able to show user as of right. This is traditionally summed up in the Latin phrase that the use must be *nec vi, nec clam, nec precario*. This means that it must be used neither by force, by stealth, or by permission, or 'putting the point more positively: the user must be peaceable, open and not based on any licence from the owner of the land'.[210] If the claimant establishes such use, nothing further is required; no further criterion need be established.[211]

12.6.1.1 **Force**

Generally speaking, the issues as to whether the use has been occasioned by force will not be difficult to establish, so, if the claimant demolishes barriers to enjoy a right of way,[212] then this will amount to forceable use. Physical force is not necessary, however, to defeat

---

[208] See Chapter 6.

[209] *R. v. Oxford County Council, ex p. Sunningwell Parish Council* [2000] 1 A.C. 335 at 349 *per* Lord Hoffmann. For interesting discussions of the merits of prescription, see C. Sara [2004] Conv. 13; F. Burns [2007] Conv. 133.

[210] *R (on the application of Lewis) v. Redcar and Cleveland Borough Council* [2010] UKSC 11 at [87] *per* Lord Rodger.

[211] Ibid. at [20] *per* Lord Walker; *London Tara Hotels Ltd v. Kensington Close Hotel Ltd* [2011] EWCA 1356 at [74] *per* Lewison L.J.

[212] *Newnham v. Willison* (1987) 56 P. & C.R. 8.

a claim to an easement; if the use is contentious, it will also be regarded as being force-ful use.[213] This was the issue before the Court of Appeal in *Winterburn v. Bennett*.[214] The appellants owned a fish and chip shop, and since 1998 their suppliers and customers had been using the car park on the adjacent land, which was bought by the respondents in 2010. A sign on the wall and in the building window had clearly stated that it was a 'private car park.' The respondents leased the land to a tenant in 2012, who obstructed access to the car park. The appellants argued that they had acquired the right to park there through prescription by lost modern grant. Richards L.J. held that any reasonable person would understand the signs to mean that they were not allowed to park there.[215] The signs were proportionate to the user, and no further steps were necessary; they constituted a clear and continuous protest against contrary use. When the signs were ignored, there was no requirement on the part of the landowner to take further steps to prevent the users from acquiring a legal right. This is surely correct; there does not need to be physical obstruc-tion or the commencement of legal proceedings in order to make the use contentious. That would set the bar far too high in the obligations a landowner is under to ensure others do not acquire rights to their land.

12.6.1.2 Secrecy

The question of secrecy can give rise to more subtle issues. If the user of the right is not obvious as, for example, if underground rods are used to support a structure, then no ease-ment will be acquired by prescription, on the basis that the use was secret.[216] Potentially a more difficult problem arose in *London Tara Hotel Ltd v. Kensington Close Ltd*.[217] In 1973 Tara granted a personal licence to KCL, who were then the owners of the Kensington Close Hotel, to use a roadway from year to year, and provision was made for payment of £1 per annum, although this was never collected. The ownership of the hotel changed hands in 1980, although Tara was not aware of this. This caused the licence to terminate, although the use of the roadway continued and, indeed, increased. It was argued that the use for the requisite period of time after 1980 was secretive because Tara did not know of the change of the ownership and consequent revocation of the licence. This argument failed. Although it was accepted that, had there been some deception as to the change of ownership the continued use of the roadway may have been regarded as secretive, this was not the case here.[218] The use was open, and it was immaterial if the owner of the servient plot mistakenly believed that the use was under a licence granted in the past.

12.6.1.3 Permission

Because the requirement is that the user is of right, a claim to an easement by prescrip-tion will fail if it is shown that the right was enjoyed with the permission of the servient owner.[219] This does not entail that the person exercising the right believes that he has the legal right to do so,[220] as the claimant's beliefs are generally irrelevant to the issue of

---

[213] *R (on the application of Lewis) v. Redcar and Cleveland Borough Council* [2010] UKSC 11 at [87] *per* Lord Rodger. See *Smith v. Brudenell-Bruce* [2002] 2 P. & C.R. 2; *Betterment Properties (Weymouth) Ltd v. Dorset CC* [2012] EWCA Civ. 250.

[214] [2016] EWCA Civ. 482. See N. Pratt [2016] Conv. 414.   [215] Ibid. at [37].

[216] *Union Lighterage Co. v. London Graving Dock Co.* [1902] 2 Ch. 557. See also *Liverpool Corp. v. Coghill & Son Ltd* [1918] 1 Ch. 307 (surreptitious discharge of effluent); *Ironside v. Barefoot* (1981) 41 P. & C.R. 326 (intermittent use of right not sufficient).

[217] [2011] EWCA Civ. 1356.

[218] Ibid. at [37] *per* Lord Neuberger M.R.

[219] *Gardner v. Hodgson's Kingston Brewery Co. Ltd* [1903] A.C. 229. See generally R. Meagher in S. Bright (ed.), *Modern Studies in Property Law, Vol. 6* (Oxford, Hart Publishing, 2011), Chapter 12.

[220] See *R v. Oxfordshire County Council, ex parte Sunningwell Parish Council* [2000] A.C. 335.

prescription.[221] If, however, the owner of the servient land simply tolerates the use without expressly consenting to it, this use will be sufficient to establish a prescriptive right to an easement.[222] 'A landowner who wishes to stop the acquisition of prescriptive rights must not acquiesce and suffer in silence.'[223] This is illustrated by the decision of the Supreme Court in *R (on the application of Lewis) v. Redcar and Cleveland Borough Council*.[224] The issue was whether a person was entitled to apply to register land as a town or village green. He was entitled to do this, if he could establish that a significant number of the inhabitants in the locality had indulged as of right in lawful sports and pastimes on the land for a period of at least twenty years.[225] The meaning of 'as of right' was accepted as being the same as is required to establish a prescriptive easement. In this case the claimant was one of a group of walkers, who would follow their pursuit across a golf course. On the facts, it was clear that it was overwhelmingly the case that the walkers would defer to the golfers so that, if a person was taking a shot, the walkers would wait until the path was clear. These acts of deference, it was held, did not make the acts of walking across the course permissive. It was merely the give and take inherent when two groups of people are using the same land. As Lord Walker put it:

> I have great difficulty in seeing how a reasonable owner would have concluded that the residents were not asserting a right to take recreation on the disputed land, simply because they normally showed civility (or in the inspector's word, deference) towards members of the golf club who were out playing golf.[226]

It was emphasized by the Supreme Court in *R (Barkas) v. North Yorkshire CC*[227] that 'as of right' is effectively the antithesis of 'by right'. Use 'as of right' occurs without the permission but with the acquiescence of the landowner, whereas use 'by right' denotes that the use is rightful—permission has been given.[228] It is acquiescence that is the foundation of prescription. If, therefore, the owner of the servient land gives an unsolicited permission for a person to use his land, then the user is not as of right, and a claim to an easement by prescription will be defeated.[229] Such permission will normally need to be express, however, as the courts will not readily accept that inaction on the part of the servient tenement owner will amount to permission. What appears to be necessary is 'some overt act which is intended to be understood, and is understood, as permission to do something which would otherwise be an act of trespass.'[230]

Finally, it should be noted that use which was originally permissive may cease to be so. This may be because the original licence was revoked, either by the act of the parties or by law. The use may also be in excess of what was originally permitted—for example, by vehicular use as opposed to pedestrian use—in which case the fact that the original use was permissive will not prevent the creation of an easement.[231]

---

[221] *R (on the application of Lewis) v. Redcar and Cleveland Borough Council* [2010] UKSC 11 at [34] *per* Lord Walker. See also *Bridle v. Ruby* [1989] Q.B. 169.

[222] *Davies v. Du Paver* [1953] 1 Q.B. 184; *Mills v. Silver* [1991] Ch. 271.

[223] *R (on the application of Beresford) v. Sunderland City Council* [2004] 1 All E.R. 160 at [77] *per* Lord Walker.

[224] [2010] UKSC 11.   [225] Commons Act 2006, s. 15.

[226] *R (on the application of Lewis) v. Redcar and Cleveland Borough Council, supra,* at [37].

[227] [2014] UKSC 31.

[228] Ibid. at [14] *per* Lord Neuberger. See also *Powell v. Secretary of State for the Environment, Food and Rural Affairs* [2014] EWHC 4009 (Admin).

[229] *Odey v. Barber* [2008] Ch. 175, applying *Rafique v. Trustees of the Walton Estate* (1992) 65 P. & C.R. 356.

[230] *R (on the application of Beresford) v. Sunderland City Council)* [2004] 1 All E.R. 160 at [75] *per* Lord Walker; *London Tara Hotels Ltd v. Kensington Close Hotel* [2011] EWCA Civ. 1356 at [86] *per* Lewison L.J.

[231] See *London Tara Hotels Ltd v. Kensington Close Hotel* [2011] EWCA Civ. 1356.

12.6.1.4 User in fee simple

An easement can only be acquired by prescription if the use is by a fee simple owner against another fee simple owner.[232] Any claim made to an easement by a tenant can only be made on behalf of the owner of the reversion. Similarly, if the servient land is in the possession of a tenant, any claim to an easement by prescription will fail, unless it can be shown that the freehold owner of the land was able to prevent the user. In this respect, it is important whether the user preceded the grant of the tenancy. If it did, it is then easier to establish the requisite acquiescence on the part of the freeholder to base a claim to a prescriptive easement.[233]

12.6.2 Prescription periods

It is unfortunate that there are three different periods of prescription.

12.6.2.1 Common law

The common law rule was that to establish a claim to an easement by prescription the claimant had to show that the right had been enjoyed from time immemorial. For historical reasons, this date, the date of legal memory, was set at 1189. Evidently, such a task would be very hard to accomplish, and so to alleviate the difficulty, the courts were prepared to make the presumption that, if a right had been enjoyed for twenty years, it had been enjoyed since 1189. As with all presumptions, however, it is rebuttable. If it could be shown that the right could not have been enjoyed from 1189, then a claim to an easement at common law would fail.[234] This meant, for example, that a claim to an easement of light would fail at common law if the buildings which were to enjoy the light were erected after 1189. In reality, prescription at common law is effectively obsolete.

12.6.2.2 Lost modern grant

Clearly, the task of establishing a prescriptive claim to an easement at common law was nigh on impossible. To overcome this difficulty, the courts invented a fiction that, if there had been enjoyment of a right for a prolonged period, set at twenty years, then the presumption would be made that an easement had, in the past, been granted but that the grant had been lost.

> Juries were first told that from user, during living memory, or even during twenty years they may presume a lost grant or deed; next they were recommended to make such presumption; and lastly, as the final consummation of judicial legislation, it was held that a jury should be told, not only that they might, but also that they were bound to presume the existence of such a lost grant, although neither judge nor jury, nor anyone else, had the shadow of a belief that any such instrument had ever really existed.[235]

This fiction, for such it is, was endorsed by the House of Lords in *Dalton v. Angus*.[236] Because the basis of the doctrine is fictitious, it is entirely irrelevant that evidence exists that no such grant was ever made.[237] A claim to an easement based upon the fiction of the

---

[232] *Kilgour v. Gades* [1904] 1 K.B. 457 at 460 *per* Sir Richard Henn Collins M.R. Despite the strong criticism of this rule by Lord Millett in *China Field Ltd v. Appeal Tribunal (Buildings)* [2009] UKCU 1650 (a decision of Hong Kong's Court of Final Appeal), the Law Commission has proposed the retention of this rule: (2011) Law Com. No. 327, para. 3.150.

[233] See *Williams v. Sandy Lane (Chester) Ltd* [2006] EWCA Civ. 1738 at [22] *per* Chadwick L.J.

[234] See *Hulbert v. Dale* [1909] 2 Ch. 570 at 577 *per* Joyce J.

[235] *Bryant v. Foot* (1867) L.R. 2 Q.B. 161 at 181 *per* Lord Cockburn C.J.

[236] (1881) 6 App. Cas. 740.　　　[237] *Tehidy Estate Ltd v. Norman* [1971] 2 Q.B. 528.

lost modern grant will only be defeated if it is shown that it was actually impossible for a grant to have been made.[238] Other than this restriction on the fiction, if the claimant can show twenty years' user as of right, and this, unlike the position under the Prescription Act 1832, does not have to be twenty years' user immediately connected with the adjudication of the claim,[239] then that claim will succeed. It appears to be the case, however, that to succeed under the doctrine of lost modern grant, stronger evidence of user as of rights is required than would be the case if the claim is made at common law.[240] If the evidence shows that the right claimed could not have been enjoyed throughout the twenty-year period, as where a claimed right of way would have been obstructed by a wall, the argument based on prescription will fail.[241]

12.6.2.3 Illegal use

A claim to an easement through a lost modern grant cannot be sustained, if the use is illegal,[242] the reason being that 'a lawful grant to do an act or acts which if done would be illegal cannot be made'.[243] This rule is not, however, absolute. So, in the welcome decision in *Bakewell Management Ltd v. Brandwood*,[244] it was held that the driving of a vehicle without lawful authority across land subject to rights of common, which is an offence unless authorized by the owner of the land,[245] could give rise to an easement by prescription. Because the owner of the land could have authorized the activity, a lost modern grant was a legal possibility.

12.6.2.4 Statutory prescription

A legal doctrine which is based squarely upon a fiction, as is the case with the doctrine of lost modern grant, is inherently unattractive. One possibility would be to replace that doctrine by legislation. That, however, has not been done. Although the Prescription Act 1832 does enable prescription to occur on a statutory basis, the Act operates in tandem with the common law doctrines. Moreover, the Act is not particularly well drafted: the Law Reform Committee having said of it that it 'has no friends. It has long been criticized as one of the worst drafted Acts on the Statute Book',[246] and its continued existence on the statute book after a period of over seventy-five years has been described as providing some support for the adage that only the good die young.[247] Moreover, the situation is complicated by the fact that a different regime exists in respect of easements of light than with other forms of easement, which means that there is a need to consider the different types of easement separately.

---

[238] *Neaverson v. Peterborough Rural District Council* [1902] 1 Ch. 557, where such a grant was prohibited by statute.

[239] See *Mills v. Silver* [1991] Ch. 221.

[240] See *Tilbury v. Silva* (1890) 45 Ch.D. 98 at 123 *per* Bowen L.J.

[241] See *Jones v. Scott* [2006] EWHC 2908 (QB). Cf. *Orme v. Lyons* [2012] EWHC 3308 (Ch), where sufficient evidence of use of a track to establish that the respondents enjoyed a vehicular right of way over it on the basis of prescription under the doctrine of lost modern grant was found even though the respondents only used the track 'sometimes'.

[242] *Cargill v. Gotts* [1981] 1 W.L.R. 441.

[243] *Bakewell Management Ltd v. Brandwood* [2004] 2 A.C. 519 at 541 *per* Lord Scott.

[244] [2004] 2 A.C. 529. *Henning v. Top Desk Travel Group* (1993) 68 P. & C.R. 14, to the contrary, was overruled. Although the decision has been criticized, M. Templeman (2005) 121 L.Q.R. 200, the better views are the supporting arguments by D. Fox [2004] Conv. 173, anticipating the decision, and C. McNall [2004] Conv. 517, supporting it.

[245] LPA 1925, s. 193(4).   [246] (1966) Law Reform Cttee, Cmnd. 3100, para. 40.

[247] *London Tara Hotels Ltd v. Kensington Close Hotel Ltd* [2011] EWCA Civ. 1356 at [20] *per* Lord Neuberger M.R. For an interesting historical critique, see *Housden v. The Conservators of Wimbledon and Putney Commons* [2008] 1 All E.R. 397 at [33]–[69] *per* Mummery L.J.

Easements other than light

To acquire an easement under the Prescription Act 1832, it must be shown that there has been either twenty or forty years' continuous user next to—that is, immediately before— the action. The reason for there being two different periods will be addressed shortly. The latter requirement means that, subject to the requisite period of interruption, the requisite period of user must occur prior to the matter being litigated. If, for example, a person has exercised a right of way for twenty-five years, but that use stopped two years prior to the action being brought, then a prescriptive claim under the statute will fail. Instead, a claim will have to be made under the doctrine of lost modern grant,[248] where there is no requirement that the use continues up until the date of the action.

Interruptions

The Act requires the user to have been without interruption. Section 4 of the Act requires the court to disregard an interruption unless it has been acquiesced in or submitted to for one year. This means that a claim to an easement can be made under the Act even where there has not been the full twenty years' user. If a person has used a right for nineteen years and one day and that use is then interrupted then, provided that the action is brought precisely 364 days after the interruption, the claim to an easement under the Act will succeed. The two periods will be added together to make up the requisite twenty-year period.[249] In the same way that acts of adverse possession can be added together by different squatters,[250] user by different owners can be accumulated to make up the requisite period under the Act.[251] The action cannot, however, be brought before that date, as taking the two periods together, there will not have been twenty years' user as of right. Neither can the action be brought after that date, because then the interruption will have lasted for more than one year, which will defeat a claim under the Act.[252]

Overriding status

The LRA 2002 has curtailed the possibility of easements taking effect as interests which override registered dispositions.[253] Easements created by the operation of s. 62, LPA 1925,[254] or the rule in *Wheeldon v. Burrows*, or by prescription, continue to have overriding status. Because, under the Prescription Act the use must be before the action, it was thought that claims could no longer be made under the Act against a purchaser, because the long use would not, until the action was brought, have caused an easement to arise, and so there would not be anything to bind the purchaser.[255] This argument has, however, been refuted on the basis that the time simply runs against the new owner of the land, against whom the action can then be brought.[256]

Different time periods

Section 2 of the Act, in setting out the prescription periods, stipulates two different periods, these being twenty years and forty years next to, that is immediately before, the action. The distinction is then made that a prescriptive claim based upon forty years' user prior to the action will only be defeated if it was shown that the right was enjoyed by written consent or agreement, or that the owner of the servient land lacks the capacity to grant an easement.[257]

---

[248] See *Mills v. Silver* [1991] Ch. 221.
[249] See *Flight v. Thomas* (1841) 8 Cl. & Fin. 231 at 241 *per* Lord Cottenham L.C.   [250] See 6.7.1.2.
[251] *Midtown Ltd v. City of London Real Property Co. Ltd* [2005] EWHC 33 (Ch), a product of the LPA 1925, s. 62.
[252] See *Reilly v. Orange* [1955] 1 W.L.R. 616.   [253] See 5.1.5.3 Easements and *profits à prendre*.
[254] LRA 2002, s. 27(7).   [255] P.H. Kenny [2003] Conv. 304 at 312.
[256] G. Battersby [2005] Conv. 195 at 205.
[257] *Housden v. Conservators of Wimbledon and Putney Commons* [2008] 1 All E.R. 397.

At common law, to acquire an easement by prescription, the user must be *nec vi, nec clam, nec precario*; that is, without force, stealth, or permission. These requirements apply also in the case of prescriptive claims under the Act, except that the final requirement, that the use is without permission, is modified in the case of prescription based upon user for forty years. The effect of the Act is this. If, prior to the use commencing, oral permission was given to the person exercising the right, then the use will be *precario*—that is, permissive—and a claim to an easement based upon twenty years' use will fail. If, however, the use continues for forty years, then the fact that its origin was permissive will not matter. It is only if the permission was in writing that the claim will fail. If, however, permission is given to use a particular right, and this permission is repeated periodically, an easement will not be acquired whether the use be for twenty or forty years, because the user has not been as of right.[258] The provision with regard to the forty-year period allows the first, verbal, permission to be disregarded. It will not affect the position if the permission is repeated periodically.

Easements of light

Easements of light are governed, principally, by s. 3 of the Act. If enjoyment of access to light has occurred without interruption for twenty years, that right will become absolute, unless it was enjoyed with written permission. As is the case with prescription in respect of other easements, the use must be next to, that is immediately, before an action. The same rule applies also in respect of interruptions. There are, however, some important differences between a prescriptive right to light and the acquisition of other easements.

Interruption to the enjoyment of light

It is relatively easy to obstruct, physically, a right of way. One simply blocks it by the erection of a gate or a fence. It is less easy to prevent the enjoyment of a flow of light. To do this would require the owner of the servient tenement to build upon his land in such a way as to obstruct the flow of light. This may cause problems, either because planning permission cannot be obtained for the building or, simply, the owner of the servient land does not want to build at the present time. He may, nevertheless, be concerned that, by inertia, an easement of light is not acquired over his land. To alleviate this difficulty, a procedure exists under the Right to Light Act 1959, whereby the owner of the servient land can register a notional obstruction to the flow of light, and this will suffice to interrupt the enjoyment of the light, thereby preventing the acquisition of an easement by prescription. If there is an actual obstruction, as is the case when the windows are boarded up, no easement will be acquired, because light is not being enjoyed, as all that is happening is the illumination of the back of a panel.[259]

Written consent

In the case of easements of light, there is only one relevant time period, that period being twenty years. A claim to an easement of light which has been enjoyed for twenty years next to an action will fail if, and only if, there was written permission to enjoy the right. The wording of s. 3 does not insist that the user was as of right. It is sufficient if access to the light was actually enjoyed throughout the period. Thus, if an annual payment is made in respect of the enjoyment of the right to light, this will not, after twenty years, prevent the right maturing into an easement.[260]

---

[258] *Gardner v. Hodgson's Kingston Brewery Co. Ltd* [1903] a A.C. 229.

[259] *Tenures (Vincent Square) Ltd v. Fairpoint Properties (Vincent Square) Ltd* [2006] EWHC 3589 (Ch).

[260] See *Plasterers' Co. v. Parish Clerk's Co.* (1851) 6 Exch. 630.

It is not necessary for the writing to refer expressly to an easement of light for it to amount to written permission sufficient to prevent a right of light being acquired. In *RHJ Ltd v. FT Patten (Holdings) Ltd*,[261] one of the terms of a lease reserved the right of the landlord to build on the land adjoining the tenant's property. This had the effect that, pending any building, the tenant was enjoying the light over the landlord's land with his written permission, thereby preventing an easement being claimed under the Act.

No grant

The easement of light does not rest upon any presumed grant. The section provides for the right to become absolute after the expiry of the requisite period. This has been held to mean that, unlike other cases of prescription, a tenant can acquire an easement by prescription.[262]

12.6.3 **Prescription rules reform**

Unsurprisingly, in its review of the law relating to easements, the Law Commission considered the rules governing prescription to be ripe for reform. Having considered, but rejected, the idea of abolishing this means of acquisition altogether,[263] changes to the existing law were recommended. Underlying the proposals were the laudable aims of simplifying the law, avoiding litigation, ensuring compatibility with land registration principles, and ensuring that the scope for prescription was not extended.[264]

What is proposed is, first, to abolish the three existing methods of prescription and to replace them with a single prescription period of twenty years of continuous qualifying use, this period to apply to all types of easement. To count as qualifying, the use must, as is the case at present, be without force, stealth, or permission. The use must also not be contrary to the criminal law, unless such use can be rendered lawful by the dispensation of the servient owner.[265]

This proposal would retain a good deal of the substantive law, while making welcome changes to remove some of the confusing and anomalous variations between different types of easement, and different time periods. One substantive change which is recommended is that the twenty-year use need no longer be next before action, as is currently the case. This aspect of the existing statutory regime is, apparently, exceptionally unpopular,[266] and is, of itself, a principal reason for the continued application of the common law fiction of the lost modern grant, where no such requirement is imposed. It was recognized, however, that this recommendation, if implemented, would potentially cause some risk to purchasers of registered land, in that prescriptive easements can take effect as interests which override registration.[267] This risk is nevertheless small, as such easements will only override if either the easement was within the actual knowledge of the person to whom the disposition was made, or would have been obvious to him on a reasonably careful inspection of the land, or, alternatively, the easement had been exercised within the period of a year ending with the date of the disposition. The proposed reforms would bring a good deal of improvement to an unnecessarily complicated area of law.[268]

---

[261] [2008] EWCA Civ. 151.   [262] *Morgan v. Fear* [1907] A.C. 429.

[263] (2011) Law Com. No. 327, paras 3.74–3.80.   [264] Ibid., para. 3.116.

[265] Ibid., para. 3.123.   [266] Ibid., para. 3.131.

[267] LRA 2002, Sched. 3, para. 3(1). Expressly granted easements cannot take effect as overriding interests: ibid., s. 27(2)(d).

[268] The Law Commission published its final report on *Rights to Light* in 2014 (Law Com. No. 356). In essence, it proposes to retain prescription for rights to light, but abolish the Right to Light Act 1959 and replace it with something simpler. It also proposes to legislate for remedies where there has been an infringement. For comment, see M. Dixon [2015] Conv. 1.

12.6.4 **Adverse possession and easements**

The existence of an easement necessarily acts as a constraint as to what the servient owner can do on his own land, because, 'Every [easement] prevents any use of the servient land, whether ordinary or otherwise, that would interfere with the reasonable exercise of the [easement]. There will always be some use that is prevented.'[269] The question can arise as to how extensive that interference can be. This is particularly relevant because of the possibility that an easement can be acquired by prescription. Now that it is much more difficult for a squatter to acquire a possessory title than was previously the case, then, provided that the use of the servient land has been enjoyed for the longer period required for prescription, the person who has enjoyed the right will find it potentially more advantageous to argue that the use of the land did not amount to adverse possession, but, instead, had led to the creation of an easement.

Although an easement is traditionally seen as the right of one landowner to do something on a neighbour's land, some rights have involved a degree of occupancy of the servient land. Until recently, the approach of the courts was to see the issue as being one of degree, and the greater the aspect of occupancy, the less likely the use in question was to be held to be capable of existing as an easement.[270] This approach has, however, recently been rejected by the House of Lords in *Moncrieff v. Jamieson*.[271] The issue, it will be recalled, was whether a right to drive a car over servient land carried with it the ancillary right to park that car on the land. It was held, on the facts, that it did. The main importance of the case was the recognition that a right to park a car was capable of existing as an easement. As such a right is occupational in nature, this led to a general, albeit *obiter*, discussion of the extent to which a right which is occupational can exist as an easement.

12.6.4.1 **Occupational easements**

Although Lord Scott stressed that 'the right must be such that a reasonable use thereof by the owner of the dominant land would not be inconsistent with the beneficial ownership of the servient land by the beneficial owner',[272] he and Lord Neuberger were both prepared to accept that a use which interfered substantially with the use of the servient land could amount to an easement. Thus, Lord Scott, in approving the decision in *Wright v. Macadam*,[273] said that, 'Sole use of a coal shed for the storage of coal does not prevent the servient owner from using the shed for any purposes of his own that do not interfere with the dominant owner's reasonable use for the storage of coal',[274] although it is not clear what sensible use the servient owner could enjoy in respect of a coal cellar filled with someone else's coal. Lord Neuberger arguably went further, saying that he could see considerable force in the view 'that a right can be an easement notwithstanding that the dominant owner effectively enjoys exclusive occupation, on the basis that the essential requirement is that the servient owner retains possession and control'.[275] This is reinforced by his earlier comment that he was 'not satisfied that a right is prevented from being . . . an easement simply because the right granted would involve the servient owner being effectively excluded from the property'.[276] The difficulty here is that it is not easy to see how the servient owner retains possession and control, if another person has the legal right to exclusive occupation of it.

Lord Scott did show some appreciation of the potential overlap between a claim to an easement and a claim to have acquired a possessory title. He referred to *Copeland v. Greenhalf*,[277] where Upjohn J. had rejected a claim that an easement had been acquired to

---

[269] *Moncrieff v. Jamieson* [2007] 1 W.L.R. 2620 at [54] per Lord Scott.
[270] See, e.g., *R. & S. Platt Ltd v. Crouch* [2003] EWCA Civ. 1110 at [45] *per* Peter Gibson L.J.
[271] [2007] 1 W.L.R. 2620.   [272] Ibid. at [17].   [273] [1919] 2 K.D. 711.
[274] [2007] 1 W.L.R. 2620 at [55].   [275] Ibid. at [143]. See also at [57] per Lord Scott.
[276] Ibid. at [139].   [277] [1952] Ch. 488.

allow the defendant to have an extensive right to store vehicles and other objects on the disputed strip of land, because 'it is virtually a claim to possession of the servient tenement, if necessary to the exclusion of the owner'.[278] Commenting on this passage, Lord Scott said:

> There may be arguments as to whether the facts of the case justified those remarks but, for my part, I would accept that if they did Upjohn J. was right to reject the easement claim and to require the defendant, if he was to succeed in resisting the plaintiff's claim to remove from the land, to establish title by adverse possession.[279]

With respect, this is somewhat unhelpful. First, in *Copeland v. Greenhalf*, although the user of the disputed strip was extensive, it is clear that Lord Scott was not convinced that the conclusion that this was an adverse possession case was actually justified. Second, it is clear from the dicta cited above that he and Lord Neuberger are prepared to allow very extensive use of another person's land to come within the ambit of the law of easements.[280] Even when the land is secured by the trespasser, it appears that for Lord Scott the matter is not free from doubt. So, when considering *Wright v. Macadam*,[281] the case concerning the right to store coal in a shed, he said:

> If the coal shed door had been locked with only the dominant owner possessing a key and entry by the servient owner barred . . . I would have regarded it as *arguable* that the right granted was inconsistent with the servient owner's ownership and inconsistent with the nature of . . . an easement.[282]

12.6.4.2 Easements and prescription

Surely, this is more than merely arguable. It cannot be the case that, in these circumstances, the owner of the servient land could be said to retain control of it. Nevertheless, it does show that there is now considerable potential for what have traditionally been seen to be possessory rights to be recognized as easements.[283] The significance of this is that, whereas the scope for a squatter to acquire title to registered land had been severely curtailed by the LRA 2002, this is not the case for easements. Instances where there may now be doubt as to whether the claim is one of adverse possession or prescription are likely to involve cases where the land in question has been used for storage purposes or for cultivation.[284] Whereas, in the past, such acts have formed the basis of a claim of adverse possession, if the use has exceeded twenty years, and the other requirements for the creation of an easement have been satisfied, one could find the counter-intuitive position of the paper owner of the land arguing that the use amounted to adverse possession, and the trespasser denying this and, instead, arguing that he was not in possession but that the use was in the nature of an easement.

---

[278] Ibid. at 498.   [279] [2007] 1 W.L.R. 2620 at [56].

[280] See *Smith v. Frankland* [2015] UKUT 294 (TCC) at [10], where the judge thought that the claimant lacked the 'character of exclusive occupation needed for adverse possession', but might nevertheless have an easement of parking on the same facts.

[281] [1949] 2 K.B. 744.   [282] [2007] 1 W.L.R. 2620 at [55]. Emphasis supplied.

[283] In any event, the claim in *Stadium Capital Holdings v. St Marylebone Properties Co Plc* [2009] EWHC 2942 (Ch) to have acquired a possessory title to airspace on the strength of an overhanging sign should, surely, have been argued on the basis of a prescriptive right to an easement.

[284] See, e.g., *Tennant v. Adamczyk* [2005] EWCA Civ. 1239. *J.A. Pye (Oxford) Ltd v. Graham* [2003] 1 A.C. 419 may itself provide an instance of this.

13

Freehold Covenants

In a previous chapter, the enforceability of covenants between landlord and tenant and their respective successors in title was considered.[1] The principal concern of this chapter is with covenants made between freeholders and the circumstances in which successors in title to the original parties to the covenant can either acquire the benefit of a covenant or take subject to the burden of it.

People at large are generally aware that if they wish to develop their land by building on it or implementing a change of use, planning permission is necessary. Applications for planning permission are publicized and people who may be affected by the development are given the opportunity to make representations. The law governing this area involves the public control of land use. It is a highly complex body of law and no attempt will be made in this book to enter into any discussion of it save to make one important point: the fact that planning permission has been granted 'does not mean that the development is lawful. All it means is that a bar to the use, imposed by planning law, in the public interest has been removed.'[2] In particular, the existence of planning permission does not override a private right to restrict a particular activity,[3] whether that right derives from restrictive covenants, contracts, or the law of tort.[4] While the principle that the existence of planning law will not of itself override private rights is well established, it is far less clear as to how such rights will be vindicated in the courts. The debate concerns whether an injunction to restrain the infringement of the right should be granted, or instead the award of damages, which effectively allows the private right to be compulsorily acquired, is more appropriate.[5] This is a debate on which the Supreme Court in *Lawrence v. Fen Tigers Ltd*[6] expressed sharply different, albeit *obiter*, views.

This chapter is concerned with the private control of land use, whereby landowners seek between themselves to regulate how land is used within a particular locality. The arrangements which people make take the form of covenants and these covenants may affect not only the parties who make them but can also affect successors in title. The person who makes the covenant is termed the *covenantor* and the person who obtains the benefit of that covenant is termed the *covenantee*. To reiterate, these covenants can operate to prevent the development of land, even when planning permission has been granted by

---

[1] See Chapter 10.

[2] *Lawrence v. Fen Tigers ltd* [2014] UKSC 14 at [89] *per* Lord Neuberger.

[3] See *Margerison v. Bates* [2008] EWHC 1211 (Ch) at [58]–[59] *per* Mr Edward Bartley Jones Q.C. See also Wheeler *v. J.J. Saunders* [1996] Ch. 19 at 26–30 *per* Staughton L.J., and *Watson v. Croft Promo-Sport Ltd* [2009] EWCA Civ. 15 at [32] *per* Sir Andrew Morritt C.

[4] *Lawrence v. Fen Tigers Ltd, supra, per* Lord Sumption. The fact that planning permission has been granted will not, of itself, lead The Upper Tribunal to grant a discharge or modification of an existing restrictive covenant: see, e.g., *In the Matter of an Application under section 84 of the Law of Property Act 1925 by Hussain* [2016] UKUT (LC). See 13.7.

[5] This debate relates to the issue of remedies and not to the essential nature of the right, the latter position being advocated by G. Calabresi and A.D. Melamed (1971–72) 85 Harv. L.R. 1089, especially 1105–6.

[6] *Supra.* See 13.6.

the requisite authority. As such, they form a type of private planning law which came into being well before the introduction of public control of land use and now operates in tandem, but not necessarily in harmony, with regulations affecting the public control of land. It is with these covenants that this chapter is concerned.

13.1 Privity of contract

As a general proposition, landowners are perfectly free to enter into any contractual relationship they see fit with regard to their respective properties. So, for example, if A contracts with B, his neighbour, to paint the outside of B's house every year, then this is a perfectly enforceable contract and if A does not do the painting, he will be liable to B for breach of contract. Again, if one house owner covenants with his neighbour that he will only use his property as a private residence then, as between the parties to the covenant, this contract is fully enforceable. The question of principal interest to a property lawyer is not so much the enforceability of the covenants between the original parties. Instead, the main issue is: if A sells his land to C and B sells his land to D, has D acquired the right to sue on the covenant and is C subject to the obligation created by A, C's predecessor in title. This issue is determined by considering whether the benefit of the covenant has run with the land, and whether the burden has run. These questions raise different issues and will be addressed shortly. First, however, attention will be paid to the extended notion of privity of contract and how it operates in this context.

13.1.1 Statutory extension of privity

In the context of land law, a key statutory provision which extended the notion of privity of contract was s. 56 of the Law of Property Act (LPA) 1925, which enables a person who is not a party to a covenant to sue upon it. The section provides that:

> A person may take an immediate or other interest in land, or other property, or the benefit of any condition, right of entry, agreement over or respecting land, although he may not be named as a party to the conveyance or other instrument.

The scope of this section was, at one time, highly controversial. In particular, it was used as authority in an attempt to outflank the common law doctrine of privity of contract, at least so far as it affected property.[7] This expansive view of the section did not, however, survive the decision of the House of Lords in *Beswick v. Beswick*.[8] Although the case did not fully resolve all the difficulties, it did leave matters tolerably clear as to the scope of s. 56 in the context of covenants relating to land.

The way that s. 56 operates is to allow a person to sue on a covenant to which he is not a party if the covenant purports to be made with him.[9] It was not sufficient if the covenant simply purported to confer a benefit on him.[10] So, if A and B entered into a covenant and that covenant purported to be made also with C, then C could sue upon it even though he was not a party to the covenants, because of the operation of s. 56. He was regarded as being privy to it.[11] If, however, the covenant between A and B was expressed to be for the

---

[7] See, e.g., *Drive Yourself Car Hire Co. (London) Ltd v. Strutt* [1954] 1 Q.B. 250 at 274 *per* Denning L.J.

[8] [1968] A.C. 58.

[9] *White v. Bijou Mansions Ltd* [1937] 1 Ch. 610 at 625 *per* Simonds J.; *Lyus v. Prowsa Developments Ltd* [1982] 1 W.L.R. 1044 at 1049 *per* Dillon J.

[10] See *Re Ecclesiastical Commissioners for England's Conveyance* [1936] Ch. 430.

[11] See *Stromdale & Ball Ltd v. Burden* [1952] 1 Ch. 223 at 234 *per* Danckwerts J.

benefit of C, but did not purport to be made with him, then C could not sue on the covenant.[12] The need for the covenant to purport to be made with the third party also meant that person had to be identifiable at the time when the covenant was made. If, therefore, a covenant purported to be made with future landowners, such people, when they acquired their land, could not sue directly upon the covenant as they were not existing, identifiable people when the covenant was made.[13]

13.1.2 Relaxation of privity

In the case of covenants made after May 2000,[14] the distinctions made with regard to s. 56 ceased to be relevant. Under s. 1(1) of the Contracts (Rights of Third Parties) Act 1999, a third party may sue on a contract to which he was not a party if either the contract expressly provides that he may, or a term in the contract purports to confer a benefit on him. The distinction which previously existed between a contract purporting to be made with a third party and one purporting to confer a benefit on him will disappear as now, in both cases, the third party will be able to enforce the covenant directly. Also gone is the rule that the third party must be an identifiable person at the date of the contract if he is to benefit from it. This change was effected by s. 1(3) of the 1999 Act, which provides that the third party must be expressly identified in the contract by name, as a member of a class or as answering a particular description, but need not be in existence when the contract was made. Because a large number of covenants which continue to affect land were created many years ago, the rules relating to the extension of privity which affected the operation of s. 56 will continue to be relevant for some considerable time to come.

13.2 The transmission of covenants

Once one has established who is able to sue directly on the covenant because they are party to it, or it was made for their benefit, the next step is to consider the circumstances when the benefit of that covenant has passed to a successor in title to the covenantee and when the burden of the covenant passes to a successor in title to the covenantor.

It will usually be necessary to consider these issues separately. If the issue in a given case is whether C can sue B on a covenant to which neither was party, two questions will need to be answered. First, has C acquired the benefit of the covenant? Second, has B taken subject to the burden? It is also necessary to distinguish between the approach taken by the common law and that adopted by equity.

13.3 Common law

In considering the position at common law, care must be taken to distinguish between the benefit and the burden of covenants.

13.3.1 The burden

It is a general rule of the law of contract that only a person who is a party to that contract can be sued upon the obligations created by it. While the doctrine of privity of contract

---

[12] *Amsprop Trading Ltd v. Harris* [1997] 1 W.L.R. 1025.

[13] For covenants made with existing neighbouring landowners, see *Forster v. Elvet Colliery* [1909] A.C. 98.

[14] Contracts (Rights of Third Parties) Act 1999, s. 10(2).

has been considerably relaxed by the enactment of the Contracts (Rights of Third Parties) Act 1999, that relaxation relates to the acquisition of contractual rights. It does not allow a person who is not a party to a contract to be sued upon that contract. The law relating to landlord and tenant represents a significant exception to this principle, in that the burden of covenants can affect assignees of either the lease or the reversion, the basis of this liability being privity of estate.[15] Other than that, the rule is largely inviolate. There is no question of the burden of a covenant running at law so as to adversely affect a successor in title to the covenantor.[16]

13.3.2 **The benefit**

Unlike the position with regard to the running of contractual burdens, the common law has never had a problem with the benefit of covenants being transmitted. Contractual rights, such as a debt, can readily be assigned to others. If A owes B £100, B can sell that debt to a debt collecting agency for, say £75, and the agency will then have the right to enforce the obligation, in full, against A. B is relatively happy, taking the view that £75 in cash is better than the right to sue for £100. In the case of covenants relating to land, the benefit of such covenants, while capable of being assigned, can also pass to a successor in title without the need for an expressly assignment.

The leading case is *Smith & Snipes Hall Farm Ltd v. River Douglas Catchment Board.*[17] The defendants covenanted with various freeholders that they would maintain the banks of the Eller Brook. One of the landowners then conveyed land to the first plaintiff, expressly with the benefit of the covenant. The first plaintiff then created a lease in favour of the second plaintiff. The river then burst its banks causing extensive flooding and the action was brought by both plaintiffs, who argued that they had acquired the benefit of the original covenant and were therefore entitled to sue for its breach. The Court of Appeal held in favour of both plaintiffs.

It was held that for the benefit of a covenant to run at common law various criteria had to be satisfied. First, before the benefit of the covenant will pass, the covenant must touch and concern the land; that is, 'it must either affect the land as regards mode of occupation, or it must be such as per se, and not merely from collateral sources, affects the value of the land'.[18] Second, the successor in title must have a legal estate in the land, although not necessarily the same estate as the predecessor in title so that, in the present case, the second plaintiff, who was a tenant, acquired the benefit of a covenant made with a predecessor in title, who was a freeholder.[19] Third, the land to be benefited must, from the deed containing the covenant, be reasonably identifiable, although such identification need not be express, and extrinsic evidence is admissible to identify the land in question.[20] Finally, the parties must intend that the benefit of the covenant should run with the land.

This last requirement was held to have been satisfied by the operation of s. 78, LPA 1925. This section, which became controversial in the context of the running of the benefit in equity,[21] provides that:

> A covenant relating to any land of the covenantee shall be deemed to be made with the covenantee and his successors in title and the persons deriving title under him or them, and shall have effect as if such successors and other persons were expressed.

---

[15] See 10.9.
[16] *Austerberry v. Corporation of Oldham* (1885) 29 Ch.D. 750; *Rhone v. Stephens* [1994] 2 A.C. 310.
[17] [1947] 2 K.B. 500.   [18] [1947] 2 K.B. 500 at 506 *per* Tucker L.J.
[19] See also *Williams v. Unit Construction Co. Ltd* (1955) 19 Conv. (N.S.) 262 at 266–7 *per* Lord Tucker.
[20] [1949] 2 K.B. 500 at 508 *per* Tucker L.J.   [21] See 13.5.6.

The effect of the section was that the covenant made by the covenantor was read as if it said that the covenant was made for the benefit not only of the covenantee, but also with his successors in title. This, together with the other criteria having been met, meant that the plaintiffs had acquired the benefit of the covenant and could sue upon it.

13.3.2.1 Nature of the covenant

Provided that the criteria referred to above are satisfied, the benefit of the covenant will run at common law. With regard to the running of the benefit, while it is essential that the covenantee owns land to be benefited by the covenant, it is immaterial as to whether the covenantor owns land himself.[22] Neither is it relevant, insofar as the running of the benefit is concerned, as to the type of covenant involved: whether it is positive or negative. While, as will be seen, this is a highly relevant consideration when regard is had to the running of the *burden* in equity, the *benefit* of either positive or negative covenants is capable of running at law.

13.3.2.2 Landlord and tenant

A recent example of the running of the benefit of a covenant at common law is provided by *P. & A. Swift Investments (A Firm) v. Combined English Stores Group plc.*[23] The defendant had stood surety for the rent payable by a tenant to the original landlord. The landlord subsequently assigned the reversion to the plaintiff and the tenant then got into financial difficulties and was unable to pay the rent. The plaintiff then sued the surety upon the contractual guarantee given to the original landlord. The issue was whether the benefit of this covenant had passed to the plaintiff upon the assignment of the reversion.

Because there had never been a relationship of landlord and tenant between the plaintiff and the defendant, the rules concerning the running of covenants in leases were of no assistance to the plaintiff. Instead, the argument was that the benefit of the covenant had run at common law. The House of Lords held that it had done so. The covenant touched and concerned the land because, first, it was only of benefit to the holder of the reversion for the time being; it was of no use to him after the reversion had been assigned. Second, it affected the nature and quality or mode of user of the land or its value and, third, the covenant was not expressed to be personal to the original contracting parties.[24] So, the benefit of the surety covenant ran at common law, it not being material that the surety did not own land and that the land benefited by the covenant was a freehold reversion.

To sum up, therefore, the position at common law is that the benefit of certain covenants can run with the land but the burden cannot. In equity, however, a quite different approach developed.

13.4 Equity

A central feature of the common law approach to covenants was that the obligations imposed by such covenants were personal to the parties who were privy to their creation. Put another way, the burden of such covenants does not run with the land. Equity, however, took a different view, the starting point of the development of this branch of the law being the decision in *Tulk v. Moxhay,*[25] a case which is the foundation stone of the modern law of restrictive covenants.

---

[22] *Smith & Snipes Hall Farm Ltd v. River Douglas Catchment Board* [1947] 2 K.B. 500 at 517–18 *per* Denning L.J.

[23] [1989] A.C. 632.   [24] Ibid. at 642 *per* Lord Oliver.   [25] (1843) 2 Ph. 773.

13.4.1 **The burden of covenants**

In *Tulk v. Moxhay*, Tulk, in 1808, sold a vacant plot of land in Leicester Square to Elms. Elms covenanted on behalf of himself, his heirs, and assigns that he would, at all times, keep and maintain the said piece of ground in an open state, uncovered with any buildings. The land then passed through various pairs of hands until, finally, it was conveyed to Moxhay, who admitted that he had notice of the existence of the covenant. Notwithstanding his knowledge of this covenant, he then threatened to build upon the land and Tulk sought and obtained an injunction to restrain him from building.

In granting the injunction, the reasoning of Lord Cottenham L.C. was quite general. He said:

> That the question does not depend on whether the covenant runs with the land is evident from this, that if there was a mere agreement and no covenant, this court would enforce it against a party purchasing with notice of it; for if an equity is attached to the property by the owner, no one purchasing with notice of that equity can stand in a different situation from the party from whom he purchased.[26]

It should be observed that the judgment in this case does not rest upon the premise that the type of covenant he was considering was a form of interest in land, the burden of which is then capable of binding a purchaser of that land. To the contrary, the basis of the decision is that, if a purchaser buys land with notice of some prior undertaking relating to that land, then it is inequitable for him to act in a way which is inconsistent with that obligation. Put in such broad terms, all sorts of different obligations could become enforceable against successive owners of land. This is something against which the law has traditionally set its face: to allow this to happen could make certain land virtually unsellable as it might be affected by a multitude of different obligations. So, although the decision in *Tulk v. Moxhay* is still regarded as the foundation of the modern law, the actual rationale of the judgment is not. Instead, the courts have taken care to fashion a new interest in land, the nature of this right being modelled closely on the law of easements.

13.5 **Restrictive covenants**

In *Tulk v. Moxhay*, the covenant to keep and maintain the ground in an open state, uncovered with buildings, reads, at first sight, as a positive covenant. The words 'keep' and 'maintain' tend to indicate an obligation to do something. In substance, however, the covenant is negative, or restrictive, as its effect is to prevent the covenantor from building upon his own land. The reasoning in the passage quoted above does not, however, lay any emphasis upon whether the covenant was to do something or to refrain from certain conduct. The issue seemed to be, simply, whether or not the successor in title had notice of the covenant. If he did, he was bound by it. This led to a view that both positive and negative covenants could be enforced as against purchasers with notice[27] and, for a time, judicial support could be found for such a proposition.[28] It soon came to be settled, however, that the only covenants which were capable of binding a successor in title to the covenantor were negative covenants. In the leading case of *Haywood v. Brunswick Permanent*

---

[26] (1843) 2 Ph. 773 at 778.
[27] See C.D. Bell [1981] Conv. 52 at 57–60. For a strong counter-argument, see R. Griffith [1983] Conv. 29.
[28] See *Morland v. Cook* (1868) L.R. 6 Eq. 252; *Cooke v. Chilcott* (1876) 3 Ch.D. 694; *Luker v. Dennis* (1877) 7 Ch.D. 227.

Building Society,[29] it was held that a mortgagee of an assignee was not bound by a covenant to build and keep in repair houses on the land, it being made clear that 'only such a covenant as can be complied with without the expenditure of money will be enforced against the assignee on the ground of notice'.[30]

Ever since this decision, it became the received wisdom that only restrictive covenants were capable of running with the land. That wisdom was directly challenged in the House of Lords in *Rhone v. Stephens*,[31] where it was held, confirming the rule established in *Haywood v. Brunswick Building Society*, that a covenant to maintain a roof was not binding upon a successor in title to the covenantor. In reaching this conclusion, considerable stress was laid, in the field of property law, on the need to maintain certainty and, in particular, not to upset established rights. Lord Templeman said:

> It is plain from articles, reports and papers to which we were referred that judicial legislation to overrule the *Austerberry* case would create a number of difficulties, anomalies and uncertainties and affect the rights of people who have for over 100 years bought and sold land in the knowledge, imparted at an elementary stage to every student of the law of real property, that positive covenants affecting freehold land are not directly enforceable except against the original covenantor.[32]

The House of Lords, therefore, confirmed the long-established rule that it is only restrictive covenants which can be made to run directly with freehold land,[33] and attempts to make positive covenants binding on successors in title have been described as 'hopeful rather than realistic'.[34] In the previous chapter on easements, it was noted that the law was highly reluctant to recognize as an easement a right which restricts the use to which the servient owner can put his land.[35] Any problem caused by this reluctance is largely met, however, by the development of the law relating to restrictive covenants, whereby constraints on land use can be imposed by the creation of a suitable covenant. There is, however, a similar reluctance to recognize as an easement any right which will involve the expenditure of money by the owner of the servient land. Here, the law concerning covenants relating to freehold land does not provide an alternative means of imposing such a liability. This lack of a direct means of providing for the enforceability of positive covenants does cause problems. These problems, and the means of circumventing them, will be considered at the end of this chapter.

13.5.1 **Land to be benefited**

As the law of restrictive covenants developed, increasingly the interest in land which was created began to take on the characteristics of a negative easement affecting land.[36] If a right is to be recognized as an easement, there must exist a dominant tenement. Before the burden of a restrictive covenant will run with the land the same requirement exists. The person seeking to enforce that covenant must retain land to be benefited.

This rule is exemplified by the decision in *Formby v. Barker*.[37] F sold all of his land subject to various covenants restricting its use. The defendant acquired part of that land with notice

---

[29] (1881) 8 Q.B. 403.   [30] Ibid. at 410 *per* Lindley L.J.
[31] [1994] 2 A.C. 310. See N.P. Gravells (1994) 110 L.Q.R. 346. See also *Thamesmead Town v. Allotley* [1998] 3 E.G.L.R. 97.
[32] [1994] 2 A.C. 310 at 321.
[33] See also *89 Holland Park (Management) Ltd v. Hicks* [2013] EWHC 392 (Ch) at [74]–[80] *per* Mr Robert Miles Q.C., sitting as a Deputy High Court judge, clearly treating the matter as one of substance not form.
[34] *Davies v. Bramwell* [2007] EWCA Civ. 821 at [8] *per* Lloyd L.J.   [35] See 12.1.4.2.
[36] See *London and S. W. Railway Co. v. Gomm* (1882) 20 Ch.D. 762 at 773 *per* Sir George Jessel M.R.
[37] [1903] 2 Ch. 539.

of the covenants. The administratrix of F's estate then sought an injunction to restrict the building on that land which, it was alleged, would infringe the covenant. The action failed on two grounds. First, it was held that the proposed building would not actually amount to a breach of covenant. More importantly, the burden of the covenant did not run because the person seeking to enforce it did not have any land which would be benefited by the covenant. This rule was confirmed in *London County Council v. Allen*,[38] where a local authority sought to enforce covenants made in its favour. The relevant land was later conveyed and the attempt to enforce the covenant failed because the authority did not own land to be benefited by the covenant. For this reason the burden of it was held not to have run.

This decision confirms the general rule that, for the burden of a restrictive covenant to run, there must, in effect, be a dominant tenement. The consequence of the rule in the present context was, however, potentially awkward and so, in favour of local authorities, the rule has been modified, to allow them to enforce such covenants despite not having land to be benefited.[39] The basic rule, however, remains.

13.5.2 **Touch and concern the land**

Allied to the rule that the person seeking to enforce the covenant must have land to be benefited by that covenant is the requirement that the land retained does benefit from the covenant.[40] This means two things. First, that the covenant touches and concerns the land and, second, that the two plots of land are sufficiently proximate to each other for the dominant land to be benefited. So, as is the case with easements, a right of way in Kent does not exist for the benefit of land in Northumberland,[41] covenants relating to land in Hampstead will not be regarded as benefiting land in Clapham.[42] The covenant must accommodate the dominant tenement.

A recent example of where this requirement was not met occurred in *Comischome Ltd v. Southampton City Council*.[43] A covenant by the BBC, made when it purchased a building from the council, that it would only be used as a broadcasting centre was held not to touch and concern the land and did not bind a subsequent purchaser. This was because, given the varied land use in the vicinity of the building, it was hard to see how its continuing use for broadcasting would have any material impact on the quality or amenity of the adjoining council land.

13.5.3 **Intention that burden will run**

It is not compulsory that restrictive covenants entered into by two landowners will necessarily create an interest in land binding upon successors in title to the covenantor. The covenant may be intended to be personal to the parties making it. For the burden of the covenant to run with the land, the parties must intend this to happen. This matter is governed by s. 79, LPA 1925, which provides that:

> A covenant relating to any land of a covenantor or capable of being bound by him, shall, unless a contrary intention is expressed, be deemed to be made on behalf of the covenantor on behalf of himself his successors in title and the persons deriving title under him or them and, subject as aforesaid, shall take effect as if such successors and other persons were expressed.

---

[38] [1914] 3 Q.B. 642.
[39] Town and Country Planning Act 1990, s. 106(3), replacing earlier legislation.
[40] See *Dano Ltd v. Earl of Cadogan* [2013] EWHC 1378 (Ch).
[41] See *Bailey v. Stephens* (1862) 12 C.B. (N.S.) 91 at 115 *per* Byles J.
[42] *Kelly v. Barrett* [1924] 2 Ch. 379 at 404 *per* Pollock M.R.
[43] [2013] EWHC 1378 (Ch) at [27] *per* Sir William Blackburne.

The expression 'relating to the land' is the familiar concept that the covenant must touch and concern the land. The reference to 'capable of being bound' would seem to be sufficient to prevent the burden of a positive covenant running with the land, as such covenants are not capable of binding the servient land.[44] Provided that the other criteria discussed above are met, then unless a contrary intention is expressed, the burden of the covenant will run with the land. In terms of finding the requisite contrary intention, while an express statement to this effect is preferable,[45] the court is prepared to construe the document as a whole to see if it was intended that the covenant is to be personal to the covenantor.[46]

13.5.4 Equitable right

The restrictive covenant is an interest in land which was developed by equity. Unlike legal interests in land, equitable interests will not automatically bind a purchaser of the servient land and, subject to some exceptions, its enforceability will depend upon registration. It is necessary to deal separately with unregistered and registered land.

13.5.4.1 Unregistered land

A restrictive covenant is, except for two types of covenant, registrable as a Class D(ii) land charge. If registered, all subsequent purchasers will be deemed to have actual notice of it and, therefore, be bound by it.[47] If it is not registered, it will be void against a purchaser of a legal estate for money or money's worth.[48] An unregistered restrictive covenant will be binding upon a squatter, who is not, of course, a purchaser for money or money's worth.[49]

There are two classes of restrictive covenant which are not registrable as land charges. These are covenants created before 1926 and covenants between landlord and tenant. The determination of whether a purchaser has notice of such covenants and, therefore, is bound by them, is dependent upon the old doctrine of notice which, in this context, will mean whether or not they could be discovered by a proper investigation of title.

13.5.4.2 Registered land

A restrictive covenant is not capable of overriding a registered disposition and, if it is to bind a purchaser for value, it must, unless it is a covenant between landlord and tenant, be protected by the registration of a notice.[50]

13.5.5 The benefit of restrictive covenants

The application of the rules derived from *Tulk v. Moxhay* indicate when the burden of a restrictive covenant has run with the land, so that one knows if a particular purchaser is bound by it. The second, independent, question then arises as to whether there is anybody who can enforce that covenant; whether the benefit of the covenant has also run. As the common law developed rules concerning the running of the benefit of covenants, so, too, did equity. In practice, the equitable rules are more important than their common law counterparts because if a person is seeking to enforce a covenant, the burden of which has passed in equity, he must establish, if he is not the original covenantee, that the benefit of that covenant has passed to him under the equitable rules.[51] If this cannot can be

---

[44] See *Rhone v. Stephens* [1994] 2 A.C. 310 at 322 *per* Lord Templeman.
[45] See *Gregg v. Richards* [1926] Ch. 521.
[46] *Re Royal Victoria Pavilion, Ramsgate* [1961] Ch. 581; *Morrells of Oxford Ltd v. Oxford United F.C. Ltd* [2001] Ch. 459.
[47] LPA 1925, s. 198.   [48] Land Charges Act 1972, s. 4(6).
[49] See *Re Nisbett and Pott's Contract* [1906] 1 Ch. 306.   [50] LRA 2002, ss 32 and 33.
[51] See, e.g., *Re Union of London & Smith's Bank Conveyance, Miles v. Easter* [1933] Ch. 611.

established, then despite the burden of the covenant having run, the position will be that there is nobody in a position to enforce it.[52] In the case of registered land, the register can then be altered to remove the entry relating to the burden of the covenant.[53]

In equity, the benefit of a covenant can run in one of the three ways, set out by Sir Charles Hall V.-C. in *Renals v. Cowlishaw*.[54] These are:

(i) annexation;

(ii) assignment; and

(iii) a scheme of development.

These three methods will be considered in turn.

13.5.6 **Annexation**

Annexation involves the permanent attachment of the benefit of a restrictive covenant to the land. Once the benefit has been annexed, it will pass automatically on a transfer of the land without specific mention. It was previously the case, and still is with regard to pre-1926 covenants,[55] that the law concerning how annexation was effected was highly complex, with meticulous attention being paid to the precise wording of a particular covenant to establish that the requisite intention had been shown to annex the covenant to the dominant land.[56] It was also necessary for the land in question to be clearly identified. There was a further complication in that, once it had been shown that the benefit of a covenant had been annexed, it was regarded as annexed to the land as a whole. Unless when the benefit of the covenant was annexed, it was annexed to each and every part of the dominant land, on a sale of only part of the land, the benefit of the covenant would not pass.[57] Happily, a good deal of the complexity affecting this branch of the law was swept away as a result of the decision of the Court of Appeal in *Federated Homes v. Mill Lodge Properties Ltd.*[58]

13.5.6.1 **Statutory annexation**

One of the issues which arose in *Federated Homes* was whether the benefit of a covenant restricting the amount of building which could take place on a neighbouring plot had been annexed to the land and had, therefore, passed to the plaintiff. Despite the fact that there were no express words of annexation in the conveyance, the Court of Appeal held that s. 78, LPA 1925 had the effect of annexing the benefit of the covenant. This section, it will be recalled, provides that a covenant relating to the land of the covenantee shall be deemed to have been made with the covenantee, his successors in title, and persons deriving title under him. Brightman L.J. held that, providing that the covenant in question related to the covenantee's land, the effect of the section was to annex the benefit of the covenant to the land. He held, further, that the section annexed the covenant not just to the land as a whole, but to each and every part of it, thereby removing the difficulty adverted to earlier[59]

---

[52] See, e.g., *Seymour Road (Southampton) Ltd v. Williams* [2010] EWHC 111 (Ch).

[53] See *Southwark Roman Catholic Diocesan Corporation v. South London Church Fund &. Southwark Diocesan Board of Finance* [2009] EWHC 3368 (Ch).

[54] (1878) 9 Ch.D. 125 at 129.

[55] See *Shropshire County Council v. Edwards* (1982) 46 P. & C.R. 270; *J. Sainsbury plc v. Enfield London Borough Council* [1989] 1 W.L.R. 590; *Southwark Roman Catholic Diocesan Corporation v. South London Church Fund &.Southwark Diocesan Board of Finance* [2009] EWHC 3368 (Ch).

[56] See, e.g., *Rogers v. Hosegood* [1900] 2 Ch. 388.

[57] *Re Ballard's Conveyance* [1937] Ch. 473.   [58] [1980] 1 W.L.R. 594.

[59] Although see the somewhat odd remarks in *City Inn (Jersey) Ltd v. Ten Trinity Square Ltd* [2008] EWCA Civ. 156 at [33] *per* Jacob L.J.

and, subsequently, in *Bryant Homes Ltd v. Stein Management Ltd*,[60] Norris J. has stressed that there is now a strong presumption to this effect.

The decision in *Federated Homes*, although advocated by some writers in the past,[61] was controversial.[62] Strong exception was taken by one specialist practitioner in the field[63] to the interpretation of s. 78 that, provided that the covenant touched and concerned the land, the benefit of the covenant became annexed to the land. Before appraising the merits of the decision, one important matter must be addressed. In *Federated Homes*, Brightman L.J. left open the question whether, for annexation to take place, the covenant must identify the land to be benefited.[64] In *Crest Nicholson Residential (South) Ltd v. McCallister*,[65] Chadwick L.J. confirmed that this was a necessary requirement. As well as being supported by authority, there is a good practical reason for insisting upon this requirement, as it facilitates the task of a purchaser of the burdened land to discover which land has the benefit of the covenant in question.[66]

Although the decision has been criticized, in defence of it, it can be pointed out, as Brightman L.J. did himself, that at common law the benefit of covenants will, as a result of this section, run with the land without the need for the intention that it should do so being expressed.[67] It would be odd for equity to take a less relaxed, more formalistic, approach to an issue such as this than did the common law. Moreover, the decision should be welcomed for having consigned to history some of the arcane learning that had been allowed to develop around this branch of the law. It is now clear that, provided that the land to be benefited is identified, whether by the conveyance or by admissible extrinsic evidence, and provided that the covenant touches and concerns the land, the benefit of it will run with the land. It will not be necessary to also show, by express words in the conveyance, the specific intention that it should pass to successors in title.[68]

13.5.6.2 Contrary intention

One of the main criticisms levelled at *Federated Homes* was that, unlike s. 79 of the Act, which relates to the passing of the burden of restrictive covenants, s. 78 is not expressed to be subject to the expression of a contrary intention.[69] So, it was argued, if the covenant in question touched and concerned the land, the effect of s. 78 would be to make annexation compulsory whatever the intention of the parties. This fear was dispelled in *Roake v. Chadha*.[70] This case concerned a covenant which was expressed 'not to enure for the benefit of any owner or subsequent purchaser of the . . . estate unless the benefit of the covenant shall be expressly assigned'. The effect of this wording was held to be that the covenant did not relate to the land and was not, therefore, annexed to it. The effect of the decision is that annexation will occur unless a contrary intention is expressed and the

---

[60] [2016] EWHC 2435 (Ch) at [35]–[39].   [61] See, e.g., H.W.R. Wade [1972B] C.L.J. 94.

[62] See D.J. Hayton (1980) 43 M.L.R. 445. For a supportive reaction, see D.J. Hurst (1982) 2 L.S. 53. For a full discussion of this decision, see N. Gravells in Gravells (ed.), *Landmark Cases in Land Law* (Oxford, Hart Publishing, 2013), Chapter 5.

[63] G.H. Newsom (1981) 97 L.Q.R. 32, perhaps vindicating the view that the decision would be more popular with academics than with practitioners: A. Sydenham [1980] Conv. 216 at 217.

[64] [1984] 1 W.L.R. 594 at 604.   [65] [2004] 1 W.L.R. 2409. See J. Howell [2004] Conv. 507.

[66] [2004] 1 W.L.R. 2409 at 2422.

[67] [1980] 1 W.L.R. 598 at 605, referring to *Smith & Snipes Hall Farm Ltd v. River Douglas Catchment Board* [1947] 2 K.B. 500; *Williams v. Unit Construction Ltd* (1955) 19 Conv. (N.S.) 262.

[68] *Mohammadzadeh v. Joseph* [2008] 1 P. & C.R. 6 at [46] *per* Etherton L.J.

[69] See also *Morrells of Oxford Ltd v. Oxford United F.C. Ltd* [2001] Ch. 459 at 466 *per* Robert Walker L.J.

[70] [1984] Ch. 40. See also *Crest Nicholson Residential (South) Ltd v. McAllister* [2004] 1 W.L.R. 2409 and the discussion and application of this in *89 Holland Park (Management) Ltd v. Hicks* [2013] EWHC 391 (Ch) at [36]–[66] *per* Mr Robert Miles Q.C., sitting as a Deputy High Court judge.

statement that the benefit can pass only by express assignment was a sufficient statement of a contrary intention.

The finding of a contrary intention is a matter of construction, and 'the parties may restrict the ambit of the benefit of a restrictive covenant to the original covenantee and whether or not they have done so is a question of construction of the instrument as a whole'.[71] In *City Inn (Jersey) Ltd v. Ten Trinity Square Ltd*,[72] various restrictive covenants were entered into for the benefit of the Port of London Authority on a transfer by it of land. The covenant referred to the Authority as 'the transferor', that term being used twenty-eight times in the conveyance. On a couple of occasions reference was made to the transferor and its successors in title. This led to the conclusion that the benefit of the covenant was intended to be personal to the Authority, and so did not run to a successor in title. The same reasoning was employed in *Margerison v. Bates*,[73] where, on some occasions, the conveyance referred simply to the vendor, and on others, to the vendor and her successors in title. As this was a professionally drawn legal document, this variation in wording was seen as deliberate with the result that the covenant which was expressed to be made with the vendor was made with her personally, and there was no intention that the benefit of it should run. What is key to these decisions is the deliberate use of the expression 'successors in title' in some references and not in others. If there is simply a reference to the transferor, the intention that the benefit will run will, as a result of s. 78, readily be found.[74]

13.5.7 **Assignment**

If a covenant has not at the time of its creation been annexed to the land, then it is possible, on a subsequent conveyance, for the benefit of that covenant to be assigned with the land. For assignment to take place in equity, the assignment of the covenant must be coupled with a transfer of the land and the conveyance and assignment must be simultaneous.[75] The assignment must identify the land to be benefited, although such identification can be done through surrounding circumstances.[76]

Once the benefit of the covenant has been assigned, the better view is that, on subsequent conveyances, further assignments should not be necessary. This view is based on the idea that an assignment should operate as a 'delayed annexation' so that the benefit of any covenants should, thereafter, pass automatically.[77] Such authority as there is on this point is, however, against this view. It would appear, therefore, to be necessary for there to be an express assignment of the benefit of the covenant each time that the land is conveyed, so that there is an unbroken chain of assignments from the covenantee to the person seeking to enforce the covenant.

13.5.8 **Schemes of development**

The final method of ensuring that the benefit of a covenant passes with the dominant land is to establish a scheme of development. The essence of such a scheme is that land, at one time owned by a single person, is divided up into lots and then sold off to various

---

[71] *Rees v. Peters* [2011] EWCA Civ. 836 at [9] *per* Sir Andrew Morritt C., a case involving a highly ambiguous document.

[72] [2008] EWCA Civ. 156.   [73] [2008] EWHC 1211 (Ch).

[74] See *Mahon v. Simms* [2005] 3 E.G.L.R. 67.

[75] *Re Union of London and Smith's Conveyance, Miles v. Easter* [1933] Ch. 611.

[76] *Newton Abbot Co-operative Society Ltd v. Williamson and Treadgold Ltd* [1952] Ch. 286; *Marten v. Flight Refuelling Ltd* [1962] Ch. 115.

[77] P.V. Baker (1968) 84 L.Q.R. 22.

purchasers. The idea is that the covenants entered into, which are for the benefit of the estate, become mutually enforceable between the various owners of the different plots of land. Although the existing rules could have been employed to achieve the required result, a different set of rules was devised with the result that, when the existence of a scheme is established, a local law is created with regard to this area of land. It should be borne in mind, however, that it has been said that: 'It may be, indeed, that this is one of those branches of equity which work best when explained least.'[78]

13.5.8.1 Origins of the doctrine

When the courts began to develop this branch of the law, quite stringent criteria were adopted which had to be met before the courts would accept that a scheme of development had been created. Four conditions were laid down in *Elliston v. Reacher*[79] which had to be satisfied. These were:

(i) the land must have been disposed of by a common vendor;

(ii) prior to the sale the land had to be laid out in lots subject to common obligations;

(iii) the common vendor must have intended the benefit of the covenants to be for the benefit of all the owners and not merely for himself; and

(iv) the land must have been bought on the footing that the restrictions were to be enforceable by the owner of other lots.

13.5.9 **A more relaxed approach**

In more recent times, the courts have been prepared to relax the criteria established in *Elliston v. Reacher* and find there to be a scheme of development to have been created when one or other of these conditions has not been met.[80] Nowadays, the courts are concerned to see that two conditions are satisfied. The first is that the area to be affected by the scheme has been properly identified.[81] Second, and of paramount importance, is that it is shown that it was clearly intended to set up a scheme for the reciprocal enforcement of obligations.[82] In order to establish such an intention, it is helpful if the land is laid out in lots, as this gives rise to a presumption that there is such a reciprocal intention.[83] It is not, however, essential to do this, as such an intention can be established by extrinsic evidence and the fact that the various covenants are identical is strong evidence to this effect.[84] No such intention to establish a reciprocal scheme will be found to exist unless its existence is brought to the attention of prospective purchasers.[85]

13.6 **Remedies**

A restrictive covenant is an equitable right and, as such, the remedies available in respect of any breach of covenant are equitable. The principal remedy which is sought is the injunction. The type of injunction sought may vary. If the breach has not actually occurred,

---

[78] *Brunner v. Greenslade* [1971] 1 Ch. 993 at 1006 *per* Megarry J.
[79] [1908] 2 Ch. 374.
[80] See Gray and Gray, *Elements of Land Law* (5th edn) (London, Oxford University Press, 2009), 283–6.
[81] See *Lund v. Taylor* (1975) 31 P. & C.R. 167.
[82] See *Juan v. Allen* [2016] EWHC 1502 (Ch) at [50] *per* Master Clark.
[83] See *Kariton v. Heun Oaks Properties Ltd* [1303] 1 Ch. 810; *Re Dolphins Conveyance* [1970] Ch. 654.
[84] See *Brunner v. Greenslade* [1971] 1 Ch. 993.
[85] See *Jamaica Mutual Life Assurance Society v. Hillsborough Ltd* [1989] 1 W.L.R. 1101.

but is merely threatened, then the plaintiff will seek a *quia timet* injunction. This is a remedy to prevent conduct which if carried out, will, it is envisaged, amount to an infringement of the plaintiff's rights, and so prevents that infringement from occurring, thereby restraining the anticipated breach. Alternatively, the breach may have occurred and the injunction is sought to prevent the continuation of the breach. Finally, a mandatory injunction may be sought to undo what has been done, such as the demolition of a building erected in breach of contract.[86]

As with all equitable remedies, the grant of an injunction is discretionary but that discretion is exercised in accordance with settled principles,[87] so that, for example, delay in bringing an action may cause the injunction to be refused.[88]

13.6.1 **Damages in lieu**

Because a breach of a restrictive covenant is the infringement of an equitable, as opposed to a legal right, there is no right to damages. This point is largely academic in that, since the time of Lord Cairns' Act in 1858,[89] the court has the power to award damages in lieu of an injunction.[90] The effect of awarding damages rather than enforcing the right by injunctive relief is that the defendant is enabled to pay for the ability to do, or continue doing, something which he does not have the right to do, and is against the wishes of the holder of the property right.[91] This consideration has, traditionally, led the courts to apply this jurisdiction sparingly.[92] This reluctance was recently disparaged, however, when, in *Lawrence v. Fen Tigers Ltd*,[93] Lord Sumption referred to a judicial reluctance to sanction a wrong by allowing the defendant to pay for the right to go on doing it as being 'an unduly moralistic approach to disputes, and if taken at face value would justify the grant of an injunction in all cases, which is plainly not the law'.

Lord Sumption's comments came in the context of a discussion of what, for a considerable period of time, was the leading case where A.L. Smith L.J., in *Shelfer v. City of London Electric Light Company*,[94] had laid down four conditions which had to be satisfied for it to be appropriate that damages should be awarded in lieu of an injunction. These were that:

(i) the injury to the claimant's legal right was small;

(ii) it was capable of being estimated in money;

(iii) damages would be adequate compensation; and

(iv) it would be oppressive to the defendant to grant an injunction.

---

[86] See *Wakeham v. Wood* (1982) 43 P. & C.R. 40; *Mortimer v. Bailey* [2004] EWCA Civ. 1514.

[87] See, generally, Glister and Lee, *Hanbury and Martin, Modern Equity* (20th edn) (London, Sweet & Maxwell, 2015), Chapter 28.

[88] See *Chatsworth Estates Co. v. Fewell* [1931] 1 Ch. 224.

[89] Chancery Amendment Act 1858, s. 2. See now Supreme Court Act 1981, s. 50.

[90] Damages are assessed on the basis of what could reasonably have been charged for the release of the covenant. See *Wrotham Park Estates Co. Ltd v. Parkside Homes Ltd* [1974] 1 W.L.R. 798; *Jaggard v. Sawyer* [1995] 1 W.L.R. 269; *One-Step (Support) Ltd v. Morris-Garner* [2014] EWHC 2213 (Ch). See D. Halpern [2001] Conv. 453.

[91] This is wrongly seen as being a dividing line within the law of property: see G. Calabresi and A.D. Melamed (1971–72) 85 Harv. L.R. 1089, especially at 1105–6. See also P.L. Davies in Bright (ed.), *Modern Studies in Property Law (Vol.6)* (Oxford, Hart Publishing, 2011), 39 at 48; M. Dixon [2014] Conv. 79 at 84. This issue relates to how a property right is vindicated: not whether it exists.

[92] It has been said that this jurisdiction should only be used in 'exceptional circumstances': *Watson v. Croft Promo-Sport Ltd* [2009] EWCA Civ. 15 at [44] *per* Sir Andrew Morritt C.

[93] [2014] UKSC 13 at [160].

[94] [1895] 1 Ch. 287 at 322–3.

Of these, the latter was seen as perhaps the most important consideration, so that when, in breach of covenant, buildings had been constructed and a mandatory injunction was sought to order their demolition, this might be seen as being oppressive. In addition, a court will take a wider view of the situation to have regard to the public interest, so that if the outcome of granting an injunction would be to deprive the public of much needed housing, the making of such an order is unlikely.[95] Even then, if the defendant had taken a calculated risk that his building activity might infringe a claimant's right, this would weaken the argument that the award of damages as opposed to an injunction was the appropriate outcome.[96]

Lawrence v. Fen Tigers concerned an action for nuisance in respect of noise caused by various forms of motor sport.[97] The main issue in the litigation concerned whether or not there was an actionable nuisance and, assuming that there was, the question of what was the appropriate remedy had not been a live issue. The Supreme Court upheld the injunction granted at trial but went on to consider the continued usefulness of the guidelines in *Shelfer*, a matter which divided the court. Lord Sumption, with whom Lord Clarke agreed, was highly critical of them. He regarded the principles which favoured the grant of an injunction as being out of date and regretted that they had been followed in modern times. In his provisional view, if planning permission had been granted for a particular activity then, as a matter of principle, an injunction should not be granted.[98] This was a minority view. Lord Neuberger started from the view that a mechanical application of the *Shelfer* principles was wrong in principle and gave rise to a risk of going wrong in practice.[99] He also accepted that the award of an injunction is always discretionary with the result that past cases tend to be illustrative rather than authoritative. Having said that, he nevertheless concluded that the starting position was that the person whose right was being infringed should be granted an injunction to vindicate his right. The onus was then on the wrongdoer to show that the right could, in effect, be bought out by the award of damages.[100] This approach was supported also by Lords Mance and Carnwarth. Addressing the appropriateness of the award of damages in lieu of an injunction, Lord Mance expressed the view, shared by Lords Neuberger and Carnwarth, that:

> the right to enjoy one's home without disturbance is one which I would believe that many, indeed most, people value for reasons largely if not independent of money.[101]

Following on from this, he did not consider that an award of damages would necessarily provide adequate compensation in the context of nuisance. The majority of the Supreme Court favoured the view that, in cases of private nuisance, once it has been established that the activity of an adjoining landowner is actionable, the starting point is that an injunction should be awarded to prevent the continuation of that nuisance. This outcome would follow notwithstanding that planning permission had been granted for the activity which is being challenged. In the case of restrictive covenants, one would anticipate, at first sight at least, that the claimant's position would be stronger. This is because the obligation not to do something attaches to a specific piece of land and is owed to a specific landowner, or small group of landowners, rather than to the neighbouring community as

---

[95] See *Wrotham Park Estates Ltd v. Parkside Homes Ltd* [1974] 1 W.L.R. 798 at 811 *per* Brightman J.

[96] See *Regan v. Paul Properties Ltd* [2006] EWCA Civ. 1391 at [74] *per* Mummery L.J (a case concerning an easement of light). See in this context P. Chynoweth [2007] Conv. 175.

[97] For an interesting discussion of which, and the relevance of planning permission, see F. Laee [2014] Conv. 449.

[98] [2014] UKSC 13 at [161].   [99] Ibid. at [119]. See also at [239] *per* Lord Carnwarth.

[100] Ibid. at [121].   [101] Ibid. at [168].

a whole. It is a right to prevent a defined activity, such as building, which may very well not amount to an actionable nuisance, and, unlike the case of nuisance, has been expressly created. Ordinarily, therefore, one would anticipate that if the claimant has been found to be in breach of a restrictive covenant an injunction would be granted to restrain further breaches. The position may, however, be complicated by the planning process. If, for example, the covenant is to restrain building and the owner of the servient land applies for planning permission, the holder of the benefit of that covenant would have the opportunity to object. The fact that he does not do so when he has a specific property right to protect, as opposed to being a nearby landowner with a general interest, perhaps shared with other neighbours, in preventing further development may well count against him if, subsequently, he seeks an injunction to vindicate his property right by seeking the demolition of a building constructed in breach of covenant.

13.7 Discharge of covenants

Some restrictive covenants affecting land may have been imposed many years in the past, when conditions were very different from those currently pertaining. Yet, they remain binding upon successive purchasers of the land, despite serving little purpose in modern society. It may also be the case that their continued enforceability is socially detrimental, preventing socially desirable development of the land. Such considerations led the Law Commission's Conveyancing Standing Committee[102] to canvass various options to curb the effect of restrictive covenants, the most radical being to abolish them altogether, although, perhaps more reasonably, less drastic proposals were also mooted, such as putting a legislative lifespan on their effect. Nothing came of this consultation paper and the only way to mitigate the sometimes doleful effect of restrictive covenants is to utilize statutory jurisdiction to modify or discharge restrictive covenants, either with or without compensation.

Application may be made to the Lands Chamber of the Upper Tribunal (formerly the Lands Tribunal) under s. 84 of the LPA 1925[103] for a covenant to be modified or discharged, and the tribunal is given the power to award compensation, a further instance whereby a person's property right can, in effect, be the subject of compulsory purchase.[104] Such an order can be made on one of four grounds:

(i) that the covenant has become obsolete;

(ii) that the continued enforcement of the covenant would be obstructive to some public or private use of the land and that the covenant confers no practical benefit or is contrary to the public interest and any loss can be adequately compensated by money;

(iii) with the consent, either express or implied, of all persons of full age entitled to the benefit; and

(iv) the discharge or modification would confer no injury on the person entitled to the benefit.

While the Law Commission has recommended that the jurisdiction of the Lands Chamber should be extended to easements, profits, and its proposed new interest, the land obligation, it did not advocate any changes to the grounds on which such modifications could be

---

[102] (1986) Law Commission Conveyancing Standing Committee, *What Should We Do About Old Restrictive Covenants*, 11–12.
[103] As amended by LPA 1969, s. 28.   [104] See 13.6.1.

made,[105] and the fact that planning permission has been granted will not, of itself, mean that a claim to discharge a covenant under this section will be successful.[106] Even where a developer has gone ahead and built on land in breach of a restrictive covenant, this does not mean that the covenants will be discharged. That point has recently been underlined in *Alexander Devine Children's Cancer Trust v. Millgate Developments*,[107] where the Court of Appeal refused to allow the modification of restrictive covenants under s. 84, LPA 1925. The covenants prevented development of land, and yet Millgate Developments had proceeded to build a social housing development in the face of those covenants, and then applied for retrospective permission to modify the covenants once construction was complete. Sales L.J. was clear that the developer's behaviour was not acceptable in these circumstances, and the public interest militated against restrictive covenants being undermined in this way:

> . . . it remains the case that in general terms it is in the public interest that contracts should be honoured and not breached and that property rights should be upheld and protected. A property developer which knows of a restrictive covenant which impedes its development of land has a fair opportunity before building either to negotiate a release of the covenant or to make an application under section 84 to see if it can be modified or discharged. That is how the developer ought to proceed. It is contrary to the public interest in ensuring that proper respect is given to contractual or property rights for a property developer to proceed without any good excuse to build in violation of such rights, as contained in an enforceable restrictive covenant, in an attempt to improve its position on a subsequent application under section 84. Put another way, it is contrary to the public interest for the usual protections for a person with the benefit of a restrictive covenant to be circumvented by a developer seeking to obtain an advantage for itself by presenting the tribunal with a *fait accompli* in terms of having constructed buildings on the affected land without following the proper procedure, and then in effect daring the tribunal to make a ruling which might have the result that those buildings have to be taken down.[108]

13.8 Positive covenants

In *Rhone v. Stephens*,[109] the House of Lords confirmed that the burden of positive covenants in respect of freehold land does not run either at law or in equity. This rule causes distinct practical problems. These problems run from the fairly mundane, to some very serious matters. To take the former matter first, it is hardly satisfactory that, under English law, it 'remains impossible to use a simple legal structure to manage responsibility for mending a fence between properties, or a single facility shared by a few properties'.[110] This is a matter of some inconvenience because, apparently, every time there is a major storm, the Land Registry is inundated with enquiries about the ownership and maintenance of boundaries and the callers are disappointed to learn that the Registry cannot say who owns them or is liable for their repair.[111] With regard to more important matters, where flats are concerned, one needs to be able to impose binding positive covenants in respect of matters such as contribution to the common parts of a building. Because it is impossible to achieve this where the flats are owned on a freehold basis, this is one of the reasons why flats are held on long leases, as covenants in leases, be they positive or negative, can bind assignees of both the lease and the reversion.

---

[105] (2011) Law Com. No. 327, paras 7.54–7.55.
[106] See, e.g., *Juan v. Allen* [2016] FWHC 1502 (Ch); *In the Matter of the Application under section 84 of the Law of Property Act 1925, by Hussain* [2016] UKUT 297(LC).
[107] [2018] EWCA Civ. 2679.   [108] Ibid, at [64].   [109] [1994] 2 A.C. 310.
[110] (2011) Law Com. No. 327, para. 5.42.   [111] Ibid., para. 5.21, n. 31.

13.8.1 **Commonhold**

The position with regard to positive covenants is far from ideal,[112] and, following the publication of the Aldridge Report,[113] the position was reformed by the invention of a new legal regime by the Commonhold and Leasehold Reform Act 2002. The Act introduced a new form of landholding, termed commonhold, whereby a collective group of people can own the freehold of a property and also own individually the freehold of their own parts of it. The scheme introduced by the Act is highly complex.[114] The system applies only to new buildings, generally blocks of flats, and entails a collaborative system of control to be exercised over the building and the individual units within it. In the first five years of the scheme, only fourteen commonholds were registered,[115] and the sheer lack of litigation or updates from the Land Registry strongly suggests that the number of commonholds remains very low—currently around twenty. The Law Commission is consulting on possible reforms to the commonhold scheme, in order to make it more attractive to both leaseholders and lenders, but it is too early to know whether it might work.[116]

13.8.2 **Indirect enforcement**

With regard to freehold land, it is not possible, by direct means, to make the burden of positive covenants run with the land. This position has long been considered to be problematic, and has led to a number of proposals for reform,[117] the most recent of which will be considered shortly. The absence of a direct method of imposing a positive burden on land has led, however, to various indirect methods, of varying efficacy, of achieving this result.

13.8.3 **Chain of covenants**

One not very effective way of seeking to impose continuing liability in respect of positive covenants is to employ a chain of covenants. If A covenants with B to maintain a fence between their two properties, A will be liable if the fence falls into disrepair. This liability remains even after A has sold the land to C. On the occasion of that conveyance A can obtain a covenant from C to indemnify him in respect of any liability resulting from the failure to maintain the fence. When C conveys the land to D he then obtains a similar indemnity from him, and so on. The covenant is enforced by B suing A, who then seeks an indemnity from C who, in turn, seeks an indemnity from D. Fairly obviously, such a chain of covenants will soon break down and this is an unsatisfactory method of seeking to impose liability.

13.8.4 **Enlargement of a long lease**

In the case of certain long leases, the tenant has the right, under s. 153, LPA 1925, to have that lease enlarged into a freehold. If this is done, the freehold is subject to the same

---

[112] For an excellent discussion of the legal problems associated with communal living, see D.N. Clarke in Bright and Dewar (eds), *Land Law: Themes and Perspectives* (Oxford, Oxford University Press, 1998), Chapter 15.

[113] (1987) Cmnd. 279.

[114] See generally D.N. Clarke, *Commonhold, The New Law* (Bristol, Jordans, 2002).

[115] See (2008) Law Com. Consultation Paper No. 186, para. 11.4.

[116] *Reinvigorating Commonhold: The Alternative to Leasehold Ownership* (2019) Law Com. Consultation Paper No. 241.

[117] See (1965) Cmnd. 2719 (The Wilberforce Committee); (1984) Law Com. No. 127. See also H.W.R. Wade [1972B] C.L.J. 157.

obligations as was the lease. Positive covenants contained in the lease would, therefore, appear to be binding on the freeholder. This method of making positive covenants binding on the freehold is regarded as artificial and has not been tested in the courts.

13.8.5 **Rentcharges**

A rentcharge is an annual payment of money charged upon land. This is enforced by a right of re-entry if the money is not paid: a means of terminating the estate. The rentcharge is made subject to the performance of various terms, which can include the performance of positive acts which, if not performed, give the holder of the charge the right to enter the land and perform those acts, charging the cost to the freeholder. The creation of new rentcharges after 1977 was, in general, prohibited by s. 2 of the Rentcharges Act 1977, but an exception was made for a rentcharge imposed to enforce the performance of positive obligations.[118] This is the most effective method of making positive covenants enforceable against a freeholder.

13.8.6 **Mutual benefit and burden**

In *Halsall v. Brizell*,[119] a purchaser of land was given the right to use various roads on an estate, it being a requirement that he contributed to their upkeep. It was held that so long as he elected to avail himself of that right, he must take subject to the correlative burden. From this decision, the principle, termed 'the pure principle' of benefit and burden, was extracted that, if one took the benefit of a conveyance, one must take subject to any burdens which that conveyance sought to impose.[120]

The adoption of such a principle would, effectively, have ended the rule that positive covenants cannot be made to run with freehold land and it was rejected by the House of Lords in *Rhone v. Stephens*.[121] It was made clear that for the principle of benefit and burden to operate there must, as in *Halsall v. Brizell*, be a clear reciprocity between the enjoyment of a particular benefit and the correlating burden, in the sense of using a road and contributing to its upkeep.[122] In *Rhone v. Stephens* itself, there was no such correlation between an easement of support and an obligation to repair a roof and so the latter obligation was not binding on a purchaser. Similarly, in *Thamesmead Town Ltd v. Allotey*,[123] a claim that a purchaser of neighbouring land was liable to contribute to the cost of repair of nearby landscaped property failed because he had no rights over that land.

As well as this initial aspect of reciprocity, the person on whom the burden is sought to be imposed must have a real choice as to whether he wishes to continue to accept the benefit to which the burden is sought to be imposed so that, if he chooses not to, he will not be bound by the burden of a covenant.[124] This element of choice as to whether or not to accept the obligation means that its enforceability is conditional and this is one reason why it is not registrable.[125] It is evident that this principle is very narrow in scope and

---

[118] Rentcharges Act 1977, s. 2(4). See *Smith Brothers Farms Ltd v. The Canwell Estate Co Ltd* [2012] EWCA Civ. 237.

[119] [1974] Ch. 169.

[120] *Tito v. Waddell (No. 2)* [1977] Ch. 106 at 289–311 *per* Sir Robert Megarry V.-C.

[121] [1994] 2 A.C. 310.

[122] Ibid. at 322–3 *per* Lord Templeman. It is now not clear whether the use of this principle as a ground for decision in *E.R. Ives Investment Ltd v. High* [1967] 2 Q.B. 379 is correct.

[123] [1998] 37 E.G. 166.

[124] See also *Thamesmead Town Ltd v. Allotey*, supra; *Davies v. Jones* [2009] EWCA Civ. 1164 at [27] *per* Sir Andrew Morritt C.; *Wilkinson v. Kerdene Ltd* [2013] EWCA Civ. 44 at [14] *per* Patten L.J.

[125] See *Goodman v. Elwood* [2013] EWCA Civ. 1103 at [34] approving the view expressed in Thompson, *Barnsley's Conveyancing Law and Practice* (4th edn) (London, Butterworths, 1996), 497.

cannot be relied upon as a general method by which positive covenants can be made to run with freehold land.

13.8.7 **Reform proposals**

If, as is clearly the case, it is desirable that, in certain circumstances, the burden of a positive obligation should be able to run with the land, it is clearly preferable for the law to allow this to be achieved directly rather than forcing people to use indirect methods. The Law Commission is of this view[126] and has recommended the creation of a new land obligation to enable this objective to be achieved.

This new form of obligation is to include what have previously been referred to as positive and negative covenants. This new obligation is intended to supersede the old law on restrictive covenants, so that those already in being would continue to exist and to be governed by the prevailing law, new negative obligations would take the form of land obligations, and old-style restrictive covenants would no longer be capable of creation.[127] In order to take the form of a land obligation, it must touch and concern the land. This would permit a distinction to be drawn between an obligation to mend a fence, which does touch and concern the land, and so could run with it, and an obligation to walk a neighbour's dog, which would not.[128]

13.8.7.1 **Legal interest**

It is proposed that this new form of obligation should take the form of a new legal interest in land, and that s. 1(2), LPA 1925 be amended accordingly. The principal reason for advocating that this new interest be legal is to facilitate the discovery of who would hold the benefit of such a covenant. By making the obligation a legal right, it would enable the benefit of it to be registered as appurtenant to the dominant land, which currently it cannot be.[129] In the case of registered land, the recommendation is that this right could not take effect as an overriding interest and would, in order to bind a purchaser, need to be protected on the register.[130] Where title is unregistered, despite the normal rule being that a legal right would bind a purchaser, regardless of notice, it is recommended that it become registrable as a land charge.[131]

This latter recommendation is sensible. While it is true that, where title is unregistered, a legal easement will bind a purchaser regardless of notice, in practice, the existence of the more common easements are frequently apparent on an inspection of the servient land. In the case of covenants, this is not so. Accordingly, for pragmatic reasons,[132] it is desirable that this new legal right should be registrable, and if not registered it would be void as against a purchaser of the burdened land, or of any interest in that land.[133]

These proposals represent a sensible solution to a long-standing problem. It remains to be seen whether they will share the fate of earlier proposals, which have been left to gather dust, or whether they will be implemented to effect an overdue reform of this area of law.

---

[126] (2011) Law Com. No. 327, para. 5.37.   [127] Ibid., para. 5.89.
[128] Ibid., para. 5.50.   [129] LRA 2002, s. 2. (2011) Law Com. No. 327, para. 5.62.
[130] Law Com. No. 327, para. 6.67.   [131] Ibid., para. 6.57.
[132] There is a precedent for this in the case of certain legal mortgages: see 4.7.1.3 Class C(i): A puisne mortgage.
[133] (2011) Law Com No. 327, para. 6.57.

14

Proprietary Estoppel

Proprietary estoppel is a doctrine of considerable antiquity,[1] which, while the subject of considerable judicial development in the nineteenth century,[2] lurked in a degree of obscurity until interest in the subject was revived comparatively recently.[3] Estoppel is seen as having two main forms. In the law of contract, it is seen principally as having a defensive function, operating to modify the doctrine of consideration to prevent one party to a contract from fully enforcing his contractual rights against the other.[4] This form of the doctrine, termed promissory estoppel, is seen traditionally as being defensive in nature: it is a shield and not a sword.[5] In land law, by contrast, it has long been accepted that estoppel can operate directly to found a cause of action.[6] When operating in this way, the doctrine is referred to as proprietary estoppel.[7]

14.1 The origins of the doctrine

Although cases of proprietary estoppel can be traced back to the seventeenth century,[8] the doctrine did not really begin to take shape until somewhat later. In *Plimmer v. The Mayor of Wellington*,[9] the plaintiff's predecessor in title had built a jetty on his land. Later, at the request of the government and at considerable expense, he extended it onto government land. The land in question then passed to the defendant and the issue was whether the plaintiff had an interest in land sufficient to qualify him for compensation under the relevant statute. The Privy Council held that he did.

In upholding his claim to compensation, it was held that the government had encouraged him to spend money on extending the jetty in circumstances when it was clear that he had an expectation of obtaining some interest in the land. Because of this encouragement,

---

[1] For early examples, see *Hunt v. Carew* (1649) Nels. 47; *Hobbs v. Norton* (1682) Vern. 137; *Huning v. Ferers* (1711) Gilb. Rep. 85.

[2] See D.C. Jackson (1965) 81 L.Q.R. 84, 223.

[3] Several books have emerged on the subject in the last twenty years. See Pawlowski, *The Doctrine of Proprietary Estoppel* (London, Sweet & Maxwell, 1996); Spence, *Protecting Reliance: The Emergent Doctrine of Equitable Estoppel* (Oxford, Hart Publishing, 1999); Cooke, *The Modern Law of Estoppel* (Oxford, Oxford University Press, 2000); McFarlane, *The Law of Proprietary Estoppel* (Oxford, Oxford University Press, 2014).

[4] *Central London Property Trust Ltd v. High Trees House Ltd* [1947] K.B. 130. The main authorities relied upon were *Hughes v. Metropolitan Railway Co.* (1877) 2 App. Cas. 349 and *Birmingham and District Land Co. v. London and North Western Railway Co.* (1889) 40 Ch.D. 268.

[5] Although that traditional view has been challenged—see D.C. Jackson (1965) 81 L.Q.R. 84; M.P. Thompson [1983] C.L.J. 257.

[6] *Crabb v. Arun DC* [1976] Ch. 179 at [187] *per* Lord Denning M.R.

[7] For arguments that the difference in terminology obscures the similarities between promissory and proprietary estoppel, see M.P. Thompson [1983] C.L.J. 257; M. Halliwell (1994) 14 L.S. 15; M. Lunney [1992] Conv. 239. For a different, highly conservative view, see P.T. Evans [1988] Conv. 346. See also *Crabb v. Arun District Council* [1976] Ch. 179 at 193 *per* Scarman L.J. who said 'I do not find helpful the distinction between promissory and proprietary estoppel.'

[8] See *Hobbs v. Nelson* (1649) Nels. 47.   [9] (1894) 9 App. Cas. 699.

and his action in reliance on that expectation, it would be quite inequitable for him to be denied some relief. In satisfying the equity which had arisen, it was held that he was entitled to an indefinite licence to occupy the land on which he had extended the jetty and that this licence was, for the purposes of the statute in question, a sufficient interest in the land to entitle him to compensation when that land had been compulsorily acquired.

A number of important features emerge from this case. First, the actual expenditure was undertaken by the plaintiff's predecessor in title. The benefit of the equity which had arisen then passed with the land to the plaintiff. Second, this was a case where there had been active encouragement by one person to another to do work on the implicit understanding that he would, thereby, acquire an interest in the land. In such cases, it is often easier to establish that an equity has arisen than in cases, to be considered shortly, where one person is mistaken as to what the true position is and acts on the faith of that belief. A third important point is that, in the case itself, it was clear that the plaintiff had an expectation of acquiring an interest in the adjoining land but that the full extent of that interest had not been articulated. This was not a problem, because:

> there is good authority for saying what appears to their Lordships to be quite sound in principle, that the equity arising from expenditure on land need not fail merely on the ground that the interest to be secured has not been expressly indicated.[10]

In other words, unlike the position in the law of contract, a claim in estoppel will not fail on the ground of uncertainty;[11] it is sufficient if the claimant can establish that he has some expectation in respect of another person's land. It is not essential that the metes and bounds of that expectation are precisely articulated. This is important, in that estoppel cases frequently arise in informal situations when it is not entirely clear what the intentions of each party are.

14.1.1 **A stringent test of certainty**

This position, which appeared to be firmly established,[12] was undermined by the dicta of Lord Scott in *Yeoman's Row Management Ltd v. Cobbe*.[13] This was a commercial case where the claimant had agreed with the defendant that he would, at his own expense, apply for planning permission for the demolition of an existing property owned by the defendant and the construction of terraced houses in its place. Once planning permission had been obtained, it was agreed between the parties that they would enter into a second agreement, whereby he would purchase the site for £12 million, and would be entitled to 50 per cent of the gross proceeds of sale of the new houses if the sales of them realized more than £24 million. A number of terms of this second agreement were, however, left outstanding. After he had done a considerable amount of work to secure planning permission, the defendant refused to enter this second agreement. Reversing the decisions below, the House of Lords held that he had no rights through estoppel, but was only entitled to a sum to compensate him for the value of his work.

That the claim to an interest in the property failed is not really surprising. This was because the parties were experienced practitioners in property transactions, and were aware

---

[10] (1894) 9 App. Cas. 699 at 713 *per* Sir Arthur Hobhouse.

[11] See also *Ramsden v. Dyson* (1866) L.R. 1 H.L. 129 at 170 *per* Lord Kingsdown (dissenting on the application of the law to the facts).

[12] See, e.g., *Turner v. Jacob* [2007] EWHC 317 (Ch) at [81] *per* Patten J.; *James v. Thomas* [2007] EWCA Civ. 1212 at [18] *per* Sir John Chadwick.

[13] [2008] UKHL 1139. See also, on similar facts, *Capron v. Government of Turks and Caicos Islands* [2010] UKPC 2.

that the original agreement was binding in honour only. The claimant was, therefore, taking the risk that there might not ever be a concluded contract between them.[14] Nevertheless, Lord Scott decided that no right had arisen through estoppel on wider grounds.

Having noted that the second agreement was insufficiently certain to amount to a contract because not all the terms had been agreed, he considered that this was also a fatal objection to a claim based on estoppel. He referred to a passage in *Ramsden v. Dyson*,[15] where Lord Kingsdown referred to an agreement that a person should have 'a *certain* interest in land', and took this to mean that there must be certainty as to what that interest was to be.[16] With respect, this seems contrary to principle, and flies in the face of the decision in *Plimmer v. The Mayor of Wellington*. As is the case with the word 'quite', 'certain' is a word which admits of more than one meaning, and that meaning is dependent upon the context in which it is used. The word 'quite' can be comparative or emphatic. An example of the former is to describe an argument as being 'quite persuasive'; an instance of the latter is to describe an argument as being 'quite compelling'. In the latter instance the word 'quite' is synonymous with the word 'utterly'. So, too, in the case of the word 'certain'. If one says that a person should be given a certain latitude, one is not seeking to define, in advance, what degree of latitude is being given; whereas, if one refers to a 'term certain' one is saying that the length of the term must be precise. It seems clear that in *Plimmer*, the word 'certain' is being used in the former sense of the word.

14.1.2 Emasculation of estoppel

The narrow meaning of the expectation expressed by Lord Scott is also quite inconsistent with the leading case of *Jennings v. Rice*,[17] to which he did not refer. In that case Robert Walker L.J., in discussing what remedy was appropriate,[18] distinguished between two types of case. The first is where the arrangement between the parties is of a 'consensual nature falling not short of an unenforceable contract'.[19] The second is where 'the claimant's expectations may not be focused on any specific property',[20] let alone any specific interest in it, because 'the claimant's expectations are uncertain (as will be the case with many honest claimants)'.[21] More importantly, if followed, Lord Scott's reasoning would limit the application of the doctrine of proprietary estoppel so severely as, effectively, to emasculate it.[22] Writing extra-judicially, Sir Terence Etherton, who had heard *Cobbe* at first instance, commented that it would be difficult to see any scope left for the doctrine if Lord Scott's approach was applied in its entirety.[23] This is because either there is a contract which is complete in all its terms and complies with the formalities prescribed by s. 2 of the Law of Property (Miscellaneous Provisions) Act (LP(MP)A) 1989, in which case there is a legally binding contract and no need to rely on any estoppel, or there is not, in which case there is neither an enforceable contract nor scope for proprietary estoppel.

In order to fully understand the tension between the doctrine of proprietary estoppel and s. 2 of the LP(MP)A 1989, this point about enforceable contracts needs to be explored in a little more detail.

---

[14] See also Lord Neuberger writing extra-judicially on this issue: [2009] C.L.J. 537 at 540–2.

[15] (1866) L.R.1 H.L. 129 at 170. He treated a passage in *Taylors Fashions Ltd v. Liverpool Victoria Trustees Co. Ltd* [1982] Q.B. 133n at 144 *per* Oliver J. in the same way. See also *Pinisetty v. Manikonda* [2017] EWHC 838.

[16] [2008] UKHL 55 at [19]–[22]. For similar remarks in the context of promissory estoppel, see *Woodhouse A.C. Israel Ltd SA v. Nigerian Produce Marketing Co. Ltd* [1972] A.C. 741 at 757 *per* Lord Hailsham L.C.; and at 762 *per* Lord Pearson, explained by M.P. Thompson [1983] C.L.J. 257 at 263–4.

[17] [2003] 1 P. & C.R. 8.   [18] See 14.5.   [19] [2003] 1 P. & C.R. 8 at [45].

[20] Ibid. at [46]. See also *Powell v. Benney* [2007] EWCA Civ. 1283 at [25] *per* Sir Peter Gibson.

[21] [2003] 1 P. & C.R. 8 at [47].

[22] See B. McFarlane and A. Robertson [2008] L.M.C.L.Q. 449.

[23] T. Etherton [2009] Conv. 104 at 120. See also Lord Neuberger [2009] C.L.J. 537 at 546.

14.2 Enforceable contracts and section 2, LP(MP)A 1989

Under s. 2(1) of the LP(MP)A 1989, contracts for the sale for the sale or other disposition of an interest in land can only be made in writing. The law that s. 2 replaced had become beset with various difficulties,[24] and the Law Commission's recommendation had been to recast the law so that oral contracts for the sale of land were no longer possible. In circumstances where the parties behaved as if there was a binding contract between them, only to discover subsequently that this was not the case, and then one party refused to give effect to their non-contractual agreement, the Law Commission was clear that the doctrine of estoppel should then be applicable.[25] So too was the Lord Chancellor, when introducing the proposed legislation.[26] Unfortunately, the LP(MP)A 1989 contained the entirely inapt and unnecessary s. 2(5),[27] which provides that 'nothing in this section affects the creation or operation of resulting, implied or constructive trusts'. One consequence of this inept piece of draftsmanship is that the extent to which the doctrine of estoppel may operate in the present context has, with some justice, been described as being 'a difficult topic'.[28]

The reason why this subsection is described as inapt and unnecessary will be explained shortly. First, one can look at how the courts have approached the situation where a relatively clear and acceptable position was thrown into considerable doubt by an ill-considered and misconceived *dictum* in the House of Lords.

At first, the judiciary seemed reluctant to accept that proprietary estoppel would be relevant where a contract for the sale of land had not been made in writing. The perceived difficulty was that, to allow a claimant to have rights arising out of estoppel when a contract had not been created because of a lack of formality would be wrong. This was because to do so would undermine the social policy underlying the legislation, that policy being to insist that contracts for the sale of land are made in writing.[29] The courts were, therefore, initially unprepared to countenance an argument that a party may be estopped by convention from relying on the lack of formality as required by the Act, [30] but that changed in the leading case of *Yaxley v. Gotts*.[31]

14.2.1 Proprietary estoppel and constructive trusts

In *Yaxley v. Gotts*, the claimant had orally agreed with the defendant's father that, if the latter bought a house then, provided that he (the claimant) did a substantial amount of building work and acted as the managing agent for the entire property, he would have the ground-floor flats. The property was, in fact, bought by the son of the person with whom the claimant had made this agreement. The son, who was the defendant in these

---

[24] See L. Bentley and P. Coghlan (1990) 10 L.S. 325; C. Davis (1993) 13 O.J.L.S. 99; B. McFarlane [2005] Conv. 501.

[25] (1987) Law Com. No. 164, paras 5.4–5.5.

[26] See H.L. vol. 503, col. 610 *per* Lord Mackay L.C.

[27] For a similar argument, see G. Owen and O. Rees [2011] Conv. 495.

[28] *Sharma v. Simposh Ltd* [2011] EWCA Civ. 1383 at [56] *per* Toulson L.J.

[29] On the importance of not undermining the policy of a statute, see *Kok Hoong v. Long Cheong Mines Ltd* [1964] A.C. 993 at 1016 *per* Viscount Radcliffe. The comments made in this case, however, were set against the entirely different context of the regulation of money-lending contracts. See *Shah v. Shah* [2002] Q.B. 35 at 42–7 *per* Pill L.J.

[30] See *Godden v. Merthyr Tydfil Housing Association* (1997) 74 P. & C.R.D. 1; *Anderson v. Antiques (UK) Ltd v. Anderson Wharf (Hull) Ltd* [2007] EWHC 2086 (Ch). For a supposed example of estoppel by convention, see *Amalgamated Investments Ltd v. Texas Commerce International Bank Ltd* [1982] Q.B. 84, discussed by M.P. Thompson [1983] C.L.J. 259 at 273–4.

[31] [2000] 1 All E.R. 711. See R.J. Smith (2000) 116 L.Q.R. 22; M.P. Thompson [2000] Conv. 245. See also *Scottish & Newcastle Plc v. Mortgage Corporation Ltd* [2007] EWCA Civ. 684 at [49]–[55] *per* Mummery L.J.

proceedings, was registered as the proprietor with an absolute title. The claimant, who was unaware for quite some time that it was the son who had bought the property, proceeded to do work to the value of about £9,000. When the defendant sought to evict the claimant from the ground-floor flats, which he occupied, the claimant asserted that he had an interest in the property. The Court of Appeal held that he was entitled to a ninety-year lease of the ground floor, free from any ground rent.

In reaching this conclusion, it was agreed that the original agreement was of no legal effect, because it did not comply with s. 2 of the LP(MP)A 1989. While it was true that the original agreement was oral, this did not appear to be the main problem in establishing the existence of a contract. Rather, the fundamental problem appeared to be that the original agreement was with the defendant's father and not the actual defendant, who was never a party to any agreement with the claimant. It is difficult to see, therefore, why s. 2 was ever considered to be relevant to the dispute.[32] Be that as it may, the Court of Appeal decided the case on the basis that the issue to be resolved was whether the claimant acquired rights in equity as a result of performing acts in accordance with an oral agreement for the sale of land: that agreement meeting the formal requirements enacted by s. 2. It was held that he did.

In dealing with this matter, there was some difference in approach shown by the members of the court. Robert Walker L.J., impressed by the argument that equitable principles should not be allowed to undermine the policy embraced by the LP(MP)A 1989, felt able to decide for the claimant by the imposition of a constructive trust. He felt, in the present context, that the principles underlying that concept were essentially the same as those underlying proprietary estoppel.[33] Beldam L.J., however, took a more expansive approach. For him, the clear policy enunciated by the Law Commission[34] was that, in cases where an agreement had been reached, but the formal requirements of the LP(MP)A 1989 had not been met, the principles of proprietary estoppel should operate. While the facts of a particular case could justify the imposition of a constructive trust, proprietary estoppel is a more flexible doctrine, and he thought that the principles on which estoppel is based should generally be applicable.[35]

Although the two approaches differ, the same result was achieved, which might indicate that there is no real difference between them. On a theoretical level, however, this is not so. Because s. 2(5) of the LP(MP)A 1989 refers to the section not affecting the creation of resulting, implied, or constructive trusts, it is entirely understandable that the judiciary should seek to employ the constructive trust to arrive at a solution in cases such as *Yaxley v. Gotts*.[36] Nevertheless, it is inapposite.[37] Section 2 is relevant to the creation of contracts relating to land. The exception to its effect set out in s. 2(5) relates to the creation of trusts and is drawn in exactly the same terms as s. 53(2), LPA 1925. That section deals, principally, with the formalities required for the creation of trusts of land and the saving provision

---

[32] At first instance, the trial judge had, for this reason, decided the case without reference to the interrelationship between s. 2 and estoppel. See Thompson,[1983] C.L.J. 257 at 247–8.

[33] [2000] 1 All E.R. 711 at 717–21. For his subsequent misgivings as to equating the two concepts, however, see *Stack v. Dowden* [2007] 1 All E.R. 929 at [36]. See 8.8.3.2.

[34] Beldam L.J. was the Chair of the Law Commission when its Report which led to the passing of the Act was published. This was a fact which was considered to be important in *Whittaker v. Kinnear* [2011] EWHC 1479 (Q.B.) at [29] *per* Bean J.

[35] See [2000] 1 All E.R. 711 at 735. Clarke L.J. agreed with Beldam L.J.'s approach to the application of estoppel principles: ibid. at 726.

[36] The same observations are applicable also to the approach taken in *Kinane v Mackie-Conteh* [2005] EWCA Civ 45 and *Kilcarne Holdings Ltd v Targetfollow (Birmingham) Ltd* [2004] EWHC 2547 (Ch) at [203] *per* Lewison J, affirmed at [2005] EWCA Civ. 1355.

[37] See in particular, *Brightlingsea Haven Ltd v. Morris* [2008] EWHC 1928 (Ch) at [44]–[55] *per* Jack J.

contained in the sub-section makes complete sense in that context. Unfortunately, it does not do so in the case of a section laying down the formal requirements necessary to create a particular type of contract. It is not surprising that the judiciary have had problems applying a sub-section which does not directly relate to the rest of the section to which it purports to be relevant. Related to this is a second problem. That is the nature of any trust which is being imposed by the courts and how, if at all, the solution being arrived at can be accommodated within the general taxonomy of the law of trusts.[38]

A trust, be it express, resulting or constructive, entails that the trustee holds property on behalf of the beneficiary. The normal conception is that the trustee is the legal owner of the property, and the beneficiary is the equitable owner of it.[39] If the contract is to purchase a freehold property, then the use of a constructive trust to circumvent s. 2 of the Act is perfectly intelligible: the result is that the vendor holds the land on trust for the purchaser. If, however, the oral agreement is to create an easement,[40] or some other right over land, then it is difficult to see how the prospective purchaser could, through the imposition of a constructive trust, acquire that right on orthodox principles, whereas there is no such difficulty in such a result occurring in a proprietary estoppel case.[41] The better view is, therefore, that cases such as *Yaxley v. Gotts* should be decided on the basis of proprietary estoppel, and this appeared to be what was happening.[42] Unfortunately, considerable doubt was then caused in this important area by the extraordinary *dictum* in *Yeoman's Row Management Ltd v. Cobbe*.[43]

In considering the claim that a constructive trust should be imposed, Lord Scott, while conceding that it is impossible to prescribe exhaustively the circumstances sufficient to create a constructive trust,[44] nevertheless focused on a line of authority which he considered to be typical.[45] The type of case which he had in mind was one where two parties, A and B, agree on a joint venture to acquire property but, for some reason, it is transferred into the sole name of A. In these circumstances, it may be fraudulent for A subsequently to deny the agreement, and a constructive trust is imposed to give effect to it. This was inapplicable in the present case, as the defendant had already acquired the property in question before there was any sort of agreement or understanding between the parties.[46]

The claimant also argued that he had acquired rights over the defendant's land through the medium of proprietary estoppel. This, too, failed. Although Lord Scott embarked on an unduly narrow analysis of the principles underlying this doctrine,[47] the real weakness in the claimant's argument was highlighted by Lord Walker: both parties to the litigation were experienced practitioners in property matters and knew perfectly well that they had not reached a position where either side was bound in any way other than in honour.[48] Consequently, when the claimant spent time and money pursuing the application for planning permission, he did so in the knowledge that his expenditure might turn out to be

---

[38] See *Cobbe v. Yeoman's Row Management Ltd* [2005] EWHC 266 (Ch) at [50]–[51] and [233], reversed without reference to this issue: *Yeoman's Row Management Ltd v. Cobbe* [2008] UKHL 1139. See also McFarlane, *The Law of Proprietary Estoppel*, 516–20.

[39] See *Paragon Finance plc v. Thakerer* [1999] 1 All E.R. 400 at 408–9 *per* Millett L.J.

[40] A similar difficulty would seem to arise if the agreement is to create a lease.

[41] See *E.R. Ives Investments Ltd v. High* [1967] 2 Q.B. 379; *Crabb v. Arun District Council* [1976] Ch. 179; *Mayor of the London Borough of Bexley v. Maison Maurice Ltd* [2006] EWHC 3192 (Ch).

[42] See *Lloyd v. Sutcliffe* [2007] EWCA Civ. 153; *Smee v. Smee* [2007] 1 F.L.R. 1123. See, also, *Oates v. Stimson* [2006] EWCA Civ. 548.

[43] [2008] UKHL 1139.   [44] [2008] UKHL 55 at [30].

[45] The main authorities, not all of which were cited in the present case, are: *Chattock v. Muller* (1878) 8 Ch.D. 117; *Pallant v. Morgan* [1953] Ch. 43; *Holiday Inns Inc. v. Broadhead* (1974) 232 E.G. 951; *Banner Homes Groups plc v. Luff Developments Ltd* [2000] 2 All E.R. 117; and *London & Regional Investments Ltd v. TBI Plc* [2002] EWCA Civ. 355. See also *Samad v. Thompson* [2008] EWHC 2809 (Ch). See M.P. Thompson [2000] Conv. 265; N. Hopkins [2001] Conv. 35.

[46] See [2008] UKHL 55 at [31]–[34].   [47] See 14.1.1.   [48] [2008] UKHL 55 at [71].

wasted, and that there might be no final contract. In these circumstances, no rights could be obtained through proprietary estoppel.

14.2.2 Proprietary estoppel and section 2

The arguments based on either estoppel or a constructive trust therefore failed in *Yeoman's Row Management Ltd v. Cobbe*. As there was no concluded oral agreement for the sale of land, s. 2 was not relevant. This was recognized in terms by Lord Walker who also commented, somewhat surprisingly given that he was a party to the decision in *Yaxley v. Gotts*, that,[49] 'I do not think it is necessary or appropriate to consider the issue on section 2 of the Law of Property (Miscellaneous Provisions) Act 1989.'[50] Lord Scott, on the other hand, while explicitly recognizing that s. 2 was not relevant because the parties had not concluded an oral agreement, expressed his views on the applicability of estoppel in a forthright manner:

> Section 2 of the 1989 Act *declares to be void any agreement for the acquisition of an interest in land that does not comply with the requisite formalities prescribed by the section.* Subsection (5) expressly makes an exception for resulting, implied or constructive trusts. These may validly come into existence without compliance with the prescribed formalities. Proprietary estoppel does not have the benefit of this exception. The question arises, therefore, whether a complete agreement for the acquisition of an interest in land that does not comply with the section 2 formalities, but would become specifically enforceable if it did, can become enforceable via the route of proprietary estoppel . . . . *My present view . . . is that proprietary estoppel cannot be prayed in aid in order to render enforceable an agreement that statute has declared to be void.* The proposition that an owner of land can be estopped from asserting that an agreement is void for want of compliance with section 2 is, in my opinion, unacceptable. The assertion is no more than the statute provides. Equity can surely not contradict a statute.[51]

It should be stressed that this passage is, as Lord Scott himself expressly recognized, entirely *obiter*.[52] Moreover, while it is manifestly of high authority,[53] it is submitted that it is wrong in principle and should not be followed, and there are several reasons for that view. First, one can point to the subsequent treatment of this issue by the courts. They have, despite what was said by Lord Scott, continued to allow equitable intervention to occur in cases where neither the provisions of s. 2 have been satisfied nor has there been a joint venture to acquire property in joint names: that situation being the one where Lord Scott envisaged that a constructive trust might be imposed. Addressing the issue head on, and acknowledging the high authority of what had been said in *Cobbe*, in *Whittaker v. Kinnear*,[54] Bean J. commented that:

> There is force in the dictum of Ungoed-Thomas in *Re Grosvenor Hotel (No.2)*[55] that a battery of howitzers off the target is more impressive than a popgun on it; but also in the retort of Salmon L.J. in the same case that a battery of howitzers off target can cause a great deal of damage . . . notwithstanding Lord Scott's dicta in *Cobbe*, proprietary estoppel in cases involving land has survived the enactment of s. 2 of the 1989 Act.[56]

---

[49] [2000] 1 All E.R. 711.   [50] [2008] UKHL 55 at [93].

[51] [2008] UKHL 55 at [29]. Emphasis supplied.

[52] It was also made without reference to a considerable weight of authority to the contrary.

[53] Lords Hoffmann and Mance simply agreed with the speech of Lord Scott. Perplexingly, Lord Brown agreed with the speeches of both Lord Scott and Lord Walker, despite Lord Walker's speech being very different in tenor from that of Lord Scott.

[54] [2011] EWHC 1479 (Ch) at [30]. See also *Herbert v. Doyle* [2008] EWHC 1950 (Ch) at [14] *per* Mr Michael Herbert Q.C., affm'd on appeal at [2010] EWCA Civ. 1095.

[55] [1965] Ch. 1210.   [56] [2011] EWHC 1479 (Ch) at [30].

Since then, the courts have continued to affirm that either proprietary estoppel or a more liberal form of constructive trust than was envisaged by Lord Scott will continue to have a potential role to play in this context.[57] Why this is right and the more restrictive approach is not must now be addressed.

14.2.3 **Void agreements?**

In the italicized part of Lord Scott's statement set out in the preceding section, considerable emphasis is laid on the effect of the statute being to make an agreement for the acquisition of an interest in land void if the formal requirements of s. 2 have not been met. Accepting for the moment that the effect of the Act is as stated, this is not a fatal objection to the operation of estoppel. In *Kok Hoong v. Long Cheong Mines Ltd*,[58] Viscount Radcliffe said that, 'On the other hand, there are statutes which, although declaring transactions to be unenforceable or void, are nevertheless not essentially prohibitory and so do not preclude estoppels.' The question as to whether estoppel can be allowed to circumvent a particular statute is determined by issues of public policy.[59] If the policy as to this issue is considered to be doubtful, then regard should be had to the Parliamentary debates,[60] where Lord Mackay L.C. simply said: 'I believe that there is nothing in this Bill to affect the operation of the doctrine of estoppel.'[61] To this can be added the decision in the seminal case of *Taylors Fashions Ltd v. Liverpool Victoria Trustees Ltd*,[62] which was cited without any hint of disapproval by Lord Scott.[63] In this case, the issue was whether an option to renew a lease had, through the effect of estoppel, become enforceable against a purchaser of the freehold reversion. Although the action failed on the facts, there was no problem with the argument that estoppel could have had this effect even though the option itself had, through the explicit effect of the statute, been held to be void as against the purchaser.[64]

14.2.4 **Formation of contracts**

As can be seen, therefore, the statement that the effect of non-compliance with s. 2 of the Act is to make an agreement for the acquisition of an interest in land void should not of itself lead to the conclusion that the doctrine of estoppel should not be applicable. The premise that this is the way that the section operates is wrong, however. Contrary to what is said by Lord Scott, it does not say that any such an agreement is void. What it does say is that 'a contract for the sale of land can only be made in writing', so that to say that the 'relevant question is whether, subject to section 2 of the 1989 Act, there was a valid contract'[65] is wrong. The section does not impose a sanction for non-compliance with the statutory formalities by making invalid something which would otherwise be valid. What the section actually does is stipulate as to how a contract is to be formed.

---

[57] See *Ely v. Robson* [2016] EWCA Civ. 774; *Matchmove Ltd v. Dowding* [2016] EWCA Civ. 1233; *Muhammad v. ARY Properties Ltd* [2016] EWHC 1698 (Ch).

[58] [1964] A.C. 993 at 1015.   [59] Ibid. at 1015–19.

[60] See *Pepper v. Hart* [1993] A.C. 593.

[61] H.L. vol. 503, col. 610.   [62] [1982] Q.B. 133.

[63] Intriguingly, Lord Scott, as Mr Richard Scott Q.C., had appeared as leading counsel for the plaintiff in this case.

[64] LCA 1925, s. 13(2). See now LCA 1972, s. 4(6).

[65] *Herbert v. Doyle* [2010] EWCA Civ. 1095 at [71] *per* Arden L.J.

Much the same point was made by Gloster L.J. in *Marlbray Ltd v. Laditi*,[66] where she said:

> The judge's variable use of terminology (i.e. 'void' in some passages, and 'not valid or enforceable' in others) is confusing. If, as he held, there was no contract at all, because the 2nd respondent never authorised the 1st respondent to sign the contract on her behalf, that was a different conclusion from finding the contract was 'void'.

To say that a contract is void for a failure to comply with the requisite formalities is no different from saying that a contract is void for uncertainty, or for a lack of consideration.[67] In each case, this is merely a shorthand way of saying that no contract has been formed between the parties in the first place. In *Yeoman's Row* itself, there was no contract between the parties, but not because the requirements of s. 2 had not been met; it was, principally, because there had yet to be final agreement as to the terms of the second agreement. The parties were in a non-contractual arrangement. Any rights which are later acquired are acquired through the doctrine of estoppel, and in principle there is no objection to this. Precisely the same argument should apply in cases where there is a concluded agreement, but there is no contract because the formalities insisted upon by s. 2 have not been met. In both cases it is not true to say that an otherwise legally binding agreement has been rendered void. What has happened is that, for different reasons, there is no legally binding contract formed in the first place. It should therefore follow that, if the agreement has been acted upon in circumstances when, ordinarily, an equity would be created under the doctrine of estoppel, it should also arise in this situation. It is not the case that rights are conferred on the parties *by that agreement*. The equity arises due to the reliance on a non-contractual expectation.[68]

It is highly unfortunate that s. 2(5) was enacted in the manner that it was. This is because the concepts of resulting, implied, or constructive trusts are not really relevant to the creation of contracts for the sale of land or of interests in land and it would have been far better, albeit not strictly necessary, had the sub-section referred to estoppel rather than to trusts. Nevertheless, after a somewhat meandering route, it would appear to be settled that, if there is no binding contract between two parties as a result of non-compliance with the formal requirements[69] relevant to the formation of a contract then, in appropriate cases, a party may instead bring an action based upon the principles of proprietary estoppel.

14.2.5 **The return to principle**

The better view is that Lord Scott's remarks should be read in the context of the particular facts of *Yeoman's Row*, where a claimant was arguing that he had rights under an agreement which had yet to be fully negotiated and was, itself, 'subject to contract'. That they should not be applied to defeat a claim in estoppel where the claimant's expectation was imprecise[70] was re-established by the House of Lords in *Thorner v. Major*.[71] The case

---

[66] [2016] EWCA Civ. 476 at [52].

[67] See M.P. Thompson [2000] Conv. 245 at 253–4. The same point is made in McFarlane, *The Law of Proprietary Estoppel* (Oxford, Oxford University Press, 2014), 6.10.

[68] See, also, in the analogous case of part performance: *Maddison v. Alderson* (1883) 8 App. Cas. 467 at 475 *per* Lord Selborne L.C. This point is also explicitly made in *Muhammad v. ARY Properties Ltd* [2016] EWHC 1698 at [47] *per* Master Matthews.

[69] Should electronic conveyancing be made compulsory, much the same argument will be applicable. See also in the context of deeds *Shah v. Shah* [2002] Q.B. 35.

[70] See *Oates v. Stimson* [2006] EWHC 1329 (Ch) (expectation of a share in profits); *Hopper v. Hopper* [2008] EWHC 228 (Ch) (some beneficial interest in a farm).

[71] [2009] UKHL 18. For a somewhat muted reaction, see M. Dixon [2009] Conv. 260.

involved two cousins, David and Peter Thorner. David began to work on Peter's farm in 1976, and continued to do so for the next twenty-nine years. David hoped to inherit the farm, and this hope became a firm expectation when, in 1990, Peter handed him a bonus notice on two life assurance policies and told him that these were for death duties. David continued to do a considerable amount of unpaid work at Peter's farm, and did not pursue a number of opportunities which were open to him. Peter did in fact make a will in David's favour, but subsequently revoked it, and died intestate in 2005. David then brought an action against Peter's personal representatives. Reversing the Court of Appeal, and restoring the judgment at first instance, the House of Lords held David to be entitled to a transfer of the land, together with other assets of the farming business.

The problems in raising an estoppel argument related, first, to the fact that both men were taciturn individuals, and it was not easy to identify quite what it was that had been promised, and, second, to the fact that the identity of the farm had changed over the years. This was because between 1990, when the conversation about death duties had occurred, and 2005, when Peter died, some of the fields making up the farm had been sold, and the proceeds reinvested in other land. In short, there appeared to be a lack of certainty which, in the light of what had been said in *Yeoman's Row*, might have been thought to have been fatal to the claim. In holding that this was not the case, Lord Walker stressed that, while the assurance must be clear, what amounts to sufficient clarity is hugely dependent upon context.[72] He also observed, making reference to Lord Scott's comments on certainty in *Yeoman's Row* that: 'All the "great judges" to whom Lord Kingsdown referred [*sc.* in *Ramsden v. Dyson*] thought that even where there was some uncertainty an equity could arise and could be satisfied, either by an interest in land or in some other way.'[73]

Lord Neuberger held that the statements made by Peter could have reasonably been understood to indicate that he intended to leave the farm to his cousin, which he regarded as sufficiently clear to form the basis of an estoppel claim.[74] He accepted that, to found such a claim, there must be some sort of assurance which is clear and unequivocal. He went on to say, however, that this was subject to three qualifications. First, it is important that any words or actions must be considered in the context in which they were made. Second, he stressed that it would be quite wrong for a court to search for uncertainty or ambiguity, and it is sufficient for the person invoking the estoppel to establish that he reasonably believed the statement or action to be an assurance on which he could rely. Third, even if the assurance could reasonably be understood as having more than one meaning, and the facts would otherwise satisfy all the requirements of estoppel, he thought that that ambiguity should not deprive a person who reasonably relied on that assurance of all relief, and that it might be right to afford relief on the basis of the interpretation least favourable to him.[75]

It now seems clear, notwithstanding what was said in *Yeoman's Row*, that it is not necessary in order to raise an estoppel that the precise ambit of what the claimant expects to receive has been spelled out.[76] Provided that the promise or assurance is sufficiently clear to justify reliance, it is not necessary that the actual interest to be acquired should be defined with precision.[77]

It is also not necessarily the case that where a contract for the sale of land fails the formality requirements under s. 2, LP(MP)A 1989, it will prevent a claim based on proprietary estoppel. Lord Walker in *Thorner v. Major* thought that s. 2 did not have any impact

---

[72] Ibid. at [56].   [73] Ibid. at [64].   [74] Ibid. at [67].   [75] Ibid. at [84]–[86].

[76] See, applying *Thorner* on that point, *Liden v. Burton* [2016] EWCA Civ. 275. As to whether any assurance must relate to specific property, see 14.3.6.

[77] *McDonald v. Frost* [2009] EWHC 2276 (Ch) at [11] *per* Ms Geraldine Andrews Q.C.

upon the claim between Peter and David, because it was 'a straightforward estoppel claim without any contractual connection'.[78] In *Ghazaani v. Rowshan*, there was a failed contract for the transfer of land. Judge Behrens noted that,

> [d]espite the observations of Lord Scott in paragraph [29] of *Cobbe* it is probably still possible to have a proprietary estoppel in the case of a contract which does not satisfy [s.] 2. However this will necessarily be an exceptional case.[79]

That seems correct as a matter of principle, but what is not clear is the basis on which an exception can be made in 'failed contract' cases. Either it is simply a question of how far the parties had progressed with their written agreement,[80] so that if the contract was sufficiently agreed, the parties could not save it through proprietary estoppel where s. 2 was not satisfied, or it is the much broader question of whether it would be unconscionable for one party to rely on the formality requirements in s. 2 and thereby defeat the claimant's legitimate expectation.[81] That second argument should not be disregarded because of a concern that estoppel would avoid the statute, as the claim would not enforce the failed contract *per se*, but would instead establish an independent equity binding upon the defendant.

In the majority of cases, the difference between those two views is unlikely to make any practical difference to the outcome: where parties contemplate the existence of a contract between them, taking steps towards that, and the nature of their relationship makes it an obviously sensible step to take in ensuring both parties do what they promise, it is not really unconscionable to rely on the statute which applies in those precise circumstances.

Attention must now be turned to the questions that are common to all proprietary estoppel cases, of which there are three: 'First, is there an equity established? Secondly, what is the extent of the equity if one is established? And, thirdly, what is the relief appropriate to satisfy the equity?'[82]

These questions will be considered in turn.

14.3 Establishing an equity

In *Thorner v. Major*,[83] Lord Walker, while recognizing that there is no comprehensive and uncontroversial definition of proprietary estoppel, said that 'most scholars would agree that the doctrine is based on three main elements, although they express them in slightly different terms: a *representation* or *assurance* made to the claimant; *reliance* on it by the claimant; and *detriment* to the claimant in consequence of his (reasonable) reliance'. While this statement does encapsulate the general gist of proprietary estoppel, it should not be taken as a literal template. This is because, as Lord Walker himself recognized,[84] the assurance element of this statement has to be taken to include cases of passive acquiescence, where the person against whom the estoppel has arisen has stood by when a person has acted in reliance on an expectation which has been acted upon by another. Although an estoppel can arise as a result of reliance on a direct assurance, it can do so in other situations as well, and so, for that reason, it is better to talk of an expectation as opposed to an assurance.

---

[78] [2009] UKHL 19 at [99].   [79] [2015] EWHC 1922 (Ch) at [192].

[80] For this approach, see *Herbert v. Doyle* [2010] EWCA Civ. 1095, applying *Cobbe*.

[81] See M. Dixon [2015] Conv. 469.

[82] *Crabb v. Arun District Council* [1976] Ch. 179 at 193 *per* Scarman L.J. See also *Macclesfield v. Parker* [2003] EWHC 1846 (Ch) at [207] *per* Lewison J.

[83] [2009] UKHL 18 at [30].

[84] Ibid. at [55]. This is recognized in the slightly wider formulation by Lord Neuberger [2009] C.L.J. 537 at 538.

14.3.1 **Active encouragement**

In estoppel cases there are two paradigm situations where an equity can arise. The first is the case where one person, A, actively encourages another person, B, to believe that he either has, or will acquire, an interest in A's land. B then relies upon that expectation and an equity arises in his favour.[85] *Plimmer v. The Mayor of Wellington*[86] is an example of such a case. So, in more recent times, is *Inwards v. Baker*[87] where a father suggested to his son that, instead of trying to buy land on which to build a bungalow, when this option was too expensive, he should build a larger bungalow on land owned by the father. The son did this and was living in the property when his father died leaving the land to trustees on trust for someone other than the son. The trustees sought possession. The Court of Appeal held that, as the son had a clear expectation of being able to stay in the bungalow indefinitely, that expectation having been created by his father, and he had relied upon that expectation, an equity arose in his favour which was satisfied by holding that he had an indefinite right to remain in the property. The trustees' possession action therefore failed.

14.3.2 **Passive acquiescence**

The other paradigm is where the landowner does not actively encourage the other person to do anything but allows that person to act upon an expectation that he has rights in the land, without disabusing him of his mistaken view.[88] In cases such as this, it is difficult to establish the existence of an equity. It turns on whether the landowner is actually aware of the other person's error[89] and consciously does not stop him from relying on that mistake. In *Ramsden v. Dyson*,[90] Lord Wensleydale said of this type of situation:

> If a stranger build upon my land, supposing it to be his own, and, I knowing it to be mine, do not interfere but leave him to go on, equity considers it dishonest in me to remain passive and afterwards to interfere and take the profit. But if a stranger build knowingly on my land, there is no principle of equity which prevents me from insisting on having back my land, with all the additional value which the occupier has imprudently added to it. If a tenant of mine does the same thing, he cannot insist on refusing to give up the estate at the end of the term. It was his own folly to build.

In practice, a dispute may involve elements of active encouragement and passive acquiescence. As Floyd L.J. put it in *Hoyl Group Limited v. Cromer Town Council*, a proprietary estoppel:

> does not have to fit neatly into the pure acquiescence-based pigeon hole or the assurance one . . . if silence and inactivity can themselves be the necessary assurance . . . they are surely not to be ignored altogether in a case which has elements of encouragement as well.[91]

---

[85] Once such encouragement has been given, the onus is on the person giving the encouragement to disprove reliance: *Greasley v. Cooke* [1980] 1 W.L.R. 1306, criticized by M.P. Thompson (1981) 125 S.J. 418. But see *Hammersmith and Fulham London Borough Council v. Top Shops Ltd* [1990] Ch. 237 at 262 *per* Warner J; and 14.3.8.1.

[86] (1884) 9 App. Cas. 699.

[87] [1965] 2 Q.B. 29. See, also *Dillwyn v. Llewelyn* (1862) 4 De G.F. & J. 517; *Mann v. Shelfside Holdings Ltd* [2015] EWHC 2583 (QB).

[88] See, generally, K.F.K. Low (2012) 128 L.Q.R. 63.

[89] See *Dann v. Spurrier* (1802) 7 Ves. 232 at 235–6 *per* Lord Eldon L.C. See also *Pilling v. Grant* (1805) 12 Ves. 78 at 84 *per* Sir William Grant M.R.; *De Busche v. Alt* (1878) 8 Ch.D. 286 at 315 *per* Thesiger L.J.

[90] (1866) L.R. 1 H.L. 129 at 168.   [91] [2015] EWCA Civ. 782, at [72].

This reinforces the point, made above, that it is better to focus the analysis on the claimant's expectation, which can arise through an assurance, acquiescence, or some combination of both.

14.3.3 The five *probanda*

The emphasis in cases of passive acquiescence is that one party has made a mistake as to what the legal position is and the other, knowing of that mistake, allows the former to rely on his mistaken view of what the position is. Although in *Plimmer v. The Mayor of Wellington*,[92] it was pointed out that cases of active encouragement and passive acquiescence involve quite different considerations, the explanation of the law came to be dominated by statements apposite only to the latter situation.

Willmott v. Barber[93] was a case where, if any rights were to be acquired through the medium of estoppel, they would arise through the landowner's passive acquiescence in the other's mistaken behaviour. Fry J., however, spoke in quite general terms of what is required for rights to be obtained. While stressing that the underlying basis of proprietary estoppel is fraud, he listed five criteria, or *probanda*, which had to be satisfied before a claim could be established:

  (i) the plaintiff must have made a mistake as to his legal rights;

 (ii) he must have spent some money or relied on his mistaken belief;

 (iii) the defendant must be aware of the true position;

 (iv) the defendant must know of the plaintiff's mistake; and

  (v) he must have encouraged the plaintiff in his expenditure or other act of reliance.[94]

14.3.4 Unconscionability and the abandonment of the *probanda*

The five *probanda* set a high threshold for the doctrine of proprietary estoppel to meet. Not only would the party who was allegedly estopped need to know what his strict legal rights were, they would also need to know that the other party was acting in the belief that they would not be enforced against him: something which is unlikely in the majority of circumstances where proprietary estoppel would otherwise operate. It was only a matter of time, therefore, before the five *probanda* were relaxed. In what has rightly been described as being 'a watershed in the development of proprietary estoppel',[95] the court in the leading case of *Taylors Fashions Ltd v. Liverpool Victoria Trustees Ltd*[96] held that it was not necessary to satisfy the five *probanda* in order to acquire an equity through estoppel. Having conducted an extensive review of the authorities, Oliver J. concluded that to establish an equity one should apply 'the broad test of whether in the circumstances the conduct complained of is unconscionable without the necessity of forcing those incumbrances into a Procrustean bed constructed from some unalterable criteria.'[97]

---

[92] (1884) 9 App. Cas. 699 at 712 *per* Sir Arthur Hobhouse.   [93] (1880) 15 Ch.D. 96.

[94] Ibid. at 105–6. Outside of cases of passive acquiescence, a situation may occur where both parties are mistaken as to the correct legal position. See *E.R. Ives Investment v. High* [1967] 2 Q.B. 379, and the discussion of it in the fifth edition of this work at p. 617.

[95] Gray and Gray, *Elements of Land Law* (5th edn) (Oxford, Oxford University Press, 2009), 1209.

[96] [1982] Q.B. 133n. For a nuanced discussion of *Taylor Fashions*, see M. Dixon in Gravells (ed.), *Landmark Cases in Land Law* (Oxford, Hart Publishing, 2013).

[97] [1982] Q.B. 133n at 151. For a broadly similar analysis, see *Ward v. Kirkland* [1969] Ch. 194 at 239 *per* Ungoed-Thomas J. On unconscionability generally, see K.R. Handley [2008] Conv. 382; H. Delaney and D. Ryan [2008] Conv. 401.

The application of a broad test of unconscionability has not gone uncriticized. It has been said that if one was to apply such a test of unconscionability, 'one might as well forget the law of contract and issue every judge with a portable palm tree. The days of justice varying with the size of the Lord Chancellor's foot would have returned.'[98] Such criticism is, however, misplaced[99] and, save for the occasional and unwelcome re-emergence of the five *probanda* as a template against which any claim must be measured,[100] the broad test of unconscionability introduced has attracted judicial approval, and is now widely accepted.[101] The reason it is preferable to the more rigid formula of the five *probanda* is that it is applicable to the wide range of differing situations which may occur and, when properly applied, does not lead to arbitrary or unprincipled results. 'It is not a sort of joker or wild card to be used whenever the Court disapproves of the conduct of a litigant who seems to have the law on his side.'[102] Neither is it 'penicillin for all types of ailments ... the last plea of the desperate and the treatment of choice for a court looking for a remedy for a deserving litigant',[103] nor 'a sort of moral US fifth cavalry riding to the rescue every time a claimant is left worse off than he anticipated as a result of the defendant's behaving badly, and the common law affords him no remedy'.[104] Rather it is a flexible and principled equitable doctrine of long standing.

It is, of course, easy to see why a test based on a broad principle of unconscionability should be viewed with some suspicion; it may be seen as providing scope for judges to apply idiosyncratic notions of fairness to different factual scenarios, the result being uncertainty. This is not, however, the case. For the test of unconscionability to be satisfied, the claimant must be able to bring his case within the broad principles enunciated in *Re Basham*.[105] These were stated as being:

> where one person, A, has acted to his detriment on the faith of a belief, which was known or encouraged by another person, B, that he either has or is going to be given a right over B's property, B cannot insist on his strict legal rights if to do so would be inconsistent with A's belief. The principle is commonly known as proprietary estoppel.

There are a number of elements in this statement which need elaboration.

14.3.5 **Expectation**

The starting point for any claim in estoppel is that the claimant must have the expectation of some right over or to another person's property. This element does not often cause difficulty but can do in some situations. Problems can arise if an expectation is considered to be unjustified. One such situation is where parties have entered into 'subject to contract' negotiations but one of them spends money, or does some other act of reliance, in the belief that the contract will be entered into but the other side later withdraws from the transaction. In this situation, it is very difficult to claim any right arising through estoppel.

---

[98] *Taylor v. Dickens* [1998] 3 F.C.R. 455 at 471 *per* Weeks J. Contrast the comments of the same judge in *Jennings v. Rice* [2003] 1 P. & C.R. 8 at para. 14, cited by Aldous L.J.

[99] Although see the interesting attempt to conceptualize unconscionability by M. Balen and C. Knowles [2011] Conv. 176.

[100] See *Coombes v. Smith* [1986] 1 W.L.R. 808 at 818–20 *per* Jonathan Parker Q.C.; *Matheru v. Matheru* (1994) 68 P. & C.R. 93 at 102 *per* Roch L.J.

[101] See, e.g., *Habib Bank Ltd v. Habib Bank A.G. Zurich* [1981] 1 W.L.R. 1265 at 1285 *per* O. *Teng Huan v. Ang Swee Chuan* [1992] 1 W.L.R. 113 at 117 *per* Lord Browne-Wilkinson; *Gillett v.* All E.R. 289 at 301–2 *per* Robert Walker L.J.

[102] *Yeoman's Row Management Ltd v. Cobbe* [2008] UKHL 55 at [46] *per* Lord Walker.

[103] M. Dixon (2010) 30 L.S. 408 at 410.   [104] Lord Neuberger [2009] C.L.J. 537 at 540.

[105] [1986] 1 W.L.R. 1498 at 1503 *per* Edward Nugee Q.C. See also *Wayling v. Jones* [1995] 2 F.L.

This is because the effect of negotiating 'subject to contract' is generally well known and so, usually, there is no justification for any expectation that the other side is in some way committed to going ahead with the contract.[106]

14.3.6 **Testamentary expectations**

A second area where problems have arisen has concerned situations where assurances have been given that property will be left to a person on death, and that person then acts on that assurance.[107] The problems have centred on the certainty of the property to be left to the claimant, and the issue of testamentary freedom.

14.3.6.1 *Certainty of property*

At the outset, the need to identify the precise property which was to be left on death did not appear to be a particular issue. Although in *Layton v. Martin*,[108] Scott J. had declined to hold that an assurance of financial security could, of itself, form the basis of an estoppel claim, in *Re Basham*,[109] a promise, in effect, to leave the residuary estate to the claimant was sufficiently certain, when relied upon, to give rise to an estoppel right. Subsequently, Robert Walker L.J. pointed to the difficulty in reconciling these approaches,[110] but appeared to favour the latter decision, noting that it had subsequently been cited with approval.[111] Given his previous approach, it is more than a little curious that in *Thorner v. Major*[112] he expressed himself rather differently. Echoing the approach taken by Lord Hoffmann that, to acquire an estoppel interest the claimant must prove a promise or assurance that he would acquire a proprietary interest in a specific property,[113] he also said that the assurance 'must relate to *identified property* (usually land) owned (or, perhaps, about to be owned) by the defendant'.[114] He then proceeded to cast doubt on *Re Basham*. Taking the view that, in the instant case, the reference to the farm was sufficiently certain in referring to what constituted the farm at the time of death, he expressly contrasted that with the more general assurance in *Layton v. Martin*, which he appeared to approve. As to *Re Basham*, he stated that it was not necessary to determine whether or not it was correctly decided so far as it extended to the residuary estate, and expressly reserved his opinion as to this.[115] Given this ambivalence, it is not surprising that, subsequently, in *McDonald v. Frost*,[116] Ms Geraldine Andrews Q.C. should state that *Re Basham* should be treated with the utmost caution and could not be regarded as laying down any general principle to the effect that assurances given about inheriting a residuary estate would be sufficient to give rise to a proprietary estoppel.

It is regrettable that this complication has been introduced. As a matter of first impression, it is difficult to see why if one person gives a specific assurance that he will leave his house to another, and that assurance is relied upon, this could give rise to a cause of action, whereas if the promise was to leave everything that is owned at the time of death, and that was similarly relied upon, it could not. Leaving first impressions aside, the principled

---

[106] See *Attorney-General for Hong Kong v. Humphreys Estates (Queen's Gardens) Ltd* [1987] A.C. 114; *Regalian Properties plc v. London Docklands Development Corporation* [1995] 1 W.L.R. 212; *Edwin Shirley Productions Ltd v. Workspace Management Ltd* [2001] 3 E.G.L.R. 16 at 22 *per* Lawrence Collins J; *Yeoman's Row Management Ltd v. Cobbe* [2008] UKHL 55. Cf. *Salvation Army Trustee Co. Ltd v. West Yorkshire County Council* (1980) 41 P. & C.R. 179 where, on unusual facts, such a claim succeeded.

[107] See, generally, M. Davey (1988) 8 L.S. 72. For a comparative discussion of this issue, see S. Nield (2000) 19 L.S. 85 and, further, S. Nield (2007) 58 N.I.L.Q. 287.

[108] [1996] 2 F.L.R. 227.   [109] [1987] 1 W.L.R. 1498.   [110] *Gillett v. Holt* [2001] Ch. 210 at 226.

[111] Ibid. *See also Jennings v. Rice* [2003] 1 P. & C.R. 8 at [45].   [112] [2009] UKHL 8.

[113] Ibid. at [2].   [114] Ibid. at [61]. Original emphasis.   [115] Ibid. at [62]–[63].

[116] [2009] EWHC 2276 (Ch) at [19].

argument in favour of such a distinction would appear to be that, in the first case, the person has an assurance of a proprietary right in specific property, whereas in the second case, because of the uncertainty in identifying the property which is to be subject to the right, he does not. This analysis is, however, seemingly predicated on the notion that the role of proprietary estoppel is limited to the informal creation of interests in land. That is not consistent, however, with decisions whereby the courts have satisfied an equity which has arisen with a monetary award, and declined to award the claimant any interest in the property which had been promised;[117] a solution which is particularly evident in a case such as *Wayling v. Jones*,[118] where, at the time of death, the person who had made the promise no longer owned the property he had promised to leave by will. It is submitted that, in principle, there is no reason why a promise to leave ill-defined property should not be capable of giving rise to an estoppel right, although it may well be the case that the courts will not be prepared to accept this.

14.3.6.2 *Testamentary freedom*

A second potential stumbling block to the operation of estoppel in the present context might be seen to relate to testamentary freedom. In *Taylor v. Dickens*,[119] an elderly woman promised her gardener that she would make a will in favour of him and his wife leaving virtually all her property to them. He then offered to work for her for nothing, which he did. Having made a will in accordance with what she had said, she later, without telling the couple, revoked it and left the property elsewhere. On her death, he argued that he had rights against the estate arising from estoppel. This claim was rejected. Judge Weeks took the view that the claimant's expectation was that the lady would make a will in his favour; not that she would not subsequently revoke such a will. As she had, in fact, made a will which she subsequently revoked, any expectation which he may have had had been fulfilled.

This reasoning is highly artificial and was regarded as wrong by the Court of Appeal in *Gillett v. Holt*,[120] and in a number of cases, including, of course, *Thorner v. Major* itself, a claimant who expected a will to be made in his favour has been able to enforce an equitable right against the estate after the will had been revoked.[121] It is, however, true that it is well known that a will, once made, can be revoked, and 'it is notorious that some elderly persons of means derive enjoyment from the possession of testamentary power, and from dropping hints as to their intentions, without any question of an estoppel arising'.[122] Because of this, it is necessary that the assurance must be in such terms, or in such circumstances,[123] that it is clear that property is to be left to the claimant,[124] and that it is reasonable for the person to whom the assurance is made to rely on that assurance,[125] and it may be that the less precise the description of the property to be left, the less reasonable it becomes for the person to whom the assurance is addressed to rely on it.

A related point is what happens to the property pending the death of the person making the assurance. In this type of case, it would appear that the person making the assurance

---

[117] See *Campbell v. Griffin* [2001] EWCA Civ. 990; *Jennings v. Rice* [2003] 1 P. & C.R. 8. See 14.5.2.

[118] (1993) 69 P. & C.R. 179.

[119] [1998] 1 F.L.R. 806. For strong criticism of this decision, see M.P. Thompson [1998] Conv. 210; W. Swadling [1998] R.L.R. 220. Contrast M. Dixon [1999] Conv. 46.

[120] [2001] Ch. 210. See also, dealing with the same point, *Sledmore v. Dalby* (1996) P. & C.R. 196 at 203 *per* Roch L.J. See M.P. Thompson [2001] Conv. 78.

[121] *Wayling v. Jones* (1993) 69 P. & C.R. 170; *Henry v. Henry* [2010] UKPC 3.

[122] *Gillett v. Holt* [2001] Ch. 210 at 228 *per* Robert Walker L.J.

[123] See *Thorner v. Major* [2009] UKHL 8 at [24] *per* Lord Rodger.

[124] For a claim which failed due to considerable ambiguity as to this, see *McDonald v. Frost* [2009] EWHC 2276 (Ch).

[125] See *Thorner v. Major* [2009] UKHL 18 at [17] *per* Lord Scott.

is not precluded from dealing with his property until death. So, in *Thorner v. Major*, the physical configuration of the farm changed during the lifetime of its owner, as some fields were sold and others bought. Nevertheless, it was held that the equity which had arisen was still enforceable against the estate. The question which can arise is what the position would be if it became apparent prior to the death, either by proposed dealings with it, or the manifestation of a clear intention that the property was not to be left in the way in which it had been promised. This latter situation occurred in *Gillett v. Holt*,[126] where, despite the fact that the promisor had not died, as it was clear from the facts that he was not going to leave the property as promised, the court awarded a remedy prior to the death. This would appear to be the approach to be adopted if it appears that the property is to be substantially disposed of prior to the death,[127] so that in a case 'where a claimant has a clear right to expect that a property will be left to him by another, an attempt to circumvent a promise to that effect by changing the will or by selling the property may give rise to enforceable rights even before the death of the promisor.'[128] If, however, as in *Thorner v. Major* some of the farm has been sold, and the proceeds spent, that, in itself, should not allow the equity to be enforced prior to death. The degree of dissipation necessary to enable the promisee to secure an early enforcement of the equity will, it is thought, be a matter of degree.

14.3.7 **Reliance and detriment**

That a person has an expectation of acquiring an interest in property is, of itself, insufficient to raise an estoppel. Before any equity can arise in his favour, it is necessary that the claimant has acted on the faith of that expectation and, in the sense to be explained, that that reliance is to his detriment.

An obvious form of reliance is to spend money. Such a form of reliance occurred in *Plimmer v. The Mayor of Wellington*,[129] where the reliance involved spending money on the extension of a jetty. While this may be the clearest form of reliance, other forms of conduct will suffice. For example, in *Crabb v. Arun District Council*,[130] the plaintiff, in reliance upon an assurance that he would enjoy a right of way over the defendant's land, sold part of his own land with the result that, when the defendant resiled from his assurance, he was left with no means of access to the property. The act of selling land was, in these circumstances, seen as a clear act of reliance. Similarly, in *Jones v. Jones*,[131] although the acts of reliance on an assurance that a house would be his included the expenditure of money, the act of giving up a job and moving from existing accommodation was also regarded in the same way.

14.3.8 **Family disputes**

A not untypical situation where claims are based upon estoppel is where the parties are in a relationship and, on the breakdown of that relationship, one party, usually the woman, makes a claim to the other's property. Quite commonly, in such situations, an assurance has been given that the person making a claim will always have secure accommodation and the difficulty is to establish an act of reliance on that assurance.[132] The nub of the

---

[126] [2001] Ch. 210.
[127] See *Thorner v. Major* [2009] UKHL 18 at [18] *per* Lord Scott; at [88] *per* Lord Neuberger.
[128] *Clarke v. Meadus* [2010] EWHC 3117 (Ch) at [74] *per* Warren J.
[129] (1884) 9 App. Cas. 699.   [130] [1976] Ch. 170.
[131] [1977] 1 W.L.R. 438. See also *Watts v. Story* (1983) 134 N.L.J. 631.
[132] See, e.g., *Vaughan v. Vaughan* [1953] 1 Q.B. 762.

problem is that the claimed acts of reliance can be seen as conduct which is an integral part of the relationship, rather than behaviour based upon the assurance which has been given.[133] The case law reveals a disparity in judicial attitude.

In *Maharaj v. Chand*,[134] a woman who had secure accommodation of her own was asked to move in by her partner. Before doing so, she sought and received an assurance that she would have a secure home in the house into which she was to move. Some years later, the relationship broke down and he sought to evict her from the property. The Privy Council held that she had, through the operation of estoppel, a personal and indefinite right to remain in the house. Her act of giving up secure accommodation of her own was regarded as being a sufficient act of reliance. In stark contrast is the case of *Coombes v. Smith*.[135] In this case, a married woman left her husband to live in a house bought by her new partner, who was also married, after being assured that she would always have secure accommodation. She also had his child. On the breakdown of their relationship, it was held that she had no right to remain in the property.

The estoppel claim was considered primarily on the basis of whether or not she could satisfy the five *probanda*, considered earlier, which the judge considered that she could not. There had been no mistake as to her legal rights. Although this approach to estoppel cases is no longer appropriate, the judge, in any event, considered that she had not relied to her detriment on the assurance which she had been given. In his view, her leaving her husband and having their child was an inherent part of their relationship. She had not done anything which could be attributed to the assurance of security in the house which she had been given.

While such a view is understandable, it is not necessarily convincing. It is true, as the judge pointed out, that to hold that the woman in this case had an equity in the house would mean that, in most cases where there is a dispute between an unmarried couple and the woman has left secure accommodation of her own to move in with her partner, quite a common event, she would be able to claim an interest in the house, or at least the right to remain in it.[136] That, however, may be no bad thing and could lead to fairer results than those which can occur when a longstanding non-marital relationship breaks down and a dispute occurs as to occupancy rights in the home.

These two cases are not easy to reconcile, and display a very different approach to what can constitute reliance. Latterly, it is becoming increasingly clear that a more liberal approach is favoured. In the increasingly influential decision in *Wayling v. Jones*,[137] a homosexual couple began to cohabit in 1971, and this continued until 1987, when the elder of the two died. When the cohabitation began, W was twenty-one and J was fifty-six. They lived in a hotel owned by J. W worked in the hotel, but received very little money. What he did receive was regarded as akin to pocket money. When he mentioned that he would need more money, J promised him that he would leave everything to him. The arrangement then continued as before, and the promise was repeated. On J's death, it transpired that the will by which he had intended to implement his promise was ineffective to do so. W then brought an action against the estate, basing his claim on estoppel.

14.3.8.1 Presumption of reliance

The difficulty was not establishing the expectation; it was showing reliance. In evidence, W said that, had no promise ever been made, he would have stayed with his partner on the same basis as before. At first instance, this statement was held to be fatal to the estoppel

---

[133] For an excellent discussion, see A. Lawson (1996) 16 L.S. 218.   [134] [1986] A.C. 898.

[135] [1986] 1 W.L.R. 808. See also *Negus v. Bahous* [2008] 1 F.L.R. 381 at [54]–[55] *per* Mr Roger Kaye Q.C.

[136] [1986] 1 W.L.R. 808 at 816 *per* Jonathan Parker Q.C.

[137] (1983) 69 P. & C.R. 170. See E. Cooke (1995) 111 L.Q.R. 389 at 391, where the disparity between the two preceding decisions is commented upon.

claim, it being considered to have shown that no reliance had taken place. Reversing this decision, the Court of Appeal held the claim to have been substantiated. Starting from the premise that once a clear promise had been made it was for the promisor to disprove reliance by the promisee,[138] it was held that this had not been done. This was because of the further evidence given that, had J told him that the promise was being withdrawn, then W would have left. This was sufficient to establish reliance,[139] and the court ordered that he be paid by the estate the value of what had been promised.

14.3.8.2 Mixed motives

This decision is significant in that it establishes that reliance can be established when a person acts with more than one motive, in this case affection for his partner and the expectation of inheritance, and when a person does not change his conduct in reliance on a promise, but would do so if the promise was subsequently withdrawn.[140] This was followed in *Campbell v. Griffin*.[141] A young man of thirty moved into lodgings with a couple who were then in their late seventies. After five years living in the house, the relationship between him and the couple grew increasingly affectionate. He stopped paying rent and, more and more, took on the role of a carer, as they became increasingly frail. He was promised that he could live in the house for the rest of his life after the couple had both died. When that occurred, it transpired that he had been left nothing and he, too, brought an action against the estate. Again, the principal problem was to show reliance. Relying on *Wayling v. Jones*, however, the Court of Appeal found in his favour. Although he was acting in a caring capacity before the promise was made, and continued to do so afterwards, this conduct was still considered to amount to reliance. The court was prepared to accept that the promise did influence his decision to stay in the house to care for an increasingly infirm couple. The fact that he was genuinely fond of them and said that, for that reason, he would not have left them on their own to suffer did not negate reliance. As was recognized, his motives may well have been mixed, and he should not lose his claim because he insisted that he was motivated by affection and altruism as well as the prospect of gain.[142]

14.3.9 Detriment

The underlying basis of proprietary estoppel is unconscionability. Essential to this is that the claimant has acted in reliance, in the sense explained in the preceding sections, on having some expectation of acquiring some right over another person's land, in circumstances where it would be inequitable to deny some effect to that expectation. This means that the acts of reliance have to be detrimental to the claimant. This requirement can easily be misunderstood to mean that the acts relied upon must, themselves, be harmful in some way to the claimant, in the sense that they put him in a worse position than he was in before.[143] This is not so. The proper meaning of detriment is that the claimant's position would be damaged if the expectation or assumption which formed the basis of his reliance were to be departed from.[144]

---

[138] See *Greasley v. Cooke* [1986] 1 W.L.R. 1306.
[139] See also *Clarke v. Meadus* [2010] EWHC 3117 (Ch) at [54] *per* Warren J.
[140] See also *Ottey v. Grundy* [2003] EWCA Civ. 1113; M.P. Thompson [2004] Conv. 137.
[141] [2001] EWCA Civ. 990; M.P. Thompson [2003] Conv. 157.
[142] [2001] EWCA Civ. 990 at 19 *per* Robert Walker L.J.
[143] See, e.g., *Coombes v. Smith* [1986] 1 W.L.R. 808 at 819–20 *per* Jonathan Parker Q.C.
[144] See *Grundt v. Great Boulder Pty Gold Mines Ltd* (1937) 59 C.L.R. 641 at 674–5 *per* Dixon J.; *Gillett v. Holt* [2001] Ch. 210 at 232–3 *per* Robert Walker L.J.

14.3.9.1 A holistic approach

The more relaxed view of what constitutes reliance, coupled with a principled view of what constitutes detriment, offers scope for solutions to be arrived at in cohabitation cases where the claimant seeks some remedy when her behaviour has not been of a purchasing behaviour, which are more favourable to the claimant than an application of the law of trusts would suggest.[145] In *Gillett v. Holt*,[146] a young boy moved into a farm owned by a much older man, with whom he had a platonic relationship for over forty years. He gave up his education, and worked on the farm, having been promised on a number of occasions that he would eventually inherit the property. When the owner of the farm sought to renege on these undertakings, the claimant was held to be entitled to a remedy in estoppel. In addressing the issue of what constituted detriment, Robert Walker L.J. made it clear that this need not consist of the expenditure of money. Rather, the case must be looked at in the round as part of a broad enquiry as to whether it would be unconscionable to go back on assurances which had been given. On the facts of the case, the giving up of his education and alternative career prospects was seen as detrimental reliance.[147] Similarly, in *Ottey v. Grundy*,[148] it was held that staying to look after an ill partner, following assurances of inheritance, at the expense of the possible continuation of a career in show business, also amounted to detrimental reliance. Giving up a career to look after children in a family home should, therefore, also form the basis of a claim in estoppel.

The correctness of this approach was confirmed by the Privy Council in *Henry v. Henry*.[149] In this case, the claimant had been promised that he would be left land. He worked that land for many years. He gave some of the produce to the landowner and sold the remainder, this in large part amounting to his livelihood. At first instance, the trial judge had held that he had not established detrimental reliance, because, for decades, he had enjoyed rent-free accommodation on the land. While the Privy Council considered this to be relevant, the Board also took the view that the position had to be looked at in the round, and regard should be had to the disadvantages which he had suffered, such as the foregoing of opportunities to move on elsewhere,[150] as well as the advantages he had enjoyed. Having undertaken this exercise, it was held that, overall, there had been detrimental reliance. The same approach to the question of detriment was described recently in *Lothian v. Dixon*:[151]

> Detriment is not a narrow or technical concept but must be judged in the round. The real detriment or harm from which the law seeks to give protection is that which would flow from the change in position if the assumption were deserted that led to it. It need not be expenditure of money or other quantifiable financial detriment but it must be substantial.

---

[145] See Chapter 9, and M.P. Thompson in Jackson and Wilde (eds), *Contemporary Property Law* (Dartmouth, Ashgate, 1999), 120 at 135–7.

[146] [2001] Ch. 210. See R. Wells [2001] Conv. 13; M.P. Thompson [2001] Conv. 78.

[147] [2001] Ch. 210 at 232–5.

[148] [2003] EWCA Civ. 1176. Contrast *Lissimore v. Downing* [2003] 2 F.L.R. 308, where the giving up of a job behind the counter of a pharmacist's shop to live with a member of the band Judas Priest was not considered to be detrimental reliance, as there was no sense that she was giving up a career: ibid., at 322 *per* Judge Norris Q.C.

[149] [2010] UKPC 3.

[150] Ibid. at [53] *per* Sir Jonathan Parker. See also *Malik v. Kalyan* [2010] EWCA Civ. 113, where such a foregoing of opportunities was not established on the facts.

[151] 28 November 2014, High Court (Chancery Division), Unreported, at [19] *per* Judge Roger Kaye Q.C. See also *Suggitt v. Suggitt* [2012] EWCA Civ. 1140.

14.3.10 **Mutuality**

For the claimant to acquire a right through proprietary estoppel, he must have acted in reliance on an expectation that he either has or will acquire rights in another person's property. Such acts, it may be said, raise an equity in his favour. For it to be unconscionable for the other person to deny some effect to that expectation he must be in some way responsible for that action, so that an equity arises against him. This was explained in *Sledmore v. Dalby*,[152] where it was said that:

> The party asserting the estoppel must be able to show that his own conduct was attributable to an expectation or mistake *contributed to by the conduct (including inaction) of the affected party.*

Finding such responsibility on the part of the person against whom the claim is made will depend to a considerable extent on the facts of each case but will be easier to find when there has been some contribution to the claimant having an expectation than will be the case where the expectation derives from a shared mistake.

In *Crabb v. Arun District Council*,[153] a council representative led the plaintiff to believe that, if he sold off a plot of land, he would have a right of way over land owned by the council. He duly sold that land and, when the council refused to allow him access, the effect was to leave his property landlocked. The Court of Appeal held the plaintiff to be entitled through estoppel to an easement. As the council had been responsible for the creation of the expectation, it was straightforward to find that, when the plaintiff had relied upon it, an equity arose against them.

14.3.10.1 *Mutual mistake*

In cases of positive encouragement, finding that an equity has arisen against the person affected is straightforward. In cases where a mutual mistake is made as to the legal position, such a finding is more difficult and can require a close analysis of the facts. Such an analysis occurred in *Taylors Fashions Ltd v. Liverpool Victoria Trustees Ltd*,[154] a decision which is illustrative of cases where an estoppel can arise where there is never an express assurance given by one party to the other.

The first plaintiff was granted a twenty-eight-year lease, which contained an option to renew for a further fourteen years. This option, unbeknown to both parties for a considerable period of time, was void against the defendants who had purchased the freehold, because it had not been registered as a land charge.[155] The second plaintiff took a lease of adjoining property for a period of forty-two years, that lease being determinable by the landlords if the option to renew the first lease was not exercised. In other words, it was intended to synchronize the running of the two leases. When the first plaintiff sought to exercise the option, the objection was made that it was void. The first plaintiff sought a declaration that, through estoppel, the option was valid, despite non-registration, and the second plaintiffs sought a declaration that the defendants could not determine the lease. The first plaintiff failed and the second plaintiff succeeded.

---

[152] (1996) 72 P. & C.R. 196 at 207 *per* Hobhouse L.J. (emphasis supplied), citing *Commonwealth of Australia v. Verwayen* (1990) 95 A.L.R. 321 at 322 *per* Mason C.J.

[153] [1976] Ch. 179.   [154] [1982] Q.B. 133n.

[155] At the time it was not realized that such an option was registrable, it being decided that it was in *Beesly v. Hallwood Estates Ltd* [1961] Ch. 105, after the option in the present case had been granted.

14.3.10.2 *Responsibility for reliance*

In both cases, the tenants had a mistaken belief that the option to renew the first lease was valid. That belief was not created by the defendants; it was a case of mutual mistake. The reasons why the first plaintiff failed were, first, that it could not show reliance on that mistaken belief and, second, even if it could show reliance, there was, on the facts, nothing to make it unconscionable for the defendants to deny any effect to the expectation. The reliance alleged by the first plaintiff was the installation of a lift in the property. Although the defendants' representatives were aware of this work, the difficulty was that the installation of the lift was contemplated by the lease itself; there was nothing to show that its installation was done on the basis that there was an option to renew the lease for a further fourteen years from the date of its determination. Indeed, installing a lift into commercial property when there were still eighteen years remaining on the original lease would be a normal thing to have done, regardless of whether there existed an option to renew.[156] The second problem was that the work done was on property controlled by the first plaintiff. While the defendants were aware of what was being done, they did not encourage it and were powerless to stop it. Accordingly, even if the work had been regarded as reliance on the expectation that the option was valid, it was not unconscionable for the defendants to rely on the strict legal position, which was that the option was void.

As regards the second plaintiff, the position was different. The whole basis upon which its lease was negotiated with the defendant was that the option in the first lease was valid. While it was true that the risk was run that the first plaintiff might choose not to exercise the option, so that the defendants could then determine the second lease, what was not the case was that the lease was being entered into on the basis that the option could never be exercised, thereby giving the defendants the unfettered right to determine the lease. As the defendants had been party to the act of reliance of the second plaintiff, the entry into the lease, they could not take the point, as against the second plaintiffs, that the option was void and could not, therefore, determine the lease.

What emerges is that, in cases of active encouragement of the expectation, for example, saying that 'the house is yours',[157] once reliance is established, there is no further difficulty in holding that an equity has arisen against the creator of the expectation. In cases where the expectation arises owing to a mutual mistake as to what the true position is, for an equity to arise against the person against whom the claim is made, it would seem that that person must either actively encourage the acts of reliance,[158] or be a party to it, as in *Taylors Fashions*. If he does neither of these things, then it is probable that an equity will only arise if he is aware of the mistake, and of the action in reliance, and does nothing to stop the other person from acting in reliance upon his mistaken expectation.

14.4 The extent of the equity

The second aspect of proprietary estoppel identified by Scarman L.J. was to identify the extent of the equity which has arisen. This means, quite simply, determining the ambit of the expectation. Where there has been an actual representation, then the expectation is defined by that representation. If, as may happen, any such representation is imprecise in scope, then it is for the court, as best it can, to infer what the actual scope of the expectation was.[159] The less formal the understanding between the parties, the more difficult will

---

[156] [1982] Q.B. 133n at 156 *per* Oliver J. [157] See *Pascoe v. Turner* [1979] 1 W.L.R. 431.

[158] See *E.R. Ives Investment Ltd v. High* [1967] 2 Q.B. 379.

[159] See *Plimmer v. The Mayor of Wellington* (1884) 9 App. Cas. 699 at 713–14 *per* Sir Arthur Hobhouse. See also *Thorner v. Major* [2009] UKHL 18 at [84]–[86] *per* Lord Neuberger.

be the task of determining the full extent of the equity, and this may impact on the remedy which has been arrived at.[160]

14.5 Satisfaction of the equity

The final aspect of an estoppel claim is the determination of the remedy to be afforded to the claimant. From quite early times, judges have stressed that, once an equity has arisen, it is for the courts, in the exercise of their discretion, to decide how the equity should be satisfied.[161] The greatest remedy available is the complete satisfaction of the expectation.[162] It is not possible to award a claimant a remedy greater than his expectation.[163] That, however, is not a necessary conclusion, and the courts have shown considerable flexibility in determining the appropriate remedy.[164] There are various possibilities, the first being in the nature of compensation, and the alternative being the enforcement of the expectation.[165]

14.5.1 Compensation

In terms of compensating the claimant as a result of his reliance upon the expectation, such compensation can be designed to reflect different types of loss. The claimant may, as a result of his reliance, have incurred expenditure, but that expenditure does not benefit the other party to the action. In such cases, any compensation simply reflects the cost of the reliance.[166] An example of this would be a claim for pre-contractual expenditure when it is anticipated that a binding contract will subsequently be entered into.[167] It is not, however, easy to establish such a claim. Moreover, in cases involving land, this may not be seen as the most appropriate response. If someone's reliance on an assurance of security in a home is to give up existing secure accommodation, while it might be possible to quantify this in terms of reliance loss, a more appropriate response may be to seek to enforce the expectation and protect the security of that accommodation.[168]

14.5.2 Restitution

Situations can arise when the claimant's act of reliance does not only involve him in expenditure; it also confers a benefit on the other party. Such cases normally involve the claimant effecting some sort of improvement to the other's land, this being done in reliance on an expectation of having an interest in that land. While, again, it may be the case that the court may seek to give effect to the expectation, there may be reasons why this is not practicable. In such circumstances, a restitutionary remedy can be effected by ordering the

---

[160] See *Jennings v. Rice* [2003] 1 P. & C.R. 8.

[161] See *Plimmer v. The Mayor of Wellington* (1884) 9 App. Cas. 699 at 713–14 *per* Sir Arthur Hobhouse.

[162] See *Macclesfield v. Parker* [2003] EWHC 1846 (Ch); *Wormall v. Wormall* [2004] EWHC 1643 (Ch). The comment in *Jennings v. Rice* [2003] 1 P. & C.R. 8 at [21] that a remedy greater than the expectation has been awarded is wrong. See M.P. Thompson [2004] Conv. 225 at 231–2.

[163] See *Jules v. Robertson* [2011] EWCA Civ. 1322 at [24] *per* Warren J.

[164] See *Roebuck v. Mungovin* [1994] 2 A.C. 224 at 235 *per* Lord Browne-Wilkinson.

[165] See, generally, L.L. Fuller and W.R. Purdue (1936) 46 Yale L.J. 52.

[166] For an argument advocating reliance damages as the normal starting point, see A. Robertson (1998) 18 L.S. 360, an argument which takes a very wide view of the role of such damages

[167] See, e.g., *Regalian Properties plc v. London Docklands Development Corporation* [1995] 1 W.L.R. 212, where such a claim failed on the facts.

[168] See *Maharaj v. Chand* [1986] A.C. 898.

return of the money expended upon the land.[169] This can be done by granting the claimant a lien over the other's land as security for the amount to be repaid,[170] or, more simply, allowing the claimant to remain in the property until the amount expended upon it has been repaid.[171]

Similarly, the reliance may take the form of conferring a benefit on a person, rather than on property. Such cases tend to involve the claimant acting as a form of unpaid help or carer for the other person.[172] In such cases, the courts can, again, choose to award the claimant a restitutionary remedy, ordering a payment to be made, the quantum of that payment representing a rough approximation of the value of the work done.[173]

14.5.3 **Expectation**

As will be seen, it is quite common in cases of proprietary estoppel for the court to make an order which gives effect, at least in part, to the claimant's expectation. This may not be possible, however, and, instead, the court may make a monetary order to compensate for the loss of the expectation.[174] In *Wayling v. Jones*,[175] the plaintiff had been assured by his lover that he would be left a particular hotel in his will. A will in these terms was in fact made but prior to his death that hotel had been sold and another purchased and no testamentary provision was made with regard to that property. The plaintiff, having been held to have relied upon the assurance made to him,[176] sought, and obtained, a judgment that he was entitled to be paid from the estate the proceeds of sale of the first hotel. In other words, although his expectation could no longer be satisfied *in specie*, he was awarded a financial payment to compensate him for his expectation interest. Such instances of money payments being awarded are rare,[177] but are indicative of the willingness of the courts, in cases of proprietary estoppel, to seek to satisfy the claimant's expectation.

14.6 **Satisfaction of the expectation**

Although any equity which has arisen can be satisfied by financial compensation, commonly the remedy which is obtained involves the actual satisfaction of the claimant's expectation. In *Pascoe v. Turner*,[178] a man purported to give a house and its contents to his partner. In reliance on this purported gift, she spent a significant amount of her savings, consisting of several hundred pounds, effecting improvements to it. He, having formed

---

[169] See *Sledmore v. Dalby* (1996) 72 P. & C.R. 196 at 208 *per* Hobhouse L.J. For an interesting discussion of the relationship between estoppel and restitution, see N.W. Hopkins in Cooke (ed.), *Modern Studies in Property Law, Volume 2* (Oxford–Portland, OR, Hart Publishing, 2003), Chapter 8.

[170] *Unity Joint Stock Mutual Banking Association v. King* (1858) 25 Beav. 72.

[171] *Dodsworth v. Dodsworth* [1973] E.G.D. 223. See also *Re Sharpe* [1980] 1 W.L.R. 219.

[172] See *Campbell v. Griffin* [2001] EWCA Civ. 990; *Jennings v. Rice* [2003] 1 P. & C.R. 8.

[173] See *Jennings v. Rice* [2003] 1 P. & C.R. 8 at [48] *per* Robert Walker L.J.

[174] See C. Davis [1995] Conv. 409 at 414–16; S. Bright and B. McFarlane [2005] Conv. 14.

[175] (1993) 69 P. & C.R. 170.

[176] This aspect of the decision was controversial. See the discussion by E. Cooke (1995) 111 L.Q.R. 389; C. Davis [1995] Conv. 409.

[177] See *Holiday Inns Inc. v. Broadhead* (1974) 232 E.G. 951; *Baker v. Baker* [1993] 2 F.L.R. 247. This may also be the best explanation of *Tanner v. Tanner* [1975] 1 W.L.R. 1346, although the case was actually decided on a different basis.

[178] [1979] 1 W.L.R. 431. See also *Dillwyn v. Llewelyn* (1862) 4 De G.F. & J. 517; *Jiggins v. Brisley* [2003] EWHC 841 (Ch).

a relationship with another woman, then sought to evict her from the house. His claim failed and, instead, he was ordered to convey the house to her.

The result of the case lends support to the thesis that the role of proprietary estoppel is to perfect an imperfect gift,[179] or, put another way, that the role of estoppel is a medium through which the claimant's expectation is fulfilled.[180] There is force in this argument; indeed, were it not valid, the actual decision in *Pascoe v. Turner* would appear to represent a remarkable windfall for the woman in the case who, for the expenditure of a relatively modest sum, was awarded the house for nothing.[181] Nevertheless, the reasoning in the case itself and in other decisions does not support such an analysis.

In *Pascoe v. Turner*, it was apparent to the Court of Appeal that the remedy awarded to satisfy the equity which had arisen might appear to be extreme and the court regarded the choice as being between giving her an indefinite licence to occupy the property or ordering a conveyance of it to her.[182] In arriving at the conclusion that a conveyance was the appropriate result, Cumming-Bruce L.J. had regard to a number of factors, which included their relative financial positions, in that he was wealthy and she was not. Moreover, it was felt that, given the nature of the relationship at the time of the trial, if she were to be afforded some lesser remedy, then the likelihood was that he would pester her in the future, an undesirable outcome which the 'clean break' solution arrived at would avoid. This was a family case,[183] where the solution arrived at was much the same as one might expect to have occurred if the couple had been married and this had been a case of reallocation of property on divorce. Because of the nature of the expectation encouraged by him, the court was able to arrive at a solution in a cohabitation case consistent with that which would have been arrived at if the couple had been married.[184]

14.6.1 **Practicalities**

In determining to what extent the claimant's expectation should be fulfilled, although it has been said that it is often appropriate to satisfy the equity by granting the claimant the interest that he was intended to have,[185] it has also been recognized that the solution to the dispute must always depend upon the circumstances of the particular case.[186] In particular, a relevant factor will be the practicalities of the situation. If the estoppel arose in a situation which involves the claimant and the other party living together in the same house, then an order is unlikely to be made which will require people, whose relationship has broken down, to continue to live together in the same house.[187] The way that the equity is then satisfied may then take a wholly different form from that which was envisaged and is likely to involve compensation for reliance.[188]

---

[179] See D.E. Allen (1963) 79 L.Q.R. 238; S. Moriarty (1984) 100 L.Q.R. 376. For an argument against this view, see M.P. Thompson [1986] Conv. 402.

[180] See E. Cooke (1997) 17 L.S. 258; S. Gardner (1999) 111 L.Q.R. 438. Both writers recognize, however, that this is not the invariable outcome of estoppel cases. See A. Robertson [2008] Conv. 295.

[181] The case has been criticized precisely on this basis. See Glister and Lee, *Hanbury and Martin, Modern Equity* (20th edn) (London, Sweet & Maxwell, 2015), 935.

[182] [1979] 1 W.L.R. 431 at 438 *per* Cumming-Bruce L.J.

[183] For the relevance of this in a related situation, see E. Cooke (1995) 111 L.Q.R. 389 at 393–4.

[184] For a discussion of this tendency, see M.P. Thompson [1984] Conv. 103.

[185] *Burrows and Burrows v. Sharp* (1989) 23 H.L.R. 82 at 92 *per* Dillon L.J. See also *Chalmers v. Pardoe* [1963] 1 W.L.R. 677 at 681 *per* Sir Terence Donovan.

[186] *Voyce v. Voyce* (1991) 62 P. & C.R. 290 at 293 *per* Dillon L.J.

[187] Although see *Sledmore v. Stallion* [2009] EWHC 1950 (Ch) at [138] *per* Ms Sarah Asplin Q.C.

[188] *Burrows and Burrows v. Sharp* (1989) 23 H.L.R. 82 at 92 *per* Dillon L.J. See also *Dodsworth v. Dodsworth* [1973] E.G.D. 233.

14.6.2 **Conduct**

A further factor which is relevant to the exercise of the court's discretion is the conduct of the parties.[189] A good example of this is provided by *Crabb v. Arun District Council*.[190] The plaintiff had been encouraged by the defendants to believe that, if he sold off part of his land, he would enjoy a right of way over the defendants' land. Having sold off the land, the defendants refused him access and he sought a declaration that he enjoyed such a right. In the Court of Appeal, his claim was upheld and it was held that he was entitled to an easement, which was the full extent of his expectation.

Although this case provides an example of the equity being satisfied in full, it is clear from the judgments that the obstructive behaviour of the defendants in the period after the equity had arisen, which occurred when the plaintiff sold his land, was a highly significant factor in the way that the discretion was exercised. Because of the defendants' obstructive attitude, the plaintiff's land had been rendered useless for a period of six years. Were it not for this, the plaintiff would only have been granted the remedy he sought on terms, those terms being that he be required to pay for the right.[191] As Scarman L.J. put it:

> Had matters taken a different turn, I would without hesitation have said that the plaintiff should be put on terms to be agreed if possible with the defendants, and, if not agreed, settled by the court.[192]

14.6.3 **Misconduct by the claimant**

Crabb v. Arun District Council provides an excellent illustration of a situation where the conduct of the person against whom the right is sought has an influence upon how the court satisfies the equity which has arisen. In the converse situation, where it is the claimant who has been guilty of misconduct prior to the court adjudicating on how the equity should be satisfied, then this will affect the exercise of the discretion and, in extreme cases such as where part of the claimant's case is based upon perjured evidence, may cause the court to decline to give the claimant any relief at all.[193] If, as in *Williams v. Staite*,[194] the misconduct occurs after the equity has been satisfied, then its effect would seem to depend upon the order which the court had made previously when deciding how the equity should be satisfied. If, for example, the court had previously ordered the property to be conveyed to the claimant, then such an order is clearly final and no order will be made for the land to be reconveyed. Where, however, the order is for some sort of indefinite right of occupation then, if the misconduct is of a sufficiently egregious nature, the protection given by equity may, it is thought, be subsequently withdrawn.

14.6.4 **Occupation**

Estoppel cases often arise in a residential setting, with the claimants being given varying degrees of assurance as to the security of their occupation in a house. In such situations, when it comes to satisfying any equity which has arisen, a principal concern, where this is practicable, is to make an order which seeks to preserve the security of that occupation.

---

[189] See M.P. Thompson [1986] Conv. 406 at 411–14.
[190] [1976] Ch. 179. See also *The Mayor of London Borough of Bexley v. Maison Maurice* [2006] EWHC 3192 (Ch).
[191] [1976] Ch. 179 at 189 *per* Lord Denning M.R.; at 192 *per* Lawton L.J.   [192] Ibid. at 199.
[193] *J. Willis & Son v. Willis* [1986] 1 E.G.L.R. 62. See also *Gordon v. Mitchell* [2007] EWHC 1854 (Ch).
[194] [1979] Ch. 291.

So, in *Inwards v. Baker*,[195] where a father had encouraged his son to build a bungalow on the father's land, the Court of Appeal, in satisfying the son's equity, held that he had an indefinite right to remain in the bungalow, for the rest of his life should he so wish.

The perceived problem with this solution, and one which was considered to have been overlooked in *Inwards v. Baker*,[196] was that such a right could be perceived to be a life interest. The consequence of this, at that time, was that the life tenant would then be endowed with all the statutory powers, including sale, conferred by the SLA 1925,[197] an outcome considered to be undesirable. In *Griffiths v. Williams*,[198] a grandmother had relied on a representation by her granddaughter that she could live in a house, rent free, for the rest of her life. Regarding the task of the court as being 'to see, having regard to all the circumstances, what is the best and fairest way to secure protection for the person who has been misled by the representations made to [her] and subsequently repudiated',[199] the parties were prevailed upon to agree that the granddaughter should grant the grandmother a non-assignable lease, determinable upon death, at a rent sufficiently low to avoid the statutory protection conferred by the Rent Acts.

This decision shows a degree of creative flexibility on the part of the courts in seeking to achieve an appropriate solution to the problem. Now that it is no longer possible to create a strict settlement, a life interest taking effect under a trust of land,[200] a court need no longer be concerned with such complications when seeking, in appropriate cases, to allow a claimant an indefinite right of occupation. It may be anticipated that when a person has assured another that he will be able to stay in a house indefinitely, and this assurance has been relied upon, an order giving effect to that expectation is a likely outcome.[201]

14.6.5 Wider considerations

Pascoe v. Turner,[202] where the claimant was granted her expectation in full by the order that the house be conveyed to her, is considered by some to be a very generous response in the light of her rather limited acts of reliance.[203] The Court of Appeal was aware of this, but nevertheless considered on the facts that this was the fairest solution, a factor in that conclusion being the relative wealth of the two parties. He was considered to be a rich man and she was in straitened financial circumstances so that, to her, the expenditure of several hundred pounds was a significant outlay.[204]

The attention paid to what has been regarded as redistributive factors has been criticized,[205] yet, within a flexible jurisdiction, the needs and resources of the parties seem to be a legitimate criterion to which the court should have regard in the exercise of its discretion. Such considerations can also work against the claimant, so that although the essential elements of proprietary estoppel are satisfied, in the circumstances, no remedy is considered to be appropriate.[206] The decision of the Court of Appeal in *Sledmore v. Dalby*[207] is interesting in this context.

---

[195] [1965] 2 Q.B. 25.   [196] See *Dodsworth v. Dodsworth* [1972] E.G.D. 233 *per* Russell L.J.
[197] See Chapter 8.   [198] (1978) 248 E.G. 947.   [199] Ibid. at 950 *per* Goff L.J.
[200] Trusts of Land and Appointment of Trustees Act 1996, ss 1, 2.
[201] See *Maharaj v. Chand* [1986] AC 898. But see *Campbell v. Griffin* [2001] EWCA Civ. 990, [34] *per* Robert Walker L.J.
[202] [1979] 1 W.L.R. 431.   [203] [1977] 1 W.L.R. 438. See also *Watts v. Story* (1983) 134 N.L.J. 631.
[204] [1979] 1 W.L.R. at 439 *per* Cumming-Bruce L.J.
[205] See S. Gardner (1999) 115 L.Q.R. 438 at 439–60.
[206] See *Appleby v. Cowley* (1982), *The Times*, 14 April.
[207] (1996) 72 P. & C.R. 196.

14.6.6 **Changing circumstances**

Mr and Mrs Sledmore bought a cottage in 1962. In 1965, Mr Dalby married their daughter and they moved into the cottage as tenants of the Sledmores. Rent was paid until 1976, when the daughter became seriously ill and Mr Dalby became unemployed. Between 1976 and 1979, Mr Dalby carried out extensive improvements to the house and was encouraged to do so by the Sledmores. Mrs Sledmore knew that her husband intended to leave the cottage to the couple and had told them of this intention. In 1979, Mr Sledmore transferred his interest in the cottage to his wife, who made a will to ensure that her daughter would inherit the cottage. In 1983, Mrs Dalby died and her husband continued to live in the cottage and refused to pay rent. In 1990, Mrs Sledmore sought possession of the cottage. At the time, Mr Dalby was employed and lived in the cottage on only a couple of nights a week, spending the rest of the time with his new partner. One of his daughters, who was twenty-seven and in employment, lived in the cottage. On the other hand, the house in which Mrs Sledmore lived was in need of repair. She was on income support and the interest on the mortgage on that house was being paid by the Department of Social Security. The Court of Appeal ordered possession.

It was clear that an equity had arisen in favour of Mr Dalby, but the view was taken that, although he had clearly assumed that he would be able to stay rent free in the cottage for the rest of his life, this was a case where he had to be satisfied with something less than that expectation.[208] A principal reason for awarding him nothing to satisfy the equity which had arisen was that he had already enjoyed considerable benefit in satisfaction of the equity, in that he had lived, rent free, in the property for a considerable number of years and so, in the circumstances, he had received sufficient satisfaction of the equity which had arisen in his favour.[209]

Although this decision has received a mixed reaction,[210] it seems to be correct in principle, in that, in deciding how the equity is to be satisfied, the court has a discretion to exercise. It can make an order which will result in the expectation being satisfied in full, but need not do so. Regard must be had to all the circumstances, including 'the subject-matter of the dispute, what was said and done by the parties and what has happened since'.[211] As has been seen, the conduct of the parties after the equity has arisen can be a material factor in how the court will satisfy any equity which has arisen;[212] and there seems to be no reason, in principle, why material changes to the circumstances of the parties pending resolution of the dispute should not also be considered relevant: 'equitable estoppel [by contrast with contract] . . . does not look forward into the future[; it] looks backwards from the moment when the promise falls due to be performed and asks whether in the circumstances which have actually happened, it would be unconscionable for the promise not to be kept'.[213] This retrospective can include a consideration of the changed circumstances of the parties.

14.6.7 **Proportionality**

An important factor which is relevant in the consideration of whether the satisfaction of an expectation in full is appropriate is whether to do so would, given the nature of both the expectation and the reliance, amount to something of a windfall to the claimant. This issue

---

[208] (1996) 72 P. & C.R. 196 at 204 *per* Roch L.J.

[209] Cf. *Campbell v. Griffin* [2001] EWCA Civ. 990 at [32]–[33] *per* Robert Walker L.J.

[210] It is supported by M. Pawlowski (1997) 113 L.Q.R. 232 at 236–7, but criticized by J.E. Adams [1996] Conv. 458.

[211] *Voyce v. Voyce* (1991) 62 P. & C.R. 290 at 296 *per* Nicholls L.J.

[212] *Crabb v. Arun District Council* [1976] Ch. 179. See 14.6.3.

[213] *Walton v. Walton* (14 April 1994, unreported), at [21] *per* Hoffmann L.J. cited in *Thorner v. Major* [2009] UKHL 18 at [101] *per* Lord Neuberger.

exercised the Court of Appeal in *Crabb v. Arun District Council*, and led to the initial view of the court being that the plaintiff's expectation should only be partially fulfilled; that is, he could have an easement, but only on the terms that he paid something for it. That he was held to be entitled to an easement without having to pay anything for it was a direct result of the obstructive behaviour of the defendant. The appreciation that to order satisfaction in full might lead to the overcompensation of the claimant has led the courts to consider only the partial fulfilment of the expectation either by effectively remodelling the understanding of the parties,[214] or simply by awarding less than the claimant expected.[215] The matter was fully ventilated in the leading case of *Jennings v. Rice*.[216]

Mr Jennings, and latterly his wife, did a lot of unpaid work for a Mrs Royle. That work progressively included some personal services. She made a number of promises to Mr Jennings to the effect that, one day, all this would be his. When she died, she had not left him anything in her will and he sued her estate. One issue which arose was what his expectation actually was. Her estate was worth in excess of £1.2 million, whereas the house and contents were valued at £435,000. At first instance neither expectation was fulfilled as the trial judge awarded him a payment of £200,000. He appealed, arguing that he was entitled to a larger award, but the Court of Appeal affirmed the original decision.

14.6.8 **Extent of reliance**

Central to the appeal was the argument that the normal role of estoppel is to satisfy, in full, the expectation of the claimant. In approaching this question Robert Walker L.J. expressed initial sympathy with the view that the courts should not exercise an unfettered discretion as to remedy, and that the starting point should be to fulfil the claimant's expectation.[217] He nevertheless upheld the original award. To do otherwise, on the facts of the present case, would be to run the risk of substantially overcompensating the claimant for the work he had done. He therefore concluded that the appropriate remedy was the £200,000 awarded by the trial judge, on the basis that this amounted to a rough approximation of the value of the work which had been done. The role of the court was to craft a remedy, which is 'the minimum equity to do justice to the plaintiff',[218] an approach which 'does not require the court to be constitutionally parsimonious, but . . . does implicitly recognise that the court must also do justice to the defendant'.[219]

The approach to be taken in satisfying the equity is to have regard to both the nature of the expectation and to the degree of reliance. Having done that:

There is a clear line of authority from at least *Crabb* to the present day which establishes that once the elements of proprietary estoppel are established an equity arises. The value of that equity will depend upon all the circumstances including the expectation and the detriment. The task of the court is to do justice. *The most essential requirement is that there must be proportionality between the expectation and the detriment.*[220]

---

[214] See *Morritt v. Wonham* [1993] N.P.C. 2, discussed by M.P. Thompson [1994] Conv. 233.

[215] See *Gillett v. Holt* [2001] Ch. 210 at 227 *per* Robert Walker L.J., commenting on *Taylor v. Dickens* [1998] 1 F.L.R. 806. See W. Swadling [1998] R.L.R. 220 at 221; M.P. Thompson [1998] Conv. 210 at 217. See also *Campbell v. Griffin* [2001] EWCA Civ. 990 (lump sum rather than a life interest awarded).

[216] [2003] 1 P. & C.R. 8; *Powell v. Benney* (2007) EWCA Civ. 1283. See M.P. Thompson [2004] Conv. 225; S. Gardner (2006) 115 L.Q.R. 438.

[217] [2003] 1 P. & C.R. 8 at para. 42, citing with approval articles by E. Cooke (1997) 17 L.S. 258 and S. Gardner (1999) 115 L.Q.R. 438.

[218] *Crabb v. Arun District Council* [1976] Ch. 179 at 198 *per* Scarman L.J.

[219] *Jennings v. Rice* [2003] 1 P. & C.R. 8 at [48].

[220] Ibid. at [36] *per* Aldous L.J. Emphasis supplied. See also *Malik v. Kalyan* [2010] EWCA Civ. 113 at [31] *per* Rimer L.J.; *Ashby v. Kilduff* [2010] EWHC 2034 (Ch) at [73]–[74] *per* Mr Bernard Livesey Q.C.

This is a principled approach, reflecting both the discretionary nature of the remedies available in estoppel cases, and the need to consider all aspects of the case when arriving at an appropriate remedy, a feature which will lead in many, albeit not all, cases to an order which seeks to compensate the claimant for the reliance.[221] Walker L.J. in *Jennings v. Rice* emphasized that,

> if the claimant's expectations are uncertain, or extravagant, or out of all proportion to the detriment which the claimant has suffered, the court can and should recognise that the claimant's equity should be satisfied in another (and generally more limited) way.[222]

It should be stressed that the courts do have, in estoppel cases, considerable flexibility in arriving at a just solution to a particular dispute. So, in *Henry v. Henry*,[223] where the claimant had lived rent-free for many years on property which he had been promised he would inherit, this benefit which he had enjoyed was a key criterion in awarding him only half of the property he had been assured he would receive. This, as well as the detriment he had suffered, were relevant in deciding the appropriate remedy.[224] In *Thompson v. Thompson*, the court awarded the entire expectation interest in the farm by giving the defendant mother a life interest with a gift over to the son on her death.[225] That was because, as per *Jennings v. Rice*, the assurance and reliance had a consensual character not far short of a contract, which meant that awarding the expectation interest was proportionate. *Davies v. Davies*[226] is a recent case on satisfying the equity raised by a proprietary estoppel claim. Eirian Davies had lived on her parents' farm for many years, working for low pay. The parents wanted the farm to stay in the family, but Eirian was their only child interested in taking it on. The various representations throughout the relationship led to an expectation, according to the judge at first instance, that she would inherit the farm. Owing to her detrimental reliance in working long hours without full payment for that type of job, and foregoing the opportunity to find a job where she would otherwise choose to work, Judge Jarman Q.C. in the High Court had awarded Eirian £1.3 million of a farm worth around £3.15 million (after capital gains tax). The sole issue for the Court of Appeal was whether that amount was correct; it was common ground that Eirian had succeeded in her claim based on proprietary estoppel, and that satisfaction of the equity should come in the form of monetary compensation, rather than the transfer of the farm itself.[227]

Lewison L.J. understood the approach to take as that laid out in *Jennings v. Rice* and *Henry v. Henry*, and in particular that 'there must be a proportionality between the remedy and the detriment which is its purpose to avoid'.[228] He noted the debate on what the essential aim of the broad discretion is, centring on two possibilities: either the aim of the discretion is to give effect to the claimant's expectation unless it is disproportionate to do so, or it is that the claimant's reliance interest should be protected, so that they are compensated for the detriment they have suffered.[229] Somewhat frustratingly, Lewison L.J. declined to decide which was the better of those two approaches.[230] Instead, he held that the

---

[221] See also *Murphy v. Burrows* [2004] EWHC 1400 (Ch) at [124] *per* Mr Richard Sheldon Q.C.

[222] [2002] EWCA Civ. 159 at [50].   [223] [2010] UKPC 3.

[224] See also *Clarke v. Meadus* [2010] EWHC 3117 (Ch) at [68] *per* Warren J.

[225] [2018] EWHC 1338 (Ch).

[226] [2016] EWCA Civ. 463; followed in *Moore v. Moore* [2016] EWHC 2202 (Ch).

[227] The press referred to Eirian Davies as the 'Cowshed Cinderella', and there was a good deal of media interest in the case. See, for example, http://www.dailymail.co.uk/news/article-3598987/Cowshed-Cinderella-won-1-3million-parents-stay-farm-sisters-want-dancing-payout-slashed-500-000.html

[228] [2016] EWCA Civ. 463 at [38].

[229] For the second argument, see particularly B. Mcfarlane and P. Sales (2015) 131 L.Q.R. 610; B. McFarlane, *The Law of Proprietary Estoppel* (Oxford, Oxford University Press, 2014), para. 7.37.

[230] Though he thought there was 'much to be said for the second approach': [2016] EWCA Civ. 463 at [39].

trial judge had 'applied far too broad a brush and failed to analyse the facts that he found with sufficient rigour'. Eirian's expectation, in Lewison L.J.'s view, was not clear, unambiguous, or consistent. Although expectation remained the 'starting point' as per *Jennings v. Rice*, this was found to be of little help where it is so uncertain: 'what is not entirely clear from [*Jennings*] is what the court is to do with the expectation even if it is only a starting point'.[231] The parents had offered £350,000 to cover Eirian's detrimental reliance, and Lewison L.J. essentially found that this covered the financial elements of Eirian's conduct based upon her uncertain expectation. How, then, had the trial judge bridged the gap between the parents' offer of £350,000 and the award of £1.3 million? Judge Jarman Q.C. had noted the parents' significant role in bringing Eirian's expectation to an end, but Lewison L.J. rightly pointed out that the promisor will always be the one to bring the expectation to an end: this is the very reason why the claim has come before a court, and 'there is no warrant (and no authority that we were shown) for increasing a monetary award on that account'.[232] Eirian may have had an expectation that she was to inherit the farm at some point, but not consistently and not 'at a high level'.[233] To ascribe a very large value to her disappointment that it did not materialize was, therefore, misconceived. Eirian's long hours of working on the farm, and the lack of freedom in the difficult working relationship with her parents, together with a much more modest payment for her disappointment, took her to a total award of £500,000 in the Court of Appeal's view, rather than £1.3 million.

One criticism of the judgment in *Davies v. Davies* is that it does not move the law forward, nor make the principle of proportionality any easier to apply. On any view, Eirian's expectation of inheriting the £3.5 million farm was out of proportion to the detriment she had suffered, and so her equity was rightly satisfied in a much more limited way (£500,000), as per *Jennings v. Rice*. The difficulty is that the trial judge had also followed that proportionality approach in awarding £1.3 million. Any award that was less than one half of the value of the farm, one might suggest, could have been defined as 'much more limited', and thus proportionate. Lewison L.J. did allude to the disadvantages of this broad discretion, admitting that the various factors were not capable of 'precise valuation', and so the court 'must do the best that we can'.[234] It is unfortunate that these issues in satisfying the equity will continue to occupy proprietary estoppel cases for the time being, as the Supreme Court refused permission to appeal in *Davies v. Davies*,[235] and subsequent cases bear that out. In *Gee v. Gee*, yet another recent proprietary estoppel claim involving a farm, Birss J. remarked that the general principles on quantifying the remedy are 'not always easy to apply'.[236] That remark is reinforced by the latest judgment from the Court of Appeal, again adjudicating in a family dispute over a farm, in *Moore v. Moore*.[237] There was no reason to impugn the trial judge's findings, according to Henderson L.J., that the son had established an equity by showing that he had detrimentally relied upon repeated assurances made by the father over many years that he was to give his share in the farm to his son, but more problematic was the satisfaction of the equity. The trial judge had attempted to replicate what might have happened if there had been no family dispute, rather than focussing on the minimum provision necessary to do justice to the son's equity.

---

[231] Ibid. at [41]. One hypothesis, offered by counsel for Eirian Davies, was that 'there might be a sliding scale by which the clearer the expectation, the greater the detriment and the longer the passage of time during which the expectation was reasonably held, the greater would be the weight that should be given to the expectation'. This seems logical, but not terribly helpful unless the sliding scale itself is given a standard unit of measurement. Otherwise, it simply seems another way of saying that the courts possess a broad discretion depending on the facts of the case.

[232] Ibid. at [62].   [233] Ibid. at [64].   [234] Ibid. at [67].

[235] See UKSC 2010/0129, 6 December 2016, refused by Lords Neuberger, Sumption, and Reed as the 'application does not raise an arguable point of law of general public importance'.

[236] [2018] EWHC 1393 (Ch) at [40].   [237] [2018] EWCA Civ. 2669.

Neither had there been sufficient consideration of the tax consequences of the order, nor was the order appropriate in the sense that it made the mother dependent upon the son for the rest of her life, when in fact a clean break from each other was needed. As such, the Court of Appeal was compelled to remit the case back for a further hearing on how the equity ought to be satisfied.

This is a rather depressing state of affairs, and arguably the law is not providing disputes of this nature with a coherent and efficient set of principles to resolve them. It is also clear that some judges simply disagree with an approach based upon compensating for the loss suffered. In *James v. James*, H.H.J. Matthews offered the view that, 'if A promises B some property right, intending B to rely on this, and B does rely on it to B's detriment, the natural impulse is (as with contract law) to require A to make good the expectation. Making the remedy proportionate to the detriment suffered would be to focus more on what B has lost, rather than on what B expected to obtain.'[238]

The effect of this uncertainty is the likelihood that claimants and defendants will use up a large amount of money in the litigation over the estate, because the remedy awarded at first instance is so easily appealable—nothing is certain or settled, because the margin of discretion is so broad, and the approach is not uniformly agreed upon or applied. This problem was alluded to by the Court of Appeal in *Moore v. Moore*:

> This is a case about proprietary estoppel. As so often, it involves a family farm, and a sad breakdown in relations between members of the family. Indeed the dispute has already been ruinous in both human and financial terms. We were told that the total costs so far incurred on both sides are estimated to be in the region of £2.5 million.[239]

14.6.9 Flexibility

The flexibility in awarding only partial fulfilment of a claimant's expectation is consistent with the flexible approaches to other, not unconnected, areas of law.[240] If a person has overpaid another and subsequently seeks restitution, then the person against whom that remedy is sought can rely upon the defence of change of position. This is a flexible defence and avoids the conclusion that, if a person has relied upon a representation that he is entitled to money which has wrongly been paid to him, the fact of reliance precludes restitution. Such a conclusion would allow the recipient of the money to retain an amount which he had been mistakenly paid, when his reliance did not equate to that overpayment,[241] a result which would result in unjust enrichment.[242] Similarly, when the reliance on an expectation is significantly less than the value of the expectation, the enforcement of the expectation in full may be an excessive response to the equity which has arisen so that, although seen by some as unprincipled,[243] it seems that the better view is that, once rights have arisen through proprietary estoppel, it is true to say that the courts have a very wide and flexible discretion as to how to satisfy the resultant equity.

---

[238] [2018] EWHC 43 (Ch) at [51]. See also *Smith-Tyrell v. Bowden* [2018] EWHC 106.

[239] Ibid. at [1].

[240] A point alluded to by Lewison L.J. in *Davies v. Davies* [2016] EWCA Civ. 463 at [67]: 'In different situations the court is often called upon to award compensation for non-pecuniary losses, and the difficulty of assessment is no bar to an award.'

[241] See *Avon County Council v. Howlett* [1983] 1 W.L.R. 605, a case of estoppel by representation at common law.

[242] See *Lipkin Gorman (A Firm) v. Karpnale Ltd* [1991] 2 A.C. 548 at 580 *per* Lord Goff of Chievely; *Scottish Equitable plc v. Derby* [2000] 3 All E.R. 793 at 804 *per* Harrison J., affirmed [2001] 3 All E.R. 818; *Philip Collins Ltd v. Davis* [2000] 3 All E.R. 808 at 826–40 *per* Jonathan Parker J. See M.P. Thompson [2000] Conv. 548.

[243] S. Gardner, 'The remedial discretion in proprietary estoppel – again' (2006) 122 L.Q.R. 492 at 463.

14.7 **Proprietary estoppel and constructive trusts**

In a previous chapter concerned with the acquisition of an interest in the home, the role of the constructive trust was considered.[244] The type of situation where such a trust is imposed occurs when a house is being acquired and the legal title is put into one person's name but, prior to this happening,[245] there is some sort of agreement that the beneficial ownership is to be shared. This agreement can be an actual agreement,[246] or one that is inferred from the fact that some pretext is given as to why the property is not being put into their joint names.[247] While such an agreement can be sufficient, where personal property is concerned, to create a trust,[248] it would be insufficient in the case of land because the formal requirements necessary to create such a trust have not been complied with.[249] If, however, relying on that agreement, the non-legal owner contributes to the acquisition of the house, it is fraudulent on the part of the holder of the legal title to plead the lack of writing and to claim sole beneficial entitlement. To prevent this, a constructive trust is imposed to give effect to that agreement.[250]

The underlying basis of the imposition of a constructive trust in this situation is the prevention of unjust enrichment. Were the legal owner to be allowed to use the lack of writing required by the statute to deny the existence of the trust, then he, having received the benefit of her contribution to the acquisition of the house, would be unjustly enriched at her expense. A constructive trust is duly imposed, which has the effect of enforcing the oral agreement between them.

More recent cases involving the imposition of a constructive trust have downplayed the aspect of unjust enrichment, and instead treated the issue to be decided as being whether the claimant has relied upon the agreement to share the beneficial ownership of the house. This has led to judicial statements to the effect that the role of the constructive trust and proprietary estoppel is the same.[251] Claimants are also increasingly testing their cases by arguing for either a constructive trust or proprietary estoppel on the same facts; *McGuinness v. Preece* is a recent example.[252]

While it is evident that there are similarities between the constructive trust and proprietary estoppel, they are separate doctrines and should not be regarded as a fused concept.[253] The constructive trust is predicated upon the basis that there is an agreement to share the beneficial ownership of property. While in an estoppel case, the expectation may be to acquire beneficial ownership of land, it may be to have some lesser right, such as a right of occupation.[254] In *Arif v. Anwar*,[255] the son had a belief that he would acquire some beneficial interest in the family home, as he had allowed money in his name to be used for

---

[244] See Chapter 9.

[245] In some cases, the agreement occurs after the house has been acquired by one of the parties. See *Austin v. Keele* (1987) 61 A.J.L.R. 605 at 609 *per* Lord Oliver.

[246] See *Re Densham* [1975] 1 W.L.R. 1519.

[247] See, e.g., *Eves v. Eves* [1975] 1 W.L.R. 1338; *Grant v. Edwards* [1986] Ch. 638.

[248] See *Paul v. Constance* [1977] 1 W.L.R. 527; *Rowe v. Prance* [1999] 2 F.L.R. 787, criticized by S. Baughen [2000] Conv. 58.

[249] LPA 1925, s. 53(1)(b). See *Lloyds Bank plc v. Rosset* [1991] A.C. 107 at 129 *per* Lord Bridge.

[250] See *Re Densham* [1975] 1 W.L.R. 1519. This line of authority derives from *Rochefoucauld v. Boustead* [1897] 1 Ch. 196.

[251] See *Grant v. Edwards* [1986] Ch. 638 at 656 *per* Sir Nicolas Browne-Wilkinson V.-C.; *Lloyds Bank plc v. Rosset* [1991] 1 A.C. 107 at 132 *per* Lord Bridge.

[252] [2016] EWHC 1518 (Ch).

[253] For an argument favouring fusion, see D. Hayton [1990] Conv. 370. For a different view, see P. Ferguson (1993) 109 L.Q.R. 114.

[254] See *Maharaj v. Chand* [1986] A.C. 898.   [255] [2015] EWHC 124 (Fam).

its purchase. No constructive trust arose because there was no agreement as to the precise extent of his entitlement, but a proprietary estoppel arose on the same facts, and Norris J. awarded the son 25 per cent of the beneficial interest.[256]

The expectation may also be to have a quite different type of right, such as an easement.[257] It is difficult on orthodox trust principles to see how the expectation of the acquisition of an easement can be achieved through the medium of a constructive trust. Third, the theoretical bases of the two doctrines are different. The rationale of the constructive trust is to prevent unjust enrichment; that of estoppel is to prevent unconscionability, which is a wider concept. In principle, to acquire an interest under a constructive trust the conduct must have contributed to the acquisition of the house in question, while reliance is a much wider concept. Finally, the role of the constructive trust is to give effect to the agreement reached. In estoppel cases, the court has a discretion as to how the equity which has arisen is to be satisfied, such remedy being tailored so as to meet the justice of the case. Part of that flexibility lies in the choice between awarding a proprietary remedy, as in *Thorner v. Major* where the farm was transferred to David, or a non-proprietary remedy in the form of compensation for the claimant, as in *Davies v. Davies*[258] and *Southwell v. Blackburn*.[259] So, while there are undeniable similarities between the two doctrines, it is preferable to see them as separate but related reactions by equity to the question of how interests in land can be acquired informally, a view endorsed in *Stack v. Dowden*.[260] This view that the doctrines remain conceptually distinct is underlined by recent cases that involve a 'subject to contract' agreement.

14.7.1 Subject to contract agreements: proprietary estoppel or constructive trusts?

Prior to the coming into force of s. 2, LP(MP)A 1989, it was commonplace when negotiations were in train for the sale of land for correspondence to be headed 'subject to contract'. There were two, related, reasons for this. The first was to prevent any correspondence from, itself, creating a contract. Thus, if A wrote to B offering to buy his house for £200,000 and B replied, accepting that offer, a contract would be created by this correspondence. If, however, the letters were headed 'subject to contract', this would indicate a lack of intention to create legal relations and no contract would be formed. A second scenario could also occur. In this scenario, C orally agreed with D to buy his land for £200,000. This, under the old law, would amount to a valid, albeit unenforceable, contract. To make that contract enforceable, a written memorandum of it was necessary.[261] Such a memorandum could be produced inadvertently, with correspondence making reference to the previously created oral contract itself constituting such a memorandum, thereby making that contract enforceable. This may have been unwelcome to the parties, particularly if a chain of transactions were involved, in that they may have become mutually bound by the contract before they actually wished to be. To avoid this happening, prior to the formal exchange of

---

[256] In *Southwell v. Blackburn* [2014] EWCA Civ. 1347, the claimant similarly succeeded in a proprietary estoppel argument even though she failed to show a common intention constructive trust, but there the Court of Appeal satisfied the equity with the award of compensation, rather than a beneficial interest in the home.

[257] See *Crabb v. Arun District Council* [1976] Ch. 179; *Joyce v. Epson and Ewell BC* [2012] EWCA Civ. 1398.

[258] [2016] EWCA Civ. 463. See 14.6.8.   [259] [2014] EWCA Civ. 1347.

[260] [2007] A.C. 432 at [35] *per* Lord Walker, recanting his earlier views in *Yaxley v. Gotts* [2000] 1 All E.R. 711 at 721–2. See also *Q. v. Q.* [2008] EWHC 1879 (Ch) at [113] *per* Black J. Contrast *Thorner v. Major* [2009] UKHL 18 at [20] *per* Lord Scott, who is advocating a new, remedial, constructive trust rather than the more conventional model referred to here.

[261] See 14.2.

contracts, it was normal practice for correspondence relating to an informal agreement to be headed 'subject to contract'.

Although the effect of expressing correspondence in preventing a memorandum of a contract from being created became a matter of some controversy,[262] it was very clear that the intention of the parties when using the formula 'subject to contract' was to avoid binding obligations with respect to the land being created. Given this context, while it is possible that a 'subject to contract' reservation can be withdrawn, either expressly or by inference from conduct,[263] it is nevertheless very difficult to persuade the courts that reliance on an expectation of gaining rights which were still the subject of negotiation could create estoppel rights.[264] It would be known to the parties that the expenditure of money or other acts of reliance, on the expectation that a binding contract will be created, carries with it an element of risk, and this is particularly the case where they are both experienced practitioners in the property market, and are both aware that either side is free to withdraw from the putative transaction.[265] Cases occurring in the present context are very fact-sensitive,[266] and the essential element is that the parties consider themselves to be creating binding obligations.[267] In a commercial context, where solicitors are involved, and it is envisaged that a formal contract will be drawn up, it will be very difficult to establish any rights arising from estoppel. In a less commercial context, it may be easier to do this.[268]

A good illustration of the usual position is provided by *James v. Evans*.[269] H entered negotiations with E for the latter to take a ten-year lease of a hill farm. A draft agreement, with one or two matters outstanding, was arrived at. All the correspondence between them was headed 'subject to contract'. E was, however, allowed into possession of the farm to take care of the flock of sheep. When final agreement had been reached, E's solicitor sent E's part of the agreement, duly signed, together with a cheque, to H's solicitor. H, however, had become seriously ill and nobody had authority to manage his affairs and so this cheque, which included payment in respect of the rent, was not accepted. H died shortly afterwards and his sister, J, as administratrix of his estate, then instituted possession proceedings and the Court of Appeal upheld a summary judgment in her favour. E's argument based upon *Yaxley v. Gotts* was regarded as untenable.

The conduct relied upon to create rights in equity were the acts of taking possession,[270] looking after the sheep, and paying half of the price of their valuation. This was rejected. Fundamental to the decision was that, as the negotiations were 'subject to contract', E could not acquire rights by estoppel because, first, he knew that the effect of this expression was

---

[262] Contrast *Law v. Jones* [1974] Ch. 112 with *Tiverton Estates Ltd v. Wearwell* [1975] Ch. 146. See, generally, Barnsley, *Conveyancing Law and Practice* (3rd edn) (London, Butterworths, 1988), 130–1.

[263] *Yeoman's Row Management Ltd v. Cobbe* [2008] UKHL 1139 at [27] *per* Lord Scott. The better view now is that any such withdrawal should now be in writing: see *Taylor v. Burton* [2015] EWCA Civ. 142 at [35] *per* Sir Colin Rimer.

[264] See *Attorney-General for Hong Kong v. Humphreys Estates (Queen's Gardens) Ltd* [1987] A.C. 114; *Regalian Properties Ltd v. London Docklands Development Corporation* [1995] 1 W.L.R. 212. Cf. *Salvation Army Trustee Co. Ltd v. West Yorkshire County Council* (1980) 41 P. & C.R. 179 where, on unusual facts, such a claim succeeded.

[265] See *Yeoman's Row Management Ltd v. Cobbe, supra*, at [93] *per* Lord Walker.

[266] See *Whittaker v. Kinnear* [2011] EWHC 1479 (QB) at [36] *per* Bean J.

[267] See *Herbert v. Doyle* [2010] EWCA Civ. 1095 at [17] *per* Arden L.J.

[268] See the comments in *Thorner v. Major* [2009] 3 All E.R. 945 at [90]–[97] *per* Lord Neuberger and in *Ely v. Robson* [2016] EWCA Civ. 774 at [41] *per* Kitchen L.J.

[269] [2000] 1 E.G.L.R. 1, although for criticism, see L. McMurry [2001] Conv. 86.

[270] In the old law of part performance, the taking of possession was always regarded as a good act: see Megarry and Wade, *The Law of Real Property* (5th edn) (London, Stevens, 1984), 594–5.

to prevent the creation of legal rights and, second, what he relied on was a normal part of the purchase of a hill farm.

The importance of the expression 'subject to contract' as a means of preventing an argument based upon estoppel has, subsequently, been stressed.[271] The rationale for this was explained as being that:

> proprietary estoppel and constructive trust must require: (a) detrimental reliance; and (b) unconscionable conduct. Since the parties must be taken to know that a party who has agreed terms subject to contract is free to withdraw, there can be no question of reliance (*particularly by a commercial enterprise involved in property transactions*) or of unconscionable conduct.[272]

As the italicized part of this judgment indicated, it is not impossible that a person may rely on a 'subject to contract' agreement as being enforceable and so the protection provided by the term may not be absolute.[273] This was confirmed in the important decision in *Matchmove Ltd v. Dowding*.[274] An oral agreement was entered into between two erstwhile friends for the sale of a building plot (Plot 1) and a 10-acre meadow. Subsequently, a written contract was entered into with regard to Plot 1 but this did not happen with the meadow. There was in existence a good deal of legal documentation, this being under the rubric, 'subject to contract.' The total purchase price for the two properties was £200,000: £120,000 for Plot 1, the balance for the meadow. At the time of the agreement the vendor did not actually own the land in question, which he needed to purchase from a third party. The purchaser, who considered the agreements to buy the two properties as being part of a composite whole, paid £66,000 as a deposit, which enabled his vendor to buy the land. In anticipation of moving to the new property, he put his own house on the market and moved some of his family into a caravan. He also helped in the obtaining of planning permission to build on Plot 1 and he was given permission to do so. He also contributed to the resolution of a dispute over a right of way. The contract for the sale of Plot 1 was completed but, after a cheque for £80,000 was tendered, the vendor declined to accept it. He was now only prepared to transfer half of the meadow for the sum of £40,000. The Court of Appeal upheld the finding of the trial judge that the vendor held the property on constructive trust for the purchaser, presumably, although this is not specifically mentioned, in return for the agreed purchase price.

Two important points emerge from this case. The first concerns the term 'subject to contract'. Although the parties in this case were both businessmen, each of them operated on the basis that their word was their bond. Consequently, as found at the trial, both parties regarded the original, oral, agreement as being legally binding. Second, despite the Court of Appeal preferring to view the case as one of constructive trust, the finding is not really at odds with that of the trial judge that this was a case of estoppel. The basis of the decision was that this was an oral agreement which both sides considered to be legally binding and had been substantially performed by the putative purchaser, who had also performed other acts relying on the enforceability of that contract. In such circumstances the decision seems to be eminently justified.

---

[271] *Edwin Shirley Productions Ltd v. Workspace Management Ltd* [2001] 2 E.G.L.R. 16; *Taylor v. Inntrepreneur Estates (C.P.L.) Ltd* (2001) 82 P. & C.R.D. 9.

[272] *Edwin Shirley Productions Ltd v. Workspace Management Ltd*, *supra*, at 22 *per* Lawrence Collins J. Emphasis supplied.

[273] See the comments in *Secretary of State for Transport v. Christos* [2003] EWCA Civ. 1073 at [34] *per* Lindsay J.

[274] [2016] EWCA Civ. 1233. See also *Saunders v. Himaly* [2017] EWHC 2219 (Ch).

14.8 Estoppel and third parties

If A has, through the medium of estoppel, acquired an equity against B, will that equity be binding on a purchaser of B's land?[275] When an equity has arisen, it is at the court's discretion as to how that equity should be satisfied. It is also the case that, until a decision is made as to how that equity is to be satisfied, the equity is inchoate in nature. How the discretion is exercised may then be affected by events occurring after the equity has arisen; indeed, in some situations, the circumstances may be such at the time of the trial that a decision not to afford any remedy at all might be seen to be the most appropriate outcome to the dispute.[276] Because the equity is uncertain in scope, this has led some to argue that rights arising from estoppel are not capable of being proprietary in nature.[277]

In cases of proprietary estoppel, the claim that is made is normally to be entitled to an interest in land and such claims are frequently vindicated. As such, the status of the claim seems to amount to more than a mere equity such as the deserted wife's equity, if such a claim could properly be described as an equity at all.[278] Certainly, there are a number of authorities where the courts have accepted that an estoppel claim is binding upon third parties. Thus, where property has been bought for value, and the purchaser has actual notice of the estoppel right, the courts have been quite prepared to hold him to be bound by that right.[279] Similarly, in cases where the person against whom the claim is made is not a purchaser for value at all, the courts have been fully prepared to enforce the claim against that person.[280] Cases such as these have led to the view being expressed in *Lloyds Bank plc v. Carrick*[281] that, at least so far as the Court of Appeal was concerned, the matter was settled that an estoppel interest gave rise to an interest in land. On the other hand, the view was expressed by Peter Gibson L.J. in *United Bank of Kuwait plc v. Sahib*,[282] that estoppel would only affect a purchaser for value who had, himself, acted unconscionably. The matter is not, therefore, as clear as it might be.

The weight of authority would seem to suggest that there are circumstances when an equity which has arisen can adversely affect a third party[283] but that the circumstance surrounding the acquisition of the property by the purchaser may be a relevant factor in the resolution of the dispute.

14.8.1 Unregistered land

Where title is unregistered, the first issue to determine is whether the claimant has a right which is capable of affecting a purchaser and, if so, the circumstances when he will be bound by it. The final issue which should then be considered is, if the purchaser is bound, what is the appropriate remedy to be granted?

---

[275] See S. Baughen (1994) 14 L.S. 147; B. McFarlane [2003] C.L.J. 661.

[276] See *Sledmore v. Dalby* (1996) 72 P. & C.R. 196.

[277] See T. Bailey [1983] Conv. 99 at 100; S. Bright in Bright and Dewar (eds), *Land Law: Themes and Perspectives* (Oxford, Oxford University Press, 1998), 529 at 544.

[278] See *National Provincial Bank Ltd v. Ainsworth* [1965] A.C. 1175.

[279] See *E.R. Ives Investment Ltd v. High* [1967] 2 Q.B. 379; *Williams v. Staite* [1979] Ch. 291.

[280] See *Inwards v. Baker* [1965] 2 Q.B. 29; *Voyce v. Voyce* (1991) 62 P. & C.R. 290, especially at 294 *per* Dillon L.J. See also *Errington v. Errington* [1952] 1 K.B. 290.

[281] [1996] 4 All E.R. 630 at 642 *per* Morritt L.J.

[282] [1997] Ch. 107 at 142. Interestingly, Peter Gibson L.J. sat in *Carrick* and agreed with the judgment of Morritt L.J. For a valuable discussion, see P. Critchley [1998] Conv. 502.

[283] See also G. Battersby in Bright and Dewar, *Land Law: Themes and Perspectives*, 487 at 504–5.

In *E.R. Ives Investment Ltd v. High*,[284] the defendant, Mr High, and his neighbour, Mr Westgate, agreed that, in return for Mr Westgate being allowed to keep the foundations of a building encroaching on the defendant's land, Mr High should have a right of way over Mr Westgate's land. This agreement created an equitable easement and, when Mr Westgate sold his land to the Wrights, this equitable easement became void for non-registration. Neither the Wrights nor Mr High were aware of this and Mr High, believing he had a right of way over the Wrights' land, did various acts in circumstances in which, had a dispute then arisen, it would have been unconscionable for the Wrights to have denied some effect to his expectation of having a right of way. The Wrights then sold the land to the plaintiff, the conveyance stating that the land was sold subject to the defendant's right of way. The plaintiff, arguing that the right of way was void for non-registration, sought an injunction to restrain the defendant from using the claimed right.

The injunction was refused for two reasons. First, as the foundations remained on the defendant's land, under the principle of benefit and burden,[285] the plaintiff could not continue to retain the benefit of having his building encroach on the defendant's land without taking subject to the corresponding burden. Second, however, the Court of Appeal held that the plaintiff took the land subject to the defendant's equity which had arisen through estoppel. It was held that this equity was binding upon successors in title[286] and was not registrable as a land charge.[287] Whether the purchaser was bound depended, therefore, upon notice and, obviously, on the facts, the plaintiff had express notice of the equity.

This was a case where the plaintiff had the clearest notice of the defendant's equity. To explain the case in the terms used by Peter Gibson L.J., that the equity was enforceable because the plaintiff had behaved unconscionably is, however, unsatisfactory because the defendant had not relied in any way upon the plaintiff's behaviour. No new equity arose after the plaintiff had acquired the land. He must, therefore, have been bound by the equity which had arisen previously. The case is, therefore, clear authority that the equity which arises through estoppel is capable of binding a purchaser. Whether or not he is bound by it should depend, therefore, on the application of the orthodox principles of notice.

14.8.1.1 Position of the purchaser

That, however, does not conclude the matter. As in all estoppel cases, once it is clear that the claimant has an equity, the question remains as to how that equity should be satisfied and it is in determining this matter that it is suggested that the circumstances surrounding the acquisition of the land become relevant. How the equity is to be satisfied is a matter for the discretion of the court and, in determining this issue, regard can be had to any relevant factors from the date when the equity arose to the time when the question as to how that equity is to be satisfied is to be answered. The fact that the relevant property has changed hands, so that the equity is being claimed against someone other than the person who was privy to its creation, would seem to be a relevant factor, as would the capacity of the purchaser and the state of his mind when he acquired the property. On this basis, it is argued that, if the purchaser has not given value, or has actual notice of the equity, then it is reasonable to satisfy the equity in the same way as it would have been had the purchase not taken place. Where, however, a purchaser for value has only constructive notice of the equity, he would still, on principle, be bound by the equity but the remedy afforded to the claimant may not be as extensive as would be the case if he had had actual notice of the right.[288]

---

[284] [1967] 2 Q.B. 379.   [285] See 13.8.6.   [286] [1967] 2 Q.B. 379 at 394 *per* Lord Denning M.R.
[287] Ibid. at 405 *per* Winn L.J.
[288] See the comments in *Re Sharpe* [1980] 1 W.L.R. 219 at 226 *per* Browne-Wilkinson L.J.

14.8.2 **Registered land**

Where title is registered, the position has now been partially clarified by s. 116, LRA 2002. This section declares that, for the avoidance of doubt, an equity by estoppel has effect from the time the equity arises as an interest capable of binding successors in title (subject to the rules about the effect of dispositions on priority). Plainly, therefore, it is the case that a purchaser of registered land can be affected by an equity arising from estoppel, although the questions will remain as to the circumstances in which he will be bound and as to how the equity which has arisen will be satisfied. Before considering this, the point can also be made that, although this section applies only to registered land, it would seem to be inevitable that a court would now hold that, when title is unregistered, an equity arising from estoppel will have proprietary effect.

For an equity arising from estoppel to bind a purchaser, it will be necessary that it is either protected by the registration of a notice or that it takes effect as an interest which overrides a registered disposition. Given that estoppel rights arise in informal situations, the prospect of the holder of such a right protecting it by registration is remote. If it is to bind a purchaser, therefore, it will be on the basis that the holder of the right is in actual occupation of the land, within the meaning of para. 2 of Sched. 3 to the LRA 2002. If the purchaser is bound by the equity on this basis, the question will still remain as to how it should be satisfied and, again, the state of mind of the purchaser when the land was acquired would appear to be relevant. This was explicitly recognized by the Privy Council in *Henry v. Henry*,[289] where Sir Jonathan Parker said:

> The Board does not rule out the possibility that cases may arise in which the particular circumstances surrounding a third party purchase may, notwithstanding the claimant's overriding interest, require the court to reassess the extent of the claimant's equity in the property.

Given that the court has a discretion as to how any equity that has arisen should be satisfied and, as the fact that the person against whom the equity is to be enforced was not a party to its creation, this seems clearly to be correct. As, however, to be an interest overriding a registered disposition, the occupation has to be obvious on a reasonably careful inspection of the land,[290] it may well be the case that the equity will be satisfied in the same way as it would have been against the person who was privy to its creation. Even if that is the case, however, if the transfer has been made by two legal owners, and the right claimed under estoppel is to a beneficial interest in the property, then, in principle, the estoppel right should not be binding on the transferee. This is because, if there had been in existence a beneficial interest under a trust, a transfer by two legal owners would overreach that right.[291] It would be a quite remarkable result if a full beneficial interest under a trust would be overreached in such circumstances, whereas the more precarious equity arising from estoppel would not be.[292]

---

[289] [2010] UKPC 3 at [56].   [290] LRA 2002, Sched. 3, para. 2(c).

[291] *City of London Building Society v. Flegg* [1988] A.C. 54.

[292] See *Birmingham Midshires Mortgages Ltd v. Suberwal* (2000) 80 P. & C.R. 256 at 262 *per* Robert Walker L.J. Cf. *Campbell v. Griffin* [2001] EWCA Civ. 990 at [37], *per* Robert Walker L.J., where this point was overlooked. See M.P. Thompson [2003] Conv. 157 at 165–7.

15

Licences

During the twentieth century, there was considerable judicial activity in the law relating to licences, how rights in land can be created, and the circumstances in which such rights can affect purchasers of land. Licences have long occupied something of an amorphous position; they are not admitted to the category of full proprietary rights, but provide an interesting area where the law seeks to afford protection to licensees against both the licensor and, in certain circumstances, a purchaser of land. It is an area of law where the courts have had to come to terms with informal relationships and seek to accommodate the conflicting pressures of the satisfaction of legitimate expectations, on the one hand, and the desire for security of transactions on the other.

15.1 The nature of licences

To date, the concept of a licence has been encountered mainly as an alternative to a lease. This concerns an occupancy right where, because the rights given by the agreement do not fulfil the necessary criteria requisite to the creation of a lease, the law considers that the occupier is not a tenant. This is not, however, the only context in which licences can be encountered. While a licence can be occupational in nature, this is not necessarily the case. Another type of licence can involve a person, the licensee, being given a right of access to another's land. Such a right can entail the creation of what is accepted to be a fully fledged proprietary right: an easement. If it does not, then it will be a licence. In this type of situation, two essential questions arise. The first relates to the position as between the licensor and the licensee. The second concerns what, if any, rights the licensee has against a purchaser of the land. In considering both issues, much will depend upon how the licence was created.

Typically, but not inevitably, a licence involves a relationship between two people which does not, for some reason, qualify as an orthodox interest in property. For this reason, the starting point in a consideration of the nature of licences is the statement of principle made in *Thomas v. Sorrell*[1] in 1673 that, '[a] dispensation or licence properly passes no interest nor alters or transfers property in anything, but only makes an action lawful, without which it would have been unlawful'.

This statement is now no longer totally accurate but serves as a useful starting point in a consideration of licences. The essential nature of a licence is that it is a personal permission given by the licensor to another person, the licensee, to use the licensor's land in some way. What is done is lawful because permission has been given to do it; were that not the case, the act in question would amount to trespass. What becomes important is the source of that permission, this being the principal means of classifying the different types of licence. Licences fall into one of four essential categories,[2] each of which must be

---

[1] (1673) Vaugh. 330 at 351 *per* Vaughan C.J.

[2] For a classification into eight groups, see Dawson and Pearce, *Licences Relating to the Occupation or Use of Land* (London, Butterworths, 1979), 21–49.

considered in turn. There are two fundamental issues which must be considered in each case: first, the effect of the licence as between the original licensor and licensee. Second, the effect of that licence upon a successor in title to the licensor.

15.1.1 Bare licences

A bare licence is a licence to occupy or use land which is given without consideration. These licences are extremely common and would include social invitations, such as an invitation given to friends to come round for dinner, or when a householder tells one of her neighbours' children that they need not ask for permission to retrieve a football every time it is kicked over the garden fence—they can simply let themselves in and get it.

As no consideration has been given, these licences can be revoked by the licensor. If the dinner guests cause offence, they can be asked to leave. If the householder tires of the children repeatedly entering the garden to retrieve errant footballs, the permission can be withdrawn. The only remaining question is how much time the licensee is to be given to leave the property. The test is one of reasonableness[3] and this will depend upon the facts surrounding the licence. In the case of dinner guests who have outstayed their welcome, a reasonable time will be short. In the case of a long-time cohabitee who, on the termination of a relationship, is found to have no interest in the house in which she lived and whose status is, therefore, that of a gratuitous licensee,[4] then a reasonable period in order to find alternative accommodation could be a number of weeks.[5]

Because it is always open to the licensor to revoke a gratuitous licence, then it must be the case that a successor in title to the licensee cannot be in any worse position than the person from whom he derives title. It follows that just as the licensor could have revoked a gratuitous licence, so can a purchaser from him.

15.1.2 Licence coupled with a grant

A person may possess a right to take and carry away from another's land some natural resource, such as game, minerals, wood, or fish.[6] This property right is known as a *profit à prendre*, and to exercise the right it is implicit that the holder of it must be able to go onto the other person's land. This does not mean that the licence itself is proprietary in nature; instead, it is parasitic upon the primary property right—the *profit à prendre*. It will only last for as long as the *profit* lasts, and will only enable the holder of the right to enter the land for the specific purpose that the grant allows. The licence is, however, inextricably linked to the property right in question, and consequently will be irrevocable and bind purchasers to the same extent as the *profit* that it is coupled with.

15.1.3 Contractual licences

Contractual licences to use another person's land are extremely common. As their name suggests, they are licences given for consideration. Common examples include when a person buys a ticket to go to the theatre or to the cinema, or books a room in a hotel.

---

[3] See *Greater London Council v. Jenkins* [1975] 1 All E.R. 354 at 357 *per* Lord Diplock. For a detailed discussion, see J. Hill [2001] C.L.J. 89.

[4] See, e.g., *Burns v. Burns* [1984] Ch. 317

[5] In the unusual but instructive case of *Macclesfield v. Parker* [2003] EWHC 1846 (Ch) a reasonable period was held to be two years. See M.P. Thompson [2003] Conv. 516.

[6] See, e.g., *Frogley v. Earl of Lovelace* (1859) Johns. 333.

Because of the degree of control exercised by the owner of the hotel, the guest does not have exclusive possession and is termed a lodger,[7] or licensee.

Contractual licences apply in situations where the relationship is commercial in nature. At one time, there was an attempt made by the courts to fit domestic arrangements into a contractual analysis. In *Tanner v. Tanner*,[8] a married man formed a relationship with another woman, who adopted his name. After she gave birth to twins, he bought a house for her to live in. She did not contribute to the purchase of the house but she did put some £150 towards furnishing it. When the relationship broke down, the Court of Appeal felt able to imply a contractual licence whereby she was to be permitted to live in the house until the children had come of age. As she had, at the time of the hearing, moved into alternative accommodation, she was awarded £2,000 damages for breach of contract.

The obvious difficulty with this analysis is that it is hard to see the normal constituents of a contract—offer, acceptance, and consideration—being present. In the factually similar case of *Horrocks v. Foray*,[9] no contract was found to exist. Megaw L.J. stressed the need for the court to be able to find the normal consensus and consideration necessary in the general law of contract[10] and, on the facts, found that not to be the case. *Tanner v. Tanner* was distinguished but it seemed clear that there was little judicial enthusiasm to try to apply a contractual analysis to informal, family relationships. It is now uncontroversial that such cases are grounded in some other part of the law.[11]

15.1.4 **Estoppel licences**

The doctrine of proprietary estoppel is fully discussed in Chapter 14, for now it suffices to say that its principal role is to enable rights to be acquired in another person's land. The underlying ethos of the doctrine is that one person, A, acts in the expectation that he either already has rights in the land of another person, B, or that he will obtain such rights in the future. A will obtain rights in equity if he has relied upon that expectation to his detriment, in circumstances when it would be unconscionable for B to deny some effect to that expectation.[12] It is then a matter for the court, in the exercise of its discretion, to determine what remedy is most appropriate to satisfy the estoppel equity that has been created in A's favour. Sometimes the court will award a licence as satisfaction, and that is known as an estoppel licence. It is important to emphasize that the rights and duties in the licence exist as a result of a successful claim in proprietary estoppel, rather than any form of contract between A and B.

15.2 **Contractual licences: the licensee's rights**

Having sketched the general nature of the different types of licence, one can now consider more closely the rights which the licensee obtains and the circumstances in which those rights may bind a successor in title to the licensor.

---

[7] *Street v. Mountford* [1985] A.C. 809 at 818 *per* Lord Templeman.

[8] [1975] 1 All E.R. 776. See also *Chandler v. Kerley* [1978] 1 W.L.R. 693, but cf. *Hardwick v. Johnson* [1978] 1 W.L.R. 683.

[9] [1976] 1 All E.R. 737, described as '*Tanner v. Tanner* in a middle-class setting': M. Richards (1976) 40 Conv. (N.S.) 351 at 364.

[10] [1976] 1 All E.R. 737 at 742.

[11] Most obviously, constructive trusts (see Chapter 9) and proprietary estoppel (see Chapter 14).

[12] See *Taylors Fashions Ltd v. Liverpool Victoria Trustees Co. Ltd* [1982] Q.B. 133n at 154–5 *per* Oliver J.

15.2.1 **The revocability of licences**

The question whether it is open to a licensor to revoke a contractual licence has met, at different periods of time, with rather different responses. The approach of the common law was robust and straightforward. In *Wood v. Leadbitter*,[13] the plaintiff had bought a ticket to attend Doncaster races. On the instruction of the stewards, he was evicted with no more force than was necessary. He then brought an action for assault, but it failed because it was held that, as the licence was not an interest in land, it was always open to a licensor to revoke a licence. The effect of such a revocation was that the licensee became a trespasser and it was then open to the licensor to use such force as was reasonable to evict the licensee from his land.

A rather different approach was taken in *Hurst v. Picture Theatres Ltd.*[14] The plaintiff had bought a ticket to watch a film and, because it was thought, wrongly, that he had not paid for admission, he was forcibly evicted. He brought an action for damages, the basis of his claim being assault. On this occasion, the majority of the Court of Appeal held in his favour, for two reasons. The first was that the licence in question was a licence coupled with a grant, the grant in question being the right to watch the performance. This is manifestly wrong. As was pointed out in *Cowell v. Rosehill Racecourse Co. Ltd*, '[f]ifty thousand people who pay to see a football match do not obtain fifty thousand interests in the football ground'.[15] No property right is created, the reason being that the transaction of buying a ticket for an entertainment does not create anything other than a contractual right in the buyer against the seller.[16] It is, however, the nature of that contractual right which is central to the question as to whether the licence can be revoked.

15.2.1.1 **The intervention of equity**

The second reason for the decision in *Hurst*, and this reason did have a lasting influence on the development of the law, was the intervention of equity. *Wood v. Leadbitter* was seen as a case decided entirely at common law. Since the passing of the Judicature Acts 1873 and 1875, the court should have regard to equity as well as law. The view was taken that equity would have granted an injunction to restrain the defendant from breaching his contract with the plaintiff. Because equity would have done this, it followed that the eviction in breach of contract was unlawful and, consequently, the use of force to evict the plaintiff was wrongful, with the result that damages were payable. The fact that an injunction had not actually been obtained was immaterial. Were the position otherwise, a person could improve his position by acting wrongfully and this is not correct.[17]

This reason for the decision proved to be influential. In *Millennium Productions Ltd v. Winter Garden Theatre (London) Ltd*,[18] the owners of a theatre purported to revoke a licence given to the plaintiffs to use it. The Court of Appeal granted an injunction restraining this action. Lord Greene M.R. held that there was an implied term of the contract that it would not be revoked and, to restrain a breach of contract, granted an injunction. The House of Lords[19] reversed this decision on the basis that, on the proper construction of the contract, no such term precluding revocation of the licence should be implied. If, however, the proper construction of the contract had been that it was not to be revoked, then it was considered that injunctive relief would have been appropriate. The House of Lords considered that the propositions of law stated by Lord Greene were clearly correct and, indeed, unanswerable;[20] the decision of the Court of Appeal was reversed simply because

---

[13] (1835) 13 M. & W. 838.
[14] [1915] 1 K.B. 1. For strong contemporary criticism, see J.C. Miles (1915) 31 L.Q.R. 217.
[15] *Cowell v. Rosehill Racecourse Co. Ltd* (1937) 56 C.L.R. 605 at 616 *per* Latham C.J.
[16] Ibid. at 617.   [17] Ibid. at 651 *per* Evatt J. (dissenting).
[18] [1946] 1 All E.R. 678 at 685.   [19] [1948] A.C. 173.   [20] Ibid. at 202 *per* Lord Uthwatt.

the House of Lords disagreed with how those propositions had been applied to the facts of the case.

15.2.1.2 Construction of the contract

The House of Lords accepted the proposition that, depending upon the proper construction of the contract, a contractual licence may be irrevocable. Unfortunately, an earlier Court of Appeal decision to the contrary, although cited in argument, was not referred to in the speeches. In *Thompson v. Park*,[21] a schoolmaster had entered into a contract, whereby he was permitted to share a school building with the plaintiff, who was the licensor. After a disagreement, the defendant was evicted and he responded by effecting a forcible re-entry, the manner of that entry, according to Goddard L.J., having the effect that he would have been 'guilty at least of riot, affray, wilful damage, forcible entry, and, perhaps, conspiracy'.[22] The plaintiff was then granted an injunction requiring the defendant to vacate the property.

In holding for the plaintiff, two reasons were given. One was that, given the egregious conduct of the defendant, and the impossibility of making an order which would require two people who were clearly at loggerheads with each other to share the same premises, it would be wrong to grant the defendant equitable relief. This reasoning is uncontroversial and, as an exercise of the judicial discretion inherent in the award of any equitable remedy, manifestly correct. What was more controversial was the reiteration of the rule laid down in *Wood v. Leadbitter*, that it is always open to a licensor to revoke a contractual licence, even in circumstances where such a revocation would amount to a breach of contract.

One of the grounds of the decision in *Thompson v. Park* is therefore inconsistent with later dicta in the House of Lords in the *Winter Gardens* case. This inconsistency occasioned Megarry J. some discomfort in *Hounslow London Borough Council v. Twickenham Garden Developments Ltd*,[23] where the issue of the revocability of a contractual licence arose again. After an extensive review of the authorities, he decided to follow the dicta in *Winter Gardens* and held that the decision as to whether or not a contractual licence can be revoked depends upon the construction of the contract and, as a matter of construction, some such licences are irrevocable.

15.2.1.3 Irrevocable licences

This analysis was followed by the Court of Appeal in *Verrall v. Great Yarmouth Borough Council*.[24] The council, when under the control of the Conservative Party, entered into a contract to allow the National Front to hold its annual conference in the town's conference hall, the period of the hire being two days. After the election, control of the council passed to the Labour Party, who refused to allow the National Front to hold its conference there. It was conceded that this would amount to a breach of contract but the council argued that the plaintiff should be left to a remedy in damages, that it was always possible for a licensor, albeit wrongly, to revoke a licence. Specific performance was ordered because damages would not have been an adequate remedy.

The argument was put, based upon *Thompson v. Park*, that a licensor could always effectively, even if unlawfully, revoke a contract. It was held that that decision could not stand with the dicta of the House of Lords in *Winter Gardens* and could no longer be regarded as good law. Certain contractual licences cannot be revoked and, in appropriate cases, may be enforced by a decree of specific performance. Such an order will not, of course, be appropriate in all cases; damages must be an inadequate remedy. In *Verrall*, the National Front would not, had the council been allowed to revoke the licence, have been able to hold their

---

[21] [1944] K.B. 408.   [22] Ibid. at 409.   [23] [1971] Ch. 233.   [24] [1981] Q.B. 202.

conference anywhere, which meant that damages would not have provided them with adequate compensation. Whether or not a contractual licence can be revoked will therefore depend upon the proper construction of the contract. Some such licences may be irrevocable;[25] others revocable only upon the giving of a substantial period of notice.[26]

Although none of these authorities were referred to in the Supreme Court decision in *Berrisford v. Mexfield Housing Co-operative Ltd*,[27] the conclusion reached in that case is entirely consistent with the view taken in *Verrall*. In *Berrisford*, the occupier had been granted a periodic occupancy agreement. Under the terms of that agreement, the freeholder could only terminate the agreement on certain, limited, grounds. Although the Supreme Court held that a valid lease had been created, consideration was also given as to what the position would have been had that not been the case. According to Lord Clarke:

> It follows that . . . even if the contract does not create a tenancy, it creates rights and obligations between the parties, so that in an appropriate case Ms Berrisford could in principle gain an injunction against Mexfield for a threatened breach of contract.[28]

The potential for some contractual licences to be irrevocable would appear to be settled.

15.3 Contractual licences and third parties

One of the reasons for the view that a contractual licence was always revocable, even if to revoke it would amount to a breach of contract, was the traditional position that such a licence could create only personal rights: it was not a proprietary right, and so could never bind a third party. Once it came to be decided that, as between the original licensor and licensee, a licence could potentially be irrevocable, the view was propounded that, if the original licensor could not revoke the licence, then neither could a person claiming through him. The effect of this reasoning would be to elevate an irrevocable contractual licence to the status of being an interest in land. As will be seen, this line of authority has now been discredited, but problems still remain in deciding what effect a contractual licence may have against purchasers of land.

15.3.1 Denial of proprietary status

The issue of whether a purchaser of land was bound by a contractual licence was considered by the House of Lords in *King v. David Allen & Sons, Billposting Ltd*.[29] King contracted to allow David Allen the right to affix posters on the wall of his cinema for a period of four years. King then leased the cinema to a third party, who refused to allow David Allen to display his posters on the cinema wall, whereupon he sued King for breach of contract. In holding King to be liable, an essential part of the reasoning was that the tenant was not bound by the contractual licence which had created rights personal to the parties to the contract. If the tenant had been bound by the licence, then David Allen would have been able to continue to fix his posters on the wall and King would not have been in breach of contract. This decision[30] provided a formidable obstacle to the development of the idea that a contractual licence could be regarded as an interest in land.

---

[25] See *Hardwick v. Johnson* [1978] 1 W.L.R. 683 (perhaps an extreme construction).

[26] *Chandler v. Kerley* [1978] 1 W.L.R. 693 (twelve months).

[27] [2011] UKSC 52.   [28] [2011] UKSC 52 at [110]. See also at [60] *per* Lord Neuberger.

[29] [1916] 2 A.C. 54.

[30] See also *Clore v. Theatrical Properties Ltd* [1936] 3 All E.R. 483, which reached the same conclusion with regard to a licence giving front-of-theatre rights.

15.3.2 **A new interest in land?**

Notwithstanding the decision in *King v. David Allen*, a theory began to take root that an irrevocable contractual licence was an interest in land which was therefore capable of binding third parties. This development started in the controversial decision in *Errington v. Errington and Woods*.[31] A father bought a house and gave permission to his son and daughter-in-law to live in it, provided that they paid the mortgage instalments. When the mortgage had been paid in full, he promised to convey the house to them. The father then died and his widow sought to evict her daughter-in-law from the property, her son having left the home to return to live with his mother.

In considering the status of the couple, it was decided that, although they had exclusive possession, they were not tenants. This conclusion seems correct as, under the terms of their agreement, they were free to leave at any time and were not bound to continue to make any payments to the father whereas, provided that they did make the payments, he could not evict them from the property. Such an arrangement is neither a fixed-term tenancy, a periodic tenancy, nor a tenancy at will and is, therefore, one of the rare situations where exclusive possession is granted to residential occupiers but no lease is created. The couple were therefore licensees and were regarded as being contractual licensees.[32]

15.3.2.1 Intervention of equity

Denning L.J. reviewed the authorities dealing with the question as to whether contractual licences could be revoked and concluded that, because of the intervention of equity, certain licences were irrevocable and that, in this case, if the couple continued to pay the mortgage instalments, their licence could not be revoked. He then went on to say:

> This infusion of equity means that contractual licences now have a force and validity of their own and cannot be revoked in breach of contract. *Neither the licensor nor anyone who claims through him can disregard the contract except a purchaser for value without notice.*[33]

In the italicized part of this passage, Denning L.J. makes the considerable leap from holding that, because the terms of the contract mean that the licence is irrevocable as between the original parties, the licence should now be regarded as an equitable interest in land. Not surprisingly, this was controversial.[34] The creation of new interests in land appears to be precluded by statute,[35] and it is also not easy to see how this dictum can be reconciled with the decision in *King v. David Allen*.[36] Again, the point can be made that certain relationships are classified as licences precisely because they do not qualify as other recognized interests in land, such as leases and easements. To admit contractual licences to the category of interests in land undermines the law's efforts to restrict the ability of individuals to create new proprietary interests.[37] If parties were free to create such interests, then land could become encumbered with an ever-increasing variety of rights, the effect

---

[31] [1952] 1 K.B. 90. Cf. *Ramnarace v. Lutchman* [2001] 1 W.L.R. 1651, where there was no payment to the freeholder.

[32] For a different analysis, see A.D. Hargreaves (1953) 69 L.Q.R. 466 and 8.7.1.

[33] [1952] 1 K.B. 290 at 299. Emphasis supplied.

[34] For criticism, see H.W.R. Wade (1952) 68 L.Q.R. 337. For more sympathetic reactions, see G.C. Cheshire (1953) 16 M.L.R. 1; L.A. Sheridan (1953) 17 Conv. (N.S.) 440 at 446–9.

[35] LPA 1925, s. 4(1).

[36] See the comments made in *National Provincial Bank Ltd v. Ainsworth* [1965] A.C. 1175 at 1239–40 *per* Lord Upjohn; at 1251 *per* Lord Wilberforce. For a more overtly hostile approach, see *National Provincial Bank Ltd v. Hastings Car Mart Ltd* [1964] Ch. 665 at 697–8 *per* Russell L.J.

[37] See the comments in *Keppell v. Bailey* (1833) 2 My & K. 517 at 533 *per* Lord Brougham L.C.

of which would be to make the process of transferring land even more precarious than is currently the case.

15.3.2.2 Life interest

Despite these objections, the attempt to elevate the contractual licence to the status of a proprietary right continued. *Binions v. Evans*[38] was a case where the merits lay entirely on one side but where it was difficult to find a convincing reason to reach the conclusion that those merits dictated so that, in the end, 'the law is as it ought to be'.[39] Mr Evans had been, like his father and grandfather before him, a longstanding employee of Tredegar Estates and lived with his wife in a cottage owned by the Estate. On his death, the Estate entered into an agreement with his widow, who at that time was seventy-three, that she could remain living in the cottage for the rest of her life, rent free, provided that she kept it and the garden in good order. Tredegar Estate then sold the cottage to Mr and Mrs Binions, expressly subject to the right of Mrs Evans' right of occupation and the price which was paid reflected this agreement. Shortly afterwards, Mr and Mrs Binions brought an action for possession, arguing that she occupied the cottage as a tenant at will. Unsurprisingly, but for different reasons, the Court of Appeal held in favour of Mrs Evans.

Megaw and Stephenson L.JJ. held that the agreement between the Estate and Mrs Evans created a life interest,[40] the effect of which was to constitute her as a tenant for life under the Settled Land Act (SLA) 1925.[41] As the purchasers had notice of this, they took subject to her interest. Lord Denning M.R., mindful that the consequence of this reasoning would be to vest in Mrs Evans all the statutory powers conferred upon the tenant for life, including the power of sale, dissented from this. Instead, he regarded her as occupying the cottage under an irrevocable contractual licence. Although on this occasion he referred to *King v. David Allen*, he reiterated the view that he had expressed in *Errington* to the effect that a licence of this type will take effect as an equitable interest in land.[42] Alternatively, in his view, because under the contract, Mr and Mrs Binions had expressly agreed to give effect to Mrs Evans' interest, for them to renege on this would be inequitable and, to prevent this, a constructive trust would be imposed under which her licence would be protected.[43]

15.3.2.3 The retreat from *Errington*

Lord Denning's views on the proprietary effect of contractual licences, while remaining controversial, were applied with evident reluctance in subsequent cases.[44] In *Re Sharpe*,[45] an elderly lady had what was held to be a contractual licence[46] to occupy a house owned by her bankrupt nephew. The trustee in bankruptcy had contracted to sell the house and, in order to obtain vacant possession, sought possession. His action failed. While taking pains not to decide what the position would have been had the contract been completed and the action been brought by the purchaser, for whose plight Browne-Wilkinson J. expressed

---

[38] [1972] Ch. 359.   [39] Ibid. at 373 *per* Stephenson L.J. See R.J. Smith [1973] C.L.J. 123.

[40] Had a nominal rent been charged, the subsequent difficulties would have been avoided as the transaction would have taken effect as a determinable ninety-year tenancy: LPA 1925, s. 149(6). Cf. *Skipton Building Society v. Clayton* (1993) 66 P. & C.R. 223.

[41] See 7.4.7.1.

[42] [1972] Ch. 359 at 369.

[43] This view continues to have some judicial support. See 7.4.7.1.

[44] Although see *D.H.N. Food Distributors Ltd v. Tower Hamlets London Borough Council* [1976] 1 W.L.R. 852. A contractual licence was assumed to be an interest in land in *Midland Bank Ltd v. Farmpride Hatcheries Ltd* [1981] E.G.L.R. 147, criticized on this point by R.E. Annand [1982] Conv. 67.

[45] [1980] 1 W.L.R. 219.

[46] For the persuasive view that this was really a case on estoppel, see J. Martin [1980] Conv. 207 at 213–14.

considerable sympathy,[47] the judge felt constrained by authority to hold that the licence conferred some sort of equity or equitable interest under a constructive trust. His lack of enthusiasm was evident, as he commented that:

> I do not think that the principles lying behind these decisions have been fully explored and on occasion it seems such rights are found to exist simply on the ground that to hold otherwise would be a hardship to the plaintiff.[48]

He concluded by expressing:

> the hope that in the near future the whole question can receive full consideration in the Court of Appeal, so that, in order to do justice to the many thousands who never come to court at all but who wish to know with certainty what their proprietary rights are, the extent to which these irrevocable licences bind third parties.[49]

15.3.2.4 The return to orthodoxy

Within ten years, this plea was answered. In *Ashburn Anstalt v. Arnold*,[50] the question was whether an occupancy agreement took effect as an overriding interest and was, therefore, binding upon a purchaser. Fox L.J., giving the Judgment of the court, wrongly[51] held the agreement to be a lease, and therefore binding. Mindful that this conclusion could be wrong, however, a full review of the proprietary status of contractual licences was undertaken. As a result of this review, it was concluded that, although the actual decisions in *Errington v. Errington* and *Binions v. Evans* were correct, the statement in *Errington* that contractual licences were binding upon all but a purchaser without notice was *per incuriam* and wrong. It is now quite clear that the view that contractual licences are to be regarded as interests in land is heretical[52] and that dicta asserting that they are will no longer be followed, it now seeming to be axiomatic that a contractual licence, while quite capable of binding the parties to it, 'is not capable of binding their respective successors, as no interest in land or proprietary interest would subsist'.[53] What remains is to explain the results, if not the reasoning, in *Errington v. Errington* and *Binions v. Evans*.

The decision in *Errington* was regarded as being clearly correct. Two of the reasons are connected. First, the agreement was seen as being an estate contract: a unilateral contract by which the couple would have been entitled, on the payment of the entire purchase money, to have had the legal estate conveyed to them. Although this had not been registered, this would not have been void against the mother as she was not a purchaser for value. While plausible, the problem is that, if for some reason they chose not to complete the payments, they would not have had the right to the conveyance. The second reason is that, by paying each instalment, which went towards the purchase of the property, they acquired a corresponding beneficial interest in it under a resulting trust. This seems correct.

---

[47] [1980] 1 W.L.R. 219 at 226. In reliance on the contract he had sold his own house and, at the time of the action, was living in a small motorized caravan on, or near, Hampstead Heath: ibid. at 224.

[48] Ibid. at 223.   [49] Ibid. at 226.

[50] [1989] Ch. 1. See A.J. Oakley [1988] C.L.J. 353; P. Sparkes (1988) 104 L.Q.R. 175; J. Hill (1988) 51 M.L.R. 226; M.P. Thompson [1988] Conv. 201.

[51] The decision on this point was overruled in *Prudential Assurance Co. Ltd v. London Residuary Body* [1992] A.C. 386. That the case was overruled on this point does not affect the authority of the dicta on the proprietary effect of contractual licences.

[52] See *I.D.C. Group Ltd v. Clark* [1992] 1 E.G.L.R. 187 at 189 *per* Browne-Wilkinson J., affirmed [1992] 2 E.G.L.R. 184. See also *Canadian Imperial Bank of Commerce v. Bello* (1991) 64 P. & C.R. 48 at 52 *per* Dillon L.J.

[53] *Berrisford v. Mexfield Housing Co-operative Ltd* [2011] UKSC 52 at [60] *per* Lord Neuberger.

Finally, the view was expressed that the true explanation as to why the offer could not have been revoked once the couple had embarked upon acceptance of it was estoppel.[54]

15.3.2.5 Estoppel

This final reason relates to the reason why an offeror, in cases of unilateral contracts, is not allowed to revoke an offer once the offeree has begun acceptance.[55] The difficulty is that, in such cases, no contract is created until the acceptance of the offer is complete; the offeree is free to abandon the acceptance if he chooses to do so and it is not obvious why the offeror cannot revoke the offer once acceptance has begun. One theory is that there is a collateral contract that the offer will not be revoked once the offeree has begun to accept it and the consideration for this is that of partial acceptance.[56] An alternative, and perhaps preferable, explanation is that the offeror was estopped from revoking the offer.[57] The basis of this argument is that the offeree, with the encouragement of the offeror, has relied on his expectation that the offer will not be revoked, with the result that the estoppel arises. In *Ashburn Anstalt*, Fox L.J. did not consider either argument in detail but simply offered the suggestion that the true explanation of *Errington* was that it was an estoppel licence which, he appeared to assume, was binding upon the third party.

While it might well be correct that *Errington* is best seen as an estoppel case, the further assumption that an estoppel licence necessarily binds a third party is not uncontroversial.[58] Although s. 116 of the Land Registration Act (LRA) 2002 declares that, for the avoidance of doubt, an equity by estoppel is capable of binding successors in title, the position of purchasers requires some scrutiny. Certainly, in *Errington* itself, the plaintiff should have been held to have been bound by the rights of the licensee. As she was not a purchaser for value, she should not be in any better position than her husband, who could not have revoked the licence. This, however, is different from saying that estoppel licences should inherently bind third parties. Indeed, it is difficult to see why an estoppel licence, once it has been awarded by the court, should act any differently on a purchaser than a contractual licence. Either they should both have the proprietary quality of binding a third party, or neither should. Assuming that this is true, it leaves open the question of what effect an equity by estoppel has under s. 116 of the LRA 2002 when the land in question is sold, but *before* the court makes an order to satisfy the estoppel. It seems possible, at least, that a court would find that estoppel equity binding upon a purchaser at the date of the disposition, even though a subsequent court order then grants a licence to the claimant, which as a personal right is *not* capable of binding a purchaser.[59] This is something of a paradox at the heart of s. 116, LRA 2002, and it is unlikely to be resolved without judicial intervention.

15.3.2.6 Constructive trusts

In *Ashburn Anstalt*, attention was given to the role of the constructive trust in this context. Reference was made to *Binions v. Evans* where, as one of the grounds for his decision, Lord Denning M.R. held that Mr and Mrs Binions held the property on a constructive trust, this trust being imposed to give effect to their contractual obligation that they would take

---

[54] [1989] Ch. 1 at 17.

[55] See the discussion of this issue in Law Reform Committee's 6th Interim Report (1937), para. 39.

[56] See Peel, *Treitel on the Law of Contract* (12th edn) (London, Sweet & Maxwell, 2007), 41, who accepts that this analysis is artificial. See also *Daulia v. Four Millbank Nominees* [1978] Ch. 231 at 239 *per* Goff L.J.; A. Briggs [1983] Conv. 285 at 287.

[57] See R.H. Maudsley [1956] Conv. 281 at 287 & M.P. Thompson [1983] Conv. 50.

[58] See *Habermann v. Koehler* (1996) 73 P. & C.R. 515 at 523 *per* Peter Gibson L.J.

[59] See B. McFarlane, 'Proprietary Estoppel and Third Parties after the Land Registration Act 2002' [2003] C.L.J. 661.

the property subject to the rights of Mrs Evans. Fox L.J. accepted that this was justified but was clearly anxious that such a trust should not be imposed too lightly, because the effect of so doing would be to upset titles to land. He accepted that a constructive trust should be imposed when a purchaser expressly undertakes to give effect to a particular interest.[60] A constructive trust should not be imposed, however, merely because a purchaser agrees to take subject to a particular interest.[61]

The restricting of the circumstances when a constructive trust will be imposed is welcome but, even in the limited situations where it is considered to be right to impose such a trust, there are problems with this solution.[62] When a trust is created, the normal situation involves the separation of the legal and equitable estate. Yet, in a situation such as *Binions v. Evans*, it is not easy to see what estate is actually held by Mrs Evans, unless it is a life estate, which would bring the case back within the confines of the SLA 1925. This difficulty would be more acute if the licence in question was an irrevocable right to cross another person's land rather than to occupy it. In such a situation, it is difficult to see how, on orthodox principles, a constructive trust could be imposed to give effect to a right of way.

A second difficulty with the constructive trust approach is that, although the trust will only be imposed when a purchaser has expressly agreed to give effect to a particular right, the enforceability of that trust against a subsequent owner of the land will not rest upon that purchaser agreeing to give effect to the interest in question. Because a constructive trust has been imposed, then, in principle, it would appear to be enforceable against a subsequent purchaser on the same basis as any other equitable interest in land. It is not clear that the courts would be prepared to hold that this is the case.

15.3.2.7 Privity of contract

Another objection to the use of the constructive trust in cases such as *Binions v. Evans* is that it appears to run contrary to the doctrine of privity of contract. The essential reasoning appears to be that, if A and B enter a contract under which B agrees to give effect to rights in favour of C, then C, owing to a contract to which he was not a party, will acquire enforceable rights against B through the medium of a constructive trust. As such, the use of the constructive trust appears to run contrary to the common law principle of privity of contract.[63]

This objection has become academic, however, in respect of contracts entered into after the coming into force of the Contracts (Rights of Third Parties) Act 1999. Section 1(1) of the Act provides that:

> a person who is not a party to a contract . . . may in his own right enforce a term of the contract if—
>
> (a) the contract expressly provides that he may, or
>
> (b) . . . the term purports to convert a benefit on him.

This seems to provide a ready solution to cases such as *Binions v. Evans* and is likely to mean that cases of this type will be decided by reference to it and the constructive trust will not be used. This is to be welcomed, as the trust was being used in an unorthodox way, largely to provide a remedy in hard cases, without paying too close a regard to normal trust principles.

---

[60] Applying *Lyus v. Prowsa Developments Ltd* [1982] 1 W.L.R. 1044. See also *Lloyd v. Dugdale* [2002] 2 P. & C.R. 13, at [52], [55] *per* Sir Christopher Slade. See M. Dixon [2002] Conv. 584.

[61] [1989] Ch. 1 at 25–6. See also *Chattey v. Farndale Hodings Ltd* (1996) 75 P. & C.R. 298 at 317 *per* Morritt L.J.

[62] See M.P. Thompson [1988] Conv. 201 at 205–6.

[63] For a more sympathetic approach to this argument, which, however, understates the privity problem, see B. McFarlane (2004) 120 L.Q.R. 667.

15.3.2.8 The economic torts

A final matter which must be considered when discussing the potential effect of a con-tractual licence is the role, if any, of the economic torts.[64] The use of tort was suggested as a possible solution to the problem in *Binions v. Evans* itself.[65] Under the tortious doctrine of interference with contractual relations, if there is a contract between A and B, and C, with knowledge of that contract, induces A to break that contract, C commits a tort. To prevent this, an injunction may be granted. In *Binions v. Evans*, if Mr and Mrs Binions had succeeded in evicting Mrs Evans from the property, the result would have been to cause Tredegar Estates to be in breach of their contract with her. As the couple had, prior to their purchase of the property, actual knowledge of her contractual right to stay in the cottage, there seems to be no reason in principle why an injunction would not lie against them to restrain them from action which would necessitate Tredegar Estates committing a breach of contract. Such a solution would have the merit of avoiding the imposition of an ill-defined constructive trust, while producing a result which the merits of the case would seem to demand.

As yet, there has been little judicial discussion of the role of the economic torts in this context and it is possible, especially since the coming into force of the 1999 Act, that the courts will be unwilling to use this method of enforcing contractual licences against third parties, particularly as the effect of utilizing the economic torts in this way could have very wide-ranging consequences.[66] To allow tort to play a role in this way would enable rights which have not been admitted to the rank of property interests to be enforced indirectly, on the basis that a purchaser had prior knowledge of certain contractual rights affecting the property prior to purchasing it and such a result may be seen to be subversive of prop-erty law principles.

15.3.2.9 Conclusions

The development of the law relating to contractual licences represents an interesting, al-beit unsuccessful, attempt to fashion a new interest in land, and it was probably motivated by two primary considerations: a desire to achieve what was perceived to be fair results in individual cases, and a wish to give effect to informal transactions when (with proper legal advice) the parties involved could have ordered their affairs in such a way so as to avoid any subsequent problems.[67] The competing consideration was the weight given to certainty and security in conveyancing transactions; a factor which clearly influenced Browne-Wilkinson J. in *Re Sharpe*. Ultimately, the importance of certainty together with the weight of authority prevailed. The failure of the attempt to create a new interest in land does not mean that other informal transactions may not give rise to rights against third parties, but it does mean that the law must have recourse to other concepts and doc-trines—most obviously proprietary estoppel—in vindicating those rights.

---

[64] For an excellent discussion of the potential impact of the economic torts on land law, see R.J. Smith (1977) 41 Conv. (N.S.) 318

[65] [1972] Ch. 359 at 371 *per* Megaw L.J.

[66] See Smith, *Property Law* (7th edn) (London, Longmans, 2011), 484–5.

[67] For example, in *Binions v. Evans*, subsequent problems would have been avoided had Mrs Evans been granted a non-assignable ninety-nine-year lease at a low rent, determinable on death.

Index